THE ALASTAIR CAMPBELL DIARIES

THE ALASTAIR CAMPBELL DIARIES

Volume 4

THE BURDEN OF POWER

COUNTDOWN TO IRAQ

Edited by

ALASTAIR CAMPBELL

and

BILL HAGERTY

HUTCHINSON: LONDON

Published by Hutchinson 2012

3 5 7 9 10 8 6 4 2

Edited extracts of the Alastair Campbell Diaries have previously been published by Hutchinson in *The Blair Years*, 2007.

First published in Great Britain in 2012 by
Hutchinson
Random House, 20 Vauxhall Bridge Road,
London SW1V 2SA

www.randomhouse.co.uk

Addresses for companies within The Random House Group Limited can be found at:
www.randomhouse.co.uk/offices.htm

The Random House Group Limited Reg. No. 954009

A CIP catalogue record for this book
is available from the British Library

ISBN 978 0 09 179628 0

The Random House Group Limited supports The Forest Stewardship Council (FSC®), the leading international forest certification organisation. Our books carrying the FSC label are printed on FSC® certified paper. FSC is the only forest certification scheme endorsed by the leading environmental organisations, including Greenpeace. Our paper procurement policy can be found at www.randomhouse.co.uk/environment

Typeset in Palatino by Palimpsest Book Production Limited,
Falkirk, Stirlingshire

Printed and bound in Great Britain by
Clays Ltd, St Ives plc

To Philip Gould (1950–2011),
because friendship matters in politics,
and team players are the best players of all.

Contents

Acknowledgements

Many thanks once more to Bill Hagerty, who took over the task of editing these diaries after the sad death of our friend and colleague Richard Stott, and to Mark Bennett, who was with me in Downing Street and has also been with me on the long and sometimes tortuous road to publication.

Both through my diaries, and the two novels and ebook I have published, I have come to appreciate the professionalism and kindness of many people at Random House. I would like to thank Gail Rebuck, Susan Sandon, Caroline Gascoigne, Joanna Taylor, Charlotte Bush, Emma Mitchell and the team of 'spin doctors', Martin Soames for his legal advice, David Milner, Mark Handsley, Vicki Robinson, Helen Judd, Sue Cavanagh, and Jeanette Slinger in reception for always ensuring one of my books is at the front of the display cabinet downstairs – at least when I am visiting the building. My thanks, as ever, to my literary agent Ed Victor, to his PA Linda Van and to his excellent team.

I want to thank Tony Blair for giving me the opportunity he did, and thank the many friends and colleagues who have helped me in good times and bad.

Finally, thanks to my family. As these diaries show, the pressures of the job I did also fell on Fiona and the children, and I thank them for their love and support. I know that they too will be happy to acknowledge our debt to Philip Gould, to whom I dedicated this volume shortly before his death, and who was an enormous support to all of us.

Introduction

At the risk of offending purists, pedants and history scholars, I have taken the liberty of beginning this volume with the same diary entry with which I ended the last one: September 11. Though this volume is the fourth in a series of the full diaries of my time working for Labour in opposition and in government, it also stands alone as a record of the most difficult and controversial period of Tony Blair's premiership. It is an intimate portrayal of Blair the war leader, with conflict in both Afghanistan and Iraq taking place during the two years covered, and September 11 is the most suitable place to begin that account.

The Taliban in Afghanistan, Saddam Hussein in Iraq, and the fear of terrorist organisations getting hold of weapons of mass destruction (WMD) with the help of rogue states, had been on TB's agenda well before September 11. Indeed, subsequently Mike White of the *Guardian* reminded me that TB had raised the issue as 'a coming challenge' at a meeting at the newspaper's head office the day before the Twin Towers fell. But without the events of that day, it is at least plausible to imagine that neither war would have taken place, certainly in the way they did. As the ten-year anniversary showed, it is a date so much now part of the public consciousness, and so central to many strategic, religious and geopolitical debates around the world, that it seems almost otiose to add the year: September 11, 2001. More than a decade on, we say 'September 11', or its American variant, '9/11', and there are very few people who don't immediately know where, when and what you mean, and summon up images of planes hitting buildings, people fleeing in terror, families grieving in all parts of the world, politicians struggling to catch up. There have been terror attacks since, but none which has made such a powerful impact, which is still felt today.

World leaders are fond of stating, in the immediate aftermath of terrorist outrages, that we must and will not let the terrorists deflect us or change our way of life. But they can, and they do. It is something I reflect on every time I go through an airport security check. But September 11 did more than see increased bag checks, belt and shoe removals and toothpaste confiscation at airports. It recast the foreign policy of major powers. It tested relationships between them. It tested the UN. It brought to a head debates which had been simmering within and about Islam. Most importantly for this book, it came to be a defining moment in Tony Blair's premiership, George Bush's presidency, the relationship between the two, the reputation of both.

The day began with TB worrying about a speech he was due to make to the Trades Union Congress in Brighton about public service reform. It was being set up as something of a 'lion's den' moment. The speech was never delivered: the first attack on the Twin Towers in New York took place as we put the finishing touches to it in a hotel suite overlooking a calm and beautiful sea. The day ended with TB back in London directing the UK end of a global crisis management response, which would subsequently see the domestic side of his job dwarfed by the consequences of the attacks.

The Burden of Power charts in sometimes minute detail what happened around TB on September 11, and every day thereafter: the initial response, the globetrotting diplomacy as the case for action was built, the decision to use military force to remove the Taliban regime in Afghanistan, a war still going on in somewhat different form today. Then not long afterwards the war in Iraq, undoubtedly the most difficult and the most controversial decision of the Blair government. In military terms, the wars were successful and, in terms of meeting the initial objectives, relatively swift. The Taliban fell. Saddam fell. But we all know that is only part of the story. The Taliban were toppled, but never really went away. Afghanistan remains far from secure, with perilous consequences for the region. Saddam was toppled, but after the initial celebrations, chaos ensued, and the controversy over the decision to commit troops to action did not disappear with the dictator those troops brought down. The stated purpose of the action was to remove what the government believed to be a growing threat from Saddam's WMD programme. Of course Saddam's long and wretched history of rule, his brutality, the wars he started, his defiance of the UN, these were all factors. But the answer to the specific question 'Why Iraq, why now?' was his continued development of a WMD programme, and the post-9/11 threat the US, the UK and others believed this posed. The fact that the weapons did not materialise in Iraq after Allied troops entered the country merely fuelled the controversy, unsurprisingly, over the original decision.

The Burden of Power seems a fitting title for a book dominated by Tony Blair's handling of these events. See the front covers of the four volumes and you see first a young and vibrant Opposition leader, then a young and jubilant prime minister taking the reins of power with an enormous landslide and huge goodwill, then a prime minister beginning to age as always they do – but still smiling – and finally, on the front of this volume, the Burden of Power. These were momentous decisions, taken amid enormous pressure and often with much else going on. It is why, though I disagree with his politics and oppose many of the things he has done, I have respect for the fact that the current prime minister, David Cameron, does the job he does. The pressures are unique to that post. Only five people alive today know what they are.

When I was asked by a newspaper to choose a defining photograph, as part of the enormous 'a decade on' coverage of September 11, I opted not for the obvious ones, but for a photo of TB sitting alongside John Monks, the general secretary of the TUC. Minutes earlier, John had said to me that it was on days like this that you realised the enormity of the responsibility that goes with the prime minister's job. The picture was used in *The Blair Years*, the extracts of my diaries published in 2007, and I have used it again in the first plate section of this volume too. TB looks focused and distracted at the same time. I know him well enough to see that his mind is whirring, thinking through the many things he will need to deal with once he has announced to the Congress that he must head back to London – his brief statement on events in the US, his expression of solidarity, his warning that the extremism behind the attacks had to be confronted, and his announcement that he would not be making the speech led to his first and last full standing ovation from a TUC event. John Monks meanwhile, also someone in a leadership position, is looking empathetically at TB, sensing the additional burdens falling on the shoulders of the man sitting next to him.

For some of his enemies, Iraq defines TB. The three election wins, a peace agreement in Ireland, record investment in schools and hospitals, Bank of England independence, devolution to Scotland, Wales and London, Sure Start, the minimum wage, civic partnerships, the New Deal, Kosovo, Sierra Leone, debt relief, securing the Olympics for London, all these and many more get parked and forgotten by those who wish only to see that when it came to Iraq, he did the wrong thing and for the wrong reasons. They see it as nothing short of a disaster, regardless of the fact that one of the most brutal dictators in history was felled after his years of defiance of the UN and brutality against his own people. It was about oil. It was about Israel. It was because TB was craven in his relationship with George Bush in particular and the US in general. It was because he had been in power too long and it had all gone to his head. For some these are unshifting and unshiftable views which, if anything, harden with time. And though TB led Labour to a comfortable third election victory even after the war in Iraq, and all the controversy that involved, I know there are people who deserted Labour on the back of it. But I hope a fair reading of my diaries shows that he took real care over all of the decisions which faced him at this time. I don't object to people disagreeing with the decisions he took. As so often in politics, things were never black and white. There was always another course that could have been taken, and I have never considered it dishonourable to hold a different view. Indeed Robin Cook expressed such a view brilliantly when he resigned from the government over Iraq. But as someone who was alongside TB as much as anyone, I know the care he took over the decisions, and the sincerity of his view that he was doing what he believed to be the right thing for Britain, British people and their security. He wasn't elected to hold views, but to take decisions based upon them, and whilst people may disagree with the conclusions he reached, they should not doubt his sincerity in the beliefs that drove him to them, not least his long-standing concerns about the threat of Islamic extremism, nor his conviction that not to have taken those decisions would have been wrong. Very little is heard in the UK media of the Iraqis who supported what we did, and who at least now have the beginnings of democracy. Those who opposed the war must at least reflect, surely, that had their position held sway, Saddam and his sons would have prospered for even longer. That was a danger TB believed the world should not countenance. It is why, despite the controversy, despite the opprobrium he has faced over Iraq, he nonetheless believes world leaders have a duty to face up to the threat of Islamic extremism, and why the conduct of Iran will at some stage have to be properly addressed too.

There was a point at which, in the run-up to the war in Iraq, I asked him if the war was really worth it if – as I feared it would – it led to him being driven out of office before his time. He said it was always worth doing what you thought was the right thing, and that Saddam was a threat the world had ignored for too long, and that included Britain. Those two insights were never far from his thinking throughout. As was clear from his evidence to the Chilcot

Inquiry into the Iraq War, he accepts mistakes were made, but he does not accept that the decision to remove Saddam was the wrong one, or that all the chaos which ensued was alone the responsibility of those who took the action to remove him. He thinks it was right, too, to be supportive of the US, not just because they came under attack on September 11, or even because we share so much in terms of values and history, but because he believed the only way to have any influence on President Bush privately – for example in getting him to take the issue of Iraq down the route of the UN, or get fresh US engagement in the Middle East Peace Process – was via maximum public support. It was to some extent a trade-off, for which he was willing to take the 'Bush's poodle' jibes.

Back in late 2001, with the memories of September 11 fresh in people's minds, and with the Taliban clearly not facing up to the challenge of helping to deliver up Osama Bin Laden and other perpetrators of the attacks, public and political support for action was stronger than it was for action in Iraq, though it is worth remembering that from some on the right in Britain, we faced the charge of being too cautious, and public support was greater at the time than it was after the event. I should make clear at this juncture that I am not linking Iraq to the September 11 attacks, in the sense of claiming Iraq played a role in them, and it was unhelpful of some in the US system to seek to do so. But where the link exists is here: until September 11, the threat posed by Iraq and WMD was one that the US and its closest allies were willing to tolerate. After September 11, the mindset shifted. To quote the phrase used often at the Chilcot Inquiry, the calculus of threat changed.

For those who think the government did the wrong thing, so much has been said and written, the arguments have been played out so volubly, that it is unlikely anything I say here, or which I wrote at the time and publish now, will persuade them otherwise. But when TB was being briefed at the Ministry of Defence on military preparedness in the event of our forces coming under attack from biological or chemical weapons, there was not a person in that room who did not consider the threat to be real. I can remember feeling a sense of fear which was matched by the looks on some of the faces in the room. I can remember TB pressing until he was as assured as he could be that our troops were as prepared as possible to face this threat if and when it came. No prime minister would commit troops to any action, let alone to the potential horror being described in that room, without thinking through the consequences, and unless they were sure there was no other way. Also, I know it is not the done thing in polite circles to speak well of George W. Bush, but I thought he made a very good observation in his book, *Decision Points*, when he said, 'If I wanted to mislead the country into war why would I pick an allegation that was certain to be disproven publicly shortly after we invaded the country?' Both he and TB, and the people working for them, believed the WMD threat was real. People are entitled to disagree with the decisions. But there was no lying, there was no conspiracy. There was a set of difficult decisions that had to be taken.

Of course the portrait of Tony Blair is the most intimate here. But I saw a good deal of Bush, of Vladimir Putin, of Jacques Chirac and other world leaders during this time. Bill Clinton still figures large, a good and sometimes critical friend to TB and his team. The night out with him and actor Kevin Spacey in a McDonald's restaurant in Blackpool was one of the more memorable meals of my life. Unforgettable too was the meeting at which he gave fellow Labour strategist Philip Gould and me a masterclass in political strategy, complete with very personal advice about my own by then difficult situation. Many on both sides of the Atlantic find it odd that TB could be close both to Clinton and to Bush, two very different leaders from different sides of the political divide. I think TB would argue that with the US the only superpower at the time, he had a duty to have good relations with its leader. Also, he genuinely got on with Bush. The Texan certainly had a cowboy touch about him, at times right down to the boots on his feet. But he has more intelligence, more charm and greater political skills than most are prepared to credit him with. It has also been interesting to note, as the Republicans have lurched through the process of trying to find a candidate to take on President Obama at the next election, that by the standards of most of the contenders, Bush is something of a moderate. Many modern politicians are more impressive in public than in private. The media age has forced politicians as a breed to communicate more and to think about how they do so. They can turn a switch and go into public mode. David Cameron is a good example of this. George Bush's switch seemed sometimes to go the other way. He would express himself less well in public than he did in private. At least he was aware that his image gave other leaders in other countries problems. I don't think the same could always be said for his vice president Dick Cheney or defense secretary Donald Rumsfeld.

Just as Iraq will always be one of the issues most associated with TB, so the issues of communication surrounding the war will always be with me, as someone somewhere reminds me online most days. As I said to the Chilcot Inquiry, I stand by everything I said and did in relation to the September 2002 dossier on WMD presented to Parliament by the Prime Minister. Being asked to give my diaries to Lord Hutton's inquiry into David Kelly's death, as this volume shows, was something of a terrifying moment. As anyone who has read my diaries now knows, I can be very frank, I can say very harsh things, I can be hard on myself and on others. I confess to being so worried about what I might have written that when I drove from our holiday home in Provence to Marseilles airport to collect my diaries so that I could transcribe them and send them to Lord Hutton in advance of my first evidence session, I had one of those momentary reflections that life might be easier all round if I just careered off the motorway. Yet as it turned out, I think the diaries may have helped our case. They showed that we took rather more care over that dossier than the BBC journalist took over his report which led to my being called to select committee inquiries, ultimately to Kelly's death, and the inquiry into that.

I never met David Kelly, but I think about him often, and whether I could have done anything differently that might have stopped him from taking his life. With the exception of the deaths of family and close friends, the day his body was found was perhaps the worst of my life, certainly the worst of my time with TB. Had it not been for Fiona, and Philip Gould who came round to the house on hearing the news, I would almost certainly have resigned there and then. I was frankly beyond caring if it meant the blame would come my way. So far as many in the media were concerned, that was going to happen anyway. I just felt the whole thing had become like a horrible, dark novel and I wanted out of it. Ironically, the night before, we were felt to be 'winning' the battle with the BBC, its reporter having been strongly criticised by the Foreign Affairs Committee. But by the morning, all that had changed. It was horrific. The feelings I had then are among the reasons why, despite always staying involved, and going back to help out in two general elections, I have never really wanted to return to a full-time position in the front line of politics.

When I gave evidence to the Leveson Inquiry into media practices in 2011, I made the point that much of today's media like to act as judge and jury on those in public life. The coverage of the Hutton Inquiry, whose deliberations are covered in this volume, but whose conclusions came after I resigned from Downing Street, is a good example. The inquiry shone a microscopic light on both the process of communication in the run-up to war, and the circumstances surrounding Dr Kelly's death. When Lord Hutton was putting government witnesses through their paces, and ministers and officials from the prime minister down were being questioned and cross-examined, day in and day out, media reporting was largely slanted to show the government in a bad light, and Lord Hutton in a good light because of the rigour of his inquiry. The bits of the evidence that suggested wrongdoing by the government led bulletins and newspapers. Anything that fitted with the government account tended to be relegated. The moment Lord Hutton concluded that the central charges against the government were not borne out by the evidence, he was condemned as Lord Whitewash. Hundreds, thousands of reports have subsequently sought to convey the sense that the BBC report was essentially true. It was not; and as Lord Hutton said at the time, even if it emerged there were no WMD in Iraq, that would not make the reporting true. It is important to remember what the accusations against us – and me in particular – were: that we inserted false intelligence into the WMD dossier, knowing it to be false and against the wishes of the intelligence agencies. To this day, I fail to see how a government can simply ignore claims as serious as that. Indeed, had the inquiry found against us, it would not just have been the end for me, but more importantly for TB. Though no WMD have been found, the BBC report is as untrue today as it was when it was first made, despite the constant attempts by many in the media to rewrite what was broadcast, or to confuse and conflate the WMD dossier with the so-called 'dodgy dossier', which was a different paper, which attracted next to no attention at the time, on which someone working for me made an error for which I apologised.

It is fair to say that in this volume, most of the personal satisfaction, even happiness I managed to get from working for TB in the early years has gone. The twin pressures of a 24–7 job of real intensity and scrutiny, and a home life where pressure was mounting on me to leave, at times felt like a living nightmare. I was glad to have discovered a new obsession in running. My sons persuaded me to go for a long run in the summer of 2002. By the end of the holiday I had decided to do the London Marathon, which coincided with a very busy time in relation to Iraq. TB felt the whole thing was a bit of a distraction; to me, it was something of a saviour. At the time I took up running, I could do the job, but I didn't feel I was doing it as well as before. I was resenting the workload, and resenting those on our own side who so often made life harder than it should have been. TB was convinced that I could and should stay, and he is a very skilful manager when it comes to getting his own way. Also, even when we fell out, as over the role of Australian con man Peter Foster and Carole Caplin when Cherie bought two flats for her son Euan, I always felt a strong sense of loyalty to TB, and I still do. It was that loyalty, in addition to the sense of being involved in such significant events, with the chance to make a difference, which made it so hard to leave. When finally I did, I knew it was the right time, even if I fell into a pretty awful depression not long afterwards.

I had forgotten until transcribing the diaries just how long I had been trying to get out. Ironically, the controversy over the communications on Iraq kept me in post for longer. TB finally agreed to my departure in May 2003, shortly before the BBC report I describe above, and yet I didn't leave until August, as the intervening months came to be dominated by the fallout. I suppose it is also something of an irony that TB hired me to take charge of his media relations and yet my own relations with the media became as bad as they did. Partly this was because I often played the role of lightning conductor. But also I was one of the few people able and willing to articulate what I believed to be a set of damaging trends in the way the media and its effect upon democratic debate were developing. I think one of the reasons I became so high profile and so controversial is that I was doing the job at a time the media age was becoming a reality. The media sought to position themselves as the sole purveyors of truth (ironically at a time when standards were falling). In their minds, what they did was truth; what we did was spin. We made mistakes, certainly, not least my colleague Jo Moore's infamous 'good day to bury bad news' email of 9/11. But in general I believe we applied far higher standards to what we said and did than many journalists applied to what they wrote or broadcast.

By the time of this volume we are certainly on the receiving end of the culture of negativity which is powerfully unique to the UK media. I'm not quite sure I would go as far as Derry Irvine's description of the press as 'Satan's people on earth' – some of them were out for Derry's son at the time – but I thought David Blunkett summed up the new media mood well when he said if TB had found a cure for cancer they'd report his failure to do anything for victims of meningitis. TB shared my analysis that the media had become a problem not just for politicians but for our culture and therefore our country. But as I said to the Leveson Inquiry, whereas I felt we had to do something about it, he continued to feel that with all the other priorities the government faced, the public simply would not understand if we launched an overhaul of press standards and regulation as another plank of reform. It was a fair point. But there was always going to come a time when the media reformed and hopefully phone-hacking has brought us to that moment. We will see.

Beyond growing disenchantment with the political media, certain other domestic themes recur in this volume: TB's frustrations at the pace of delivery; something of a culture clash with parts of the Civil Service; continuing difficulties with matters Royal; another media frenzy erupting from false charges that TB sought a bigger role in the Queen Mother's funeral, clearly being fuelled by members of the establishment, some of whom never quite reconciled themselves to a long-running Labour government; TB and his fashion sense – my determination not to let him wear a coat Cherie wanted him to put on in Russia led to one of my biggest rows with her; and of course the TBGBs. John Holmes, formerly TB's foreign policy adviser, made an interesting observation: that TB's problems are caused by his relations with two GBs – George Bush and Gordon Brown. They certainly figure large in his thinking and in any history of this remarkable period. Yet again the two sides of Gordon Brown – the brilliant and the impossible – are on show. But by now TB seems to feel the impossible outweighs the brilliant. Even at the height of international crisis, GB is asking TB for a date of departure (much as Fiona was asking the same of me). The battleground is as much about policy as simply the ambition to be PM. The euro, for example, with TB still keen that Britain should step up preparations to join the single currency, and concerned that GB's scepticism is a tactic to court the right-wing media, the left already supportive of him because of his approach to poverty. There are some fairly extraordinary scenes resulting from GB's attempts, often without consultation with the ministers concerned, to direct policy in other departments. Ministers are often unsure of what their instincts are expected to be, always a sign of division at the top.

The policy differences are exacerbated by what became a largely dysfunctional working relationship, the management of which consumed extraordinary amounts of time and energy. TB talks of GB waging a war of attrition. Jonathan Powell at one point says it is like watching a failed marriage disintegrate. John Prescott says it is all about TB's guilt at becoming leader ahead of GB, and GB's never forgotten sense of betrayal. At times GB could not even bring himself to look at TB in meetings. It all got so bad that TB, fed up with what he sometimes called GB's 'destabilisation strategy', came back from one holiday determined to sack him. It never happened. At another point a small number of his inner team are asked to reflect on what became known variously as his '*grande stratégie*' and '*le grand projet*' (he and I often spoke in French for some reason, particularly when he was nervous) – namely announcing that he would not fight the next election, but would stay on until that point. I think it is possible that had GB been more co-operative and more of a team player, TB might have executed that strategy. But things seemed to get worse not better. More even than in previous volumes, TB, his ministerial colleagues, I and my colleagues in the TB team are worrying about what GB would be like as PM. Yet when it came to it, there was enough of the good amid the bad to have most of us supporting him when he took over. TB says at one point that GB is a 'malign force but head and shoulders above the rest'. Back to the 'brilliant and impossible' prism.

There have been plenty of books written about the Blair/Brown era, and the Blair/Brown relationship, and there will doubtless be many more. Most of the memoirs, biographies and autobiographies of our time in government have been written with the benefit of hindsight, and some of them to suit a single view or perspective. I hope that one of the advantages of a diary from the centre, in terms of its potential contribution to historical debate and analysis, is the lack of such hindsight.

This volume brings to an end the detailed daily account of my time working for TB, in opposition and in government. I have kept a diary ever since, continue to do so and one day may publish my post-Number 10 diaries, where from a slightly different perspective I took part in and recorded two more election campaigns, between them the transition from one PM to another, and many of the ups and downs along the way, as I sought to build a different sort of life, but found myself drawn back in again and again. Re-reading this volume now, and gathering the impressions of those who have read it during the editorial process, I do understand why some people ask the question: 'Why on earth did you go back to help GB?' I understand too why they point to some passages and say it was obvious he was not temperamentally suited to the job of prime minister, or to leading Labour through a general election campaign. But look elsewhere, and it is not quite so evident. He had huge residual strengths and a political appeal which made him hard to resist when, despite all the differences between the Blair and Brown teams, as Prime Minister he was asking me, Peter Mandelson and Philip Gould to return to the fold to help him out in the run-up to the last election. Peter Mandelson returned full time, and full on, back in the Cabinet. Partly because of my views on the Lords, and partly because I didn't want to go back full time to the front line, I turned down the offer of a peerage and ministerial post but did go back to help plan the election campaign, and support GB during it. And despite being ill for much of the time, Philip made his usual big contribution on polling and strategy. As Philip wrote in his revised *Unfinished Revolution*, published shortly before his death last November, I had predicted a hung Parliament from some way out. For much of the campaign, however, I had felt the Tories were on their way towards securing a majority, and I think we surprised ourselves in preventing them from getting one. But when, after several days of post-election wrangling, the time finally came for Gordon to leave Downing Street for Buckingham Palace to offer his resignation to the Queen, I did get the very strong feeling that, politically, we had for the time being run our course. Shortly before, he spoke on the telephone to TB, from the desk in the corner of his office. It was my old office, which he had taken over when he turned 12 Downing Street into what he believed was a more modern set-up for a PM. As he and Tony chatted, Peter Mandelson and I sat and listened. All of the relationships had been tested at times, but there remained a togetherness of sorts, and certainly the sense of a remarkable shared journey that changed Britain, and British politics, for good and, in my view, for the better.

That moment also reminded me of another insight that has deepened with time and experience: that politics, at its best, is a team game. TB once said we were at our best when we were at our boldest. In what was widely seen as a dig at New Labour, by way of response GB said we were at our best when we were Labour. I felt we were always at our best when we were together, united, pulling in the same direction. When it happened, it felt like we were unstoppable. But it didn't happen all of the time; far from it.

Whenever I was under the cosh, my mother-in-law was fond of reminding me of the old Harry Truman quote, 'If you want a friend in Washington, get a dog.' But friendship in politics is possible, and can be real. Teamship is vital. It is because Philip Gould was both a great friend and a great team player that I chose to dedicate this volume to him. He more than any of us understood that politics is a team game, and right up to his death was trying to heal some of the wounds that came with the pressures of power. He died proud of the role he had played in helping to get Labour back into power, and in helping TB and his team do the job we did. I publish this full account humble enough to know we didn't get everything right, but proud of the overall story it tells, and happy to share it.

Alastair Campbell
January 2012

Who's Who

September 2001–August 2003

The Cabinet

Tony Blair	Prime Minister (TB)
John Prescott	Deputy Prime Minister and First Secretary of State (JP)
Gordon Brown	Chancellor of the Exchequer (GB)
Jack Straw	Foreign Secretary (JS)
David Blunkett	Home Secretary (DB)
Margaret Beckett	Environment, Food and Rural Affairs Secretary (MB)
Charles Clarke	Labour Party Chair 2001–2, Education Secretary from 2002
Estelle Morris	Education Secretary 2001–2
Patricia Hewitt	Trade and Industry Secretary, Minister for Women (Pat H)
Robin Cook	Leader of the House of Commons 2001–3 (RC)
Clare Short	International Development Secretary
Alistair Darling	Work and Pensions Secretary 2001–2, Transport Secretary from 2002 and Scottish Secretary from 2003 (AD)
Stephen Byers	Transport, Local Government and the Regions Secretary (SB)
Alan Milburn	Health Secretary 2001–3 (AM)
Tessa Jowell	Culture, Media and Sport Secretary
Geoff Hoon	Defence Secretary
John Reid	Northern Ireland Secretary to 2002, then Labour Party Chair 2002–3, Leader of the House of Commons 2003, Health Secretary 2003–5

Paul Murphy	Welsh Secretary 2001–2, Northern Ireland Secretary from 2002
Helen Liddell	Scottish Secretary 2001–3
Lord (Gareth) Williams	Leader of the House of Lords 2001–3
Lord (Derry) Irvine	Lord Chancellor 2001–3
Hilary Armstrong	Chief Whip (Commons)
Andrew Smith	Chief Secretary to the Treasury 2001–2, Work and Pensions Secretary from 2002
Lord (Bruce) Grocott	Chief Whip (Lords)
Lord (Peter) Goldsmith	Attorney General

Additional Cabinet changes 2002–3

Peter Hain	Welsh Secretary from 2002, Leader of the House of Commons from 2003
Paul Boateng	Chief Secretary to the Treasury from 2002
Baroness (Valerie) Amos	International Development Secretary 2003, Leader of the House of Lords from 2003
Hilary Benn	International Development Secretary from 2003
Lord (Charlie) Falconer	Lord Chancellor from 2003

10 Downing Street

Andrew Adonis	Head of Policy Unit
Alison Blackshaw	AC's personal assistant
Cherie Blair	Wife of TB (CB)
David Bradshaw	Special adviser, Strategic Communications Unit
Alastair Campbell	Director of communications and strategy
Magi Cleaver	Press officer, overseas visits
Hilary Coffman	Special adviser, Press Office
Kate Garvey	Events and visits team
David Hanson	Parliamentary private secretary to TB
Jeremy Heywood	Principal private secretary
Robert Hill	Political secretary
Anji Hunter	Director of government relations
Peter Hyman	Strategist and speechwriter
Tanya Joseph	Press officer
Tom Kelly	Prime Minister's official spokesman (with Godric Smith)

Liz Lloyd	Special adviser, Policy Unit
Sir David Manning	Chief foreign policy adviser
Pat McFadden	Deputy chief of staff
Fiona Millar	AC's partner, aide to CB (FM)
Sally Morgan	Director of political and government relations
Jonathan Powell	Chief of staff
Terry Rayner	Driver
Catherine Rimmer	Research and Information Unit
Matthew Rycroft	Private secretary, Foreign Affairs
Martin Sheehan	Press officer
Godric Smith	Prime Minister's official spokesman (with Tom Kelly)
Clare Sumner	Private secretary, Parliamentary Affairs
Sir Andrew Turnbull	Cabinet Secretary from 2002
Simon Virley	Private secretary
Anna Wechsberg	Private secretary
Ben Wilson	Press officer
Sir Richard Wilson	Cabinet Secretary to 2002 (RW)

HM Treasury

Ian Austin, Ed Balls, Spencer Livermore, Ed Miliband, Sue Nye	Special advisers

Whitehall/Security Services

Admiral Sir Michael Boyce	Chief of the Defence Staff 2001–3
Sir Richard Dearlove ('C')	Head of the Secret Intelligence Service (MI6)
Sir Jeremy Greenstock	UK ambassador to the United Nations
Sir Stephen Lander	Director general of the Security Service (MI5)
Dame Eliza Manningham-Buller	Lander's successor, 2002
Chris Meyer	UK ambassador to Washington
Sir Richard Mottram	Permanent secretary, DTLR
Sir David Omand	UK security and intelligence co-ordinator
John Scarlett	Chairman, UK Joint Intelligence Committee
Sir John Stevens	Metropolitan Police commissioner

United States

Dan Bartlett	Communications adviser to GWB
George W. Bush	43rd President of the United States (GWB)
Andrew Card	White House chief of staff
Dick Cheney	Vice President
Bill Clinton	42nd President of the United States
Hillary Clinton	US senator and wife of Bill Clinton
Ari Fleischer	White House press secretary
Karen Hughes	Communications adviser to GWB
Colin Powell	Secretary of State
Condoleezza Rice	National Security Advisor (Condi)
Karl Rove	Senior adviser to GWB
Donald Rumsfeld	Defense Secretary
George Tenet	Director, CIA

International

Kofi Annan	UN Secretary General
Yasser Arafat	President of Palestine
José María Aznar	Prime Minister of Spain
Silvio Berlusconi	Prime Minister of Italy
Osama Bin Laden	Militant Islamist, founder of al-Qaeda (OBL)
Hans Blix	Chief UN weapons inspector
Jacques Chirac	President of France
Jean Chrétien	Prime Minister of Canada
Catherine Colonna	Chirac's press secretary
Mohamed ElBaradei	Director general, International Atomic Energy Agency
Saddam Hussein	President of Iraq (SH)
Lionel Jospin	Prime Minister of France
Hamid Karzai	Chairman of the Afghan Transitional Administration from December 2001
General Pervez Musharraf	President of Pakistan
Mullah Omar	Taliban leader, Afghanistan
Romano Prodi	President, European Commission
Vladimir Putin	President of Russia
Gerhard Schroeder	Chancellor of Germany
Ariel Sharon	Prime Minister of Israel

Hutton Inquiry

Gavyn Davies	BBC chairman
James Dingemans QC	Senior counsel to the inquiry

Greg Dyke	BBC director general
Andrew Gilligan	Reporter for the BBC's *Today* programme
Lord Hutton	Law Lord, former Lord Chief Justice of Northern Ireland
Dr David Kelly	Biological weapons expert, Ministry of Defence
Richard Sambrook	Director of BBC News
Jonathan Sumption QC	AC's, and later government, lawyer at the inquiry

The Labour Party

Douglas Alexander	Minister of State, DTI, and party strategist
Stan Greenberg	US pollster
Glenys Kinnock MEP	Wife of Neil Kinnock
Neil Kinnock	Labour Leader 1983–92
Michael Levy	Businessman, Labour Party fundraiser
Peter Mandelson	Labour MP for Hartlepool, former Cabinet minister
David Triesman	General secretary

Parliament

Iain Duncan Smith	Leader of the (Conservative) Opposition (IDS)
Charles Kennedy	Liberal Democrat Leader
John Major	Former Prime Minister (1990–97)
Margaret Thatcher	Former Prime Minister (1979–90)
Lt Gen Sir Michael Willcocks	Black Rod, House of Lords

The Media

Guy Black	Press Complaints Commission
Adam Boulton	Sky News political editor
Rory Bremner	Impersonator and satirist
Michael Cockerell	BBC political documentary maker
Paul Dacre	*Daily Mail* editor
Richard Desmond	Owner of Express Newspapers
Sir David Frost	Broadcaster
Trevor Kavanagh	*Sun* political editor
Donald Macintyre	*Independent* political commentator
Andrew Marr	BBC political editor

Piers Morgan	*Daily Mirror* editor
Rupert Murdoch	Chairman, News Corporation
Andrew Rawnsley	*Observer* political columnist
John Sergeant	ITN political editor
Rebekah Wade	Editor, *News of the World*
Philip Webster	*Times* political editor
Michael White	*Guardian* political editor
David Yelland	Editor, *Sun*

Family and Friends

Donald and Betty Campbell	Parents of AC
Rory, Calum and Grace Campbell	Children of AC and FM
Alex Ferguson	Friend of AC, manager of Manchester United
Philip Gould	Political pollster and strategist, adviser to TB (PG, Philip)
Audrey Millar	Mother of Fiona
Gail Rebuck	Publisher, wife of Philip Gould

The Diaries

Tuesday, September 11, 2001

I woke up to the usual blah on the radio about TB [Tony Blair, Prime Minister] and the TUC [Trades Union Congress] speech, all the old BBC clichés about us and the unions, the only new thing GMB [trade union] ads asking if you trust TB not to privatise the NHS. Peter H [Hyman, policy adviser and speechwriter] and I went up to the [12 Downing Street] flat. TB had done a good section on public-private, an effective hit back at the John Edmonds [GMB] line. With the economy, public services, Europe/euro and a bit on asylum which was really worrying, we had a proper [TUC] speech. We sharpened it and honed it a bit. He was furious at the GMB ads, said he intended to give Edmonds a real hammering. We finished it on the train to Brighton, were met and driven to the hotel. We were there, up at the top of the hotel putting the finishing touches to the speech, when the attacks on the New York Twin Towers began.

Godric [Smith, deputy press secretary] was watching TV in the little room where the Garden Room[1] girl had set up, came up to the top of the little staircase leading to the bit where TB and I were working, and signalled for me to go down. It was all a bit chaotic, with the TV people going into their usual breathless breaking-news mode, but it was clearly something way out of the ordinary. I went upstairs, turned on the TV and said to TB he ought to watch it. It was now even clearer than just a few moments ago just how massive an event this was. It was also one that was going to have pretty immediate implications for us too. We didn't watch the TV that long, but long enough for TB to reach the judgement about just how massive an event this was in its impact and implications. It's possible we were talking about thousands dead. We would also have to make immediate judgements

[1] Offices of the Downing Street secretarial support

about buildings and institutions to protect here. TB was straight on to the diplomatic side as well, said that we had to help the US, that they could not go it all on their own, that they felt beleaguered and that this would be tantamount to a military attack in their minds. We had to decide whether we should cancel the speech.

There was always a moment in these terrorist outrages where governments said we must not let the terrorists change what we do, but it was meaningless. Of course they changed what we did. At first, we felt it best to go ahead with the speech but by the time we were leaving for the venue, the Towers were actually collapsing. The scale of the horror and the damage was increasing all the time and it was perfectly obvious he couldn't do the speech. We went over to the conference centre, where TB broke the news to [John] Monks [TUC general secretary] and Brendan Barber [Monks' deputy] that he intended to go on, say a few words, but then we would have to head back to London. We would issue the text but he would not deliver the speech. John Monks said to me that it's on days like this that you realise just how big his job is. TB's mind was whirring with it. His brief statement to the TUC went down well, far better than his speech would have done.[1] We walked back to the hotel, both of us conscious there seemed to be a lot more security around. We arranged a series of conference calls through Jonathan [Powell, Chief of Staff] with Jack S [Straw, Foreign Secretary], Geoff Hoon [Defence Secretary], David B [Blunkett, Home Secretary]. We asked [Cabinet Secretary Sir] Richard Wilson to fix a Cobra[2] meeting as soon as we got back.

We set off for Brighton station. He said the consequences of this were enormous. On the train he was subdued, though we did raise a smile when someone said it was the first and last time he would get a standing ovation from the TUC. Robert Hill [TB's political secretary] was listening to the radio on his earpiece and filling us in every now and then. TB asked for a pad and started to write down some of the issues we would have to address when we got back. He said the big fear was terrorists capable of this getting in league with rogue states that would help them. He'd been going on about [Osama]

[1] Blair told trade union delegates 'This mass terrorism is the new evil in our world today. It is perpetrated by fanatics who are utterly indifferent to the sanctity of human life and we, the democracies of this world, are going to have to come together to fight it together and eradicate this evil completely from our world.'

[2] The committee intended to lead responses to national crises; named after the Cabinet Office Briefing Room.

Bin Laden for a while because there had been so much intelligence about him and al-Qaeda. He wanted to commission proper reports on OBL and all the other terror groups. He made a note of the need to reach out to the British Muslim community who would fear a backlash if this was Bin Laden. Everyone seemed convinced it couldn't be anyone else.

We got back and before Cobra he was briefed by Stephen Lander [director general of MI5], John Scarlett [chair of the Joint Intelligence Committee], RW. DTLR [Department of Transport, Local Government and the Regions] had closed airspace over London. There had been special security put around the Stock Exchange and Canary Wharf. The general security alert had been raised to Amber. Three hundred companies were being contacted to be given advice. Scarlett said OBL and his people were the only ones with the capability to do this. Neither he nor Lander believed other governments were involved. TB said we needed a command paper of who they are, why they are, what they do, how they do it. He said at the diplomatic level he felt the US would feel beleaguered and angry because there was so much anti-Americanism around. Lander felt the pressure on the Americans to respond quickly, even immediately, would be enormous. Afghanistan was the obvious place. Iraq, Libya, Iran, the Americans will be trying to find out if they helped in this. He said there were a lot of people sympathetic to Bin Laden, more than we realised. TB said they will move straight away to the international community and their response. If I were [US President George] Bush, I would demand the Taliban deliver him up.

Scarlett and Lander were both pretty impressive, didn't mess about, thought about what they said, and said what they thought. Scarlett said this was less about technology than it was about skill and nerve. Lander said this was a logical step up from the car bomb. Turning a plane into a bomb and destroying one of the great symbols of America takes some doing but they have done it and they have been able to do it because they have any number of terrorists prepared to kill themselves. TB's immediate concern, apart from the obvious logistical steps we had to take, was that Bush would be put under enormous pressure to do something irresponsible. If America heard the general world view develop that this happened because Bush was more isolationist, there would be a reaction. He felt we had to take a lead in mobilising diplomatic solidarity in the rest of the G8 and the EU We had to start shaping an international agenda to fill the vacuum. He spoke to [Chancellor of Germany, Gerhard] Schroeder, who wanted a G8 meeting, [President of France, Jacques] Chirac and [Prime

Minister of France, Lionel] Jospin, who were not so sure, and then [Vladamir] Putin [President of Russia], who had a real 'I told you so' tone, said he had been warning us about Islamic fundamentalism.

TB and I both pressed Scarlett and Lander on why they were so sure there were no rogue governments involved in this. They said because Bin Laden was able to do it himself and that suited his purposes better. We all trooped over to the Cobra meeting, which was a bit ragged, but that was to be expected given what people were having to deal with. There were contingency measures that had gone into effect. Private flights had been stopped. There were no commercial flights to go over the centre of London. All small-plane flights were being grounded unless they had specific clearance. Security was being stepped up around financial centres and major computer sites. The Met [police] were raising numbers on visible patrols, particularly at Canary Wharf, Heathrow and in the North London Jewish areas. We had upped protection on our premises in the Middle East. There was talk of moving some of the planes based at RAF Leuchars to London in the event of a hijack. Jack S said the EU GAC [European General Affairs and External Relations Council] was planning to meet. Geoff Hoon gave a briefing on what troops were where in the Middle East.

TB did a very good summing-up, first going through all the different measures that I should brief, then on the specific reports he wanted to commission, then on the importance of a diplomatic strategy to support the US. He said they would feel beleaguered and all the tensions that had been apparent before would now become more open, whatever the warm words around the world. He asked Jack and Geoff to come through to Number 10, said it was vital that we worked up an international agenda that went beyond the US just hitting Afghanistan. He felt NMD [National Missile Defense] would quickly rise up the agenda.

He intended to say to Bush that he should deliver an ultimatum to the Taliban to hand over Bin Laden and his people and then hit them if it didn't happen. He had been reading the Koran over the summer. [The Prophet] Mohammed had lost battles but there was a belief that if you died in the cause that you believed in then you went straight to heaven. That was a very, very powerful thing to work against. TB's public words were very much in total support of the US. He said this was going to be a nightmare, as big and as bad as any we had endured. It was interesting that he had not asked GB [Gordon Brown, Chancellor of the Exchequer] to come back for the smaller meeting. I asked him why and he said because in their recent discussions he had been monosyllabic. The Israelis were making massive attacks on the terror groups. TB said we were going to have to work exceptionally hard on the international response. Bush was getting it in the neck for not being in Washington.

Everyone was in bed when I finally got home, and Fiona [Millar, AC's partner and adviser to CB] had fallen asleep watching it all on the TV. I did a call with Jonathan to go over how much we would need to kick out of the diary in the coming days. Pretty much all of it, at least for a while. Jonathan said the Americans would be unlikely to let Bush travel – it was a bit much that he couldn't even go to his own capital – but the fallout from this was going to need an awful lot of diplomatic activity. I think we're going to be seeing a lot of the insides of planes, he said.

I turned off the TV in the bedroom and went downstairs to channel-hop while writing it all up. The TUC felt a bloody age ago. Some of the footage of the aftermath, clouds of dust and debris literally rolling down streets, was extraordinary. So were the eyewitness accounts. Gut-wrenching. What was amazing about this was that people like Bush, TB, Chirac and the rest were having to react and respond in exactly the same time frame, and with pretty much only the same knowledge of the incident as people watching on TV. The difference was they were going to have to take some huge decisions about it too.

Wednesday, September 12

Bush did a broadcast at 2am, said all the things you'd expect but looked a bit shaky. TB was generally thought to have handled it well yesterday and also got a fairly good press for the TUC speech that never was. I got in early and read the overnight intelligence reports, everything pointing now to Bin Laden. TB was starting to think about the long term and what to do about the whole terrorism agenda. It had clearly moved up to a different level. The day was taken up almost exclusively with the attack. TB wanted as much information as possible and he wanted to be in a position to work out Bush's likely reaction. He felt it likely that Bush would feel the pressure for an early response. The full enormity of what had happened was only now really sinking in. TB was pretty clear that we would end up going for the Taliban. At Cobra there was a review of the security procedures put in place. RW [Richard Wilson] and others wanted to reopen City Airport but [Stephen] Byers [Transport Secretary] objected and TB, with GB and JS [Jack Straw] in full support, agreed to keep the airport shut and the flyover path over London shut too. GB at Cobra contributed when asked to, but otherwise pretty much sat there, or muttered out of the side of his mouth to Jack. He clearly hated it, possibly hated the fact that TB was so clearly in charge in these crisis management situations.

Lander said that Bin Laden was last thought to be in Kandahar three days ago. John Stevens [Metropolitan Police commissioner] said there were more than a thousand extra police officers on the streets. TB said he had talked to the Governor of the Bank of England [Eddie George] and they were keeping in contact about how to maintain confidence in the financial system, while the supply of oil was also being constantly monitored. Jack said that we should not get ahead of the US in terms of what we say. He felt our best role was to stay close and try to exercise influence privately. Afterwards there was a smaller meeting in TB's office with Richard Dearlove (C) [chief of the Secret Intelligence Service (SIS), MI6], Lander, Hoon, Jack and Kevin Tebbit [permanent secretary, Ministry of Defence]. C said there was a significant international operation going on by us and the Americans and others that he was confident would show who was behind it.

TB commissioned a note on what Bush's options were, saying he had to get inside his mind if he could. Hoon said al-Qaeda tentacles were all over the place – Africa, Chechnya, this wasn't just about Afghanistan. There was also the view that the intelligent thing would be to wait several weeks but TB pointed out things were likely to move much more quickly than that. If the Americans are as convinced as we are that this is Bin Laden, there should be pressure put on to yield him up and if they refuse to co-operate, then he would be entitled to hit them. TB warned, following on from his phone call with Putin, that the Russians would essentially co-opt this whole event as justification for what they were doing in Chechnya. There was a discussion about recalling Parliament.

Later TB saw Scarlett and Lander and others to get a fuller briefing on Afghanistan and Bin Laden and how he operated. One of the experts from the FCO [Foreign and Commonwealth Office], a total Arabist, came very close to saying the attack was justified, saying the Americans should look to their own policy on the Middle East to understand why so many people don't like them. Scarlett said it wasn't clear that OBL controlled all the training camps, but what he did know was that there was a very large supply of young men ready to die for the cause. It was also clear that there were likely to be would-be terrorists here as asylum seekers. Both C and Lander were very good on big picture and detail. They both felt Bush would need a few days for the Americans properly to assess all this stuff. TB and I agreed he should do a press conference, saying that Cabinet would meet tomorrow and Parliament on Friday. We worked on the script and went through various options of how to express the support he would give to Bush, which was pretty full on.

We got a message that Bush wanted to speak to him. It was a good call, Bush was pretty calm and TB very supportive. Bush said he was the first foreign leader he was speaking to and he would value staying in touch. He said the American people would give him a bit of time. TB said there might be a case for a G8. TB went over some of the things he had been saying to us, and Bush said he was grateful for the help and would appreciate if he put some of those thoughts in writing. Bush said the UN and NATO statements were 'useful cover for the work that we would have to do', by which I think he meant continuing intelligence gathering and then attack. He said this was 'a new war, Pearl Harbor in the twenty-first century'. He said these people had to come out of their holes sometime. TB said he felt for him personally and Bush replied 'I know what I've got to do. I'm not a good mourner. I'm a weeper. I'll weep with the country but then act, but I don't just want to hit cruise missiles into the sand.' TB was a bit worried that the longer he waited, the more he would be expected to do.

TB wrote off a note for Bush's eyes only, which spelled out some of the problems we were facing and where Bush might go to build useful alliances. I felt Bush was almost Zen-like, almost too calm. Maybe he had decided he could wait longer than we thought. TB was sure we would need to do a lot more than just take out OBL. There was a second Cobra meeting with another discussion about whether to lift some of the restrictions. John Stevens said that the casualty figures were very vague but the UK casualties could be up to a thousand. TB agreed we should get out the possibility that figures could go into the hundreds. TB and Blunkett had a meeting on asylum with DB pushing hard for ID cards and detention centres. The general feeling was that TB was doing well. He was constantly telling us about bits of the Koran. Earlier we got the Muslim Council to condemn the attacks. Ben Wilson [press officer] started in the press office. What a day to start.

Thursday, September 13

TB's worry was that GWB would turn inwards. He had sensed a bit of resistance to the G8 idea, which he felt was a big mistake. He felt now was the time to bind in as much international support as possible. He felt a big military hit combined with a big international effort of support and a long-term agenda for terrorism was the way to go. There was a whole load more intelligence all pointing towards OBL.

We went through to the Cobra meeting where we agreed we could wind down the emergency response. TB's note to Bush was strong but he was not sure he would be receptive. TB had a meeting pre Cabinet with Jack S, Geoff [Hoon], [Admiral Sir Michael] Boyce [Chief of the Defence Staff, CDS] – who had replaced [General Sir Charles] Guthrie. I felt that with all the focus on the States, there was a danger we would neglect the Brits involved, and the fallout, which would be substantial, so suggested Tessa [Jowell, Culture Secretary] be used to sort out all that logistically etc. but also to be a kind of minister for helping families and victims. Jack was worried it would cut across the FCO stuff but I felt it needed a specific minister, specifically deputed. The Palace played the US national anthem at the Changing of the Guard while Prince Charles was visiting the embassy to sign the condolence book.

Cabinet was very sombre, though Clare [Short, International Development Secretary] did her usual bit. TB was very much in charge. He said it was an act carried out in America which should be seen as an attack on the democratic world. Of the thousands killed, he feared several hundred would be British. He said all the evidence pointed to OBL. He said long term there had to be a strategy for dealing with Islamic fundamentalism but for the moment the focus was on finding the perpetrators, putting in place the security measures needed here, and assessing the financial implications for the world economy.

Jack went through the diplomatic activity, said the UNSC [United Nations Security Council] had been easier to mobilise than the EU in some respects. On security, he said the problem was security is only as good as the weakest link. Blunkett went through all that was being done to protect public buildings, big computer installations and infrastructure sites. He said suicide bombers are notoriously difficult to plan for. He pointed out, as did others, the importance of reaching out to decent British Muslims. TB said there were three areas to focus on – whatever US military response is made, and our participation within it. Politics and diplomacy and in particular trying to get impetus into the Middle East peace process [MEPP]. And practical security arrangements. Clare said the real problem was lack of progress in the Middle East, the fact that so many people were willing to be suicide bombers, and she asked if we had the will to improve life for the Arab world. Patricia [Hewitt, Trade and Industry Secretary] briefed on oil and energy supplies, and was fairly confident. It was a good meeting, and I think people sensed TB was going to have an important role, not just here. Jack was doing fine on the media but agreed we would need to broaden the field.

TB and I then spent a while working on his statement for tomorrow, though getting the right balance and tone would be the hard bit. Both Hilary Armstrong [chief whip] and Robert Hill warned him that the PLP [Parliamentary Labour Party] may be a bit dodgy on this and TB said 'Are they mad? Do we just let these people get away with killing thousands of people?' He said if this had been on British soil, just imagine the pressure for a swift response. Jonathan had brought in some interesting books on the Taliban which we were trying to read in addition to the material being provided by the spooks. TB sent a message to all Arab leaders. We did a TB article for about fifty regional newspapers in areas with large numbers of Muslims. There was the beginning of talk in the States about how TB's response was better than Bush's, which made him a bit anxious, and he recalled how [former US President Bill] Clinton had got a bit jumpy during Kosovo.

Friday, September 14

David Manning [Blair's newly appointed senior foreign policy adviser], who had been in the States at the time of the attacks, was now back. Quite a baptism. He gave a very good assessment of where the various bits of the American set-up were. He felt Bush was being fairly restrained but at some point that would stop. We had a meeting with TB, C, Lander, Francis Richards [director] of GCHQ [Government Communications Headquarters, intelligence monitoring agency]. Everything pointed to OBL, training camps, possibly some help from the Taliban. The US clearly believed there was real evidence but we agreed it would not be possible to publish much of it. We left for the Commons, got the tone of the statement right and went over the difficult questions. TB did fine. IDS [Iain Duncan Smith, new leader of the Conservative Party] was OK but there were too many clichés and not enough smart questions. TB felt he was perfectly bright but lacking in real imagination. Our backbenchers were fine, and the Tories and Lib Dems basically onside for the approach he set out. TB was sure that ultimatum followed by attack if no response was the right way. Anji [Hunter, head of Downing Street presentation and planning] took a call from Will Farish, the new US ambassador [to London], specifically inviting some of us to the service at St Paul's. We travelled up with Richard Wilson and John Gieve [permanent secretary, Home Office] and ended up in the front row, which was a bit embarrassing. [John] Major, [Margaret] Thatcher and [James] Callaghan [former Prime Ministers] were all there. GB was sitting next to IDS. It was a nice service. I chatted with Jamie Rubin [former

US State Department chief spokesman, 1997–2000] at the end, who said the American right would use this as an excuse to do all sorts of things right round the world. Be very careful of these people, he said.

Back at Number 10, TB, Jonathan, David Manning and I had a session pre TB's phone call with Bush. TB was worried by the reluctance to have a G8, felt it showed they were looking inwards when they should be looking outwards. They should be using now to bind in Russia and France. He also felt we had to do more to bind in Pakistan, who were going to be absolutely vital in all this. The call took place at 1.45. It was clear that the wobbly Bush of the last call had become the hawk again. He said this was a war and they would win. They wanted OBL dead or alive. Afterwards TB seemed a bit alarmed, said 'My God, fasten your seatbelts.' He said people would understand Afghanistan, but if he went for Afghanistan and Iraq together, it would be absolute madness. He was quite troubled, said we had to think of a way of getting to the US for a face-to-face meeting. He said he needed to see him in a room, and look in his eyes, not do all this on phone calls with fifteen people listening in. Bush would be getting lots of conflicting advice, and TB said he could sense that in the change of tone from call to call. We had to persuade Bush that we had to go for OBL and the Taliban but if he went for Iraq the Russians and the French would peel off. He asked DM to make sure he stayed in permanent contact with Condi [Condoleezza Rice, US National Security Advisor] and make sure they did nothing too rash. We got over Geoff H, Jack S and CDS.

TB went through his assessment of the US plan – ultimatum to yield up OBL and then let outside body move in to get rid of the camps. Alternatively, hit OBL straight away possibly going for the Taliban. And the next step is to look to other countries, including Iraq, and other countries not even linked to OBL. He said their instinct was to resolve the WMD [weapons of mass destruction] question quickly. We needed to consider what such a strategy would be and what part we would play in it. He said his advice very strongly will be to deal with Afghanistan very distinctively, whereas to go for Iraq would be certain to lose Russia and France from any international support. He said they had definitely moved to action mode but we still had an opportunity to mould things in the right direction. He said he was confident he could persuade him that to go beyond Afghanistan for four countries at once was World War territory.

CDS asked if there was any indication of how they intended to hit Afghanistan. TB was not aware they were currently planning anything beyond missile attacks. Geoff said there had been talk of special forces going into Afghanistan. CDS said it was possible to attack mountain camps as a way of showing we were not scared of putting our boots on their soil. Geoff said [Donald] Rumsfeld [US Defense Secretary] had been looking for reasons to hit Iraq. They definitely wanted regime change and that was the channel of advice that Bush had been getting since the election. Jack said they would be mad to do Iraq without justification because they will lose world opinion. TB said 'My job is to try to steer them in a sensible path.' He said we had to separate these two missions. He said their line of argument will be that it does not matter whether you did the Trade Center, if you are in the business of terrorism, then we are going to put you out of business. It's possible to be sympathetic to that but the political consequences are all too obvious. We cannot ignore that's where they are. We are talking very big issues here. He said even in the most benign circumstances this is going to be difficult.

TB said they all needed to keep in close touch with opposite numbers. He was worrying about which camp would be having most influence on Bush. We also agreed it might be sensible for Guthrie to go to see [General Pervez] Musharraf [President of Pakistan]. TB said afterwards he felt Bush was getting bad advice, that we had the right strategy and we had to persuade him of that. He would feel so much better if he could see him face to face. It was a bit alarming just how different the two calls had been. After the first, TB was worried he wasn't doing enough, and now he was talking about taking out anyone who might harbour terrorists. TB asked CDS to refine the paper on military options. Ed Richards [senior policy adviser on media business issues] came to see me about Gavyn Davies[1] getting the BBC chairmanship, which was likely to break next week.

Saturday, September 15

The aftermath of the attacks was still totally dominating the media, stories moving more to the human tragedy as well as the diplomacy. TB had a meeting first thing with C, Lander, [Francis] Richards, Scarlett, Wilson, Jonathan, Manning and me. They kept saying there was more and more evidence pointing to OBL. But as TB and I agreed later, nothing that would stand up in a court of law. There was real unease among our side now, that the Americans would do something to fracture the coalition that was being built up. Scarlett said there

[1] Goldman Sachs economist, unofficial policy adviser to Blair, and husband of Sue Nye, personal aide to Gordon Brown.

was evidence of real tensions in Pakistan. Lander reported three people arrested with false passports at Gatwick. Manning said Colin Powell [US Secretary of State] had spoken to Jack and sounded worried. There was no doubt some in the US had an agenda, led by Rumsfeld and Paul Wolfowitz [Deputy Defense Secretary], to see this as a revenge against Iraq for not finishing the Gulf War. Lander briefed TB on some of the difficulties we were facing on the issue of people using the UK to plan terrorism. TB just sat shaking his head when he told him about someone who we knew to be planning terror in India, that this was accepted by the tribunal, but we couldn't kick him out. We discussed the need for changes to human rights law and civil liberties. DM had mentioned to Condi that TB thought they should meet soon. TB, Jonathan and I were all casually dressed. The spooks were all in dark suits and carrying their battered briefcases. TB said to them, if I didn't know you were all so young, I'd say there was a generational gap.

He felt he should probably see Schroeder on Wednesday, Chirac Thursday, then the US. He called a couple of times later when I was out running, was now at that stage where he was testing his own thoughts by constantly setting out the same position and trying to find weaknesses. It was basically ultimatum, act, follow-through short, medium and long term. But we would need to be building support at every stage and he was obviously worried about the American capacity on that front. TB was getting a good press here and even more so overseas, especially the States. I couldn't help thinking that though this was a total disaster, and was going to wipe out chunks of his domestic diary, if leadership was important, here was a real opportunity to show it. The Sundays arrived, wall to wall on the attacks. The main live news story was Bush's meeting at Camp David, where he said the US must get ready for war and that OBL was the prime suspect. TB was getting a good press, GWB a bad press. [James] Naughtie's second instalment [of his serialised Blair/Brown book, *The Rivals*] was running which focused on me, and GB's fears about my diary.

Sunday, September 16

TB was doing CNN so I went in for a pre-meeting with him and David Manning. DM said they were looking at an ultimatum followed by a 48- or 72-hour wait. The noises from the Taliban were getting more and more aggressive. Thousands of refugees were pouring over the border. Pakistan was clearly going to have a hard time whatever. Robin [Cook, former Foreign Secretary, now Leader of the House of

Commons] was on *Frost* for us and the BBC were really pissed off that TB did CNN. It was a good interview. We went over all the really tough questions, but a few of them never came. I had an argument with CNN who were initially refusing to release the whole interview to other broadcasters but in the end they did.

TB said he sensed Bush would end up in the right place, that some of the stuff on the phone calls had clearly been for the benefit of internal consumption, which was why he really wanted to meet him soon, without anyone else there. 'I hope to God he's not listening to some of the people round him, because we need to be wary of them.' He was more confident. Chirac was pretty clear that they could hit Afghanistan but no further. Schroeder was in a bit of a problem at home and not quite so strong. Jospin was all over the shop because of his coalition [government] situation and Chirac was going to make it as hard for him as he could. TB wanted to get a message of support for Musharraf. He later called me to say we must get out the message about how closely the Americans were consulting us, as whatever they thought about them, that would make the other Europeans want to get closer.

Monday, September 17

Up to the flat to see TB and told him that the US were suggesting that he went to Congress with Bush. 'Oh yeah,' said TB. I said it was serious and I was worried about it because it would play into the whole poodle thing. John Kerr [permanent secretary, Foreign and Commonwealth Office] called to say it would be ghastly, that the whole thing would become an orgy of US patriotism, with TB in a kind of nod-along role. I felt we should only do it if TB also spoke, but wasn't sure if that was even doable. Charles Clarke [Labour Party chairman] told him later that there were real anxieties around about Bush and that people around the world saw TB as the only person who could restrain him. He said it was an awesome responsibility. Clare Short had gone on [Andrew] Rawnsley's [BBC Radio 4 *Westminster Hour*] programme last night and had said something that let them write government split and tension headlines. TB later wrote to her. He was really angry, said it sent exactly the wrong signal to the Taliban about our seriousness of intent. Jack and I had a long chat before his *Today* programme interview and agreed he should move the story on by echoing the line on OBL and saying that we had our own evidence that all pointed his way.

TB spoke to Musharraf later who said the risks he was taking were real and he needed real help. He seemed keen on the suggestion of

Guthrie going out. At the 8.30 intelligence meeting, there was no real knowledge of where OBL was. Lander reported on some of the people under surveillance here. There was a really gloomy mood. There was talk from the US of concerns that OBL had acquired some kind of basic nuclear capability, and worries of a possible chemical, biological or radiological attack. At TB's military meeting, Geoff Hoon and CDS were both focusing on the difficulties of any military offensive. Boyce was very unlike Guthrie as CDS, who had always been pretty can-do. Boyce was quite soft-spoken, very polite, but I wondered if he wasn't something of a fellow depressive. Geoff said he had had some difficult chats with Rumsfeld. CDS said only six per cent of Afghans have electricity. They don't even have fuel dumps that we would recognise as such. There's nothing really there, very few targets. TB said they had to know that we would hurt them if they don't yield up OBL. David Manning said we had to do more to help the Northern Alliance.[1] Lander and CDS said the heroin trail should also be hit. They said more people had been killed by heroin than died last Tuesday.

We were now planning a series of visits for TB, Berlin, Paris, Washington, New York. He was worried about Congress unless he spoke. Then came news there would be an EU summit on Friday. All a bit of a nightmare. TB had lunch with [Italian Prime Minister Silvio] Berlusconi who was wearing a pile of make-up and his hair was dyed jet black. He was reasonably supportive on the idea of military action 'provided not too many people die'. TB said there was no such thing as a painless war. He said either the US will see the international community rallying to them or there will be a battle internally and the isolationists will win. His worry was people show support up to the point where the shooting starts. He said we had to divide this into two – Afghanistan, and the broader terrorist apparatus. In respect of the second part, the decisions are for the long term.

Berlusconi emphasised that we had to make clear this was not a war against Islam. TB said it was important we got Arab countries as part of our coalition. The best signal of all would be a restart of the Middle East peace process. There was a real risk that [Israeli Prime Minister Ariel] Sharon sees this as an opportunity to say that [Palestinian leader Yasser] Arafat equals OBL. He said it was important we all made clear to Israel this should not be an opportunity to settle scores but on the contrary we should have the objective of reinvigorating the peace process. There was something very odd about Berlusconi. He didn't seem quite in control of his body, his arm

[1] The coalition of disparate opponents of the Taliban.

movements were a bit weird and most of the time he addressed himself to the interpreter rather than TB. They had a fairly lacklustre discussion on Europe and the euro. The Federal Reserve cut interest rates while they were having lunch. TB then had a big Africa meeting and we had a discussion of sorts on his [party] conference speech.

Sandy Berger [former National Security Advisor to Bill Clinton] was in town. He was looking a lot thinner, younger and happier, said he was exercising five days a week. He felt TB was doing well, that a position of total support was the best because he could influence from that position in private. He felt TB had a lot of respect because of our experience re the IRA and we should be saying this is not a war that you just win or lose, but a war you constantly manage. The New York Stock Exchange reopened but the economic impact was growing.

Tuesday, September 18

TB was at Chequers for a meeting with a group of officers. He had a chat with Jiang Zemin [Chinese premier]. He was getting a very good press as a kind of international interlocutor. Bush was going down pretty badly everywhere apart from the States. We were getting more and more work done on the nature of the Taliban. There was a bit of a discussion as to whether it was the kind of trip Cherie [Blair, TB's wife] should go on. I did the morning meeting. Geoff Hoon was doing fine. Tessa told me relatives were getting more and more angry but not with us so much as with the general situation. GB went up after interest rate cuts and the economic scene was getting more and more difficult. I started work on a note for Karen Hughes [AC's opposite number in the White House] about the system we had put in place for Kosovo. If anything, this situation was going to be even more complicated and difficult. There were a stack of meetings to plan visits, particularly the US. I was really worried about him looking like a poodle at Congress. There was to be a church service and also a visit to 'Ground Zero'. The main news story of the day was the toing and froing of the Taliban about whether to hand over OBL. They prevaricated by saying 'clerics' would decide.

TB saw Guthrie to brief him on his mission to see Musharraf. I suggested he tell him that his visit was the first step towards Britain moving to Pakistan-style rule. TB did the World Service, trying to push the line that the coalition was strengthening. David Blunkett was round for dinner. He was a bit down about the whole asylum mess and was vicious about the inability of the Home Office to do what we asked them to. He was convinced reception centres and ID cards were the answer. He said he hoped TB would stay for a long time but also asked when I thought JP [John Prescott, Deputy Prime Minister] would go. I asked if he ever thought he could be leader of the Labour Party. He said no, he could be deputy. Deputy leader or deputy PM with a department? He laughed. It was basically the latter, and I imagine he wanted it fed back. He believed we had lost our way a bit and were slightly losing the plot on public services but he was very pro TB at the moment. He said [Alan] Milburn [Health Secretary] was probably the best current bet as a non-GB [leadership] candidate. The anti-Bush feeling in the press was getting way over the top. The liberal press was revolting, the *Mirror* moronic, the *Mail* poisonous.

Wednesday, September 19

I went to see TB who was with Jack Straw discussing MEPP and saying farewell to [John] Sawers.[1] John was telling him he was going to the Middle East and he didn't want Michael Levy [Lord Levy, Labour fund-raiser, Blair's personal envoy to the Middle East], anywhere near him. I was winding up Jack [a supporter of Burnley's local rivals, Blackburn Rovers] about Burnley's latest win – eight out of nine – when Geoff Hoon and CDS came in, looking grave. CDS said that on a very unofficial net he had got hold of what the Pentagon were proposing – Tomahawks followed by 1,000 missiles raining down on various targets. He was very sceptical, said it sounded basically political and it would mean hitting a lot of sand. TB was keen for their take on what we should advise them militarily. He said he was clear what needed to be advised diplomatically but we needed to give them a military plan too. CDS felt what was needed was surgical strikes and special forces.

Then to a broader meeting with C, Lander, Scarlett, GH, JS, CDS, RW and our lot. Depressing. Lander felt that if there was a big attack we just could not predict the response. He said there was a definite rise in Islamophobia since the attacks. Nobody had a clue where OBL was and nobody was hopeful about finding out. They were also checking whether the Pennsylvania plane [United Airlines Flight 93] had been designated to hit a nuclear power plant.[2] There were quite

[1] Sawers, Blair's foreign affairs adviser, had been appointed UK ambassador to Egypt.

[2] The intended target of the hijacked plane remains unclear. It has been assumed that the four terrorists intended to crash into Washington's Capitol building, or perhaps the White House. The most likely nuclear power plant would have been Three Mile Island, south of Harrisburg, Pennsylvania. However, passengers, aware of attacks on the World Trade Center and Pentagon, overwhelmed the hijackers. The Boeing 757 crashed in a field at Stonycreek, Pennsylvania, killing all forty-four people on board.

a few OBL people in the UK and Europe and they understood they were currently planning attacks. We were also worried that Bush's 'dead or alive, head on platter' type of rhetoric would not be helping in Pakistan, which had the potential to be a tinderbox.

We could only get at Mullah [Mohammed] Omar [Taliban leader] and OBL with Taliban and Pakistan co-operation and even that was doubtful unless we gave them Kashmir. As the discussion wore on, CDS finally articulated what I had been thinking – namely that we had to start to prepare people for a very long-term operation, possibly taking years and years. OBL was travelling most of the time. There was no sign of a shift in the Taliban's position and any plan to divide them would take an age. I asked whether there was a public enemy number three, four, five so that the focus and the judgement wasn't solely on whether we got OBL.

Afterwards, I had a meeting with another expert just back from Islamabad, who said that the only thing OBL feared was the opprobrium of clerics. He could not care less about Western opinion because he hated the West. He said OBL had a tough, nasty, dedicated group of people around him which was virtually impossible to penetrate. They were ultra careful, especially in their travel and communications. He could probably slip to Pakistan but it was unlikely. He agreed with the guy on CNN yesterday who said the only way to get to OBL was through saying, and getting clerics to say, that he was not Islamic, that what he was doing was contrary to Islam.

TB saw some of the delivery ministers and had a meeting on Railtrack before we set off for RAF Northolt.[1] I told him what Blunkett had said about being deputy leader. He said JP had said that if it helped with Gordon he would stay on. JP was pretty down on GB at the moment, said he had told him he would support him if he sorted himself out but not if he carried on the way he was. TB admitted there was a part of him that felt it would be irresponsible to back GB for the succession. On Bush, TB said he's basically bright but he's just not good with words.

We flew out to Berlin and TB and [Gerhard] Schroeder spent most of the meeting one-on-one with an interpreter. They did a brief doorstep together, and Schroeder was very strong, considering how difficult this was for him with less than one in three Germans supporting military response, but he said he was keen to lead them towards it.

[1] Railtrack plc, the company operating much of Britain's rail infrastructure, had been bailed out by the government after reporting a huge loss following extensive repairs to the network – a result of the Hatfield rail crash in 2000. It was about to be placed in administration by Transport Secretary Stephen Byers.

He gave a very good description of his own situation and felt they had to be part of the response. But for sixteen years, he said, the SPD [Social Democratic Party of Germany] was basically a peace party. Ditto the Greens. The churches were against war and culturally it was very difficult for them to go for conflict but he felt they had to. He said his situation was very different to Britain. 'You have polls where seventy-five per cent condemn the attacks and seventy-five per cent say yes to action. We have seventy-five per cent condemn the attacks but thirty per cent saying yes to action.' He was pretty relaxed and philosophical about it. We had dinner up at the top of the new swanky building that housed his new office [the Bundeskanzleramt, eight times larger than the White House], much nicer than Bonn, with great views. He talked about his own political situation. He could always go for a grand coalition but he preferred what he had and said he owed a lot to [Joschka] Fischer [Green politician, Vice Chancellor and minister for foreign affairs in Schroeder's coalition government] because he took the Greens with him. They had a bizarre love-hate relationship but they basically knew they could rely on Fischer. He said that whilst TB was building a coalition of nations, he had quite enough to do in building a coalition inside Germany.

He was much more likeable when he was open and expansive, as he was on Europe as well as Afghanistan. He had nice friendly eyes, a warm smile and easy manner, and seemed to understand and appreciate the scale of what TB was trying to do. His lovely interpreter was with him who told me not to lose any more weight. I was definitely becoming addicted to running. We got back on board the 146 to a message that Cherie had spoken to Laura Bush [George Bush's wife] who was keen for her to go to Washington. Flew to Paris.

Thursday, September 20

Paris. Up for a run in the embassy gym. Over breakfast, TB set out the approach he intended to take with Chirac, the need to separate the short-term response from the long-term agenda to deal with the deeper problems. Chirac had coincidentally been to the States and Catherine Colonna [his spokeswoman] suggested it had been helpful in that he had got a real sense of how deep it went for the Americans. For a while, he would probably curb his basic anti-American feelings. It was clear he wanted to be involved but it was also likely the Americans had remained suspicious. They did a brief doorstep together and there was a flurry of excitement because TB said at one point 'within the next few days' and we had a major job to smooth it over, make clear he was talking diplomatic not military.

We headed for the plane to meet up with Cherie, the rest of the staff and the press corps coming with us to New York. I had just about finished the note I was doing for Karen [Hughes] setting out the need for really tight co-ordination structures between all the key players, and the need for a really thought-through strategy for reaching moderate, mainstream Muslim opinion. Before dinner, TB had a long session with C and the military planners. They were looking at specific targets based on information they had obviously garnered from their various discussions with opposite numbers. What was very clear was that the US were well advanced. These were detailed plans. After an hour or so with them, TB said at least he got the sense that these guys knew what they were doing. I had a good chat with C, who said that in some ways the brave thing would be to do nothing, hold tight until we were absolutely sure of where OBL was. I was worried that the focus was so much on OBL that success or failure would be judged solely according to that.

TB did a briefing on the plane, cranking up the sense we were heading towards action and playing up solidarity with the US. TB worked on a new note for Bush with two aims – first, bringing OBL and al-Qaeda to justice, and second, going after international terrorism in all its forms. The ultimatum, and help for the Northern Alliance, remained central. He felt we should use air strikes to demolish the camps, support the NA, gather intelligence to designate high-value targets, hit the drugs trail, go for OBL, strong forward base in Uzbekistan and the Afghan border, a deal for Pakistan, help Musharraf, help Afghan people, new relations with Iran, support from Russia and Arabs. He set out too a number of things in the practical fight against terrorism – the disruption of groups from their travel. Extradition laws. He said we needed: 1. an integrated and streamlined military planning operation, binding in other allies too; 2. detailed work on the long-term agenda; 3. a well-staffed US–UK-led propaganda team, and 4. the political, military and media operations linked between us.

We landed in New York and though we had an escort, the combination of bad weather, dreadful traffic and continuing post-September 11 chaos meant that sadly we had to cancel the visit to a fire station. I was able to rescue it a bit when Clinton agreed to go instead of TB and take Cherie with him. TB was getting frantic because we were so late but we finally reached St Thomas' Church and then a mild panic because there were suggestions that the reading, which had been suggested to me by Paddy Feeny [Tessa Jowell's press officer], was not appropriate because it was about bereavement and some of the people there did not believe they had yet lost their loved ones. It suggested they were all emotionally shot to pieces. TB was in the front row with CB, Kofi Annan [United Nations Secretary General], Bill and Chelsea [Clinton]. TB's reading[1] went fine as did the message read out by [UK ambassador Sir Christopher] Meyer from the Queen, including the brilliant line 'Grief is the price we pay for love.' Bill C asked me if I wrote it. I said I'd love to take credit, but no. He said find the guy who did, and hire him.

After the national anthems we had a brief meeting with Bill and Kofi who both warned of real dangers from Pakistan if we weren't careful. Then we were taken up to the room where all the relatives were gathered. The contrast, the moment you entered the room, was palpable. We had been engaged in the normal diplomatic chat that goes on even in these circumstances, humour included, and now into this dreadful, dreadful atmosphere, haunted eyes, faces drained of blood, lips quivering. Most said it was all made worse by the fact they had no bodies to take home. Most carried pictures which they showed to TB and Bill as they moved through the room. Bill was absolutely terrific when he stood in for TB at the fire station. By now we were running really late and I felt terrible constantly reminding TB, but it was impossible to leave without him going round to speak to everyone. And they all just wanted to pour out their stories. These were in the main just ordinary people caught up in one of the most extraordinary things ever to hit anyone.

We finally got out to the airport and discovered that all the press luggage was being thoroughly searched so we were delayed even further. Meyer was next to useless at trying to cut through it. David Manning was on the phone trying to organise helicopters and warning them how late we might be. TB said he wanted a real inquiry into how we had managed to get into a situation where we spent half an hour sitting on a fucking plane while the president was in Washington waiting for us. Meanwhile Jonathan sent Meyer off the deep end when he had told him that the White House had said the meeting was one plus three, and TB wanted Jonathan, David Manning and me. Meyer threw an absolute tantrum, said he would be a laughing stock in Washington, threatened to resign on the spot. Jonathan did his usual

[1] Blair read a passage from *The Bridge of San Luis Rey*, a 1927 novel by American author Thornton Wilder. Prefacing the reading, Blair said 'We wanted to be here today, to offer our support and sympathy to the families of the lost ones. Many are British. Amid the enormity of what has happened to America, nobody will forget that this was the worst terrorist attack on British citizens in my country's history.'

unflappable bit, just let him let off steam and eventually it was resolved by David M asking Condi if she could slip in an extra place. It was all a bit silly and as TB said, leaders couldn't give two tosses which officials from the other side were there, but it made sense to him to have the three people he would be working most closely with not just here but everywhere.

When we landed, we headed straight to the White House to be met by GWB, Powell, Condi and Dan Fried [senior director for European and Eurasian affairs, National Security Council]. We were taken upstairs to one of the bigger rooms and TB went over to the corner with Bush and they clearly embarked straight away on a very tough conversation. He said later it had started fine, GWB saying how dreadful the events had been but now something good had to come out of it. The focus was OBL and the Taliban and tonight when he spoke to Congress he was going to deliver the ultimatum. But he also talked about how they could go after Saddam's [Saddam Hussein, President of Iraq] oilfields. TB emphasised the need for a measured response. Jonathan said later it was funny how [Margaret] Thatcher had gone to see Bush Senior to say 'This is no time to wobble' while TB was visiting Bush Junior – 'This IS a time to wobble.'

We went through for the dinner, scallops, veal, salad, Bush and TB doing most of the talking. Powell, Condi, Fried, Jonathan, DM and me, with Meyer stuck on the end desperately taking notes. I couldn't work out if he was embarrassed or not by his tantrum. Bush was pretty much directing the conversation, said he was grateful for our support, said Britain was a true friend and we were going to win. He said anyone could join the coalition provided they understood the doctrine – that we were going after terrorists and all who harbour them. Obviously the wider the coalition the better, but they were going to do this anyway. When the scallops arrived, there was a thin ring of pastry on top which he picked up and said 'God dang, what on earth is that?' The waiter said it was a scallop. He said to him it looks like a halo and you are the angel. I think he meant the waiter. It was a bit alarming how loudly they all laughed, including Powell, at his jokes, like when he said he wouldn't do questions at the doorstep because he had his speech later and he was never allowed to say more than one thing a day. I sensed sometimes he was taking the Mickey out of himself, other times out of his team.

When he chose to be serious, he was fine. He said it was interesting Putin himself made sure the Russians didn't react last week, a clear sign the Cold War was over. Both he and Powell were really worried about Pakistan and wanted TB's take on how best to help. When we were talking about Uzbekistan, he said some of their people were 'throat cutters extraordinaire' then said don't write that down, then said if it ever came out he would say it was Powell, and they all started laughing again. He said they were going to go for the Taliban after the ultimatum, said the country was run by a bunch of nuts and we had to get a new government in there. He said he had really beaten up on Sharon who was clearly trying to use this to go after Arafat. 'I said Arafat is not Bin Laden and you do nothing.' Putin wanted to use it to go after Chechnya even harder. He said they feared Hollywood was the next target because it was high-profile, Jewish and decadent. They also had intelligence they would go for Air Force One [presidential plane]. He talked us through a fairly graphic account of what happened, how he was told of the first attack at the meeting at the school and he thought it was an accident at first, then how Andy Card [White House chief of staff] whispered to him about the second attack and said to him 'America is under attack, sir,' and he said he knew there and then this might be the biggest challenge he ever faced. We agreed the need for written shared objectives and a big public information campaign stressing the long haul.

He told the story of one day when he was playing volleyball and his dad came in and said they had got [Manuel] Noriega [dictator overthrown following US invasion of Panama] and it was 'like VE Day' and the truth was it had never just been about Noriega. On Iraq, he said there was no point denying there were differences in the administration. TB said it was easy to sense that every time the subject came up. Reading between the lines, I sensed Bush was with the doves but he enjoyed teasing Powell. I think the mood might have been different if Cheney and Rumsfeld had been there.

TB talked about the need to be sure of his ground, that we needed public opinion with us the whole time. Bush said yes, but when I am speaking tough I'm speaking to Middle America, most of whom have never heard of Bin Laden, they just know someone attacked their country and killed their fellow citizens, and they say hey, Mister President, go get someone and why ain't you done it the day before yesterday? He was in some ways much more impressive than the image, and very straightforward and self-deprecating, which is always a good trait in a leader, but the cumulative effect of the jokes, the asides and the trivial points left you feeling a bit uneasy by the end. It was the cowboy bit. He did, however, as he had over Putin when we first met, show signs of adaptability and intelligence. When TB said he had spoken to [Mohammed] Khatami [President of Iran] on the plane, Bush laughed out loud, assumed it was a joke. But when

TB said he was sending Jack S to Iran on Monday, Bush suddenly got serious, discussed Iran in some detail and then set out the kind of message he would like Jack to deliver. TB was making a point of praising Powell. He was going to be key in keeping strategy on the right track. It was still hard to work out who was calling the shots.

Bush was also graphic on the sophistication of the attacks and the technical ability of the pilot who hit the Pentagon. He seemed to have a certain admiration for the fanatic. Said the timing and the execution were sophisticated, brilliant. He said there are Muslims so dedicated they are prepared to drink to pretend to people around them they are not Muslims. They did a brief doorstep, TB fielding most of the questions and then he and GWB went up to the Bush flat before heading out to Congress. Bush and TB travelled together in the presidential limo. Jonathan, DM, Meyer and I were taken up to the First Lady's box, with the press gallery to our right, the Congress down below. TB came in with Laura, [Rudolph] Giuliani [mayor of New York], [George] Pataki [governor of New York] and the guy who was going to be the new homeland security minister [governor of Pennsylvania, Tom Ridge]. It was all a bit Politburo, standing ovations constantly interrupting the speech, rapturous applause for good lines, off the radar if they were really good. Because TB was next to Laura, he had to get up every single time that she did, which was every time anybody else did. Anji was watching me from the other side of the gallery and said I looked like I had swallowed a lemon. It was grim. Poodle-ology gone mad. But it was an excellent speech for all that, very well crafted. The story was ultimatum and telling the US troops to be ready. We met up with Bush afterwards, and he gave TB an enormous bear hug. This was getting worse. He was very warm to me as well but I couldn't wait to get out. Things hadn't been made easier by a couple of dreadful conversations with Fiona who said she could see Kosovo coming all over again, and I'd never be there. TB was drained by the whole thing. He kipped a bit on the drive out to the plane. We had a bit of debrief and TB said I had to seize the opportunity to co-ordinate strategy. It was now 4am UK time and everyone was shagged out. I slept most of the way back.

Friday, September 21

TB liked the note I had given to Karen Hughes and wanted me to get going on it. C wanted a copy, saying there was all manner of stuff they could do with us. We landed in Brussels and drove to [UK ambassador to the EU Sir Nigel] Sheinwald's residence. Stryker McGuire called from *Newsweek* and said there was a buzz going round that someone had overheard one of our people saying it was all a bit of a disaster, Bush was really alarming and planning to do far more than we wanted. I just about persuaded him it wouldn't have been any of the key people. But I agreed with Godric I should probably do a briefing, and we also pushed the line about changing UK law on terrorism. I was trying to pull them back from the sense of imminent military action. I went for a run and then back from TB's TV interviews where he was very good on the empathy and some of the personal stories from New York.

The summit [European Council emergency meeting on terrorism] was straightforward enough, and the text OK. TB wanted me to work on the US press to get them to see it as significant. Jack arrived and agreed to do the press conference rather than TB, who, thank God, wanted to leave early. I got home about midnight. Chris Patten [former Conservative Cabinet minister, now a European commissioner] hitched a lift back with us and said he was really worried about the Tories now but resisted my blandishments about defecting. The trip had gone well. TB was getting an amazing press at the moment. GWB had also turned things around with his speech which most of our media thought was very powerful, and some printed the whole thing in full.

Saturday, September 22

We were really just in military build-up mode now, plus I was keen to get coverage in the mainstream media for what we were trying to do to reach Muslims at home and abroad. TB called from Chequers and clearly thought now we should probably go to Pakistan. We set off for Norwich vs Burnley and met Charles Clarke and family for lunch. Charles felt that our politics were fine and TB was getting real strength out of this. He felt Clare should have been sacked years ago, that he never saw why Neil [Kinnock, former Labour leader] tolerated her and the same went for TB. Almost two weeks on now, the media was still totally dominated by the attacks, particularly now the anti-terror laws and military build-up. I did a conference call for the ministers on programmes tomorrow stressing that we praise Pakistan and talk up OBL as being un-Islamic. We lost 2–1. Generally, I felt the mood was pretty good considering. Certainly no grief and if anything a sense that TB had done well. The Sundays arrived late, millions of words of fuck all.

Sunday, September 23

TB called before a round of calls with Kofi [Annan], [Jean] Chrétien [Canadian Prime Minister], [Atal Bihari] Vajpayee [Indian Prime

Minister]. We briefed up TB's meeting with the chairs of select committees tomorrow, Home Affairs, Defence, Foreign Affairs, International Development. We needed to show we were building a domestic coalition as carefully as the international coalition. TB was sure now he needed to go overseas again but both of us were worried we were losing sight of the domestic agenda. Philip [Gould, pollster, strategist and adviser to TB] did a good note on the conference speech. We had dinner with the Goulds, Tessa [Jowell], David [Mills, Jowell's husband] and Jessie [Mills, their daughter]. David and Jessie were both very heavily against military action. Jessie was very anti-American, and said most young people were.

Monday, September 24

At the intelligence meeting, John Scarlett presented more evidence of OBL's involvement. But they were still no clearer on exact current whereabouts. He went through what they knew of the kind of security operation that existed around Bin Laden, which meant he basically never stayed in the same place twice, and apart from a few who were with him the whole time, the others would rotate. The intelligence picture was very patchy and I had a lot of doubts about whether we could get to the stage where any of this was publishable. The feeling was military action next week rather than this. Boyce said the US were realising they did not have the targets they thought they might have. TB was interested in what more we could do for Pakistan. Lander briefed on the people who had been arrested, also on the intelligence that the UK could be the next threat, up to and including anthrax.

TB and I had a long chat later re GB. TB had asked him what he thought of what was happening, and got the monosyllabic treatment. Eventually he said 'How am I supposed to know what to think? I don't know what is going on.' TB said there was not a word of support, or a hint of understanding of how tough this was. He even got back to the point of demanding a date for TB's departure, at which point TB snapped, said he was fed up of the way he spoke to him, the way he treated him. 'You say I have a choice about when to go. It's you that has a choice, about whether you work with me or against me, and get it into your head that if you work against me, you'll get no help from me.' He said GB was also urging him to cut loose the IRA from the peace process, which was ridiculous. I sometimes wondered whether he wouldn't actually be a total disaster as prime minister and whether in fact we weren't duty-bound to ensure it didn't happen. John Rentoul had a very good line on the 'psychologically flawed relationship' and it wasn't far wrong.[1] The main issue to be resolved today was the recall of Parliament, and what to do about party conference. TB wanted it all kept under review. He was worried about the meeting with the Foreign Affairs, Defence and Intelligence select committees but in the end it went extremely well.

TB went through four separate areas – diplomatic, action being taken, evidence re the attacks, implications for domestic law. He said we were sure the Taliban knew something was happening. He made clear military action would follow if they do not comply in yielding up OBL. He went over some of the long-term issues, money laundering, shutting down the camps, the trade in WMD capability, including the involvement of what he called responsible business people. He said a lot of people had expected the US to go straight in but they didn't. They want to get it right. Even the Tories were effusive in their praise for his handling. Questions were intelligent and sensible and as an exercise it was definitely worth doing. Chris Mullin [Labour MP, chair of the Home Affairs select committee] said afterwards he had found it extremely useful. TB was on good form and they sensed he was in charge and in control of all the arguments. On conference, we agreed it would be difficult to do normal traditional conference-type announcements but we should not imagine the whole flavour had to be foreign affairs.

TB had a meeting with IDS, who did a very supportive doorstep. TB felt he was a reasonably nice guy but very right wing, e.g. already trying to link OBL to Iraq. I went home for a run with Rory [AC's elder son] then back for TB's dinner with Blunkett, Milburn, Estelle [Morris, Education Secretary], Steve Byers, Cherie and Sally [Morgan, political secretary]. Both Alan and Estelle felt they didn't have the money to deliver and needed to press for more, that the tax credits agenda was doing them in. They both seemed demoralised. They also feared that even if we met the targets, people would not see it as a transformation of public services. Blunkett had a right old rant at the Civil Service.

Tuesday, September 25

Jack Straw was involved in a diplomatic row with Israel as he arrived in Iran because he talked about Palestine in an article for an Iranian

[1] Rentoul, author of *Tony Blair: Prime Minister*, wrote in the *Independent* that while Blair was successful and feted abroad 'at home his style is cramped by his psychologically flawed relationship with Gordon Brown'.

newspaper. TB said the FCO sometimes lacked subtlety. Sharon cancelled his meeting with Jack and it took a call with TB to get it back in his diary. We needed TB up today so I spent much of the day putting together a script in three parts: 1. Taliban are our enemy as diplomatic effort intensifies; 2. we are addressing the humanitarian crisis, and 3. we will report on any change to domestic law within two weeks. We announced the recall of Parliament.

At my morning meeting, I asked who was the minister responsible for the civil contingencies situation and was told Chris Leslie [junior minister]. Lovely bloke, but the public would be shocked, I reckoned, that it wasn't a big hitter. I spoke to JP after speaking to TB and we agreed Blunkett should lead on the issue. JP came to see me later, concerned he had not been visible, but there was going to be plenty of deputising work to be done, for example CHOGM [Commonwealth Heads of Government Meeting] if TB didn't go. TB was talking to Sharon, [Syrian President Bashar al-] Assad and later giving a polite bollocking to Jack. He then spoke to [Junichiro] Koizumi [Japanese Prime Minister] before he did a doorstep with the main political editors out on the terrace overlooking the garden. He was on form, strong on the Taliban and good on the humanitarian too. I did a background briefing for the broadcasters. We were having to chop and change his diary the whole time.

Wednesday, September 26

Jack called from Israel, convinced that we were briefing against him and that the idea of Number 10 charging in to rescue ministers was bad for everyone. I think I managed to assure him that we weren't, and he accepted there had been a fuck-up but wanted me to make it more clear that Sharon called TB, not the other way round, and that there had been no question of him having to apologise. Jack and I usually managed to straighten things. TB had done a draft outline for conference and we were now into pre-speech mode, what was the argument, what was the idea, what was the narrative. I really liked the power of community as a force for change at home and abroad. I was getting more alarmed about the lack of civil contingencies planning.

I had a meeting with heads of information [Civil Service communications chiefs], did my usual spiel about the need for co-ordination, did a Q&A, but it was pretty clear we were going to need to strengthen things again. The MoD and the FCO were basically OK, though the FCO had a real problem with gabbiness, everyone thinking they needed to get their own point across to the press. Within two hours, the *Guardian* had been briefed on the meeting and what I had said to them. TB spoke to Major and Thatcher, thought there may be a role for Major in this. He said Thatcher had totally gone off on one, said 'the English-speaking peoples' would have to win this despite the weakness of the continental mainland. 'We will win this like you and I defeated socialism, she said.' TB replied he would have to give her exclusive credit for that.

Thursday, September 27

Sixteen days on, after all the bellicose talk, there was still no sign of US action. Bush was leading the news with talk of tougher airline security. Our main story was going to be TB's meeting with Muslim leaders. The press had been complaining about lack of access and with Philip's note saying that TB was being seen by the public as 'a rock', and calling for him to be more not less visible, we agreed that he should do a press conference. He was worrying about Clare. I was trying to get her to do something publicly on the humanitarian front, possibly on the lines of building a humanitarian collation alongside the military coalition. I worked on TB's script – not a war on Islam, humanitarian collation, domestic work goes on. There was some polling showing quite a dip in economic optimism. Julian [Braithwaite, press officer] was due off next week on a management course which was bad news because he was generating some terrific stuff on the anti-OBL front.

TB's meeting with the Muslim leaders went pretty well and his message was clear at the press conference. Then a somewhat alarming meeting with the defence chiefs and the spooks. It was pretty clear the US remained undecided, could not find that many good targets, and didn't have the bases in the region. Hoon said there was a lack of clarity which made it difficult to plan. TB was getting a bit alarmed that the Yanks didn't seem to get why they needed better co-ordination. TB said we needed joint planning cells, not just with the military, but the political and the propaganda, and we needed something similar with Europeans. Equally, the humanitarian effort was going to have to be co-ordinated internationally. TB said the humanitarian operation was every bit as important as the military. Boyce said the only viable bases will have to be in a contiguous country. Iran is a no-no, the Americans won't go near Pakistan. The 'Stans were being difficult, messing us around. Condi Rice was sure the Russians were playing games. Boyce warned that the Taliban were brutal if they got their hands on enemy forces, capable of skinning them alive. It's called a hair-shirt policy. General [Anthony] Pigott [Deputy Chief of the Defence Staff (Commitments)] did a really interesting presentation setting out the concept of military action working at various levels, including the psychological and the need to win hearts and minds, but again there was no sense of the Americans getting how to do that in a joined-up way.

TB felt that Bush could afford to wait if he gave a sense of forward strategy but it was lacking at the moment. We went straight from that to Cabinet which was really TB, Jack, Clare, Geoff and DB briefing them. TB on the overall strategy, Jack on the Middle East peace process, Blunkett on civil contingencies and race relations, in which he expressed his anger at the BBC constantly giving lunatics a platform, and Clare on the humanitarian effort, and Geoff giving a military update. Then GB doing a big number on the economy, including, as he had already briefed to the press, that the reserve was pretty much gone and they would have to stick to their spending plans. Foot and mouth had already cost us £2 billion extra. He rattled through some bad figures from Europe and America, said we were better protected than most economically but we still had to bear down on spending. TB's view, expressed on the basis of what they briefed, was that it was a silly message because it would add to public concern and lack of confidence.

I grabbed Clare as she left and said we needed her out motoring on the humanitarian effort. Later she announced more money for Pakistan. Just as GB was demanding a date for TB's departure, so Fiona was asking me for a date too. She feared we were heading for another period of international crisis when I would be anywhere but home. She had become really bitter and angry about TB, and I wondered if that wasn't just an easy way of making it not about me.

Friday, September 28

Went in to work on the conference speech, worked up the script for the Sundays to keep the focus on the nature of the Taliban. There was a growing sense of drift, that the US didn't really know what to do. Peter Hyman and I went home to work on the speech.

Saturday, September 29

TB spoke to Bush and felt he was still unclear on his own strategy. The media here and there was pretty much geared up, with wall-to-wall war build-up. TB was working on the speech at Chequers and felt comfortable with the draft so far. I took Rory to Spurs vs Man U who came from behind to win 5–3.

Sunday, September 30

Up at 6 and off at 7 to Chequers with Peter H. We arrived to the sight of TB still not dressed and fretting about difficult questions of domestic terror and what more we could do to deal with those successfully abusing our laws here. Peter and I had worked up a new ending for the conference speech and TB was by and large perfectly happy with what he had done. Peter was trying very hard to get him to drop stuff that he felt was basically just whacking the party but TB was adamant there had to be sense of him challenging the party. We set off for *Frost* and in the car went through the lines on extradition, asylum etc. Chris Patten was there reviewing the papers.

TB had his frightened-rabbit look up to the last minute but the interview went fine even if he got a bit jargonistic, e.g. talking about 'UBL' (OBL). We stayed on for breakfast and TB gave Patten and Edward Llewellyn, his right-hand man, a bit of advice about what to do with the Tory Party, basically stay in there and make them come to their senses. He thought Patten was absolutely top drawer, and if we had a few like him, we would be in much better shape. Back at Chequers, he, Peter H and I went through the speech line by line. At one point he admitted that part of the purpose of constantly challenging the party was to remind the public that he was not a traditional Labour leader, and that was in many ways his main selling point. He wanted a more forward section on the euro, including the prospect of it happening in this parliament. He had done a good section about the notion of solidarity as an international doctrine. The speech was a lot better for the fact that we didn't feel the need to touch every policy base going. Later we left for Brighton.

Monday, October 1

Most of the day stuck in the hotel, working on the speech, and also on a briefing script which I wanted to push out as interdependence/power of community. We had fallen back on the speech and having spent the weekend thinking we wouldn't have the usual last-minute bollocks, that's exactly what we did. I got Hilary [Coffman, special adviser] to do the briefing and by the time the press had finished with it, it was taken as a declaration of war. The main arguments we were still having were just how close to be to the US, and how to frame the public services section. TB wanted to hit the reform message, whereas I was arguing for a greater focus on the values underpinning the reform. It was very much his speech though, much more than any other conference speech we had done. He was comfortable in the argument and confident about the way he was putting it. Most of the speech team went over for [the speech by] GB. I carried on working and had it on in the background. It would be seen as a pretty good and wide-ranging domestic speech and because he allied himself to the main domestic ministers, it was likely he would get written up as the domestic PM to TB's foreign affairs PM.

We had the usual toing and froing, writing and rewriting, but TB only wanted polishing and honing from us now. It was his speech, and it was pretty well done. I had a semi-altercation with JP just before midnight when he popped in. Cherie and Sally were also there and I made a crack about GB being the domestic PM and JP snapped that even in these circles, we shouldn't be slagging him off. It was a bit much on one level, as he and I had had a session in the afternoon where he had been raging about him every bit as much as I did, but he had a point. He was worried that the tensions and the frustrations both between the principals and their teams meant that the divisions just became a given. [Gerhard] Schroeder was the main international speaker and got terrific applause for his reference to Old Labour. He went down pretty well and I think enjoyed coming over.

TB and Bush agreed TB should go to see Putin to try to secure bases and then to Pakistan to try to get a proper fix on Musharraf. It was a perfectly friendly conversation with the usual joshing and laughter amid the heavy stuff, but TB admitted he was worried they didn't seem to have a grip on things. Schroeder had felt Putin would help if we really pushed and if there was a gain in it for him. The pre-speech briefing led ITN ahead of GB which was likely to have pissed him off big time. The big message of the speech was coming together fine, international solidarity, the power of community at home. I didn't leave the hotel all day. We got to bed just after 2, which was early by comparison with most of these conference speeches.

Tuesday, October 2

TB was up at 6 and I went in to find him with the usual mass of paper all over the place, but he seemed OK with things. He had reordered things, cut down a lot of the middle section on domestic policy. There were still one or two bits that read too much like they had been done by committee, which we fixed. It was a very New Labour speech, and authentic for his voice. The overnight briefing had gone very big on the idea we were declaring war on the Taliban. It was leading the news not just in the UK but in the States too, so much so that as we were going through the autocue rehearsal at 12, Jonathan came in to tell us that David Manning had read the words on Afghanistan to the White House, who were worried about what we were saying about the nature of military action. They felt it was too forward, too clear re what we intended to hit, with the reference to camps and military installations. But that was the section we had briefed which would make it hard to pull back even if we wanted to. We toned it down a little and got it just about in the right place. TB asked Jonathan and I to go through to his room and go over the final version with the words on Afghanistan. He was getting a bit exasperated with it all, said this was like Kosovo all over again. 'What on earth do they think we are going to hit? They just aren't clear about what they want to do.' I think Hilary [Coffman] was feeling a bit stressed out at the thought that a briefing I had written and she had read out to a few journalists was now leading the news here and in different parts of the world, so much so that we had a sudden blitz of TV channels in the US and elsewhere wanting to take the speech live.

It was inevitable that foreign policy would get the main coverage but it was a strong domestic speech too. We also had extensive discussion about whether we should show the euro section to GB. It was a sign of how bad things were at the moment. The basic view was GB would take it, demand a change, then brief that he had done so to show that he could, so in the end we agreed simply to send the text through once the speech was pretty much done. As ever, his people were assuming a great plan had been unleashed to draw attention away from his speech. In reality, the briefing we did was pretty minimalist. TB had not spoken to him, so far as I knew, since we got to Brighton, which was ludicrous when I thought of the issues he was addressing.

When it came to the delivery, he got the tempo right, a bit slower and more measured, not worrying too much about reaching the heights. [BBC political editor] Andrew Marr's reaction was that it was as though he had levitated above the party, and indeed just before I left the hotel, I had said to him I got the sense that this year he needed us less, and he needed his colleagues less. The clap lines were good, the mood was good, nobody seemed to get overly alarmed at the public services section and all in all, it went down fine. The party loved the stuff on Palestine, Africa, the environment and the central idea of community driving through the whole policy agenda was strong. The euro was the only bit I felt tricky at the briefing afterwards. We left not long after to get the train back. TB called later, worried about the advice we were getting on security re the trip to Pakistan. But he was pretty keen to go, and very keen to go to Russia. The speech was getting huge play everywhere, including one headline in the States that it was TB's 'pitch for world leadership'. We would have to watch it.

Wednesday, October 3

Extraordinary press for TB's speech, though some found it a bit preachy and there was a real danger of overreach. We had a real problem with the Indians over the planned visit to Pakistan. Vajpayee was on the phone, totally adamant that if TB went to Pakistan without also visiting India, it would be a real disaster for him. He was normally so quiet and soft-spoken but there was both panic and a bit of anger in his voice. TB said that having listened to him, there was no way we could do one without the other. It was not impossible that if OBL successfully launched another hit then the Indians could launch a strike at Pakistan. The security committee, which advised on TB's own safety, had met yesterday and basically would prefer that he didn't go to Pakistan, but if he did, they wanted us to use the [Royal Air Force] VC10.

We had endless coming and going on that, including at one point Cherie coming to see me, quivering with rage, bottom lip trembling, telling me I was mad to allow it and 'Do you want to be a martyr or what?' She said it was the most stupid visit there had ever been and I should be telling him I'm not going. I pointed out that we had all seen the advice, but that he had decided to go, that therefore I should probably go too, and that if we all went down, I didn't think it would be me qualifying for martyrdom. Fiona later discovered TB and CB had had another row about Anji, which maybe explained why she was so angry. At 2.40, TB saw Geoff H and CDS. There was an outside chance the Americans might go in the next twenty-four hours because of intelligence on OBL's whereabouts.

At 4pm, the top defence and intelligence people went through what the US were asking for from us on the military side and TB gave his go-ahead. C, Scarlett and Jack set out the thinking about India/Pakistan. Jack felt we had to go for Musharraf over the help given to terrorists in Kashmir. Scarlett felt that any heavy pressure at the moment on Kashmir was a deal breaker and if our aim was to keep Musharraf on board, we should avoid it. Lander said that the Indians and Pakistanis effectively fought a proxy war over Kashmir and if you removed the proxy, there was a danger they would fight a real war with nuclear weapons. The VC10 plan meant that we had to cut down on the number of journalists we could take which led to lots of rows, all a bit pathetic. The VC10 was a bit of a nightmare because it was so old [first flown in 1962] and slow. I wrote to all media outlets pointing out that there could be no speculation as to where we were going.

Thursday, October 4

Fiona was demanding a date again, and it was obvious there was going to be an awful lot of travelling. TB and I had worked on his Commons statement late but the US intelligence agencies had taken out four of the seven pieces of information we had hoped to put in as evidence. TB was still keen to do it. We went through the statement one more time. The story was the assertion that it was definitely Bin Laden and al-Qaeda.[1]

I had running battles through the day with the BBC over them constantly saying where we were going in Pakistan. I travelled out to the airport with TB. He was very up for the visit. He had just briefed JP who told him he was really taken aback by my attitude to GB at Brighton. TB said I had to watch what I said, which was fair enough. TB had filled JP in on all the diplomatic manoeuvring and the military planning, with the strikes planned for Saturday. We went over what we needed from Putin. Something strong on OBL's involvement would be a start. TB was looking at it also from the point of view of developing a deeper relationship.

TB said he feared the Indian leg of the trip most. We were warned that the point of maximum vulnerability on the plane was on arrival and departure from Pakistan. C joined us on the plane. He would be seeing his opposite number in Russia later, as well as [Russian defence minister Sergei] Ivanov. I picked his and David Manning's brains on Kashmir. I had read up some of the disasters on previous visits. The problem was that both sides regularly just briefed that we shifted our line even if we didn't. The general feeling on the evidence document was that it was OK but there was no smoking gun. Both IDS and [Liberal Democrat leader Charles] Kennedy said they were convinced though.

On arrival, Rod Lyne [UK ambassador to Russia] came on the plane to brief us, then off to the residence and a brief meeting on Putin. TB

[1] Blair told the House of Commons 'Our findings have been shared and co-ordinated with those of our allies, and are clear. They are: first, it was Osama Bin Laden and al-Qaeda, the terrorist network which he heads, that planned and carried out the atrocities on September 11; second, that Osama Bin Laden and al-Qaeda were able to commit these atrocities because of their close alliance with the Taliban regime in Afghanistan which allows them to operate with impunity in pursuing their terrorist activity.'

was beginning to wonder whether the conference speech hadn't put him too far out in front. I said I feared it did and he was going to have to do this stuff anyway. We set off for the Kremlin. The meeting was largely one-on-one, plus interpreters, and then David Manning in for a bit before Tom Kelly [AC's deputy], Magi [Cleaver, press officer] and I were taken to meet him. Putin spent a lot of the time talking about how TB might go tomorrow to Tajikistan to persuade them to let us use their bases. The problem was the US would be opposed because it would mean the Russians effectively controlling our bases.

The joint press conference was OK if a bit dull but TB warmed up towards the end. Putin was very warm about TB, though his interpreter was poor and the press couldn't really hear him and when they did couldn't really understand him. Tony Bishop [interpreter], who had done them all right back to Stalin, was a different class by comparison. TB then set off for Putin's dacha while I went for a run with Rod before dinner. TB got back at 1am, Russian time. He said they had a good time, if a bit surreal at times. They played some form of Russian snooker and he said he won. Bush had called halfway through and spoken to them both. TB reckoned they were deadly serious about helping but felt that the US didn't really want them closely involved.

Friday, October 5

Very little sleep. I had breakfast with Rod who was not just very good at his job but very human with it and willing to engage on different levels according to different needs. TB was up late and we set off immediately for the airport. He said that Putin's problem was that he felt he was pushing out the boat but the Yanks were not responding and it made life difficult for him. On the flight to Islamabad, he said he was glad to have made the initial investment in Putin and felt they got on well. He was trying to work out what outcomes we wanted from Pakistan. I felt there was a danger now that the British public started to ask what is this all about, and why is he spending all his time on the needs of other countries not our own?

I really felt for David Manning on the flight out. He had pages and pages of notes to do on the Putin meeting, plus trying to debrief TB, who was always notoriously difficult to debrief because he would be straight on to focusing on the next thing. TB briefed the press on the plane, talking about the trap we were laying around the Taliban. TB's words in Pakistan were going to be important and we took a bit of time to work on that. I talked to C about what might follow any military attack. He believed there would almost certainly be some kind of al-Qaeda retaliation, possibly London, more likely a lesser-known European city. We flew over Everest at one point. The arrival was covered live with TB, straight into the cars and off to Musharraf's palace. They seemed to have shut down pretty much every road and the crowds were also kept well away. It was about as big a security operation as we'd had. They started off one-on-one.

TB reckoned him [Musharraf] to be a very tough character. I think their basic hope was that we wipe out the Taliban leadership, felt that if we did the whole show would crumble. They seemed pretty keen to get OBL, but you could never be absolutely sure who was saying what for what reason. He told TB we shouldn't underestimate how unpopular the Americans are here. He said Mullah Omar was impossible to talk to because he is a mystic, constantly talking about the afterlife. TB's impression was that he was determined to hold firm but it would get very difficult once military action started and he would need a lot of hand holding. Guthrie had done a good job laying the ground for the visit. He thought it sensible not to come to India with us because he was keen to be seen as Pakistan's man within the equation. It was amusing to watch him operate. He had been placed on the seating plan next to TB. When I suggested he might not want to be spotted, which he clearly would be as the cameras were due in, he was clearly not keen to move. And then when he and I were chatting and I asked him why he wasn't coming to Delhi, he said, just loud enough for them to hear, 'I think it's very important that the Pakistanis know I'm basically their man.'

There was something of an irony in Musharraf saying military takeovers and military dictatorships were not accepted in the world.[1] He talked over his road map for the introduction of democracy. TB did lots of warm words, made clear how important Pakistan was to this situation. We then got ready for a joint doorstep with a joint lectern which was a bit weird. I said to Musharraf he would be asked about the evidence we had presented and whether he accepted it. When he came over as a bit equivocal TB immediately stepped in at the lectern and said he strongly welcomed what Musharraf said.

At dinner I was between two five-star generals who spent most of the time listing atrocities for which they held the Indians responsible, killing their own people and trying to blame 'freedom fighters'. They were pretty convinced that one day there would be a nuclear war because India, despite its vast population and despite being seven

[1] Musharraf, as a general, had led a military coup in 1999, deposing elected prime minister Nawaz Sharif.

times bigger, was unstable and determined to take them out. When the time came to leave, the livelier of the two generals asked me to remind the Indians 'It takes us eight seconds to get the missiles over,' then flashed a huge toothy grin. We arranged it so that we had an early dinner there and then flew to Delhi but I sensed they were holding us back as long as possible. The service was unusually slow, especially after the starters, and I could sense that they were sensing that we were getting a bit impatient, and wanting to move on. We started to chivvy TB a bit, and he did his 'Oh, is it time to go, I'm having such an interesting time' look, which they took as the chance to start up a whole new strand of conversation.

As we took off, there was a lot of black humour flowing around about the prospect of us being downed by a stinger [anti-aircraft missile]. I think all of us, other than the experts, had been a bit taken aback at just how much Kashmir defined their relations and just how deep the mutual hatred and obsession was. We arrived in Delhi and TB, one of the cops and I got in with the ambassador [High Commissioner Sir Rob Young] and drove into town. TB motioned to the ambassador, asking if the car was bugged. He gave a kind of non-committal no. I was given my own valet, Sunil, who just would not leave me alone. He followed me to the gym and I literally had to tell him to disappear. He was waiting at my door when I got back.

TB, Anji and I had a chat over a drink but it was odd. I didn't feel as much part of things as I was, how often I was thinking and asking myself whether I really wanted to be there, or whether I was only there because he wanted me to be, and because I had grown used to it. As ever, we ended up talking about GB, TB saying he was biding his time, knowing that in politics, nobody walked on water forever. C and I had a great laugh about the name of the Indian security service – namely RAW [Research and Analysis Wing]. I said I intended to rename R&I [Number 10 Research and Information Unit] and we would have RAW Domestic, RAW International, and the really secret stuff would be handled by a tiny elite team called RAW Hide. He was a bit like Guthrie in the way he had got himself close to TB and used that to generate support at the top for the service as a whole. He was astutely political in his grasp of issues and very good at sorting the point that TB would most likely want to zone in on.

Saturday, October 6

Sunil was driving me bananas. Everywhere I went, he was there. I was beginning to wonder whether he had been put there either by the spooks or a paper. I told him at one point I was a tea-aholic, and he kept making me tea after tea and bringing it in. When I came back from the gym, by the time I got out of the shower, my running gear had been picked up and folded. We set off for the prime minister's residence, yet another purpose-built, well-equipped building, far better and more practical than Downing Street. Vajpayee was frail and his voice was weak, but in part because he had no fear of silence, there was a quiet force to him when he spoke. TB went through the mantra about military, diplomatic, humanitarian, and the need for restraint by India to build stability in the region. He said he had been very forceful with Musharraf over the attacks on the Kashmir Assembly.[1] The Indians were very steamed up and you couldn't help feeling that if a real refugee crisis absorbed Pakistan's forces, the Indians would go for them on the other front.

TB said that what had happened to the US had the same psychological effect as if we had lost Parliament or Buckingham Palace. It had touched every nerve. Vajpayee was pretty frank about what he thought of Pakistan and Musharraf and how he came to power, kept emphasising he on the other hand led a democracy, and TB said 'With humility, I think it's important to continue with restraint.' Jaswant Singh [foreign affairs minister] said it was not possible to separate the Taliban and OBL, they were totally interdependent. This was, as the general told me last night, a two-front war.

Singh did a lot of the talking. I sat next to him at the breakfast later and he was enormously charming. The joint press conference was in a beautiful garden setting which was home to all manner of exquisite brightly coloured birds flying around and singing. TB and Vajpayee were such different breeds of politician, TB all drive and words and desperate to get everything right, Vajpayee calm, something almost mystical about him.

We set off for the airport and, using the Kosovo statement we did in Berlin, I started work on a draft of a TB statement in the event of military action. TB was pretty anxious about the India–Pakistan situation. We were also still unclear when the US were going to strike. TB slept for a good bit on the way back and I had a chat with C who told me we were very loose on our mobiles during the Kosovo crisis. I chatted to Manning and enlisted his support in persuading the Americans, not least in his link to Condi and TB's to Bush, of the need to get far better media co-ordination in the coming days. TB

[1] On October 1, Pakistani terrorist group Jaish-e-Mohammed had killed thirty-eight people in a suicide and car bombing attack on the Jammu and Kashmir State Legislative Assembly in Srinagar.

had found the visit absolutely fascinating, said it was one thing to read all the briefs and listen to all the experts but you didn't have to be there for long to get a sense of just how dangerous and volatile it was. And it was clear too that we were able to exercise some influence in stopping them. They were adamant that, helped by Pakistan, OBL had successfully made Kashmir terrorism worse than ever.

They were coming up to local elections in India in which 160 million people would vote. C said to me he saw TB's strengths as many and varied but one of them was his ability to be nice to people whoever they were, however much was going on. We got back into Number 10 for TB's phone call with Bush which began with GWB saying we were definitely going to launch the strikes tomorrow, that he would get his speech over and Karen and I should discuss the various statements and timings. I faxed over the TB draft. TB briefed him on the last couple of days and laid it on thick about his worries re India and Pakistan and the importance of trying to calm it all down. He suggested to Bush he speak to Vajpayee.

Fiona was in a foul mood when I got home, said she assumed that I was going to be off fighting another war again. I had a laugh with the boys about Sunil. About the only time he left me alone was when we left and he had disappeared and despite him driving me crazy, I had been hoping to see him to give him a large tip for at least enlivening the visit.

Sunday, October 7

I was out playing football with Calum [AC's younger son] when TB called, really worried about Pickett's Lock[1] and what it said about Britain and our potential for sport. I agreed with him, but it was an odd thing to be obsessing about given what else he had on his mind. Karen Hughes called and said my note had really got them thinking about how to do the media in what was obviously going to be a cross-national media operation. I went in for Geoff Hoon's PINDAR [Ministry of Defence crisis management centre] meeting in the bunker. I chatted to CDS about exactly how to pitch our involvement. We had three Tomahawks let off and support staff not yet being used. I set out the timing of the Bush and TB statements. Then news came through that they were going early so we had to cobble together the final drafts taking in a few of Condi's changes, including them not wanting to say that action would be proportionate. I was up and down to the

[1] Abortive site of a National Athletics Stadium. Cost and inadequate transport links made the site, in North-East London, unviable.

flat to get the final changes in and signed off and then downstairs to do the statement to the media.

JP, Jack and Geoff were there to flank him and it was going to be important to get away from some of this presidential stuff that was surrounding him. He looked absolutely fine, but just minutes earlier, as Bush was starting his speech, TB was not even dressed, his hair was wet. He was pretty nervous about the whole thing, was sweating and later beating himself up over not having prepared properly for the statement. At least it suggested there was still humility in there. I was sure he had made the right decisions though but as ever, nobody could accurately predict exactly what would happen when the shooting started.

Monday, October 8

Several of the papers ran TB's words alongside GWB's and noted the similarity of language and message. The coverage was wall to wall of course. I was in early and the first meeting was with the intelligence and defence people. I was beginning to feel a bit sorry for Lander at the way TB asked him whether there was any sign of an attack on the UK, as though Lander was expected to know the answer in yes or no terms. He had a mischievous little face, a bit of a cross between Ian Hislop [editor of satirical magazine *Private Eye*] and Richard Stott [former tabloid editor turned irreverent *Sunday Mirror* columnist]. He said there were a large number of people 'who worry us', that sixty had been interviewed in the past three weeks, that the ones they were really worried about were under permanent surveillance. [Admiral] Boyce went over some of the thirty-two attacks launched in the immediate wave, and some of the planned targets tonight. These were likely to go on for three to five days in the first instance. Scarlett said all planes came back safely.

There was a pretty clear impression the operation had not been as effective as being hoped. [Sir John] Kerr said the Israelis were not being helpful. There were also real concerns about what reactions there might be against some of our [diplomatic] posts, especially in Indonesia. There were legal difficulties being raised re targeting some of the Afghan TV output. Both Harriet [Harman, Solicitor General] and the Attorney General [Lord Peter Goldsmith] had seemingly raised concerns. TB was clear post Kosovo that their media machine was a part of their military machine and a legitimate target. Afterwards, Richard W, Jonathan and I persuaded TB that there should be regular meetings of a War Cabinet – TB, JP, GB, JS, GH, Clare, RC, CDS and the main agencies. TB was reluctant at first, probably because of his ongoing arguments with GB. RW said he was worried about the 'presidential' tag, and he was right, though his concerns – that his structures were not always being followed – were maybe not the same as mine, though they were linked – namely that we needed a cadre of ministers bound in to the decision-making and able to go out and explain properly to MPs and public.

I got TB to agree to do Al Jazeera [Arabic news network] whose coverage was causing a lot of concern. What with that, Church leaders coming in, Cabinet and a statement in the House, there was plenty going on to brief the media and keep them busy. The Al Jazeera interview was difficult, as expected, and with a lot of focus on the Palestine question. It pretty much went to the heart of every question and managed to create the sense TB was on the defensive, though he did get over some of the key messages for the Arab world. In the pre-briefing, a couple of ultra-Arabists from the FCO had been urging him to use the interview to dump on Israel, or at least distance ourselves as much as possible. I spent a fair bit of time working on the statement for the House, in which he was able to announce the second wave had started. He did fine, though it was all a little bit flat.

Cabinet was largely just TB and the other ministers involved reporting to the rest of them. By and large they were supportive. TB went through the three different planks – military, diplomatic and humanitarian. The aim was to put a ring round the Taliban regime, undermine them militarily and politically, and meanwhile show this was about the regime not the people. He went through how we were working with the Northern Alliance, but stressed any future rule had to be broad-based. On the diplomatic front, we had a lot of allies wanting to join up in some way. But we had big problems in the Arab world and there was going to have to be a major propaganda effort to reach them. We cannot say often enough that 'This is not a war on Islam.' He said the strong message from the Church leaders, and from many Muslims, was that now we had started it, we should finish as quickly as possible. He also emphasised that we had continually to make the link to domestic policy – that this had implications for our fight against drugs and terrorism; that it was important to restoring confidence in the economy; the sooner we act, the more likely we will be to contain a refugee crisis. Geoff made clear we were able to study all of the targets because some of the planes came out of Diego Garcia [Indian Ocean military base].

Clare reported on the humanitarian situation, said even before all this Afghanistan was heading towards famine. Five million were going hungry, nothing like enough food was getting through and in six weeks the roads will be impassable. Air drops and leaflets were not enough. We must get back to convoys. She said the US were being 'more generous than usual', and money was less of a problem than logistics. GB, just back from the G7 meeting, said consumer spending was holding up, but recent company performance was not good. Tessa said the latest estimate had 120 British people killed on September 11. A lot of relatives and the process of identification and the return of remains was clearly difficult. I sent through a follow-up note to Karen Hughes on co-ordination. I saw GB re the PBR [Pre-Budget Report]. At TB's office meeting, he was just railing at the lack of progress on the domestic agenda and worrying that because he would be forced to focus on the international, departments would be taking their feet off the accelerators again.

Tuesday, October 9

I was getting into a much better rhythm with Karen Hughes. If anything, the need for proper co-ordination was going to be even greater than Kosovo because there were more and different communications challenges. For Kosovo, we had a bigger alliance, and we were fighting for Muslims. We now had a lot of anti-Americanism running around, despite Sept 11, and we had a particular problem with some of the Arab media and the way they were fuelling the idea of a war on Islam. It was going to be important to get the Americans not to think they were just talking to America the whole time. We got big play home and abroad for the Al Jazeera interview, and we were going to need to do a lot more with the Arab media. TB was seeing [Gerry] Adams and [Martin] McGuinness [leading Sinn Fein politicians in Northern Ireland] at 8 and we had to choreograph the arrivals to avoid any crossover with the War Cabinet – not what we needed right now.

At the morning meeting, there were two immediate problems to address – the first was that the BBC were reporting TB was going to Oman. They just would not listen to our concerns on this. And the second was the leak of a Jo Moore [special adviser to Stephen Byers] email from September 11 saying that it was a good time to 'bury bad news'. I didn't allow much discussion of it at the morning meeting. It was perfectly clear someone inside had leaked it and it was a classic Civil Service move on a special adviser. It was a stupid thing to say, and knowing Jo she would be mortified, but I didn't like the idea of her being hanged, drawn and quartered for it. I also knew it would unleash another avalanche of bollocks about spin, me, culture of blah.

I spoke to Byers and he asked if I thought she would have to go. I was worried it might end there. But after talking to TB, we agreed there should be a reprimand and an apology. TB felt Jo was basically a decent person, very committed and professional, and it was a bit much to destroy her career over one leaked email that she should never have sent. Tom [Kelly] came back from the eleven o'clock a bit taken aback by the ferocity over it. TB was clear that she had given us great service down the years, and it was not a hanging offence.

I did a conference call with her and Steve and we agreed there would be no budging from that line. My only question mark was whether she was really up to facing the shit that was coming her way. She sounded OK, and she had always struck me as pretty good under pressure, but who knows? I got SB to organise [Richard] Mottram [permanent secretary, Department of Transport, Local Government and the Regions (DTLR)] to do the official reprimand bit. I wrote to Greg Dyke [BBC director general] complaining about the BBC – Kate Adie [BBC chief press correspondent] – doing a number re TB and the forthcoming trip to Oman. The War Cabinet was OK. It was remarkable how quickly these extraordinary meetings became almost routine in their nature, TB wandering in with us lot, ministers chatting a bit, the spooks and defence guys sitting up straight and getting ready to do their stuff, Scarlett, C, Lander, CDS, all chipping in, very matter-of-fact and straightforward. Scarlett was meticulous in his presentation. It was again not exactly clear how successful the strikes had been. They almost got Mullah Omar. He was injured, might be dead.

Jack S and Clare both pressed Lander on what was happening re suspects here, and he was clear that though a lot of them were covered, there could be no guarantees, because a threat might well be coming from people we do not know about. They were both worried about Pakistani opinion in the UK really becoming inflamed. Blunkett really went off on one about the cops, e.g. John Stevens wanting to surround shopping centres with machine-gun-toting officers. He really let rip, and there were a few raised eyebrows, including TB's. David clearly didn't take much to the cops, made a point of saying the Security Service had been terrific, but there had to be better co-operation with the Special Branch and the police more generally. There was a lack of hard-headed clarity, and it was really annoying him, he said. The US was in the lead for attack but the UK and Israel were not far behind. The US were in no doubt there were a number of al-Qaeda 'unexpired events' still to be completed. TB said to Lander he should give us a shopping list of anything they felt would help. He didn't want them to hold back for fear that things would be politically difficult. He said give us a list of what you would want in an ideal world and we can decide what is politically possible. There was a discussion of the Saudi oilfields, what would happen to the oil price and the world economy if they went up under attack. Lander and C both said it was as well to be prepared for something pretty serious, up to and including WMD.

Ed Balls [special adviser to Gordon Brown] came to see me. He was worried re where TB was on the euro, said some of the recent noise about it was 'dangerous'. He felt TB was trying to set a political timetable for an economic union. I asked if GB was on a different track to TB. He said he didn't want to make the same mistake as the last lot made re the ERM. GB thought we had an agreement to shut down debate on the euro and couldn't understand why we had opened it again. I said it would help if they could discuss it without shouting at each other about every slight, real or imagined, going back years. Ed said we would get brownie points from the Hugo Young [*Guardian*] and the Phil Stephenses [*FT*] for opening it up again, but did we really think it was the right course to go down at this stage?

There was a review of security in the event of a major attack. Fiona and I were both in the red team that would be taken to the underground place with TB, but we agreed we should not be in there together, that one of us should be with the kids if at all possible. TB did the BBC World Service Pashto service, who were clearly thrilled to be asked. The interview was done by a young woman called Nijiba who afterwards told us some horrific stories re the kind of thing that went on inside Afghanistan. TB suggested I try to get her out on our airwaves too. I was determined that TB keep up a voice on the Arab and Muslim media.

We left for the airport at 6, and in the car TB asked me when I thought was the best time for Anji to leave. I felt soon. It just hadn't worked out as he had hoped for the second term. There was too much baggage in all the difficult relationships and the recent trip had shown that for all she brought to the table, Anji needed a clear role to be effective and it wasn't there at the moment. I felt he had been wrong to stop her leaving earlier when she had basically wanted to. He said how impressed he had been with David Manning. He was doing a superb job with Condi, and he was also such a nice guy to have around. TB was still worried that the Yanks were on a slightly different track, wanting to broaden this out. He was worried re the domestic agenda suffering with all of us focused elsewhere. The Jo Moore furore was really building and the hacks on the plane were trying to get us going.

We landed [in Geneva] and set off for the Intercontinental to meet Sheikh Zayed [al-Nahyan, President of the United Arab Emirates]. He was around eighty, surrounded by zillions of hangers-on, one or two of whom had a bit of a gangsterish feel to them. In the meeting, SZ said it was a battle of humanity and inhumanity, sanity and insanity. There was a TV screen in the background with pictures of a giant green parrot and some pretty girls. The parrot squawked regularly. After a while, one of the sheikh's flunkeys got up and motioned for David Manning, Anna [Wechsberg, private secretary, foreign affairs] and I to leave so that they were one-on-one. Christ knows what they would talk about. TB came out with a huge grin, and said they had resolved the problems of the world. They had brought an Abu Dhabi TV reporter with them, having promised him a TB interview and when I said nobody had mentioned it to me, they started to cut up a bit rough and unpleasant. One of them said, we are aware of your reputation but I should know the sheikh would take it as a personal slight if this didn't happen and there would be a diplomatic incident. Then another came in with a rather menacing smile and muttered something about whether the IRA really were quiet, and whether they were linked into Bin Laden and so on. In the end, partly because it allowed us to keep going with the Arab media strategy, we agreed. As it happened, it was his best interview yet and gave us live words for the travelling hacks too.

Wednesday, October 10

We landed [in Oman] in beautiful sunshine with a full red-carpet welcome, bands, national guard, the Omani works. We then headed for the guest house, set way back in its own grounds close to one of the sultan's residences. The place itself was about as ornate as anything we had seen. My bedroom had two gold-plated chandeliers hanging from a ceiling that must have taken months to paint. The bath was surrounded by more perfumes and toiletries than I knew existed. It was apparently the room normally reserved for visiting spouses so God knows what that made me. There was a lovely open-air swimming pool so I had a quick swim before doing a note to the MoD on my plan to brief the travelling press on the overall strategic direction based around the 'objectives of military action' document. We were running into a problem with the sense being communicated by the US that they were constantly trying to link Iraq into the equation.

TB was keen to pull it back and through a mix of my briefing and his interviews at the army base, we just about did that, but it was difficult to do while simultaneously avoiding US–UK split stories.

TB's room was even more luxurious, a carpet that your feet seemed to disappear into, paintings and statuettes that were both gaudy and somehow conveying a certain style. We went out to the poolside to go over what he would say to the UK troops, then set off by helicopter. I was always impressed by the way the military could set up home anywhere. Their base was pretty much a desert, but you had the sense of being in a very British, very well-organised operation. While TB was shown around, I did a background briefing on the objectives document, which they saw as substantial and newsworthy. But I stupidly referred to it as a 'policy bible' which had a touch of Bush's 'crusade' reference, which I tried to pull back from later. We rejoined TB who was getting a good response from the troops. There were several Burnley fans there, including one with the club crest tattooed on his shoulder. The speech to the troops was excellent, both in terms of its actual impact on the troops, and in media terms.

Flew back by helicopter. It was now almost unbearably hot. We got back to a couple of immediate problems. It emerged TB had told some of the squaddies, who had passed on to the press, that he had said one of the kids was thinking about the military as a career. I got Godric to call around and try to get them not to run it. Meanwhile, the BBC was reporting already that we were going on to Cairo. The others were not unreasonably pissed off that they were abiding by the agreement while the BBC seemed to be making a point of breaking it. Also, TB had been pictured with a guy wearing a T-shirt with the slogan 'We came, we saw, we kicked ass', which might go down better in the US than the UK.

I was getting pressed the whole time about the Yanks and Iraq, which was difficult. We got a report through on Battle Damage Assessment which showed the strikes had not been as effective as planned, but TB's bigger worry was the overall strategy. Then news came through that Iraq had shot down a Predator [unmanned surveillance plane]. The Americans were bound to react. The Taliban told OBL that he was free to fight Jihad. Bush publicly raised fears that OBL was using videos to send coded messages to terrorists already in the US. He also announced the '22 Most Wanted'.[1] I went out for a run on the sultan's private beach. It was hot, but that wonderful dry heat that meant that once I was into a rhythm, I was running well and felt privileged to be out on my own in such beautiful surroundings. I had a quick swim in the sea before going back for TB's bilateral with the sultan and then

[1] FBI list of twenty-two terrorist hijackers and bombers, including Bin Laden. Bush said 'Eventually, no corner of the world will be dark enough to hide in.'

an extraordinary dinner where wave upon wave of food came towards us. I noticed for the first couple of courses the sultan and his colleagues just picking, and after a while it became clear why. We were on the fifth course before I realised we were still on the appetisers. By the end, we had been served twenty-one courses. The sultan said he had a little surprise for us and out of nowhere came a pipe band, Omanis dressed in kilts serenading us with pipes and drums from the balcony above the dining room. They weren't bad.

On the substance, the Palestine problem came through every part of the discussion. He said Israel had to give. He was obviously aware of the tensions over Iraq, said they were happy to support us for now, re Afghanistan, but if the US went for Iraq, they would flake away and so would others, pretty quickly. David, Jonathan and I later had a go at TB, tried to get him to speak to GWB, but he felt he should wait for a face-to-face meeting. His bigger concern was whether they had thought through the military strategy, that they had been bombing without putting troops in sufficient numbers near the targets, or thinking through counter-attacks.

Thursday, October 11

I went for a run on the beach first thing. I hadn't slept well, partly because I felt a bit uncomfortable with the over-the-topness of the luxury. I was used to sleeping in some big beds, but this was like sleeping in a field with a duvet. TB was in the gym when I got back, again a word which understates its luxury. He was worried about the Americans, worried about the military campaign, concerned the CIA were actively looking for reasons to widen and hit Iraq. The damage was being done by bombing but where were the ground forces ready to move in and mop up? He also felt the US were paying insufficient attention to pubic opinion outside America. He felt he should go to Washington soon. He, Jonathan and DM thought there was a case for me going ahead to try to get them in a better place on their global communications strategy.

After breakfast, we set off for the airport surrounded by outriders with machine guns and tanks carrying anti-aircraft missiles. We had to have a meeting with one of the sultan's courtiers as part of the protocol, then on to the plane and on to Cairo. TB did an on-the-record briefing broken down into three parts: 1. a strong hint about the use of ground forces; 2. we had to do far better at the propaganda war in the Arab world, and 3. as important as anything, that the Middle East peace process was the key to solving all this. We had a problem with the Saudis apparently putting it out that they had postponed

TB's visit after the bombing started because it was too difficult for them. We tried to make the case that it was more about logistics than diplomacy, but they were pretty unshiftable and the Saudi snub story was a big part of the media mix.

TB was doing well and was still getting a very good press, still showing strong leadership, but he was also very conscious of the danger that he was setting himself up for a fall by being in such a position of international leadership. But he felt he was getting somewhere with Bush, and also felt strongly that he had to do it. He spent much of the flight writing a personal note to GWB to send when we got back to London. We were never quite sure how widely these notes were circulated in the US system. He wanted to be as frank as possible, but was always conscious of the strains in Washington. He was clear that we needed more special forces and more ground troops quickly. We needed bases in Uzbekistan and stronger links into the Northern Alliance. He was emphasising as well the need to deliberate with colleagues and strengthen the coalition at every phase of the campaign. He really laid it on about the importance of MEPP, and also that if there was any sense of trying to use this to go for other countries, it would play into Bin Laden's claim that this was not about September 11, or about the Taliban, or about him, but a war by the West on the Arab world. Get that wrong, and there was a danger of losing any chance of support from Russia, the Arab world, half the EU. HE also felt, whatever they thought, we should not be lumping Syria in with Iraq.

On MEPP, he stated clearly it was the single biggest thing to get right, and his rebuke of Sharon had helped him in the Arab world, but that he needed a major new initiative, that talks had to get going again, that there had to be an acceptance at the outset that there would be two states at the end of it. He recommended a role for the EU as a way of lifting some of the load on the US. On the issue of propaganda, he said we needed to understand that the Arab world was on a different media planet, and Palestine was at the heart of it. He said we needed a dedicated, tightly knit unit for the war generally and for the Arab and Muslim world in particular. We have to reframe the way we think about reaching out to them. It was a very strong note, quite difficult to write because he had to be firm without seeming to be talking down to him, or not deferring to what was clearly a stronger power. We got back to London and I wrote a note to Karen to develop what TB was saying on communications. Bush did a press conference in the early hours and the story was he was giving a second chance to the Taliban, that the bombs would stop if they handed over OBL. They were slightly getting their messages mixed again.

Friday, October 12

I spoke to Byers and said he had to get out and do the media on Railtrack, even if it meant taking questions on Jo [Moore]. I felt the best thing was to do clips before the Railtrack meeting, where he could say something on Jo, then go out again after the Railtrack meeting, but only talk about rail. He sounded down and the press on this had been worse than I had realised just from the media brief. His clips were fine but I could tell from how often he was calling how nervous he was. I was starting to put my mind to a much bigger operation re the Arab media. We just weren't at the races on this. We had had the occasional reasonable one-off hit, but a strategic operation was non-existent. Julian was nagging me about it and was right. I planned a brainstorm on it.

Colleen Harris [Prince of Wales' staff], called saying that Charles was really keen to help. I said what about a visit to Bahrain, UAE, etc.? They said what about Saudi? I said we were already planning to go there. It would be great in some ways if they went together but would it mean TB could not do the politics properly. That would be the fear. I also suggested that in the UK, he could do more regional visits, mosques in particular, as we could not say often enough that it was not a war on Islam. TB, Jonathan and I met and agreed we should aim for a Saudi visit this week, Washington the week after. Re Byers and Jo, he said before leaving for Chequers that they had to tough it out.

Jonathan Prince [US Democrat adviser] called from Washington, said Hillary Clinton [former First Lady] had suggested he call because the Americans just were not at the races in the media war at the moment. She was worried the administration was constantly putting out mixed messages, e.g. when Bush had said on the same day both that it was safe to fly, and that we were facing a one hundred per cent threat. TB felt the problem was they lacked absolute clarity in their aims and strategy. He and Bush chatted on the phone for fifteen minutes or so but didn't achieve much. We had heard the Taliban were planning to invite in selected film crews, and I put in a warning about the importance of them being aware of the dangers of being used.

Saturday, October 13

TB was at Chequers and he and I both had the same feeling, it just wasn't clear where this was heading. He said Bush would be getting fed up about all the talk of splits between [Colin] Powell and the Pentagon, so it was hard for TB to push himself even further in the task of trying to get GWB in a better place. He said there was a real danger he was beginning to be seen as a pain in the arse. The sooner they met the better, he said. I had a couple of conversations with Colleen Harris and then with the creepy Mark Bolland [deputy private secretary to the Prince of Wales] who emphasised that the prince was really keen to get more involved. I sensed there was a bit of an operation to try to get back in with us a bit after all his countryside outbursts. I did a note to TB on what Charles might do, from articles, speeches and visits to a fully fledged joint visit to Saudi which would clearly be a very big step.

On the Jo Moore front, he felt that part of the problem was quite a lot of our ministers probably did treat civil servants like dirt, so when the more malign of them saw the chance of revenge, they would take it. He said we were fine because he always tried to be nice to them and they saw me as a character who at least had ability to match authority and who was always nice to the support staff and messengers. But a lot of the real civil-servant types would not take kindly to a lot of our people. He reckoned Boyce [CDS] was someone who probably believed a lot of the propaganda against us, that we basically listened the whole time to focus groups, that I was just a brutal apparatchik, etc.

On the Americans and their communications, he said it was so obvious what they needed to do. He said the sooner I went out to Washington the better, but he was conscious of not wanting to impose me or it all become part of a narrative about him overreaching himself. Condi called David Manning at 5pm to alert us that they were about to admit to a stray missile. I said we would put out the line that it was the right thing to admit it. She also said the Americans were worried about TB's security because he was right out there in front of the assassination queue. I worked on a note on Arab opinion, really laying it on the line about how far removed we were from a proper operation. I got into my stride, set out five pages' worth of possible ideas then called Karen Hughes to discuss it. She always sounded grateful for support and surprised at how many ideas it was possible to generate, but equally she always sounded annoyed when you got into the territory of the need to understand why anti-US feelings were so strong. I picked up, for example, a kind of revulsion in the Arab world at the sight of Bush urging American kids to send a dollar for the Afghan children. She couldn't understand it. I told her the *Guardian* had reported on this as being all about America and the mighty dollar, and they just had to understand better how they were seen outside. I agreed to send her my note, she said she would hold a similar brainstorm and we would swap notes afterwards.

Sunday, October 14

Chris Meyer sent a telegram from which it was clear the State Department were also worrying about the scale of the Islamic opinion problem. I did a note to Chris and sent him a copy of my letter to Karen Hughes. I went for a run with Rory and missed JP on *Frost*. JP called me afterwards beating himself up, saying he had been bumbling. Audrey [Millar, Fiona's mother] had watched it and said he was fine. Byers was on the phone, as was Jo [Moore], and I told them both they should keep their heads down till Tuesday and his statement on Railtrack should be sufficiently robust and substantive to get above the noise. He sounded very fed up and isolated. I was also busy sorting through a few problems pre Arafat. TB said he was willing to do a joint press conference provided he didn't just use it to trot out all the old lines about Israel. I felt if we could get Arafat to echo strongly what his spokesman said, namely that OBL could not speak for Palestine, that would be progress. We were getting heavier warnings about TB's own security. Jack called me re my note on Arab opinion, said we were on exactly the same wavelength and I should use whatever FCO resources I needed.

I went out to play football for an hour with Calum, then in for TB's War Cabinet meeting, TB, Jonathan, DM, AC, RW, AH, C and CDS. TB said he did not want the full War Cabinet daily, maybe two or three a week, but he would speak to Geoff and Jack separately. CDS was going to Tampa tomorrow and was hopeful we would get a fuller and better assessment after that. TB was pretty open about his worry about a lack of a clear overall strategy. There had to be ways of showing progress being made according to an understood plan. He was clearer than ever after the recent visits that our role had to be being in a position to give the Americans advice which they accepted, and adopted, as we were currently doing on Iraq, humanitarian, propaganda.

CDS set out where our forces were operating, and how we were liaising with the Russians. TB felt the division between Powell and Rumsfeld was raw and difficult. He said on the military, humanitarian, diplomatic, propaganda, post-Taliban planning and MEPP, there had to be far greater clarity and unity. I did a conference call and agreed with the Palestinian team that TB would push the boat out re the Palestinian state question if Arafat would condemn OBL, say he had no right to speak for Palestine and that this was an important message. The Taliban took a group of journalists into Afghanistan to Karam [village near Jalalabad, Nangarhar province], which they said had been destroyed by the US. The press were sceptical but even so I called Karen Hughes and said they must get out a response on it. It was perfectly clear after a while that she didn't know what I was talking about. I was surprised she hadn't been told, and a bit worried about whether they were really at the races.

Monday, October 15

The press was all a bit ragged but it felt like we were losing the media battle. I was determined to get going on a proper operation for Muslim and Arab opinion, and also to strengthen US–UK operations. 8am, War Cabinet. Jack was worried that we were too lax on targeting and said that at the risk of being unpopular, he felt we should be thinking about it more carefully. TB listened for a bit and got a bit irritated, said our job was to set the overall strategy but you could not have a campaign run by committee because it will not work. John Vereker [permanent secretary, Department for International Development (DFID)] gave quite a positive report on the humanitarian front. Lander said there was a worrying increase in talk of threats to the US and UK, while TB was also a current target. There was no real sign of fracture within the Taliban, and also we still had mixed messages about the Northern Alliance. Both CDS and Geoff Hoon said there was no real clarity of where it was going. Our special forces were obviously key but we needed far greater clarity about what they were required for. C was very helpful on the Arab–Muslim opinion front, and agreed one of his best people would come to my meetings on it.

We had a pre-meeting with TB re Arafat [visit]. It was tricky, in that in the current context, things that both of them had said hundreds of times, might resonate differently. We really didn't want Arafat just to go off on one on Israel. There had to be real substance coming out of this. Because TB was clear that getting the peace process going again was perhaps the single most important thing we could do. But it wasn't hard to see how you could go from that to a position that pushed the Israelis off the other end. Arafat arrived, with the usual large entourage, but they did most of it one-on-one, with David Manning in there taking notes, and TB seemed to have given him a pretty straightforward message. We had the extended meeting which was really just an opportunity to finalise the scripts, agree pretty forward language on Palestinian state but also be clear it should not be pitched as a change of policy, which is what Arafat really wanted. Arafat wasn't looking particularly well but as before, he managed to lift himself. The press conference went fine. TB had felt it wasn't a great idea for the media to see Michael Levy [Labour fundraiser and adviser on Middle East], as they would make it all about party funding.

So he wasn't very happy when Michael got himself into the departure shot. He just could not resist it. TB said he had only one thing to do – stay low profile – and he didn't do it. Michael had a real desire to be recognised for what he was doing on MEPP, and put funding behind him, which was understandable.

I had my meeting with the broadcasters. I went through the issues, pretty gently, not remotely bullying, absolved them of blame for most of the stuff I was talking about. I told them about our worries on the videos and emphasised that the security issues around TB were very real, and it wasn't on to report his movements in advance. Richard Sambrook [BBC director of news] said they would prefer I hadn't done this through the lobby. I said that was because we were exasperated by their continued reporting of his movements. I had a very good meeting with key FCO and SIS people on Arab–Muslim media. I said I wanted somebody monitoring this stuff for me full time, saying what we got right and what we got wrong. John Kerr had given me a very bright Arabic speaker called Gerard Russell who would be able to go out there on the Arabic TV and speak for us.

George Tenet [CIA director] was coming in to see TB with C, who brought him round to see me to discuss the notes I was sending through to Karen and enlist his help in persuading them of the need for much better communications. I told him we feared they were putting out messages that were very good and positive for the American audience, but not for the broader community, including here, but also above all in the Arab world. He said Richard [Dearlove] had talked to him about it, that Condi was the key to this, that I needed to get her on board to persuade Bush they needed to crack down on the mixed messages (the latest today, [Dick] Cheney [US Vice President] and the Health Secretary [Tommy Thompson] saying different things on bio-terrorism) and run a properly co-ordinated international structure. David Manning felt he and I should go there next Tuesday. Tenet said the US was totally fixated on the anthrax scare.[1] Tenet was bright, but had a slightly irritating habit of playing with a large cigar when he was listening. He said he totally bought what we were saying and he would feed it back. He agreed we needed more [Colin] Powell and less Department of Defense. Mum phoned later, saying Dad was going to have to get tests for a possible brain tumour.

[1] An outbreak of anthrax in the United States, intentionally spread via the postal system, caused five deaths and a total of twenty-two infections between September and November 2001.

Tuesday, October 16

There was a growing sense that things were not going brilliantly. TB was doing a speech on public services so I went up to the flat to work on that with him. He had pretty much done the draft himself. The Jo Moore thing was still big and we agreed she should do something to camera, which she did in the afternoon, apology then back to work. She did OK, looked fine but sounded very fed up. Colin Powell was going to Pakistan but the backdrop was the division between him and the Defense Department. David Manning spoke to Condi and said she was very excited at the idea of us both going out there and felt on the media side, I would be pushing at an open door. The aid agencies were calling for a pause in the bombing.

Wednesday, October 17

The general feeling was that Jo's public statement had backfired and made matters worse. Also, there was a real feeling media-wise that Afghanistan was not going according to plan. At the 8am meeting, CDS reported back from Tampa that they intended to carry on bombing at this intensity for a couple of days, then really push on for the fall of the Taliban. He said [General] Tommy Franks [commander-in-chief, US Central Command (CENTCOM)] was fine and strong but there was no clear political direction. Rumsfeld was felt to be very erratic. TB felt there were some critical decisions not being faced up to, e.g. on the Northern Alliance, we either get behind them or not. His view was we should go full steam ahead with them but at the same time put other groups alongside them. But it wasn't as simple as that, the Northern Alliance was not cohesive, there were eight or nine tribal chieftains in varying states of control. TB said the Northern Alliance must be sitting there thinking the Americans were just scared of suffering casualties.

TB said the Taliban will not fold unless there is someone moving in to drive them out. He also felt we were losing the battle on the humanitarian front, that somebody really strong had to be in charge of it. Chris Patten's name was floated. He also wanted more pressure on the Russians for the use of bases in Uzbekistan. David Manning pointed out that Ramadan began on November 17, which would be another complicating factor.

Karen Hughes called from Air Force One, said she had discussed my note with Bush and I should go out next week. TB spoke to Bush at 2pm. Bush said the anthrax there was weapons grade and probably given to OBL by Saddam. Later in the conversation he said he hoped

TB was in the loop about targets in other countries. TB made three main points: 1. we had to go for the Northern Alliance, let them do what they could, put them on a leash if need be and hold them back later. Bush said he agreed, that 'You are right as always', the Northern Alliance are the best people to help us but they have to be able to share power later. 2. get other countries involved, however small their commitment, e.g. Jordan, other friendly Arab nations. Bush said in fourteen days we would have Mazar-e-Sharif [city in north Afghanistan] and Kabul [capital of Afghanistan] in friendly hands. 3. on the humanitarian, TB said some truly awful pictures would start to come through and it was important people understood the bigger context first, otherwise there would be a bigger backlash against us.

They then discussed the propaganda side and Bush said he had heard that I was really discouraged after our visit to the Middle East and I had really got Karen and her people going. He switched between serious statesman and Texan redneck pretty quickly, e.g. when after a serious discussion on public opinion in the Arab world, he suddenly said 'We got the asshole on the run and we're gonna get the bearded one soon.' He also said 'I ain't got much credibility on this peacekeeping stuff so I want those Scandinavians involved.' I wasn't sure what Prince Charles wanted to do. His office having asked how he could help, now Stephen Lamport [private secretary to the Prince of Wales] wasn't clear what kind of visits he would do. TB called late after his call to Chirac and was plucking his guitar rather annoyingly. He was very pleased with himself that he had managed to fix a three-way meeting with Chirac and Schroeder before the Ghent [EU] summit.

Thursday, October 18

The *Mirror* was wall-to-wall offside, and other papers/chatterati were starting to get very flaky. Not even two weeks into the bombing and they were all very jumpy already. I did a briefing for the Arab–Muslim media, the first briefing I had done with three Special Branch in tow, though thankfully none of them seemed to notice. It went well and I enjoyed doing it, partly because I could feel that they realised there was a point. The questions were the obvious ones, MEPP, Iraq, protests. I promised them far greater access to ministers.

At the War Cabinet, Scarlett said the Americans seemed to be upping their support for the Northern Alliance and were starting to probe positions at Mazar-e-Sharif. CDS said CENTCOM had said they would give whatever support the NA needed. TB was back saying we needed to construct a leash to pull them back in. As he listened, I could see Blunkett getting more and more agitated.

Eventually he said it was incredible that we were all sitting around basically saying there was no clear strategy. He said I don't want to shoot the messenger but where is this all going? He said we were coming up to Ramadan and even bigger problems and if we weren't careful this would all turn against us. Kerr said [Lakhdar] Brahimi [UN special representative for Afghanistan] had to get his skates on. We went through the humanitarian side of things. Clare was up on the border today and doing OK. Lander reported on a specific threat to TB. TB was a bit irritated at Geoff and CDS who both seemed to have lost confidence and therefore weren't inspiring it. Afterwards, the full Cabinet in which they went over pretty much the same ground.

Then to TB's press conference where he was working from notes and we were trying to get up the line about the next two weeks being the most testing period. There was a bit of resistance from the Foreign Office that I was trying to take premises, people and resources, but John Kerr was being extremely helpful. We were starting to get the backlash following the announcement of the three-way trilateral with Chirac and Schroeder. Catherine Colonna called to say they were very keen to hold their press conference at 7, but Berlusconi in particular was throwing a total wobbly. There was a danger tomorrow's summit would be a total shambles. TB said to me he wanted me to try to take over the propaganda side of things because what it lacked at the moment was total single-mindedness.

Friday, October 19

Richard W came to see me, said there was a really bad feeling around the place re Jo Moore. I said it would get a lot better if civil servants weren't constantly briefing against her. At the morning War meeting, Scarlett said there was a clear sense of Taliban morale crumbling. The chief of the air force was among the Taliban waverers. A fair number of defections and confidence Mazar-e-Sharif would fall soon. The Northern Alliance were far more bullish. CDS reported that the Americans were getting a bit fed up with us for not agreeing to all the targets. TB said if there was any target that we believed should be hit and there were legal problems here, he wanted to know about it. He said if I was Bush, I would be going spare about this. Later he called [Lord] Goldsmith over. RW gave a word of caution in relation to the *Belgrano*[1] and TB said the problem there was not the legality,

[1] Argentine Navy light cruiser, controversially sunk in 1982 by a British nuclear submarine whilst outside the 200 nautical mile exclusion zone around the Falkland Islands. 323 Argentine sailors died.

it was the attempt to cover it up. I couldn't resist adding 'A failure of spin over a discredited Tory regime.' Richard smiled.

I did a conference call with Jack and all our ambassadors in the Arab world to get them bought into the need for a more proactive approach. Most of them seemed to get it, though there were one or two whingers who basically said there was nothing much we could do. But it was an OK call and I felt we were making progress. We left for Ghent on an RAF flight, the only real story the Big Three summit. TB seemed fairly relaxed about it. I was worried it would end up as a coalition fracture but TB felt the risk outweighed the benefit of Chirac wanting us involved in this way. We arrived and went straight to the meeting in the cellar room of a chapel. Chirac seemed a bit pissed off that it was TB plus three – DM, Jonathan and I – whilst he and [Lionel] Jospin were plus one. Schroeder was a bit late so Chirac kicked off going through what the French could offer, mainly AWACs [airborne warning and control planes] and special forces, reconnaissance and refuelling. He was clearly keen to get involved quickly. TB told him we had people working alongside the NA. Chirac felt pre winter and pre Ramadan we had to step up the pace. TB said at the moment we had no option but to work through the NA but we would need to bring them back in if they became too difficult. They were vital to taking Mazar-e-Sharif.

Schroeder's contribution was more about how they could help build a post-Taliban government. Jospin chipped in with a question about the post-Taliban regime and before he had even got the words out, Chirac interrupted and in the most patronising way imaginable said 'Can we finish on the military phase first please?' Chirac also asked Schroeder direct whether they would send special forces. Schroeder said if I was asked, I'd say yes, but I hope not to be asked. Germany was in a particularly difficult position and he pointed out that it would have to be put to parliament first as a fundamental change in their foreign policy. Even when he was onside though, Chirac would always make sure we knew his real opinions about the Yanks in particular, as in when he said that 'irrefutable proof' of anything was not necessarily proof if it came from the CIA.

It was a pretty odd meeting, not least because of the rather poky venue, the fact that there was not enough coffee, that the carpets were a bit thin and the noise from outside loud. TB said he felt there had been a shift in Israel's attitude to the UK and the US, and a big change in the US attitude to Israel. If Arafat made a positive move, e.g. handing over detainees . . . Chirac interrupted again, saying he would be assassinated. Schroeder said he had spoken to [Ariel] Sharon who referred to Arafat as 'my Taliban'. That is how they see them. It was by now like Babel's tower, with so many interpreters translating between three languages at once. TB still felt we had to construct a gesture from Arafat.

The rest of the day was by and large a waste of time for me. I had Tom Kelly to deal with the Ghent business and so instead I focused on planning the Saudi visit. Then a call from the *Mail* asking whether it was true that Prince Charles was to be a special envoy to the Saudis. It was frustrating. They clearly wanted to help, and to get a 'Charles joins war effort' story out there, but it was an odd way to go about it – briefing that we have asked them to do something when actually we'd talked about something else.

TB was bored with the summit deliberations and came out for a chat. As ever, they had not skimped on the food for all the under-worked hangers-on, with national dishes from each of the fifteen member states. We watched Louis Michel [Belgian foreign minister] stuffing his face. I reminded TB it was part of the deal that I didn't have to come to these wretched European summits any more. He said to see this as part of the Arab media brief. The main story was the Big Three summit upsetting everyone else but TB was unapologetic. The press conference was straightforward, they did the future of Europe over dinner, then off to the plane. TB said Chirac had been interesting because he so clearly wanted to be on the same page with us on this. TB recalled what [Margaret] Thatcher had told him – 'The Germans are big but they feel so guilty they don't use their power, you can't trust the French, the Italians are only good for clothes, the Dutch are the most like us but too close to the Germans. But I do like the Danes.'

Sunday, October 21

Up early and off to see Dad who was looking very frail. TB called as I drove up, still adamant we should stay robust on Jo Moore. I agreed it would be even worse to get rid of her now, but she must be miserable as hell. He was really worried about the Middle East, feared after his conversation with [Ariel] Sharon that after the seven-day mourning of the tourism minister [Rehavam Ze'evi, assassinated by Palestinian gunmen], the Israelis would go into real battle against the Palestinians. I got Godric to brief the Mondays that we were closer to seeing UK ground forces in action. I hadn't read the papers first thing, and I had a flick through when we got back home, a bit alarmed at how much 'spin' was back in the news because of Jo.

Monday, October 22

Godric's briefing went big, and alongside the Americans' weekend briefing on the [US Army] Rangers going in, there was a feeling of the temperature rising. However, the feeling of drift in the War Cabinet was grim. It must by now have become clear to John Scarlett, C etc. how different the mood was in the meetings with the broader group of ministers. John did his best to put over a sense of progress, with hints that Mullah Omar was worried, and reports on the sense of shock among the Taliban about how the attacks had intensified. CDS gave his usual very downbeat assessment, focusing mainly on problems. He said we were not advancing as fast as we should be, but we were looking at at least five more days for Mazar and that Kabul would not be taken before winter/Ramadan. John Vereker said we were still not talking catastrophe on the humanitarian front but we were just two and a half weeks from winter.

Afterwards, TB said he felt that the morning meeting was becoming too big, and he was worried about what might be leaked. He also said he felt Geoff and CDS were too negative, constantly saying what they couldn't do. 'I want my military to be straining at the leash, us having to hold them back.' He then told me to get a story planted somewhere that Boyce was doing a great job. He said my visit to the States tomorrow was vital, that I had to persuade them of the need for a central hub. It was like putting together a general election campaign, required that level of organisation and detail. I had to persuade the Americans how important it was to think beyond their own public opinion.

I was now working close to flat out on getting the Arab media unit up and running properly. Arab opinion was saying this unit would have no impact and was just propaganda. Julian Braithwaite's view was the SIS, or some of them, were feeling vulnerable, wanted to feel they were the only people who really got this stuff. It certainly read like something designed to deter us. John Kerr had been a fantastic support. I went over with him to meet the new team, who seemed pretty bright but I made clear we would need more still. Jo Moore was moving up the agenda again and my worry was that she would weaken in the face of all this. I got home fairly early as it was Rory's birthday tomorrow, but was dead tired again. The news was all [Gerry] Adams after he had called on the IRA to disarm which was a big moment.

Tuesday, October 23

BBC were getting more and more outrageous, Taliban claims were being treated pretty much the same as anything we said followed by endless Fergal Keane [journalist] emoting. At the 8am meeting, John Scarlett said all the terror camps had been demolished and I said why on earth haven't we done a big presentation on that? TB asked CDS at one point what size of an area was covered by 'the front line'. There was a long pause and he said quietly 'I don't really know I'm afraid.' TB asked him what kind of advice he should be giving to Bush. Boyce said it depends if they are prepared to go through Ramadan. TB said let's assume they are not. 'Mmm, mmm, it's very difficult.' If you were to sum up his contribution it was to say we couldn't take Mazar, the NA were impossible to deal with, the Americans were not being totally open. He had the top special forces guy there who sounded much more like he knew what he was on about, but who was also none too optimistic. The NA were finding it harder than we feared to take Mazar and we didn't necessarily have all the people there that we needed. On the military, the diplomatic, and the humanitarian, we just weren't where we needed to be.

Kerr felt Colin Powell's Middle East vision was wishful thinking unless they have a lot better intelligence than we do about the current state of Israeli thinking. TB asked David Manning and me to go through at the end of the meeting and said he was seized by how important our visit was. 'You have got to get a grip of the show.' I was tying up loose ends before getting ready to leave. Robin Cook came to see me before doing his first on-camera briefing for the Arab press. He was clearly a bit baleful about not being Foreign Secretary. I told him I was going to Washington with Jack and he said 'Don't jump on my grave.' He did one of his chirpy 'won't let you downs' and off he went.

I left for the Savoy where I was doing a 'turn the tables' interview with Jeremy Paxman [BBC *Newsnight* presenter] and had decided on a twin track – keep asking about his earnings and throw in general-knowledge questions about people from the smaller countries involved in the crisis. It seemed to go fine. Lots of nice charity types there. I teased him into whacking [John] Humphrys [BBC *Today* presenter] a bit, accepting the superficiality of TV as a medium, and he wasn't great on the general-knowledge stuff.

TB was at a session at the Commonwealth Club with all Cabinet ministers and their permanent secretaries in a kind of big bonding session. I went to meet up with Jack. He said TB had been excellent, really thought about it and the whole event had been a huge success. He then added that it had all been the idea of Alice [Perkins, Straw's wife, a civil servant]. In the car, and later on the flight, he and I had a series of really good conversations. He was very down on GB, felt that the mad streak had got worse and the combination of TB rising into a different league to the rest of them plus economic worries had put GB in a very bad frame of mind. Said he was loathed by many of his colleagues. On TB, he felt he didn't do enough in Parliament. A lot of our chat was about kids, football, stuff unrelated to politics and Jack was definitely still a fully paid-up member of the human race. He, I, David Manning, Simon McDonald [Straw's private secretary] and one of the coppers were up in first class when Alison [Blackshaw, AC's personal assistant] came down from club to do some work, some of the other passengers complained – tossers – so I went back with her to club.

I did a note to TB re his *Telegraph* interview and PMQs [Prime Minister's Questions] tomorrow in which I felt he needed to give a longer than usual update on overall strategy, the military, MEPP, thinking on the Taliban. For the bulk of the flight I was working on a note for the White House setting out ideas on a draft communications plan and structures. I said in terms the thinking needed to be on a par with the thinking applied to elections with many of the same functions. Jack and David read it through, made a few comments and were basically both happy with it. It was largely modelled on Kosovo with the Arab–Muslim angle meaning a different kind of response was required. Jack travelled with his own polish and made a big play of shining up my shoes.

We landed to be met by Tony Brenton [deputy head of mission, UK Embassy] and two pieces of news – the IRA had delivered, and Burnley had beaten Crystal Palace [1–0]. We went briefly to our ambassador's residence before I went out to a restaurant to meet Dan Bartlett [deputy to Karen Hughes] who with Karen and Ari [Fleischer, White House press secretary] was part of the press triumvirate during Bush's campaign. He seemed a bit nervy but seemed a nice enough guy. I had not really been aware of just how much the anthrax situation was convulsing the system and it meant Afghanistan was not nearly so much in the news as it was at home. I did feel though that I was pushing at a fairly open door. He said Bush was up for it, realised we had to make change. At one or two points he stated openly that they knew they were not up to their game, that they thought too much on American lines, not enough about opinion outside, and they were happy to take all the advice and help going. He was good at analysing problems – e.g. how the Arab media viewed us and why – but their solutions weren't that great. He gave me a paper from Karl Rove [senior adviser to Bush] that I think was meant to be their response to the brainstorm I had given to Karen, but it was not what

I expected. I think the basic problem was that they genuinely didn't understand anti-Americanism. They couldn't see how, given that in this instance they had been the victim, and given all the help they had tried to administer around the world, they were not more popular. So it made them more insular, and a lot of their ideas were actually about things that would simply strengthen their standing at home but do nothing for them overseas necessarily.

I was walking a fairly difficult line, because basically TB wanted me to try to take this over, but at the same time it was important not to give them the sense we thought they couldn't do this. I got a bit close to the mark when I showed him a polling presentation from Philip [Gould] which showed that quite a lot of Bush's statements had gone down really badly. He seemed surprised, even a little hurt. He said Condi was totally on board for trying to improve presentation and if I had her and Karen onside, I would get the president. I was in two minds about giving over the various papers I had done there and then but in the end did so and agreed they would form the basis of our discussions tomorrow. I got back to the residence, felt I had made a good opening. Stayed up for a long chat with Jack and [Sir Christopher] Meyer who said that the US military gave no clear sense of strategy. Sounded familiar. Alison came in with the cuttings from home, including some pretty big reviews of my session with Paxman, widely judged to be a straight win.

Wednesday, October 24

Washington. I couldn't sleep so I was up and about at 4.30 and chatted to TB in London before his *Telegraph* interview. The American papers underlined how totally obsessed they were with anthrax. It took up the first fifteen minutes of US bulletins. It confirmed me in the view that they were unlikely to have been thinking enough about the stuff I was trying to persuade them of. My first meeting was with Karen Hughes. I was accompanied by Bob Peirce [embassy press staff]. We arrived at the White House, a brief wait then up through the warren of steps and little offices and through to see her. It was a fairly small office, lots of pictures of her and GWB. She looked a bit shell-shocked, sounded it too. She said this was all very different to running a Texan political campaign. We went through the notes I had sent over, the importance of third parties, who their key communicators were, how to improve message co-ordination between the various bits of government, polling, Muslim outreach, the UN. I said why didn't GWB visit a few mosques? Who did they have in the US Muslim community who could be built up into being the kind of people

TV wanted to hear? Who were the right people to put on the Arab media and would they understand the need to use a slightly different language?

I went through the note done on the plane which she pretty much bought into but my heart sank a bit when she said Rumsfeld would in fact be agreeable to doing a lot of this. She said how can we set this up quickly? I said you just do, top down, all the way. Then to lunch with Condi Rice. She was already with DM and C, Dan Fried. Sebastian Wood from the embassy and Steve Hadley [US Deputy National Security Advisor] joined us later. Condi was a lot more relaxed than Karen and we started out laughing about the pictures of the Northern Alliance on horseback, suggesting we may have overestimated their military capabilities. She and DM had already gone over the problems caused by conflicting signals coming out of the different bits of government, the lack of a clear military plan. Condi had seen my paper and was pretty much signed up straight away. The concept I was pushing was a 24-hour cycle in which Washington, London and the region, probably Islamabad, were in permanent contact, and driving the news proactively in all the different time zones. There was some discussion about who and how to get into Islamabad. Condi said Bush believed the PR so far had been dreadful and had told her and Karen 'go fix it' and I was definitely pushing at an open door. Once or twice the conversation slipped into anthrax but it was important to keep that separate, not least because of the dire effect it had on their morale.

Condi was impressive, had the same kind of grasp of detail as DM did, good manners, pretty straight talking. I noticed no wine, just water on the table. She said she would give Karen the backing she needed to make this happen, and agreed Karen would chair a team here which liaised with me in London, and that we would send a Brit to them and get one of their best people to us. It was proving very straightforward to get them signed up to the kind of operation we needed. Then to the Pentagon, by now it was hot, and we had a fair old distance to walk before we finally reached [assistant secretary of defense for public affairs] Torie Clarke's office. She was nice, smart, also spoke in a very fast, clipped manner like Karen. She felt Rumsfeld was doing too much and agreed we weren't getting out enough pictures that showed progress. I also said it was important that she did what she could to stop the Pentagon/State Department public divisions and the best way to do that was to agree a very concerted 'White House in charge' strategy. She seemed up for that too though clearly one of her problems was the number of people who spoke to the press on background. I told her what Steve Hadley had said, that the State Department had a war room, the Pentagon had a war room. I said they seemed to be at war with each other. I started to push on the idea of maybe [UK General] John Reith [chief of Joint Operations at Permanent Joint HQ] getting involved in a cross-national way. She said Rumsfeld had committed himself to doing daily briefings with the bureau chiefs and could not get out of it. I suggested they could get out of anything if they were busy enough, but told her that in the European and our context, he scored last behind Powell and Bush in terms of the buttons he pressed.

Then to the State Department to see Charlotte Beers who had been hired as undersecretary of public diplomacy and whose background was advertising. I had been warned she was a lot older than she looked, maybe well into her sixties, and had picked up some opposition to her. She instinctively seemed to get what I was on about and also had some clever ideas for how to spend the money she had won for advertising. Her basic pitch was that the Arab world had a very narrow view of America based upon wealth, politics, films and music, and all the big companies. She showed me a portfolio of absolutely stunning photographs of mosques, most of which looked at first glance as though they were in the Arab world, but all of which were in the States. Then some wonderful pictures and stories from ordinary American Muslims. She was clearly going to be useful on the soft stuff in particular. I could see why she was getting up a few noses there, but I liked her style.

Then back to the White House to link up with Jack and have a meeting with Cheney. Jack told me my communications paper had gone down well with Rumsfeld and Powell. When Cheney came in with his people – Scooter Libby, his chief of staff, Mary Matalin, his press woman, and three military advisers – Mary and Cheney both had the note in their hands. On the military campaign, Cheney was bullish. Jack asked him outright what the strategy was. He said NA should take Mazar, then he went over some of the whys and hows and wherefores of what might follow vis-à-vis Taliban, al-Qaeda, Bin Laden, but it wasn't really an answer to the question what is the strategy. Jack said UK support was strong but could we hold the coalition together if this thing went on longer than expected? He said he thought so. They did the Middle East and Jack asked how difficult it was having such a strong pro-Israel lobby. Cheney said its influence is sometimes overstated and that at the moment they were pretty subdued. Jack said [Ariel] Sharon was doing things which were dangerous and could not be part of our strategy. I had always assumed that Cheney would be more open and forthcoming when he was in charge of meetings rather than, as when Bush was there, clearly comfortable playing second fiddle. But he was not one to speak too much for the sake of it. He had cold, slightly menacing body language, listened very intently without giving much away, and usually paused before giving a thought-through answer. I went through the concept I was trying to get him signed up to and he was fine about it, said we should just do it.

Mary said on the way out she was so pleased I had sent over the note and gone there because they had been pressing for this kind of approach for ages. She was a real bundle, as you'd expect from someone hitched up with James Carville [Democrat strategist]. I was fascinated how that all worked. I just could not imagine living with someone from the other party. She said it just about worked, but they were able to separate out different parts of their lives and they just got used to having good arguments. We definitely made progress though. Jack did a brief doorstep while David and I left from a side door and headed back to the residence. We had a couple of hours at the residence. I chatted with Meyer about things we would need to keep the pressure on over. I spent the first two or three hours of the flight back writing up notes with Alison [Blackshaw] out of the various meetings. We had got the cuttings through at the airport and Northern Ireland decommissioning was getting big play, but positive.

Thursday, October 25

I didn't sleep well. I drove in from the airport with Jack, mainly small talk, how hard it was getting the time you needed for kids and family. I had really enjoyed his company, and his manner. Sometimes, because of the nature of the job, there was just too much stuff going on around TB, whereas I felt in the last couple of days, we had clear and limited aims, and pretty much met them in full. He was very sound on schools, and the need for kids like ours to go to schools with a broad mix. We got back for the War Cabinet, which was all a bit grim, not really going anywhere, not really making the progress we needed, CDS as ever telling us what we couldn't do rather than what we could, weather bad, not enough agents alongside NA, not clear where key Taliban people are. TB said we must take Mazar before Ramadan. Boyce's understanding was that the Americans did intend to continue bombing after Ramadan. TB said we have to be absolutely single-minded in the next two weeks. He asked for a paper on how it would be taken if all available resources could be found. RC said we would lose support quickly without real progress. I filled them in on the media plans we had agreed with the Americans and TB was still banging on about the need to do more with Muslim opinion here. Scarlett said Al Jazeera had an OBL broadcast that had not been put out possibly because the interviewer had been asked to do certain questions, soft questions, and hadn't.

Full Cabinet was pretty much the same as the smaller group, and I sensed people beginning to get a little bit low and worried. I started phoning round and organising volunteers to go out to Pakistan and the US. Karen called me later with Dan Bartlett and a guy called Jim Wilkinson [White House deputy director of communications] on the line. Jim was going to run their war room. We went over what they needed there, and what we needed in Pakistan. I called Hilary Synnott, our high commissioner in Islamabad, and got him on board for trying to find premises. I called George Robertson [Secretary General] at NATO to get him signed up, then a few UK-based ambassadors. The German guy was helpful as ever. We had applied a catalyst and things were finally starting to move. When I did a meeting of GICS [Government Information and Communication Service] staff, I got more volunteers than we could initially handle. TB was pretty down about the military side of things. There were going to be redeployments of UK troops from Oman tomorrow which would be big news, but we had a problem with Rumsfeld saying something interpreted as an admission we would never get OBL. I got home to see the kids, and Fiona and I went out for dinner, and she was desperate for me to leave, and couldn't understand why now was not the moment.

Friday, October 26

I gave the morning meeting a miss and took Grace [AC's daughter] to school. TB said he wasn't sure he could cope with many more of these meetings where all he heard was things going wrong and things everyone agreed needed to be done but weren't being done. I spent most of the day working on setting up the new media operation. We were talking about whether we could use the spiked Al Jazeera interview [with Bin Laden], then a note to Karen. The need for what we were doing in Pakistan was shown up every time I turned on the news. The Taliban were getting far too easy a ride. I chatted to TB about the pressure I was under at home to leave. He said it was the worst possible time. He thought the problem was that I had an enormous job and Fiona felt undervalued by comparison. But she was extremely bright and able and we should try to build up what she did.

George Robertson called with some names. I went over to see John

Kerr who was trying to find me premises for our war room. He greeted me in a ludicrous plumed hat he was supposed to wear when he went to see the Queen. He was very funny, very friendly, despite everyone saying how devious he was, my experience so far was that when he promised something, he delivered it. I got Anne Shevas [Downing Street chief press officer] working on turning the offices he was offering into a proper war room. I called Will Farish, the US ambassador, to beg for Lee McLenny [press counselor, US Embassy]. I had Deborah Hermer [GICS] heading out to Washington and briefed her. Tessa [Jowell] was due out in New York for a ceremony and I fixed her to do some media before and after. I went to see Fiona in the office and tried to assure her things would get better, but she wasn't convinced. TB was obviously worried about what I had said about Fiona. But he said I had one of the best jobs in the world, I did it brilliantly and I would hate it if I was not involved. I was worried with all the trips coming up that Fiona would really decide she had had enough of it all.

Saturday, October 27

We had computers brought into the war room. Mary Matalin called and said Jim Wilkinson would be fine, that he was one of those people who 'walks through walls'. She said James sent his regards and was relieved that the Brits had finally kicked them into shape! I spoke to TB and agreed some lines for Tom [Kelly] to put out re moral fibre, this being a long-term battle. Boyce's briefing of yesterday was going big.[1] Boyce's interview and the gloomy photos of him played into the idea, gathering too much pace, that the war was 'going nowhere'.

TB was wondering whether I should take an upfront spokesman role either here or Pakistan and was worried 1. that we would lose sight even more of the domestic scene, and 2. that the media would not be able to resist turning it into the AC show. I felt we needed two different people to do it, one heavyweight, serious, big picture, maybe an ambassador, someone else doing the nitty-gritty. Paddy Feeny was out with Tessa and I persuaded her to let me redirect him to Washington to join the Jim Wilkinson effort. Boyce was still fretting about Guthrie's profile and about Rumsfeld criticising him. TB asked me to advise him to stop reading the press.

I had to leave for Chequers for TB's 9am meeting with him, David M, Jonathan, [General] Pigott plus two, C and the head of special

[1] Boyce had said that fighting the Taliban was not like fighting an army, but fighting an idea like communism, and may take fifty years.

forces. We met in the Hawtrey Room.[1] The message that came through from all of them was that the Americans were a bit all over the place. TB ended by saying that we had to become like an extra strategic mind for them, give them a real plan. Pigott said the Taliban obviously had to be attacked physically but we also had to attack their morale and attack the concept. For the moment their morale was quite high and the NA's was low. A lot of this was about changing mindsets there about how this was all going. He said if the Americans were here, they would explain their current thinking as follows: 1. assemble all the hardware they needed; 2. initial strikes and create conditions for the third phase – we are well into that; 3. march onwards to decisive action; 4. sustained effort, fall of the Taliban, humanitarian and post-Taliban really steps up.

TB said what would Tommy Franks say if I asked him what was going on. 'I'm building up, I'm looking to get the total picture by spring, I'm continuing air strikes, I'm giving sixty per cent support to NA at Mazar, twenty-five per cent Kabul, fifteen per cent Herat. I'm keeping the coalition engaged.' He said there was also confusion about Ramadan and it was important not to let the sense build that there would be an automatic pause. We should see Ramadan and winter as opportunities. There had been a very long conference at the Pentagon, the seventy top brains including five C.-in-C.s, and it was very frank. The main complaint was that there was no central plan, no real strategic clarity from the Pentagon. One had said 'We're still working to the president's speech on TV.' TB lightened the mood, by saying 'Christ, I hope you lot aren't following my party conference speech.' The special forces guy said they were.

Pigott went on, said the inter-agency machinery wasn't working, that there were constant arguments about who was in control, info ops not working, no clear understanding of how properly to use the coalition. He said there was a lot of praise in the American military for TB and the UK operation by comparison. TB said the Taliban would be feeling that they had a better chance than they thought as we go up to winter. He too did not like the idea of a pause because it indicated this was going on for a long time after and that would put pressure on the international coalition, including Pakistan who were getting worried that things were not going as they should.

He was still keen to step up the operations to take Mazar-e-Sharif. We kept being told it was about to fall. He said if nothing happens

[1] Named after an Elizabethan occupant of the house, William Hawtrey, whose family had owned the Chequers estate from the thirteenth century.

between now and the half-time whistle, and by the time they get back on the pitch, we will be in difficulty. Pigott said we should not encourage half-time thinking. We need to be thinking of more harrying, looking at this not just in terms of bombs and territory but total domination. TB said it would look like the Taliban were tougher than we thought and the NA more of a ragbag than we thought. He said if we were the NA we would be thinking 'Do these guys really know what they're doing and might I be better off watching my own back?' C said the US were using some pretty heavy power. That he had been at the CIA and seen live pictures of the C130 [gunship] attacks and that those big powerful drops had a big psychological impact. TB said he had used up a lot of political chips on Mazar-e-Sharif. Chirac and Schroeder both believed we would have taken it by now, but what were they using there? 2,000 horses! The SF guy said it was a mistake to think of the NA as an army in the conventional sense. He said it would take months to train them and even after that you wouldn't want to risk your lives on them.

I said we had to get away from the idea that progress was only measured in bombs and territory, that we had to do more to shape the perception of events inside and outside. TB said GWB would soon surely be getting the fear in the pit of his stomach 'that I've been having for the past two weeks'. The SF guy said Americans never lost a battle in Vietnam but they did lose a war. TB said again we had to strategise for the Americans. They were against using the Al Jazeera interview. It was classically the kind of thing that would give us a big media hit, and also unnerve them, but they were cautious.

TB was now more seized than ever that the information propaganda effort had become more important, not less. He summed up – first stage air superiority, better use of intelligence, reshape perception of progress, step up special forces operations and get alongside NA more, get them off the ground properly, start planning post-Taliban regime. He asked for a detailed list of everything these guys thought was needed to ensure success so that he could prepare another note for Bush. He and I went out for a walk in the garden. He said this was scary stuff but he couldn't understand why the Americans weren't focusing more on what needed to be done. Then the news came through that the US had hit an NA village. Another bloody mistake.

Sunday, October 28

Spoke to Jack several times before *Frost* and we agreed it was time to crank up the line that the media had very short memories and next to no humility about their predictions that had been wrong. We had to be getting the focus on the long term. Charles Guthrie agreed he would speak to Musharraf about making sure that our media centre out there would be allowed to operate properly. Tanya Joseph [Downing Street press officer] had volunteered for Pakistan and I briefed her before she left. TB sent through a nine-page note based on the meeting yesterday, setting out where he thought every aspect of the operation should be improved and tightened. Jim Wilkinson called, said that he had premises and was setting up units to cover liaison with us, central desk, terrorist funding, humanitarian, Internet, Grid [diary mechanism to co-ordinate announcements], Muslim opinion, key opinion formers, writers. They were on the right lines and said they would take as many of our people as they could get. The Americans were saying they would reconsider on the Al Jazeera interview if we could give them a real reason, but he was not sure.

I drove up to Wolverhampton for the Burnley game. The phone hardly stopped on the way up and it was difficult to talk, TB on re matters in general, Tessa re some of her concerns about how the families of September 11 victims had been handled, C re Al Jazeera and personnel for Islamabad, Guthrie and Geoff H re the same. TB spoke to Bush later and started to talk through some of the points in his note. Bush mentioned twice how grateful they had been that I had gone out there and was sorting out the media. DM felt it was in some ways the best call yet, because GWB sounded more mellow, keener to listen, more on the same wavelength again. But Rumsfeld was still going on about Iraq the whole time. We lost 3–0. I got home to do a note for us and the Americans on why I thought we should use the Al Jazeera interview.

Monday, October 29

The press was wobbling even more. I told an 8.30 meeting that it was time for us to get more robust, challenge the fundamental flakiness of the media. TB was at Chequers, in full cry about the need for improved rebuttal. I had a good meeting with Jamie Shea [director of information and press] and Mark Laity [senior spokesman] from NATO and put together a note for George Robertson trying to persuade him to give us more people. Paddy Feeny and Peter Reid [press attaché, UK Embassy] were already installed in Washington. Jim Wilkinson had pretty much got the thing up and running and we had our first properly functioning conference call. Another round of calls on a regular basis was another big chunk out of the diary alongside all the meetings already in there, added to which today I was trying to draft TB's Welsh Assembly speech for tomorrow. I had forty minutes on the phone with Piers Morgan [editor, *Daily Mirror*], who was basically driven by spite re what he saw as favoured treatment of the *Sun*. I had an hour with the South-East group of [Labour] MPs and was beginning to curse Robert Hill for having talked me into doing these groups, though the feedback was pretty good.

TB's note had further galvanised people, and was useful to me in making clear around the system that the demand for this new centre of operations was his, not mine. I fell in the road and ripped my suit and badly bruised my leg running back from a meeting at the FCO. I was also late home and walked into another huge row after I told Fiona I would probably have to go on the trip to Israel. TB, as was clear from the office meeting, was also frustrated about the public services stuff. He had seen GB for a meeting on tax credits, now costing £4 billion.

Tuesday, October 30

TB had left by the time I got in to go to Bristol, then Wales for the speech. He had married my draft to his and it worked fine. I did the usual morning meeting then took one separately for all the people in the new CIC [Coalition Information Centre]. I felt things were starting to motor. [Lee] McLenny had arrived. [Mark] Laity was starting, though there were one or two concerns about how much he seemed to want to be the front man. I spoke to the Australian high commissioner [Michael L'Estrange] to get some of his people. I was disappointed that Karen Hughes had not yet been on one of the conference calls. I got Phil Bassett [head of Number 10 Research and Information Unit] to agree to go over to the FCO war room. I wanted him to be circulating agreed lines to take on all the difficult running issues to the three centres and relevant capitals. It would take a bit longer before we had a real grip, but I felt it was coming. I went over and did a pep talk, felt they were a good bunch. I said it was almost impossible to imagine us losing the military battle but perfectly feasible that we could lose the battle for hearts and minds. There was definitely a mood in the media, who were talking up anything that went wrong. Nick Soames [Conservative MP, former Armed Forces minister] called and said TB should make another Commons statement before long. He felt we were doing well and said we should ignore the press who were just 'loathsome creeps'.

Wednesday, October 31

I was starting to motor again but was also agitated that actually getting the three centres moving was too slow. I was still pressing on the Al Jazeera [Bin Laden interview] front but Condi wanted to wait because the president was going to try to get the Qataris to make sure it wasn't screened. I was sure it would get out there at some point, and as we knew the content, and the Al Jazeera worries, far better we got it out there first. I spoke to Karen about the idea of generating big women's events to talk about how ghastly the Taliban were. Bush had written to TB today and amid the other stuff had said explicitly how grateful they were for what we had done to change the approach. So it was beginning to work through and hopefully within a day or two we would be properly up and running. Mark Laity wasn't getting on with some of the others and slightly driving people mad.

TB was out in Syria, and got a total banjaxing by President Assad, which was a bit of a problem.[1] Assad had basically said enough for it to be seen as lambasting our entire approach. TB was giving him the benefit of the doubt, he said it was as much a clash of media cultures as anything, which was the line we tried to push to the hacks when we saw them on the plane later. I wasn't wholly sure why we felt it worth him going there in the first place. TB was in danger of getting hooked on the international stuff, having at first promised to take it easy, though Jonathan was probably right in pointing out that he was as well placed as anyone to do this, and that a lot of people round the world would rather see TB doing it, even on Bush's behalf, than Bush himself.

We were starting to get press calls about the CIC, so I put together a line. [David] Yelland [editor, *Sun*] was pitching for an interview with Bush. I sent him a blind copy of the letter I sent to Karen making the case for it and he sent her the most over-the-top CV-type letter I have ever seen, but he was basically being helpful at the moment. Also the *Mirror* seemed to be a bit more positive on the domestic front. I was flying out to meet TB for the Jordan and Israel part of his trip and was hoping not to be noticed because they would want to use it as part of the Syria crisis jigsaw they were trying to put together after Assad's big whack at him. When I spoke to TB about it before leaving for the airport, he seemed OK about it, said it had

[1] After repeating Syrian condemnation of the September 11 attacks, Assad defended 'resistance fighters', saying 'Resistance to occupation is an international right. Nobody can deny we have many organisations, many people who support the resistance fighters who seek to liberate their land.'

actually been quite comic to stand there having been promised the guy was going to be supportive and then watch him deliver an attack totally lapped up by our lot.

On the flight out, I did a stack of notes with Alison [Blackshaw] on things we needed to do at the three centres, areas for brainstorming, note to Geoff H re helping the *News of the World* with a shock issue on the Taliban. We arrived in Jordan and were driven to the palace where we had last been for the king's funeral.[1] TB was now talking about going back via Rome because there was a trilateral planned for Sunday and he was keen to keep Berlusconi vaguely on board.

Thursday, November 1

Amman. TB got an absolute mauling in the press for the 'Syrian humiliation', 'Disaster in Damascus' etc., way over the top in some ways, but there we are. I went out for a run round some of the hills near the palace, and loved the sounds of the city starting to wake up, particularly the calls to prayer. TB once said if I was religious I would probably end up as an Islamic fundamentalist, and I think I know what he meant. TB was trying to put his best face on after yesterday, and was comical in his description of it – 'It could have been worse, he could have taken out a gun and shot me' – but we also had a long chat with Jonathan and Tom K, later with the ambassador, Edward Chaplin, re how to retrieve the situation. All we could do was emphasise his willingness to take risks, get his hands dirty, do whatever it took, to work up and see through a plan. There was clearly no point trying to make out Assad had been anything but unhelpful, though TB was still of the view it was as much a clash of political and media cultures as a deliberate act of hostility.

We left for breakfast with King Abdullah. In common with others we had spoken to, he was worried about the impact of Al Jazeera, which was developing real sway among the broader Muslim community. We talked about the need to get clerics out emphasising the un-Islamic nature of OBL's words and deeds, and the need to reframe the argument from Islam vs West to moderate vs extreme forms of Islam. He was in two minds about whether we should engage more fully with Al Jazeera. He felt we had to be careful not to be exploited, or get to a situation where the more we did, the more they felt they had to represent 'the street'. It was an interesting take. He said that looking at the latest unbroadcast OBL tape, the problem was he 'looked the part', and we should not underestimate his appeal. The original

[1] The funeral of King Hussein, February 1999. See *Power and the People*, pp 652–6.

plan had been not to do media but in the end we did, and got him to push the line about the need for moderate Muslims to defeat extremists in argument.

It was a useful and very friendly meeting, and he certainly seemed like someone who grasped what TB was trying to do and wanted to help. His father was a hard act to follow, but he cut it as king, even if he could come across as being quite nervous at times. I sensed he agonised a lot, and at points I saw similarities with Prince Charles, though Abdullah has raw power. We boarded the helicopters and set off for Jerusalem, on the way discussing with TB how to develop this argument about moderate vs extreme, and how to challenge the assumptions, how to win round those countries basically supporting extreme views even if not always extreme actions. While he was seeing Shimon Peres [Israeli foreign minister], the Al Jazeera OBL interview was already circulating amongst his supporters in Pakistan. So it was out. I got DM to call Condi, and I called Karen H. She was very stroppy about being woken, while George agreed with me that we should just go for it, just do it. I was furious because it was now twelve days since we first knew of this interview, we had had all this time to sort it, and it just didn't happen. Here we were discussing how we were going to react WHEN it came out. The Americans were negotiating with the Qataris to suppress it, which was crazy, as all that would happen was that it would get spread underground and in its own way have even more impact, whereas I was sure if we had got it out in our terms, we could neutralise it in the Middle East and turn it to our advantage in the West. I was particularly fed up with it because it meant in a way I had lost the first battle to mount a serious media job on a tricky issue, and I was worried they didn't really get it.

TB and Peres overran, then I travelled with him to the [Ariel] Sharon meeting, before during and after which I was struck just how much heavier the security was for him and TB, not just the number of bodies around, but the barriers and the closed roads. Even we had to go through a weird series of obstacles before arriving at a kind of back door and in to see him. Sharon was less belligerent than usual and the lunch in many ways went fine, but they really just wanted to whack the Palestinians the whole time. At the press conference he was very uncompromising and I could sense our press getting very excited, building up for 'rebuff for Blair' Day 2. In fact, set against what he often said and how he said it, it wasn't that bad, but it was enough to give them what they wanted. Even accepting how difficult the politics were and even remaining conscious, as I always tried to, of the reasons why Israel existed in the first place, it was very hard to warm to Sharon. And this was him in fairly mellow mode. TB felt there was a lot more to him than he showed and agreed these exchanges were difficult. But TB had his own mantra, commitment to the right of Israel to exist alongside a Palestinian state.

We left for another long helicopter flight and drive to Palestine, handover at the checkpoint and then on to see Arafat, struck as ever, as it was impossible not to be, by the immediate switch from First World to Third. We had the usual over-the-top welcome and guard of honour and then in to see Arafat and Co. TB was urging Arafat to be more constructive in his comments on the Israelis, but of course it was like dealing with a mirror – the things we'd heard Sharon attacking them for, now we got the reverse view, equally forcefully. I was tired and hungry by now, knew that if I started eating the selection of nuts laid out on the tables I wouldn't stop, and so it proved. We had another helicopter flight to get us to the airport later and we were running late, TB moaning about being away so often, yet he was the one who now wanted to go to Genoa to see Berlusconi.

Friday, November 2

I spoke to Wes Clark [retired US general, Supreme Allied Commander, Europe, during the Kosovo conflict] to suggest we stay in touch and that he did regular media. He felt he was excluded from some circles because he was close to Clinton but he felt he had a lot to offer. I saw the SpAds [special advisers] from all the departments, did the usual spiel, then a very long briefing with the foreign press. I felt totally on top of the issues and in command of the arguments but they were beginning to pick up on the gap in a strategy based on hammering the Taliban whilst not fully supporting the Northern Alliance. Guthrie called, said Musharraf was a bit alarmed about the use of the word 'war', felt there were better ways of describing the situation. I always enjoyed talking to Charles who had a grasp of the issues that went way beyond the military. I was also talking to the Americans about an agreed Grid format and process. TB called as I was on the way home, said he was sure he had the makings of a plan to take the Middle East peace process forward. I said we cannot get so focused on the international but then lose sight of the domestic.

Saturday, November 3

The main story of the weekend developed into a diplomatic fiasco. While we were in the Middle East, Chirac had suggested another Big Three meeting and TB had agreed. That was really why he had wanted to go to Genoa on the way back, to try to keep Berlusconi sweet. With the papers starting to talk of the Big Three again, Berlusconi called TB to protest, and TB relented. That meant asking the Spaniards too. So while we were busy briefing that there was to be a meeting between the five major European military contributors to the effort, the Belgians bullied their way into it to, leaning on the Germans to say they would not do it without the Belgians. So that was them plus [Javier] Solana [Secretary General of the EU Council] now involved. Then [Wim] Kok [Netherlands Prime Minister] called TB to say if the Belgians were there and he wasn't, it was a political disaster. It was a total shambles, and by tomorrow we would have problems with the rest and TB would be getting the blame for splitting Europe. He felt we could emphasise that it was a good thing they all wanted to come, which was pretty lame. Throw in Syria, [Ariel] Sharon and now this, and it wasn't a great diplomatic picture.

TB remained torn about whether I should go up front as one of the CIC on-camera spokesmen. He felt I was probably the best person to do it but it would make spin a problem again. And this time possibly not just with the media but with the public. It was probably a bad idea all round because with all the travelling, and the long hours, I was already walking on eggshells at home. I asked the conference call to get a figure from the Pentagon of the percentage of Afghanistan land space that was being bombed. It came back pretty quickly – 0.0002536. I got John Reid [Northern Ireland Secretary, former Armed Forces minister] up deploying it as a way of trying to counter the media impression of the blanket bombing of the whole country. John was very good at communicating strategy – lay the ground, go for the front line, then further options which we were not going to flag up. I was starting to get not great feedback from Peter Reid and Paddy Feeny about Jim Wilkinson's operation in Washington. They felt he kept stuff to himself, didn't delegate and didn't really appreciate what we were doing. Peter described him as a human dynamo, real bundle of energy, but not a manager and so people didn't really know what they were meant to be doing.

Sunday, November 4

There was still too much focus for my taste on the Taliban claims, and not enough scepticism about them. The dinner at Number 10 was growing more and more farcical and ridiculous as the day went on and the guest list grew. By the end of the day, some of the hacks were calling it a bring-a-bottle party. I spoke to TB and we agreed he shouldn't do any media, partly because he'd find it so hard to keep a straight face. He had given up on trying to pretend there was a way of saying it showed Britain strong in Europe. What it showed was a reality – namely that France, Germany and Britain were more powerful than the rest – that others didn't like the reality and that we didn't feel sufficiently comfortable with the French and Germans just to be able to tough it out. Most of the foreign leaders actively wanted to do media, which was fine, and even the big guys like Chirac I think liked doing stuff outside Number 10, but there was something very comic about the whole thing. I was working up a briefing on the CBI [Confederation of British Industry] speech. GB had done a pretty positive section on EMU [Economic and Monetary Union] but then the *FT* claimed the spin on it was anti euro. GB flatly denied to TB there had been an operation to do him in on the euro.

Monday, November 5

TB called, first asking whether we 'got away with the dinner' – just about, though Christ knows what the other leaders made of it – but also, and more seriously, worrying about where we were on the euro. I saw him as soon as I got in, and he was still going on about it. 'It's so obvious what is going on – he [GB] is trying to get the right-wing press behind him by seeming to be anti euro, and the left-wing press by being pro the poor. My problem is in not being able to trust what he's saying on the euro.' The problem when the two of them were mistrustful was that it spread down through the operation. I went over to the CIC and they were now pretty much clear about the different functions, and who was doing what. TB set off for the CBI in Birmingham and his speech seemed to go down OK.

The US conference call was better, more focused and confident. We collated all the different Arab leaders and voices criticising OBL and started placing them more widely. They were also starting to involve us more in working through GWB's basic messages. I was arguing for him to be closely involved in this argument about extremism vs moderate Muslims. Peter Reid said Bush had visited the Washington CIC this morning which gave them a real boost. Also, after the conference call today, they had had for the first time a proper follow-through meeting. But some, notably the NSC [White House National Security Council], were still a bit antsy about us being involved and sometimes telling them what to do.

Tuesday, November 6

TB got OK coverage for the CBI speech, but it was seen in part as a rebuff to GB on the euro. I went up to see him in the flat and he told me of his chat with GB yesterday when GB denied doing a spin job on the euro but then went into an elaborate thing about how it was TB's fault because he had got the *Telegraph* to do a story about Roger Liddle [special adviser, European affairs] saying we were going in at a certain date as though the tests were irrelevant. TB said what worried him was that their bizarre understanding of how we operated meant it was almost certainly how they operated. He said he didn't mind madness but he minded madness that had a policy read-across. He thought there was something almost comic about GB pumping out the line about TB being too presidential when he was the one arguing for decentralisation and GB was in practice the great centraliser. GB had been at him again, saying he promised to help him become leader to which TB said, I did, and I will, but only if you are going to help me do what I need to do while I am here. His worry now was so deep that he actually had moments wondering whether Gordon wanted him to succeed at all, e.g. on public services, or with the euro. 'He wants to be the prime minister that finally delivers excellent public services and the prime minister at the time we make the decision on the euro. What irritates him about the war is that it might just see me build a reputation too big for him to handle.' This was not good. The way each thought of the other was not healthy.

I asked Scarlett whether we could divulge some of the material they had on the Taliban running out of money and he came back later saying we could. The papers had calmed down again and I think we were beginning to see the benefits of a properly organised strategy. TB said 'My ass is right out there and we just have to pull this off.' Jack had done an interview on OBL in *The Times* and we tried to push on that. I was constantly toing and froing between Number 10 and the Foreign Office, had a quick meeting with TB before leaving for the airport with Alison [Blackshaw], Phil Bassett and Lee McLenny.

I was at the airport to do the conference call, the focus on Taliban lies, the need to do more re opinion in Pakistan, and generate more moderate Arab voices. On the plane, I worked on a draft script for TB for tomorrow. I was met by Peter Reid and drove in to the embassy. Chris Meyer had put together a good group for dinner – Dan Bartlett, Jim Wilkinson, Charlotte Beers, Richard Boucher from the State Department, Tucker Eskew [White House media affairs], who was going to be coming over to work in the CIC in London. It was a good discussion and I felt they were more or less buying into our approach. But there was still no sign of the Pakistan spokesman and the tension between the White House and State [Department] was pretty clear. I quite liked Charlotte because she was different and thought a bit laterally, but I sensed she was driving the traditionalists a little crazy. She left reasonably early, and once Richard left both Dan and Jim really tore into the State Department. We agreed to there effectively being one 24-hour Grid that we all operated to. Meyer raised the question of when Powell was going to make the MEPP speech that had already had a lot of build-up, even without a date. There was still no sign of a date. Dan said that my last visit had been a catalyst to get them going properly, and now we had to start producing results, and above all get the military plugged in better. That was the other big lesson from Kosovo.

Wednesday, November 7

Slept pretty well, out for a really good run in near perfect temperature, then back for breakfast with Meyer, Phil Bassett and Lee McLenny. What we had all picked up last night and again today, was the tension between the White House and State. It was clear this wasn't just about the Pentagon. I had a stack of meetings lined up, first with Victoria ['Torie'] Clarke at the Pentagon. We did the conference call from there. She was very easy to talk to, very open and receptive and agreed we had to find ways to help them off the hook Rumsfeld had landed them on of having to brief every day. We had to get the media to understand there was more to a media plan than media briefings, and that they couldn't expect to see the same people all the time.

Then to the CIC, which had been really well set up, with beautifully designed signs above desks saying what everyone did, the office well laid out, atmosphere OK, Jim Wilkinson very dynamic, a bit introspective. Then over to see Mary Matalin to discuss the *Sun* and BBC interviews we were hoping Cheney would do, and how best to project message from them. She was an interesting character, had a rich voice, an accent I couldn't place on the class scale. She was attractive in a very unclassical kind of way and could be very funny, e.g. about what life was like in the 'secure undisclosed location' they go to in times of crisis. I so couldn't get my head around how she, committed Republican working for one of the real hate figures of the Democrats, could live with James Carville, a committed Democrat even more driven and obsessive about politics than her. But she was adamant it worked. Of all of them, I felt she was the one who most shared my understanding of the difference between strategy and tactics.

Then over to see Karen, via Karl Rove. She had a bad cold. My main worry was the slowness with which we were going for the Pakistan operation, and the lack of a spokesman yet. I didn't feel

Karen was totally on top of things. She was obviously very focused on Bush, but probably not as plugged in across the system as I had hoped, and of course it was probably, almost certainly, a harder machine to drive. In between times, I was talking to Anji [Hunter] whose departure day was now set, and we talked over how to deal with any fallout. BP [Hunter's new employer] would be doing the basic announcement. She said she was relieved that she was finally going, but also upset at the way things had panned out. Then off to the State Department and the guy sent down to escort me up was clearly pretty disaffected. I was making small talk in the lift and before long he was saying he didn't like what we were doing, that it wasn't really diplomacy. Fair enough. I later told [Colin] Powell that we needed to see more of him and less of Rumsfeld in Europe.

I bumped into the [House of Commons] Foreign Affairs Select Committee who were on an official visit and chatted to some of them. Then back to the White House and over to meet TB. He, Jonathan, DM, Meyer and I went in to see Bush. They did most of the meeting one-on-one. [Retired US general] Wayne Downing [Deputy National Security Advisor for combating terrorism] said to me 'Ah, you are the infamous Alastair whose name I now see on everything.' I couldn't quite work out if he was being friendly or not. Jonathan and I were both talking to Powell to suggest he upped his profile a bit. He didn't do much to dispel the idea of pretty considerable divisions.

TB and Bush had pretty much done most of the heavy stuff by the time they called us in. They ran through things but in a fairly prosaic way. Bush cracked a joke about not being intelligent enough to meet the head of Pakistani intelligence, but apart from that there was not much of note beyond them both preparing lines for the media event. It went OK but Bush gave a really poor answer on the Middle East. TB by contrast was on form, as Powell told him as he came off. Over dinner, TB came close to being very irritating because he was in his full-on statesman mode, almost lecturing on the lessons from Northern Ireland, the advice he had given to Putin etc. Bush at one point was going on about going after OBL to kill him – 'I mean bring him to justice.' On the plane back, TB said he felt Bush had been a lot more focused, had thought more about the future of Afghanistan, relations with Russia. He had not been much impressed by his dealings so far with Europe.

Thursday, November 8

As we landed, Robert Hill called to say Henry McLeish [Scottish First Minister] was about to resign. This was what Peter MacMahon

[McLeish's spokesman] had called about last night when we were waiting to leave the White House, to say they believed the *Herald* had another story that was about to be a killer blow, which indeed it was.[1] I got TB to speak to him and he was very warm. We got in to Number 10. TB was a bit angst-ridden re Anji going. Cabinet was all Afghanistan and with GB at Treasury questions, the mood was a lot better than usual. The CIC was much more into its stride now. King Abdullah [of Jordan] was in for lunch and was pretty sound, privately and in the doorstep afterwards.

As during Kosovo, I was getting annoyed at the sense of moral equivalence [in the media] between what we said, in systems of democracy founded on the duty of politicians to tell the truth, and regimes like Milosevic and the Taliban who felt no such obligations, and yet whose word, even when proven to be false, was often given exactly the same weight. Musharraf came in and while he was talking to TB one-on-one, I had a long session with his finance minister [Shaukat Aziz] and press secretary [General Rashid Qureshi] who said they were supportive of the CIC in Islamabad and would help. The press guy and I were called in to see TB and Musharraf to go over basic arguments to push at the press event, again focusing on moderate vs extreme, and talking up the basic decency of the vast bulk of the Pakistani community in Britain. I was feeling the workload very heavy at the moment, because I was now more plugged into the American side, and had these three centres of operation, all of them producing their own paper flows, bad ideas amid the good, and personnel issues, some of them a screaming pain.

Friday, November 9

I felt bad at not having gone to Anji's farewell last night, but it would have been a step too far to have come back from yet another trip and then gone out, to Anji's farewell in particular. Kate [Garvey, events and visits team] came on in tears, said I was the only one of the old team who hadn't been there and it was terrible when people fell out. TB's big media event of the day would be a press conference with [José María] Aznar [Spanish Prime Minister], which would coincide with the news that Mazar-e-Sharif finally was about to fall after what sounded like some pretty heroic stuff from some of our guys out there. I was due to do a foreign press briefing at 12 and wanted to focus again on the unbroadcast Al Jazeera [Bin Laden] video. I got TB, DM and Scarlett

[1] McLeish resigned later the some day, saying he accepted full responsibility for mistakes in the subletting of his constituency office.

to agree to it and say we would use it to do a revised evidence document. I called Jim Wilkinson just before the briefing, said I was going to do it and he said hold on so he could speak to Karen H. The president had been against it before and that was a real reason not to do it. I said try to get clearance and let me know during the briefing. I left Julian [Braithwaite] outside to wait for the call while I started the briefing, largely on the MEPP discussions and TB's visits. Julian came in and said go with it provided I don't mention Al Jazeera, just that it's a video circulating, so that was fine. But because I did it in the middle of the briefing, it didn't fly as I hoped.

Before the press conference, TB said to Aznar 'What do you want me to say on Gibraltar?' to which I said 'Don't answer that.' Aznar was pretty strong on the war. Also the Dutch were preparing to send troops so I tried to organise the newly arrived Tucker [Eskew] to get some positive US reaction. The [*Evening*] *Standard* splashed on a picture of TB looking a bit tired under the headline 'Shattered', which at least communicated how much he had been doing. Geoff H was on the rampage because the *Mirror* had changed the words of an article he had done and totally misrepresented it. I gave the *News of the World* material on the Taliban running out of money and teed up the *Sunday Telegraph* to use the OBL video material to incriminate him more and highlight the stuff about him being genocidal vs the Jews and other races.

By the end of the day, [the capture of] Mazar-e-Sharif was a big story but I went ballistic about [BBC correspondent] Rageh Omaar's piece, called [Richard] Sambrook saying it was a fucking disgrace, really lost it with him.[1] TB was off to Chequers with Aznar. Cheney did his interview with Yelland which they planned to do over five pages. I was home by 8, tired, but feeling things were moving our way a bit.

Saturday, November 10

The main story was Mazar and an interview from OBL claiming he had nukes, but the best line from our perspective, which we got running in the US and Pakistan straight away, was the line that it was OK to kill thirteen-year-olds, and also that Afghanistan was the only truly Islamic country. One of the lines we had been trying to get up was that their basic desire was to 'Talibanise' every country, and this allowed us to do that. TB was due at the [Labour Party] National

[1] Campbell would fax a lengthy letter to Sambrook asking if he was satisfied that his reporters had not fallen 'foul of . . . [BBC] guidelines on scepticism, terrorist claims, speculation, staged events or the guideline which says reporters should make it clear when they have not been able to witness events themselves?' Sambrook defended their reporting.

Policy Forum and we agreed he should do a clip on that part of the interview, try to isolate OBL from more reasonable governments and opinions. I did a [Foreign Office] telegram to all posts saying they should generate reaction. TB said he felt for the first time things moving our way a bit, and the Americans deploying a strategy.

The White House/State problems had flared up a bit in the open, Karen Hughes reacting very angrily to an interview by Charlotte Beers in which she had spoken about Bush as a 'product'. We were still having trouble getting things off the ground in Pakistan. The Pakistanis were still asking for delay. I wasn't feeling terribly focused today, but a combination of Mazar, military momentum, and OBL's own remarks being used against him had us in a far better place. I managed a few hours off whereas TB, as well as the NPF, also had an Armistice event.

The *Sunday Telegraph* splashed on the OBL [Al Jazeera interview] words 'Yes I did it' which helped push it on into Sunday. I also had to get involved with the *Mail on Sunday* chasing Alastair Irvine.[1] Derry [Irvine, Lord Chancellor] had spoken to the paper and they were splashing on his words and that was that. I said to Derry, why didn't you phone me? He sounded very down. 'Don't persecute me, this is bad enough already.' Alison [Derry Irvine's wife] was very low, obviously because of Alastair and also because of all the coverage about them around the time of Donald's death [Donald Dewar, First Minister of Scotland and former husband of Alison Irvine]. 'I think we pay a heavy price for being in power. I sometimes wonder what is the point of being in power when we are powerless to do anything about the evil that the press bring into the lives of our families. When I say evil, I mean evil. They are Satan's people on earth, no compassion, no decency at all.' We agreed a tough line about this being despicable and their attempts to pretend it was a story about drugs policy as being utterly transparent. We had done an article for the *Mail on Sunday* by TB and I called them to pull it, saying I didn't want to see his name on an article that they would use to give credibility to a rag I viewed as being total scum.

Sunday, November 11

There appeared to be a bit of difference opening up. Bush saying to the Northern Alliance not to take Kabul, Hoon in the *Sunday Times* saying we were moving on to Kabul. I spent a lot of the day helping Derry

[1] The 24-year-old son of Lord Chancellor Derry Irvine had been exposed by the *Mail on Sunday* as a crack-cocaine addict seeking treatment in the US.

deal with the press trying to do stuff on Alastair. He called me at 8 to go over the letter he wanted to send to [Lord John] Wakeham [Press Complaints Commission chairman], who coincidentally was on *Frost* attacking a judge's decision to gag the *People* about a footballer's sex life. TB's basic take was that they were scum, but we had to deal with them, and he wasn't convinced that meant through legislation. Derry said he strongly believed there should be a privacy law and the requirement in law to strive for accuracy. He believed, and I shared his view, that they now actually do damage to the standing and reputation of the country, because serious people think there is something odd and a bit disturbing about a country with a press like ours. GH did *The World this Weekend* [BBC Radio 4] and said we had UK forces on the ground, which was bound to go big and would raise questions about why they were only mentioned now. I spent some time working on a letter to Sambrook. Catherine Rimmer and Chris McShane [Number 10 Research and Information Unit] had done some excellent work showing where specific reports broke their own guidelines. TB called after the Cenotaph, said he was surprised to see IDS wearing his medals. The Royals had been very friendly, especially the Queen Mum.

Monday, November 12

The news had turned right round because of Mazar-e-Sharif and there was a real impression of there being a strategy unfolding so there was a much better mood around the place. OBL saying Afghanistan was the only truly Islamic nation opened up a whole host of opportunities and we brainstormed on how to make sure it struck right round the Muslim world. At TB's office meeting, we tried to stay focused on the domestic and public services in particular. He was worrying that departments were slowing and slacking a bit whereas now, with so much media focus on the international, it was the time really to be driving forward. I sometimes wondered whether we weren't victims of what might be defined as success. For example, TB wanted a more centralised system, or at least one where Number 10 could pull levers more effectively in departments. But did it mean that when we weren't focusing so much, they were waiting for the levers to be pulled? Don't know. Also, had we to some extent been responsible for some ministers thinking things only mattered if there was profile attached to them? Again, not sure.

TB was also worried that Anji's departure would leave gaps – she did give him a particular Middle England kind of view, and she was particularly good at schmoozing those people that Jonathan and I didn't have much to do with, particularly some of the right-wing opinion formers. RW came to see me to say he was really angry at the dreadful press he was getting. I said I hadn't really noticed it. He said it was worse than anything I ever got. I said don't be ridiculous, I've been savaged so many times in the press I've given up even noticing. He said beneath the nastiness in the headlines, they sort of acknowledged I was brilliant whereas with him, they just wrote him off. I said this is what they do, try to undermine anyone who is doing a good professional job because they want to render us illegitimate. Papers like the *Mail* felt it was wrong for anyone to serve a Labour government. They had done it to Guthrie, and they will do it to him because he is doing a perfectly good job and he shouldn't let it get to him. I had to do the eleven o'clock because both Godric and Tom were late in. It went fine, and the main focus was the advance of the Northern Alliance and I got up the idea of Taliban morale crumbling. Vajpayee was in for lunch, mainly the two of them, then a doorstep.

As we began the 2.30 conference call a plane was crashing in Queens, New York, and it appeared to be on our television before theirs.[1] I could hear Mary Matalin calling James [Carville] to turn on the TV. But actually, considering, they were pretty calm and we discussed Ramadan and also how to build up the women's events we were planning. TB spoke to GWB around 4, reviewed military strategy, discussed Ramadan and how to use an evidence document. I called George Robertson and said Mark Laity was maybe too senior and was becoming a bit of a problem for some of the guys over there. I asked for someone more junior. Tucker [Eskew] was making a difference, hard-working, supportive, he seemed to be able to make things happen pretty well. I really wanted us to get up a humanitarian story now though, so it wasn't just about dropping bombs and fighting. The New York plane crash was pretty huge. Ari Fleischer was doing fine on it, but not a nice thing to have to deal with. The general feeling was that it was an accident but who knows?

Tuesday, November 13

I woke to the news that Kabul had fallen, with John Simpson [BBC world affairs editor] seeming to claim that he had liberated it.[2] All

[1] American Airlines Flight 587 crashed shortly after take-off, killing all 260 people on board and five people on the ground. Though al-Qaeda claimed responsibility, a subsequent investigation found that the crash had been accidental, caused by overuse of rudder controls during turbulence.

[2] Simpson, one of the first journalists to enter Afghanistan, having disguised himself as a woman in a burqa, declared on entering Kabul 'It was only BBC people who liberated this city. We got in ahead of Northern Alliance troops.'

the armchair generals now moved on from saying the military strategy hadn't worked to saying that we had fucked up the diplomatic channels. And that was what was worrying TB when I got in. He looked tired, had not slept much. I told him that GB was meeting all the church leaders downstairs and he just rolled his eyes. TB called a meeting of the inner War Cabinet. CDS was still pretty gloomy though he did at least have detailed plans for going in. TB wanted ideas on how the military plan should now be taken forward and extended and how we get the diplomatic channels moving faster. He also wanted specific ideas on the humanitarian side of things and he wanted to put forward military, political/diplomatic and the humanitarian plans to Bush by lunchtime. He wasn't sure they would listen but he said this was the time to build out with a real plan of action. I saw the Scottish group of [Labour] MPs where Tam Dalyell went off on one re TB being presidential and I really got stuck in. There were amazing pictures from Kabul, and now it was on to Kandahar and also get in a better position on the humanitarian front. Burnley beat Watford 1–0.

Wednesday, November 14

The news overnight was our troops on standby. I complained first thing about today's poll from the Muslim community.[1] The *Mirror* and the *Mail* led on a picture of the Northern Alliance butchery of a Taliban solider and it was obvious we were going to cop it for any brutality on the way in. There was plenty of 'What now?' stuff. Polly Toynbee [*Guardian*] did an excellent piece about our media culture. TB called as I was driving in and agreed that he should do a statement. He shared my amazement at the ability of our press to turn yesterday into a problem. I said to Tucker at the morning meeting 'Hey, great news, we lost.' He had been genuinely shocked by the desire of most of our media, or so it felt to him, to fail. TB spoke to Bush and then Schroeder then worked on the statement. The top line was that the Taliban was defeated. TB was still pushing to go faster and further on the political front but it was so difficult mobilising international action on the back of fast-moving events. The coverage out of Kabul was extraordinary though and there was a sense of people's lives changing instantly. PMQs was OK. The statement was fine content-wise but TB was really tired and not really on form. I think both of us felt a bit that you work your guts

[1] A BBC poll suggested eighty per cent of UK Muslims were opposed to military action in Afghanistan.

out, you strive with everything you've got to make something happen, every step of the way people are saying you can't do it and then when it happens, they are just straight on to saying you can't do the next thing. It wasn't even about a desire for recognition of achievement. It was just the feeling of grind that went with the situation that our media made everything feel like swimming through treacle.

There was going to be a UN presence by Friday and the UK diplomatic presence by the weekend. There was a fantastic story to be told about the role played by a small number of our spooks and special forces, if C and Co. were up for it. John Scarlett had also been superb, calm, clear, always meticulous about the material he assembled and put forward to the PM, but just as willing to give bad news as good. I had a meeting with David Puttnam [Labour peer, former film producer], who I like and think is one of the rare cases of people adapting from success in one world at a very high level to success at a different level in politics. He told me both the BBC and *Guardian* had said to him they were genuinely worried about their relations with us. He also wanted to say that Estelle [Morris] was a real star but she needed boosting and she needed help that she would never ask for herself. I got Tucker in to say hello to TB. He told me afterwards he had never seen a politician who thought so quickly on his feet, who could assimilate big arguments quickly and make them simple.

Thursday, November 15

The news was dominated by [eight Western] aid workers being released [after three months held captive by the Taliban]. Mullah Omar did the BBC World Service. At the War Cabinet, there was a bad scene with Clare because she was totally opposed to putting in a senior humanitarian figure in overall charge. The obvious assumption was her worry of being overshadowed or outperformed but her argument was that there were enough tensions between the various agencies and organisations and this would make it worse. Cabinet was obviously largely dominated by the events in Afghanistan and the diplomatic follow-through. Then I had a session briefing Clare before she did the press conference on the humanitarian side of things. She really was ghastly to deal with. She would give every impression of agreeing with you, and then do or say something different; or she would just have an argument for the hell of it, but in that whiney 'everyone but me is wrong' voice that made me want to seal my ears with hot wax.

Friday, November 16

We had to hope that the real story of yesterday didn't come out, namely that our our guys had landed but the FCO had forgotten to ask the Northern Alliance for authority and protection so that Abdullah Abdullah [soon to become foreign minister, Afghan government-in-exile] went crazy and at one point they were even asking our guys at Baghram [airbase, Kabul] to leave. The Americans had finally settled on a spokesman for Islamabad, former ambassador Kenton Keith, and he came in for a meeting. Nice guy, fairly quiet but intelligent and he seemed to be on the right track. I then had a meeting with David Manning and the NATO experts while David and I did a very good briefing on the new moves to bring Russia closer to NATO, which was very much a product of TB's thinking and DM's detail and drive. He was such a nice guy, and so absolutely professional. Often at these briefings, with a Foreign Office policy expert, I would just have at the back of my mind a worry that they would say something that would give us a problem. But with David I had absolute confidence.

Conference call was largely about the women's events, plus I was pushing for the *News of the World* to get a piece from Rumsfeld. The Americans were still focused almost totally on the military campaign. Rumsfeld did a briefing showing pictures of Northern Alliance forces with American special forces on horseback. Rumsfeld had definitely emerged as one of the characters of the campaign, was much more popular in the States than here but in his own way had been more impressive than Colin Powell who had come over as a bit weak and dithery. Then, from left field, Mo [Mowlam, former Cabinet minister] had done a [Michael] Cockerell film [BBC political documentary, *Cabinet Confidential*] and said TB was presidential, had killed Cabinet government and the TB/GB relationship was unhappy. JP was asked about it in front of cameras and used the line 'She's daft.' He called me afterwards. I felt he wasn't far wrong.

Saturday, November 17

The *FT* second lead, part inspired by Mo and part by the usual chat around the place, talked of an 'all-time low' between TB and GB, included the stuff about him doing in Byers, messing around on the euro, generally very anti GB. TB was exercised about it, said it was bad anyway, but also that the party really wouldn't like it if they felt TB was going for GB. It was one thing for the guy at the top to be under attack but it would look bad for TB if it was reciprocated. I spoke to Ian Austin [Brown's spokesman] who did his usual ludicrous 'we never brief the press' routine and descended into a lot of inarticulate rambling. The problem was there was a reality fault-line problem and it had to be addressed. But the thing was that other ministers were starting to take a lead, starting to think this was the way to get on.

TB felt Afghanistan was going better so far as we and the Americans were concerned but he couldn't understand why Brahimi was not more proactive. There was also a Reuters report of the Northern Alliance asking our troops to leave Baghram, so we had to deal with that. I went to Coventry vs Burnley with Calum, and did the conference call in the car park, regularly interrupted by supporters coming over to shout down the phone. Laura Bush was doing the broadcast out there as part of the build-up to the women's event. The Sundays were wall to wall and not much to worry about, though there was far too much TB/GB stuff. We were obviously heading for another wave of it.

Sunday, November 18

John Scarlett had been to the US and said they were more hopeful of finding OBL. He said it would be easier if he stayed in Afghanistan, so I suggested we have a plan to brief round the place that as Afghanistan is 'the only Islamic country on earth' it would be a terrible defeat and loss of face for him to go elsewhere. John felt that departure to Pakistan via the North-West was his only possible option for leaving but even that, it wasn't clear he could do. I had a long run, then took the kids to see *Harry Potter* [*and the Philosopher's Stone*, the first film in the series]. I couldn't quite understand the ballyhoo, and I slept through the second half. The GB stuff was running big again. There was no science to this but sometimes a mood just developed and a combination of Mo and the *FT*, then fuelled by others off the record, got us in a bad place. GB came out of it badly but so did the whole government. It felt dangerous.

Monday, November 19

I was really tired, and emotionally drained after a weekend split evenly between working, time with the kids, and arguing with Fiona. The news was ragged and there seemed to be real confusion over what our troops were doing. The American focus seemed to be almost entirely getting OBL, with the future of Afghanistan barely getting a look-in. So it looked like our troops were sitting there for no purpose, with neither the NA nor the Americans really wanting them there, so it was a bit messy. I probably underestimated how hard the last few weeks had been and maybe I was going in for a crash period. I had to find some energy from somewhere. TB said we had to stop any attacks on GB. He didn't think I was doing it directly, but the mood music he and I generated gave others licence, and we had to do everything we could to stop it. I spoke firmly to my lot while Jeremy [Heywood, principal private secretary] sent round an email saying the markets would react badly if this stuff went on. Later he, GB, Balls and Simon Virley [private secretary, economic affairs] had a PBR meeting with TB. TB said Balls was 'unbelievably rude' to all the Number 10 people, including him.

I had lunch with Andrew Marr at Christopher's [restaurant]. He said the problem was the reality – we could talk all we want about how well they work together, but they all knew GB was angry and smouldering because he was consumed with ambition for the top job. TB was back to his point about the danger of 'policy read-across' in what was essentially a personality thing. He had asked GB what he called a few polite questions about the tax credits and he was met with a bombardment. I had quite a nice time with Marr who, though self-obsessed, at least thought about things and I think appreciated how hard government was, and how comparatively well we did it. The Pakistan CIC was due finally to open tomorrow and the planning on that dominated the conference call. I saw Pat McFadden [former Number 10 deputy chief of staff] and persuaded him to go to Pakistan.

Tuesday, November 20

I didn't feel great and stayed in bed till 10. I wouldn't have gone in at all but I had a couple of meetings it was difficult to move. Clare gave us a bit of a problem when she told a select committee that the US record on aid wasn't good.[1] TB called re Clare and said 'Just try to finesse it.' I said finessing Clare Short was beyond anyone.

Wednesday, November 21

We were still communicating a sense of split with us wanting to put more troops in and the US not, us wanting the focus to shift to the future of Afghanistan, and the US not. Added to which Clare's comments to the DFID select committee gave us a continuing problem which was on the conference call, the Yanks clearly a bit agitato. Dan said to me later, how much money do we have to spend overseas before people start to recognise who the biggest donor in the world is? Jack Straw came through for the morning meeting to go over his press

[1] Short told the House of Commons International Development Select Committee of communications between aid agencies and the US military 'not being taken seriously enough at a high level'.

conference in the [Downing Street] Pillared Room re his trip to Iran and Pakistan and a bit more on the humanitarian push. The Taliban did a press conference with a 'No surrender' top line, also saying they didn't have contact with OBL. Rumsfeld's basic position was that they didn't want anything that detracted from the hunt for OBL, so having had out troops on 48-hour standby, they had to be let down again.

Halfway through the main PMQs meeting at lunchtime, Godric came through to say Clare had done *The World at One* [BBC Radio 4] and had another whack at the US, saying the UK and France were ready to go in but they were holding things back.[1] TB rolled his eyes, shook his head, muttered 'She's just not serious' but the truth was every time she did it and got away with it, she knew she was able to get away with it next time. She had been indulged too much for too long. I reminded him how virtually everyone, including Neil [Kinnock], who had ever worked with her, had said she should be one of the earliest casualties. [David] Yelland came to see me prior to his meeting with GB and I did my best to persuade him the TB/GB relationship was OK.

Thursday, November 22

I could feel myself going down with flu and losing my voice. GB had done an interview in *The Times* about how great the Cabinet was. It was all a bit much, protesting too much, and the general take around the place was that it was embarrassing. TB/GB was without doubt the government fault line, as well as part of its strength. But we had to do something about it. We couldn't allow it just to become a given, another Number 10/11 relationship going wrong because of personal rivalries. Prior to the War Cabinet, GH and CDS briefed TB on the operations going on in the south. CDS was looking tired and grey, and I didn't feel got any real satisfaction out of his job. He and Geoff were not in the same place about what to do with the troops who had been on 48-hour standby. John Scarlett said at the War Cabinet the Americans were putting massive effort into the hunt for OBL, and we had to be careful not to take our eye off other parts of this that needed very careful attention. I did a briefing for the foreign press on tomorrow's Europe speech and Afghanistan, using the line from the Taliban yesterday that it was 'time to forget' as a way of getting up facts about the nature of the regime. I had agreed with Tim Livesey

[1] After Short told the BBC radio programme of the 'regrettable' delay in deploying US troops to protect aid convoys, Downing Street commented 'Clare Short speaks for herself.'

[press officer, foreign affairs] we should use it to do a big number on the EMU section of the speech tomorrow. I had to persuade TB first though. I was rapidly losing my voice, and by the time I had done an interview with the 'Mind Out' mental health campaign [to raise awareness of mental health problems], I was washed up and went home.

Friday, November 23

Felt dreadful, and stayed in all day. My briefing of yesterday went big, leading several papers and the radio, the BBC doing the 'most pro EMU yet', usual bollocks. TB was happy enough with it, and did want to press on, but was pissed off at the *Sun*, which splashed on the line that we would have a euro referendum to coincide with a general election in 2005. Trevor [Kavanagh, *Sun* political editor] called early, claiming he had written it based on something I had said to Yelland, which was bollocks. The big problem with Europe was that most of the papers had a line and no real interest in setting things out as we said them. Despite feeling crap, I did the conference call but they were lacking energy and at the moment had just become glorified 'lines to take' discussions. The new common line coming out of the media re Afghanistan was 'bloodbath fears'. I turned on the telly to watch TB's speech, the start of which was delayed because a member of the audience collapsed, and TB called afterwards and said the poor guy had 'lost his bowels', said it had taken a while to clear the place up and it was the first time he had rushed through a speech because of the smell. The speech went fine, good mood music without anyone really going for it as a change of policy.[1]

Saturday, November 24

I took Rory to do his cross-country race. TB called and said we were still discovering things they [Brown's Treasury team] were trying to sneak by us in the Pre-Budget Report. It really was unacceptable the way they operated on these big Treasury moments. He was fine about the way the Europe speech panned out, worried about the PBR, and not sure where the war stuff was all going. He was also still anxious about the briefing going on re Anji. I was really fed up with all the soap-opera stuff. The conference call was all about the difficult questions re the siege [of Kunduz in northern Afghanistan, where the Taliban were besieged by the

[1] In the speech to the European Research Institute in Birmingham, Blair criticised the 'embarrassingly long history of Euroscepticism' in the UK, saying that whilst the economic tests for entry into the euro should first be met, it was time to recognise that Britain's future was 'inextricably linked with Europe'.

Northern Alliance] and whether we were responsible for prisoners. We agreed we must not make ourselves so in anything we said, whilst it was legally checked out.

Sunday, November 25

The war coverage in the Sundays wasn't so bad. Stewart Steven [*Mail on Sunday*] was apparently saying I should go. Crap stuff on public services clearly coming down the rails. Charles Clarke did the *Westminster Hour* and said some parts of the NHS were worse than before, which would go a bit.

Monday, November 26

Pat [McFadden] and Tanya [Joseph] both called me to say the briefing in Pakistan had been poor, because Kenton had been unable to say anything much about the Marines and Kandahar.[1] We were clearly going to have a problem getting all bits of the American machine to see the CIC operations, particularly the one in Islamabad, as a place where anything and everything could be briefed. I spoke to Jim Wilkinson [in Washington], and we agreed we had to be more punchy about the message, faster in prising information out of the military, and more disciplined in the deployment of lines to take. I took up the same theme in the conference call, said that the point of these was to set communications strategy, not just discuss the issues of the day. The other theme coming up, as well as the division in troop deployment, was 'where next?' I wasn't on good form. I felt that after a good start, we were no longer making the weather. The processes were the right ones but not being followed rigorously enough, and the calls were too unstructured and meandering. We went to the launch of the book on Neil [*Kinnock*, by Martin Westlake and Ian St John] with Calum and Grace. Neil got very emotional in his speech, and it was a nice enough do.

Tuesday, November 27

It was the start of the Bonn [inter-Afghanistan] talks under [Lakhdar] Brahimi, and also the battle of the Mazar-e-Sharif fort [Qala-i-Jangi prison] was still going on.[2] The main focus of the day was the PBR.

[1] The first of a major deployment of US Marines had landed by helicopter south of the Taliban stronghold of Kandahar.

[2] At the end of the prison revolt, eighty-six Taliban prisoners would be alive, out of an original 300–500, after seven days of fierce fighting with Northern Alliance and American and British special forces. The Taliban prisoners had surrendered at Mazar-e-Sharif believing they would be set free.

TB came down from the flat, having finally got GB to deliver more for health. It was ridiculous that we had to go through this rigmarole the whole time. We probably ended up pretty much where GB expected us to in the first place, maybe with a bit more on top, but surely we could have got there without what had been a very difficult process. It had been crazy. What's more, there was only one story that was going to dominate, namely that taxes would have to rise to pay for a better NHS. Possibly the biggest strategic decision we would take this parliament, and though we had all known it was coming, we were catching up late in terms of the strategic discussions that we should have had ages ago. But again, it was a result of having conceded too much to him early on. After the PBR Cabinet, I had a meeting with Ed Balls, who came in with all the published documents. I asked him when they went to the printers, and he said he didn't know. I said one thing's for sure, that GB was still getting his ear bent by TB about what was in it after it had gone.

At Cabinet, GB did his usual stuff, plenty of big message, plenty of figures and it went down OK, though this was an easier audience than the public would be. Taxes up for a better NHS was a pretty strong Labour line, and most Labour people would like it, but we were going to have to engage in a pretty big argument, not least around value for money, to win it with the public. If we did though, it would be a significant shift and an important win. Pat seemed to be making a difference in Pakistan and was pretty much in charge of Kenton's words. I had been hoping that once we got the CICs up and running, they would go on autopilot, but I was having to do a lot of hours every day re all three.

The PBR went OK, albeit surrounded by too much tax and spend. TB said GB's problem was that he sometimes lacked subtlety and everything was so obviously political. He had announced [Sir Derek] Wanless [banker] to conduct a review of future NHS funding but most people would see him as a stooge there to do what GB wanted done. I quite liked that, but there was a danger the only message was tax and spend.

DTLR put out minutes of the Byers Railtrack meeting but only four pages.[1] Crazy. I told Byers I thought it was a bad plan and they should never have hired Martin Sixsmith [DTLR director of communications]. Byers thought I had given my approval. It turned out he had asked his office to check what 'Alastair' thought of Sixsmith, and they had

[1] The government had decided in October to put Railtrack in administration.

asked Alistair Darling [Work and Pensions Secretary], who seemingly said he thought he was fine.

Wednesday, November 28

TB/GB relations were so bad that it was currently almost impossible to get either of them to say anything good about the other. TB felt there was a personal/political motivation to pretty much anything GB did. He was 'diddling' the whole time. TB said maybe he had always been like that, but when we did less important jobs, and when so much of what we did was about campaigning, it didn't seem to matter so much. He said we had to try to harness his ambition with the national interest. A lot of the time, it coincided, but not always. We had a meeting with GB re PMQs and how to handle the PBR fallout. The tax and spend argument was the obvious one for the Tories to go on, but we could take it easily to investment vs cuts. PMQs went fine, and style-wise, TB was getting more relaxed, less reliant on notes, getting the big arguments in his head and then finding ways of pushing them out there. I ran home, first proper run for almost a week.

Thursday, November 29

PBR coverage was going a bit awry. After a pretty low-key War Cabinet, TB saw GB and Alan Milburn, who was livid, said that basically GB was trying to use his position to take over NHS policy [via Brown's Wanless review], and he wasn't having it. He was not alone in feeling departments had not been properly involved in the PBR preparations. TB said we had to get an agreed strategy going forward and asked me to do a meeting with the Treasury and Health, which I did, and tried to make a start but there was no doubt Number 10, the Treasury and the Health department were not all in the same place, nothing like it. It did sometimes feel like there were two governments, and when TB had so much of his time and energy focused on foreign affairs, that feeling was maybe stronger. CDS was really steamed up about the arguments they had had to get involved in yesterday re SAS identification [an injunction had been taken out against the *Sun*]. For him, he was quite emotional, really felt that newspapers that couldn't see why it was important that these principles were adhered to were beyond the pale.

The mood at Cabinet wasn't good. TB was a bit late, GB was not communicating, the departmental ministers were largely pissed off because of the PBR. Robin [Cook] got rolled over on his paper [White Paper on reform of the House of Lords] and ended up looking a bit bruised. There was a discussion of sorts on health but it was a bad atmosphere and I was glad when they all trooped out. The *Mirror* came in for lunch, Piers Morgan behaving like a child. TB let it go for a while but then put him down heavily once Morgan started to get on his high horse about the *Sun* and his claims we gave them the election date. He went on and on until eventually TB said that he had better not be calling him a liar. Chirac was in later but I missed a lot of it because I was doing the conference call, which was mainly Bonn [Afghanistan talks]. We were slightly losing our way strategically. I had to motivate myself to get going again.

Friday, November 30

GB's latest thing was an interview with the *Sun* yesterday, done to try to show the PBR was not the end of New Labour, but he ended up going contrary to the strategy we had agreed yesterday and playing into their line that we had done nothing and that the NHS was all crap. TB told him it was a direct result of him doing his own thing, seeing everything through his own political prism rather than agreeing a strategy and seeing it through. Milburn, unsurprisingly, was incandescent. He said he knew how he worked, because he had seen him when he had been at the Treasury. He saw it as his right to trample on everyone else's territory. 'Can I go out now and make a speech saying that the economy ought to be doing a lot better?' Yesterday at Cabinet Geoff Hoon had dared to suggest we would have to look at NHS charges and GB had carried on the conversation afterwards and ended up jabbing him in the chest.

JP called from [a ministerial visit to] New Zealand to discuss *Frost* and I filled him in on how things were going – not well. He said he had always told GB he would be willing to support him as next leader but only when TB decided to go, never at a challenge. He felt there was an arrogance about him in feeling he could say when TB should go. JP believed that TB and GB effectively did come to some kind of deal way back, but TB denies it now and feels guilty, while GB remembers it only on his terms and feels betrayed. But he said the party will suffer, and will not wear it, if they fall out badly. He also agreed with TB's analysis that a lot of the time the personality differences didn't matter but when they affected the policies and the direction of the government, it became very dangerous. I spoke to Byers about Jo [Moore]. She was away with her husband, but [Number 10 Grid co-ordinator] Paul Brown's email expressing frustration with the department [DTLR] had leaked and it was all a bit of a mess. I told Godric to shut it down as best he could. I said to Steve he had to get out there and deal with Railtrack, try and close down this other agenda.

Pat McFadden called and said Islamabad CIC reminded him of a 1980s by-election campaign, no real resources, no real drive. We were giving them OK material and decent scripts, e.g. today on Bonn, but then the Americans would worry, think we shouldn't be straying beyond the region. Pat said the Pakistan-based press were getting a bit fed up with it all. He said we had to be more aggressive, not least in rebuttal and forcing the media to take the agenda. GB's *Sun* article was running on, *The World at One* doing a big number. It had definitely been a mistake.

Saturday, December 1

George Harrison's death [the ex-Beatle had died of lung cancer] was massive across the media. Politically though, there was a bad, febrile atmosphere. TB had a long conversation with GB, called me afterwards and said it was very difficult. He said the post-PBR problems were the direct result of lack of proper planning between us, the fact that we weren't working together well. GB's argument was that it was a direct result of him being briefed against and of us not having a grip of the government machine. His evidence for the second point was an admittedly silly interview by Charles Clarke in *The Times* giving the impression we should go for a euro referendum even if the economic conditions weren't met. So the Treasury, never slow to overreact or find out what exactly was said, went off on one on that. What they did, and seemed to believe, was to present themselves as victims, saying they bent over backwards to be helpful to colleagues, but were constantly attacked in return.

Milburn's rage had not abated with the passage of twenty-four hours. He told TB direct that if he went to the *Sun* and slagged off the work of another department, he would expect to be sacked, so why was GB allowed to slag off his department? I told both Ian Austin and Ed Balls that this arose both because of their propensity for acting in secrecy and also because they overreacted and overcomplicated things. They overdid the tax message, then worried about it, so ran off to the *Sun* but overdid the reform message in a way that allowed the *Sun* to ally GB to their own 'tax-funded NHS crap' agenda. Milburn was strongly of the view that we should whack back and at one point said if we didn't, he would. But TB was adamant that would be a mistake. He said when I make a move, I'll make a move but it has to be me that decides, nobody else. I went to [Crystal] Palace vs

Burnley with Calum, Gavin [Millar, Fiona's brother] and [David] Bradshaw [special adviser, Strategic Communications Unit]. 2–1 [to Burnley], and for once hardly any calls.

Sunday, December 2

The papers were full of TB/GB/health. GB was on *Frost* doing OK on health, but then a very odd answer when asked whether they had a deal about when TB would go. 'I'm not going to talk about a private conversation' was his basic line. He said it twice, and even though he said good things about TB, it was clearly going to be the story out of it. I was watching with Fiona and both of us felt it was deliberate. TB hadn't watched it and when I told him, he said 'What on earth does he want to do that for? Even by his own lights, it's pointless.' I could only think that he was trying to take the rather weird moral high ground from TB, give the impression that there was a deal, that TB reneged on it, but he had better things to worry about, like running the economy and helping the poor. TB again said though that it was important we didn't react, and did what we could to close it down. But I'd be very surprised if ministers weren't out and about. Milburn was calling regularly, fed up with the whole thing, feeling excluded from decisions with material effect on his department. I was pretty sick of the whole thing, told Ian Austin he could get on and brief what the hell he wanted. He did the usual victim act, how they were always being asked to respond because they were being briefed against the whole time and they were very restrained. I said if GB involved other ministers, and you covered bases properly with departments, you wouldn't have these problems with people like Milburn and Clarke. They need to be brought in, not kicked out.

He obviously got straight on to Balls who came on ten minutes later, and we went round the same block. As ever, he was blaming others – notably Peter M [Mandelson, former Cabinet minister] of course, who they always put close to the root of all evil, Milburn, Clarke, Blunkett – for trying to split TB and GB, and we had to close it down. I said they hadn't done enough to get colleagues in the right place, and to get the politics in the right place. He claimed he tried to call me five times on the day of the *Sun* interview but I was too busy. I said that was bollocks, that I was assiduous in returning phone calls. The problem was GB was in a different place, and actively wanted to be. And his anger was so great that it did have an impact on direction and policy. The TB/GB fault line had hurt us recently on the euro, on the NHS and the tax and spend argument. He realised that, he also said, 'To lose your Chancellor is like putting two balls in the back of your own net.'

I had sent JP a digest of some of the press and he was pretty appalled. I filled him in on GB on *Frost* and said I really felt at the moment it wasn't TB vs GB but very much GB vs TB, that though Tony was pretty fed up with him, he was adamant we did nothing to undermine him and was trying the whole time to get things on a better keel. JP said it was one man's guilt meeting another man's betrayal and they had to sort it out themselves. He agreed he would speak to GB on his return and tell him to get his act together, and speak to Alan to tell him to keep his cool. JP said he knew I had my ups and downs with GB but accepted my main interest was the same as his, which was ensuring the third term and if we didn't stop this nonsense pretty soon, there would be a risk it never happened.

Monday, December 3

I used the day to take stock re Pakistan [CIC]. It just wasn't working in the way it should. I felt the structures were right but we were weak on output. At the morning meeting, I skipped over TB/GB and health and instead suggested in briefings we just bulldozed through it. The coverage of *Frost* was predictable enough but we just had to play it down, say GB was just refusing to get into all the personality stuff. We also had a problem re TB's stuff on the EU average [pledging to raise NHS spending to the EU average by 2005], though as TB said to GB 'Look, I made a mistake, now let's talk about how we can get it right.' I think sometimes GB and his people totally underestimated how many issues TB had to be on top of at any one time, and how infrequently we actually screwed up. But whenever we did, he went on about it as though it had all been planned. Things were looking pretty poor and confused. We needed greater unity and focus on the domestic front, greater unity, purpose and imagination on the international. Alan Milburn was still really pissed off with GB and needed to calm down a bit.

I was feeling tired, feeling that life was yet another problem, yet another meeting, yet another plan to deal with the problem, then on to the next one. I felt like I had been doing it too long. Iraq was still featuring too much in American thinking, they were still going on about December 11 [marking three months since 9/11] and the idea of a major event with national anthems and the full works. I know it affected them more deeply than anyone, but they were in a different place to everyone else on this, and we couldn't keep having memorial after memorial.

Tuesday, December 4

People as varied as Fiona, Pat [McFadden], Sally [Morgan] and [David] Bradshaw were all pointing out that I was bored and looking for something new and different to do. Although I didn't miss the grind of the briefings at all, and certainly didn't miss the press, I probably had lost something of my edge by not having that actual need to be on top of everything all the time. The conference call was all about December 11 memorials again and the idea of every country in the world playing national anthems, which I felt was all a bit much, but they were very keen. I went up to see TB in the flat and he said maybe we just had to resign ourselves to GB putting himself in a slightly different place, and operating differently.

Wednesday, December 5

A deal was being struck today in Bonn which would be a pretty amazing achievement. We were also getting reports of defections from the Taliban which we agreed on the conference call we should try to push. I had a meeting with [BBC] Radio 5 bosses, feeling we should be doing more with them, rather than everyone thinking the world listens to the wretched *Today* programme and the other Radio 4 news programmes. Fiona and Sally were seeing Yelland but I don't think either of them really had their hearts in humouring the commentators from the right-wing papers as Anji did. TB did fine at PMQs though IDS was a bit better. TB's preparations were certainly easier. We got a new poll in showing pretty good figures on the parties, but not great on public services. Paul Marsden [Labour MP] attacked 'Labour thugs'.[1]

Thursday, December 6

There was more and more intelligence suggesting pretty high-level defections around Mullah Omar, including some of his closest people, and also an account of three al-Qaeda advance scouts killed trying to work out an escape route from Afghanistan. GB was in a rage early on because Milburn was going further than agreed on the 'choice' argument with his proposals on patients being promised a choice of going to another hospital. Alan was doing a GB-style bounce and then trying to row it back a bit, and probably enjoying giving GB some of his own treatment. I had a session with TB pre Cabinet to make sure he was OK with the general thrust of what I was trying to get sorted re health. Cabinet was mainly a discussion on health

[1] An opponent of the Afghanistan war and Labour's anti-terrorism legislation, Marsden claimed several Labour MPs had physically and verbally threatened him.

which broadened to the public services more generally, and an update on Afghanistan.

At the War Cabinet, Scarlett was excellent, really clear exposition of what was going on, without being over-optimistic or over-pessimistic. Lander was warning in a rather less relaxed way of real fears of more attacks, including here. Boyce was almost becalmed and though he was nice to him, TB had become a pretty fierce opponent of the service rotating 'Buggins' turn' system of appointment. TB asked him about how something had gone and CDS gave all the reasons why it had been a bad idea and difficult, and a soldier had had his leg blown off yesterday. His worry, not unreasonably, was the idea that you had Brits in one part of Afghanistan killing Taliban, whilst in another we were like a police force. He said it was dangerous, not at all benign. Clare said the Americans didn't really want troops involved in the humanitarian effort at all. There was a difficult issue looming quickly, re whether Mullah Omar could get amnesty [on condition of renunciation of terrorism and disassociation with al-Qaeda]. The Americans were saying no, whilst we were a bit more equivocal. A difficult one. I had fallen behind with paperwork, hoovered through it. Philip [Gould] and Stan [Greenberg, US pollster] had a new poll. TB doing OK, the Tories absolutely nowhere, public services not as bad as we feared, apart from transport which was a total disaster.

Friday, December 7

I spoke to TB re counter-terrorism and agreed that we needed to get more political. I got Blunkett to do a letter to IDS asking how he could square his claim that they were shoulder to shoulder with us with the fact that they let their troops go through the lobbies in the Lords to do us in. The general sense re Afghanistan was that it was going pretty well for us, what with the fall of Kandahar, but the press were now looking for us to 'lose the peace'. The continuing hunt for OBL and confusion over what we would do with Mullah Omar were getting just as much attention.

The conference call was partly how to counter that, also about December 11, whilst I was now pushing for a big hit out of the football match in Kabul, trying to get some names out there to really make it fly.[1] I also made sure the Yanks knew, and that it got through to Bush, of the political problems the Tories were trying to give us.

[1] On December 15, the first post-Taliban football match would be played in the Kabul football stadium, once the scene of public executions. Kabul Red Crescent played Pamir, the latter team wearing West Bromwich Albion kit donated by BBC Radio 5 presenter Adrian Chiles. Red Crescent won 2–1.

I was pushing for publication of another al-Qaeda tape that was doing the rounds, which had yet more admissions re September 11. They said it was going to be discussed at a meeting with the president on Monday. I was amazed that something like that went to him. I would have thought it was a middle-ranking handling issue. [Paul] Marsden [anti-war Labour MP] was on an inexorable path to the Lib Dems, which was obviously the best place for him. We had a session with TB and Hilary Armstrong [chief whip] earlier in the week trying to get to a position where there was no fuss when he finally went.

Saturday, December 8

TB was worried that Alan Milburn was beginning to brief against GB as a matter of course. And whilst he understood how angry he was, didn't think it was sensible. I was pushing the Blunkett counter-terrorism attack on the Tories. Out with Fiona to [*Express* proprietor] Richard Desmond's party at the Roundhouse [North London performing arts venue]. It was handy enough, though neither of us really wanted to go and in truth were only going because TB couldn't. It was all a bit over the top, everyone photographed with *OK!* magazine photographers and backdrops. I had a long chat with Jonno Coleman [radio presenter], who was totally on board and who I reckoned we could use in the run-up to the campaign. I was chatting to Ulrika Jonsson [TV presenter] and Melanie Cantor [her agent] and Ulrika was all over me like a rash, which was all very well but Fiona was a few yards away and looking a bit askance. Sven [Göran Eriksson, England football manager] walked in, and I assumed she would know him. I asked her if she had met 'Britain's other famous Swede'. She said no, and I got him over and introduced them. He was pretty robotic when the four of us were talking in English, but then the two of them got going in real hurdy-gurdy [Swedish] and he was altogether more animated. Fiona and I were next to the Ronsons [Gerald, businessman, and Gail, charity fund-raiser] at dinner, and we were both surprised by how much we liked them. Gail was really lively, clearly big on family but also seemed to have a real heart. Gerald was totally open, quite interesting about his jail experience,[1] but also quite knowledgeable on the political front, very pro Israel, not keen on politicians generally but liked TB. I had an interesting chat with Tony Ball [BSkyB chief executive] and his absolutely gorgeous wife Gabriela.

[1] Ronson had served six months of a one-year prison sentence in 1990, for his part in the Guinness share-trading fraud of the 1980s.

He was another one who had a good feel for politics, and thought the TB/GB situation would become a problem for us. Desmond got up on stage. Though clearly a bit of a wide boy, he did have a certain charm and there was clearly part of him that just liked having loads of money to spend on his friends. They had Jim Davidson [Conservative-supporting 'comic'] as the comedian. Really bad choice. He completely, totally bombed, and deserved to. It was pretty vile and once the grave opened, he couldn't stop digging. It took Tony Blackburn [veteran disc jockey] of all people to rescue things by getting up and being DJ for the night.

Sunday, December 9

I did next to no work all day. Geoff Hoon had ballsed up on *Frost* when he said that if UK forces landed OBL, we would have to have assurances about the death penalty not being used before handing him over. It shouldn't have been difficult to have danced around it, and was a case of GH thinking legally rather than politically. TB was exercised about it, and made clear he didn't want it running as a problem. Of course, if we were too heavy it would become a TB/GH bad scene so we did a gentle ring-round trying to calm it without making it a calming story. I called Dan Bartlett to alert him and he told me the *Washington Post* had revealed, via the CIA he thought, the existence of the new OBL video and said that Bush would decide tomorrow whether to release it or not. I called Trevor Kavanagh, knowing the *Sun* were planning to do Hoon quite big, and gave him the story of OBL boasting about September 11 in the video, and the fact that only one hijacker per plane knew what they were going to be doing when they got on those planes. Blunkett called, a bit worried about the way his 'debate' on race was going after he told the *Independent on Sunday* that races had to become more integrated by being more British. These were tricky waters, and I wasn't sure we were sensible diving into them right now.

Monday, December 10

The OBL hunt was still going big, the DB race row likewise. The *Sun* splashed on the video and there was continuing coverage about the UK to provide troops for a security force etc. The [Paul] Marsden strategy was going OK. It was becoming a given that he would defect [to the Liberal Democrats], and though there was a fair bit of press coverage about our so-called thugs, people didn't really buy it as the reason. We had been talking over the weekend of defection as a fait accompli, and when it came, we all felt relief and the pretty certain knowledge that he would be forgotten within a week. I went up to see TB in the flat. He was totally relaxed re DB and race, felt that David had thought through his position. On Afghanistan, he wanted to get the MoD in the same place as us, then agree with the US a force to go there later and hand over to Muslim troops. Nigel Griffiths was the other story in town, another expenses/fees so-called scandal and TB said get the facts before we make a decision.[1] Good meeting with Charles Clarke and David Triesman [Labour Party general secretary]. The party was £8 million in debt. David said he was confident he could get the finances sorted but it would be tough. We also had a good session with TB on membership, message, ideology, etc. TB was encouraging Charles to generate more political and ideological debate. Charles and I both felt we should be making more of the way our media culture damaged debate but TB remained resistant. I went briefly to the *Guardian* [Christmas] party but I really couldn't be bothered with it and left after a few minutes and went for a run. The football match in Kabul had become my latest obsession. I really wanted it to go big. I was also very keen to push on the OBL video. I thought it was unbelievable that Bush himself would take the decision on that. We had put a lot of planning into tomorrow's 'We refuse to forget' [9/11] event which would get a lift with [Colin] Powell coming through.

Tuesday, December 11

Boyce did a speech at RUSI [Royal United Services Institute] yesterday, which was going pretty big today, where he basically said that the US were in a different position, that we had to choose between being part of a stabilisation force, and taking part in the wider war on terrorism. I raised it with TB, who just shrugged his shoulders and rolled his eyes as if to say 'not much we can do about it'. Later I raised it with CDS. I said it was good to see that we cleared the speech, an ironic reference to the fact the *Telegraph* reported that we had done so. 'Did I?' he asked. And I said 'No, you didn't.' 'Should I have done?' 'Well it is the normal practice that we see speeches likely to make news, which a speech by the Chief of the Defence Staff at a time like this might well do.' I couldn't tell whether he was

[1] The Small Business minister had been claiming rent through the House of Commons Fees Office on the Edinburgh South constituency office he owned, without declaration in the Register of Members' Interests. He insisted that monies paid were used to benefit his autistic sister. A 2002 Standards and Privileges Committee investigation would rule that although Griffiths had made 'technically defective' claims, he would face no further action.

irritated, worried or indifferent. He wasn't the easiest guy to work with, but he probably felt the same about us. TB raised the speech with GH who said he had tried to tone it down but the MoD was so leaky there was a limit to what he could do without it becoming an issue.

Then Colin Powell gave us a problem. In Paris, he did a doorstep saying he was pleased that the UK had volunteered to lead a security force. Given that Tom Kelly had been pushing the line that no decision had been taken and discussions were still going on, which all sent Adam Boulton [Sky political editor] into an absolute bilious frenzy in which he said it was extraordinary that the British public learnt of this kind of thing from a US politician and that Powell was coming for a 'bizarre event' to remember September 11. I sometimes wondered if Adam didn't let a lot of his own anger about whatever come through on issues like this. I got him in after his report in the street, and said it was outrageous that he editorialised like that. He held his ground and after a pretty robust exchange, went off in a huff.

Powell arrived and as they came in [William] Farish asked Straw to tell me that Powell didn't want press people in the meeting. We were called in at the end to make sure lines were in the same place before the press conference. TB was on pretty good form, bounced away the CDS stuff and put over a general message well. I felt that our event to commemorate September 11 struck the right note, dignified and respectful, not over the top. The US school band I thought was better than the New York trumpeter and I thought GWB's people made a mistake in having him in front of an Israeli flag. Not many would notice that it was an alphabetic point, as the flag was between the Irish and the Italian, but I suspected it would give them problems. I did a local Labour Party meeting, and got a fair amount of grief, particularly on faith schools.

Wednesday, December 12

The Yanks were still dithering on the OBL tapes, saying they were worried about quality, about translations, worried about the impact on relatives of victims at seeing him gloat. We had already got third parties lined up on reaction, but I was beginning to wonder whether they would ever see the light of day. We were also still in the same position on troops and the security force. TB was going through the terrorism bill in detail and said there were some real holes in it and it needed a lot of work. I took him over to the CIC, which was a real boost for them all. There was still a real impact on people when he walked into a room just to say hello, even if he did slightly give the impression of not having a clue what they did. We thought IDS would do war, sleaze and public services at PMQs. He did health and transport but the nervous cough was getting really bad, and he just lacked impact, even if he made a strong point. TB said afterwards he would be amazed if he survived the term. I ran into GB at Number 11 who was having one of his receptions. There were lots of other people around so he did one of his big, friendly 'How you doing?' greetings. I found it odd that he could paint it on like that, whereas if there had been nobody else there, it would have been the usual growl or heavy discussion, depending on mood.

Thursday, December 13

[Bill] Clinton was over making a speech and was up in the flat with TB. He was losing his voice so we sent out for some medicine and I chatted to him and Chelsea Clinton in the kitchen while TB got changed. He was clearly a bit worried re Bush, not convinced he was doing the right things, but even with us, he was pretty discreet. He had time to kill and TB had work to do. I took him for a little wander round the building to see some of the people these big cheeses wouldn't normally see, like the switchboard and the messengers, and of course he was brilliant with them. The War Cabinet was gathering outside the Cabinet Room and Dearlove and Scarlett were clearly pleased to see him. I took him round to see the press office and the Grid team and he made a total beeline for Harriet Quinlan [Strategic Communications Unit]. As I took him out, he said 'Gee, you got some great women.' Later Doug Band [Clinton aide] called in a bit of state because Bill had referred to 'Prime Minister Brown' in his speech on AIDS at the QE2 [Queen Elizabeth II Conference Centre in Westminster]. I assured him TB wouldn't mind.

I got back for the War Cabinet. There was discussion about whether OBL was now in Pakistan, but it was clear nobody on our side really knew. Our bottom lines were that any operation had to be under CENTCOM, the US had to provide lift and extraction if necessary, but it was already becoming clear that the French didn't want to be formally under CENTCOM. The Germans didn't want to be under CENTCOM for different reasons, namely it would suggest we were going to fight rather than keep peace. TB later met Jospin when we arrived in Laeken [European Council summit in Belgium], and he was very clear that the French couldn't operate like this. TB was clear that if there were no French or German forces, that politically and presentationally it was difficult. He felt we might have to call their bluff, say we would go ahead without them.

Cabinet was pretty short, John Reid on Sinn Fein offices in the Commons, DB on the fallout from the Sarah Payne case,[1] TB briefing them on the war situation, then a political Cabinet. TB did his usual script, at some length. Maintaining economic strength and stability, investment and reform, what type of society we want to live in, international strength, pro-European, strong on defence. In all of them, emphasising we had broken free from traditional positions, we can manage the economy but also attack poverty. We can invest in public services but also do difficult reform. Strong on people's rights but demanding responsibility. Tough on defence but proud of helping others in the world. All this matters for giving the party a sense of what we believe in, confidence in what we are for. He felt the Tories were in real trouble, and that the Lib Dems were becoming ridiculous, saying to anyone what they wanted to hear.

JP was basically defending himself on delivery, speaking almost exclusively about transport. GB said we were doing some difficult things and we had to get the party behind us on them. The press and Opposition were trying to demoralise people, make them think what we call progress was all spin. Jack was worried about cynicism, declining faith in politics. DB made a similar point, said the Tories were deliberately trying to erode confidence in politics. He said the papers were constantly trying to set us at each other, but in fact this was the most unified Cabinet ever in political terms. Tessa talked about a generation becoming disengaged. Alan felt the right wing were still better in some ways at conducting ideological battle. He felt we had been overly cautious about the country's desire for change and fairness. On public services, we have to be careful we don't revert to old-style command and control, that we have confidence in our own programme for change. And he argued strongly for under-promising and over-delivering. Darling was worried about the Libs. He said we all know they are wankers but out there it is not considered a bad thing to vote for them. Estelle echoed something Alan said, said we still have a language of caution when people are desperate for us to be more radical. Clare said this was a good government. She thought the Labour bit was good but the New bit wasn't. She felt the policies were good but the presentation was useless. She said everywhere she went she was getting this stuff

[1] Child sex offender Roy Whiting was convicted and sentenced to life imprisonment for the murder of eight-year-old Sarah Payne, who had been found dead near Pulborough, West Sussex, in July 2000 after disappearing from a field close to the home of her paternal grandparents. The case prompted a campaign, led by the *News of the World*, for the government to allow controlled access to the sex offenders register, which in 2010 resulted in the adoption of 'Sarah's Law'.

about Tony and Gordon, that it was stupid and dangerous and it had to stop, that we had to pull together politically. Charles spoke well, particularly on the need for more debate within the party, better relations with the media, and with academia. We need to get more out of the Civil Service.

TB said it was important to understand why the media was like it was. A lot of them believe we are omnipotent, that the Opposition is useless, that they have to do the job for them. They don't conduct a policy debate, drowning out the policy debate through scandal and controversy. It makes it hard to get definition. They deliberately breed cynicism. But New Labour, a modernised centre-left party, is strong enough to defeat that. Centre-left parties lose when they move out of touch from where people are on the basic economic and social issues. If we remain rooted in the instincts of people, we can defeat cynicism. It is not the left that is in retreat. He said we could be confident that we were in the right position, that the Tories had not yet learnt how to adapt, and that the Lib Dems, driven by opportunism, were storing up real problems for themselves in the future. Sally had worked on people, even on Alan and Charles, to be nice about GB. But, as TB said, 'Was he gracious? Was he hell.' Eventually, by 4pm our time, the OBL video was being played out and we got a good hit on it and had the third parties really going for it. We were into ping pong on the counter-terrorism measures [Anti-terrorism, Crime and Security Bill, which would receive Royal Assent the next day], dropped the religious hatred bit but finally got it through.

On the plane [to Laeken], TB, Jack and I carried on the discussion about cynicism in the media. I felt that unless the press bought into the idea that they have at least some responsibility, it was not going to be easy. The conference call was largely how to take forward the material in the video. Tucker [Eskew] had the idea of making a direct appeal to al-Qaeda people to realise they were working for someone who mocked their suicides. I watched [Sir] Ronnie Flanagan [Northern Ireland chief constable] on *Newsnight* when he was given a really hard time [Flanagan had been accused of 'flawed judgement' over the Omagh bomb inquiry], a really unpleasant interview. I felt so strongly about it that I wrote to him, said I thought he had handled it incredibly well and that the public would have ended up respecting him far more than the interviewer.

Friday, December 14

The OBL video was a massive hit, though there were still doubts being spread in the Arab world about its veracity. We were now co-ordinating third-party responses from around the world to show that opinion was changing. CDS was chairing a contribution conference in London but the problem was the French and the Germans not wanting to be under CENTCOM command, the French because they are French, the Germans because their parliament would only support peacekeeping forces. It was tricky, because our red line was CENTCOM in charge because it meant they would have to stay involved and make sure our troops were got out if things got really tricky. In fact it was clear from the overnight telegram from Washington that the Americans didn't mind as much as we did. After TB spoke to Chirac, who was adamant that the French could not be under CENTCOM, David M and Co. negotiated with the French and then TB personally negotiated a text, which they felt was OK, namely saying the UK would be in charge but working with CENTCOM. DM then spent much of the afternoon speaking to people in the MoD, eventually including GH, to emphasise it was what the prime minister wanted. He was getting quite stressed up and angry about it. I was even beginning to wonder whether CDS was looking for a reason to quit. Even though TB was very careful with him, and always polite, he probably knew the relationship was not as strong as with Guthrie, and he probably didn't much like us either.

TB and Chirac spoke again and TB said, to laughter at the other end, that he was having trouble with his military. Chirac was in good form, and was retelling the story about when a microphone picked him up saying he loved Scotland but the haggis looked like shit and tasted worse. There was a lot of talk about who we would get to chair the [Future of] Europe convention, Giscard [former French President Valéry Giscard d'Estaing] or [Wim] Kok. TB was planning not to waste too much capital on it. Kok would be an obvious choice for us, but TB wondered whether Giscard might not be better because he was from a big country, and though he liked Kok, he would be more minded to put the interests of the small countries first.

The discussion in the morning was Afghanistan, and at the lunch the ludicrous Louis Michel briefed the historic decision that there was to be an EU army of 3,000–4,000 people in fifteen different countries, massive development, blah blah blah, what a lot of nonsense. I was at lunch with Peter Hain [Europe minister] who was about to do *The World at One* so I briefed him to go very hard for it, as did Jack at the press conference. However, Jack had also had a private chat with Hugo Young and said we would go into the euro by 2003. They turned it into a splash, so we had GB on the rampage again. TB came out for a chat at one point. He said he thought GB's problems were deep and it was a shame because he was brilliant in many ways but in the end maybe he didn't have the breadth. So perhaps he was a great Chancellor and that was that.

I left TB etc. to meet up with the family at Neil and Glenys' [the Kinnocks] in Brussels. Neil had a real downer on most of the Cabinet, including GB. He also felt Charles was overdoing the 'openness and honesty' bit, because it was being done at the expense of others. They were both reasonably OK re TB, but very down on Hoon, Clare, Milburn. Neil was on his best form for ages though. But he felt GB was in danger of blowing it and that Balls was a bad influence on him. Ronnie Flanagan called me while we were having dinner and said that my letter to him 'meant more to me than you'll ever know. That someone like you could be bothered to say that with all the other things you have to deal with.' He sounded very emotional, and was clearly feeling a lot of the pressure, but I thought he was basically a very decent bloke.

Saturday, December 15

I managed to avoid going back to the summit, and stayed in touch by phone with Godric. TB did the press conference early and it was all a bit of a non-event, though he was doing well on the substance. He had settled on the view that Giscard was best for the convention because we would be able to influence it more. I got a very different take from Glenys and Helle [Thorning-Schmidt, Stephen Kinnock's wife, Danish MEP] who were really steamed up about it.

Rory and I went for a run then down to the Grand-Place. Carole Walker [BBC] was there filming and couldn't believe her luck at bumping into us there. She interviewed both Neil and Glenys before we had lunch. We went for a wander and I was sad to discover that the Stock Exchange pub where I based myself when I was a busker here had gone. Godric was calling pretty regularly to keep me abreast of the endless rubbish from the summit. They had meant to agree the sites of the planned new agencies, but had to defer it to the Barcelona summit. Berlusconi was arguing that the food agency should go to Parma because of the cuisine there. TB said he really did seem to believe that it was a food agency, like a kind of glorified restaurant. The favourite was in Finland and Chirac had asked TB 'Why do we want to send the food agency to a country that only eats reindeer?' TB said somehow Europe seems to work, but if we are being frank, a lot of it is haggling, deals and people missing the point.

Sunday, December 16

Someone was at it in the *Sunday Times*, with a headline 'Generals warn glory-hunting Blair'. There were clearly people at the MoD briefing against us the whole time. TB wasn't happy about it at all. We travelled back on Eurostar after what had turned out to be a really nice weekend. I went for dinner with the Goulds and David Triesman. We had a lot of problems in the party, but I felt David was a genuinely nice man who would make a difference.

Monday, December 17

Yesterday's *Mail on Sunday* had some crap about a so-called bugging scandal involving Lord [Nazir] Ahmed [the Labour peer, opposed to the Afghanistan war, alleged that his phone had been tapped during conversations with Foreign Office minister Denis MacShane]. I called Denis MacShane to say I thought he should go up and deal with it. By the time I got to the office Jack Straw was on in a real fury. They are my ministers, not yours, and I'm not having it. He said he was 'fucking angry'. I said he knew I directed ministerial traffic in the media, this was a situation when we had to move fast to kill it. And when I heard the *Today* programme was still doing it, I knew it had to be dealt with. He said they had agreed at the FCO last night to put nobody up and I should have called him. He said the first he knew Denis was going on was listening to it on the news. I apologised to him, though it would have been avoided if they had communicated yesterday on their decision not to go up.

TB was working on the [Laeken] statement for the Commons. He was very pissed off with the briefing against him [in the *Sunday Times*] from the MoD, which was clearly born out of their being in a slightly different place. Friday had been very difficult for David M [re CENTCOM], and later for TB with Geoff Hoon. As a result of their calls, the MoD agreed to speak direct to the DoD [Department of Defense] to try to agree what was going to happen. TB had negotiated the words direct with Chirac but every time the MoD came back with a new objection, their line was CENTCOM would not put up with it. TB was suspicious that our own people were winding up [General Tommy] Franks. Also, at the end of the morning war meeting, CDS said to me that if Laeken was as bad as everyone said 'That's the end of ESDI' [European Strategic Defence Initiative]. Another revealing statement. TB said he was giving us the impression that troops would not want to do this 'and I just don't accept that'. He felt it would be wrong if the UK was not properly involved in this. The Franco-German problem was a real one though.

Russia was also wanting to be involved, and winding up [General Mohammed] Fahim Khan [leader of the Tajik Jamiat-e-Islami party within the Northern Alliance] to say not many troops should go in. CDS took delight in saying he had witnessed a video conference in which Bush briefed Franks on the force and said 'I've spoken to the PM and I've made no promises at all.' CDS was really doing nothing but give TB headaches at the moment. He defended Franks by saying that Chris Meyer spotted immediately that the US would not buy the language TB agreed with Chirac. I suggested to TB that he had a private word with Boyce. After the Laeken statement he got him in with Geoff Hoon and 'cleared the air' and said we needed more questions to be answered than we were asking.

If ever we needed evidence of TB not focusing on the domestic, it came in a meeting with Hilary [Armstrong] and Charles [Clarke] when he asked whether we could get a piece of legislation through to be told it went through on Thursday night because our MPs stayed up all night. It was amazing he didn't know that and I could feel him thinking he was getting out of touch. He also wanted to get out of a dinner on Africa with ministers tonight but we pushed him into it by saying he was in danger of not being taken seriously on it. He agreed reluctantly but when it came to it, it was Bono and Bob Geldof [rock stars campaigning to write off Third World debt] who got the invitation up to the flat. He was happy enough with the outcome of Laeken and Giscard's appointment and felt he was far less federalist than people imagined.

On the conference call, we discussed plans for a 'one hundred days on' paper of some sort. Torie Clarke was on, warning after Rumsfeld's visit to Kabul that we should be very much in the 'this is far from over' territory. I was still having to deal with personality and personnel issues in the various CICs.

Tuesday, December 18

TB was back arguing for a big New Labour kick, feeling we had lost a bit of momentum on all the main domestic areas and needed it back. He was quizzing me about whether the operation missed Anji and what to do with Peter M. He said he wanted to bring him back if he could but his fatal weakness was the press and his belief that if his profile was low he would get nothing and nowhere. He was worrying about the Americans, felt that they liked our support but in the end felt they could do what they wanted. He felt Rumsfeld and the right were in the ascendancy. TB was fretting as ever re holiday cover, who would make things happen while he was away.

I went to Grace's school play and then for a long run on the Heath. Then out for dinner with Tucker Eskew and his wife [Lisa]. He felt that apart from NMD [National Missile Defense] and Kyoto [climate change protocol, 1997], there was a lot shared between the two countries' agendas and TB had more influence than maybe we thought. He thought our media was mad but that we dealt with it pretty well. I still felt the second-phase questions hadn't really been dealt with and also that 'where next?' was far too prevalent in Americans' thinking.

Wednesday, December 19

TB had dinner last night with GB and said he had been on best behaviour but it was still difficult. TB had given him a pretty frank assessment of why he (TB) was generally thought to be an OK PM – because he had breadth, could deal with a stack of different things at once, and get on with a range of people. He felt GB had breadth but was too narrow in the field of people he related to. He told him he still believed he was easily the best person to follow him but he was not going to support him in circumstances where he felt he was being forced out. They had also discussed the euro, where he felt GB was more open-minded but that Balls was pouring opposition into his head the whole time. TB was looking a bit downcast again, probably worrying that a basically bad set-up with GB was something of a reality.

The US conference call was largely about one hundred days on. I needed to talk to Karen [Hughes] about where the whole CIC operation went now. The *Sun* had a story that Byers was to be sacked so I called Steve to say it was balls. There were continuing problems re ISAF [the UN's International Security Assistance Force, agreed in Bonn that month] before Geoff's statement and we were busy getting all the words sorted with the Americans and the French. The Germans seemed to have an even bigger problem than the French with the idea of serving under CENTCOM. There was a lot of briefing against us going on. Meanwhile the Wembley [national stadium] issue was flaring up again. The FA [Football Association] were going to announce that Wembley was their favoured option and they didn't want to refer to the James report.[1] Called Tessa [Jowell] to warn her to be very careful in her choice of words, that she could end up having to resign if she allied herself to someone else's version of events that didn't

[1] The investigation and report by consultant David James into the viability of the Wembley Stadium rebuild and the legality of the procurement process.

turn out to be right. In the event she was even tougher than I would have been. I had both Adam Crozier [FA chief executive] and David Davies [FA executive director] on the phone trying to get me to persuade her to spin the James stuff as dealing with Wembley. Out for dinner with Tessa and family. She was in quite good form considering how badly Wembley was playing out. Earlier I had a pretty tough meeting with the BBC over their plans for their 'Your NHS' day [a day of programmes, 20 February 2002], which they said was meant to be a fair, balanced look at the NHS, but everything we heard around the place suggested that they were just looking for the bad the whole time. I left them with a clear impression we were thinking of not co-operating at all.

Thursday, December 20

I was due to have lunch with Peter M, which had been my suggestion after he emailed me re an article he was doing. I asked Hilary C to find somewhere discreet and she had booked La Trouvaille in Newburgh Street. I arrived first, Peter a few minutes later and we were put in the window. Who should walk by, just seconds after we sat down, but Andrew Marr, but he was so busy window shopping on the other side of the passageway that he didn't see us. Peter did most of the talking early on, re what he had now taken to calling his 'defenestration'. He was very calm and friendly, said he wasn't blaming me directly but described the whole episode leading to his resignation as a 'road accident' in which everyone accidentally conspired. I said if it had been anyone else, we would probably have survived but he had baggage that weighed us down. On the whole Geoffrey [Robinson, former Paymaster General] loan episode, he felt it was a case of the circumstances of one period being different to those of another. When he took out the loan, Geoffrey was not *persona non grata*, was not a media bogeyman, was a friend who had always taken an interest in helping Peter. Peter said he had always wanted a nice home and to find someone to live with. He hated [his former flat in] Wilmington Square [Bloomsbury] because it didn't feel like a home. The themes of his loneliness, and his sexuality making him more lonely, or certainly more secretive, came through. He hated being away from Reinaldo [da Silva, his partner]. His private life was happy, but why because he was a politician should there have to be comment about it at all, why? It was he who was the politician. Nobody ever disputed he was a good minister and he felt he had to get back to top-level politics. I said it was true, he rarely got criticised on ability grounds. He accepted a return to the Cabinet was difficult, so the options were probably Europe or the UN and he was intending to develop his international profile.

I discussed the lunch with TB in advance. He said he didn't rule out Peter coming back but he had to lower the personal profile. He was a phenomenal talent but flawed and the heart of the flaw was his relationship with the press. When I relayed that, Peter did the usual thing of saying he hardly ever spoke to the press, only read the *FT*, it was the media that had created the persona, not the other way round. He clearly couldn't accept he had done much wrong, certainly felt wronged and tried to come to terms with it every day, and said he found it difficult. He said he knew I thought his problem was the profile but it wasn't. His problem was that others, including me and TB, couldn't make the shift from seeing him as 'Bobby'.[1] He felt he never recovered from that, that he could never be seen as a legitimate politician, that it was cruel that even as a minister, TB and I often saw him more as a behind-the-scenes person. Add in his worries about the media constantly probing re his sexuality, add in GB 'always there, as a presence intent on destroying me', and it wasn't a happy mix. He felt the rift with GB, contrary to legend, was not when he supported TB. It was at Chewton Glen [country house hotel in the New Forest], when he, TB and GB had had a meeting before the dinner and GB, to everyone's astonishment, produced a blueprint of everything to be done, including personnel issues in the party. TB was visibly taken aback and asked Peter his view. Peter stalled and said we needed to think about it.

After TB went to bed, Peter asked Gordon 'Why on earth did you do that?' GB said between them they could control TB and all the big decisions. Peter said again, why did you try to bounce him like that without warning? GB asked if Peter supported him on the substance of the proposals he had made, which were a mix of policy and personnel. Peter said he needed to think about it and discuss it with TB. GB replied 'You've made your choice,' and stormed off. He said it was a pretty blatant attempt to use him in undermining TB early on. He felt one of GB's weaknesses was that he underestimated TB's steel. He saw me and Peter as the two strong people and had always felt if he could get us over to him, he could deal with TB. He underestimated our loyalty, but also TB's steel.

[1] Mandelson's 'code name' during the 1994 Labour leadership election, a name often revived by those seeking to paint him as a Machiavellian figure. See *Prelude to Power*, pp 42–3.

By now, there were more guests in the restaurant who had noticed us and we were virtually whispering across the table. Peter told me of a meeting he had had whilst the Hammond Inquiry was going on.[1] He wanted to explain to GB why he was fighting so hard for his story to be heard. They met in Gordon's office at the Commons. GB put him at ease straight away, asking with seeming sincerity how he was. Peter said bruised and hurt and really trying to come back. He said he told him the story as dispassionately as he could, his role, Jack's role, my role, Mike O'Brien, TB, the Civil Service, 'I was as dispassionate as I could be, tried not to blame, no individual's fault, just a terrible set of circumstances ending in a road crash.' GB listened and said the problem was that I had created the context on the Monday by saying that was the only contact between you and the Home Office (via his private office) and it meant an elephant trap was laid. 'Then you fell into it. The only way out is for Alastair to say he misbriefed and apologise but he won't do that.' He said TB had always been a weak personality and he needed strong personalities to support him. First, it had been Peter/GB and then it became Peter/AC. But AC wanted to be the main voice 'so he conspired to push you out, it's obvious.'

Peter was in full flow, vivid, and I sometimes felt he had a photographic memory for these key moments and his key relationships. He said he told GB he didn't believe it was like that, pointed out 'You have to remember Alastair is different to us, he would happily walk away from politics, he has a different life he can lead, family, money to make beyond our dreams, he never chose this path, he was pursued, we poached him and a large part of him didn't want it.' Then Peter spoke as GB again. 'Yes, but once he chose it, he wanted to be number one and he's done it by getting rid of you at a time TB and I are seen as rivals.' Even aiming off for possible exaggeration, and I'm not sure there was that much, I was mildly shocked. Peter claimed he had remained supportive of me and said it was all too obvious that GB was just trying to use the circumstances of the time to get Peter to move in his favour. He said that TB was in a different class as a

[1] In January it had been claimed that Mandelson had helped wealthy businessman Srichand Hinduja's application for a British passport, and Mandelson resigned as Secretary of State for Business, Innovation and Skills. An inquiry headed by Sir Anthony Hammond QC was asked to establish what approaches were made to the Home Office in 1998 in connection with an application for naturalisation by Hinduja and the full circumstances surrounding the approaches and the later grant of the application. The inquiry found that neither Mandelson nor Home Office minister Mike O'Brien had acted with impropriety of any sort.

politician 'I love his deviousness, his selfishness, the way he is able to turn everything to his own advantage. His genius as a politician is his understanding of people, but also the fact that he is totally selfish and people either don't see it or if they do, they don't seem to mind because of what he brings to them and the job.'

I reminded him of the time TB had told us that Labour governments always foundered on issues of ego and personality, and that we had to be different. I agreed with his car-crash analysis, felt that if it hadn't been him, we would have handled it differently, felt that we both made mistakes. I felt sad that he was out of things, and sad that I had played a part in that. He was right that I could probably walk away. He wasn't able to, yet had had to. Despite it all, we were still able to talk openly and I still considered him to be a friend whose judgement I value. We went out, and stood there, in the middle of Carnaby Street, with a couple of bodyguards, passers-by shooting the occasional odd look and Peter said 'Happy Christmas. I had better do some shopping.' And off he went.

The conference call was all one hundred days, then we did a selective briefing for the broadsheets and the BBC, really greasing up Putin. Then a meeting with Crozier and Davies from the FA after yesterday's fiasco. They wanted assurances we were still up for it and they wanted me to persuade Tessa to put out something more supportive. I pointed out that politically we had to be very careful to cover our backs re the James report and anything else that may emerge. They also had to understand the political considerations concerning Birmingham missing out on a major national project. Crozier seemed a nice enough bloke, a bit looking after number one maybe, a bit pushy. I reported to Tessa that they felt there were senior people in DCMS [Department of Culture, Media and Sport] really trying to kill off the project. Tessa seemed keen on the idea of the stadium, but not keen on the FA, and she wasn't keen on pushing the boat out.

Peter had given me a lot of food for thought. It was, as he said, crazy that he wasn't in government. We weren't exactly blessed with A-league ministers. He pointed out that he may have made mistakes on the personal front, but he never fucked up on policy and he always gave real direction to whatever department he was in. It was true. All the departments he worked in said the same. He could make decisions, and he could run things. I tried to work out whether he had gone second time around because it was him, or because of what our media operation and media relations had become, and his role in that. In a way, the strength he had brought to the modernisation of our media relations was what made him the bogey figure he was, and that status plus baggage was what made us turn a mistake into something far bigger. It was the same reason so many in the media felt about me as they did. He also seemed more resigned to things. He believed that the new papers he had discovered for Hammond to look at showed that he was done in. But he had no desire to push it, felt it would only be worth it if it led to a change of attitude by the public and that would only come about if TB and I said that it changed things materially. And neither of us would want to do that because the world had moved on.

I was struck by how much he, and from his reported comments GB, believed I meant to TB, far more than I felt myself. He had said that both he and GB felt I was by far the closest, that he felt hurt because we had been such close friends, not so close any more, whilst GB just hated me and feared me in equal measure and saw me as someone that had to be dealt with. He really enjoyed the story of my row with GB during the election with Bob Shrum [Brown's polling adviser] trying to calm things. He was making enough money and travelling a lot but when he listed the countries he was due to be visiting, he said 'I'm busy, but it's no life.' He also wanted to dispute my line, which he had heard me say more than once, that he had dumped his old friends for a new rich set. He said he found his life very lonely at times and people like Carla Powell [socialite, wife of former Thatcher adviser Charles] gave him friendship and support and also a lot of fun that was missing a lot of the time.

I watched him wander off before going to do a bit of shopping of my own. In some ways, we'd grown apart, but I felt that between us we'd given something to TB, and the party, that really mattered, and that meant there would always be a bond there. I talked to Philip, and Grace [Gould], who was listening to the conversation, said she thought we would always be working together in some shape or form.

Friday, December 21

[Vladimir] Putin was coming over. TB was up north and flew back. I went down [to Chequers] to meet him so that we could prepare a proper script before Putin arrived. The only real announcement was a bilateral working group on terrorism, and the main interest anyway was Afghanistan. The trail for OBL seemed to have gone cold and that was casting a cloud over the whole scene. But we had the inauguration of a new administration in Kabul to look forward to tomorrow, and today the first Marines arriving there, so the media backdrop of the TB/VP press conference was OK. The MMR issue [questions over whether the Blairs had chosen the measles, mumps and rubella vaccination for baby Leo] was going from bad to worse, and in addition Fiona, Hilary [Coffman] and Magi [Cleaver] were trying to work out how to handle the Egypt holiday. Fiona had done a brilliant job getting CB in the right place with the public, and could see it being undone. She feared a combination of yet another fancy holiday, with questions over who pays, and MMR, could produce a bit of a tipping point.

The Putin meeting was largely Afghanistan, also Russia/NATO, a lot of it just the two of them. We were definitely more confident. Tucker [Eskew] had given me a baseball cap for Christmas with the words 'Media scum' on it, which I showed to Putin. TB said 'Don't encourage him' I think talking to VP about me rather than the other way around. The press conference at RAF Halton was fine, pretty low-key, but it looked good and the co-operation and warmth was strong. There was some interest in the terrorism issue. I went back for the office [Christmas] dinner but Hilary and I were still dealing with MMR. I did a little speech thanking them all, saying they were the best possible team, but afterwards admitted to Godric I felt we were coasting a bit and needed to up our game in the New Year, especially on story development and narrative.

Saturday, December 22

Up early to head for Burnley vs Millwall. The new administration in Kabul was leading the news all day. But I spent a lot of the journey dealing with MMR. We had got ourselves into a bit of a mess on this. We had had to hold a privacy line, and I did feel that it was the thin end of the wedge, that every time they had to do something like this with the kids, it became a big media thing. But the reality was that the doubt was being used to fuel doubt about the safety of the vaccine, with potential serious knock-on effects, which would be a lot worse if it emerged Leo hadn't had it. I spoke to TB, and we agreed that we should emphasise both of them supported the policy one hundred per cent but they didn't see why they had to talk about their children. I went a bit further with some of them, dropping a very strong hint in the hope they wrote it as fact without attribution.

Through the day, this took up the time and energies of Fiona, Hilary, Tom [Kelly], John Shields [press officer] and me, all dealing with it because of Cherie's views, and TB's disengagement. He was just angry, said it was monstrous that the press could get into the family like this, and it was, but we had to deal with it. I said to Tom we should put out a statement from TB making it clear he was pro MMR vaccine but if he commented on whether his child had taken part in one government medical campaign, he would be expected to do them all. It was all running pretty big by the time we finally got the words out. I spent the whole of half-time dealing with [Lord] Wakeham, and after a crap match [0–0], most of the journey home trying to get the press in a better place on it. Once it also came out they were spending $10,000 on a few days' holiday in Egypt, we would be in major out-of-touch land.

Sunday, December 23

TB's statement was being seen as a hint that Leo had the jab, though they were still saying we would neither confirm nor deny. Frank Dobson [former Health Secretary] called, and agreed, which was good of him, to take up the bids he was getting, and was on the robust end of the market re their privacy, also saying TB and CB clearly backed the policy. This was beginning to do us quite a bit of damage. The big story was a Brit caught on a US plane with explosives in his shoes.[1] I went for a massage and bumped into Rachel Stevens of S Club 7 [pop group], so got Grace to come over and she was incredibly nice to her, called us in while she was having a pedicure, her jeans rolled up and her tiny feet in a bowl of weird-looking stuff. She was so nice to Grace.

Wednesday, December 26

I worked on TB's New Year message, euro, public services, commentary on the war. TB called as he left for the airport en route to Egypt. He said he knew he would take a hit, he was desperate for a break and said he intended to come back firing on all cylinders. I had been approached by a TV company asking me to make a film on a year in the life of Burnley if we got promoted. Fiona was really pressing me to go for it. It was tempting but only as a halfway exit, not a real alternative.

Thursday, December 27

Jeremy [Heywood] sent through some good suggestions and additions [to the New Year message] on public services. TB changed the euro section, but otherwise it was fine. We agreed to get it out for the 30th,

[1] Richard Reid, a radicalised convert to Islam with links to al-Qaeda, had been discovered on an American Airlines flight from Paris to Miami attempting to detonate explosives hidden in his shoes. Pleading guilty to eight charges, in 2002 he would be given a life sentence without parole.

ahead of the honours briefing. The problem with the MMR issue was that it was such an obvious and easy talking point and people sensed the vulnerability.

Friday, December 28

I went up with Calum and Rory to Mum and Dad's. Fiona called saying Cherie had been on to say she had got a message that GB and Sarah [his wife] had had a baby [Jennifer Jane, born seven weeks early, weighing 2 lb 4 oz]. We had known nothing about it so I had to get Anne Shevas to track down Ian Austin so that we had a line ready when all the calls started. There's no doubt it would give GB an added positive dimension. There was already around the place a feeling that he was the real character of the government, and this would show that in a way.

Saturday, December 29

GB did a doorstep, looking pretty happy and human. TB's New Year message went fine, the odd splash, a few page leads, not massive. I wasn't convinced these New Year messages were worth the effort.

Sunday, December 30

I took Rory to Man U vs Fulham. Saw Alex [Ferguson, Manchester United manager] beforehand. Clearly thinking about staying another year. JP was on, pissed off, felt he wasn't getting proper support, e.g. before his *Today* programme interview. I sometimes wished politics could just all shut down during these holiday periods. I put in a couple of calls to get him where he needed to be. We went for dinner at the Milibands [David and Louise]. Lots of chat re GB. The baby would hopefully do him some good. I gave them a cut-down version of Peter M's account [see December 20]. David seemed pretty shocked too.

Monday, December 31

TB called to wish us a happy New Year, and also tell us what a great time he was having. I did my best to tell him it was cold and miserable and the country was falling apart. It seemed from the way he was talking about [Egyptian President Hosni] Mubarak, his sons, Egypt generally that he assumed he was being bugged. He was relieved the NHS annual crisis had not materialised, though I told him rail [safety] was running as a pretty big problem. He said he felt ready for the fray, public services and Europe were what really mattered and there had to be absolute focus on them. Kenton Keith was in town and came to see me at home at 3pm. Kenton was a lovely guy, but I think his way of dealing with the obvious tensions between the different parts of the US operation, and the scale of some of the issues we were talking about, was to retreat a little bit. He was due to leave, said he had enjoyed it, felt they had made a difference, in large part thanks to the people we sent. He felt the White House never really understood the need for Islamabad [CIC], and he was pretty scathing about Karen [Hughes]. He was intending to write a book and it would make clear she was only really interested in Bush's re-election, that there was no real understanding of the need for a broader approach on foreign policy and public diplomacy. The tensions between Pakistan and India [military standoff including movement of troops and missiles to borders] were dominating the serious news, and getting very difficult.

Tuesday, January 1, 2002

We saw in the New Year at Terry's [Tavner, friend] and had a perfectly nice time though I was feeling tired a lot of the time. It was also difficult to be open with anyone really. I was taken aback a bit by the bitchiness re GB, and the idea he was deliberately having a baby to soften his profile. It is the kind of thing people say joking, but here were people not centrally involved in politics who seemed actually to believe it. I spent most of today with Calum, football, cinema, just hanging around, and had a nice time. Mentally I was trying to crank up a couple of gears into work mode but was wishing I was somewhere else.

Wednesday, January 2

Fiona seemed genuinely happy with all her birthday presents and the way I and the kids were treating her, though I could sense her feeling that I had been more engaged over the holiday but was about to disappear again before the day was over. We had all her family around during the day and I managed to avoid doing too much on the work front. I'd written some half-decent lines for Tom Kelly to brief out re the visit to Bangladesh, India and Pakistan but Jack Straw called to say he was worried we were raising expectations too high and that we would not be able to meet them. Jack was a real team player at the moment, genuinely wanting to help and not making points like this unless he really felt he had to. But I sensed he worried TB was overreaching himself. I encouraged him to do a note to TB, which he did, saying we had to be careful not to let the Pakistanis get away with too much, that they did at times get too close to terrorists, and that we had to be fairly tough with them. We went out for dinner then I headed to Heathrow.

I tried to sleep all the way to Cairo, where it was 3am UK time when we picked up TB and CB. They were full of their usual post-holiday bonhomie and we were all feeling like shit after a sleepless flight and body clocks a bit screwed. TB seemed to have got a lot of his energy back. He knew not to push too hard on how marvellous a time he had, but clearly they had been looked after well. He read the voluminous briefs, then we did a briefing and afterwards a series of taped interviews. We had agreed that for the first leg we should be aiming news-wise for the agreement of the Bangladeshis to send troops as part of the ISAF. But the press were more interested in the euro and TB/GB and after pushing him several times on whether they had spoken while he had been away, his answers were evasive enough for them to realise they hadn't and that was good enough for some of them to run away with it.

TB told me afterwards he had tried to speak to GB three times about the euro in recent days. He felt that the baby, contrary to the general feeling, was unlikely to change him at all. I relayed to him Peter M's view that GB had somehow managed to alienate every single one of the people who might be able to persuade TB to move over at some point. TB felt Gordon just had too much time on his hands, and he had always over-calculated. He relied on calculation not instinct and feel, and he assumed others operated in the same way. On the euro, he did not feel GB was totally opposed as such, but a combination of natural caution and over-calculation took him to the wrong conclusion. It was a pretty grim start to the year though, if even a baby could become a source of tension.

TB said he was very clear where we needed to be focusing in the year ahead – Europe and public service reform, but on both he had ceded too much power to GB already and every step forward was going to be difficult. He said he wasn't overly worried, but I sensed he was. We then sat down to work out day by day what we were doing and what we were hoping for on the visit. The FCO briefs on the Kashmir background were fascinating. How one issue came to dominate the political and diplomatic relations of two major countries [India and Pakistan], one of them a future superpower, was a great lesson in how not to do diplomacy, but what the solution was heaven knows. TB's NI experience led him to be tempted to think he could sort it, but if anything it was even more intractable than NI. We finally arrived in Bangladesh around early evening their time.

Thursday, January 3

Bangladesh. The visit got off to a potentially embarrassing start. TB's suit was badly crumpled after his car journey in Egypt and not nearly smart enough to wear as he left the plane. But all the other suits were in the hold and it would take a while to find them. So Magi [Cleaver] was despatched off the plane first to find someone wearing a smart suit that would fit TB. We watched her through the windows walking up and down the lines of people eyeing them up and down. None of them were suitable. Then she spotted a young man at the back of the crowd and went over to him. His face was a picture. I think he thought it was some kind of spoof but then Magi was doing her best 'this is fucking serious' look and seconds later the two of them were coming up the stairs. 'Ah, the body double,' I said. He was a DFID official and gobsmacked to be on the plane with TB, CB and the rest of us. TB said 'Sorry about this but as you can see my suit is not in good shape.' So then this poor guy is stripping off so that TB can try on his suit. It wasn't perfect but it wasn't far off. The swap was done and then we were ready to disembark.

There was a full-on welcome and then straight to the president's residence. There were some pretty overwhelming scenes of poverty on the way and once we got into town the open sewers took some getting used to. But the people were by and large friendly and welcoming. Also, whereas the leadership of some countries lived in inverse proportion to the poverty of the people, with the president [Professor Badruddoza Chowdhury] and PM [Khaleda Zia] too, you were always aware of this being the Third World. They did not overdo their own luxury. The president's trousers barely reached his feet. Yet the brief had talked of this being a deeply divided and corrupt country. The divisions were clear enough at the broader ministerial meeting where various ministers had a series of arguments right in front of us, constantly interrupting each other and point scoring.

The PM was good, she was just about able to calm them down and she was up for the idea of Bangladesh being part of the ISAF in the future so that was fine. They were all pretty upfront about pitching for money for bridges and roads and the like. We had a brief and very chaotic doorstep before the official dinner, which was like a low-budget wedding reception. The room was a bit dingy and with huge spaces around the edges. The food was OK but not your usual official dinner extravagance, and the cheap tablecloths and paper napkins were a world away from some of the fineries we saw in other parts of the world. I was sitting with our rather loud high commissioner [Dr David Carter], who I quite liked because he was out of the usual cut, though it was odd he spoke no Bengali. I watched Man U vs Newcastle on Bangladeshi TV, which was more than Rory was able to do because it wasn't the live match at home.

Friday, January 4

OK coverage out of yesterday but Gus O'Donnell [Treasury permanent secretary, former press secretary to John Major] had given us a bit of a problem. He had done a meeting with students and the papers were mangling it to say that he said effectively that EMU was a political decision and the economics were never likely to be clear and unambiguous. TB was pissed off not just at GB's general behaviour and modus operandi but also that Gus should be saying this kind of thing and talking about this kind of an issue in a way that gets to the media. I felt, to be fair to Gus, that it was just a statement of the obvious, in that ultimately politicians would have to make a political judgement based on the economic analysis, but TB felt it was where GB was currently parked, namely in a position to say, whatever the economic analysis was, that it was not clear and unambiguous.

The guy from DFID had another clothing mission to perform because I suddenly discovered a hole in my shoe, and he got a shoemaker to bring in a stack of different shoes, none of them terribly nice. Events in Kashmir were the backdrop to the next stage of the visit. TB, David Manning and I met to discuss how we choreograph a sense of TB playing a part in trying to get the immediate problem solved. DM had a paper, making clear our belief that the Pakistanis would 'go nuclear' and if they did, that they wouldn't be averse to unleashing them on a big scale. TB was genuinely alarmed by it and said to David 'They wouldn't really be prepared to go for nuclear weapons over Kashmir would they?' DM said the problem was there wasn't a clear understanding of strategy and so situations tended to develop and escalate quickly, and you couldn't really rule anything out. The Kathmandu Asian summit should at least be a chance to calm things down, but the tensions were pretty strong.

After dealing with all that, we then went from the sublime to the ridiculous, with a long discussion about whether TB should wear his Nehru suit. I was marginally in favour provided it didn't look too ridiculous, partly because hopefully it would be seen as showing respect, but also because if we could generate pictures, we were more likely to generate coverage. We got to the [Windsor] hotel [Bangalore] and he put it on. It looked fine. We went for dinner at the governor of Karnataka's residence [Raj Bhavan, residence of V. S. Ramadevi], terrific food, and I enjoyed talking to our high commissioner [to India], [Sir] Rob Young, about the enormity of their democracy, the four million electoral officers for example involved in the actual logistical running of an election.

Saturday, January 5

Bangalore. I went out for a run, partly through the affluent upper-middle-class parts, also through some of the new industrial bit, and then through some of the poorer parts, and the feel you got in all three was a real sense of energy and dynamism. There was a phenomenal amount of building work going on, and the high-tech centres were as high-tech as anything back home. I got back for a final run through the speech with TB. He was now beginning to worry whether it was a bit over the top to describe the UK as 'pivotal' even though he had said it before. The central argument, that a combination of Britain's history, current strengths within all the major international institutions, and vision for the future, made us uniquely placed in some of the big international arguments was right. We set off on the long drive out to the university campus in an old Raj-era car, which gave us both backache by the time we got there. The setting was good, though there were too many introductory speeches including one from a minister that was taken as a bit of a go at TB, but his speech went down fine.[1] At lunch, I was with some of the people in the big international financial institutions. It really brought home how the scale of development here was going to impact on First World economies.

There was a discussion about TB going to Baghram for a brief visit. Magi wanted to drop the ceremonial part of the Indian visit but David [Manning] and Rob [Young] were both worried about it. MoD security were advising against going there in daylight, so we settled on a rather grim set-up that would mean a long flight back overnight. Magi was really in Magi mode, very tough with both David and Rob, partly out of revenge against the Indians who had cut Cherie out of the [forthcoming] Vajpayee dinner. DM said it was not the same. TB not going to see their president because he wanted to go to Kabul was like Vajpayee cancelling the Queen because he wanted to go to Dublin.

On the way back to the hotel, TB was chatting away about how quickly India's power was going to grow. He had been quite impressed by some of the British business guys who were down here in Bangalore. We also talked about who was going to fill the gap Anji

[1] Blair told the audience of politicians and business leaders 'Today, inevitably, I speak against the background of September 11 and the tension here in this subcontinent. But I want to set even these events in a wider context: how Britain and India work together, with others, to confront terrorism; but also how we build support for the policies and values that promote peace and justice and mitigate against extremism and terror, in all nations everywhere.'

had left in relation to what he called 'personal care and attention', the problem about the suit on the plane being a classic example. There were obviously difficulties with GB's baby and TB spoke to him briefly after the baby was transferred to a special care unit.

Sunday, January 6

Gordon's baby was clearly dying. TB and CB were both genuinely upset. So was Alison [Blackshaw]. Fiona called a couple of times from home to say we had to be careful on the various visits not to look too happy, because the media were obviously trying to set up shots of TB not seeming to care about this developing tragedy at home. Through the day, it was announced that the baby was deteriorating and had had a brain haemorrhage. After Fiona's second call, we put out a line re TB and CB thinking of them. The Sundays were even more ridiculous than usual, most of them taking as the nose to their stories the throwaway remark by an Indian minister [Pramod Mahajan, parliamentary affairs minister] yesterday that 'We are cool enough' as a great snub, India saying fuck off as a response to him re his Nehru suit.

I was more convinced than ever that we had to articulate this business of us having a press that actively wanted failure. The Indian press had been overwhelmingly positive about the speech, about him and CB, about our role. I went to the gym, where the little guy in there insisted on giving me a workout on the weights, and I was in agony by the time I got back to see TB. We went out on the rooftop of the hotel for a chat and he was clearly a bit down. He was putting enormous effort into trying to get progress on various fronts at home and abroad and all the time we had this media shit to swim through.

We flew to Hyderabad. Vajpayee and Musharraf had met yesterday but every account we had underlined how difficult any progress would be. TB was trying to get the focus on to two key principles, that Pakistan restate and more importantly show their seriousness in renouncing terrorism, and then India say yes to dialogue. TB was taken straight off by helicopter to look at some education projects while DM and I headed for the hotel to work up a proper script for TB to use post Vajpayee. David said he was shocked, even knowing what he did about our media, at the way they seemed to want us to fail, when we were actually dealing with political/diplomatic issues that were literally life and death. TB came back and, as often happened, his mood had improved by going out and about and talking to people outside the usual mix.

We flew up to Delhi where TB did Indian TV, some European

media. We got to the hotel, then a pre-meeting before Jaswant Singh [foreign affairs minister] arrived. He was pretty much signed up to TB's general approach and agreed to try and get Vajpayee on that two-principles pitch. Several times he said we needed to know where the Taliban leadership were, implying that they were in Pakistan and the Pakistanis knew where they were. He said that Musharraf had implied to Vajpayee that they could turn the terrorist taps on and off. It was so like listening to the sides in Northern Ireland.

TB told him the Indians were on strong ground and provided they said they would have meaningful dialogue, they could use us to pressure Musharraf to take the first steps. He said the Americans had to hear loud and clear that India was prepared to have a dialogue and then the pressure on Pakistan over terrorism would grow. We left for the Hyderabad palace for the talks. TB pushed hard but got very little change out of Vajpayee. He was holding out for a lot more from the Pakistanis. He was pretty shrewd, and his total lack of embarrassment at long silences was a real strength. It meant others had to go running for him. He said he would only do a brief opening statement and then say in answer to questions that he was happy to go for dialogue but by the time it came to it he was so quiet and meandering that there was no clarity.

People were more interested in the huge contrast between his near-mystical manner and TB's boyish enthusiasm. Also, bizarrely, he wore interpretation headphones the whole time even though the entire proceedings were conducted in English. He did in fact explicitly say that he would go for dialogue if the Pakistanis renounced terrorism in word and deed but it wasn't done with the force and clarity required for our dunderheads to see it as a story, so it didn't really fly. Tom [Kelly] and I did our best to push it as him giving TB a message to Musharraf, but it wasn't easy.

At the official dinner, I was for some reason seated next to Vajpayee. He was an attentive host, but so quiet. I asked him whether it was a strength or a disadvantage to have such a quiet voice, and whether he used silence as a political weapon. He said he liked to think his authority came from within, as well as from the position he held. When he spoke in his native tongue, he could raise his voice to great levels and had regularly addressed crowds of half a million during the election. But words were precious, and there was little point speaking when nothing was to be said. He said Gandhi fasted to preserve his strength, and he too had learned the value of rest and peacefulness. TB was across the table talking to [Lal Krishna] Advani, the interior minister, and George Fernandes [defence minister]. At one point he joked across the table to

Vajpayee re me, 'Be careful, he's a bad man,' and Vajpayee said 'I don't think so.' Fiona called several times to keep me up to date with GB and the baby, which was obviously desperately sad.

Monday, January 7

Really, really heavy day. Breakfast with TB in Delhi. Both he and CB sensed that the GB situation re the baby was heading for disaster, and he said it will change GB, but he didn't know whether for the better or the worse. It might give him a different sense of priorities, but it might also feed the dark side of his character. We were starting to get more criticism re TB focusing so much on foreign affairs. He felt the answer was to build the logical argument re why these issues mattered at home. We set off for the airport and boarded the C130 for Islamabad. TB and CB were up on the top deck sitting just behind the pilot who had a paper cup fixed by a rubber band to his head and 'I am a Sunderland fan' written on the cup. TB was worrying about how to get Musharraf on to a tougher line on terrorism. The flight was uncomfortable and it wasn't easy to work. We landed, similar huge security, then left for the CIC.

I was travelling with David M and [Sir] Hilary Synnott, who knew his stuff. We got to the CIC, a nice, modern set-up but it did, as Pat [McFadden] had told me, feel more like a library than a communications hub. TB had a meeting with a group of Afghan women while I met Kenton Keith to discuss who should stay and who should go. Tanya [Joseph] had been winding me up about the American guy who called himself 'the hawk' and now I could see for myself why he had driven her so bonkers. He was the archetypal over-the-top US patriot. When TB thanked them all for the work they were doing, the hawk piped up 'It's easy, sir, when your children are at risk.' They were a pretty good bunch though, just hadn't gelled to make the difference I had hoped they would.

TB was on good form at the press conference. We were being lobbied by the American ambassador, Wendy Chamberlain, for the UK to become a mediator re Kashmir. TB was attracted, I could tell, but resisted nonetheless. I was worried about TB taking on yet another huge international commitment. She was adamant that only TB could sort this out. We went to the hotel and down to the pool to discuss how to handle the meetings. TB felt step one had to be Musharraf getting tougher with the terror groups, use that to press the Indians to engage. There had to be an absolute break with the Taliban and any of the groups they supported. But Pakistan also had to know there were benefits out of that.

We left for Musharraf's place and most of the talks were one-on-one, afterwards described by TB as 'very, very hard going'. I talked to [Shaukat] Aziz, the finance minister, who was very urbane and very charming, really trying to convince me that Musharraf wanted to break the terror groups. There was clearly a concerted effort going on as David M was getting the same message just as hard, hearing Musharraf had said before the December 13 attack on the Indian parliament that they would crack down on them. We were called in after a while and went over familiar ground on Afghanistan, then some bilateral stuff, and TB, clearly feeling the meeting was getting a bit rambling, suggested the two of them plus their press people should go through the difficult questions for the press conference. Musharraf went through what he intended to say, which was pretty much OK, then TB did the same and Musharraf clearly baulked at him saying 'Support for terrorism must stop for talks to begin.' He said he didn't like it because it suggested that Pakistan and its government supported terrorism. We persuaded him that the best thing to do then was for him to say right at the top that he opposed terrorism in all its forms. We also persuaded him not to talk about Kashmir as a 'freedom struggle' because that would not be understood by our and by US opinion. Better to say it was an indigenous struggle. We spent an awful lot of time toing and froing on it but eventually he agreed.

It was a pretty tortuous exchange, indicative of how deep-rooted the problems were, but it did mean we got what we wanted in terms of a tough anti-terrorism statement and even our media took it as a bit of a breakthrough for TB. The media event was strong. Then drinks, then dinner. I was next to General [Muhammad] Aziz Khan [chairman of Joint Chiefs of Staff, Pakistan] and the finance minister. Their general feeling was that India was in a box and didn't know how to get out of it. It was funny too how both sides seemed to talk of the other as equals, even though India was so much bigger and more powerful.

We had done pretty well though on both legs, then to the airport and back on the C130 for the flight to Baghram. The troops were loving it and the press were genuinely excited about the trip. We flew in total darkness to Baghram, with only the occasional flash of green from night sights. As we arrived, it was pitch black. TB and CB went out to a red carpet, [Hamid] Karzai [chairman of the Transitional Administration], the band playing the barely discernible tune of welcome, and general chaos to which I added, stepping down from the plane, when my briefcase, even though the combination lock was on, suddenly opened and papers were flying all over the place.

Thankfully, the hacks were all being taken off the other end and didn't notice as David [Manning], Anna [Wechsberg] and I scrabbled around using hands, feet and anything else to trap the paper and get, hopefully, all of it back. TB was now standing with an Afghan shouting into his face in what seemed to be part of the welcome. We were then taken to a line of armoured vehicles and the Special Branch advance guy introduced David and me to the special forces who were going to be looking after us.

The drive was slow, over endless tank traps, eventually reaching the old Russian barracks. TB had a one-on-one with Karzai, said he was very upbeat, probably too much, but he was clearly pleased that TB had come, particularly given the genuine security risks, and there was a good atmosphere between them. As we came out of the meeting, into the darkened corridor, Keith Lowe [protection officer] took me to one side and said 'You should probably tell the PM that the Chancellor's baby has died.' There is something about a baby's death. Even the cops, who can turn pretty much anything into a source of laughter, seemed really saddened, and were explaining to the Afghans what had happened. I told TB in between meetings. I said I'm afraid there's bad news, and he knew straight away what it was, and asked us to try to fix a call.

We had to move to a bigger room for a meeting with eight of the ministers from the interim government. One look around the room was enough to tell you what a nightmare job Karzai had trying to hold things together. TB and Karzai said a few words of welcome and then opened things up. They were a pretty aggressive bunch. One of them was the double of Orson Welles [heavyweight actor] and said they needed long-term help. His tone of voice suggested he didn't think we would deliver it. There was another guy who looked like something out of the Taliban and who spent most of the meeting trying to stare us out. One or two were dressed in Western-style suits but they said little. Karzai was definitely a cut above but he really had his work cut out. They had cobbled together from somewhere a collection of chairs and tables, and laid out a rather sad collection of sweets that nobody touched. TB said Britain would stay with them for the long term, and work to make sure that the reconstruction conference in Tokyo [January 21–22, to be co-chaired by Japan, US, EU and Saudi Arabia] went well.

Karzai said Afghanistan was well rid of the terrible leadership that went before. Abdullah said they were effectively reconstructing a country from scratch. Karzai obviously picked up on the somewhat negative tone of some of the ministerial contributions and concluded the meeting by saying they were all 'so glad that such a distinguished person has come to see us, taken the risk, you have demonstrated such goodwill. When the Afghan people get to hear that you visited us, they will be proud and thrilled.' One of the special forces guys said to me 'Welcome to bandit country.' We drove, as slowly and painfully as before, to the special forces HQ, to put a phone call through to Sue Nye [GB's personal aide]. She confirmed that the baby was dead and that it had now been announced publicly. TB was genuinely cut up, said it was a horrible thing to have to go through, and even worse with all the attention on it. He was having to talk quite loudly to be heard. I could sense that this collection of real hard nuts from the SAS and the SBS were a bit bemused to have their prime minister in there having a near-weepy phone call. He was due to be doing the press, so we went over how to respond to the baby's death whilst also covering the substance of the visit. He was pretty discombobulated and wanted further confirmation and assurance that it had been announced. Karzai arrived and we filled him in on what was happening, explaining why he would have to address it. Karzai showed a deft touch, taking his hat off when TB spoke later re GB.

We were taken to meet some of the real heroes from both SAS and SBS. The first presentation was from a guy who had been part of a team following a tip that OBL was in a certain cave. They had ended up living for days without supplies, having to make do with what they found, including a thirty-hour period in which the only consumption between four of them, apart from stuff off trees, was a small bottle of water. They had been calling on bombers and fighting their way, hand to hand, towards where they were going. But he had gone by the time they got there. Then a Geordie who had been at the fort at Mazar, buried under rubble after an American bomb went astray, got out, involved in all sorts of fighting, got out the body of the American guy who had been killed there, eventually flushing out the al-Qaeda people by pumping in freezing water. He told it all with a mix of real pride and deadpan humour. These guys were genuinely impressive people. Their living quarters here, let alone when they were out and about, were incredibly basic and yet there was an enthusiasm there that was incredible. None of them seemed boastful, or demanding of credit or praise. They just explained very factually what they did. One of the most impressive was the smallest, a Scottish guy so small I was surprised he was even allowed in the Armed Forces. We were then given a presentation by [Major General John] McColl on ISAF [of which McColl, a UK soldier, was leader]. He too was impressive, not least the way he worked out the details of the military technical agreements and the way he was establishing authority in Kabul, e.g. by troops being visible at DFID projects, being seen to do good infrastructure work. Once again, we were confronted by the ingenuity and the resilience of our troops. TB said he needed a pee and we were taken out, up a field, to a series of upturned tubes into the ground.

Back on the C130, I met the SIS guy who had actually been the first person into Kabul, even if John Simpson had never met him. He too combined modesty with a very matter-of-fact ability to describe astonishing events. We flew out in total darkness, with a flare going by every now and then. Eventually, I managed to sleep. We landed in Oman and were glad to be transferred to the million times more comfortable 777. I called Ian Austin, and later wrote a letter to GB, as did TB and Cherie. TB briefed us on the one-on-one parts of his various meetings over dinner. He felt we had achieved things in India and Pakistan that actually made conflict less likely. But he was beginning to take seriously the stuff about him being more abroad than home, and talking about pulling out of his Africa tour. I felt that would be a mistake because it would look weak and defensive.

Wednesday, January 9

We landed, straight into the office, and back to all the crap. TB had told Jonathan he wanted to pull the Africa trip. Liz Lloyd [policy adviser] said the four leaders [of Ghana, Nigeria, Senegal and Sierra Leone] had cancelled a dinner with Chirac in Paris to be there for him, so he couldn't. My first morning meeting of the year, as we went through the media brief, was like swimming through shit. Virtually every paper over every story in knocking mode. TB, the great man abroad as seen overseas, was being whacked at home over absolutely everything. It was easy to dismiss as the usual media frenzy, but it must be causing us political problems.

I went up to the flat to discuss PMQs. He said we had to resist the *Groundhog Day*[1] feeling, that it was the greatest danger we got bored or started to let these bastards get us down. It had always been a struggle, always would be, and we had to stick at it and really get going. PMQs was OK if not brilliant. Transport was going big and then it emerged [Peter] Hain had said we had the worst railways in Europe, which went straight to the top of the news. Very annoying and stupid. JP livid, said what is it with people like that? TB had spoken to GB who wanted him to go to the funeral on Friday.

[1] 1993 Hollywood comedy, in which the same day repeats ad nauseam.

Thursday, January 10

At the morning meeting, I made sure the Foreign Office knew how pissed off everyone was at Hain, which was still getting a fair bit of play. War Cabinet was largely India/Pakistan, where is OBL, and some domestic stuff. CDS said if India and Pakistan go to war, we will be up the creek without a paddle. Geoff said there may have to be limited compulsory call-up of Territorial Army reserves. TB gave a pretty gloomy assessment re India/Pakistan, said Vajpayee was really upset at the way Musharraf treated him. Military dispositions remained the same, with more than a million troops there [Kashmir]. He assessed that the Indians believed that they could absorb 500,000 deaths. Pakistani capability was far greater than the Indians believed.

Cabinet was mainly a discussion re public services, and lots of people defending Byers. TB said the media were determined to give us a rough ride and would focus not on things we had done but on things we hadn't done. We shouldn't pretend everything is perfect but we shouldn't let them get away with the impression nothing is being achieved. We should be confident. Byers said the attacks over rail were an attack on the whole reform agenda, we had to be robust, emphasise the decades of underinvestment and failed privatisation and stick to the ten-year plan. He said he was delighted to have given colleagues a bit of a break from media heat. Both Reid and Jack Straw said the attacks on Steve were attacks on all of us and it was important we didn't allow these issues to be personalised but stuck together. Milburn echoed that, said it was railways today, could be any other service tomorrow because this was about an ideological assault on public services. Blunkett felt the Tories were beginning to get their act together and IDS was deliberately undermining confidence in the public services as a way of showing us as out of date. He felt they had hit on something and that disillusion went quite deep. It was a good discussion. And people were very supportive of Steve.

TB felt we had two years of struggle and provided improvements were clear at the end of that, we would win this argument. Their desire is to say the public services are hopeless and therefore we should return to the agenda of the 80s. Our argument is that through investment and reform we can build them up. In the afternoon, we had a four-hour strategy meeting with my main people plus other heads of department, but I felt just as I kept doing the groundhog stuff, so did they. TB chaired. We did agree TB should chair four new informal ministerial groups, on Europe, public services, rights and responsibilities, and also what someone called an 'ism' group, the need to knit everything we are doing together round a coherent set of beliefs. People kept arguing on the need to be more radical without being specific or clear as to what they meant.

TB felt that in health Milburn had come out clearly as a reformer and that had changed things within the department. He felt there was a danger Estelle [Morris] was opting for a quiet life. He was tempted to go back to a big speech on the lines of the one he had planned to make last September 11 [to the Trades Union Congress], about why [public service] reform was so important. Fiona and I both said afterwards it was the same people making the same points they had been making for years. We needed new people and we needed new ways of working. A lot of it was about the way TB worked with Cabinet colleagues. He was collegiate in some ways, and they would all say pretty easy to work with, but he didn't really let go. The meeting drifted into a discussion of specific areas like [banning fox] hunting and Lords reform. On both, TB was worried about buggering up the whole of our programme if we weren't careful.

Jeremy [Heywood] did a fascinating presentation showing that we were actually spending less of our GDP on public spending than [Margaret] Thatcher, if you looked at the figures in a certain way. Andrew Adonis [head of the Policy Unit] said we were wasting billions on GB's pet projects. Peter Hyman [policy adviser and speech-writer] felt we were deluding ourselves if we thought that TB would change his ways. He was wedded to his informal style, he let colleagues roam free only provided they were roaming in the direction he wanted, he would never go full frontal on the media, and he would always be as interested in positioning as in policy or people. He was what he was, and he would never change.

TB spoke to GB a couple of times, said he sounded devastated. He said it would change him fundamentally, but nobody could be sure how. Alistair Darling told me that GB had spent the whole time she was alive talking to the baby. He too felt this would change GB. Fiona and I were not so sure, felt it would increase his anger, his belief that TB got everything easy and he was a victim. Chris Meyer came to see me, lobbying for a seven-day trip to the US with lots of big events, speeches, TB being showered with prizes. It all sounded totally OTT, and not necessary.

Friday, January 11

TB called me on his way back from the baby's funeral to say it had been a nice service but with a very odd audience. He had been quite shocked to see how many journalists were there, including [Paul]

Dacre [*Mail* editor]. I said I couldn't imagine why they would have wanted anyone but really close friends there, and TB said different people react differently in grief. He said he went back to the house after the service and GB had been very warm, and that it almost reminded him of the days when they had been genuinely close.

Saturday, January 12

To the Goulds' for dinner. Gail [Rebuck, publisher and wife of Philip Gould] asked whether Philip and I had ever had a discussion that did not cover TB, GB, Peter M and their varying relationships. The answer is probably not, at least none that lasted more than a minute or two.

Sunday, January 13

In for the *Frost* interview, chatting to TB on the way, but we lacked a real hard story and I felt we were tired in our communications. Partly it was because [Sir] David Frost [interviewer] didn't really push him hard, but also both of us lacked the energy that we used to put into this sort of thing automatically. I felt that I was playing the old tunes but to a lesser effect. TB felt it was just that the press were in the mood to give no quarter.

Monday, January 14

The papers were dire and TB wanted to go on a blitz. I said I was not so sure, felt they would just say it looked like panic and this was maybe one of those periods we just had to take. What was clear was we needed to fight back better on public services. I called Piers Morgan who said to me that the *Mirror* was 'no longer a Labour paper', which not long ago would have been a big statement that would have made real waves. He also argued that we ought to raise income tax. I pointed out that we had made clear in the manifesto that we wouldn't. 'Nobody will mind if you break a promise like that.'

I had dinner with Blunkett at Simply Nico [Westminster restaurant]. He made pretty clear he felt he should be the next Chancellor. He said TB should stay as long as possible, and he should stay at home more. He felt both TB and I should do more to talk up the rest of the Cabinet. He understood why we had to keep GB sweet, but he doubted he was ever going to change, whereas the rest of them by and large responded well to being treated well. He was very down on his department. Something had to be done, he said, about the quality of people going into the Civil Service, because a lot of them were absolutely useless. He was very onside with TB but worried about the impact of the clear decision made by most of the media to turn against him. Someone in his constituency had said that if TB found a cure for cancer, the press would all ask why has Blair done nothing for meningitis? I put to him TB's notion that what the press were reflecting was that the public wanted to see us tested and survive, but he shared my view that public opinion was bound to be affected by the incessant media denigration.

David also said Jack was totally obsessed with the idea that he was dumping on him when in fact he was just putting through necessary policy changes. We had a nice evening, and David was reasonably relaxed for him, but it was sometimes worrying how much of the talk focused on the personal divisions. I had also noticed this morning that Charles [Clarke] had gone from being very engaged to being really pissed off quite quickly. TB had noticed the same thing and took him aside afterwards. Charles was feeling he just had a party management job without a real say in the politics. We clearly needed to involve him more.

Tuesday, January 15

There was growing disquiet about the Americans' treatment of al-Qaeda/Taliban 'prisoners' and Tom's eleven o'clock was pretty grim on the subject. I chatted to a number of commentators like Polly Toynbee, David Aaronovitch [*Independent*], Alice Miles [*Times*] trying to engage them in argument about defending the NHS. We were lacking strategy at the moment but we were also lacking freshness. The same people were coming up with the same solutions to the same old problems. Milburn was doing well today on his NHS reform stuff, and how to deal with failing hospitals. Dobbo [Frank Dobson, Milburn's predecessor] looked pretty bitter in his attack. TB felt basic message and policies were right but the media mood had changed again and we had to just think through how to deal with that.

Wednesday, January 16

The Rumsfeld interview last night was giving us problems because he basically made clear he couldn't care less about the condition of al-Qaeda/Taliban people in Cuba [Guantanamo Bay].[1] I wasn't sure whether this was a problem or not as a general issue, but I was pretty sure talking about it the way Rumsfeld did was not sensible. On the

[1] Donald Rumsfeld has been reported as saying 'I do not feel even the slightest concern about their treatment. They are being treated vastly better than they treated anybody else over the last several years.'

conference call, I was asking whether it wasn't possible to give a proper explanation of real conditions there, but Torie Clarke pointed out the questions they were getting were why any money was being wasted on these people at all. The story out of the PLP meeting was lots of critics rounding on TB and it was also clear the media were desperate to give IDS a lift to even things up a bit. I also felt, e.g. at PMQs meetings, that we lacked the obvious themes that tended to be clear when we were strategically strong. TB did OK on Guantanamo, but IDS had enough good lines for the press to give him the write-up they wanted to.

TB said afterwards he knew he hadn't been brilliant but he said he wasn't yet ready to go for IDS big time, that he wanted to wait and be sure he was going on the right line of attack. I was probably a bit harsh on him but felt he had been complacent. We weren't motoring at the moment. I felt I hadn't yet knitted together the various parts of the communications operation. We had been going through a bad phase and it was bound to show up in the polls soon. People were making comparisons with the Tories in their second term but there were big differences – the Tories basically had a supportive press, their people were less prone to panic and more up for a fight.

Thursday, January 17

The mood in the media was now pretty nasty. TB told Cabinet that while it was difficult, it gave us the opportunity to get up definition for reform. There were a number of interesting contributions, not least JP, who made clear that if we pushed too far on private sector involvement in health, we wouldn't be able to take the party with us. TB did at least steady nerves a bit. People were asking for a core script and I was clearly going to have to get back to doing the weekly strategy notes.[1] Charles Clarke felt he was being blamed for the lack of coherent strategy, but it was largely my fault, because I had been so demotivated. DB raised the need to stage prison pay. TB was emphasising that we were not going to improve public services without real change. We should be pointing to education as the area where reforms had most obviously yielded benefits. But in health now, virtually every indicator was moving in the right direction. So do not be apologetic or defensive.

There was a comic moment when TB started a sentence: 'If JP had come to me in '97 and said renationalise the railways, it would have been a short conversation.' 'It was a short conversation,' JP interrupted.

[1] 'The Week in Strategic Context', a strategic communications note drawn from the Grid, addressed to John Prescott but copied to all ministers.

Byers pointed out, and he was right, that since September 11 we had lost political definition on the domestic agenda. But it doesn't mean we don't have the right arguments. Jack said we were caught in a spiral of rising expectations. People's point of reference was not always their own experience but the national media. TB said that post '97 we were perceived to be on a massive burst of activity but actually to a large extent we were feeling our way. He felt that this term we had a clearer agenda and we just had to stick to it. Ed Balls called and later came to see me. He said GB had been pretty badly affected but was intending to come back to London next Monday.

We were still getting hit on Guantanamo with the ICRC [International Committee of the Red Cross] going today, and a UK team, including spooks, going tomorrow. I was frankly taken aback at the scale of the media opposition there seemed to be. On the conference call, Torie [Clarke] said it was time to get some steel in our spines re Cuba. We won the PCC case re Euan/Oxford, but Neil Wallis [editor, the *People*] told me a lot of key people at the PCC weren't happy.[1] The *Mail* were really gunning for CB at the moment and TB was worried about it, felt they were trying to do her in on a grand scale. I had a meeting with Byers, Jo Moore, Darren Murphy [Milburn's special adviser] and Sian Jarvis [head of communications, Health Department] re Tuesday's debate and the idea of a Byers/Milburn briefing for Monday showing the modernisers were still in charge. Byers was taking a hit at the moment but Milburn's stock was still high. I had a long chat with Mark Malloch-Brown [United Nations Development Programme] to try to co-ordinate Tokyo [Afghanistan reconstruction summit].

[Rupert] Murdoch [head of News Corp] was coming in for dinner, and along with Les Hinton [News International executive chairman] brought James and Lachlan [Murdoch's sons]. They arrived a bit early, and I took Murdoch upstairs because TB wanted fifteen minutes with him, then entertained the others in my office before we went up. I was interested to see how Murdoch related to his kids. Lachlan seemed a bit shy of expressing his views whereas James was anything but. Murdoch was at one point putting the traditional very right-wing view on Israel and the Middle East peace process and James said that he was 'talking fucking nonsense'. Murdoch said he didn't see what the Palestinians' problem was and James said it was that they were kicked out of their fucking homes and had nowhere to fucking live. Murdoch

[1] The Blairs had complained to the Press Complaints Commission about reports in the *Daily Telegraph* and *Daily Mail* about Euan Blair applying for a place at Oxford University. The complaint was upheld.

was very pro Israel, very pro Reagan. He finally said to James that he didn't think he should talk like that in the prime minister's house and James got very apologetic with TB who said not to worry, I hear far worse all the time. Most of the discussion was a run round the main foreign policy blocks, Israel, Saudi, Iran, Indo-Pak, a little bit of why does Britain have to bother so much? We didn't get into Europe at all, which was a bit of a waste. TB said afterwards he was quite impressed with the way Murdoch let his sons do so much of the talking. Murdoch pointed out that his were the only papers that gave us support when the going got tough. 'I've noticed,' said TB. I gave them my culture-of-denigration argument and was probably a bit over the top but I felt frustrated that we had to pander so much.

Friday, January 18

I took the morning off to go on Grace's school trip to a museum, which was a real reminder that it's not just people in jobs like ours that live in permanent stress. God knows how teachers do it. The kids were a handful, albeit very good fun. The teachers at least had a laugh when a teacher from one of the other schools at the museum pointed over to me and said 'That teacher is the spitting image of Alastair Campbell.' I did the conference call, after which the news moved on with a number of al-Qaeda related arrests in the UK [eight suspects had been arrested in Leicester].

Saturday, January 19

I took the boys to play football in Regent's Park, and TB called, emphasising again we just had to keep going because we had the right arguments and the right policies. But media-wise we had the *Mirror/Guardian* on one end of the spectrum doing us in from the left and the *Mail/Telegraph* doing us in from the right, and we weren't very good at fighting back. The *Mail on Sunday* had a Pentagon picture from Guantanamo Bay which they put beneath the headline 'Torture'. The issue had been bubbling up for days now and I suspected this could be the tipping point. Our problem was the Americans didn't seem to get how bad it was for them. We were in danger of losing the moral high ground, though of course they didn't seem to see it like that. They only ever looked at the US audience, which was a big mistake.

Sunday, January 20

Dad had another turn, and broke his shoulder falling, so I set off with Grace. I asked Tom Kelly to stay on top of the Guantanamo situation as best he could. Sebastian Wood [UK Embassy, Washington] and his security service people were only there yesterday and only able to do interviews today, so it was going to be tricky. Tom called me on the train, said Jack S wanted to put out a statement calling on the US to clarify. I said to Tom to get TB to speak to him. They spoke, then Jack called me saying TB had agreed to him putting out a statement. I was a bit dubious but didn't think it was worth a great fight and instead toned it down a bit, taking out any reference to TB having raised it with GWB.

Jack said that Colin Powell had said to him on an open line from Kathmandu that he was beside himself at the way Rumsfeld and the Department of Defense were handling the issue because it was giving him so many knock-on problems. The statement went out and needless to say within minutes it was US–UK rift. TB denied to me that he had given JS the go-ahead to put it out. Jack said it was important because it was right in principle to push for the basic human rights of any UK citizens to be protected, and we had to watch out for TB being made to look weak by being complicit through neglect in bad things the Americans did. Tom did a ring-round of the lobby and managed to lower the heat on it.

Dad was a lot less sure on his feet than before and Grace a bit taken aback by how much weaker he was, but he was pleased we went up. Grace was playing cards with Mum and when Dad fell asleep in his chair, I sat down and worked through a response to TB's note re strategy, which I felt was a bit tired and weak. I set out a note based on four phases, Opposition/term one/term two/legacy; taking the same fundamentals to all – economy, society, public services, international – but trying to revive each for the different phases. I also felt TB's language was becoming a bit distant again.

Monday, January 21

Guantanamo was running big and bad, and we were not in shape to deal with it. At the TB office meeting, we were discussing his strategy paper and my response to it. It was the first one with Charles C present, one of the responses to his pissed-off mood last week, but he was constantly putting up objections to things being done, saying why things couldn't happen, e.g. lack of resources, or we didn't have an agreed core script or strategy, or ministers would not let him perform the cross-cutting role we asked him to do. He was slowly moving into my area too which funnily enough didn't bother me too much because I was conscious of not doing the job as well as I should be at the moment, and also I'd felt since he got the job that if I raised my game a bit Charles and I could do a good double act on the media. It was clear TB was talking to Peter M more and not happy with me that we had not filled the post-Anji gap re taking care of the right-wing media.

At my morning meeting, I said we had to start pushing back on Guantanamo. Once we got the Sebastian Wood report [on Guantanamo Bay], I got Ben Bradshaw [FCO minister] to do one [on detainees]. The draft done for him by his office was so poor that I found myself at 3.20pm, ten minutes before he was due on his feet in the House, rewriting it with him by phone. He did fine though and looked and sounded confident and on top of things.

I had lunch with Peter Kellner [political commentator and pollster] who wanted to help us more. He felt the *[Evening] Standard* would stay where it was politically under Veronica Wadley [editor]. He volunteered the view that we lacked the coherent narrative of the past, and he was right. I had a meeting with [Sir] Michael Jay [former ambassador to France] who was taking over from [Sir] John Kerr as permanent secretary at the FCO and I think persuaded him of the need for new structures ready to be properly activated in the event of a genuine international crisis. We had done fine re Kosovo and Afghanistan but we lost so much ground early on when actually setting up the structures from scratch. There ought to be a structure in place, ready to be manned fully if needed. I was spending a fair bit of time fixing things for the football match in Kabul.[1]

Tuesday, January 22

At the morning meeting I read the riot act re DTLR, and gave the same message at a meeting re the Tube later, re whoever was doing in [Stephen] Byers. It was clearly coming from inside the department. I was trying to sort out timing of teachers' pay before leaving for a very nice lunch with David Frost at Le Caprice. Whatever was going on, he seemed to give us the benefit of the doubt, and he felt TB was just in a different league to most of the politicians he dealt with.

More evidence of the Yanks' uselessness and lack of touch when DoD [Department of Defense] said on the 2.30 conference call they intended to announce today they [Guantanamo detainees] were 'unlawful combatants' and release another picture. They were clearly being driven by the insight that US opinion would just about take

[1] A 'unity' football match would be played on 15 February at the Afghan national stadium between Kabul Olympic Football Club and troops of the International Security Assistance Force, the latter including players from the UK, Denmark, Norway, France, Italy, Spain, Holland and Germany.

their word for it, and also the feeling that there was no reason why they should be treated properly, but they didn't seem to see through the implications elsewhere. Jim Wilkinson, who at least seemed to get that part, joined me in talking them out of doing the picture, and that then led to them suffering a hiccup on the other part of the plan. Rumsfeld then went off on another one re Guantanamo. He just lacked subtlety.

TB called an internal meeting re the domestic situation. He felt the key was the CSR [Comprehensive Spending Review] and the Budget and he and GB working together closely. PG said the Tories were nowhere but that had led to expectations on us being higher and we were really expected to fulfil them. He felt we had the basic script right but we needed a better communications plan. At the Tube meeting, I was arguing for Steve [Byers] to go head to head with Ken Livingstone. [London mayor]. The DTLR crew were a pretty hopeless and unconfident lot.

I did the East Midlands group of [Labour] MPs, who were the best yet in terms of engagement. Dennis Skinner was on good form. I got home for Man U vs Liverpool, where I'd fixed for the ball for the match in Kabul to be handed over. Karen Hughes called during the match. She apologised for having been a bit out of touch, agreed we should scale down London and Washington, put Tucker Eskew in charge over there, leave Islamabad to please Musharraf, then use three or four others as a roving team going at short notice to different parts of the world where we felt we needed a presence. But the longer we talked the clearer it was she was really just focused on the US audience.

Fiona was close to the end of her tether, fed up with me, fed up with the pressures I brought into the house all the time. She thought I had changed, that I cared more about the job than her. She said I never seemed to take her feelings and concerns into account as I went about the job in the way I did. She accepted I was good with the kids, but after the job and them, there was nothing left, and it made her unhappy. I tried to do my usual, say that this was not going to go on forever, that I had to do it this way, that we should be proud of the difference we made, but it cut no ice. She said it was all about me, she was only there as an appendage.

Wednesday, January 23

I slept badly and when I did had all manner of awful dreams, including one where a pack of lions and hyenas were hunting me down in the corner of a field. I woke up, my whole body in a sweat. The mood in the house was bad as I left for the morning meeting. I got a call from one of the hacks saying IDS was going to do health at PMQs, the *Standard* having done a big number of the treatment of a woman called Rose Addis.[1] TB was up for really going at him. IDS used the line from the woman's daughter that she had been treated 'worse than a dog'. TB stayed calm, just presented the hospital's denials, but it was their toughest exchange so far and the manner in which IDS put it meant it was going big. TB felt it was a mistake, that the public would instinctively see the difference between the role of a relative and the role of a politician putting them in the spotlight deliberately, but I was not so sure. The press would now do IDS' work for him, and if we were not careful we would be into a new season of personal case histories presented as the big picture. TB said he felt real heat in there. Equally it did allow us to get up definition of what we were doing, the idea of a struggle for the very future of public services. Some in the media were arguing the Tories can never win on health, but they can hurt us if all the public hear are bad case histories like this.

Milburn came into TB's room at the Commons and we agreed we had to get the doctors at the Whittington Hospital out there. They did the *PM* programme [BBC Radio 4] and were excellent. It then turned out the main one was a Labour Party member – so what, in a sane world, why shouldn't he be? – but we got him pulled for later media. Unfortunately at the four o'clock, Tom gave out personal details of the people covered in the *Standard*, material which had been prepared for TB's PMQs brief, and although it was already all in the public domain, either from the hospital or the family, it was a tactical error because it allowed the Tory papers to make it a 'Labour dirty tricks' story, rather than being about IDS getting his facts wrong. I felt provided we held our nerve, this would be OK for us, because it allowed us to get up dividing lines rooted in values. Tucker had an interesting take – said that it was the best example yet of our crazy media and political system. The idea that one elderly woman's care was the big political story for the entire country was ridiculous.

Thursday, January 24

The papers were full of the health row, with the doctors pushing back. I briefed Hazel Blears [junior health minister] for the 8.10 slot on the

[1] Addis, a 94-year-old, had allegedly been neglected in the Whittington Hospital in North London. Her daughter made a complaint to her MP – Conservative leader Iain Duncan Smith.

Today programme. She was calm and rational and did well. Up to see TB who felt even by our standards the press had been ridiculous over this, us being put in the dock over the so-called leaking of details when the family went to the press and the Tory leader raised it on the floor of the House. But the press loathed us at the moment and were just desperate to give IDS a lift. I wrote to Piers Morgan whacking him for taking the Tory line on health. Probably just frustration at TB refusing to take them on more vigorously.

Cabinet was interesting, in that it was clear the exchanges with IDS yesterday had really got them up for a political battle on the NHS. But there were some worries expressed, not least by TB, at the idea IDS could somehow set himself up as the friend of the patient. There was a brief discussion of the Lords where JP railed at the idea of an elected chamber, said it was only of interest to 'Charter 88 or Charter 99 or whatever they call it'. TB gave a very strong message on public services and the dividing lines and they clearly felt better afterwards, speaking to one or two outside. The BMA [British Medical Association] put out a rather unhelpful statement on the back of the Rose Addis case. TB and Alan agreed we needed white coats rather than politicians out there at the moment pushing back. We went to do the *Jimmy Young Programme* [BBC Radio 2 talk show], Jimmy complaining to us before the interview at the way he was treated by the Beeb. He was still pretty good and they got through a fair bit of ground. TB was good on overall message and was clearly feeling in his stride.

On the train to Darlington, TB was working on the speech [to health workers in Newcastle], did a very good section on the current row and set it in the context of the debate going to the heart of the parliament. We got to Myrobella [Blair's constituency home], worked some more on the speech, then I went for a run. We had dinner at Myrobella after a brief trip to the [Trimdon] Labour Club and I pointed out to TB that virtually everyone we had met today, including on the train, had complained about the way the media covered the country and then political debate. It was an issue waiting to be tapped. He didn't feel we were the people to do it though. TB asked how things were with Fiona, and I said not good. He said I had to involve her more but also be nicer to her. He said he had realised with Cherie that it was really hard for her. We were blokes, he said, and we were doing big difficult jobs and taking a lot of heat all the time. So we felt CB and FM ought to realise that, because they lived with us, and be totally supportive and understanding. But it was hard for them too, and we had to do better at understanding that too.

Friday, January 25

The NHS row was probably a messy draw, but the TB speech was at least reasonably well set up. I was sleeping in the room next to his and he woke me up at 6, asking if I wanted a cup of tea, meaning he wanted me up to work on the speech with him downstairs. He felt we just had to shut down the Rose Addis row as best we could so we removed the lines that would most obviously be taken as a reference. With the opinion formers, we were running the argument that IDS scored a tactical hit but it was a strategic blunder because it got him back to an arch-Thatcherite position. I had worked up some good lines on my run yesterday re what being on the side of the patient meant, including being on the side of the staff, who in the Addis case felt really angry. TB was in very jokey mood, saying what kind of political victim will the dirty tricks operatives go for next – nuns, Sunday school teachers, war heroes?

Tom was a bit worried about the briefing he did but I told him not to worry and it was one of the good parts of TB's leadership that if staff screwed up, he encouraged them not to let it fester. We set off for Newcastle, and though it was a bit flat, the speech went fine.[1] The medics and the managers both seemed to feel IDS had made a bit of a blunder, but of course it was always hard to tell at these kinds of gatherings how much was politeness and how much was real. At Darlington, we met up with Neil Wallis and Nigel Nelson from the *People*. TB did a crap interview, just didn't get engaged, and we didn't have a top line. He said to me afterwards when I pointed out how crap he had been that he assumed I would cook something up with them so he wasn't really concentrating. He said he was bored and irritated at the way they used anecdote to make what they thought were serious judgements, e.g. going on about what 'Mrs Wallis' would want to know. We talked about the press again. He said he was the one person who hates the press more than I do, but 'I should not be the person who takes them on the whole time.' He said we don't have a [Norman] Tebbit [Margaret Thatcher's Cabinet 'attack dog'] figure, which is a problem, but even if we did, he was not convinced it was the right way to go. Where I agreed with him was that they matter more to Oppositions than governments, but they are really up for damaging us at the moment.

[1] After telling the audience that each negative media story about the health service was 'tomorrow's fish and chip wrapper', Blair said 'This is the decade when we look to public service professionals as the new byword for can-do innovation and dynamism. For shaking things up and getting things done.'

Saturday, January 26

TB was off to Paris with CB and called for a brief chat re the NHS before he left. He felt we could win the argument and had moved to a position, as it was clearly going into the Sundays, of saying it was in our interest to keep this whole thing going. I took Calum to Regent's Park to play football but Neil Wallis was pressing me re TB's NHS words and wanted them harder and harder, basically to run the line that if we didn't fix the NHS we wouldn't deserve to win again.

Sunday, January 27

PG called to say he felt we needed a new sense of drive and strategy, that it all felt a bit stale. He was right. He didn't feel Charles Clarke spoke the same language and strategy as us, was too conceptual, not hard-edged enough, felt he was deliberately placing himself off centre as a way of building up a 'not TB' positioning. I was pissed off with myself re the *People* which as I expected went on a very hard line re the NHS and TB was concerned that it made it seem that unless we met any and every expectation re the NHS we would be admitting to failure.[1] Not surprisingly, he was not one hundred per cent happy that it came from something he didn't say, but that I said for him. He agreed that as it was the *People* it was unlikely to fly, but we prepared lines on it in case. The worry was that it became one of those statements that stuck and which the Tories could ram down our throats at the next election, exactly the argument I had used with Wallis before I got fed up and gave up.

Monday, January 28

Health had died down but the *People* interview was worrying both of us. I apologised to TB for pushing it too far. He was fine about that, just wanted to make sure it did not become an enormous hostage. It had the feel of something that could become big at a later date, and I was amazed the Tories weren't pushing it. If they had any sense they would keep it running till PMQs. My hope was it just went away but it nagged away at me because it was a mistake and I was angry with myself. TB wanted a transcript to see what he actually said but of course we were talking about 'add-on words' agreed between me and Wallis.

[1] Blair was quoted as saying 'If the NHS is not basically fixed by the next election, then I am quite happy to suffer the consequences. I am quite willing to be held to account by the voters if we fail.'

At his Monday office meeting, TB said so much depended on how he and GB operated together and that depended on GB. He said he was willing to co-operate in every which way, but Jeremy said the current vibes the other way were not good. We talked about Charles [Clarke], me saying we really lacked a politician attack dog who did not mind putting the boot in big style. I could only do it up to a point. I was constrained by the position and by the fact I didn't go on camera. Peter [Hyman] was very down on Charles, said he sometimes felt we had a party chairman who was against party campaigning. The Tories were vulnerable. They were just going negative negative negative, talking the country down, willing everything to fail, and without real policy prescriptions, and that was not a great position for them, but we didn't have the firepower to hurt them for it.

I had a visit from one of Crown Prince Abdullah's right-hand men, wanting advice on how to improve the Saudi image in the West (not knowing at this stage the *Guardian* were on to a story of Brits being tortured there). I was as frank as I could be within the confines, even at a meeting like this, of diplomacy. But I said they would need more than a few ad campaigns to win people over. They needed the reality to change. The look in his eye suggested that was not certain. I had a stack of meetings planning the Africa trip, then Peter Hill and Hugh Whittow [editor and deputy editor of the *Daily Star*] came in to see TB. They were very straightforward, said they didn't want much politics in the paper, but they were up for stories if we thought of them once in a while. As to what kind of story, Peter said what people really wanted was fame and if they couldn't have fame they wanted to feel close to it. He suggested we try to get the spirit of *Pop Idol* [TV talent contest] into politics. TB asked me afterwards if they were for real. I said they were. I had been trying to persuade them to draw *Mirror* readers over by starting to be more pro Labour.

I was also working on my speech on public diplomacy for tomorrow, which I had been getting ideas and comments on from around the place. On the conference call, I told them the Powell/Rumsfeld splits were bad for everyone, and asked if they couldn't do more to contain them. I also felt they should be getting a lot more out of the [Hamid] Karzai visit [to Washington]. I felt the calls were becoming a bit vague and waffly, not least because the top Americans were not always on them. Jim Poston [FCO] was doing a good job progress-chasing in the London CIC though, was really making a difference.

Tuesday, January 29

The *Mail* splashed on Enron, totally overlooking the fact that the Tories took money from them.[1] This was clearly the latest smear zone for the scummy end of the media. When I went up to see TB, he said maybe there is a case for resurrecting 'Mailwatch'. He really hated them, he said. It didn't feel like a scandal to me and I was confident the public would see through it but you couldn't be sure. DB was struggling to get up his ASBOs [antisocial behaviour orders]. I went over to Lancaster House [government building] to speak to the conference of all our ambassadors from Arab and Muslim countries. I was arguing for a deeper engagement and urging them to badger us for more, not just leave it to Gerard Russell [Islamic Media Unit, FCO] and Co. I said TB took this seriously. I argued that we should stop thinking purely in country-to-country terms but see the need to put the case pan Arab. There was actually a case for some of these guys becoming spokesmen across the piece, not just in their own posts. Some of them had gone totally native, others felt we were wasting our time, but some of them seemed to get it and wanted to engage more. Julian said as we left, the problem is the clever ones realise you are taking over a chunk of their jobs, and the really clever ones realise that might help them take a chunk of their colleagues' jobs.

I was trying to get on top of Bush's State of the Union address and eventually Peter Reid got hold of an advance copy. It named Iran, Iraq and North Korea in the context, or so it would be taken, as possible targets of attack.[2] Karzai was doing well out there. I got hold of his draft itinerary for his visit here and it was ludicrous – forty minutes with TB and lunch with Robert Cooper [UK special representative in Afghanistan] for heaven's sake. I put a note round saying it was being revised and we went for Karzai coming to the end of Cabinet, proper meeting with TB, joint Al Jazeera interview kind of thing. Also we should get Afghan exiles in to see them.

GB was back in action again and TB said they had one or two nice conversations, almost like the old days, but that he was currently totally paranoid re Milburn, Clarke and Hain, felt they were all positioning as rivals. I asked TB if he felt he had come back a changed

[1] Allegations that collapsed energy company Enron had offered financial support to Labour in return for a change of policy on gas-fired power stations. The allegations were denied.

[2] In what would become known as his 'axis of evil' speech, Bush specifically homed in on three nations he claimed were developing weapons of mass destruction.

man. He shook his head. Ed Richards [senior policy adviser on media business issues] came to see me re the media ownership policy discussions. He said in the end it boiled down to a decision about whether we were prepared to see Murdoch become more powerful. He felt that we shouldn't. I got a crazy letter from [Piers] Morgan in response to mine, saying I had misquoted him on saying the *Mirror* was no longer a Labour paper, but I could always rely on [Neil] Wallis to 'squeeze in Blair press releases in between Jordan's tits and kinky sex spreads'.

Wednesday, January 30

We assumed IDS would do health at PMQs but without an individual case, though the *Sun* had a story about a baby that got lost in the laundry. IDS majored on rail and was a lot better. He had definitely improved, and TB didn't really think on his feet. I was working on the speech for [the Labour Party spring] conference, trying to turn the strategy paper into a speech that could be used to disseminate strategy. After PMQs I went with Geoff Hoon to the MoD to meet the air commodore and his deputy in charge of the team responsible for the Mull of Kintyre Chinook [helicopter] crash [in 1994].[1] They realised this would come our way and they wanted to persuade me of their case that the two pilots, whatever their supporters said, had been guilty of gross negligence. There was a Lords committee report coming up so it was going to be back up in lights and they felt they had to make their case better than before. GH let them do pretty much all the talking. I listened, asking questions as we went, for about ninety minutes, at the end of which I was pretty well convinced, though the unanswered question remained why they made the error they did. Their theory was that the pilots believed they were in a different place, above water, and also that they realised too late that they should not have been flying in those conditions [too low, in heavy fog]. I got back to work on the speech, then up to see TB to tell him I thought he had been poor at PMQs, and we had a bit of a post-mortem.

Thursday, January 31

Before Cabinet I went round to see TB who was in with GB. It was the first time I had really seen Gordon since he came back. I said

[1] The helicopter was carrying twenty-five British intelligence experts from Belfast to a conference in Fort George, Scotland. A 1995 RAF board of inquiry ruled that the crash was caused by gross negligence, a judgement challenged by families of special forces pilots Jonathan Tapper and Rick Cook.

hello. He kind of grunted. Not 'Thanks for your letter', but a grunt. Fiona had also sent them a present which I know must be really difficult for them now, having all these kids' clothes and other presents, but I found it odd he couldn't be civil at a time like this. TB said at the earlier ministerial meeting, he had sat there scribbling notes, refusing to engage even though the others were trying to bring him in. At Cabinet itself, his presence transformed the mood from Cabinets where he had been absent. There just wasn't the engagement from others when he was in this kind of mood, and TB looked disengaged and distant. They were going through the motions, and then at 11.15 TB had to leave early to meet Karzai.

As we walked down the corridor to the front door, TB said 'I'm afraid he hasn't changed. If anything, he has changed for the worse.' He said people were feeling sorry for GB, and trying to express it, but he was just pushing back the whole time. Karzai was in one of his long capes, and when I told him he was getting as much coverage for his fashionability as his politics, he said he had started wearing it one day because it was cold, and he just kept wearing it. Now it was part of his make-up. In Afghanistan, he said it was a very conservative form of dress. TB had a tête-à-tête with Karzai. I was chatting to [Ahmad] Wali Massoud [Afghan ambassador] who was very shrewd, pushing the line we needed more ISAF forces there. As they met Afghan exiles, Tom warned me the big talking point was Karzai saying Sharia law had a place in Afghanistan. I raised it with him and he said he had said no such thing. Welcome to our press, said TB.

They both did fine at the press conference, though the story was Karzai asking for more troops and TB saying there had to be a limit. They did a joint [BBC] World Service interview, where they were asked about GWB's axis of evil. At the lunch, you could see them trying hard to adapt to this new way of life. Karzai had his wits about him, and looked and sounded the part, if a bit forced at times. But [General Mohammed] Fahim Khan [new leader of the Northern Alliance], a real brute with enormous hands and a big growly face, could barely hold a knife and fork. It was an interesting lunch, Karzai now moving on to drugs, and explaining the help they would need to change crop production patterns. They were virtually rebuilding a country and its infrastructure from scratch, as when he said they would be grateful for advice on how to establish a new central bank. Khan was even more straightforward, said we had been giving a lot of help to the regional warlords but now we had to start giving more help to the centre – i.e. him.

On the conference call with the White House, I told them there had been an overwhelmingly negative reaction round Europe to the GWB ['axis of evil'] speech. They seemed surprised. It wasn't a good call. TB and I had another session re the press. I said I was convinced we needed to make them part of the debate much more than they were. He said he was in two minds but in the end he would decide. I said fine but there may come a point where I can't do it this way. He said we had to be clear that if we were effectively declaring war on them, that was a big decision to take. I said three-quarters of them had declared war on us and too much of the time we just took it. TB said remember Machiavelli, kill or hug, but don't wound.[1] He felt I was landing the odd blow and leaving a few wounds. I said maybe I wanted to kill and I could no longer pretend with papers like the *Mail*, and some of the chatterati, that that is exactly how I felt. He said when we were at media dinners together, e.g. with Murdoch recently, it was clear to everyone how I felt and I needed to be cautious. I said I hated having to pander to these people, and that they took it as weakness not strength. I had said the same to Blunkett re his greasing up to Dacre. TB gave me a look that suggested he was fed up hearing the same old song. I said it is no good just being fed up. I'm fed up too, fed up with the fact we are in power and doing nothing to change the poisonous media culture which is actually damaging the country now. I said I couldn't stand the *Mail*, most of the *Telegraph*, a fair few of the broadcasters, most of the Sundays, and now Piers [Morgan] was on my list of barely worth talking to. Fiona was back on at me to quit if I felt strongly, and disagreed on a fundamental strategic point. Fiona and Sally [Morgan] both felt he was still talking to Anji the whole time and she was winding him up re us not doing enough with the right-wing media. Fiona said she just could not do what Anji did, grease up to all these people and pretend we liked them. In Kabul, they were talking of tens of thousands for the football match, which cheered me up a bit.

Friday, February 1

TB was at Chequers and I spent most of the day working on the upcoming speeches. TB asked why I was so low. I said I felt I was doing the same old stuff the whole time, and I was frustrated we were not really changing things as I thought we would. I took Calum

[1] Blair paraphrased a line in *The Prince* (1532) by Niccolò Machiavelli: 'Men ought either to be indulged or utterly destroyed, for if you merely offend them they take vengeance.'

to tennis, and TB called again. He said he knew how frustrating it was, but we had to keep going on the things that really mattered.

Saturday, February 2

TB still felt we were not winning the basic arguments on public services, or shifting the dividing lines to where we needed them. He did not like the mood in Cabinet on Thursday, felt there was a grumpiness and a grunginess that could not be allowed to fester. It wasn't just about GB, though his mood did not help. I spoke to JP about it too, and he felt there was just a bit of unease around at where we were going, and also people getting used to the media being so much more hostile. He was trying to do a bit of work as a go-between between TB and GB, to get them engaging and working together better, but it wasn't easy. He too felt GB had come back worse not better after his baby's death. There is a lot of distrust there and he is not the kind of guy just to get over it. Andy Grice [*Independent*] wrote definitively that Leo had had the MMR jab and there was a strong feeling we must have put it out there deliberately. I certainly hadn't but I wondered if someone else had done it for TB. It ran as a main broadcast story most of the day, alongside the measles outbreak in a London nursery.

Sunday, February 3

Down to Chequers, TB ranting against the media. We finished the speech and the main line was meant to be this being a fight between wreckers and reformers. There was a political problem though, Jo Moore calling me to say Byers had used the same line and indicated at the time he meant the unions when he referred to wreckers. It meant that despite our efforts, that was where the story was heading. It was clearly going to be tricky. We had an OK line re small-c conservatism but of course that too was likely just to get played straight into the tricky political angle they would all want. We flew down to Cardiff [Labour spring conference] by helicopter and the speech went down really well with the audience.[1]

Halfway through, I always try to find time to pick out half a dozen or so average-looking people and see 1. whether they are really listening, and 2. whether they seem to be going along with it. They were all pretty rapt, and as the argument developed, the head-nodding

[1] Blair told delegates 'Forget the nonsense about privatising public services . . . if we are to win the argument for collective provision, defeat the wreckers and secure the future of our public services, then we must be prepared to use all available means to make the improvements that patients and pupils and passengers demand. And we will.'

became more pronounced. TB went off script towards the end and did a good section on how at every stage of reform – expelling Militant, policy and party changes under Neil [Kinnock], the difficult changes we had made in Opposition and government, there were always voices saying don't do it and others crying betrayal. But only through change do we advance, etc. But even though it was pretty obvious he had the Tories in his sights when he talked about wreckers, the unions couldn't resist doing the victim thing and making it seem as though he meant them. I did a quick briefing, reminding myself how glad I was I didn't do them all the time.

Helicopter back and then home. Later, I was really hacked off with Fiona when TB called to speak to me about something, she answered the phone and was nice as pie to him, said none of the things she was constantly saying to me, and I thought at least I tell him when I'm pissed off and I tell him why. It made me think that actually a lot of the attacks on him made to me were surrogate attacks on me for doing the bloody job in the first place. I was also back in a depressive mode, I was sure of that, which didn't help. She felt I just didn't want her to take on a bigger job because it threatened me somehow. I didn't buy that but I did feel it wasn't on for both of us to be full-on working the whole time, and that we both should be spending more time at home whenever possible. He called back later and said what was I on about, telling him Fiona was pissed off, she seemed fine! I told him I was totally hacked off. He said I was frustrated because I spent so much time clearing up after other people, but never lose sight of the things we were getting done, and in the end they were the things that were important and would be remembered. TB did the [*Evening*] *Standard* drama awards and was amazed that Natascha McElhone [actor] went up to him and asked him to ask me to give her a call. 'She is gorgeous,' he said.

Monday, February 4

The public services speech was all in the wrong place, thanks to the dunderheaded unions taking the whole speech as an attack on them. Then John Monks [TUC general secretary] was wound up by the unions and the media and he was leading the news with comments re TB making 'juvenile remarks'. DB did pretty well whacking back but our overall message was a bit confused. TB insisted we had to hold absolutely firm, that we were doing the right things for the long term and we would hold firm. He seemed a bit down, worried we could not actually get our own people properly to understand what was needed.

I raised MMR with TB. We both felt it was yet another case of the media stirring to try to make the story even worse, because that was then an even better story. The problem was if this did become a huge public health issue, there was a real danger he would get the blame and it would stick and inflict real damage. CB was adamant she wanted to take the *Independent* to the PCC for the Leo-had-the-jab story and I was adamant that was crazy, even though she had a case. TB had been telling all sorts of people he'd had the jab and was probably in some ways, maybe one removed, the source and he seemed relieved it was out there. I felt we were going to need a really strong MMR campaign to get over the benefits and the risks if people did not have it.

I met Tessa [Jowell] who wanted a bit of advice on her image/profile. Her great strength was her niceness and her enthusiasm but I said sometimes the Florence Nightingale touch could grate a bit. She needed to be more wedded to policy issues linked into real people. I bumped into GB as I took her out. Another monosyllabic grunt. Peter M called from South Africa, denied he had got up the Hammond [Inquiry reopening] story, said on the contrary he had not wanted it to happen. He could tell I was unconvinced. He said originally he had pressed for it then TB said he didn't think that would help him. Peter then agreed but by then TB had changed his mind and RW told Peter the new inquiry was going ahead. He sounded OK but he was clearly very fed up with his lot. Condi Rice slapped down Jack over his remarks that Bush's axis of evil speech was about electoral US politics. Not a great day, but I had a long chat with Natascha McElhone which cheered me up.

Tuesday, February 5

TB's 'wreckers' [speech] was still running big and bad. The GMB and UNISON [unions] took out full-page ads attacking us. There was now no sense anywhere of it having been about the Tories, but there was also a feeling that it was just a phoney row. I was really down again, struggling to get out of bed, struggling to get through the front door, feeling demotivated all day. TB later asked me if I was fed up. Very, I said. Why? A mix of things – grind, GB making life more difficult than it should be, being expected to do too much, including work others should be doing, the media, feeling that so far as my particular skills were concerned I had done my bit and we were now in a different phase requiring different skills. 'You're not thinking of leaving are you?' he asked and I said maybe I was. He said he felt I had a massive contribution to make and also that I would miss it more than I thought. Nothing else will ever replace this professionally, he said. But the grind gets me down. The media were a screaming pain in the backside and I had such contempt for most of them, I couldn't hide it and maybe he was damaged by that.

He said you are not just a media person, you do far more for me than that, don't worry about them, let the others take care of them. He said he had a lot to do and he couldn't do it without a strong team to help him pull the horses. The GB problem was graphically on display again this morning. He did *The Times* on his Commonwealth Education Fund [overseas education advocacy project], which was fine in that it was on two of TB's areas – education and Africa – but GB did it without any consultation and without any reference to TB or the broader Africa agenda at all. I told TB that in both the *Today* and *GMTV* interviews, GB did not even mention him and he seemed taken aback. He said the one thing capable of destabilising me is the lurking presence waiting to do me down when the opportunity arises. The truth was if these two worked together, this government would be fifteen per cent better than it is. That was a margin worth worrying about.

What was clear from any reading of the media was that GB's people poured poison vs TB the whole time – how they were the real radicals, how TB didn't care about the real issues in the way GB did, how GB was the substance and TB the style. There was clearly a plan to get him up on development issues to ensure TB did not get too much out of Africa. If they worked together on this, they would be unstoppable. But it wasn't happening. MMR was running big. As for 10,000 extra nurses – no fucking coverage at all. Milburn was ballistic about it. I went with TB to a young people's event at Westminster Hall organised by the Lib Dems. TB was OK but a bit passionless. [Liberal Democrat leader Charles] Kennedy was predictable and his speech a bit dull. IDS surprised a lot of them by being pretty good and was well received.

The top story politically was the Chinook inquiry [see January 30] on which we just had to hold firm, though the Lords was coming out pretty hard against us. It all looked nakedly political and maybe people saw that. I had lunch at Wiltons with [Field Marshal Lord] Peter Inge and [Air Marshal Sir] Erik Bennett [adviser to the Sultan of Oman] which was good fun. Both were lively and engaging, and pretty gossipy. [Nicholas] Soames was at the next table and when he got up to leave I made a point of saying, very loudly, 'Can you get the car round, I'll be there in five minutes.' Inge [a former CDS] said he hoped I was being nice to Boyce. I said I was. He said I should tell him we valued him because he tended to get down on himself.

Both he and Bennett felt the US would become a real problem for us and that TB was really the only person who could hold things together. They seemed to feel he had real influence and that he had to use it.

Wednesday, February 6

The *Sun* yesterday did a front-page campaign pitch on giving everyone the choice of three [individualised MMR] jabs not one, and today led on a story that TB was wobbling, and had ordered a review of the costs of three in one. Because [David] Yelland had been in yesterday to see FM/SM and briefly seen TB the buzz went round that it came directly from us. We denied it last night but then the Tories jumped on the bandwagon and by this morning it was leading the news. The media were really whipping this into a frenzy but it was one with potentially serious consequences now, and the Tories ought to get hammered, but they wouldn't be, at least not the way we would have been in Opposition for something of this kind. We had some good facts to get over, like there were ninety countries using the vaccine, like the fact that in the US you had to have it to be able to go to local schools. I warned Yelland we were going to dump hard on their story. Both the *Sun* and the *Express* agreed to take rebuttal articles on it.

Dacre said he would only do so if it was TB or CB writing re Leo. I wrote telling him I thought their coverage on MMR was irresponsible and dishonest. I bumped into Piers [Morgan] coming out of a meeting with GB. We said hello and later he called, said he wanted to be more supportive re MMR, but we ended up having another argument about the nature of their war coverage. TB left for the airport [for Africa], called from the car to go over how much media he should do on the way and once he got there. He kicked off by dropping another hint Leo had had the jab. I left early, collected the boys and off to Watford for a fantastic match, which we won in the last minute, Marlon [Beresford, Burnley goalkeeper] having saved a penalty at 1–0. It was one of those wonderful matches that makes all the crap ones seem worthwhile.

Thursday, February 7

I felt a bit odd, both good and bad, that I wasn't on the Africa trip. Good because hopefully it would show to Fiona I was serious about trying to do things differently; also because I could have a bit of time to sort some of the personnel issues; bad because I would be worrying whether things were being handled properly, and whether in fact I ought to be there. TB was getting good if low-key coverage for the speech [to the joint national assembly] in Nigeria and it was definitely the right thing to do to stick to our guns and go. JP was standing in for TB at Cabinet, and as when he did PMQs, the massive differences came over – TB who would want the minimum of fuss and preparation pre Cabinet, JP who wanted to over-prepare, almost rehearsing what he would say and how he would handle things. As well as Joan Hammell [Prescott's special adviser], Jonathan and Richard W were brought in. JP stumbled over a few words and I suggested he just take the agenda and see how things go, as there were no real big decisions to be made.

There was a seemingly endless conversation in Cabinet itself re [reform of] the Lords. JP said he intended to be clear outside that the party did not want an elected second chamber as a rival to the Commons. He told me earlier he was fed up with 'the little red gnome' (RC) briefing the press about some of his moves re Parliament and then expecting the Cabinet to be bounced and I think the Lords gambit – out of nowhere – was his warning shot. Cabinet lasted far longer than usual, again reflecting an earlier comment by JP that TB did not let discussions flow enough, but you would be hard pushed to refer to any decision or new point that was made. They also got into a discussion re the Speaker [of the Commons, Michael Martin]. They were worried re MM saying the Tories couldn't attack TB over his role as leader of a party, because ultimately that would constrain us more than them. John Reid was the only one really to speak up for Michael, saying he felt there was a lot of snobbery around re the fact a working-class Glaswegian got the job but we should support him. I noticed GB muttering under his breath to himself. We got a letter from Sarah [Brown] re our letters and gift today, so I was trying hard to be understanding of GB's situation but he really didn't help himself.

DB was doing his immigration White Paper, which was going OK, but was a bit too pitched to the right-wing media for my taste. I had just concluded the highly vituperative exchanges with Dacre. I went home early to collect Grace from school, then Fiona and I went out for dinner at Les and Mary Hinton's, a fair old crowd there. I was sitting next to Zeinab Badawi [Sudanese-born BBC newscaster] who was nice enough, and interesting on Islam. Rebekah [Wade, *News of the World* editor] and Ross [Kemp, her actor fiancé] were there but fairly quiet for them. Jeff Randall [BBC business editor] was anything but, full of right-wing views dressed up as fact and wisdom. I liked Mary Hinton, a real good old working-class type who struck me as someone who saw through the lot of them. Les told me he had been shocked by Rupert's tolerance of James [Murdoch] swearing so much in front of TB. I said TB rather liked it of him. He said afterwards they had gone to a pub for a drink, James had started up again and the barman told him to shut up and stop swearing.

Friday, February 8

Alex [Ferguson] came in and he and I went for lunch at the National Portrait Gallery. It was always good to get his take on things because he followed politics closely, but with a very outside-the-beltway view. He felt we were doing OK, but he thought immigration really picking up as an issue. I told him re my current doubts about the job, and he still felt I would regret it massively if I went. He wondered if the press were getting to me more than I realised, but it was more the stuff at home and the feeling at the office I was doing too much of the stuff I had now done for years. He was glad he had stayed, said it was as much Cathy [his wife] as he who had made up his mind on it, because she realised just how much he would miss it. He was still fit and relatively young and he just would not be fulfilled without it. We both had fish and chips, the most amazing chips I've had in yonks, identically shaped. He said [David] Beckham [Manchester United footballer] was becoming more and more difficult to deal with. He now had four different agents who came in last time with forty-nine different demands related to his new contract. He [Beckham] was also beginning to commute a lot more between north and south, flying up for training, which was OK once or twice, but ludicrous as a long-term thing.

I did a conference call to plan next week's football match in Kabul. They were reckoning on 30,000 people turning up for it. TB called from Ghana, said he was enjoying it and glad he had gone. He said the president of Ghana [John Kufuor] had introduced his press officer as 'my Alastair' to which the press guy [Kwabena Agyepong] said 'I wish.' 'Your notoriety has spread to the continent of Africa,' he said. He seemed in relaxed mood, at one point asking me 'What are the Sundays up to?' then before I could answer 'Aw, who cares?'

Saturday, February 9

Nick Matthews [senior duty clerk] called before 8 to say that Princess Margaret had died. TB was currently being told and it would be announced by the Palace shortly. There was no need for him to come back, but he would need to say something so I might want to start thinking about that. I reminded Nick that he was the one who called me re [Princess] Diana's death. 'That was a bit more dramatic than this one,' he said. TB called as he waited to leave for Sierra Leone.

Tanya [Joseph] had done a draft statement that was OK so things were basically under control. I said it was important he didn't try too hard, or appear emotional, just say she was basically a good thing, thoughts with the Queen, Queen Mum, rest of family, etc. [Sir] Robin Janvrin [the Queen's private secretary] called to go through the statement they were putting out. He said the Queen actually saw it all as a bit of a release and a mercy because she had been in a good deal of pain. Her instincts were to carry on with her (fairly light) duties next week, and to make the funeral private. He said the Queen would probably want to speak to TB later.

TB set off for Sierra Leone, met the troops and the government welcoming party and then did his doorstep on Margaret. It was a bit actorish for my liking, but OK I guess. We had to watch any sense of this being anything like Diana. Janvrin was thinking the same thing though perhaps for different reasons when he called pre TB's call with the Queen. He said she wanted advice on how to avoid the comparisons with Diana in terms of tributes, flowers, mood etc. I felt the simplest thing was to say it, to make clear this was different in part because it was expected. I also felt people would respond to the fact the Queen and Queen Mother would take this differently and there was a case for them being seen fairly soon, showing she was still up and about and doing her duty, but also showing some emotion at the loss of a younger sister. She would clearly be thinking of her own mortality, not to mention her mother's. [Prince] Charles went to Sandringham 'to comfort the Queen Mother' and also did a broadcast, which was OK but he was not a natural presenter and he shifted around too much, creating constant distractions from what he was saying.

I spoke to TB again after his press conference in Senegal. I suggested he advise the Queen that she needs to be seen, because that would attract support and also crowds, albeit nothing like on the scale of Diana's death. 'How can I advise her to do that?' I said just say the country needs to see she's OK and bearing up. They want to find a way of expressing sympathy for her. He also needed to make sure they were aggressive in dealing with any media attempts to make Diana comparisons as a way of reflecting on the Queen. Burnley 1, Barnsley 1.

Sunday, February 10

The only political story running out of the Sundays was the *Sunday Telegraph* reheat of the *Western Mail*/Plaid [Cymru] story on [Indian industrialist Lakshmi] Mittal's donation [£125,000] to the Labour Party. The donation seemingly came a few weeks before TB wrote to the

PM of Romania [Adrian Năstase] to welcome a deal with a Mittal company, which was basically Dutch rather than UK. Our line was that this was something done following a request by our ambassador, but it was clear this was going to be the next media frenzy to deal with. I took Rory to his mini-marathon heats, which he won easily, then to Charlton vs Man U. We met up with Alex F pre match. Rory was loving it, down the tunnel as the players warmed up, Alex talking to him about why he was picking the team he did. There was a minute's silence for Margaret, well observed. Janvrin called to get my take on how I thought things were. I felt fine, but still thought there should be more focus on the Queen if she was up to it at all. Rory Bremner [TV satirist and impressionist] had a sketch on 'me' telling 'TB' why I wasn't going to Africa.

Monday, February 11

The Mittal situation was tricky.[1] Jonathan had been through all the papers and realised that he (Jonathan) had advised against doing anything on the grounds that Mittal was a known Labour donor and supporter. For some reason that did not appear to have been communicated to TB and the letter as prepared was put in his correspondence folder. It meant we could stick to the line that he had merely done something as asked by our ambassador for sound reasons to do with his assessment of Anglo-Romanian relations, no big deal unless people were determined to make it so in retrospect. TB was totally dismissive of the whole thing, saw nothing wrong with it at all. I said it was a bit odd that he was writing letters to the Romanian PM about what was in the end a Dutch deal, even if Mittal ran the company. He found it bizarre, as did Jonathan and I, that he did not see the point made by Jonathan – rightly in my view – but even so he was clear we just had to ride it out and tell them to get stuffed.

I went over to the DTI for a meeting re the Post Office. Pat [Hewitt, Trade and Industry Secretary] didn't seem totally on top of it. We had allowed the debate to develop in a way that suggested the Post Office was a public service on a par with health and education, so the idea the country was ready for what would be seen as privatisation by a Labour government was self-kidology. The timing was tough and the Dutch were going to be the bigger party. Weird that the two tricky

[1] The situation, which Blair would dismiss at PMQs as 'garbage', became known as the 'Garbagegate' affair. Mittal, a substantial donor to the Labour Party, had been seeking control of Romania's state steel industry, and despite one per cent of his company's workforce being based in the UK, Blair's intervention was seen as decisive.

issues I was dealing with involved the Dutch. Back for a meeting with TB and Alan M on health communications. TB felt we just were not getting over the reality of the progress being made and we were not getting over the scale of reform planned or required. There was a conflict though between a message that said 'things going well' and one which said 'lots more to do'. The *Guardian* splashed on how GB was going to 'stand up to Europe' on the Stability Pact [safeguarding fiscal discipline of EMU], and warn they would not get in the way of our plans for investment in public services. It was a classic piece of GB spinology, a phoney row if ever there was one, launched without our knowledge, but one we would have to row in behind.

Tuesday, February 12

Brian Groom [*FT*] called to ask whether it was true that there had been an earlier draft of TB's Mittal letter which referred to 'my friend', and that the reference to 'friend' had been deleted. It transpired that there had, and that Michael Tatham [private secretary, foreign affairs] had – again, rightly – deleted it. This was getting a bit weird and was obviously being briefed out by someone. So our line that TB had not changed the draft was true. But it wasn't true to say that 'we' had not changed it. TB was adamant we should not engage, not get into drafts, simply say TB signed the letter as requested, end of story. I suggested we get our man in Bucharest [UK ambassador Richard Ralph] to write a letter to *The Times* explaining why he had wanted to get the TB letter but though he was keen Jack and, even more so, Michael Jay were less so. I had a meeting with the Northern group of [Labour] MPs at 5, and there was something really sad in seeing Peter M there as just another back-bench MP [for Hartlepool] listening to me blather on about the message and the machinery. David M [Miliband, Labour MP for South Shields] was there too, and seemed to be getting on fine with the real Northerners.

I then got back to learn Jonathan had spoken to Jack in Istanbul, and then to Michael Jay, who were adamant it would be bad for the diplomatic service if an ambassador was personally placed at the centre of a diplomatic controversy. I called Michael and said, jokily at first, that he mustn't feel got at by the right-wing campaigning elements in the press, and whatever happened to the great FCO, scared of nobody? He said he was totally against doing this, because it put an ambassador right at the heart of it. I said he was already, and there were plenty of situations down the years where others had been. I said it would help him and it would help us. He was adamant though. I was impressed at the way he stood up to me, if unpersuaded by the reasons. I suspected they just felt a bit beleaguered and said as much to Jack when he called. He said no, it wasn't that. It was simply that they felt they should protect a member of the service.

As TB came back from the Palace [Royal Audience], I told him the *Guardian* were on to the fact Mittal had been at [Labour fund-raiser] Michael Levy's party for high-value donors on June 24. Again, he was totally dismissive, and said I needed to stop giving off worried vibes about it. His mix of bluster and head in the sand was really irritating. He was irritated when I said so, said he was not prepared to take this seriously, it was a fuss over nothing and we should not be getting our knickers in a twist. I said my knickers were not in a twist but it was a frenzy and we had to have answers to questions even if we thought the questions were ludicrous. He would not be able to dismiss it in the House. He would have to answer questions on it.

Wednesday, February 13

I was in early, and up to see TB in the flat. It was dark up there and he seemed a bit down. He asked me if I was depressed. I said yes. Clinically I mean, he said. I said I think so. He said my problem was I was agonising – stay or go. He felt I would hate it if I went, no matter how much I sometimes hated it now. I needed to see the press as the inevitable downside of a job that had a huge upside, namely doing an important job and being part of a huge process of change for the country. He came back to the theme over at the House pre PMQs, said I should remember what Leon Brittan [former Conservative Cabinet minister] said about leaving power, leaving powerful jobs – for a year you feel better, eased of pressure, able to do normal things, but then you realise what you miss, the ability to make change. He said 'If I die tomorrow, they would say he was the guy who modernised the Labour Party, made it electable, won two landslides, sorted the economy, improved public services, Bank of England, Kosovo, Northern Ireland. They would barely mention the frenzies we have survived, so always remember the big things, the big reasons why we're doing it.'

He accepted Mittal was a problem for us, the focus moving to Jonathan's role as gatekeeper to TB and how that fits with any political or party role. The ticking timebomb that worried me was Mittal's letter to Levy, and Jonathan's notes. I was angry with Jack and Jay for their refusal to let Ambassador Ralph set out the case, because I felt it was what our current argument lacked – the reason why it mattered to him. TB looked tired, Jonathan looked nervous. They both hated this kind of thing. We had to decide how heavy TB should get [at PMQs], and we agreed – heavy. PMQs was not as bad as we feared, because the Tories were not forensic enough, and TB really went for IDS and we avoided the question about whether he or Jonathan knew Mittal was a donor. Back to a press event with [Rudolph] Giuliani [mayor of New York] where TB managed to avoid any Mittal questions. TB spoke to Jack to emphasise we needed the ambassador's reasoning out there. He was also worried after his meeting with Eddie George [governor of the Bank of England]. He had not liked what he heard re the euro, where Eddie seemed less and less keen. TB felt if we didn't go for it this parliament, we would lose out a lot more in the long run.

Thursday, February 14

The *Mirror* and *Express* had stories that Jo Moore had suggested that DTLR put out railway indicators on the day of Princess Margaret's funeral – another 'bury bad news' situation. They denied it last night. I missed the 8.30 meeting because I was at a *Guardian* breakfast with TB. Godric was agitated when I got back. Martin Sixsmith had said at the meeting that Jo had indeed said something like that and though the email referred to in the *Mirror* did not exist, there was another one – which he gave to Godric. It was an email FROM Sixsmith TO Byers and which suggested Steve HAD suggested using the cover of Margaret's funeral to get out bad news. I smelled a very large rat. It was already known – because Byers had announced it – that we were planning to do the railway indicators. It was hard to get a full picture, not having been at the meeting, but both Godric and Tom felt there were some really funny games going on. It looked like Jo was being totally done in. Given what they had been through, politically and media-wise re Jo's 9/11 'bury bad news' email, it was pretty much unthinkable that they'd have done a version of the same thing again, so I didn't buy the idea Byers would have done this. Tom and Godric both thought it odd that Sixsmith had brought the email to the meeting, and on reading it they saw it was not clear that Steve had suggested doing this. It was Sixsmith suggesting he had.

We got back from the *Guardian*, where TB did fine on the war, despite them pushing the whole time re Iraq and a bit on party funding. I told Godric that at the 11.30 he should make clear what balls the stuff on Jo Moore was. But Godric was really concerned something odd was going on. He, Tom and I met with Byers before Cabinet, and agreed we should say the email in the *Mirror* was a total fabrication, but point out there had been an e mail exchange between Sixsmith and Byers pointing out that as Friday was the day of

Margaret's funeral, there was no question of doing railway indicators then. It was another load of old balls really, but with the potential to do real damage. I got the feeling that if ever there had been any trust between Byers and Sixsmith, there was none now.

At lunchtime Anne Shevas took a call from Jon Smith at PA who said he'd had a call from someone claiming to be a press officer from DTLR who said Sixsmith wanted it known that Godric had got it wrong at the morning briefing, that there was indeed an email that had the words 'Margaret, burial etc.' in. It was hard to disagree with Godric's analysis that something very odd was going on. Byers had been complaining that he had parts of his department out of control and Richard Mottram [permanent secretary, DTLR] seemed unaware how to resolve it. I called Mike Granatt [Head of the Government Information and Communication Service], said clearly things were going on there which were inexcusable and he had to get involved. He drafted a letter making clear officials simply could not brief against ministers. Godric went off to the four o'clock and came back to say they were going crazy, and based on the weird call to Jon Smith had accused him of lying, having yesterday accused us of lying over Mittal.

I had to leave for a Q&A with permanent secretaries and a few business people at Chevening [in Kent, official country residence of the Foreign Secretary], which I could really have done without. It was basically about crisis management communications. When I worked on the speech, I found myself trying to work out how many genuine, genuine crises we had had and it was probably fewer than half a dozen. Yet we had hundreds described as crises and dozens that felt like it from time to time. But most of these guys had never actually been involved in a real full-blown crisis, and yet felt they were in one every time they were in the papers.

I got back to find Mittal on the news and the Jo Moore situation back running big. Godric was really angry that his honesty was being questioned. I spoke to Byers again and said it was obvious he couldn't work with his own press team, but I also felt this was heading towards Jo's departure. It was totally unfair on Jo who though she had made a dreadful mistake on September 11, was basically loyal and a good person. My sense was that Jo was fed up with the whole thing anyway.

Friday, February 15

Godric texted me just before 7 to say he felt we should put the Sixsmith email out to set the context. I talked to Byers who agreed. He had felt strongly yesterday that I should stay out of this but it had to be gripped. Godric spoke to Sixsmith who agreed that Jo had never suggested using the funeral. Godric said he was given a different impression yesterday. TB was heading to Italy and had finally agreed this was damaging us. I told Steve it had to be brought to a head quickly. I talked the whole thing through with Richard Wilson who was seeing Mottram at 9.45. Richard was pretty good on this. He knew that there was funny stuff going on inside the department and he didn't much like it. I took Calum to tennis and RW called to say he had been 'very heavy' with Mottram, had told him there were only three routes – muddle on (not acceptable), lose one of Jo or Sixsmith, or lose both, or possibly suspend them while it was sorted out. I was trying to play tennis with Calum but got call after call on this bollocks.

Sixsmith saw Mottram at lunchtime and seemed to be in agreement to go, provided he got money, Jo went too, and we did not dump on him. So by the time I got in – around 2.30 – we seemed to be ready to go with it. Jo wanted to get her kids home from school so the plan was then to go for 5pm. Then Byers called to say Mottram was now not so clear that Sixsmith had actually resigned. He had seemingly gone out for treatment on his eyes, and come back to say he was still thinking about it. This was being so badly handled. It seemed Mottram had not actually got a bloody resignation. So we now had a situation where we thought both had resigned, Byers had now said so on TV, Jo had gone, but Sixsmith hadn't and was, like as not, liable to pop up and say this was like Soviet Russia, where his resignation was announced when in fact he had never resigned. TB called from Italy and said that whilst this was all crap, it was dangerous crap and we had to be careful. I said I was fed up with the whole thing. Byers, to be fair, was amazingly resilient and had a bit of the Zen about him, but he was damaged.

The Kabul soccer match had been an amazing success, spoiled by crowd trouble among the thousands who couldn't get in. There were about 42,000 inside to witness a stupendous goal, thousands more outside. Lawrie McMenemy [Football Association special ambassador] did fantastic interviews in his trad Afghan cap. Simon Wren [MoD] called me, said it was the most exhilarating thing he had ever been involved in.

Saturday, February 16

Another crazy day. TB called as I was going out of the house to take the kids to Regent's Park. We had talked briefly last night but now I filled him in on the whole madness of yesterday. He said he would speak to RW and they agreed we should play it a bit long. I said it would be too much for Byers and probably for Godric too if Sixsmith was allowed to stay in the GICS, just move on to another job. The trust issue was a problem. Steve [Byers] was quite clear an agreement was reached on the basis both Sixsmith and Jo would go. Then Granatt called me to say TB/RW seemed to think Sixsmith could stay. This was getting ridiculous. Mottram then spoke to Sixsmith to work out a deal.

I spoke to Sixsmith, the call taped by Martin Sheehan [press officer], and played along with him, just tried to get a sense of where he was. I said both Godric and Tom felt they had been misled by him. He was apologetic for the mess, but said he had not deliberately done anything wrong. Of yesterday, he said he had had an assurance from Mottram he would not be 'sacked' while he was out at the eye doctor. Byers called to say Jo had gone on the basis they were both going, and he was not prepared to let Jo go and him stay. TB was pretty fucked off with the whole thing, as was I, and felt there were real problems at the top of the department. Mottram had been clear with me he [Sixsmith] would go if the money was right, Jo went and he got a testimonial. Now he was apparently in a position where Jo had gone, he was staying and he was getting a glowing tribute from Mottram.

I spoke to Alistair Darling, who knew Sixsmith better than I did and who had spoken to him earlier. He said Sixsmith seemed to think he was being offered gardening leave [instructions to stay at home] and let's see what turned up. Mottram called around half five to 'pick my brains'. I said I felt we should let it calm for a bit and see where it went. Sixsmith was going to be seen as a hero in the press, because they love the damage being done to Byers in all this, and he may want to go back to the media. It was ridiculous TB even had to be bothered with this. Byers was livid we were even thinking about Sixsmith staying. I said let's sleep on it and see where we are tomorrow. He said if he stays it means 'they have won'. He felt that the whole episode risked sending the worst possible signal: that ministers and special advisers can be done in by anyone with an agenda. I was now way beyond the end of my tether and thinking fuck the lot of them. Godric was the one I felt for, because he really cared about his integrity, and he felt he had been dropped in it.

Sunday, February 17

Byers called again late last night, after having told TB he would have no option but to resign if Sixsmith was allowed to stay in the Civil Service. TB told him it was simply not worth resigning over.

TB felt Mottram had clearly not handled things well, but that Byers also had to take responsibility for relationships between key people in the department. He said part of the job is building an *esprit de corps* and he clearly failed to do that. But what do you do if people inside are doing you in? TB's view was you don't let it get to that. Easier said than done. Byers felt if Sixsmith stayed, then because of the way this was playing out, it would be felt within as a great victory for the right of civil servants to undermine ministers and they would just move on to the next one they don't much fancy. Sixsmith called, claimed Byers was not taking Mottram's calls. I had now reached the point where I was very cagey in what I said, assumed he would be taking his own legal advice, so said little, advised him to bide his time and not do anything too rash. He said he had been offered thousands by the papers to tell his story, which I guess was a way of saying he had other options if he didn't get a decent deal. I told him Byers was hostile to any kind of deal but we just had to wait and see whether once he got a new team in there he was less bothered.

On the media, TB felt there may be a case for a new ethics commissioner, tougher rules for MPs alongside a statutory watchdog for the press, including re accuracy. He felt we should go for the liberalised view on media ownership, and encourage European companies to get involved in taking over parts of our press. I said when he told me he had been thinking re the press, I was hoping he was going for PCC on statutory footing with fines for inaccuracy, VAT on newspapers, privacy laws, really put it to them. He felt it wasn't worth all the aggro. Godric was still very steamed up re Sixsmith, sent me a five-page note setting out why he believed he had been misled, and how.

Monday, February 18

At TB's morning meeting, he was mainly focused on the war again, feeling he was going to have to get back in the saddle more. Byers came in to see TB and we just about persuaded him Sixsmith wasn't worth resigning over. We had to bide time then move on and we were better leaving RW to manage the process. Byers was adamant we would regret it big time if Sixsmith was allowed to stay in the system. I met [Mike] Granatt and Sue Jenkins [GICS] to put together a hit team to go to DTLR. The best part of the day was when Rory came in and we went for a run through Hyde Park. Stan [Greenberg] and Philip [Gould] came in with a new poll. Not brilliant. Down on state of the parties and on right/wrong direction. Trust and openness bad. TB felt it could have been worse given recent events and the tone of the media debate. Stan felt we had endured a lot worse but I didn't like the feel of it.

We went in for a meeting with the *Observer*. Mary Riddell [columnist] making a big thing of saying to TB 'Of course nobody is saying yoooooou are corrupt' when [Andrew] Rawnsley [*Observer* political commentator] had done just that and had his piece bought up by the fucking *Mail*. I saw the BBC team re NHS Day and finally agreed we would co-operate as best we could. I had a meeting with TB/CB re the US trip. I thought it a bit odd she wanted to be on holiday in the States when Euan was doing his A levels. TB said there was no way in the world he could have a holiday at the moment. CB was pissed off but adamant she was going. I even felt TB going out early for a couple of days was not a good idea, but she just felt I was being too puritanical and worried re the press. I said I wasn't bothered about the press, I was worried about the public. She said we should not let the press run our lives. TB said we have to apply common sense and at the moment it is not on for me to be seen taking a holiday.

Tuesday, February 19

Godric was getting a small taste of the media shit I endured most of the time, and I felt it was getting to him a bit. TB had a 'Phase 2' war meeting with David Manning, C, Peter Ricketts [FCO], Tom McKane [Cabinet Office], Jonathan and me. TB was not sure if the Americans had taken all the decisions. He wanted to be in a position to influence their strategy, which we would project as being about fighting poverty and taking aid, but which they would see as fighting for their values. He also wanted to commission papers on Iraq, Libya, North Korea and the European trade in WMD. He wanted work done on how to rejuvenate the MEPP. He assumed by the time of our visit to the States in April, there was a chance the Americans would be casting around wider, and he wanted all the facts at his fingertips. He felt that the political situation would be different and internationally a lot harder for the Americans than things were post September 11, if they were thinking of going for any of these other countries.

I had a meeting with Tucker [Eskew] and Jim Poston. Tucker was due to go back [to Washington] on March 13 to replace Jim Wilkinson and set up a new Office of Global Communications. He said he was phenomenally grateful for the opportunity he had had to work with us. I was still having to deal with the Byers/Sixsmith fallout. Byers adamant Sixsmith had to leave. Sixsmith telling me that SB had cut a deal with Mottram – a new job and a mild testimonial. Byers read to me what he called a 'threatening letter' from Sixsmith, still describing himself as his director of communications, saying he didn't want to damage him, saying AC didn't want 'collateral damage'. Sixsmith was constantly dropping hints to me about how he was being offered money to 'tell all' in a way that would damage the government. TB had clearly led SB to believe he would be sacked, RW that he could ease him out. RW was telling Mottram to play it long. Byers was sure Sixsmith was taping all calls, possibly with a view to doing a big thing about it all afterwards. Piers Morgan was adamant they'd been within their rights to run the story they did, not least because they ran it by the department's press office. TB told me Peter M had said to him it would be a disaster for the TB operation if I left. TB felt I just had to rise above the day-to-day.

Wednesday, February 20

NHS Day was in fact nothing like the stitch-up we feared. Jack S came over for a chat. He was strongly of the view that TB should do something that would symbolise a greater respect for Parliament, maybe appear at the PASC [Public Administration Select Committee]. He asked how I was, and I said pretty fed up. Why? Because I spend so much time clearing up the shit, and I don't always feel I get the support in return. Number 10 is seen by departments as interfering, and yet they are on to us the whole time to sort things that go wrong. Jack felt we had made Number 10 more powerful but not necessarily more effective across government. He felt there were too many of our people who called departments and said they were 'Number 10'. If it was me or Jonathan, people knew that mattered, and in any event we would deal with ministers. But departments had any number of people calling up and saying what TB wanted, or what Number 10 wanted.

Sixsmith was calling me all day, but I decided not to engage. The *FT* were on to the story again and I suspected he was trying to bounce us into a deal. The phone logs apparently showed both Sixsmith and Ian Jones [DTLR head of news and Sixsmith's deputy] called the *Mirror* and *Express*. Hardly earth-shattering. It would be very odd if they didn't call them pretty regularly. Sixsmith was not wanting to say he was talking about the terms of his departure. He wanted the line to be he was going to another department without a stain on his character. Byers, Mottram and I did a call at 6, and we agreed Mottram would say to Sixsmith that he had clearly resigned on the Friday and we were now working out the terms of his departure, and this is what we would be saying. But after they spoke, Mottram backtracked on that as well. Philip was doing [focus] groups tonight specifically re the press and called after the first one to say maybe I was right, that they really didn't like the press, and they liked TB when he was strong. They wanted more not less leadership. The RCN [Royal College of Nursing], King's Fund [health think tank] and others, including [Sir] John Stevens from the Met [Police], had written an open letter to TB which was going to be seen as a big attack re public services, low morale, pay and conditions etc. I spoke to TB who agreed we would do an 'open reply', full of praise for them and setting out some of the things we were doing. TB was alarmed that DB had bitten off more than he could chew re the cops. He had always seen the police as something of a touchstone. If you have them offside, that is not a good place to be.

Thursday, February 21

We were about to leave Number 10 [for TB's constituency] and as I walked to the foyer with Helena [Hopkins, duty clerk], Sixsmith literally charged through the front door. He didn't see me but headed to my office. I was determined to leave Mottram to sort this out, so I went to the car to avoid him and left Anne Shevas to deal with him and try to calm him down. She said he was clearly on the edge, that she had just let him talk and didn't engage much at all. He was saying our line in the *FT* that he had resigned from DTLR was wrong and we had to correct it. If not, he would, or he would have to get the deal agreed. I spoke to Richard Wilson and said we should not be having to deal with this. Mottram should be dealing with it. RW called later, said Mottram had made clear if he didn't resign he was sacked and they started to talk about a deal. The *FT* story didn't go too big. It was going away and Mottram was finally getting the message to Sixsmith that he was not on very strong ground.

We got a small plane up north. TB then did a series of visits around Sedgefield while I worked with Anne-Marie [O'Brien] from the Garden Rooms [offices of the Downing Street secretarial support] on the speech [for the Scottish Labour Party conference in Perth], working up the public services sections, and the interdependence theme. I felt we had got things back on a proper agenda. Philip said people were crying out for a plan and a proper sense of direction and would be relieved simply to hear us talking about issues they understood and cared about, not all the bollocks from inside the Westminster village. TB went out for dinner with John Burton [constituency agent] while I worked on the speech, and tried to make sense of the clashing drafts we now had. I got TB to do a Good Luck letter to the UK curling team at the Winter Olympics in Salt Lake and then stayed up to watch. It was brilliant, really exciting, and we won gold. Myrobella was the usual chaos but we just about managed to get the speech for tomorrow sorted.

Friday, February 22

The speech was just about finished. Felt a bit flat and uninspiring, though it was OK for the job of getting up investment and reform again. We signed it off on the flight up to Perth. Nice hotel, but he was in real witter mode re what the line was, and did we have the argument right? The *Record* ran a quote from TB saying 'If the unions want a fight, they can have one', which he never said. I asked for, and got, a correction and apology. They said it was a 'production error'! TB finally spoke to GB who was livid at what we had done re NHS Day. He argued that it was totally counter to HIS strategy. Even by their standards, it was a grim conversation. Basically, so far as GB was concerned, TB was only the PM and he should not be talking about tax, NHS spending, any spending really.

We did a visit to a science company and then to the conference. TB tried to ad lib but it didn't really work. In his peroration he talked about winning a third term and how we should dominate the next hundred years like the Tories did the last hundred, so most of them had a headline out of that. It was probably a mistake. We flew back, I did a box in the car then out to Rachel's [Kinnock] for dinner. My lot were late but Neil and Glenys were there, and I had a chat with Neil re TB/GB. TB had been down on GB today, said he was currently impossible; that the way he tried to present the [EU] Stability Pact as a public spending defence of our schools and hospitals was 'pathetic'. Neil agreed, also said he noticed how TB always talked up GB but it was never reciprocated. Both he and Glenys were also incredulous that [Paul] Dacre had been at the funeral of the baby.

Saturday, February 23

We went to see *The Lion King*[Disney stage musical]. Halfway through the play Anne Shevas texted me to say the *Sunday Times* were splashing on 'Sixsmith not resigned' and they had a massive write-through, clearly well briefed from the Sixsmith perspective. I went out at the interval, spoke to Anne then to Mottram, said there had to be a statement out from him making clear Sixsmith resigned TO HIM on the Friday. It was ridiculous that so much time and energy was going into this. He couldn't possibly stay as a departmental spokesman after all this. It was clearly going to be the start of another great blah but we just had to get through it.

Sunday, February 24

TB called, said the Sixsmith stuff looked like a spin doctor using spin to complain about spin. He felt we should stay out of it. I called RW to say he should get Mottram to deal with it. Mittal was still running too. We had lost the agenda again to a heap of crap. I briefed Helen Liddell [Scottish Secretary] who was on the media rounds, to be totally dismissive of the lot of it. I spoke to Byers before his [Jonathan] *Dimbleby* [ITV] interview to make sure we were saying the same thing. During it he appeared to suggest he had no role in personnel issues and denied he had blocked a deal to allow Sixsmith to get another job. That wasn't a hundred per cent true and would cause us real problems. Godric and Tom were dealing with the lobby on it, but the media were determined to see Sixsmith as a creature of probity and honesty and anyone who disagreed with him was a liar. Godric was in a total rage about it. Byers called me a couple of times for reassurance. It was difficult now, he having suggested he had no say in whether a deal could be done to move Sixsmith to another department.

Monday, February 25

TB called me early re Byers' statement he had nothing to do with personnel, and Sixsmith's position. 'Isn't this a bit of a problem?' Both he and RW said it was simply untrue. TB felt the only person who could put this right was Mottram and he would speak to RW to get Mottram to put out a statement. Mottram was reluctant but agreed and set to work on a draft. TB had now reached a judgement there was a problem at the top of the department, ministerial and civil servant. He was clearly moving to the view Byers would have to go. I still felt he had been victim not villain. He had been done in by civil servants operating from within, and screwed up his handling of it.

At the morning meeting I just skipped through the Sixsmith situation, didn't allow discussion, though Ian Austin couldn't resist a dig at [Ian] Jones over Mottram's 'We're all fucked' line in the *Sunday Times*.[1] Phil Bassett [Number 10 Research and Information Unit] made a crack about Sixsmith's homes, and within hours something was running on PA, friends of Sixsmith saying he was being smeared over his 'property portfolio'. Sixsmith was meanwhile doing little photo-calls with 'Liar Byers' headlines draped over his arm as he went home carrying a pack of bacon.

TB and I had lunch with the *Express* lot. TB was really motoring on crime. [Richard] Desmond was indicating he wanted more favourable coverage of the NHS. TB said to me afterwards I had to do

[1] Sir Richard Mottram reportedly told Sixsmith 'We're all fucked. I'm fucked. You're fucked. The whole department is fucked. It's the biggest cock-up ever. We're all completely fucked.'

better in curbing my contempt for the media. He said it was hard to charm them when your main press man sat there radiating a clear desire to wipe them off the face of the earth. I got back to the office to see the Mottram letter which needed strengthening. As drafted, it made matters worse for Byers. He needed to be clear that Sixsmith had agreed to go in the meeting last week, and also something that left open the possibility that Sixsmith was negotiating with Mottram and so Byers could not actually veto a deal any more than he could deliver one. This was clearly the point of vulnerability though. RW got the Mottram letter strengthened, removed some of the earlier ambiguity. TB agreed it could go, but I could tell he was mulling over whether SB could or should survive. He had failed to grip the department. He had failed to pin down events on Friday. True, he was only dealing with a difficult situation because people who were supposed to be working for him had created the difficulties, but TB felt the basic failure to grip the department was the problem. Steve was clearly worried, raised the situation with me several times through the day and all I could say was that his statement yesterday was the most difficult thing. I was now getting anonymous text messages saying things like 'You're losing 8–0.' The press was also in total kill mode and though things seemed relatively calm when I left for home around half seven, I still had very bad vibes. Martin Sheehan had taped my call with Sixsmith but the tape was wiped, so I asked for a note as detailed as possible. TB was the usual mix of exasperation, irritation and determination. He had had dinner with JP and GB last night and said it went well, though I would believe any progress when I saw it.

Tuesday, February 26

Papers grim. The *FT* had been briefed that Byers did indeed block the deal and Sixsmith was about to do the rounds playing the victim. TB called at 7.15 and said 'How difficult is this?' I said very, but if SB went it would be totally unfair because he had been done in from within. What was also clear was that there would be some who would try to move on to me/Jonathan straight away. The problem was it was not possible to square what Steve said on *Dimbleby* re not being involved. It was a big problem. TB was clearly thinking he should go. Sally, Jonathan and I were pushing hard for SB, and Peter [Hyman] was manic about it, saying he had only been put in the position he was in because he was done in from inside.

TB took a long meeting where everyone, including Jeremy, Tom and Godric, agreed it was unfair for Steve to go but TB kept saying he could not answer the question about how he came to say something that was not true. Steve called and I suggested the only way round this was for him to apologise for giving the impression he did. RW came in for the end of the meeting pushing for Steve to go. Also both Charlie [Falconer, former Solicitor General, now housing minister] and Derry [Irvine] had been sent the papers and transcripts and both called me to say they thought he would have to go. I still felt if he apologised, possibly in the House, and we went on the offensive against the internal operation against him, we could get through it provided the PLP remained supportive. As Jonathan said, we were going to have to throw him into the gladiators' ring and see if he survived. It was not the best way to deal with it, but there was a reluctance to toss him overboard given the background.

We watched him do the statement in the Commons and as Peter Kilfoyle, Tam Dalyell [senior Labour backbenchers] and others got up to back him, there was at last the feeling that we could fight back. The main thing was that SB was thought by MPs to have done well. I was impressed by his Zen-like qualities today. He didn't panic. It could so easily have gone the other way. TB was just about OK with the way things went, but clearly felt there was something odd, which of course there was, about the *Dimbleby* interview. What was clear was that without today's statement, TB could not have got through PMQs tomorrow defending what Byers said on Sunday. We had to get back on the big picture pretty soon.

Wednesday, February 27

TB called and I said though the press were in full cry, the party was fine and the issue was subsiding. TB was still worried about forensic questioning. The key problem remained why Byers said what he did and the extent of his or his office's involvement. If IDS did a proper forensic six-question job, it would be difficult. In the end he didn't and he was as hopeless as Theresa May [Shadow Transport Secretary]. Andy Grice got hold of Sixsmith's 18,000-word dossier but people were bored with it now.[1] One or two said it would only fly if they could somehow move it towards me. TB had said at PMQs that the hunting [ban] vote would happen shortly, which led the BBC *Ten O'Clock News*. Inevitable suspicion that we put it out because we wanted a diversion. Would that we were that well organised.

[1] Sixsmith had kept detailed contemporaneous notes and verbatim accounts of conversations with Campbell and others.

Thursday, February 28

TB did OK out of yesterday but though the mood was calmer, you could still feel the anger in the media. Loads more pieces on me, notably a big one in the *Mail* about my so-called army of spin doctors. TB was doing an interview for ABC in the States, very forward on Iraq and pro GWB. He had decided that was the best position to adopt to gain influence. At Cabinet, he said it was important to emphasise that nothing re Iraq was planned and that we were a long way off taking decisions. Blunkett referred to the unsettling speculation and said a lot of people had difficulties with Rumsfeld. TB said Bush was in charge, not Rumsfeld, and David said, to some laughter, 'That's mildly reassuring.' There was a lot of support for Byers. TB said there were two agendas, the policy agenda we were trying to address and a media-only interest in the scandal and sensation, with the Tories preferring that agenda as a way of avoiding questions about policy. They had been on a tour of Europe to look at public services and come back with no great insights.

Byers said he was grateful for the support of colleagues, said the PLP had been superb. Also, we shouldn't forget there were a lot of dedicated, hard-working civil servants. John Reid said the media will want revenge. What was interesting about most contributions, e.g. Margaret [Beckett, Secretary of State for Environment, Food and Rural Affairs], was that the press and media were as much the Opposition as the Tories. This had been a media-driven frenzy, with the Tories playing shotgun. TB said we were more spinned against than spinning. They cannot find a full frontal policy assault so this is the substitute for it. It makes it all the more important to stay on a proper policy agenda. DB said the role of special advisers had to be properly understood and defended. He said at the Home Office there were serial leakers. Without his SpAds, he wouldn't have got a White Paper finished. He said he was lucky to have good press secretary who got on with the SpAds but it wasn't the same story everywhere.

The Peter M situation was also back with us. I ran a line past him re our response to the second Hammond report.[1] It didn't go far enough for him. He said why can't you just be honest and straightforward and say that if we had known everything then that we know

[1] Anthony Hammond had reopened his investigation into the Hinduja passports affair after Peter Mandelson submitted correspondence between himself and his private secretary, Mark Langdale. Hammond conceded that though the correspondence offered 'some support' for Mandelson's account of his conduct, 'it is still not possible to reach any firm conclusions about the contacts which took place between Mr Mandelson and Mr O'Brien'. Hammond's main findings, and Mandelson's situation, were unchanged.

now, he wouldn't have left his job. I said we couldn't have a situation where we were saying TB got it wrong. He said we could say we all got into a muddle. He was calm but firm, said he wasn't prepared to haggle or beg for us to do the decent thing. TB spoke to him later and said that 1. he didn't believe the new papers necessarily helped him because they showed he had been more involved not less, and 2. he didn't accept he did the wrong thing because Peter had misled us and therefore allowed us to mislead the public.

We had an office meeting about how to frame this and TB redrafted the statement to take it closer to what Peter M wanted, namely that things, including his resignation, could have been different. The other problem, as Peter Hyman pointed out, was the clear contrast to draw between Peter M being sacked when we were saying he hadn't lied, and Byers not being sacked when people were saying that he had. I left early for Rory's parents evening then afterwards to [outgoing *Times* editor] Peter Stothard's party where GB was pretty much monopolising the new editor [Robert Thomson]. I had a nice chat with Ken Baker [former Conservative Cabinet minister], who advised me to get out at least a year before TB.

Friday, March 1

The Peter M report, Hammond Mark 2, was the main political story and we bent over backwards to be nice about Peter, to the extent that the story effectively became TB apologising for him being sacked. I felt sorry for him. The reality was if it had been another minister, he or she probably wouldn't have paid with their job. Also, though we could present it in the way we did, it wasn't the case that the report fully exonerated him.

Saturday, March 2

TB was phoning fairly regularly from CHOGM [Commonwealth Heads of Government Meeting in Australia] and was pretty fed up – first, because it was raining and second, because they just weren't serious about dealing with Zimbabwe [impending presidential election]. It was coming over as black vs white. He said he was thinking a lot about the press. No to jihad, yes to a tougher stance. But the note he sent through was the usual mix of pandering and using different groups of people to deal with them. I was a bit alarmed by it. We needed a big message that blasted through to the public. Calum and I set off for Burnley vs Norwich, crap match [1–1]. Home by half nine. The *Sunday Times* had another 4,000 words of Sixsmith, used as 'evidence' that Byers had misled the Commons. IDS weighed in re TB, me and trust. Not good. The *Mail on Sunday* did a big number on pictures of nude women allegedly inside TB's cuff on his shirt.[1]

Sunday, March 3

TB was doing interviews pushing a very hard line on Zimbabwe [human rights], whilst on Iraq, he was making supportive statements for Bush and hotting up the rhetoric for action.

Monday, March 4

I spent part of the day working on a note responding to TB's note on the press. We had to break the herd instinct. I had lunch with Richard Wilson. He clearly believed I had been briefing against him during the Peter M affair, which I hadn't, and we cleared the air on that. He seemed pretty down, said he had just about had enough of the job and really hated recent events, as had I. I felt he had done pretty well and that TB was probably right, that we should have involved him more, but Jonathan basically felt he was hostile. He said he felt I was exceptionally good at the job but perhaps the GICS had withered a bit under my weight. He liked Tony, felt he was an extraordinary character and the way he used the impact he made on people was a real gift. But he wished he could have done more to help him.

He thought maybe it was a generational thing, but he never felt that he got into the inner circle. He felt Jonathan despised him. He said permanent secretaries felt real respect for GB. He sometimes thought Tony believed he could live with GB on the back benches, but he didn't think so. He gave me the impression of someone who felt he hadn't succeeded. He was keen for a Civil Service Act but didn't seem sure what he would want to do with it. There was something very sad about him today. It was in its own way an enjoyable discussion in that for once we had been very frank, cut through some of the crap that sometimes surrounded us. He talked a lot about his kids and in particular how proud they were of their deaf son, and what perspective his deafness gave them. The nonsense about TB's shirts was getting out of hand. He was now getting more coverage for his bloody clothes than we were for policy.

Tuesday, March 5

We were doing an article for the *Express* on Iraq, which TB had toned down, though one paragraph he had written was totally

[1] At the Commonwealth summit, Blair revealed Paul Smith-designed shirt sleeves featuring a naked, kneeling woman holding a telephone on each cuff.

incomprehensible. I took in some changes from DB, the FCO and John Scarlett and then got it signed off by TB. TB was disappointed about CHOGM, both the outcome and the lack of real commitment there had been re Zimbabwe. Sally was worried about the Iraq article, felt that we were in danger of getting into a real mess with the party on this. Jack was also cautious, said he felt TB was more vulnerable than he had ever been and had to be really careful. Jonathan, though totally supportive on the substance, made an interesting observation. He said he couldn't put his finger on it but he felt we could be at the point of the beginning of the end. The big problem domestically was GB looming large, difficulties in driving through the changes in the public services, and the international agenda developing in a way none of us had planned or predicted.

Wednesday, March 6

It still felt like we were swimming through treacle. TB called just before 7, having landed at 6.15 after a 24-hour flight via Singapore. I was down on him at the moment, annoyed about all the stuff about his clothes. He felt we were far too defensive about it and I thought in its own way it was damaging, suggested out of touch. He believed our problem was one of communication. I believed there was also a problem with reality and that currently we lacked purpose and direction and when that happened, the trivia and the shit took its place. Clinton had told him that the press and the Tories were doing exactly what his opponents had done to him – drown out policy debate, attack integrity and persuade the public that we spent all our time dealing with all the shit, not worrying about the things people cared about. TB believed we did have a real strategy, and it was the right strategy, but the press were just trying to distort it the whole time. I felt we weren't disciplined enough at agreeing to a strategy, sticking to it and driving it through.

We had a good meeting with Charles Clarke, David Triesman, Douglas [Alexander, DTI minister], Ed Miliband [special adviser to GB] etc. going through Philip's latest groups. They were neither bad nor good, just indifferent. We agreed on 'Investing in strong communities' as a basic local election message and agreed TB would have to go out campaigning to show we meant business. We had to get back to values-based politics, which meant handling better the frenzies when they came and using them to emphasise the two agendas. TB was tired at the PMQs preparation meeting and very pissed off that we were all so pissed off at all the coverage of his clothes. We were finding each other irritating at the moment. I ran home, then to Rory's GCSE options evening. TB had a stack of different meetings but he didn't seem to be up for anything at the moment. He was a bit spooked by GB.

Thursday, March 7

I drove in with Philip who felt we needed a plan to deal with spin and sleaze. He said switchers had been getting jittery, no sense of delivery, nothing going on in the debate that they identified with. TB leadership and the economy, commitment to public services and the Tories were what kept us going but we weren't in good shape. TB felt this was the effect of the press drowning the real agenda. I felt he was a bit head-in-sand, couldn't see, or didn't want to see there were reality as well as perception problems and they couldn't all be addressed by a communications plan. Blunkett was in a foul mood because someone had briefed the *Guardian* against his spending bid. TB felt David was slightly losing the plot with the police.

Cabinet was mainly about Iraq. Not exactly division, but a lot of concern, where is it going? DB saying he didn't feel there was much support. Several saying the real concern was the Middle East peace process. Charles [Clarke] said the party would support provided the case was real and properly made. Jack pointed out it was untrue to say sanctions had stopped food going to Iraq. Geoff H said that if action was taken it would be because of UNSCRs [UN Security Council resolutions]. DB raised the international and legal basis for action. He said that support for Kosovo and Afghanistan had been pretty overwhelming. He felt a military assault on Iraq would carry less weight. It would depend on the role of the UN. Robin started off by saying that Saddam was a shit, a psychopath, who resolved their prison overcrowding problem by shooting 15,000 people with the longest sentences and who gassed the Kurds. On military action, he said there was a fine balance to strike. Saddam will not listen to Kofi Annan [UN Secretary General] unless he believes there might be military action. He said he wasn't convinced that action three years ago had been productive. He doubted whether it would be worth taking action if he was still standing at the end, and said he will be much cleverer than the Taliban. He said the best way of isolating Saddam from the rest of public opinion there was progress in the MEPP. He also warned that Britain could end up isolated, with a number of EU governments sounding sympathetic but on past form would not sign up. Charles C felt the judgement that would be applied would be one of success or failure. He felt people understood TB's position of support in exchange for influence.

TB said people's concerns were justified. 'I do want to assure you that the management has not gone crazy.' What are the dangers? US unilateralism. Bush doing it for the wrong reasons. Lack of progress in the Middle East. Taking action which proves to be ineffective. He said post September 11 there was a huge dialogue over a new UNSCR. Russia is owed a lot of money by Iraq. Egypt said Iraq had the most dangerous leader we have ever come across. [Hosni] Mubarak saw him as a real and present threat. He said we had to try to influence and shape US strategy. But we have to try to put ourselves in the right position. Get the weapons inspectors back in. He said the only thing Saddam responds to was real fear. If we had regime change it would make a huge difference to the whole region. It wasn't a row as such, but it was immediately briefed to the [*Evening*] *Standard* as such and that would frame it for the rest. It was a good discussion. TB said nothing decided.

Later we saw Milburn who said the problem was we were still behaving like a first-term government. We were too timid. We should be bolder, risk more arguments, more enemies. John Monks had written a bad letter to TB, saying we were in danger of losing our roots. Alan felt GB was the problem, that he spooked TB and we were paralysed on the economy, euro, public services.

Friday, March 8

Cabinet awayday at Chequers. Mood not great. The papers were full of division, threats of resignations over Iraq which even though untrue was clearly being flammed up from somewhere. TB and I were not getting on at the moment. I was fed up with the whole business, and he knew it. He was probably going elsewhere for advice, notably Peter M and to be fair, I could see why because I was giving him very little by way of ideas and support at the moment. I was down on him and down on the job. TB emphasised the need to get through this difficult phase with direction focused on values and delivery. He was still on the basic message mantra focused on the economy, society, public services, the international agenda. He felt the crime agenda was the most important at the moment. People needed to know we got it.

GB was looking odd, his face often contorted, his lips pushed out like he was blowing the whole time, his hands often clasped together over his eyes. He couldn't bring himself to look at TB when he spoke. TB said we were currently facing a test of mettle and maturity and had to hold our nerve. He was worried about yesterday's briefings out of the meeting. But after three months of sustained onslaught, we were still in a pretty strong position in the polls. The strategy against us was to assault our integrity because that goes to trust. Then it was to say that public services were crap and it makes no difference spending more money.

On the Civil Service, be careful not to be in a state of war with it. Win them over for reform. He said the fundamental positions we took were right, the specific programmes were right and the values were right, and though government is tough, what we've been through is nothing like as tough as other governments have, so we need to exude a sense of leadership and confidence, hold firm, take the tough decisions, drive the programme through. JP said whoever briefed yesterday's discussion on Iraq had behaved appallingly, that we worked hard to unite on policy and we should protect that unity. He said yesterday was a good discussion but then loose talk, nonsense about hawks and doves and threats of resignation had damaged us. Blunkett said it was rare he disagreed with TB but he disagreed with him about the Civil Service. They put SpAds on the back foot. They were in the strongest position they had been in for ages. There needs to be more Civil Service reform. Clare said the Cabinet was not ideologically divided. The '45 government achieved a lot but there was a real bitterness there. Of course there are differences here, but there is no big ideological divide. Our values are different to Tory values that have dominated in the last century. Our kind of values can become the norm, she said, which will be phenomenal.

Margaret B warned that though IDS was hopeless, we shouldn't underestimate because he may have a certain appeal. She said the mood in the party was terrible, they think we are growing out of touch. She also felt we needed to do a better job of challenging cynicism. The press are more poisonous than ever before, churn out all sorts of stuff that's untrue, unchallenged. Byers felt the Cabinet was too pessimistic. Strong economy, good record on jobs, inflation and interest rates. Robin lightened things a bit, started off by saying if JP was blaming him for briefing on Iraq 'he can step outside'. He said he totally supported TB in saying we needed to use Parliament more. We were not using Parliament enough to set the agenda. He said the problem with disengagement was one affecting the whole of Europe. Politics is now seen as a matter for politicians not people. We must convey a sense that we are not an elite constantly rubbing shoulders with the rich and famous. He said GB has been a very distributionist Chancellor but we never talk about it. We don't talk enough about the changes we are making.

John Reid said he could remember a time when the press was more poisonous, when Neil was leader. It will get worse than this. But what they prey on above all is division, and we should do nothing to feed it. He said we needed to be more political, less managerial, emphasise values, struggle, change, then delivery. GB said we had a historic opportunity to dominate for a generation, and deliver full employment. He felt we should worry less about the media, get the strategy right and shape long-term expectations. He said the Budget would further establish a strong economy, fairness agenda, solid foundations for the public services with the stress on reform as much as money. Alan M said values-based politics, being politicians not managers, was what was needed. When we were doing difficult things, explaining why according to our values, that was when we are strong. We had allowed ourselves to be projected as being on the side of the wealthy as well as the poor and sometimes the people in the middle didn't feel we were on their side.

TB summed up at some length. He said that after yesterday's Cabinet Richard Wilson had said to him he had never known a Cabinet with less malice in it and it was important we stuck together. When colleagues are in trouble, we support them. There was no doubt the press was in a different mode to the public, who wanted to see us with our sleeves rolled up, getting on with the job, doing the things they elected us to do. Our opponents remain frustrated because we have a strong coalition of traditional Labour and aspirational Labour, and we have to hold that together. He said the reason centre-left parties have lost in Europe is partly because they allow different parts of their coalition to erode. They don't get the importance of the anti-social behaviour agenda, rights and responsibilities. He spoke well, and the mood at the end was better than at the beginning.

Saturday, March 9

Middle East, Zimbabwe and Iraq the main issues at the moment. I took Rory to a race at Chelmsford where one of the coaches came over with some kids and said they were studying me at school.

Sunday, March 10

TB called re the [Dick] Cheney [US Vice President] visit, not sure what we were meant to get out of it. On the domestic front, he was worried we were losing the tough-on-crime bit. We went out for dinner with Tucker [Eskew], Lisa [his wife] and their son Thompson. He said basically we had been responsible for his new lease of life.

Monday, March 11

We had a meeting with Julian Miller [Cabinet Office intelligence and security official] on the idea of a WMD document. Cheney arrived for talks with JP, then a tête-à-tête with TB during which they went over Iraq. So far as Cheney's mood music was concerned, he was when not if, and though they hoped for a lot of support, he didn't consider it to be essential. The Americans claimed to be conscious of the importance of the MEPP but we were not sure they really got it. At the lunch, Cheney had a quiet manner, was pretty calm and although he had gravitas, somehow the whole wasn't as impressive as it ought to be. They started on Afghanistan. It was clear the Americans wanted out as soon as possible. He said if we were still there in a year then questions would be asked. The aim was try to help the Afghans get themselves a proper army and security force. TB was clear we had to be in it for the long term. Cheney felt building the new regime could be tougher than taking down the old one and that the poppy crop remained a real problem. He was worried about Saudi and its fundamentalists and felt the regime's deal with the fundamentalists made it harder for them than for Pakistan to keep control. On the MEPP, TB went through the similarities with Northern Ireland. Cheney was very down on [Yasser] Arafat [Palestinian leader]

They discussed NATO expansion and TB said re Putin that the key to understanding him is that he is a Russian patriot. At least Communism got them noticed. He's not a Communist, far from it, but that colours his thinking. He wants to be at the top table. He raised steel tariffs and got very little response. Cheney was one of those politicians not embarrassed to say nothing. After lunch we took Cheney over to the CIC where he said a few words. After he left, I went for a run but had bad asthma and cut it short.

Up to the flat for dinner – TB, Peter M, PG, Sally, Jonathan, Robert Hill [Blair's political secretary] and I. Peter M was on better form and we had constant references to his own demise, and my/TB's roles in it. His analysis was that we came in after a pretty unedifying election, had a bad start, lacked clarity on the agenda, then Afghanistan drowned out domestic issues. Now there was a different mood where anything we did was being turned against us. TB insisted the problems were perception not real. Peter, Philip and I argued that some of the problems had been real. We had lacked clarity. We had lost the clearer sense of purpose we had before. Jo Moore staying was a mistake. So was the Mittal letter but TB always defended our basic position. I said there was a real problem, not just one of perception, even if it was a succession of different perceptions that created the problem. He said no, this is dangerous thinking which has to be resisted because what they want is to stop us being effective.

Peter felt TB had certain blind spots. He should do more in Parliament. He should do more in Cabinet. We should try to generate an intelligent debate within the media about the media and its relations with politics. Philip felt that in some ways perception had become reality, but it was reality that had to be dealt with. I said just because our opponents said we had lost direction or that we were out of touch, didn't automatically mean it was untrue. And then there was GB. I said the reason TB was so confident and commanding on foreign policy was that he didn't have GB getting in the way the whole time as he did on public services and Europe. Philip asked him direct whether he enjoyed dealing with foreign policy more than domestic, because that's what he felt. TB felt, particularly post September 11, they couldn't be separated in the same way as before, but his main focus was always domestic and at the moment specifically crime. He agreed on the need to do more in Parliament and develop a better media strategy. TB no longer really bothered to hide the way GB was affecting his thinking, e.g. when Philip said it had to be a Budget for crime, TB said he won't get that because GB won't want Blunkett to come out well. Jonathan's view was that the media were just bored with us. Mine was that we lacked clarity and conviction. Peter's that we lacked the bigger narrative, so the drip-drip had to some extent worked and people no longer believed us in the same way as before or respected us in the same way.

Tuesday, March 12

We decided not to brief the speech in advance. The result was there was nothing in the papers and the result of that was the broadcasters concluded it couldn't be newsworthy and didn't do much with it.[1] It was extraordinary the extent to which they let the papers decide the agenda for them. TB was up at 5 to work on the speech. Though he didn't change it much, he did enough to make it less values-based. He was strangely lacking in confidence at the moment.

Wednesday, March 13

Crap press for the speech. Not trailing it hadn't worked at all. Up to see TB early. We had a cup of tea in the kitchen and as he made it, he said he was alarmed at the damage GB had been doing recently. Tube, Post Office and Railtrack were all 'disasters waiting to happen' and he felt they were disasters made in the Treasury. Yet he felt we

[1] In the speech, delivered at the London School of Economics and entitled 'Next Steps for New Labour', Blair said 'Remember ten years ago: we were on our knees, out of office and out of hope. Now look forward ten years and imagine what could be possible . . . imagine too what we could achieve pulling together if we show our determination, stick to the values we believe are right, stick to our plans and see them through.'

should be involving GB more in strategy. This was real groundhog-a-go-go. He felt there was a shape to every parliament and we were just going through a bad patch. We would come out of it. Murdoch was in for breakfast, friendly but still very anti euro. Philip had a session with GB and said he was pretty pro euro at the moment. He felt that we were useless on strategy and that we should stop talking about public service delivery and just do it. Philip pointed out to him that was the opposite of TB's approach, and that we wanted the two running alongside each other and said 'Why on earth don't you talk about it? If you work together properly, we would be unstoppable.'

Thursday, March 14

Stan came in with a polling presentation that showed things shifting towards the euro. But better public services and higher living standards were what people wanted now. Cabinet was nearly all foreign, mainly Zimbabwe[1] and MEPP. GB sat there the whole time looking phenomenally pissed off and at one point appearing to be asleep. Jack was a lot more confident than before. I had a meeting on media ownership with Ed Richards. TB was keen for total liberalisation as a way of getting more Europeans into our market but it could lead to Murdoch getting ITV news. TB's general view was that we got nothing worse out of Murdoch than we did from anyone else. Ed was with me in bemoaning the lack of focus on the cultural impact, the fact that content regulation was virtually non-existent and these people had too much unchecked power. He said that Pat [Hewitt] and Tessa [Jowell] were also opposed to TB's view. They wanted controls on it. Then to a meeting with TB and DB re the blitz on street crime we had been pressing for. DB was using it to push for more money. TB wanted something that was visible, that worked, and that sent out the right signals. He set off for Barcelona [EU summit] and said he wanted me to focus totally on crime and the Blunkett package.

Friday, March 15

The riots in Barcelona were taking off as the main story there.[2] I was working with the Home Office to get up some decent crime stories

[1] Following Robert Mugabe being returned as president in the election of March 9–11, the Commonwealth Observer Group's preliminary report on the way it was conducted claimed 'a high level of politically motivated violence and intimidation' by supporters of the ruling party, Zanu-PF, had marred and influenced the poll.

[2] The EU leaders' summit was disrupted by anti-globalisation protesters in Las Ramblas.

pre DB on *Frost*, but they weren't motoring. TB was clear he wanted a proper blitz on this but even DB was now irritated by it all, the feeling that Number 10 was intervening the whole time. Natascha McElhone came in for a cup of tea and it was nice to hear her say the kind of thing I said the whole time, so often I was never quite sure whether I believed it or whether it was just a line to get me through, namely that by the time we were gone all the press frenzy would be forgotten and people would see we had delivered real things that mattered. John Monks was leading the news with an interview in *The Times* attacking TB over being too close to [José María] Aznar [Spanish Prime Minister] and [Silvio] Berlusconi. TB, GB and JS all went up and hit back on it. It was the main story out of Barcelona. TB's basic line was that the press were going through a mad phase and we just had to wait till normal politics could be resumed. He was quite chipper but the mood was bad.

Saturday, March 16

West Ham vs Man U. I saw Alex F beforehand who, a bit like Natascha yesterday, felt things were not nearly as bad as we seemed to think. Astonishing match, 5–3 to United, with a stunning goal by Beckham. I was amazed how many people from overseas there were in the crowd, seemingly just over for the day.

Sunday, March 17

TB had been on several times yesterday and today re Blunkett on *Frost*. He was OK without being brilliant and later did a lobby briefing. I worked on a note to put round the party on the public services argument. Then to Gavin's [Fiona's brother] for Burnley vs Preston on TV, with Paul Gascoigne [former top-flight midfielder] having signed for us. We went to the Hodges' [Margaret, minister for universities and husband Henry] for dinner with DB, who was a bit down. I said he shouldn't have referred to TB talking about the management losing their marbles re Iraq. Margaret H was pretty down as well, felt that GB had got himself into a much stronger position and TB was slightly losing the plot. I said I could easily see circumstances where GB never became leader. David claimed that he would never work under GB other than as Chancellor and in any event GB would be his own Chancellor. It was a very jolly dinner, as they always are with Margaret and Henry. But the backdrop was TB in a bit of trouble, GB and Co. at it more than ever and DB feeling he was a contender too. TB had said to me earlier that there was too much knicker-wetting going on in the Cabinet. They had to get tougher. He said he'd had Clare on talking about what her 'bottom lines' were on Iraq.

Monday, March 18

Heavy news day. SRA [Strategic Rail Authority] bad figures, hunting[1] and an 'out of the blue' Geoff Hoon statement on 1,700 fighting troops going to Afghanistan. The DB interview plus briefing led to some pretty grim headlines, e.g. Blunkett saying our streets are not safe. Up to the flat on arrival. He seemed about as up as I was down. He said we came out of the election with the press trying to do us down, they wanted to give the Tories a lift but have given up on IDS so are now trying to build up GB. TB said all that mattered was that we delivered. He was frustrated at lack of delivery, at departmental slowness and the poor quality of cross-cutting work. He wanted to set up Cobra-style groups to tackle pinch points in the public services like bed blocking, Internet crime, weaknesses in the transport system.

The morning meeting was more meandering than ever, tired and lacking in drive. Ian Austin was pissed off that our crime meeting was going to get in the way news-wise of GB's speech on the NHS. I made little effort to dispel the impression that it had been deliberate. TB also had a difficult meeting with Tessa and Patricia [Hewitt] on media ownership. Their approach was fairly liberalising but he wanted to go the whole hog and said again Murdoch was no better or worse than any of the others, and what the media needed was real competition, takeovers galore. Patricia said this would go down badly with the party, the media and the public. TB said he didn't think the public obsessed about it. Jack called me to say he was worried about our direction on WMD. If WMD alone was the issue, Iraq was not as bad as Iran and Korea.

Tuesday, March 19

The Treasury was still gibbing at the crime meeting tomorrow because it would hit GB's speech coverage. Hunting was going big and so was the follow-up to military deployment and the growing political row about our failure to brief in advance. We had taken our eyes off the ball and not covered the bases. TB was not feeling great. I went with him to the stocktake on health with Alan. Then a communications meeting with DB and team. DB was clearly pretty beleaguered at the

[1] MPs voted for a complete ban on hunting with dogs when asked to choose between three options: a complete ban on fox hunting; the preservation of the status quo, and the compromise of licensed hunting.

moment. TB was far too nice about the Home Office being dictated by events. Yes, they had to deal with a lot of stuff that just happened, but it didn't mean they couldn't be more strategic.

[David] Yelland was in to see TB. Quite interesting, because Yelland was very down on the press, saying something had to give, the negativity had to stop somewhere. Then out to do Zimbabwe's suspension by the Commonwealth, at last. [John] Howard [Australian Prime Minister], [Thabo] Mbeki [South African President] and [Olusegun] Obasanjo [Nigerian President] did their thing. TB wanted to do a Cobra-style meeting for tomorrow's effort on crime, which I thought was a bit silly but there we are. TB had a one-on-one with GB and said afterwards he now felt he was operating the whole time, positioning himself in slightly different places all the time.

Wednesday, March 20

A row between GB and DB re who was doing what today. GB's NHS speech was fine but DB's crime summit, as planned, was going to get far more coverage. DB agreed not to do the *Today* programme as a sort of peace offering to GB, but he did breakfast telly and it was pretty much leading the news. GB's 'tough choices' message was seen as a hit at other ministers. I had a very frank discussion with TB after the crime meeting. He said GB was operating the whole time. It is nothing new in politics but at the moment it is particularly bad. He was setting himself up as Mr NHS now, trying to divide and rule e.g. between Alan M and the other ministers. The worry too was the idea that education was no longer number one priority. Ian Austin was in a major strop and at the end of the day we had a real row, me saying at the end I couldn't care less what they thought; that this was payback for years of them treating people like shit, including GB's Cabinet colleagues. He said it simply wasn't true that they were 'at it' and I had to believe that. I replied then all the journalists who said they were at it were liars?

TB was good at the crime meeting, closed it really well, drew in the centre of gravity of the comments. He felt DB was too emotional about it, saw it too much in personal terms. We had good ideas but we needed to know we had the systems and people to put them into practice. [Sir John] Stevens was pleased and did clips with DB that went fine. TB was raving about the crime meeting, felt it had been a really useful exchange and that if we listened to the cops more, we could get more done. On the hunting vote, Hilary [Armstrong] called and said TB was in some bother on this. TB wanted to push on and was in real 'fuck off' mode. All a bit grim at the moment.

Thursday, March 21

TB/GB relations getting worse. Then an extraordinary thing later when George Pascoe-Watson [*Sun*] read to me the opening sentences of the draft of TB's [planned education] speech, accurately. It had gone to the Treasury and DfES [Department for Education and Skills] private offices earlier. Ian Austin, Ed Miliband and others denied it was them, claiming it must have been Education. All very odd. After Cabinet, TB had a meeting with GB, Margaret Hodge re student finance. GB was arguing strongly for a graduate tax, TB for top-up fees and it all ended a bit ugly when TB seemed to put his foot down, said eventually we have to make a decision and this is the decision we are making. GB said nothing after that and walked out as soon as it was convenient.

Our immediate problem for the day was [Labour MP] Alun Michael's hunting statement. TB was in a rage at not having followed his instincts, having voted for when he hadn't really wanted to. Deep down, he wished he had never let this thing on the agenda. Alun's draft was long, rambling, a bit unclear. But when he came in to discuss it at 9 and we went through it, the more you pressed for clarity, the more obvious it was the only way to get it was to come down on the side of the ban. The solution was a new bill. TB didn't really want that. He wanted more delay, more consultation and was in a foul mood on it. [Margaret] Beckett and [Alun] Michael were perfectly calm but getting a little bit exasperated. Before the statement, Gerald Kaufman [veteran Labour MP and chairman of the Culture, Media and Sport Select Committee] called me to say he would never see himself as a loyal TB supporter again if we backtracked on this. I said I never realised he was so passionate about it and he said he was, adding 'If the Tony who stood up to Milosevic and Bin Laden can't stand up to the Countryside Alliance, I can't support him.'

The mood with GB was poisonous. At the start of Cabinet, when TB read out the absences, he said in a perfectly friendly way 'It says here you're in Monterey, Gordon.' GB didn't even look up, let alone smile. TB said later he found his behaviour at times weird. I said we just had to accept there was a counter-strategy. Cabinet was largely foreign affairs, a bit on CSR/Budget. Milburn was good, emphasising the need for a more collegiate approach. TB saw Clare earlier and told her to watch this stuff about her being offside on Iraq. He said she had been very disarming, saying she had been done in on it and would not be a problem, but then at Cabinet whacked Geoff on Afghanistan. Then to Northolt and the flight up to Manchester with Tessa. TB wasn't sure what to push in the speech but we worked up education still the number one priority, tough on truancy. We visited the Commonwealth Games stadium which looked great, fantastic atmosphere, then to Bolton Arena, where he did an OK Q&A. There was a group of councillors from Burnley lobbying me to be their MP.

Overnight at the Lowry hotel in Manchester. Another discussion re strategy over dinner. He had had dinner with Clinton last night who had suggested I pick his brains on how to deal with this changed media mood. He had said the danger was doing the wrong thing instead of the right thing. Keep listening to your instincts that got you there in the first place, not the press who want you out. Keep getting out with people. TB and I were still disagreeing about the extent to which this was a reality or communications problem. What I did agree was that we needed more imagination in our communications. TB said there was a danger he, TB, was just becoming boring because people were so familiar with him. Bill's great appeal, or part of it, was his celebrity. He felt we had become too defensive about TB the phenomenon. He said this isn't your fault because everyone says you're the best in the world at what you do but we need new thinking, new ideas. I said it was about reality, lack of texture and enrichment. It's about you, drawing on real interests, real passion, real experience. I said we could do all manner of new interview ideas, pictures, talking points, but in the end it was about how he spoke about what he really felt. It became quite a tough exchange but we both felt better after it. After the others left, he filled me in on his earlier conversation with GB. He said Gordon's view has always been that when the going gets tough, I [TB] should disappear in a puff of smoke and he'll come in. He doesn't really get me. I do this job better than he thinks.

Friday, March 22

IDS had done a local paper interview in which he said TB ruthlessly exploited his children. I filled in TB who said IDS would regret this. If he had any sense he would apologise, but probably he wouldn't. Yelland called and, bizarrely, IDS had called him to say he didn't recall using those exact words, he felt really bad and he wouldn't do it again. I said to David that that was more about the desire to stop the papers whacking him and if he meant it he should call TB. Off to Abraham Moss High School. Good speech but limited coverage.[1]

[1] In a speech focusing on secondary schools, Blair said 'We should be proud of our education system, our teachers and staff. There is, however, a lot more to do. We want to be the best. And we can be. The challenge is to educate not just the top twenty or thirty per cent well but all our children.'

We flew back, and I met up with Fiona and the kids on the M4 and headed for Devon.

Saturday, March 23–Friday, March 29

We were staying in an area where the mobiles didn't work, so I had limited contact with the office to a couple of calls a day, and did very little work. When I bothered collecting any papers, the theme of TB in trouble was developing pretty fast. I felt we had a clear difference in how to deal with it, which meant I felt I wasn't really offering solutions at the moment. He had been clear he didn't see the current situation as my fault, but I found his obsessive belief that it was about communications rather than policy or overall positioning a bit odd. We were staying in a house near Totnes and the local pub was run by a couple of party members who were generally OK about things, though there was nevertheless a sense that we weren't on top of things like we used to be. We went back to Tavistock a couple of times including a visit to the *Tavistock Times* office.[1] As often happened when we were away, usual suspects and others were lining up to whack us on various policy areas – Iraq, Post Office, tax and spend, TB's relations with Berlusconi. We got into a routine fairly quickly. There were some great hills around and I ran every day as well as playing tennis with Calum and swimming. We had a couple of days on the beach. The kids were an absolute joy at the moment.

Saturday, March 30

Jeremy [Heywood] called to tell me, in total confidence, that the Queen Mother had died. Although she had been frail, the actual death came as a surprise. The Queen was there [Windsor] now and they were trying to tell Charles who was in Klosters [ski resort]. They hoped to announce it soon. They were aiming for around 6. TB came on the line and we went over what to do. Unlike with Diana's death, there were well-laid plans which swung into action pretty quickly. But it was evident from the call I took from Robin Janvrin early evening that they were a bit worried, unsure that there would be crowds to justify three days' lying in state, or that there would be the level of interest necessary to fill nine days of news. I felt that it would develop a strong momentum of its own and that they were worrying unduly, though I could see why. TB, Jeremy and I agreed that we should go

[1] Campbell and Fiona Millar had met as junior reporters on the Mirror Group training scheme, and worked together on the weekly paper.

for a recall of Parliament before people started to call for it, and got Hilary Armstrong on the case.

TB worked on his words and as soon as it was announced formally, we got a crew to Chequers. He spoke well, and all the better for it being all his own words. The atmosphere was very different to Diana's death. It was not a Diana moment. TB felt there would be quite an outpouring of grief but I felt more that it would become one of those moments where people simply reviewed the past. Cherie was out in the States on her holiday and we had to make a decision about whether she came back or not. She clearly didn't want to. TB spoke to the Queen around 7 and told me afterwards she was 'very sad but dignified'. I spoke to Janvrin again, who agreed we should go to the US as planned and Jeremy H successfully pushed them for a Tuesday funeral so we could get to the US and back. I spoke to JP, who agreed to do the media on the Queen Mum tomorrow. Jeremy was doing a fantastic job with the Palace.

Sunday, March 31

TB called re the fact that cameras were still hanging around. He was volunteering to do more extended interviews today but we took the judgement it would look like he was muscling. Maybe another time. We did a couple of conference calls to agree what we should be saying about the visit to the US going ahead, recall of Parliament, receiving the body to Westminster Hall. TB, Jeremy and I went through the draft guidance on national mourning and took out a reference to businesses closing down on the day of the funeral, instead putting in the idea that schools do something to respect it, also give guidance on how practically people went to see the body. Our input was fairly minimal compared to Diana's death, but there was nonetheless a steady traffic between us and the Palace. I felt Charles should do something public fairly soon, the Queen maybe later in the week. JP did fine on the lunchtimes. Once all the amendments were put into the guidance, and some of the more antiquated language was taken out, we put it out. There were the beginnings of chat about the Royals coming under more scrutiny, how long would the Queen stay, would she abdicate kind of thing, but it was still pretty low-key.

Monday, April 1

Philip [Gould] gave a hilarious account of TB's behaviour last week at the various strategy meetings, that whenever he was challenged or under attack he just curled up into a foetal position. He said he was wearing the most extraordinary collection of brightly coloured shirts and ties whilst GB was always in a plain white shirt and red tie. 'It was a classic style meets substance moment.' He said GB hadn't really engaged. TB finished his note and as I had told him we were at Philip's, he sent it through there. The fax ran out of ink after page three, which ended 'Here is what we should do.' There then came through seven blank pieces of paper. When I finally got it, it was fine, but the kind of note I had seen so many times and we never really fully delivered on them.

Tuesday, April 2

Chequers. I was working on a response to TB's notes. He asked me what I thought of his note when we got there. I said good in parts. He said I really had to read it carefully, because it meant a lot of change from him, and he was serious about making that change. We both felt we needed new blood around the place. I said he could only get new blood if he got rid of the old blood and if he was looking for volunteers, I'd be happy enough to go. He asked if I actually wanted to go. I said I'd stay if he really wanted me to but I wasn't enjoying it and therefore wasn't doing it as well as I could, or possibly vice versa. I felt I was stuck in my own tram lines and so were others. He asked who could replace me and said he couldn't just take a chance. At one point we thought of Adam Boulton [Sky political editor] but coincidentally today we had the TV political editors in for lunch at Chequers and he thought Adam lacked judgement. I said people may emerge if they knew there was a vacancy. Most of the hacks would be amazed we were having this discussion. He said so was he, that I was too important to the operation and gave it strength which would be impossible to replace. I said all I was saying was that if he was looking for space for new blood he should feel free to look for a replacement. Later we were talking about Manchester United. He said that I was his [Roy] Keane[1] and he was very loath to lose me.

On Iraq, the meeting started at 10 up in the Long Gallery. It was a repeat of the smaller meeting we'd had on Afghanistan. Boyce was looking very tanned and smartly dressed and mainly set out why it was hard to do anything. He even talked up the Middle East peace process as a problem, as if TB had never thought of that. TB wanted to be in a position to give GWB a strategy and influence it. He believed Bush was in the same position as him, that it would be great to get rid of Saddam and could it be done without terrible unforeseen

[1] Aggressive and highly competitive central-midfielder, hugely successful captain of Manchester United.

circumstances. We were given an account of the state of Iraqi forces, OK if not brilliant, the opposition – hopeless – and Saddam's ways – truly dreadful. CDS appeared to be trying to shape the meeting towards inaction, constantly pointing out the problems, the nature of the administration, only Rumsfeld and a few others knew what was being planned, TB may speak to Bush or Condi but did they really know what was going on? TB said in the end Bush would take the decisions. CDS said so far he had followed the Rumsfeld (he always pronounced it Rumsfield) advice. He said apart from Rumsfeld, there were only four or five people who were really on the inside track.

There was also a different understanding on UNSCRs, the US thinking they have existing cover, us believing we need a new one for foolproof legal cover. Both C and John Scarlett kept saying co-operation was better, e.g. on intelligence, but CDS would keep coming back to the problems. I recalled his dire warnings about the Taliban skinning people alive. Now he was saying this would not be as easy as the Taliban. General Tony Pigott did an OK presentation which went through the problems realistically but concluded that a full-scale invasion would be possible, ending up with fighting in Baghdad. But it would be bloody, could take a long time. Also, it was not impossible that Saddam would keep all his forces back. He said post-conflict had to be part of conflict preparation. The Americans believed we could replicate Afghanistan but it was very, very different. There was a guy there called [Lieutenant General] Cedric [Delves], our military man based in Tampa, working with the US inside CENTCOM. He was sunburned, wearing American lace-up boots, and said Tommy Franks was difficult to read because he believed they were planning something for later in the year, maybe New Year. He basically believed in air power plus special forces. CDS said if they want us to be involved in providing force, we have to be involved in all the planning, which seemed fair enough. TB said it was the usual conundrum – do I support totally in public and help deliver our strategy, or do I put distance between us and lose influence? We discussed whether the central aim was WMD or regime change. Pigott's view was that it was WMD. TB felt it was regime change in part because of WMD but more broadly because of the threat to the region and the world. On WMD, people will say that we have known about WMD for a long time. He said what was sure was that this would not be a popular war, and in the States, fighting an unpopular war and losing is not an option.

C said that the presidential finding, based on an NSC paper, made clear it was regime change that they wanted. Pigott kept coming back to the point that Saddam could pull forces back to the cities, put them among civilians, meanwhile reinforce the CBRN [chemical, biological, radiological and nuclear] sites. There was a discussion about who would replace Saddam and how could we guarantee it would be better. Scarlett said it couldn't be worse. There was a discussion re Kabul which CDS said was getting more and more dangerous, and Turkey, who, CDS said, were taking over ISAF but basically leaving us to do the work. The Beeb was in the news because of a row about Peter Sissons [BBC news anchor] not wearing a black tie during the Queen Mum death coverage.

Wednesday, April 3

Amazingly, the row about Peter Sissons' tie was still raging. Of course it was a mistake, but in the end so what, but the *Mail* et al. were in total fulmination mode. Peter M had responded to TB's note in not dissimilar terms to mine. TB had obviously been talking to him about my state of mind. He said he felt he knew how I could regain happiness through work: 1. be nicer to TB, 2. get new blood around me, and 3. manage my time better. The lack of cohesion with the Treasury was really bothering me. TB was anxious that we get the focus for the meeting at Crawford [Texas] off Iraq simply and on to the Middle East. Second, how do we get the Americans to do more re the Middle East peace process without it looking like we are criticising them for not doing enough? He had told Bush a year ago that he should get more involved now because he would have to and he would eventually be playing catch-up.

The [pre-US trip NBC] interview was fine, pretty straight, Middle East, Iraq, Afghanistan, about thirty-five minutes in total. TB was thinking hard about the visit, said his job was to give Bush a strategy, and to get the political processes up and running. It was clear both from David M and Chris Meyer that the US government was in a divided state, bordering on chaos. Cheney and Rumsfeld vs Powell, with Condi trying to get Bush engaged more, possibly with Powell. Bruce [Lord Grocott, Blair's former parliamentary private secretary] did some good lines for TB's [Commons] statement on the Queen Mum and between us we got some half-decent anecdotes. TB just about caught the moment.

Thursday, April 4

I ran in, thirty-six minutes, up to see TB to go over Crawford/Middle East. DM wanted him to speak to Bush who coincidentally came through later in the day and they had a pretty good conversation. Bush was about to do a speech attacking both sides and saying he was sending Powell to the region. That gave us plenty to brief around. TB had an hour with GB on the Budget but Gordon was still on his kick that we shouldn't be talking too much about public services, a view TB described as absurd given that was the platform we were elected on. GB said you never heard the Tories talking about unemployment. They never said they would sort it, said TB. It's like saying we should never talk about asylum. If it's a problem, people know it's a problem, and we have to deal with it. I saw what Philip meant about their clothes. GB was wearing a dark suit, a white shirt, a red tie, shoes that weren't cleaned properly and socks that fell down round his ankles. TB was wearing Nicole Farhi shoes, ludicrous-looking lilac-coloured pyjama-style trousers and a blue smock. After GB left, I said he looked like [spoof 1960s spy] Austin Powers. He said you are the second person who's said that. Gordon wasn't the first. Probably one of the kids.

He was clearly not hopeful we could get GB any closer onside at the moment. But he still wanted me to try to work with him on strategy. I was in with him when he spoke to Bush and he was happy after the call, felt Bush was far more engaged and on the detail than we had been led to believe. I left to take Calum to a tennis match but then had to deal with a little flurry about TB/CB's Egyptian holiday last Christmas. TB's entry in the Register of Members' Interests said it had been paid for by the Egyptian government and that he had made a donation to charity. But it seemed the money never went, partly because the Egyptians never said what charity it should go to. This would be the next crapola to deal with.

Friday, April 5

It was the day of the procession of the Queen Mother's body to the lying-in-state. A beautiful sunny day, wall-to-wall coverage for the Royals, OK crowds, nice atmosphere. Up to see TB in the flat. Another Austin Powers moment. Yellow/green underpants and that was it. I said what a prat he looked. He said I was just jealous – how many prime ministers have got a body like this? Re the Egyptian holiday, he thought they had paid, but it seemed there was a mix-up at the Egyptian end and the cheque never went. Fiona spoke to John Sawers [UK ambassador to Egypt, Blair's former foreign policy adviser] who was out in the desert and we told him it had to be sorted and we would get the cheque sent off today. Just before we took off for the States I did a conference call with Fiona, Anne Shevas and Martin Sheehan. We wanted to rectify the inaccurate Register [of Interests] points. I reminded TB that Henry McLeish [former Scottish First

Minister] ended up resigning over an inaccurate statement in the Register.

TB was seeing Jack later who suggested walking over to Westminster Hall. TB agreed and asked Gordon to go too. I said I thought it was a bad idea because it would look like they were trying to get attention. In the end they went by car. They went off as the procession came through. The crowds were far bigger than expected.

On the plane, we worked on the speech for tomorrow, pretty much wrote it himself, having decided he wanted to be totally supportive but also push for more US engagement. He would make clear we would support them on Iraq but also make the point about UN inspectors effectively as an ultimatum. We chatted around it for ages. I was worried it was too sugary re the Yanks but he insisted we had to do that to get them engaged in other ways. For example, he thought it was fair to say Bush's speech on the Middle East yesterday was, at least in part, influenced by us. For the first time I could recall, he did his own written checklist for the meeting with Bush. He wanted to do Iraq and MEPP first so that he knew where he was. We arrived and TB was met by Condi and flown off to the ranch. We were taken to our hotel. TB was having a one-on-one dinner and we went out for dinner with Condi, Andy Card [chief of staff], Karen [Hughes], Anna Perez [press secretary to Barbara Bush], Karl Rove [senior adviser]. A lot of it was small talk, and Karl Rove trying to persuade us to get fitted up with big Texan boots. Meyer was the only one who did. We were eating in a steak house which served obscenely large steaks. They seemed a bit more tense than the last time and it might be they were just starting to feel the pressure more, or more likely that they knew this was a bit trickier.

Saturday, April 6

Crawford, Texas. I went down to the gym in the hotel. There was an enormous woman on the only treadmill. Robin Oakley [CNN European political editor] called and she heard me speak and then, as she padded at the slowest possible pace, asked me if I was English, then if I knew Tony Blair. I said I did. She said she was so happy that the world was run by two God-fearing young men, Bush and Blair. She asked if I was his bodyguard and I said no. She said she prayed for Tony every day and she prayed for his bodyguards, for him to keep the world safe and for his bodyguards to keep him safe. She asked if I believed in God and I said no. She gave me a rather pitying look and then told me she was a member of the George W. Bush email prayer group and she was happy for me to be added to their list. Eventually she got off the treadmill. I ran for half an hour but then got called up because TB had asked for me to go out to the ranch with David and Jonathan. I set off with Magi [Cleaver] for a 45-minute drive down dull roads through pretty dull scenery. The rain started. The security checks were fairly light and we were driven down to the guesthouse where TB, CB, Leo [Blair], Kathryn [Blair], Gail [Booth, Cherie's mother] and Jackie the nanny were due to stay. It was a nice enough place but not exceptional. A flat bungalow with three bedrooms was the main residence. I hung around for a while in TB's room. TB and Bush had talked mainly about Iraq last night and today had been more focused on the Middle East peace process, about how to deal with [Ariel] Sharon [Israeli Prime Minister] and Arafat. Bush felt they were tired and old and with no new vision. He thought Arafat was weak and useless. They were turning their minds to the press conference and Bush was someone who liked to prepare for these events carefully.

We were doing the press conference at a school in Crawford and the toughest questions were why had there been no response from Israel and did TB agree Saddam had to go. Bush's posture and delivery were a lot better, more confident. We talked about it at the ranch before dinner. He said in the early days he got really knocked by the way they took the mickey out of the way he mangled words, and it made him hesitant, like when he said infitada instead of intifada and got mauled for it. Now he had given up caring what they think and it had made him more confident. He said the truth is I have a limited vocabulary, I'm not great with words, I have to think about what I say carefully. They had both been pretty heavy on Iraq and that was the story for most of them. The atmospherics were pretty good though. As we left the school, TB and I were walking to his car, GWB waiting and he shouted over 'too late for fine tuning now'. I said I hear you didn't like Trevor McDonald [ITN journalist who had recently interviewed Bush]. He said it just maddens him the way they all ask the same questions, so it's a pain.

When we arrived back at the ranch, we chatted in a little group outside the bungalow. Barney his dog came over and he said 'This is my Leo.' I said hold on, Leo's not a dog. Yes, he said, but Barney's the substitute for the little boy I never had. They went back to talking about the Middle East, David [Manning] and Condi having spoken earlier to Colin Powell to try to get him to the Middle East earlier. TB was setting out steps that could be taken. He was convinced that Bush valued our input on this at least. I left with David and Jonathan. We went for lunch at the coffee station in Crawford with some of the

White House staff including Andy Card. They were certainly doing their best for us.

We were driven back out to the ranch for a drinks reception and dinner. It was very relaxed, a three-piece band playing in the corner, waiters and waitresses in jeans and work shirts, no starters, tournedos and a selection of puddings. GWB and Cherie were at one table with a set of guests and TB and Laura were at another and then other tables all around. Bush was wearing Texan boots and jeans. I was with Condi, Karen, a very right-wing former ambassador [Anne Armstrong, first female US ambassador to the UK] who was going to the Queen Mum's funeral and one of the Bush daughters' boyfriends.

Over drinks before and after dinner, I had a couple of long chats with GWB. He asked me why I wasn't drinking and I said I was a recovering drunk. Me too, he said. I asked him how much he drank. He said two or three beers a day, a bit of wine, some bourbon. He gave up in August '86, a few months after me. I went through the kind of quantities I was drinking at the end and said they dwarfed his efforts. I said that having a breakdown and not drinking had been the best thing that ever happened to me. It was like seeing the light. But you still don't believe in God? he asked. No I don't. We talked about his axis of evil speech. Karen had said to me earlier they had had no idea it would impact quite as hard as it did. He said that was bullshit – he knew, and he was serious. We talked about running. He could still do between 6.45 and 7.15 a mile and was thinking of doing his own race for charity. He was also a member of a club, qualification for which rested on the ability to run a sub-seven-minute mile when it was a hundred degrees in the shade. He had dragged TB out for a run and said he had had to hold back a bit. TB said it was the first run that far since he left university. After a couple of toasts, Bush then just got up and said everyone could leave because he wanted to go to bed. Everyone signed the menus. They were always extremely respectful in front of him. I couldn't see any of them suggesting he had a touch of the Austin Powers about him. TB thought that was why he seemed to enjoy the banter with us, because he didn't seem to have anyone there who really stood up to him and just had a laugh. On Iraq, it was clear they genuinely hadn't decided what to do, or even whether to do anything at all.

Sunday, April 7

TB called early to give me a few final changes for the speech. I could hear Bush rushing him in the background. They went off to church, which was a three-hour round trip. We both reckoned Bush had been quite a lad in his youth, both on the booze and the birds front. But they got on, there was no doubt about that, and they were both people not afraid to face down critics. They both seemed to view Iraq and Saddam as an issue of conviction. We finished the speech, which was now strong, putting in a few final changes strengthening the references to the UN and also strengthening the use of the word 'justified' when talking about regime change. Most of the world's media was on the Middle East, but our lot would be on Iraq because that was the better political story.

The big thing was trying to get the peace process going again but Bush was very down on both Arafat and [Ariel] Sharon, who he had bollocked in a phone call yesterday. The drive down to the speech venue was much more scenic, including past some of the most incredible wild flowers any of us had ever seen. TB was speaking at the [George] Bush Library [at College Station, Texas]. While we waited for everyone to gather, I did a note to him on the advisability of doing a statement to the Commons on Wednesday. He was concerned it was setting a precedent that he would do one every time he went abroad and we were being pushed to do things no other prime minister would do. But I tried to push the positive reasons. He was the only leader really plugged into Bush and able to exert influence. He was far better than Bush at empathy and explanation. And it was important that we set this out as British foreign policy not theirs, and Parliament was the best place to do that.

George Bush Sr [former President] came through to say hello and ask us if we wanted to change his introductory remarks. Maybe it was just age, but he seemed a lot more comfortable in his own skin than Bush Jr, though less jokey. The only change I made was to delete England for Britain when he talked about us losing the Queen Mum. TB and I went through the speech one last time. He got a very warm reception, the speech went well[1] and although he got some tricky questions in the two separate Q&As, he was on form. I heard Bush Sr say to the people he was with how impressive he was. He had definitely made an impact. The argument was clear, he set up difficult questions, and answered them. JP called and said he really liked the speech.

On the plane I had dinner with TB and Jonathan and we discussed where we were going to find new blood for the office. I suggested a minister or senior MP getting involved in managing and motivating.

[1] Blair said 'Leaving Iraq to develop WMD, in flagrant breach of no less than nine separate UN Security Council resolutions, refusing still to allow weapons inspectors back to do their work properly, is not an option.'

Neither of them seemed keen. The reality was Jonathan wasn't a traditional chief of staff, in that he didn't manage a lot that went on, and I wasn't a traditional communications director. What we did was largely driven by what TB wanted us to do and what our personalities best allowed us to do. But it meant gaps that sometimes led to lack of clarity. Also the Policy Unit was badly managed and not properly integrated. TB was clear he wanted it sorted and wanted the game raised.

We debriefed him on the private sessions with Bush. He had been surprised how relatively positive he was about the idea for a big push on Africa. He had not enjoyed his contact so far with Europe. He liked Schroeder, loathed Arafat and had a total reversal of view of Putin. He now liked him. Bush had told him he had learned a lot from talking to his dad about success and failure. Bush Sr had told him he had not been nearly ruthless enough with his appointments and the people around him. He was trying to learn from that. He was also trying to learn the lesson that no matter what you did, you had to be out talking to the people that elected you. We got a few hours' sleep, landed and straight to the office. He had agreed to a [Commons] statement on Wednesday.

Monday, April 8

I called [Sir Robin] Janvrin to say I thought they had handled events incredibly well and today's broadcast by the Queen was the crowning glory of a very good PR campaign. They had done well every single day. Today, as well as the broadcast, they had the [Westminster Hall] vigil of the four grandsons. I spent a lot of the day working on Wednesday's statement with David Manning and Matthew Rycroft [private secretary, foreign affairs] Peter Hyman was nagging me to set up a Budget strategy meeting every day from now on in. Fat chance. GB just wasn't engaging. He was clearly trying to position himself as the saviour of public services whilst TB was fighting hard for more money for defence.

Tuesday, April 9

The Queen Mum's funeral would be a media wipeout so the morning meeting was brief, though I did relentlessly take the piss out of Ian Austin who had said a few days ago that nobody would be interested in the Queen Mum's funeral. I went upstairs to watch the cortège go through Horse Guards and towards the Mall. Big crowds, real solemnity and the BBC did a good job on it. I went to TBWA [advertising agency] who did a terrific presentation on the idea of segmentation, targeting campaigns to specific groups of people. They were very good on overall branding but their basic take was that we needed to isolate groups and direct our communications to them through policy that impacts upon them rather than through the media they consume. Trevor Beattie [chairman of TBWA] gave me a copy of *PR Week* which had said that New Labour, New Britain was the best consumer PR campaign of all time.

Wednesday, April 10

GB had got hold of a tape of Liam Fox [Shadow Health Secretary] making very unwise comments on the NHS. GB got the *Mirror* to splash on it. Philip felt opinion was moving back to us a bit, with health improving, education not as good as it should be, crime worse. We worked on the Middle East statement which was fine, and it was right to go for Israel and the Palestinian Authority equally. The statement on the Middle East had definitely been the right thing to do. The right-wing press were trying to cause trouble. The *Telegraph* were trying to link the success of the Queen Mum's funeral with hostility to New Labour. The *Telegraph* were also saying we tried to change the arrangements for the funeral, and Peter Oborne [columnist] was saying the same thing in the *Spectator*. I got Jeremy to write to them to complain. I had a meeting with Ed Balls on the Budget. He was happy where expectations were. I was less happy. We worked out what message TB should do in setting it up. They didn't want too much focus on health yet but we did need to start a campaign to stand up for the NHS. We were going to be putting up taxes but it was vital that a New Labour message runs through it all. PMQs was fine, the Middle East statement OK, the PLP not too dreadful.

We had a reception for [former Labour Prime Minister] Jim Callaghan's ninetieth birthday at Number 10. He made a really warm speech, terrific about his wife in particular, Audrey suffering from Alzheimer's, and he said how he sat with her and talked to her every day and sometimes she said a few words that made sense and it was magical. Michael Foot [Callaghan's successor as Labour leader] and I talked endlessly about Burnley and Plymouth [Argyle, supported by Foot]. Tony Benn [former Labour Cabinet minister] was filming the whole thing. Betty Boothroyd [former Speaker of the House of Commons] was there to call everyone to order. There was a good turnout of ministers though JP was angry he hadn't been invited. Denis Healey [former Labour Chancellor of the Exchequer] and I nattered about Keighley [where AC and Healey grew up]. Merlyn Rees [former Labour Home Secretary], Bernard Donoughue [head of former Labour Prime Minister Harold Wilson's Policy Unit, 1974–76], Tom McCaffrey [Callaghan's former press secretary], [Roy] Hattersley [former Labour deputy leader], Margaret and Peter Jay [Callaghan's daughter and former son-in-law]. TB said afterwards they were a good bunch of people but in the end they had failed to stay together.

Thursday, April 11

We were due to have a meeting on Budget strategy. TB was delayed at an NHS seminar. GB arrived on time but because TB wasn't there, he buggered off for ten minutes, came back and said 'What's this meeting about?' What became clear was that he didn't intend to expand on what was in the Budget. He said I wish we could do a presentation based on delivery but we don't have any. Puzzled looks all round. He told us about a campaign to be fronted by [Sir] Magdi Yacoub [pioneering heart surgeon] that was about getting up third-party support for the NHS. We would involve doctors and nurses in a fight for the future of the health service. I said that's all fine, but are we clear that taxes up to pay for health is going to be the main line out of the Budget? He was, but felt we needed this bigger campaign to lay the ground.

GB also wanted enterprise talked up and investment dividing lines laid down. As ever, he was a mix of strategically clever and clear – as in keep the Tories out of the centre, stop them becoming New Conservatives – selfish and exclusive – as in clearly not wanting TB too closely involved – and unrealistic, as in imagining that tens of thousands of doctors and nurses would come out to make the case for us. TB was weak at the meeting, looked tired and fed up. After half an hour GB just upped and left. Ed Balls treated TB with a bit more respect, but not much.

Then Cabinet. TB started with a contextualisation of the Budget, with a focus on enterprise, the need for a big battle on investment and tax, the need to get up delivery and reform. He said these are the areas where political battle will be joined, that this is far more important to the PLP than Iraq. He spoke for a few minutes, then said 'Anything you want to add, Gordon?' No, he said. So there was no discussion at all. I slipped a note to JP saying that they would all be very pissed off if there was no discussion at all on Budget strategy, saying why didn't you come back in the context of the local election launch today, but by the time he did GB said he had to leave for Treasury questions. TB had also slipped a note to GB saying he should say something. He said nothing. Absolutely ridiculous.

Later GB, Charles C, Alan M and I met to discuss the strategy for the Budget. GB set great store by his 'Say yes to the NHS' campaign, though I remained to be convinced we would get all the professionals properly involved. Likewise, Charles seemed nervous about how readily the party would get involved. GB was claiming he didn't want to rewrite the local election campaign but clearly wanted this to be a big part of it. I left with TB for Northolt [en route to Sedgefield]. I said GB could be a total pain but he still had amazing strategic energy and drive, that nobody but him or us could have motored on the NHS Fox story like that. TB did the *Northern Echo* when we got to Myrobella, then to the Labour Club for a Q&A where he was excellent. Don Macintyre and Andy Grice [*Independent* journalists interviewing Blair] stayed for it, and it ought to give them plenty of decent colour. We took them for dinner at the Dun Cow pub and TB talked about how much he enjoyed the Callaghan event but also how sad it was that this group of people seemed the best of friends now, but how they had split apart and how history might have been different if they had stayed together and the left of the party hadn't made the right feel that they had to leave.

Friday, April 12

We left for a business Q&A, which was pretty dull, and then to a much more interesting Q&A with leaders and others working in the public services. The cops seemed the most onside, health and education less so, but the basic message was that things were getting better but money was tight. Then to Darlington Memorial Hospital, where again the mood was OK but they said they needed more [investment]. We flew back and I got in for a meeting with Number 10 and the Treasury re GB's NHS campaign. My worry was that they didn't have the infrastructure to mount a campaign and also that they lacked anything to campaign against. I was ready to go to war with the *[Evening] Standard* over Oborne refusing to accept we didn't interfere in the lying-in-state arrangements. I had a meeting with Clare Sumner and Simon Virley [private secretaries], who had handled arrangements with the Palace, to go over it all. I sent a letter off after talking to TB and Guy Black [director of the Press Complaints Commission], to the PCC, who said if everyone is going to be clear that the report was wrong, it's fine and we should go for it.

Saturday, April 13

[Policy adviser] Liz Lloyd's wedding, TB came to the church service and briefly to the reception where he did a nice little speech, referring to the ghastly process of conference speech-writing and also to our 'dysfunctional relationship'. Tim Allan [AC's former deputy] and James Purnell [Labour MP, former Blair adviser] did a very funny song about Liz's past and Tim said that the new people he worked for [in public relations] were all totally indifferent to the fact he used to work for TB, but dead impressed that he worked for me. Most of the old office were there, and Ed Miliband turned up late for a while. Work-wise, fairly quiet though later on a rash of calls about Mo [Mowlam] in the *Observer*, extracts from her interview for a documentary to go with a book which was the usual over-the-top bollocks about her being smeared.

Sunday, April 14

We went out for dinner with the Goulds and Bob Shrum [Brown's polling adviser], who had probably worked on the Budget speech far more than we had. He said he would really like to get a better relationship between me and GB because he felt our politics were actually quite similar. I said I feared it was pretty hopeless.

Monday, April 15

TB was in pretty much constant dialogue with GB. The papers were full of Budget trailers. There was very little left and they had not done much by way of holding things back. The basic problem was no acceptance of a minimum delivery, not least because GB didn't talk about delivery, possibly preferring for him to get credit for the economy and TB none on delivery. His latest line was that we had delivered nothing, despite the strong economy. On sleaze, TB was moving towards an ethics adviser. I was chasing the *Standard* and the *Spectator* re the Queen Mum lying-in-state. I spoke to Boris Johnson [*Spectator* editor] who tried to be all jokey saying he would consider correcting it if I did a piece on the Blair/Bush relationship. TB wasn't feeling well and had picked up the bug that Leo had. The Tories had done a health document and Alan M and Darren Murphy put together a very good response on it. The *Guardian* was running a two-part series on the Treasury, its power and how it was built. Real self-aggrandisement with the help of two of their fans, Larry Elliot and Kevin Maguire [*Guardian* journalists]. Cherie and Fiona visited Holloway jail, which Fiona said was about as depressing as it gets.

Tuesday, April 16

Met Ed Miliband to go over the Budget broadcast script which was OK but lacking in a reform message. TB and GB were going through the final meetings both on policy and the tone of the statement. Magdi Yacoub finally got his article in the *Mail* but I didn't feel the 'Yes to the NHS' campaign was properly cooked at all. All the bulletins were leading on our troops fighting in Afghanistan. Some of the squaddies gave tremendous interviews. The pre-Budget coverage was cranking up, GB out with young kids. TB saw Hugo Young [*Guardian*] and then Peter Riddell [*Times*] trying to win the argument for tax for the NHS. I had altogether more difficult conversations with the *Sun* lot.

TB called a discussion on the ethics adviser idea. The worry was it was merely a response to a spasm of 'something must be done' which in fact would give us nothing but problems. TB felt that we needed something that gave us a bit of distance and a bit of time. He felt that for example with Peter M we might not have lost a very good minister if there had been a process one removed from us. But what both the Americans and [John] Major's government had shown is that just about every time they set up new bodies and structures to look at these kind of issues, they seem to make matters worse not better for themselves. We had an internal meeting to work out how best TB could take forward the Budget message in the coming months. TB was happy enough with the Budget and GB clearly did not want to be seen as Old Labour.

Wednesday, April 17

The Budget was reasonably well set up but the dominant story was clearly going to be tax for a better health service. TB was clearly a bit nervous, said we were doing something very few people in politics ever did successfully, openly advocating tax rises. I felt it could be the thing that gave us the definition we needed. At Cabinet, GB did a very good presentation. TB looked really tired and a bit out of it. Jack slipped me a note saying he thought TB looked ghastly and we needed to get him in better shape before this afternoon. GB did his usual mix of big message and factual rat-tat-tat. On the big message, what I liked about it was it was all the same arguments coming through, and the spending figures were fine.

TB said it was a crucial moment for the government. There were three things to get across. Strong economy the basis of everything we do. Continuing determination to get people off benefit and into work. Strong economy plus more people in work means more investment in public services. He said that there should now be a critical argument on the NHS. The issue is not whether we spend more but how. We have to win the argument that our system is better and more efficient than the French or German social insurance systems or the

Americans' way of doing things. This issue about whether more money in this way delivers better services will dominate this parliament. There was an odd moment in GB's summing-up when he referred to the NHS campaign and said 'I think' it's called 'Yes to the NHS', as though it had nothing to do with him. But he did a good job, and it went down well with colleagues.

TB was on great form at PMQs, GB did well, IDS was crap. The immediate business reaction wasn't great. The PLP was fine. A lot of the vox pops of families were positive, though there was quite a lot of 'broken promises' re tax. I did a ring-round and certainly they saw it as pretty epoch-making that we were openly going for a tax rise as the top line. We had a strategy meeting, TB plus the internal team. He agreed finally to appear at select committees and agreed also that we should move to cut down on briefings. I was arguing for a real shake-up in the way we communicated. Peter M felt we needed to change things gradually, both in terms of policy substance and presentation, a lot of it just do unannounced and build towards people realising that there was such a thing as New New Labour developing.

Thursday, April 18

Press as expected. The *Mail* a total parody. The *Sun* grim, *Guardian* OK, *Mirror* not great. GB came over at 9.15 to leave for a visit with TB, complaining that there was not enough reform in Milburn's follow-through statement. TB said that the thing to watch was people thinking this is a return to Old Labour. GB up in arms. 'God almighty, you can't say we didn't deliver on the message yesterday.' 'No, but . . . ?' The line was running a bit that it was an own goal because as the NHS was such a huge employer, the NICs [National Insurance contributions] rise would have a disproportionate impact there. The press were pretty determined to make the general Budget story a problem for us, but the Tories were hopeless. TB told Cabinet that as he saw it, the two big areas for us in the next phase were health and dealing with antisocial behaviour. Reform was every bit as important as money. He said if we can't feel confident about these arguments, we don't deserve to be in business.

As GB arrived, TB said it was a brilliant Budget, brilliantly delivered and these arguments would dominate politics for some time. DB said we again had the opportunity to emphasise values, our belief in mutuality, the belief that we have obligations to others. TB felt the media could have been worse and on the TB/GB stuff, building up GB at his expense, he said to us it didn't matter, they are going to do that. He felt the public took the view that GB was good at what he

April '02: . . . and congratulates GB on Budget

did but they also wanted me here checking him. He also felt it was good to have a range of big figures around the place.

Sally [Morgan] and I went to see TB to say we were worried, that he looked ill, wan and grey. He said he was tired, feeling stressed and more than usually discombobulated re GB. I was working on a letter to the PCC, Clare Sumner having worked out what happened. It was clear that in her dealings with Black Rod[1] [Lieutenant General Sir Michael Willcocks] she had set out what she thought the guidance for the PM and the government was, and Black Rod had taken that as us complaining about it, which was then passed on in distorted form. Black Rod was clearly tricky. Both Clare and Simon Virley were adamant they had done nothing more than get clarification on what TB was meant to do.[2]

Friday, April 19

Business was attacking the Budget a lot now, and when TB did a round of TV interviews there was a lot of stuff about trust, whether we should have been more up front at the election that we would need to raise taxes. The *Mirror* led on Sven's [Göran Eriksson] affair with Ulrika [Jonsson], which was truly gobsmacking for all sorts of reasons. I told a few people in the office that I had introduced them [see December 8, 2001] and not long after Tom Baldwin [*Times*] called to ask if it was true. I had told only a handful of people so it was extraordinary that he knew. I stalled and spoke to Melanie Cantor [Ulrika's agent] who confirmed that the [Richard] Desmond party was the first time they met, when I had been talking to Ulrika. She said it was amazing but true. The *News of the World* was going to do something and the *Mirror* was basically a spoiler, her role having been essentially just not denying it. She said she had been amazed when Sven called her for Ulrika's number. The dreadful thing was that the FA was pressing him to put out a statement, but it seemed Nancy [Dell'Olio, Eriksson's partner] hadn't known. I just could not fathom who would have told Baldwin. I tried really hard to work out who told him, but he was giving away nothing. The only

[1] The Gentleman Usher of the Black Rod, the sovereign's parliamentary attendant, sergeant-at-arms and Keeper of the Doors in the House of Lords.

[2] The *Spectator* having claimed that Blair had tried to 'muscle in' on plans for the Queen Mother's lying-in-state, the *Mail on Sunday* asserted that a Downing Street aide had telephoned Black Rod to ask if the Prime Minister would be able to greet the Queen and the coffin as it arrived at Westminster Hall. Downing Street confirmed the call, but maintained it was only to clarify the Prime Minister's role. A complaint to the Press Complaints Commission resulted in the regulator finding there was no evidence that the Prime Minister had done anything wrong, but Number 10 dropped the case.

person I had phoned on seeing the *Mirror* was Fiona, so it must have been one of the handful of people in the office.

I spent part of the day finishing the letter to the PCC. I had sensed from the earlier conversations with Clare that maybe Black Rod was playing games here. She called him again and had the exact same feeling. He told Clare he felt we were just keeping it going, that it was a mistake, and he clearly didn't want it to go to the PCC. As far as TB was concerned, even if someone had said it, it was one hundred per cent wrong and if the PCC couldn't deal with something like this, what on earth was it for? I also had another chat with TB re Gordon. He felt there was a real problem of temperament. He felt it may just be the case that he's a great Chancellor but that doesn't necessarily mean he could do the job of prime minister.

TB had clearly taken to heart our strictures about him needing to do more spontaneous stuff with people. I was talking to Jonathan in the private office. The door opens, TB comes out and says 'Hey, this guy doing the marathon in a diving suit, he's about to finish.[1] Shouldn't I go there, or get him in for a cup of tea or something?' Peter Hyman fell about at this sudden conversion.

Saturday, April 20

The Times page 1 and the *Mirror* splash were on me supposedly playing cupid between Sven and Ulrika. Talk about being in a fucking soap. I spent the morning working on a note for TB who was doing *Frost* tomorrow, on the need to get back into big message and the big promises kept, notably stability, jobs, constitutional programme, the specific tax pledges. I wrote it in the car on the way to Stamford Bridge [Chelsea football ground]. Philip had spooked me a bit, saying that after the Budget GB had definitely moved up a few notches at TB's expense, and we had to get the focus back on TB being the guy leading the big driving agenda. We met Alex before the Chelsea–Man U match [0–3], he and just about everyone passing by mercilessly taking the piss re Sven and Ulrika. Thank God he got us tickets with the fans because then I discovered Sven and Ulrika were both there, separately.

Sunday, April 21

The *Mail on Sunday* ran something about GB being against a full-scale war in Iraq, followed up by the *Mirror* despite GB office denials. [Sir

1 Lloyd Scott completed the London Marathon route in five days and eight hours, wearing a deep sea diving suit weighing 110 lb. He and Blair would appear on *Breakfast with Frost* on April 21, though not together.

David] Frost wasn't on form, TB didn't really get going but it was OK as a post-Budget message interview.

Sven was massive in the tabloids but thankfully I was fading out of the story. Sunday's coverage on the Budget wasn't as bad as I thought it might be, though there was a bit too much 'GB the Colossus'. Calum and I set off for Burnley vs Coventry [1–0], on the phone most of the time.

As we drove home, Jonathan called. John Holmes [UK ambassador to France, former foreign policy adviser to Blair] had been on, saying it was [Jean-Marie] Le Pen [National Front candidate] second and [Lionel] Jospin third in the French elections [determining a run-off election between Le Pen and Chirac]. Political earthquake time. I chatted to John Holmes about how we should react and then briefed Jon Sopel [BBC] who was covering it, to make sure he got over the message that it was unlikely for the hard right to rise like this here because we did take crime and other issues on the respect agenda seriously. TB felt we should stay out of it as far as possible but there were definitely going to be spillover problems from this.

Monday, April 22

TB's interview came out OK but Le Pen was dominant. TB's worry was that it gave the BNP [far right British National Party] a boost by allowing them to be seen as the British equivalent of Le Pen. Sven/Ulrika was still massive and Sven did a press conference, pretty Zen-like, refusing to say much, did OK, but I guess it all depended what was happening behind closed doors both with him and Nancy, and him and the FA. Melanie told me it was real love as far as Ulrika was concerned. The PCC situation was dragging on. Jeremy sent my letter to Janvrin who was happy to say that the *Mail on Sunday* story as it referred to the Queen was rubbish. TB was due to do an interview with the *Guardian* tomorrow, focused on more personal stuff. He showed we were still able to have a laugh. As when he said he thought he'd say that the people he really related to now after a few years in the job were the Royal Family, that Prince Charles was really his kind of guy, and that both of them were much misunderstood and took great solace from each other. 'Think that should satisfy the *Guardian*, now what's next?'

Tuesday, April 23

Some of the right wing were trying to present the Le Pen outcome as a sign of the left across Europe under attack. But there was a general understanding that New Labour was different and that we had taken the right course on crime and immigration. With so much focus on Europe now, because of the French elections, there was also an opportunity in the fact that e.g. the Dutch and the Germans were desperate for a TB-type figure. I finished the PCC draft that Clare [Sumner] took to see Black Rod at 2. She came back and said he had said to her that there had been other calls, suggested there was something to it and he had had no problems with the *Mail on Sunday* story where it referred to him. We were clear that the only calls had been from Clare and Simon and that Jeremy had dealt with Janvrin. Godric was asked about it at the four o'clock so having got the draft statement to Guy Black (who by 4 knew that Black Rod had seen Number 10), put out a line that we were lodging the complaint. There was a line developing that this was the Establishment against us. Yet we had cleared the whole thing with the Palace.

The morning meeting was mainly a discussion of the BNP. I spoke to Charles Clarke who was visiting Burnley and felt they might win one seat on the council and wanted TB to stick to his Blackburn programme. The PCC story took off on the *Ten O'Clock News*. TB watched it, for once, and said we seemed to have lit the blue touch-paper and we had better win this. He still thought it was the right thing to do, but thought Black Rod was going to be a real problem. [Peter] Oborne was moving the goalposts to this being about us and the press rather than the facts of what happened. I had a meeting on Iraq with John Scarlett, Tom McKane [Cabinet Office] and Martin Howard [MoD] to go through what we needed to do communications-wise to set the scene for Iraq, e.g. a WMD paper and other papers about Saddam. Scarlett a very good bloke.

Wednesday, April 24

The PCC stuff was running straight. Guy Black called to say he thought my statement was masterful, that he felt we had a strong case anyway but it was even stronger when it was laid out like that. I met with Jeremy, Jonathan and Martin Hurst [Number 10 adviser on agriculture] re the FMD [Foot and Mouth Disease: Lessons Learned] inquiry to get me ready for when I gave evidence. Re PMQs, I was worried about people going for us on David Blunkett talking about schools being swamped with asylum seekers' children at schools near reception centres. I thought it was a stupid thing to say and called to say we needed to let the heat out of this, but David was very high horse, said he was not going to apologise and he believed in calling a spade a spade. PMQs went fine, TB setting a new cat among pigeons saying that we would get on top of street crime by September.

Guy Black called again to say he had advised Black Rod not to talk to the press now that it was all under investigation. Back for a meeting, me, Peter M, Philip G and Peter H re TB. Peter M thought our problems were 1. sleaze, so-called; 2. the charge he was hollow; 3. the feeling that he wasn't in charge. I said we had to get back to TB being seen as strong, on people's side, in charge, delivering, the same TB that they elected. PG felt we had to decide what we would do, almost as if it was a leadership election, what were the things we would emphasise, experience, tested in a crisis, rounded, gets people's lives, capable of leading a team. GB had his issues and never tired of hounding them. TB had become too managerial again.

Thursday, April 25

There was quite a good discussion at Cabinet on the Le Pen situation. Robin [Cook] said there had been a genuine miscalculation re the two rounds of voting. Jack said Jospin had fought a terrible campaign. What it showed was that post the collapse of the Berlin Wall, asylum and immigration were big problems for a lot of countries, and governments would get judged on how they handled them. He said there was a lot of racism in France and there was a problem with Muslim youth feeling disconnected. Then, in a very Jackish kind of way, he referred to an article he had written for *The Times* in 1985 in which he said PR [proportional representation] would lead to the rise of Le Pen. John Reid, warming to the anti-PR mood, pointed out that Hitler was elected by PR. TB summed up, saying asylum was a problem to be dealt with, not exploited. People want to know there is a fair system, rules with integrity. He said up to now, EU colleagues had been reluctant on this and we had been something of a lone voice but now they would realise more. GB was at UNISON, and it was noticeable how much lighter the mood was.

To Windsor for the Queen's Golden Jubilee media reception. It was a beautiful evening, about 700 journalists there. Oborne and [Simon] Walters [*Mail on Sunday*] both tried to engage me in conversation but I pushed them off. The general feeling among most of the hacks was that we shouldn't have gone to the PCC but that's because they were self-serving. I had a chat with Janvrin who said he really hoped Black Rod would deliver for us, but he didn't think we should put our house on him. The event was a huge success for the Queen. There was something truly pathetic about these so-called hardened hacks, many of them self-proclaimed republicans, bowing and scraping the whole time. She moved effortlessly between them and left grown men in little puddles of excitement as she moved on to form the next one.

She was such an old pro but there was something mildly sick-making about the way they fell about in front of her.

Friday, April 26

TB did the PEB [party election broadcast] last night in the margins of a visit to Dudley, and today was off to Blackburn [local elections to be held on May 2], allowing me to complain all day that he had never ever been to Burnley. Jack was in his usual Blackburn–Burnley wind-up mode, and sent me a message that the road into Burnley had been blocked by a broken-down banana lorry taking in the food for the natives. The visit went OK without too much focus on the BNP. TB was back mid pm, had enjoyed getting out, and felt the mood out there was better than we thought. Boris Johnson wrote to say would I do a letter next week setting out our position re the lying-in-state, which suggested they were looking for a way out.

Saturday, April 27

Someone had briefed, or possibly the Sundays just picked it up from Mary Ann Sieghart's column in *The Times*, the possibility of child benefit withdrawal from parents with persistent truants who veer towards crime. The problem was that whoever was briefing was doing so by saying it was TB against GB and others. Amazingly, TB had been asked about it when filming for the PEB in Dudley on Thursday, but there was no way it could have been briefed out of that. It was possibly a sensible idea to look at, though at first blush I didn't think so, but in any event there was no point getting it out in a time or in a manner that would send the party neuralgic. Once the papers came in and we basically said it was being looked at, we were facing an ill-discipline problem – ill discipline of those who briefed it with a particular slant, then the ill discipline of not standing up for it properly so that in the end it looked like a gimmick.

Sunday, April 28

JP was doing interviews and I briefed him to hold firm on the child benefit issue, but he was clearly uncomfortable and didn't. GB called TB and complained both about the policy but also, and this made me suspicious, said that it was being deliberately fuelled to do him in, totally overlooking the fact that it had been pitched as a hit on TB. Jeremy, listening in, said it was a truly dreadful call. Even when TB said he wasn't prepared to put up with this any longer, GB was unmoved, kept at him. TB was also struck by something Charlie Falconer had said, namely that Balls had briefed DTLR officials to bid over the odds on housing because 'Number 10 are not interested in housing'. It was beginning to feel a bit too warlike. During the day I briefed variously TB, JP and Estelle [Morris] who would all be expected in their various media appearances to say something on the child benefit row. Estelle was fine, JP wasn't. TB was angry and frustrated, said it only became a problem when we sounded like we were in retreat. GB was currently working on Cabinet, party, press, the voluntary sector, the lot, just getting himself in a slightly different position.

Monday, April 29

Child benefit story was still raging on, with lots of split-ery around the place. The take generally was that the Cabinet was against it. TB was a bit head-in-hands mode. We put it round that the story was clearly put there by someone who wanted to kill the policy, which was probably true. I suspected GB's people were responsible for the *FT* story saying that [Rupert] Murdoch would be shafted by the media ownership bill. So I called Les Hinton simply to say don't believe everything you read in the papers.

TB's big concern re the GB situation was the feeling that ministers were unsure what their instincts were meant to be, because though we were the present, they realised GB was the future. TB needed to be clear that they were answerable to him. I said there was a case for sacking one or two Brownite ministers like Nick Brown [minister for work], tell them it was unfair but it was needed to shake things up a bit. He was more up for it than I thought he would be. I told the morning meeting that the real story here was not [child benefit] policy but ill discipline. TB intended to go up and defend it big time on his local election visit, which is exactly what he did.

I had a few meetings then up to 9 Whitehall to give evidence to the FMD inquiry. Quite tough, and maybe I didn't prepare enough for it. I gave them a paper on the media and how hard it had been to put over what we were trying to do. He [Dr Iain Anderson, chairman] clearly felt that we had ballsed the first stages and never really got over it. He suggested that maybe in future we should bring journalists in as part of our team, which was an interesting idea.

Back to get changed for the Number 10 dinner for the Queen, which was being attended by all her PMs or, in the case of those who'd died, by family reps. Terry O'Neill [photographer] in to do pictures. Ted Heath [former Conservative Prime Minister] complaining about the seating plan. A bit of a problem re Stockton [the 2nd Earl Stockton, former Conservative Prime Minister Harold Macmillan's grandson] taking the place of Macmillan's daughter [Lady Caroline Faber]. But it went well enough, nice pictures of her with all her surviving prime ministers which we got out by 8.45. TB's kids were downstairs to meet her when she arrived then up for drinks. The Queen said 'Isn't it wonderful not to have to be introduced to anyone?' [John] Major and I had a very civilised conversation, re Chelsea, cricket, small talk. But there was always a tension there and Norma [Major] was very distant. Thatcher was complaining loudly about the decor and the paintings, how some of the carpets and furnishings looked worn, and the colours in the Green Room weren't properly co-ordinated, tut-tutting, not exactly saying 'wouldn't have happened in my day' but not far off it.

The Queen, the PMs and their descendants went into the State Dining Room whilst Robin Janvrin, Jeremy, Fiona and I had a very nice dinner in the White Room. Robin was a thoroughly decent bloke. There was another drinks do at the end and I had a long chat with Mary Wilson and Robin [widow and son of Harold Wilson]. At one point Ted [Heath] was sitting on one sofa, Jim [Callaghan] on another, just having an old man to old man conversation about how things used to be. Ted could barely bring himself to look at Thatcher but she teased him a bit, tried to make him laugh, without any apparent success. Prince Philip was deep in conversation with TB, the Countess of Avon [widow of former Conservative Prime Minister Anthony Eden], Macmillan's and [former Conservative Prime Minister Alec] Douglas-Home's families, and there was lots of reminiscing about life in Number 10. It was interesting to see the difference between the Queen's demeanour at the do at Windsor, when she had been doing her professional small-talk thing, and here, where she seemed genuinely happy.

I said to Fiona that nobody else had really had the kind of access and contact that she had had and yet while everybody thought they knew what she thought of them, nobody could be sure. But I don't think I've ever seen her smiling so much. TB occupied pretty much a back seat, wanted the others to be talking to her and enjoying it. I also knew he was worrying about the question he had asked earlier, whether he had already ceded too much power to GB, and whether it was too late to get it back.

Tuesday, April 30

The *Mirror* splashed on a poll, figures bent and twisted against TB. He was almost minded to scrap the interview with them but we went ahead and it was OK, Brian Reade [columnist] basically onside but there was little point dealing with Piers at the moment. I called Byers who said there was an agreed statement going out today effectively exonerating Sixsmith. He had delegated to mediators and the lawyers had totally caved in. We got RW to stop it going out today because it would look like we were burying it under the Queen's address to both Houses of Parliament. I couldn't believe this was still dragging on.

We had a long-term diary meeting based on the plan Peter H, Philip and I had put together. They all basically disagreed with it and it turned ugly and I said I was fed up with being surrounded by commentators who were great at criticising other ideas but didn't deliver their own. Then to a meeting with GB and the Eds [Balls and Miliband], which was better than usual because TB was much firmer. There was a big disagreement though, TB and I strongly believing we had not only to deal with crime and antisocial behaviour, but be seen to deal with it because in part the signals you sent out were important actually to dealing with it. Their basic take was that to talk about crime was to alarm the public that it wasn't being dealt with. Ed Balls felt we had lost the 'causes of crime' part of the argument. TB said that we always had to do both. GB thought the Tory strategy was to say they were moving to the centre now but they would become more right wing later. TB not sure, though at least on that there was a civilised and sensible discussion.

Sixsmith was clearly threatening to go to the press if things were held up any longer. TB kept going on about how incompetently it all had been handled. Godric was more wound up than ever. I told Richard W we were fed up having to cover up the incompetence of people who should have sorted this out. He looked really hurt, said the senior Civil Service really tried to work with us. I said a lot of them used the SpAd issue to hide behind. He got really angry at that, said that he was happy to resign if we thought it would make it better. I said nobody was talking about that, or even thinking about it. I calmed down a bit, said I was sorry that he and I had ended up shouting at each other. The truth was with the combination of the *Mirror*, the whingeing at the diary meeting, still having to deal with Byers and the ludicrous discussion with GB about crime, I had just about had enough.

Wednesday, May 1

I was in a foul mood with everyone. The *Mirror* interview was fine but there was a big factual error about TB's kids which we got a correction for. I spent most of the day locked away, and most people knew to avoid me. Yesterday's diary meeting sparked a flurry of emails, Sally M and Robert [Hill] in particular feeling I had just dumped a long-term plan on them without consultation and was trying to bounce them. It was more that I was just trying to get some proper direction and movement and was fed up of the endless circular conversations without agreement. Creativity was dead, had been for some time, and there had to be change.

Thursday, May 2

Up to see TB. He said the row he had had with GB at the weekend was as bad as it got. He was effectively fighting a campaign of attrition, wants me out and thinks he has to wear me out to get me out. In the end 'I'm quite stubborn.' He said he had called back to apologise and GB had been nicer since. I said that's how he works. It's the banging-head-against-wall theory. He forces you to lose your rag, you feel bad, he feels a bit more empowered. Interestingly, though, the undertone for a lot of the five-year coverage was that GB might not be rounded enough for the top job. Things would be so much better if they could work together. GB had been a bit better but when I bumped into him this morning getting a coffee pre Cabinet it was the usual total non-communicado.

Cabinet was mainly Middle East and Afghanistan. Charles C was looking for reassurance on his recent whacks on the media. I advised he keep going, but get himself some cover by making clear there was a lot of good amid the bad, and engage other ministers on it too. Then we got ourselves into a bit of a mess re changes to the lobby. I had floated the idea at the meeting with the BBC and then Tom Baldwin called to tell Godric that Simon Walters was planning to present it as a great attack on the media, so I decided to go upfront on it now. I called James Hardy [*Mirror* political editor], the chairman of the lobby, and suggested he get together a group of people to do a meeting with me, Godric and Tom [Kelly]. I told them we were going to change things. TB would be doing more in Parliament. He and other ministers would be doing far more press conferences and on days they did, we would cut down on lobby briefings. We also intended to open the briefings to others, including more foreign media. They were suspicious but some, like Patrick Wintour [*Guardian*] and to a lesser extent Trevor Kavanagh [*Sun* political editor], seemed OK on it.

Meanwhile Andy Marr [BBC] had been on broadcasting that we were scrapping the lobby which put them all into a total tizz, and they were disappearing into real media wank. They couldn't quite work it out. The meeting went on for about an hour, some genuine concerns, which we could work out, few real complaints but by and large I think it was OK. I called JP to talk it through, he having earlier complained to me that we didn't seem to be in touch as often as we used to be, when changes were happening. TB called later from Ireland and asked if I had sparked a meltdown. I left early for Calum's parents evening. Tom and Godric were having to deal with the immediate fallout and Godric was a bit stressed out that the briefings would if anything become even tougher in the short term. Our aim had to be to make the briefings themselves less newsworthy and also extend the range of people there. Ludicrously, it was the second item on the *Ten O'Clock News*.

The local election results started coming in and it was clear we were not going to do as badly as some of the predictions.[1] But the BNP won three seats in Burnley, including in a beautiful leafy village, so that was going to take a lot of the attention, and was pretty grim. Most people seemed to think though that the big picture was us OK, Lib Dems OK, Tories pretty poor, plus embarrassment over elected mayors re the monkey in Hartlepool and Robocop in Middlesbrough.[2] Good news in that turnout was better than expected where there was full postal voting.

Friday, May 3

RW came to see me, said was I sure I knew what I was taking on with the changes to the lobby? He said lots of people had tried this. The scale of the coverage on it was ludicrous, a further sign of their self-obsession and their obsession with me, which in part was what we were trying to address. Once we talked it through, he was pretty supportive, and said he would help to find premises so that we could do the bigger briefings with the foreign media included, and any other accredited journalists who wanted to turn up. JP called, said that he had premises in his office, in the room that used to be [former Conservative Prime Minster Winston] Churchill's cinema. The general feeling on the local elections was pretty good for us. TB was at Chequers, pretty chipper. We were under pressure on elected mayors, farce thereof, but TB was adamant we just hold firm.

[Bill] Clinton called me at 1am to go through some changes in the article he was doing for us re all the attacks on TB. He didn't want

[1] Labour: 2,402 council seats and control of sixty-three councils. Conservatives: 2,005 council seats and forty-two councils. Liberal Democrats: 1,263 council seats and fifteen councils.

[2] Stuart Drummond, who played the local football club's mascot monkey, was elected mayor of Hartlepool, while former 'zero tolerance' chief superintendent of Cleveland Police, Ray Mallon, won the mayoralty in Middlesbrough.

to attack the motives of our critics, just attack the attacks. It was a good piece though, and worth the effort. He was always good to talk to, because he had such a good feel for our politics, and for how best to position TB. He felt we were just going through one of those phases where people wanted to see us tested and pressured and coming through. TB must have said something, or his instincts told him something, about me going a bit offside, because he said that in these top jobs like president and prime minister, you really need people close by that you can trust and rely on one hundred per cent. He said it was important that I hung in and kept helping TB through.

Saturday, May 4

I chatted to a few columnists and the general take was that a combination of the local elections and people taking stock in a measured way five years on was pretty good for us, bad for the Tories. The conference call was mainly Middle East and the lead-up to the French election second round. Papers arrived.

Sunday, May 5

French elections were dominating the news and it was pretty clear as the results came through that Chirac had won. We put together a line fairly straightforwardly and got that out. I had a nice day out with the kids, tennis with Calum. Went to see *About a Boy* [film], lunch, then Rory won his race.

Monday, May 6

Bank Holiday. Pretty quiet until later with news of [right-wing Dutch politician] Pim Fortuyn's assassination [in Hilversum, Netherlands]. Conference call with TB, Jonathan, [Sir] Stephen Wall [EU adviser]. We agreed to cancel the planned visit tomorrow and put out a short statement. We were already getting a bit alarmed by all the focus post elections on the politics of the far right, and this wasn't going to help.

Tuesday, May 7

Up to see TB in the flat. He was clearly thinking about bringing back [Ken] Livingstone [into the Labour Party]. Also wanting to get back into the antisocial behaviour agenda. TB set off for Scotland for the Donald Dewar [former First Minister of Scotland] memorial event. The Sixsmith pay-off deal was an absolute outrage – big pay-off, Byers in deep shit. I did an interview with [Tom] Baldwin for *The Times* re our relations with the press.

Wednesday, May 8

Massive suicide bomb in Israel. TB said the problem now was that Israelis were stating as a fact that [Yasser] Arafat was behind the latest bombings and even though there was no direct evidence it was very difficult to counter and it would push the US into a much harder-line position. We spent some time working on the right response. TB wanted to keep the balance but felt that basically we had to tilt towards pro-Palestinian. He was really worried about the impact in the States – another bomb, another massacre, [Ariel] Sharon back from the US successfully able to make it look like it was impossible to negotiate with Arafat.

Thursday, May 9

The *Times* interview went quite big and got too much pick-up in later editions and on the broadcasts. I was a bit concerned about the stuff at the end re not being sure about staying. TB called me at 7.10. Said he felt that Byers was pretty shot. He said he was going to give him a chance to step down of his own volition before a reshuffle which he planned for the next few weeks but wanted total radio silence for now. He felt it was monstrous the way Steve had been treated internally but ultimately ministers have to be responsible for their own departments, and he would have to go fairly soon. TB said GB had asked him if it was true that I was going to leave and TB had said no. I said his boorishness yesterday, not just with me but with Vera [Doyle, Number 10 messenger] when she was trying to pour him coffee, was Olympian.

TB took a strategy meeting with the internal team to go through the big strategic overview paper I'd done. It had caused a lot of anger, people feeling I'd bounced it on them, but Peter M was totally supportive, which was important, and would help with TB. TB's meeting with JP didn't get off to a great start. As we walked in, TB didn't realise JP was right behind us as he said to me 'What on earth are we going to talk about in here?' JP was pressing him on the need for greater involvement of Cabinet committees. Cabinet was largely a row about select committees, and Clare going on about every issue she could think of. Later meeting of [departmental] heads of information to go over the lobby changes, which was more productive than usual. TB off on a visit to South London and back for a visit to Number 10 by Sven, [David] Beckham, Gareth Southgate, David Seaman [England footballers] and the suits from the FA plus some kids from Southwark. Big media turnout in the street with kids having a great time though CB was monopolising Beckham, or possibly vice versa.

Friday, May 10

TB at Chequers working through a stack of boxes. Called a couple of times to discuss German TV and *Newsnight* [BBC] interviews planned for next week. I was putting together a series of briefs re *Newsnight* when news came in of a bad train crash at Potters Bar. The early indication was that it was a points failure, seven dead. TB wanted us to rebut some of the coverage of last night's David Beckham event, and in particular the widespread regurgitation of the story of him claiming to have seen [former Newcastle United footballer] Jackie Milburn, which was one of those annoying urban myths.

Saturday, May 11

We were dealing with the train crash aftermath, then up pops another sleaze situation. This time re [Richard] Desmond offering free ads, which we then said should be a financial donation which we could use to buy the ads. The claim was that this was all agreed at a meeting of me, TB, Margaret McDonagh [former Labour general secretary] and Desmond. One thing we knew for sure was that no such meeting ever took place. But it was the usual Saturday problem of getting all the facts together. The direct allegation seemed to be that the donation was made as some kind of thank you for nodding through the *Express* takeover. In fact, there was no need for ministerial reference because the OFT [Office of Fair Trading] would do it and he had no other newspaper interests so reference up didn't apply. But it was one of those stories that whatever the facts would be made to look bad. I spoke to Desmond who confirmed he had never discussed funding with TB.

The Express group put out a statement confirming a donation but it fell in the period before the Electoral Commission rules on disclosure came in. The *Mail*, *Observer*, *Sunday Times* all going big, so needless to say the BBC followed it up big. We got John Reid straight on to Radio 5 as the papers dropped and he was excellent. Another Saturday taken up dealing with nonsense. These funding stories were actually born of the fact we were more open, but got no credit for it at all. This one was not a scandal at all but they could make anything look like a scandal. I was really impressed with Reid today. He could assimilate facts quickly, get the point quickly, and express it on the media having thought it through rather than simply parroting a line.

Sunday, May 12

The fightback re [Richard] Desmond had gone OK. We had successfully shut down the allegations re a meeting. So it was basically a

May '02: Potters Bar train crash kills seven

question of whether we should take money from someone who made money from pornography and the Beeb found a few MPs, after a lot of trying, to say no it wasn't. Gerald Kaufman called to say he had been asked for his view and as soon as he made clear he didn't intend to be critical, they made clear they didn't want him on. I called Desmond from Northolt. 'I wouldn't have your job for all the money in the world,' he said. I was a bit pissed off that so much of this was again focusing on me, because I was a so-called 'friend' of Desmond's when all I had done was go to his birthday party because TB couldn't. The *Mail* of course had two interests here, do us in and do him in.

On the flight to Germany, we went over the interview TB was to do with Sabine Christiansen [German television talk-show host], which Schroeder had asked him to do, but which had the feel of something a bit eccentric. On arrival, we went to meet Schroeder. He looked tired, said that he was doing OK but his party was not and it was tough to change it. He and TB went out for a quick chat on the balcony and then back in for the broader meeting – Europe, world economy, Afghanistan, Middle East, on which Schroeder said 'You know more than I do,' and TB said 'What I know is that it's bad.' He said he was trying to persuade the US to keep on engaging. They both agreed nothing could happen without the Americans, but their opinion was in a very different position to ours. Democrats as well as Republicans are lined up behind [Ariel] Sharon so Bush was in quite a difficult position. Schroeder said the Jewish people in Germany tended to present any criticism of Israel as anti-Semitism, which was a dangerous route. He said they were fairly lucky in avoiding a big debate about right-wing extremism in their election, 'which given our history is a good thing'.

We had a long and pretty tedious session with bureau chiefs and then the Christiansen show. The German translation was played over speakers above the audience's heads as TB spoke so it became quite hard for him, but he did pretty well. We flew back late in one of the smaller RAF planes, wondering whether the visit had been worth the effort. What was absolutely clear was that the Europeans saw TB as the number one star of European politics at the moment.

Monday, May 13

Spoke to [Richard] Desmond again. He said he had paid 'only' £75k for the Beckham party [publishing rights]. Some of our MPs were going on about him not being a fit person. Godric was feeling pretty jaded at the moment as well and was needing more than usual support. I decided we should not do a four o'clock, which produced the expected tantrums. Fuck 'em. Desmond still running as a big negative for us.

Tuesday, May 14

Sally M sent a note to TB of a conversation with Frank Dobson, who was seriously offside. He said our current difficulties were being made worse because 'TB and AC have lost the plot'. The main news running today was the three new asylum centres, with lots of attendant nimbyism ['not-in-my-backyard']. Media-wise, our main focus was the extended *Newsnight* interview which he had agreed to do as part of our strategy of doing more sustained and serious interviews, which *Newsnight* have agreed to run over three nights. TB looked pretty knackered first thing, then had [Thabo] Mbeki at 7.30, [Jean] Chrétien [Canadian Prime Minister] at 8.30, before we got down to briefing for the interview. He was sure [Jeremy] Paxman [interviewer] would want to do lots on [Richard] Desmond, but they pretty much stuck to the deal – three sections, public services, foreign policy, society and belief. Paxman was tough but fair and TB held his own. As an exercise, it definitely worked. TB said he thought it was odd that Paxman was always lumped in with [John] Humphrys [BBC *Today* programme presenter]. He thought the big difference was that Paxman was actually interested in the answers.

Wednesday, May 15

The general view of *Newsnight* was that it was a strong interview. Good coverage. We thought the Tories might come on [Richard] Desmond at PMQs, but IDS did NHS and crime and TB was able to hit him hard on investment. TB was OK, though he didn't think it was one of his best. Also, Robin [Cook] seemed to be asleep on the front bench. I had a meeting with the whips and went through the lobby changes, the determination to do more in Parliament and the need for them to be fully engaged in what we were doing re message and strategic communications. Charles C was also focused on the need to work up a 'new politics plan' basically an end to top-down command and control message work, more about how we develop MPs as local ambassadors, and how we make a link between politics and liveability issues. Charles was really enthusiastic, really wanted to motor. I was in favour but worried that a lot of the MPs wouldn't be as enthusiastic as he was.

Thursday, May 16

Newsnight getting lots of coverage, euro the lead in several papers, big coverage in the Middle East for what he said about that. There was a bit of a flurry when the BBC put out the transcript of the stuff being broadcast tonight which seemed to show he was saying he would stay for a full third term, which he actually hadn't meant that way. Cabinet, without JP, and also without Clare, which in her case made a big difference for the better. Nepal, Dutch elections, rail, bits and bobs. The *New Statesman* had a line claiming Charles C and David Triesman wanted an inquiry into the Desmond donation.

Guy Black called through the morning and said there was a snag. He came to see me at 1.30. He had been to see Black Rod and asked him for a draft of what he would say. He said he would prefer it if nobody knew that he had been to see me, and he showed me the draft statement. It was dreadful. It backed the *Mail on Sunday* story. Guy said 'We have to stop that letter going to the PCC.' I think Guy was trying to be helpful. I said all I wanted was acknowledgement that TB had done nothing wrong or disrespectful. Then came news Byers had done a lunch with the women's lobby [of parliamentary journalists] and talked about a paving bill [allowing for further reforms in the next parliament] on the euro being planned and saying fifty-one per cent was enough in a referendum. He was wrong on the paving bill and I'm afraid we had to say he was plain wrong. What a prattish thing to do, as if he didn't have enough problems. Phil Webster [*Times*] called to say the Tories were putting it around that Byers was about to be sacked, so we had to deal with that, say it wasn't the case.

Friday, May 17

Up very early, in to meet Robert Thomson [*Times* editor] and Bronwen Maddox [*Times* foreign editor] who were coming to Spain with us to do a TB interview. Re Byers, in the car out to the plane, TB said Steve was becoming accident-prone and would probably have to go. I said what about splitting the department, as we had discussed before, and leaving him with one part of it. TB shook his head. The *Newsnight* interview was still producing positive coverage elsewhere, though the Beeb had 'accidentally' sent the full tape to the *Telegraph*, including at the start where I interrupted TB and got them to refilm which unleashed the latest storm of bollocks. It was interesting spending the day with Robert Thomson, who was not really immersed in the UK media culture. The interview was serious and fair, whereas most interviews these days are purely designed to get a story. He struck me as being a quirky but decent character. We were in Spain purely as a favour to Aznar who had really wanted TB to go to the EU–Latin America summit. While he went off to that, I went with Robert and Bronwen to a cafe in Madrid. I don't think he was clear yet what he

(*Right*) The moment that changed the world: the al-Qaeda attack on the Twin Towers.

(*Above*) George Bush is told the news by his chief of staff Andy Card whilst listening to schoolchildren reading; (*above, right*) Tony Blair is about to tell the TUC that he must return to London; and (*right*) Bush speaks to Blair by phone the following day as Condoleezza Rice stares out through the Oval Office window.

(*Right*) Bush waves the Stars and Stripes and shows solidarity with rescue workers at Ground Zero.

The Blairs in the US:
(*left*) Tony Blair, Laura Bush and New York Mayor Rudolph Giuliani applaud President Bush's speech to Congress; Cherie (*below, left*) looks at the helmets representing some of the firemen who lost their lives; and (*below*) Tony and Cherie Blair, Kofi Annan, Hillary and Bill Clinton join in singing a hymn at a memorial service in New York.

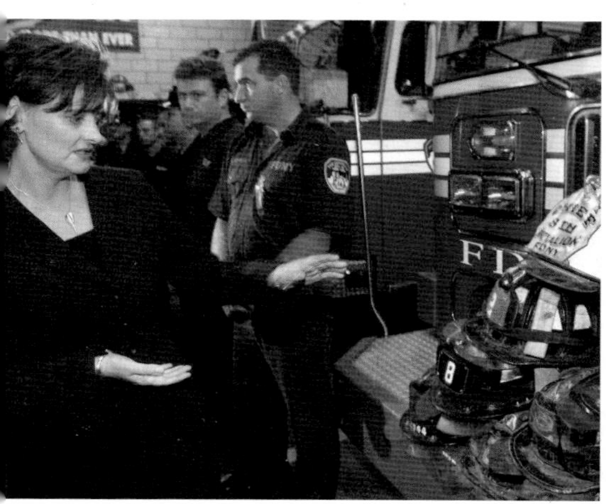

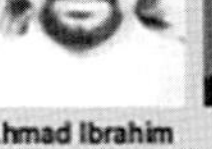

(*Right*) Osama Bin Laden is one of the FBI's twenty-two 'most wanted' members of al-Qaeda; (*below, left*) Saddam Hussein, President of Iraq; (*below, right*) a headline greeting Bush's labelling of Iraq, Iran and North Korea as 'the axis of evil'.

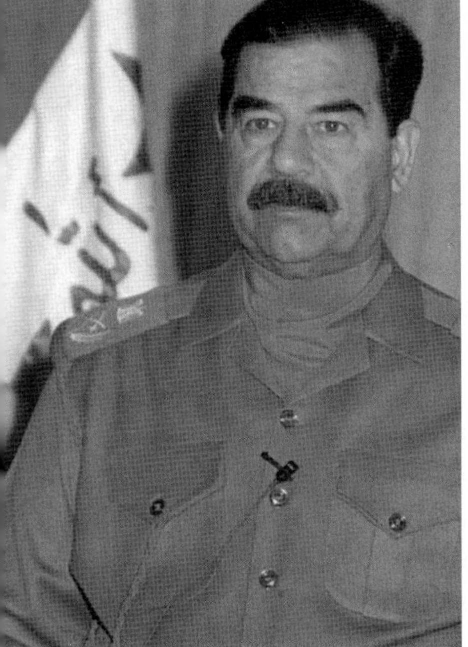

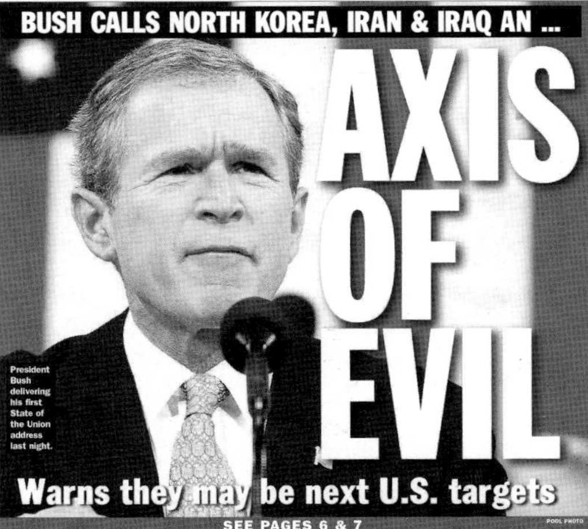

GHOULS' GOLD

Families outraged as WTC steel sold as souvenirs

EXCLUSIVE – PAGE 3

NOELLE BUSH

Jeb Bush's daughter busted

STORY PAGE 5

SPORTS ★ ★ ★ ★ FINAL

DAILY NEWS

www.nydailynews.com NEW YORK'S HOMETOWN NEWSPAPER Wednesday, January 30, 2002

BUSH CALLS NORTH KOREA, IRAN & IRAQ AN ...

AXIS OF EVIL

President Bush delivering his first State of the Union address last night.

Warns they may be next U.S. targets

SEE PAGES 6 & 7

POOL PHOTO

TB and his two GBs: (*right*) together in Washington on the day Bush hailed Blair 'a true friend'; (*below*) a cartoonist's take on Gordon Brown's troubled relationship with Blair, which at times (*bottom*) could not be hidden from the cameras.

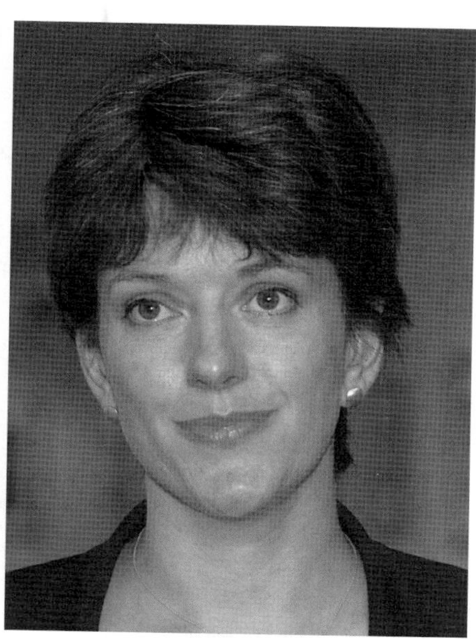

(*Above, left*) Transport secretary Stephen Byers and (*right*) his political adviser Jo Moore, whose political career came to be defined by one email about 'burying bad news'.

(*Below*) The Queen with five of her prime ministers: Tony Blair, Margaret Thatcher, Ted Heath, Jim Callaghan and John Major.

(*Above*) US actor Kevin Spacey adds a bit of showbiz sparkle to Labour's 2002 conference, here with Tony and Cherie Blair and Bill Clinton. (*Below*) The former US president and his actor friend later enjoyed a night out in Blackpool's McDonald's. (*Right*) Tony Blair with weapons inspector Hans Blix.

(*Left*) Carole Caplin and Peter Foster, the Australian fraudster who sparked a crisis over two flats bought by Cherie Blair, and strained relations further between the Blairs, AC and his partner Fiona Millar (*below*, with Cherie Blair).

(*Right*) Strategists together: Peter Mandelson, Philip Gould and Campbell at a meeting with the German ambassador.

Me and my shadow: (*above*) Campbell and Blair in a lift in Brussels, before a very difficult conversation over Iraq with Jacques Chirac (*left*). And another difficult conversation, th time with President Putin (*below*)

wanted to do for the paper, but he was definitely an interesting addition to the media scene.

Saturday, May 18

Very depressed. One of my major glooms. Went for a run but lost the will after half an hour and came back. Work-wise, trying to get Aznar meeting on Monday focused on asylum rather than Gibraltar [sovereignty]. I never felt less like working.

Sunday, May 19

The *Sunday Telegraph* splash said GB was supporting TB's push for an early [euro] referendum, which they went into overdrive to rubbish, prompting me to wonder if they had set the whole thing up. Some of the papers got hold of John Birt's [former BBC director general, now Blair's 'blue skies thinking' adviser] report suggesting massive new toll roads which ran. I took Rory to Basildon where he was racing and had a long run myself round the town centre and some of the estates. I went into a shop to buy some water and the guy behind the counter said he couldn't believe I was in there, at which point TB rang and I got him to speak to the shopkeeper, who practically fainted. I said you now have to promise me you'll vote Labour for the rest of your life. He said he would. Rory ran well, won the 800 metres, second in the 1,500. The news was dominated by Afghanistan and another suicide bomb in Israel. The Sundays had loads of *Newsnight* follow-through and though they were contaminated by the thing about me interrupting TB, the overall impression was good. JP called from China to agree a statement confirming he had diabetes, which the *Mail on Sunday* had run.

Monday, May 20

We were hoping to get the Aznar focus on asylum, along the lines of the letter Stephen Wall had done for TB on the need for the Seville summit to address the issues. But Gibraltar was running pretty hard. Charles C seemed very het up at the office meeting. He tended to go from being superconfident, quite strategic and clear one day, to being a bit hyper and all over the place the next. TB was emphasising that all that mattered was policy, making the right decisions for the longer term. Aznar arrived for lunch, first just re Gibraltar, which was really difficult and on which zero progress was made. Jack S had said on the radio that if the Gibraltarians rejected a deal that would be the end of it, which the Spaniards felt was a shift. They were very suspicious, a bit paranoid, and so didn't really accept the truth, which was that it was a bit of a cock-up. Aznar was fine at the lunch, said he was over for a speech at Oxford and said he intended to say that there should be a president of the European Council, elected by the members of the council, who should be a former PM. 'That's why I'm putting you forward,' he said to TB, who replied 'I'm putting you forward as well.' A short press conference, half Gibraltar, half asylum and off they went. Meeting with Mark Bennett [Labour press officer], trying to get him in for a while to help out.

Tuesday, May 21

The CBI speech was in OK shape but he wanted to do a lot of it from notes, so all I did was draft a few clips and put together a release based on extracts. The best line was probably the straight passionate defence of the Budget, especially as we heard Iain Vallance [CBI president] was intending to go for the Budget tax rises and say we were on a yellow card re the economy. Stupidly, despite having an enormous blister on my foot, I ran in and later in the day was unable to walk. IDS was making a speech on equality and opportunity and how he would stand up for the poor and vulnerable so I got Fraser Kemp [Labour MP] out motoring re his kids going to Eton.

I spoke to Guy Black and then sent over the latest letters on the case. Charlie Falconer's view was that if Black Rod was being this difficult we should just get out of it. We now just have to get shot of the whole thing. I went to the Gay Hussar [Soho restaurant favoured by politicians and journalists] with Fiona and Fraser Kemp and had a very nice lunch at which I was being drawn for a cartoon to go in a book of cartoons of regular Gay Hussar customers. Martin Rowson's cartoon was pretty good, though I looked alarmingly like Jeremy Paxman. He had Fraser peeping out of the corner of the page. I got back for a series of meetings, including the main TB/GB strategy meeting. GB and the two Eds arrived late, walked in surly and it was as bad as it gets.

They seemed genuinely to think that the more we talked about crime, the worse it was politically. TB was convinced, and I was sure he was right, that we had to be seen to address crime, antisocial behaviour, respect, order, the basic-values issues that flowed from them. He said to GB that he had a point but he was totally exaggerating it. Of course we shouldn't be going on about crime the whole time but it was ridiculous to say that we shouldn't talk about it. People have to know that we get it. GB said it was far better to do things first, do them properly, then say they had been done, rather than announce what we were going to do, then do it, then have everyone say it wasn't working. He was obviously referring to the child benefit situation. But it was a totally unrealistic approach.

The combination of TB's lack of focus, GB's combination of sulking and aggression, Ed Balls' near contempt for TB, my and Philip's near exasperation at the whole thing made it a particularly bad meeting. You would also have thought we were in an election campaign. GB said why are we fighting the election on crime? Sally M pointed out we weren't fighting an election at all. TB said don't see it as crime, see it as respect, community, values. I asked GB to explain what he meant by doing things without getting coverage for them. He gave me the death stare, said nothing. I said you got up a big message on the economy by making difficult decisions, announcing them, arguing for them, then seeing the benefits through. We had to do the same in every other area. He said the economy was different. I said we had a big agenda on public services and on the state of society, and they required a similar political strategy. TB was pretty gloomy as the meeting ended and he set off for the CBI. The speech was strong and went down fine.[1]

Wednesday, May 22

Not much out of the CBI speech, mainly TB vs Vallance et al. The *Mail* really getting stuck in re Carole [Caplin] as personal trainer to CB, TB etc. Party funding went as well as it could, though [David] Triesman wasn't too great when asked about [Richard] Desmond, who would now get a bit jumpy. My foot was now in a really bad way. Alison [Blackshaw, AC's PA] suggested the NHS walk-in centre at Soho which was absolutely brilliant. Another Labour success. They drained off some pretty ghastly looking liquid inside the blister, patched it up and I could walk pretty well straight away. I had a nice chat with the nurses who showed me round. Fantastic facility. Back for a PMQs meeting, not clear what IDS would do but we were set for possibly TB's worst ever with a real cock-up when he got a factual answer wrong re which department was responsible for elections and referenda. Fall-about time for the Tories, though it wouldn't get through to the public much.[2]

[1] In a speech reported as Blair taking on business critics, he told the CBI dinner 'Nobody likes paying taxes. Even after the Budget we remain a relatively low-taxed economy and one of the best of the world to do business. But I was elected to fix our public services, schools and hospitals first, and that is what I intend to do.'

[2] Asked by Iain Duncan Smith which Cabinet minister was responsible for referenda, Blair indicated the Home Secretary. However, responsibility for referenda had been passed from the Home Office to Stephen Byers' department (DTLR) a year earlier.

TB had Jonathan, Sally and I in for a chat afterwards, said he didn't really know how to take things forward with GB at the moment. I was now having regular weekly meetings with Peter M, Peter H and Philip, which were useful, proper strategy discussions not always getting sucked down into what was going on day to day. Home via the gym, and TB called, joking about the earlier disaster at PMQs, agreeing that next week if the Tories had any sense, they would turn it into a general knowledge quiz.

He was worried about the way they [the *Mail*] were going for their connections with Carole. He said the problem is you are under such scrutiny that you become a kind of prisoner and you can't actually do a lot of the things you want to. He said I know there are lifestyle issues that are a problem but I can't stop Cherie having a life and there are things I ought to be able to do without everything being an issue for the press. I said maybe, but there are plenty of upsides, e.g. running the country, being involved in all the major decisions affecting the country, the kind of people you meet and the places you go to, people at your beck and call. I was trying to persuade him that we needed to be much more forward thinking about new communications, use of the Internet, direct mail, more genuine interaction. He felt it would take a long time before we were in a position where the press was not setting the agenda for the rest of the media.

Thursday, May 23

Asylum took up a lot of the day, and the French so-called deal re Sangatte [refugee camp] and the *Guardian* getting a leak of the paper written by Olivia McLeod [policy adviser] on 'radical' asylum measures. Everyone assumed Clare Short had been responsible. The story made clear she was opposed to some of the plans, as indeed she later made clear on *Question Time* [BBC TV programme]. Cabinet was mainly Kashmir with a feeling sometimes that we had five Foreign Secretaries – TB, JS, Geoff H, Robin C and Clare. GB as ever saying nothing unless he had to. Afterwards I had a long chat with [Alan] Milburn who felt we had to move to a different sort of political discussion, get definition less according to events than arguments and values. Philip had been to see him and was pretty down about public opinion, trust.

On the way home I had a row with Michael Levy, who, with Charles C's and the party's backing, had decided to do an interview with Rachel Sylvester [*Times*] tomorrow. I said I thought it was a mistake, we had just about managed to park the issue of funding and we should let it lie down. He got very emotional, said he had been put in a box for eight years, done everything asked of him, yet was treated like a leper. I said the Lords was not a conventional home for lepers. He said he was determined to have his say and defend the line that we had to keep on raising funds. I had pretty much the blue mists both with him and with Charles, who also thought he should do it, and my mood got worse watching Short on *Question Time* making clear she wouldn't have taken the [Richard] Desmond money and attacking us over asylum.

Friday, May 24

The SPD [Social Democratic Party] team came in from Germany for a series of meetings with me, Jonathan, PM, PG, SM, RH [Robert Hill], DA. They were similar to us but also very different. They didn't really have a clear strategy or message. When you asked them what it was, a huge great jumble came out, and when you implored them to get the focus on the economy and less on the cultural issues that they seemed drawn to, they sort of said they agreed but I don't think they did. TB joined us at the end of the lunch and when we filled him in on the discussion so far, he said it was obviously, keep the focus on the economy, and in relation to the straight Schroeder vs [Edmund] Stoiber [Chancellor candidate] battle, try not to go too head-to-head and do it almost indirectly and through policy. They seemed a bit beleaguered, also said that because Stoiber was successfully 'hiding' from some policy areas, they couldn't really get the political debate going. I said it was always possible to get the debate going, it's how you frame the debate and then generate the arguments.

Philip got very aggressive, saying it had to be economy first, social second, cultural issues third. It seemed so obvious to us and yet ask them what their strategy was and it was thin, clearly designed for the party, words like innovation and justice, rather than the public. TB was going to have to speak to Schroeder if these were his top campaign people. They wanted TB to go to Germany for two days' campaigning, which would pretty much kill any relationship with Stoiber at birth if he won.

Saturday, May 25

Birthday. Forty-five today. The herald for a weekend of gloom. Feeling really down again. Best thing was that Rory was running in the South of England qualifiers, so he and I went out to Watford. Fiona had bought me a pedometer and I ran for over an hour to get it working. The Roy Keane/Mick McCarthy drama was for some reason really draining me too, even though I knew neither of them well.[1] I felt a real sense of empathy with Keane, felt he was driven but also haunted by demons, depression, violence, an inability to share all the same emotions as everyone seemed to have around the big moments. TB, coincidentally, said he had had friends over for dinner, one of whom asked what I was like. TB said he is the Roy Keane in the operation, driven, doesn't suffer fools, expects everyone to match his own standards, flawed but brilliant.

Sunday, May 26

I ran for an hour then had a heart-to-heart with Fiona, who was finding my depressions harder and harder to deal with, which I completely understood but it didn't exactly help. At the heart of it was probably stuff that had always been there, and also a feeling at the moment that I hated the job but I couldn't work out how much of that was because of the pressure she put me under to leave, and the pressure TB put me under to stay. Charlie [Falconer] called me about the Dome because they were close to a deal that was being presented as giving it away. So another hour trying to help deal with that.

Monday, May 27

Up to see TB early. He had been thinking over the weekend about a reshuffle, perhaps on Wednesday, with Steve [Byers] out. He didn't want a major reshuffle but he knew Steve had to go. There were others he would like to get rid of, notably Clare and Nick Brown, to a lesser extent Robin, but he knew he couldn't, certainly not all at once. He was thinking of AD for transport. TB agreed with me that Steve had been the victim, but he did feel a lot of it was his own fault. But I think we both felt sorry for him where it was ending. He was totally fed up with Clare and intended to see her to make clear she understood she was far from being indispensable. These reshuffles, like pregnancy, dentistry and exams, were further proof that pain has no memory. I didn't know how many we have done now, but until a new one starts, you forget how awful the process is.

First the usual and occasionally random discussion of who could go where. Then the unstructured remembering by different people at different times of reasons why such and such a move was unwise or

[1] A public row between Republic of Ireland football captain Keane and manager Mick McCarthy during preparations for the World Cup in Japan resulted in Keane leaving the squad. The Irish team was defeated by Spain in the second round.

even impossible. With each reshuffle also came the realisation that the PM's power and room for manoeuvre is more limited than people might think. In an ideal world, there was no way people like Short, Nick Brown, Michael Meacher [environment minister] would survive. But there were balances to be considered, and you couldn't make all the personnel changes at the same time. We also knew with absolute certainty that today's broadly loyal minister was tomorrow's bitter and backbiting backbencher, their only hope of salvation in their mind turning against the government, giving the impression it was out of principle rather than bitterness. We had seen some already, and there would be more after tomorrow. He was pretty clear he couldn't get rid of Nick Brown. He thought of making him chief secretary [to the Treasury] but it was interesting that GB rarely wanted in his own team the people whose claims he pressed hardest with TB.

Then a couple of quite extraordinary serendipitous moments. JP came in, and TB told him he was thinking of making a few structural changes, and JP said he shouldn't rule out hiving off parts of DTLR. Then Byers came in and said to TB that he wanted to go, if TB felt that was the right thing to do. Steve said he had had enough, and he knew it was the right thing for him. We agreed to separate the Byers announcement from the rest of the reshuffle so that we could genuinely say it was his decision. He was still extraordinarily Zen-like, very calm, only very rare flashes of emotion. He said he passionately believed in what we were trying to do as a government and now felt he was a liability and that was something he didn't want to live with. We chatted with TB for twenty minutes or so and Steve and I walked round to my office to sort the detail. I got Godric in, who was really angry. We agreed the best thing to do would be a short statement to camera in Number 10, which would show he was not being forced out, no questions. I said I was astonished how calm he was. He said politics is a rough trade, but we love it, and I found myself replying 'Do you know, I'm not sure that I do any more.' Yeah, he said, maybe not. He said he had spent so many years working for a Labour government, had been proud of what we had done, but he knew this was the right time to go. He asked me if I thought he should have gone earlier. I said probably, yes. But I was like him, I really didn't want those fuckers to get a scalp. I was worried even now that TB would look weak out of this because in the end it was Steve deciding to go, basically driven out.

We agreed that Milburn and Blunkett should do the rounds for him, speak up for him. What he needed to get out of this was a bit of dignity and self-respect. He went off, and I think the people in the outer office could tell from the body language what was going on. I joined a TB office meeting plus Hilary Armstrong to go over the rest of the reshuffle. I was still pressing for Clare to go, but TB really felt it wasn't possible yet. There was a bit of pressure for Paul Boateng [financial secretary to the Treasury] for chief secretary. Hilary agreed that if he sacked Nick Brown, he was just setting up a rival GB whips operation. We made a bit of progress, and then TB said we should prepare a list to send to him in Rome tomorrow so he could work on it on the flight back, by which time we would be announcing Byers. I saw Michael Levy who said he had been really upset at our conversation the other day, that I'd been thuggish towards him, that nobody ever spoke to him like that. His interview went fine and he would never do anything to harm TB.

Tuesday, May 28

TB left for the NATO summit in Rome, which was genuinely historic on one level but when he called in, it was to tell me inter alia about Berlusconi getting some dolly bird to hand out watches to all the leaders while Chirac made a speech attacking him over his pronouncements that NATO was the key to our defence. We had an internal meeting plus Hilary A to go over the reshuffle options for TB. We persuaded ourselves that [David] Miliband could go straight in as a Minister of State because he was nice enough and popular enough for the inevitable jealousies to be contained. Just how big a twat Sixsmith was became apparent when he appeared at the gates after Steve went, wanting to be let in, saying he was still his director of communications.

Steve was more nervous than I had ever seen him now that the moment was coming, Jan [Cookson, his partner] was fine, relaxed about it, happy even. His mother felt he was doing the wrong thing. With Mark Bennett working at my computer we finished the statement. Steve read through it a few times, kept in 'friends who knew me know I am not a liar and try to behave honourably'. I got the office to call round the media to tell them to come to a briefing without telling them what it was about. We thoroughly enjoyed the spectacle of [Adam] Boulton blathering from Rome for ten minutes about all the things it might be – referendum on the euro, declaration of war, TB illness. Others were speculating it would be me resigning, one or two that he was going back on some of the decisions in the reshuffle.

Nobody mentioned Steve. He was still fairly calm but not quite so Zen-like. I left him for a while to compose his thoughts and he asked for a glass of water. I went back in, asking him if he was ready, then took him up the long route through the basement so that nobody would bump into him. We got to the side door, he took a deep breath, said 'Here goes then', and in he went. He did well, held it together but as he came out he was a bit choked. I took him back to my office where Boulton was still blathering away, now saying it was evidence of how few friends he had that the news didn't leak. What total scum these people are. Couldn't bring himself to admit he hadn't heard a whisper, and all his speculation had been for the birds. We sat around chatting with Hilary Armstrong and Sally M while Mark B tracked down Mike White and Lucy Ward to do the *Guardian* interview. Again, he was pretty good. He seemed happier in himself already. He looked grey as he started but the colour came back as the interview went on. We knew the press would be pretty merciless about both him and TB, but we just had to get through it.

I joined the TB meeting on the reshuffle, the usual agony. JP was worried it would look like he was losing part of his job rather than gaining. Hilary A and Robert Hill said his reputation in local government was not good, but TB saw no way of changing what he had agreed with him. Jeremy gave TB a long list of what JP wanted. Fiona and I went out for dinner at the Mannings' [David and Catherine] but I was in and out the whole time. Estelle [Morris] was worried she was being heaved because she had a call that TB wanted to speak to her first thing. I called David Miliband to tell him to be in London. Milburn called to get briefed on Byers for the *Today* programme. The whole thing was a bit draining and I didn't much enjoy dinner despite David and Catherine being very good hosts, the Master of the Rolls [Lord Phillips] interesting and a Frenchwoman there [Christylle Rouffiac, wife of Lord Phillips] who had a good take on our media culture. At one point I looked out of the window and saw a druggie breaking open a pay and display box where the car was parked.

Wednesday, May 29

The press was vile about Steve. 'Liar for hire' in the *Star*. The *Mirror* was merciless. It's like they get a corpse, but then are disappointed there is nothing left to try and kill, so they kill the dead body too. TB had to get on with the reshuffle. [David] Miliband could scarcely believe he was going to be a minister let alone in charge of schools as Minister of State. Estelle not totally happy and had wanted Margaret Hodge out, but TB resisted on that. He had a number of difficult conversations with GB. TB wanted to move Yvette [Cooper, junior health minister, wife of Ed Balls] but GB was resistant. 'You can't do that. She won't accept it.' To which TB said she would get very short shrift. GB described the LCD [Lord Chancellor's Department], where TB was planning to send her, as a graveyard, which was rubbish. She had also gone AWOL but eventually came through and was clearly expecting a big job. When he told her she said straight out 'What do I have to do to become a Minister of State?' He should have said 'Not talk to me like that for a start', but instead said these reshuffles were very difficult. Doubtless helped by Ed, they were out spinning straight away that she was going to be the minister in charge of referendum administration.

We now had the ever-changing grid of all the ministerial changes, Jonathan trying to keep a grip of the master copy. He started the calls to ministers. He was certainly tougher than in the past, usually saying 'There is no easy way to say this but I need your job to make space for changes. It doesn't mean you haven't done well or can't come back.' Seven sackings in all. We got it all done in time for Tom to do a briefing at 3. Alistair Darling and I had a chat about how to grip his department [Transport], and also how to avoid becoming a pawn between TB and GB. Alistair was pleased TB had entrusted him with a pretty big challenge, said he intended to get on top of the detail, worry more about doing than talking about it. [Paul] Boateng [as chief secretary to the Treasury, becoming the UK's first black Cabinet minister] came in and I warned him against getting trapped by the GB machine.

There was a fair bit of 'blow to GB cronies' around the place, so I got Tom and Godric to call round and get that in a better place. TB and I went upstairs and Peter M was there, playing with Leo. He was clearly annoyed for three reasons – first he was not back in government and nobody had called him to say so. Second, he had been brought back from Korea for another meandering meeting. Third, Douglas [Alexander] was there for the strategy part of the meeting. He was very snappy, ate very little and was the first to leave, though as ever made some sensible and telling contributions amid the histrionics. TB was very solicitous of Douglas, and clearly wanted him to feel he was part of the inner team. He failed to persuade TB that he should do more to deal with some of our negatives, like Parliament, greater interaction. Then another argument about how to deal with the press who were in total kill mode most of the time. TB was looking a bit frail, physically and politically. I ran home around 10.

Thursday, May 30

TB called first thing after reading my note on the PCC which warned him how Black Rod was behaving, and we had to look for a way out of this. He asked me to send all the papers to Derry [Irvine], who quickly came to the view that we should try to get the papers involved to write to me around a deal that we would drop it on the basis they accepted TB had not been involved, which had always been our concern. TB was torn, as was I. On the one hand TB didn't particularly want a great row with a senior official of the House, but nor did he want to back down. I went in to see him first thing to go over the options, then had to leave because I was having breakfast with C at SIS HQ. I liked Richard [Dearlove] a lot. He was witty and engaging, and also had a real strategic understanding on the big foreign policy issues. Kashmir, it was a disaster waiting to happen. He was really worried about the Americans' lack of proper engagement in the Middle East. Lots of small talk re Cornwall, where he had a house, as well as big talk on the foreign policy stuff.

Some of the papers, most adamantly David Yelland at the *Sun*, were saying that Sixsmith was lining himself up to do a deal on his story. Yelland was really steamed up about it, said he held no candle for Byers but he didn't like this. I did a note to RW, Jonathan and Mottram, setting out what was being said, which, if true, would seem to be a breach of the agreement I thought Mottram struck.

TB called a few times from his visit to East Anglia, pretty perked up at the reception he was getting. He was pretty exercised re the PCC. I had a good chat with Douglas. I was very frank re GB, said he had been a nightmare to deal with of late and I was reaching the point where I couldn't be bothered with it. He agreed to be a conduit if it was helpful. On the TB/GB front, he felt it would only work if Philip and I were properly involved. I said I thought the Eds were a problem too because they were constantly pushing GB in a different direction. He said he hoped he could help there too.

Guy Black came in. I went through his various Black Rod meetings. The *Spectator* and the *Mail on Sunday*, post Guy's meeting with Black Rod, had gone from wanting mediation to wanting adjudication. Guy had told him he didn't want to receive his letter. Black Rod said he wanted the truth to come out. As Guy said, it was inconsistent, and a lot of it irrelevant and it would lead to a massive public row. Both RW and Jeremy said they totally believed Clare Sumner on this. I left it with Guy that we would either go to adjudication or settle through an exchange of letters. I had a quick lunch with Andy Marr at Orso's [Italian restaurant, Covent Garden] and back to work on Sixsmith. The cheque was stopped for now though he would almost certainly get his money in the end. Godric was in an absolute rage about it.

Friday, May 31

Start of the World Cup. Mottram had a 10am deadline for paying the cheque to Sixsmith. But on the back of a story in *The Times*, he got counsel's advice that there would appear to be a breach of agreement if the story was true and therefore we had good reason not to pay it. Sixsmith had obviously been told that I was trying to stop the cheque. He started to put stuff out over the weekend about me running a smear campaign against him. I was also trying to work through the PCC situation. Guy Black called and I said I would try to get TB to a position of an agreed exchange of letters. It was going to be messy but the sooner we were out of it the better. TB was in a real fury about it. The idea that Clare [Sumner] would get on to him [Black Rod] and try and get us a bigger role – it just doesn't merit a moment's thought.

Later, TB called to say he had agreed Michael Wills [Labour MP and GB adviser] should be minister in charge of the criminal justice service IT systems! I really couldn't be bothered with it but I eventually spoke to Michael at 6 to agree a line to put out on PA [Press Association], but it transpired that PA didn't think it was a story and then Joe Murphy [*Evening Standard*] got on to it and turned it into a TB/GB row splash.

Saturday, June 1

Dominated by England vs Sweden – good first half, dreadful second half. A short letter came through on the fax from Sixsmith – 'Alastair, we haven't spoken since February 21. Perhaps we should.'

Sunday, June 2

Michael Wills came on to say the *Mail on Sunday* story re him and a row between TB and GB must have come from Number 10. I thought he'd been wound up by GB and I gave him very short shrift. GB's other claim, that Peter M was behind it, was ludicrous. Sixsmith sent a long letter to Mottram, copied to me, with all manner of claims about us smearing him. I dictated a response to Mottram which stuck to the facts. Darling had an interview in the *Telegraph* which was taken as a hit on [John] Birt, who went into a really precious tantrum. Jeremy called to say we needed to be very nice about Birt, which we were, and could I get AD to speak to Birt. I was helping David Miliband with his first big [ministerial] speech for Thursday.

Monday, June 3

Darling called me after speaking to Birt, said it was the most extraordinary call he had ever made. 'I said I wanted to have a discussion with him about transport policy and he said it was very important that I built a bridge to him. He was unbelievably difficult.' I did a note for TB suggesting how we take forward the PCC case and talked it through with Guy Black. Then, with all the family and the neighbours out to St James's Park to watch the Golden Jubilee concert on the big screen. There was a fantastic atmosphere and the Royals had handled the whole week brilliantly. It was interesting to see how much more enthusiastic older and middle-aged people were compared to the kids. Certainly for our lot, the Jubilee meant pretty much nothing compared to the World Cup.

Tuesday, June 4

Another bank holiday, so a quiet day, and I felt sorry for TB having to go to St Paul's for the Jubilee service. Then back to the Guildhall where he had to make a speech about the Queen. Not easy, getting the balance right, trying to say something significant whilst also trying to avoid just sounding like a creep. He had written a passage comparing her commitment to that of a cleaner or a doctor, which didn't ring true. He asked me to work on a passage about the reception she got at the concert when she walked on, which had certainly been impressive. Fiona and I were both worried, having been there, that there would be a lot of comment on the reception for him which had been cool by comparison, especially when the cameras panned to him as Ben Elton [comedian and author] made a joke about the NHS and transport being no better than when she first became Queen. What a tit. TB had said to Prince Andrew we could have done without the Ben Elton jokes and Andrew said surely politicians just have to live with that kind of thing. It was clear every time he talked about it, though, that TB liked the Queen, rated and respected her but he felt that Charles' speech, the way he framed the argument about traditional, the un-pc second verse of the national anthem, was meant to be a dig at us.[1]

Wednesday, June 5

TB was seeing [Hosni] Mubarak and Rumsfeld at Number 10, and I wanted to get up to see my dad in this relatively quiet period. I took the boys up and watched Ireland draw with Germany with him. Also working on [David] Miliband's speech.

Thursday, June 6

The *Independent* led on an email which was misrepresented as an attempt to dig dirt on Pam Warren [survivor of the 1999 Paddington

[1] In his speech at the Jubilee party, the Prince of Wales had referred to the 'politically incorrect second verse' of 'God Save the Queen', which asks God to 'Confound their politics, frustrate their knavish tricks', etc.

rail crash]. AD wanted to put out an apology from Dan Corry [former special adviser to Stephen Byers] and from Byers straight away, as a way of showing this had nothing to do with him and he condemned it.[1] He also wanted to publish the emails which in fact showed something different to what had been reported. I was a bit worried we would set a precedent, and also reluctant to be issuing apologies for things that had not been done. Why shouldn't political parties try to check if there are any political affiliations of people who suddenly become part of public debate? I consulted TB at Chequers and he felt that AD should do what he wanted and it was probably right. The facts were actually on our side but that didn't stop the papers going into total blah overdrive. Mike White pointed out to me that we had now definitely passed the point where newspapers allowed facts to get in the way of a desire to hit the government.

Friday, June 7

I had pretty much finalised an exchange of letters with the PCC. TB added two points – first, an even more staunch defence of Clare Sumner, and second, we reserve the right to come back on this if any of the papers suggested that he had tried to muscle in on the arrangements. I took a very chatty call from JP but he was pretty menacing as well about the planned Third Way event [policy discussion organised by Peter Mandelson] coming up tomorrow, saying that 'If it's a beautiful people, New Labour, pointy head, Mekon kind of thing, there'll be a backlash and TB should know that.' He said there were people in Number 10 who never bothered to think about him or the party in this and he wasn't happy. Trying to play down its importance, I said I wasn't even going to it and it was a Peter M, Andrew Adonis [head of the Policy Unit] thing, which got him going even more, divisive and stupid, chickens would come home to roost, etc.

Dan Corry was tracked down at the World Cup in Tokyo and we agreed a statement for him to put out as an apology. The *Independent* had a partial account of our dealings with AD yesterday, presenting them as Number 10 not happy with an over-the-top apology.

[1] Corry had emailed the Labour Party asking for information on the political affiliation of the Paddington Survivors Group, which Pam Warren co-founded. The email was sent the day after Mrs Warren had publicly accused Stephen Byers of misleading Parliament over the decision to take Railtrack into administration.

Saturday, June 8

I was trying to get the Sundays focused on TB's welfare speech next week. The Corry email died down pretty quickly with a few pieces saying it was actually an OK thing to do. I had dreadful hay fever and was feeling a bit ground down again. I was reaching the point when I really couldn't be bothered listening to the news, reading the papers or talking to journalists. TB was at the Third Way conference with Clinton et al. and seemed to think it was worthwhile. I think he was surprised I didn't go.

Sunday, June 9

I briefed John Reid for *Frost*. He had been at the Clinton/Peter M wonkathon and said he had had a terrific conversation with Clinton re Ireland. JR was totally up for going for the press, so we had now reached a stage where all communication was dismissed as spin, all funding was sleaze, all attacks were smears. Gwyneth Dunwoody [Labour MP] did an interview saying she had been smeared. IDS was on the broadcasts really going for us. There was a real nastiness and poison about where we were at the moment and I wasn't quite sure how we dealt with it.

TB came back from his weekend policy wonking seeming very up and energised. Clinton had been through something similar to the attacks we were getting. His view was that they went on character because they couldn't win on policy. The challenge was to use that to build a position of confidence and strength. The challenge for modern politicians was understanding change, developing and implementing policy but also shaping and winning arguments. He said we were seen around the world as probably the best and most successful modern left-of-centre party in terms of winning and doing, but we rarely came over as being confident in our own position. TB felt too there was definitely something about people on the left, that sometimes power scared them, or troubled them, and they started to believe the message from the right, that actually they were the people best able to handle power.

Monday, June 10

The welfare speech wasn't badly set up. A couple of pieces of spin by media. First my letter to the *Indy* was used on page 1 for a 'We will learn lessons' headline, burying the fact that it was about their story being wrong. Also, the *Sunday Express* made-up spin on TB's speech was described by the broadcasters, without any knowledge at all, as our handiwork. I finalised the exchanges with the PCC, toned them down a bit at their request, and then, after Guy Black told Black Rod that it was on, the rumour mill started. Then a truly pathetic meeting with Mavis MacDonald [permanent secretary, Cabinet Office], Jeremy and Godric to agree what to do re Sixsmith. TB told us not to go against the legal advice. We should seek to establish what we could legitimately do to get the assurances we sought and if the QC thought we were not within our rights we should not go beyond that. It was pretty clear everyone just wanted shot of it. We left it that we would see what he was prepared to do by way of assurances but the reality was if the answer was nothing, they were going to shell out anyway. As I said to TB, he would get his cheque and then there would be nothing to stop him building a career attacking a government that paid it to him. The message to everyone in government would be fall out with elected ministers and you can make a lot of money out of it. TB said it may be unjust, but it was time to leave it.

I told the Monday morning meeting there was more departmental leaking than ever, there was a culture of acceptance of it and it meant we looked weak. On the press generally, Charles C wanted to campaign in defence of politics. Everyone agreed we were being damaged by all of this, as Clare Short so kindly pointed out on the *Westminster Hour* last night, and none of us were really clear how to get out of it.

TB went off for the welfare speech wearing his glasses for the first time delivering a speech. On his return, he said that whenever he was talking about policy, he felt strong and confident. It was dealing with all the shit that ground us down. The key to re-engagement was as much about policy as anything – particularly public services but also red tape, crime, causes of crime. Godric was also feeling worn out, ground down. Philip was worried that TB and GB were in very different places and we had to get them closer together. The new media environment was definitely something in which we had to agree and implement the strategy. Their view was pretty much now that a story about the government was only really a story when it was a bad story, and that even when the facts didn't fit the bad story, they were made to. It was a cultural shift, born of the impact of 24-hour news and the press, which had forced them to change their role. It required a strategic response but we spent hours over months talking about it without agreeing what that response was. Mine was to make them part of the debate, confront them with the reality that they are players as well as spectators. It was risky, it might make them worse, though it's hard to see how much worse it could get. TB still seemed to think we could muddle along, charm and cajole a few from time to time, divide and rule. We were miles apart on this.

Tuesday, June 11

[Roy] Greenslade [journalist and former editor] had a piece on page 1 of the *Guardian* re the PCC, which was about as good as we could get in terms of where it was pitched. I knew the next few days were going to be grim. TB called as I was running through Green Park on the way in. He said if the press were going to say this was a climbdown, they would give the sense that the original stories were true, in which case we might as well have gone for a full PCC judgement. We released the letters, then Tom did the 11 and they were on the rampage. What was clearer than ever was that the *Mail* and the *Telegraph* were going to crank up into an even bigger gear in terms of going for me personally.

We had a dreadful TB/GB plus key people strategy meeting in which we were trying to sign him up to the six-month strategy paper. Every time we put forward a specific idea or thought, GB would say something slightly different. When he read Philip's analysis, which was not new to him and with which he basically agreed, he feigned shock and said he would now have to rethink the CSR strategy. His basic line was that going on about crime had been short-termist and we needed long-termism. If TB said responsibility was a key theme, GB would say what about opportunity? If TB had said opportunity, he would have said what about responsibility? This was hopeless. Thankfully I was called out to take a call and afterwards went back to my office. Douglas called me afterwards and said he couldn't believe how bad that had been. The truth was GB was winning the ghastly war of attrition.

Earlier, even before that meeting, TB had called in Jonathan, Sally M and me and asked if we thought it was possible for him to announce publicly that he wouldn't fight the next election and tell Cabinet that if ministers wanted to fight a leadership election, they would have to do it outside. Sally feared it would make him a lame duck straight away, though Aznar had seemed to survive a second fixed term pretty well. I said he had to decide whether it was the right thing to do, and that if it wasn't, he was simply caving in to psychological warfare. Did he really want to go? And was it really the right thing? He said that's exactly what Cherie would say. What he'd like to do was win an election, win a referendum, then go after getting the new leader in place or, if a referendum were possible this side of the election, win that, stay to the election and get a new leader in place.

He said all GB ever asked him these days was when was he going. There was a real sense around that GB was at it the whole time. Sally said disgruntled former ministers and disappointed backbenchers were being given strong hints of jobs. He was courting JP the whole time. He was going more and more sceptic in his dealings with Murdoch and his papers. TB had devolved too much power in the areas he really cared about like public services and the euro. Godric felt that on the press front, the new level of nastiness was a direct response to the changes to the lobby. They really did believe we were trying to do them in the whole time. There was no doubt that now with Byers gone, and with TB still pretty impregnable, I was the next best target. Charles Clarke did a piece for *The Times* attacking parts of the press, which would fly a bit.

Wednesday, June 12

The *Mail* and *Telegraph* absolutely vile about me, the others a bit more balanced. Charles' attack was going big and I admired his guts in doing it but GB and Co. were straight out saying it was a mistake to attack the press. TB was still in an absolute fury about Black Rod. We had agreed to try to close it down but it was clear we would not have long to wait before more Black Rod-ery came pouring out. I was managing just about to hang in there but I was going through a mega down phase, worried I wasn't being terribly effective, worried about being strung out by sustained attacks. Even Fiona was adamant I couldn't leave now because it would so weaken TB. Peter M said if I went GB would be home and dry and the Tories would be jubilant, so I just had to hang in there. He said TB relied on me as a brute force able to drive the machine. He said he too was worried about the extent to which they wanted to go for me, but still felt I had no choice but to stay.

At PMQs, TB thought IDS might do the PCC business. In the end, nobody raised it. IDS did Pam Warren then welfare but didn't land a blow. TB had a good tone. Our side better. Weekly meeting with Peter M, PH [Peter Hyman] and PG. On the euro, we went over the various scenarios. Don't go for it, and TB is weakened. Go for it and win, and TB could successfully bow out, though GB would be likely to think TB would use it as an excuse to stay longer and so might block. So option three, do a deal, but GB is unlikely to trust. Option four, do the euro and lose, then GB is home and dry. PH felt that just going for it would show courage and conviction, but I was sure it would be the end of him, if he went for it and lost. Peter M was a real strength at these meetings, seemed to worry less about status or how he was perceived by us, and was most of the time giving very clear and concise strategic advice.

Starting to get calls from journalists who were picking up on Black

Rod's evidence. TB said if Black Rod had had a genuine complaint, why had he not come straight to him or RW? He said he was totally satisfied civil servants did nothing wrong. He said things were going to get very tough and we had to be strong. Tessa [Jowell] called, asked if I was thinking of going, said I mustn't.

Thursday, June 13

[Roy] Hattersley and [Trevor] Kavanagh were both saying I had to go, Kavanagh in quite a friendly way. Piers [Morgan] had actually been pretty good about me on Channel 4 last night so I dropped him a friendly line. Alex F called, said it must be serious because he even had people phoning him to say how hard I was getting it at the moment. He said don't let other people think for you, because they'll all have their own motives. If there is doubt, he said, then there is no doubt. He said it was an old Irish saying. I thought about it through the day. When it came to it, I didn't just want to run away. I still had a job to do. It was pretty heavy though, evidenced by the kind of people sending in letters of support. Not just people I'd expect to like Bruce [Grocott], but also Alice Mahon, Ann Clwyd, David Clark [Labour MPs]. I even had Gwyneth Dunwoody defending me on the radio. Jonathan at his weekly meeting tried to be chirpy as ever, said it was a 'Save AC Campaign' meeting. People looked a bit shot, particularly Sally.

David Manning was genuinely shocked by Black Rod's behaviour. The *Spectator* cover had me and TB getting spanked by the little fucker. We were of course building up to the *Mail on Sunday* who would no doubt publish the memo from Black Rod to the PCC so we had to decide whether to put our version out, with our own dossier of evidence. I felt we had to because Sunday was in danger of being a massive event with only one side of the story there. Tom had forty-five minutes of it with the lobby. This thing took up hours through the day. Meanwhile, perhaps the most dramatic Cabinet yet. TB meandered through the Grid in the usual way, bit of chat, bit of Middle East and Afghanistan, then GB came in about the Tories doing an opposition day debate on world poverty. He said it was strategically important because they were trying to become New Conservatives, position themselves in the centre through mood music but we should be wary because in policy they would be very right wing. He said their weakest point is health. The unspoken message was that TB does Grid, spin and foreign whereas GB does substance and strategy.

But then JP came in with a virtual declaration of war on TB. He said he knew we had to do the press stuff and he wasn't knocking that but it was interesting that the Tories were trying to echo New Labour and avoid substance. But he said we have a very good compromise between Old and New. He said we all have to be involved in future policymaking but 'I'm bound to say if we're going to have weekend retreats for some at Hartwell House [Buckinghamshire hotel, venue of Peter Mandelson's Third Way event], and Mandelson giving interviews saying we're all Thatcherites now, then we're going to have some very serious discussions in here.' He said the compromise between Old and New means we're Labour again and there will be real division if we try to replace policy structures.

TB was looking at him with a mix of steel and humour whereas others in the room clearly sensed it was quite a moment. GB had the beginnings of a smile on his face which was as broad as I've seen it in years by the time he left. JP said the Labour Party has always been lousy on the back foot. There needs to be more forward strategy and it has to be discussed right here. TB hit back pretty hard, said it was time for a little reality check, time to stop believing everything people read in newspapers. He said we are on our sixth year in government and sometimes government gets difficult. The way not to deal with it is to wet our knickers every time it gets difficult. We are in a strong position. The economy is good, we have the right agenda on public services, the right approach on social exclusion. The Tories were coming at us on character because they had nothing else to go on. They had lost on policy. We have to stick on policy, not get distracted or irritated. He said we had been uniquely blessed as a government, to a large extent free of many of the problems other Labour governments had faced. Our mettle was being tested and it's at times like these that we had to hang together, not fall apart.

The history of Labour governments, he said, is that they make themselves fail rather than others make them fail. We are winning all the arguments, so let's get a sense of perspective. He then looked around, smiled, said 'I've got the Indonesian president coming in now, so that's the end of that.' JP put on his real sour look and walked straight out. GB smiled. The rest were blank. It was Paul Boateng's first Cabinet and Bruce's [Grocott] first actually at the Cabinet table. Paul looked really shocked. RW came to see me later. He said that was a big, bad moment. TB was pretty calm afterwards, convinced it needed saying. He had had a pretty heavy session with JP earlier, who was going on about the Hartwell business. It was now an open thing around the world that GB was doing in TB. Yesterday he had spoken to Chrétien, who referred to having a Brown problem, namely that his Treasury minister was after his job and he had told him to fight for it from the outside. But the message out of Cabinet had been pretty clear – from JP, I've had enough and I'm going to throw my weight around, and from GB, I'm moving in. From TB, I'm staying. From the Cabinet, confusion and concern.

Alan Milburn was worried enough to wander over later, bring in some sandwiches, said TB had to face up to the fact that GB was killing him, and if he didn't stand up to it, his supporters would get very demoralised. He said there was no way I could think about going and if anything I should go back to doing the briefings. But TB had to get back rooted in more substance and politics, cut the crap. He was very calm, clear and strong and I was grateful that he came over like he did. Meeting then with TB, Derry [Irvine], Charlie [Falconer] , RW etc. to go through PCC/Black Rod again. Agreed to a strategy with TB, covering note plus evidence dossier to put out pre Sunday. Fraser [Kemp] was fantastic, organising support for me in the PLP.

I collected Fiona from Sarah Brown's book launch [*Magic: New Stories*] and we went to a very nice Robert Thomson dinner with the Scardinos [Marjorie, chief executive of Pearson plc, and Albert, her journalist husband], James Baker III [former US Secretary of State] and his wife [Susan], Ian McEwan [author] and his wife [Annalena McAfee], who was literary editor of the *Guardian*. Baker was impressive, particularly on the Middle East. He felt that Bush was moving in the right direction but had made a huge mistake in giving DoD an equal seat at the foreign policy table. It meant Powell and Rumsfeld were at odds the whole time whilst Condi was less a full-time National Security Advisor to the president but a mediator between the two. His view was that one day there would be a land-for-peace deal but he felt it likely it would only happen under a Labor government [in Israel]. Baker had picked up on the scale of coverage and the level of nastiness around me and once we got through all the jokes was very supportive, said I should take it as a compliment. I liked Ian McEwan too once he opened up a bit, while Marjorie Scardino's husband shared a devotion to a struggling league club [Notts County]. Marjorie said this is a good government, I was doing a great job and I had to keep at it. TB called late for a chat. He said JP would be reflecting and would come back a bit now. He hadn't liked the mood today, which was why he had really gone for it.

Friday, June 14

Most of the papers had some sort of editorial comment about me. The *Guardian* – I should go. [Richard] Littlejohn [*Sun* columnist] snide.

Telegraph snide. *Independent* not so bad. *Mirror* bad. TB said 'That's it for Piers with me.' I wrote a short statement for TB to go on the front of the dossier. I got the staff together after the morning meeting to explain what was happening. Jeremy then called, said there was a real problem. [Lieutenant Colonel] Malcolm Ross, comptroller of the Royal Household, had told Charles Moore [*Telegraph* editor] yesterday that they too had been told TB wanted to walk [through crowds from Downing Street to the Queen Mother's lying-in-state] and they had said it was a bad idea. If true, it was dreadful. But it was not true that Number 10 had said to the Palace that he wanted to walk. I had put in TB's statement that nobody from Black Rod's office had complained to TB or Richard W. RW didn't want to be in there. He told Clare he was fed up of being a human shield, to which she had said, 'You are supposed to be a human shield, protecting and defending me.' She was really upset about the whole thing. But I took out the reference to RW and instead put 'me or anyone on my behalf'.

Richard came to see me. I offered him tea but he said he wouldn't stay. He then said 'I just want to say two things. The first, you are probably not fully aware of how stressful and traumatic this has all been for you personally. Second, I don't think there's much support for you around the Cabinet table.' I said I think I'm a better judge of those at the Cabinet table than you are and apart from GB from time to time, and Clare who doesn't matter much, I have no real problems with any of them, and I'm one of the few people who gets on equally well with TB and JP. So what are you saying? That because the Tories and the press are after my blood, I should get out? No, no, no, he said. But just be very careful. There was a hint of menace there. He stayed for a matter of minutes and unlike previous such visits, my antennae told me the intention had been to unsettle me. If so, it didn't work. On the contrary, I felt strengthened because I drew a contrast between those who were calling and writing to express support, and those who were going on the airwaves to say they wanted me out. What sort of people were calling? RC, Jack S, Margaret B, Brian Wilson [energy minister], Kim Howells [culture minister]. Lots of backbenchers. Family, Fiona's family, Alex F, people at Burnley. PR people like Matthew Freud or Melanie Cantor. At one point Alison [Blackshaw] was just coming in with lists of names. My team was totally solid too. TB did a clip on the whole business from Jersey which was strong, and Godric did the briefing, followed by the honours briefing and we were in a much better position. We briefed ministers and MPs going up on it and I felt the machine starting to roll, but even better Oborne was out saying that he had never said TB did anything wrong.

The other big drama was JP. He called me at lunchtime. I said 'That was pretty dramatic yesterday.' 'What?' 'What you said in Cabinet.' 'Well, you've created camps and you're in one of them and you've pushed me to the other. There you go.' 'Oh well. I just wanted to say I was taken aback. Me, not him.' He told me that just before Cabinet TB had accused him of messing around with GB and said he wasn't having it. JP said he wasn't prepared to be excluded from strategy and he wasn't having all this Third Way/Mandelson policy stuff bypassing the party. He let off steam, said he had warned him again and again and he thinks if he strokes my arm I'll be fine, but it goes much deeper. He has to do things through the Cabinet and his ministers and not his own little Loya Jirga [Afghan Grand Council]. He then said 'You've withdrawn from all this anyway.' I said that I'd tried to pull back because of the attention I was getting, but it hasn't worked, has it? He said no, you've got your own problems. I've never had a problem with you but we've grown distant again. I'm loyal to TB and you both need to understand that. I always will be, I'm not going over to GB, but Tony has got to start treating people better than he does. I know he has a lot to deal with, a lot of problems, a lot of difficult people, a lot of big decisions. But he knows he can do it better. We chatted for close to an hour and I think both felt better at the end of it. We agreed to have dinner at our house tomorrow night. TB called later and said JP had been transformed, which showed I should keep close to him.

As ever, JP then started to worry about tomorrow, about taking up all our time at the weekend, said he would get a takeaway. I said 'Aw, aren't you sweet?' TB spoke to GB who was on his way to Canada. GB said he was thinking of him and if there was anything he could do to help either of us, he would. I was almost minded to write to him to thank him for all the support he had given and to say if he ever ran into difficulties, his support would be reciprocated in full. TB was pretty feisty about things but at the end of the day it was all pretty tough. He got back from the BIC [British–Irish Council] in Jersey. He said Northern Ireland was a mess and we may lose [David] Trimble [Ulster Unionist Party leader and First Minister of Northern Ireland].

Fiona took Grace to the ballet and I had a great chat with Rory and Calum who were developing similar views to my own about the press. Calum said something really sweet, that I'll still be standing after all these people are gone. Richard Desmond called and asked if there was anything he could do to help. I suggested a piece from Jack Straw defending me. Desmond came back saying Jack's office had said he didn't want to do it. I called Jack, who said he hadn't even been told about it and was more than happy to do it.

Saturday, June 15

We agreed re the *Mail on Sunday* that the best line would be to point out the inconsistency with the statement at the time. Once the papers dropped, we had a quick conference call to agree the lines and Martin Sheehan put out a statement. Most felt the whole thing was overblown bollocks, Black Rod says AC must go. Nothing much to it.

JP and Pauline [his wife] arrived about 8. After all the small talk, JP with some anecdotes on his trips, taking the mick out of Pauline's hats, then we got down to it. He liked TB, felt he was the right guy at the right time and a good leader. But he wanted to be properly involved in decision-making. He only felt he was in the areas for which he had direct responsibility but if he was going to be a proper deputy, he had to know a lot more about what he was up to and where we were going. He said he sometimes felt TB stroked his arm, patted his head, that it was about managing him rather than using him properly as a DPM [Deputy Prime Minister]. He had used the line on Thursday about 'the snake leaving the skin behind', that TB seemed to have this ability to lose people but not necessarily lose his strength. He said that he felt I had pulled back and that meant people in Number 10 didn't always feel there was a proper understanding of JP's views. I said that was true, but it wasn't personal. The personality clashes did my head in. GB was in TB's head the whole time messing it up.

He said TB had directly accused him of playing around with GB, building an alliance to isolate him, but that misunderstood things. He had told GB he would support him to take over but he would not be part of any plan to force out TB. He agreed with me that it was almost like a failed marriage, they had fallen out but they knew they had to live together. He felt there was a deep belief inside GB that they did have a deal, that GB had done his bit and he felt TB was doing the dirty on him. He felt TB was still popular in the party and the country and he couldn't see any pressure for him to go. He also felt that on the policy front, and again he felt my partial disengagement had something to do with this, the balance had tilted too far towards [Andrew] Adonis and what JP saw as a very right-wing agenda. We both agreed how much we missed David Miliband there [i.e. as Adonis' predecessor in charge of the Policy Unit].

I tried to give him a sense of what it was like for TB getting his head pummelled every day by GB. I tried to explain too why sometimes TB didn't want JP at some meetings. I said when TB is making a big decision, he prefers an endless series of circular conversations with different people rather than full-blown confrontational sessions that are supposed to reach conclusions. It's just his style. I suggested a weekly meeting of TB, JP, Charles C and I to keep JP more involved with political strategy. It was a really good evening, because we both laid things out very frankly, both also knew we needed both of us to raise our game again, and in a bizarre sort of way we needed each other to do that.

JP warmed up as the evening wore on and was in full flow by the end, totally open about himself, his background, his chippiness, why he felt as proud as he did of where he had got to, why he was so desperate to play a role getting TB and GB to work together better than they did. He said he would do nothing to damage the party and even though they had different views about lots of things, he felt TB was in the same place on that. He said between us all, we have put Labour in the strongest position ever and a lot of that has been down to TB and GB hanging together. I said don't underestimate the impact GB is having on him for the worse at the moment. I said he had not exchanged a single civil word with me since the election. They stayed till close to midnight.

Sunday, June 16

TB called, even more outraged and angry about Black Rod than ever. I filled him in on the JP dinner. He said the only question is whether an open and admitted two-term strategy weakens me or gives me more space. He said that even though GB had behaved abominably towards him in many ways, it was really important that leaders did not try to get successors in their own image, but go for the best on offer. He said it was important to his own legacy that the party does well after he's gone. So if GB was the best option for delivering a third-term Labour government, it's the right thing to do. But he admitted he had doubts about him temperamentally, that he worried what he would actually be like. He thought that perhaps two full terms is pretty close to the limit for jobs like this. But what really mattered was what we did policy-wise. He felt if he could get GB working with him properly on policy, we would be unstoppable. He said JP was key because he was the one politician that GB feared and the idea of a black spot being put on him, JP saying he wasn't fit for the job, he would really worry about that.

The *Mail on Sunday* stuff didn't go very far, and though there was reams of it in the papers, nothing deadly. I briefed Margaret Beckett for *The World at One* and she was absolutely brilliant. Haughty and dismissive. Reid was excellent on *On the Record* against Tim Collins [Conservative Party vice chairman], whom God preserve. The story was going nowhere but it didn't stop the BBC leading on it most of the day. We went out for dinner with the Goulds and the Milibands, all very supportive though Gail [Rebuck, publisher and wife of Philip Gould] said, probably rightly, that it was worth me trying for a concerted period of being nice to the media and then getting out.

Monday, June 17

Only the *Mail* with 'the smearing of Black Rod' led on it, but the mood was definitely different now. I agreed with TB we should just shut up shop, say we had said all there was to say. There was an excellent story in *The Times*, saying the Palace were worried Black Rod was dragging them into a political row, but it was dropping down the agenda. At the Monday morning meeting, TB was worrying about how we get back on the front foot. He was very nice to Clare Sumner. She was so manifestly nice, and professional, and mortified to have been accused in the way she had been. I saw TB on his own later and he was clearly thinking a lot about this two-term plan, moving to the view that if he did it soon it might give him more freedom. His only worry was his fear that GB would not change, and continue not co-operating properly. He said it was extraordinary to think that GB discusses the euro more openly with Murdoch than he does with him.

Tuesday, June 18

The Black Rod story was dying, yesterday's *Times* pretty much the turning point. David Davies [Football Association executive director] called as I was in a cab to the Eurostar, asking if TB would go out for later rounds of the World Cup. We agreed he would certainly come out if England got to the final, possibly before, and we also had to think about receptions etc. afterwards. He said they were having a fantastic time. What was clear was that if Japan went out, most of the Japanese would swing behind England. I explained some of the recent madness re the Queen Mum, so it was important it was clear the invitation came from them to TB, rather than TB 'muscling in'. We agreed both to speak to the Palace to find out their plans, which looked like [Prince] Andrew for the semi, Charles and Andrew for the final.

I left for Brussels with Danny Pruce [press officer, foreign affairs]. We went to [Ambassador Nigel] Sheinwald's residence where I briefed the Brussels hacks on the summit, pushing hard on asylum and immigration. The mood was fine and it was definitely worth doing. Then to the EPLP [European Parliamentary Labour Party] where I pushed the line that the Tories had moved out of policy, were trying to turn politics into a policy-free zone and make character the issue, which required a fresh approach to communications again.

Godric called to say Cherie had given us a bit of a problem. Without knowing there had been nineteen deaths in the morning in the Jerusalem suicide bombing, she said something that was taken as a defence of suicide bombers.[1] She was with Queen Rania of Jordan to launch a charity. And after Rania said something fairly balanced, Cherie said something that appeared to offer justification for suicide bombers and off we went on the next great frenzy. We needed a statement out from CB, plus Rania's words to give the context, plus getting Labour MPs attacking Michael Ancram [Conservative deputy leader and Shadow Foreign Secretary] for making a big issue of it, plus we needed prominent Jews out defending her and putting a more balanced message. After the Black Rod/AC spin row, this was the next one and it wouldn't be very nice for CB.

Wednesday, June 19

CB row died down quickly, more support for her than I expected. All the country really cared about was the World Cup, which was great. We were starting to think about going to Japan if they got through. David Blunkett did a pretty heavy attack on the press which though it was fairly light-hearted would probably prolong the Black Rod/AC/CB stuff. TB was off to Paris for dinner with Chirac, called afterwards, said he had been good on beef, Sangatte and the general need for more co-operation before summits, so he was pretty pleased with himself.

Thursday, June 20

Ran in, thirty-five minutes, 4.4 miles. Whizzed through the morning meeting, need to get the focus totally on TB's [televised] press conference. He was over at a Cobra meeting, back really late, eating into preparation time. I had worked up the script pre Seville [EU summit] but it was all going to be about his demeanour and body language under questions. The only strategic decision was whether he engaged in all the current debate about the press and the nature

[1] Mrs Blair said young Palestinians felt they had 'no hope but to blow themselves up'.

of the debate. He was minded not to and I didn't particularly want the Black Rod business reopened so we agreed just say he wanted to be judged on substance, that he was prime minister, not commentator. The backdrop for the media was a *Telegraph* poll saying fifty per cent didn't trust him. Cabinet, better mood than last week but a bit meandering. They discussed foot and mouth, the Tube, a lot of foreign affairs stuff. Clare made even by her standards a ridiculous intervention, saying could he make sure that if Bush sent in Saddam death squads, there was a proper discussion here in Cabinet before they went. He and several others flashed identical looks of disbelief.

He went up [to the press conference], with only Saeed [Khan, Number 10 press office] for company, and we stayed back to watch it on TV in his office. It was very long, he was solid and serious, with a few really good moments but it was definitely worth doing, though the coverage was as much about the wretched hacks and what didn't happen as about what he had said.

Friday, June 21

Good coverage for the press conference, even in some of the hostile press. He was good at them, but we needed more colour and texture. TB was off to Seville via Scotland. England vs Brazil was all anybody cared about. One up, then lost 1–2 and the whole country was deflated. TB called afterwards and sounded pretty down about it. I was also feeling a lot more disappointed than I thought I would. Godric had spent three days working up a proper communications plan on asylum and we now discovered we had been holed by Clare Short doing a pre-recorded *GMTV* interview, recorded after the meeting at which we had agreed we would not tie aid to asylum. It was a mad idea which we had somehow allowed to get away from us.

Saturday, June 22

TB in Seville, going OK but he was a bit bored and in any event the media was wall-to-wall World Cup. I watched a lot of soccer, slept, then we went out with Philip G and Gail to Chequers for dinner to raise money for a Roald Dahl museum. I had an interesting chat with Jackie Stewart [former world champion racing driver] on how useless the civil servant he had dealt with re Formula One had been.

Sunday, June 23

DB called Fiona for what turned out to be a very difficult chat. She had said to Tessa she was really angry about a line in the *Mail* that Blunkett didn't rate me. He was adamant he had never said it, and

I was perfectly prepared to believe him, but it was clear Fiona didn't believe him at all, and made sure he knew. She said whenever ministers were in trouble, they came to me for help, so it would be nice if it was reciprocated. I spent most of the day at various sporting events with the kids, which is what I like doing most at the moment.

Monday, June 24

Coverage of Seville crap. Lots more GB-ery around the place. At his morning meeting, TB was tired, vacant, had nothing to say. At one point he asked Charles [Clarke] if he had anything to say and Charles said 'Yes, cheer up a bit.' It was mainly a discussion about G8 [forthcoming summit in Canada], but with no real focus. Peter H and I left pretty appalled and later had a long session to go over it. We just weren't professional enough. We had slack in the system. We didn't prepare him properly. There was no sense of grip. The real problem, as I'd said to JP, was that TB was spooked by GB at the moment. Even when he wasn't pummelling, there was a part of TB's mind given over to worrying about him. Bad start to the week. Calum came down to the office and I took him to Wimbledon [tennis championship] and we had a great time. Bush's speech on the Middle East was going big. It was taken as 'Arafat must go' and it was going to be quite hard to work out a proper response.

Tuesday, June 25

The Bush Middle East speech was making big waves right round the world but it didn't seem terribly thought through. It seemed the White House was too consumed with the squabbles and struggles within the government, particularly Powell vs Cheney/Rumsfeld, than in really thinking through a plan on the Middle East. Also, truth be told, Bush had a surer touch on domestic than international. I pointed out that Bush calling for the Palestinians to reject Arafat was the surest way to ensure a boost for Arafat. TB didn't really want to end up in a US–UK rift situation, but we said it was up to the Palestinian people to elect their leaders, which was taken as an attack on Bush so we were heading for the rift headlines, even though TB was really in agreement that Arafat was weak, and that there had to be more sympathy for the Israelis.

We had an office planning meeting re September, at which Fiona said they were thinking about going to the Strozzis [Prince Girolamo and his wife Irina] again and also going to Aznar's daughter's wedding. He knew my views on holiday with the Strozzis, but I thought the wedding was equally ridiculous given he didn't know the daughter. Aznar really wanted him to go, but this was behaving like royal families. If I raised it with him he said, OK but I do need to have some kind of life as well. Going to a politician's daughter's wedding in Spain did not strike me as being life.

GB called, said he wanted to come over and go over the Mansion House speech which was a very sceptical speech, lots and lots of focus on the tests, the combined weight of which would ensure very sceptical headlines. He came over and was also trying to go back on the idea of the £1 billion commitment for Africa which we had agreed yesterday and which had been leaked to the *Guardian*. TB wanted it changed to tone down the scepticism, a discussion that continued in the car on the way to the airport [en route to Canada]. GB said he thought it was quite positive. TB said it most certainly was not. Godric did a briefing on the Middle East but it was hard to answer the direct question: if Arafat was re-elected did we expect the US to deal with him? The answer was yes, but what we didn't know was if they would. We landed, got taken by helicopter to Kananaskis, up in the mountains where you could feel the thinness of the air as soon as you arrived. It was perhaps an indication of how unfocused I currently was that my immediate thought was to call Brendan Foster [former Olympic runner and friend of AC] and get some tips on altitude training. We went straight to the [Jean] Chrétien bilateral where he was clear he wanted to make sure Africa remained the main focus. He had seen Bush and said he would need pressure putting on him. He wasn't keen on the extent of commitment we were trying to get. He was good on the detail both of what was happening in Africa but also realistically what we could expect from the other countries. But it was clear his worry was that the Middle East stuff would just keep raging away. I went out for a run along a mountain road through some fantastic scenery, but it was pretty tough going because of the air.

Wednesday, June 26

G8 summit at Kananaskis. TB had bumped into GWB at the gym and they had forty minutes in there, mainly just the two of them. TB felt that they could tolerate Arafat as a titular head but not as the man who led the negotiations. They just didn't trust him. Bush wanted to do media at the start of their bilateral, not least because there was another fraud-related company crash [WorldCom]. But I was worried that if it went to the Middle East, which it would, TB would get put into the poodle position. TB said we must not change the line, and instead should let them move to us a bit. But Bush was basically someone who said what he thought. It's a quality people always say they want in a politician but when the politicians are in the really big jobs, I think it's sometimes the reason they turn against them. In Arafat's case, he thought the man was a terrorist. Listening to him later, I felt sometimes he imagined he could just say things away, just as he had said to us he thought Bin Laden was dead but he daren't say it in case Bin Laden popped up again. We worked through and thought we got to the right position, namely the Palestinians should elect their own leaders but they should elect leaders who could be relied upon to negotiate.

Then off to a very dull [Junichiro] Koizumi [Japanese Prime Minister] bilateral, lots of football talk, Koizumi saying everyone in Japan thought England would win. He did a big tribute to TB's leadership post September 11, said he had read biographies of Churchill and applauded his and TB's efforts to get the Americans properly involved in world peace. TB was equally flattering about Koizumi's reform programme. They went over debt, aid, Afghanistan. Then off to see GWB. The little doorstep they did was OK. I got the feeling that Condi was a bit put out that I was there as well as David Manning. She was pretty status-conscious and I don't think had got the point that I was more to TB than Ari Fleischer [White House press secretary] was to Bush. Bush was on good form, but you did worry whether he had thought things through. He said the problem with Israeli politics is that they tend to unite around the toughest lines. As to why he was so hard on Arafat, he felt he had lied about the money he gave to families organising terrorism. He did seem to have the outlines of a possible step-by-step process, but nobody seemed terribly confident. He felt neither Arafat nor [Ariel] Sharon were capable of delivering peace. TB felt there had to be improved security structures, otherwise they were at the mercy of suicide bombers. GWB said 'I think I've stopped Sharon from killing Arafat – I don't know if that's a good thing or not.'

Bush was pretty scathing on some of the Africa stuff. He said he liked the plan, but then through the discussion came out with hard lines on corruption, conflict. He said 'I'm enthusiastic about Africa. What pisses me off about Africa is that for every good intention there appear to be more bad actions.' TB felt the issue was leadership. He strongly felt the debt issue wasn't just moral, but ultimately we had to get these countries on their feet for sound political and economic reasons too. Bush said he was putting up half a billion dollars for AIDS in Africa but he wanted to know there was strategy. GWB was a weird mix, much wittier than people would imagine, quite self-deprecating, very open for someone in his position. At times too, you felt he had a real grasp of issues, but then he would just go off on one like 'If Chirac pushes me on trade, I'm going to crawl over his chilli' – a new one on all of us. He couldn't pronounce 'Yemenis', when he was telling a story about how Yemenis were taking out lots of US thermos flasks filled with honey. Then he'd give a clever and broad-ranging analysis of the dangers to America of reliance on Saudi oil, how to get out of that. TB and GWB went off to the heads-only session and later Putin arrived and scuppered the $20 billion deal to sort the issue of Soviet WMD, because he had decided at the last minute he wanted something different to what we thought was agreed. Inside the summit, there were a couple of massive bust-ups, first Chirac claiming the US didn't really care about Africa, and Bush hitting back hard. He was being exposed to the kind of anti-Americanism they didn't really understand. TB played a bit of tennis with Schroeder. I had a drink with Schroeder's interpreters and got the very strong feeling they thought he was going to lose the election.

Thursday, June 27

The summit was going fine and the Africa plan resolved better than expected. TB and Chirac were also getting on better. A number of the African leaders were in for part of the summit and although there was an inevitable feeling of poor men coming to the rich men's table, the Africans were pretty positive and TB started his own press conference with a quote from Obasanjo [Nigerian President] that it was a historic turning point for Africa. TB's press event was a bit weird, one camera, one reporter, the pictures being beamed back to the hacks miles away in Calgary. Tom felt it was fine. TB wanted another discussion about his future, or '*La Grande Stratégie*' as he now called it. The only question that mattered was whether it strengthened or weakened him. I veered to the lame-duck side of the argument, putting GB in an even more powerful position on the euro, but TB felt it would allow him to be himself more. I was worried that all that had happened was that GB had effectively worn him down to force him out ahead of his time. It was true that he had always imagined only doing two terms, but I wasn't convinced it was remotely time for him to go yet. I also shared his worries about the GB temperament question. TB still felt that two terms was about all you get in the modern world. But if it took a couple of years to do the euro, he would be happy to hang around for that. I asked him what Cherie thought. The same, he said. But I have to resolve the question whether it weakens or strengthens me.

The more he talked about it, the more I feared it was one of those things that had a certain immediate appeal but which would go in the box marked 'things I wish I hadn't done'. He said it wasn't a case of being fed up, but eight years was roughly what you got, and if we couldn't see the sort of progress we wanted in public services in that time, there was a bit of a problem. We started to talk about the conference speech, and I got the sense he was thinking about using it to indicate departure. I felt the conference speech should be about explaining change and communicating change, answering the question 'Was the country really changing for the better?' We believed it was, and if we were right, then we could communicate the vision of a better country out there in the future, nobody left behind.

He talked about Cherie, said she was very hardy, tough, could endure the rough-and-tumble and was certainly not pushing him out. He said nice things about Fiona and what she had been doing, said she was important to the operation and it was important I kept her happy. We spent what seemed like hours driving to the plane because there were demonstrators clogging the motorways which pissed him off. But overall it was a good visit, we got in the right place on the Middle East despite Bush, Africa was OK and in our private conversations we had got back some of the old working relationship and warmth. But I was a bit worried that mentally he was moving towards the exit door with only the euro to hold him back. As we arrived at the airport, he got even more pissed off to hear Oxfam said the deal was peanuts so I got the office working out how many peanuts you could buy with all the millions that had been pledged. The flight home was fairly uneventful apart from when I lost my credit card down the side of the seat and they had to take the thing apart to get it out.

Friday, June 28

Jackie Stewart came in to see me about the Silverstone Grand Prix situation, genuinely concerned we were going to lose it. It was a long, convoluted story of how the British Racing Drivers Association, of which he was chair, lost the rights to Bernie Ecclestone [Formula One supremo], how Bernie had built and accumulated power. He controlled all the TV, advertising, corporate revenues and he and Max Mosley [President of the Fédération Internationale de l'Automobile] just took an aggressive view that in all sorts of ways the BGP [British Grand Prix] wasn't good enough. Jackie's big worry was that we would lose the centrality of the UK to the whole motorsports industry if we lost grip of the grand prix. He was an interesting bloke and I enjoyed talking to him about his career. He said he thought TB looked really tired and was losing his sparkle. He said it was really important we didn't push him too hard and also he should think about having a personal trainer with a daily regime.

Saturday, June 29

The whole weekend ruined by hay fever. Not much on the work front, the usual Sunday newspaper shite, the *Sunday Times* on some fiction re Number 10 refurbishments, *Mail on Sunday* rather hopelessly trying to link CB's Palestine charity [Medical Aid for Palestinians] to Hamas [Islamist political party with military wing]. Part of the day taken up dealing with Steve [Byers] in Greece. I tried three or four times to talk Rebekah [Wade, *News of the World* editor] out of doing the Byers story [about a relationship with a woman in a hotel] on the front but in the end she did and it was pretty grim reading, though she said it was a lot worse and tackier before they spoke. I fixed up for Steve to have a chat with her. Rebekah said she felt sorry for him. He sounds really nice and I wish we weren't doing the story. 'Well don't then. Just dump it, bin it.' She said they couldn't, but they were taking the woman to France for a week to stop her talking to anyone else so hopefully it would die down fairly quickly. I did a call with JP to go over everything pre *Frost* tomorrow. He was a lot more onside after our dinner.

Sunday, 30 June

JP on *Frost*, followed by a conference call, but with the World Cup final on [Germany 0, Brazil 2], I wasn't keen on working too hard today. The Byers story didn't really run so I think we had handled it reasonably well. TB sent over a note on forward strategy. He emphasised yet again that getting the policy right was what mattered above all. On political positioning, he was worried that the 'Nobody left behind' slogan was too exclusive, not New Labour enough. It suggested we were only concerned with the people at the bottom of the pile, not everyone else.

Monday, July 1

TB used his Monday morning meeting to hammer home his determination to keep the focus on policy. He felt there was a danger that because of all the noises off the whole time we became a bit timid. He had a meeting with Charles C, David Triesman and Hilary Armstrong about the trade unions. TB felt they were becoming an even bigger nightmare than ever. Hilary felt the problem was that GB was running a counter-strategy with them. TB agreed reluctantly to do another dinner for them but felt we needed to divide and rule a bit. The leaders of the big unions were indulged by the media because they attacked us, and they were capable of talking the most meaningless drivel. Simon Heffer [*Daily Mail* columnist] came in to see me for lunch. It was the usual jolly chat but he also said that 'as a friend' he would advise me to leave fairly soon because the *Mail* was really going to go for me personally from now on in. I told him to 'take a message back to your leader [editor Paul Dacre] that I gave up long ago worrying where his bile was poured'. We were still trying to find a venue for the press briefings out of Number 10. The QE2 [conference centre] was the best option but it would cost four grand a day. Ten-mile run.

Tuesday, July 2

Ran in. TB called me up as soon as I arrived, in a stew. GB had done an interview in *The Times* suggesting massive investment in EMAs [education maintenance allowances], on the day that we were pushing the antisocial behaviour strategy. He said it was complete news to him, and typical of the way GB did his own thing without regard to others. GB was complaining the whole time that we didn't have a strategy. But the problem was we did have a strategy but he had a counter-strategy as a counterpoint to TB's profile. TB was now of the view that GB was just doing him in the whole time. What would it do to the country if he took over? He felt that the tragedy for GB was that they were both actually in the right jobs for them. TB was now going through the CSR bids from different departments, then saw GB who complained we were operating on a different set of figures. In fact the figures had been agreed between Jeremy, Ed Balls and 'Mr Adonis' as GB called Andrew. But GB said these were different figures to the ones they had been working on. The EMA move was a classic exercise to get up a big GB story to counter TB doing something different. TB then did the *TES* [*Times Educational Supplement*], for which he was pretty good, much better than Channel 4 later.

With the *Sunday Telegraph* in for lunch, he was back on pander mode, and I felt a bit queasy at some of the things he was saying, particularly about public services. I also felt he talked too much about focus groups and what they said. Later off to Channel 4, which we had agreed to do on the basis of real interchange with viewers but it wasn't great. He didn't really drive the message about this being a CSR for schools as he had done with the *TES*.

Wednesday, July 3

PG called, said that for the first time there was polling, bad for TB, that had the idea in there that GB would be better. I felt this had been a media thing but clearly it had got through, because GB was fortunate that people didn't focus on him in the same way. Philip was worried about it. Yet when I had a meeting with Jim Naughtie [BBC *Today* programme] I was quite taken aback by just how negative he was about GB, felt he wasn't a serious option, that he was 'so strange, humourless, simmering with such resentment that I couldn't see him being a good leader'. He said he found it incredible that the second most powerful person in the country felt such a compelling need to have people think he was able to duff up Estelle Morris. Jim was on good form, very lively, said that he felt our recent problems were partly because people felt we, particularly TB and I, were too big for our boots, a bit arrogant, always thought we knew best. He felt, and funnily enough it was one of the points I made in the notes done last weekend, that we needed to take the lead in generating more honest and realistic debates, because the media wouldn't do it for us.

After PMQs, I saw TB to agree a line to give to the *Spectator* who had some story about TB and CB using private-school tutors for Euan and Nicky. It was odd how virtually every bad argument we ever had tended to be in the area where public life and private life collide, and often related to education. He said most normal parents would sympathise. I said you are not a normal parent, you are the prime minister, and if you are that you have to think through the politics of everything you do. Out of school lessons, fine, but given how many decent teachers there are what was the point in sticking your chin out to say 'Hit me, I'm getting private school teachers'? He said if Rory and Calum were struggling, we would get them help. I said I sure as hell wouldn't go to a private school for it. I had a long meeting with Peter M and Peter H. Peter M felt that the real damage was being done below the surface, that we were not in as good shape as we wanted or needed to be.

Thursday, July 4

Philip had briefed TB on the latest poll which showed the trust problem growing. TB felt the lack of a clear strategy driven through in communications was the central problem. I felt it was more that GB was running a counter-strategy which meant we were being presented negatively from the left and the right. And the party was picking up the idea that on policy substance, we had moved to the right. As John Reid said to me before Cabinet, Number 10 had lost Pat [McFadden, former Number 10 deputy chief of staff], [David] Miliband, Jon Cruddas [Labour MP, Blair's former deputy political secretary for union liaison], and 'the only person left who would bleed a hundred per cent red blood if you cut him is you'. He said TB was losing his networks in government, Parliament and party. He also felt JP was not as powerful as he was, GB basically hostile, RC on his own kick in Parliament, plus he had people like Clare offside anyway, so TB was becoming more and more isolated. TB looked a bit wandering at Cabinet, which was mainly GB going through general state of the economy, said the spending review would be the week after next. He said our underlying position was sound and he was cautiously optimistic about growth, industrial production rising, the job situation pretty good.

I had lunch with Jonathan Dimbleby to discuss TB doing a solo *Any Questions* [BBC Radio 4]. Dimbleby said he was struck by how TB always looked tired. Back for a brainstorm with Philip, Douglas, PH, Michael Barber [head of the Prime Minister's Delivery Unit], Andrew Adonis and some of the key policy people. How to address specific issues of delivery on the public services in London. Some of the best and worst was in London, but the fact that the national media was based here tended to skew things towards the worst, added to which virtually none of the senior media people used state schools or the NHS and so had a vested interest in running them down to justify their own decisions to themselves. Douglas and I were both a bit worried about the idea of specifically identifying London in terms of its special problems. But we agreed to do a region-by-region report on the public services setting out good and bad.

Phil Bassett [Number 10 special adviser] had been over briefing JP for *Question Time* and he had gone mad at the *Spectator* story on private tutors. He said I ought to call JP to try and calm him down. He was in a total rage, said it wasn't about tough choices for parents, because we all had tough choices. Pauline was always telling me we should use better schools and I felt we had to use the local school. So does virtually every Labour MP. He said Cherie does all that Liverpool stuff and her poor background, but when it comes to schooling for her own kids, there's this snobbery about the best schools and now private-school tutors. JP called after the programme and said he hadn't done well, so I made a point of watching it and he was fine. Called him to say so and he said he just felt tired and jaded at the moment.

Off to the US ambassador's residence for their July 4th do. Usual mix of politicians, media, great and the good. The best moment of the evening was when I was chatting to [Sir] Roger Bannister [first athlete to run a mile in under four minutes] about Rory's running, introduced him to Fiona as 'the former athlete', and she asked him what his distance was. 'Lots really, but I was probably best known as a miler,' he said without a hint of embarrassment, while she blushed when she realised what a daft question it was.

Saturday, July 6

Another quiet day. Only work-related thing was the *Observer* getting hold of the fact we were selling HUDs [eye-level 'head-up' displays for F16 combat aircraft] to the US, knowing they would go on to Israel. Had a series of calls with Jack S to agree what to say in the morning interviews – not a new policy, but addressing a new reality of multinational assembly lines. The vice president of Afghanistan [Haji Abdul Qadir] was assassinated [shot in the head in Kabul], so we were scrabbling around a bit on that too.

Sunday, July 7

Patricia [Hewitt] was on *Frost*. She was fine but was not even asked about arms [sales], which surprisingly didn't take off. There were a few GB/CSR stories around, but all a bit incoherent. We lacked a strategic theme that was drawing policy together at the moment. Out for dinner with the Goulds. Philip was worried TB didn't really get what our weaknesses were at the moment.

Monday, July 8

At TB's Monday meeting, TB was baulking again at 'Nobody left behind' as a theme for conference. He felt reform was the most important focus, that conference should be about the remodelling of the welfare state around the themes of rights and responsibilities. I felt we needed to be bigger than that, that we were going through a bad time and we lacked clarity about how to get through it. TB also wanted to go into another round of persuasion with the right-wing media, and we just disagreed on this. I felt that if we isolated the *Mail*, we would gain leverage with the press on the left, one of whose main angsts was the feeling we had courted the right too much. There was also something so putrid about these papers that culturally it was right to challenge them rather than keep trying to win them round, which in the *Mail*'s case was an utterly lost cause. But the key to everything was to get up a bigger message about where we were going. Thatcher always had a sense of direction, even when the shit was flying. Often we had it, but at the moment we didn't. Charles C was in very grumpy mood at the meeting and later told me he hated the job.

I listened in to a couple of bad TB/GB calls. First, with lots of dicking around on the date of the CSR, TB feeling he was trying to bounce us into the 15th. TB made clear he was not signing it all off until he was happy with the Home Office budget. It had not even been taken to Blunkett yet. I pointed out that again, important detail was being held back from him. He said he was so used to being abused and mistreated by him that he had almost stopped caring, and just wanted to make sure the final package was OK. We had all sorts of CSR follow-up planned, e.g. visits, but we still didn't have a date. I had a meeting with Afghan journalists, which was interesting not least for the way that they saw Britain's role, namely far more positively than our media did.

Tuesday, July 9

TB called an internal meeting to run through the final difficult bits of the CSR. He was playing far tougher with GB than before. TB said he was pressing for yet more for education and we would get it. The Home Office settlement still needed to be improved but he was confident we would get there in the end. The process was crazy. Jeremy [Heywood] and Ed Balls would agree, only for TB and GB then to reopen and disagree. To get where we needed to be on education, we were going to have to take something out of JP's and Milburn's budgets. The outstanding issues were becoming small in number but very difficult and the TB/GB bilateral this afternoon was the most difficult yet. Nothing was really agreed. They both had to leave for the Barbara Castle [former Labour Cabinet minister who had died in May] memorial, and even that had its own TB/GB-related problem. The initial suggestion had been that TB and GB do readings but GB had seemingly insisted on doing a big speech and in the current climate, it would look odd for him to do a big number and TB a little reading. So quickly we had to work up a speech for TB who until this point was not even aware he was doing it.

I went to retirement parties for Geoffrey Goodman [*British Journalism Review*] and Michael Jones [*Sunday Times*]. I got TB to come to Geoffrey's and make a nice little speech about integrity in journalism. Betty Boothroyd was at Michael Jones' and told me there was quite a lot of disillusion out there now. Charlie F was in to see TB re the Home Office and popped round for a chat. I made the argument that it was possible, and at times I felt probable, and very occasionally felt certain, that GB would never be leader. Charlie was not convinced, felt there was nobody else really emerging. Mike White called to say Stephen Bates [*Guardian* religious affairs correspondent] was doing a story that TB had rejected several names for the new Archbishop [of

Canterbury]. In trying to rebut it, I helped confirm it would be [Dr] Rowan Williams [Archbishop of Wales].

Wednesday, July 10

Ran in, up to see TB in the flat, who was hugely seized of the importance of IDS and [Michael] Howard [Shadow Chancellor] making clear they didn't intend to match our spending plans. It was classic Hague-ism.[1] He [IDS] had tried compassionate conservatism but now he had moved back to where his instincts were, on the right, a hard-line cuts agenda. It was a defining moment for Parliament and we had to pin it on them big time. But the big government story of the day was DB reclassifying cannabis [from Class B to C]. Keith Hellawell [government drugs adviser, or 'drugs czar'] went on *Today* and 'announced' he had resigned in protest. I had always tried hard with Hellawell, tried to boost him re his communication skills, but he had never quite cut it within the government machinery. I had to calm Blunkett down, say the most important thing was getting cops to back us and by and large they did. But I felt a bit uncomfortable both with the policy – but also the clear mixed messages of saying it was OK to take it but dealers could get fourteen years.

TB and GB met, and it was a collector's item. GB constantly complaining there was no strategy. Why did we do a crime initiative on the day he had done his NHS speech [see March 20]? TB saying 'I cannot believe you are still going on about it.' GB blaming TB for the *Telegraph* attacking him and when I pointed out that the *Telegraph* tended to attack TB a lot harder, he was having none of it. After he had left, TB said we just had to keep managing him. It's a pain, but he is still the best politician in the government, 'with the possible exception of me'. He said 'I've thought long and hard about whether I could put him out, and I don't believe I can. I feel a sense of duty to leave the Labour Party in good shape and the two of us as avowed enemies would be too bad to contemplate. I've thought about it but it's just not realistic, because whatever his faults, which are many, he is still the best qualified to take over.'

He said one of his weaknesses was that he forced others to adopt his own failings. He said Nick Brown would probably get hit hard in the FMD [inquiry] report [he had been agriculture minister during the 2001 foot and month crisis] and why? Because he didn't go to the centre for help when he most needed it because GB, as we knew, was

[1] Labour had attacked former Tory Leader William Hague for tacking to the right under pressure.

urging him to ignore all the presidential bullshit, so-called. I felt GB was trying to force him out by wearing him down. There was no doubt in GB's own mind that TB had reneged on a deal of some sort, but perhaps more significant than that, TB was moving to the view that GB was not temperamentally suited to a bigger job.

Fiona had a meeting with Jan Taylor [Number 10 Correspondence Unit] who had noticed a lot more disaffected mail coming through, the feeling that TB wasn't trustworthy. It chimed with what Philip was saying. PMQs was OK, and TB managed to get up the Tory cuts plan. IDS not great. I got Godric to say at the four o'clock that TB had to cancel his regional visit tomorrow because he had more CSR meetings. The Treasury went bonkers about it and I told them that was their problem. If they worked to a proper agreed strategy, there wouldn't be a problem.

Thursday, July 11

TB called me through and we went out for a chat on the terrace. Philip had briefed him on how his trust ratings had really dipped. He said 'In truth I've never really wanted to do more than two full terms. I could fight a third election *in extremis*, but it would have to be *in extremis*, namely that my worries about GB were such that I feel it would be wrong.' It was pretty clear to me that he had just about settled his view, that he would sometime announce it, say that he was going to stay for the full term, but not go into the election as leader. The big question was the same as before – does it give him an authority of sorts, or does it erode that authority, and do people just move automatically towards GB? He felt it was possible that it would strengthen him because he would be able to move people without anyone saying it was because he feared a rival. I had noticed, and he did it again today, that he had started to think about legacy, and how his premiership would be viewed, another indicator that he was moving psychologically to the exit door. He said 'I think even if I went now, it would be pretty good. Clinton-plus, certainly Clinton without the baggage.'

He felt in terms of transforming the party, winning, and the big policy changes we had made, there was a lot to point to. 'But the euro does matter a lot to me. Not because of a place in history but because I think it is the right thing for the country. The only question is whether it would just be seen as a deal with GB, that we do it, I go, he takes over. If I said I was going, sometime in the run-up to the next election, it would actually give me more power over him. I could move him. The question is whether politics would just want to move on to the next story. Maybe, but it would release me to do all the things I want to do. Really drive the public services agenda, really go for Europe and other foreign policy issues.'

He had mentioned the idea to Peter M, thinking he would be totally hostile, but he wasn't, because he could see the logic. It seemed to me he was definitely moving towards it. We walked in from the terrace to the Cabinet Room, and I asked him whether he really thought this was the right thing to do, or whether in fact he was being intimidated into doing it, and thinking it was the right thing, by a mix of GB and the press. He said, I don't think so. 'You have to know when to go. I also think the history of leaders trying to choose their successors is a very bad one.' So far as I was aware, only Jonathan, Sally, Cherie and I, and now Peter, were aware he was even thinking about this. As we walked back to his office, I said 'Christ, how much could I get from the press for this one?' He smiled, then stopped again and said 'Is it the right thing or the wrong thing? I want your best brain on it.'

At Cabinet, TB asked GB to speak on the economy pre CSR again and he warned it was going to get tougher and that there would be a need to reshape perceptions and expectations re pensions and house prices in particular. He said that problems in the American economy were going to have a big impact here and we would be 'severely tested'. TB spoke briefly about pensions and asked for a note. GB, very deliberately as part of the current style vs substance line they were running, said he would be happy to provide a note on this for Cabinet but 'It's very important that we focus on next year not next week.' In other words he was long term, TB was short term.

DB briefed the White Paper on criminal justice reform. Derry showed once more why he is not the most natural of politicians when he followed DB's presentation by saying 'I counsel caution about rebalancing the system in favour of the victim. This needs a more balanced approach.' Everyone knew what he meant, but it was the sort of statement that if made publicly would be a pretty full-scale disaster area. Joan Hammell [Prescott's special adviser] came to see me, said we really needed to watch JP, that he was very pissed off again, the bilaterals were not really serious. He was talking about not doing the visit with TB next week. GB had shown him the *Mail*, said that we cancelled the regional visit for CSR meetings and he said to Joan 'I'm just a pawn in their game.' TB, JP and GB were due to have dinner next week and I told her JP just had to understand how grim GB makes it for him from time to time.

Friday, July 12

Up at 5 to head off to Nottingham to see Rory running in the English Schools [athletic championships]. He had to stay with the rest of the team so I had hours to kill and worked up a speech for TB to set the tone for the CSR. It worked well as a newspaper story. Over to see Mum and Dad, and he was looking really ill.

Saturday, July 13

Back to the stadium for the finals. Really hot, nice atmosphere, but considering these were meant to be the best young runners in the country, the facilities were dreadful. Tom was doing a ring-round re the CSR briefing I had done and I was topping up with a couple of them to push education. The other situation we were having to deal with was Anji [Hunter] and Adam Boulton [in a relationship]. Anji called me about it last night, and Adam this morning and we agreed it was probably best that they let the *Mail on Sunday* do their worst and just say nothing. Sky wanted Adam to put out a statement and I called Nick Pollard [head of news] and said it was best not to. If they did, everyone would feel they had to run it. It was quite a turn-up for the books. Adam was very apologetic at the fact we were having to advise him on how to deal with it. TB called about the leak of the criminal justice White Paper to the *Mirror*, the *Independent* and *The Times*. Blunkett was livid, and demanding a leak inquiry which TB agreed to.

Sunday, July 14

We were getting into a much better place on the CSR, but why had it been so difficult? Peter M had noticed a shift, called to say 'For once the Treasury seems to be in the right place.' He was calling about a story in the *Observer* that he might become ambassador to the US. 'Please kill this at birth because it has clearly been put there to damage me.' We still didn't have agreement on DB's budget. Tessa called to say that she and other ministers were appalled at the letters being sent to them by the Treasury which were essentially telling them not just how much they were getting, but what to do with it.

Monday, July 15

Ran in, 31.03 minutes, personal best. TB had spent a lot of the weekend trying to influence GB's CSR statement to the House, felt it was too much focused on 'spend, spend, spend', not enough on reform. But we definitely had it set up in a better place, and GB was working for a good parliamentary and media response and by and large he did it. He delivered it fine, if a bit monotone, and he was effective in dealing with [Michael] Howard's not brilliant response. Education was running big out of it, but though there was reform in there, it didn't come through strongly. The CSR pretty much took care of itself so we had plenty of time to prepare for TB's meeting with the [Commons select committee chairs] Liaison Committee tomorrow. It would be like PMQs but without the noise and with more than just the Opposition party leader able to follow up forensically. So TB was mainly focusing on fact whereas I wanted a discussion of message and texture. We had the annual Labour Party reception in the garden but TB had to leave to take a call from Bush. Nothing much of substance, Bush saying he understood TB was taking a fair bit of stick for being supportive, and he was grateful.

Tuesday, July 16

Press OK for GB. Up to see TB in the flat, another chat about his future. You only get two terms, not sensible to choose a successor, usual stuff. I said what I couldn't work out was whether he really thought this was the right thing, or whether he had been pushed into it by bullying. He felt not, but though GB could be very difficult, he always tried to put that to one side when he worked out what to do. His big worry was still whether GB was suited for the job. We went through the Liaison Committee briefing, maybe an hour or so on that before he said he now wanted to prepare on his own and we left him. It was getting a big build-up from the media but he was pretty much on top of things by the time we left for the Commons. He was a bit nervy and faltering at first, and the interchange with the MPs wasn't terribly relaxed, but he picked up when they got on to serious policy, particularly foreign policy. They didn't really go for him, though there was far too much focus on the centre. It was definitely worth doing, was getting big play and good reviews both for him and for the MPs.

I went as [*News of the World* columnist] Chris Buckland's guest to the IDS press gallery lunch. I got a good look at IDS. He was much more personable than I thought, also more presentable. He told a couple of OK jokes at the start of his speech, mentioned me four or five times, which was far too often, because it suggested they were the ones obsessed with communication not us, and his main point was to attack the BBC over scrapping political programmes. Also said he would reverse our lobby reforms. It was OK without being brilliant. What I didn't feel was a big political or intellectual challenge to us.

I got back for a meeting with Tom McKane, David Manning and Jonathan re Iraq and when to do the documents. TB had raised the temperature another gear by making clear publicly we intended to do something and also saying that Saddam had to be dealt with. We agreed not to go for it yet, because it would look like we were going to go to war if we did, TB having made it clear that it would be the start of another phase. TB was pretty pleased with the way the Liaison Committee went, felt it had been worth doing because it was possible to engage in depth. The main news running out of it was Iraq. Philip called after the recent groups, which were grim. GB's CSR was just seen as more promises and the real problem was they didn't really feel there had been proper delivery yet. So the trust problem was real and deep. We really had to watch it now. The general judgement, fair or not, seemed to be not good enough, too many promises, not enough delivery.

Wednesday, July 17

Ran in, bang on thirty-one minutes. Union strikes [council and public transport workers] and the criminal justice White Paper were running big. TB was fine at PMQs, but frustrated that they didn't really go on the CSR. We agreed 'Schools and hospitals first' as the slogan for conference. I had a very interesting meeting with Carol Fisher [Central Office of Information] who felt there was a system of apartheid in the Civil Service, that people who came in from outside were tolerated but not welcome, and though she felt she had had some success in making change, her life had been something of a misery there. She clearly couldn't stand the old-style directors of information. It was quite an interesting take on things.

I read the FMD [inquiry] report which was pretty devastating, basically said every major decision was wrong. Although he [Dr Iain Anderson, chairman] was by and large OK about TB, it was clear he felt we should have done more early, should have called in the army and set up Cobra earlier. It was well written, well argued and all the better for that. It was a considered piece of work and I felt the sustained impact was pretty awful. Jeremy and I reacted pretty much identically. We showed it to TB without comment, and he felt pretty much the same. TB got a good press at the Liaison Committee but of course the apology from the IRA yesterday was a massive story and took over.[1]

To the Roof Gardens in Kensington for Ross [Kemp] and Rebekah [Wade]'s marriage party. Anji and Adam [Boulton] there together,

[1] The IRA issued an unprecedented apology to the families of those 'non-combatants' it killed during the thirty-year campaign of violence in Northern Ireland.

which was all a bit weird. GB and Sarah. Mo [Mowlam], Chris Smith [former Cabinet minister], DB came later. I enjoyed talking to Mark Bolland [press secretary to the Prince of Wales] who was incredibly indiscreet, not least in the way he talked about Prince Charles. He was scathing about the Palace establishment, said they hated him and they distrusted Charles' whole operation because they felt he was a threat to the Queen. He was pressing me re TB and GB, and also re what TB thought of matters royal, but I was rather more circumspect than he was.

Thursday, July 18

Fiona spotted a photographer in the street when she came back from swimming. He was from the [*Evening*] *Standard* trying to get a picture of me running. Up to the flat to see TB. He had not seen the *Spectator* interview with Piers [Morgan] which was a total diatribe against him and CB and had called for GB to be leader.

Went through to Cabinet with JP. He had had a couple of differences with GB over policy. As we walked through, he told me he was going to get rid of the RMT flat because it wasn't appropriate to have his own house becoming a story while he was doing a lot of difficult stuff on that front.[1] JP talked about the housing issue at Cabinet. TB did a bit of general spiel, but what was interesting was that he didn't really do what we discussed beforehand, instead went off on one on ministers' failure to deal with red tape and bureaucracy. He said if the Tories had any sense they would latch on to this, create a political narrative around the fact that we are demanding more in the centre whilst at the same time pursuing policies of devolution, and sometimes businesses feeling we have tied them in knots.

GB didn't speak, which again was a bit odd a few days after the CSR. Fiona had given a lift in to Ed Miliband and just as we felt GB and Co. were doing us in the whole time, they felt we were. GB didn't like the drift of policy but Ed said he felt powerless to do anything about it. Fiona felt GB now feared he was running out of time and the question was no longer whether he would take over but what there would be to do when he did, would he just come in on the back of failure re public services? Fiona had told Ed that if TB and GB worked together as a team, TB would be far more likely to be happy to let him take over, but the more it looked like GB was trying to

[1] Prescott was paying rent of £220 a month under a protected tenancy for a flat subsidised by the Rail, Maritime and Transport Workers' Union.

force him out, the more TB would dig in, and the more his people would be loyal to him even if they disagreed with some of what he did. She said Ed presented GB as a victim. But he had to use his power to be part of a team. She said why not just do the job, be nice, work with everyone else, and wait in the near-certain knowledge that before too long he would be prime minister? She said Ed had said it would be great if I worked with GB, but Fiona told him GB had barely acknowledged us for months now.

I went for lunch with David Frost at Le Caprice. He felt TB could pretty much stay as long as he wanted because he was in a different league, could probably win four elections if he put his mind to it, could certainly beat Thatcher's record. Then in for a meeting with TB, Margaret Beckett, RW and all the FMD people. TB had read the [inquiry report] introduction thoroughly, skimmed through the rest and felt it was pretty damning. But neither he nor Margaret were really up for saying someone should go for it. I said the overall sense as you read through it was of chaos, near panic, all the big decisions badly taken and there was bound to be a real drive for resignations and if we felt that was the case, and that's where we would end, we should do it now. Margaret felt that wasn't right, that Nick Brown was popular in the House and there would not be a real demand. I felt if the Tories got their act together, and really went for this, then we would be in difficulty. We would either lose people, or it would become a real symbol of arrogance. Billions wasted. Total fuck-up all round. But nobody says sorry and nobody resigns.

Margaret was pretty clear, said the Tories didn't resign over BSE. I felt if we were serious about the new politics, there had to be heads rolling, but Margaret was totally opposed and TB was a bit flaky about it. Margaret was very robust about the need to tough it out, felt it would be wrong for there to be sackings out of this. I totally disagreed but in the end if TB wasn't going to push it, there wasn't much we could do. I said if we are complacent or unapologetic we will be killed on this, and if the Tories or the Countryside Alliance can't put together a decent summertime campaign on it, they are totally useless.

Friday, July 19

Got in and TB called me up to the flat. He was wearing the most extraordinary collection – a white collarless Nicole Farhi shirt, plain blue trousers and England football slippers with the three lions on them. I said I find it very hard to take him seriously wearing kids' slippers and that shirt. He said I had a bias against style. He asked if I had thought any further about his '*grand projet*'. He felt it was nonsense that the Cabinet was moving towards GB and he really thought this could give him strength. He would announce it in the autumn, pre conference, make clear to the Cabinet that if anyone sought to exploit it or organise a leadership campaign, he would sack them. He felt it would actually allow him to move GB e.g. to the Foreign Office, because the charge could not be levelled that he was doing it to damage a rival. It would allow him to do what he thought was right without people saying he was simply interested in staying in power. Bill Clinton had said to him 'Whatever you do, go when they're still asking for more. Don't go like Thatcher.' TB said if she'd gone in '88, it would have been very different for her. Her last two years were just a downward path.

He had also decided that GB would not like it. It would mean the curtain on him would open more widely and the spotlight would fall upon him more. Deep down, he felt GB probably was flawed, not right for the top job but it was not a good idea for leaders to pick their successors and the party and the country had to discover these things for themselves. I had quietly discussed what he was saying both with Fiona and Sally and both were adamant it would make him a lame duck overnight, but he was persuading himself it would give him extra authority. There was also the possibility of space opening for another successor to emerge. I wasn't sure about that but for now he seemed set on it, constantly saying to me 'You only get two terms in this job.' I told him what Frost had said, namely that he could easily go into the record books for longevity. He said the great difference between him and other politicians was that he could walk away from it.

He then walked over to the wall, leant against it, laughed and said 'There's another complication I need to tell you about.' He said 'I think Cherie is pregnant.' He said they were both absolutely gobsmacked by the whole thing. But it did mean it was forcing him to think about the future. 'I've effectively got two families with the same woman.' He had known she might be pregnant for a few days and it had clearly had an impact on his thinking about the *grand projet*. I felt a big weight carrying two pretty major secrets from the same conversation, his apparent decision to go before the election, and Cherie pregnant again.

Saturday, July 20

I slept really badly, lots of different worries just floating around, couldn't decide whether TB was right with his *grand projet*, was trying to separate out my own feelings about my own position, which would probably welcome it. As for CB being pregnant again, it was mind-blowing. It was a nice morning and I went out into the garden to dictate some notes to the office, and was stung by a bee, much to the Garden Room's amusement.

Sunday, July 21

Conference call re FMD. Jeremy and I both felt that the FMD draft statement from Defra [Department for Environment, Food and Rural Affairs] was poor and both of us made various efforts through the day to get it improved but the department was very resistant. There was something of an irony in it, as one of the subtexts of the whole report was that they had been slow to exploit necessary help from the centre. It was only when I spoke to Margaret B herself that we started to make some progress. Jeremy and I still believed TB was slightly head-in-the-sand about the potential impact, but TB felt it might not be the total disaster we feared. I found myself beginning to wind down and think about the holiday.

Monday, July 22

Ran through the parks, six miles in just over forty-two minutes. I bumped into Michael Martin [Speaker of the Commons] in Green Park, where he was out walking, and had a really nice chat with him, about bagpipes and about Scotland. Through the day, a series of meetings with the policy people on the pamphlet we were planning for September. The balance to strike was between reform and values. I wanted the focus on values, as a way of saying we were New Labour delivering Old Labour goals. TB was on reform for a purpose. I was really impressed with Douglas [Alexander] at the moment. Of all the GB people, he was the one least wrapped up in the whole TB/GB thing.

TB had a conversation with Iain Anderson [FMD report author], then spoke to Margaret B, then to Nick Brown to tell him that he was not going to have to resign and we would tough it out. He went [to the Commons] for the [FMD] statement, which was just about OK. He filled in Sally and me on last night's dinner with JP and GB. He said it was pretty awful, GB doing his usual complaining that there was no strategy, what was going on, who does what, with the unions his latest area for complaint. TB told him to calm down, said we had a problem and we had to deal with it but let's not get our knickers in a twist. He said it was quite useful for JP to see so clearly the extent to which GB failed to hide the fact he could hardly bear to be in TB's company. JP had said at the end that a lot of the attacks had been personal dressed up as political.

TB and I went for lunch at the *Guardian* and he was on good form, but Iraq was clearly going to be a major problem with everyone, though helpfully Mike White reminded us that TB had talked about WMD, and his worries about the link with Iraq, when he last went for lunch there last September. Later I had a meeting with SIS re Iraq. C had just come back from the US and had reported from his discussions with Condi and George Tenet [CIA director] that as far as they were concerned it was when not if, with or without us, and they did not feel the need for a new UNSCR. TB was right out there and was going to be very exposed. Then to the farewell dinner for Richard Wilson, which was a nice enough do. TB was fulsome in his praise and though Richard and I had had a few ups and downs, he was actually not a bad guy, and I liked his kids. You can tell a lot about people from the way they react to their children and the way their children react to them, and I was really impressed by their relationship with Tom, their deaf son. I sat next to him at the dinner and really liked him.

Tuesday, July 23

TB chaired a big Iraq meeting, JS, GH, CDS, C, Francis Richards [director of GCHQ], Peter Goldsmith [Attorney General], plus the key Number 10 people. C reported his strong feeling that the US had pretty much made up their minds. Steve Hadley [US Deputy National Security Advisor] was saying there was no need for another resolution, and how many more times do we hang around watching the Iraqis stiff Kofi? Condi was a bit better but not much. TB was asking whether the Iraqis would welcome an invasion or not. Jack felt the regime would appear to be popular until it tips, but when it tips, it will happen quickly. All the signs out of Washington were that their thinking had moved forward, as per Bush's remarks about taking the battle to the enemy, taking him on before he takes us on. Boyce set out military options. These would vary from provision of bases, maritime support and special forces, right up to the provision of thousands of troops. Geoff felt the preparations either for a generated start or a running start were well advanced. Kuwait was essential to the plan, so is the UK because of Diego Garcia and Cyprus [airbases].

On the heavy side of things, we could be looking at two armoured brigades entering via Turkey. Jack set out the political difficulties. He said it was all being driven by DoD and NSC, and Powell and the State Department were not fully involved. Apparently Powell would not be at the August 4 meeting at which all this was being thrashed out. Boyce thought CENTCOM would be briefed on August 1 or 2, Rumsfeld on August 3, Bush on August 4. TB said he did not want any discussions with any other departments at this stage and did not want any of this 'swimming round the system'. He meant the Treasury, because Boyce had been talking about the need for new money, e.g. for tank desertification. Jack said that of the four powers posing a potential threat with WMD – Iran, Korea, Libya and Iraq – Iraq would be the fourth. He does not have nukes, he has some offensive WMD capability. The tough question is whether this is just regime change or is the issue WMD? TB was pretty clear that we had to be with the Americans. He said at one point 'It's worse than you think, I actually believe in doing this.' He was acutely conscious of how difficult it would be both with the PLP and the public, but when Jack raised the prospect of not going in with the US, TB said that would be the biggest shift in foreign policy for fifty years and I'm not sure it's very wise.

On the tactical level, he felt maximum closeness publicly was the way to maximise influence privately. Geoff pointed out the Americans' clear view that they already had legal justification. They had a different take to Goldsmith, who did not see regime change alone as having a legal base for force, and also that self-defence/humanitarian were not current overwhelming arguments, which leaves UNSC. TB said he needed to be convinced first of the workability of a military plan, and second of an equally workable political strategy. Jack said we could probably get the votes for a UN ultimatum, but the Americans may not want to go down that route. TB saw regime change as the route to dealing with WMD.

As if to go from the sublime to the ridiculous, TB, having spent much of the morning dealing with Iraq, spent part of the afternoon doing an interview with readers of *Chat* magazine, including a ventriloquist and a fortune-teller. There were some days I wondered how he kept going with all the different things he had to do, because sandwiched in was a meeting on euro preparations plus a stack of different policy issues. On the euro, TB was keen that we crank up but Roger Liddle [special adviser, European affairs] said that most of Europe thought we were not going to do it because GB was blocking him.

Wednesday, July 24

TB at the PLP, PMQs and the Northern Ireland statement at which we were raising the bar on a ceasefire judgement [amid renewed violence in Belfast]. He did well at the PLP and at PMQs and we were ending pretty well. IDS had not covered himself in glory with his reshuffle and as he came back from PMQs TB said 'That is a dead man walking. We should be thinking when, not if, and who's next.' TB had chatted with JP about his own future and had said that if he went at the election, JP should go too so they could let in a new broom, and he was pretty much up for that.

We were picking up signs that Clare was at it over Iraq. TB called her in to say he did not want her messing around on Iraq. She said she would be supportive and that she was not out to cause trouble. Yeah, sure. At Richard [Wilson]'s main farewell, he [RW] told a story about Leo pulling on his trouser leg and saying 'Alastair'. It was a nice enough do and I was tired. I also noticed there was not a single black face apart from his old driver. This was the never-changing Establishment.

Thursday, July 25

Today the second of TB's new monthly press conferences. He called me up to go over tricky areas, mainly Iraq, Ireland, unions. We had got Michael Barber lined up to do the press conference with TB to try to get some focus on public service delivery. On Iraq, he said he didn't really want a big fight on this unless he has to have it. TB ran up the stairs for the press conference so started out of breath. Michael Barber did well and it was interesting enough. Questions mainly Iraq and Ireland. Hopeless on the personal stuff, e.g. would the 21-year-old TB approve of the TB of today, and he just muttered about being less radical. Then he was off to Manchester [for the opening of the Commonwealth Games].

I had a long session with JP re August [recess] but we mainly talked about GB. I said TB was at the end of his tether and really didn't know what to do about him. JP said he could see that and after Sunday's dinner he understood better what I meant. GB just raged at him, at one point asked him the same question ten times. JP asked him afterwards why he behaved like that. He said he just got an outpouring of bitterness and anger and mistrust. 'It really is like a lover spurned.' JP said he saw his job as trying to make sure the party held together and came out stronger. He had told GB he would support him but not if he took on TB, and nor would the party, so he had to bide his time. He shared our view that GB was in part using the euro to do in Tony. He said if it was true that he spoke more to [Rupert] Murdoch about his thinking on the euro than he did to TB, it was an outrage. He told GB it was make your mind up time.

His assessment was that TB wanted to do the euro and get out. He didn't really want a third term for himself but he did want it for the party, and that's what JP wanted too. If TB and GB split the party they will not be forgiven and that's why we have to do all we can to keep them together. But it was going to be difficult. I said I was glad that he had seen for himself what TB had to contend with in the face of this hatred. TB was growing almost immune to it. JP said I have to keep TB onside for an approach based on working together, and he had to work on GB. He said obviously some of these things are too sensitive for wider discussion, but he intended to get his own assessment of the two of them on their own intentions. Also, TB had to involve him and GB more on discussions of strategy.

I asked him about his own intentions. I said TB felt that if he went before the election maybe they should step down together and maybe that would make transition easier. He said that was probably right. He said he had been very angry when TB directly accused him of siding with GB. He said he will always be loyal to the leader because 'that's my job'. GB had said he would keep him on but 'I'll have to make a judgement. I can see how a clean break might be best.' He said if GB waffled on about the fourth quartile of the economic tests then he would know he was messing about and he would say no. He intended to get to the bottom of GB's euro intentions. He agreed with me that GB was probably panicking, that he was running out of time, but also he was worrying about the economy. 'He took all the credit when credit was going, so now he worries that he gets the blame,' he said. It was a good, friendly discussion and I think we both knew we would have to work together pretty well to keep the two of them in some kind of partnership.

TB called a couple of times from his visit to the Commonwealth Games. I watched the opening ceremony, which was excellent, and after all the bollocks in the media that Manchester would be a disaster, it was looking pretty good. TB raised his *grand projet* again. I said I don't know why you keep asking me, because you've basically made up your mind. He said no, depends on a lot of things, and I really want you to think over the holiday about whether there is a way I can use it to strengthen myself.

Friday, July 26 – Wednesday, August 28 (holiday)

We had a great start to the holiday, driving to Paris for the last day of the Tour de France and staying with John and Penny Holmes. It was a beautiful hot day and Grace was having a fantastic time in the garden with Bonny the dog, and just looked as happy as I had ever seen her. The cycling itself was less exciting than the stages, just a procession, but there was a nice atmosphere. The first time I was really bothered was when we got to Pizay for our second overnight stop. The *Mail* were on to the story that Alastair Irvine [son of Derry Irvine] was in jail [for drugs offences in the US]. It had been hard enough for Derry just to deal with the fact of what had happened, but having to deal with these fuckers could make it worse. I did a conference call with Godric and Alan Percival [Lord Chancellor's Department] and put together a statement and an outline strategy. Derry agreed to it. He said things had been pretty unbearable recently. I said I thought people would think it odd that they hadn't gone out and he said he didn't want to create a UK media circus around him. He was pretty clear that the only real route to rehabilitation was to stop taking drugs. The *Mail* did it big a couple of days later but the follow-up was relatively limited.

Philip and Georgia [Gould] joined us in Paris and on the drive down Philip typically left his passport at a service station. TB called as I was driving down to discuss Iraq. It was clearly going to be a problem and we were not on the pitch. We agreed that we should start to push out some of the Saddam material. He and CB went on their mini-break in Cumbria and she had a miscarriage. By now we were down in Puyméras, from where Fiona and I sorted out with the detectives how to get them in and out of hospital without anyone knowing. Keith Lowe and Charles Lindsay [detectives] did a great job, got them in, got them out the next day and as when Leo went in, the hospital didn't leak.

TB sounded pretty down about it though he was philosophical. He said Cherie was feeling very low and sad. They were also worried that it would crank up the media interest in their holiday. We decided against actually putting something out and instead waited for calls from the press once they noticed what was going on, which they did when the kids went to France without TB and CB. We had a statement ready with the bare facts plus an appeal for them to be allowed a quiet holiday. Coverage was big, fairly sympathetic and once they got away the next day, they were basically just doing captions stories. The local French paper said that Britons had been '*stupéfaits*' at the news of the pregnancy. The main news back home was two young girls who had gone missing.[1]

The Commonwealth Games had become a real success story but

[1] Two ten-year-olds, Holly Wells and Jessica Chapman, had gone missing in Soham, Cambridgeshire. After a search lasting two weeks, their bodies were found and school caretaker Ian Huntley was arrested and subsequently convicted of murder.

Brendan [Foster] called me to say people would go apeshit when we ripped up the track at the end. The boys and I were pretty hooked to the European athletics. I was playing tennis most days with Calum but just as Rory was now way ahead of me on running, so he was way ahead of me on tennis. We had a little running drama for the holiday when Anne Messelink [holiday agent] called to say that a friend of hers had been approached by a *Sunday Times* journalist trying to find me. The next day, he appeared at the bar in the village and Eva, the bar owner, called me to warn me. She then set up a little network of people round the village who kept tabs on him and for the next two or three days I was able to dodge him. On the Friday morning, when I was out in Marseilles collecting Gail [Rebuck], the reporter arrived outside the house and later came back with a photographer. Fiona told them we did not want to be disturbed. I called [John] Witherow [*Sunday Times* editor] to ask what was going on and he said it was a piece about how New Labour was taking over the area and turning it into the new Tuscany. 'It's the price of fame. You do know you're a bit of a fashion icon don't you?' I said I reckoned Murdoch was a lot more famous than I am and I bet they are not doorstepping his holiday.

TB was due to do a meeting and photocall with [Jean-Pierre] Raffarin [new French Prime Minister] after their lunch in Cahors on the 12th. The French wanted a real big-licks press conference but TB and I were worried we would simply end up with totally different positions on Iraq. Totally counterproductive. Neil [Kinnock] was very down on GB at the moment. He had told him that he was the only person in history who could say with almost total certainty that he would be the next PM and the only person who could stop him was himself. If people felt he was trying to shoehorn Tony out, there would be a real reaction against him. Neil had his own problems through the summer, namely a woman in Brussels from the court of auditors attacking him, making all sorts of allegations, which he was pushing back on.

I had a series of conversations with TB re the US. Bush had suggested that he go there for the September 11 commemorations and they have a discussion about Iraq around that. I was worried about it, felt that people would see through it and also it ran totally counter to the strategy we planned for September. We agreed to keep it on hold for now. There had been stories about how Robin was leading Cabinet moves against our position and when I told him TB said 'Well, they can just calm down.' I had to get a bit involved sorting the French re his meeting with Raffarin, which they wanted to do bigger than we did. He felt that working with the French was a bit easier now that it was clear who was in charge, without the uncertainty of cohabitation.

I was running most days and one day Richard Eyre [theatre director], who was staying nearby, wanted to come out with me and we did about eight or ten miles, and at one point I thought he was going to pass out, and suggested we stop. Eventually, I ran ahead. We spent a lot of time with the Kinnocks as well as the Goulds and did a better job at avoiding political talk. Philip was very excited about a Milburn article in the *Spectator* which he felt took him into a higher league and showed some of the qualities that had got TB to the top, notably guts. Philip's general view at the moment was that TB could come back really strong but he had to resist being spooked by GB. Neil felt GB was capable of throwing it all away, but did anyone really think Milburn was the answer? I doubted it. Hugh Hudson [film director] came over for a night and it seemed so, so long ago that he, Neil and I had worked on that election broadcast.[1]

Cherie called Fiona on the 17th and said TB's dinner with Alan Milburn recently had had a profound effect on him. It was one thing to hear from me and Sally that GB was at it, but Milburn, given his experience as chief secretary, was another thing. He had given an assessment of how he [GB] operated in the Treasury – the secrecy, the divide and rule, the briefings. He felt TB needed to strengthen his team and he wanted to help him do it. Jack Straw was on a few times towards the end of the holiday as he was due to visit Powell in the US and we discussed whether to announce it, given it would be seen as a big Iraq thing. After a bit of toing and froing we decided not to. Jack was keen that we push the Yanks towards accepting that there had to be a UN mandate re Iraq but the noises from Cheney and Rumsfeld were very much focused on 'do it whatever'. There were a number of articles in the States, e.g. from Jim Baker and Richard Holbrooke [senior US diplomat], voicing real caution. Philip came home a couple of days before us to do some groups on his first night back, which were dreadful, particularly on delivery. The end of the holiday was hit by some pretty bad weather which washed out the village fair, and although we had a nice time, I had not been sleeping that well.

[1] The 1987 broadcast, popularly known as 'Kinnock: The Movie', mixed footage of Kinnock's speeches with shots of the Kinnocks walking on a coastal path in Llandudno, Wales. As part of Labour's highly professional, but ultimately unsuccessful election campaign, the broadcast strengthened and broadened Kinnock's leadership profile.

Thursday, August 29

First day back. Didn't feel like going in. JP called from South Africa, wanting reassurance about how he had handled the summer, also saying I had to get some more passion into TB's speech for the [Johannesburg] summit [on sustainable development] and only I could do it, and he was really worried that we wouldn't get a proper agreement without TB doing the real hard negotiations towards the end. TB spoke to Bush. He had sent him a long note in late July and David Manning had been to see Condi. The next day he had been called in to see Bush himself. He had been pretty frank and made clear that this was very difficult for us. Equally TB's note said we would have real public and party problems and things would be even worse in Europe. David's worry was that there seemed to be no thought-through political or public information strategy and too many difficult unanswered questions. He also felt Condi was far too optimistic about the Middle East and prospects for progress. Their meeting had been earlier and David had said we needed to exhaust the UN route but in the ensuing weeks Rumsfeld and Cheney had both made what were seen as fairly belligerent speeches. David had put the case forcefully that they had to understand the difficulties of other countries. He believed that on the idea of an ultimatum the Russians, Chinese and even the French would support or acquiesce. David's strong sense was that though they might go it alone, they didn't want to. They valued TB's advice. They needed to be persuaded on UN/ultimatum and on the need to do more re the Middle East. Bush felt that it was possible to see a quick collapse of the Iraqis. He had also talked up evidence of links with al-Qaeda, which our and US intelligence were not convinced of. We were pushing the idea of a tough, time-bound ultimatum. Bush had said he was 'evangelical' re getting rid of Saddam and was a 'good vs evil guy'. He felt equally strongly about Korea. But David felt it was not a lost cause to push him down the UN ultimatum route. TB's note had made clear our basic support but also said we had to be blunt about the difficulties. His note went through the need for an agreed strategy on six fronts – UN ultimatum route/evidence/MEPP/post-Saddam/Arab Muslim worlds/Afghanistan. Finally and fairly briefly he addressed the military plan and of the running start vs generated start, he preferred the latter.

When they spoke, TB sensed Bush was a bit nervous about the UN route but equally he wasn't happy about the Cheney/Rumsfeld comments, which he tried to justify by saying they had been reacting to [Brent] Scowcroft [former US National Security Advisor] and Jim

Baker. Later though I spoke to Mary Matalin [Cheney's press secretary] who was adamant that Cheney had not 'gone freelance', by which I assumed she meant he had been speaking with Bush's knowledge and approval. David was not so sure. TB was now clear he should see Bush as soon as possible and felt that we had to get at it before he was making his UNGA [UN General Assembly] speech, and preferably whilst Bush was still having his 'Council of War'. He was clearly getting a lot of competing advice.

TB still felt confident we could turn the argument. He felt the left had got itself into a ridiculous position by appearing to be standing up and protecting Saddam. The reality was people had let him get away with it for too long. Everyone felt that if we could get the UN route it would be a lot easier. TB, when I first saw him today, was wearing the full Rio Ferdinand [footballer] look – shorts, his FA slip-ons and the trendy vest. He said he had been thinking a lot and the most important thing now was that he did what he thought was right, on foreign and domestic regardless of what the focus groups or anyone else thought.

Friday, August 30

TB had decided he wanted to delay the EMU referendum to 2004 so we had lots of time to make the case. He wanted to calm Iraq and we spent some time working out what he should say to the press on the plane tomorrow. He had done an exceptionally long note on the general position, the need to get a big political argument re the individual and the state, the need for much greater radicalism re reform in the public services. It contained a few barbed criticisms about what was coming out of the Policy Unit and his continuing frustration at the lack of strategic capability in the main departments came out of virtually every note he wrote. I think we both felt frustrated that so much fell upon the centre, whilst departments complained that it was because we took things away from them. If they were more competent and capable, I think everyone would be happy.

TB also said, though we had heard it after holidays before, that he wanted to change the way we worked, so that we became more formal, with a proper approach modelled on a company board. We went through his note page by page, general direction, radical reform the answer not the problem, discussion about the pamphlet. Jonathan was pushing even harder than TB on the radicalism front, re diversity, choice of provider [in public services], Civil Service reform. He thought the Tories would come in and take a big-state argument against us.

TB had also proposed trying to establish a cross-party commission on pensions and transport. He felt both were issues that would require several terms to sort and we should try to build support across the board. But why, we all thought, would the Tories go for it, taking away two of the most potentially difficult areas for us?

TB was also banging on even louder than ever about crime and asylum. Felt that if we weren't careful asylum would become the next fuel-protest situation, and for obvious reasons have the potential to be even worse. There were more bad figures out today and he felt that the Home Office just weren't on top of it. Nor did they get the need for the message on this to be so widely understood that it had an impact on behaviour. On Ireland, he was more not less worried than when he went away. On Europe, he had really gone through the detail of the IGC [EU Intergovernmental Conference] negotiations, and said that whilst on the big message we were standing up against the superstate ideas, it was in the detail that these arguments were won and lost. The one big surprise out of his holiday was him saying he didn't want to do the [euro] referendum before 2004. On GB, he felt we had to keep trying for an agreed strategy but at the same time broaden his efforts with the rest of the Cabinet. He was worried about the party but totally dismissive of the unions, felt they were just misreading what was happening in the country. Finally on the office, he said he wanted fresh people but didn't go beyond that. I got David Manning to tell Condi that we would like to announce the TB visit on Tuesday but it would be difficult to pin down re dates. I was also concerned that the mood music going out from us about the need for a UN resolution was being picked up by the US as evidence of us diddling them.

Saturday, August 31

Up at the crack of dawn to go to Number 10 and meet the TB convoy. The *FT* splash said TB pressed Bush for a UN mandate, which could be a problem with the Yanks, while the others were saying TB would break his silence on Iraq on the plane to Mozambique. We both wanted to avoid talking about Iraq, but it would be difficult and we agreed we would have to say he was not letting it overshadow the [Johannesburg] summit. If pushed, he'd say that doing nothing was not an option but he didn't particularly want to go beyond that. Privately, he was growing more and more dismissive of the critics. He found it unfathomable that even the [Church of England] bishops almost appeared to be defending Saddam as if he was some great liberal. Equally, he was clear that the Yanks had not handled it well over the holiday. Condi had admitted as much to David, that they had allowed the game to run ahead of them, and Cheney and Rumsfeld had just made it worse.

We spent ages on the plane working on the three speeches he would be making on the trip, including one in which he intended to be very forward on Kyoto [climate change protocol, 1997]. He was clear that he wanted to be more and more himself, but also that we did need fewer papers and fewer journalists who were basically out to kill him. He was a lot steelier than when he went on holiday. Clear that getting Saddam was the right thing to do. Barely mentioned GB. Very strong language on climate change in the speech. He saw the press and it was going to be hard for them not to make Iraq the story. We arrived [in Maputo] and a somewhat chaotic and noisy motorcade took us to the hotel. Clare Short arrived and TB was pretty chilly with her.

We drove out to the presidential palace where they [TB and President Joaquim Chissano] had a tête-à-tête and I talked with the finance minister [Luísa Días Diogo], the daughter of a nurse. The dinner was pretty ghastly, cold soup that was meant to be hot, cold prawns that were meant to be hot, a strange-tasting turkey and a fruit salad out of a tin. I'd love to know if Chirac, should he ever be here, would do his usual over-the-top 'look at all this wonderful food' routine. I liked the politicians. They had a directness that was appealing. There was a lot of talk about Maria Mutola [800 m runner, nicknamed 'the Maputo Express'] and the president told us she was so good at football that the boys demanded she was sex-tested to see if she was a girl. She was a major national heroine though.

David had got Condi to get GWB to offer TB next Saturday for a meeting in the margins of his so-called war counsel. I think they realised they had messed up the presentation and had to get into a better position, so it seemed clear Bush did want TB there, but heaven knows what Cheney and Rumsfeld would make of it. TB was up for it. JP was in total summit mode and calling the whole time from Johannesburg.

Sunday, September 1

Iraq was becoming a frenzy again. TB was becoming more and more belligerent, saying he knew it was the right thing to do. He said the US had to be managed. Obviously the best thing to do would be to avoid war, get the UN inspectors in and all the weapons out. It was obvious too that the US had to be managed into a better position.

That is what we have to do, he said. But we won't be able to do it if we come out against the US the whole time. He was developing the line that the UN route was fine if it was clearly a means to resolve the issue, but not if it's a means to duck the issue. Equally, it was clear that public opinion had moved against us during August. I worked on the speech while he went to church. He came back to sign off the speech, including the very strong line on Kyoto.[1]

I went out for a run, first through the diplomatic compound then drifted into what looked like the middle-class area of town, and eventually into a shanty town, where the kids were surprised to see someone like me running through, and joined in for a bit. They were incredibly friendly, and parts of the countryside were lush and rich. But the signs of extreme poverty were everywhere amid sporadic signs of wealth. Later we flew to Beira [second city of Mozambique]. We had *Marie Claire* magazine with us and I got them to interview the finance minister. We visited the hospital. The kids' malarial ward was pretty depressing, several kids to a bed, helpless-looking parents. One of the little girls was called Grace so I phoned home and told her about it. Then to a town called Dondo, TB pretty much mobbed going round the market. Watched a children's show, then a school visit before flying back to Maputo. The hotel seemed obscenely nice after some of the things we had seen. Up to see TB and finalise the speech. Spoke to Fiona who had received an email from Cherie about discussions she had been having with Cate Haste [author, wife of broadcaster Melvyn Bragg] about a book she was planning to do on PM's spouses.[2] Fiona sounded very fed up about the whole thing.

Monday, September 2

Flew down to Johannesburg, finished the speech on the way. It was one of these difficult little five-minute jobs, where everyone was trotting out the same clichés and we decided to concentrate on the big-vision message. TB had a chat with Clare at the hotel. She said that if she had a problem with Iraq, she would tell him. She said too that she was very surprised when TB had said GB did not always work closely with him. I had an example, the *Mirror* doing a story re

[1] 'Kyoto is right and it should be ratified by all of us . . . the facts remain, the consequences of inaction on these issues are not unknown, they are calculable. Poverty and environmental degradation, if unchecked, spell catastrophe for our world, that is clear.'

[2] *The Goldfish Bowl: Married to the Prime Minister 1955–1997* would be published in 2004.

GB warning against the cost of an Iraq war. We reached Johannesburg and set off for the usual summit bollocks, I could tell TB was a bit nervous about the speech because it was one of those where he and a small group of others were expected to make the biggest impact, but it was a pretty tough audience. He was also livid at all the stuff appearing in the media about the UN and now, the *Mail* splash on TB going out there to see Bush. He spoke to David [Manning] and Jonathan, saying he wanted a message round the system that all this loose talk had to stop. And he wanted the Americans to know how angry he was. He thought it might be Sally thinking she was protecting his internal position, saying he was pushing Bush, but TB knew it would be damaging with the US. Condi had said it looked like we were trying to push them, and they didn't like it.

Iraq scene was a bit grim and all building up to the press conference. Condi liked the argument that the UN was the route to dealing with it, not the route to avoiding it. TB's speech got a pretty good reception but the Namibians whacked him [Namibian President Sam Nujoma demanding sanctions on Zimbabwe be lifted] and when [Robert] Mugabe [President of Zimbabwe] had a go as well, that was the news for the day. We had a bilateral with Zhu Rongji [Premier of China], who agreed we had to deal with Iraq but said he felt strikes would be bad and dangerous. He said 'wisdom and patience' were required. Then Chirac, and we agreed to get the focus not too much on Iraq, had a short press event, which was a bit chaotic. TB had a warmer conversation with him than usual, sensed that Chirac was worried about a Schroeder victory because it would mean bad relations after his backing for Stoiber.

We left for Alexandra township, where we had been before. Plenty of progress to see, lots of change amid all the problems. They had set up a huge marquee with music playing, dancing, nice food, where TB planted a tree and made a little speech about how steadily this place was changing for the better. He was good at this type of event and it came over well on the media here but by now Mugabe was the main story at home, at least as far as the main papers were concerned, though Fiona said he was coming over really well on TV. He did clips on the tour of the township saying Mugabe etc. did not represent the true voice of Africa and he was worried that other leaders would look at these comments and say why should we help them? On the edge of the township, new homes had been built which were being shown to us as evidence of the great progress, though in reality homes housing large families were of a size a modestly well-off single person would expect at home.

We got back for a reception hosted by the British delegation to the summit, I spent most of the time chatting to Jack McConnell [First Minister of Scotland]. TB had a stack of bilaterals with Kofi [Annan], [Thabo] Mbeki who was very weak on Zimbabwe, [Jean] Chrétien and Helen Clark [New Zealand Prime Minister]. Although a lot of the talk was about the summit business, most conversation turned to Iraq at some point and TB was clearer by the end of the day that we had to get the Americans down the UN route. President [Abdelaziz] Bouteflika of Algeria told TB he wanted Algeria to be able to join the Commonwealth. TB was so taken aback that he said yes, I'm sure that's fine. He felt that all the angst that was coming our way about Iraq would strengthen our hand as it was clear that a lot of them would come with us down the UN route and we'd set that up with the Bush speech to UNGA. On the way back, we went over the lines for the press conference tomorrow. TB said he intended to be on the tough end of the market as we ran through some of the questions. I went to bed and slept almost till we landed. The summit outcome was OK but the general take was that it hadn't delivered all that was promised or hoped for.

Tuesday, September 3

Landed 7.15 at Teesside, and drove to Myrobella with TB. Press working themselves into a lather re press conference. I finished the script and TB decided in the end to do very brief opening remarks on the North-East, Johannesburg outcome and then Iraq, but the bulk of the argument was going to be made during questions. He came back and we went through some of the hard questions on Iraq. The hardest was 'Why now? What was it that we knew now that we didn't before that made us believe we had to do it now?' It was not going to be at all easy to sell the policy in the next few months, especially because GWB was so unpopular in the UK. TB, Tom Kelly and I went through it all again in the garden. He said several times he was going to be on the tough end of the market, and he was. He kept going for ninety minutes, really hitting the ball in the middle of the bat, top lines very clear – dealing with Saddam was the right thing to do and we would stand by the US. Major bulletin coverage. The *Sun* thought he was brilliant. Even critics said he was on top, committed and passionate about it. Definitely worth doing.

He then did a call with GWB who was planning to tell Congress leaders TB was going to Camp David, so I got an operational note ready to go. The toughest question was what new evidence was there. He said the debate had got ahead of us, so we were going to do the dossier earlier, in the next few weeks.[1] The problem was this was going to raise expectations massively. Today was about beginning to turn the tide of public opinion and it was going to be very tough indeed. We went to Trimdon Labour Club for a reception mainly for the foreign media. Then Tom and I headed back to the airport. Good trip overall, strong press conference but a long way to go.

Wednesday, September 4

Generally positive press for TB. The problem, as shown by [now FCO minister] Mike O'Brien's dreadful interview on the radio, was the dossier and the massive expectations. TB felt we could make the case. The story today was going to be Bush saying he would consult widely and go to the UN. Meeting on September 11 [anniversary], agreed we should be low-key, no minute's silence other than at St Paul's. Then I left for home and had a conference call with Condi and the White House team. Not brilliant. We agreed we needed a way of telling the whole story from the word go, maybe year by year. They were making fairly small presentational points. But we agreed we had to get CIC structures back up soon, and that there must be much better co-ordination of message than in August. We then discussed what message they wanted from Bush's speech [to US Congress representatives at the White House] e.g. challenge to UN, bad stuff on Saddam, make clear he was going down the UN route, but it could not obstruct and divert. It was an OK call but I didn't really feel we were at the races yet and it wasn't clear how we were going to get there. The Commons would be important, but it was not going to be easy. Robin Cook called because he was doing press tomorrow re Commons modernisation and was clearly up for causing problems on Iraq. He said he would 'try to stay on message' but then said 'I hope Tony and you don't want a shooting war.' He said Bush and Co. had screwed it up and we should not be held responsible for that.

Thursday, September 5

The Bush [White House] speech went down OK. At the office meeting, out on the terrace, ostensibly to talk about follow-up to TB's note, we

[1] Blair also undertook to publish a dossier on Iraq's WMD development, saying 'Originally I had the intention that we wouldn't get round to publishing the dossier until we had actually taken the key decisions, but I think it is probably a better idea to bring that forward . . . a lot of the work has already been done. There needs to be some more work and some more checking done, but I think probably the best thing to do is publish that within the next few weeks.'

just talked about Iraq. All of us were pressing TB to go with the flow on the demands for a recall of Parliament, but he was very resistant. We were saying it would let off steam and show he was serious in our Parliament strategy. But he said there were too many questions that we could not really answer, added to which there was not really much to say at the moment. The press conference had settled things but the media were determined to keep a sense of frenzy going on this. Agreed to put out the line that there was no question of troops being sent without Parliament being consulted. But the idea of a 'Council of War' had taken hold. Added to which [Michael] Cockerell [BBC political documentary maker] was today screening his special-relationship documentary [*Hotline to the President*] in which TB's answer to a question about 'blood price' was the big story.[1] TB said we had to get the UN route but could not do it too much. We were pushing him on dossier timing.

JP was very loyal, said he was totally supportive. There was a lot of angst around. I called Robin C to give him the line on recall of Parliament and he said I hope you are not going to go down the road of war because I believe it could mean the end of the government. Meeting with John Scarlett, Tom McKane, Des Bowen [MoD], Edward Chaplin [FCO], Julian Miller [Cabinet Office intelligence and security official] to go over 'the dossier'. It had to be revelatory and we needed to show that it was new and informative and part of a bigger case. John Williams [FCO director of public and press affairs] was offering to write it full-time. John Scarlett was clearly aware of the responsibility, he was so serious. I felt he was very human. He warned us that there was very little re nuclear. JS called to say he had seen C who had agreed to go through all the relevant material.

Friday, September 6

In late. TB meeting with Hans Blix [head of UN Monitoring, Verification and Inspection Commission, UNMOVIC], plus David Manning, Jonathan, AC. He went through what they had to do, said that WE were the military threat and there was no movement by Iraq. But also, said that if the Iraqis felt the US had decided to do the military

[1] Asked if Britain was prepared to 'send troops . . . to pay the blood price', Blair replied 'Yes. What is important though is that at moments of crisis they [the USA] . . . need to know, are you prepared to commit, are you prepared to be there when the shooting starts?' He added 'We are not at the stage of decision on Iraq, and there are all sorts of different ways in which we might decide to deal with this Iraqi problem in the end.'

option come what may, they would not move. DM spoke to Condi and got the sense they were going to be sensible re UNSCR. TB talked to Putin and Chirac who were OK.

Saturday, September 7

In to chase TB up to be ready to leave by 11, CB fretting over his clothes and hair. Cherie said she felt we were fine on Iraq provided we could go down the international route. TB said he believed we had materially influenced GWB and that DM was worth his weight in gold for the way he framed the argument. Despite the negative public line put out by the Russians, both he and GWB were encouraged by the Putin calls. Felt that he was saying the UN had to deal with it, though he was not keen on war. On the flight out, TB meeting DM, SM, Jonathan, Matthew Rycroft [private secretary, foreign affairs] and [General] Tony Pigott. TB did his usual thing, of going through things with a pad and pen and then calling us round. He set out what we should get into a UNSCR. Query over whether there should be a specific timeline. And the toughest question was whether we would have to go back to the UN for a second resolution if the first one was rebuffed. DM's view, which TB came round to after a long discussion, was that it was probably best to get a tough first mandate by promising to go back to the UN, but make clear the UN had to face up to this. About half an hour or so going through all the tactical considerations, what the French and Russians would live with, how to get the US not to put in things that they would see as unreasonable, e.g. elections.

TB was clearly trying to get GWB in a more doveish position, all the more necessary when we heard that Cheney would also be at Camp David. When we did the media, TB pushed the IAEA [International Atomic Energy Agency] report on potential activity at nuclear sites and we briefed the Sundays re threat to UK, dodging questions re the UN. On the plane, after the diplomatic run-through, Tony Pigott went through the US military thinking. There was a build-up going on now. The timelines were quite short because once we got to the really hot season it was impossible to fight. He said the Saudis would not give their territory so they had to go through the Gulf and Kuwait. But they also wanted to go in from the north, with our and Turkey's help. He said there was a plan for a fifteen-day air build-up, followed by a massive ground force, which would be the moment of maximum danger because that would be the point at which he might use chemical/biological weapons. Tony Pigott said there were three packages on offer for the UK. One, weakening

Iraq's ability to fire off at Israel. That was the most strategic. Two, a bigger land and air package. Three, a huge – possibly 15,000 troops – force as part of the northern advance. It would mean calling up reservists soon as well as doing something visible eg movement of warships. TB was clear that the threat of the build-up had to be real for the Iraqis to respond at all, though they may respond with madness.

Pigott was clear that the US were gearing up for it but didn't want to do it alone. They would probably get a few others, e.g. Australia. TB was keen that we emphasise the Dutch had come out for it. He was clear the UN route was the best route but equally clear that if that was used for delay, we should not tolerate it. TB got changed at Andrews Airbase and we got on to the Marine 1 helicopter with Will Farish [US ambassador to London], Chris Meyer [UK ambassador to Washington], [John] Negroponte [US ambassador to the UN] and Bush's main protocol guy. Forty-minute flight, going over what TB should say at the arrival doorstep with GWB. We landed, TB out the front, us out the back. They walked through a line of soldiers to where the doorstep was set up. Bush was his usual rather faltering self. TB OK, both talking up the threat. We went up to the main building and TB, Bush, Cheney, Condi and David had an initial session. TB felt that his job was to sell the case for the UN route to Cheney. Jonathan and I met with Karen Hughes [AC's opposite number in the White House], Dan Bartlett [her deputy], Andy Card [chief of staff], Steve Hadley and Farish and went over the communications issues. I told the Bush advisers there was a lot of scepticism about motive, including people feeling it was about avenging Dad [Bush Sr]. I also said the sole superpower status of the US raised anti-Americanism and they didn't understand that. Karen was pressing the usual stuff re visuals, Dan [Bartlett] saying we had to get Saddam's story up, the abuses, etc. We gave them an honest assessment of where EU/Arab opinion was. I said our domestic problem was 'poodle' but also why now? Why only Saddam? What about the Middle East? On why now, the case had to be built on evidence. On why only Saddam because he was a unique threat.

On Middle East, TB was clear to GWB he really had to engage on that. Karen was asking if we could help the Middle East peace process by dealing with Iraq. [Steve] Hadley was pretty hard over, talking about the importance of promoting democracy and freedom, and I said we had to be careful we were not talking about Americanisation. After some of us were called in to the TB/GWB meeting, and asked to brief on our own discussions, I said to GWB I felt they had to GET this anti-Americanism. A lot of it was jealousy and some of it resentment that they felt obliged to feel sympathy and solidarity post September 11. But some of it was just fear of their power. When I said we were worried about some of the language they used, Cheney looked pissed off and said 'You mean we shouldn't talk about democracy?' I said not if what people take out of it is not a message about democracy but a message about Americanisation. GWB seemed to get it. At one point we had a break and Bush shouted out across the room 'Hey, big guy' to me. TB was not there at the time but I went over and Bush said 'I'll say this, and I don't want it on the record, and with apology to the mixed audience, but your guy's got balls. But it's the right thing to do and future generations will surely thank us. I really believe that. I really believe the world has to get rid of Saddam and I really appreciate y'all coming over.'

When TB came back in, GWB said he'd decided to go to the UN and put down a new UNSCR, challenge the UN to deal with the problems for its own sake. He could not stand by. He would say OK, what will you do? Earlier, not too convincingly, Karen had claimed GWB was always going to go down the UN route. Cheney looked very sour throughout, and after dinner, when TB and Bush walked alone to the chopper, Bush was open with him that Cheney was in a different position. Earlier, when we had said that the international community was pressing for some direction but that in the US there would be people saying 'Why are you going to the UN, why aren't you doing it now?' Cheney smiled across the table, making it pretty clear that was where he was. The mood was good. As we left, Bush joked to me 'I suppose you can tell the story of how Tony flew in and pulled the crazed unilateralist back from the brink.' He said he was going to make clear that if the UN didn't deal with it – no hesitation. He said he didn't commit troops lightly, nobody would. Said TB totally understands link between WMD/Iraq and terrorism. Condi said the Cold War was about our values winning and we should push that. I said it was important they didn't come over as ideologues.

DM said the TB/GWB/Cheney meeting was quite extraordinary, a US president using a UK prime minister to persuade an American vice president. Cheney had not looked happy but it was clear Bush had made his mind up. He was very clear on the threat, and the need of the UN to deal with it. He said he would get something on the Middle East. 'That's a promise.' He was, as Sally said, far more impressive close up. At the dinner, a lot of politics having been done, there was a fair bit of small talk. He was quizzing TB about what Balmoral was like. Also filling us in on the row at Augusta golf club [in Georgia] where women were trying to win entry against the rednecks. He said they would have to let them in so the sooner the better. He and I discussed our running. He had done one marathon and his mum and dad had come out to cheer him at nineteen miles and his mother had shouted out 'There are three fat ladies ahead of you.' Cheney said next to nothing over dinner, ditto Hadley. TB got very bad stomach cramps. On the helicopter, TB and I agreed the top lines for the media waiting at Andrews Airbase. Shared strategy, shared determination to deal with it. The press conference went fine, TB feeling a job well done. I slept right through the flight to Aberdeen [where TB was visiting Balmoral]. First thing, TB, Godric and I discussed the line from the [forthcoming TUC] speech to push. The argument that the UN was the route provided it was dealt with was perfectly strong. Briefed on that. Maybe went a bit far for the Yanks, but TB and DM had done a bloody good job.

Monday, September 9

The press on the trip was OK and there was a sense we were in a different position but we were still facing a lot of press and public hostility. I did the morning meeting, then chatted to TB up at Balmoral re the speech. He was a bit alarmed that the story on Leo singing the national anthem to the Queen had been leaked to the *Sun*. He remained of the view that we would get there in the end, and also that it was still possible to avoid war.

Meeting with John Scarlett on dossier before being joined by three senior SIS people. They were all pissed off at reports in the *Telegraph* and *FT* that MI6 were unhappy at being asked to do the report and put intelligence material in it. They said that was not the case, and they believed it was the FCO setting them up for the blame if the report was not good enough. We agreed a process for writing the report. Scarlett agreed with me that the FCO was trying to take it over and I said I will chair a group looking at it from the presentational point of view. Jack Straw called me about it and I said John Williams should be part of the team, not the writer. John Scarlett felt there was an ownership issue. He said he must feel he will have ownership of it. He and the SIS guys were really helpful. Went over some of the issues, Arab media, links with CIC, agreed there should be a permanent plug-in. Good meeting and felt they were basically OK to deal with. Then did a note to JS [Scarlett], copied very widely, setting out the process. JS to own. AC to help.

Left for the train to Preston. Had to drop out of the US conference call. I worked on an overnight script on TB's [TUC] speech, which

Tom briefed, main focus on Iraq but also the hostile atmosphere with assorted union leaders getting on the news with real criticism over Iraq and much else besides. TB was in no real mood to be nice to them. We drove to Blackpool, then up to see a very downcast John Monks [TUC general secretary] with a very downcast Brendan Barber [his deputy]. I think they were worried that their modernising legacy was vanishing amid the noise of the dinosaurs. TB was definitely going to get a hostile reception tomorrow. He spoke by phone to Chirac who really went off at the Americans again, said they didn't understand the Middle East, or how they brought anti-Americanism upon themselves.

Tuesday, September 10

The overnight briefing went pretty big on the line that he intended to be very robust. It was being built up as real lion's den stuff. The speech was in three parts – Iraq, which would improve by being clearer about the balance between UN and determination to deal with it. It was measured, calm, serious. Second, public services, which was all a bit samey and listy, and third, partnership with the unions. We were a bit worried that some of the lines were so hostile – e.g. indulgence or influence – that he might get booed but he wanted to do it and felt it would strike a chord with the public. Monks wanted him to tone it down, which he did but I still felt it lacked clarity. TB got a much better reception than we feared, was even applauded for the attack on indulgence, and a fair few got up for a standing ovation, so he was pretty pleased with himself as we went back to the hotel for meetings.[1]

Alex F called, really worried about Iraq, said he thought it was a very dangerous situation for TB. I said TB had a real sense of certainty about this one. He was really on the rampage about the press as well, said we had to do something, they were out of control. We had very little time before [Labour Party] conference and we hadn't done a lot of the planning we normally do. The Tories were clearly going to reposition as being more interested in domestic policy than Europe, and they were going to try to get up compassionate conservatism. They would try to do us as being distracted by foreign policy, and divided on Iraq. There was a bit of a flurry later on when Charles C

[1] After telling union leaders that his door was open to any of them, Blair told TUC delegates 'Partnership doesn't make headlines. But the vast majority of trade union leaders and members know that it does far more good than a lot of self-indulgent rhetoric from a few that belongs in the history books. Indulgence or influence. It's a very simple choice.'

said the recall of Parliament was under review. TB was still not keen, but I was sure we were going to have to do it. Got Iraq dossier draft, read it at home.

Wednesday, September 11

Good press for the TUC speech. TB was with Robin C, even more puffed up than usual. Robin said we had to recall Parliament and better we do it sooner rather than later. We were behind the curve. He was making clear he felt we had to avoid military action, saying he didn't want to serve twenty years under a Gordon Brown premiership. He even mentioned Suez. This is not Suez, said TB. That was not thought through and the US were not there. I'm not going to let the US go unilateral. It would be wrong and this way I get to influence them. RC spelled it out, said the US didn't understand the Middle East peace process. They were doing Iraq for the wrong reasons and they were hugely unpopular. He welcomed the fact TB had been able to restrain Bush, but they were clearly determined to go to war. 'I'll put you down as an unenthusiastic then,' said TB. RC said he feared it would be the end of the government. TB really was isolated at the moment and yet he kept going on this. We agreed that I would draft the letter from TB to Michael Martin setting out our thinking, saying it would be connected to the dossier and unrelated to UN thinking. Then we had to square MM. David Hanson [Blair's parliamentary private secretary] got him in New York, read him the letter. Later Jack S called me from NY, he was with MM, who said maybe we should think of a two-day debate instead, because lots would want to speak.

Meanwhile I was working on the Iraq dossier. Long chat with John Scarlett. I said the drier the better, cut the rhetoric. The more intelligence-based it was the better. There was a need to separate IISS [International Institute for Strategic Studies report] from what was new in this one. I gave some suggestions later re a different structure. We had the basic story and now had to fill it out. TB looked at it and felt it was pretty compelling stuff. He was in a bit of a strop re recall of Parliament, said that it was a new precedent. He also didn't want Cabinet until after a recall. Ridiculous. No wonder Betty Boothroyd said it was becoming more presidential. I watched the St Paul's [anniversary of September 11] service, to which I was invited but couldn't go, while reading the Iraq dossier. Then meeting with TB to sort lines on the recall of Parliament, and briefing. Philip had now done ten groups since the holiday and the pessimism was dreadful. They were close to a turning point, and really angry about Iraq. Robin put out a line effectively claiming he persuaded TB to do the recall.

Thursday, September 12

GWB speech to the UN [General Assembly] was leading news all day, up to delivery at 3.30 NY time. They sent a draft through yesterday but though good in tone, it lacked the crucial point that they would go for another UNSCR first. It just wasn't there. This was what Cheney/Rumsfeld wanted. They felt that more 'UN-ery' was just a way to give Saddam the chance to mess them around. So David Manning sent through a passage from TB and spoke a couple of times to Condi. But it was only at the last moment that we heard he WAS going to include reference to UNSCR and in the end he delivered it in plural. That meant that others would be able hopefully to welcome it more than they would have done. RC was on the *Today* programme, diddling like crazy both re his alleged influence persuading TB to recall, and also on the issue of whether there would be a vote. Nobody pointed out there was no vote when he was Foreign Secretary re Kosovo, Gulf, and the attack on Iraq a few years back.

I had a long chat with Alan Milburn. JP had had the same conversation with him as he had had with me, namely saying he would support GB but not if he went for TB. 'There can only be one prime minister, and we have already got one.' But Alan said TB was very isolated and Iraq was going to be very difficult for him. He said he and John Reid would be there totally. He put down DB as 'cautiously supportive'. We were hoping to get Margaret B fully on board. But he felt there was quite a lot of dicking around. TB, at the political strategy meeting, was beginning to focus on his conference speech. Douglas and Peter M both made the point that we lacked a narrative for this phase of New Labour. TB wanted to make 'reform the route to social justice' a big theme.

Meeting with TB, Jonathan, DM, AC, C and an SIS colleague re chemical and biological weapons, and what Blix would be looking for if the inspectors went in. It showed what was going on was really bad and getting worse, that he was determined to keep WMD for reasons of regional power. They were strategically vital and he was going to keep them come what may. C said we could use some of the material through assertion.

They were confident this stuff was real, not being run against us. SIS believed the regime would collapse and there would be lots of defections etc. Very interesting meeting. TB saw Charles Kennedy and then IDS who immediately went out and said we were publishing the dossier before the debate. IDS was basically just diddling about with it. GWB speech going OK. David Davies came in and asked if I wanted to be chief executive of the Football League. He thought they would definitely go for it and I would enjoy it.

Friday, September 13

Meeting with Julian Miller on the dossier to go through the new structure. I was worried that it was going to have to rely too much on assertion. We also had a flurry with an overnight telegram re Scarlett's US trip, because he'd been told the US were going to publish their own dossier using US material and we worried it would undercut ours. I raised it on the conference call. There were also persistent reports of problems re Cheney and Rumsfeld pushing for much more robust, less UN-related lines. GWB speech had gone down well and seemed to shift opinion around the place but they were arguing for such a tough UNSCR that it would not be acceptable to anyone.

Geoff Hoon called me last night before *Question Time* and said it was going to be tough, not least, as he first intimated and later confirmed, the US were on the point of asking us to upgrade [RAF] Fylingdales [radar base] for National Missile Defense. Otherwise we were working out how to 'park' Iraq pre Parliament recall. I was worried that the dossier was going to be too assertive and that even though the agencies presented it as their work, it would be seen as us trying to spin them a line. GB did an *FT* interview saying he supported TB on Iraq. I called JP in Thailand and said it would be good to get him out there in similar vein. He agreed I could brief out his support whenever I wanted. I briefed Phil Webster [*Times*] who got it on to page 1, and we got a bit of broadcast play too.

Saturday, September 14

Burnley vs Stoke. Good win, 2–1 after going one down. TB called after his visit to Peter M's Progress [New Labour policy pressure group] event. Philip said TB was on great form. Lots of Iraq in the Sunday papers, but a bit of a lull. We killed the story in the *Sunday Telegraph* re TB demanding from each Cabinet member what their view was on Iraq.

Sunday, September 15

Up at Mum and Dad's, eight-mile run, lunch, then back with Calum. Göran Persson [Swedish Social Democratic Party] won the Swedish election. TB had given him Clinton's advice about looking hungry to the end, even if you already know they want you to win.

Monday, September 16

Chat with Scarlett re dossier. He was still worried the US were going to do their own version first. It came up on the conference call again, and I had to pin down Dan Bartlett afterwards to try to get it back out. We were really needing to get some focus back on the domestic agenda but it was going to be hard. At his Monday meeting, TB was going on about parking Iraq, and then getting proper focus on Home Office and asylum. This was real groundhog day, him just railing and railing at their inability to grip these issues properly. Yet again, he said he wished we could get out of hunting. Today was the tenth anniversary of the ERM.[1] We were blessed with the current Tory lot being so useless, but he really felt that on some of the toughest issues, departments just weren't delivering. They lacked cutting policy edge.

Tuesday, September 17

I was in bed after midnight and Dan Bartlett called. Kofi had announced a letter from Iraq saying they'd let the inspectors back in. Dan wanted us to share a sceptical line, making clear the issue was disarmament. That was fine. We put out a fairly tough line. Needless to say our media was on the case straight away saying how that clever Saddam had done us in. I commissioned the CIC to do a paper on his past dicking about. TB wanted to be on the very tough end, saying we needed a tough new UNSCR and that had to be about maximum inspections, etc.

Meeting about Iraq's 'offer' of inspections, as on conference call later. I agreed with Jack he'd do a doorstep on it. I bumped into RC who said 'great development and we should claim it as TB's success'. Jack said to me he felt Robin was on an exit strategy and he was going to cause us real problems. I got the new dossier draft and did detailed comments on that. TB also read it and made some comments. Nuclear was the most difficult part. Scarlett and I chatted away re that. Then a meeting with Jack and [Sir Jeremy] Greenstock [UK ambassador to the UN] to go over tactics on the UN negotiations. Greenstock was very good on the detail. TB felt the US hawks would be trying to say to GWB we should never have gone the UN route and now it becomes a mush and we had to be really hard over on them. Debate meeting with Hilary Armstrong, who said there were massive expectations re the dossier. On hunting, she

[1] Black Wednesday, when the then Conservative government withdrew the collapsing pound from the European Exchange Rate Mechanism at a cost of £3.3 billion.

said it simply wasn't possible to get out of it. TB said he would rather be humiliated for doing a massive U-turn than stay in a position he believed to be wrong.

Wednesday, September 18

Iraqi move being seen as blow to us. The overnight briefing on TB's [poverty] speech and the commitment to 'redistribute power, wealth and opportunity' was seen e.g. in the *Mail* splash as a hint at more tax rises and a sop to Old Labour. TB called at 7am. 'What on earth is this?' I said we just had to stick to the same message that we had agreed yesterday, that we were back on the domestic agenda, doing the things we have to do and being open about it. He was not overly pleased. The Treasury were in a real flap about it. TB's speech went OK,[1] then he did some clips on Iraq which were seen as keeping up the pressure, then did five minutes for BBC crime day. I was still working on the dossier. I got Jo Nadin [Number 10 special adviser] to read it with a fresh eye. She felt it was very convincing, apart from nuclear. I made a few more suggested changes to John Scarlett and went through the nuclear section with Julian Miller, which was OK. JS was keen to keep in the very downbeat assessment. Got TB foreword signed off, then to meetings re dossier production. Charles Clarke came to see me to say he was worried there had been friction between us at recent meetings. I said no, but we had a basic disagreement re ways to attack the Tories. I felt also he had been too focused on so-called attacks on him. He said he didn't see politics as his sole job. His job was to get the politics done by others. On the dossier, the Tories were making clear they felt we should have something on the link to terrorism.

Thursday, September 19

TB was down at Chequers hoping to get going on the conference speech. The A-level exam row was in danger of getting out of control.[2] Estelle Morris decided on an independent inquiry. TB spoke to her at length and sensed a bit of panic around the department. After the criminal records [vetting of education employees] issue post Soham

[1] Speaking at an East London school, Blair said 'Our goal is a Britain in which nobody is left behind, in which people can go as far as they have the talent to go . . . in which we continue to redistribute power, wealth and opportunity to the many not the few, to combat poverty and social exclusion, to deliver public services people can trust and take down the barriers that hold people back.'

[2] A new two-level exam system, filtering out less able students at the halfway stage, led to accusations that exam boards had fixed grades to avoid much higher pass rates.

[child murders], a decision allegedly taken by officials, and now this, she was in danger of becoming tainted goods, not reforming fully, not competent. We were also getting bad coverage at the moment on crime, asylum and transport. As I said to the Yanks on the conference call 'Joy to be back on the foreign agenda.' Most of my work at the moment was on the dossier. Nuclear timelines just about sorted. Jo Nadin had one or two good thoughts and I put them through. I agreed to drop the conclusion. Some people reasonably convinced, others not. We'd end up convincing those who wanted to be and not those who didn't.

TB spoke to GWB yesterday and got him on to the same strategy. TB said we had to hang tough. He later spoke to Putin who was very wary re a UNSCR. Blix was at UN saying he could be in there soon but being quite conciliatory with them. The Iraqi foreign minister [Naji Saberi Ahmed] was at the UN saying, via letter from Saddam, they had no WMD programmes. I signed off on the dossier before John S' final meeting on it. DB came round for dinner. He was getting whacked by the *Express* in particular at the moment and it had made him a bit paranoid re the press in general. He was also defending his relationship with the *Mail*. I could see no purpose for the government as a whole in his courting of Dacre. He was interesting on his visit to GB's house in Fife at the weekend. He said neither had really acknowledged any difficulty between them. TB was barely ever mentioned. GB had not really engaged on the euro, on Iraq, or on the future. On the Sunday they had asked him to go to church. DB said TB had to stay for the next term because there was currently no one else ready to challenge GB. He said I had to stay too.

Friday, September 20

The French food standards authority said UK beef was OK [and the unilateral ban should be lifted in France], which ran quite big for the whole day. On Iraq, the US were making it clear they would go it alone whatever. They also published their new security strategy document, full of the theory of pre-emption and their determination to make sure they are never again rivalled as the world's foremost military power. Tricky. I did a final meeting re how to do the dossier arrangements. I spoke to Jack Straw and said I was really worried about him briefing foreign governments in advance. Jack had promised it, and said he was a bit hacked off because he'd had Number 10 backing for it when he suggested it. I was worried that they would leak and there would be a Parliament problem. So we agreed a compromise: that our ambassadors would brief host governments from a speaking note. We agreed no media briefing in advance. John Williams not very happy with it. I was sure it was better that it was written by spooks not spin doctors.

Saturday, September 21

We went to the cinema to see *My Big Fat Greek Wedding*, but I couldn't get into it at all. Lots of A-level stuff around, plus Iraq, and the massive build-up for the countryside [pro-hunting] march. We then learned that Prince Charles' letter to TB re hunting was being leaked to the *Mail on Sunday*. It could have been really bad but thankfully they didn't have the text, just a briefing on it, and the line that if we banned hunting he might as well go skiing all year round. Then we learned that Clare Short had pre-recorded *GMTV* and there was plenty in it to make news – no second Gulf War, protect Iraqi children, so on and so on. What a self-indulgent bitch. I didn't bother TB with it. What with her, the march, and Schroeder expected to lose the elections, it was shaping up to be a big and bad news day tomorrow.

Sunday, September 22

TB called after church. He was praying for Schroeder to win, not least because Stoiber had communicated to us how angry he was at TB's pro-Schroeder *Tagesspiegel* interview. The exit polls suggested Stoiber winning, which he found a bit alarming. He said Clare was a pain in the arse but it was still better off keeping her inside 'So I'm afraid we just have to bear it.' But what with Robin as well, there was certainly a sense of ill discipline on Iraq. On Prince Charles, he thought it damaged him more than us. He had said to Robin Janvrin at Balmoral that he has to learn the difference between short and long term. He felt it was OK for him to give us a bit of a kicking now and then but that if he started to get too political, eventually the next generation will think who elected you to talk about all this stuff? The [Countryside Alliance] march was big [estimated 400,000 people]. We went to Jamie Rubin [former US State Department chief spokesman] and [CNN journalist] Christiane Amanpour's house. They were very down on GWB. Jamie felt that TB was basically the articulate voice of the Western world, but that the right in the US was bad and dangerous and we should be very, very careful getting too involved with them. TB had done a near complete [conference] speech draft, which was good news.

Monday, September 23

Massive coverage for the march, and TB adamant that we should be trying to find a way out of this. Schroeder had a narrow win

[Bundestag elections], which cheered us up and by the end of the day, they had been on saying he wanted to come for dinner tomorrow night, which was one in the eye for Chirac. On Iraq, post Clare's interview there was a lot of focus on division and before Cabinet TB got her in for a little chat, though again was not as tough as he should have been. Meeting with Jack re UNSCR and also votes. We agreed we should make UNSCR the focus of HoC [House of Commons] vote. TB was working on his statement for the Commons.

DM said over the weekend TB had to work on GWB in a thirty-minute call because the US was going down an impossible road again, basically a route that was unsellable. We were worried that Rumsfeld and Cheney were pushing for the idea that we get in conditions that we know Iraq could not meet. Chris Meyer popped in and said 'Beware these right-wing people in the US government. They are bad news for us. They see TB as a bit of an irritant, a complicating factor, and though they like the articulate support if they felt the need to hang us out to dry, they would do it.' He said he had recently seen Scooter Libby, Cheney's chief of staff, who was virtually dismissive of the whole UN route. Geoff Hoon came in to go through all the military options with TB.

TB had just seen GB. 'He was totally ridiculous. Even Balls looked shocked. He was basically just saying we could not afford a military conflict and making clear he had to be consulted on every piece of spending.' TB felt he was getting worse, in part because he didn't react much other than by making clear he thought these outbursts were ridiculous. At Cabinet, TB did the intro, went through what the dossier was based on, emphasised the need to put over the history of UN resolutions and also the nature of the regime. The dossier brought together accumulated evidence about Iraq's attempts to build WMD, part historical, part intelligence-based. We were not saying he was about to launch an attack on London but we were saying there was an attempt to build a WMD programme in a significant way. He made clear we were still focused on the UNSCR route and if he doesn't comply there will have to be international military action. He will not comply unless he thinks the threat is real. Meanwhile, we have to redouble efforts on Afghanistan and MEPP.

Jack Straw went through where we were on resolutions, then JP came in with quite a hit on Robin and Clare, said we could all do our bit of positioning to make our own views heard, and get a few plaudits, but we were in this together. He said TB had done a brilliant job moving the US down the UN route and we should stick with him and stick together. He said it's easy to do, a briefing here, a word there, and it's not on. Go down that road and we're in real trouble. One or two do it and it's indulgent. He said Tony had an incredibly difficult job at times like this and we should support him. He said he had been asked by the BBC if he agreed with Clare about killing innocent children and 'I said I'm not very keen on killing innocent children either.' Clare sat looking out of the window with a face like thunder, but didn't interrupt him.

GB came in with a few long-term points for the US, the need to think through post-Saddam, the importance of MEPP. Patricia Hewitt suggested the Attorney General came to Cabinet to explain the legal position. Robin was pretty creepy. Both Jack and JR had a bit of a dig at him. Even after her performance yesterday, and even after JP, Clare was still full of herself. She said if we are going to have collective responsibility we should have a collective decision. There was no doubt Saddam was dedicated to possessing WMD but re the UN, there's a double standard vis-à-vis Israel. She said she admired TB for the way he had got the US to go to the UN, but then she went off about Afghanistan being a mess. JR said 'I think we can all make our points without giving the impression that some of us have a monopoly on caring and humanity.' Most of them said what we would expect them to say, though I was quite impressed by [Paul] Boateng's speech, during which Clare spilled tea over Andrew Turnbull [new Cabinet Secretary and head of the Civil Service].

It was a pretty good discussion, though focused as much as anything on the idea that we were having to deal with a mad America and TB keeping them on the straight and narrow. JP referred to the idea that TB would have sleepless nights, that we knew it could go to a difficult choice between the US and the UN. TB said he believed it would be folly for Britain to go against the US on a fundamental policy, and he really believed in getting rid of bad people like Saddam. The discussion was serious and sober and hard-headed and TB was in control of all the arguments. Several of them praised him and his leadership without it sounding sycophantic. Milburn had one or two interesting observations about anti-Americanism. He too felt there was a problem re double standards, and the lack of drive on MEPP. Charles C said the mood in the party was apprehensive. GH said the ultimate objective was disarmament and that weapons inspectors are a means to an end. The clearer we are that we would use force, the likelier it may be that we don't have to. On the question 'Why now?' he said his record, his use of them, and his continued development.

TB said if he fell, the people who would rejoice most would be the Iraqis. It is basically a wealthy country whose people live in poverty. He said the US can go one of two ways. It can go unilateralist, and there may be some who want that, but he was sure Bush was not one of them. Or they can be part of a broader agenda on Africa, MEPP, Afghanistan. Funnily enough, I think TB won the Cabinet over more easily than the public. A poll tonight showed us below forty for the first time since the fuel protests [in 2000]. After Cabinet, Jack did clips on the idea that we were not talking about leftovers from when the [UN weapons] inspectors were in but an ongoing programme. I put out TB words which led the bulletins, but as I briefed [Andrew] Marr and others I realised once more it was not going to be easy.

Tuesday, September 24

Dossier day after months of waiting. Adam Boulton was good all day. [Andrew] Gilligan [defence and diplomatic correspondent, BBC *Today* programme] and [Tim] Marshall [Sky News foreign affairs correspondent] and the so-called experts went on about nothing new, but a combination of TB's Commons statement[1] and the gradual serious build-up re the dossier got us into a better position. TB had to go to the NEC [National Executive Committee of the Labour Party] but had done the statement pretty much himself, gone through most of the difficult questions and was OK on it all. The only really tough question was, if the UN did not sanction war, would the US and UK go along with it? The Iraqis put up their culture minister [Hamed Youssef Hamadi] to deal with it, and he was crap, his main line that it was all a Zionist plot. TB did well. He came back from the NEC laughing because Mark Seddon [NEC member and editor of left-wing magazine *Tribune*] said he had been to see Tariq Aziz [Iraqi Deputy

[1] Blair told MPs 'As the dossier sets out, we estimate on the basis of the UN's work that [in 1997] there were: up to 360 tonnes of bulk chemical warfare agents, including one and a half tonnes of VX nerve agent; up to 3,000 tonnes of precursor chemicals; growth media sufficient to produce 26,000 litres of anthrax spores; and over 30,000 special munitions for delivery of chemical and biological agents. All of this was missing or unaccounted for.' Blair concluded the statement saying 'Look at Kosovo and Afghanistan. We proceeded with care, with full debate in this House and when we took military action, did so as a last resort. We shall act in the same way now. But I hope we can do so, secure in the knowledge that should Saddam continue to defy the will of the international community, this House, as it has in our history so many times before, will not shrink from doing what is necessary and right.'

Prime Minister], that he was a nice man and it was easier to get in to see him than it was to see TB!

Couple of Q&A sessions before statement, but he was so good on this now. The general feeling re the dossier was pretty good. Massive around the world. Leading almost every bulletin in the world at lunchtime. TB's statement was really strong and I felt Jack did OK yesterday after Cabinet and again today. I called John Scarlett a few times and he was OK too. The conference call was largely about the dossier. Chirac, Bush, lots of others responding to it going well. TB saw Piers Morgan but Sally sat in because, as TB said, it would be like a red rag to a bull if I had been there. Sally said he was reasonably tough, saying it simply wasn't true when they said they supported us on the domestic agenda, and he had a real thing about Cherie. Meanwhile Fiona had a meeting with Cherie and Cate Haste re this ridiculous book project. I felt it was just wrong that she was getting money out of this and we shouldn't do it. Schroeder arrived at 6.15. It was quite a thing for him to come to see TB rather than Chirac after his election and it was playing big in all our countries.

Wednesday, September 25

Massive coverage round the world and, apart from the *Mirror*, doing pretty well in UK media. Really big hit but still pretty difficult. TB/Schroeder meeting went OK and he was very much trying to get into a better position re the US. The *Mail* did something on letters from Prince Charles to Derry [on the legal system encouraging a US-style compensation culture]. The LCD were clear that they hadn't leaked them. But it was a very difficult situation, à la Black Rod, and they were clearly fighting back. I got Godric to speak to Colleen Harris in Charles' office and she said they were clear it had not been leaked by government, as alleged by the *Mail*. But through the day lots of Charles surrogates were up saying he was being attacked by us.

TB and I had several conversations on it through the day. He felt Charles had been captured by a few very right-wing people. TB felt the only line we could take was to make clear it was not government who leaked it and express total respect for Charles' right to speak on these issues. Some of our MPs were wading in but there had to be a worry he would come over as the man speaking up for 'ordinary people' against an over-mighty government. The *Mail* was revolting even by its own standards. It led the bulletins most of the day until Estelle [Morris] came under attack for undermining, allegedly, the [Sir Michael] Tomlinson inquiry [into A-level standards]. TB said it was all very unfair but if this thing becomes the fiasco it risked

September '02: Dossier leading news bulletins worldwide

becoming, Estelle may well lose her job. She just wasn't gripping it and was getting bad advice. Jeremy [Heywood] saw David Normington [Department for Education and Skills permanent secretary] to find out what was going on and Bill Stubbs [Sir William Stubbs, chairman of the Qualifications and Curriculum Authority] took that as us interfering with the inquiry.

Conference was really looming now. I had a long session with Philip to go over our difficulties, ended with me saying I wanted out and him saying I would never have such a great job and that maybe if I needed a new challenge, I needed to grip the party stuff as I had the government. JP was on the rampage, he had clearly been wound up by GB over foundation hospitals. TB was clear it was the right thing to do but GB was almost ideological about it.

Thursday, September 26

Stayed in all day with Peter H to work on the speech, namely re optimism/boldness and the forward vision section. Sent a vile letter to Dacre, and got one back, re their continuing to suggest that we were involved in the leaking of the Charles letters. Philip called, urging me to get involved in stopping Britain in Europe [pro-European pressure group] from publishing a pamphlet that was going to be 'Labour's case for the euro'. Also pulled an idea from the party that we get Clinton sticks of rock made.[1] TB was at Chequers, called a couple of times to say he was struggling with the argument for the [conference] speech. He also felt a dark cloud of GB over him the whole time. He said GB was getting desperate and now was acting as a destructive force much of the time.

Later Andrew Adonis called to say GB had sent a 44-page letter to all Cabinet ministers attacking foundation hospitals, under-delivery by the Department of Health, as well as some of the proposals [on NHS funding and structures] coming from Adair Turner [former CBI director general] and Simon Stevens [health policy adviser]. Earlier, Alan Milburn had said to me that GB was positioning himself as reforming re PFI [Private Finance Initiative] but totally against anything that looked like private sector provision of public services. Not surprisingly, Alan was pretty ballistic about the letter, and said what it showed was GB's determination to kill any real progress. When I told TB about it, he paused for a long time and then said 'He's brilliant and ambitious but he's also bonkers and I just can't be bothered with it.' I spoke to Balls and asked him what plans they had to ensure this letter, written

[1] The former US president was to attend part of Labour's conference in Blackpool.

for leaking, didn't leak. JP was also of the view that if Cabinet ministers suddenly found themselves hit with fifty-page letters about another department's work, when he had not even gone through it with the minister, they would think he was mad. But JP also felt TB had brought this upon himself by hitting the reform buttons so hard and by not having proper discussions. I said he avoids it because he has GB sitting there absorbing anything he can use to do him in. He said that debilitates all of them. He was friendly, basically sympathetic but did repeatedly make the point that a lot of it was TB's making.

Friday, September 27

The GB situation was really serious now. On close reading, GB's letter to ministers was, as both Jonathan and Sally said, a declaration of war. TB spoke to him when he got up in the States [Washington DC, where Brown was meeting fellow governors of the International Monetary Fund]. TB said I view this as really very serious, to which GB said 'It is very serious,' and he made clear it was deliberate too. Alan [Milburn] was on the *Today* programme, and when asked re GB's opposition to foundation hospitals, said that TB backed it in the Fabian pamphlet [*The Courage of Our Convictions: Why Reform of Public Services is the Route to Social Justice*] today. It was a bad scene. TB felt GB had reached the point where he felt TB was not going to move over so he had to do what he could to bring it about. JP came to see me, and said he felt this could end with GB going, that TB could not back down on foundation hospitals. Alan said that TB had to establish command, that GB was looking for a fight and we needed to understand this was a fight with TB, using him as a surrogate.

TB was still working on the speech at Chequers and felt it was kind of getting there. The QCA [Qualifications and Curriculum Authority] report on A-level results came out, which cleared everyone, but then Estelle sacked [Sir William] Stubbs. Conference was going to be tricky and tomorrow we had the massive march against the war in Iraq. I had a series of exchanges with Ian Austin [Brown's spokesman] to establish an agreed line to take on the policy issues in GB's letter, in which he just sent back the Treasury line. I sent back some changes and he said the line said nothing about the NHS being free at the point of use. They were now being puerile about the whole thing.

Saturday, September 28

Woke up to one of those rare and totally gobsmacking revelations that newspapers very occasionally produce, namely that John Major had a four-year affair with Edwina Currie [former Conservative minister]. It was one of those 'cor, fuck me' jaw-dropping moments. How on earth did he get away with it? I had never heard so much as a whisper. I went in to discuss the *Observer* interview with TB. We had worked up a pretty good message note, but he wasn't on form. We wanted the story to be a mix of confidence plus reform but it didn't really work. Bill Morris [general secretary, Transport and General Workers' Union] had done a big attack on foundation hospitals in the *Observer*. The anti-war march was big and the coverage enormous. TB was in no doubt what we were up against. He was still exercised re GB. 'My worry is that he is so ambitious, and so keen to bring me down, that he might bring the whole show down.'

In recent weeks, he had found him impossible to deal with. He was sure GB had effectively decided to stop us doing the euro, even if it was the right thing. He felt he had nobody close in giving sensible advice. He said he had said to GB after the election that he was happy to help him become leader but he had to work with him. But TB stopped short of thinking he had to strike against him. What works, we have to keep it working. What doesn't, we have to manage it. He had told GB that if the foundation hospitals memo leaked he would hold him personally responsible. He said he had tried all reason with GB, but it was hopeless.

He'd seen Prince Charles who was raising concerns about the equalities legislation for the disabled and what it meant for the armed forces. Later we flew north to Blackpool and TB went off to do a visit in Manchester while Peter Hyman and I went to the hotel to work on the speech.

Sunday, September 29

The papers were quoting Prince Charles re a letter of apology to TB over the leaked letters but we hadn't got one and they told Jeremy that none were sent. TB was pretty supportive of Charles though, and said it was really important we should not let them think they fazed us.

I stayed in the hotel all day apart from a run out on the beach. Speech meetings on and off all day, honing lines with Bruce [Grocott], David Miliband, Peter H. At 10pm, I said I felt the structure had gone backwards and TB went into a major rewrite mode, working for a couple of hours on his own. He had said after the holiday he wanted to be more his own man, and of all of the speeches, this had the most of him in it, on Iraq – worried but clear – on EMU – keen to get out there – and on public services – resolute and determined on reform. There was a narrow dividing line between confidence and arrogance and I think we were just about on the right side. He wrote a very clear and passionate attack on anti-Americanism. GB was on his way back from the States and we didn't even see a copy of his speech through the day. Foundation hospitals wasn't really taking off, and I was amazed the letter from GB hadn't leaked. TB did a Q&A in Blackpool, and was on really good form, though he nearly let out a couple of the best lines from the speech.

Monday, September 30

We were pretty much there now, though TB still wanted better lines, more colour and texture, and we also needed to take out about 1,000 words. It was a bit meandering in places, and the public services section wasn't hanging together. But he was determined to do it his way, much more than usual, was far more resistant to making changes, unless the case was absolutely overwhelming. GB's speech was OK without being great. It played too much to the party, wasn't modernising or challenging enough. It was GB's attempt to cover the waterfront but it lacked boldness and was not memorable. TB read it after the event, said it wasn't a great speech. Lots of people were noticing that GB just looked a little diminished at the moment.

Clinton called me from Number 10, having gone there with Magi [Cleaver, press officer], having flown in early, and was clearly enjoying himself. He read me a very funny spoof draft, said he was going to do a 'never give in to Tony' speech. He said the US press were giving the Bush people an easy ride. 'Our press is either right wing or Establishment so they don't care too much about the economy, jobs, health care, because they are all OK. They know that the Democrats want to be on the economy and Bush wants to be on the war.' A Karl Rove [senior adviser to Bush] memo was leaked saying that 'war is the only issue that excites our base'. He said if Labour or the Democrats had ever done something like that, there would have been a total outcry. He was worried that TB was being used. I told him what TB had said a while back about 'really believing this'. He said a lot of Democrats were up there asking 'Why is Blair helping Bush so much?' We talked over how his speech might fit into the general pattern of conference, and help lift the mood. He was clear about how he could help, and looking forward to it. I told TB later what he had said about the view of Democrats. 'But what do I do about it?' He believed we were doing the right thing, and also that Britain basically had to be with America at these really difficult moments.

Tuesday, October 1

Philip, Liz [Lloyd, policy adviser] and I had been up till 3am going through the speech line by line and trying to get in more colour and texture. It was in good shape. TB was up around 6, and I went in to see him at 7, and he was pretty happy with it. He felt it was the most rounded intellectual speech of the lot. The overnight briefing had not gone particularly well, it didn't matter much. We did the read-through and it felt pretty good. We made the right cuts and it was fairly lean. The big argument that we were trying to recast the 1945 welfare state settlement came through clearly. There was the usual last-minute cutting, minor chopping and changing, the running up and down the corridor with last-minute changes for the typists, and also a very annoying last-minute fuss over his shirt, most of us thinking after the sweat pictures [wearing a blue shirt for the conference speech in 2000] he should wear a white shirt. Cherie for some reason was desperate for him to wear blue or purple, and even got Carole [Caplin] to call. Total waste of time. At least ten minutes wasted on it. Then off we went. TB was less nervous than usual going on, and the audience was pretty much with him the whole way.[1] GB's body language was unbelievable. At times his face and his body seemed to contort in pain, and he found it virtually impossible either to laugh or applaud in the same way his colleagues were. The briefing afterwards pretty much took care of itself and people seemed to think it was strong and confident and very much himself. It was a hot day outside, bit too humid but I walked back to the hotel feeling we had done pretty well.

I got Robin C to meet Clinton on arrival, which seemed to chuff him up no end. Bill arrived to a great scrum. He was just what we needed to take us through the next twenty-four hours. I took him up to see TB. On Iraq, he said the Republicans were really hitting the Democrats hard and using TB. He said TB had to keep the US going down the UN route. Clinton was pretty bitter about [Al] Gore, felt he should have won convincingly. He had been a great vice president but ran a poor campaign. In politics, you are dealing with a mix of reality and rhetoric. What we did was speak to our base through our values and have policies that went to the centre. Al did the opposite. He had right-wing policies but left-wing rhetoric and it was a mistake.

Clinton was still at his best when defining the big political sweep, the strategic big picture, and his analysis of our situation was pretty good too. He was also brilliant at talking in big geopolitical themes, but then bringing them down to stories and pictures of people in their lives. We got him down to the gala dinner where he made a good little

[1] After paying tribute to 'the brilliance and vision' of Gordon Brown, Blair told Labour conference delegates 'We are at a crossroads: party, government, country . . . I believe that we are at our best when at our boldest. So far we made a good start but frankly we have not been bold enough.'

off-the-cuff speech, then down to Northern Night [regional reception] with TB. Clinton was loving it now, big crowds gagging to see him and get near him and he was turning on the full charm, really hit the buttons when he spoke about TB, about the UK, how important we were, how the world looked to us, blah blah. TB got a bit carried away, said something in his speech about the world needing the philosophy and leadership of Clinton right now, which could easily be turned into a big hit on Bush. I could tell as soon as he said it that he was worried. On the way out, he asked me if I thought it was a problem. I said it partly depended who was in there, but I would put in a call to the Yanks.

Of all the visitors we had had to conference, Clinton was the one with the most star quality, up there with Mandela. As we were heading back to his suite, BC said he fancied going for a walk. It was windy, a bit cold and it was starting to rain, but he was like a big kid enjoying the lights. 'I love this place. I love Blackpool.' The security guys were clearly used to these kinds of eccentric excursions. We passed a big bingo hall, which advertised itself as the biggest amusement arcade in the world. 'Hey, I wanna go in there. Let's go play the machines.' We got to the door and it looked a lot less inviting close up, so we walked on. We were trying to find somewhere to eat. He said he wanted some fast food, nothing fancy, but we walked past two or three places that were closed. By now the rain was getting a bit heavier. Kevin Spacey [actor and friend of Clinton] was with us, having been on a trip with BC. We must have walked on for a couple of miles. Eventually we found a McDonald's that was open. Bill was now on the phone to Hillary, a mix of heavy politics and small talk, going on with her too about how great this Blackpool seafront was. He made quite an interesting point when he came off the phone. All the delegates and the conference people are inside the security bubble, but more of them should get out here with the real people. The tighter the bubble, the more you should try and get out of it.

The staff were gobsmacked when we trooped in. There was a young kid behind the counter who was shocked enough to clock Kevin Spacey, but then saw Clinton and went a funny shade of pink, before getting everybody out of the kitchens to come and see. Doug Band [Clinton aide] ordered massive amounts of burgers, chicken nuggets and fries while Bill went round saying hello to the small number of customers in there. There was a fringe event going on at a pub or hotel over the road and word went round there. [Former Labour minister] Margaret Jay's daughter Tamsin came back with a few journalists including Matthew d'Ancona [deputy editor, *Sunday Telegraph*] but they just sort of gawked, pretended they had just been

October '02: . . . and goes to McDonald's on the seafront

going out for a night at McDonald's. I got them over to say hello a bit later on. Meanwhile a crowd was building outside, some of them classic Blackpool landladies out of the postcards, looking and pointing and then when he occasionally turned round and waved at them, they were waving back in a state of high excitement.

So there we were, sitting in a Blackpool McDonald's, drinking Diet Coke and eating chicken nuggets as he poured forth on the theme of interdependence, the role of the Third Way in progressive politics. He was also quizzing me about GB, and could sense that GB didn't really want to acknowledge TB's peculiar skills and talents, just as Gore hadn't used him properly in the campaign. He spent a while talking to the crowd on the way out, then we got driven back in a little van. He was like a man replenished, not because of the food but because he had been out with real people, and got something out of it. It was probably the single biggest difference between him and TB. They both loved political ideas, wrestling with policy problems and the rest of it, but of the two, Bill was the one who most saw politics in terms of its outcome in people's lives.

We got back to see TB who had been doing the rounds of receptions and was on a bit of a high, chilling out after the speech, which seemed to have gone down really well. They talked about Bush and it was pretty clear that though Clinton didn't go for him in public, he didn't rate him much and thought he stole the election. 'The problem was that we let them,' he said, and then gave another pretty negative analysis of the Gore campaign.

Wednesday, October 2

I went to the office meeting, then did a few bits and pieces for Bill's speech, including the suggestion he kick off with 'Clinton, Bill, Arkansas CLP, New Labour'. He needed assurance that it would work. He also asked me to work on a few lines on Northern Ireland, and on the Third Way. Hans Blix seemed to be making progress and looked like he was trying to do a deal which would not necessarily include palaces. It wasn't good enough for the US but the UN were pushing it and suggested that we didn't need another UNSCR. Powell was very hard line that there could be no new inspections without a new UNSCR. We were saying the same but TB and Jack had a very difficult meeting early on, Jack explaining that the US were getting very jittery re the UN route. As Bill said, Rumsfeld and Cheney didn't want to go the UN route, Powell did, and Bush was not so sure. Jack said the French were simply making clear they would not support war at all. The Chinese didn't care, the Russians were playing hardball.

TB was also conscious that he had told Bush that Blix was a good guy who knew what he was doing and he was worried Bush would doubt his judgement. TB would speak to Bush later, after Clinton's conference speech, and it became quite fraught because the Americans wanted one resolution that would allow them to hit Iraq at the first sign of Saddam lying or causing trouble. TB came off the phone around 4pm and said 'That was difficult. He is beginning to wonder whether we are going down the right road.' The Americans basically felt that Saddam was fucking them around and they were getting more and more impatient.

TB and I had the *Mirror* lunch to endure, which considering recent events was reasonably friendly. [Sir] Victor [Blank, Trinity Mirror chairman] made his usual spiel about the *Mirror* being a constructive friend. TB did his usual stuff, Piers [Morgan] being cocky, then we left so that I could hurry up Bill. He had put a fair bit of work into the speech and it went down a storm. He was very good on TB, the best exposition of the Third Way I had heard, awesome on the purpose of politics and on the big geopolitical questions. He did a terrific denunciation of so-called compassionate conservatism, got very close to the mark on the Republicans' domestic agenda and was fairly heavy on them on the international stuff too. Some of our press were seeing it as a big attack on Bush's policy, whereas we wanted it pitched much more as his expression of support for us.

The real line Clinton was pushing was that we should appreciate the fact that TB was in a position to influence US policy vis-à-vis the UN route, and get Bush to side with Powell versus Cheney and Rumsfeld. Earlier, when we had been running through the speech in his room, he was scathing about the American press, and the corporate corruption they didn't pursue, the laziness of their coverage. Jonathan and I both felt there were likely to be reverberations from Washington, and TB made sure he was the one who briefed Bush on it on the call. He got fantastic coverage on our news, and the top line running was that he was backing TB to keep going down the UN track. But it was becoming more and more difficult. TB was less confident we could get the tough resolution we wanted. Peter H suggested earlier that we get TB to do a press conference before leaving Blackpool and we got TB up for it, so then we had to sort a venue, backdrop etc. Word had got out about the McDonald's trip, which was also running big. Jack and Powell had talked five times and Powell was worried that Bush was struggling to keep on the right side of the line. Bush himself had told TB that 'I'm having trouble holding on to my horse' but what was clear was that GWB was trying to get TB to agree that if Saddam was found to be lying that was *'casus belli'* [case for war]. David Manning and Condi spoke to try to get things back on track, then TB spoke to GWB again. Bush was clearly being assailed by his right wing at the moment. TB felt his problem was that his rhetoric was aimed at the Republican right wing but it would stop him getting to the right policy positions. Perhaps it was the Clinton influence, but he seemed to be moving to the view that this was a government which was ruthless about its own power and position. Jack had told him, and we assumed this was in part based on American intelligence, that Chirac was basically intent on avoiding military action come what may.

The GB situation was no better. TB and I both noted that Clare Short had looked like death warmed up after Bill's speech, presumably because it had been so fulsome about TB and his unique position. Ditto GB. While TB said Ed Balls had brushed shoulders with him when he walked by, like kids in a schoolyard do. Fiona and I went out for dinner with the *Independent*. They were all swooning re Bill and felt TB had done really well yesterday. But there was still resistance there and one or two of them were really pushing for GB. Then a flurry of calls, including from James Blitz at the *FT*, re foundation hospitals. He had been told that GB had seen TB and the policy had been sorted in GB's favour. In fact it hadn't and I told James so, which led to the *FT* splash 'Blair and Brown at loggerheads over foundation hospitals'. TB was neither angry nor upset, just said he really had to sort it. He agreed with me that GB or Balls must have set Blitz up to try to bounce us. He felt Gordon was now so bitter and jealous that it was hitting his judgement. GB was worrying he was running out of time. If it was going to be resolved, then maybe TB ought to press the advantage now, the week definitely having strengthened him.

Thursday, October 3

Awesome coverage for Bill. Not least the *Mirror* front page – the *Mirror* salutes you, sir, an American leader who says everything we have been waiting to hear. Up early and in to see TB pre the *Today* programme interview. The hard question was whether the conference vote meant that we could only take military action with a specific UN mandate. TB felt we just had to dance around it for now and point to the UN process. He was actually more worried about the A-levels issue. He could not find the rationale as to why, if it was an accident waiting to happen, and then it happened, no minister carried the can. He felt that nobody had really thought through it all and gripped it. For the press conference, I drafted very brief opening remarks on reform, Iraq and the French beef ban being lifted. On Iraq, the Americans were saying today they were putting out a dossier on [Saddam's] palaces, which they never did. But we used the line that it was no good going for ninety-nine per cent of Iraq being inspected if the WMD were in the other one per cent.

TB was OK on foundation hospitals, said there was agreement on principle but technical details needed to be worked out, Milburn was right to want greater autonomy, GB right to press for value for money. The truth is that both had cocked it up by overzealous briefing which we had allowed to get out of hand in the crazy conference atmosphere. He was good on *Today* and [James] Naughtie said he looked like he had got his second wind. TB said he had never been clearer about the direction of the government, a theme picked up by *The World at One*. A lot of the journos were pissed off at having to stay in Blackpool for his press conference but he was on a roll. He was amazingly bouncy for the end of such a heavy week. On Iraq, he said Saddam would be disarmed come what may, but we must have a new UNSCR before inspections go ahead. Then lots of regional questions for those stations that didn't get full interviews. And though it wasn't chart-topping stuff, it was definitely another win for us, 4–0 I would say. We went down to the conference centre and I watched John Reid who had real presence on the podium, could deliver a joke and a message. Good mood at the end. I listened to Reid on *The World at One*. He was absolutely superb.

I spoke to a number of columnists on the drive out to the airport and they all seemed to think TB had had a particularly good week. GB could win the lesser races but he wasn't in the same league. We were in a great position. The Iraq row never really took off. TB had been commanding and strong. GB had put himself around everywhere but had not been brilliant. And the Tories were gathering against a backdrop of worries about Jeffrey Archer,[1] Major shagging Currie, and growing concern over IDS.

Friday, October 4

Iraq still really tricky. TB just wished the Americans would do more to put over a proper message to the world and worry less about their own right wing. First, a meeting in the garden, TB, AC, Jonathan, Andrew Adonis, later joined by David Manning. First we had to work out how to respond to the breaking news that Sinn Fein members

[1] Lord Archer, former Conservative deputy chairman and London mayoral candidate, was serving a four-year sentence for perjury and perverting the course of justice. Despite being imprisoned, he was continuing to attract a lot of media coverage.

were being arrested for arms offences and the obvious worry the ceasefire was breaking. Just had to play it along. Then foundation hospitals. There was a plan for a major presentation on this to ministers on Monday but Andrew said the Health department and the Treasury just could not agree on the facts. It was clearly going to have to be sorted at political level and I suggested a TB/GB/JP/AM meeting with no officials at all. TB said he was worried GB was just looking the whole time to position himself slightly to the left on everything. He felt Balls was a real problem, clever but often giving him wrong strategic advice.

Then A levels, on which he was persistently worried, saying we had to find some good people to put round Estelle. On student finance, again a GB problem, with AA saying the Treasury were preparing to undermine it as 'the university poll tax'. TB said 'I'm afraid there does rather appear to be a pattern here. It could be he is getting desperate and maybe preparing to bring the show down.' David Manning joined us, said we were in a much better position with Blix having said yesterday he was keen to get a tougher resolution with no inspections till then. TB felt there was a case for trying to get Putin more firmly on board and then get him to work on Chirac. He felt the Americans simply had no strategy for the French because, as Bill [Clinton] had said, it was all being driven by his [Bush's] own domestic politics.

David Manning felt that Saddam was probably going to make positive noises about inspections and try to drag things to February because then the 'window of war' would close because he couldn't expect troops to fight in fifty-degree heat. I got a message from Godric that Charles Reiss [*Evening Standard*] was picking up on a line from Mary Ann Sieghart's [*Times*] column that GB was 'insanely jealous' of TB. TB wanted us to put out a very pro-GB line and make clear he would never sanction such a statement being made. But it was worrying, given he had said those very words, and I wondered to whom as well as to me.

In the conference call with the Americans I stressed the worries from here that Bush needed to get out a message to the world, not just the US. Tucker Eskew [White House media affairs] said Bush had said that war was his last choice not his first choice. Then spoke to Blunkett to get him signed up to do the first of the planned new briefings to be done by ministers rather than officials. Jeremy did a note to TB on EMU, saying that even Gus O'Donnell [Treasury permanent secretary] did not know what GB was really thinking but Jeremy's guess was that GB would come to us in the next six months and say that four out of the five tests were met or being met but that one, sustainable convergence, was not. TB said that on everything, even these vital national interest issues, he was just using them to position himself in a different place to TB. However, surely the lesson of the week had been that the party had changed and it was GB who was not properly adapting to it. TB remained adamant that we should not go after GB and his people through the press, because the party would not like it and would get confused. But the GB fog was clouding everything.

I called Doug Band in Germany to fill him in on the coverage of Bill's speech, and Bill came on the line and said 'Hey man, what is going on in Northern Ireland?' I explained how some of the SF people were stuck in the arms game. He said if there was anything he could do, he wanted to do it, and he would go there at the drop of a hat. He asked if Bush's people had reacted to his speech. I said not officially, but my sense from Dan Bartlett and Tucker was they weren't terribly happy about it.

Saturday, October 5

Ran a half marathon around the Heath. Papers moving on to the Tories. Iraq fairly low-key, focus on trying to get the UNSCR. I took Grace and her friends to the cinema but was called out by TB, really obsessing at the moment about GB and what he was up to. He feared it was coming to a head.

Sunday, October 6

Philip called, said it was obvious that Jonathan did a lot for TB, particularly foreign and Northern Ireland, but that I basically held it together and I could not possibly leave. Also, he said, what else would I do? He felt TB was moving to a different phase, developing in an interesting way and I should be part of that history. Silly briefings on foundation hospitals still going on over the weekend by Treasury and Health. As a policy problem, it was one easily sortable behind closed doors but they were at it.

Monday, October 7

The Tories were in pretty dire straits. They had had a dreadful press over the weekend, were now trying to get up the idea of twenty-five policies being announced in the week, but IDS was looking vulnerable. They briefed overnight that he was going to go for the Thatcher mantle on public services, which totally played into our hands, allowed us to attack on lurch to the right and cuts. Quite a big news day with

Northern Ireland still very difficult, Blunkett up with some tough new asylum measures.[1] At the morning meeting, I told everyone we say absolutely nothing on foundation hospitals other than that the principles were agreed and the details being worked out.

TB saw JP to get him on board. JP was pretty much onside at the moment. TB told him that he felt GB not only wants him out of the job, but was also trying to make sure we don't succeed while he's doing it. It makes him even madder when people say that TB's doing well. He was genuinely concerned GB would bring the whole show down. At TB's morning meeting, he said we needed a strategy to build up the better union leaders. 'I can't believe I find myself saying this, but [John] Edmonds [GMB union general secretary] is about the best we've got.' Peter H was saying that for once we had the chance to drive real momentum forward from the conference and the key was the Queen's Speech. Philip had done an excellent note pointing out that on four fronts we faced the toughest battles – Iraq, EMU, public services and economy – none were easy but TB had strengthened his position on all of them. TB wanted a big, bold Queen's Speech but that was not what was going through the system at the moment. We just didn't have the big theme and it was all too piecemeal.

I did a staff meeting to explain how we should now be more focused on strategy and less on day-to-day news, and what that meant in practice. TB was still on about seeing [Viscount] Rothermere [chairman of Associated Newspapers] to try to get the *Mail* neutralised a bit. I felt they were a total waste of time and we should go for them harder. On Iraq, we still felt that Bush was looking to TB to move Chirac, but TB was sure he could only be moved by Bush, if at all. I saw Alan Milburn to discuss foundation hospitals. Alan was very down, and I tried to persuade him it wasn't as bad as it seemed, that all that mattered was the policy that was agreed in the end and he should ignore the rest of it. He felt we underestimated the negative impact GB had on progress. I said we didn't, but we had to try and make things work. I felt GB had made a mistake in allowing himself to be presented on a par with Alan because it was clear where TB needed the policy to go. I went to a meeting on asylum where DB and Derry had a few rather lively exchanges, Derry accusing Blunkett of taking cheap shots at judges for the sake of a few headlines.

[1] Blunkett proposed denying support to asylum seekers unless they claimed asylum at a port or airport and declared how they entered the UK. He also proposed that failed claimants should be less likely to be granted exceptional leave to remain.

Tuesday, October 8

The Treasury couldn't resist doing a bit of briefing on foundation hospitals. Basically TB supported GB in that he felt Alan was using this to try to get more money for his CSR settlement. But he supported Alan in that he wanted foundation hospitals with the ability to borrow, within overall Treasury controls. TB was happy enough with the policy outcome but of course GB had to insist that he had won.

Bush's speech [in Cincinnati] of late last night was leading in the news and was a bit more aimed at the international community, so maybe they were listening a bit more.[1] I had a meeting with Dickie Stagg and Asif [Ahmad] in the Foreign Office, and then all the CIC staff, to get a bit more direction into their operation. Asif was going to the US tomorrow so we needed him to keep going at the Americans to be more international in their message. I had a conference call with Peter Reid [press attaché] at our embassy in Washington re the same.

TB did a brief doorstep on Ireland after his meeting with the Bulgarian president but wasn't happy with it. Then [David] Trimble came in for a shouting match. TB was going to have to go over there soon. We had a long-term diary meeting, desperately fighting to get more domestic stuff back in the diary but it wasn't easy with all the foreign commitments in there already. There was a lot of dithering internally and with the FA over whether we should have cameras in for the World Cup reception. Eventually we agreed to have a pool [media sharing]. They [England players] arrived by coach, most of them with wives and girlfriends, though Beckham was solo because she [Victoria Beckham] was at a birthday party for one of [their son] Brooklyn's friends. Of all the people who had been into the building in our time here, these were the ones getting the most rubbernecking, particularly him. I spent a lot of the time chatting to Emile Heskey as we had both gone to the same school [City of Leicester], also trying to make Paul Scholes and Nicky Butt feel more at ease than they looked. Nancy [Dell'Olio, partner of Sven-Göran Eriksson] pretty much stole the show from all of them when she arrived in an amazing red outfit that was bound to be all over the front pages and very much seen in the context of sending a message to Ulrika [Jonsson] that she was history. TB did a little speech and then off he went.

[1] Bush laid out in detail, for the first time, his case for disarming Iraq, saying 'If we know Saddam Hussein has dangerous weapons today – and we do – does it make any sense for the world to wait to confront him as he grows even stronger and develops even more dangerous weapons?'

Wednesday, October 9

I ran in, a bit sluggish. Nancy totally stole the show last night with the plunging neckline on her scarlet trouser suit. David Davies [FA] called to say he was really sorry that that was about all anybody knew from last night. I said it was fine, I thought she was a real character. Lots of people in the office were saying how unimpressive they had found most of the players. TB, JP, GB and Alan M were due to meet to resolve the foundation hospitals policy. Andrew Turnbull had been asked to try to draft a compromise. As of last night, it was far too close to the Treasury view but had been improved overnight. Simon Stevens had drawn up a press release making clear we were going ahead with foundation hospitals in the Queen's Speech and they would enjoy substantial freedoms, which was OK for Alan. But, with TB's support, it was going to be 'on balance sheet' which was enough for GB to claim victory. We should never have got to this at all. At the start of the meeting, GB indicated how he intended to carry on by saying the previous minutes didn't accurately reflect the last meeting. Rolling eyes all round. TB was clear he wanted to support GB in not letting Alan use this to reopen negotiations but he did want to be able to press all the reform buttons. Once the meeting finished, we decided to put the press release out straight away and do the briefing speaking for everyone. But because it didn't suggest GB had 'won' he went mad that the press release had gone out. Also Balls was going berserk because he had not been in on the process.

Meanwhile Northern Ireland was going bad. TB saw Mark Durkan [Social Democratic and Labour Party] and later Bertie Ahern [Taoiseach of Ireland] and it was pretty clear that we were going to have to suspend the Executive. Philip called having done some groups on the Tories last night. They were beginning to break through a bit. They were getting somewhere with the idea of modern Thatcherism. Major was basically out of the political script, but the idea of a softened and modernised Thatcher had appeal. Philip and I both felt that TB was being too complacent about the Tories. Both he and Peter M felt the public would not be impressed with anything they had seen, but I sensed the media still trying to give them a lift. The big problem for IDS was an incoherent economic policy – where was the money coming from? – and silence on Europe.

Thursday, October 10

Foundation hospitals worked out as a bit of a score draw but it was perfectly obvious GB was going to keep at it and cause more trouble. I felt though that he had really messed up the handling of it. It hardly helped with their presentation of him as lord of the domestic manor while TB and JP had to sort it out, with Alan and GB seeming to be equals. TB saw [Gerry] Adams, [Martin] McGuinness and Bairbre [de Brún, Sinn Fein]. I went in at the end of the meeting and GA was giving TB the usual rather patronising history lesson. TB did though believe that Adams and McGuinness were genuinely trying to move towards non-violence and there was little chance of the IRA going back, but they had real issues in dealing with their own people. McGuinness and I had a long chat about football while TB and Adams had a little session in the corner of the room. Adams did a big number in the street.

Then we left for the airport and I listened to IDS' speech, which I thought was really poor, no real argument and very negative about Britain. I did a quick conference call with the party people to agree lines on it. TB had a brief session with the hacks on the plane to Moscow and they were winding up the line that he accepted Russia had legitimate financial interests in Iraq. Over dinner, he and I had another little argument about how to handle the Tories. He denied being complacent but felt IDS was just useless and that the Tories had not faced up to the change they needed to make. I agreed it was hard to take IDS seriously but felt that some of the strategic moves they were making might have appeal. The Tories were pushing IDS' line about 'the determination of a quiet man' but it was pretty woeful.

TB felt the press conference with Putin tomorrow could be tricky because we were in such different positions and there was little point pretending otherwise. We flew out in a crappy little airbus, then TB, CB, David Manning, Tony Bishop [interpreter], cops and I were flown by helicopter to the hunting lodge [at Zavidovo] forty-five minutes away. Pretty bleak landscape on the way, and the odd ramshackle home in the middle of nowhere. TB and CB were taken straight away to see Putin for dinner. I went for a run around the lake inside the grounds. TB came back a bit more confident that Putin would be in the right position re the UNSCR but there were other problems to come. On the way out to their dacha for dinner, Putin had taken them on a diversion to go and look at wild boar.

Friday, October 11

TB spent several hours one-on-one with Putin, so David and I were hanging around a lot of the time. They seemed to be getting on fine, though at the press conference, Putin took a bit of a pop at our dossier.[1]

[1] Putin remarked that the dossier 'could be seen as a propagandistic step' to influence public opinion.

Earlier we checked what he would say about a UNSCR, namely that he might consider one, but on the dossier there had been no prior discussion, so the perfectly avoidable problem became a story for some of our lot. I was kicking myself, thinking maybe I wasn't as alert as I used to be, not to have spotted that one coming. TB was less bothered about it than he was about actually sorting the UNSCR situation. Putin took me aside at the end and said he hoped they realised he had just announced a change of position in saying he would consider going for the UNSCR.

But the press were happy for the wrong reasons and we were slightly on the back foot. The one thing we lacked, during the brief time we had the hacks in the compound, was a picture so [press secretary Alexey] Gromov and I agreed TB and Putin would do a little walk through the trees by the lake. We went over to meet TB and VP who had just been having breakfast with their wives. TB was wearing what I can only call an Afghan hippie coat. I said there was no way he could wear that. Mohni Bahra [protection officer] had a fairly ordinary-looking sheepskin and I suggested they swap. This is ridiculous, Cherie said. Just ignore him. I said my job was to stop him looking ridiculous and try to get the press focused on real issues and not his bloody clothes. I said if he walked out in that, they would fall about and we'd have endless blather about his coat rather than the substance. Putin was looking on a bit bemused and TB, a bit embarrassed, said 'He doesn't like my coat very much.' Putin smiled and nodded in a way that made me think he thought I was right not to. He then tried on Mohni's coat, which just about fitted and looked fine and unremarkable, at which point Cherie said to me 'You are a total fascist.' I said I think that's a bit over the top but he would look a complete clown going out in that. Mohni meanwhile was trying on TB's coat and launched into an impersonation of Elvis Presley. Godric, Magi and the cops were all totally on my side, really felt it was over the top but it was all a bit bloody. The walk-by went fine. They had another meeting, then off on a boat trip, stopping at a field for lunch where a marquee had been set up and they served barbecued wild boar.

TB liked him. I got the sense he was still a bit isolated. Putin told him he was pretty much alone in the leadership re pursuing a very pro-Western policy, and he felt he was getting very little in return from the US. TB told him he thought Bush got it but he wasn't sure about some of the others. As the day wore on, TB seemed to buy more into the Putin charge. He said he would have to talk to Bush about it. Putin said that if there was something the Americans were worried about, they expect the whole world to share their concerns and drop everything, but if it's something that the rest of the world are interested in, like the Middle East peace process, they don't get the urgency. He was clearly pretty pissed off and the rhetoric cranked up through the day. But he was making an impact on TB, who was even saying to us by the end of it we had to get the Americans on a more multilateral track. On Iraq, VP said to TB 'Do you really think Iraq is more dangerous than this fundamentalism? Course not'. His bottom line was the oil price. The Iraqi debts were one thing, but if the oil price went too low, he was in trouble with his electorate. We had to remember he was putting through big reform and he was not always going to be popular. But he felt the US didn't sufficiently understand the problems other countries had. I think TB was beginning to feel the same, for example on missile defence.

On the flight back, we discussed it further. They were about to go public with the demand re [RAF] Fylingdales and we had a discussion about whether to go on the front foot. I felt we had to. TB said he was more confident than ever that the Tories didn't have a thought-through strategy. He said that before we went snap on New Labour, we had gone through a thorough intellectual examination of values, policies and the means. The presentation came at the end of all that. They had gone for presentation first. If they really wanted to signal change, they would go for Europe as the issue. It had definitely been good for him to have had as much time as he had with Putin on his own, away from some of the more conservative elements. Putin had also suggested setting up a secure line between the two of them. TB and VP had been swapping notes about other leaders and both confessed to a great fondness for Vajpayee [Indian Prime Minister]. Putin said that he sometimes felt that if he asked a question on Wednesday, he had to wait till Friday for the answer.

Saturday, October 12

Quiet work-wise. I settled down to watch the England game [European Championship qualifier, England 2, Slovakia 1]. The car bombings in Bali were totally dominating the news agenda.[1]

Sunday, October 13

Jack seemed to be handling Bali fine, it was apparent early on that there were quite a lot of Brits involved. I put out TB words after he

[1] Three bombs detonated in the tourist district of Kuta killed 202 people from twenty-one countries, including eighty-eight Australians and twenty-six Britons. Various members of Jemaah Islamiyah, a violent Islamist group, were later convicted and three sentenced to death.

spoke by phone to John Howard. I was working on a speech for the media correspondents lunch tomorrow.

Monday, October 14

Bali still absolutely dominant. Today was the first of our new-style lobby briefings, with Blunkett on street crime. The lobby was still very pissed off. The venue, a room upstairs in the Foreign Press Association [Carlton House Terrace], seemed fine and the mechanics seemed to work but to our annoyance, Jack Straw did a doorstep on the Bali figures just before DB was on, which took away the point of the whole thing. The morning meeting was largely Bali, A levels and Northern Ireland, with JR about to suspend the devolved institutions, so it was a pretty big news day.

At TB's meeting, he was pretty dismissive about some of the policy ideas being put forward by AA and others. He felt they weren't being radical enough, not motoring, going along in the comfort zone. But as we went through the various problems, it was clear that the common link was still GB, and on the euro, TB was in no doubt now it was being sacrificed to their internal difficulties. We had a meeting on the Queen's Speech and TB was still not happy about the radical edge. The big things seemed to be fines for child truancy, foundation hospitals, housing benefit, student finance. Hunting was still a problem. If there was one thing he could just wish himself out of, this was it. I was pushing for a statement on Bali tomorrow, which he eventually agreed to. The basic line coming over was that you could not do the war on terror and Iraq. He however said it all showed up the dangers of the modern world.

I went off to Christopher's restaurant to do a speech and Q&A with academics, opinion formers and media correspondents, the bulk of whom actually seemed broadly to agree with my analysis of media/politics and the questioning was far more supportive than I expected. I felt I had a proper argument to put to them, also accepted our share of the blame and said that the press had to face up to their responsibilities too. Even Stephen Glover [columnist], for all the bile he pours out in print, asked a very tame question. Charlie Burgess [*Guardian*] wanted me to do a piece for them based on what I had said. I felt what it showed overall was that I was at my best when defending and promoting politics in general, strategy and policy, and not when getting down into the areas for a dogfight.

The lobby meanwhile were whingeing and whining about the changes. What a bunch of tossers. Blunkett was a bit pissed off because he felt he had had to take the heat. We just had to persevere with this.

It was right to try to broaden the range. It was right to try to involve ministers, and it was right to try and do it outside Number 10.

Tuesday, October 15

Ran in, thirty-two minutes. Home in 31.37.82, a homeward personal best. During the day I formally signed up for the [London] marathon. Up to see TB in the flat. Anna Wechsberg [private secretary, foreign affairs] had done a good draft of the Bali statement. I did a new ending, then he did his own with a couple of over-the-top lines, e.g. a reference to 'satanic struggles' then a tacit comparison with the Second World War. He was meant to speak to President Megawati [Sukarnoputri, of Indonesia] but she was on answering machine, and the ambassador in Jakarta [Richard Gozney] couldn't find her! He seemed to be fretting a lot about it when it was actually quite straightforward. But the question was growing how can we do terrorism and Iraq and TB was keen to build the argument that they were part of the same coin. TB had lunch with the Danish PM [Anders Fogh Rasmussen] then over to the House, no real problems out of the statement.

Back to meet Jeremy and Sally and go for a meeting on the honours list with [Andrew] Turnbull, Hayden Phillips [permanent secretary, Lord Chancellor's Department] and people from the [Cabinet Office] Ceremonial Branch. It was a really dull list and we were creeping back towards more Establishment dominance. We wanted more head teachers in there. We fought for George Best [former footballer].[1] OBE for Anthony Buckeridge [children's author]. The thing had actually gone backwards and though we had lots of ideas, it was too late for most of them, and it just felt like one of those fights not really worth having.

Jeremy said the TB/GB meeting today had been absolutely disastrous. They had gone through the most difficult issues – euro, pensions, child and housing benefits, university finance. He said the atmosphere was dreadful, that he had never seen a more difficult TB/GB session. On the euro, GB effectively refused to discuss what was happening inside the Treasury. He ended by saying that TB was not the only minister in the government and he didn't have a veto. It was very hard to see how we could sustain this position much longer. Relations were if anything getting worse.

[1] Belfast-born Best, a world-renowned winger who succumbed to alcoholism, would die in 2005 without receiving an honour. He has been honoured by a saying in Northern Ireland, 'Maradona good; Pelé better; George Best.'

Fiona was losing patience with Cherie, over the Cate Haste book, but also the trip to Bermuda next week where she was staying with the governor [Sir John Vereker].

Wednesday, October 16

One or two potential problems developing out of Bali. It emerged that we did put out local warnings about the danger of visiting night clubs, but didn't put it in our [FCO] travel advice. I spoke to JP re doing the briefing tomorrow and he was clearly a bit nervous. I said don't rise to the bait if they try to wind you up. He said they would probably succeed because 'I bloody hate them'. We assumed IDS would come on A levels, which he did, and when he said they weren't worth the paper they were written on, TB really picked it up and went for it as an insult to people who passed exams. The press felt it had been a huge mistake and TB came back convinced IDS was a goner. I had quite a good meeting with Charles C on the Tories, tried to get him signed up to a big push on the Tories so that we could get dividing lines in place so the election was not a battle between us and perfection, but between us and them.

Philip's groups were very down on IDS at the moment and up on TB. Philip's new thing was that Theresa May [chairman of the Conservative Party] was a great hope for them, which was ridiculous. The TV news [re Bali] was dreadful, and I sent a message through to the FCO that all we could get in these situations was empathy and competence. We should have put Tessa [Jowell] on the case. We were also getting into a muddle on Bali intelligence, with the Americans and the Australians indicating that they did get specific threats, but of course it was always very easy after the event. I was worried this was not being gripped. Saddam won his elections with one hundred per cent.[1]

Thursday, October 17

I made contact with Leukaemia Research [charity] re the marathon and they sounded very up for it. I spoke to [Andrew] Turnbull and Jeremy about generating sponsorship and they were fine providing I wasn't using government facilities. At the 8.30 meeting, I read the riot act re the general lack of grip re intelligence warnings, especially now as the Australians were saying all Aussies should leave Indonesia. Later saw TB and asked if there was any point thinking of TV [election]

[1] Of 11,445,638 eligible voters, it was reported that every one of them voted for Saddam Hussein, the sole candidate.

debates. He said no, that it was totally one of those that just placed you on the at-risk register. On the Tories, we all agreed IDS was probably dead meat, we had to stay focused on the character and ungovernability of the Tories as a whole. We also needed to get up delivery through definition rather than through lists of statistical claims, e.g. 'I'm not prepared to put at risk the smaller class sizes we have delivered by accepting a Tory approach based on . . .'. Douglas [Alexander] was really impressing me with his strategic mind at the moment. Philip said the Tories were nowhere and IDS was just the worst message carrier they could possibly have.

Then a meeting with TB, Jack S, Geoff Hoon and CDS. First Jack went over where we were re the UNSCR, with TB feeling he was too close to caving in on the two-resolution route. Then GH and CDS re the military options, which included substantial numbers of 'boots on the ground'. CDS said he would have a real problem with his army if they were not properly involved and also TB would have far greater influence with the US if we were there on the ground. Sally was totally against. I was probably for, but the costs, around £1 billion for Package 2, and £2 billion for Package 3, alongside the far greater risks, were pretty horrific. The question to resolve was really whether we went in for the whole hog.

CDS said that [US General] Tommy Franks was going to a meeting in Ankara with the Turks next week and really needed to know what our answers may be. TB said it was not no, but it was not yet yes, and he wanted more work done analysing the cost. Then to Cabinet. The discussions were almost all foreign, with incessant interruption from Clare including a real display of rudeness to TB on the Middle East. She said Palestine was getting worse and worse and what was he going to do to make good what he had said to conference? TB said he was continually pressing the US and she said 'Is that it?' with real disdain and contempt. She and Jack then had another little spat re India and Pakistan. Then a discussion on Bali, then where we were on Iraq, then JP on fire, then GB re the need to be very firm on the pay awards. The atmosphere wasn't great. We briefed hard out of it. TB's warning that there could well be more attacks.

Hilary Armstrong said to me afterwards that Clare was angling to become deputy leader under GB. She was a totally ridiculous figure. Today had been like listening to someone on a bus, chipping in comments about other people's conversations, totally unable to see why people wouldn't see that she was right about everything. I saw JP before he went over to the briefing, told him not to say that there was no Bali warning, and not to rise to the press bait. He did fine and later we had a bit of a post-mortem on the week.

Adam Crozier and David Davies came in to see me, said that the FA was moving towards a position of support for a regulator to bring order to football. They wanted to sound me out. I said I felt there were fundamental design flaws in the game, with the FA in charge of the national team and the grass roots, but not the bits in between, and it really made for chaos. TB was off to Northern Ireland and his speech went really big, and we were pleased that Sinn Fein were not too dismissive.[1] The French were winning the day at the UN and watering down resolutions.

Friday, October 18

TB, now in Sedgefield, got very good coverage out of Belfast. The main story today was the Fire Brigades Union strike ballot [over pay], Bali, and the UN with the French claiming they were pushing things to a different position. Adam Boulton called, said he was doing *The Week in Westminster* [BBC Radio 4], and why didn't I do it with him on the lobby changes. I decided to do it to put over the points of principle – more access to ministers, more access for more media, expert briefers. On the US conference call, I was still pushing for more CIC reform. The [Fire Brigades] ballot came out nine to one in favour of strike action, so that was going to be the main focus domestically for the coming period. Alex [Ferguson], Mark and Jason [his sons] came round for dinner. We'd all done pretty well sorting things out when a couple of lowlifes had tried to set him up in South Africa last week. Mark was saying Alex owed these journalists nothing, that he kept some of their careers afloat by talking to them. He said he felt Alex should cut himself off from them, that he was the best club manager ever, a historic figure in football, and he should be rising above them all the time. They were very nice kids, clearly adored their dad but were worried for him. Jason said that when he had been in trouble last week, 'the people at this table, not journalists he might think he could trust, sorted it'. Alex said 'That's what friends are for. They are the people who walk into the room when everyone else is thinking of walking out.'

[1] In the Belfast speech, Blair asked Northern Ireland politicians 'Do we have the courage as politicians to do what the people want us to do? Do we trust each other enough to make the acts of completion happen? I can only tell you as British prime minister that I have that trust in all the parties I have worked with. We must implement the [Good Friday] Agreement in full, because it is the choice of the people; the people here, the people in the South and the people of the United Kingdom as a whole.'

Saturday, October 19

Calum and I left early for Leicester. I had a long chat with Estelle [Morris], trying to persuade her to do the ministerial briefing on Tuesday, partly because she had something to say, but also because it would show she had guts and was prepared to fight back. But she said her confidence was low, one more mistake and she would be in real trouble, and she didn't feel up to doing it. We got to Leicester fairly early and I took Calum to see where we lived and went to school. Both the house and the school looked very different to how I remembered them, and the street seemed wider and the whole area seemed more prosperous than I imagined them to be. Then to the Aylestone Leisure Centre where I was doing an anti-racism event and a couple of interviews. I had lunch at the ground, then over to the away end for the match itself [Leicester 0, Burnley 1]. Our lot were generally OK, but when the anti-racism stuff was mentioned, there was a minority started singing 'You're just a town full of Pakis', indicating how far there was still to go.

Sunday, October 20

I was trying to persuade TB to make the speech to midwives part of the general strategy on public services staff, trying to bind them in. I got Godric to do a very tough line on the FBU, no going back to bad old days. TB was still worried we needed the Queen's Speech to be stronger, particularly on [higher education] top-up fees and child benefit conditionality. He was worried about the intelligence issue and the handling post Bali, so when I heard Jack wanted to make a statement tomorrow, I felt it was an opportunity to put out the broader picture re intelligence and warnings, drafted a section for Jack making clear that there had been no warning, that we had to assess this stuff the whole time. And to overreact to every warning, every piece of intelligence, would be to do the terrorists' job for them. TB said we had to be very wary of the French, watch they didn't do us in on the UNSCR, maintain the position of broker. Jack, a pretty rare thing this for ministers, called later simply to thank me for it.

Monday, October 21

Someone had briefed the Cobra meeting on fire [strikes], so the media coverage was giving a sense almost of national emergency. It was all a bit chaotic, and [Nick] Raynsford [minister] gave us a bit of a problem by saying that the army would not cross picket lines. There was just no need to get into that yet. My day was rather overshadowed by illness. After a few days of low-level colitis, it was back with a vengeance. By the evening, I was back on the steroids. [Professor] Michael Farthing [gastroenterologist] thought it was a mix of stress, lifestyle, plus maybe a bug from Russia. He was sceptical about me doing the marathon though he conceded I looked fitter and better than before. TB's other worry was the [EU] Stability Pact. He and JP had both been putting pressure on GB at least to discuss the euro properly, and JP had warned him he was thinking of making a speech about the Stability Pact. It led to GB then briefing the *FT* that he was looking into the issues. JP came to see me to discuss fire and whether he should meet [Andy] Gilchrist [Fire Brigades Union general secretary]. We agreed that for now it should be left to Raynsford.

TB asked me, David Manning and Jonathan to think through a strategy to avoid Chirac being credited with sorting Bush. It was TB who had persuaded them of the UN route, got it up and running. At TB's weekly office meeting, his big worry as ever was public service delivery. We had a bit of an up-and-downer on schools when he said he wanted to replace the word comprehensive with specialist. What on earth was the point of that? Post Bali, he felt that on issues of intelligence, we should take the public much more into our trust and explain how we make these judgements, set out the difficulties we face in doing so. There were calls for an inquiry but our feeling was best to let the ISC [Intelligence and Security Committee of parliamentarians, appointed by the Prime Minister] look at it. As if to underline how difficult all this was, a new JIC [Joint Intelligence Committee] paper came in showing there were lots of different areas considered liable for attack – British schools abroad, airports and airline desks, bars. We were tightening security on official buildings and more vulnerable soft targets, but if we actually put up warnings about every target that might be considered vulnerable, should the terrorists be able to do it, the whole place would shut down. They also thought Bin Laden wanted to do a few high-profile assassinations.

Tuesday, October 22

David Miliband called late last night to say Estelle had pulled out of the 8.10 *Today* programme slot because the Tories had dug up her pledge to resign if Key Stage 2 targets were not met. It was pretty black and white and DM and I discussed a line to help them through it, which was not brilliant but would have to do. But as she had a press conference later it was going to be pretty tough for her. Estelle asked to see TB and having been with him for a while, he asked me and Sally to pop round. She was basically saying she felt that her integrity and honesty was what made us value her and if TB felt she should go, either because of this, or because of the cumulative effect of recent events, she felt that they should have that conversation. TB said he didn't think this latest thing on the 'pledge to resign' was serious enough. I said it all depended deep down on whether she felt she was up to doing the job. She was clearly stressed, fiddling aggressively with her hands, her neck was bright red and at times she seemed close to tears. Sally felt that the team around her wasn't strong enough. It seemed to me that deep down she maybe felt she wasn't up to it. TB said we should all think about it. I had a couple of long conversations with her later in the day, during which I felt she was moving towards leaving, and I started to draft an exchange of letters. If it was going to happen, it was best to do it before a head of steam built up, and for her to say what appeared to be the case, namely that she found the pressure and realities of modern politics very difficult. We had the *Times* team in for lunch, during which I wrote the [exchange of resignation] letters, Alice Miles [columnist] constantly asking me what I was writing, was it newsworthy, and at one point, is it a reshuffle?

I spoke to Estelle around 6pm, having said I would take TB's mind on things. He basically didn't think she should go, but that only she could know if she was really up for it. She said to me that she just was not capable of coping with the nasty personal stuff in the media, like her nieces at school being approached, or a boyfriend of fifteen years ago being looked into. The growing sense I had was of someone who was looking around for reasons to go, but didn't want to say that actually she was just finding it very difficult. When I next spoke to TB, he felt she probably would have to go and the only question was when. We didn't particularly want tomorrow because of PMQs. In any event it was worth her sleeping on it again, thinking about it for a day or two, so maybe Thursday. She sounded pretty confused, very down, kept asking the same question – what do you really think? What does Tony really think? TB called when we were having a party for Rory's birthday, and he was already thinking about a reshuffle. I felt maybe Tessa [Jowell] or Pat [Hewitt], not Charles [Clarke] because I felt he was beginning to get the hang of the chairman's job, and also was it a good precedent in a sense to reward the fact that he had spent most of the time doing the job making clear he didn't want it. TB felt he might be the right person for now. Peter H was particularly down on Charles, felt he was all problem, no solution. And he found his meeting style, which was basically get everyone to make random points, deeply irritating. JP's statement on fire [describing threatened strikes as 'completely unnecessary and completely unjustified'] went fine.

Wednesday, October 23

Fire dispute really picking up strong. The FBU was seeing the TUC but we were in a much better position than we might have been. The first meeting of the day was a rather alarming security meeting with Jack S, GH, CDS, DB, John Scarlett and the agency chiefs. There was a lot of specific threat stuff around, particularly re Heathrow. We agreed that there should be visible stepping up of security at airports. Then to a fire meeting, TB being ultra nice to JP, who was glad not just to be involved, but that TB seemed to be trusting him fully with the negotiations. He was so on board that in the Commons office after PMQs, when TB was doing his usual whisky-bottle and photo-signing session, JP was organising the bottles. We agreed it was far better for now we stay very calm and reasonable, lots of public information stuff.

At the pre-PMQs meetings, for obvious reasons TB and I were more worried than the others about questions on Estelle. After the meeting I went to my office and called her. She had just made a speech in Birmingham [to secondary-school heads]. She said she had slept on things, and now she had made up her mind and was clear that she was going to go. I had suggested yesterday that she might think about going back to being schools minister, and she said she would think about that. She said she had worked out what she was good at and what she was less good at. She was good with people, and she was good on policy but she couldn't run a big department strategically and she just couldn't cope with the modern media and its intrusiveness and nastiness. She said there was something I had said yesterday which had made a real impression on her, when I pointed out that compared to others, she hadn't really had a hard time in the media and I had said 'Maybe Tony and I are just so used to it that we have grown immune.' She said 'I don't want to be immune, because it would mean I would stop feeling.' She asked me repeatedly if I thought she was doing the right thing, and what TB really thought. I said he basically worried that she had lost her nerve, and that if she didn't feel up for it, there was no point hanging around. He also felt she was an asset and he wouldn't want to lose her, but if she had decided, he would respect that. She said she yearned for her old job in a way, but maybe it was difficult going back. I filled in TB who was still keen we did nothing pre PMQs but felt he should see her later, go ahead with it tonight, reshuffle tomorrow. Sally, Jeremy and I were arguing for Alan Milburn. TB was concerned because he had promised Ian McCartney [minister for pensions] the next Cabinet job. He called Peter M for views and he said we would be made to let her go.

TB was on great form at PMQs, hit IDS hard both on fire and on health, but was also strong on Northern Ireland. He didn't like having to defend the line about the army not crossing picket lines. I arranged for Estelle to come in just after 6. TB's view was that if she had decided to go, she should go now, which was also JP's opinion when I spoke to him after PMQs. I was honing the resignation letters but also beginning to sink in a sea of unread paper, re the GICS review, Queen's Speech. It always seemed to happen when I was drawn into the day-to-day again. TB had a call with Bush. It was clear the Americans were getting more and more impatient about the UN and at the way the French in particular were slowing things down. TB made clear he really felt we were best to stay on that course, and he would talk to Chirac again tomorrow. Estelle arrived and Sally and I had a long session with her in my office. She said she felt she was really good with teachers and she could do that part of the job great. She was hopeless with budgets and figures and there was too much of the department for her to stay on top of it all the time. She said it was the right thing to go but if we wanted her to stay to Christmas, that was fine, or if we wanted her to go back to the old job under David M – who she clearly thought was going to get the job – that was fine too.

I showed her the letters I had drafted, she read hers first, and said yes, that's right, it sums it up fine. When she looked at the one I had done for Tony, she started crying. Sally went over to her and hugged her and after a minute or so she regained her composure, but she looked broken, She said it was just very tough for her and she hated the media side of things and she never felt able to cope with it. By the time we took her round to see TB, she was fine, very strong now, clear she was doing the right thing. TB was not sure it would be possible to put her back to the old job straight away, but maybe later when he moved David [Miliband] on. We finished the letters, TB changing the draft of his to be much warmer and making it clear that he was keen to have her back. We got Sue Littlemore [social affairs correspondent] in from the BBC to do an interview in Sally's office.

We finally got the letters sorted and out by 7.45 after Estelle had called her parents and her permanent secretary. Her private secretary came in and was crying. I briefed Tessa [Jowell] to get her round and about on the interviews tomorrow. I sat in on Estelle's [BBC] interview and she was excellent, really open and candid, saying she had decided she was not doing as well as she wanted to. It was a really strong, quite moving interview that would do her and politics some good. Afterwards she came over and gave me a big hug, said she had always

October '02: TB hits Duncan Smith hard at PMQs

enjoyed working with me and hoped we would again in the future. Chris Woodhead [former Chief Inspector of Schools] was out dancing on the grave straight away. TB was going out for a dinner and came to see me before he left. He said it was important that I moved Estelle away from the idea she was coming straight back, because he would probably leave David M where he was. He wanted to take time on this and get it right. How many resignation letters have I now written? It's a bit alarming how easily they flow from the pen. Estelle didn't change a single word, TB just inserted a little bit of extra support. He felt people would find it odd that she went but it was 'for the best'. It sounded pretty ruthless and probably was. I had said to Estelle 'Sometimes I feel like the executioner. I always seem to be there at the death of a ministerial career and I find it unbelievably draining.'

Thursday, October 24

Estelle got a good press. David Puttnam [Lord Puttnam, friend of Morris] sent me a message saying that she had been really grateful for all the support I had given her. I was in early, did a note to JP on his fire interviews and also a message note on the Queen's Speech [November 18]. Sally M and I went up to the flat. She had spoken to Alan who was adamant he should should stay at Health, but after speaking to Darren Murphy [Milburn's special adviser] and others, came back to say he could see the merit of a move to a big challenge that was behind the curve on modernisation. TB was moving towards Charles Clarke. I had doubts about how modernising he was on education and whether he would work properly with the centre. Peter Hyman said that Charles was constantly decrying the [Prime Minister's] Delivery Unit and was also opposed to targets. John Reid was up for the chairmanship, so once the main decision was taken, the rest should flow quite easily. But TB wanted to take his time. He said there were four possible names – Milburn, Hewitt, Clarke, Jowell. He got Hilary A and Andrew Turnbull to join us. Andrew said he felt Milburn was the most proven, was more respected than liked by officials. TB wanted to speak to JP, then see Charles. We arranged for Charles to come through 70 Whitehall in case he said no. JP was OK re Charles, if not terribly enthusiastic, but not OK re John Reid [becoming party chairman], largely because TB had made a promise to Ian [McCartney]. TB didn't even tell him what he was planning to do with [Peter] Hain [Europe minister], namely Welsh Secretary. He didn't consult GB at all, largely because he couldn't face the usual nonsense of GB trying to promote his own people way beyond their abilities. He did consult JP, Blunkett and Jack, who said yes to Charles provided he got a warning about being more disciplined. The general feeling was that Charles had not done the last job particularly well and it was a risk. TB accepted Charles had not been a great party chairman but education was a job he really wanted, he was a big personality and he thought he could do it. He felt Alan needed a year to get critical mass on [NHS reform] delivery. So we got JP in to agree, then Charles, then Paul Murphy [replacing John Reid as Northern Ireland Secretary] then the Cabinet meeting. TB saw Charles privately and said he had given him a real warning about the need for reform, the need to work better with other people. Charles looked shell-shocked on the way out, as if congratulations were falling on deaf ears.

It was education questions at 11.30. We had to decide if Charles went to the House for questions. David M and I put together a script but once TB got into Cabinet, he wasn't keen for us to announce the names. But with the lobby waiting, and all but Peter Hain now announced, what was the point? In Cabinet, GB, rarely, spoke several times, first on the need to stand up against the French attack on the [British EU] rebate. He also chipped in on Lords reform and on Iraq. With Charles due to leave any moment for questions, I slipped a note to TB saying he needed to announce the first three changes, otherwise they would all hear it first on the media. GB went virtually white. While others were nodding approval, he looked around with something close to hatred. He puffed his cheeks out, his eyes narrowed and he just scanned the room. He knew he had been hit. He went to see TB afterwards and as we waited outside in the private office, GB's raised voice, and TB's attempts to calm him down, could be heard.

As GB left, thunderstruck, he said nothing to any of us, just stormed out. I asked TB what he had been saying. 'He was mad. The whole thing was a conspiracy against him. Every single one of them is a disastrous appointment. All designed to damage him.' He said he had also railed against me [AC] and my diary and said he wanted to raise it in Cabinet! He had railed at Cherie, said that she hated him and wanted to do him down. He told TB that his office was full of Tories. Later, I was talking to Tessa in the foyer when GB came by, still storming. 'That man is fucking insane,' she said. I told her she had been in the frame for education, which cheered her up. Neil called, thrilled at the appointments. All very Kinnockite. He was also supporting my push for Kim Howells [culture minister] to get Europe. TB got to Brussels and was immediately upstaged by Chirac and Schroeder doing a deal on [EU] enlargement/CAP [Common

Agricultural Policy] and saying that the UK rebate would have to be looked at. This was payback time for Schroeder going to see TB rather than Chirac after winning. The French were gunning for us again.

Friday, October 25

Ran in in the pouring rain. Really like running in the rain. Good press re reshuffle. John Reid had been excellent on *Newsnight* last night and I called to tell him so. I called Andrew Turnbull re whether we could use John for briefings and he was clear we could provided we didn't make them party political. He felt the reshuffle was strong too, that we had good people in the toughest departments. JR said he would take his time to build a proper relationship with JP, but he saw little point trying to build bridges with GB at the moment as he seemed to be in a total rage the whole time. Did the 11 and was being pushed on why Robin said Estelle was 'hounded out' of the job. TB spoke to Putin to offer our support after Chechen gunmen took the audience in a Russian theatre hostage.[1] He called from the [Brussels] summit. Said that Schroeder had been taken in by the usual Gallic swagger. He said after the bilateral between the French and German, Chirac had called him in, totally patronised him, tried to say the whole thing was sorted because France and Germany had decided and that was that. 'I'm not having this,' he said.

In the discussions through today there was a lot of angst about taking radical CAP reform, as per Berlin, off the agenda. Chirac waded in and said that was exactly what was happening. Jack gave TB the passage from the Berlin outcome that committed them to further CAP reform and TB made clear that they had to get on with it. Chirac said this was a personal attack that in all honour and all morality should not happen. TB said 'I've been very polite' and insisted. Others then backed him. Chirac later walked up to him and said that was an all-out attack, he would not tolerate it and maybe we should call off the Anglo-French summit. TB said fine, no problem, but there will be CAP reform and we are not going back on the rebate. He said he had stayed really calm, as he always tried to when people are losing their temper, but what it means is that they will really come at us on the rebate. They had also had some pretty fiery exchanges on Iraq, TB telling him the US were going to do it so it depended if he wanted to be part of the equation or not.

[1] Armed Chechens claiming allegiance to Islamist separatism had taken 850 hostages in a Moscow theatre and demanded the withdrawal of Russian forces from Chechnya.

Schroeder's interpreter had said to TB afterwards, 'Wow, what was all that about?' as Chirac stormed off, and TB said he didn't care about him losing it. The French had to accept that they should treat the UK as an equal in Europe. 'He can present me as an American poodle if he wants, but we're not putting up with his shit any more. We do it on our terms now.' Sounded like it had been fun. I agreed with Godric we should brief a couple of the Sundays that Chirac's real anger had been Schroeder coming to the UK first after his election, that this was all about that, and he had to get the message that the UK should be treated as an equal. On the Europe job, TB was moving towards Denis MacShane [junior FCO minister]. Had a bit of a comic moment on the fire front when a Green Goddess [auxiliary fire engine] crashed and had to be rescued by the fire brigade.

Saturday, October 26

TB was a bit pissed off at the way it came out in the media that somehow the French had 'won'. All the more reason to get out what had actually happened, and the fact that this was Chirac's revenge for Schroeder coming here after the election. TB strongly felt the real significance of the last couple of days was that the Franco-German gambit had not worked. The Russian [theatre] siege ended, all the Brits were safe, and TB spoke to Vlad. I spoke to JP and suggested we had radio silence on the fire dispute. [Andy] Gilchrist was beginning to make mistakes. JP agreed, felt he was beginning to behave like an old-fashioned general secretary. JP offered four per cent back on the table with talks on modernisation. He called me around 5 to say it seemed to have worked and the FBU executive had agreed to call off the first two strikes. He had done a good job on this. TB called, still angry about Chirac, said that once they started speaking again, it would be to have strong words, that we were not going to be 'treated like a dog' in the way he had tried on Friday. 'I love Jacques, but he can be fucking arrogant and needs to be taught a lesson.' The Sundays had loads of write-throughs on Estelle, and maybe I should have talked to them more, because they were all just the usual clichéd stuff about the fact that women couldn't survive. Education were also briefing stupidly, that it was actually all about top-up fees and that I had asked her to stay.

Sunday, October 27

Conference call re the post-summit fallout. For some reason, our media just did not want to acknowledge that TB had actually stopped the French gambit from working. The weather was dire. Mum had been staying and her train north was cancelled so I drove her up, briefing a bit on the way. Charles Clarke called re the Sundays. We agreed he should use his first speech on Wednesday to set the full strategic picture.

Monday, October 28

TB working on the statement, including re Russia, though the Russians were causing a bit of concern by refusing to say what gas was used in the attack to free the Moscow theatre hostages.[1] The death toll was now a lot higher than first thought, but TB was instinctively sympathetic to Putin. It was one of those damned if you do, damned if you don't situations where whatever the outcome some would find grounds to criticise. At TB's office meeting, we went over the merits and demerits of the various contenders for Europe minister, and ended up going for Denis MacShane. TB did not want a lasting stand-off with Chirac, and though he was glad we'd stood up to him and seen the strategy through, he did not want to see Chirac go through with cancelling the Anglo-French summit.

Then a meeting re the FBU and how we get them off the sixteen per cent [phased pay increase] figure. At some point this was going to become a big communications job. For the time being, JP was handling fine behind the scenes but he said too at some point it would take off in the wrong direction, and we would have to be ready. I had a stack of meetings, including re top-up fees, which David Miliband was warning me had the potential to be political disasterville. A good Queen's Speech meeting, which I felt was beginning to hang together better, then another pretty dire meeting on the euro. I felt a bit for Douglas [Alexander] because people were looking at him almost as the GB presence but he knew, as we knew, that he could not really speak for him, and we all knew that this thing was undoable without TB and GB playing on the same pitch in the same way.

Interesting meeting with the French ambassador [Gérard Errera] who wanted to explain to me why Chirac was like he was, and why we should not let these bust-ups affect us too deeply. He said Chirac felt he always had to stand up for the French national interest. I said why should anyone imagine TB does not always have to stand up for the UK national interest? Yes, he said, but sometimes we seem to think they are the same. I wasn't quite sure what he was on about. 'And then there is Iraq,' he said. Yes there is, and TB again thinks he

[1] Russian special forces pumped an unknown chemical agent into the theatre and raided it, killing thirty-nine of the attackers and upwards of 130 hostages.

is standing up for what is right, and for the UK national interest. Unconvinced grimace. Then there was ESDP [European Security and Defence Policy], he said, where Chirac felt we were not European enough . . . then there was Kosovo . . . then there was Macedonia. I said at least it was best to be open about the differences, and try to sort them, but I made sure he knew TB really did not think a cancelled summit was a good idea.

Then to a meeting with Cathy Gilman of Leukaemia Research, who was very jolly and seemed to know what she was on about, and was really keen on the idea of the marathon, with Amanda Delew [campaign director, the Giving Campaign] who agreed to help out with ideas on the fund-raising side. Fiona joined us for a while and when Amanda suggested a whole load of 'meet AC' sponsorship ideas, Fiona said she couldn't quite see why anyone would want to pay to meet me. I pointed out that she does not always share the high view of me that others seem to at times. But I was convinced we could raise at least half a million. Then to the opening of the new party offices [16–18 Old Queen Street] across the park where TB made a very funny little speech, watched by an unsmiling let alone laughing GB, followed by an even funnier little speech by Richard Wilson [actor and Labour supporter].

Then to dinner at the German ambassador's [Thomas Matussek] residence, with Peter M and PG the other guests. The ambassador's wife [Ulla] took pictures of the three of us and I think it was the first time we had ever been photographed together, having always tried to avoid it when the media were asking. I liked the ambassador, though I suspect he was a bit less of an Anglophile than the last guy [Hans-Friedrich von Ploetz], and he had certainly done his research on us lot. Peter was on very good form, very funny, taking the mick out of the ambassador and me in a way that nobody could find offensive, talking as though it was a matter of fact that I had gone out of my way to destroy him. He was also pretty caustic re Schroeder and the way the German left had responded to modernisation here.

We also had some pretty heavy exchanges on Iraq. We knew the Germans had pretty much the same intelligence as we did, but were pursuing a very different line. We felt that Schroeder's stance during the campaign had been so crass that he would have a real job getting back in with the US at all. The ambassador took it all in good spirits, but also took a serious message from it. Towards the end, Peter said what should he say in the speech he was due to make in Berlin? The ambassador said you should say Germany should show more leadership, carry out far greater reforms and do a lot more to co-operate with Russia. He was pro TB but also believed he was at his zenith and the only way now was down. He thought the Tories were hopeless. As we left, PG said to me we had to find Peter M a job. He was a wasting talent. He had so much more to offer than most members of the Cabinet and we had to find him something proper to do. It was true that someone like the ambassadors would listen more to Peter than to most ministers, and he did cut a sad figure at times, because he knew he had a certain authority, but no express power to deliver anything.

Tuesday, October 29

The French row was in danger of escalating out of control. TB called as I was running in. On the one hand, he wanted to be on good terms but equally Chirac had to know his recent behaviour was intolerable. The line from the French was now that this had all come out the way it did because of our briefing. TB wanted the message fed back that we had to be treated as equals, and would not accept anything less, but also that he wanted to calm things. I spoke to Peter Hain before he did *Today*, and agreed the basic line that we fight our corner as aggressively as any other country. David Manning, Jeremy and I had all spoken to the ambassador in the last twenty-four hours, so he knew this was serious. He also knew we didn't want to inflame further. But he knew that to us there had been a cumulative effect building over time.

I spoke to Catherine Colonna [Chirac's spokeswoman] at 11.10. I always liked dealing with Catherine. She was very French in her style and elegance but there was something Anglo-Saxon about her directness and I was always able to have frank conversations with her. Jesus, I said, we left them for ten minutes on their own and they started a riot! She said she felt Chirac had lacked *'politesse'* with TB and now, probably because he knew it, he was *'têtu'* [stubborn]. We agreed to try to calm. But then ninety minutes later up it popped on AFP [Agence France-Presse], that the Anglo-French summit was cancelled. David Manning and [Sir] Stephen Wall [EU adviser] were both up for a big counter-attack, but TB was more of the view he go up to do media and try to settle it down. I was not sure about that.

It rather dominated the Tuesday strategy meeting, but we did manage a decent discussion re the euro, and convinced TB that there were some very live questions that had to be addressed. But we couldn't get going until we had some sense of direction from him and GB, but all GB was doing was saying he would do nothing to compromise the tests. TB said again that he believed we could win a referendum, but Peter M, PG and I all felt we needed to know the shape of a plan sooner not later, e.g. could we have a positive assessment pre election and a referendum after? Did we envisage the assessment and referendum close together? How did we put together a campaign? What are the rules? It was all a bit high-wire and yet I did not feel we knew where GB really was, other than probably not in the same place as TB.

On the Queen's Speech, the focus on crime, rights and responsibilities was strong. We then discussed the politics of tuition fees, which seemed to be getting worse not better. It was almost without doubt the right thing to do, and there was a perfectly good argument for it in terms of the long-term benefit to the country, but it was not easy to persuade people that education was anything other than a right that should come free. I felt we needed a much bigger communications strategy around the bigger arguments. We also had to ensure there was not a diminution of access, and we were not yet convinced the work on that had been done either.

After I got home, JP called re a visit on Thursday, and also to go over the Fire Service situation. I asked how things were with GB. He said he was at a crossroads. He didn't much like some of what TB wanted for health and education. He felt he had been bounced to some extent on foundation hospitals. Also he was not going to get himself into a position where because he was being used to shift GB on the euro, that was used to say he was anti GB on big domestic issues too. I sensed JP was back to a 'plague on both houses' mood and he sounded a bit more menacing than usual, though we did end with a laugh when he heard the doorbell going in the background and he said 'Go on, that'll be Tony popping round for a nightcap.' Catherine Colonna called late, said she was trying to calm things but suggesting there were *'d'autres dans la forêt'* [others in the forest] who were still stirring things.

Wednesday, October 30

TB called at 7, said though the French row was calming a bit part of him felt it had been good to have it. He had been trying to get into a proper position with the French for five years and maybe this was the only way to have done it, now we can work out what we really agree on and what we don't. He felt he understood Chirac's position on most things but Chirac did not understand his, or really try to. He wanted to fix a proper summit meeting for February now and work through a really substantial joint programme. He felt there was a lot more we could do on defence. He felt even on Iraq it was possible to get to a closer position. He was growing a bit disappointed with Schroeder and saw Anglo-French relations as important in part because the Germans were a bit flaky. I spoke to Catherine a couple of times to try to pin down a date for a proper meeting but we didn't get there in the end. Things won't have been helped by [Labour MP] Tony Wright's question at PMQs.[1]

Because we pretty much all felt now IDS was a goner, and because we all would prefer he stayed, the PMQs meeting was full of black humour about how good he was, but TB was finding it harder to get up for these encounters because he just didn't feel IDS had it. The papers were full of stories that there were now enough people up for a challenge. In the end IDS and [Charles] Kennedy both went on tuition fees trying to pin TB on the manifesto commitment not to introduce them. This was going to be difficult, because TB had pretty much decided this was the right thing for the country, and the right thing for the universities, but politically it could be as difficult as anything we had yet done, especially as GB had now pretty much admitted he was putting together a slightly-to-the-left platform and this would be part of it. At PMQs TB effectively had to stand by the manifesto whilst making the case for a different position.

After PMQs I told TB and Sally M re my conversation with JP last night, his general offsideness. 'This is all pressure from GB,' TB said. Yesterday's GB meeting had been dreadful. 'I said to him at one point, sorry but I'm not listening to this any more. You've lost it.' In the pensions meeting, GB did the old trick of identifying the position of others, misrepresenting it and then having a non-argument so that the real positions were not addressed. I said to TB he had a limited period of maximum strength and he had to use it. He knew what I meant but said 'If he walks, or if I push him, we have to be very careful because the party will not like it and blame will not just fall to one side.' GB was making mistakes though, because he was growing desperate his time would never come. TB said he had no idea if it was all going to end in divorce but we had to be on the right side of the arguments if it did.

John Reid's first meeting re party issues, and he was good, if a bit loquacious. The thing I liked about him was his ability to think things through quickly and articulate them clearly. Philip gave the

[1] Wright said 'Could I ask the prime minister to tell us exactly how rude he was to Monsieur Chirac? Did he perhaps remind him that if the French president was not in the Élysée he would almost certainly be in jail?' Blair responded 'No, I didn't say that.'

most positive polling readout for a while, and some of the deeper strategies – e.g. anti spin, focus on long term – were getting through and making a difference. Pat McFadden came in halfway through, having finally decided to take Robert Hill's job [as Blair's political secretary, Hill having been appointed special adviser to Charles Clarke]. Pat had to decide if he was going to pursue a serious political career now or meander into middle age. I had an hour with David Wilkinson [Cabinet Office] for his GICS review and was perhaps too frank. I said I felt the GICS was to a large extent a barrier to good communications and that leading people were obstructive to change.

I had a good meeting with Peter M, who was pro John Reid and up for a more political role at some point, and PG. I was working on a fund-raising letter for Leukaemia Research and read through all the old cuttings and speeches re John [Merritt, Campbell's late best friend who died of the disease]. TB called a couple of times later, really turning over top-up fees in his mind. He knew this was going to set the next phase of the domestic context. He was up for being 'at our best when at our boldest' and up for a debate taking off in that direction. He agreed to do a press conference on Monday to get up pre-Queen's Speech messaging on crime and antisocial behaviour.

Thursday, October 31

The day didn't start very well, Fiona repeating her view that she didn't see why people would pay money to talk to me at sponsored events, which was her way of saying she didn't really want the pressure of the marathon adding to the pressures of the job. But I was sure I wanted to do it, could do it, and needed a new challenge like this. I left in a pretty foul mood though. First meeting re European defence where Jonathan and I both thought TB was kidding himself if he thought we were going to get a decent deal with the French any time soon. Another meeting re top-up fees. Surely, I said, there must be another way of doing this. TB said ultimately not. You could fiddle at the edges, rename and repackage but ultimately it was a top-up fees system we were proposing and it was right. In which case, there was a big job to be done in winning the argument, and we were going to need the universities to carry a lot of the load. If this was genuinely the only way they could keep developing in the way they needed to in order to remain high quality and compete with universities around the world, then they had to be making that case too.

John Reid was at the political strategy meeting and was a bit more focused and less anecdotal than Charles. He had a good line re the Tories playing the man not the ball, going for TB personally because they were scared of the policy debate. The general view was IDS was a goner and we went over the various [Conservative leadership] contenders and worked out the outlines of a strategy for each. It was an excellent meeting. JR was clear, and very, very political, and Douglas was developing a real grasp of what was needed for the mechanics of the euro campaign. We also agreed to go for a much simpler, clearer Queen's Speech message so I spent part of the day working on that, as well as TB's press conference script for Monday.

GB was being pretty difficult re the ASB [antisocial behaviour] agenda, trying to run the line that the more we focused on it, the more people felt we were failing on it. TB tried to explain that he needed to stop seeing it as a political issue. It was a REAL issue, about people's lives, and they wanted us to GET it. Milburn came in to discuss the [NHS] consultants' contracts with TB who told him GB was now deliberately winding up JP to see all difficult reform as being essentially driven by Tories in Number 10. AM said JP had been at him the whole time re foundation hospitals, but he was determined we had to press on.

A TB meeting with JS, GH and CDS who said the Americans seemed to be cutting us out of some of the military decision-making because we had gone for Package 2 not Package 3, and also reporting that some inside our army were pissed off not to be more involved. God, he was hard to read, sometimes giving the impression none of them wanted anything to do with this, then at others giving the impression they all wanted to be off to the front line. Cabinet – discussion re Europe and the CAP, with Jack clearer than ever we had to mount and win an argument re CAP.

Clare's interruptions were even worse and more irritating than usual, because she was doing her serious questioning act rather than the holier-than-thou bit. At least with the holier-than-thou bit, people knew how to deal with it, which was basically ignore. At the end she came over to me, all smarmy, and said 'Well done for doing in Chirac,' then added 'I love him on Iraq but I hate him on Africa . . . We have to think about the world!' Really? I said we all think about the world and I for one would prefer a world in which Saddam does not have weapons and does not terrorise his own people. To be fair to her, she did a decent presentation to Cabinet on what was happening humanitarian-wise in Afghanistan. GB waded in pretty heavily on Europe. Alan was excellent on the consultants, really on top of it, and political, but I could see GB looking very darkly at him as well as TB.

I had a get-together with the staff from the media team and I was pretty heavy with them, said too many of them were operating in the comfort zone and we needed all-round game-raising. I think one of the reasons I was tired and down was because they all kind of felt I would come up with the creative stuff in the end, and they just had to deliver. But I wanted all of them to be thinking more creatively and strategically. Two or three of them looked a bit hurt, but I feel it needed saying. I showed TB my marathon fund-raising letter and he had reservations. He felt it would get me up in lights as a target again and I had to be careful about the donors. He also thought I should not state explicitly I was trying to raise a million, but maybe aim for £100k to start. It was all good advice but I wondered if he was also worrying that I was focusing on this as a substitute for work.

Friday, November 1

The [Paul] Burrell [former butler to Diana, Princess of Wales] trial was about to collapse, meaning a welcome news sponge for the weekend. Burrell had told the Queen after Diana's death that he'd taken some of her possessions for safe keeping, so the prosecution case that he never told anyone was debunked by Her Maj. TB had been told on Tuesday and then the Attorney General had to broker a prosecution statement between the CPS [Crown Prosecution Service], the police and the Palace, and which was due to be read in court this morning.[1] The AG had had to go to see the Queen yesterday, to alert her to some of the difficult questions that would flow, but in any event to alert her to the fact the case was being dropped. It was going to be seen as a total fiasco, though the Queen had been through far worse.

I was working on TB's words for Monday re the ASB bill for his press conference, the plan having gone a bit off track yesterday with a consultation paper containing the idea of £50 fines for dropping chewing gum in the street. It was total bollocks, and annoying, though I suppose it did at least get over the kind of issues we were talking about. I took the office through the plan for the Queen's Speech, then did a session with SpAds. I felt we were strong on message at the moment, and also that the changes re the media operation were beginning to bed down well. We were certainly hearing less about spin than for a while, and TB was finding his voice better.

[1] Burrell had been accused of stealing more than 300 items belonging to Diana, Prince Charles and Prince William. Late intervention by the Queen, who recalled a 1998 conversation with Burrell, raised questions as to whether the trial should have gone ahead in the first place.

Fiona was very down on Cherie at the moment, having discovered she had already signed a contract on the book [on Prime Ministers' spouses], TB having told us she hadn't. Cherie basically admitted to Fiona that she hadn't consulted us because she knew we were hostile to the project. Fiona said we were hostile to people coming in and potentially landing her in difficult circumstances through their own ambitions for the 'project'. I said to TB that I could not see the advantage to HIM of this happening, I could see plenty of possible downsides, and in the end it was him and his reputation we had to be focused on. He just had to accept Cherie was not going to get the same kid-gloves media treatment that Norma [Major] got. TB was at Chequers, pretty unbothered by it all.

Saturday, November 2

The *Telegraph* had the MoD saying GB was blocking cash needed for Iraq. Then I became worried that the government role in the Burrell trial would become an issue so did a conference call with [Lord] Goldsmith and his team to agree the best lines to take if it did, emphasising the AG was the only member of the government with any active role in this. The CPS took the decision to go with the prosecution. The Queen told [princes] Charles and Philip last Friday about her conversation, the prosecution then realised they'd had it, told the AG, who then told us. It had all been a bit classic Establishment for a while, running around rather than sorting quickly.

Goldsmith was very conscious of his position. When I said we should be saying this was in no way a government decision, he said we have to be careful not to imply he is not a member of the government. He is, albeit independent when it comes to legal advice. When I asked why he personally had had to see the Queen, he said 'Because I am HER Attorney General and HER senior lawyer.' We were all pretty clear he had done nothing wrong, but it was one of those with plenty of scope for media mischief around the edges and we just had to get the lines cleared. Frank Dobson [former Health Secretary] had a big go in the *Observer* and *Mail on Sunday* re 'elitist' policies on health and education, which would run on the broadcasts. There was something sad and a bit bitter about Frank, but in truth we had not done a good job at keeping him on board.

Sunday, November 3

Eight-mile run with Rory and some of his mates. Conference call to pin down the detail on tomorrow's press conference. I had a couple of long chats with Douglas and Gus O'Donnell re the GICS review, and both felt a proper outside review was needed. Gus felt we almost needed to start from scratch, get rid of the GICS and start all over again with an outsider in charge. An ex-Health permanent secretary was being suggested, but I called Alan who felt it was a bit old school, as did Godric. Gus was clear this was the one opportunity we would get to be radical and we needed to get [Andrew] Turnbull signed up for that too.

TB called when I was at tennis with Calum. He was unaware of the Dobbo attack, and when I said he had gone for Andrew [Adonis] in particular, he got pretty angry, said it was a way of attacking New Labour without saying so. 'If we followed the lead of people like Frank we would be straight out of power again. They do not get how the country has changed.' He felt that with David Miliband leaving [as head of the Policy Unit, to become an MP in 2001], we had lost a very deft political operator – which Andrew was not – but he felt he got more policy drive from Andrew, whilst we had to do the politics. He said David was a good Policy Unit head, but so is Andrew, in a different way. I said he cannot just ignore the political fallout though. Andrew lacks certain political skills and the Policy Unit has become too managerial, with the result that the party sees it as soulless and right wing. Fair or not, we have to deal with that. I said your friends as well as enemies think it is sending out conflicting messages and is not sufficiently political or Labour. I was worried he was just becoming stubborn about this, when with a few modifications we could deal with the problem. It was not as though anyone thought he was not constantly looking for the modernising options. But seen as it was, it was also giving the GB lot a good deal of licence to cause trouble in the PLP and the party.

TB said there were elements who wanted to slow down or stop the process of reform and we just could not let them. I said I am not arguing for that. I am arguing for a more political policy unit to help us make sure they cannot win that argument. Andrew is just a surrogate for attacks on you, I said, but don't get angry or stubborn about it, work out how we deal with it. The answer is better policy and better communication of the arguments. If it all sounds managerial, we lose. It has to be about values all the time, and that is where we are not as strong as we were. It is nobody's fault, it is just where we are. The GB point was brought home again when Darren Murphy picked up from some of the hacks that the Treasury were briefing fairly aggressively against top-up fees. I called [Ian] Austin to rail at him but he did his usual. He dropped in that [Ed] Balls was doing an interview with Jackie Ashley [*Guardian*].

I dropped in that GB had effectively told TB he was putting together a left-wing positioning strategy and we would be watching for the signs. I was never sure whether Ian was really at the top table so maybe I was wasting my breath, but I told him I was really sick of their modus operandi.

Monday, November 4

The *Guardian* splashed on the Balls interview and a not very uncoded attack on TB's policy direction, which all tied in with Dobbo. TB was furious but it was difficult to respond without provoking a TB/GB row publicly and there was just no point. He said the worst thing about all this is that 'I still try to help him and he basically treats me like shit.' He felt that they were now running a basic destabilisation strategy, though one without a clear outcome. Every time they did this, they tended to reinforce rather than weaken TB's resolve, though they definitely had an impact on morale and effectiveness. He said this was all about trying to portray TB as being in love with markets, and therefore effectively not Labour. TB said if people knew the truth about how GB treats him, they would be appalled. He felt that GB was trying to push him into trying to get rid of him, and he would then seek to mount a challenge. But it was impossible to be sure.

I pointed out that GB tended to back off whenever it looked like becoming too public that he was up to this kind of stuff. I felt the loss of the baby had also had a profound effect and in its own way added to GB's hatred of TB. It all added to the sense that everything came easy for TB and hard for GB. Leo was such a cute kid and added to the idea TB got everything. Austin fed back my comments re GB's left-wing platform because GB raised it later, trying to make a joke of it. TB was at a loss how to handle things at the moment. He said GB was operating as though he were part of a different operation, not the government. There were plenty of problem areas to go through at the press conference pre-meeting – Royals, Iraq, Chirac. TB wasn't brilliant, not as bouncy as usual, but OK.

Tuesday, November 5

Press conference coverage fairly low-key though TB was pleased that the *FT*, which most of Europe's leaders take a look at, led on the row with France. He was fairly big in most of the papers though on a mix of subjects and the original intention, of driving through a message on ASB, didn't really come off. The main political focus of the day was meltdown for IDS after the rebellion against his three-line whip on gay adoption [the Conservative whip being to oppose]. There was a swirl of rumour that he was about to quit.

There was very little interest in us today. We had the first of the new 'board meetings', part of TB's efforts to get a bit more managerial focus into the working of the office, but I didn't hold out much hope of this lasting. The style didn't suit him and some of the discussion was below his pay grade. Cast of thousands. The bulk of the discussion related to his continuing unhappiness about the lack of strategic and delivery capability, both at the centre but above all in driving progress in departments. He felt there was a big disconnect between radical policy thinking and front-line delivery. There was no strategic economic narrative. We went over the 'traffic lights' review, a [Michael] Barber innovation showing [red, amber, green] how well each department was doing on the main public service projects. It was a mixed picture, but not enough green for my liking. TB was also exasperated at the general failure on major IT projects. Several people said in their different ways that departments did not respond well to calls for change. [John] Birt ['blue skies thinking' adviser] said departments see the centre as something to be worked around. But I felt they now had so many different voices representing Number 10 that they were able to play us off against each other. The key had to be getting ministers signed up to a shared vision and then wanting to put it through with the same vigour as we did. But departments were complaining all they ever got was pressure from us without clarity or follow-through.

We had far better discussions on Europe and Iraq. TB was still worrying away about the French, said this was 'Macmillan–de Gaulle all over again, but we have to think our way through it very carefully.'[1] They basically think we are too close to the US and we think they are too old-fashioned and blindly anti-American. We needed to keep improving alliances with others, not just Germany. He felt there was also a personal element to Chirac's current stance, that he resented how TB was seen as the great white hope around the new EU.

I watched IDS [press conference] and his basic line – 'Unite or die' – was simply going to add to his problems. First, unite around what? Second, the unity call came very badly from someone who had helped do in [John] Major. There was a hypocrisy attached to it and also something absurd saying the fight was about modernisation, coming

[1] Then French president Charles de Gaulle vetoed the British application to join the European Economic Community in 1963 because he thought the UK, under the premiership of Harold Macmillan, lacked the necessary political will to be part of a strong Europe.

as this did on the back of what he did re gay adoption. I had lunch at the Savoy with John Witherow and David Cracknell [*Sunday Times*]. Witherow was starting to bid for my post-Number 10 book! He was pretty positive re TB, very up on Milburn, felt GB OK as Chancellor but not convinced beyond that. I drove back with Michael Jay [FCO permanent secretary] who was having lunch there. We discussed the UNSCR state of play and though we were still on course for tabling tomorrow he seemed pretty pessimistic. On the euro, I said TB was as keen as ever but GB was making it virtually impossible, and I didn't think it could happen unless TB moved him.

TB saw Fiona re CB. She felt we were totally hostile to the book idea which is why she hadn't involved us. He felt it was not about her making money but trying to do something useful. Fiona felt Cherie had not been open with any of us, including him, about the project. She was happy not to work for CB, and do something else, but needed to know the lie of the land. She had tried to rub along with Carole [Caplin] but she had no idea how involved she was. I met Nick Robinson who had been made ITN political editor, full of the usual stuff about wanting to do more serious in-depth analysis blah. I'll believe it when I see it. We were in OK shape at the moment. The reshuffle had worked out well. Charles Clarke was starting to motor on policy. John Reid was a breath of fresh air at the centre. GB's currency was a bit low, which had its upsides and downsides. As TB said, if only he could get that relationship back on some kind of keel, we would be in very good shape.

Wednesday, November 6

We were going to get the UNSCR tabled today. TB didn't quite know how to handle PMQs with IDS in the state he was in. He was very focused on the GB situation at the moment. He had a euro-specific meeting with him, and got Gus [O'Donnell] along too, but said it had been as grim as grim can be. I called Gus later who said the lack of GB communication was almost comical. We thought re PMQs that IDS would do top-up fees and Gibraltar, and indeed he did, but the mood around him was so bad at the moment, it was like a dead man walking. I was beginning to feel sorry for him.

We had a good political strategy meeting, working on how we get definition out of their current situation being a problem about the Tories as a party, rather than just IDS as a leader. John R said we had to watch out for the line that we were too powerful. There was an even greater mood around in the media at the moment that with the Tories so useless, they had to go even more into Opposition mode. I wanted to see and hear a big argument out there, possibly a JR speech, making clear that to a large extent we had created this turmoil, and we were very proud of it. After PMQs, weekly meeting with Peter M, PG and Peter H. Peter M was really motoring on the line that the City felt TB was being weakened at GB's expense, and also that they sensed GB was basically Old Labour. Later I bumped into GB, the Eds and Gus in Number 11. GB grunted a kind of greeting, but friendly it was not. The best thing that happened all day came later, Burnley 2, Spurs 1.

Thursday, November 7

UNSCR was the main news all day and we were building up Jack's role. TB had a long call with Bush yesterday, who had been celebrating his election win. TB said he was much clearer about what to do and more interested in trying to get better relations with Chirac and Schroeder. He couldn't deny that he had felt personally affronted by Schroeder, and he wasn't going to hide that, but he did want to build things up. Today TB spoke to Putin who said he would vote for or against, but would not abstain.

IDS was finished. TB was starting to think that [Michael] Portillo would be OK for us, that [Kenneth] Clarke [both former Conservative leadership candidates] would give them a lift but in many ways present an even bigger target. Today's Cabinet was straightforward – Iraq/UN and fire, which was getting difficult again, and asylum/Sangatte [refugee camp], DB saying [Nicolas] Sarkozy [French interior minister] was being helpful. TB said Jack had done really well on the UN situation. Jack did a very Jackish explanation of the background. I went for lunch with Gus Macdonald [minister for the Cabinet Office], Barry Cox [deputy chairman, Channel 4 and government adviser on digital television] and Richard Tait [former editor-in-chief, ITN] to discuss a few ideas re elections. I started to feed in the idea that there would be none of the old battle-bus routine. I was also quite keen to move away from the expectation of a press conference every morning. The 24-hour media beast had been an absolute bastard to deal with last time, so much effort for so few viewers and it would be even worse next time.

I got back for a very alarming terrorism meeting. Eliza Manningham-Buller [new director general of the Security Service, MI5] gave an overview, then Julian Miller re some of the voluminous stuff out there, then a specific discussion re Heathrow airport and the London Underground. The top-level worries were chemical weapons in the Underground, a hijacked plane into Heathrow, suicide bombs on high-profile targets. Alistair Darling was pushing quite hard on it, asked if we were prepared for the kind of blind panic that would follow. He for one did not feel we were. TB said it was important to strike a balance. Milburn and Liam Donaldson [Chief Medical Officer] wanted to put out a lot of factual material on 'what if'. There was also clearly a need for more training re major incidents on the Tube. There was a fiasco later when the Home Office released the wrong version of Blunkett's statement which meant the media got the draft that had the section in about a dirty bomb that we thought better out.[1] I called Huw Evans [special adviser] to ask how on earth could that happen? But I suppose it did get up the focus on terror.

I chaired a two-hour meeting on Iraq communications. Went through a lot of different scenarios and planning. We agreed that the crunch was likely to come quickly. We needed communication plans ready for all the different scenarios. I went to meet Alex [Ferguson] at the Hilton and travelled with him to a charity dinner. GB was there with Gus O'Donnell and I took Alex and George Graham [former football player and manager] over to say hello. Even in those circumstances, GB and I barely acknowledged each other. I spoke to Gus and Sue Nye [GB's personal aide] and said they had to get their boss to stop treating TB like a hate figure. Gus said it takes two to tango. I said TB tangoes all day long with him. Alex coughed up five grand for my marathon. I shared a car home with George Graham who clearly wanted to be back in the game.

Friday, November 8

I didn't sleep well, but ran in, up to see TB to discuss political Cabinet. I filled him in on the encounter with GB and Co. last night, his inability even to look at me when I was taking over Alex and George Graham, and also the subsequent discussion with Gus and Sue. Alex noticed the vibes. Philip had spoken to GB last night and asked why all the communications channels had closed, and he simply said 'A lot has happened since last year.' TB was more open than ever, said he was thinking about the denouement on this, but it was important if it ended in a fissure that people genuinely understood he had tried

[1] Blunkett took responsibility for the error. The statement as released said: 'Maybe they [al-Qaeda] will try to develop a so-called dirty bomb, or some kind of poison gas; maybe they will try to use boats or trains rather than planes.' The revised statement, which Blunkett said had been amended to avoid creating panic, said: 'If al-Qaeda could mount an attack upon key economic targets, or upon our transport infrastructure, they would.'

everything. He felt he would at some point have to move him over or out, go out and say that he had been willing to stand aside before a third election, but even that had not been enough for him, that he would not work with me. The only other job he could realistically offer him was Foreign Secretary and he felt he would refuse that and walk.

TB said the reason 'psychological flaws' had been so damaging was because it rang so true with people who knew GB, and it rang true with GB himself. TB felt he was beyond repair. I said he had maximum power for a limited period, and it usually drained with time, and he had to use that power, not let more drain away before he decided and acted. I think the general feeling now, not just in Number 10 but around the Cabinet table too, was that GB was pretty hell-bent on TB's destruction. TB said he still felt we had to try to get it back together but he didn't hold out much hope. What was really important was that the upper echelons felt he had tried, and GB had refused to co-operate. JP was the key to this, and he was currently of the view that they were as bad as each other, even if GB had started to take the thing off the rails. TB felt it would be wrong to cave in to the kind of psychological and political pressure GB was piling on.

The main focus of the day was the UNSCR being agreed later in the day and I worked up a script for the UK on that. The morning meeting was largely about clearing up the dirty-bomb fiasco of yesterday. Political Cabinet was a good discussion. PG did a presentation which was realistic without being too downbeat, and on the fundamentals we were in a very strong position. TB did an overview – public services, antisocial behaviour, economy – and was very strong and clear on reform in particular. GB spent most of the time with his head down looking at his papers, but looked up a bit angrily when TB said there was a missing ingredient to the economic argument, its relation to the new economy and the developing economic giants, the whole science and research area. JP raised one or two concerns on the public services, and the fears of reforms leading to two-tier services, but he was OK generally. Hilary A spoke as well as I had ever heard her speak, said we had got into a rut on this two-tier thinking, said that a drive to uniformity had let millions of kids down. Schools and hospitals in the poorest areas were the ones that would benefit most from reform. Blunkett said two-tier exists now. In Hackney twenty per cent of parents send their kids private. People are opting out of the system and we have to attract them back. They won't come back to an unreformed system.

Reid, Milburn and Charles C were excellent on reform. The centre of gravity had definitely shifted to the reform end of things, which made GB's contribution a bit odd. It was a verbal version of Ed Balls' recent article, and he said the coming argument was about the limits of the market. It was reasonably politely put but the coded message was fairly clear. The impact was muted though because he did not put the case with his usual vigour, and he sounded a bit old-fashioned and out of touch. It was as though he had decided what he was going to say in advance and couldn't adapt to the discussion, and he didn't resonate as he had planned.

Milburn spoke at length and in detail on the health reforms and how they related to other reforms and he had a good line, that if independence was good enough for the Bank of England, it was good enough for schools and hospitals, which brought a thin smile to GB's lips. Margaret B said the message we put out on this was unclear, and there was a lot of confusion in the PLP about what we were actually saying. TB made clear that if we lost the ground on reform, we were giving the Tories the opening they needed and we must not give it to them. He said re markets that we would end up in an 'absurd situation' if we allowed our opponents to present this as an argument about privatisation. It is about choice and empowerment. If that wasn't a big enough hint to GB, he then said we needed to learn lessons from Al Gore's failure and defeat. Gore got himself into the wrong position on the role of the state. The Tories want to do us as the big-state party, holding the individual back and we must not let them. He was really on form today and a number of them commented on it during the break.

They came back for another good discussion, this time on ASB. Peter Hain said he had been told so many times that Cabinet meetings were boring, but he had felt this was a really strong discussion. 'Who told you?' snapped TB, joking, and they all laughed, with the usual exception. The mood generally was good. Even Clare was broadly on message on the ASB agenda. Only Alistair D came in on the GB point, saying that if we focused on excellence there could be a problem – the elitism point. JP said at the end that it had been a breath of fresh air to have a longer, broader-ranging discussion that went into themes rather than just policy. TB said he would look to do this more often.

The only bad note, as TB and JP discussed afterwards, was what he saw as GB's diddling on the markets argument. It had merely been an attempt to disrupt the flow. JP felt it wasn't that bad, but he came to see me before leaving and said though he was going to have one more go on Sunday at getting them working together, he felt things were as bad as ever. He said TB had guilt. GB had hatred. And though TB was a more generous spirit, there was wrong on both sides. But he felt TB was the more rounded and complete politician. He was brilliant at winning arguments and he should do it more with the whole Cabinet like that, rather than just let these things simmer. He should force a proper Cabinet discussion on the euro and the five tests, let's see where people really are, including Gordon.

JP said he had raised with GB why he had gone incommunicado with me and GB said he knew I was keeping a diary and he was sure I would publish it while he was still in power. I said why doesn't he fucking ask? It's not really that, said JP, it is all about the trust broken between them and he sees you as an extension of TB. I said if he spent more time building bridges and less time knocking them down, alienating people, treating them like dirt, he would find he had a lot more support than he thinks. JP felt TB should involve the Cabinet more, stop handling so many issues, particularly the euro, bilaterally with GB, and he would tell GB to stop demanding a date because it was counterproductive. He said both of us were important to getting them to the right place, and we should have one last go for peace. I said it was beginning to sound and feel like a peace process between enemies, like NI or the Middle East. JP laughed, said you're not far wrong, but these are the two giants of the Labour Party and if they do not work together, the party suffers.

Saturday, November 9

The best part of the day was [Burnley] getting Man United in the FA Cup draw. Also watching *Bend It Like Beckham* [comedy-drama film] with Fiona, Calum and Grace. Fantastic little film. I worked with TB on his *Observer* article [on rights, responsibilities and criminal justice] and did a conference call with JS, GH and DB who were doing media tomorrow. David didn't sound good and I think the terror fiasco had hit him a bit. He hated it when he was being blamed for cock-ups, even though this was clearly not his fault personally. The issue had subsided a little but there was still the mood in the media that we were hiding something. I was feeling back on form and worked on TB's Mansion House speech for Monday, using some of the lines and arguments that came out of yesterday's discussions, getting up arguments pre Queen's Speech as well as on the international agenda. TB was off at the Albert Hall [British Legion Festival of Remembrance] tonight but also working on the speech. Meanwhile the Royals story was going from bad to worse and TB was worried about it.[1] The idea of the Royal Family being run by a load of gays was taking hold. Did an eleven-mile run along Regent's Canal. Sundays full of Royals, Iraq and the Tories who were progressing steadily towards meltdown.

Sunday, November 10

TB called at 9 to go over where we were on the [Mansion House] speech. His basic message was that we could not defeat terrorism by security measures alone but we needed a coalition of common ideas and a shared agenda. He was really concerned re Chirac, felt that he was likely to be hostile for some time, and it would be difficult to rebuild. He felt JC was in the wrong on a lot of these issues, but he was sure we were heading for an extended bad time with him. On Iraq/WMD I said I felt we needed to be much more open and take people into our confidence much more about the information and arguments he was having to weigh up. He thought the Royals situation was damaging them. I felt what it was exposing was that the Queen was solid as a rock but beneath and around her things were a bit weak. He felt Charles should be staying above it all like the Queen if he wants to be seen in the same league.

TB was due to meet JP and GB later, ostensibly to discuss the fire dispute. I told him JP was pretty much in the 'both as bad as each other' camp at the moment. TB said deep down he knows that isn't true but he has to maintain that to be in a broker position. He thought GB will have gone away from Friday's Cabinet a bit worried, because it was so clear that the body of opinion wasn't with him. He thought he might come back to the idea of some kind of deal based on co-operation and departure. When TB told Jeremy he was still thinking he might go before the election, Jeremy said the senior Civil Service would be up in arms if they thought GB was taking over any time soon 'and for once they would be right'. Jack Straw was so horrified at GB's recent behaviour that he had asked TB 'Has he got something on you? How else do we explain to ourselves why you tolerate it?' TB's answer was the usual – that although he can be maddening, he has a brilliant side to him. TB was thought to be on such good form at the moment that his colleagues were clearly thinking GB could be moved. JP called re the fire situation. Gilchrist had heard [Professor Sir George] Bain [chairman of a government-funded independent

[1] During the Paul Burrell trial it had been revealed that Diana had secretly kept tape-recorded conversations in a locked box. These reportedly included details of an alleged rape in 1989 of a male member of Prince Charles' staff.

review of the Fire Service] would be publishing tomorrow, and he was worried that we were pushing it out. I said no way, and we would just keep radio silence on it.

Monday, November 11

We were well set up on the CJS [criminal justice system] reforms and on the speech, and on Iraq TB was at least getting some credit. There was still huge coverage for the post-Burrell Royals fallout. Bain put out his review, which the FBU rejected immediately needless to say. It was a good piece of work and I think serious people would wonder why on earth they could throw it out so quickly. We had a brief discussion on the Queen's Speech debate and also truancy, where it was clear TB was moving to the idea of fixed penalty notices with child benefit sanctions. David M, Jonathan and I went through the speech to work on the balance between warning and assurance. I think we just about got there, though it was one of those that could go either way.

We were also having to get the balance right re Bush. There was no point him [TB] just getting up there and putting the US line but he did not want to be seen as anything other than supportive. The question was how you weave in the argument about maximising influence without being explicit. The problem was, as he said to the morning meeting, that Bush did not really seem to take account of different concerns. President [Vicente] Fox [of Mexico, visiting Downing Street] felt the same. The speech came together OK though and he had done some strong stuff on MEPP and on the Muslim community. I had a ninety-minute meeting re the GICS review. Gus [O'Donnell] made it clear from the off he was on the radical-change end of the market, which was good news for me. He said he did not feel what was currently envisaged as change was nearly radical enough, and would not be seen as such. What was slightly depressing was that some of the people and arguments were exactly the same as those we had in '97.

Tuesday, November 12

[Andrew] Gilligan was doing a big number on security at Posts [UK embassies], clearly on the alarmist end of the market. Lots of 'intelligence says this, intelligence says that'. I called [Sir] David Omand [permanent secretary and security intelligence co-ordinator, Cabinet Office] who said there had been a warning in Australia re an attack on Posts, which had been checked out through Cobra and found to be nothing. We agreed a line that there was no general new threat to Posts and people should not change their plans. Then after I ran in, John Denham [Home Office minister] called, to say there had been a warning that went out via Transec, that part of the Department of Transport responsible for security, which did say there had been intelligence, though it did not say put out a new level of vigilance. The Gilligan report was outrageous and we used it to set out how difficult it was to make these judgements.

Up to see TB in the flat. He was more worried about fire and the FBU claim that we had been spoiling for a fight. Another discussion re GB. He said JP was the key and I really had to work on him. He knew deep down that we were in the right and he also knew he was in a powerful position and was using that. TB said 'The crazy thing about all this is that I never wanted to fight a third election but I may have to because I don't feel I can trust him to take over when he is as impossible as he is now. The only question is whether I can move him or get rid of him.' He said we were strong on policy substance but GB hung over everything like a shadow. I had a chat with C on the phone to take forward what we had been discussing about use of intelligence in the public diplomacy campaign. The Palace were setting up an inquiry into the post-Burrell issues, rape, gifts etc., which was a massive story. I had lunch with Jeremy Vine [BBC]. There was something very positive and likeable about him. He was desperate for an interview with TB on the whole God thing. Then to the Newspaper Press Fund at Australia House, lots of the old crowd from the *Mirror*. I went for a drink with Rebekah Wade [editor, *News of the World*], interrupted by a call from Gerard Russell [Islamic Media Unit, FCO] re an OBL audiotape where he seemed to be taking credit for the Bali and Russia attacks. We got Hoon up.

Wednesday, November 13

Queen's Speech was running fine, but drowned out by fire, Iraq and the Royals, particularly after last night's interview by [Sir] Michael Peat [private secretary to the Prince of Wales] on the so-called 'St James's Palace inquiry'.[1] Morning meeting largely on the OBL video. Then I met some of the Middle East experts who had been looking for the kind of thing that could be surfaced publicly, for example only one in three actually voted in the recent referendum. Also, the fact that Saddam seemingly listened to Radio Monte Carlo [Arabic service],

[1] The Prince of Wales had announced an internal inquiry to be headed by his private secretary. Sir Michael Peat had responded to criticism of the limited scope of the inquiry by saying it would be conducted 'without fear or favour'.

so we agreed it was worth trying to fix a TB interview for any direct messages we wanted. We agreed that the Middle East guys should come more regularly to our meetings. In between Queen's Speech meetings with TB, we had the first fire-strike meeting with JP, Nick Raynsford, Omand and Hoon. JP had done well and the next phase was going to get particularly tough. Omand and Jeremy were both pushing for a programme of training of new people or moving on anti-strike legislation but we were still in a position of saying that we didn't want to inflame. At the political strategy meeting, we were trying to hone the local elections message to get local parties motoring more on crime and community campaigns. I went over to Derry's rooms in the Lords for his Queen's Speech reception, where I came face to face for the first time with Black Rod, all dressed up in his finery, his face too pinkish for my liking, and a rather smug grin. 'We meet after all this time,' he said. I said that he had caused us a lot of grief. He said he had only been trying to help. I was pretty short with him. Derry was thoroughly enjoying himself, delighting in introducing me to all the men in tights as 'the prince of darkness'. He asked me if I had hit Black Rod. It was quite a jolly do, a mix of ministers from the Lords and Commons, officials, ambassadors. I asked Derry if he hated all this flummery and nonsense as much as I did. He made a jokey little speech about how he came into politics so that he could preside over ceremonials, walk backwards in front of the monarch, listen to a Labour legislative programme being delivered to rows of tiaras. David Hanson [Blair's parliamentary private secretary] was telling me around a hundred MPs would vote demanding a UNSCR second time around. Queen's Speech was going OK, but Iraq plus fire made sure it was surrounded more with a sense of problems than solutions.

Thursday, November 14

TB really tired. He didn't get a great press out of the Queen's Speech debate and in any event fire was getting much more attention. He said if we had a Tory government, they would not be getting attacked in the same way. Also the notion of industrial unrest was being taken to the Tube, with Mick Rix [general secretary of rail union ASLEF] out there. JP was doing a statement which I rewrote during Cabinet, giving him some cover by making clear that if we moved from a two-day to an eight-day strike, we were in a different ball game and some of the issues that had been kept off the table to suit them when we were trying to avert the strike would then be on the table. JP was up for doing the tough stuff if we had to. He was very on board at the moment, just took the changes, including a sound bite that said we had bent over backwards and been met with a response that was wrong, irresponsible and puts lives at risk.

The morning meeting was mainly Iraq to go over TB's interview and the response to the Saddam statement. We needed to get out as well the fact that only one in three voted in the 'election' for Saddam. I was very pissed off at the GICS FCC [fire co-ordination centre] and the lack of co-ordination in ministerial interviews. I got TB to say at Cabinet that we needed volunteers to go out around the regions. Cabinet was largely about fire, JP making clear that we would shift gear now, especially if they moved their position to an eight-day strike. I was outraged at the way they were using Fire Service buildings to plan the strikes, to protest, but then go inside when it rained. The employers were totally useless, the TUC not much better. Our MPs broadly OK. Cabinet also discussed Iraq, and TB was looking tired and fed up.

He did the Radio Monte Carlo interview, got up a few strong clear lines – not about oil, not going to push in an exiled government, only one in three voted. We had a meeting with Tessa on sports policy. The presentation was too long and TB wasn't really engaged. I said I had no real sense of a grass roots sports strategy. Then did a visit with other key Number 10 people to PINDAR, the three-storey underground bunker [below the MoD]. Very basic living quarters, internal TV station. A bit alarming in that before these kinds of emergency sites had always seemed a bit fanciful, but at the moment they didn't.

Friday, November 15

The tougher message on fire strikes was coming through but the press was so desperate for us to fail, that they couldn't resist trying to turn it into a story about mixed signals. To lunch at MI5. We discussed the US, these guys seeming as frustrated as SIS at the Americans' inability fully to understand why they needed to motor more on the Middle East. There was clearly a lot going on, much greater threat closer to home, and they said it was sometimes difficult for Western minds to come to terms with the added dimension of terrorists who in many ways didn't mind if they were disrupted because they didn't fear dying, but welcomed it. I said we had better relations at the centre of SIS than with them and we needed to keep more closely in touch because I was sure that as they spent so much of their time thinking strategically and thematically, there was a lot of their work that could dovetail with public communications. They were clearly worried that they were having to move resources from organised crime because of the growing need to keep tabs on Islamic fundamentalism, added to which for all the progress, Northern Ireland still took up a lot of resources, they clearly felt under pressure.

Then did a speech and Q&A for the staff. There were about 400 people there, generally a lot younger than I would have expected, pretty poor on the ethnic mix front, but very welcoming, good atmosphere, good reception. My main theme was the gap between messages being pumped out daily in the media, and the reality of most people's lives, and how that impacted upon the way governments operated and communicated. Quite a good range of questions, from the obvious – how did I assess the Security Service's profile, was spin our fault, how do you deal with 24-hour news – to the less obvious, e.g. on hunting. The last speaker had been the Archbishop of Canterbury who had managed to speak for a whole hour without mentioning God. I said I think I would find it impossible to go for an hour without mentioning TB, not that TB is God. TB had gone off to Warsaw and was due to do the *Mirror*. He called afterwards, said it was a crap interview. It had been arranged on an agreement to get the focus on crime, but he said crime was barely mentioned. On fire, he said if e.g. the RMT [rail union] went for secondary action, or the FBU went for eight days, we would have to go for them big time.

Saturday, November 16

TB at Chequers. [Sir George] Bain called to speak to him, to say in his view they [FBU] didn't deserve much at all, and he was worried JP just saw this as an old-fashioned split-the-middle negotiation. He felt it would be bad all round if we caved in at all. The other thing we had to track all day was the *Sunday Times* story on a plot to attack the Tube.[1] I did a conference call later on the Sunday broadcasts with JP, Hain, [Margaret] Hodge [minister for universities] plus the spooks to get lines squared, but it was going to be difficult to keep the press under control, not least because they would want to know if this was the reason we changed the 'poison gas or dirty bomb' warning by DB [see November 7]. The current game by the media was to get us into confusion stories, mixed messages whether on fire or terror. TB felt that for the next phase, basic competence was going to be the issue – on fire, asylum, PBR – plus of course we had Iraq to deal with. He was still saying that the US did understand the need to move on the Middle East peace process.

[1] Three men had been arrested in London on terror charges and the *Sunday Times* had speculated that they had planned to release cyanide gas on the London Underground.

Sunday, November 17

The *Sunday Times* story was going big all day and the broadcasters were taking it into mixed-signals territory. JP was OK on *Frost* but I was a bit worried that he said there was no threat to the Tube as reported. The papers as ever were being irresponsible and stupid.

Monday, November 18

Hans Blix going back to Baghdad. Fire difficult. On fire at least, the media were on to something re mixed signals, e.g. JP saying let's talk, TB focusing on money for modernisation, GB there's no more money for anything. TB's *Mirror* interview was crap, total waste of time. Fire was the most pressing issue. We still didn't have a grip of it. While the softly, softly approach was right in the early stages when trying to avoid the strike, we definitely needed a change of gear. What we had to watch was a sense of division, and the idea some would willingly put in lights that TB was being urged to take them on and defeat them. He and JP had to be in the same position, focusing on the need for long-term reform, but we weren't there at the moment.

Top-up fees was also a bit of a disaster area at the moment. AA said at TB's Monday meeting that we needed a while to sort it. Philip warned he thought it was a potential tipping-point issue. TB's weekend note had been largely devoted to a plan for dealing with the French, relations with Chirac still causing him a lot of concern. Media-wise, our main event of the day was the Trevor McDonald [ITN journalist] interview, and though we had managed to get a fair bit of preparation time in the diary, TB wasn't really fired up, didn't really engage or have edge, so on balance it was a negative. They had wanted a line on fire and on terror for their news coverage, but the exchanges on crime were pretty average. Planning meeting on the Prague [NATO] summit, then on the euro and Britain in Europe [pressure group], where yet again we agreed they had to do more work independent of us, but it was a pretty hopeless situation. The news coverage out of Trevor McDonald was a lot better than I thought it would be and the reactions to the interview as a whole pretty positive.

Tuesday, November 19

Called JP to discuss fire. I felt it was all a bit ragged, that we had GB tough on public spending, TB tough on modernisation, JP basically just wanting a settlement. We also had word through the *Mirror* on the elitism front that GB was against top-up fees. We then got filled in on GB's breakfast meeting at the *Guardian* where it seems he had been off-centre on EMU, top-up fees, and Iraq. Peter M called, said he felt the ground was moving somewhat. There was a distancing strategy going on.

JP said his basic approach had been to try to stop the fire dispute whilst preparing for one anyway, then get very tough if it came to an eight-day strike. I drafted him a few sections for his speech in the [Commons] debate, which broadly he was happy with. Later the employers offered sixteen per cent with modernisation. The FBU rejected it, wanting twenty per cent without modernisation. TB had a speech on e-commerce, which was actually quite a good speech, though it was never going to fly and we put in a few lines on fire. I had a meeting with SIS on some of the anti-Saddam activity inside Iraq.

We had the *Express* lot in for lunch, which was a pretty weird event, largely Richard Desmond [proprietor] and Peter Hill [*Daily Star* editor] talking about the business of newspapers, as if we were supposed to find it as endlessly fascinating as they did. TB was OK, good on fire, but as with the Trevor McDonald interview yesterday, he wasn't really pushing out message in these media encounters. Peter Hyman felt we were a bit complacent and that we had slipped back from the [Labour] conference success on public service reform.

At our 6pm strategy meeting with TB, PG went through the recent groups and said the mood was uncertain, and with the potential to turn sour. We then got to an interesting discussion on TB/GB, Sally M feeling even more strongly than I did that Gordon was effectively running a daily strategy against TB, and we had no counter-strategy. TB said he admitted that he had moved on this, that he now accepted that GB was a largely malign force, but we had to understand that the party would make a judgement about who was responsible if there was a split which led to a schism. Also, he was in ability terms head and shoulders above the rest, and he really didn't want TB/GB to be THE story of this government. It will always be a story, but we should all do what we can to ensure it is not THE story. Peter M and Pat [McFadden] both said that the crux question was what was his plan for GB? TB said the ideal was to work with him on the programme we have got, but it's getting more not less difficult. 'It's almost like he pours concrete on top of the policy areas.' It even crossed his mind that he was trying to stop us reforming as a way of setting himself up as the reformer for the future. Peter M said it was absolutely clear from the recent briefings to the *Mirror* and the *Guardian* that he was up to no good.

I was arguing that we should get out there his modus operandi, the fact that he said different things to different audiences in a way that he wouldn't be able to if he had the top job. TB looked very down, and also said he still felt we should try to keep managing it. We have managed it successfully for several years and we needed to think very carefully before rushing into anything rash. Peter M said their game was deliberately to put TB into a box marked 'right wing' so that where progressive change was made, it was seen as theirs, whereas all the difficulties and controversies had been made to stick to TB. I felt that if TB really believed it was going to end in tears one day, better to get it dealt with now. Peter M sort of agreed, though his worry was whether it would be sufficiently clear that it was GB's doing that brought us to this, not ours. Jonathan said his concern was that GB was not beyond bringing the whole show down.

Wednesday, November 20

Kevin Maguire had a piece in the *Guardian* doing in TB on our handling of the fire strike, as did [Paul] Routledge in the *Mirror*. Jonathan Freedland [*Guardian*] had a big piece on how the fault line was now opening for sure, while Patrick Wintour's [*Guardian*] news story, also based on yesterday's breakfast, was GB coming out against top-up fees. It was pretty tricky stuff. When Jeremy spoke to Balls first thing, he denied GB had spoken against top-up fees and said the problem was in the current febrile atmosphere, anyone who was anything other than totally in favour of top-up fees was seen as anti TB. Classic Balls. The reality was there was a deliberate strategy going on to put us into a right-wing construct in the eyes of the left – foundation hospitals, top-up fees, pro US on Iraq.

Peter Riddell [*Times*] also had a piece saying it was time for GB to speak out re the limits of the market in the NHS. There was no doubt that there was a major operation going on. But TB, who called me up as soon as I got in, said his instinct remained to let it run, not to respond, just let them get on with it. But he accepted it was serious and that the most serious point was that policy issues were being blocked. My belief was that GB had been gifted a policy cover for what in reality was a personality battle and something of a vendetta against TB. TB was adamant that if it came to a split it had to be absolutely clear who was responsible. But I felt we had a strategy being run powerfully against us, and we were doing nothing in return. TB said I had to trust him on how to deal with this one. I said the problem was the party didn't see him coming out with enough that was seen definitively as Labour.

We got a bit of a problem out of the Hoon/CDS briefing, where

CDS said something pretty daft, making clear he felt it was bad for the Armed Forces to be involved in the fire dispute. We were getting ready for Prague but first had to endure a pretty useless political strategy meeting with John Reid, Douglas etc. where Spencer Livermore [special adviser, Treasury] was meant to do a Pre-Budget Report presentation, but pretty much said nothing that wasn't already known to a reasonably well-informed member of the public. Catherine Colonna called to say if TB asked Chirac for a summit date he would offer one probably. I said it was a pretty silly way to work. When we finally got there, TB said Chirac was so cold that there was no way he was going to risk humiliating himself, so they just had a cordial handshake and that was that. He said he was happy to hang tough for a while longer.

PMQs preparation was focused on fire and Tory calls for a director of homeland security, on which IDS did six questions, though not terribly well. TB did OK but missed the opportunity to do a values-based answer on top-up fees to Tony Wright [Labour MP]. I don't know why he won't do it. He said afterwards it wasn't the time, and he didn't want to look like he was making a U-turn. I felt the only way to win this argument was to make it about values and opportunity, whereas he was more on the idea that the status quo wasn't an option for the universities, as if they as institutions rather than people as individuals were more important.

I drove out to Northolt with TB. I had dinner with Dan Bartlett [now White House communications director] once we got to Prague. We went through why the US was so unpopular, the need to understand it and broaden the agenda. He was very down on the State Department, which of course outside America was the one part of the US government that was seen as vaguely bearable. The Americans currently thought it was seventy to thirty that there would be war, but that the thirty was genuine. We needed to set up a proper operation in Qatar, not least to have people able to make an impact on Al Jazeera. He was pretty down on the new [White House] Office of Global Communications, which of course the State Department were pretty much opposed to because it cut across much of what they did. He said the problem with State's communications was that some focused on long term, some on three metres at a time and there was not much in between. I said I strongly felt they should try to keep Rumsfeld off the international airwaves, and broaden their messages beyond America. He told me GWB intended to visit Africa, which I suggested was a great opportunity for a much broader repositioning of their global message.

Thursday, November 21

I had agreed with Dan last night that TB and GWB would do a short media event together, so we went through key messages on Iraq and fire. GWB arrived for the summit, was met by a beaming GR [George Robertson, NATO Secretary General] and then through for a meeting. Bush had the most extraordinary pair of cowboy boots on, and was full of the usual hail fellow well met, how ya doing? They did an OK doorstep, including on the latest bombing in Jerusalem. But the press were all focused on Iraq, and on the line that the US had pretty much decided. Bush felt there was a need for real pressure to build through troop movements, international condemnation, really tough and unpredictable inspections, to get Saddam off balance.

He said that once we made that phone call that agrees Saddam's in breach, we had to do something militarily, and quickly. Quick sustainable bombing raid, and boots on the ground. He said if Blix gets dicked around, while a US or UK plane is shot down, we go for him. He was clearly not keen on Blix, said he was wringing his hands and talking war and peace but 'That is our judgement. He is not going to get between us and freedom. Once we strike we go for it, we don't wait for the world to sing "Kum ba yah", to hold hands and wait for Saddam to develop a better karma.' TB said he felt there was a twenty per cent chance Saddam would co-operate, but Bush said he didn't know what co-operation meant. TB believed the regime would crumble pretty quickly, and Bush said both our secret services needed to be put to work to help that. They were thinking of a list of the top ten most wanted as part of a divide-and-rule strategy, e.g. put some members of Saddam's family on there, not others. He felt Saddam was making Blix and the UN look like fools. He also felt that if we got rid of Saddam, we could make progress on the Middle East. He reported on some of his discussions with [Ariel] Sharon, and said he had been pretty tough with him. Sharon had said that if Iraq hit Israel, their response would 'escalate' which he took to mean go nuclear. Bush said he said to him 'You will not, you will not do that, it would be crazy.' He said he would keep them under control, adding 'A nuke on Baghdad, that could be pretty tricky.' He was also clearly worried about the stability of Saudi Arabia.

I then left for the airport. The fire scene was pretty bad. On the flight, I did a note on the dinner with Dan Bartlett and what we needed to do to take things forward. There was some interesting stuff around on deception programmes, for example [Iraqi] officials being forced to put papers and materials in their homes with the warning that they and their families would be harmed if they were lost. JP was doing a fire statement at 7 with the strikes due to start, making clear that there was no more money, and that pay must be matched to modernisation and that in the meantime, preparations go on. We had to start getting a bit tougher in our language on modernisation.

Friday, November 22

The unions and the employers did a deal in the early hours which they sent through to ODPM [Office of the Deputy Prime Minister], we said no and they got out to say we had scuppered it. The problem being exposed was that we weren't in control of the negotiations but we would get the blame. The FBU and the employers both came out to say we had scuppered the deal but the problem was we were being asked not just to bless a deal but to fund a deal. JP was doing the *Today* programme and I tried to get hold of him but was in the shower when he came through and missed the call. It was pretty grim. He was clearly tired and took everything too personally and the message was pretty mangled.

We agreed at the morning meeting to get more on the offensive and we put together some aggressive lines for Godric at the 11, that it beggared belief the employers had signed up to this, that the unions were determined to avoid modernisation. We had to get back on the front foot because the FBU were making all the running. JP though was still putting out different kinds of noise because he was saying ultimately we would have to do a deal. He was also wanting to get the TUC more involved though they had been pretty unhelpful and difficult. We did a conference call with TB in Prague who was wondering whether to do media on it. He felt it was best not to because JP would feel undermined, though we got JR on to the lunchtime bulletins, who was excellent. TB flew back later and was in one of his irritating 'all that matters here is the facts' moods. His basic argument was that we would have to foot the bill and yet the talks had led to all the modernisation measures being removed.

We had a meeting with JP and GB at which we agreed to publish a paper on the economic impact, the Treasury having done a paper on the figures with £4 billion for local authorities and £16 billion for the public sector, making clear that if this was applied across the economy, it [the settlement] would cost hundreds of millions without modernisation attached. GB's main point was that we had to get the local authorities to negotiate this, but it wasn't clear what we were meant to do to achieve that. TB and JP both said afterwards it was a very Gordonic point, focusing on something that wasn't actually central. JP had become more seized of the TB/GB problem, and we both agreed it was surprising that the media weren't currently making more of what GB had been up to recently. It was not a great meeting. JP wanted to do interviews. I suggested he did one-on-ones, but he got a bit ratty and wasn't clear enough. We were not in a very good position. TB was pretty clear there was no way we could give in on this.

Saturday, November 23

TB called at 9. He wanted to do a press conference on Monday to set out the whole case, make clear why we couldn't give in, make a direct appeal to the firefighters. He was worried JP would react badly to that, wouldn't want him to do it, and asked me to speak to him. JP and I chatted for an hour or so before I sensed the moment was right to raise it, and he was fine. He was really fed up though with some of the personal vitriol he was getting from some of the papers. He was scathing about [John] Monks, who was leading the news today saying the TUC 'supported the FBU'. I said we needed to use the next few days to set basic expectations, and he should see the TB press conference as part of that. He wanted to know if TB would let the TUC have a role in trying to sort this. The *Mirror* had been pretty vile, and he said he would like to have a go at [Piers] Morgan publicly re the DTI investigation [into share dealing by journalists at the *Mirror*]. I said that would be a mistake, and he mustn't let them think he was taking any of it personally. He said that's the way I am, I can't help it, what am I supposed to do, if someone whacks me unfairly, I want to whack 'em back. He did think I should be toning down the really heavy messages because in the end we would have to negotiate. We seemed to have a cast of thousands on the ministerial conference call. JP was down at Dorneywood [official country residence] and was clearly having dinner because at one point, as we were discussing Iraq, we could all hear him saying 'I'll have rhubarb on mine.' The main message was all about getting the talks back up and focused on the right issues.

Sunday, November 24

JP called several times pre *On the Record* [BBC]. Tried to get him on the broader economic message. TB was getting more focused on it, wanting greater clarity. The plan had been for JP to say in the interview that TB was doing his press conference tomorrow, so that nobody thought it was him being bounced out of the picture, but he forgot to mention it. He did very good clips that were used for the bulletins. We briefed out a pre-press conference message on today's pay rise being tomorrow's rise in interest rates and inflation. The press were picking up on GB and JP saying slightly different things re sixteen per cent [settlement]. The Sundays were cranking up the idea of the unions now being at war with the government and John Monks was not exactly covering himself in glory. I went out for a seventeen-mile run, stopped a few times to take calls.

We did at least now have a bit of process story re fire and I felt if we got through today and tomorrow properly, on the comms front we would be in better shape. The FBU and the Tories were both out on mixed signals with GB making clear there was no more money and JP saying the deal on the table last week was still worth talking about. JP had been fine yesterday about the press conference but he was now getting worried it looked like TB was taking over. JP called me at 7.15, really down. He said he was thinking about handing it all over. He thought the soft-cop routine would work, but it hadn't and maybe he should put out a statement or go up on how sixteen per cent was no longer a runner. He said he had always felt he could do a deal of some kind with [Andy] Gilchrist but maybe he was wrong, maybe we should just go hardball. I said there was no need to change his role, and we would make sure there was no question of tomorrow being seen as sidelining him. I said if he suddenly put out a clarifying statement, they really would have a field day. He agreed, but he was clearly very down. He said he felt it deeply, in his heart, and he absolutely hates it if people think he has fucked up.

Monday, November 25

News leading on press conference and the line that TB would speak direct to firefighters and their families. We needed a stronger process story. Pat McF was talking to [Sir] Jeremy Beecham [chairman, Local Government Association] to get a line on the streamlining of discussions. He also wanted TB to speak to Monks which he did just before the press conference. TB wanted to get up modernisation and the need for change in working practices as the issue. JP came over for a meeting and asked for a private word with TB and me. He said he felt dreadful. Because of his background, he really wanted to think he could handle these kinds of disputes, and thought he had got some kind of agreement worked out with Gilchrist but it couldn't happen. He felt like he wanted out of the whole thing. He wanted GB to make clear in his opening statement that he and GB were not at odds. TB was very good with him, said he had worked incredibly hard on it, and done the right things, and don't let the press play the game they are playing and unsettle him by attacking him. Put it behind him and don't worry.

We went through the draft script I had done yesterday, toning down some of the rhetoric. We had three aims. First an economic message about the potentially dire impact of the FBU winning; second, get up what we meant by modernisation, and third, process. TB was on pretty good form [at the press conference]. The economic message came over and for the first time we really got the modernisation proposals on the agenda. I called JP in the evening, after he had finished the [Labour] NEC awayday in North London. He had pretty much had it with Monks on this one, felt he had been gutless, but said he had found more support than he expected among the union guys on the NEC, including the RMT. I said we had started to turn things and we could turn things more quickly if we kept things focused on the modernisation agenda. He sounded happier, said he was thinking about doing the government evidence to Bain tomorrow to keep the modernisation message going and give a sense of what a modern Fire Service should look like. I had a meeting with Tessa on sport. On the [2012] Olympics bid, the sooner we made the decision the better. I also felt we should get Patrick Carter announced [as chairman of Sport England] soon.

Tuesday, November 26

Struggling to get a grip on Iraq co-ordination. There was definitely now something of a turf war between the FCO and the CIC operation, driven by John Williams' [FCO] genuine and loyal belief that Jack was a key communicator. TB had definitely got fire into a better place. Before he left for his education speech in Birmingham, we agreed to take out all the stuff on top-up fees, which in the current atmosphere would just set off a different neuralgia, and the speech didn't actually need it. I was taking a hands-on interest in story development on fire. We were starting to bank them up, e.g. a report on joint control rooms, as well as some of the specific modernisation issues, e.g. the shift system, second jobs. We got up more modernisation messages through the publication of our evidence to Bain. Anecdotally, we were being told support for the FBU was weakening. JP's statement was OK but in questions he pointed up that twenty per cent were due to retire, which led to headlines about 10,000 job losses. But we were still in a far better position than before. TB called a couple of times, and said that you couldn't keep dancing around the jobs issue forever but it was good in a way that JP blurted it out. Then to the FPA [Foreign Press Association] dinner. Clive Anderson [broadcaster and comedian] hosted it extremely well, though Jack's speech didn't quite hit the notes. We were shortlisted for press office of the year though thankfully didn't win. I quite enjoyed the event but I hate these late nights.

Wednesday, November 27

I was working pretty much full time on fire, trying to keep going on modernisation. PBR Cabinet was very dour, and I didn't get the sense ministers were terribly impressed. We had a whole series of fire meetings over lunch. I stayed over at the House afterwards for the PBR. [Shadow Chancellor Michael] Howard's response was pretty good. Fiona called to say that our cops had a piece of paper from Cheshire cops about someone who had gone to them warning that Carole Caplin's partner was a fraudster. Peter Foster, the boyfriend, was apparently once involved in a tea scam in which he used Samantha Fox [former topless model who had dated Foster]. We saw TB later and of course he was in denial about it, said that her mother was marvellous. If Carole was now in cahoots with someone trying to set themselves up on the back of them [the Blairs], things could get tricky. Fiona said she had felt increasingly frozen out by Cherie and Carole, whose choice of men was a bit worrying, and yet all we ever heard from TB and CB was that she was marvellous.

Thursday, November 28

Dreadful press for GB on the PBR. I wrote to Ed Balls, said we should have kept in much closer touch in the build-up and needed to keep in close touch re a strategy to improve on the very negative day one. We were winning back a lot of ground in the fire PR battle, but with the talks due tomorrow we needed a strong line. So after Cabinet, TB, JP and officials met and we agreed to a very tough line, namely no commitment for government cash, nothing to risk stability, money tied to modernisation. JP was still very sore, said that he would never forgive the way the TUC denounced him. We were worried that Bain was coming under a lot of TUC pressure and was heading closer to sixteen per cent over two years. TB told JP that we had to break them on this, not in a rub-your-face kind of way, but simply making clear they did not win anything for their strike action. He was still pissed off that that red fire engine issue was not being handled properly.[1] TB spoke to Bain and was a bit concerned at his tone. We agreed to put out a tough statement at 4. TB had also been working on the

[1] Rather than elderly Green Goddess auxiliary fire engines, in the event of industrial action by firefighters, a reserve of modern red fire engines should be available to military crews.

Europe speech, which was a big one, but lacked a fundamental driving point, was a bit too nerdy, and with everything else going on, unlikely to get much coverage. We were getting up the notion of joint [Fire Service] control rooms with JP doing a visit with Bob Ainsworth [Home Office minister] to Devizes.

The other thing taking up a fair bit of time through the day was the Peter Foster issue. TB had told Cherie that she and Carole had to go through it all with me and Fiona, but it was pretty clear they weren't keen. Cabinet was mainly fire, with the general sense we were in better shape, NHS pay deal, and the bombing in Mombasa [Kenya], on which there would be the usual post-event finger pointing about what we knew of any threat.[1] We then left for Cardiff with the speech almost done, and agreed we would get cameras in for the Welsh Labour Party fund-raiser. We flew down, got driven to the hotel, which was besieged by firefighters and supporters, making a phenomenal amount of noise with Klaxon horns. TB was worried he wouldn't be heard, and the police had turned the venue into an island site, about as heavy a policing presence as I'd seen outside conference and summits. We were feeling a bit besieged. The speech was an OK piece of work[2] but we ended up getting more coverage overseas than we did here, when we got more for TB's piece in *Paris Match* saying happy birthday to Chirac.

As TB was speaking, I took a call from Ian Monk [PR consultant]. Ian had always been perfectly friendly, but my guard was pretty much up from the word go. He said that Carole, Foster and a lawyer had been to see him to get advice re their protection. I took the call from the stone staircase going down from the floor where TB was speaking, and could hear the applause for his speech at various points. Yet here I was, talking to a former hack turned PR about what was clearly going to be the next self-inflicted frenzy.

I did a two-page note for TB saying the Foster story was clearly going to become public and that we had to have defensive lines ready making clear that he had never met him and that it was not true, as he was saying, that he was their financial adviser. I said we had to

[1] A vehicle drove into the Israeli-owned Paradise Hotel and exploded in the lobby, killing thirteen, and two surface-to-air missiles were fired at but missed an Israeli charter aircraft. A previously unknown group, the Army of Palestine, claimed responsibility.

[2] Blair referred to the fire dispute at the fund-raiser, which had been boycotted by up to seventy trade unionists, saying 'It's better to do the right thing even if it is the unpopular thing, than to do the wrong thing and have the country pay the consequences of it.'

be very careful not to be thought to be, let alone seen to be, giving any advice to Foster. Monk had told me CB called Carole twice during his meeting with her. Fiona said Cherie had told her that she had not been able to get hold of her today and was really pissed off that we were being excluded, not least because neither of us trusted the people involved to grip it properly. TB called CB when we got back to the hotel and said it had to be gripped and Carole had to understand this was about us every bit as much as it was about her. As he understood it, the guy was a total conman, and dangerous. Monk had told me Foster [an Australian] had lost his deportation case and we had to hope he went. I could tell that after the initial insouciance of yesterday, TB was genuinely worried, though he was pretty soft with CB. Re GB, we agreed that if only we had a proper co-operative operation at every level, they would have got a far better media out of the PBR. On fire, the FBU were much more on the defensive, being forced to defend questionable working practices.

Friday, November 29

TB called before doing clips at a temporary fire station near Sedgefield. Richard Boucher [assistant secretary for public affairs, US State Department] was in town. On Iraq, even the State people were pretty clear they were going for it. On the Middle East, they were currently against a conference. Richard was clearly up for working together more closely, and it was almost as if he was trying to build alliances outside the government to improve the operations within it. I set out how I thought they could do quite simple things to do with Bush's profile abroad. In the end most questions came back to the need for a broader agenda, and a strategy that clearly went beyond merely American interests.

Chirac called TB to offer February 4 as a summit date. TB's birthday present and the *Paris Match* piece had obviously worked. Then a fire meeting to work out the next stage in communication terms, working up the idea of the MoD reviewing shift patrols, more public safety campaigns, more red fire engines. TB was angry because the squaddies were clear they needed more red fire engines. He was very clear that we had to get really heavy if they went for a second eight-day strike, that we would have to take the negotiations over, give them a take it or leave it deal, and if they left it, tough.

Had a very interesting discussion with TB about the nature of these jobs and friendship. He said he felt part of the problem of his life was that it's not possible to make real new friendships once you get to a position like his. It meant that if you are already close to people, you got even closer to them, both at work and outside work. So people like me, Sally, Anji [Hunter] and Kate [Garvey, events and visits team] he felt very, very close to, felt he could trust us. But even if he met new people that he liked, it was always difficult because in the end he was the prime minister, and that was bound to affect the way people think about him. Carole had come on the scene fairly early on, and they had both liked her. She was a bit wacky, fun and interesting. But don't worry, he said, I do realise how dangerous this is. I said it came to something that we were worrying about a professional conman close to the heart of the whole bloody operation.

Saturday, November 30

I was up through the night, vomiting several times. But I still had the Cobra paper on the fire dispute to finish, and took a couple of conference calls to get into really good shape. Then Gilchrist, who was not operating terribly well under pressure, made a big mistake, did a speech attacking us over Iraq and New Labour. I felt he was already losing a fair bit of support, and if the public thought he was actually out doing this as part of a general political kick, he would lose a lot of support across the spectrum. On Foster, the *Mail on Sunday* sent over more than twenty questions. We decided not to answer question by question and instead gave them a short statement making clear TB had never met Foster, he had never been to Number 10 or Chequers.

The real problem was over the flats.[1] TB admitted to me he was always against the idea of a flat on political grounds, but also that until today he had no idea they had bought two. I felt people would just about understand a mother wanting to get a decent place to live for their son, and might just about understand that she didn't trouble TB with all the detail, but they would find it a bit weird to think they had got two flats with the help of this guy Foster. He was still, however, very defensive about it all, said Carole was basically nice, and maybe this guy wasn't so bad after all. For crying out loud. Anyway we got through it and when the papers dropped, the others seemed to see it as much a story about Foster as about TB, though Cherie didn't come out of it too well. All very messy but in some ways could have been worse. In a way it was probably best that the *Mail on Sunday* had done it, because the other papers tended to think the *MoS* would have flammed it up as they were so oppositionalist. I was still feeling wretched by the evening and stayed in.

[1] Foster had assisted CB when she bought two flats in Bristol, where Euan Blair was at university.

Sunday, December 1

I felt much better after twenty-four hours' illness. The Gilchrist overly critical speech gave us a big opening. But there was clearly a bit of briefing around on a strike ban, which, as TB said, made it look like we were lurching around again, just when we didn't need to, because Gilchrist was on the run. The *Mirror* was the only paper left on his side now. JP was being pretty tough while TB was making clear we should move towards taking over the FBU negotiations, making a final offer and if it was not accepted making clear they would be fired and new personnel hired. There was lots of GB in the press post PBR, and some pretty major diddling on the euro. TB still felt his strong card remains that the public wanted him, not GB, and he felt that even if he became unpopular, that would remain the case. The PBR had included a euro reference but was now being seen as blocking the euro and TB was in no doubt GB was trying to thwart it.

On the flats, he denied they had evaded stamp duty or that Foster had helped them get a mortgage, though he later did say Foster had been to the flat in Bristol with Carole, and sent Cherie an email about the building society and the mortgage, so TB accepted Foster was able to present himself as an adviser. He said he had formed the view that Carole was basically decent but naive. I said I felt she had pretty much got them where she wanted them. She also had very bad judgement about men and while this guy was around we had a potential problem the whole time. It had to be sorted. He said he had left her in no doubt what he thought and she was going to reflect on it. Carole had said to TB that maybe the best thing was if Foster got deported, but that was just another excuse to be a victim. How people like this got into the system was beyond me.

Monday, December 2

The Iraq human rights dossier [containing information from human rights groups, government sources and the United Nations] and the fire report were doing well on the bulletins. Only the *Mail* were really going at Carole. The other big story was TB/GB split on the euro with several following up the *FT* splash of Saturday suggesting that the PBR report on macroeconomic stability should be read as being clear we were not joining the euro. TB called me up to the flat, had toughened his mind on fire, felt we should get to the position where we put down an offer, that was it, and if they kept on striking we make clear they would be sacked and others hired. He said his real concern was GB. Maybe he had been too naive for too long but he realised we now had to have a real strategy for him. He had one big card, namely that he was the elected PM. He believed it would become more and more clear that GB was responsible for a lot of our problems. But he had the ability to hold us back on policy and he felt at every level he was going at us in a pretty big way. He wanted to play long.

He was making tea while I was leaning against the oven and Cherie came in wearing her nightdress to get herself a drink, not totally hostile, but we didn't discuss the issue in hand. I went off to my morning meeting and there was too much going on – fire, Iraq human rights, plus Blunkett and Sarkozy meeting on Sangatte. I was trying to get a line agreed with TB that Foster gave no help in getting the mortgage on the flats but TB admitted we couldn't really say that. There was a real problem re CB's judgement on Carole, who could do no wrong. TB was also a bit all over the place. I told Tom [Kelly] and Godric to be very careful because I wasn't confident in the robustness of the case we were putting, and feared the facts on Foster would come back on us at some point.

The FBU did a four-hour meeting at the end of which they said ACAS [Advisory, Conciliation and Arbitration Service] had asked to intervene. The press took it as the first sign of crumbling so we pushed hard on the line that our position was as before. TB saw Monks and [Brendan] Barber with JP, said he felt they [TUC] had behaved really badly on this, that if they kept pushing out all this stuff about the link with the unions broken, it would be self-fulfilling. Fiona spoke to Carole and said she was back to thinking Foster was victim not villain. Ian Monk was still on the case advising her.

Tuesday, December 3

TB/GB thing was messy, one or two reports suggesting GB would get chopped. TB felt GB had overreached again and was now trying to pull back. He felt he was moving to a different mode, and the problem was he did have real reach in the party and was doing it on policy issues of substance. I was amazed by the fact the press weren't going bigger on it. TB said I had to leave it to him to sort with GB. But he did accept that there was a reality problem. He said GB had raised me again, and my diary, and had asked TB to discipline me. TB had said to him that if you treat serious people like shit, don't be surprised if they are not exactly rushing to help. Also, [Ed] Balls was about to make a speech about the history of the euro. That would inflame further and risk things getting out of control. I did a few meetings on fire, top-up fees, sport strategy, then home to collect the boys and off to Burnley vs Man Utd. I did the US conference call on the way, which was poor. Saw Alex briefly before the match, which we lost 2–0, but it was a terrific night to see the ground [Turf Moor] full and humming.

Wednesday, December 4

Student march on top-up fees included Will Straw [son of Jack and President of the Oxford Student Union], and by the end of the day we were in a different position, TB ruling out 'upfront fees' during PMQs. Crap day. At the John Reid party meeting, I had a real pop at Spencer Livermore, who was resisting any message focus on ASB, saying schools and hospitals were all that mattered. TB was fairly relaxed after a not very good PMQs but top-up fees was going to be seen as a U-turn and a victory for GB. Pat [McFadden] had lunch with Sue Nye yesterday and said GB's lot were totally convinced we were doing him in the whole time, me in particular. They felt I was trying to disable him as a possible successor to TB. They denied having any strategy against TB at all.

There was a flurry before I left. The *Mail* called to say they had an exchange of emails between Foster and CB which totally debunked the idea that he was not an adviser. Even though I had half expected this, I was absolutely livid, and Godric was worried he had been put in a position of misleading people. TB and Cherie were at the theatre. Bloody hell. I told the *Mail* I couldn't find them and we would have to deal with it in the morning. We were being hit again because we didn't get the full facts out. I dictated a note to TB saying this was likely to be big and bad. He called me at ten to twelve, said it was ridiculous to say Foster was their financial adviser. He was still in denial about it. He said at the weekend he had said that Foster had sent Cherie an email but CB did not even reply, so it was ridiculous – one of his favourite words at the moment – that this was a big story. I said we had given, in his name, the clear impression that Peter Foster had had nothing to do with the whole thing, but these emails would show very clearly otherwise. I said this was a problem born of Cherie going to a different place getting bad advice. I also felt he was far too tolerant of the whole Carole scene. As we were speaking, I got a message that the *Mail* had done three pages, all pretty grim. I told him, and he said he was going to have to get to the bottom of it. He went off and got all the emails from Cherie and was up most of the night going through them and working up a response. I went to bed but was unable to sleep. Why the fuck should I spend so much of my life digging them out of shit of their own making?

Thursday, December 5

Carole had been a disaster waiting to happen, as I had said for years, and it was happening. I called TB who had been working on some kind of statement overnight. We both knew there was no point going over the old ground. This just had to be sorted. I got a cab in and was hugely cheered up by the driver who said the reason the media went at the government was because we were doing a good job on the main things, and the reason they went for me was because they hated people who stood up to them. I got in, up to the flat, where TB was sitting at the table in the window, a welter of emails spread out in front of him, having written a draft statement. There was no small talk, no banter. Cherie came in wearing her pyjamas, could barely look at me and we didn't speak. TB and I agreed that the problem was going to focus on the fact that we misled the press. They continued to insist that this guy was not their financial adviser, but based on these exchanges, they were deluding themselves if they thought we could persuade people of that. When it suited the media to treat Foster as a conman, they would. When it suited them to take things at face value, they would do that too. This problem arose, like others before, because TB and CB so often wanted to believe the best and ended up doing so. But we were going to get the blame for this.

I said there was a case for turning the draft into a CB statement and she agreed to that. We spent ages going over it. As the day wore on, I could see TB was becoming more and more worried. He and I went up to the little changing room by the bedroom and he said his instinct was to fight it out. I said if we gave nothing on this, we'd be dead. He said it was only because we lived in a world infested with this media scum that we had to get into any of this. Cherie joined us, looking very downcast. I then worked on a Number 10 statement followed by a CB statement which said she would have been more circumspect if she had known and that she regretted causing misunderstanding. TB saw the Danish PM while Jonathan, Sally, Tom and I went to CB's office in the flat with the latest version. We had to fill in some of the gaps with copper-bottomed facts. I read it out. At the end she looked to Sally and said 'Alastair hasn't looked me in the eye since the weekend. He thinks I'm a fraudster.' No I don't, I said, anything but, but I do think you can be a bit daft and have some odd friends, but we are where we are. We went through it, and Fiona joined us, Cherie didn't change much and then she had to leave for court. She was very emotional, bottom lip quivering when she spoke to me, but otherwise OK.

TB came back and was fine with it. He said we had to clear up the idea we had misled the press. He was worried we were going to end up with the worst of all worlds, which of course we were, but I felt we just had to get the facts out as best we could. We finally got it sorted, TB taking out the reference to the *Mail*'s 'vicious personal campaign' and agreed it before Cabinet. I left Cabinet early to put in an extra couple of lines and then spent some time with Tom before he did the eleven o'clock. He went off armed with the best answers we could muster but it was going to be pretty grim. He came back to say it had been particularly torrid, that they didn't really buy the idea that we didn't mislead them. The hacks were also moving to the idea that it was me and Fiona who were responsible for the misleading.

TB spoke to CB and she agreed we could make clear she alone was responsible for any misunderstanding. Through the day the story developed into one about Cherie's judgement re Carole and re them not telling us that Foster had indeed had a lot to do with these transactions. TB called Tom and me round and Tom filled him in very honestly on how hard the briefing had been, and said it was moving to a great row about us and the press, focused on me in particular. TB said he was sorry we had been dropped in it like this. Sally said he really had to sort her out, that he was far too tolerant. She should not be doing the book. She should take proper advice. Carole had to be off the scene. TB was clearly worried about the impact of all this on Cherie, said it was monstrous that she was being done in like this, that she is a far better person than all this suggests. I said he should worry less about Carole and more about his own position. Later he set off for Bristol where he was due to do a Q&A and see Euan. I worked the phones, mainly editors and columnists, all feeling pretty sore about it all, and we were heading for an orgy of stuff about the Number 10 media machine again. This was a massive setback to the new media strategy. Tom did the four o'clock, gave out the CB statement that she alone was responsible for misleading the press, which helped us. Foster did a little doorstep, protesting innocence. He was clearly going to be around for a while. We were going to take a real hit on this, and as I said to Godric, pretty much the whole day taken up with dealing with this bollocks.

Friday, December 6

The papers were dire for CB, while the *Mail* and the *Telegraph* were really going for me – Liar-in-Chief. The storm was probably at its height and would blow out before too long, but TB was really worried. Cherie had been very frosty with Fiona last night. I explained that Fiona had a lot of sympathy for CB, but there was no point disguising the fact we felt this was a problem of their own making, and in part the result of Cherie relying far more on Carole than Fiona for advice on things which ultimately could impinge on him. He said I was talking about his wife, whose character was being assassinated. He said they were trying to do to her what they had done to Diana. I said it was nowhere near as bad as that yet, but why give them ammunition? It doesn't mean you have to totally change your lives, but you just have to be more careful about who is around. It was not a warm conversation. These character issues, where the political and the personal collided, were always difficult, and it must at times have felt like they both had me and Fiona on their backs the whole time, trying to cut out what they would regard as any fun or escape out of their lives. I said we were trying to help navigate through shitty waters. He said I know, but we are talking about my wife here.

I asked how Euan was. Fine, he said, but he won't be fine when he sees what this is doing to his mother. He accepted she had not been totally open with us, and also that we should have been able to go through everything as soon as this issue emerged, but it was clear he still felt they were more victim than villain. I was feeling crap all day because Grace and I had a rare flare-up in the morning, the kids as ever picking up on the tensions from elsewhere. TB called from Bristol and said he was worried we had no line out to Carole. He wondered if Hilary [Coffman, special adviser] shouldn't speak to her, but Hilary felt Carole would just see her as my agent.

TB called again from the train and said of course there was one person – GB – who would be loving all this. I had a few ministers on saying they would happily go out and defend Cherie – Hilary A, Robin C for example – but in the end we settled on Paul Stinchcombe [Labour MP] who was a genuine friend and who did well in making the case for some perspective in all this, and saying her faults were excessive loyalty and protection of her children. TB called again to say he had now spoken to Carole, and he sounded a lot better. He was talking about her like a doctor talking about a patient – she was stable at the moment, but she would need attention. Foster and Monk were still with her, so the dangers were still there. He felt she knew Foster had to go. He said you have to trust me on Carole. I honestly believe she would never sell her story, she is a good person, just naive in many ways.

Today's broadcast story was to a large extent about me, which was a pain, and a total joke in the way I was being collared on this. Meanwhile, there were all sorts of ridiculous rumours swirling round the Sundays, the most outlandish of which was that Cherie, Anji and

Carole used to take showers together. It was beyond belief the way some of the Sundays operated, literally just made it up. TB said we had to get to a position where we were saying, and the public was believing, that there were two very different agendas, a press agenda and then the issues that really mattered to people. But we were not there yet. And my next worry in all this was [CB's] clothes and discounts.

Saturday, December 7

Went for a run, but couldn't get going. The media were kind of on hold waiting for the Sundays. The whole day was a series of conference calls as the various sets of questions came in, mainly from the *Mail on Sunday* and the *News of the World*, a few from the *Sunday Times* and the *Observer*. I was buggered if I was going to be tarnished any more with this nonsense. People knew that I had always been warning about this woman. TB said that we had to be professional and focused. But I feared there was a lack of professionalism and focus coming from his desire to believe the best not just of Cherie but also of Carole. He said that Cherie was the subject of a vicious character assassination. I said I thought a lot of this was self-inflicted. He said that was really unfair, Cherie didn't deserve this. I said I had been warning about Carole for years. He said that's not true, that I had stopped a few years back. I said that was because it became pointless, the more I tried the more difficult Cherie became, to the point where I was worried neither of us were wholly rational about it.

He said you have to understand the pressures I operate under. I said I do, probably better than anybody else, but you also have to understand how damaging this kind of thing can be. It's been building up, and you also need ways to defend the individual situations to do with lifestyle, and by and large that can be fine, people will tolerate it but then sometimes there's a tipping point and that's where we are now. In all we must have had ten conference calls through the day. He said he resented having to deal with all this nonsense when he was also having to worry about Iraq. I continued to say it was all avoidable. We got the *Mail* questions in the afternoon and they related mainly to Foster and Carole being invited to things with Cherie, plus the issue of a trust that bought the flats, plus Fiona's role. We were dismissive of the invite stuff, fairly detailed on the trust. Then the *News of the World* came in with various groups of questions, first the claim that CB definitely knew about Foster's past so her statement on that was false, second that Carole tried to do a deal on clothes as we had always suspected, and third the wacky stuff about them having mudbaths and showers together.

By now, we were at Catherine MacLeod's [political editor, the *Herald*] farm in Essex to get a Christmas tree, but I spent most of the time on the phone up in one of their boys' bedrooms, Fiona popping in and out. TB had Cherie with him though she wasn't on the call, and he was saying to her 'This has to be one hundred per cent accurate' and it was easy to hear she was on the edge of it all, crying and saying why do you believe him not me? What a fucking mess this was. The fact of the purchase was politically grim, the sense of a cover-up and misleading was disastrous for our media relations, and the whole image being created of CB was appalling. When the *News of the World* stuff came through, the lack of a direct channel to Carole became an issue and in the end TB had to speak to her himself. She was denying that Cherie misled anyone about Foster and also denying she did deals on the clothes, which I didn't believe. TB wanted Fiona to act for Carole and put out a statement for her, which we refused to do.

Catherine and her family all seemed to be of the view that our life was absolutely crazy. Even when we went out to the field to pick a Christmas tree in a howling wind, I was called by Switch [Downing Street switchboard] for yet another conference call. The *News of the World* stuff came from someone who used to work with Carole but helpfully she used a different name so we could be fairly dismissive. Again, I was struck by how blinkered TB could be re some of the central allegations. For example, Carole saying she didn't do deals on clothes was enough for him but there was no way we could become their defenders. I was also angry that the press office had been put in a position where this shit was taking up all their time.

I was also sick of so much of the flak flying my way. I didn't mind when it was over things that really mattered, or when it was things I'd done that people disagreed with, but I hated it when I was copping it for things I had always been against doing. TB said, when I pointed it out, 'This is not very nice for me either you know.' I said yes, but at least you have some control over your own life and how you spend your time. At one point during the day, CB came on the phone, thinking I was Tom. 'Oh, it's you,' she said, and gave the phone back to TB. She really was resentful of us at the moment. Fiona's theory was that TB was so tolerant with CB because he had fallen for some of the Carole stuff himself. We had the worst of all worlds at the moment. I got Stephen Pound [Labour MP] out publicly asking [Paul] Dacre if the *Mail* had paid Foster for the emails. There wasn't too much to worry about in the various Sunday stories but the compound effect of a great morass was difficult.

TB and I were both feeling the pressure, and finally snapped in the evening when I said the whole fucking thing was their fault. He came back pretty heavy and the call ended badly. He called a bit later to say he understood this was difficult for us too, but we always did best when we hung together. The low point though had been when he was calling me and then calling Carole in quick succession to get her responses. The idea of a prime minister talking to this ridiculous woman who was sitting next to some ghastly conman was absurd and degrading. We got through the day somehow but I felt bruised and fed up.

Sunday, December 8

I did a long conference call with Jack Straw and Alistair Darling last night but amazingly neither was asked about CB in their interviews. Jack was doing fine on Iraq. I went for a six-mile run, then a swim, then a few calls, the press basically focusing in on the trust and how could they buy a flat through a blind trust, whilst my fears about the clothes issue were not yet realised. TB didn't call me during the morning which was rare. Philip was worried about the *Sunday Telegraph* because it looked like I was dumping on TB and CB. It's true that in some quarters I had let my anger get away from me. But I felt entitled to be angry when our advice was ignored with this kind of effect, and we were now having to deal with it, something that should have no government significance at all. I also felt that if they didn't change their ways, there would be more of this kind of stuff to deal with and I had just about had enough of it.

TB was down at Chequers seeing [Bill] Clinton, and it was pretty obvious as the day wore on he was not in contact, presumably because he was feeling I had distanced myself and briefed against Cherie. Philip, Gail [Rebuck] and Peter M came round to discuss the whole picture. Peter M took out his yellow pad. Must be serious then, I said. Fiona and I were in a state of real anger about the situation, and we had to try and work out a way out of it. Peter M had no idea of the extent of the problems we potentially faced, e.g. clothes, discounts, all the New Age stuff. We agreed we needed 1. to get Foster out of Carole's life, and 2. to manage Carole out of theirs. Gail said it would mean us giving massive support to Tony and Cherie, and also embracing Carole. I said there was no way I could do that, or let any of my staff do it. Fiona said even they had no real idea what our lives were like having to deal with this for so long. I feared that a lot of the really positive side of TB's image was eroding.

It was a good discussion and at the end we agreed we needed a proper audit of clothes, freebies, Carole's access, any use of government facilities, and we needed to put the fear of God into TB and make him understand the political precariousness. TB was fed up of hearing all this from me and I agreed with Peter M he would go with a warning that this was a real disaster unless gripped, that CB had to be reined in, Carole managed out over a six- to twelve-month period, and meanwhile we had to be very supportive. Peter was horrified that I was even thinking of going, but I really did feel the time was coming. He then called TB and arranged to see him tomorrow. Philip and Gail felt this could be the beginning of the end if not gripped. Peter believed if we did grip it, we could then repair, rehabilitate and move on, but it was difficult while Foster was still there.

Sally M called to say that Cherie had called her to say that AC/FM were briefing against her. Sally believed there was real damage to be done to TB by all this. TB had said yesterday this was not why he came into politics. I felt exactly the same. Cherie later called Fiona, was very frosty, said it was very clear Fiona disapproved of her, and intimated that maybe it would be better if she didn't work for her. Pretty unpleasant, after all Fiona has done for her.

Monday, December 9

I said to Fiona I felt we could be out by Christmas. I sensed a denouement. I said I wasn't going to be in a position where I was defending the indefensible. I took enough blame without taking it for things that weren't of my making. At the morning meeting, we skipped over CB, Iraq the main focus, while at the TB meeting we were mainly on asylum, NHS and fire. TB saw Sally, Jonathan and me, later joined by Hilary [Coffman] and Fiona. We agreed we needed a full audit of the clothes situation, and we would probably have to register retrospectively any discounts. TB kept trying to persuade me that Carole was basically a decent person and would do nothing wrong, e.g. on clothes. I said this had to be copper-bottomed, and I'm not sure I believed it. He got very defensive and we had another row about it, saying that we had a real problem because he took what she said at face value and I didn't. It was not an easy conversation. All of us felt he was not being quizzical enough.

The main area of press interest was the blind trust, but Andrew Turnbull backed TB's view that it was in accordance with the ministerial code on blind trusts. He was also OK about the Number 10 press office being used because we were only being asked any of this because she was the PM's wife. TB did the *FT*, and was on very good form, really pushing the New Labour reform agenda, definitely worth doing. But there was only one political story in town. There was an awful lot of [broadcast journalists'] two-way chatter about me and Fiona, while [Trevor] Kavanagh [*Sun*] had a big piece re how TB couldn't afford to lose me. Hilary was up seeing CB, came back and said she was not exactly on the same page as TB. She had also spoken to Carole who said she had not kept receipts. He said he obviously understood Carole could not come into Number 10 but then Hilary discovered she was coming in to see Cherie at 4.30. We put a block on that.

I had several meetings with TB, who was looking more and more depressed about the whole thing. Then Tom got totally banjaxed at the four o'clock – Foster's solicitor put out a statement which showed that CB had taken part on a conference call with Carole and Foster's solicitor. It sent the media into a frenzy. I went to tell TB, who looked grey, angry and sick. Cherie was due to be turning on the Christmas tree lights outside, but TB called for her to come down to the office, told her the questions that had now been put to Tom and she said yes, she spoke to the lawyer because Carole was worried Foster's case wasn't being handled properly, and what was wrong with that? She had a look of injured innocence. TB looked really angry, was close to the end of his tether. This is the worst possible nightmare, he said. She talked us through it and we put together a line which said she didn't know his past and she had made a short phone call.

TB said the whole thing was ridiculous, the media just moved from one charge to another, and when one fell down, another came up. We had gone from stamp duty evasion via slimming pills and now this. The problem was he saw nothing wrong in her making such a call, and I did, because she was the PM's wife, a QC, a judge, and she should have better judgement. TB said OK, she's maybe been daft but does she really deserve this kind of treatment? TB didn't raise my briefing against CB but Hilary came to see me, said it was the right thing to do for the credibility of the office. IDS was now writing in about the blind trust, about my role.

I had a long chat with Peter M before we went to see TB. He felt we could fight back harder and I said the solicitor's statement was a tipping-point moment. The politics on this were getting worse and worse, elitism while top-up fees was the issue, a real sense of out-of-touch lifestyle. [Conservative deputy leader and Shadow Foreign Secretary Michael] Ancram was out and about on it. TB was keen for us to get people up so I briefed Stephen Pound and later Clare Short. She did a good job on *Newsnight* but it wasn't great having to ask people to do this. TB did at least apologise to my team, or at least tell me to tell them that he had, for what they were having to do. He came through later to say a milder version of the same thing. God knows how many hours and how many people this was taking up at the moment.

Tuesday, December 10

Ran in. Papers grim, and the news leading with the Tories calling for an inquiry. Up to see TB, and we did a conference call with Peter M who had seen both of them last night to go through the facts of it all and was confident that CB was OK on it and there were no real new problems to worry about. I argued there *was* a problem in CB making a call to a lawyer, because she was a QC and his wife. TB was getting very agitato. He said 'I'm not having my wife treated like this and we have to fight back on the basis we have done nothing wrong.' He wanted to go up and do a big defence of her, but I said if he went up and just stated nothing had been done wrong, he would be more tarnished by it. He was so angry that I felt it would backfire if he went out now. TB's anger was affecting his judgement on it. He really seemed unable to see anything wrong in it. I felt that unless we let some air out of the situation, this was just going to go on and on. We also had to divide and rule, isolate the *Mirror* and the *Mail* from the rest. Peter M was keen for CB to do something today. Fiona, who later also saw Carole, felt too that CB should do something. I wasn't so sure. I chaired the first Iraq Strategy Group meeting and we agreed to do an objectives document. It was an OK meeting but we needed to get to a position where we were far more in control of the agenda.

Fiona came back from her visit with Carole, who didn't want to say she was dumping Foster, and had moved towards thinking as I did, that Cherie should do something public. TB was off to see the Prince of Wales for lunch, and new questions came in from the *Mail*. They were now suggesting 'judge nobbling'. It was time to go for it. It was a tipping point and we were all now up for CB doing a big number. I put calls out to Peter M and Charlie [Falconer] to get them to come over and we went through things line by line, making sure that all the difficult questions were answered in there, why the flats, how Foster, what she knew, why Carole. Fiona was terrific today, so was Peter M, saw things really clearly, but we had to fight back and that meant changes in the dynamic. An interview would be no good, because then someone else would set the agenda with it. It had to be bigger to break through. We decided that in the end Cherie was going to have to go up on this, break through, let the public see it and judge for themselves. She was due to do an event [Partners in Excellence children's services awards] over at Millbank, with a ready-made audience, who would be sympathetic.

I called a few ministers to line them up to do supportive media on the back of a statement from Cherie. I think we all felt that though there was a risk in this, it was probably the best way to blow the storm out. Writing the statement, Fiona was sitting at my computer, while I dictated the draft, Tom chipping in, then we were joined by Peter M, Charlie F and Sally and we did a bit of writing by committee. The first draft was too long, but we had cut it by the time Cherie came down. She was a lot calmer than yesterday, though she and I were still finding it hard to engage. I gave her the draft and she had a few minor changes which she explained to Peter M and I put them in. We suggested she did a read-through to ensure she was happy with it and also so she would be aware of the points where emotional intensity might take over. Peter M said she should pick out people in the audience, look in their eyes and speak to them direct. She looked at me and said 'I certainly don't want to look at him.'

We all said good luck and off they went. She looked very pale, said she was worried about crying and went upstairs to compose herself. It was a minuscule drive to Millbank, but Fiona called to say they got stuck in traffic. She got through the scrum, she read the statement pretty well, looked very emotional, pretty close to tears.[1] After the event everyone felt a lot better. TB had been with the Queen when she did it and they hadn't watched it. He caught it on the news later and said he was really proud of the way she stood up to it. He really felt there was an opportunity to go for the *Mail* now, and to a lesser extent the *Mirror*, because there would be a market in the rest of the media to do so. He was finally angry about the state of the media and realised there was no way papers like the *Mail* were going to be anything other than hostile. TB did for once thank us for what we had done for him. As Peter M said, he had a real fright and we had to make sure he did not go back, and that Cherie didn't either. The news ran fine, and the centre of gravity of the story had moved, so that it now just looked like journalists with an agenda rather than

[1] Cherie Blair said 'My immediate instinct when faced with the questions from the *Mail on Sunday* ten days ago was to protect my family's privacy, and particularly my son in his first term at university, living away from home . . . I am sorry if I have embarrassed anyone, but the people who know me well know that I would never want to harm anyone, least of all Tony or the children or the Labour government.'

genuine important questions that needed to be answered. Everyone agreed today had just about paid off. The old team had got together and done it again, but it had been a very tough few days and the press would be reluctant to let go of it entirely.

Wednesday, December 11

The papers were much better, the *Mirror* the only really vicious one. Margaret Beckett went for the press in general and was wonderfully dismissive of [BBC *Today* programme presenter John] Humphrys. TB much happier. We had to decide whether to do a doorstep or wait for PMQs. We agreed he should do a doorstep, support CB, attack 'parts of the press' and say there were more important things to focus on. We were all feeling a bit battered but in stronger shape and there was definitely an appetite among some of the media to go for the *Mail*.

Then a meeting with TB, GH, CDS and C. C and David Manning were just back from the US and they reported the mood there was far tougher. They felt Saddam was just messing about and that Blix was hopeless and too soft. There was a hilarious headline in the *Süddeutsche Zeitung*: 'Rumsfeld promises patience as Blair threatens war'. We went over the various military options. It would be possible to do something fairly quickly but TB didn't believe GWB wanted 'an ugly start'. I presented my idea of a strategy document to clear objectives which they agreed, but later Jack and GH put out some signs against it. Geoff was very much on the Rumsfeld end of the market at the moment. CDS was a bit more engaged. David felt the US were in a very different position.

The news was still leading on CB but it had a very day-after feel to it. Fiona was in touch with Carole who claimed she was easing Foster out. TB's doorstep was running big. Then a meeting with Peter M and Peter H. Peter M felt TB would learn from this, that he had had a genuine scare. Fiona and I headed up for dinner with TB and CB and the Yellands [*Sun* editor David and wife Tania]. We had a nice enough time, mainly chit-chat, but I'd have preferred to have been at home with the kids. It was pretty clear there was no real change at the *Sun* re the euro. But Yelland was still broadly supportive, clearly liked them both personally. TB was out hard on Iraq/WMD. The other big story today was Yemen and Korea exporting WMD materials. Later I discussed with TB whether I needed to go to Denmark [EU summit]. Part of me wanted to, but a larger part didn't. A lot did depend on whether TB and CB really were going to learn from all this. The PLP had been terrific in the main. The *Mail* and the *Mirror* had been vile but some of the others pretty reasonable.

Thursday, December 12

If we thought it was all going away, we were wrong. Radio 4 was leading on a *Scotsman* story that CB had been more involved than admitted before in the Foster case, with lots of detail based on a fax that he had. It was running wild again. Tom [Kelly] called and we agreed we needed a line very quickly. Tom spoke to CB, FM spoke to Carole. Both said it was Foster who faxed pages to CB's flat at Carole's request, but with the current microscope on it, it was going to be difficult to explain as innocent. Really grim again. I ran in and did a quick conference call, including with TB. There was so much in the story that was wrong that we ought to be able to explain it away quite quickly. But the problem was because of recent events, the media had an excuse constantly to say our word could not be trusted. Very difficult to deal with. On the call, TB said that CB, who was due to leave for Warsaw at 9, was adamant she never saw these papers or Foster. Godric and I went up to see TB. Godric was confident these issues could be explained, but it was like there was an equivalence, a moral equivalence, between us and Foster. TB was getting exasperated. He looked tired and grey and could not work out where it would end. Fiona was talking to Carole, saying she needed to put out a statement, which she did, saying that she had initiated this, Cherie did nothing wrong and she was sorry. I was worried it was all getting to TB again. He was desperate to get closure on it.

In the margins of Cabinet I was trying to persuade Jack and Geoff of the need for a campaign objectives document as an important piece of strategy if and when things happened. Cabinet was mainly fire, and Turkey [US support for Turkey to join the EU]. TB thanked colleagues for their support. Clare for once shipped in with something supportive and sympathetic, said the whole thing must have been horrible for him and Cherie. The Turkey discussion was interesting and important and I wrote a script for GS to try to get it up at the 11. But he had yet another pretty torrid briefing and he and Tom were pretty pissed off about the whole thing. I did a fresh statement for him for the four o'clock, to try and shut it down, but it was probably too aggressive, and after a conference call with TB and Peter M, I toned it down. TB felt Cabinet had been supportive but jittery. He was looking wan.

TB popped in a couple of times, pleased when Foster's solicitor backed up our story. It was now beginning to feed into broader questions. Philip did groups later and said the link was lack of trust in institutions that were supposed to work. It hit authority to govern. Peter M sent over a note saying we needed these three things: 1. us clearly focused on real issues; 2. the sense of a media vendetta; 3. Carole had to dump Foster otherwise we were linked in through her to a conman.

Charlie [Falconer] came over and he and I went through it again from square one trying to work out a way through. The *Scotsman* story was pretty comprehensively knocked down but they were all still going with it and the *Sun* tape wasn't as exciting as it first seemed. TB did a brief doorstep in Copenhagen, and he looked pretty rough. I went to Rupert Murdoch's party, nice enough do, usual News International lot plus the likes of [Sir] Alan Sugar [businessman], [Paul] Dacre, Victor Blank. Dacre was at one point talking to IDS and I walked by and said to Iain 'How nice to see you talking to your leader.' Philip called and said that despite the *Sun*, the bulletins had been dire and it had definitely broken through to the public. What a fucking nightmare.

Friday, December 13

The *Sun* tapes story helped on one level in that it put more of the focus on Foster. The BBC led on Foster saying that Carole covered up for CB. The whole thing was absolutely ghastly. Andrew Neil [editor-in-chief, the *Scotsman*] was on the *Today* programme at 8.10 blathering away rubbish about Watergate. The frenzy was still raging, but both Tom in Denmark and Godric here were saying very little. I was exhausted and fed up with the whole thing. The *Mirror* was saying I was increasingly demented. I agreed with Tom and Godric we should not defend the *Sun* over its story but simply emphasise this was a story about a conman. I finished the Syria article we were doing to set up President [Bashar al-] Assad's visit. I went home early and was at the school when it came out that Foster was planning to make a statement on Monday.

I said to TB that we had to work out the worst possible stories that Foster could come out with. So long as there was that link to him through Carole, there was damage being done because we were being asked to defend the indefensible. Turkey and accession was the big issue for the meeting in Copenhagen and it was resolved OK for us, though the Turks weren't terribly happy.[1]

[1] It was resolved in Copenhagen that if political criteria were met two years later, negotiations for Turkey to join the European Union could begin 'without delay'.

December '02: AC, Duncan Smith, Dacre at Murdoch party

Saturday, December 14

For the sixteenth day running, most of my time was taken up with Foster and Caplin. Peter M called, very Peterish, pretending nothing much was going on, asked how I was. Spitting tacks, I said. 'Do you like anyone?' he asked. I said Rory, Calum and Grace, and Fiona when she's not disagreeing with me. The rest can fuck off. TB called as I was out on a run, and said that we just had to shut it down, not answer any more questions, and tough it out, I said something that made both of us snap. I was at the top of Golders Hill, had just got my breath back and said to him the real problem was that whether you like it or not, you are linked to a conman. He said I resent that. 'You are. You're married to a woman who is determined to protect and keep a woman who is in love with a conman so you are linked to a conman.' He shouted at me down the line 'I am not linked to a conman.' You are, and until Cherie dumps Carole or Carole dumps Foster, or preferably both, that's the way it is. And every day it's like that it hits your authority more, both with the rest of the government and with the public.

TB was having none of it. 'We have a fundamental disagreement. You think Cherie has done something monstrous and I don't. You think Carole is monstrous, and I don't.' I said there was a difference between monstrous and wrong. 'Well, I disagree. She is not a bad person and I'm not going to dump on people just because the press tell me to.' I said it was time to do the right thing despite the press, not the wrong thing because of stubbornness about the press. 'Well, if you're going to take that attitude, we have a problem.' I agreed, and said I wasn't going to defend Carole or anything to do with her. 'Fine, don't then. Just say nothing about it.' Fine, I said, but if this goes on much longer I'm off, out of here, goodbye. There is only so much of this shit I'm prepared to deal with. 'Well that is hardly the best attitude at a time like this.' He then went into a spiel that our opponents were always trying to divide us, we had to stick together, that this would blow over soon and we would be back on a proper agenda again. It was a very difficult conversation, among the bloodiest we had had and devoid of the humour that usually laced difficult conversations between us. I was basically saying I felt their judgement on Carole was terrible.

TB called later and we had another half-hour on the phone, this time a lot more friendly. I explained that one of the building workers we had in recently had said 'Mr and Mrs B were floating off to a different world.' He said 'Look, I know how difficult this is for everyone, but in the end we have to hold together and get through it. We've actually done nothing wrong other than live in a country with a totally insane media. Without the media we have this would not be the madness it is, and we cannot let them drive us apart.' I said I agreed, but he knew I needed to let off steam now and then, and also we really did need to rethink his modus operandi. PG spoke to TB, told him the public was bemused and not really giving us the benefit of the doubt. Sunday paper write-throughs were OK-ish, but the whole impression left was of a total mess, not at all pretty.

Sunday, December 15

Neither of us spoke to TB or CB today. We had both had enough of dealing with it, and they had probably had enough of hearing our complaints about lifestyle and out-of-touchness. We went out for dinner with Philip and Gail. Philip was very down about things while I was just plain angry. He felt there was a problem of trust anyway and this made it worse. Even though the press was vile and ridiculous, people felt there was something in it all.

Monday, December 16

I felt a lot better running in. Foster fairly low-key. The *Mail* ran a story that TB called Carole's mum from Copenhagen. There were pictures in several of the papers of Foster driving Carole, her filming the media. Bits and pieces about me, generally negative of course, and lots about CB's judgement. The feeling was the heat was going out of it though. Assad's visit and Iraq were the main focus of the day. We were in an OK position on the Blix dossier but it was going to get more difficult. Good piece from Phil Stephens [*FT*] on the press destroying the political discourse.

The mood at TB's office meeting was a bit muted. Sally told him that people felt let down. We were going over his weekend note on public services and Iraq. You had to hand it to him, that even on weekends as bad as the one he must have had, he still found the time to set out the forward plan and the arguments on the public services. I felt on Iraq we ought to have a slightly different line to the US, not become an extension of them. TB wanted me to work more on Iraq, possibly go to the US. He spoke to Bush re the UN process. The Americans clearly felt Blix was a problem, his dossier was poor.

TB had a private chat with Assad and agreed lines on suicide bombers/Israel. The lunch was OK if a bit dull and the communications minister [Bashir al-Munajid] gave us a long lecture about their different IT systems. Assad was very odd-looking, tall but with quite a weak chin. TB was pushing on Iraq, making clear that if the US went for it, they wouldn't stop until the regime fell, also saying it was clear to us that Iraq was concealing and not being open. He said that David Manning was in constant touch with Condi Rice, 'who is Bush's American adviser'. 'As opposed to his French adviser . . .' I whispered to Jonathan. Assad said they believed any US attack in that region would strengthen the country under attack. He said a lot of people were against Saddam in Iraq, but all of them were against the USA. Jack said that it was 'five to midnight' and both of them were pretty clear about how serious Bush was about it. TB said Bush understood better than they thought about the impact on the Arab and Muslim world. Leo came in, which had the usual effect of warming things up and Assad was clearly up for a rather more friendly press conference than the last one [October 31, 2001]. It was actually a pretty good event. TB saw them off and then left for the House.

Foster had done his statement, said he was going to write an autobiography, had a bit of a go at me. We decided just to ignore it. Later TB called me in for a one-on-one chat. We gave each other the eye and he asked me what the problem was. I said I felt there was a reality problem. We had to change ways out of this. He said he didn't believe the damage was long term, that it would blow over and we would get back to a proper agenda soon. I said I know, but I sometimes worried that we didn't do enough to counter the out-of-touch problems. He was clearly angry I had been dumping on Carole and by implication CB in the press. 'Your great strength is that you feel things deeply and you think things clearly. You are the Roy Keane of the operation, but like him you sometimes stamp people on the head without meaning to. That's how Carole and her mum have felt and they are not like us, they are not used to it. I know that you and Fiona basically just want to protect the show. But you can come over as being unbelievably hard, Cherie needs support. She will listen to you and Fiona more than anyone, but only if she feels you are being supportive.' I said I never felt that he did not appreciate what I did for him and I sometimes felt Cherie should be far more appreciative of what Fiona does for her, that it's hard to feel warm towards someone you think is taking you for granted. As over the weekend, it was pretty frank stuff. He said he knew that if Carole stayed with Foster, they could have nothing to do with her. Also, even if she dumps him, he has to be more careful. 'I have been reckless and foolish and paid a price. So has Cherie, who had a terrible shock. But she is a good person not a bad person. And you have to take us as we are, strengths as well as weaknesses.'

I said what had been frustrating was that Fiona and I felt so clearly we were giving the right advice in these lifestyle issues and yet we were really just seen as irritants banging them round the head. Now we felt vindicated, but no satisfaction in that in any way, because we also felt let down. And there was a lot of that feeling round the building which he had to put right. He said we all had to learn from it, and never forget that the only people who want us divided are our opponents. The Tories, because they fear our professionalism. The press, and also GB who would love it if you and I were at odds, so we have to hang together.

Tuesday, December 17

Foster was down the agenda and we were getting back to proper domestic issues, e.g. pensions, GPs, transport plan update. Good press on Bain,[1] very good press for the Assad visit. So things felt better though we were all still bruised. We had the office strategy meeting up in the flat. TB said we had to have a strategy for rebuilding trust and connection. I said another foreign holiday is not the best start. Even though they were paying, it would not be billed like that. TB wanted the focus for the next stage on antisocial behaviour and public services, but the reality was Iraq and terrorism plus Northern Ireland meant we faced a tricky New Year. I felt we may as well play into that reality and put together a plan for TB on Iraq communications. It was the usual end-of-year feeling. What do we do for the New Year message, what have we got planned when we get back, who's around over the holiday, everyone feeling tired.

The MoD were doing a background briefing on Iraq military build-up which was going to move things up a gear. The American conference call was pretty hopeless, not very strategic if the big players were on it and not at all strategic if they weren't. TB was looking pretty grim. During the meeting, Peter M slipped me a note to say I had to be more supportive, that I had an ability to make him feel very low if I wasn't. Yet when Fiona called Cherie for a chat, she was curt and dismissive, even rude. TB had another bad meeting with GB who was arguing for a two-year delay on university [top-up] fees. NMD was running quite big, the US making the formal offer for the upgrading of [RAF] Fylingdales [radar base], and the PLP were a bit jumpy. JP came in for a chat, said that TB was too prone to letting

[1] The final Bain Inquiry report recommended an eleven per cent pay rise over two years, compared to the FBU's demand for a forty per cent immediate increase. It also proposed replacing an automatic wage mechanism, dictating the level of pay, with a new formula which would simply inform the bargaining process.

guilt run his whole life, that he was maybe too tolerant of some of the things CB did because of it, same as he was too tolerant with GB some of the time. He also feared TB and CB were both a bit too much into the celebrity bollocks and GB would use that against them.

Wednesday, December 18

The Cherie stuff was almost totally gone now, but Hilary [Coffman] was still pursuing the questions of the clothes. She called CB to discuss it, and CB said, to Hilary's utter amazement, 'Why don't you pop up, Carole's here, and you can talk to her direct.' This after TB assured us she would not be going back in. Of course Cherie was getting lots of letters of support and this made her feel that we had overreacted. She was still not speaking to me, nor I to her, every effort having been rebuffed, and I was making no secret of the fact I found the whole thing absurd. It seemed TB didn't know that she [Caplin] was coming in.

The MoD's briefing on Iraq had gone big and [Sir David] Omand was doing a terrorism briefing, with all manner of dire warnings, which would be leading the bulletins by the end of the day. At the political strategy meeting, David Triesman [Labour Party general secretary] told me that Piers Morgan had said to him 'The country is being run by two couples and I'm at war with both of them.' Spencer Livermore made the ludicrous statement that tax rises would be popular. Philip put his finger on the problem when he said we had two political strategies running against each other, opportunity versus security, and we should be wedding them together. But GB really saw his job almost as frustrating our political strategy. We had a whole succession of non-arguments. It was perfectly possible to link jobs and education to a strong society founded on values and respect, but we went round in circles on it.

I left for Grace's school concert then back home to work on the New Year message and the Iraq note to TB. The reports of chaos out of the various briefings were soon coming in. Geoff H having a statement on Iraq forced out of him, Jack S conflicting with TB on Iraq dossier response, plus the Omand briefing. As Mike White [*Guardian*] said, if that was all meant to calm things down, it didn't exactly work.

Thursday, December 19

I started the day in a rage because Omand's briefing was unplanned big news and [John] Williams' [FCO] briefings re Blix were a hardening of our position. Both had almost caught out TB in the House yesterday, so I did a major bollocking at the 8.30 meeting, said there was no point trying to co-ordinate if we had this kind of thing. Then to see TB re the *Guardian* interview where we wanted to get up the New Labour message again. He was OK, but not on sparkling form, as Polly Toynbee [journalist] noted. Interesting on Rowan Williams [Archbishop of Canterbury], who TB felt was intelligent Old Labour.

I chatted to Milburn and Charles Clarke who were both sympathetic but also said it was a real problem if I went offside on anything. TB mentioned to me later that three or four ministers had raised me with him, not in a critical way, just a bit worried. He asked 'Have you reassessed recent events?' 'What do you mean?' 'I think you slipped the reservation for a while. You went for Cherie and Carole. I know the reasons, you wanted to protect your people, but you should have discussed it with me. If this kind of thing ever happens again, we just have to have it out.' I said a lot of people, and Fiona and I are among them, felt we make pretty big sacrifices and get taken for granted. There is a lot of give and not much take. I didn't mind so much with him, because I knew the pressures he was under and basically supported what he was trying to do. But he always knew that I was not prepared to defend what I thought was indefensible. True, he said, but in the end we could discuss these things. But if he decided something, he had to be able to make those decisions from a position of leadership and we couldn't have a situation where his senior press person was briefing against his wife. He thought it all led to the impression that we had lost the plot. I held my own, saying the people around him weren't machines and he and CB had to take into account what they thought. They had asked an awful lot in the last few days, of Tom, Godric, Hilary. He said they were fine. I said not so. They might not say to you what they say to me. They are not happy about it. He disagreed, but I knew. I said I really felt they had to change their ways.

He said I was such a big personality and so forceful that if I was pissed off, everyone felt it and it dragged the whole show down. It's why he made the Roy Keane analogy. He said you lead by example which is great, but if you're pissed off, everyone around you gets pissed off. You wear your heart on your sleeve and give out very powerful vibes, and I'm just saying that in the last few days, that's not been a good thing. Now we have to put it together. I think both of us felt better afterwards but I really felt it was ridiculous that Cherie was still seeing Carole, and not protecting herself sufficiently on the freebie front. Milburn was sympathetic, said hold firm. Charles said you have to let Cherie be herself, whatever that is.

Cabinet was low-key, fire, Iraq, Clare as ever pointing up the need for more discussion. Jack on Blix. He was going to the UNSC today and we and the Americans were both going to be saying the process was holed. Bad political strategy meeting with John Reid, Douglas etc. at which TB said he felt we lacked real strategy at the moment and needed new structures. I said I felt he was looking for new structures as a way of avoiding dealing with the personal/political problem, namely that the TB/GB schism was growing. Things had got worse without Ed Miliband there.[1] Not only were we not on the same pitch most of the time now, but if we ever tried to get on the same pitch, one side would pretend that in fact we were apart. Douglas felt polling was the way to engage GB and then get some kind of agreed plan out of that. John R and Douglas both called me afterwards to say how grim they thought things were. John was beginning to realise what a difficult job it was. TB called on his way north and I briefed him re Blix who had been pretty negative on the Iraqi declaration.[2] Jack called again to agree a line and we agreed he should do a doorstep outside Number 10. He did fine. There was no doubt the mood music was clearly building up to war.

Friday, December 20

Guardian interview OK. Got TB up on a clip on Iraq when he was in Hartlepool. He was worried about Blix's comments that we had not been helping enough with the intelligence. Cleared my desk, shifted loads of paper, then left for the *What the Papers Say* awards at the Café Royal. I was sitting next to Jane Moore [*Sun* columnist], who said didn't I find it irritating that they kept panning the cameras on us? Some of the awards were ridiculous and I said to [Alan] Rusbridger [*Guardian* editor] 'Your profession is in trouble.' The 3am Girls [*Mirror* gossip writers] – columnists of the year. Picture of the year was a fake. The Paul Burrell reporter [Steve Dennis, *Mirror*] got reporter of the year. Dacre won 'scoop of the year' for 'Cheriegate' and he very sarcastically thanked me for all my attacks on the *Mail*. I told him I had only just started. I did manage to get a few marathon cheques, including from Annie Robinson [broadcaster, former *Mirror* colleague]. TB's interview for Forces Radio was now leading the bulletins as a warning of war.

Saturday, December 21

Eleven-mile run, averaging eight minutes ten. Drove down to Gillingham vs Burnley, lost 4–2. The big US build-up re Iraq was going

[1] Miliband had taken a year-long sabbatical to teach at Harvard University.
[2] A 12,000-page weapons inventory given to the United Nations by Iraq maintained it had no nuclear, chemical or biological weapons programmes.

on. The Egyptian press printed details of TB/CB's holiday [in Sharm el Sheikh] and the security committee decided to meet to reconsider. I felt the best outcome would be if they didn't go.

Sunday, December 22

The *Observer* splashed on TB saying no to the Olympic bid, which immediately became a broadcast story. We put out a line making clear no decision had been taken. We got Dick Caborn [sports minister] on to Radio 5. In saying he had barely discussed it with TB he was trying to say no decision taken, but it was taken as a signal of lack of interest and commitment. Sarah Hunter [policy adviser] had done a good note on it which made clear it was potentially winnable, though we lacked Brits in the right places on a lot of the international sporting bodies.

Monday, December 23

TB called and signed off the New Year message. I went into the office, cleared my desk and brought home a stack of paperwork. Patrick Diamond [policy adviser] had done a good paper on New Labour renewal. Stephen Wall had done a big note on Europe, which suggested to me we had far more problems than previously imagined. I felt in general that we were not in great shape. Iraq was building up pretty big now. The Iraqis shot down a US drone. There was no way they were not going to go to war now.

Friday, December 27

Thirty-five minutes on the treadmill, pretty fast. Kamal [Ahmed, *Observer* political editor] and a photographer here for four hours to do a piece on me doing the marathon. Saw an osteopath who said I had one leg slightly longer than the other and my right knee was inflamed. I had a really vivid dream about Dad dying. Mum and I were out in the field and then we went back into the house and Dad came through from his bedroom, sat down and said 'I'm absolutely buggered. I'm not sure I can go on much longer like this.' Small trickles of sweat and blood started to come down his face and I just hugged him and said he was a great father and I hoped I was too. Mum was crying.

Saturday, December 28

Took Grace to Brighton for her first solo Burnley match. On the way down, a call saying Clare [Short] had done Radio 5 and said it would be deplorable if England played [a cricket World Cup match] in

Zimbabwe, how she intended to press Tessa [Jowell], etc. More evidence of how Clare just stirs. It was a difficult line to tread this one, making clear what we would do if it was our decision, but also making clear that it's not. The difference between having a view and being able to make a decision. Jack S and Tessa both livid at Clare and her usual moral-conscience stuff, as though she was the only one who had one and the only one who says what she thinks. Tessa said we could all go out and say things to please certain constituencies but we don't because that is the deal on which a system of collective responsibility works. It was bloody cold. We went 2–0 up, then conceded two in the final two minutes. Dreadful.

To the Milibands for dinner. David had quite a detached view these days, felt the government was losing its way. We were both very frank about recent events and our belief that we were talking about rather ridiculous people who had somewhat left the planet. Fiona was feeling it much more than me at the moment and I was also finding it hard to get up much enthusiasm. And TB/GB was a total, probably irredeemable fault line. In the *Sunday Times*, the Olympic bid was the latest issue seemingly to be the focus of TB/GB division. It was all dispute and difficulty by proxy.

Sunday, December 29

Conference call with Jack Straw, Mike O'Brien [FCO minister] et cetera re Zimbabwe and we agreed that Mike should do clips making clear that the decision was for the cricket authorities but if it WAS our decision we would say do not go. It was a tricky one because on the one hand there was a clear political message to send, and on the other it wasn't the job of government to say where sportsmen should and shouldn't play. The problem with a compromise position was that it tended to land you in the worst of all worlds. Clare and now Nasser Hussain [England cricket captain] were saying that we should set up a body to decide on these things. IDS wrote to TB urging him to 'clear up the confusion' and take a lead. Jack though was very unkeen to move the line. I reminded him that the last time he, Mike, Tom Kelly and I were on a conference call it was followed not long after by a ministerial resignation, namely Peter's. Tessa was seething at Clare, felt she was just stirring on this and she intended to write to her rather than speak to her, so that the argument could not be misconstrued and spun against her. TB called for a general chat which seemed mainly to consist of telling me what a marvellous time he was having. 'How lovely,' Fiona said when I told her.

Monday, December 30

Zimbabwe ticking over. Finished the New Year message. It was pouring all day so Calum's tennis was off again. Instead, I went for a long run, 8.7 miles in one hour ten. The *Sun* had a two-page spread in 'Bizarre' [gossip column] on me allegedly dumping Britney [Spears, American singer] for Ms Dynamite [award-winning British singer], seemingly based on the fact that I listened to Ms Dynamite when running, though in actual fact I was mainly listening to the Lighthouse Family [British musical duo] on long runs. Godric was doing the honours briefing, plus Zimbabwe. Went to see the new James Bond film [*Die Another Day*], which was total crap.

Tuesday, December 31

Agreed with Anne Shevas [chief press officer] to put out the New Year's message for tomorrow. But no doubt that I was letting my own mood affect it and the overall impact was pretty downcast and gloomy.[1] Fiona and I both agreed we could not recall feeling less like the New Year mood you were meant to feel. It was largely because we knew that TB and CB had to change but saw little sign of it happening, and had very little belief that it would.

[1] In the message, Blair said 'With the world economy, Iraq, terrorism, the Middle East, Africa, the environment, Europe, the euro, this is a big and difficult agenda . . . the world economy will intimately be affected by world events on peace and security, for good or ill.' The *Daily Telegraph* described Blair's words as 'unusually grim and distinctly unfestive'.

Wednesday, January 1, 2003

Very quiet on the work front. The New Year's message got big coverage, but there was no doubt I had allowed my own somewhat gloomy view of events to colour things, so the coverage was pretty much on the 'we're all doomed' lines. As Mike White said when he called me to discuss it, 'Don't jump.' Fiona and I were both pretty down about the thought of going back. Partly it was the weather, partly the thought that actually the tone of the message was pretty much where things were, and also the fact that TB, whenever he phoned, went on and on about what a marvellous time they were having, and how energising it all was for him. I said there was a time when I felt natural warmth to his irrepressible enthusiasm and zest for life. But it can sound unbelievably irritating and selfish when he's basking in sunshine and we are swimming through floods.

He was mulling over the various pressing problems and they were pretty much the same as a year ago, if a bit more advanced and a bit more difficult in some cases – US–UK, terrorism, MEPP, Northern Ireland, public services, Europe and the euro. We had to get through it as best we could, but within that list there were a lot of complicated and interacting problems. I felt out of sorts personally, not motivated by much other than the kids and the marathon training. I had stopped doing the weekly strategy notes, and in trying to analyse why, I feared it was largely because he and I were in slightly different strategic positions. I felt we needed to be more on reconnection with party and public whereas he was still pressing on all the controversial buttons, often with right-wing positions flying from them.

Thursday, January 2

Had a nice enough day for Fiona's birthday, got her plenty of decent presents, out for dinner and also had an OK session at the track. All quiet on the work front.

Friday, January 3

David Davies came round to sound me out about the FA chief executive job. He wanted to mark my card about the politics, and to go over why he thought it was a good idea for me. It was clearly a highly political organisation and very difficult to reform, but he felt even the non-modernisers would be impressed and flattered if I was interested and he reckoned I had a good chance of getting it. He felt the job would be as big as I wanted it to be, and that above all the organisation needed greater focus and clarity about priorities. It sounded tough but Fiona was very keen and at the end of a few hours mulling it over, I was quite keen as well. I liked David who was pretty straightforward, and a very good ally. I then headed north with Calum and on the way fixed David Hill [former Labour Party chief spokesman], Howell James [former political secretary to John Major] and Richard Tait for the GICS review team. Dad was a bit worse but still hanging in there. I went to the local gym, did seven miles on the treadmill.

Saturday, January 4

TB back, called on his way from the airport to Number 10, said he was really fit, full of energy and ready for the fray. He said he was clearer than ever about all the problems but we just had to hold firm. On GB, he said he had a plan. I asked if it was cautious or radical. Radical, he said. He added there was no point being in the job if you couldn't do it properly, so the situation has to be resolved. On the euro he was still of the view we should try to go for it. He was chirpy enough but keen for a realistic take on our problems.

I felt we had slipped back on Iraq, slipped back on Europe, enjoyed no real breakthrough on public services, crime and fear of crime were a bigger problem than the figures suggested, the GB relationship had become a fault line, and I felt we needed a fresh and discrete TB strategy too. Overall, I said I didn't think we were in great shape. Also, though it could be rectified, I felt our own relationship had changed as a result of the CB/Foster saga. Most of the time, I couldn't give a fuck when the press turned on me, but I really resented it over shit like that. Calum and I left for Grimsby vs Burnley. We were two up, then blew it and drew. It was freezing cold. Drove back, very little traffic from the press, the Sundays were full of crap, mainly on gun crime.

Sunday, January 5

Alice Miles called from *The Times* to say that [former Labour Cabinet minister and co-founder of the Social Democratic Party] Roy Jenkins' death had just been announced and would TB do a piece? I said maybe, but later spoke to TB and said I felt not, but maybe he should just do his own short tribute. He sent it through. It was very warm and personal, I felt the combined effect was over the top. I called TB to say so and he agreed to take out 'mentor' and instead talk of his support. I also pointed out he should at least say he disagreed with the formation of the [breakaway] SDP. 'But won't people think I'm just doing that for the Labour Party?' I said 'You are the leader of the Labour Party, and they did try to kill us.' 'Yes, but he was right in a lot of what he said, do you want me to say that?' Laughter. I said no. 'Surely the party is used to my little eccentricities by now.' Yes, but one day they might decide you have gone too far and rise up against you. I just feel it's a bit over the top. He said I thought you would but OK, take out the word mentor and put in something about me disagreeing with the formation of the SDP, but I do think he was a great figure and I am very sad about his death. At least he took the changes and agreed not to do *The Times*.

Andrew Adonis [Jenkins' biographer] called to get the go-ahead to do his own big tribute piece to Roy. *The World this Weekend* had yet another discussion of the New Year's message, which must be the first time it was still being covered five days after it was published. Mike Granatt [head of GICS] called from Scotland Yard to say there had been some arrests, possibly related to a ricin factory.[1] Out for dinner with the Goulds. Philip really not keen on the FA idea. Gail thought it was a useful bridge to a new phase. All of us felt that TB was not in a strong position and really needed a new approach. Philip felt I should make clear I would only stay if there was a real onslaught on spin, a real effort at rebuilding trust, a new modus operandi and with him leading by example, e.g. on the lifestyle issues. The only other people I discussed the FA with were Godric, who felt it would be a good way out, and Alex F, who was also very positive, felt it

[1] Six men were arrested after a police raid in Wood Green, North London, on suspicion of manufacturing ricin with the intention of attacking the London Underground by releasing the poison in airborne form. The only subsequent conviction was of Kamel Bourgass, who had already been sentenced to life imprisonment for the murder of Stephen Oake.

was a real job that I could do well. He felt [Adam] Crozier made too many enemies because he was too much of an empire builder. They were both very positive about the whole thing, and I respected their opinions. But both Fiona and I felt guilty at the idea of leaving just at a point when we knew things were going to get very rough.

Monday, January 6

Papers full of gun crime and Roy Jenkins. We got a bit of stick for the focus on crime looking like a response to recent events, which it wasn't. Derry was on the morning media re courts and sentencing, and Tam Dalyell [senior Labour backbencher] was on re Iraq. I called Jack S to discuss the best way to handle it. He was pretty much echoing [Colin] Powell's line that it was 40–60 [more likely that there would be a war]. He had called me a couple of times over the holiday and emphasised the importance of TB not positioning himself so that no war looked like failure. TB was pretty sure that there would be a war, or that in any event Saddam Hussein would go, and war remained the likeliest if not only way of that coming about. I chatted to him first thing, and then did a conference call to agree we would publish the Iraq policy objectives paper. John Williams rightly said it would get lost with all else that was going on but I felt it was important to have it out there at the moment. These strategy papers were as much about internal understanding as publicity.

TB's morning meeting with the office went on for two and a half hours as we worked our way through the twenty-page note he had sent to us at the weekend. Much of it could have been written for any other year ahead – prioritising public services, Europe, crime and asylum, delivery and trying to get the Civil Service to modernise more, relations with GB and the lack of proper economic narrative. So it went on, and we all had our usual position, all a bit stuck in tramlines. TB was not for giving an inch to the party, wanted to be even more modernising than ever, at the cutting edge of reform. I said he didn't need to keep winning modernising spurs, and I was worried that whilst he was identified so personally with all the controversies, it was being put together against us as being right wing, and he had to be careful. On Iraq, pretty much everyone was emphasising how little support there was, how little understanding there was of a real threat, but he was in pretty defiant mood on that too, said the threat was real and people would come round.

Later he called me in, was very friendly, and said he just wanted to know how I was. I said fine, up to a point. 'But only up to a point?' he asked. Yes. I couldn't deny that I felt pretty ground down by things.

I asked what he was going to do about his 'friend next door'. 'I'm going to sack him. I've come to a settled view that he has to go. There was a time when I could make the case that the tension was creative. But it has reached the point where it is destructive and it can't go on. I'm not prepared to be in a position where I have got the job, but I am not allowed to do it properly. It could be that it ends up with me being toppled but I would rather that than this situation. I remain of the view that the party will not get rid of a leader if they think the leader is doing basically what the country wants and needs.' He seemed fairly set on it, but doing it would be harder than saying it. He was also keen for Ken Clarke to become Tory leader, feeling it would waken up our lot and also help the country on Europe. The general feeling was that IDS was fucked.

Then we had a meeting with the political team in the flat. Hilary [Armstrong] said that John Healey [economic secretary to the Treasury], Jon Cruddas [Labour MP, Blair's former deputy political secretary for union liaison] and others were really organising now over the 'elitism' issue and trying to get TB on the wrong side of the divide. She was very fretful on Iraq and hunting. TB seemed much more relaxed after his break but in a way that just added to the sense that he was slightly losing the plot. Sally said she would go bonkers if she heard him say one more time that he was clearer than ever. It was all a bit groundhog day. Later we had pretty lengthy discussions on his speech tomorrow to the FCO heads of mission conference, where he wanted to say we were a unifying force around our vision of the world and that we had to get influence with the US and use it to broaden out our agenda. I asked him if he genuinely thought that our role was to keep them on the straight and narrow. Too damn right, he said, but if we say that's our role, we lose any influence. He said he only wanted to make speeches that really made a point, which meant we could strip out a few in the forward Grid.

Tuesday, January 7

I ran in the long route with Hugh Jones [former international marathon runner and first British man to win the London Marathon] but I was struggling. TB called me up to the flat just before 8. He was worried about the Palestinian reform conference. The Israelis' response to the latest suicide bombing was to prevent the Palestinians from coming to the London conference, so the conference was effectively scuppered. He was not happy with Jack's saying the chances of war were now 40–60, thinking we should not get into that type of running commentary. And he was livid that Derry gave us a batch of dreadful headlines from his *Today* interview on how we would let burglars go free, just as Blunkett was up doing his tough anti-gun crime stuff. We were a bit ragged generally, and he intended to make clear to Cabinet we couldn't tolerate some of the looseness we had been enduring of late.

I had an Iraq strategy meeting, and took them through what TB had said in his note and we discussed how we needed to do more on WMD education, e.g. the dossier, the need to communicate more what was happening on concealment. We had a good discussion about the basic distilled message, namely that the reason Iraq WMD was so important and linked to terror was because one day terrorists would get them. Then the John Reid/AC party meeting. Greg Cook [Labour polling expert] said we were at our lowest lead since TB became party leader and moving down on all issues and attributes. People seemed a bit down, but both JR and I made the point that we were in a remarkable position for a third term midterm. We had been defying gravity for too long. Then a discussion on the Lib Dems. I felt we were missing tricks in not going for them hard enough. JR still felt it best to leave them alone.

A lot of the day was taken up with the ricin issue. Since the arrests on Saturday, lots of tests had proved negative but there had been a Cobra meeting this morning which was told ricin had been found in Wood Green. Mike Granatt came to see me to say they had agreed to do a joint Met/Department of Health briefing while DB wanted to do a written statement to the House. I was fine with that, provided it was mainly all operational, police security story with some health backup. That was all agreed, but Mike called back two hours later to say DB had really gone against the idea of a police press conference because he worried they always went over the top. Instead he had agreed a joint Blunkett/Milburn statement. I felt it set a bad precedent, that ministers would have to go up on every potential terrorist situation. I called Milburn who was fairly relaxed, but agreed that if ministers were to do it, it should be to the House, and backed me. DB agreed provided there was no massive briefing around it.

We sorted the final version which went out at 3.15. Once it was out there, it was pretty much an all-day news sponge, which massively ate into the coverage which had been planned for TB's speech. Perhaps that was no bad thing in view of the fact following our overnight briefing of the speech, the US Embassy came on, alarmed at the way it was being presented as us trying to get them to broaden their agenda. I spoke to David Davies, and said I didn't rule the FA job out. He felt there was a way of doing it quietly if I went for it, which I doubted. We had a PMQs meeting on tomorrow being the first occasion for an earlier time. TB said if we had a decent Opposition, they really ought to be able to land some blows tomorrow. He said I must not discuss what he had said re GB yesterday with anybody. 'It can only happen when the waters are calm and it's least expected, and it must be a totally ruthless operation.' Like me, he had been shocked yesterday by Hilary saying, in front of civil servants and others, that GB was openly organising, and naming some of the people doing it for him.

Wednesday, January 8

Ricin enormous coverage. Up to the flat for PMQs meeting at 8. The new time slot of noon would change the rhythm of the day. We were expecting them to go on crime/burglary and the differences between Jack S and Geoff Hoon on Iraq, which was indeed what IDS did, though he was pretty crap. TB was still in pretty much of a rage about Derry and the burglary stuff, much more relaxed re GH/JS. I drafted him a note pre Cabinet tomorrow, saying that he had to reset the basic discipline and order, that there had been far too much thinking aloud, far too many politicians as commentators, and that we had to make clear again that the price of the privilege of serving in Cabinet was collective responsibility.

I had little input into PMQs, apart from one line, namely that what was one hundred per cent certain was that Saddam would be disarmed, as a way of getting round the slight problem Jack had given us with the percentage game. I made clear to the morning meeting that TB was pissed off both at the initial 40–60, also at Geoff's reaction and we had to get basic discipline back. We went over for PMQs and he successfully got up the public spending/cuts dividing line, then back to Number 10 and an amazing snowfall. TB, David Manning, Jonathan, Matthew Rycroft [private secretary, foreign affairs], Sally and I met to discuss Iraq. David was back from Oman and said he felt we had to give the inspectors more time now, but the US were impatient, felt the UN worked too slowly. TB said that if Blix found nothing, and the UN gave no specific sanction, it was going to be very hard to do. David said the Americans were very keen for a visit by TB at the end of the month. TB knew how difficult this was all going to be and felt we had to be out there fairly soon making the case, that it was only a matter of time before al-Qaeda get their hands on WMD unless we show how serious we are at dealing with the WMD issue.

TB was clear it was the right thing to do, and was on pretty good form, but also accepted there was not much support. Philip said to me later that there was next to no support for the war and the domestic agenda was in poor shape too. I had a meeting with Charles Clarke re some of his trickier issues. On student finance, he was confident it could be sold as an opportunity measure and we could get it done fairly quickly. He said he had been round to see the whole Cabinet one by one and that he had a lot of support, e.g. from Jack, Blunkett, Andrew Smith [Work and Pensions Secretary], Tessa, most of the others. The problem would be JP, because of the process, and GB because of the politics. But Charles was very confident, both about the arguments and the process. He was clearly a lot happier than when party chairman. He was also up for telling the NUT [National Union of Teachers] that no minister would go to their conference because they were not serious and did not properly represent teachers. Piers Morgan was apparently on *The World at One* describing Saddam as 'a benign dictator'.

Thursday, January 9

Very snowy, very icy, so ran in slowly. Iraq was running big with Blix to do 'minor' UN reporting today. The *Mirror* splashed on 'What is the point of Jack Straw?' The *Express* had a scaled-down version of the same thing, claiming to have been told TB had said Jack was extremely stupid re the 60–40 remarks and had authorised the Geoff Hoon attack. Even though TB was indeed pissed off, he did no such thing. Later GH apologised to TB, said he had just lost concentration and made a mistake. It was relevant to the Cabinet discussion. TB made the point that we were in much more difficult waters and that our opponents were constantly on the lookout for differences between us. He did a very tame version of the note I put to him suggesting he really lay it on the line and impose basic discipline. Instead, he said that we were a very tight and disciplined unit, but some resented that and we had maybe eased up a bit and got a bit lax. JP was a bit tougher, said there was simply no room for Cabinet ministers going out and giving their personal opinions and streams of consciousness. JP was very firm and very supportive but I could tell from the look on some of their faces, that they felt damage was being done to TB's authority by the fact it had taken John really to hit the message.

Then on Iraq, TB said that with Jack away in Indonesia, there was not much point in a major discussion and we wait till next week, yet he then allowed a discussion in which Clare accused Geoff and the MoD of briefing against Jack. She said she wanted a discussion of the military options because she did not believe that UK forces were needed. Yes they are, said Geoff. Well I don't think so, she said. Again,

TB just smiled rather weakly at her. I said to him afterwards that he had been really weak in there today, and his supporters left very pissed off. He just shrugged and looked irritated.

TB then had a very difficult conversation with GB re student finance. Charles was successfully winning round the Cabinet but GB was opposed and ready to move against by saying it was elitist because potentially it would punish the poorest first. He was making clear that TB could just plough on if he wanted, but he was adamantly against it. Charles was all bouncy and convinced he had cracked it, not knowing the depth of GB's determination to stop it. GB's view was that there was no real crisis in university funding, that it was just a way of them getting more money, and we didn't really need this big reform. Cabinet also had a very testy discussion on the Lords, Robin pushing at the 'democratic' end of things, JP, JR and DB very much against major reform that included an all-elected second chamber. Blunkett said we were sleepwalking towards constitutional gridlock which would stop governments doing the things they were elected to do and the public would give up on politics.

JR said we were not sleepwalking, but heading to disaster with our eyes wide open. Bruce said the reform and the make-up of the Lords was irrelevant without reform of the procedures, for example with no guillotine they could really screw us up. But again TB was not really directing the discussion so all we got was a collection of very different opinions. GB said next to nothing and left with Clare. Then to a meeting on health communications. We still lacked a clear top-line message. I was moving towards a 'personal NHS', also saying the statistics were hopeless for communications, which had to be rooted in the personal experience of patients. Milburn took me aside at the end, said people were getting really fed up of TB's tolerance of Clare in Cabinet. He said it was like having a bag lady in there just speaking out on everything.

TB saw Adams and McGuinness pm, then C came in. He told us that the Brits got on with Blix pretty well and we were a good buffer for the US, who were much less subtle. Blix knew that he was being 'cat and moused' but he was not on a mission. He was sure Saddam was lying but still felt he had to establish that for himself. C felt we had a better chance of finding the breaches than the US. TB, half in jest, said 'My future is in your hands.' The nightmare scenario, or one of them, was that there was a discovery that was sufficient for the US but not for us. C said the other risk was that we found the evidence of the breach before the US were ready to go to war. C felt that if the inspectors had another month with genuine access, the picture would be pretty clear. We were now pushing the line that they needed time and space to do the job.

I had a meeting with the Al Jazeera general manager and news editor who were over visiting the BBC. It was an interesting discussion. They did not appear overly hostile, but they said we had to face up to the fact that none of our arguments were really getting through to the Arab world at all. We were helped a little by the current row between TB and Israel over the Palestinian conference, but we were kidding ourselves if we thought our arguments were getting through at all. They said Gerard Russell was good and popular, but that they wanted and needed more access to ministers and military. They had been turned down for a facility on the [HMS] *Ark Royal*, which I sorted for them. They said we were not the US, and we should establish our own space. But nobody believed Saddam had WMD, or that he had any link with al-Qaeda.

Friday, January 10

The *Observer* sent me the magazine piece on me doing the marathon and Fiona went absolutely mental because of the ironing board being in the picture. God knows what that's all about. Crime figures – dreadful coverage, and there were the beginnings of the notion in the media that TB would get so fed up he would go. He was certainly pretty fed up and I went up to the flat just after 8. Cherie was there, much friendlier than before they went away, and neither of us mentioned those events. TB felt we had to make real changes. Even in front of the others now, he was talking about 'major reconstruction of the government', which was clearly code for GB. He also felt quite a few permanent secretaries should go. I said I felt he underestimated the negative impact upon him in looking weak as he had yesterday. He felt the problem was that the government was not sufficiently New Labour. We had defeated the hard left, but the instinct of most of them was to settle for that, not go much further, go for consensus politics with internal vested interests. That wasn't good enough.

We had a meeting – him, me, Jonathan, Peter H, Sally, Hilary C and Fiona – specifically to discuss him and his profile. Yet another discussion about how we reconnect him with the public. This couldn't be about gimmicks, initiatives so-called, and all the rest of it. It was about endeavour, constantly speaking the language of people's lives, but also being seen to be in charge and being seen to be on their side. It was yet another circular conversation of the kind we had been having for years. I said the question people were beginning to ask was whether he could change and do the on-your-side stuff in a way that broke through. He said that the big decision was whether to make the changes that would allow us to go for broke, but the truth was we could just end up with the 'broke' bit. He felt GB's game plan was to make him feel so miserable and paralysed that he would quit while he was ahead. But he was too strong to get rid of him right now.

Saturday, January 11

11.19 miles in. Ran round Islington, the Barbican, Embankment area and back up through town. There was a real sense of problems building up. Iraq obviously, with the party going offside, [anti-war] demo again, and the papers really hitting us on crime and public services. The *Telegraph* had a page 1 story headlined 'Campbell more spinned against than spinning', which spoke of a rift with TB and had a fair bit of accurate stuff, for example the row over the New Year's message, some of the background on Cherie/Foster. At first flush, it looked like Peter M's work, and there was a hint of that in their editorial looking forward to my leaving. Peter called later and said he thought it was probably Sally. My hunch was that it came from the Treasury. Peter M called and said I had to make it absolutely clear I was there for the long haul. TB called around 9 and said it was the usual lightning-conductor crap and nothing to worry about. We were going through a difficult period and it was far better we were seen talking about serious issues than the usual personality crap. We went over an outline script for Monday's press conference on the line of holding firm and sticking to our course. I was worried Clare would go off on one tomorrow so did a conference call with her and JR to go through the papers later. TB called again after returning from Germany [a private visit to Hanover]. He said the dinner with Schroeder had gone fine, but as the pressure grew on Iraq, the differences became more obvious.

Sunday, January 12

IDS was on *Frost* going for TB for 'wobbling' on Iraq. TB felt we just had to hold firm and take the difficult decisions needed. He said the Sunday papers were now beyond parody, not really worth bothering with, but that there would be a reckoning upwards before too long. We needed to decide whether to do a WMD dossier. He was in two minds about it, and so was I. John Scarlett told me on Friday he was keen, but the FCO less so because it gave rise to other difficult questions. TB was still going on about Derry's interview and said that of course, the liberal press would back him and therefore Derry would think even more he had done the right thing, when in fact he had given us a big problem with the public. He felt that on crime, Derry was not so much New Labour as Old Liberal. The *Independent* had a big story, including on page 1, on alleged concerns in the Civil Service about my diaries. The only person who had ever raised any such concern was GB, both with TB and Turnbull.

Monday, January 13

Clare Short's interview went pretty big as a combination of division/warning to TB and the backdrop to the press conference was clearly Iraq. The tough question was whether there could be any military action without a second UNSCR. It was going to be difficult, lots of party in turmoil, diving polls stuff. The latest flurry about me was by and large confined to the *Guardian*, in which a minister was quoted as saying it was nonsense, and the *Mail* which did a full-page cocktail of bollocks, including yet another [Peter] Oborne piece saying that if I went it would presage the end of TB. There was a nice little leader defending me in the *Sun*. I texted [David] Yelland but then a bit later Rebekah [Wade] called to tell me she was the new editor and David was going to the US to do a business course.

At TB's Monday meeting, we were going round in the same circles. We just didn't have the necessary cohesion at the moment. PG did a very good note over the weekend identifying lack of trust, lack of a coherent narrative and lack of teamwork as our three big problems. I felt all the narratives in the world were not going to bring together the poor, weakened operation. Bruce [Grocott, Lords chief whip, Blair's former parliamentary private secretary] did me a note on the pros and cons of my leaving, said that the pros were all for me and the family, and all the cons were for others, especially TB. Tessa called, said she would do anything to support me, and to remember that if it hadn't been for me, we would not be in the strong position that we are. TB did fine at the press conference, no real news story, just pushing the line that we were backing the UN and we had to give the inspectors time. He also got up a good defence of tax rises.

He called later and said he had felt very strong at the press conference, felt that once we stood up to their arguments there was nothing much there. All that matters is making the right decisions. He felt that if we failed as a government, it would be because we were not doing enough fast enough, we were not being New Labour enough. I pointed out he still had to resolve GB. He said I can deal with that and if I have to I will. Dan Bartlett and I went over some of the projects they were engaged in.

They had similar but also different PR challenges, and the sense of the split between Powell and Rumsfeld was strong. They were also being criticised for not doing enough on North Korea because they were distracted on Iraq.

Tuesday, January 14

Six-mile run in, four-mile run home, sub eight-minute miles for the first time in ages. The press conference had done the trick in calming things down, and the Middle East conference was going far better than it might have done in terms of turnout and presence. GB was doing a tax credits launch and came out pretty hard for the line on Iraq. At John Reid's party meeting, we went over how to do the Tories on twenty per cent cuts, lines on the Lib Dems and a discussion of local elections slogan where we wanted the focus on crime and GB's people wanted schools and hospitals. JR was getting more and more confused about what we were meant to get out of these meetings. I had a meeting with Craig Reedie of the BOA [chairman, British Olympic Association], but my sense around the place was that we were moving away from supporting the [2012] bid. He gave me a big sell about the prospects of winning. I asked a fair few tough questions, and felt much more disposed to it afterwards than before, but I still felt it was going to be difficult to get Cabinet onside for it. Rebekah had gone to ground and the *Guardian* ran a line that she intended to be less close to us than Yelland. I did the conference call with the Americans, then fire, then diary meeting. Later to [broadcaster] David Frost's party. Lots of people I tapped for marathon sponsorship. A policeman was murdered in a terrorism operation in Manchester.[1] I made a few calls to get our response and handling agreed.

Wednesday January 15

Got a cab in, ran home. Thirty-three minutes. The murder of the policeman in Manchester dominated the PMQs meeting at 8. It emerged that an asylum seeker who had had his case turned down was involved and so we assumed that would come out pretty quickly. The Tories were already on to the theme of border safety. As well as the obvious sympathy for the policeman and his family, TB was worried about the backlash, that this could be a tipping point re asylum and the public. We arranged for him to speak to the chief constable and also to write to the family. He had one of his regular

[1] Special Branch officer Stephen Oake had been stabbed in the heart by Kamel Bourgass, in a raid connected to the January 5 ricin raid. Bourgass received a life sentence for the murder of Oake and seventeen years for his involvement in the ricin plot.

sessions with the PLP, which went a lot better than it might have done, and which set us up for a much better than expected PMQs.

He filled me in on another bad meeting with GB yesterday re tuition fees. He felt GB's problem was that he saw everything through politics rather than life, so the child tax credit was a policy aimed at women, but actually showed a lack of understanding about how modern families work. I went back for a long meeting with David Wilkinson [Cabinet Office] and Bob Phillis [chief executive, Guardian Media Group], who was going to chair the GICS review. Bob felt, probably rightly, that I was not seeing Mike Granatt enough. David was very supportive, saying that I was expected by the PM and others to deliver strategy but didn't have all the levers. Mike had said I was on the bridge with TB when he was in the engine room. But I still felt it didn't really work.

At 5.15, TB, Jonathan, David, Sally and I went over to the MoD for a briefing on Iraq. CDS and all the other chiefs were there in uniform. We sat round three sides of the room. CDS said they expected Bush to make a decision for February 15 and they would go within twelve days or so to a massive air, sea and land operation. It was going to be called 'shock and awe', and the scale would reflect that. There would be hundreds of plane sorties from day one, aimed at wiping out his infrastructure and playing for a 'house of cards' effect. They went through where UK forces were most likely to be involved, taking out his defences close to the border. Substantial numbers of our ships and planes. A total of 42,000 UK forces possibly, 300,000-plus from the US. Then a slideshow briefing showed the scale of the attacks on the whole country, moving up to the capital. Oilfields were to be seized straight away, which, with the conspiracy theory about oil, would be difficult presentationally. [Admiral Sir] Alan West, ex-intelligence now naval commander [First Sea Lord], said there would be so much going on in the first day or so, that the international media would not know where to go.

TB pressed on whether Saddam would use chemical or biological weapons. They said they were buried so he might not be able to activate them quickly, but that was the reason [General Tommy] Franks had gone for the doctrine of overwhelming force. They believed Saddam was working on an assumption that it would be done by air strikes first, and then move in on land. It was interesting to see how much more fluent and confident Mike Boyce was in this setting. They knew the oilfield situation was difficult, and would require careful presentation. They said it was the right thing to do to prevent ecological disaster because Saddam might well go for blowing up his own oilfields as a way of causing chaos in the markets.

The planning was clearly well advanced, but it was still unclear whether the politics would allow any of it. But if this was going to happen as quickly as it seemed, TB said, then the work on aftermath questions had to happen now too. The intelligence people, including the defence guys, were pretty strongly of the view that Saddam would use WMD if he could. They warned of the inevitability both of civilian deaths and casualties of our own, but they felt in the initial attacks it was likely we would lose more through normal exercises than by being killed by Iraqis. They felt we would be able to strike very accurately but acknowledged the Attorney General might have difficulty in agreeing to some of the targets we would expect to hit. The scale of bombing meant that there were bound to be civilian deaths. TB also emphasised the need to get in place proper humanitarian support.

It was a pretty heavy-duty scene. It took place in the new MoD buildings, with everything very carefully laid out, typed name plates, tea and biscuits that nobody seemed to touch. On the way in, it had been like one of those scenes from darkly lit political thrillers where politicians and military and entourage are marching purposefully down a corridor, very little conversation, the only noise heels on floor, people walking too fast. It was pretty clear as we got into the cars and headed back to Number 10 that the Americans were going for this and TB had looked more nervous, particularly about the idea of UK military casualties and the possibility of large numbers of civilian casualties. It was pretty clear the Treasury were at it again. There seemed to be a pretty clear briefing against Charles' student finance proposals in *The Times* and against the Olympic bid in the *Guardian*.

Thursday, January 16

Jonathan's weekly meeting mainly on asylum and more 'why can't we just sort this out?' TB had met with front-line [Home Office] staff yesterday and regaled them with stories of people who were simply taking the piss in their attempts to come in, including the current fashion, which was to say they were from Iraq when they couldn't even speak the language. The main focus later would be the Iraq situation as Blix inspectors found shells and, though not yet public, notes of the nuclear programme. Stan Greenberg and Philip came in to do a presentation on polling. We were still seven points ahead, though the Tories did better on certain to vote. On the thermometer ratings, GB was slightly ahead of TB, while Bush was nestling between IDS and asylum seekers. When we briefed TB, his reaction was to say it could be a lot worse. We had been kicked about for months. The Cherie business had dominated pre-Christmas. On education we had been hit by the A-levels fiasco. Crime and asylum are gut issues that the people don't feel we get. And on Iraq, millions think we aren't listening. He said we have to win in Iraq and we have to be seen to be winning on crime and asylum.

Cabinet was fine. On Iraq, TB set out where we were. Trying to make the UN route work. Inspectors in there. Report back on January 27. He said the Russians were closer to the Americans than they say publicly, while the French do not particularly want to be left on the outside. But it was going to be tough. In the meantime, we build up the troops, and make sure that if it does come to conflict we are able to get it over quickly. Jack was pretty confident about the UN process, pointed out that a lot of people said we would never get a resolution in the first place but we did, on the strength of the case. Robin C said IDS had really sunk to a low point. He [RC] said we were in a tremendous position on the UN, 'thanks to you', he said to TB. He said the prospect of getting a second resolution was stronger if we do not rule out saying we may do it without one. One or two of them talked about the problem that Bush gave us with public opinion, but TB was clear we had to stay close publicly to maximise influence privately. There was a bit of criticism of communications strategy, with a feeling that because only two or three people were out there talking about it, the assumption was that the rest of the Cabinet were opposed.

At the end of the discussion JP did a very passionate wind-up. He said the discussion showed there was no real division 'so let's stop pretending there is'. He said the briefings and the 'talking out the side of the mouth' have to stop. He said the party doesn't like the idea of intervention but sometimes we have to make difficult judgements. If TB has the courage to put the case, we should get behind him and not give the press the opportunity to say there is division. Even Clare was reasonably measured. TB closed by setting out where he had asked for more work to be done, in three different areas – first, what offer we can make to the Iraqi people, e.g. re territorial integrity, lifting of sanctions, future prosperity; second, aftermath and the UN role in that; third, the unexpected and in particular the risk of WMD being used against our troops, or environmental catastrophe around oilfields.

John R left early to do the FPA briefing. TB was in a stronger place after a combination of the press conference, the PLP and PMQs. But the real discussion today came at the committee on the student finance review. Fourteen ministers there, with JP in the chair. Charles C put his case, and then a lot of the others expressed support. But then GB really laid into it, non-stop for twenty minutes, saying it was unfair, regressive, wasteful and not what the Labour Party was about. Charles gave as good as he got but was shocked when DB came in and backed GB. JP said it was clear they couldn't resolve it, it would have to be referred to TB who would have to decide. The whole thing had got very bloody. A lot of the things that GB said to TB privately were now coming out publicly for the first time, and the circle having been so wide, it was bound to leak soon. JP wanted to brief TB, said there were real differences and he would have to decide on the basic questions of fairness and the politics. TB was clear that GB was now really just on a mission to stall, paralyse, hold back. Charles then came in, really angry, said he had just told Ed Balls that he saw GB's intervention as a declaration of war. He told TB it was totally unacceptable behaviour and he should not allow it. GB was just trying to bulldoze his way to a solution that Charles strongly believed was wrong, and he felt TB had to stand up against him. TB headed off to [address Labour Party members in] Scotland after lunch.

I was working in the office when Charles called just after 4 to say that the details of the discussions had been leaked to the BBC. He was all a bit garbled and hyper but he wanted to go up and do a lobby briefing to put his perspective. I said he must be careful that this didn't just become a personality spat, but a serious issues-based analysis. I called JP who was in Milton Keynes. He agreed to Charles' briefing plan so long as it was treated as a genuine leak that he had to deal with, as opposed to the deliberate flaming of a row. When it came, it was actually not that bad for us. TB was reasonably calm about it. The storm passed fairly quickly before the news broke that Blix's people had found shells.[1] I spoke to Dan Bartlett and we agreed we would respond cautiously and let the media do the hoo-ha. Earlier, on the conference call, there was a pretty torrid row between Torie Clarke [assistant secretary of defense for public affairs] and Richard Boucher re next steps on the WMD debate, no doubt reflecting the argument going on higher up the food chain.

Friday, January 17

If it hadn't been for the UN inspectors' discovery of chemical shells, and TB meeting Blix today, the student finance row would have given us massive problems. Ian Austin claimed that the Treasury were really angry, that GB was furious that the discussions had been leaked, but nobody believed him. The fact that the *Guardian* was leading with a

[1] UN weapons inspectors had found eleven empty chemical warheads at the Ukhaidir depot, seventy-five miles south-west of Baghdad.

GB triumph, and that JP was wrongly stated as supporting him, left little doubt where it was all coming from. I had a long chat with JP who was outraged, and happy for us to let it be known he had not taken sides. He said GB had always operated like this and of course it was being put over as a pretty acute political problem between TB and GB. GB was setting himself up as the protector of the 'real' party interest. We chatted for an hour or so and he was clearly very onside at the moment, provided we kept in touch with him.

We did a conference call – TB, Jonathan, Sally, Godric and I – and 1. agreed we would say that we press ahead with publication next week, and 2. the arguments to put, namely that we had pretty much agreed everything, that universities could be able to charge more, that payment would not be upfront and the question was whether the individual paid back through future earnings or whether it was done through a collective pool. I did a visit to the CIC to get them better geared up on Iraq. OK but not brilliant. The FCO were not engaging as well as they had been. Later, Colin Powell said things would be clear in two weeks.

JP called me later, after I had gone to bed, said that he had spoken to GB after our conversation and things had to be resolved. The leaking of the discussions, and the nature of them even more so, had made it a very political issue and TB had to be supported. GB said to JP he intended to write something down overnight as a possible solution, and clearly wanted to calm it all down now. JP said he would talk to TB tomorrow. He was back in the referee role and clearly pretty fed up about it.

Saturday, January 18

Five miles on the treadmill, knee and ankle really bad. JP called again, said he had a pretty clear idea that GB had done the lion's share of the briefing. He said the problem we were getting into was that TB was worrying about legacy and GB only really cared about taking over and was frustrated the whole time. We had to get them to get their act together. Charles C put round an excellent note on the access issue, and the White Paper itself was in far better shape now. It also became public that the Blix inspectors had found nuclear papers which went pretty big.[1] We were in a much better place all round than a week ago, but it still wasn't great.

[1] 3,000 pages of documents detailing the process of producing enriched uranium had been removed from the Baghdad home of a leading scientist. The notes – on creating the substance using lasers – dated back to the 1980s.

Sunday, January 19

David Hill did us proud on *Frost*, plugging the *Observer* piece on the marathon and the [paper's] leader on Iraq. He was very nice about me, saying it was because I was good at my job that I was maligned. 'Agreed, agreed,' said Frost. Charles C was fine [on *Frost*] but he gave the figures people would have to pay back which was likely to cause a storm. There was a rash of dreadful asylum stories in the Sundays and DB decided to go on *The World this Weekend* to face them down. TB said he was looking forward to 'my reconstruction of the government'. He said he hadn't spoken to GB over the weekend and didn't intend to. He was simply not going to be halted any more, but it wasn't possible to do anything pre any action in Iraq. It was a terrible thing to say, he said, but he really did believe now that GB did not want him to succeed. Tessa came round later and said that when she finally got to see GB about the Olympic bid last week, she felt like she was being beaten up behind the bike sheds. He took her to bits, blaming her for getting the issue up in lights so that he would get the blame. She said he was so vile that even he recognised it and phoned her later to apologise.

Monday, January 20

Charles Clarke's interview on *Frost* had got up the issue of £21,000 and put TB in a total flap, made worse because during the day GB sent a long letter to members of DA [Cabinet Committee on Domestic Affairs] setting out objections, and a side letter to TB on the politics of it all and how we were 'getting it all wrong'. Andrew Adonis, Peter H and I went over to see Charles. You got the sense developing of something a bit personal between them, which we had to calm. Charles admitted that he had made a mistake on *Frost* by saying £21k. We needed to get over a message about opportunity and access and also spell out scenarios of how it would all work for different kids from different backgrounds. It also needed to be clearly in the box marked 'tough decisions', to which Charles added 'Like the euro, which he also wants to duck,' before laughing uproariously.

At TB's morning meeting he was seized about the whole issue, but also becoming increasingly worried about Iraq. The key question was what we did if and when the US went without the UN. There was a good response to the *Observer* piece [on AC's marathon run] and lots of cheques coming in now. TB felt that GB had effectively declared war and now intended to let him take the rope and put him out when nobody expected it, which is why he emphasised again that nobody said a word. He was in a total rage about asylum, felt the Home

Office just didn't get it. He was absolutely enraged by the fact that we kept pressing on this but it just didn't happen. We had a women's media reception, at which the women from the lobby were unbelievably aggressive towards TB, whereas the magazine editors were much more like human beings. Nice enough do, though. Then TB, CB, Fiona and I went off for dinner at DB's government flat at Eaton Place. David had been on at us for ages about wanting to return some of the dinners we had given him, and he was very proud of the house, the way he kept it, the way he managed on his own, though obviously he had help in for dinner. It was a bit of an odd evening though. Cherie, with me at least, was in a very odd, chilly mood and I reckoned relations with her were pretty well beyond repair. She was probably just responding to the fact that earlier we had tried to tone down her speech [to King's College Law School] for Thursday on children's rights. TB had said that if we thought there was a problem, and it needed changing, just change it, but she was not really up for listening. David was on OK form, though rather overdoing the host bit, while TB was being more serious than he might normally be at a social event, really wanting David's take on things. The conversation wasn't really flowing.

On student finance, I said nobody would believe that parents paid nothing if upfront fees went, because parents would feel responsible for the debts of their children. Cherie, perhaps not clocking the irony post Bristol flats, said she didn't believe that was the case. David seemed a bit ground down by the Home Office and by the crime and asylum agenda. He really never held back these days when complaining about the Civil Service, the lack of real grip and momentum, the difficulty in getting them to change their ways.

Tuesday, January 21

Five-mile run in, averaging 8.10 per mile. Up to see TB, really exercised about student finance now. He felt the exchange of [Cabinet committee] letters with GB had exposed the deep personal and political loathing coming from Gordon. GB was setting out a stack of objections in the policy, which he said was unfair and regressive and anti opportunity. He had spotted the way the *Mail* was going with it, £21,000 splash headline yesterday, and he was moving towards an argument that this was an attack on Middle England and therefore a political disaster. TB had a fair bit of time to prepare for his appearance at the [Commons select committee chairs] Liaison Committee. He kept coming back on the need to get together a proper political strategy on student finance. He wasn't clear we had it. I felt it lay in a mix of tough choices plus a dividing line on access. He feared the Middle England attack would really hurt, that there were just enough elements of the poll tax in this for it to be a disaster.[1]

He went off to the Liaison Committee, where he tried to get up the message that Saddam was weakening, also did lots on counter-terrorism. I had an OK meeting of the Iraq strategy group. There had been a discovery of lots of al-Qaeda documents seized in Afghanistan. One of the SIS guys felt there was more in there about a potential al-Qaeda link with WMD. We also had a discussion about what if anything we could do to build a better image for Bush and in particular break down the European hostility towards him. There was no doubt that though he was different to the caricature, as the main message-carrier he really hurt us. The conference call was a bit all over the place. I was trying to get a proper discussion going about oil, whether in fact we take on the argument about it all being about oil by saying that in part it is, because of its importance to economic stability, but it just wasn't the forum for a proper strategic discussion. We did however have a bit of proper discussion on Bush, where they needed to know the depth of the problem they had in Europe.

After TB came back, we had a long meeting on student finance, GB now trying to take out the proposal that they also be charged interest on the debt. TB was now demanding to see all the research from all the different systems round the world, also the comparisons between our richest and poorest universities. Then a meeting on the Olympics, where TB and I both made the point that we didn't seem to have the firm basis on which to make a decision. TB wanted clear advice but people were blowing hot and cold not according to hard fact and analysis. Tessa had definitely moved towards yes, others had moved away. The worry I sensed was that we would say no simply because it was easier than saying yes, and then regret it.

Then over to Derry's at the Lords to launch my appeal for marathon sponsorship. It was Derry's idea to hold it there, and it paid off with a terrific turnout, including some big cheques at the end of it. Dickie Bird [former cricket umpire] was an absolute hoot and ended up going back on the train with Mum, talking loudly all the way back about how much he liked TB, me, the government, etc. David

[1] The Community Charge, or poll tax, was a system of local government funding that moved away from the rateable value of property and placed a blanket levy on individuals. It was introduced by Margaret Thatcher's government in 1989 in Scotland and 1990 in England and Wales. It provoked significant anger, even leading to riots. Thatcher had chosen to front the policy herself. Her stridence on the issue contributed to her political demise.

Sainsbury [science minister and party benefactor], John Browne [businessman], David Frost, good turnout from News International and *Mirror* old and new. TB popped in and didn't look all that comfortable being photographed with me, and I sensed he was a bit bemused about how big the whole thing was going, he probably found it a bit odd when he wasn't the absolute centre of attention. Tessa, Peter M, Jackie Stewart [former racing driver], Trevor Beattie [advertising executive], Tony Ball [BSkyB chief executive] and his beautiful wife Gabriela. Did a little speech about John [Merritt], Lindsay and Hope.[1] Fiona and I found it a bit stressful but the kids were great, and we hoovered up not just cheques but some terrific auction items as well.

Wednesday, January 22

Cab in, but ran later, eight miles, after seeing Mel Cash, a physio who had been recommended, and who spends a lot of his time doing ballet dancers. Tuition fees and asylum were TB's big concerns pre PMQs. For once, he had watched last night's *Ten O'Clock News*, saw GWB saying he was sick and tired of the line, a clear message that he was losing patience with the UN, and they had pretty much decided it was going to happen and that was that. He felt there had definitely been a change in mood and it was pretty bad, and in addition the Franco-German forty years love-in today was more than symbolic, but also carried substance.[2] Stephen Wall had done an interesting note on it. TB read it, said what it means is that the French will get Schroeder into a basic anti-American camp, which is why Bush needs to do more to make it an international coalition.

Sally [Morgan] and I banged on at him again about the need to get them on a broader international route and even he, today, was saying how tough the situation was. He sensed that the inspectors would not necessarily come out with what was needed for absolute clarity, so we would have to face the prospect of going in without a UNSCR. Chirac was making it clearer than ever that he would be against war come what may, even with a smoking gun.

The anti-war mood was definitely growing and I raised it on the US conference call and pointed out the difficulty it was causing. It

[1] John Merritt, Campbell's closest friend, had died of leukaemia in 1992, as had his daughter, Ellie, six years later. Merritt's widow, Lindsay Nicholson, and Hope, their surviving daughter, attended the launch of Campbell's marathon run, which would raise funds for Leukaemia Research.

[2] At a press conference marking the fortieth anniversary of the Franco-German post-war friendship treaty, Jacques Chirac and Gerhard Schroeder announced their decision to co-operate against a US-led invasion of Iraq.

led to a rare proper discussion. I said they were going through all the gears for their domestic audience, and saying what Bush said yesterday, that gave us problems over here. Tucker [Eskew, White House media affairs], [Richard] Boucher and [Anna] Perez [now spokeswoman for Condoleezza Rice] all asked, genuinely as opposed to in irritation, what we felt they should do. I said it was back to the big picture about the UN standing up for itself, him being the guy that went the UN route, but are we serious or not? David also spoke to Condi to say the politics had got a lot harder and they had to be more sympathetic to international issues, pressures, concerns.

Dan Bartlett called and we spent half an hour or so kicking it around. We faced the same danger we had had re Kosovo and Afghanistan, namely moral equivalence, this time between US and Iraq. Dan realised they had a problem and wanted to do something. I was very frank, but he took it well enough. Condi told David that Bush wanted to spend some of the dinner discussing communications. Sally said to TB if we didn't take real care, this was the end of him. So far as the PLP was concerned, there had to be UN support, and they had to see real evidence. TB was pretty clear though that we couldn't peel off from the US without very good reason.

The other problem today was [Robert] Mugabe [President of Zimbabwe]. Unbeknown to me, on Christmas Eve Jack Straw had got TB to agree we would try to do a deal with France re EU sanctions on Mugabe.[1] He would come to the France–Africa summit in exchange for France agreeing rollover sanctions so that he didn't come to the EU Africa summit. I tried to get TB to look at it again, but he felt the other Europeans just didn't care enough about it. At the PMQs meeting, he was back raging about Civil Service performance, particularly re asylum. He was pretty poor. He then stayed in for Charles' statement on tuition fees, which he didn't feel had sufficient political message. He didn't feel we had set the expectations right. I worked on his speech for tomorrow and got Matthew Doyle [Labour Party press officer] out briefing the line that reform is the key. The message was becoming tired though. Godric came back from the afternoon lobby, having had a real hard time over Zimbabwe, because we had learned by then that TB and Jack having done a deal with the French on it, Clare [Short] and [Peter] Hain were both on record saying it was wrong.

[1] Though no agreement had been reached, France was pushing for EU travel sanctions against Mugabe to be eased to allow him to attend the Franco-African summit in Paris.

Thursday, January 23

Six-mile run with Hugh Jones. At Jonathan's meeting, we agreed now was the time to motor on the big argument on student finance. Charles C was up for it, but stupidly pulled out of *Dimbleby* [ITV]. I was really annoyed at the Mugabe decision, it was realpolitik at its worst and I was amazed that Jack had signed up to the deal. Robin was now lobbying hard against. Jack was in the US seeing Powell. We persuaded TB he would get absolutely fucked over and why on earth were we helping out the French like this? TB said his recollection was that Chirac was going to ask Mugabe, otherwise the others would not come, and then get TB to veto it. TB said he was OK with that, but Anna Wechsberg's [private secretary, foreign affairs] note on their chat didn't say that. TB had scribbled on it and his note was misinterpreted as going hard for the deal. He wanted Jack now to unravel it.

At the political strategy meeting, Philip said we needed more simple messages. TB asked Douglas, John Reid and me to put together a strategy paper focused on outcomes, and also wanted us to get a grip of a crime and asylum communications strategy. The recent [focus] groups had been poor, disconnected, not delivering, trust a problem, crime and asylum really bad, only the economy really accepted as doing OK. Cabinet was pretty low-key, Iraq, most people treading water before tomorrow's political Cabinet. Good stuff on the marathon front, *The Times* wanting a column on the build-up in exchange for cash for the fund, ten grand from Gavyn Davies [BBC chairman]. TB lunch with Bertie Ahern, cooked by Jamie Oliver [TV chef]. I was just trying to plough through paperwork as they talked over where we were with the IRA. They were still thinking it was possible for a big-bang solution to end the IRA.

I left early for Rory's parents' evening. He was doing well but apparently talks about Manchester United too much. Ken Clarke on *Question Time* came out against our [Iraq] policy and said we were the fifty-first state of America. I called TB to make sure he knew. He said there was no doubt we were going to go through a bad phase, be more unpopular, but we were doing the right thing and would come through it. At our best when at our boldest, etc.

Friday, January 24

Ran in, thirty minutes. Brief meeting with Douglas on the draft communications plan we had worked up on asylum. The *Today* programme had an Iraq story about chemical weapons which went OK, and we didn't overdo it. Probably came from the CIA. One of those days when there was too much stress and pressure, too many things to deal with. Cabinet was pretty poor in terms of the discussions. TB flat, GB a bit tired, Milburn and Reid probably the best contributions. JP strong re discipline but also saying we needed more Cabinet committee discussion on policy. Clare offside, the rest pretty average. Hysterical moment at the start. Someone in the previous meeting had broken the back of a chair. JP carried it round to where GB sat and said 'Let's see if he notices, and let's see if he laughs.' He didn't want me to change it back, said leave it, and let's see what happens. When GB came in, JP was watching to see how he reacted. He sat down, the broken piece fell away and again he showed himself pretty much incapable of laughter.

TB said we were strong on the surface but get beneath it and on the issues – Iraq, crime, asylum, public service delivery – we faced a lot of problems. He felt now was the time to be facing up to the tough decisions, not ducking them. The background, Iraq and tax rises coming in, would make it difficult, and we were in for a testing time. GB said they were the biggest tax rises ever under Labour, £12 billion, and we faced a number of important economic challenges. He warned fifteen per cent of the extra money would go on public sector pay. We just had to defend the tax rises for health. He felt taxes were now set at the right level, and we could campaign against the Tories on cuts. He said the main theme running up to the Budget is modern prosperity for all. He went into no detail, said it would go through an economic subcommittee. He felt we needed to decide department by department the key achievements of the government. And on the euro, he emphasised the comprehensive nature of the tests.

Jack pointed out that we were coming up to six years in power and we were still more popular than past Labour governments. They failed because of division and lost momentum. JP said it should be possible to discuss and debate policy differences without Cabinet committees becoming a battlefield. Honest debate is good, division and briefing is bad. Milburn felt we were losing trust and momentum. He felt we were being protected by the uselessness of the Tories and politics would be transformed if they got a half-decent new leader. He felt that would help because it would challenge the massive sense of complacency in the PLP. He said we needed a course to stick to but we need the political sense of purpose. Charles on tuition fees, Alan on foundation hospitals, Andrew Smith on welfare reform, we had to tie it together around our values. 'We have thousands of administrators, but we are the politicians and we have to lead, get back to locating policy and values.' He felt the Tories were trying to place us as big state, and the values of public service were the answer to that. He said that Blunkett had the most difficult job in government and that crime and asylum were not just his issues, they were health issues, education issues, housing issues, and we need to restructure government systems to recognise that. Margaret [Beckett] said virtually everyone who came to her surgery last time was an asylum seeker. Peter Hain diddled a bit, said he wasn't advocating jettisoning New Labour, but said we had to accept we weren't new any more, do a better job at talking to party and public.

Helen [Liddell, Scottish Secretary] said she felt there was a corrosive sense of division and self-indulgence. Cue Clare. She said the record of the government was fine, but the style and presentation damaged us and the PLP was troubled. JR said the basic narrative – strong economy, fairness, public services, rights and responsibilities, Britain strong in the world – is still a strong one for us, and does relate to our values. The PLP was a problem because too many of them do not get the narrative and yet they are an important messenger. TB said that we could win on jobs, health and education. We couldn't win on crime and asylum, but we can lose on them and we have to deal with them or pay a big price. But it was a basic tough-decision message, if not put over terribly energetically. A pretty desultory discussion re the Olympic bid with Tessa in favour but far from clear where the rest of the Cabinet were, and a real lack of clarity about whether we thought we could win.

On Iraq, TB was due to speak to Bush and sent through a note in advance. He was clear that so far as international political support was concerned, we did not have it without Blix finding a smoking gun and we needed more time. His proposal was to give them another month during which Blix would do two more reports. He was sure that in time we could turn opinion. Bush was pretty clear there would have to be a war, because he did not believe Saddam would ever comply, or that the inspectors would ever be allowed to do the job. As TB said, this was Bush in a different mode. They have very different problems to us. We are getting criticised for being too gung-ho. They are criticised for not being gung-ho enough. Condi explained Bush was going down in the polls because he was keeping the troops out there too long. TB and I felt it was more likely he was getting hit because he was not winning support for going without the UN. TB, who was wearing shorts and tennis shoes and about to go to the gym, was a bit taken aback. Also the Saudis were saying that the US didn't need a second resolution, and were saying something different to us.

TB wasn't terribly amused by Jonathan's characterisation of his current position, as set out in his note, as 'wobble and delay instead of shock and awe'. TB was confident we could get Bush to the position where he stayed long enough for a second UNSCR. There was also a real danger the Attorney General would resign if he thought the plan was disproportionate force. He was clear with the Cabinet it was important to stay with the Americans, and emphasise that closeness as a way of influencing the debate there, and he wanted to do a big pre-Camp David diplomacy round. He set out what he saw as the political and other realities. He felt Bush deserved praise for showing strength in forcing Saddam to the position of getting the inspectors in, but said we didn't have enough international support and we needed time to build it. He was also clear with Bush that not only did he not have support in the country but as things stood he couldn't really call on a majority in his own Cabinet. He set out the case for delaying military action to give the inspectors more time, during which it would be clear they were being obstructed. Blix would report two or three times up to March, which would almost certainly show they were not being given full co-operation, and meanwhile we would carry on the military build-up and meanwhile build diplomatic and public support and get Arab leaders to push hard for Saddam's removal. He still believed it would be possible to get him out without war, but the option had to be there, and the threat had to be real.

It was a very well-made, carefully constructed argument that made sense and it was clear Bush had read it. When I asked TB if he thought Bush had basically decided there was going to be a war, TB said if that call was anything to go by, pretty much. He remained hopeful he could keep things on a multilateral track but it was not going to be easy. He was facing a very tough call indeed, about as tough as they get.

Saturday, January 25

Sixteen-mile run with Hugh, steady then slow. [Bill] Clinton was in town and explicitly told TB something I felt already, namely that Bush was not winning support for his strategy because people in the States felt it was a political strategy dreamt up by Karl Rove [senior adviser to Bush], not a principled foreign policy. We put together TB's briefing for *Frost* and in particular on asylum where he wanted to signal change to our obligations under the UNHCR [UN refugee agency] and ECHR [European Convention on Human Rights]. He felt, particularly on the back of the BNP win in Calderdale, that we had to get a grip of this and be seen to get a grip.[1] He was worried that

[1] The far-right British National Party had won a council by-election in Calderdale, West Yorkshire, pushing Labour into third place.

DB had too much on his plate and was unable really to crack it. He was in no doubt that we had to toughen our approach and he intended to send out a very strong signal. On Iraq, he was clear about the message, that we had to set out a pre-Blix positioning, to show that the onus was on Saddam.

On the Olympics, TB was warming to the idea. We had received a whole stack of handwritten letters from some of the athletes, and it definitely had an effect on him. He now felt it was the right thing to do but we would see where the Cabinet flowed on it. Then to Brentford vs Burnley with Neil [Kinnock], Calum and Charlie [Enstone-Watts, Calum's friend]. We didn't deserve to win but took all three chances. Good day. Back for [Fiona's mother] Audrey's birthday party, mainly talking about Iraq with Glenys [Kinnock] and Lindsay [Nicholson]. Lindsay had written me a really nice letter after the event on Tuesday, saying she couldn't have got through everything without me and Fiona, that John always worried about me but if he had seen me on Tuesday he would have stopped worrying, that the persona there on Tuesday night was my political and personal beings coming together as a whole, saying this is what I am, and if the breakdown was the low point, now I have planted a flag on the summit of recovery. Kind of how I felt, and a really nice letter.

Sunday, January 26

Up before 7 and in to see TB to go over all the running stories pre *Frost*, and agree messages on Iraq, Zimbabwe, asylum, GB/TB. He was, despite the real difficulties we faced, much more confident. Strong on tuition fees, very good on Iraq and asylum, and generally empathetic with pumping out message. His body language on GB was not great, but he didn't mind that. He didn't much like the way the press were presenting the TB/GB situation as six of one and half a dozen of the other. As Neil had put it, it was more like three of TB and nine of GB's lot. I went back with him, and did a conference call with Tom and the press team and agreed we would push out more intelligence on concealment and push in certain quarters the idea of radical action on asylum including looking at the ECHR.

Most people I spoke to seemed to think TB did fine, some that he was back to his best, which was probably overstating it. Neil and Steve Kinnock were at home when I got back, dropping off Grace who had been staying with them, and Neil said something interesting, that TB always seemed more comfortable when he was defending something thought to be unpopular. News-wise, the interview ran fine but our problem was that GWB seemed hell-bent on war and we looked like we were doing things from a US not UK perspective. TB was talking about going to Spain and Italy to show that Europe was not just France and Germany. During the afternoon I spent hours signing Leukaemia Research letters to appeal for funds.

Monday, January 27

Clocked up close on forty-five miles last week, did ten today. *Frost* came out as a mix of Iraq in most of the heavies, with the briefing on intelligence going well, ECHR in the right-wing papers but lots of doubt as to whether we would do it. TB cancelled his morning meetings and called in experts and lawyers from the Home Office and the Attorney General's office and spent literally five hours non-stop being taken through the system from start to finish. At the end of it, it looked even worse than when we started. As Jonathan said, it was like the NI peace process in that every time you thought you had it sewn up, you could pick a thread and pull it for miles. The only interruption he allowed during the five hours was an 'encouraging' Putin call in which it was clear Vlad was really losing patience with Saddam. Despite yesterday people were still applying the yardstick that the inspectors would have to find WMD rather than simply that Saddam had to co-operate.

On Zimbabwe, Liz Lloyd [policy adviser] was blaming me for getting us into a different position, she hadn't felt the original deal was defensible. I was up to £76,000 on the marathon front, and today I finalised my deal with *The Times*, also cheques in from Sarah Brown and Sinead Cusack [actress]. The *Sun* was getting a lot worse on asylum. There was a piece by [Trevor] Kavanagh which DB condemned as racist. Rebekah [Wade] came on about that. She had just had her weekend with Murdoch getting her orders. I said she was being totally irresponsible by inflaming asylum as an issue and pretending there were simple solutions when there were not. It was pretty clear she was going to be difficult, probably more difficult than she actually wanted to be. Blix came out at 3-ish and it was OK. It made clear that Saddam was not really co-operating.

Probably the most noteworthy meeting of the day was when Ed Balls came to see me at 3.30. No small talk. I asked him what he intended to do to help get TB/GB on a better footing, because things are really bad and a lot of it is down to their modus operandi. I told TB I was seeing him and he agreed I should say he had never imagined fighting three elections, that he had always imagined he would hand over to GB during this term but that GB would not have that conversation. He felt that GB did not want to work with him, particularly on public service reform and the euro, and the relationship had become – my word – dysfunctional. Ed agreed it was bad and dangerous. As so often before, their view was that Peter M was responsible for a lot of the bad stuff that appeared in the media. I dismissed that. He talked about the coverage today as if we had planned it deliberately. He insisted there were people around TB who saw GB only as a problem.

I said it was only happening because the relationship between the two of them had become more dysfunctional. If they worked together, and JP was on board with them, we could do pretty much anything, but it simply wasn't happening. The meetings were dreadful. The so-called strategy discussions weren't strategic. He said GB felt that TB was tolerating and even promoting factionalism, as with foundation hospitals – for which again he blamed Peter M as well as Milburn – and now top-up fees. GB profoundly disagreed with the policy. There had been no strategy for its preparation. We didn't need it. It was right wing and would give us a problem right up to the election. GB just couldn't understand why we were doing it.

I said TB felt that GB believed he could do the top job better, that he now neither liked nor respected TB, and that made it hard to feel they could work together. It would be a lot harder to help him get the job if he thought he was being pushed out. Ed said that GB of course wanted to be PM but it was nonsense to say he had an operation to achieve that or that he was trying to undermine TB or his legacy. He said I only heard TB's side of the story. I said maybe if GB spoke a bit more, that wouldn't be so. He intimated, and later said outright, that GB was offended before the last election, and afterwards, because TB was making clear that his departure was conditional on GB saying yes to the euro and us going in. It sounded to me like a line they were developing in the event of GB being forced out.

I said between us we ought to be able to do something to improve things because what was happening now was mutually destructive. He said that he had offered regular meetings with me but he sometimes felt I didn't think he was senior enough. I said no, we just do different jobs. I would like to have better relations and of late I've had no relationship with GB at all, and that is his choice. I said I felt he was playing a dangerous game placing himself to the left of TB, to which he retorted that it was TB who was placing himself to the right, with some very Tory policies. I said he always wanted to be cutting edge, but before they had been able to do it together and that is what we had to get back to. I said they had to cure themselves of their obsession with Peter. He said I was blinding myself to the obvious, that Peter was wreaking revenge on all of us.

He denied they had an operation and said there was no way the Labour Party would ever allow someone who was disloyal to be made leader, so it would be crazy for GB to do that. He had genuine policy and strategy differences. He couldn't believe that TB had not replied properly to his note on tuition fees. We agreed we had to get back on a proper TB/GB footing, and he and I would mull over how. We had had a proper frank discussion for the first time in a while, and both had shared analysis if not entirely shared views about how to address it. Then to see TB who was still talking about asylum, even more worried after a meeting with some of our MPs who had told him it was raging. His big worry was that it was going to turn the country against us.

Tuesday, January 28

Blix had changed the dynamic a little but it was still very difficult. TB was pretty well geared up for the US trip but realised we were in a very tight spot. We got up the idea of 'material breach' [of obligations under UNSC resolutions] which Jack did today, and later at the press conference. We really had to motor on Blix, get out lots of material about what it meant, the potential capability of the materials he was talking about. The morning meeting was a lot chirpier than recently, though asylum continued to be really grim, particularly in the *Sun*, where Kavanagh was now clearly driving the policy of the paper, hard, in a pretty inflammatory way.

I had a long chat with Dan Bartlett re Bush's State of the Union address. David Manning had a couple of difficult calls with Condi because they were getting really impatient now. TB felt that there would be more Blix reports revealing greater non-cooperation, and then there would be much more solid international opinion. But they [the US] were clearly growing tired of waiting, already felt they had bowed to us on this and now they were going to be hard to persuade. TB and I agreed that probably what made us most angry was that they were doing the right thing but in the wrong way. Another good Iraq strategy meeting. At least we were using these meetings to develop proper strategic message, on Islam, outreach, oil. The SIS guys were very good on this, John Scarlett a bit more cautious. But everyone seemed to think we were heading for war, and it was only a question of how and when. We had got hold of all the Iraqi 'lines to take' and when I said they weren't great, one of the SIS guys said that Iraq lacked meetings like this.

I saw Philip, told him about my meeting with Balls. He said I had to get a grip or TB was going under. He had noticed I was more detached and assumed that the marathon was part of an exit strategy, raise my profile then get out. I said maybe it was a strategy to keep me in, give myself other challenges that weren't just the ones that did my head in here. He said I had to imagine what it would have been like five years ago if we were in this state – you would be motoring, working out plans, getting people going, firing them up, really going for it. We were tired and worn down. He felt we used the TB/GB thing as an excuse not to motor. There was something in what he was saying.

Balls sent me an email saying that Gordon had been 'encouraged' by our meeting and should we do the same next week. Yes. I put to TB what Ed had said about the euro being a condition of succession. TB said 'That's a lie. He always says that. He says to me, so are you saying you won't go unless I do the euro and I say no, I'm not, I'm saying that I'm entitled to be able to have an honest conversation with you about it.' I asked if he thought it was worth it me trying to develop relations with Ed to put something political back together again. He said yes, but it must be on the basis that whilst we must discuss everything, ultimately he must be allowed to decide. Also they have to get over their paranoia that we are somehow responsible for anything bad that appears about him in the press. He felt Ed's claim that they didn't have an operation was ridiculous. He felt GB was worried, now realised that TB might just dare to move him. 'I know what I have to do. If I don't do it, I won't get the job done in the way I have to do it. This is the key to reconstruction and renewal.'

TB spoke to Chirac later and Chirac was doing his usual high-falutin' stuff, lots of blather. At one point, TB held up the phone with his hand over the mouthpiece, turned to me and said 'I can't be bothered with this any more. Bullshit.' He talked to John Howard [Australian Prime Minister], who was really worried we wouldn't get a second resolution. Then to [Costas] Simitis [Greek Prime Minister], who was hopeless and totally with the French. [Peter] Foster deported.

Wednesday, January 29

Having tried to develop a better relationship with Ed, the first test came today with the *Telegraph* front page, saying GB was constantly asking TB to step aside. GB/Ed wanted us to issue a total denial. I said that was difficult because TB was clear to me that it had happened often enough. Ed said not. I also said TB had disputed their version of events re the discussion on the euro, that he never linked the idea of the job to this or any other policy. Ed was sceptical. We agreed to be totally dismissive of the *Telegraph* story. PMQs meeting was largely about asylum. TB felt he had been right to deliver the signal he did on *Frost* and wanted to signal more now. For obvious reasons, Iraq was worrying TB more and more. He wasn't sure Bush got just how difficult it was going to be without the second UNSCR, for the Americans as well as us. Everyone TB was speaking to, including the tough guys like [John] Howard, was saying they needed a second resolution or they wouldn't get support. TB felt that was the reality for him too, that he couldn't deliver the party without it. David was in the US today and saw Condi for three hours to go over the whole scene, tried to make her see that rushing our fences was not sensible, stating in terms that TB would not be able to deliver Cabinet or Parliament as things stood. We did however have a rare, for these times, PR hit in the form of an article signed by, eventually, eight European leaders about standing alongside the US in standing with us for Resolution 1441 [on the return of inspectors to Iraq].

I had a long chat with Dan Bartlett re the European signed article and also going over what we hoped to get out of Camp David. I was trying the whole time to get over to them just how bad the politics were. TB really exercised at the moment, said he sometimes wondered if they really got it at all, spelled out some of the risks of going without a resolution. 'What on earth do we say or do if something goes wrong, which it's bound to, e.g. there's nothing to stop Saddam killing kids and saying it was us.' He was gearing up to be very frank with Bush. He had an OK meeting with [Silvio] Berlusconi [Italian Prime Minister], full of the usual flouncing.

Thursday, January 30

Matthew Rycroft, Danny Pruce and Steve Morris [Number 10 officials] had done a terrific job on the *Wall Street Journal* article which was leading the news, and lots of the other papers followed up. But the build-up to Camp David was going to be tricky. The sense was that the US were totally decided and we just had to go along with it. I did the morning meeting, and chatted with the SIS guys re the report on Iraq's infrastructure of concealment. Lots of meetings with TB, first on asylum. He was worried by DB at yesterday's meeting, felt he had been floundering a bit, was just raging at people, not clear what the plan was. CDS, GH, JS and JP came in for a meeting re Iraq. Jack said several times TB had to make clear we couldn't do it without a UNSCR. He also felt that the Attorney General would not let us hit most of the 'shock and awe' targets because he would feel disproportionate force was being applied. The politics of all this were dreadful.

CDS warned that he was worried the Americans felt they would be seen as liberators. It just wasn't so. They would be resented. We went through the strategy for the next phase. [Colin] Powell's speech to the UN, then the next Blix report, TB clear that he wanted to try to get GWB to a second UNSCR, clearly getting the message that we couldn't do it without one. He felt we needed two or three Blix reports, and more time for Arab leaders to push Saddam out. Even Geoff, much more than before, seemed worried, telling us that Rumsfeld was saying inside the administration that the problem with the UN route was that it was open-ended, that other countries just used the process to ensure nothing ever happened. JP and I exchanged very worried looks.

The Iraq discussion in Cabinet was a bit scratchy. Jack said the Blix report was pretty devastating for the regime, and it covered missiles that were banned, weaponised VX [toxic nerve agent]. Clare said we were losing the public because people thought the Americans were hell-bent on war. TB was clear that his role was to pull the Americans into the right position re the UNSCR. GH said 1441 changed the terms of the debate. Clare and JR snapping at each other, Clare having a go and John saying why was it she could say what she liked but if anyone said anything she disagreed with, all she could do was heckle. Robin chipped in to support Clare. Robin was very spiky, in part perhaps because he was sulking over TB and the Lords yesterday.[1] Then JP on fire, making clear he didn't favour anti-strike legislation. GB said the unions had been totally behind the curve. He said the trade union movement does not understand what is happening to it out in the country. 'There's a shock,' said TB, to laughter.

Then a discussion on the Olympics. Jack reported on the committee meetings so far, the £2.6 billion estimated costs, the rise in London council tax, some of the pros and cons. JP said we were more experienced than we were at the time of the Dome but what was absolutely essential was that if we went for it, we all went for it, that there could be no division on this. He was broadly positive. When he mentioned the Dome, Clare chipped in 'Most of us were against it,' and he gave her one of his snorts. TB said he was struck by how pro the London MPs were. Nobody was saying go for it irrespective, but we had to pin the details down. GB said, very finance director-ish, that it would be desirable to go ahead if the finances are sustainable. DB was

[1] To Cook's chagrin, Blair had said the true options on Lords reform were either a wholly elected or wholly appointed House of Lords. He told Labour MPs 'I personally think a hybrid between the two is wrong and will not work.'

sceptical, Paul Murphy [Northern Ireland Secretary] pro. TB had to leave halfway through to take a call from Bush, from which he returned looking very worried. Overall the Olympic discussion was more negative than I thought it would be. Tessa pro, Charles pro, GH pro, Alan M basically pro. Lots of yes-buts, but the buts were very heavy, particularly on finance, with Andrew Smith and [Alistair] Darling both very clear no's. John R very opposed. JP less sceptical than before.

It was snowing as we set off for Madrid [for talks with Spanish Prime Minister José María Aznar, en route to Washington]. On the plane, TB worked on a new note on strategy for Bush. He was clear in his own mind about policy and strategy, but worried Bush would not go for it. David [Manning], back from the US overnight, reported they were really impatient with the UN. TB saw his challenge as persuading Bush that it was in America's interests to stay with the UN. He felt it would be total madness not to, and he was right, but it was not going to be easy. He was aiming to persuade Bush to wait till the middle or end of March and support a second resolution before action. He went through it all in his note, the military, the diplomatic, the propaganda questions, plus early planning on aftermath. Very simple lines and questions that we had to get answers to.

He was worried after the phone call today because Bush sounded much more frustrated re the UN, definitely listening more to those saying he had to go for it. He wanted to be able to take him to one side and go through the whole thing. They may not like it, but Blix was the key, and they had to see that. They couldn't just bully here. Blix had to get the evidence of non-cooperation and we had to get the argument round to non-cooperation being a breach, but we needed two or three Blix reports to get that. He also emphasised that the 'other agenda' was important, particularly MEPP. He had pretty much given up on Schroeder as being opportunistic, felt that Chirac was going to use whatever happened to do us in, so was keen to build up the other Europeans, hence off to see Aznar.

Landed, helicopter to Moncloa [palace], meeting then press conference, then back on to the plane for the flight to the States. TB was now focusing his mind on crunching down the arguments. He said this is the toughest spot yet. I have to persuade him to stay on the UN route. He wrote another note, said that Blix could put down questions, report on February 14, then again on February 28. If co-operation gets harder and harder to achieve, by March 5 we declare Iraq in breach and maybe go for another UNSCR. We give the Saudis ten days to mobilise Arab opinion to get rid of Saddam. March 15, military action. He then laid out the potential problems on the way

– e.g. Saddam uses WMD, attacks Israel, destroys oil wells, or there is major civil unrest. He went through the aftermath questions, organisation of humanitarian aid, role of the UN. On propaganda, Powell at the UN, the history of Iraqi non-cooperation. The WMD threat more generally, the link to terrorism, the growing worries in the intelligence. They have to understand that Blix is key – I lost count of the number of times he said it during the flight. We were also feeling the beginnings of the global split, Chirac trying to get a little group going of France, Germany, Russia and China, saying the priorities were Afghanistan, MEPP, AIDS, poverty.

TB then set out the forward diplomatic strategy, then asked me to fill in on communications. He also asked me to draft what we would view as ideal GWB clips out of the meeting. I felt we had to get him as close as possible to a second UNSCR, and tone down the rush-to-war talk. TB was in OK mood, but really worried. He just didn't know how Bush would be. He said he wanted as much time on his own as we could get, to persuade him he was more vulnerable than he thought. There was a risk of hubris. He needed world support more than he thought, especially if something went wrong. Shock and awe, then Iraqi kids dying, Saddam would stop at nothing and would happily inflict civilian casualties and we would be on the back foot straight away.

We went round the Cabinet one by one to assess who would support him without a second resolution. We could probably just about get to a majority but it would be difficult. It was pretty much 'future on the line' time. On Clare, TB said he knew the Cabinet hated the way he tolerates her but he didn't want her outside, as that would be even worse. I said appeasement never worked. He said sometimes it worked better than the alternative. David Manning was telling him we had to fight hard for more time, that we should persuade them it was in their own interests.

Friday, January 31

Poll in the *Mirror* said two per cent felt a war on Iraq would make the world a safer place. I made sure Dan [Bartlett] knew and made sure he told Bush just so he knew we were up against it. TB had also slept badly and was up and about, going over the same questions again and again, kept saying we needed a clear intellectual construct which was that 1441 focus should be on the co-operation issues, if the Iraqis didn't co-operate and Blix makes that clear repeatedly, we should say so and then we go for a second resolution and action could follow. We had allowed the goalposts to be moved to the smoking-gun issue, and instead it had to be about the inspectors not getting co-operation. We typed up all the relevant past resolutions, so he could read from them, particularly 1441. I had a long chat with Dan, made clear the issue for us was the second resolution, that that was where the press would go for the gaps and therefore we should try to close them. It was difficult because of course in the US the UN was not popular. Also Peter Reid [embassy official] was worried that the UK stories of TB trying to press GWB would backfire. 'They hate being pressured.'

We had a long chat in TB's bedroom with him, DM, Jonathan, Sally and I. The French officials were apparently really worried about France being left behind and some evidence that the Germans were looking to get into a different position. David had been shuttling between us and the Americans and they certainly had the message that we had to keep pushing for a second resolution. They felt 1441 was all they needed. Goldsmith was making clear that he didn't agree. Over breakfast, TB kept asking what we wanted out of today and I kept saying 'Bush moves towards second resolution.' We joked about this being his last visit to the States as prime minister. [Sir Christopher] Meyer [UK ambassador to Washington] said TB could make a fortune doing lectures.

Blix's interview was a bit iffy but he did have the line that there had been no change in Iraq's attitude. TB went off to the gym. I read a JIC note that made clear they held out little hope of Saddam just giving up, whilst there was every prospect of him doing something crazy like setting off the oilfields. The weather was apparently terrible at Camp David and meant we couldn't go there by helicopter so we were grounded in Washington and at 1 we left for the White House. While TB was seeing Bush, Tom Kelly and I saw Dan and I gave him a very frank assessment of the politics for us, said that our balls were in a vice. He said they believed that both politically and legally they could go without a second resolution. Again, we went over the issue of anti-Americanism. 'My guy's not doing you a lot of favours is he?' No, I said, it used to be Rumsfeld, now it's the president but I can see why you can't keep HIM off.

We went up to wait for TB and GWB. The question to resolve pre the press conference was what to say about a second resolution. GWB and Condi were both up for the idea of him saying he was 'open' to a second resolution, but Ari Fleischer [press secretary] pulled him back, said it would be seen as a shift in US policy, and then tried to push him back the other way, said that I was worried after what TB said in his interviews earlier, it would be a split story. It was a very odd scene. Me standing next to Bush, Condi and Ari next to TB, Ari and I trying to push each other's leaders in a different direction. Bush said he could say a second resolution would be 'welcome but not necessary'. TB and Bush having had a lot of the discussion without us there, it made it harder to push back without them stating the nature of the discussion they had just had, and in any event Bush was impatient to get on with it. As a result, we didn't really have the lines properly prepared. 'Let's just do it,' said Bush.

They both dispensed with opening remarks, which I think was a mistake because they gave no real context. The overall impression was poor. TB didn't really answer the question about a second resolution. And though Bush said it would be 'welcome' he looked uncomfortable and the body language was poor. Whatever people said about him, he is actually a very direct personality, which meant that he wasn't good at hiding what he thought or felt. Even though the words were kind of OK, the overall impression was not. As they wrapped up, Sally and I caught each other's eye. She grimaced. Tom managed to spin our lot [travelling UK media] to a more positive position by saying Bush was making clear he was open to a second resolution. TB said afterwards that in fact it had been the best meeting they had had in terms of substance, that they got on well, that Bush had read and digested his notes and was more on the same page than we thought, said he intended to work hard to get a second resolution and work to get a majority for it. TB repeated that if we didn't have the cover of the UN, when the Iraqis were bringing dead babies out of bombed buildings, having killed their own people, we would be in real trouble, so we had to go for it. But the politics of the UN on this were the opposite for him. David's note on the meeting made pretty clear they had made their minds up and that the campaign was going to start March 14, later than originally planned. For Bush, the diplomacy had to be based round the military campaign, not the other way round. We had very short timelines now.

The press conference over, we went to the family dining room for dinner – Bush, [his wife] Laura, Condi, George Tenet [CIA director], [Dan] Fried [National Security Council], [William] Farish [US ambassador to London], Dan [Bartlett] – TB, C, AC, Jonathan, [Christopher] Meyer, David M, Sally M. We talked a bit about the Democrats. He reckoned [Senator John] Kerry was the front-runner [to be Democratic presidential candidate in 2004], the guy who was married to the Heinz heiress [second wife Teresa] who would be able to put up millions from front organisations. He wasn't impressed by [Senator John] Edwards [another Democratic contender]. We had a good laugh on the Olympics when I persuaded him to say that London would be a great choice. Jonathan ruined the whole thing by pointing out that New York was going for it. Bush reckoned Hillary [Clinton] could go for it [the presidency] in 2008. Laura was pretty quiet all evening. Bush was playing up his daft image again, saying his favourite leaders were Who and No because he could pronounce their names properly.

TB was due to do a couple of interviews at Andrews Airbase so Tom and I travelled back with him. He said he was confident of getting a second resolution. We had to cancel an interview with [George] Stephanopoulos [TV journalist, former Clinton adviser] because of the fog. George was in a terrible state so I agreed he could come over to do it in London or Chequers on Sunday morning, though that eventually got cancelled because of the space shuttle crash.[1] I had told Dan that people in Europe really questioned their motives, and TB came away feeling their motives might be questionable, but he was adamant that it was the right thing to do to get rid of Saddam and send out a message that we were determined to deal with WMD. But he knew how tough it was going to be. Expressing confidence on a second resolution was the best way of dealing with that.

On the plane, as we flew home, I was taken aback by the extent to which the press thought the body language between them had been bad. We briefed hard that this was the US playing hardball, the message directed as much at the French and the Russians as anyone else. What was really annoying was that both Bush and Condi seemed fine about saying they were open to the idea of a second resolution, but that Ari [Fleischer] had pushed him back, and by the time he was out there, his body language was terrible. TB felt things had gone about as well as they could have done, but still felt they were doing the right thing in the wrong way, and just wished they could improve the way they put their case to the world.

Saturday, February 1

Got home, felt ill, went to bed. Space shuttle crash pretty much overwhelmed the media agenda. Out for dinner at Tessa's. David Mills [her husband] massively against the war. There was definitely a feeling there that we weren't doing the right thing, or if we were, we weren't doing it for the right reasons.

[1] The space shuttle *Columbia* disintegrated over Texas during re-entry to the earth's atmosphere. All seven crew members were killed. President Bush addressed the United States, saying 'This day has brought . . . great sadness to our country . . . the cause in which they died [space programme] will continue.'

Sunday, February 2

Did fourteen miles in just over two hours, took the total for the week to forty-seven. Press very low-key on Iraq because of the space shuttle. Spoke to TB who wanted to make clear he had no problem with Robin and others criticising his position on reform of the Lords, the Sundays having a few stories about Robin shaping up to quit. He wanted to go out early to Le Touquet for the Chirac dinner, but Chirac didn't want to move it. Tuesday was going to be tough. Spoke to Catherine Colonna to discuss how we avoided *la bagarre* [trouble].

Monday, February 3

Space shuttle still huge. TB's statement on Iraq was running fine, alongside the Pentagon briefing on the scale of the military attack planned. GB was making a speech [to the Social Market Foundation] emphasising we were OK on the economic front, though there were a few pieces around on his reputation falling, which was a bit of a current theme. Andy Marr [BBC] called, claimed that he was being wound up by the Treasury to present GB's speech as a split with TB, with a big attack on markets and a different tone on Europe. I called Ed Balls and we agreed a line to push, that it was pro market, pro reform, pro PFI. TB read it, all forty pages of it, and felt it was fine but it just didn't take on the arguments in the way that he needed to.

We had another firefight re Zimbabwe. TB was calling Chirac at 11 who mentioned that *Le Monde* had got hold of a telegram that revealed that Straw and [Dominique] de Villepin [French foreign minister] had agreed to Mugabe going to Paris and that TB was aware. Our immediate suspicion was that the French had done it deliberately. Catherine Colonna called me after the call and said please believe me, this was not an official leak and they were very embarrassed about it. It clearly put TB in a bad light and she said they would probably say nothing about it. Our line was basically that there had been discussions at various levels but we had been unable to agree, which was why there was continuing discussion in Brussels and our bottom line was sanctions rollover. The money was beginning to come in for my marathon appeal – £5,000 from [David] Sainsbury, £2,500 from the GMB [union], £500 from Jackie Stewart.

TB felt on Iraq we had finally got the focus where it needed to be, on the issue of co-operation with Blix. He did calls with Putin and Simitis, which were better. The joint article had had the desired effect of the French and the Russians taking us a bit more seriously. [French ambassador Gérard] Errera's brief for the summit was that TB was weakened but still the only show in town because the Labour Party needed him more than he needed them and his prediction was that TB would be PM for some time. We went over to the House for the post-US visit statement and spent longer than usual going through the difficult questions, many of which just didn't come up. In any event he did well, a lot of passion and personal commitment, making clear he was doing this because he felt it was right.[1] I got back for an honours meeting, usual bollocks where anything too radical was blocked and the usual Establishment lot put forward. I sometimes wished TB took more of an interest in changing all this, but at the same time could see why he didn't want to spend time on it. His hopes for the Chirac meeting tomorrow seemed a bit unrealistic. He wanted a really positive outcome, but it was hard to see where it would come from.

Tuesday, February 4

The Anglo-French summit at Le Touquet was being built up on the assumption of a big bust-up. Catherine Colonna and I were talking the whole time, and were on the same track in trying to get things in a better place. We were both using the line that more unites us than divides us. We left at 8.40 for Northolt, flew out on a tiny plane that Chirac wouldn't be seen dead in. Stephen Wall had done a good draft for the press conference which I topped and tailed. TB was convinced that the pro-US EU leaders' joint letter had been the right thing to do and would find Chirac in a better position vis-à-vis us, because if there was one thing he understood, it was strength. It was very cold on arrival. We were driven to the town hall, a huge scrum of media and public around TB and JC. Then in for the main bilateral, [Jean-Pierre] Raffarin [Prime Minister of France] also there, in the room normally used for marriages. It was when you saw French president and prime minister together that you were most aware of where the real power lay. Chirac, who could be overbearing at the best of times, was even more so in the presence of his prime minister, and although TB was his political opposite number, I think psychologically he tried to make TB think in terms of being Raffarin's opposite number.

They went through some of the difficult non-Iraq issues first, defence, CAP [Common Agricultural Policy], climate change, Africa.

[1] Blair told MPs 'Eight weeks have now passed since Saddam was given his final chance. Six hundred weeks have passed since he was given his first chance. The evidence of co-operation withheld is unmistakable. He has still not answered the questions concerning thousands of missing munitions and tonnes of chemical and biological agents unaccounted for.'

On EU institutions, Chirac claimed close agreement, at one point even claiming that on the reform of the institutions his position was '*plus Britannique*' than German. He said we had to convince the smaller countries that they do not lose by having a full-time president of the Council and we had to strengthen the Commission and Council at the same time. TB said he had had lunch with Giscard [d'Estaing, former French President] last week and that he had done a good job. Chirac – '*Je t'ai dit que c'était le meilleur.*' [I told you he was the best.] TB – '*Tu avais raison.*' [You were right.] Chirac – '*Comme d'habitude.*' [As usual.] Things got trickier on CAP, Chirac absolutely clear that he wasn't going for the kind of major change we wanted. He said the British view and the French view of farmers was very different, that France was the second biggest agricultural exporter in the world, that in England agriculture was not popular, that in France it was. Chirac was at his patronising best or worst, depending how you look at it, and TB had a big smile as he spoke. 'I think you are a very fair man, Tony, and it would be good to see if we can get you in a better position on this.' '*Si non, on arrive à un moment où on s'engueule. Tu comprends s'engueuler?*' [If not, we reach a point where we are rowing. Do you understand 'rowing'?] TB – '*Je comprends très bien. Surtout maintenant.*' [I understand very well. Especially now.] The joint letter had definitely got to him, and he emphasised that prior to the spring summit there should be a joint letter from UK, France and Germany, even though '*je me méfie des lettres*' [I mistrust letters]'.

On Zimbabwe, he [Chirac] apologised for the leak, said there would be a leak inquiry 'which will not find out anything'. Again, he gave the impression that we were opposing for the sake of it. On the Middle East, Chirac was sceptical that the Americans would do anything, said power was not in Washington but in the Jewish population in New York. When TB said he believed Bush would do something, Chirac looked upwards rather dramatically. '*Que Dieu t'entend.*' [May God hear you.] They weren't much closer on Afghanistan. Chirac pessimist, TB trying to see the bright side.

Then Iraq, where Chirac said 'I'm not going to convince you, you won't convince me, so we can explain that one easily.' He said tomorrow we get the 'famous American revelations, namely *rien du tout* [nothing at all]'. 'Is that because they are American?' asked TB. No, but if there were real revelations, we would know them too. He said they would listen with respect to [Colin] Powell, then Blix and [Mohamed] ElBaradei [director general of the International Atomic Energy Agency]. He said there was no point pretending we were in the same position, other than agreeing that we wanted to disarm Iraq.

They thought 1441 and more time for the inspectors. If Powell has important things to say, he should let the inspectors examine it. On a second resolution, if there was a war, we would need one but we do not need one at the moment because we are going through 1441. He came back to the letter, and TB said there was little point commenting on it. 'But it created a lot of noise. We should show some humour on that, otherwise we will appear imbecilic or hypocritical.' Catherine chipped in and said sometimes your humour does not travel with the press, Mr President. He asked what she advised. *'Dire rien.'* [Say nothing.]

He said war had to be absolutely the last resort because the consequences – political, human and economic – were terrible. It was a tense, pretty spiky meeting and at the plenary as well, though people were pretty much going through the motions of saying what they discussed at the various bilaterals, the atmospherics were poor and flat. Only the chiefs of defence seemed to have got on. When the French CDS [General Henri Bentégeat] said that Boyce was shortly leaving his job, it set Chirac off into a huge, obviously pre-planned, and for us rather embarrassing, tribute to Boyce. Chirac was even more full of Gallic gesture than usual. His face seemed to get more lined with every meeting. TB was tougher than usual, felt the letter had had a genuine and desired impact, that he now knew if France and Germany tried it again, we had the wherewithal to build alliances elsewhere. TB and Chirac had lunch together.

I was with Catherine, who had been with him about the same time I had been with TB. We agreed to get them away from the others before the press conference to try to get the focus on the need for Saddam to disarm, and the importance of the UN, also to try to minimise the differences on the tough questions, e.g. second resolution. Both did pretty well, good body language, no attempt to deny differences, but Chirac brilliantly fobbed off the really difficult questions, e.g. on material breach, US–UK. TB was keen to get back to vote on the Lords, so we got some of the ministers out doing end-of-summit interviews. Chris Meyer sent over a bootlegged version of Powell's presentation. Tony Benn [former Labour Cabinet minister] had done an interview for Channel 4 with Saddam [in Baghdad], which was nauseatingly toadying.[1]

TB was pleased with the way the day had gone, felt that particularly over lunch Chirac had been warm and making an effort. TB called

[1] Benn described the interview as 'Very historic for all of us' and asked Saddam to 'Help me see what the paths to peace may be.'

again later, said he felt he could now see a way of getting to the same place with Chirac. I said surely the best thing for Bush was to get Saddam out without a war. TB said that was his whole strategy, get the Blix report, then a second resolution, then get the Arabs to press him to go.

Wednesday, February 5

The Powell presentation to the UN was going to be the focus of the day but [Andrew] Gilligan [BBC] had a so-called secret DIS [Defence Intelligence Staff] paper suggesting there was no real link between Iraq and al-Qaeda.[1] Up to see TB for PMQs preparation and we were assuming they would do the Lords after last night's debacle.[2] And maybe Iraq pre Powell. We had a meeting of the Iraq communications group to go over how we dealt with Powell. I saw Ed Balls who returned to the theme of the so-called leadership/euro deal, allegedly done by intermediaries, by which I presume he meant Anji [Hunter] and Sue Nye and from which, he said, he and I were to be excluded. I said for God's sake, let's get real. He said GB was still obsessing re why TB did not reply to his note. The reality was there were real policy differences between them.

I said we needed proper structures for discussing strategy and we had to be honest with each other about the problems. I felt he, Philip, Douglas and I should meet regularly. He wanted to add Spencer Livermore. I said the most important thing was that we agreed things and then stuck to them, instead of constantly moving the arguments to slightly different places. I'd had a session with Arnab Banerji [recently appointed economic adviser to Blair], who I think was finding it difficult to work out exactly what his role was meant to be, but he said the Treasury was full of angst and vibes that TB would try to move Gordon. I sensed from Ed that GB was a bit more nervous. He kept saying we stand or fall together. His line about TB doing a deal, that he would go if GB helped him do the euro, was probably the line that they were developing for public use if TB did try to get rid of him. It was a good meeting though, and we always worked better if we worked together. Then a meeting with Peter M, Philip and Peter H where we agreed that things had got a bit cavalier and slipshod, that we weren't properly knitting together policy, politics and

[1] The three-week-old 'top secret' document stated that the 'aims [of al-Qaeda] are in ideological conflict with present-day Iraq'.

[2] Both Houses of Parliament had voted on the future make-up of the House of Lords. Eight reform options were defeated in the Commons, while the Lords voted for the status quo.

communications. On the GB front, Peter M was against my closer co-operation strategy, said that all they did was use these meetings to hoover up intelligence and use it against us.

Thursday, February 6

The Powell presentation to the UN re WMD had gone well and there was a sense of things moving back to us. The first meeting of the day was with JS and GH who had a bit of a spat about the DIS leak. Then CDS, C, Eliza [Manningham-Buller], John [Scarlett] and the main MoD targeter. They took us through a presentation of 'shock and awe' making clear that the aim was an overwhelming immediate effect. Jack and I both felt the words 'shock and awe' were ghastly and I spoke to Dan about it later. Boyce said it was the first time we had done an effects-based campaign. The aim was to isolate Baghdad. Hit bridges, deny WMD capability as the risk would be at its highest early on. Some of our guys to go forty-eight hours before the air campaign starts. They envisaged sixteen days between the start of the air campaign and a ground campaign, but want to get that down to as low as five days if we can get the regime to collapse early. Scarlett warned that there would be civilian casualties and that Saddam would use them to create political problems here.

TB asked about the assessment on collateral damage. Geoff said some was inevitable but the missiles were far more effective, even since Afghanistan. It had to be clear we were targeting Saddam and the regime, and also focusing on the aftermath and the humanitarian. When Geoff said that Rumsfeld was going to be running the humanitarian side, he was met with laughter mixed with shock all round the table. Shock and awe humanitarian. C reported that Blix was making clear there could be no aggressive inspections in mosques and cemeteries. He also said no serious interviews had really taken place at all because there had been so much intimidation. Eliza gave a very gloomy picture of the terrorist scene here, said that even though al-Qaeda were not directly linked to Iraq, they would use an attack on Iraq to step up activity here. TB was looking really worried at that point. There was also a lot of intelligence around on a planned hit on Heathrow. TB said he had no doubt that trying to remove Saddam quickly in the event of action was the best way, but he wanted to know what he was in for. C and John said there were suggestions that the Republican Guard were to be kept out of Baghdad because Saddam didn't trust them fully. Then to Cabinet, after a brief wash-up session with a worried-looking TB.

Cabinet was fine though as Tom Kelly said to me, Clare Short was like the granny who sat in the corner talking through the important bits when the family was trying to watch TV. TB reported on Camp David and the Chirac talks, put a pretty optimistic face on both. Jack went through what was happening at the UN. Robin was quizzing on the parliamentary process, Clare on India/Pakistan and rebuilding Iraq. JR said he was troubled about the lack of domestic consensus, that there was a sense of people losing their moral compass about the nature of the Iraqi regime. Tessa said she didn't know anyone under twenty-five who supported action and we had to do better at countering the scepticism.

Then Blix and ElBaradei came in. TB asked Blix how he was with the weight of the world on his shoulders. 'A lot is on yours,' said Blix. He felt Powell had done well but he was avoiding comment. He was pretty cagey all the way through, made clear his job was to be sceptical. TB said the issue was whether they were co-operating or not. At the moment there appears to be some, but there must be full co-operation. Blix said they had discussed the idea of enhanced co-operation. They were trying to resolve the issues of anthrax and VX. On the remnants of old programmes, they should be able to tell us. TB said that the reason we believe they are not co-operating is that we have no more documents, and they are resisting proper interviews. Blix described it as a moment of truth, but also said he did not want to be put in a particular arena. He felt the 14th of February was a little early to report to the UN [Security Council] and that they had a meeting of the College of Commissioners [of UNMOVIC] on the 12th.

TB said he felt Iraq would come up with some surprise to split the international community, that intelligence showed he would regard giving up WMD as a total humiliation, that it was essential to his internal grip. Blix said the South Africans were sending a delegation to tell them how to give up WMD. Blix said Iraq had definitely been hampered by inspection. He said they had been to some of the places named in the dossier, and it could be they had been sanitised, but they found nothing. The indication was that come February 14 he would be saying they had not found WMD but there was no real co-operation. He didn't want to name scientists for interview for fear that they would be killed. He was a lot less bullish than last time and clearly fed up with the feeling he was being bullied by America. He didn't want to pose any new questions because they would take so long to answer.

Then TB saw ElBaradei. He was quite open and chatty, less nervy than Blix. He said the Iraqis claimed they had never tried to get uranium but it wasn't true. He didn't think many tears would be shed in the Arab world if Saddam went. He was worried that Iraq would claim they were being attacked not because of weapons but because they were a Muslim country. He felt it better if TB and Bush could say it was part of a vision of a zone free of nuclear weapons. Also, it was important the aftermath was a UN administration, multilateral, not the US. He said their strategy was to force him into co-operation, though he doubted it was possible. But he came back again and again to the theme that American public diplomacy wasn't working.

TB said we had to sort out Saddam in as peaceful a way as possible, but above all sort out MEPP. He said Saddam's duty was one hundred per cent co-operation, not hide and seek. ElBaradei said we needed intrusive inspection but it can't be done without active co-operation. TB said if there was a breach, there would be a second resolution and then we could build pressure on him to go. I caught the news later, ElBaradei making clear that the Arab world wanted Saddam out and they would help him on his way if they could. Blix was less impressive, came over as very ponderous and bureaucratic.

TB and I left for Northolt to fly to Newcastle where he was doing a two-part [BBC] *Newsnight* special, first on Iraq with an audience of critics and then on public services. It was a good setting, with a view out over Gateshead and Newcastle. He was very strong on Iraq, not so good on public services. Meanwhile Channel 4 ran a story that the CIC paper on the infrastructure of concealment, which I'd commissioned, had included passages plagiarised from a Californian document, and claiming we had made it look like intelligence.[1] It gave them another spin story, which was a real pain.

Friday, February 7

The CIC dossier was causing a lot of embarrassment. Seemingly whole chunks were lifted off the Internet. I wrote a note to the CIC to emphasise the importance of quality control and to make clear that this shouldn't have happened. It was a bad own goal, especially as we didn't need it given the very good intelligence and other materials

[1] *Channel 4 News* had broken the story of what was dubbed the 'Dodgy Dossier', a briefing paper compiled for the Sunday papers by CIC civil servants. Cambridge academic Dr Glen Rangwala recognised plagiarised passages from writings available on the Internet, particularly 'Iraq's Security & Intelligence Network: A Guide & Analysis', an article written by political scientist Dr Ibrahim al-Marashi, and published in the *Middle East Review of International Affairs* in September 2002.

we had. Definitely no more dossiers for a while. I called John Scarlett who was very nice about it, but also rightly emphasised how careful we had to be. Then another major PR problem emerged, namely Derry's pay rise as part of the pay review bodies. Derry's pay was linked to the Lord Chief Justice who was linked to the performance-related pay of permanent secretaries and it meant he would get a £22,000 rise. The feedback from *Newsnight* was good, though the dossier was a real setback. It also came to be stated as a fact that it had been put together by Alison [Blackshaw, AC's PA] and John Pratt [press office assistant]. Ridiculous, but a sign of how difficult it was going to be to get our message across. *Newsnight* had pulled in 4.2 million viewers, way up on usual, almost matching BBC1.

Then to the LSE [London School of Economics] where I was speaking to Philip's students. There were a few Trots around but nothing like the trouble they had feared. During my speech about twenty came to the stage and held up banners urging NO to conflict, but I was perfectly polite to them and they just stayed there, largely ignored. I felt the Q&A session went fine. At the end Philip called one of the protesters to ask a question and I really laid it on the line about Resolution 1441, the authority of the UN. I asked him if he believed the UN was the best place to resolve it. He said the UN was a front for American imperialism, at which the audience groaned, and he was dead. I went through the whole Iraq story as reasonably and dispassionately as I could, and was surprised to get very warm applause for it, as also for a passionate defence of politics and the centrality of communications to any programme of progressive change.

Saturday, February 8

Times magazine did a good piece on the marathon with a good appeal at the end. TB called early on in a rage, adamant he had not signed off Derry's pay rise. We didn't quite know how it had happened, but when I called Derry it was pretty clear to me he had no intention of giving it up because of what he saw as a hoo-ha in the tabloid press. Derry was very clever but sometimes lacked very obvious politics. JR called to say he was confident we could fight our way through Iraq but how do you defend this when you are telling soldiers, teachers and firemen to settle for less? JP called, asking if it was worth us trying to get him to change his mind. I said I didn't think so but we could try. JP spoke to him, said he wasn't just the head of the judiciary, but a member of the Cabinet that was agreeing the pay of other public sector workers, that he had to get political because this was damaging government and party. JP said Derry put the phone down on him. JP was also asking GB to call him but he never did and then I had Ian Austin on asking if I could get it sorted because GB was on *Frost*.

Jeremy [Heywood] was on the case and worked a way out, namely to review the salary link in the light of performance-related pay and also review whether in fact the Lord Chancellor's salary did have to be higher than the Lord Chief Justice's. Derry still didn't want to budge, saying to me 'I'm buggered if I'm going to do something because of the tabloid press.' But as TB said, we all hate the press, but it doesn't mean they are always wrong and they are right about this. It is indefensible in the context of our overall policy on pay. JP made clear that both he and GB would find it impossible to defend in their various interviews tomorrow. But it took two more very difficult conversations.

I then spoke to JP, JR and Ian Austin to tell them about an hour before the statement went out. It missed the first editions, apart from the *News of the World*, presumably tipped off by Austin, who headlined it as 'Brown blocks Derry rise'. I raised it on the conference call later, said to JP we didn't want this to be anything other than Derry's decision, that nobody should spin it to damage him. JP called GB and said it must be his camp who had tipped off the *News of the World*. GB of course denied it and even claimed he had told us to deny the story.

Sunday, February 9

The CIC dossier was still rumbling on. Alison even made Rory Bremner [TV satire show]. Following JP's call last night, GB denied he had pressured Derry, telling [David] Frost that it was all Derry's idea. But of course the story that ran was GB denying putting on the pressure, which increased the sense that he probably had. It was not a great interview for either of them. GB a bit predictable. TB called to complain that he had so much work to do over the weekend. He cancelled his morning meeting tomorrow, and said he wanted to talk about how we get more politics back into the office. Blix was in Baghdad and ElBaradei came out with more positive comments re co-operation. The other big story was the Franco-German 'peace plan' and there was a lot of build-up to the march next week.

Monday, February 10

TB called me up with David Manning and Jonathan as soon as he arrived. He looked very pissed off, for once grumbling that Jonathan and I were both in sweaty sports gear. He was harassed and fed up. The Franco-German plan, which presumably Chirac knew all about when we met at Le Touquet, had wrong-footed us. It looked reasonable and the Russians seemed keen to support it. David M said the French denied saying there should be a UN force, the Germans had denied it, but still it ran. We also had a problem in NATO with France, Germany and Belgium blocking Patriot missile defences for Turkey. TB thought it unbelievable that these countries were putting the transatlantic relationship at risk. It had definitely been a few steps forward and a few steps back, Colin Powell and TB on *Newsnight* taking us forward, a combination of the dossier and international division taking us back. TB said we needed a proposal. I said the problem was people felt we were driven by a timetable dictated by a desire for war rather than by a desire to disarm Iraq.

TB was looking more worried and harassed than I had seen him for a while. I looked at his diary and really felt for him for once. Today alone he had meetings on Iraq, on asylum, where Blunkett was giving him grief, feeling he was weakened by TB driving the policy, a big meeting on terrorism, a difficult meeting with the military on Northern Ireland pre Wednesday's plan, Ruud Lubbers [UN high commissioner for refugees] for a meeting re refugees, the trade unions re two-tier workforce, and a lot more besides. I went to his meeting on the Olympic bid. He was still keen but we agreed that a combination of Cabinet opposition, the usage of political capital, uncertainty about costs, GB likely to be against made it very difficult. But he remained keen.

At a party meeting with Hilary A, JR etc. Hilary said it was really grim in the PLP on Iraq. TB did his 'Oh well' look but beneath it I could tell he was concerned. Then to a meeting in the Cabinet Room with a huge group of ministers, spooks and police. TB, JP, GB, DB, AD, Lewis Moonie [parliamentary undersecretary for defence], C, Eliza, Scarlett, GCHQ, [David] Veness [assistant commissioner for specialist operations] from the Met. There was a mildly embarrassing moment at the start when JP walked in and said to me 'Did you see Gordon's first answer on *Frost*? What a laugh.' I then nodded to the other side of the table where GB was sitting, staring down at his notes, pretending not to hear, JP not having seen him. There had already been a Cobra meeting on the threat of a surface-to-air missile attack on Heathrow on Wednesday at the end of Eid.[1] The choice was

[1] Eid-ul-Adha, 'Festival of the Sacrifice', the Muslim festival commemorating the prophet Abraham's willingness to sacrifice his son for God.

a difficult one. Carry on with the programme of arrests that was underway; do that, plus step up security at Heathrow, visibly and overtly with a public announcement, or three, close the airport. As far as TB was concerned, the last of these was unacceptable, though we had to be clear about all the things we had said about how we would respond to specific threats in intelligence.

DB was very grumpy, clearly had very little confidence in the ability of the police and security forces to handle the public communications on it, constantly warning how their briefings went wrong. His basic pitch was to say as little as possible. AD talked about the need to make sure our political flank wasn't exposed. He was also worried that once we announced it, we didn't have the airlines and insurers all going crazy. Eliza was very clear that the threat was serious and the decision that had to be made now was whether TB/MoD authorised the operation for the airport tomorrow. We then agreed that Veness rather than ministers should announce it. Afterwards, Veness and I went to my office to agree words and lines to take and then planned the Q&A. Then a mountain of comments came through, including AD not wanting to say in the Q&A that Heathrow was safe, DB, ludicrously, not wanting to mention Heathrow at all.

On Iraq, Putin and Chirac put out a joint position. TB's 'bridge between Europe and America' was looking pretty shaky and the media was working itself up into going crazy about TB being isolated. People were even beginning to say that his premiership was now on the line. In the conference call with the Americans, I briefed them on the dossier problems and tried to get a proper discussion of all the different divisions, but all we got was the usual crap about who was doing what today.

The fallout from the CIC dossier was continuing. C and John Scarlett both said they were getting a bit of grief from some of their clients who were less signed up to the openness strategy than they were. Michael Jay [FCO permanent secretary] came to see me to say he felt we had to tighten up, get the CIC people more closely bound in to the FCO on policy, go easier on 'product-led material'. TB could barely be in a more exposed place now. PLP tricky. Massive march being planned. France and Germany right out there now, open in their hostility, Russia difficult. We were in danger of looking like we were the bad guys prepared to disobey international law. It was one of those days when I really felt for TB. Any one of the issues he was dealing with – Ireland, security, terrorism, asylum, some of the diplomatic stuff – was enough to lose you sleep, and he had a stack of them. He looked absolutely shagged out and was clearly feeling a bit isolated.

Tuesday, February 11

The Heathrow situation low-key at first but became huge once they had pictures of troops and tanks at the airport. The briefing on it was OK but got a bit too detailed. Godric was stitched up at the four o'clock, his words on the specific threat twisted. I had another Iraq communications group meeting, and a bit of an inquest into the CIC dossier. John Scarlett and Nigel Inkster [SIS] said there was some dismay among colleagues but John was clear they still understood the need for the [intelligence] agencies to help in public communications. But it was a blow, not least because it was being pinned at my door and would be used to change the general modus operandi. At least TB was being robust about it. He was about to speak to Bush. He had looked at the Mirage report in *Der Spiegel*[1] and decided that maybe we took the wrong line, that maybe we should say it was interesting because it accepted that conventional inspections would not work and was effectively arguing for taking the country over without saying so.

We grasped our way to a plan that was basically wait for Blix, then surface the elements of a second resolution that included the ultimatum, then Saddam to go, and if he didn't we were going to go for it. He spoke to Bush at 12, who was very solicitous re TB's political position, said he was determined to help get a second UNSCR. He was livid with the French and Germans, less so with the Russians. But he was just as worried as TB was. TB could not quite believe that the French and Germans were so flagrantly damaging their relationship with the US. He said the problem was everyone accepted Saddam was bad, evil, and a threat, but they didn't necessarily believe that gave you a reason to go to war. We had to be the people putting forward one last push for peace. TB also wanted to get European leaders to our cause in advance of Monday's council meeting. But we were looking shaky. I had a good meeting with Jack who was on form at the moment. Ditto Jeremy Greenstock [UK ambassador to the UN], who filled us in on where everyone was re a second resolution. He said the sense of America vs France and Germany was really big. David Omand, with whom I had a perfectly civilised discussion on

[1] *Der Spiegel* reported a Franco-German plan, 'Project Mirage', to prevent war by sending UN regulars into Iraq to strengthen weapons searches, declare the whole country a no-fly zone and increase trade sanctions. Iraq would have become, de facto, a UN protectorate, forced to disarm.

the CIC document, sent round a letter re new rules on the handling of intelligence which was fine, if an obvious attempt to retrench.

Wednesday, February 12

At the PMQs meeting, we reckoned it would be a mix of dossier and asylum. Iraq was grim at the moment, we just weren't making headway. TB said again that the problem was people couldn't see the case for war based on a threat to us. We went over to the House and then heard that JR had said we were facing a threat on the scale of 9/11. In fact he hadn't said that, but it was how it was taken, and we had to wrestle with it all day. Then both Blunkett and [Sir John] Stevens [Metropolitan Police commissioner] said we had considered shutting Heathrow, which added to a feeling of raggedness. The build-up to the march was growing and clearly it was going to be huge. TB was still saying he could win people round. With TB gone, I tried to clear the mountain of paperwork that had built up. I didn't feel like I was motoring at the moment. I had done my first marathon column for *The Times*, which they liked.

Thursday, February 13

I ran in with Lauren Taylor [ITN] and a camera crew on a cycle rickshaw. 6.3 miles. Later did another 9.2, running back from seeing the podiatrist at Roehampton, who said I had totally flat feet and needed orthotics. The terrorism stuff was being covered ludicrously, cranking up the idea of 'mixed messages' and also still pumping the idea that we had basically sent tanks to Heathrow to scare people re Iraq. I got in for the end of TB's breakfast with John Howard. UNMOVIC had found a missile in Iraq that breached the allowed range. Howard was impressive if dull. They did a very good joint doorstep on Iraq and terrorism, though the media were getting a bit frenzied again.

I took Howard to say hello to [Rupert] Murdoch, Les Hinton [News International chairman] and James Murdoch who were in for a meeting with TB. After he left, we kicked a few things round on the international scene before TB looked very sharply at Les, and said 'What about all this other stuff then?' and we got into a pretty spiky exchange in which TB said it's not much good supporting us on the international agenda if the domestic coverage is so hostile. We argued our corner on health and education and I felt TB did it too much from the perspective that this was an agenda they should back, e.g. a liberal market in public services rather than these were the issues we really believed in and they should support us because it was right for their readers. TB went off for a meeting with Clare, trying to get her back in line, though there was no doubt where it was going to end.

Then a meeting with Jack, GH, Clare, CDS on the humanitarian aftermath planning. Jack was giving me a very hard time re the dossier which had indeed done us some harm. I was prepared to take responsibility for it, but truth be told it was as much a failure of internal quality control. But his point was that they saw themselves as answerable to me, and therefore tended to work outside FCO systems. Cabinet was pretty heavy, DB on terror, TB and JS taking them through where we were on Iraq pre Blix. Then RC reporting on a meeting of the PES [Party of European Socialists] . He really played up the extent of the opposition and I sensed he was putting down a marker that he might actually bugger off. He was clearly very offside and had become more so. Clare was chuntering away the whole time. Then Northern Ireland, which was also tricky. Then TB called in AD and DB to say we had to learn lessons from the handling of the Heathrow threat. Gently, but they got the message.

Life seemed to be a never-ending round of meetings on really difficult issues. Next Jack on tactics re a second UNSCR, and whether to table it before the European Council. I was impressed by Jack at the moment. He was really on form, on top of the detail, but not in that obsessive way that he sometimes gets. TB, like me, had sensed that Robin had moved to a different position, a different tone, and was gearing up to go. TB went off for a visit in Yorkshire, then called about whether to do media on the security situation after IDS went on the rampage. Then a Venezuelan was caught with a hand grenade at Gatwick. TB called again from Yorkshire while I was at the podiatrist. He felt we had to get up the humanitarian theme and at least give the marchers something to think about, and something to put them on the defensive. They may not like to think of it in these terms, but they might like to reflect on the penury, the poverty and the cruelty, and that as far as Saddam was concerned, these big explosions of public protest were seen as helping to keep him in power.

Friday, February 14

At the morning meeting we agreed we needed to get up more of the humanitarian side of things ahead of the march. Catherine Rimmer [Number 10 Research and Information Unit] had a good line, that even if there were one million people on the march, it was still less than the number of people whose deaths he had caused. But it was going to get very tough. Left for City airport [for Edinburgh and the Labour Party spring conference in Glasgow], the plane slightly delayed. Matthew Freud [communications executive, husband of Rupert Murdoch's daughter Elisabeth] called to say that Murdoch had left yesterday hugely impressed and telling everyone TB was the man, not GB. I did the conference call on landing in Edinburgh, then up to see TB who was working on the speech.

I watched Blix [deliver his report to the UN Security Council] on the TV in my hotel room. He leant this way one minute, the next way the next, but it was obvious he was not going to come down as clearly as he had before. There was not much co-operation, yet he was not saying so. You definitely got the impression that he was deliberately siding with France, attacking us and the US. At one point he picked apart some of Powell's presentation. And even though he said there were clear issues of breach, for example proscribed weapons, he was signalling that inspections could work. I went through the main points with TB who said he wanted to read a full version, did so, said it was a total disgrace, that he should just have told the truth and the truth was Saddam was not co-operating. We were in a very tough place now. TB felt the Americans had fucked it up by failing to manage relationships properly. But the French would now be cock-a-hoop. TB showed no signs of changing tack though, said we were doing the right thing. But whether we liked it or not, we were moving towards a regime-change argument.

TB felt we had to make more of the moral case but we agreed he could not really set out the forward plan he had devised on the back of this, because it would look like weakness. We were getting very close to the argument, which itself was politically dangerous, that the marchers were pro Saddam, that they plus international community divisions would keep him in power. He, Sally and I had dinner in a private room downstairs at the Caledonian. It was our favourite Scottish hotel, but there was something odd and rather dingy about the room and it was all a bit sad and depressing. Then when we started to work on the [spring conference] speech, he couldn't find his glasses and was scrabbling around on the floor. We worked pretty late. There was a lot of American reaction to Blix, with Powell very emotional, Bush on much the same line. We were told there would be big protests tomorrow. TB was clear we just had to hold our line and defend ourselves from a moral point of view. But we were already into the black humour, speculating about what he would do in a few weeks when he was out of a job.

Saturday, February 15

The first thing TB said was that he had slept badly. So had I. He knew that he was in a tight spot. 'Even I am a bit worried about this one,' he said. The problem was that for the moment it looked every part of the strategy was in tatters – re the EU, re the UN, re the US, re the party, re the country which was about to march against us. We rewrote the speech to get even more focus on the humanitarian side of things. We had had letters from Iraqis urging him to carry on, which we decided to use in a strong passage pushing the moral case for action. One of the people who had written was a Glasgow doctor who we got to come over and see him. We had to involve Iraqi exiles much more. The moral case for peace was being put on the march and that gave us the right backdrop to make the moral case for action. I put in the final bits in the speech about the inhumanity of keeping Saddam in power doing the dreadful things he does. We struggled to get the broadcasters to take the Iraqi exiles and I wrote a letter of complaint to the BBC and Sky that important voices were being ignored unless they opposed the government.

We drove through to Glasgow, went over where we thought weaknesses in the Cabinet were, who we had to win round. The speech was pretty strong and we joked about it being his last as leader. There was massive security around the conference centre. The speech was heard in near silence. He wasn't playing it for applause but to put over a rounded argument. It was well received, not least because it was so serious.[1] Meanwhile TV was wall-to-wall, uncritical coverage of the march and the usual over the top claims about its size.[2] What was clear was that it was very big, and I got more and more angry about the claims being made for it, e.g. the *Mirror* front page with a dying Iraqi child and the headline 'March for him' as if he was starving because of us.

The speech went down well with the media and we got as many front-page leads as the march, which was a surprise. TB was confident and felt we had the right argument and we now needed a big strategy to put the case properly. I got home, then later down to the canal and did an eighteen-mile run at just over 7 mph. On the route back, I bumped into no end of people coming back from the march, placards under arms, faces full of self-righteousness, occasional loathing when they spotted me.

[1] Blair told Labour delegates 'It is still possible for Saddam Hussein to prevent military action by co-operating, and fulfilling his obligations as set out by the United Nations.' Blair dismissed Saddam's invitation to South African officials to visit Iraq to advise on disarmament. 'The concessions are phoney, the weapons are real.'

[2] Police estimated that at least 750,000 people had taken part in the London march. Organisers put the figure at nearer two million.

Sunday, February 16

Carole [Caplin] had done an interview in the *Mail on Sunday* but TB was in so-what mode, said it would only blow up if we responded, that he was absolutely sure she would not set out to harm us. I said the problem was that people would question his judgement over it. Fiona had pretty much lost respect for both of them, and a lot of it because of Carole. He said she wasn't a bad person and he didn't accept she was trying to damage him. On Iraq, he felt more confident than he had for some time, because he felt confident in the argument he made yesterday, that it gave us a chance to get back on higher moral ground. The press on the march was not nearly as bad as it might have been. But that was an awful lot of people who took the trouble to go out, which meant that there was a hell of a lot more who thought about it. We really had to push the humanitarian arguments harder.

Monday, February 17

The media on Iraq was still an uphill battle, but the commentary was a lot better and I think the serious people were thinking the coverage of the march had just been too one-sided. TB was really nagging me about getting out more on the humanitarian side, getting better material out of DFID and the CIC. At TB's weekly Monday meeting, we went through the usual and continuing irritants – red tape, complexities of the asylum system, lack of drive in departments on public service reform. On Iraq he was keen for a major upgrade of our communications and believed we could win the argument as set out at the weekend. David M reported Condi as saying that we could go for a second resolution, that she had been told by Blix he felt it was unfortunate his report had gone too far the other way. I did TB a long note on the need to get the US to talk in our language. A lot of the antagonism they caused was by the manner of what they said as much as content, Blix was a case in point. I got the very strong impression that he thought we were OK and they were anything but, yet we were pretty much saying the same things.

We left for Brussels [EU summit] at 3 and agreed that TB would do a doorstep setting out the basic line that now was not the time to weaken. It was one of those summits that nobody really wanted but we were there and we had to get a recommitment to 1441. We did so, and then Chirac was doing the usual posturing, saying there could be no second UNSCR. It was interesting how keen some of the other countries were to make clear they were basically on our side – Spain, Italy, the Dutch, the Danes and the Irish. Jack was taking notes of the discussions which he was getting sent out to me and enabling us to brief as we went. Later more and more people were out on our side. Chirac was slightly losing it, later issued a pretty clear threat to the enlargement countries trying to come in, said they should be careful, they were too pro US and may not be able to come in. Things were going our way much more than we had expected and it was quite a productive day, Jack getting the notes out to me, me turning them into briefings for Godric and Danny [Pruce], who were just working the press centre the whole time. It definitely gave us the feeling that with momentum, we could turn the argument.

Tuesday, February 18

Chirac was widely felt to have made a big mistake attacking the ten candidate countries who felt they were being bullied.[1] Of course he was getting a great press at home and reviving a sense of Gaullism. Needless to say our press were keen to build him up at TB's expense. Our plan was to consolidate the actual success of yesterday, restate the basic case and get going re Iraqi exiles. I had a meeting with the Iraq communications group. There was a clear understanding that we were widening to take in the bigger dimension of the moral and humanitarian side, and we had to be clear about whether this was shifting to a regime-change position. We had to be clear that it didn't, that the basic rationale hadn't changed, but equally we were entitled to make the case that the world would be better without him in power.

I was worried about the CIC which was not working as well as it had been. Gerard Russell's Islamic media unit was doing fine but the CIC as a whole was not producing as it should. We were beginning to get good email responses from Iraqi exiles. At the press conference, TB was relaxed and confident, even though the story was building that his own future was on the line. He seemed relatively unconcerned. Then another meeting on Iraq. The US was still giving out the message that it was going to happen and the rest was just giving us cover, e.g. saying that a second resolution wasn't absolutely necessary but they would try to get it. Maybe they were just getting irritated with us for having taken them down the UN route in the first place.

Wednesday, February 19

TB called on the way to Chequers after what he described as a truly dreadful meeting with GB. He said it wasn't even worth talking about.

[1] The ten East European and Mediterranean countries due to join the European Union in 2004 had signed a letter of support for the US stance on Iraq.

He was at a genuine loss to understand why Chirac was prepared to go so far out in damaging his relations with America. It could be Chirac had just decided to go for it as a way of building national identity, but it was a high-risk strategy and he thought it would backfire badly. John Reid was doing a tour of local parties and said he genuinely felt we could persuade people. I spoke to Piers [Morgan] to try to get him to take a piece from John as I knew they were meeting tonight. Of course he wanted TB, but agreed to take JR as a first step. This followed our meeting with Victor Blank [*Trinity Mirror* chairman] yesterday who had suggested JR as a possible link to Piers. TB was pretty frank with Victor, told him he found it very difficult to have a serious conversation with Piers, as the only thing he was really interested in was himself.

TB sent a note through to Bush setting out the basic strategy – that we put down a UNSCR, not push to a vote, instead use it like an ultimatum, give him two weeks or so to take us to the French date of March 14. He spoke to Bush later, said we couldn't dispute that public opinion was against us but he strongly felt the French and Germans were in the right place for public opinion but in the wrong place for the world. Dan [Bartlett] was clearly feeding in our conversations because Bush referred to the fact that I had said he was giving us real problems because they just didn't speak our language. TB felt it was a good call, which ended with Bush raging at the churchmen, this on the day that our church leaders were having a go at us too.

Thursday, February 20

TB was getting more and more worried on Iraq, and with good reason. He called from Chequers saying we really had to think through the strategy on the theme of 'the last push for peace'. He wanted a strong media plan to underpin it. Dan Bartlett was in agreement we had to tone down the war rhetoric and tone up the push for peace. I said we couldn't emphasise enough how we needed the sense that we were trying to avoid war, not rush towards it. TB called later, asked for a call on the Brent [secure phone], later joined by Jack, to discuss rumours that Blix had been saying he intended to report that Iraq was complying when our evidence pointed in the opposite direction. TB later spoke to him. He felt we needed to get the US, UK and Spain putting out a second resolution. I felt we also needed someone unexpected on it, like Mexico or Chile.

Jack wanted to do a parliamentary debate next week and we went over when to announce it and what kind of motion. We now had to get the second resolution, and put down the ultimatum, that amounted to Saddam being forced to answer the questions he had not yet answered or even been properly asked about the leftovers, interviews with scientists etc. We had to get the tone straight prior to the Bush/Aznar meeting on Saturday. Andrew Adonis had sparked another flurry with the Treasury. Ed Balls was complaining about a story in the *FT* based on TB's progressive governance article about co-payment.[1] Andrew was adamant it referred to what we were doing on tuition fees, but the Treasury were cranking it up as a threat re the NHS. I explained all that to Ed but he was equally adamant it was a hostile act.

David M's conversations with Condi were getting more and more scratchy. Condi was keen to be pushing towards conflict whilst we were emphasising the peaceful route still. Dan and I spent quite a while working on an agreed script.

Friday, February 21

TB called en route to Rome. He really felt everything now had to be set in the context of pushing for peace, that we wanted to resolve it peacefully. He said he really wanted me to work on Dan Bartlett, and get properly agreed message scripts, which I had been doing much of last night and this morning. By the end of it, we had a very strong four-page Sunday briefings script, which if everyone stuck to it, would get us in a far better position. He called me later and I gave him an example of where words that seemed commonplace to them gave us major public opinion problems here. Rumsfeld leading the news here simply by saying 'We're ready', that totally cut across our message that we were trying to avoid war not rush into it. I had the idea of the ultimatum in the briefing note. TB was happy with it and so was Jack until he spoke to Powell who said that the real ultimatum would be made just before action when we tell Saddam to get out of town. I was fine with cutting it, though it weakened it.

Late pm I got a message that the Americans wanted a conference call – Condi, Dan, Steve Hadley [Deputy National Security Advisor] on their side, with David M, Jonathan and me. They clearly had worries. I set out why we wanted to frame it this way, set out the process including a side statement directly challenging Saddam. But Condi feared that setting it out as a final chance – again – or a challenge to Saddam, suggested there was something here beyond 1441. She said 1441 was all that we needed. We tried to use the call

[1] Payment made by an individual, usually at the time a service is received, to offset some of the cost.

to get over the need for a different sort of language on this, but they really didn't get it.

During the day I had had three long calls with Dan, a difficult but productive conference call with Condi, a totally useless thirty-minute conference call, yet despite all that we were not really in the same place. I could sense Condi felt we were weakening. She really didn't like the final, final opportunity line, couldn't see that it was simply a way of trying to show we preferred peace to war. TB had done a very strong message at his press conference with Berlusconi, strong on the moral case again. He called to say he felt much better placed on the arguments but it was all still very tricky. John Williams [FCO] had already suggested prior to the Condi call that we say the gap between tabling a resolution and a vote was the closing of the final opportunity for 1441. It was a bit convoluted but we went for that, though Condi kept coming back with noises and a voice that seemed to get shriller as the call went on, that she was concerned we weren't firm enough. I said she had to understand that we were hit hard here because people felt we were rushing to a timetable set by others. The ITV programme on me and the marathon was fine and seemed to get an OK response.

Saturday, February 22

TB was seeing the Pope [John Paul II]. He called but then said as he was on a mobile, to say nothing. Bit of a pointless call really. Tom briefed strongly on 'the last push for peace' while I listened in to a TB/Bush/Aznar/Berlusconi call, livened up a bit by Bush saying he planned to get out his biggest guns and cowboy hat to help Aznar's rating in Spain.

Sunday, February 23

TB was full of it re the Pope, had clearly found it very special. He was for once asking about the marathon. 'Are you really going to run twenty-six miles?' That's what a marathon is. He wanted us to keep pushing on the push for peace, but said we kept being undone by the Yanks and their mode of communication. I called Alan Milburn to suggest he try to cool the public spat going on between him and GB. I watched Rory Bremner which had me and Condi swapping places and was moderately amusing.

Monday, February 24

Iraq was totally dominating, but at TB's morning meeting it was the usual whinge about asylum, crime, health and all the dreadful figures that were coming out. He was really fed up with it all, in a rage at departments who he felt took their feet off the accelerators once we were all occupied with something else. On Iraq, I said I felt we needed to add some substance to the 'last push for peace', which at the moment just sounded vacuous, something to say to get us through a bit more time. We needed something concrete, like signs of Arab pressure on Saddam, or a new diplomatic effort that meant something. He said the last push WAS the pressure being applied, or the pressure was the last push. But I still felt it looked like we were trying to meet a US timetable, not genuinely trying to avoid war. But all the US politicians did was communicate an impatience to get to war. Hilary A was a little bit more confident about the Commons [vote], but said it was all going to be tough. She, Jack and I negotiated the final motion, which was fine, not explicit re military action or UNSCR.

I think TB was beginning to think I was a bit distracted by the marathon, and maybe I was, though I felt the training was on balance a bonus for the job. It was the focus on the event itself, the build-up and the fund-raising, that was maybe taking my attention away. I discussed Carole [Caplin] with him again. The *Mail* were doing a string of stories at the moment that seemed to be coming from her or someone close to her. He was still maintaining she was a victim in all this and that she would do nothing to harm them, and was upset by the way these stories were coming out. Even after the TV documentary, he was saying she was victim in all this.

I had a meeting with some of the SIS people, including a former member of the Iraqi government who had some good insights into the way we were putting our case, the messages that were likely to get through, and those which didn't. He was clear a lot of the US messages were undermining what we were trying to do. We also needed to emphasise we didn't want to be there for long, and that the commitment to the MEPP was absolute. No matter how closely you read all the briefing and the intelligence, it was always a help to get this kind of verbal face-to-face analysis. He was interesting on the way the regime worked, and felt we should be getting messages into Iraq re that – how they worked against the interests of business, against families – e.g. by using them to spy on each other – and against women. He claimed Uday [elder son of Saddam] raped a different woman every day.

I went to [David] Yelland's farewell [as *Sun* editor]. TB popped in briefly. [William] Hague [former Conservative leader] very nice re my marathon efforts and sponsored me, along with a few others there.

The SCR [draft UN Security Council resolution] went down. Jack and [Sir Jeremy] Greenstock were both out on it but what the French would do was not clear. We put it down with the Americans and the Spaniards, while the French put down a memorandum with the Germans and the Russians. TB was keen to rubbish it but not go OTT. But the main perception of the whole thing was a riven international community and the perception for TB was pretty grim.

Tuesday, February 25

Saddam interview with Dan Rather [American TV news anchor] was going big, both saying he was NOT going to destroy al-Samoud [missiles, with a range in breach of UNSCR 1441] – though we knew he would – and also challenging GWB to a TV debate, which was hilarious, but also a good way of getting up a clear and straight line. I went up to see TB who was fairly relaxed re the French, just wanted us to keep making the case, setting out the whole background. At the Iraq communications group, both John S and I were stressing that the regime-change argument was more productive than the technicalities of 1441. Over to the House for the statement [on Iraq].[1] He was on form, and had a lot of Tories strongly supporting.

Later, TB had a meeting with GB and Balls on the euro. Yet again, he said at the end it was the worst yet, that 'I just can't be bothered with it any more.' He said GB talked to him like he was a five-year-old. If it was serious, he would be worried, but it's a total joke. If he had any sense, he would just be totally, absolutely, totally supportive on the war. GB had sent a copy of TB's progressive governance [*FT*] article to JP, with bits underlined, and was saying a lot of it could be said by a Tory. JP was onside at the moment. TB said 'I'm afraid I have reached the position where I trust nothing he says because everything is worked out through the prism of his own position.' There was real contempt in his voice.

TB called during the Juventus vs Man U game. He said it was going to be really tough from now on in. The truth was we may well have to go without a second UNSCR, or even without a majority on the UNSC. The Bush poodle problem would get bigger. We were giving the Lib Dems a big opening, but he was adamant it was the right thing to do, and worth the political consequences. I said what

[1] Blair told MPs 'The intelligence is clear: [Saddam Hussein] continues to believe that his weapons of mass destruction programme is essential both for internal repression and for external aggression. It is essential to his regional power. Prior to the inspectors coming back in, he was engaged in a systematic exercise in concealment of those weapons.'

if a hundred of our own MPs are voting against the government and he said fine, they're mainly the dispossessed and disaffected. He knew it was more serious than that but was pushing the argument now that those against us had to face up to the fact that the consequence of their actions was Saddam staying in power. Hilary Armstrong called and said things did not look good. He must be worried about the growing talk of his job being on the line over this. He was getting a good response for doing well in the House, but an awful lot of our side were already publicly committed to rebellion. The question they were asking was is Iraq a threat to us, and now? TB was dismissive of Blix. He said his job was to set out the facts, but he now saw his mission as to stop war.

Wednesday, February 26

Jack went a bit loopy re a JR interview in which he seemed to suggest today's [Commons] debate would be the last vote before action – it wasn't. With the debate straight after PMQs, that was almost all we discussed at the PMQs meeting. I did though have a meeting with Alan M and Darren Murphy [Milburn's special adviser] to try to get them in a less confrontational position re GB, which was doing nobody any good, and to try to get the dividing lines back to being about us and the Tories, not internal. On Iraq, Alan was very much of the view that we should get on with it.

TB was good at PMQs, and [Charles] Kennedy [Liberal Democrat leader] was so opportunistic it would begin to damage him soon. JP meeting, where he was very supportive, and urging TB to do more of the direct communication, both with MPs but also on the media. There was a sense among most people that if the uncommitted and unsure could hear the arguments direct, unmediated by a cynical media, we would win over more people.

Then all eyes on the vote. Through the day, we got the indications the majority would be bigger than we thought initially. Dan Bartlett sent through lines from Bush's MEPP speech for us to start briefing from midnight to try to build it big from the morning. It was imperative our people felt there was something substantial involved in this. Then back for Burnley–Fulham [FA Cup replay at Turf Moor, Burnley]. We were on great form, 3–0, and I had avoided the nightmare of not being able to go. The Iraq debate itself was good, though the dangers were very clear and there was a growing sense of menace in the voices of the disaffected, particularly former ministers. Frank Dobson [former Health Secretary] was now pretty determinedly anti, and as Alan M said, we had handled him disastrously. There was also Chris Smith,

Tony Blair (*seated*) before the Commons debate on going to war with Iraq; with him are (*left to right*) Jonathan Powell, David Manning, Peter Hyman and Alastair Campbell.

Campbell watches Blair's speech live on television from the Prime Minister's office.

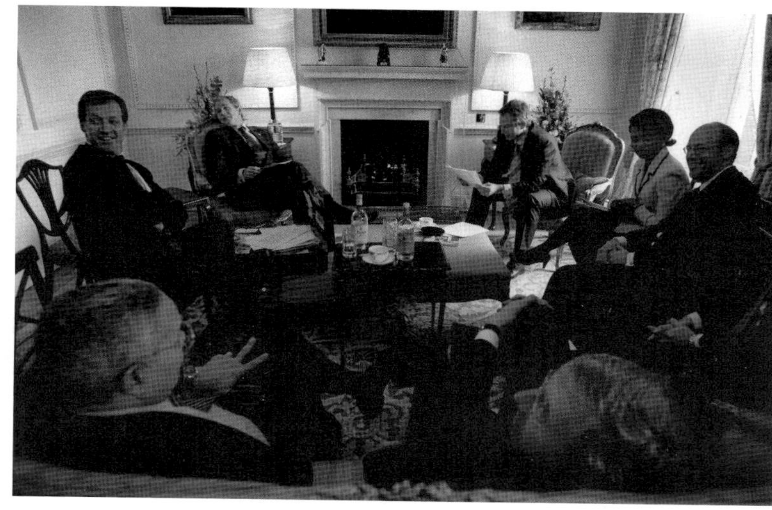

US–UK talks at Hillsborough Castle; clockwise from bottom left: Colin Powell, Alastair Campbell, George Bush, Tony Blair, Condi Rice, Ari Fleischer and Jack Straw.

MERIDIEN
NO
DON'T ATTACK IRAQ
NOT IN MY NAME
MAB
Freedom For Palestine
NO WAR ON IRAQ
STOP THE WAR
ATTACK
NO WAR

'hough the run-up to war preoccu-
ied everyone, Campbell found
me to train for the 2003 London
/larathon (*above, left,* at the finish-
ıg line with Fiona), raising half a
nillion pounds for Leukaemia
Research in memory of his best
riend John Merritt (*above, right*),
nd prompting the charity to
emind him of his day job (*right*).

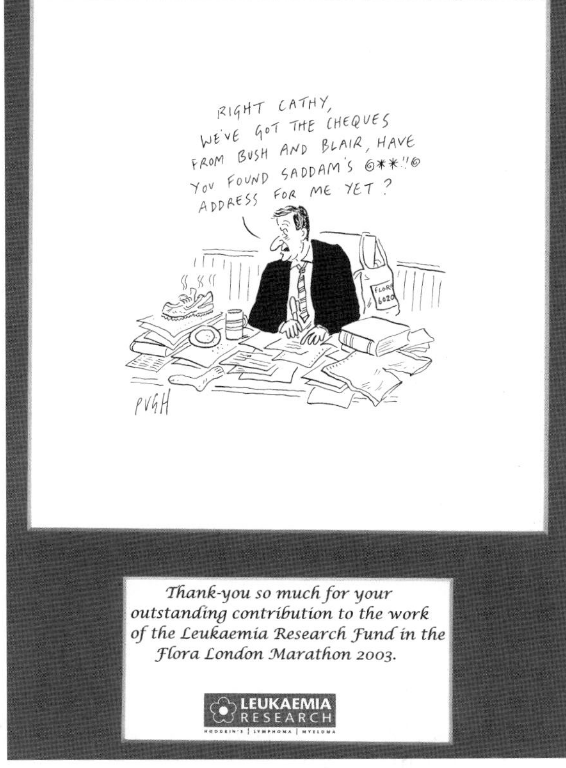

RIGHT CATHY, WE'VE GOT THE CHEQUES FROM BUSH AND BLAIR, HAVE YOU FOUND SADDAM'S ©**!!© ADDRESS FOR ME YET ?
PUGH
Thank-you so much for your outstanding contribution to the work of the Leukaemia Research Fund in the Flora London Marathon 2003.
LEUKAEMIA RESEARCH
HODGKIN'S | LYMPHOMA | MYELOMA

Facing page) The march
gainst the war, February 2003;
nd two ministers who
ventually resigned in protest:
Clare Short and Robin Cook.

Saddam is toppled; Blair thanks the troops.

Bill Clinton (*above, far right*) works on a speech with (left to right) Peter Mandelson, Philip Gould and Alastair Campbell; and (*right*) a cartoonist links Clinton's past problems to Campbell's current ones.

DENIES SEXING UP...
I WANT YOU TO LISTEN TO ME... I DID NOT HAVE SEXUAL RELATIONS WITH THAT DOSSIER....
MAGIC FOR DUMMIES
THE BIG BOOK OF EUPHEMISMS
24·6
MORLAND 03

(*Above, left*) John Scarlett, the spy forced out into the open by the row over (*above, right*) weapons inspector David Kelly.

(*Left*) Alastair Campbell, with Jonathan Powell behind him, leaves Number 10 to give evidence (*below, right*) to the Foreign Affairs select committee.

Lord Hutton (*left*) headed the inquiry into David Kelly's death. BBC reporter Andrew Gilligan (*above*) and Campbell (*below*) arrive to give evidence. The artist's impression (inset) shows Campbell being quizzed by the inquiry's counsel, James Dingemans QC.

PRIVATE EYE

£1.30

CAMPBELL QUITS

Campbell arrives home on the day of his resignation, 29 August 2003, an event enjoyed by *Private Eye* (*right*).

Peter Kilfoyle, Kate Hoey, Glenda Jackson [all former ministers], the list went on. At least we ended up with a majority of the PLP, though David Miliband said to me he reckoned there were about ten backbenchers who were actually totally supportive of TB's position on this. Jack did a good job in the debate and probably helped keep a few on side. Ann Clwyd [Labour MP and Iraq expert] was absolutely terrific and we needed to hear more of her. She brought a real passion to the debate and everyone knew it went back a long way. But the result was pretty tough.[1]

Thursday, February 27

TB was exercised re the French. 'They are really going for it now. This is war by other means.' TB remained reasonably chirpy, said he felt comfortable with the arguments and we just had to keep making them. Philip told me that the groups were far less cynical than the media. They were looking to hear TB more, and when they did, they just about gave him the benefit of the doubt. There was an instinctive understanding that no prime minister would do anything as difficult and unpopular as this for the hell of it. The public wanted a deeper sense of engagement. They were actually ready and willing to listen to deeper arguments on it. There was a hunger for debate on the substance, not just the media headline stuff. TB felt we had to be pushing on two main arguments – the moral case, and the reason why the threat was real and current, not because he could whack missiles off at London but because he could tie up with terrorists and others with a vested interest in damaging us and our interests. But we should understate rather than overstate, a point I made on the conference call. The Americans' saying there was a direct link was counterproductive. Far better to be saying this was a possibility and one we were determined to ensure never came about.

TB, JP, Jack S meeting at which we went over the distinct possibility of no second resolution because the majority was not there for it. TB knew that meant real problems, but remained determined on this, and convinced it was the right course. He said later that he felt only now was Bush really aware of the full extent of the stakes here. This had the potential to transform for good America's relations with Europe and the rest of the world, and in a worst-case scenario was a disaster for everyone. He wanted to get the thing done quickly, but he also wanted them to understand better the broader agenda. He

1 The amendment arguing that the case for military action against Iraq remained unproven was defeated 393 to 199.

felt Bush had moved a good deal on that but was less convinced it permeated throughout the administration.

At Cabinet, things were pretty much rock solid. TB looked very tired and I could sense a few of them only fully realising, when they saw him close up like this going through the arguments, the enormity of the decisions, and the enormity of the responsibility involved. Robin was the trickiest, and was delighting in giving the sense of how isolated we were from normal traditional partners. Clare was doing her usual interruptions and mutterings but a bit less provocatively and for her was relatively onside. She wanted to do a big number on aftermath preparations but TB was there ahead of her. He was very calm, matter-of-fact, just went through where we were on all the main aspects of this. Margaret Beckett, who had been excellent on the radio this morning, made a very strong intervention. She was a useful barometer and she was very supportive. Nobody was really looking to make TB's position more difficult out of today, with the possible exception of Robin, who was moving towards exit.

Later I headed with Sally for the airport to meet TB, who had been at the archbishop's enthronement at Canterbury.[1] There was a cock-up over the planes but we finally met at the Hounslow Suite after a long bus journey and went over themes for the speech in Madrid tomorrow. He had a cold and was surprisingly OK considering the delay. He did an OK interview with Jackie Ashley [*Guardian*] on the flight, and was strongly putting the moral case, but whether it was his cold or her rather irritating manner, he didn't really get into his stride. It was OK but no better and would be unlikely to change Guardianista opinion. I'm not sure anything will at this stage. When I told him that Fiona felt he was on some kind of kamikaze mission on this, he said sometimes when you were in the top job, you just had to do what you thought was right, even if you knew so many people thought you were wrong. We finally got to Madrid, then by helicopter to Moncloa [palace]. He said he knew the risks but he was clear we were doing the right thing.

Friday, February 28

The Ritz Hotel [Madrid] was a bit faded and jaded, and for various reasons I didn't sleep as well as I had hoped to. I went out for a run early on, and gave up after three miles, just couldn't get going. I had worked late on TB's speech for Wales, in particular trying to explain in ways that would connect why he cared so deeply about this, why

[1] Dr Rowan Williams had been anointed as the 104th Archbishop of Canterbury.

he was willing to face potentially disastrous personal and political consequences for this one issue. I was struck more and more by how many people, mainly but not limited to critics, said they couldn't understand why it seemed to matter so much, and that was what we needed to explain. All the rational arguments were out there and yet for a lot of people this had become emotional as much as rational. It had to be in the area of the nature of the threat, but also the lessons of history when it came to failing to stand up to danger.

Blix was now causing us significant problems. He was talking now about Saddam's line on [potential decommissioning of] al-Samoud missiles being a significant piece of disarmament. TB was raging again, said the man was supposed to be a civil servant, but had decided to behave like a politician. He is just desperate not to be seen as the person who allowed a war to start, but his job is to present the facts. He felt Blix was being bullied successfully by the French who, he was now convinced, wanted as their main foreign policy objective to build Europe as a power rival to the US, and determined to shaft TB as the, or a, main player in Europe. He was also worried that Kofi [Annan, UN Secretary General] was getting closer to the Franco-German position from where we thought him to be. At last night's dinner with Aznar, he told TB that Chirac had said directly to him that there were two possible visions for Europe – in one, close to the US; in the other, as a rival. Chirac knew which he wanted. Aznar knew which he wanted too, he said, and it wasn't that.

In Spain there was four per cent support for action without a second UNSCR, twenty-three per cent with it. TB said to Aznar that four per cent was roughly the number you could get in a poll for people who believed Elvis was alive, so he had a struggle! Aznar seemed as determined as TB though. TB's cold had got worse and he had stayed late in bed. The Jackie Ashley interview disaster went on. After all the travel nightmares of yesterday now it transpired the tape hadn't worked, so TB had pretty much wasted his voice. Godric, Sally and I tried to help her out from notes and memory, but it was another pain we could do without. His cold cannot have been helped by all the nonsense of yesterday, broken planes and buses to get scheduled flights and the rest of it. As Jack Straw said, 'He is effectively vice president of the free world, and has to travel around like a cost-cutting tourist.' I had a similar feeling at the Moncloa, which was a beautifully designed and expensively built complex for the PM and his staff and the kind of thing that would provoke an absolute outcry if we went for something like it. Downing Street had a lot of advantages, but set against this, it had a lot of disadvantages too. The Aznar breakfast was the usual going through the motions on a communiqué which would get very little attention at all, and then focusing on the questions likely to come up, which were all pretty obvious. It helped that generally on Iraq they were in the same place, and able to offer a bit of mutual support. Aznar was determined to reshape Spain's relations with the US. The press conference was good, and between them they got up the right message.

We set off for the airport, TB now turning his mind to the [Welsh Labour Party conference] speech, in between continuing to vent his spleen at GB. He was convinced that GB and Co. were running the line to the media that the reason TB couldn't persuade people was because of the general TB-trust issue. 'It is actually wicked.' There was another story in *The Times* today about TB planning to overrule GB re foundation hospitals which sparked another little wave of Treasury briefing against Milburn for having stirred it up. Back on to the small plane taking us to Wales where TB wrote out in long hand the Iraq section of the speech for Swansea. Very strong. The nature of the threat plus the lessons of [Neville] Chamberlain as 'a good man who made the wrong decision' [appeasing Nazi Germany]. I reordered it and we signed it off on the thirty-minute drive to the conference centre. Fairly big demos. His voice was really bad now but he just about held it together for the speech, which went OK, both in the hall and media-wise. On the plane back we were talking through general positioning. Blix was not making things easy in one direction; the Yanks were making it difficult in the other. This is tough, he said, very tough, about as tough as it gets. He asked what I thought the chances were of it killing him off. Twenty per cent, I said. 'I'd say nearer thirty the way things are right now.'

Saturday, March 1

I did a twenty-mile run, my longest yet, stopping only once when TB called for a chat re Blix. A combination of Blix and the recent moves by the Iraqis had got us on the back foot again. He felt it was all now about the politics of the UNSC, and would come down to a hard-headed argument for votes. It was all going to ebb and flow but we just had to keep going. He was clear that the consequences of not being with the US now were incalculable. I said I felt there had been various points where we could have done something different vis-à-vis the US. He said no, the only way to have had influence with them was to be clear from the start we would be with them when things got really tough. He was clear our interests were aligned.

Sunday, March 2

Yesterday's news of the arrest of al-Qaeda's Number 3 kept the media off our backs for most of the day, but in general I felt things moving away from us again.[1] Saddam was definitely outwitting us on al-Samoud missiles and getting us in the wrong place. We didn't have the armoury to hit back hard. It was partly my fault because I hadn't been motoring as I had in previous full-on communications situations. We were doing OK on the sustained arguments material, but on the quick tactical stuff I didn't feel on form, and I think that hit TB's confidence on some of this too. I had to decide re the FA [chief executive job] because they were starting interviews tomorrow, but I had pretty much reached the conclusion it wasn't possible. PG said it would be seen as a disaster for TB, just when he didn't need anything to add to his problems. The latest polling was not as bad as it might have been considering.

Monday, March 3

TB called me up at 7.45 as he was due to leave for Belfast at 8.15. He was even more worried than he had been on Friday. He felt things just were not where they needed to be. David M and John Scarlett came back from their weekend trip to Mexico and Chile and felt both countries were very firmly on the fence and could see no reason to come off it. TB said it was still possible we could get a majority on the UNSC but if it was in circumstances where people felt we bullied and arm-twisted, the French would be less worried about putting down a veto. The Americans were frankly alienating people by their tactics. David M said the message these smaller countries got was the basic assumption from the Americans that they would come over in the end.

I said to TB that our problem on the communications front was largely caused by US friendly fire. Just when we started to get a message through, they would come up with something different which would pose a real problem for us. They looked the whole time like they were desperate for war. We at least didn't look like we were desperate for war, but we did look like we were desperate to be with them, so to a lot of people it amounted to the same thing. TB said he would have to tell Bush that it was not possible to get the votes at the moment. It was totally what they didn't want to hear but they had to hear it from someone. He was very down on the Americans

[1] Khalid Sheikh Mohammed had been captured by the Pakistani secret service in Rawalpindi.

at the moment. I was feeling much as I had done for some time, compounded by another totally useless conference call which was becoming little more than a telephonic multinational diary meeting. Also I sensed they were becoming irritated with us. I told David I wanted to be frank with them that Bush, not just Rumsfeld, was the main communication problem. With TB away [in Northern Ireland] for the next day or two, I did a series of meetings on the structures we had, and also trying to analyse which of our key messages were actually getting through, both here and in the regions.

I had a meeting with Ed Balls, still going on about Peter M urging Milburn to be a rival to GB, still claiming that we were encouraging columnists to write that GB could be for the chop. He claimed GB wanted to do more on Iraq, and I said the more he did the better. But I always felt he would only do it on his terms. I also suggested he and Milburn do something public together in the run-up to the tax rise. TB called in once or twice re Iraq. Blix had effectively become a commentator as well as a player. Saddam's games were playing well for him and whether they tried or not, the Americans just weren't helping us in public opinion terms. Sally felt the party was with us up to the point of the destruction of missiles, which tipped the balance towards giving the inspectors more time. TB was moving to the Canadian position of a bit more time to get the questions finally answered.

I was beginning to fear that if we went to war without a second resolution, TB would fail to get it through the Commons, and he would be dead in the water. 'I've just got to tell Bush clearly that if he does this wrong, he'll have governments toppling all over the place and cause absolute chaos.' There was a poll in Spain showing ninety-five per cent opposition. Opposition in Turkey was enormous.

Tuesday, March 4

TB still in Northern Ireland. The Iraq meeting was fine though I felt we needed to do more to get up the bigger argument about democracies versus dictatorships. We were in a very odd period where there was a strong sense of momentum towards war come what may, but with the dynamics feeling as though they were totally against us. He was doing OK in Belfast, though [David] Trimble [First Minister of Northern Ireland] walked out at 7 and Sinn Fein kept chiselling away. They kept at it till gone midnight and TB didn't get back till 3am. I had some good cheques coming in – [Michael] Heseltine [former Conservative Deputy Prime Minister], [Jeremy] Paxman [BBC]. Ed Balls called, clearly having spoken to GB, and said he thought if he did something with Milburn, the story would be division not unity. Depends how you do it.

Wednesday, March 5

TB had just a few hours' sleep before his meeting with [Igor] Ivanov [Russian foreign minister]. David M had raised with Condi the idea of TB going to Chile and Mexico and trying to get them to co-present on the day of Blix the idea of a final ultimatum and taking the clusters document [a paper setting out where Iraq had not complied with its disarmament obligations] from Blix to get out what needed to be done. She was not dismissive, though they may be sensing that we felt they lacked the subtlety required. TB felt strongly these countries needed to be given a reason for coming on board more than fear of US bullying. The idea would be to say after Blix reported that it was clear Saddam was not co-operating and now we would set a date by which the UNSC would decide it was clear he had not taken the final opportunity to disarm. Ivanov was clear that Putin would like to be more involved. David felt there was a case for going to Chile as early as tomorrow.

TB was pretty good in the House today, considering how little sleep he had had and how difficult the issues were. France, Germany and Russia issued a joint statement, de Villepin driving it mainly. Earlier Jack came over for a meeting with TB and told him 'If you go next Wednesday with Bush, and without a second resolution, the only regime change that will be taking place is in this room.' Written down, it sounds more menacing than it was. He was trying to be helpful. TB's call to Bush was OK, though as I stayed in TB's room, I only heard his side, saying we had a real problem with world opinion, that these countries needed a reason to come round, that he wanted to go to Chile and set out the outlines of an amended resolution with a deadline so it was clear there would be war if Saddam hadn't responded. Blix was out again today, as much commentator as civil servant. TB felt the UNSC had to take control of this now, not Blix.

When the call ended, Jonathan walked in and said that was a 'fuck me' call, in that they actually seemed far apart. TB said it was not as bad as that. He told Bush we would be with them come what may but these other countries needed help to come over. He also said Bush needed to work more on Putin, not just write him off. TB then did the [Chilean President Ricardo] Lagos call and put the same idea. Lagos didn't totally go against it but was not exactly wild and we certainly had to put on hold the idea of going tomorrow. By the end of the day, not only did he think he should go to Chile, but also

Moscow and another visit to Bush. So the wanderlust was on. 'We are in this, and nobody must think we would ever wobble.' But the Americans were not helping. They claimed they had already slowed down as a result of TB, that Bush had wanted to go as early as yesterday but TB had made sure he didn't. It was a pretty grim scene, and no matter how grim, TB was still saying constantly it was the right thing to do.

Thursday, March 6

I ran in, slightly different route, almost five miles, then up to see TB in the flat with David and Jonathan. He was looking a bit more worried. He said the frustrating thing is that he felt that if we were in charge of it all, we would have sorted it by now. David said the Americans were much more confident they had the votes for a second resolution. TB was keen the Americans reach out far more, especially to Putin. He was also keen that we 'rise above Blix' and a meeting with Lagos might be the way to do that. Jack came over and we discussed pre-Blix positioning. We needed to get out the idea that we wanted the clusters document out there, also the sense that Blix was just inhaling the politics in all this. We agreed we needed to publish a version of the clusters document which would help turn round the argument. I was impressed with Jack at the moment. He could sometimes be very nerdish, and wood-for-trees, but his grasp of the detail was a help, and his political feel was currently good. We discussed with JP the idea of going to Africa to see the three leaders there.[1] He was off to New York on Concorde at 9 with the message from TB that we needed to turn the Blix clusters document to our advantage.

Cabinet was scratchy, Robin and Clare both a bit bolder in setting out their concerns, Clare saying that the idea of horse trading and bullying was bad for the authority of the UN. TB hit back quite hard, said it was not just the US who were bullying and intimidating. What about the French telling the Bulgarians they would not be able to get into the EU if they sided with America? Robin was diddling rather more subtly whereas Clare was just doing anti-Americanism. John R hit back hard as well as TB. I walked through with TB to his office at the end. He said 'God, you wouldn't go into the jungle with them would you?' The mood had generally been OK, though there was clearly a lot of concern about our position.

[1] Angola, Cameroon and Guinea supported continued inspections, but were thought to be against taking a stand on disarmament by military action.

We set off for a studio in Wembley, where he was doing an MTV special. He was fairly relaxed and it helped put out a tough message, the idea that it was going to a vote and people had to decide.[1] The audience was pretty good, not the usual rent-a-crowd. He spoke to the Cameroon president [Paul Biya] in the car on the way back and offered him a visit to the UK. Then the call to Lagos, and the idea of the visit was clearly not on as things stood. There was a rumour doing the rounds that Bush was about to address the Americans to say they had captured Bin Laden. I called Dan. It wasn't true. He intended to say they were confident of a second resolution and he intended to be positive re MEPP. We agreed there may be a case for going for Blix tomorrow.

With the Chile trip off, TB was keen to go and see Bush soon. I said we had to be clear about a purpose, because there would be such focus on the visit. He said it was to get them to do the right thing. I said but they were already very clear about their purpose, which was to go for it. I said 'Are you not sure that your frustration at the way others are dealing with it is just producing a kind of wanderlust?' He said no matter how many times you spoke on the phone, there was no substitute for face-to-face meetings. He said don't worry, we'll get through this fine. I asked him, if at the end of this he was history before his time, was this issue really worth sacrificing everything? He said it is always worth doing what you think is the right thing to do. Iraq is a real problem, Saddam is a real problem, for us as much as anyone, and it's been ignored too long.

Friday, March 7

Up to the flat to see TB with David, Jonathan and Sally. Condi had told David overnight that Putin had been clear with Bush that they would veto the second resolution. Also we still didn't have a clue whether Chile and Mexico would come over. The mood was gloomier than ever. TB was keen to get up the clusters document and also move towards the sense of an ultimatum. He and David were both now expressing their irritation at the US. David was even of the view that we should be pushing the US to a version of the Franco-German idea of inspections with force, a blue beret [UN] force involved in disarmament. TB spent hours on the phone, including an hour with Putin, a long call with Jack and later with Bush. He wanted to give

[1] Blair told the MTV audience 'If we don't act now, then we will go back to what has happened before and then of course the whole thing begins again and he [Saddam] carries on developing these weapons . . . dangerous weapons, particularly if they fall into the hands of terrorists.'

him a clear message about the political realities, namely that we could not do this without a Commons vote and it was not going to be easy without a second resolution, or with a resolution that was vetoed. The Russian veto was a new element. Everyone expected the French to be ultra difficult but thought the Russians might be more prone to be neutral, but Putin's position had clearly hardened. During their call, Putin was very clear that he felt taken for granted by the Americans, and he felt he got a lot of talk from them but very little delivery. Jack was doing his UNSC speech and did it well and with passion. Bush was agreeing to a slightly later deadline, March 17.

TB, Jonathan, Sally, Pat [McFadden] and I had a meeting to go through some of the what-ifs, including him going if we lost a vote. TB said he felt that there had to be a vote on a second resolution and if it was about the use of troops and he lost a vote on that, he would have to go. The Tories were making clear they would support us on a war motion but not on a confidence motion. Andrew Turnbull was quietly looking into how a JP caretaker premiership would operate. Even though we were talking about his own demise, TB still felt we were doing the right thing. He said even though we were all rightly irritated by the Americans, it was the French we should be really angry with. Bush told TB he would certainly go for a vote. He was still making clear he didn't feel he needed a UNSCR but he wanted to go for it.

Jonathan described the whole thing now as an enormous game of diplomatic chicken. TB said we could not flinch now, that if any weakness was signalled, we've had it. He was making clear to Bush, not in personal or moaning terms but as a reality, that his job was on the line, that if we didn't get the Commons vote, there could be no using UK troops, which the Americans needed. Black humour was setting in. TB said his future was now in the hands of the dying president of Guinea [Lansana Conté] and the diplomatic judgement of Jeff Ennis [Labour MP]. We were sending JP to a president's deathbed to keep the British government alive.

Bush was at least conscious of the difficulties they gave us. He said to TB don't worry, I'll be more subtle than you fear. 'I'm not going to say to Lagos – hey you mutha, I'm gonna crush you like a Chilean grape.' TB said afterwards that the reason he liked him was that he was actually so straight, and understood his own weaknesses as well as strengths. He happened to be right on the issue even if they didn't always handle it well. I said all that being said, TB did need to think about his own position, not get pinned into just doing what Bush wanted. TB was clear with him that we needed a bit more time. I reckoned the chances of him being out within a week or two were about 20–1 now. Parliamentary arithmetic was complicated, and not yet entirely clear.

Jack called from New York and pissed me off when he referred post CIC dossier to the 'discredited Downing Street machine' and said he didn't want to put out our short clusters document. We did it anyway, with Tom going over to the gallery after Blix. We were all outraged at the Blix report. TB said it was political and dishonest. Dan Bartlett said we don't care what he thinks, his job is to tell us what he knows. Scarlett said he was wrong in saying the Iraqis were trying to co-operate more. TB was very philosophical about it all. As I sat listening to him on the phone, I lost count of how many times he said: 1. we are right on the issue; 2. we have to see it through; 3. I'm philosophical about what it means for me and whether I survive or not. TB was keen to push the idea that the only reason the concessions were coming was because of the pressure we were applying. But there were real divisions and dangers and the UN was on very dangerous terrain. There was a very clear picture, clearer than ever, of the US in one place, us in another, the French in another, the Russians in another, and the UN as an organisation really worried about where it was heading.

Saturday, March 8

Blix didn't come out as badly as it might have done. In a sense he was almost irrelevant now. I spoke to TB to agree the lines to push for the Sundays – namely there are two routes by which he can avoid conflict: 1. he disarms, or 2. he goes. TB was working the phones pretty much flat out, especially Lagos but also the Chinese and keeping in touch with Bush. We were pushing hard for the second resolution. We were discussing whether JP should go to Africa to work the African countries on TB's behalf. I tried to get Jack out for the *Frost* programme but he said he was desperate for a day off. I spoke to JP who agreed to come down from Hull to do it. JP was totally onside at the moment. TB felt the PLP was at best shaky. He remained sure we were doing the right thing and it helped internally that JP was as solid as he was.

Later I did a conference call with JP, [Patricia] Hewitt and [Peter] Hain who were also on the [Sunday] programmes and went over some of the problem questions e.g. on second resolution and also the issue of a Commons vote. By the time the papers came in, the main story was a mini wave of threatened resignations by PPSs [parliamentary private secretaries]. JP was totally scornful, said they were cowardly and pathetic. When it was pointed out that Anne Campbell was one of them, JP said 'Who is she PPS to?' 'Me,' said Patricia. 'Who is me?' said JP. 'It's Patricia here, John.' I managed to get in a long run earlier, twenty-one miles or so, and was feeling in good shape pre marathon. But Rory was racing at Brighton and had a massive allergy attack which had Fiona really worried for a while. Again, I felt bad that work had kept me from going down there with him, but he seemed a lot better when they got home. The key now was winning the necessary votes at the UN but in some ways the situation was in limbo. TB was clear we just had to keep our nerve and keep striving to get their votes.

Sunday, March 9

Up to watch JP on *Frost*. He was fine on the basic lines we had agreed though the resignations were the main news out of it. Andy Reed [PPS to Margaret Beckett] duly resigned as I was driving with Calum, Philip [Gould] and Georgia [his daughter] to Watford. I was troubled all the way by the possible clash between the marathon and the [FA] Cup semi-final if we got through and were playing on the Sunday. But the problem never arose as we played poorly and went down 2–0. I had agreed to do a piece for the *Mirror* which I dictated rather half-heartedly on the drive back.

TB spoke to Jiang Zemin [Chinese Premier], and the Chinese put out the line that they were calling for more time for inspections. Then at around 5.30, just as I was settling down to do some work upstairs, Clare Short called me. She hardly ever called me, so I was surprised when Switch came on with her. She was friendly enough as we did a bit of small talk, but then got to the point. She had done an interview with Andrew Rawnsley for the *Westminster Hour* and had said she would resign if we went to war without a second resolution; that we were allowing our own policy to be dictated by the US; and that we were not doing enough in the Middle East. She said it all very matter-of-factly, as though she was telling me a few football results. I was conscious of myself shaking my head as she spoke, and then making a mental note to myself not to let my loathing of her pour out, but I said I was at a total loss to understand how she thought this kind of public conversation helped the government make and implement sensible policy. I also reminded her that nobody, as she herself had said, had done more than TB to get this down the UN route.

She said nothing at first. Then I said I also thought it absolutely extraordinary that she should be saying this to me, rather than to TB. 'I thought I would call you because I knew you would be angry and

I thought I'd rather get the anger direct than through the media.' The whine in the voice was whinier than ever. As if TB was going to be doing fucking cartwheels. I said I found the whole thing extraordinary. I thought the deal was that if you were a Cabinet minister, you spoke up in Cabinet if you had concerns, that was the place to do it, and then a policy or a line was agreed and everyone stuck to it. I said I had never heard her say in Cabinet she would resign. She said – rich this, considering how often she spoke – that she tended not to speak in Cabinet in case she was briefed against. I said there was no point her talking to me; she would have to speak to TB. I would call him to see if he wanted to speak to her. She said she was going out shopping with her mum but she would take her mobile with her. How considerate.

TB was at church so I sent through a note to be given to him when the service ended. I called JP, who was due to meet TB at 7. He said the whole thing was typical of her – she was a coward, couldn't cope with pressure, and so ended up doing it like this, hanging her conscience out to dry. Jack called after learning Mike O'Brien was going to be played the tape of her interview on the programme. He said this was the result of years of her being allowed to do what she wanted. It was a disgrace. I spoke to Mike and we agreed he would simply stress the line we were working for a second resolution and not get drawn into a detailed conversation re Clare. TB finally called after he got back to Chequers from church. He was as appalled as I expected him to be. 'It is disgusting, totally disgusting.' It was the same word virtually every minister who called to complain used. TB said he was appalled for a whole stack of different reasons: 1. at what she had said and done; 2. that she had done it on the radio rather than talking to him; 3. that she had called me rather than him, and 4. most importantly, that it totally undercut his strategy to build UN support. He felt it showed there was a willingness among some – her included – to push him out over this. I was less sure it was a thought-through thing at all.

I said I cannot see how you can keep her without looking weak. He said in process terms, there was no doubt about that. The BBC had told Mike O'Brien that she called them up and volunteered to go on. He spoke to her later, and said simply he would reflect. We agreed to a public line that simply made clear she had never spoken in these terms within Cabinet or to the PM. There was no point rushing on this. JP spoke to her a couple of times. He said what she was saying was that she didn't have confidence in the PM's strategy, or his ability to pursue it. She claimed it had not come out as she intended, which was bollocks. I now had the transcript and went through it with JP. He said he didn't see how he could keep her in those circumstances. She was clearly limbering up to go. He thought it was not impossible GB knew what she was planning and that she might be thinking in terms of a stalking-horse challenge at conference. I went with Fiona and the kids to Pizza Express, but the phone just never stopped, usually another minister to go on about how beyond the pale she was and had to go.

TB called again, said Saddam would be laughing his head off when he heard about it. Later a secure conference call with Jonathan, David M with Condi, Dan and Andy Card [White House chief of staff] to go through the various scenarios: majority with no vetoes – fine; majority plus veto(es) – manageable but difficult; no vote; no majority. We said if we got a second resolution we would put it to a parliamentary vote quickly. We could live with a French veto, because people expected it, but we couldn't live without a majority. If that happened, we would probably have to put it to a vote, and if we lost it, there was a danger we would lose the prime minister. The Yanks said that if we got a majority with vetoes, Bush wanted to go straight in, within days, even short of the March 17 deadline, would say the UNSC had failed to act, and get going, on the basis of 1441. We made the point that we needed the second resolution. Without it, we had real problems in Parliament. They said continually they wanted to help us but of course what they really wanted was the use of our forces.

Jonathan and I continually emphasised we needed the second resolution. We had seven definite votes still, but Condi was less confident re Chile and Mexico. She said [Vicente] Fox [President of Mexico] was in a state of torture because it was such a big thing to stand up against the US. They basically wanted by Tuesday/Wednesday to say we had exhausted every effort and now the diplomatic window had closed. We said if we got the majority for a second resolution, even with vetoes we would have to go through it, including with the timetable. Andy Card said he feared the president's response would be 'Here we go, another final opportunity, a final final opportunity and this time we really mean it.' I said TB's job was on the line and we did not want to lose him. 'No, nor do we,' said Condi. I think our concern was probably deeper. I called Jack Cunningham [former Cabinet minister] who was doing the media in the morning. He was scathing re Short, Chris Smith, Kilfoyle, Dobson. There were two groups ranged against TB, he said – those who never wanted him, and those who felt he didn't share their own high view of themselves. But the mood out there was not good, and this was a 'dangerous moment' for TB. I listened to Clare's interview and the disgusting self-indulgent whine made the words even worse to the ear than they were in print on the transcript. It was clear she was asking to go, but wanting the moral high ground when it happened.

Another rash of ministerial calls after it went out – JP, JR, JS, DB – all saying she was an outrage and there had to be decisive leadership about this. JP said to her afterwards that he had been sitting in the room with TB as he called some of these leaders and she totally undercut his strategy. Phil Webster [*Times*] told me every single broadsheet had been planning to lead on TB trying to go the UN route, and then Clare does this. I listened in later to the TB/Bush call. TB started by saying he was 'fighting on all fronts'. 'Attaboy,' came the reply, a bit too patronisingly for my tastes. TB said one of his ministers was threatening to resign, also that Chirac told Lagos that the Africans were 'in the bag'. I hope that's bullshit, said Bush. TB had spoken to the four leaders who made up the 8 plus 1. [Pervez] Musharraf [President of Pakistan] was with us but it was difficult for him. Cameroon said absolutely. Guinea's foreign minister coming tomorrow. [José Eduardo] Dos Santos [President of Angola] solid.

TB was doing most of the talking, said he felt Lagos was trying to move. We had been working on the idea of laying out a series of tests re what we meant by full co-operation. He felt Bush needed to work some more on Fox. He felt if we could get them to accept the idea of the tests, other countries would also come with us. But Bush said he was already putting enormous pressure on Mexico. He said he had also been twisting Lagos' arm, 'but gently because I respect you'. GWB said he could be in no doubt that if there was a vote, they would have to use it. TB said the Chileans felt any tests should be agreed through Blix. Bush not happy. Bush said Saddam was very adept at exploiting weakness and Blix was weak. These countries need to see we want to do this peacefully. He wants the vote to go through but not on an unreasonable basis.

TB said the public opinion problem stemmed from people feeling the US wanted a war. We have to put up the genuine tests of disarmament, show the determination to try to do this peacefully. Bush said he had never come across a situation where the dividing line between success and failure was so narrow. He said we want it done peacefully, or any other way. His tone was very different to TB's. Bush was talking the diplomatic talk whilst clearly irritated by the whole thing. His worry was that we were negotiating with ourselves, that we get a resolution with a timeframe, everything they want, and we get nothing for it. He said he couldn't believe Chirac said he had the Africans in the bag. 'I can,' said TB. 'I have a lot of experience of them.' He [Bush] was clearly aware of how tough things were getting for TB. He said if the swing countries didn't vote with us 'my last choice is for your government to go down. That is the absolute last thing I want to have happen. I would rather go it alone than have your government fall.' 'I appreciate that,' said TB. 'I really mean that,' said Bush. TB said it was also important he understood that he really believed in what they were trying to do. Bush – 'I know that but I am not going to see your government fall on this.'

TB said 'I've got our troops there too. If I can't get it through Parliament, we fall, and that is not exactly the regime change I want. We have to work out what Mexico and Chile need.' They agreed to speak again to Lagos and Fox. TB said we were in high-risk, high-reward territory. Bush said he was being eroded domestically by inactivity. He also said he felt the hardest part would be after Saddam. Then Bush did a number on the changes in the Arab world that could follow. TB said the biggest concern in not going with the UN was the lack of support if things went wrong. [US General] Tommy Franks had said ninety per cent of precision bombs are precise. That leaves ten per cent. But Bush was left in no doubt TB would be with him when the time came. Bush said 'I'm not going to let you down. Hang in there buddy. You are doing great.' What had been interesting was that Bush listened far more intently to TB. TB did not make too much of his own problems, and was stressing he thought we were doing the right thing.

Monday, March 10

Needless to say Clare was leading the news, amid lots of assumptions we would sack her. The papers, as expected, were fairly grim. I went up to the flat where David was briefing TB on Jeremy Greenstock's meeting with Blix. Blix was just about up for the clusters plan. TB wanted Jeremy to work on Blix and [Dimitri] Perricos [Blix's deputy] to get them signed up to it. It was the only show in town and the only one likely to lead to a majority of the UNSC. He was still working on Lagos and worried about him. Re Clare he said he viewed it as an act of personal betrayal to do what she did, without warning, when he was in the midst of negotiating on this. TB's real anger with the French had been the sending of mixed messages to Saddam, and that is what Clare was doing too. He was minded to sack her but on the other hand felt there was no point in doing anything other than being totally hard-headed and ruthless about the issue, in which she was something of a sideshow.

I got Jack Cunningham, Bev Hughes [Home Office minister] and Alan Milburn up all making the point that it was odd to do this on the radio rather than speak to the PM about the threat to resign. JP spoke to her twice last night and again this morning and sensed she had concluded we were definitely going to war and she was going to position herself to resign with maximum damage. He even wondered whether she wasn't setting herself up as a possible challenger to GB. I took JP up to the flat. He said it was on balance not sensible to help turn her into a martyr, which is what she wanted, but instead leave her hanging in the wind for a while. He went off to speak to her again and later TB spoke to her, told her she had committed an act of gross betrayal, that he was at a total loss to understand how she could do that. Her defence was that she felt in recent weeks his approach with her was to listen politely but take no notice. He said to her who do you think got us down the UN route, who is the one still pushing on that, who is the one trying to use this to get the MEPP going again? She was totally beyond the pale. He had decided however that he was not going to sack her. JP and I were usually at the front of the 'get rid of her' queue but agreed that on this it would be a mistake. JP said it was all about her position, nothing else. She did say sorry at the end of her conversation, but in that whiney, drippy way that was designed to convey she was sorry that he couldn't see things as clearly as she did.

Jack C was excellent on the media. TB and I prepared for the ITV programme which was pretty dire because the usual so-called representative audience was packed with the usual activists. TB meeting with Hilary A, John R, David Triesman. Hilary said that if we didn't get a second resolution, or if there was a French veto, we were in trouble. So the PLP was willing to subcontract foreign policy to Chirac? We headed over to the FCO for the ITV special. I knew the moment we arrived the audience would be a problem. You could smell the mood. They were not so-called ordinary people but a group put together to give TB as hard a time as possible. Trevor McDonald didn't chair it very well and the whole thing became not just difficult on the substance, but also pretty undignified. When all is said and done he is the prime minister and one or two of them were talking to him like he was a piece of shit on the pavement. He kept calm and dealt with it fine, deciding in the end just to absorb it all but as he came out he gave me a look that could kill. It was a pretty shoddy operation and Peter Stothard [former *Times* editor], who was following us around for the *Times* magazine with [photographer] Nick Danziger, reckoned that not only was the audience slanted, but they had wound them up beforehand.

Then a meeting to discuss whether we could get going on a revised amendment with the challenges to Saddam. [Igor] Ivanov had said the Russians would veto and Chirac did the same. Pakistan indicated abstention. TB told Lagos that if Chile and others moved, the French would pull back but that looked doubtful. Chirac was clearly up for the kill on this, really felt he could damage TB and alarm some of his traditional allies. Chirac was now out with the veto message. TB was on and off the phone to Lagos who said he was eighty per cent there but worried about France and Russia. TB spoke to Greenstock, then at 9.50 did a long call with Bush. GWB kicked off 'Did you save your Cabinet woman?' TB said she was still in for the moment, that she met every description of self-indulgence 'but we have to carry on'. TB did most of the talking, set out where he thought all the different players were. GWB reckoned seven votes solid 'locked up' but Pakistan and the Latins were difficult. He felt Chirac was trying to get us to the stage where we would not put to a vote because we would be so worried about losing.

TB said he felt Lagos wanted to come, but he needed to be able to say he had achieved something, even winning a few days more. But I could sense in his voice and the manner of the discussion that Bush was less emollient than yesterday. He felt Fox would do whatever Chile did. TB said Lagos wanted to come with us but he was very nervous. TB had spoken to him several times. He was biting but wanted to know what the inspectors would say. Lagos was asking do we have to accept military action if he fails these tests? Bush asked re timeframe. TB said they would want to kick us back a few days as a way of showing they got something out of this.

The French and Russian strategy was to play it so hard that we end up thinking we cannot even dream of getting to nine or ten votes. But TB said if we can shift Chile and Mexico, we change the weather. If we can make these tests the basis of an ultimatum, and then the French and Russians have to veto, with Chile and Mexico behind us, and the numbers right on the UN, I think I have a fighting chance of getting it through the Commons. Bush was worried about rolling in more time. TB held his ground, said the Latins had to be able to say they got something out of all this talking to us. They need to be able to point to something that they won last minute that explains why they finally supported us. Bush said the first resolution was also tough – total and complete disarmament. 'We can't weaken.' 1441, he said, we should just put it down again.

TB felt the second resolution was important and this was the best way to get it. He felt that we needed UN backing, or at least a majority, on the assumption France and Russia would veto. Bush said 'Let me be frank. The second resolution is for the benefit of Great Britain. We want it so we can go ahead together.' His worry was that we would get rolled over on timings and also the inspectors would get used by Saddam again. There was something crazy and random about what was going on. It was a pure accident of timing that suddenly made Chile and Mexico the focus of so much diplomacy, TB working on Lagos, Bush on Fox. TB said when this is over, we need to take a long hard look at the reality of how the UN works. These countries suddenly had a lot of power but seemed unsure how to use it. TB felt the Russians, French and Germans now had a bit of a swagger, felt they were showing that the Americans can be taught a lesson. TB felt if we swung over Chile, Mexico would come, then we could go to Putin and say let's be reasonable.

Bush said he'd had a bad conversation with the Turks. [Recep Tayyip] Erdogan [new President of Turkey] had basically given him a lecture on world events when Bush called for [military] overflight rights. He said he would have to go to Parliament. Bush said 'It was not friend-to-friend, far from it. Maybe the interpreter didn't get the nuances, I don't know, but it was a bad call, no camaraderie.' He said again we must not retreat from 1441 and we cannot keep giving them more time.

I was by and large signed up for the policy but it did make me feel a bit sick the extent to which our problems were US-created, and our politics now so dominated by their approach. TB had not really wavered at all but as the time got nearer the politics got tougher. Bush said 'It's time to do this. We have sent tough signals and he knows that. So no more deals.' He had told Rumsfeld to move the ships. We had Schroeder coming over and Bush told TB the Germans needed to know the real lie of the land. He said he took Schroeder's election antics personally.

Bush said again he had no problem with TB presenting him as the US hard cop against his persuading soft cop. He then said 'It makes me sick the way these people are trying to divide us so that we help save Saddam's skin.' Bush said 'If you ran for president over here, you'd whip my ass.' Laughter. TB said he was sure we were doing the right thing and we had to see it through but it was going to be really tough. Bush signed off with 'Hang in there friend.'

Tuesday, March 11

Growing sense of crisis, what with the Chirac veto, talk of a challenge to TB and the dynamic moving away from us the whole time. The press was about as OK as it could be re Clare, but generally things were getting more not less difficult. TB was seeing the Portuguese PM [José Manuel Barroso]. I missed the start because I was doing the morning meeting, but went in for the end, and said there was the case for going at the French with the concept of an 'unreasonable veto'. TB laughed and said to Barroso 'He is the Roy Keane of the operation.' When he said that Barroso would be more diplomatic, I said I know, because he is the Eusébio [great Portuguese footballer]. The doorstep was fine, TB saying Chirac risked letting Saddam off the hook by saying they would veto *'quelles que soient les circonstances'* [whatever the circumstances]. After Barroso left we had a meeting with JP, JR and Hilary A to try to get more politics into all this. The party was going to be important and we were neglecting things.

TB asked if we should not be a bit nicer to Clare and was met with a row of uniformly horrified looks. JP looked at him as though he was mad. TB briefed them on the diplomacy and we agreed I should do a briefing note to go to the whole of the PLP. JP and I also agreed, having persuaded TB to do more difficult TV, that there was a danger it was going too far, that Operation Access had become Operation Masochism and there was something a bit undignified about him getting beaten up too much. [Peter] Goldsmith had done a long legal opinion and said he did not want TB to present it too positively. He wanted to make it clear he felt there was a reasonable case for war under 1441. There was also a case to be made the other way and a lot would depend on what actually happened. TB also made clear that he did not particularly want Goldsmith to launch a detailed discussion at Cabinet, though it would have to happen at some time, and ministers would want to cross-examine. With the mood as it was, and with Robin and Clare operating as they were, he knew that if there was any nuance at all, they would be straight out saying the advice was that it was not legal, the AG was casting doubt on the legal basis for war. Peter Goldsmith was clear that though a lot depended on what happened, he was casting doubt in some circumstances and if Cabinet had to approve the policy of going to war, he had to be able to put the reality to them. Sally said it was for TB to speak to Cabinet, and act on the AG's advice. He would simply say the advice said there was a reasonable case. The detailed discussion would follow.[1]

[1] Lord Goldsmith was later to tell the 2010 Iraq Inquiry that he had strengthened his legal view of the Iraq War after a visit to the US, for discussions with lawyers there. He described suggestions that he did so because of political pressure as 'complete nonsense'. The former Attorney General said he had believed it was 'safer' to get a new UN resolution but gave the 'green light' after deciding force was justified by UN accords dating back to 1991.

Alan Milburn called me later to say RC told him he would resign if we didn't get a second resolution. Of the two, RC was easily the more serious and the more thought through. Peter G told TB he had been thinking of nothing else for three weeks, that he wished he could be much clearer in his advice, but in reality it was nuanced. I had a polling meeting with Stan Greenberg. The Lib Dems were on the up a bit. Tuition fees was a growing problem. The figures on right/wrong direction were not great. Asylum was still number one problem area, then crime, and the two were becoming linked in some people's minds. We were losing young people, London swing voters, plus middle class. The Tories had the beginnings of a message that was getting through. Of those who voted for us last time, only sixty-three per cent were still solid. Stan was very sceptical about what we were doing with the Americans. He felt we were being used as part of a US strategy.

TB did a call with Lagos, who was still moving about, then to a meeting with JS, GH, CDS and the AG re the military plan. GH said he would be happier with a clearer green light from the AG. Andrew Turnbull really irritated TB when he said he would need something to put round the Civil Service that what they were engaged in was legal. TB was clear we would do nothing that wasn't legal, and gave him a very heavy look. Peter [Goldsmith] did a version of the arguments he had put to TB, on the one hand, on the other, reasonable case. GH raised the US request for use of Diego Garcia and [RAF] Fairford, saying we should not say it was automatic but had to go round the system. TB said he did not want to send a signal that we would not do it. GH and JS were trying to press on him that the Americans were thinking about doing this very soon, i.e. even at the weekend, and that some of our forces would have to be in before.

CDS said his formal military advice would be that it was not sensible to go on the 17th because of the full moon. We would have to get in before any bombs with night vision and buggies. Our forces were to be involved in the operation to secure the oilfields and prevent the Iraqis setting off an environmental catastrophe to hit the oil markets. We desperately needed some change in the diplomatic weather. The best thing may in the end be to go in without a vote because of the timings, and that once troops are in there the mood changes. But short of that, which was risky enough, it was hard to see how the dynamic changed. There was another small step back with the news Guinea would not be coming with us because they were now in the chair. The system is crazy, like pot luck as to who is in a voting seat at any one time, though I guess it is just about the only way they can make all countries feel more or less involved.

Then came another Rumsfeld disaster. He did a press conference at which he said he and Geoff Hoon had just spoken and went on to indicate that we would not necessarily be in the first wave of attacks because of our parliamentary difficulties. It was not entirely clear whether it was deliberate – i.e. a warning shot that they could and would do it without us – or a fuck-up. We all assumed the latter. He just didn't get other people's politics at all. David M said it made it virtually impossible to have a shared strategy with them. Hopeless. Yet another communications friendly fire. TB went bonkers about it, then called Geoff, who admitted he had put the thought in Rumsfeld's head because he was trying to be very explicit about our difficulties as a way of reining him in. Rumsfeld must have thought he was being helpful, God knows. GH got on to the Defense Department and got them to put out a retraction, making clear we were with them. But it was all very ragged, and indicative once more of the difficulties.

TB had an audience with the Queen at the Palace which usually cheered him up a bit, but he came back still in a real fury re Rumsfeld. He spoke to Geoff, then Lagos, before going to JP's flat where he was having dinner with him and GB. As if he didn't have enough on his plate he was also in the midst of another 'let's sort GB and the future' phase. He said afterwards it was all very odd because they didn't really get to the point. He said he felt something close to contempt for GB at the moment, the way he was manoeuvring even on this. Hilary A had told him earlier that there were people in the PLP not sure which way to go because they were unclear where GB was, and whether it would affect their future chances if he took over. It was a bad scene, really bad, and one which TB felt reflected badly on GB's leadership credentials.

Sally and I were both working late and waiting for his 11pm Bush call. We saw him in the flat when he came back. He said he couldn't believe how the US kept fucking things up, the Rumsfeld thing just the latest. TB was pretty mellow, probably a bad sign. He had suddenly had a load of energy drained from him. He also took a call from Murdoch who was pressing on timings, saying how News International would support us, etc. Both TB and I felt it was prompted by Washington, and another example of their over-crude diplomacy. Murdoch was pushing all the Republican buttons, how the longer we waited the harder it got.

TB/Bush call, 11pm. Bush referred to Rumsfeld's latest gaffe. 'I want to apologise for that – one of those attempts to be helpful that wasn't very helpful.' These things happen, said TB, but with enough irritation in his voice for the message to be clear. GWB described his latest calls with Fox and Lagos as 'difficult'. He had said they had to give us their votes, that we had to get this over with. There were two options – the soft resolution, or no resolution, but there needs to be an up-and-down vote. He was determined we could not let the date slip. He told them they could have a week. He said the Africans were under huge pressure but solid. Pakistan looking for a way back. 'I just don't understand these guys.' He said Lagos and Fox were clearly happier with no vote. TB said we needed to hold their feet to the fire. Bush 'I'm waiting your instructions. If it falls apart I'm going to make a speech to the American people saying I tried, and now Saddam has forty-eight hours to leave the country.' TB said he still felt Chile would come round and not walk away.

Bush felt seven days was too big a stretch to give them. He said Congress was getting restless and all the polls were showing criticism of the UN for inaction. 'We just got to go.' TB said we had to do something to change the diplomatic weather and get on the front foot but if we can't get anything, we're in real trouble and there is no point pushing the UN beyond what it will take. Bush said 'We know he's not going to disarm. We already had benchmarks. I said to Ricardo [Lagos] that it is time to stand up and be counted. I want your vote. He said no. I said I'll tell Tony and he said no, I'll tell him.' He sounded pretty much at the end of it. TB said he would speak to him again and that a week's delay was the top end for us. As Condi had said, the danger is losing altitude but if we were on the front foot we would gain it again. But Bush said these guys were just playing for time. He felt maybe we stand on Thursday and say there could be no new UNSCR, that it had failed in its mission so Saddam has forty-eight hours to leave. He did not feel the need to buy more time. He was more impatient than ever. TB said he felt a bit more give on the last Putin call but Bush wasn't really listening to this stuff now. TB felt the problem was that the Chiles and Mexicos were not used to making decisions as big as these. But he felt Mexico was making a big mistake siding with the French against the US. Fox was less like a leader than an official. All we got was 'I'll get back to you.'

Wednesday, March 12

Jack S said that Rumsfeld's idiotic comments gave us a way out, namely that we could not be involved at the start but could do humanitarian afterwards. TB was not keen but Jack was very blunt. He said we were dealing, however right we thought it was, with a

US 'war of choice' and we had to understand, as Powell told him the whole time, that some of these people around Bush could not care two fucks about us whatever, and that went for TB as much as the rest of us. Jonathan and I agreed that last night had effectively been a pincer movement. Rumsfeld fucking up had forced us to come out strong. TB felt the Murdoch call was odd, not very clever. Jack had clearly been wound up big time while he was over there. He said we were victims of hopeless bullying and arrogant diplomacy. David M also felt yesterday had been a rather crude attempt to shaft us. He came to see me later and said we really have to work hard to keep TB in position. He was so earnest about it but adamant that both America and France were so capable of doing the wrong things for the wrong reasons that TB was absolutely key to keeping the international community together. David felt he was in a different league to the rest and could not be sacrificed in all this.

David felt we should say to the Americans they could only use our troops after the first effort and also on humanitarian duties. TB did not want to go down that route, no matter how much he agreed the Americans were not being helpful. Jack was absolutely vituperative about Rumsfeld and said we were being driven by their political strategy. TB said maybe, but it was still the right thing to do. After Jack left, we went down for a meeting with JP, HA and JR. TB admitted things were not going in the right direction at all. We agreed we were going to put out six tests[1] for Saddam today and also emphasise we were in this because it was right, not because the US wanted it. That was a point I made on the conference call where I didn't hide how pissed off we were with Rumsfeld, and said we couldn't have a situation where they were commenting on our politics.

TB had a couple of meetings with GB who was being brought in more closely on Iraq now, thanks to JP's meeting with him. We agreed that we really had to put it to a vote in the Commons even if we didn't get a second resolution because that was what we had promised and TB would just have to go and fight for his life on it. JP and Hilary both felt the note I did for the PLP was helpful and suggested I do

[1] The tests demanded: a statement from Saddam admitting the concealment of WMD and undertaking not to retain or produce WMD in the future; that at least thirty scientists and their families should be delivered for interview outside Iraq; the surrender of anthrax, or evidence of its destruction to be provided; all al-Samoud missiles to be destroyed; all unmanned vehicles to be accounted for, including details of any aerial devices for spraying chemical and biological weapons; all mobile chemical and biological production facilities to be surrendered.

another to update facts and arguments. I also put round a note to Cabinet on arrangements and structures for communications in the event of war. At PMQs, TB was on form and IDS was awful because he tried to exploit the Clare Short situation. There was a suggestion that the French may try to put down a resolution based on our tests. TB agreed my note on the tests. Jack at the PLP set us up well and we were now clearly saying 1441 gave us the legal cover we needed.

Chirac had effectively said he would veto anything, so even though we were continuing to work for it, it was hard to imagine getting one. The French were clearly worried. Just before PMQs, Matthew Rycroft took a call from [Gérard] Errera to say the Elysée wanted to make clear that 'whatever the circumstances' was being taken out of context. They were clearly backtracking. Then to the secure room to listen to the Bush call. Bush said his people had watched TB at PMQs and said he was brilliant. TB said he had spoken to Lagos and the Chileans were buggering about. Bush said Fox had told him he would get back to him within an hour, and then went off to hospital for a back operation. TB laid it on the line that we had to have a vote in the Commons. He said we couldn't pull the plug on UN negotiating because the bigger the gap between the end of the negotiation and a Commons motion, the worse it was for us. We had to keep trying. Bush said when do you anticipate a vote? TB said we had pencilled in next Tuesday. Bush: 'Erm.' Long pause. TB: 'You want to go on the Monday?' Correct. TB: 'My military have given me formal advice re the full moon.' It's not a problem, said Bush. 'What – are they taking away the moon?' TB said he would have to check it out. There was clear tension between Bush wanting sooner and TB wanting later.

Bush was clear that the French position meant no UNSCR. But we were still trying to be reasonable. He felt that on withdrawal of the resolution he would give a speech saying the diplomatic phase is over, issue a 48-hour ultimatum to Saddam, say late Friday, which takes us to Sunday. TB went over the politics here, how we were pulling out every stop. TB said there was a danger the Tories would see this as their chance to get rid of him, support us on a war motion, but not a confidence motion. Bush said they would make it clear to the Tories that if they moved to get rid of TB 'we will get rid of them'. He said he wouldn't speak to 'Iain Duncan Baker' himself – TB didn't correct him – 'but he'll know my message'.

The French had definitely allowed themselves to be presented as the unreasonable ones, which was probably swinging opinion our way a bit, but it was still very difficult. TB said it was important we still showed we were trying to be reasonable. But he said if Bush could delay his broadcast till after our Commons vote, it would help. Sunday, say you've tried, the French are being impossible, we are working the phones. Monday, we take it to Parliament and say we must bring this to a conclusion. Vote Tuesday. Forty-eight hours you go to their people and say war. The best argument we had is that we don't want our foreign policy decided by the French, though TB was clear again that Rumsfeld's comments had given us a problem.

He then started to press on the Middle East and said that if Bush would commit to publishing the road map, that would be a big breakthrough. We needed a fresh UNSCR on the humanitarian situation post conflict. Nobody doubts us on the tough side of things, but it's Middle East, humanitarian, democracy in Iraq, that people here want to hear about. TB spelled out the symbolism in the road map. Bush didn't quite get it but was willing to do it. He said if you took a poll here they'd think the road map was a local atlas. He said he had never shaken hands with [Palestinian leader Yasser] Arafat and he was never going to kiss him either. But TB really pressed on him and he got it by the end. Bush said we had to watch out for the French, that they would be worried they had got themselves in a ridiculous position.

I then had a long call with Dan Bartlett, who said there was some talk of a Bush/TB/Aznar meeting on neutral territory at the weekend to show continuing commitment to diplomacy. TB was now worried that the French would put down their own resolution aimed at getting support for delay and forcing the Americans to veto it. We were now in a position of not having a second resolution put to a vote at the UN, but then having a vote in the Commons for military [action] without a second resolution on the grounds everyone knows the French would veto it. I was very frank with Dan, said that the chief American voices had been doing us real damage. Hilary Armstrong came in for a chat. She was very stoic about it all and said it was going to be difficult.

Thursday, March 13

Greenstock put down the six tests at the UN at 2am. Before anyone had even had time properly to discuss them, de Villepin rejected them, allowing us to go to an aggressive position re French intransigence and their 'whatever the circumstances'. We needed to keep going on the tests through the day. We also wanted it that Blix wanted the TV address rather than us. I had a brief chat with IDS before he saw TB for a Privy Council talk re where we were. I just could not imagine him in there as PM. Jack and JP had both spoken to Robin and were clear he was going to quit if we didn't get a second resolution. It was a matter of when, not if, now. TB was due to see Robin and Clare before Cabinet and JP emphasised how important it was to make clear today was not the final Cabinet before any action, that there would be another one if the UN process collapsed. The political argument we needed now was that the French had made it more not less likely that there would be conflict. This was the way some of our MPs could come back. The other thing all of us were pushing on our US counterparts was the importance of publication of the road map. Dan and I had taken to calling it 'the Detroit A to Z' as a way of me trying to get them to understand why it mattered so much to us. Jack agreed to go out and do clips on the French.

Cabinet was delayed while TB saw Robin and Clare. When he came in he said 'Good morning,' and they all – or almost all – did a schoolkids-type 'Good morning' back which at least lowered the temperature a bit. TB talked through Iraq. Gareth Williams [Leader of the House of Lords] said there would be a debate on the legality. Clare said the AG should come to that. TB said of course he would. He said that the French had exposed fully how intransigent they were. Chirac's 'whatever the circumstances' was a mistake, and the wrong approach, and people were angry about it. They had also now rejected the basis of the tests we were proposing without any discussion or consideration. He felt Chirac's desire for a 'bipolar world' was leading him to turn away from discussion of any kind on this. He promised another discussion before a vote. Jack reported on UN activity. Clare chipped in 'Why can't the US give more time?' GB came in very strongly later on, on the French in particular.

RC said we should not 'burn our bridges' with the French, made clear that though there may be a legal base for action, there was no political case without a second resolution and we must keep working for it. He spoke very deliberately, as though he had rehearsed and of course everyone was listening for tone as well as content. It was a very clear marker that he would quit if there was action without a second resolution. He felt that without it we did not have the moral, diplomatic or humanitarian cover. Clare was even heavier, said we needed the road map published, lambasted the 'megaphone diplomacy' but as ever gave the impression it was just us and the Americans who engaged in it. She said the world community was split because the Americans were rushing. We should not be attacking the French but coming up with a different kind of process. 'If we can get the road map, we can get the world reunited behind it.' She was calmer by the end and my sense was RC would definitely quit, but she might stay.

I did a secure call with Dan. They were still keen on another meeting. Bush was prepared to come to London. I said I was not sure that was the right thing to do. The best thing you guys can do for us is publish the road map. I mentioned the idea of the Bush visit to TB. He was tempted but finally agreed GWB on UK soil in the run-up to the vote was not what we needed. The satirists would have a field day, 'I've come over here so that Tony and I could hold joint prayer sessions with your troubled backbenchers, so they can see the light. I like Tony so much because he is so much not a socialist,' etc. Definitely not what we needed right now.

TB was sure the French had something else tricky lined up. I did a note for TB post the chat with Dan, emphasising the need to keep driving a hard bargain from the position we were in. We agreed a plan – road map Friday, maybe visit Saturday. Talks expected to collapse Monday. Tuesday vote. Action begins immediately after the vote, then war declared, though no bombing yet. Then bombing and the POTUS [President of the United States] call. I went over to SIS to go over a few things, and what they could do to help once we got going. They were focused on the need to make sure the MoD documented properly all the atrocities, WMD, torture incidents etc. They were a pretty impressive bunch. We went over a lot of the obvious stuff, but once the discussion got going, I felt they got far better than other parts of the government machine the importance of dominating the media battle and also the need to stay robust whatever else was going on.

He was due to speak to Bush. Bush said that they could do the road map, give it to the Israelis and Palestinians once Abu Mazen [about to take over as Palestinian Prime Minister] accepts the position. TB said that could make a big difference, anything up to fifty votes. 'It'll cost me 50,000,' said Bush. TB said he had just seen a group of 'wobbly MPs' who were all clear the road map would help. There was a totemic significance to this. TB said it might also help him hang on to a couple of Cabinet ministers. GWB suggested he might be better off without them. He clearly could not fathom why the road map mattered so much. He had been reluctant because of Arafat. He then said 'Tell Alastair, like I'm telling my boys, that I don't want to read a word about this until I've said it. It is in our interests that I come out and say this, and it's clear I mean it.' TB said the French thought they had lost the initiative and were getting worried. He felt we had to keep in very close touch with Mexico and Chile over the weekend. He was worried the French would come up with a counter-proposal and win them over. Bush referred to the discussions Dan and I had been having. 'I guess me coming to London might create a stir.'

They kept going back to the parliamentary arithmetic. TB said it was knife-edge, that we were maybe twenty-five short of comfort. He said I know you think I've gone mad about the road map but it really will help. Bush said that Rumsfeld had asked him to apologise to TB. He said after the diplomatic process collapsed he would do his ultimatum speech. Nothing military will happen before our vote. After our vote, if we win, the order goes to Rumsfeld to get their troops to move. Ops begin. He said he would not be doing a declaration of war. Wednesday 8pm in the region, 1pm US, 6pm UK 'They go. Ten hours of operations before anyone finds out what is going on.' He intended to wait as long as possible before saying the troops were in action.

Dan called later to say they were postponing the meeting to Sunday because Spain had big demos on Saturday and Aznar felt he should stay for that. Aznar didn't like the idea of Bermuda so we settled on the Azores.[1] I had a meeting with GB and his people to go over all the difficult lines and to engage him in more media. We had to pin this on the French now. Then another chat with Dan to work out how we fill the void in the coming days. I asked him to make sure Bush did not wear any of his bomber jacket-type stuff. Things were pretty rocky with Fiona, who was really pressing for departure now, and I was feeling pretty stressed. I called Neil [Kinnock] in Rome and asked for him to have a word with her, and just spell out the kind of pressure I was under, and why I needed her to hang in just a while longer.

Friday, March 14

A real sense the diplomatic scene was going nowhere but we kept going with the line we were working flat out for a second resolution. To a meeting with TB, JP and GB. Gordon was far more engaged, pressing for constant meetings, election-type hours, working with me on the arguments and lines, agreeing to do more media. I was keen we somehow avoid the Azores meeting being seen as a council of war but it would be hard. A message came through that Chirac wanted to speak to TB. It was a lot friendlier than it might have been and he said we should strive for good relations. He was straight on to the point TB expected, namely he could see a way of co-operating on the tests but it must be the inspectors who decide if Saddam is co-operating.

[1] A special summit would be held at the Lajes airbase on Portugal's Azores islands, attended by Bush, Blair, Aznar of Spain and Barroso of Portugal.

He said he could not support an ultimatum or anything taken as support for military action.

TB said the problem with that was that it meant he could have as many last chances and as much time as he wanted. There had to be automaticity [trigger for attack]. Chirac said there could not be automaticity. They agreed Jack and de Villepin should talk but TB issued instructions to Jack to concede nothing. There was intelligence suggesting the French were seeking to get the undecided six to go for tests plus more time. TB suspected Chirac would move to a position of automaticity but inspectors are the sole judges of compliance.

Robin called to discuss 'rules of engagement' in the event of his resignation. I got Sally to join us when he came over. We were pressing him to stay, saying we couldn't have the French running our foreign policy, telling him Bush was about to do the road map. He said it would make a bit of difference but not much. He said this went deeper. He felt we were too close to a unilateralist right-wing US government that didn't care two hoots about the UN and didn't care two hoots about Tony, other than for his skills as a better politician and communicator than they are. He felt it was dishonest for him to pretend he supported them any more. He couldn't. He said he did not want to be awkward and was clear he wanted TB to stay. 'I do not want to be part of a process that sees Gordon become prime minister on the back of this.'

I said I thought if his mind was made up we should tie it all up before Monday's Cabinet. He said fine, that he was sad but felt a great peace of mind having made the decision. He wasn't questioning the integrity of those with a different view but he was doing what he felt was the right thing. He said he valued the good relationship we had and 'Could we agree a pact of no rubbishing on either side?' Absolutely. 'Can you ensure John Reid is part of that? The man can start a fight in a paper bag.' He intended to do a personal statement and speak in the debate. We agreed to consult re draft letters over the weekend. I said I would ensure TB was warm about him and he should be warm about TB.

I then went to another meeting with TB and GB. TB said it was extraordinary how much more dangerous the world seemed, when in fact more people were enjoying peace and prosperity than ever before. He had to leave for a few minutes and GB and I watched Bush doing his road-map statement. He did it pretty well and put the tone in as we had been suggesting. GB asked me what I really thought of Bush. Complicated, I said. Bits of him I like, bits I don't.

But he has got a long way by being underestimated. I was conscious of putting a bit of a line, even with GB, because you never quite knew how he stored these things away and used them. We spoke fairly openly but there was none of the old flow and warmth and laughter. Sad really. I worked on TB's draft words for the MEPP press conference. The Palestinians were being negative post Bush. TB said if they carry on like this they will lose the opportunity they've been given. It had a feel of Northern Ireland about it.

Then to the secure room to listen to another TB/Bush call. He kicked off with a 'Tell Alastair we're grateful he didn't leak anything. Tell him we're watching his every move, heh, heh.' He and Cheney had spoken to eight Arab leaders. TB reported on his call with Abu Mazen. Bush said 'If he plays his cards right he will be here in the Oval [Office].' Then on to the vote. It was already in the US press that it was on Tuesday. Bush said he was predicting a 'landslide, baby!' TB said it was too close to call. Bush was pissed off with Clinton, felt he was being difficult. The Azores was on. TB said we had to be seen striving all the way even if we felt the French had made it impossible. Bush said it was a 'moment of truth' meeting after all the previous last chances. TB said we must not let it be built up as a council of war. The more we talk about the UN and the aftermath the better. Bush said Dan and I were working on the outcomes for the media and we were getting Cheney to set the context on the Sunday shows.

TB briefed on the Chirac call, said the divide was between those prepared to consider military action and those who were not, who would give him as much time as he wanted. Bush said he did not trust the French but we had to do a slow waltz with them in the next few days. He felt they thought America was more guilty than Saddam. TB said the French appearing to be so unreasonable had been a big mistake by Chirac. I did another call with Dan re the arrangements for the Azores then a stack of calls, a last meeting with TB and headed home. TB saw Clare again and was confident he could keep her in. He was resigned to losing Robin.

Saturday, March 15

In for 8.30 meeting. Up to see TB in the flat. He was in the bath and Jack was pissed off not to be able to speak to him when he called in from Blackburn. TB was in very odd-looking shorts as he finally came down, said right, sorry I'm late, sat down and got going. He said it was clear now what the French would try – yes to the tests, even to the possibility of military action, but they would push for a later date.

We had a pre-meeting with JP, GB and DA downstairs before all the officials came in. GB was beginning to motor a bit, firing with good media and political lines. He also felt we needed to explain more clearly why we had been so keen to get the second resolution when now we were saying we didn't need one. The answer lay in the pressure we had been putting on the Iraqis, through the building of international support. He also felt we should be pressing publicly over some of the questions he still felt Blix had not fully answered.

Goldsmith was happy for us to brief that in the coming days he would make clear there was a legal base for action. We now had to build up the Azores as a genuine diplomatic effort, which was not going to be easy. It was running as a 'war not peace' situation. John Scarlett joined us, reported signs of the Iraqis really hunkering down, said there were reports of summary executions. Godric and I were briefing ministers and then the media re the coming AG advice. A few decisions having been taken, the travel of direction clear, we felt in a stronger position. Robin sent over his draft letter which was pretty negative. I worked on TB's, set it in a place that would make Robin want changes in both. TB went off to call Lagos. I got home in time to listen to a very long TB/Bush call. 'Hey Tony, how are you?' 'I'm very well.' 'That is what I want to hear every time.' He accepted we had done the right thing pushing him on the road map. 'Good advice and it has helped a lot.' The *New York Times* had it as 'Blair insistent, Bush responds' but it was a good move.

Bush was pretty vile about Fox, Chirac and Schroeder and to a lesser extent Lagos. He wanted to go for a 'coalition of the willing' meeting next week, but exclude France and Germany. He was venomous re Fox, said he could not believe they were not supporting us. He had guys like the Danes saying they were trying to help but had constitutional difficulties. Or Musharraf with all his problems saying let's get it over with. TB said it was time for the UN to show it could do its job, Bush that anything that weakened 1441 was not on. His plan now was: 1. get through Monday; 2. get through our vote, then 3. coalition of the willing. He and TB then came up with the idea of doing the press conference before rather than after the meeting in the Azores. I was opposed, felt it would fuel the idea that this was all a bit of a charade. There was the odd flash of Bush humour in there. He said he would call some of our backbenchers and tell them he was converted to Kyoto, planning to go vegetarian, would legislate so that all fertiliser could only come from cows and horses and campaign for an agrarian society.

His main line was that anything that takes us back from 1441 was not enough. This was the final stage of the diplomacy. TB said the UN had to be seen to do its job. Bush felt the TB line re the divisions being between those prepared to use force and those who were not would come best from TB not him. 'People kind of know where I am on force.' He said we have come to a conclusion at the UN. If we issue an ultimatum and the prospect of force, and France says no, it becomes impossible. TB said he still thought Chirac might say yes, but with a delay. Bush said if he went for yes with twenty-one days, he would reject it. They are the ones being unreasonable, not us. TB said he would definitely lose one minister, RC. 'What does he do?' Was Foreign Secretary, now Leader of the House. Bush said the ranks of the disaffected swell after a time.

Then going over the various timing issues again. TB said he was not sure where Kofi was. Bush said he had totally different problems to us re the UN, that the pressure in the States was to bury it. Then 'I told Fox he has seriously messed up. He has really let me down on this.' He then went off on one about the just demands of the free world. Was the UN really serving the world as it should? It had been pathetic in Rwanda. Then a discussion about anti-Semitism in Germany. TB said as things stood he was probably the only EU leader whose natural instincts were to go out and defend Israel. TB said the view here was of an all-powerful Jewish lobby in the States which could prevent a president moving on MEPP. Bush reckoned he had ten to fifteen per cent of the Jewish vote so it was all a bit of a myth. He had a lot less to lose than a Democratic president would.

Briefly they discussed proliferation of nuclear weapons. We do not need Saudi Arabia popping up with nuclear weapons, said Bush. The IAEA is pathetic. It's got Cuba on its board. He said he was convinced we would help world peace and at the end said 'It has been a great conversation. Let's get a bit of exercise and rest up for the Azores summit. It will be historic. And I'll be nuanced, I promise.' TB: 'We don't want anything unnatural now.' I went out for a longish run before getting back for Neil and Glenys coming for dinner. Neil was pretty much with me on Iraq, Glenys against, but we managed to avoid a big flare-up. Neil told me he had written to Robin saying don't resign, that he ought to stay in there and be part of the dealing with the aftermath.

Sunday, March 16

In for a long meeting in David Manning's office after TB came back from church. First just David, Sally, Matthew [Rycroft] and I, then GB, JR and HA joined us. We were trying to boil down the central arguments and dividing lines now. I suggested we say we intend to go back to the French and test their position – do they support any element of what we are saying? Are they really saying there are no circumstances in which they would support anything seen as a threat of military action? If they are, we go. If not, we have to look again. David M said there was no indication the French intended to shift. GB did *Frost*, and came back saying the really tough questions were in the field of legality. GB also said if we are saying this is the final shot at diplomacy, what are we actually saying we are going to do after today? Bush didn't want a process story but I suggested one, namely a last round of contacts at the UN post the Azores meeting. I spoke to RC. He said he had thought about the changes I had suggested to his letter. He was happy to say TB had helped keep this on the international, multilateral track. He was happy to make clear he felt TB should remain as leader.

It was now time to leave. There was the usual last-minute stuff to do before we got into the cars and set off for the airport. Pretty big media turnout in the street but we pretty much ignored them. I travelled with TB in the car to the airport and first he spoke to Margaret B, then a call with [Jan Peter] Balkenende [Dutch Prime Minister]. Then we just chatted a bit. This was as tough as any decision we would have to make, he said. He felt it very deeply. It was a tough, tough call. He was still angry at the way the US had handled it. 'If we had been totally in charge of this, I am absolutely sure we could have won the French round,' he said. I felt the US and France both, for different reasons, did not want to meet on this. We got on to the plane and for most of the flight were working on other papers and TB's message for the press event after the summit. It felt a bit insubstantial, especially given where it all now seemed to be heading. It was an opportunity though to set out the whole story, how we got to here, the French intransigence and so on.

It was a four-hour flight and the media were pretty much in 'council of war' mode. It was hard to sell this as a genuine diplomatic effort. Clinton sent through a draft of an article for the *Guardian*. He was trying to say he supported TB but the unspoken message was that he didn't support the war. TB asked me to work on a different version. I was also working on the Iraq vision document and the RC letters, and shifting paper. Alison [Blackshaw] said she was always amazed how much work we seemed to get through on planes, and this one was particularly prolific. Re RC I put in a reference to his support for Operation Desert Fox [1998 bombing of Iraq], and Kosovo, and also hinted he could go on to another big role, having successfully got the

Sunday Times to do a story saying he might go to Europe as a commissioner. We were also still negotiating the texts for the summit. DM felt there were too many references to terrorism and the language – e.g. peace-loving people – was too American. Also on the road map, they were saying it was a prospect. We needed it clearly there as a fact, something that was happening. They were pretty low-key re UN aftermath involvement and David was getting very fed up with them. I said why can't we just say we will work for new UNSCRs on appropriate post-conflict government? We arrived in the Azores for what was going to be a fairly odd meeting. At the airbase we had a meeting with Barroso, then joined by Aznar. TB spoke by phone to Kofi who was pretty much in agreement that the French had fucked up. He agreed to see him in New York later in the week. Then we heard Chirac was intending to set out a new proposal, but it turned out simply to be calling for more time, thirty days. It was clear now, said TB, that the French did not intend to move.

We hung around for Bush to arrive and once he did we all moved to the US part of the base. TB travelled with Bush in the presidential limo and the ludicrously large motorcade. We sat around a fairly small square table. The mood shifted regularly from serious, e.g. going through texts, running over difficult arguments, to light-hearted. Bush at one point just looked over at me and said 'You're just like a faucet. Can't stop leaking.' I said we called it tap. Barroso did a long and ponderous opening and said we had to make the last effort for peace. Everyone kept going on about it being 'the last effort for a political solution'. But there was a more than slight feeling of going through motions. The meeting itself was in an odd room, way too big for the numbers, with a kind of weird grey crazy paving-type set-up on the walls, thick white tablecloths.

Bush talked about it being a last effort. But he said it was important the world saw we were making every effort to enforce 1441. He said everyone had to be able to say we did everything we could to avoid war. But this was the final moment, the moment of truth, which was the line most of the media ran with. He stressed he wanted the UN to play an important role in the post-Saddam era. He was clear we had to emphasise Iraq's territorial integrity. He was emphasising he would really move on MEPP. He said again TB had been right to push him on the road map, and said he intended to spend a lot of time on this. He said re Chirac 'I don't want to provoke him into unreasonableness.' He was however keen to say he wanted the UN properly involved in the post-Saddam era. He would not deal with Arafat though. Condi and Karen [Hughes, AC's opposite number] later showed me the current draft of GWB's ultimatum speech which I felt was a bit too warlike. Too much war, not enough ultimatum.

TB said we had reached the point of decision for people. We had been here before, but there really had to be a decision. How many times could there be a last chance, serious consequences for material breach? He reported that Kofi had said the French and Russians would not rule out force but would not agree to an ultimatum, which was an odd position. He really hit the UN buttons post Saddam, and was trying to force Bush to go further on that. 'It has to be a UN-authorised government.' He was also hammering home the advantage on MEPP, but I wasn't convinced it would happen. We needed some kind of process story. I suggested to TB they all instruct their ambassadors at the UN to have one last go, see if the position of the others has changed. TB was constantly emphasising final appeal, final opportunity for the UN. Bush was scathing re the Turks, said Erdogan 'just doesn't get it. The Turkish military are setting him up.' He was pretty keen to get on with things now, wanted to pull down the SCR now. He then said he would address the American people tomorrow – say diplomacy had failed, issue the ultimatum. He said to TB we should say we were issuing one last set of instructions to UN ambassadors to have a go at securing agreement. Aznar said he was concerned the French, Russians and Chinese would come up with a proposal. Bush said he would be happy to veto if they did. He was even talking about not going to the G8 summit.

Aznar was really pushing the importance of the transatlantic alliance, but he was in even more political hot water on this than we were. I introduced Bush to Godric, said he was our Ari Fleischer. 'You gotta be bald or something to do these spokesmen jobs? Or is it the job makes you bald?' TB had vanished to the loo. I said we've lost the PM. 'I hope not,' said Bush ''cos he's the reason we're all here on this island on a Sunday.' He asked about the vote, said he was confident we would win. I said Robin C might shift a few. As we left I said to Bush, if I do a sub-four-hour marathon will you sponsor me? He said 'If you win the vote in Parliament, I'll kiss your ass.' I said I'd prefer the sponsorship. Over to the press conference and now he went into 'bastards' mode in a kind of imitation of me. Dan said he was amused by the fact I dealt with the press in the way I did. He saw them as bastards too, but in the US nobody dare say it.

The press conference was very well set up and at least the Yanks knew how to do these kind of things. They did their statements, then one question from each country, and all on-message though Bush went off on one a bit re Chirac. He did his 'moment of truth' well, but there was something very odd about his manner today. Bush had just about had enough of the serious talk and we had another half-serious, half-jokey conversation re marathon training. The last hour or so dragged a bit and we were basically just chatting, filling the time while the hacks all filed before getting back on the plane and heading home. In the car to the plane TB seemed to think it had gone OK, though we were all pretty clear the US had decided and nothing that came out of the French or anyone today would have changed their approach. I told him re the kiss-ass threat. He laughed, but then said it is not that often that a major US policy depends on a UK parliamentary vote. Sally reported from Hilary A there had been some movement our way.

We saw the press on the plane, and we were making clear the French had to come back and say whether there were any circumstances at all in which they might support military action. I lost it with the staff when I learned the texts and documents had not been issued at the right time. TB was seeing David Margolick [*Vanity Fair*].[1] TB was still saying it was the right thing to do. I had lost count of how many times I had heard those same words. We started work on his speech for Tuesday, which was going to have to be one hundred per cent.

Monday, March 17

The summit came out not too bad, Bush's 'moment of truth' the best top line, the overall sense that the diplomatic process was going nowhere and now we had to gear up on the military side. There was the not insignificant matter of our vote, mapping out in my head a note to send to Dan with an overnight press summary, schedule for the day and stressing how important it was that Bush's 1am speech did not create problems for us. I said GWB was unlikely to pull any of our people back, but he could push them the other way. I leavened it a bit by telling him the *Guardian* had said Bush was better than Blair yesterday. He called later, said they had built up the ultimatum as I suggested and also injected a lot of conditional material so that it was not simply seen as a declaration of war.

Then to a meeting of TB, JP, GB, JS, JR, HA plus the usual lot to go through the day. Jack was irritating TB a bit by going on about process the whole time and irritating JP who was trying to get a

[1] This was the interview from which would emerge one of Campbell's most oft-quoted statements. When, at the end of a long interview, Margolick asked Blair about his religious faith, an impatient Campbell interjected, 'We don't do God.'

straight answer to the question of whether RC should do a statement tomorrow or today. Jack and I both felt today was better, on a day of massive events, then GWB in the morning, rather than before TB's speech. We agreed Greenstock would put down the SCR at 10.15 New York time, that we would say at the 11 there would be a Cabinet at 4, Jack's statement later and also that the Attorney General would publish his view that there was a solid legal base for action. Jack would go through the motions of talking to his opposite numbers but basically the game was up. De Villepin had rejected it again. GB said we needed to get up the Blix unanswered questions as well. TB was fairly quiet, worrying about his speech and about rebels. We agreed Margaret B should do media so I spoke to her to brief her, then sent over the AG's opinion and our various texts from yesterday.

I was working on a draft exchange of letters with Clare in case she went. JP went off to see her and reported back that she was probably going. It was all playing totally to her attention-seeking. Jonathan emailed me about the draft exchange of letters, saying 'Probably better not to have them drafted by someone who so clearly despises her.' Probably true. Robin called re my draft. I had mentioned the various military situations we had been involved in – Operation Desert Fox, Kosovo, Sierra Leone. He was very funny about it, said 'I can see why in these circumstances you want to present me as a heroic war leader, but I wonder if you couldn't put in one or two of my humanitarian triumphs as well.' He was keen that we make mention of Lockerbie and the International Criminal Court, and also wanted to make clear that he wanted TB to stay on as leader. It was so different dealing with him rather than Clare. He felt she was in a totally ridiculous position. TB was working to keep her in, even suggesting we get Kofi to call her. RC came to see TB and they agreed there was no point in him staying for Cabinet. So Robin and I went round to my office to agree the process. We agreed we wouldn't put the letters out until 4.15, once Cabinet was in.

We joked about the fact that it was the first resignation letter I had not written. 'I'll race you to see whose memoirs that appears in first,' he said. He was very friendly, seemed liberated, also clear that he had a strong if very different political future ahead of him. He was also very nice to me personally, said we had been through some very difficult times together and he always valued my advice and support. He said there was something oddly fitting about the fact that we had worked so closely at the end of his marriage and were working so closely again at the end of his ministerial career. He wanted to leave by the side door so I walked down with him, we shook hands, he said 'I really hope it doesn't all end horribly for you all,' and headed off to Birdcage Walk.

TB started Cabinet, introduced Goldsmith, then Clare came in and asked Sally where Robin was. 'He's gone,' said Sal. 'Oh my God.' TB's only reference to Robin was to say that he had resigned. He said French intransigence had made it impossible to get a resolution. We were at an end of the diplomatic process. We intended to issue an ultimatum and seek an endorsement for action if it was necessary. He said we had tried everything to avoid this course. The other big issue was MEPP, and the US had undertaken to publish the road map. He also emphasised the planning that was going on on the humanitarian front. He said Jack and the FCO team had done a brilliant job but an impasse is an impasse and the French block is not conditional but absolute. Jack said nobody could have done more than TB did to keep things within the UN.

I was in and out agreeing final changes to the article Bill Clinton was doing for us for the *Guardian*. I got back in as Peter Goldsmith went through the answer on legal authority to use force. Clare asked if he had had any doubts. He said lawyers all over the world have doubts but he was confident in the position. One by one, a succession of colleagues expressed support, then Clare said she owed them 'a short statement', that she intended to reflect overnight. She said publication of the road map was significant but we shouldn't kid ourselves that it means it is going to happen. She said she admired the effort and energy that had gone into getting a second resolution but there had been errors of presentation. 'I'm going to have my little agonising overnight. I owe it to you.' JP, John Reid and one or two others looked physically sick.

JR spoke next, said never underestimate the instincts for unity and understand that we will be judged by the Iraq that replaces Saddam's Iraq, and by the Middle East. Derry said he felt we would have got a second resolution if the French hadn't been determined to scupper it, and said we had made so much effort to get a second resolution that it had led to people thinking we actually needed one. Paul Murphy was just back from America and said what an amazing feeling there was towards us there. 'It's not quite the same here,' said TB. JP pointed out we were on the eighteenth SCR dealing with Saddam and it was about time we moved to uphold the UN's integrity. He said the only reason the Americans went down the UN route at all was because of TB and now he is getting them down the road of the Middle East peace process and deserves all the support we can give.

We had agreed JP would speak in the street post Cabinet. I had drafted a script and he went through it with me and Jack. He went and did well. TB felt Cabinet had gone well. JP had been terrific. Only Clare was ridiculous. Fittingly, when she spoke, huge gusts of wind had blown through the open window. TB had another call with Bush, fairly inconsequential, mainly about the vote. TB said at the moment we had 190 backbenchers against us and we wanted to bring it down to 150. Bush seemed genuinely surprised when TB said his comments on the Middle East had helped. They both felt the French had mishandled things. He was in very folksy mode, said that TB had 'heart in your voice and a spring in your step, so that's fine by me'. He asked TB if he had to be in there in Parliament for ten hours of debate. TB said you get the odd comfort break. GWB laughed. TB said it was tough and would be tight and that French intransigence, plus the Middle East moves, had helped, but also we had to keep the UN in play. He said a lot of our backbenchers were mildly obsessive about the UN and the post-war issues. Robin did his resignation statement, did it very well, a really powerful Commons moment and got a fairly widespread standing ovation. Margaret [Beckett], who was about to do *The World Tonight* [BBC Radio 4], was unimpressed. She called me, felt it was typical Robin, said he would support TB and then call directly on people to vote against action, which, if carried, would defeat the PM and the government. She wanted to go for him but I said it was better simply to say that TB would also be going to the House and would make a case that was logical and powerful and strong. I was surprised at how angry she was with Robin. She said she hoped she could hold her tongue. TB was working on his speech for a good part of the day and it was in good shape. Neil [Kinnock] called and said Robin was one of a very small number of people who could bring catastrophe to the government and even though it was difficult, we should try to keep a bridge out to him. It was pretty clear by now that Clare would be on her way too, if with a lot less impact.

Tuesday, March 18

Debate day dominant. GWB's statement overnight had come out fine. They had taken in all our changes, the ultimatum was calm and strong, the tone towards Iraqi people compassionate, the commitment to the Middle East peace process was in there strong, and all the bellicose stuff either taken out or conditional. So to be fair, they had delivered big time for us. The Robin resignation speech, and the standing ovation in parts of the House, was still getting a lot of play but I sensed that was the high point of the rebellion. I ran in, then up to see TB in the flat. He was on the phone to Blunkett who was warning him that John Denham [Home Office minister] would resign. Also Philip Hunt [Lord Hunt, junior health minister] went on the radio to resign. That seemed to be about it at the moment. TB was in a pretty calm mood. He felt we were winning some people over on the arguments, but we had a problem in that there were a lot of our MPs who had promised their local parties that they wouldn't support without a second resolution. This was the unintended effect of the point Derry made yesterday, that we fought so hard to get one that people assumed we needed one before action.

TB had been up early and had rewritten the speech so it was much more his voice. The only ongoing discussion was about whether to keep in the passage about the 1930s [appeasement], or whether really direct comparisons might backfire. It was not yet clear what Clare intended to do. Then we heard a rumour that she was planning to make a statement, which we assumed was a resignation but then learned was to be an announcement she was staying. We had a meeting to organise a pretty much all-day blitz of the airwaves including getting GB live on some of the bulletins. We had Margaret out and about all day doing well. Whether in the House or out, we were at least making the arguments but Hilary said it was still too difficult to judge the outcome. I worked on the Queen's message to the troops, and spoke to Dan [Bartlett] a couple of times to go over the exact timings of military action. There were going to be a lot of special forces operations around the oilfields, then wait till Friday for a proper announcement. Clare was making a complete fool of herself. TB had done very well keeping her there, but she was now viewed as humiliated. She was pretty much finished. [William] Hague was on to it, had an absolutely brilliant line in the debate, how TB had 'taken his revenge and kept her'.

TB's speech in the House was one of his best.[1] Very serious, full of real argument, confronting the points of difficulty and we felt it moving our way. He did a brilliant put-down to the Lib Dems ['unified, as ever, in opportunism and error'] which helped the mood behind him. I did another secure call with Dan. It looked like Wednesday late, special forces. Thursday, preparations underway. Friday, 'A' day, first Bush, then TB, recall Parliament. By the time I got back in, Sally said there were definitely some people turning

[1] Blair told MPs 'This is the time for this House, not just this government or indeed this prime minister, but for this House to give a lead, to show that we will stand up for what we know to be right, to show that we will confront the tyrannies and dictatorships and terrorists who put our way of life at risk, to show at the moment of decision that we have the courage to do the right thing.'

back to us. I got GB out on the media again. He called me into his office for the first time in ages to discuss the line to take on Clare. Stay nice to and about her and not put the boot in. TB's speech had gone fine and the reaction was good. It was one of those days when people out in the country were actually following what was going on. IDS and Charles Kennedy had both been poor. There had been some excellent back-bench speeches but the interventions didn't really zing, TB had definitely come out on top.

There were a lot of protesters outside, so I faced a bit of abuse going in, then up to JP's office to agree the line that we push from the moment the vote was over, that we won the vote, because we won the argument, and now the country should unite. JP asked me to stay back and asked if I had a problem with him. I said no, why? He said he felt I was angry because he screwed up this morning in going for Robin and Hunt and I had kept him off through the day. I said not at all, but it was one of those days when GB seemed up for it and I wanted him out and about as much as possible. We had also used Peter Hain a lot as well. We ended up having a very friendly chat, then going down to wait for the vote, which for the government motion was 412 for and 149 against, and for the rebel motion 396 voting against and 217 for. 139 Labour MPs rebelled. I called Dan B with the result as it came through.

I was in the front office of TB's Commons office, MPs coming and going, the staff all pretty relieved. TB came back and called everyone in to say thanks. He said we had pulled out the stops and we had to. His own performance today had been superb. All of us, I think, had had pretty severe moments of doubt but he hadn't really, or if he had he had hidden them even from us. Now there was no going back at all. He had to give authority for our forces to go in and by tomorrow night it would be underway. Everyone was assuming the Americans would start a massive bombing whereas in fact the first action would be some of our forces acting to prevent an ecological disaster. I got to bed by 1am.

Wednesday, March 19

TB got the best press he had had for ages, because of the quality of the speech and the fact that he had seen it through. As Bush said on their call later, other leaders would look at what he did, and the power with which he did it, and really learn lessons from it. 'Landslide,' he said, referring to the road-map publication as 'genius'. He referred back to what he called 'the *cojones* conference' at Camp David. 'You showed *cojones*, you never blinked. A leader who leads will win, and you are a real leader.' He said the object is regime change and once Saddam is in hiding, that is the beginning of the change. TB felt the next stage after winning the war would be to work out the geopolitical fallout and repair some of the divisions. Bush said Condi had this line that we should 'punish the French, ignore the Germans and forgive the Russians', which was pretty glib. TB didn't comment at the time but later said he didn't agree. We should try to build bridges with all of them. We finally got Bush to agree that there was no point TB going to the US at the moment, that we should wait until the fighting starts. 'You're one of the few leaders they let me see,' said Bush.

De Villepin called JS to say that Chirac was 'pained and shocked' at the way we had misrepresented what he had said, that this was not what was expected of an ally and it showed TB lacked courage. Chirac was clearly going up the wall and we were getting a lot of signs that he had basically been hoping TB would fall on the issue. Bush said that the Iraqis would now be 'shredding documents like crazy'. When he heard about the prisoners who had had their tongues cut out, it 'made me vomit'. He said the road map would be published today when Abu Mazen was confirmed. He would call and congratulate him.

I went to see David Manning then chatted to C and John Scarlett. Desertions were beginning in Iraq. The Republican Guard was moving to Baghdad. Nobody seemed to have a clue where Saddam was hiding. It was possible to feel the planned operation moving through the gears. First we had the ad hoc ministerial meeting where John S went through the intelligence, and CDS was clearly reluctant to go over the military plans in detail. I also found myself holding back with Clare there. TB saw her afterwards to tell her not to worry about the savaging she was getting in the papers at the moment. I felt her credibility was now totally shot but he still wanted to keep her on board and she was off to New York.

Fiona came to see me, said she couldn't stay in the job any longer and started crying. She said it wasn't the war per se, but it had been the last straw. She felt it was a waste of time her being here, that she wasn't happy doing what she did. I said she should go if she wanted to, and if she didn't support what we were doing, to try not to do it in a way that makes us an issue. She said but you are a big issue, which meant that there was never a right time to go, but she really didn't want to stay. She went to see Sally, got very upset. Sally said she felt it was as much about Cherie/Carole as being about me. It was about not being valued. I didn't quite know how to deal with it. It's true there was never a right time, but this was about as unright as it could be, in terms of us being made an issue. It didn't exactly help that the message from the security people was that patrols around the house would be stepped up while the conflict was going on.

I wrote letters of complaint to the BBC, first from me to [Richard] Sambrook [director of news] on various issues re [John] Humphrys, [Andrew] Gilligan and Rageh Omaar [BBC journalists] on the nature of their coverage. Then drafted a letter from TB to Gavyn Davies [BBC chairman] and Greg Dyke [BBC director general], attaching articles from David Aaronovitch [journalist] and [John] Simpson [BBC]. PMQs was low-key after all the drama of yesterday but TB did fine, pushed the general vision stuff, also explicit about regime change for the first time. TB called me in later to discuss France, what to do at the summit with Chirac. He was clear we shouldn't go running after them, that they should come to us. But there was no chance of that at all.

I told TB about Fiona. He reacted, as I knew he would, by saying he couldn't understand why people got so emotional about this. I said well, it's going to happen so I have to work out how to handle it. I said it's true she wasn't happy with the war, but there were other issues too, chief among them that she now had a bad relationship with CB, despite having successfully helped build a very positive image for her. She felt we had next to no life outside work, and that I gave too much for too little in return. He went into 'this is ridiculous' mode. I said Tony, you are talking about Fiona and I won't have it. He said for God's sake, I was always saying things about his wife, but this stuff was very difficult, when big political issues were swirling around and they got mixed up with relationships. But if she went and said it was about Iraq, that would look very odd for me because people would think that was my position too.

I said it's probably a consequence of a build-up of neglect, some of it mine, some of it Cherie's. He said it was a bit much to have all the things he had to deal with and be expected to keep everyone happy all the time. I had the weekly meeting with Peter M, PG, PH. Peter M was interesting on GB. He felt GB had come back to us a bit because he was worried about Clare, in that if she went it was his last out-and-out support in Cabinet. Whatever the reasons, he was a bit more back on board. TB called me out for another chat on his way up to the flat and we went into the Number 11 study. He said he felt Fiona was probably fed up with being in my shadow and needed a role independent of me. He asked me what I wanted to do. I said if he was going before the election, I may as well go sooner rather than later because I couldn't imagine working in the same way for a different leader or prime minister. He said in the big moments, like now, I gave real added value, and I shouldn't underestimate how important that was to him. So all he asked was that if I did go, I helped find someone who could replace me.

I asked what his plans were. 'I really don't know. I've never really wanted to fight a third election, but I don't know, I might.' I asked if he had done a deal with GB. Not at all, he said, but he didn't rule it out. He said it was interesting that GB had been more co-operative recently and said JP had been the key to that. JP had basically told him that if TB didn't want him to get the job, and JP was agin it, it would not happen. In the end, he said, I think it's wrong for me to think I can pick the next leader, or control what he does. But I do worry about him. I worry about the party and do want it to be well led. Things were definitely in flux again, and it was odd how often it was the really big moments that brought out these situations.

It was a friendly enough chat and although inevitably he was thinking about his own interests too, he did seem to be applying his mind to a decent way out for Fiona. As for me, I said I wasn't that excited about the euro, which might be the next big thing, and I wasn't sure I could face doing another election in exactly the same job. Maybe I could leave and come back for that. I told Godric about the Fiona situation. He felt it was potentially bigger than Cook going, because it played into so many different parts of the soap opera, which in the end is what the press love most.

Thursday, March 20

After going to bed late last night, then another row with Fiona over my leaving, and her demanding a departure date NOW, I was woken at 3am by Godric. Did I know action had begun? Then media calls started. GWB had gone on TV to say that preparatory action had begun, taking the MoD totally by surprise, and most of us in Number 10. It transpired that Condi had indeed told David [Manning], who had passed it on to TB, but neither thought to pass it on. It meant we were not ready in the way we should have been. We put together a line that said TB was told just after midnight, and when there were operations with substantial UK involvement, we would say so. GWB later apologised to TB who said all he really cared about was that we now got on with it and won. It turned out the US had some late, sudden intelligence re Saddam's whereabouts and took the decision to go straight away. They reckoned later he may have been injured, and certainly there was real angst and turmoil being reported from his inner circle. I was up most of the night, got a couple of hours' sleep and then in for a 7.30 meeting.

TB had a meeting of his inner team (Jonathan, DM, SM, AC) with C, CDS, John Scarlett to get a military and intelligence briefing before being joined by JP, JR, GB, DB etc. John said there were reports of growing internal strife, e.g. pilots being ordered to carry out suicide missions; one-fifth of the Republican Guard deserting. We discussed whether TB should do a broadcast. With our Marines due for action taking a peninsula towards Basra tonight, it was madness to think we could wait another day before TB did a broadcast, so we went ahead with setting it up. Peter H had done a draft but TB was keen to do his own, into which I wrote a couple of clips, but it was basically very much his own voice.

We got hold of the Speaker and GH offered a statement. We were clear we would not be giving a running commentary but statements in the House were going to be an important part of the overall communications. Cabinet was fairly sombre and subdued, and so much better without Clare's constant muttering and interruptions. Sally and I were chatting about what I should do re Fiona. TB, JS and GH all did a fairly basic reporting job on what was happening. Lots of praise for Hilary A on the whips' operation. There was a pretty united mood and a lot of understanding for the enormity of the decision, and the pressure on TB now. He still hadn't decided on RC's replacement. I was feeling the stress today, just a bit wired, and burdened. When these big moments were on, everyone seemed to want to call, or pop in, and it all just added to the sense of pressure.

We recorded the broadcast at 3pm. TB did fine, though he was blinking a lot. We did it in two takes, and I was watching the camera crew to get a sense of their response. They were definitely following the argument, and I sensed the effect was positive. Then straight to the Bush call. GWB reported on the strike, said they very nearly struck lucky. They were still hopeful. They had another discussion re France and Russia, and Bush signalled he really wanted to go over all that in detail at Camp David. He felt it would be a vital discussion for the future of the world, because these relations were central to the direction the world took. He wanted to get back on decent terms with Putin in particular. Then, apropos of nothing, he said 'And tell Alastair I am NOT going to kiss his ass, even though you won the vote.' TB laughed, and said 'I think he'll be relieved. He was not exactly looking forward to it.'

On the flight to Brussels [EU summit], Jack S and I were chatting re the French. His basic view of Chirac was really negative. At the meeting, Chirac seemed to be avoiding TB, and wanting it to be noticed that he was avoiding him. Later, with Chirac sitting at his desk in the meeting room making a call on a mobile, TB went over and shook him by the hand. But it didn't exactly warm things. When we left the building at the end of the session, we had to walk by Chirac and his entourage to get to the cars, and on seeing TB, he just turned away. De Villepin did likewise. The atmosphere generally was dire. The meeting room was being kept pretty tight so I was relying on Jack's notes to follow what was going on. Jack came out to tell us that Chirac was trying to remove any reference to Iraq being responsible for the crisis, and [Costas] Simitis [current EU President] was letting him. TB did not say much, and on the occasions I popped in, they seemed to be splitting into groups rather than getting things sorted round the table. It was not a nice atmosphere at all. But in terms of outcome, it was OK for us, and the French did not have as much support as they had hoped for. I had a chat with Schroeder's team who thought TB's speech had been 'brilliant'.

Friday, March 21

Nick Matthews [senior duty clerk] called me early to say that eight UK Marines and four US servicemen had been killed in a helicopter crash inside Kuwait. Worst possible start to the day. I went out for a run, then back to see TB in his bedroom. He was getting dressed, and reflecting on the news we'd just had. We agreed he should not say anything about it till the press conference. He said that people will be saddened but they understand that these things are going to happen. I sensed he was hiding how he actually felt. He said what mattered now was that we saw through the military campaign. At the summit centre, Schroeder was the first to come over and offer condolences, followed by others. Chirac wrote TB a little note, which was nice of him, and his words were totally devoid of any side or politics. It was interesting how many of the smaller countries were just not prepared to take the Franco-German line on things, and Chirac was definitely weakened around the place.

TB and I discussed euro/GB. GB had definitely been more co-operative recently, and that was largely down to JP. But GB was now keen to include the euro assessment in the Budget, and TB felt he was going to be in a 'yes but' position, that there were a number of changes that had to be made, e.g. to the housing market, before we could consider it. We were in the middle of this conversation, just outside the main meeting room, when Chirac came out to have a pee. He walked past us, went to the Gents, and when he came out he and TB both smiled warmly at each other. Chirac went back into the meeting room, but then came straight back out and walked over to us. *'Tony, est-ce qu'on peut avoir un mot?'* [Could I have a word?] I stepped back a little, Chirac put his hand on TB's back and steered him a little way down the corridor, where there were fewer people. But most were looking on, whilst trying to look like they weren't. They chatted for ten minutes or so, and the body language of both was tense.

Chirac said it was time to calm the atmosphere, lower the temperature, that there was nothing to be gained from the kind of mutual aggression we had been showing. He said he could not understand why we had been so aggressive towards him and it was time to call off the press attacks. TB said he could not understand why they had been so aggressive diplomatically. They agreed it was time to make up. But Schroeder's people were clear with me that Chirac had been hoping to destroy TB on the back of this, and failed. TB had been down at one point but bounced back quickly and won a surprisingly high number of plaudits from fellow leaders here. On the way out to the airport, he said 'God, it is awful, this war business.' 'Yes, that's why it is usually best to avoid it.'

Then to the Bush call. He said he was sorry about the deaths, then added 'It's called sacrificing for peace and freedom.' He said he thought they had secured the southern oilfield. Rumsfeld reckoned eighty-five per cent of Iraqi oil was secure, so the danger of a self-inflicted environmental attack, or a huge impact on the markets, was limited. We occupy thirty-five per cent of the country. The Scud baskets are under our control. The ground campaign started early. 45,000 troops, US, UK and Australian forces marking the way. Basra should be surrounded today. The Iraqi Army in the north has surrendered. Inside Baghdad there is chaos. There are defections. Saddam's circle is fracturing. It all sounded a bit too good to be true.

There were worries re Sunni/Shia divisions, worries re minefields, worries re oil platforms, though he said the Brits had done a brilliant job securing the offshore platforms. Bush sounded very bullish, said that where there had been combat, the force had been overwhelming. TB said it was important that we underclaimed and overdelivered. Bush said 'Yes, we only have forty per cent of the country.' It had gone up five per cent in two minutes. TB felt most Iraqis would not be waiting for Saddam to topple, that they did not need to flee. Bush said the Brits had been great. He said Clare Short had been given a briefing and was apparently surprised that the Americans only had one horn coming out of their heads. TB filled him in on the summit, and said how strong the accession countries were generally. TB felt the French were trying to come back to us a little bit. At the War Cabinet, C said there were some suggestions – alluded to by Bush earlier – that Saddam had been hit. He may be injured, and there were definitely signs of the inner circle turning on each other.

Saturday, March 22

In for the War Cabinet. Another helicopter crash, and also Terry Lloyd of ITN [correspondent in Iraq] was missing. News-wise, things had moved to the region and the overall sense was of things going pretty well. TB set off for Chequers, saying he felt we were in much stronger shape than we might have been. I went home, set off for a run but had a bad asthma attack and walked back after a mile or so. Whether it was the air, stress or both, I don't know.

Sunday, March 23

I got up early, flicked through the papers, but as often when there was a real and moving international story, the impact of the papers was lessened as events drove the agenda. TB called and he wanted to change the planned broadcast to the forces into an interview, so Emily Hands [press officer] and I worked on that. There was a spate of stories of troops being captured, tortured, etc. In the end, we established there were ten US soldiers captured [in an ambush at Nasiriyah] and later they were paraded. The big battle seemed to be taking place around Umm Qasr [port in southern Iraq], and there were pockets of resistance elsewhere. ITN, not surprisingly, were going crazy re Terry Lloyd. Stewart Purvis [editor-in-chief] called to say that the MoD were being hopeless but it seemed that Terry had gone too far behind enemy lines [near Basra] and was shot by US special forces dealing with Iraqi troops at the time. Purvis called again later and said they now had pictures of the body and would be putting out a statement shortly. I said I would organise a TB tribute. I knew Terry reasonably well and liked him.

In then for a War Cabinet meeting. CDS on the military update and the latest on casualties. GH explaining what they had tried to do re Terry Lloyd. C still not clear on Saddam's whereabouts or well-being. CDS said things were pretty much on track but there had been a number of accidents and the going was hard. As we wound up, the Iraqis were parading the [captured] American servicemen on TV. Dan called to say Bush was intending to go on TV and say this was a flagrant breach of the Geneva Convention. We agreed TB would echo that in his forces interview with BFBS [British Forces Broadcasting Service]. He said to me as we came away from the interview 'How do you really think it's going?' I said from everything we could gather, fine, but it is going to be really tough. There were too many signals that the US did not really want the UN to lead on the humanitarian effort. TB said his next meeting with Bush was going to be vital in terms of all the big strategic questions, and how we planned for the future. He was clearly worried.

At the end of the War Cabinet he had taken Boyce aside for ten minutes or so, just to try to get a real fix on his analysis and how he thought the Americans were doing. Boyce did not hide the difficulties ahead. There had been a bit of street fighting going on. Then we heard that a Red Crescent [medical aid] hospital may have been hit by an RAF bomb, with possibly as many as seventy dead and fifty injured. In briefing, I was simply saying things were on track despite the accidents but there was inevitably a lot of focus on the accidents and less on the 'on track'. The truth was the strategy was on course, but they were meeting greater resistance than anticipated.

Monday, March 24

Four days in and our ridiculous media were all on 'setbacks'. As I said to TB, if we had had 24-hour news during World War Two, we would all be German by now. The main news overnight was two UK soldiers missing, big stuff on PoWs paraded, so all quite tricky. I got the cab in, and up to see TB and Jonathan. He was generally worried. Jonathan and I were both pointing out that this was the fog of war, and it would take time for a rhythm to be established and we had to hold our nerve. The media were pushing hard at the limits of what they should know and then deliver instant comment on everything. At the pre-meeting CDS said things were still going pretty much according to plan though there were Fedayeen [Saddam paramilitary] fighters in Basra causing a fair bit of trouble. C said there were some reports, as yet unclear, of an enormous civilian disaster in Basra, with dozens possibly killed. In general, the bombing campaign was more low-key than people had expected, and very targeted, but the fighting was going to be tough, especially when our forces reached the Medina troops on the road to Baghdad.

Then through to the broader meeting, where John Scarlett ran through things and there was a run round the block on the issues already discussed in TB's office. These meetings were not great. John and CDS obviously felt they were being asked to repeat themselves; those not at the earlier meeting assumed there was something else going on they didn't know about. David Blunkett was in a pretty bad mood and went off on one, saying he needed to know whether Basra was going to become like a medieval siege. TB just said 'No.' David was so down on his own civil servants most of the time that he had slightly got himself into a habit of messenger-shooting, and these guys didn't particularly like it. John R asked whether we shouldn't be moving to messages and tone that suggests longer not shorter term. He felt we had been caught a bit behind the curve and needed to get ahead again. I picked him up on it at the party meeting later, said 'Aah, the man losing his nerve.' 'No,' he said, 'just keen to ask questions because we have to make sure we can sell this policy to party and public.'

I said we had to communicate that there was a plan, it was unfolding, there would be mishaps and accidents but the basic plan would be seen through, and this was not a time to communicate nervousness to generals, which I fear is what they took away from the meeting this morning. He and David B both denied panic but it seemed close to it to me. Later another meeting with C and CDS who assured TB things were generally on track, but there was going to be heavy resistance and a lot of fighting. He and C both said that the 24-hour news was making it much harder in the field. We discussed with CDS and GH the idea of the main Baghdad switchboard being bombed, as it was central to the working of the regime. We also discussed a new missile that could wipe out the power to broadcast on Iraqi state TV, but GH was worried about it.

Then working on TB's statement to the House. He was very focused, but also worried and wanted to walk round the garden to go over it. He was starting to think ahead to the meeting with Bush. He felt Russia had behaved really badly, and though there was an explanation he felt it showed they could not really be trusted to be strategic partners. It was sad, he said, but there we are. We were also picking up all kinds of signals that Cheney and Rumsfeld in particular were not that keen on us being too involved in the UN/aftermath issues. TB felt there was some sense to the really hard US approach. Why should the French and the Russians come in at the end and clean up? Condi was giving the French a very hard time. We were in for a very foggy few days and we were going to need a lot of nerve around the place. I had a long chat with Dan B re the visit and how we intended to handle the public side of things.

Tuesday, March 25

I still felt we did not have a big picture out there, and the problem with the embedded media was that they were just putting over little snapshots from where they were, all competing to get on, but with no sense of an overall strategy. I also felt the military were going a bit native with the media, giving them too much access, letting them get in too close. GB asked to see me, and we met next door. He said the War Cabinet meetings were hopeless. You had Clare just blathering away, DB and JR behaving like armchair generals and giving out weakness vibes to the real generals. He felt we needed to structure things much more like a campaign. We needed to be clear what it was we were pushing every day, e.g. today would be push on Baghdad with a line out on humanitarian and reconstruction. The problem was there were currently too many places and people capable of setting an agenda from somewhere. I asked if he thought the party was OK on this. He said the party is fine on Iraq. 'It's other things they are worried about.' He said there were real worries about the direction of domestic policy and I needed to rein him in a bit.

I got back to the pre-meeting at Number 10. There were more friendly fire incidents today, including UK on UK. The Saddam broadcast on Iraqi TV had the effect of pushing the message he was still in power, which might set us back on the internal opposition to him, which had been growing in confidence a bit.[1] TB and I agreed that we had to reimpose a big-picture message, and he would have to be the one to do it. I had done a script overnight that set out the overall mission and purpose, update on the military front, humanitarian. The War Cabinet was possibly the worst yet. John S and CDS went through the motions of telling us what they had already told a smaller group of us in the pre-meeting and then we meandered around for a bit, with Clare, JR and DB asking a few questions. I scribbled a note to John S 'How many of these would you take into the jungle with you?'

They reported that the Fedayeen were being organised by Chemical Ali.[2] CDS reported continuing difficulties with the Turks re requests for access. He also warned operations may have to be scaled down because of the weather. David B had a go at one of the UK military spokesmen who had been on. 'I would get him off the airwaves if you can.' GB said to me afterwards that TB needed to take DB and JR aside, tell them these were supposed to be meetings on military strategy and we should have a separate meeting on political strategy. John's and David's questions did tend to be about the politics of where

[1] Saddam had urged Iraqis to attack the US and British enemy: 'O Iraqis, fight with the strength of the spirit of jihad . . . strike them, and strike evil so that evil will be defeated.'

[2] Ali Hassan al-Majid, military commander and chief of the Iraqi Intelligence Service, who had deployed chemical weapons in attacks on the Kurds. Later convicted of war crimes and hanged.

we were, but the overall impression for the military and intelligence guys was not good. TB went off to the NEC, then back to prepare for the press conference. They were all going to be on the 'Why is it all getting bogged down?' theme, which was easy to deal with. The tough questions related to differences with the US on the UN role, where we were not in the same place. We had stated clearly there would be a UN role in the aftermath, but the US signals were not as clear. We just had to go back to the Azores words on this. It would be so much easier if Powell, not Cheney and Rumsfeld, was driving the policy in the States. The press conference seemed to last an age. I watched downstairs. They were running a split screen with TB on one side, and bombs being loaded at [RAF] Fairford on the other. One of the girls in the office said the whole thing was being presented like another form of reality TV show, round-the-clock coverage of anything and everything and the prism was 'setback' and 'bogged down'.

On the conference call, I was pressing for more strategic communication and less focus on one part of the picture. There was next to no context out there for the briefings and pictures. They were like random scenes. The briefings in Qatar, and at the Pentagon, kept taking us to our weak points, e.g. PoWs and casualties. TB did the big picture OK today but there was precious little sign of it anywhere else. Also we had real problems on the diplomatic front, particularly re the UN. We had a good meeting of the Iraq communications group, and we agreed to get a message to all those with access to media in the field about the need to stay plugged in to bigger message and overall strategy. We also agreed to press internally for strikes against Saddam's TV output, which was integral to his command and control, part of his infrastructure of fear, and a legitimate target.

We had a lot of problems – sense of setback, bogged down; UN role; humanitarian crisis growing; Basra very tricky. It was a good meeting though and I felt if this group was in charge of the whole communications operation, we would be in a better position. We had to step up even further the contacts with the US. I commissioned a message note justifying attacks on their TV station. Then to the Bush call, and lots of comforting noises to each other, TB saying things were going as well as they could be expected to, Bush saying our troops were so much better than theirs and it was going well. TB said there was a chance the whole thing would collapse quickly like a pack of cards, but we shouldn't bank on it. There would be a lot of fighting, but eventually people would notice change happening, different people in control and if we handled the relations with the

Iraqi people well, change could come quickly. Bush said that if the word went round that Saddam was incapacitated, and also when we 'kick the crap out of the Republican Guard', that will have a profound effect around the country. He was in pretty bellicose form. They discussed Putin, and Bush said he was going to be looking for advice on how to deal with him from now on in. TB said [Hosni] Mubarak [Egyptian President] was nervous and what these guys wanted more than anything now was for the job to be done quickly.

We then left for the MoD for a presentation by CDS, [General Sir] Mike Jackson [Chief of the General Staff], [Admiral Sir Alan] West, [Air Chief Marshal Sir Peter] Squire and [General Sir John] Reith from PJHQ [Permanent Joint Headquarters]. Reith was very impressive but it was absolutely clear this was going to be a lot tougher. Reith felt the US had been excessively optimistic about the collapse of the regime. The hard core and the Fedayeen were absolutely up for the fight. They had nothing to lose, and would not just give up. TB asked about Baghdad. They said it would be split into forty sectors, and our forces would try to take them one by one, before sending in regulars. It would take several weeks, and there were a lot of dangers attached. Jackson said it was the only possible plan. Reith was excellent on the overview, but said that at Basra for example, it was not yet clear the best way to proceed.

The most important thing for TB was to communicate to the Iraqis that we would see this through, that they would benefit from the fall of Saddam. But we should not expect them to welcome with open arms, because they will find it hard to believe the Saddam era is ending. We were doing OK with public opinion in our own country, but we were nowhere in Iraq. Reith said we had to separate regime from people, and that meant taking out his media. The march on Baghdad was going OK, but they expected a lot more fighting. Our forces were busy in the Western Desert dealing with his Scud facilities to prevent them trying to draw Israel in. West went through the navy role and said [trained] dolphins were being used in minesweeping. Back at Number 10, TB was clear it was going to take longer than anticipated. Shock and awe had not really happened. So we had taken the political hit of a stupid piece of terminology, and then not actually had the military benefits. He felt reassured by the expertise of our military.

Wednesday, March 26

More delay in Basra. War Cabinet was awful. C told me later he found the whole thing ridiculous, and it was. It was necessary to involve the key ministers and keep them up to speed with everything, but the nature of the discussion did not inspire confidence. Clare blathered away, DB was a bit better today, whilst JR did come over a bit as an armchair general. The truth was we were not totally clear about the picture out there. TB had a bilateral with JP, who said Clare's behaviour at these meetings was intolerable and he should not put up with her for too long. TB never quite agreed with us on that and he had another meeting with her later, going out of his way to keep her involved and on board, as much as she ever would be. His concern at the moment was that there might be more support for Saddam than we thought, and that explained the level of resistance. Then later, when a bomb hit a Baghdad market, and the Iraqis started to pump out pictures of it, we were looking a bit shaky.

I was doing an email exchange with Dan on the visit, and it was clear Bush was pissed off at the *FT* story suggesting TB would press him for a bigger UN role. They were sensitive to the idea that TB was shaping their strategy, which was understandable. TB asked me to send a message back that this was our media seeking to open divisions. We knew of a Rumsfeld memo to Bush saying that TB would demand a bigger role for the UN, but that they should resist. Jack said Powell was on our side in this, and was trying to put a halt to the neoconservative stuff. TB's worry was the military campaign. He felt the Americans lacked the absolute single-mindedness needed to get the job done quickly. He said it was beginning to remind him of Kosovo. As we headed to the airport, the market attack was really taking off as a media and political issue, though there were suggestions the Iraqis may have been involved themselves.

TB was working on a long note for Bush on the plane, and I left him to it and had a long chat with Jack, going through all the difficult areas. He was worried just how far out on a limb TB was pushing himself, but was still totally on board for where we were. The main message in TB's note, when you boiled it down, was that there was a lot of support for the aims of the campaign, and we totally believed the policy was right, but there was real concern at the way the US put over their views and intentions, and that rested in people's fears about their perceived unilateralism. He was urging him to do more to rebuild with Germany, then Russia, then France, and saying he should seize the moment for a new global agenda, one to unite the world rather than divide it. A distorted view of the US was clouding everything – look at how much cynicism there was at their efforts in the Middle East. We had to break that down. Why had Mexico and Chile gone the other way? Why did so much of Europe?

In the end he wrote a twelve-page note that was both subtle and blunt at the same time. It was a good piece of work and if Bush took it on board would have a good effect. But he still had his own internal battles to deal with. I didn't really feel Bush had the will to deliver on this new international agenda TB was talking about, but we would see.

We landed in pretty miserable weather conditions, then flew down to Camp David, Bush seemed more nervous than usual, and it came out in that over-cockiness that sometimes spills out. 'We're gonna win. I'm sure of it. Basra will fall. The people will rise up, and choose freedom.' Overall, he was confident we were going to win. He made a jokey little reference to the *FT* story, when TB said we had not been pushing that line. 'Don't worry, I blame Alastair.'

Thursday, March 27

GWB had clearly read TB's note and was going through it virtually line by line. He was fairly strong on MEPP. He said he knew there would have to be a reckoning in their relationships with others. He seemed a lot more on top of the detail and in the discussion on the complexities of the Arab world seemed less one-dimensional than before. TB's note was saying that in essence the US had a choice about what it wanted to do with its power. They had to face up to that choice. The power was a given but how it was used was a series of choices. Jonathan and I were staying in Redwood – the cabins were all named after trees. We went over to see TB who was worrying about the whole UN scene. I felt we had it parked fairly well and there was no real need to take it forward at the moment. We walked down to Laurel where the meeting was to be. At first there was just me, TB, Jonathan and DM. TB felt on the war that we had reached the point we did in Kosovo where it felt like we were holding back slightly and not really going for it. In Kosovo the point came a bit later but it did feel similar.

On the UN Bush had said last night he was happy for a UN role but he was pretty scathing, said their handling of some issues was woeful, that some of them couldn't run a garbage service. It was a recurring theme. He just wasn't up for it really. It was interesting how Bush liked to take in different views and experiences round the table. He wasn't status-conscious in these meetings. He was also prone to go off on conversational tangents, asked me a few times re my running, and telling me he had been doing seven-minute mile pace round the Camp David track, which was faster than I could. They had another confined session then came out to discuss how we dealt with the press. Condi said we should go over the aftermath issues.

Bush said he understood there had to be some kind of role for the UN but he didn't trust their competence. He said on Kosovo the UN had been all over the place. Jack said 'With respect Mr President, Kosovo is not the only model. There is Bosnia, where the UN was light touch. There have been others which they have done well.' They agreed Sérgio de Mello [UN high commissioner for human rights] would be a good guy to do the UN job [Secretary General's special representative in Iraq] but Kofi may want him to stay on human rights. Pre the press conference TB was worried re the body language. I said the most important thing was the issue of resolve, and a message to the Iraqi people about seeing it through and being with them for the long term.

As TB walked back to Dogwood cabin afterwards he said to Jonathan and me 'He's not wrong about the UN you know.' I said he may have a point but it doesn't mean he is a hundred per cent right. We were driven by buggy up to the hangar where the press conference was being held. Dan had told him that I referred to them as 'the bastards' and Bush was saying 'bastards, bastards' loudly. I had done a script for TB and created a bit of a problem maybe by referring to the dead soldiers being 'executed'.

TB and Bush went off for a walk and then came back for lunch. Fairly relaxed and informal. GWB was geeing me up re the marathon, said I would love it, that it was one of the best things he ever did. TB and Bush then went out on the terrace for a genuine one-on-one. TB said afterwards they had discussed US politics and the pressures from the hard right. Bush had changed into a tracksuit. He did casual gear a lot better than TB but I guess the White House logo on everything helped a fair bit. He looked very fit for his age though the media had felt he looked tired at the press conference. I had an interesting chat with Dan about how Bush worked. He was a real early to bed, early to rise man. He was obsessed about punctuality and would really go for people who arrived late for meetings. He liked to read a brief, then discuss, then decide. He was open to ideas. He was very religious. He was loyal to friends but once you fell out with him, that was that. We were just whiling away the time while Bush and TB chatted. After half an hour or so they came in and we walked up to the helipad. TB was pleased and excited that Bush seemed to have moved on the road map. He was saying not only that he would publish it but take the lead in implementing it. We had a nice enough journey to New York with a fantastic view out of the helicopter. To the UN to meet Kofi. The main focus was post-conflict and Oil for Food.[1] Kofi was really pleased TB had gone to see him rather than the other way round. It was clear the politics were getting harder and harder. Bush was heavy enough but Cheney and Rumsfeld were even heavier. Back to the plane by chopper.

Friday, March 28

There was definitely a changed mood, lots of it media-driven. The morning meetings were developing a rhythm. First a pre-meeting with TB, GH, JS, C, CDS, John S and the key Number 10 people and then through to the broader meeting. CDS was confident things were going OK though it would be a while before there would be a commonly understood acceptance of military success. The weather was not helping and there had been more resistance than predicted. Not all bad news but there had been another friendly-fire incident. TB felt the Bush visit had been good and yet again today we saw how the propaganda could quickly go wrong. There was another attack on a Baghdad market. No evidence it was ours but the Arab media were straight out saying it was. At the morning meeting, we had a long discussion about how to improve outreach to the Arab media and also how to deal with the embedded media. As I said to TB, the problem was that the military had gone native on the media, rather than the other way round. They were all getting too much access and putting over little snapshots, so that there was very little communication of a big picture.

War Cabinet was pretty grim, with Clare blathering on about the UN. It was quite clear she was going to quit. She kept saying the issue was not fudge-able because it was a question of legality. TB said nobody was saying we were going to do something illegal. But she said there was a US draft that did suggest that. She said it was a matter of principle for her, and it should be for all of us. TB and Jack both had a go, not really clear what she was on about. C and John S said to me afterwards it was extraordinary that she behaved in the way she did. James Harrower [Number 10 security] and Mohny [Bahra, protection officer] called about how to handle demonstrations at home. James said the police were also discussing the possible need

[1] The UN Oil for Food programme had been set up in 1995 to enable Iraq, despite economic sanctions aimed at demilitarisation, to sell oil on the international market in exchange for food, medicine and humanitarian supplies. The programme was suspended by Kofi Annan prior to the invasion, and eventually terminated in November 2003.

for security on the marathon route. TB was planning to speak to Chirac and Schroeder tomorrow. He said we needed to start putting together the main European relationships again. [Royal Fleet Auxiliary ship] *Sir Galahad* finally docked at Umm Qasr [delivering humanitarian aid, after being delayed by mine clearance].

Saturday, March 29

In for the 9am meeting. The head of the Iraqi air defences had been sacked because of malfunctioning air defences, which may have caused two explosions in Baghdad. 24-hour news was a bit of a nightmare at the moment, as they covered it like any other story, with a mix of hysteria and comment the whole time, and the settled view was that it wasn't really happening. They seemed to think wars should only last a few days and then they should get on to the next thing. There were suggestions the public were getting sick of all the comment though, and making up their own minds. But a combination of dead soldiers, friendly fire, lack of progress towards Baghdad, Rumsfeld mouthing off re Syria [warning Syria not to aid Iraq] was not great. Dan told me they were delighted that Richard Perle [Rumsfeld-appointed Pentagon adviser and neoconservative lobbyist] was having to resign as chairman of a defence group [Defense Policy Board Advisory Committee, Department of Defense], though he was staying on the board.

At the War Cabinet Jack said we would be in a better place if Bush was not surrounded by 'loonies'. ORHA [Office of Reconstruction and Humanitarian Assistance, established by the US to become a caretaker government in Iraq] was in a state of chaos because of internal US difficulties. They appeared unable to agree on anything. TB asked me afterwards if I thought the propaganda effort was working. I said not. He agreed. The problem was the US were pretty much doing their own thing, and they lacked coherence at the centre. The embedded media were treating the whole thing like scenes from a war movie, and there was no place for the big picture. The media here were pretty much set on presenting things in the worst light. So the mix was not good. We had to raise our own game, but also get the US and the military to raise theirs, and co-ordinate better. The pressure for instant comment and analysis was a real added problem in modern conflict situations.

Sunday, March 30

The papers were not good. The overall impression was that things were not really going our way. TB and I had both come to the view over the weekend that we needed to beef up the whole communications effort. If we were moving from 'shock and awe' to a message of steady progress, it required a different communications plan and approach. I went to Greenwich to run the first half of the marathon course with Hugh Jones [runner]. Did 14.08 miles in two hours flat. I quite liked the course and could see no real problems in it.

TB called a couple of times later, as he was preparing another note, including on the media, and we tossed around a few ideas. The Americans were still causing us problems on the media and political front, e.g. Rumsfeld suddenly turning on Syria had apparently also been a shock to the White House. Things not great with Fiona, and were unlikely to improve until I was out of it. Even with all this going on, there was a large part of me wanted out. I had pretty much lost it with the media, had very little time or respect for any of them, which was not a great position to be in, and maybe it was time for someone else.

Monday, March 31

In for the usual morning meetings, with both CDS and C more hopeful. John Scarlett also reported that the general picture was a lot better. TB later saw CDS and a general from the campaign and said he got more talking direct to the general than he had from weeks of meetings. The truth was that the military and intelligence campaigns had not been wholly successful. The morning meetings were not very productive, and the mood at the War Cabinet was the usual mix of sullen and concerned. Then to TB's meeting with JR, HA, DA, Peter H, Jonathan, Pat McF, Sally, David Hanson [Blair's PPS]. TB went through what he wanted on the political and media fronts. It was basically a war room à la Millbank, with all the main tasks being overseen from there, and everyone knowing what was going on in all the different parts of the operation.

I then spent most of the day in a series of meetings working out how to put it into practice. I called in the key people from CIC, FCO and MoD, and explained we needed much more centralised co-ordination. We were heading for another version of the Kosovo model, though as I pointed out to TB, getting real co-ordination with the Americans wasn't easy because their own internal co-ordination was not there. Another TB/Bush call, which was basically just going through TB's note. A lot of the discussion was about presentation and Bush said he would speak to Dan 'who is kind of responsible for this'. He did so, because Dan called later and said TB had really got GWB 'spun up', because he was asking what we were going to do to grip it. I said we had to have a real exchange of people and we also needed them to get their act together internally. He said the reality was they had no real grip of Rumsfeld. The main story of the weekend was division between Rumsfeld and the military over the way the campaign was being waged.

TB called later and asked if I thought it had been OK to raise the comms and media issues like he did. I said it was, but don't underestimate how hard it will be to grip. We have our own internal problems but they are nothing compared with the Americans'. He had to be more direct with Bush because at least he tended to get things done when he cared enough about it. I sensed on the call today that Bush was maybe sharing TB's feeling that the military campaign was not quite right. They were both desperate for better communications. The BBC was a bit better today but we had to do more to slow the rhythm. Shock and awe had to become steady progress.

Tuesday, April 1

I did a note overnight on the communications effort for TB. Last night had been better but we were still having real problems with the BBC, particularly the reports out of Baghdad and the embedded reporters. TB was involved in a series of meetings with GB re EMU. GB had suddenly announced last week that he wanted to do the euro assessment in the Budget, and say that four out of the five [economic] tests were met, and set out how we intended to meet the fifth, plus there was the suggestion, from us, that we could do the [euro] referendum bill. Andrew Adonis and Peter Hyman in particular were against it, felt it would be seen as sneaky. I felt it was big and bold and TB should use GB's desire to do it now to extract maximum leverage for a pro position. But then after one of the sessions, TB said 'God knows what he's up to. I just can't work it out.'

The military campaign was going better. There was a classic Clare moment at the War Cabinet when she asked CDS if we shouldn't be talking to the local military down there. 'We're killing them, not talking to them,' he said. She was more and more ridiculous at these meetings. At the pre-meeting TB raised the *Guardian* splash that the US was going to run Iraq from Kuwait. We worked up a line 'Iraq for and by the Iraqi people'. But most of my day was taken trying to set up TB's war room. I got him to raise it at the War Cabinet so ministers and top brass knew we would be changing things on the comms front. GH said he would like to have it at the MoD.

I chaired a ninety-minute meeting to work through all the things we would need for it and started to bring in the people we would need to drive it. Anne Shevas [chief press officer] found premises at the FCO and rebuttal in MoD. Things were feeling better at the moment, and it was also the case that sometimes if we got the communications right, and the PR situation settled, things then improved in reality because people could focus better. We had intelligence, which I wanted to use, that Saddam was planning to attack holy sites as a way of generating real anger against us, not exactly difficult in the Arab world at the moment. CDS said we had to wait for the US to agree never to attack holy sites, even if they were being used to store weapons.

We had an internal meeting on some of the domestic policy issues, foundation hospitals, asylum, health and NICs. There was a lot to be sorting on the domestic front but most of our time and energies were going on Iraq. At the lobby we were starting to use the basic narrative set out in TB's note – 1, strategic grip, 2, steady advance then 3, end of regime. It was the best way to slow the media rhythm. I was working on humanitarian stories for tomorrow. Clare did [Jonathan] *Dimbleby* on ITV and was talking about the illegality of the US approach. We were making good progress finding out what happened at the first Baghdad bombing, enough for Jack to say it was 'increasingly probable' it was caused by Iraqi missiles. The sense of strategy was finally beginning to get communicated through the media. I lodged another complaint with the BBC re their output from Baghdad from [Andrew] Gilligan and Rageh Omaar.

Wednesday, April 2

Definitely a sense that the military campaign was going better, plus we had a strong humanitarian message running alongside. The major news overnight was the battle getting closer to Baghdad, and also the rescue of a female US PoW [Private Jessica Lynch] by the Marines. Jack sort of got up the holy sites issue on the *Today* programme. I got a cab in and on the way up the street Alisdair Macdonald [*Mirror* photographer] showed me a picture he'd taken of Geoff Hoon yesterday as he left Number 10, with a 'Top Secret' paper facing the camera, and with the text legible. I thanked him and later spoke to Geoff about it. We had a fairly brief PMQs preparation meeting. TB now had maps of Iraq in his room. At the pre-meeting the picture given was a lot better, particularly in Basra. CDS made a revealing comment when he said in Basra we were using lessons from Northern Ireland. Troops were getting to know people, finding out who the ringleaders were, then seeking them out. 'Did you do that in Northern Ireland?' I asked. Laughter.

The War Cabinet proper was the usual blather. At the political meeting we agreed: 1. big push on holy sites; 2. pull back the military narrative so that it did not appear like we were about to win any day now, and 3. more out there re Iraq vs Iraqi people. I was working on a TB speech re a future vision for Iraq. Jack S called to say he was intending to go to ORHA. He said not to mention to Clare because she would want to come and it would change the whole tone and nature of the visit. Then to a meeting with John Reid and Douglas [Alexander] to see how they would fit in the war room. We agreed Douglas would be semi-permanent, JR in and out, though later TB told me he was thinking of moving JR to Leader of the House and Ian McCartney [pensions minister] to party chairman.

Over for PMQs which was fine though it was interesting that there were no questions on the conduct of the war – it was all about the post-conflict questions. I got back and started to insert people into different parts of the war room. The conference call was a mix of wandering conversations and pipe dreams about how well we were doing. I just didn't see it. I had a separate chat with Dan re the Northern Ireland visit. We were thinking about a joint interview, and also getting over their guy from Homeland Security. TB saw GB again re EMU and was clearly now thinking he was being stitched up to do something he didn't particularly want to do. I saw Peter M, PG and PH and discussed the BBC coverage. I got a nice letter from Neil [Kinnock] saying his favourite game at the moment was imagining how the BBC of today would have covered World War Two. 'Hitler would have lived to 1978.' PG felt the public were making up their own minds and that TB was in OK shape. The public liked TB being so big in the States and he felt we should build that side of the profile even more. My big worry was the Arab media. We were kidding ourselves if we thought we were making real inroads.

Thursday, April 3

TB had issued instructions to ministers in the War Cabinet that they couldn't go on holiday at Easter. When I mentioned it to Fiona, and said we needed to work out how to handle it if the press came after me when we were away, she snapped back 'I suppose that's a polite way of saying you can't have a holiday.' I couldn't understand why she felt we both had to leave. We still had a lot going for us. But she didn't really believe we could get our lives back until we were both out of their [the Blairs] shadow, and maybe there was something in that. I got Sally to speak to her, and Peter M. Both felt that her anger with me for being a driven, obsessive, selfish bastard had boiled over but because she basically wanted us to stay together she preferred to express it as hatred for TB and CB who in turn gave her lots of ammunition. But it was really grim at the moment.

On the war front, things were going better. The movement towards Baghdad was quickening, more people were deserting, and more was coming out re the nature of the regime. TB was late for the pre-meeting because he had another euro meeting with GB. He was now firmly of the view that GB was trying to bounce him while his eye was off the ball because of Iraq. GB was now trying to make out that he had always intended to do the assessment now, and that TB had agreed to it a while back, which he hadn't. Also that it was somehow TB's fault Iraq was 'taking so long'! And he was back on to a Peter M kick, saying that Peter was responsible for foundation hospitals and the division they were causing. So it went on.

There was an established meeting rhythm now – TB with me, Jonathan, DM, sometimes Sal, then pre-meeting with CDS, C, John S, then the War Cabinet, then a mop-up, and today full Cabinet as well. The mood was OK. TB went through the whole picture and was emphasising steady progress. I helped GH with his Commons statement and then went over to the war room. Dickie Stagg [director of public services and information, FCO] had done a great job and it was pretty much all there now, now needed the fine-tuning and the drive. It would definitely make a difference and we had some good people in there already. I worked on TB's 'message to the Iraqi people' and we brainstormed on the different ways to get it across. TB was out on a troops visit so I tried to clear my in tray.

TB had asked GH and others to work on a counter-plan on the future of Iraq to offer to Bush that was not Rumsfeld's eccentric ideas. TB said there was no point just going on about Rumsfeld the whole time. We needed a counter-plan. David M, Jonathan and I did a secure videolink with Condi, Dan and Karen. They agreed that on Tuesday we should publish a joint statement similar to the Azores. We also discussed [Bush visiting] Northern Ireland. I asked what the US media would make of GWB pitching up there. They said their approach was to say it was to show those involved in the MEPP that peace processes can work. Good idea. It was a good discussion, pretty frank about each other's difficulties, so at one point we joked about swapping Rumsfeld for Clare. But I sensed we were at least gripping some of the post-war issues and had a sense of a stronger strategy going forward. Then a rash of calls on the euro, as GB's lot seemed to be putting it about that there would be something on it in the Budget, which confirmed the suspicions this was an attempted bounce. TB got back at 6 [from Aldershot and RAF Lyneham] and we went through the outstanding issues. HC [Hilary Coffman, special adviser] said he had been terrific with the troops.

Friday, April 4

More EMU meetings and TB was reverting to his original view that it would be seen as sneaky to do it in the Budget while a war was going on. Jeremy [Heywood] had been up until 1.30 negotiating with Ed Balls and trying to make the language more positive. After all the morning meetings TB called an office meeting and he looked pretty fed up. While GB's rationale to TB was glass more than half full, it was the empty bits that would get the attention. TB saw him again later and said it was the worst meeting yet (again). GB said the assessment was done and he was not having it rewritten 'for political reasons'. He was back to speaking in code again. He said 'I know what your plan is' – i.e. you are going to sack me. TB tried to get him to say that was what he meant, but he didn't. TB said he was not prepared to be bounced into something that he felt was wrong. His instincts were telling him this was the wrong way, and the wrong time. He had discussed it with JP who had said he should follow his instincts, and also that there had to be more time for the Cabinet to be brought properly into the discussion.

GB said he was not prepared to let them rewrite the assessment and if that was what we intended, he would have to go. 'There's the door,' said TB. GB claimed he had been trying to have these discussions for ages, which was total balls. The Treasury had already prepared for printing, and now sent to the printers, 3,000 pages of background material. TB said he had been trying to discuss this for months and GB had resisted, all the time preparing for this decision and announcement, and we had to wait for something written by someone called Dave Ramsden![1] Sally said it would be hard to win a referendum campaign without GB. But what he was doing was ensuring there wasn't one for the foreseeable future.

TB and I went out on the terrace later. 'One thing is for sure,' he said. 'At the moment he is crackerjack. My big worry is that he will bring the whole show down.' I saw Ed Balls later and although we were able to talk in a civilised way about it, there was no getting away from how grisly things were between them at the moment. I

[1] Treasury official then leading work on the assessment of the five economic tests.

had told TB I was seeing him and he asked me to get over the message that he didn't want to sack him, they had to work together but he did not fear him any more. I discussed my own situation with TB. He said if things were bad and I was feeling demotivated, I had to decide what I really wanted to do, but he felt I would regret it if I left. The truth was I didn't really know if I wanted to leave or not. He had a lot on his plate at the moment. Iraq, then the euro suddenly thrown in and I felt bad adding to the problems, but I really need to resolve in my own mind what I intend to do.

The Iraq situation was better. The airport at Baghdad was eighty per cent under control. The Republican Guard was on the run. The broadcasters there were finally beginning to accept that we were doing well. There were signs now of regime collapse. Our main media focus today was the [BBC] World Service Arabic Service and Abu Dhabi TV. The Islamic media team were doing well. We also had some good Iraqi exiles in who were able to talk about the regime far more convincingly than we could. We signed off the TB letter to the Iraqis which we were going to be getting out through the military. The main message for the interviews was that it was a war on Saddam not Iraq. We were also pushing the line that Iraqis wanted to see money spent on schools not palaces. Pictures came in of Saddam out on the streets but it was not entirely clear that it was him rather than a lookalike.

TB did a video conference with Bush. Dick Cheney, Condi and Andy Card were also in the shot. Cheney said next to nothing, just sat there looking menacing. I couldn't work out whether he always looked like that or it was an effect he sought to create. They went over the Middle East again, Russia, military update, but TB said afterwards he preferred the one-on-one phone calls to the video conference. There was something about it that made him feel constrained, unable to speak freely. There was also something a bit surreal about the fact that while we could see them on the main screen, there was an ordinary TV screen to one side, Peter O'Toole starring in some old-style Zulu war film [*Zulu Dawn*, 1979].

I saw TB again before he went up to the flat. He was concerned GB was setting himself up to walk by claiming TB had sought to rewrite the euro assessment politically. TB's view anyway was that it was a political process based on economic judgements. The assessment per se could not decide. That had, ultimately, to be a political judgement. Dan B called as I was leaving to say AP [Associated Press] were on to the Belfast visit. I knocked up a quick briefing note with Ben Wilson [press officer] to use it to get out basic message on Iraq, MEPP and NI.

Saturday, April 5

The military picture was changing fast. As I arrived at the office for the 9am meeting, Sky was showing US tanks going through Baghdad. Things were also going a lot better in Basra and the mood was much improved all round. The regime was refusing humanitarian help. However, the post-conflict issues were looking really ragged. Though we were trying to minimise the differences, the truth was there were differences between us and the US, and differences between the White House, Powell and Rumsfeld. TB said to me he couldn't understand how I could think about leaving when we were in a position to sort the big geopolitical questions for the next generation, and surely it was right to see the whole thing through.

At the War Cabinet, issues to do with the future of Iraq were becoming more difficult. Clare's tone was becoming more menacing. Scarlett said there was a possibility Chemical Ali was dead. I went up to Mum and Dad's with Grace and did the conference call from Robert's [Templeton, sick relative] bedside. I raised the issue of a planned ORHA briefing for Monday which I said would be a bad thing at the time TB was seeing Bush. Dan and Tucker [Eskew, White House media affairs] both agreed and we would try to move it. The military situation was getting better all the time but as the prospect of winning came closer, the aftermath issues became more pressing.

Sunday, April 6

David M and Matthew Rycroft were pulling together the post-conflict arguments for TB. It was difficult. David called when I was on the train home and said we were meeting a fair bit of American resistance. I got home and Fiona and I had another heart-to-heart. She thought the kids were fed up with it and she was determined that we should leave together. I don't suppose I handled it very well, just raged about how I hated being pressurised like this when I had so much on my plate at the moment. The reality was I was unsure what I wanted to do. I was very torn.

Monday, April 7

Fiona picked a fight this morning as soon as I went downstairs with some jibe about 'the thought police'. I said it was time she got a grip of herself. She ended up calling me a bastard and throwing a cup at me, which smashed on the floor at my feet. She was more angry than I had ever known her and taking it all out on me. Part of me understood. Part of me resented it. But I had a terrible sense of foreboding about it. I left for the office feeling like shit. At the intel meeting, the news was overwhelmingly good. Basra was going according to plan. Around Baghdad the US troops were really going for it now. All our problems really related to the future of Iraq. [Ahmed] Chalabi [expatriate Iraqi dissident], a friend of Rumsfeld and [Paul] Wolfowitz [Deputy Defense Secretary], was putting himself around the whole time as a key player, possible future leader, when the reality was he would be unacceptable.[1] The nature of a UN role was becoming the key difficulty. The Americans didn't want the French in particular to be involved, and because of the reality of the P5 [permanent UNSC members – US, UK, France, Russia and China], that meant the UN. Their general take was that they had given the UN the opportunity to deal with this, the UN had fucked it up, and didn't deserve to be straight back in the game. But TB was firmly of the view they should be rebuilding relationships, not keeping them broken. He said at one meeting of the inner group 'I did Iraq because I thought it was right and I am prepared to take whatever comes my way to do what I think is right. But I'm not prepared to stand up for something I think is wrong.' He was back to the notion that they were doing the right thing in the wrong way. We wanted an interim authority that was mainly Iraqi, then a truly representative government. TB felt his job was still to keep the US focused on the UN route but the pressures in the States were all the other way, to present the UN as a bad thing that shouldn't be allowed near the place. Dan called to say Bush had agreed to our idea of a joint Iraqi TV broadcast with TB so I worked on a script. Then domestic problems took another bad turn, Fiona sending Jonathan an email saying she intended to resign. TB said he would see her on Wednesday when we got back.

On the flight to Belfast TB worked on a note for Bush setting out why it was so important to get the UN properly involved – to show our commitment to rebuilding after the divisions in the international community, for the Arab world, for Europe. It was a two-page note, very clear and rational. We landed, got a helicopter to Hillsborough. As I was making a few calls in my room, TB called me through to

[1] Chalabi and his organisation the Iraqi National Congress provided the US government with intelligence material about weapons of mass destruction and links to al-Qaeda, the majority of which was used in good faith in making the case for military intervention. It later turned out to have been fabricated by an Iraqi defector codenamed 'Curveball'. Chalabi would be appointed president of the interim governing council of Iraq in September 2003. He would later dismiss the fabricated intelligence, saying 'We are heroes in error. As far as we're concerned, we've been entirely successful. That tyrant Saddam is gone and the Americans are in Baghdad.'

his room. He asked how my situation was at home. I said that unless I had an exit date, I had no 'marriage'. He said he was really saddened and disappointed, but he understood. He would not put me under pressure to stay. He felt it was a bad move for me, that I would forever regret not seeing the whole thing through to the end. 'But you need to know you have done more for me than anyone, more than I could have asked for, I could not have done it without you, and I will not feel let down, so let me relieve you of any pressure you may feel on that front.' But I did feel it, because I knew he valued the close team around him and I knew I made a difference. I felt it very strongly here at Hillsborough because there had been so many good and bad moments here, but I knew I had helped with both.

We stood at the window and I reminded him of the time we came here in Opposition and he looked out over the grounds at Hillsborough and said the Tories were not going to give it all up without a real fight. We had won that fight and I knew a lot of that was down to me and the work I'd done for him, and it was not easy to walk away from it. He asked me when I wanted to go. I said summer at the latest, maybe conference, maybe before. He just nodded. We went round in circles for a while and then he said I would have to help him find a successor. I felt David Hill [former Labour Party chief spokesman] was possibly the only option. We went downstairs to wait for Bush and Co. to arrive. They flew in, then drove up, GWB, Powell, Condi and Andy Card in Bush's car. TB and Bush having a fair bit of time together. At one point they came back from a walk and Bush was talking about his favourite presidents – Washington, Lincoln, Roosevelt, Reagan. He said Reagan made the country feel good again and he saved the Republican Party.

I tried to go out for a run but was stopped at every second tree by bloody American security men jumping out from trees. Gave up after a couple of miles. Bush seemed to be going in the right direction on MEPP, said he intended to put real pressure on Sharon. He was still not in bridge-building mode elsewhere, said that he didn't want TB to accept Putin's invite to meet VP, Chirac and Schroeder at St Petersburg. Meanwhile Clare had sent through a note listing all sorts of points she wanted TB to raise with Bush. Jack was of the view that it didn't matter too much if she went. TB felt it was a good discussion but he was concerned that Bush was in such a different position re the UN and trying to rebuild relations. Jack felt they really were pressing for a right-wing government there, though Bush seemed to be pretty clear [Ahmed] Chalabi was a non-starter.

TB said 'this neocon stuff' was crazy. I had asked Dan last night what 'neocon' meant and he said it was the belief that government had a moral purpose. I said does that mean moral purpose can only be right wing? TB felt today's meeting with Bush was going to be tough. It was clear Condi was pushing a fairly hard line re the UN. We had a fight on our hands to keep in a 'vital role' [in the press conference script]. She wanted 'important' which sounded too grudging. 'It's meant to be,' she said. My other worry was that it might be briefed they had downgraded it. TB was determined we had to get something out of this and in the end, largely thanks to Bush, we did. Bush was excellent on Northern Ireland, and on MEPP, linked the two well by saying he would spend as much time and energy on MEPP as TB did on NI, then excellent too on the UN role. He was good on the war message too. The general feeling afterwards was that it was the best media performance he'd done.

It was interesting to watch him in the main meeting today, where he was letting TB do a lot of the talking, then taking in Powell's and Condi's views in particular, then more or less saying what we expected him to in the first place. He seemed restless too, a bit fidgety. He and TB were in the big armchairs by the fireplace, the rest dotted around the room, Jack and Powell on the sofa together. Powell was talking at one point when Bush got up, got himself a coffee, asked me if I wanted one and came over to talk to me about the marathon. When is it? What time will I do? How much money will I raise? Dan pointed out that I had a piece in *The Times* on it and Bush picked it up and read it, getting to the end plug for Leukaemia Research. 'You doing it for leukaemia? Did you know my sister died from leukaemia? Would you like me to give you a cheque?' I certainly would, I said.

He went to the door giving on to the lounge, opened it and shouted out 'Blake [Gottesman, aide], get my chequebook.' Later the cops said he created an absolute stir because nobody had a clue that he had a chequebook with him, let alone where it was, though they did find it eventually, and he wrote out a cheque there and then. He said his sister was called Robin and died aged seven when he was four. 'I will do this because you are my friend,' he said, 'but I am also doing it for her.' I asked if the charity could publicise it. Sure, he said. TB came over and asked what I was up to. I said the president had just given me a cheque so where's yours?

Bush seemed seem to buy into TB's line that he had to develop a bigger international message that was not just terrorism but MEPP, world poverty, environment, etc. He was pretty vile re Chirac, said he felt betrayed, that Chirac had gone against him not on the merits but as part of a general anti-US strategy and he would never forgive that. 'The only thing that would swing me round to France is regime change.' Bush said he would maybe rebuild with Schroeder first but he wanted TB to make sure he knew he felt personally affronted and he would only think about putting things back together with them on the clear understanding German foreign policy was not run by the French.

TB seemed to have worked a fair bit of influence on him because the general reaction from the press conference was that Bush went well beyond what was expected. He also tore a bit of a strip off Condi at the pre-meeting when she was still picking away at him, and he suddenly said 'There is too much tension in here.' He asked everyone to leave apart from me, Blake and Magi Cleaver [Number 10 press officer]. TB and Bush also had a fairly long stroll, just the two of them while Jack continued to work on Condi, Powell and Dan Fried [National Security Council], saying that the warmer the words re the UN, the greater the influence within it. Jack and I both fought very hard to keep 'vital' in the text, and eventually they agreed to it. Later Dan said, only half in jest I think, 'Can we win any of these arguments at all?' He obviously had the counter-worry, that if Bush was too warm re the UN, he would get hit at home. TB said to Bush 'that was a very rash promise' – to spend as much time on MEPP as he had on NI.

Bush knew he had done pretty well. I was trying to get them up to do the Iraqi TV pieces to camera straight away while they were still in the mood. Bush's crowd were gathering round him clearly telling him he had gone too far in our direction. Both Condi and Dan looked slightly panicked, though he was holding firm and seemed not to be bothered. During the press conference Powell had slipped a note to Condi saying they would have to send a 'Rummygram', to warn Rumsfeld of what he was saying. Jack was trying to joke with Condi about it but she was clearly not happy. She said he had risked bad US reaction re the UN and they would have to make some calls to see how bad it was. Bush overheard and snapped back at her 'I don't want any pulling back on this.' We were due to do the broadcast recording on the same floor as the bedrooms. I went up with them, and went in to TB's room while he tidied himself up. Bush came in after a while. 'Hey, they didn't make your bed yet.' He said he was getting a bit of grief from his people but he was fine with what he said. TB said it was the right thing to do. We sorted the filming logistics, then down to meet Bertie [Ahern] who was arriving for lunch, and then the other parties. The press conference was running pretty much word perfect for us.

We gathered the parties, including [David] Trimble, [Gerry] Adams, [Martin] McGuinness, [David] Ervine [leader, Progressive Unionist Party] etc., in a rough circle inside the main dining room. Bush did the rounds and was pretty good at it, and did a little general number, saying he was there in the hope he could put some wind in their sails, and that when NI finally moved to lasting peace, it would be seen as a symbol of hope around the world. I was chatting to Powell about the French. He said even he found them impossible to deal with, that he found de Villepin arrogant and condescending. The meeting went fine, and they all seemed to think it had been worth him coming. TB and Bush then walked down the hill to the helicopters. I was following on behind with Condi. We joked about the next venue, maybe Cyprus. I said I thought it had gone pretty well, but said she seemed a lot more wound up than before. They flew off and TB went back in for meetings with Bertie and the parties.

TB was full of himself on the flight home, really felt it had been good and positive, pretty much on all fronts. GWB was definitely moving a bit on the international agenda, and buying into the need for a new approach, but the tensions internally had been very clear. TB felt Schroeder had a chance of getting back in with Bush, but not Chirac. TB was even more firmly of the view now that Chirac's world view built around rival poles of power was crazy. Chirac had put himself out on a limb and would see France's power diminish. The question unresolved from today was when to declare victory.

Wednesday, April 9

Today was the day when things really started to turn. While we were having a meeting on the humanitarian issues, which I wanted to badge as a return to normal life, the US forces were now motoring big time, and the Iraqis were spilling out on to the streets in greater numbers and with more confidence. The BBC reporters and David Chater [Sky] were beginning to change their tune. The main focus for the media was the toppling of a statue of Saddam, all the more dramatic for the time it took, but the effect ruined in many ways by an American soldier getting up there to put a US flag round his face. They just don't get it sometimes. I could appreciate the emotion that led him to do something like that, and these guys are soldiers not diplomats, but even so, surely someone nearby would have reckoned on how what plays well in the States goes down like a lead balloon elsewhere. The PMQs pre-meeting was strangely flat and desultory and they could tell TB's mind was elsewhere now, moving on to the next set of problems.

War Cabinet. Signs of regime collapse were all around now. It was still not clear where Saddam was but they believed both he and Chemical Ali were alive. Clare was rabbiting on more than ever. I slipped TB a note about the time Saddam shot his health minister at a meeting because he was annoying him and did he want me to get a gun? Yes, he scribbled. We came out of the meeting straight into another GB-inspired mini crisis. Jeremy had discovered late yesterday that GB planned to include in the Budget a review by [Sir] Derek Wanless [banker] on health inequalities, obviously with a view to making big changes in the future. He hadn't discussed it with TB or with Alan Milburn, who hit the roof when told about it, and demanded it be removed from the Budget. Of course GB being GB, it was too late to unpick fully, the background documents having been printed we assumed, and Wanless having been lined up. We did though get it pulled from the statement and got the Treasury to agree Milburn would be in charge of the review.

TB and I were in many ways so used to it that with everything else that was going on, we didn't let ourselves get too wound up, and we were trying to make light of it when Alan came in to see TB pre Cabinet. He was totally on the rampage. He said it was just unacceptable to have a Chancellor behave like this, to announce major change in someone else's department without even discussing it. He could see TB was not going to get too wound up and so added 'And it weakens you in the eyes of others that you let him get away with it.' He said the NHS was more monitored and reviewed than any other part of government and if this was to be another great review, he would put out a statement denouncing it. 'I am just not having it.' We tried to get him down from the ceiling but he said he intended to raise it in Cabinet.

I had to leave to chair my Iraq morning meeting which went on a bit so I missed the start of Cabinet. GB was in full flow when I got back, going through the Budget. He got an OK if not overwhelming response. TB said we were doing better than most countries, but there had to be a continuing emphasis on the changes we needed to make for the future. DB made a joke about being upset at the rise on wine. GB said sparkling wine was frozen. 'I don't like that. I like red,' said David. Charles asked about 'the speculation that we would be doing the euro tests today and what is the answer on that?' 'The answer is no,' said TB. Then Alan got in there, made a few political points, e.g.

that as the Tories tried to stake out a low tax position, we had to win on value for money and he would circulate a paper to colleagues about where the money was going in the health service. He then said he wanted to raise a process point, that there was to be a second Wanless report announced in the Budget. He said that at ten to nine he got a call from Paul Boateng [chief secretary to the Treasury] to say there was to be this review, and it was totally unacceptable and it was unnecessary for the Treasury to operate in this way. Of course having been there as chief secretary, he knew that for something like this to be included in the overall package it will have been known about for some time, and he stated several times it just wasn't necessary to behave like this.

Ian McCartney [newly appointed party chairman], who was at his first Cabinet after the mini reshuffle involving him and John R, came in with his first intervention, which was pretty telling. He said it was important that colleagues (i.e. GB) did not make things even more difficult than they already were for other ministers. He felt there were sufficient reviews of the NHS going on already. He was not clear what the purpose of this one was, or its agenda. And though at times he was coded, he laid down a marker that he thought GB was exploiting the foundation hospitals issue to be divisive in the party. GB totally ignored the point when he was summing up. As the meeting finished and we went through to TB's room, TB sat down in the chair by the fireplace, shaking his head. 'I just don't know what you do with him. On the one hand, there is nobody else there who has the breadth and the reach that allows you to put together a Budget like that. On the other, why is he incapable of working with other people unless they are wholly owned disciples?'

PMQs went fine. The Budget a bit of a monodrone. Peter M came over for a chat re my situation. The TV was on in the background, Saddam's statue coming down. He felt Fiona in some ways resented the way I was seen as such a big figure, when she was every bit as political, and she felt let down personally by TB and CB. We perhaps had more realistic expectations because when all was said and done he was a politician and a human being with weaknesses as well as strengths. Fiona was very unforgiving of others' weaknesses, he said. Also she had got herself into a mindset that could only see the downside. He said I was a figure in political history and that only came about because TB gave us that opportunity.

TB was seeing Fiona and seemingly told her he was sad things had reached this point, that she had done a good job, and he knew these were very high-pressure positions. She felt he was fine about us leaving but not yet. She told him she thought the political side of our operation was weak, that too much fell on me. She said it was fine on one level, but the reality was she didn't much like him or respect him any more, and she was convinced we had to get out. I felt that considering everything else he had to deal with at the moment, it was a bit much to expect him to be on top of all the internal personnel issues too, even those involving us.

He had a stack of calls post PMQs, including Chirac and Kofi and he was clearly going to be a feature if not the key player in the aftermath. David Blunkett came round for dinner and Fiona was now pretty open about how she felt about things. He said to me when she was out of the room 'You must not let her push you out. TB has to have you there, and so do the rest of us.' He was making clear he thought TB had to grip GB. He realised he couldn't sack him but he could swap him with Jack. GB might see it as a downward step but you cannot be Chancellor forever and Foreign Secretary is the other big job he could do.

Thursday, April 10

Jonathan had stayed out in Northern Ireland trying to get the final pieces in place for a deal but it didn't work out, so we aborted the plan for TB to fly out. Jonathan called early to say that they couldn't do it. TB worked on it for a while, tried out various forms of words, but in the end the IRA were not going to deliver. GB got a fairly good press out of the Budget but on Iraq, the media were moving effortlessly from 'victory' to lawlessness and humanitarian disaster. Their determination to ensure TB got no credit at all for Saddam's fall was pretty intense. Jack was chairing meetings on the aftermath issues and said to me later that having Clare there was like having a fifth column, that he felt the whole time she was trying to sabotage.

The mood in the War Cabinet and Cabinet itself was better but still not great considering the progress made. We still had major problems ahead – e.g. where were the WMD? What do we do to repair the divisions in the international community, particularly between the US and the EU? TB had another difficult call with Chirac.

De Villepin told Jack that as far as France was concerned, the US and the UK were 'the demandeurs' so they clearly felt it was up to us to make the running in trying to repair things. Schroeder was trying to get back onside. There were signs of Putin doing the same, but they all would delight at the fact that 'victory' was messy and not universally seen as such, and that now we had to involve them more. GH said there were plenty of other countries wanting to help but they needed UN cover for their internal politics. It was blindingly obvious and yet we were still struggling with the US on this.

John Scarlett's military and intelligence update was overwhelmingly positive. By contrast Clare was exacerbating problems as much as she could, winding up the International Red Cross, or being wound up, and the DFID website was pretty much unadulterated bad news, dreadful about everything. After Cabinet I left with Charles Lindsay [one of TB's protection officers] for the Tower Hotel. Charles was doing the marathon and at the security review it had been suggested he run with me, whilst the cops on the route would also get an alert when I was in their area. Deep down I did not imagine anything would happen, but you couldn't be sure in the current mood. I did a photocall at Tower Bridge, then a press conference and interviews. The organisers were a good crowd and seeing the HQ brought home how close it was now.

Then an Iraq update meeting. CDS was very clear that a near-philosophical difference between us and the US was responsible for some of the disorder problems we had. We believed in peacekeeping. They believed in war fighting. We were good at both. They were only really focused on one, so didn't adapt quickly enough to changed circumstances. *The Times* had done a story re Bush's sponsorship cheque, and having seen it, TB said 'I suppose I'd better sponsor you too then.' He was totally at a loss re GB at the moment. JP had told him it had to be sorted one way or the other, that it could not go on like this much longer. TB agreed in theory but was unsure in practice what that meant he should do. He felt the euro business had become a bit of a nightmare now, and could easily have been avoided if there was genuine trust between them.

Friday, April 11

A few OK pictures from the marathon photocall. The main news overnight was lots of looting going on in Iraq, the BBC hyping for all it was worth. Gilligan was saying there was more fear there now than there had been before. The main focus both of the pre-meeting and the War Cabinet itself was the disorder, and there were still problems re ORHA. [General Sir] Mike Jackson was saying that if only the US would operate in Baghdad as we were in the south, we would all be better off. But they didn't, so things were becoming very messy. In reality, the operation had been an enormous military success, but it didn't seem like that. We were having to dance around perfectly legitimate questions re when ORHA was going to be up and running and what we were supposed to be doing there. I could hardly believe the marathon was just a couple of days away, that I had all this other stuff to keep me awake, but the one recurring dream I had been having was that I lost my race number on the way to the starting line. TB went off to Sandhurst [Royal Military Academy] where he was speaking at the passing-out parade. Geoff Hoon called re Terry Lloyd. It was pretty clear US forces had killed him. Amid all this, we then had the people from *The Simpsons* in to record TB. The writer [Al Jean] was a really serious type who clearly worried himself a lot about his work. He and I had been batting scripts back and forth and it was fine really, though as TB said, there would be plenty of people willing to slag him off for doing it. But hell, he said, there aren't many perks to the job worth having, so how can you say no to a bit part on *The Simpsons*?[1]

Saturday, April 12

I was determined to be in the best possible shape for the marathon tomorrow so rested up a lot of the day, didn't go in for the morning meetings, watched Man Utd vs Newcastle on the TV and took Grace to see *Maid in Manhattan*,[2] which had a seriously silly plot, though the relationship between the politician and his spin doctor was moderately amusing. TB left me pretty much alone, though he did call to ask why I hadn't been to the meetings. I said I really wanted to get my head in gear for tomorrow, and in any event Jonathan had filled me in. Baghdad was still looking grim, though things were getting better in Basra. I was getting loads of Good Luck messages and I was getting really psyched for it. I ate a ton of pasta, then went to bed, after laying out all my gear for the morning. I was really pleased to have got this far, and pretty confident. I think part of me was glad to be doing something to keep John's [Merritt] memory alive, but part of me was glad too to be doing something that was in a way independent of the job, even though I had managed to raise as much as I had because of that, though the biggest donation was £50k from the Bridges [neighbours].

Sunday, April 13

I had my recurring dream about losing my race number, only this time there was a different twist. It rained at Greenwich, the ink on the number ran and it became illegible and I was stopped from

[1] Blair became the only head of government to guest star in the animated comedy series, welcoming the Simpson family to London in the episode 'The Regina Monologues'.

[2] Romantic comedy film starring Jennifer Lopez.

running. Relieved to wake up, I turned on the radio and they were talking about me doing it, which I took as an omen I would do OK. It was a nice day, fresh but looked like it was going to be sunny, and the mood up at the start was terrific. There were two starting points and Charles [Lindsay] and I were starting from the one with the smaller numbers, which was a bonus. We were taken to the VIP tent to wait and I chatted to the Slovak PM [Mikulas Dzurinda] who asked me if I would do a race out there. I was peeing every few minutes, a mix of nerves and all the fluids of the last couple of days.

The start felt great, and I reckoned I was in OK shape for sub four hours, which is what I really wanted. I did the first mile well below eight minutes without even really trying, which was probably the adrenaline getting me to start too fast, the second mile bang on eight, and then into a fairly steady rhythm for a while. After three miles Charles said I ought to run on ahead on my own. The hardest points were nine miles, fifteen and twenty-one, but the bands and the crowds were great. 'Rockin' All Over the World' [hit record by Status Quo] got me through one tricky part. A Jennifer Lopez song playing made me think of Grace at another and got me through. The crowd were fantastic all the way. I didn't get a single adverse comment, which surprised me considering how much war divisiveness there had been, and loads of encouragement. Philip and Georgia [Gould] popped up a couple of times on the route. Andrew Turnbull, Alun Evans [Cabinet Office], others from the office though I missed Alison [Blackshaw] and her crowd at Canary Wharf. I had been warned Canary Wharf would be quiet but it was about as noisy as anywhere on the route and I got a great lift there. There were no quiet and lonely miles at all. Also, on a couple of occasions when I was struggling one of the other runners would come alongside and help push me on, including a woman from Dulwich who suggested I 'lock on to her' and follow step by step which, as she had a near-perfect bum, took me through another tricky mile before I recovered my strength and eventually left her.

The last few miles from the Tower were hard and exhilarating in equal measure. I hit twenty-two miles with fifty minutes left to break four hours so I knew I was going to do it and could relax a bit. The crowds by now were just a wall of sound and encouragement. I was worried I was going to cry on crossing the line, so forced myself to do it as I ran towards Big Ben, lost myself in a crowd of runners, and just let the emotion come out, imagined friends on one shoulder, enemies on the other, friends pushing me on, enemies failing to hold me back; thought about John, thought about how long left my dad had, thought about the kids, really piled it on and cried for a bit as I ran, and then felt fine on the last mile.

I had trained hard in really difficult circumstances work-wise and I felt a real sense of achievement. I wondered around twenty miles if I could beat Bush's time, but as I tried to pick up the pace, the pain in the hamstrings really intensified and I just went back to my steady plod, and settled for sub four. I didn't realise the cameras were on me for the last couple of minutes, by which time I was swearing at myself the whole time, push yourself, faster, fuck it, keep going, push, etc. The last few hundred metres were a mix of agony and joy. The pain was pretty intense but by now virtually every second someone was shouting out encouragement, from 'Do it for New Labour' to 'I forgive you everything Tony Blair has done' to endless 'Go on, you can do it, not far to go.'

I was siphoned off at the turn into the Mall and could now hear the commentary. I spotted Fiona and the kids right at the end in the stand and ran towards them. They were screaming at me to head straight to the finish but I was seven minutes inside my target and just so pleased to see them. My legs buckled a bit as I stopped and my voice was unbelievably weak, but it felt fantastic to have done it. I posed for a few pictures for the snappers, did an interview with Sue Barker [former tennis player turned sports commentator], dictated my column to *The Times*, and also did a briefing at the ICA [Institute of Contemporary Arts], by which time my legs had pretty much seized up. We got home, by which time I had a massive dehydration headache, and was drinking gallons of water. We went out for dinner with the Goulds. Philip had reminded me of the Woody Allen character[1] today, popping up in incongruous places along the route. But I felt really happy at having done it. Grace said she had felt so proud of me, and did I know what a fantastic thing I did for John? I was really touched, especially as she had never known him.

Monday, April 14

Good enough coverage of the marathon, including some nice pictures with Fiona. TB was seeing the Slovak PM, and said he hoped that now I would get back to getting HIM good media coverage, rather than me. He said it with a smile though and the response in the office was really warm. Loads more cheques were coming in today on the back of the recent interviews. The war meeting was fairly low-key.

[1] Zelig, the mysterious title character in Allen's 1983 mockumentary, who sidles into camera shot for most of the major events of the twentieth century.

TB was getting more and more exasperated with Clare. When CDS and Mike Jackson said that the humanitarian scene was not as bad as the [International Committee of the] Red Cross were saying, Clare snorted and said 'I believe the ICRC.' TB said she was a total burden. He also felt that now, if he got rid of her, there would not be too much of a fuss. There was still no sign of WMD, no sign of Saddam, and a considerable humanitarian challenge. A little boy named Ali was getting a huge amount of media attention, and becoming something of a symbol.[1] We were going to have to resolve his case pretty quickly.

I missed the Bush call but TB said GWB had said to congratulate me on the marathon and to say that my 'bleeding nipples' were all over the US media. TB told him that I had also been covering my balls with large amounts of Vaseline. Bush said 'I think I have heard enough about his body now.' The conference call was not great. Syria was a problem[2] because it was clear we and the US were in a different place on substance and on how to handle it. Then a TB/Milburn meeting on foundation hospitals. TB felt the whole thing was looking very ragged, that we had made clear the direction of travel we wanted, but the Health/Treasury conflict was forcing us to a bit of a muddled compromise.

Tuesday, April 15

Nice email from Keith Blackmore [*Times* sports editor] who said he thought my pieces for them had been the best marathon column he had ever read, and if ever I wanted a career in sports journalism, I knew where to go. My legs were still stiff and sore and I had to walk downstairs pretty much sideways. I got a cab in and the driver was really friendly, and full of congratulations. He was also totally onside re Iraq. The War Cabinet was OK, though Clare was still causing us as many problems as she could. It was perfectly obvious she was going to end up going. TB wanted me to go on the trip to Germany, but agreed I could come back after that. He wanted to discuss the media and political plans for the next phase, and we often managed to get some decent work done on these plane

[1] Ali Ismaeel Abbas, a twelve-year-old Baghdad boy, had lost both arms when an American rocket fell near the family home, killing most of his family. His case became a symbol for media and other commentators of the suffering of ordinary Iraqis during the invasion. He would later be flown to Britain for treatment.

[2] Syria's President, Bashar al-Assad, had urged non-Iraqi volunteers to take up arms in support of the Saddam Hussein regime.

journeys. By the end of the day I had put together an OK plan for the next few weeks.

As we drove to Northolt he must have said three, maybe four times, that he was just at a loss to know what to do about GB. He felt that he was now of a mindset that he needed to wage war on pretty much every front. To create the circumstances to depose him, he felt he had to create and win power struggles. I felt if that was the case, it was totally the wrong approach. If I were him, I would love TB to death, support him so closely that TB felt a certain pleasure in handing over power. As things stood, he was making it harder and harder for him to do it. He seemed to want not only to get rid of him, but also destroy any sense that TB had a legacy worth the name.

At the War Cabinet, Clare had said she had been talking to the French and German development ministers and 'they just need lots and lots of talking to', to which TB replied 'Well I'm all in favour of therapy but I'm not sure it constitutes a policy.' I asked if he finally accepted my long-held view that she was bad news. He did. He said what she did re 'reckless' was an act of treachery.[1] He believed GB was now calculating the potential implications of her resignation, that he wanted her to resign over 1441. TB said he was still of the view he didn't really want to serve a third term but he couldn't see how he could hand over to GB.

I was urging the MoD to do something about the young boy who had lost his arms, Ali, who was getting enormous media attention. We flew up to Scotland with Helen Liddell [Scottish Secretary] and Catherine MacLeod [*Herald*] who was interviewing TB. We landed, drove to the Burrell Collection [Glasgow art museum], where the speech [for the Scottish Parliament elections] went fine, then off to RAF Leuchars [Fife] to see the families of pilots out in the region. The people there seemed genuinely appreciative of the support TB gave them. Of all the various services we came in contact with, I would say the military were consistently the best to deal with. Then to see the team on permanent standby for a terrorist incident or a hijacking. A great bunch of blokes, who admitted that a lot of the time they were bored stiff, but they knew they could be called on any second, and had to keep mentally alert the whole time.

Back on the plane and off to Germany. TB was reading the

[1] In a BBC radio interview, Short had been asked if she thought Blair had acted recklessly. She replied 'I'm afraid that I think the whole atmosphere of the current situation is deeply reckless; reckless for the world, reckless for the undermining of the UN in this disorderly world, which is wider than Iraq . . . reckless with our government, reckless with his own future, position and place in history.'

intelligence and briefings pre the meeting [EU summit] in Athens. Chirac was up for causing as much trouble as possible on Iraq and ESDP. Schroeder was seeking to be more constructive, and even to become the bridge to France/Russia. But Chirac basically wanted us to be left out as much as possible. TB felt it was as though Chirac had 'found religion', that he had become fixated on a multipolar vision of the world, and it was a recipe for disaster. 'It is madness. It is like a rerun of the Cold War, and yet there is no real balance. If you say US or France, what is he talking about, what is the choice?'

Chirac was intending to try to stuff the Americans over ESDP by backing a ridiculous Belgian idea of a four-way defence summit with France, Germany, Belgium and Luxembourg. The French were assuming that we would not want to upset them, and so were intending to try to push the whole defence debate in a different direction. It was the wrong assumption, and the wrong time to make the move. Luxembourg for God's sake. TB had a good meeting with Schroeder in Hanover. He said he did not subscribe to the Chirac multipolar view and also that he was looking for better relations with the US. Then a three-hour flight to Athens, during which I worked on a note to get TB back focused on some of the domestic issues that had gone off the boil during the height of the Iraq business.

Wednesday, April 16

Overnight in Athens and I woke up to open the curtains of the hotel room and behold the most beautiful blue sea imaginable. It was hot without being unbearable, and I sat out on the terrace and finished the note I had been working on on the flight down. Then the media monitoring note came through and Short had given us another problem, this time saying time will tell if TB made the right decision and whether we should have given Blix more time. TB was pretty close to the end of his tether with her.

TB had a breakfast meeting with [Romano] Prodi [President of the European Commission] who was mumbling and rambling more than ever. At the end of the meeting, even his own spokesman said to me 'What on earth was he talking about?' TB spent a lot of the meeting just nodding and I don't think he could hear much of what Prodi was saying either. Very odd. Then to a meeting with Kofi, who made a beeline for me on arrival, said 'Ah the marathon man, and such a good time.' I think TB was getting a bit pissed off with the attention it had been getting. To be frank, I was beginning to feel a bit of a void without the training routine and the day to aim for, and would need something else. I had been kind of hoping work would fill it again, but things at home made that difficult. We were due to go off for a week in Majorca and tonight I had promised to take Rory to Arsenal vs Man United and was fretting about getting back in time, particularly when the plane back was delayed. I left the summit early with Kate [Garvey, events and visits team], got to the airport and just made it back. I told Kate I was feeling myself heading towards the exit door.

Thursday, April 17 – Thursday, April 24

We had a nice enough week in Majorca, but Fiona and I had said too much to each other that was hurtful in recent weeks and we weren't really getting on that well. At one point she said in terms that she sometimes felt that I had left her for TB, that that was where all my emotion and energy went, and that any left over went on the kids but not her. It was a pretty harsh thing to say, but I knew what she meant. I could only do the job full on or not at all, and full on meant staying on top of things round the clock. Whenever I didn't, I felt things slipped backwards. Her view was that I had been to some extent brutalised by politics, that I had put up so many barriers around me as a way of making myself immune to the attacks that came my way, but it had carried over into our home life too.

The kids were brilliant though, and seemed to have a great time. I had a couple of heart-to-hearts with Philip, but his main concern really was that I stay involved. TB called a few times. He had had another session with GB at Chequers which had been better, but then it was all briefed into the *FT* as a discussion of the euro tests, saying how TB had agreed it would be very difficult to do this parliament. It was intolerable if they could not have private discussions on issues like the euro without it all being spilled into the media.

Friday, April 25

We got back last night and to Fiona's annoyance I went in today for a whole stack of meetings, first on health policy, one on foundation hospitals then PCTs [NHS primary care trusts], then Charles C in for a session on the choice agenda for schools, where he and TB pretended to be in the same place but weren't in reality, then on the euro. TB was determined to ensure a more positive tone to the assessment. He had read all the texts now and felt it was OK and reasonably positive. Arnab [Banerji, economic adviser] was of the view that it would and could be presented as a case for entry. TB also went through how it could be presented positively. But GB would present it in a negative light. TB said we needed to get the focus on fact – he would be saying four out of five tests were met, measures would be taken to meet the fifth, there will be a changeover plan and a referendum bill. Provided there was warm body language alongside that, it could be a big step forward. But it was not clear to any of us that he and GB were on the same pitch. He did the *FT* interview and though we didn't really want the euro to be the story, he was pretty forward on it.

Iraq was looking a bit messy though Tariq Aziz [Iraqi Deputy Prime Minister] was in the hands of the US. I went to another meeting on Iraq but wasn't really focused, and I suddenly realised how much of my thinking was about leaving. When Phil Stephens [*FT*] pointed out to me earlier that TB had been leader for almost nine years, it came as something of a shock, stated in those terms. I liked a lot of the people in the office, and was pleased with the team I had built, but was that enough to keep me? I don't think so. Was the closeness to TB and all that meant enough? Not any more.

Then to a reshuffle meeting, TB, Pat McF, Sally, Peter H and I. TB was clear Clare would go, so would Scotland and Wales as separate jobs. He was also intending to reshape the Lord Chancellor's Department and say farewell to Derry [Irvine], which would be quite a big thing to do. He was clearly feeling in bold mood. But he still felt the difficulty on public services was the paralysing effect of GB when he didn't want to go with TB's agenda. Home, and another humdinger of a row. Fiona said either she leaves and I stay, which she thought was a recipe for disaster, or we both go and I always blame her for forcing me out, which did not exactly make her feel good about the future either. A story came in later which would reinforce her view of how CB had changed for the worse, namely that she had been invited to a store [Globe] in Melbourne [Australia] and walked out weighed down by stuff. 'I wish she didn't have this thing about a bargain,' TB said when I told him.

Saturday, April 26

Grimsville at home. I was feeling really down. I couldn't let things get so bad we split up. I went out for a run, and came across a scene in Golders Green that underlined how much I didn't want it to happen. A young boy was screaming as his mother tried to hand him over to his dad, because it was 'his weekend'. We had another flare-up on the way to the Landmark Hotel, where we were due to meet Alex [Ferguson]. We managed to have a nice time despite it all. We met Carlos Queiroz [assistant manager, Manchester United] who seemed a decent sort, Tony Coton [goalkeeping coach] and some of the players. Alex was clearly losing it with [David] Beckham. 'He's upstairs preening himself.' He said when he dropped him Real Madrid knew about it within minutes. He felt Beckham was addicted to the press profile, couldn't exist without it. He said even Gary Neville [teammate] was losing it with him a bit.

It was a nice enough hotel but he ended up complaining about the wine. 'Govan boy complains about the wine,' he said. 'That's New Labour.' Fiona said she held him responsible for me still being there, because he had been so adamant at the time of the election that I should stay. He said 'No, what I said was do what you're good at and if you're still good at it, carry on, but always be in control.' He reckoned if I knew what else I would rather do, and I would be happy away from it, I should go. Fiona was a lot calmer talking about these things when it wasn't just the two of us and now she was saying she'd be happy for me to stay till the next election provided she was absolutely clear that that was it. Alex was talking through who might be his successor. Maybe [Roy] Keane [Manchester United captain] – 'the most intelligent player I ever worked with'. On GB, he felt he was clever but lacked Tony's presence.

Sunday, April 27

TB called first thing, after two long conversations with GB, and said they'd been awful. On foundation hospitals TB said to him 'Am I supposed to believe that Frank Dobson and Bill Morris [TGWU general secretary] just stumbled across these arguments against foundation hospitals?' For example Dobson had written to MPs on foundation hospitals and referred to the J-Curve theory [of how nations rise and fall]. On the euro TB thought that GB was buying into the idea of a rewritten assessment of the euro but when Jeremy went through it with Ed Balls, it went nowhere. It had taken TB almost forty-eight hours to get hold of him. When he did at least they were talking but he said GB was just creating non-arguments. It was draining and on the fundamentals they couldn't agree.

TB felt GB clearly believed that TB was going to move or sack him and this was all about protecting himself. He'd said to him 'I know what you're up to. I know your plans.' TB said to him 'I don't have a plan. I would like to work with you.' He said it then went into a 'no you're not, yes I am' routine. He said to me later that he was really unsure about fighting another election but he said there were a lot of people in the party saying to him 'You cannot hand over to this guy. You've made your mark but we have to live with him after you've gone.' TB had read the euro assessments himself and actually felt they were broadly positive, but Balls had put enough in there to present as anti. TB said the second of the conversations was 'monosyllabic'. He said he really didn't know what to do. He said he had never wanted to fight a third election, but it was difficult to hand over to someone who was behaving in such a crazy way.

We also had the problem of Melbourne and CB's shopping spree. A clothing company had asked her to look at some goods and she ended up with sixty-eight items and we had another freebie story to deal with. TB suggested to her that she get someone else to help her with the PR and she called David Hill. He, Hilary C and I were all of the view that it was best to do nothing, say nothing, and just wait till it went away. She had told TB that she hadn't asked for any of this stuff and it just turned up at the hotel. We were heading for a rocky patch all round, and this didn't help.

Monday, April 28

Iraq meeting. We were being warned of the possibility that Saddam had got rid of WMD and certainly most of the documentation, before the conflict. How big a problem was it if it turned out to be the case that we found none? Very difficult. It seemed the best we could do was defectors saying that it had all been destroyed. WMD were not being found and that was a problem. At the War Cabinet, Jack S and Clare had their standard row about the ORHA [post-conflict] operation. Clare said Jack wanted to throw people at the organisation 'regardless of effect' and Jack said she was talking nonsense. Clare was looking and sounding more and more ridiculous. TB did OK at the press conference and though the BBC decided early on that WMD was the story, later they moved to the domestic agenda stuff. Peter M called me, said re EMU he felt GB was doing the wrong thing for the wrong reasons. He felt we were being cowardly.

Tuesday, April 29

Iraq, and where were the WMD, was back as a problem. Yesterday John Scarlett called and asked me how big a problem would it be if we didn't find any and had to rely on ex-scientists telling what had been there and what they knew. Big problem. I got a cab in to meet up with TB then into the car and off [to Russia]. He said he felt good at the moment but the GB situation was like a permanent dark shadow. 'I just don't know what to do about it.' He said the problem was he just didn't believe what he said to him any more. 'I cannot fathom why he has to be so destructive.' We had a tiny but revealing example. John McFall [Labour MP, chair of the Treasury Select Committee] told us – simply as a matter of fact, no agenda and no reason why it shouldn't have happened – that he had discussed the TSC report with GB. GB told TB he hadn't. Why? TB said surely Gordon must realise he is making it harder not easier to hand over to him. What is unfathomable is that it is such a not clever strategy.

The visit had been Putin's request and it was an OK thing to do but there were some very difficult issues, particularly divisions over the UN role. Iraq generally would be difficult. TB saw the press on the plane and I was warning them not to expect major league front-page stuff. But unbeknown to us Putin was gearing up for a direct big whack on WMD and plenty else besides. TB's basic case at the moment was that the world had to come together. That the US was the only superpower and it was better that we tried to work together rather than try to be setting ourselves up as rivals. But France, Russia, maybe China and India wanted to check that power as a matter of policy.

On arrival TB, David M and Tony Bishop [interpreter] were taken up to the Putin dacha while the rest of us were taken to another building. We were hanging around with some of the Russian officials and it was a pretty tough atmosphere. When we did the pre-meeting with TB and Putin I was very clear that our press would be looking for the differences on Iraq and WMD. I asked Putin what he was likely to say. He said he would simply say we should carry on looking. But he definitely had the steely look in his eye and TB was looking a bit on edge. When it came to the event he let rip in the opening statement, made clear he doubted WMD were there and painted a comic picture of Saddam in a bunker somewhere sitting on his arsenal. TB was doing his best to look unfazed. The press were suddenly all terribly excited. Trevor Kavanagh [*Sun*] and Charles Reiss [*Evening Standard*] had big smiles over their faces as they took notes of what Vlad was saying. They sensed a diplo-disaster which of course it was, especially as Putin had invited TB and we thought we'd agreed lines.

David Manning was taken aback and angry, said he felt it had been deceitful of Putin to agree what he intended to say then go off on one like that, clearly pre-planned. He said the one-on-one session had been very tough and that Putin was in no mood to listen to pro-US messages. I noticed too when they came down that he just looked angrier than before, was less chatty and relaxed. He was also putting on a bit of weight and acting in a much grander fashion. He had his own stables now and had showed off the horses to TB who felt he was showing signs of becoming the traditional Russian leader in terms of interest in lifestyle, luxury and so on. The press conference was pretty stunning. The mood when we regrouped was very chilly. TB took me to one side, said how do we deal with that? I said not much we can do to stop them going into overdrive.

TB said 'I almost felt like interrupting him and saying "Hey – you invited me out here. I didn't expect to get stuffed by you like that."' Then TB, Vlad, the interpreters and I were taken into a little side room. TB said to me, very deliberately and inviting absolute honesty, 'What did you make of that?' I said it was very explosive, our media would be very excited. Putin looked a mix of surly and worried. He could sense TB was angry but he was also totally unapologetic. He said the US had created this situation. In ignoring the UN they had created danger. They were saying there may be rules, but not for us. Time and again he made comparisons with the situation he faced in Georgia, used as a base for terrorists against Russia. 'What would you say if we took out Georgia or sent in the B-52 bombers to wipe out the terror camps?' And what are they planning next – is it Syria, Iran, Korea? 'I bet they haven't told you,' he added with a rather unpleasant curl of the lip. 'Also there is no consistency. Saudi and Pakistan are problems but for different reasons the Americans prop them up'. He said other parts of the world felt pressure to go for Israel. He said he didn't support that 'but these are dangerous games'. He said the Americans' enemy was anyone who didn't support them at the time. Anywhere from Algeria to Pakistan. Then what about the new powers like India and China, do their views matter, or is it only America?

TB had given as good as he got at the press conference and did so again at the dinner once he realised that the diplomatic approach was not exactly working. He said there was no grand US plan for global domination. There was a series of choices. On MEPP they were deciding whether to engage or not. On Korea they were deciding whether to engage diplomatically. On a lot of other issues they were deciding whether to approach them on a unilateral or multilateral basis. 'We have to help them choose the multilateral route. But you have to understand that September 11 changed their psychology and it changed Bush's psychology personally. Before, anti-Americanism was just an irritant that they put up with. Now it became a threat.' Putin said that meant anyone who disagreed with them on these choices was a threat. 'That is ridiculous. I am a Russian. I cannot agree with the Americans on everything. My public won't let me for a start. I would not survive two years if I did that. We often have different interests.' TB said but you have to build a strategic partnership with them. He said he was tired of trying. 'They don't listen. They only hear what they want to hear. Some of them are crazy.'

Putin said the South Koreans had told them the Americans had said they were prepared to use nuclear weapons on the North. Crazy. He said they would end up killing people in the South too, 'and that is on our border'. Vlad was in full flow. He said they had asked to run reconnaissance flights along the Russian border during the Iraq crisis 'as a counter-terrorism measure – what nonsense. It was to intimidate us. We told them it was an unfriendly act. They did it.' TB asked him if Bush knew and Vlad said his people knew, but the question was why did they do it? Because they think they can do what they want. Others have to operate by the rules but not them. China might feel it should be able to sort out Taiwan. But it feels constrained by the UN, by international opinion. India and Pakistan might like to set off nuclear weapons at each other but they feel constrained. Time and again he referred to Georgia and Chechnya and said 'Why can't I go in alone – because of international pressure. Yet there are people threatening our people, killing people on our streets.' TB said Iraq was different because there were nineteen outstanding UNSCRs on Iraq. The UN had made its demands and for once they should be upheld. Putin said the US was thousands of miles from Iraq. So was the UK. Saddam was a monster but he was not a direct threat.

TB went back to his argument about September 11. Putin went back to his line that if we were saying anyone who disagreed was a threat that was ridiculous and dangerous. TB was pretty taken aback by the vehemence. Normally there would be a bit of levity, a bit of banter, or if things were heavy I might throw in something lighter. But this was not that kind of meeting. I could see David [Manning] feeling more and more intense about the whole thing. We agreed afterwards that it had been a real privilege to have been in on a discussion like that, where the raw politics and feeling of a country like Russia came pouring out. There were even short periods of silence as we ate – caviar, a nice enough fish plate then some horrible cold meats including one that looked like dogshit and tasted pretty dreadful too. Then a nice mix of ice creams. Lots of vodka being poured into different glasses but little of it was drunk.

There was no give at all. Putin's face was tight and his eyes really piercing. His cheek muscles clenched whenever TB defended the US or the policy on Iraq. He said partnership was a two-way thing and the Americans care only about themselves. There had to be a role for both partners, not just one partner doing whatever they wanted. That was the central message, again and again and again. TB kept asking him – so what do you do, how do you resolve it? – and then would come another wave.

I kept thinking of Fiona when she was really angry with me, telling me it was all one way, all on my terms. I took her for granted and she'd had enough of it. This was someone who felt he deserved to be treated as an equal, and he wasn't being treated as an equal and he was angry, and TB was the person who was going to cop the anger. At one point Putin said the whole post-September 11 response was designed to show off American greatness. They don't care what anyone else thinks. TB was about to respond but he didn't let him 'Don't answer – there is no answer. That is the truth Tony, and you have to know it. There are bad people in the administration and you know it.'

David said as we left 'Fascinating, absolutely fascinating.' I said that was the death of diplomacy. It certainly was, he said. There was no effort at all. TB was a bit subdued as we went to the plane. He said he thought ultimately Putin would do a deal on the UN but he felt Iraq was clearly going to have to be sorted as a coalition of the willing. He felt we should put together a plan that tried to meet the points the Russians were making, but if they were basically just going to bugger about we should say OK, we will have to do it on our own. TB had been taken at one point to see Putin's private quarters and what he saw worried him. He said it was like something out of the Roman Empire, that it had been transformed. An Olympic-sized pool for his own use only. Stallions. Horses with butlers! I had felt too that Putin was far grander than before, much more up himself, a bit peevish.

I drove to the airport with TB and though we assumed the car was bugged, we had a pretty frank discussion. He was less shocked than David and I had been and said they had an argument different to ours and it was far better we have it out like that. But in the end they are wrong. You cannot just walk away from the US. It is a mistake. The reason they will go it alone on some things is because they can. He was blaming Chirac a bit for getting Putin more wound up. Chirac was even saying the US was a bigger threat than al-Qaeda. He was really keen to see TB fall flat on his face over this one. What was very clear was that it was going to be difficult to put things back together again. These were pretty deep fissures we had been witnessing. By the time we were flying home, TB was saying 'what a day. He invites me out there. I go. He insults me publicly and privately. Then I come home. Bloody brilliant.'

He thought a lot of it was driven by Russia no longer being seen as a superpower and the anger that aroused. They were angry and humiliated and they needed to let out the anger. I said though that

Putin had a point – the truth is the Americans do tend to treat people like shit unless they agree with them and that their vision of democracy was stars-and-stripes-coloured. Everything was seen through their own prism. TB said that the answer was not to rival them, because they were now the only superpower, but to build a partnership, support them but in exchange for support be listened to and gain influence. Tony Bishop felt Putin had missed an opportunity to build bridges and he seemed genuinely disappointed that Putin behaved as he did. The press were as shocked as we were and had loved it.

TB said what it showed was real deep anger but the question was how was it to be channelled? How do we use it to get the world on a better footing? He could see some merit in Putin's argument but he seemed to be saying the Americans were not entitled to use their power for their own ends. I said he wasn't saying that, he was saying others had the right to be treated with respect. That their status as the only superpower – something Vlad never actually acknowledged, I noticed – gave them an added responsibility to think of others. I had sat in on so many TB meetings but this had been one of the most memorable. David M and [Sergei] Prikhodko [Putin's foreign affairs adviser] both agreed afterwards they might as well not have been there because the normal diplomatic niceties were out of the window.

Wednesday, April 30

Grace's birthday, stayed home to do her presents etc., then took her to school. It reminded me how rarely I had done so, whereas with the boys it had been pretty much an everyday occurrence, particularly Rory. The [Middle East peace process] road map was finally being published today but all a bit overshadowed by a suicide bombing [in Israel].[1] Then it transpired it was carried out by two men with UK passports, which gave it an added difficult dimension here. TB apparently told the PMQs pre-meeting that he felt yesterday was not as bad as it came across on the media, but though the Russian media was not quite so bad, it was certainly not a diplomatic success story.

I went straight to the Commons where TB was doing the PLP. He said it was better than expected, also that it was more obvious than ever that the anti-foundation hospitals argument was being run out of the Treasury. Hilary A told me that John Healey [economic secretary

[1] Three people were killed and sixty injured in the blast at a bar in Tel Aviv. Asif Muhammad Hanif, the suicide bomber, and Omar Khan Sharif, his accomplice, were both British citizens. Hamas and the al-Aqsa Martyrs' Brigades of the Tanzim Fatah declared joint responsibility.

to the Treasury] had apparently told Jon Trickett [Labour MP] to vote against it. GB was using Healey, Ann Keen, Kevan Jones, Doug Henderson [Labour MPs close to Brown] and others to get up the argument that this was two-tier, divisive. I saw Peter M later and we agreed the time was coming when this had to be exposed for the operation it was, that it all depended on those who knew what was going on remaining silent, including the hacks who got fed this stuff the whole time.

PMQs was a score draw on public services. TB was strong on foundation hospitals but GB was lukewarm at the Treasury Select Committee which was going to spark another TB/GB rift round. Back for an Iraq communications meeting. We agreed to keep them going. I was worried though that ORHA lacked strategic message and capability. Emily [Hands, press officer] was back, and now Ben Wilson was out there and both were saying how hard it was to grip it. But I still felt there were very basic things we could be doing to communicate very basic messages, whatever the security nightmares. Rumsfeld made a visit to Baghdad and [US General Jay] Garner [director of ORHA] did a big chest-thumping number all about being proud to be American. All yuksville stuff for audiences outside the States. Margaret Tutwiler [US State Department] was in charge of the media side of things there and I fixed a call with her for tomorrow.

TB was heavily focused on Northern Ireland, where we were in a bad place again, heading towards cancellation of the elections, which we would do tomorrow. TB said he was determined to treat Sinn Fein politicians like any other. His big worry was that SF would not deliver on the final steps. The other big story was the *Times* exclusive on Special Branch transcripts of calls between McGuinness, Jonathan and Mo [Mowlam, former Northern Ireland Secretary], clearly genuine.

Peter M had been attacked in the *Sun* and wanted to do an article. He sent over a draft which said that both TB and GB had said we MUST join the euro and that it was a matter of when, not if. It took me twenty minutes to persuade him this was not the time, that the second line was an important strategic plank of the assessment, and he should wait. He finally, if reluctantly agreed. He was clearly fed up though. Another discussion about the Olympic bid. TB moved from very pro to neutral and back again. He feared a big hit on the whole Pride in Britain theme if we didn't go for it. On the way out I bumped into Sarah Brown with a group of wives of Norwich City footballers. She introduced them to me as wives of Norwich United players.

Thursday, May 1

Back running regularly, twice today, feeling a lot better after first reasonable chat with Fiona for ages. She had seen Jonathan yesterday to say she was leaving definitely in September, whatever I did. At my morning meeting, Ian Austin [Brown's spokesman] reacted very defensively when I asked why GB didn't simply say that he supports the policy on foundation hospitals. Ian protested that he did, and said people were briefing against GB. Both the *Sun* and *The Times* had leaders today attacking him for not being reformist enough, leaning to Old Labour, which was clearly Murdoch's line.

We had a brief political meeting, with TB and the core political people, back to the argument why public service delivery isn't happening at the rate we want, why no overall narrative, where is the sense that education is still the number one priority, where are the values driving what we are doing? We were also still miles apart on the euro. The Treasury sent over a draft structure for the statement, which was hopeless.

Cabinet was pretty dire, a fairly desultory run around the block on European elections, Northern Ireland, fairly lacklustre discussion about Iraq where Clare made even by her standards a ridiculous intervention, that seemed interminable, about a museum in Baghdad.[1] JP was barely containable. TB then had a meeting with Milburn who was in a total rage re GB. 'It's fucking not on. He's actually encouraging people to vote down a government bill [Health and Social Care Bill, containing plans to introduce foundation hospitals] that's been agreed. He's just sent over a long document with new queries and problems which in fact have already been answered. You wouldn't tolerate it from anyone else but you have to realise this is an attack on you, Tony, and you can't just stand there and take it, you have to do something.' All TB could do was say he had spoken to GB who had assured him he would get in there and support the policy. Alan's face betrayed the reality, that it was wishful thinking. Hilary A said it was becoming a settled view that GB was using this to damage Alan but it was also damaging TB.

Alan came round to see me afterwards and said if this kind of thing happened again, he would walk. I had the phone call with Margaret Tutwiler in Baghdad. She had a very broad, slightly weird accent and was prickly and defensive. I got the impression she didn't

[1] Short suggested that, by failing to prevent looting at the National Museum, US troops had violated the 1907 Hague and 1949 Geneva conventions, which required occupiers of countries to maintain civil order.

really understand why she had to speak to me. I tried a bit of charm and flattery, but all I really got back was a litany of difficulties, how the lack of communications and security made it all very difficult. The impression I got was of a pretty chaotic approach. I said I just wanted to help as much as I could because I feared there was a lack of positive strategic communication and the media would fill the vacuum. She said she thought the best thing would be if we could persuade the press to leave because everything was so chaotic! It was a pretty hopeless discussion.

We had Rumsfeld due in tomorrow. I agreed with his office that there should be no media. TB with Rumsfeld was the last thing we needed right now. We went out for dinner with the Kinnocks. On Iraq, it was very much Neil and I on one side, Glenys and Fiona on the other. Neil had a great line, said he thought we had the best possible outcome, that Saddam was both dead and alive. The only point he slightly lost it was when Glenys said we were following the Bush doctrine. He was pretty down on GB at the moment, said he had told him that the only thing that could stop him becoming leader was himself.

Friday, May 2

The local elections were better for the Tories than expected. BNP strong in Burnley [from three council seats to eight]. We did badly without it being a disaster.[1] TB felt that for midterm, second term, it was OK. I ran in and at the morning meeting had to contend with Ian Austin's anger at the coverage on foundation hospitals. Both the *Sun* and *The Times* ran stories that GB allies, with John Healey named, were orchestrating the opposition. The Treasury put out a denial and Healey called me later to say it wasn't true. 'You know me well enough to know I wouldn't do that.' He said he had been accused of stirring both Dobbo [Frank Dobson] and Doug Henderson but was adamant he had not spoken to them about it. TB, though he had asked us not to stir it, didn't exactly complain about the coverage. It was interesting to note again that it was only when their antics risked being exposed that they occasionally started to pull back.

TB was seeing Rumsfeld at Chequers. But I emphasised to TB he needed to make clear to Rumsfeld how urgent it was that they got their act together at every level. I had been alarmed by the Tutwiler

[1] Labour lost 833 council seats, the Conservatives gained 566, taking control of Birmingham and Coventry, and the Liberal Democrats gained 193. The far-right British National Party gained eleven nationally, giving them a total of thirteen.

call. She was very defensive. Dan [Bartlett] called me later, fresh from the spectacular impact of Bush landing on an aircraft carrier in a flight suit to deliver a victory speech, and said she [Tutwiler] had never really wanted to go there.

On foundation hospitals, I met with my team to plan the next few days, with Darren Murphy [Milburn's special adviser] sure we would win the vote, Simon Stevens [health policy adviser] less confident. We hadn't really got up the argument well about how this was helping to deliver Labour goals. TB had a pretty daunting workload at the moment, Iraq, UN, euro, NI, asylum, public services, European Convention, all of them really eating into his diary, with the GB business constantly in the background. Looking back at the week, I didn't feel we had achieved much.

Saturday, May 3

The *Times* magazine ran Peter Stothard's piece [on TB at fifty] which was pretty fair. The other thing running was follow-up to the line in *Vanity Fair* of me saying 'We don't do God' when I tried to shunt David Margolick to the back of the plane [see March 16]. Allied to Peter Stothard's line that TB had wanted to say 'God bless you' at the end of his Iraq broadcast, there was a bit of a running theme in the media about me trying to stop him talking about God. TB seemed reasonably relaxed.

His current refrain was that the only radical policies were coming from the centre. Even the departments we felt were pretty good, like Health under Alan and Education under Charles, didn't really drive forward change. The machine at the centre was trying to push forward all the time, and the bureaucracies in departments trying to push back. It was really frustrating him. He was disappointed that Charles and David Miliband had allowed the schools funding situation to deteriorate. Whilst he had been so focused on Iraq, others had taken their foot off the accelerator.

I spent part of the day drafting a note on all the strategic challenges we face, viewed through what goals we would like to meet by the summer, just twelve weeks from now. Iraq, MEPP, Afghanistan, Africa, on the geopolitical front, the polar world division with the French, euro, IGC [EU Intergovernmental Conference], all the big domestic issues, also trust, TB. I did it partly to force myself to think it all through but also to draw attention to what I thought was a gap between the scale of the challenges and the lack of capacity in departments and at the centre to meet them. I was trying to get TB to shake up the system, not just rest on his being so sure that it was all about policy. I sent the note through and he called a couple of hours later. He said he had been thinking the same thing. Six years in, almost to the day, we were facing more or less the same problems. It was all about delivery of the machine.

He felt re the politicians, that we had some OK ministers but too many of them were basically European social democrats, who tended to look for partnership and compromise rather than face up to really difficult decisions. He didn't like fighting on too many fronts. He felt re the argument on foundation hospitals that it actually wasn't that radical. He felt that the controversy of the schools agenda was also not matched by the radicalism, that we were being held back by forces of conservatism. I said again I felt we should have stuck with that argument. I put a worst-case analysis – at best what could be called the variable quality of ministers, GB paralysing reform, senior civil servants often resistant to change.

We also faced a big loss when Jeremy [Heywood] went [to join Morgan Stanley investment banking division]. TB had deliberately sought out David Manning and Stephen Wall and that had made a difference. He had to do the same with Jeremy's replacement. If the Civil Service wasn't so status-conscious, it would be possible to get one of the best permanent secretaries, Gus O'Donnell or Michael Jay even, but neither would be keen because it would be seen as a demotion. But at least he was focusing on these personnel issues.

Sunday, May 4

Calum and I went to Wimbledon vs Burnley, last game in the season, Wimbledon's last game at Selhurst Park and a bit of a sad affair all round [Wimbeldon 2, Burnley 1]. Leeds beat Arsenal, leaving Man United the champions. Alex F and Rory both mildly delirious. I watched a bit of [political journalist] John Sergeant's BBC programme to coincide with TB's birthday. It was very funny in parts, though Mo [Mowlam] and [Peter] Kilfoyle were exceptionally bitter. Overall TB came over fine.

Monday, May 5

TB called first thing, wanted to talk again about the strategic challenge note I had done. He said it was the right analysis. He wasn't sure how widely we could discuss it because it was about policy and personnel. He was aware that things weren't working as well as they should be. He reckoned we had a year really to get it moving, really to be in a position at the next election where it was accepted that public services are much better. We agreed we were nowhere near that. Education had gone backwards. Health is better but it's patchy. Ditto crime. Transport is a disaster. He then said he was thinking about making this a five-year term, really get these issues sorted, 'particularly if I decide I don't want to fight a third election'. He still hadn't decided but said he couldn't understand why there was now this assumption that a term was four years when the option of five was there. He was also thinking about a reshuffle just before Whitsun followed by a major drive on reform. He knew we would lose some of our coalition over the euro but was confident we could win over others on reform.

He was also still making up his mind about GB. He acknowledged he had ceded too much to him. He said it sometimes felt like we were driving with the handbrake on, because he thwarts reform, not necessarily because he is against it, but because he wants to make life difficult. It was obvious that TB wanted to go a lot further on public services, open them up to real innovation and competition. He was working on a note of what he wanted to see in the statement on the euro assessment. As far as he was concerned, this was a big test of whether GB was serious about working with him. 'If he's not, then I'm prepared to do the deed. I'm not prepared to be held back from making a change I believe it may be in Britain's interests to make.'

The note had at least provoked, or at least brought to the open, some pretty big thoughts. What we actually did about driving change in these big departments was less clear. He felt the Foreign Office was pretty good, Treasury good but limited and sometimes malign, but that overall we didn't have good domestic departments. What he was signalling was that 1. he intended big policy changes, 2. a big reshuffle, 3. longer term, he seemed to be keeping open the option of someone else leading us into the next election. He said he had not ruled out standing again but 'I kind of think eight years is enough for this kind of job.'

Tuesday, May 6

We were building up to the foundation hospital vote tomorrow and used TB's speech to the Newspaper Society to get up some of the arguments on that.[1] [David] Bradshaw wrote in quite a funny section

[1] Blair warned the audience of newspaper executives that Labour rebels voting against NHS reform and foundation hospitals would be 'a collective mistake of historic proportions', and that reforms would give more freedom to bring 'new providers into elective surgery to reduce waiting times for NHS patients, whether those providers are from the NHS, the private sector or abroad. For the first time giving patients real choice to go elsewhere for treatment, paid for by the NHS, if they are waiting too long.'

on TB being fifty. TB started his day with a ninety-minute session, one-on-one, with GB on the euro. He said afterwards that it was a 'real crackerjack job'. He had asked him for a completed copy of the draft statement on the EMU assessment. GB said not until they had sorted out their differences. So here we were, a few weeks before what might be the momentous decision of the parliament, possibly of TB's premiership, and his Chancellor wouldn't tell him what he intended to say. 'It's like dealing with a child,' he said. 'I said to him that I wanted him to work with me. He says I am working with you. Then, no you're not, yes I am. Then he's back into "I know what you're up to" and he does all this stuff about me wanting to get rid of him.'

TB said he had told him that it felt at times like driving a car with the handbrake on. 'That's a very significant statement,' said GB. No it's not, it's obvious, said TB. He said he just couldn't see a way out of it at the moment, also that he believed GB was actually intent on destroying the health bill. Alan was making clear he would resign if we lost the vote tomorrow. We signed off the speech, then into the car where Putin called him to say happy birthday, which suggested he was trying to calm things down a bit after recent events.

Wednesday, May 7

Ran in and the morning meeting was pretty much all taken up with foundation hospitals. The whips were still worried that if the Tories really went for it, we could lose. The rebellion could be bigger than we thought. TB had breakfast with John Howard [Australian Prime Minister], mainly Iraq and Zimbabwe, then to a meeting with Charles C on schools funding. Charles was clear it could be sorted but he may need more money. We went over for PMQs and though TB did well, and IDS was crap, the signs were still of a very big revolt. I got back for an Iraq communications meeting and we were really focused now on how to try to get a UK operation properly inserted into Baghdad. I called [Major General] Tim Cross [senior British officer, Coalition Provisional Authority] who said that he couldn't properly express to me just how useless the Americans were. They had no idea. He said there were people working hard but who couldn't deliver. He felt we should try to get a CIC-type operation inserted in there. I had been led to believe he was very protective of the US there, but in reality he could barely conceal his contempt. 'I'm afraid they are very capable of snatching defeat from the jaws of victory because they are just useless at the things they now need to be doing.' On the communications side, he said somehow we had to make it work. We agreed to try to get more of our people there. It would help when we got John Sawers [UK ambassador to Egypt, Blair's former foreign policy adviser] there as the UK envoy.

Then it was a case of hanging around for the vote. TB said 'This is classic. The Labour Party and a group of bone-headed MPs making historic errors that will help put us out of power and leave others to do the reforms that we should have done.' He said it was a different issue but a rerun of *In Place of Strife*.[1] If we lost, he wanted us to come back with a bill that was more reformist, not less. He felt it was crazy for Alan [Milburn] to talk about resigning and that he was far too prone to the cavalier and dramatic. But I spoke to Alan who said he had thought long and hard about it and he would definitely resign. 'There have to be rules. This is my bill and if it's rejected I will have to go.' When it came to the vote, it was 304 for the bill to 230 against. The wrecking amendment was defeated 297 to 117, with sixty-five Labour rebels.

Thursday, May 8

The foundation hospitals vote was fading away but it emerged during the day that Clare hadn't voted. She claimed it was because she thought the vote was at 10pm. Nor did she come to Cabinet, claiming that she had to read intelligence briefs before a meeting with the leader of Rwanda [President Paul Kagame]. TB had another euro meeting with GB, who seemed a bit troubled. Last night's vote was not great for him. TB told him that the reshuffle would be after the euro statement, which he hoped would bind him in a bit. TB seemed a bit more confident on the substance.

Cabinet was awful, even without Clare. Iraq, Northern Ireland, then a truly awful discussion of the local elections. Ian McCartney was not too bad, very factual about the results, where we had done well, where we had done less well, some quite good analysis, but then a whole load of interventions displaying considerable knicker-wetting. Alistair D was clearly in a bit of a flap about the Libs letting the Tories in, Blunkett on the BNP and the need to reinforce what we were trying to do on the crime agenda, and above all the need to tackle asylum. Patricia [Hewitt] saw it all through the prism of the electoral behaviour of women. JP left before the discussion had finished, muttering that he couldn't stand any more of this.

[1] In 1969 Harold Wilson's Labour government issued a White Paper, *In Place of Strife*, that proposed the reform of industrial relations. Divisions in Cabinet and the Parliamentary Labour Party over the proposals led to them being dropped.

TB agreed afterwards that it was a pretty awful discussion but equally he should have given more of a lead. I went off to speak at lunch for all the EU ambassadors. I was on good form at the Q&A, where the questions were mainly on the euro, fallout from the local elections, TB's future intentions, EU–US, and defence. It was definitely worth doing. The German [Thomas Matussek] and the Greek [Alexandros Sandis] asked afterwards why I didn't do TV briefings because they felt that apart from TB, nobody really explained foreign policy so clearly. Only the French sent a deputy rather than the actual ambassador.

Back to Number 10 for TB doing another series of public services meetings, first health, then education, really trying to press his own people and the departments to think more radically. I was also worried that what Jonathan, Jeremy and Andrew [Adonis] were badging as ever more radical, felt to me like radical right wing. We had a brief political strategy meeting, at the end of which Philip said to me he thought TB had been a bit too unyielding – he was right, everyone else was wrong, he was now going for broke. I think it was just an expression of his frustration at lack of delivery. Fiona was having a dreadful time with Cherie, first of all, Cherie seemed to hold her responsible for TB not having a birthday party, whereas in fact all of us had been clear it was the wrong thing to be doing, no matter how privately intended, while Iraq was still as intense as it was. Now, another problem. We had *Marie Claire* [women's lifestyle magazine] in for an interview and picture session and Fiona had told Cherie not to let them in the flat without her being there. Not only did Cherie have them up in the flat but allowed them to photograph her in the bedroom with Carole [Caplin] putting on her lipstick. Fiona was convinced she would be better out of it sooner rather than later. The way I was feeling, I was keen to get out pretty soon too.

Friday, May 9

TB was up in Sedgefield and called a couple of times. I was more conscious, after Philip's observation, of how regularly he said 'I know I'm right about this.' In truth, often he was, and I was as down on departments as he was, but equally I was beginning to get less and less motivated. We were already beginning to talk about elections and it just didn't hold out the excitement it once did. Also Rory had an interesting take. He said he reckoned I wasn't as good as I used to be, that if I left soon, I would be a legend, the first person really to take communications to a level that made an actual difference to politics, whereas if I stayed, it was downhill all the way. 'You're not enjoying it as much as you did, you're not doing it as well as you did, and never forget that the reason [former Manchester United footballer] Eric Cantona's a legend is because he left at the right time.' I had a long call with Dan Bartlett, who was as seized as I was with the need for change in ORHA's modus operandi. I offered to put a team of UK people at his disposal. Paul Bremer was replacing [General Jay] Garner [as director of ORHA], [John] Sawers was going soon so it was possible we would improve things but we really needed to up our game. Calum finished his SATs [Standard Assessment Tests] and was particularly happy with a question about Henry V being a lower-league football manager, and how would he prepare to play Arsenal in the Cup Final.

Saturday, May 10

I spent most of the day taking the boys to various sport events, then later the Goulds came round for dinner. Philip, who could normally be relied on for a bit of optimism, said that for the first time he could see TB losing the election, that he seemed a bit out of steam, not getting things like he used to.

Sunday, May 11

The *Mail on Sunday* had stuff on Cherie and Bermuda.[1] It seemed to us that whether knowingly or not, Carole was shipping stuff to the Mail group.

Monday, May 12

TB was seeing GB the whole time, trying to get him to be more positive about the euro assessment or at least be positive about the idea of a referendum this parliament remaining a possibility. TB called me to the flat first thing to say he was really worried about Cherie. There was someone very close in putting stuff into the press, this weekend again with the freebie story in the *Mail on Sunday*. He noticed for the first time that the kids were getting worried about it. He wanted to know if I thought Fiona was still able to help her. I said Fiona felt she had been let down, that Cherie had changed and that Carole was a bigger problem than either of them were prepared to concede. I said Fiona was definitely leaving. He asked what she would do. I said that depended in part on me. He asked what I wanted to do. I said I would like to go fairly soon. I wasn't enjoying the job anything like

[1] Cherie had agreed to give a speech to the Bermuda Bar Association and intended taking her mother and children.

as much as I did and I wasn't doing it as well as I could. He said he thought I had done it well during Iraq, and he was sure I was doing it better than anyone else could. I said the public service reform agenda was not really my thing, and in any event I wondered whether some of our media problems might be helped if I went. He said he realised why I felt the way I did, because there weren't that many really high-pressure jobs, but he had one of them, and I had another. He really wanted me to think it through very carefully. He was not sure yet whether he would fight another election. A lot depended on GB.

Later, when he saw Fiona again, he said he was unlikely to stay but he couldn't be sure. She spent an hour with him and though he started off very defensive about Cherie, he admitted that in part because of the pressure of the job, he had neglected her, but he also knew that things had to change. TB and I had been talking about it just before 10 and Jonathan and Andrew Turnbull came in.

Suma Chakrabarti [permanent secretary] had called from DFID to say that Clare was about to resign. From then on we were set for a day in which she would do as much damage as possible. She got a line out to PA as soon as she resigned, then interviews, later a statement. Every part of it was very bitter and designed for maximum damage. TB though felt it was the best outcome. He was intending to sack her, she probably knew it, so she walked, but with little credibility. Her letter of resignation was pretty bitter. I worked on TB's reply, conscious of the fact I had waited eight years for this, but now it came to it I felt very little satisfaction from it. She wasn't worth it. I watched her Commons statement and she got more and more bitter as she went on, spreading the attack on Iraq to the whole style of government. She was heard in near silence with the occasional gasp as the boot went in.

TB said afterwards that he had bent over backwards to be nice to her and about her, and if there was a criticism to be made of him, it was why he let her stay so long. 'I doubt that any Cabinet minister has ever been indulged so much by a prime minister.' There was no point pretending it wasn't a bad day but she was such damaged goods that it wasn't that bad. Adam Boulton [Sky] said few people could swallow it all without gagging. She was pretty powerful as a speaker but nauseated a lot of people. Valerie Amos[1] took her job. The main thing the politicos were on to was any input GB had. She said on TV that she had discussed her position with GB which begged

[1] Baroness Amos, FCO minister, became the first black woman in the Cabinet.

the perfectly fair question, why he hadn't mentioned that to TB. We were going through a pretty vulnerable phase. GB, euro, reform, rebellion, Iraq.

Tuesday, May 13

Al-Qaeda bombings in Riyadh [Saudi Arabia, thirty-five killed] which were pretty massive. I spoke to John Sawers through the day about ORHA. He was due to have dinner with Paul Bremer and I suggested that he proposed to Bremer that we send a UK team to support their media operation. The papers were needless to say full of Short but the commentariat wasn't greatly in favour of her. I felt CS herself was not so damaging but the GB resonance was and there was a bit of focus on why he hadn't alerted TB to what was going on. We were trying to persuade TB that he did have to do more to get back in with those parts of the party drifting off, but he was more and more determined that reform was really all that mattered. The BBC called me out of the blue to ask if I would do a documentary on Paula Radcliffe [world record-holding marathon runner]. I obviously couldn't do it now, but it underlined again that I wouldn't be short of offers of work if I left.

Sawers called me after his meeting with Bremer who had asked if I could go out there and help set up the new system I was proposing. Lunch with Piers Morgan. We met at the Savoy Grill. He was in appeasing mood, said he had ballsed up the war, had lost 60,000 readers through that, 120,000 to the price war and he accepted he had fucked up. He knew he wasn't in a strong position with us but said he wanted to come back in a bit, needed to get rid of [John] Pilger [journalist and polemicist], cut down on [Paul] Routledge [columnist], stop whacking CB, get back to being more positive on the domestic agenda. He denied there was a pro-GB agenda at the *Mirror*. He viewed TB as a formidable politician who won things through argument. He was sure that if ever it did go to a TB/GB war, TB would win and the *Mirror* would be on our side. Back for a meeting on the Olympics. I sensed we were moving in the yes direction. I had a chat with Sally who said TB didn't believe that I would go, so if it was serious, I maybe ought to have the conversation again.

Wednesday, May 14

Alison [Blackshaw] spent much of the day trying to sort flights to Iraq while I was talking to John Sawers, then a series of meetings and conference calls on what we needed to do if I got out there. I was starting to ask some of our people, like Simon Wren [MoD] and

Darren [Murphy], if they would go to Baghdad. I got the sense that with Bremer there to replace Garner there was the chance to move in properly, though everyone agreed it would not be a good story if I actually went out and ran it.

TB was still thrashing out the euro with GB. He wasn't at all happy with the process and nor were we, but it was about all we had. Charles C had a bit of a rough time at the PLP because MPs felt the Tories were on to something re tuition fees. Fiona had a face like thunder when I told her I might have to go to Iraq. Then a problem with the Olympics. Yesterday we were clear that we had sorted out the answers to all the financial questions we needed to be clear about for now, but today GB told Tessa that it was definitively not sorted. Both Andy Marr and Martha Kearney [BBC] were chasing me on the euro. Then Simon Buckby [pro-euro campaigner] called me at 9.30 to say the BBC were getting him on to respond to a report by Marr that the assessment had happened, it was negative and it was definitely not happening this parliament. This was clearly the next stage of the bounce. I called TB who said I should call Marr and say he could end up with egg on his face if he was definitive about this parliament.

Andy said he had been briefed by someone with 'iron authority', which I assume was his way of saying it was GB. GB denied briefing Marr. I put in a call for Ed Balls who came back just as the bulletin began. He was on a train. He said unless GB was a kamikaze pilot there was no way they would do this the day before a Cabinet meeting that was already going to be difficult. He was adamant that neither he nor GB had spoken to Marr. I said Andy could not have done a story so definitively unless it was one of us four, or Jeremy or Jonathan. I knew it wasn't me or TB and I didn't for one second think it would be Jeremy or Jonathan, both of whom were in a state of outrage.

The upshot was that I was taking calls till well past midnight. The best line we could deploy was that a very small number of people knew what would be presented to Cabinet tomorrow, Marr was not one of them and whatever he said the final position was not decided. TB felt GB was worried at the moment. He knew that Clare had damaged TB, but felt she damaged GB too. 'If this thing ever was pushed to a contest, the fact is I would win. People would not want him if he was trying to force me out. He also knows now that if I wanted to, I could get rid of him and I've decided unless he starts being more co-operative and more supportive, I will do that.' He sounded pretty steely. When I finally got to bed, the phone went again and it was TB again, saying he was sorry I had been kept up late.

The euro stuff was not taking off in the press, but it was still leading the BBC and we had to get ourselves in a better position. TB came down from the flat and after the usual bound down the corridor, we got into his office, sat down, in the armchairs, and he looked really fed up. I asked him what was wrong. He said he and GB were in a different league to the rest of the Cabinet as politicians, and GB was the only one who got anywhere near him in terms of ability, which was why he still felt he had to be next. But he couldn't see a way out at the moment. He felt if they fell out terminally, and he felt he had to get rid of him, that was the nuclear option. 'I would probably be left standing but there would be plenty of big holes in the floor around me and the party would be damaged for quite a while.' He sat down at one point with a pad and made a joke of it, saying let's do the pros and cons.

Cabinet was going to be tricky. Jeremy had worked out a stage-by-stage process. They had to have a sense of involvement in the process. So we would give them the eighteen documents, and follow it with a series of trilaterals with TB and GB, followed by another Cabinet and finally TB's statement to Parliament. JP and GB came over and we signed them up to the process. TB believed that GB now thought that if he didn't do what he wanted on the euro, he was prepared to move him. He said he would still be a pain in the arse at the FCO but he couldn't do as much damage there. They had another one-on-one after which TB claimed GB was on the same pitch, but we doubted it.

Into Cabinet. First FBU/troops, then Iraq/MEPP, then TB set out the process on the euro and you could sense the relief round the table. He said that everyone within the Cabinet would be engaged in this discussion and whatever the press briefings coming out, he said the final decision had not been made. A number said explicitly how pleased they were at the process. It meant TB was wrestling back some of the control in this, though GB couldn't resist saying there would also be meetings of the economic affairs subcommittee. TB said there would be another full Cabinet on June 5 or 6 and his statement would probably be on June 9. He urged them to ignore anything they heard in the media until this process was through. TB chaired the discussion well.

Then on to the Olympics decision. TB set out the basic case, Tessa the process and also the need to learn lessons from the [Millennium] Dome and Wembley [Stadium]. JP said everyone had to support it if a yes decision was taken, that there could be no mixed messages.

Both Blunkett and Straw, then McCartney, said what a huge benefit it had been to Manchester to host a successful Commonwealth Games. GB then said, in a pretty barbed way, that it was important the business community get the message that things will be asked of them. We had agreed that JP would do the media at lunchtime on the euro. JP went through to see GB at Number 11 and shortly afterwards Joan Hammell [Prescott's special adviser] came out and asked me to join them. We went over what JP would say, then GB said to me 'Where do you think the BBC story came from?' Before I could answer, he said it was not him or Ed – 'I absolutely guarantee you.'

I did a note to John Sawers on what we could offer Bremer, and on what approach I should take. I had another long chat with [Margaret] Tutwiler who seemingly had delayed her departure by a week in case I went out there. I was really trying to help but practically anything I suggested she would say that they already had it, even if I knew they didn't. I got the very strong impression she saw me simply as an irritant. Charles Heatley [FCO spokesman in Baghdad] told me that whatever John Sawers said out there, there tended to be an immediate US push back. He also said there was a lot of chatter there about me trying to take over the communications side of things. He felt there was no way I would get them to accept everything we wanted.

Tutwiler gave me a long list of all the things she said were being done, but in the end what mattered was output and in so far as opinions were hardening, they were hardening against us. She was due to be the next undersecretary for [public diplomacy and] public affairs [US State Department] and was going through the approval process, so clearly didn't want to be seen as part of any failure. Her attitude was 'we're not doing perfect but we're doing OK considering'. John fixed a call with him, me, Bremer and Tutwiler. I did a five-minute pitch, then said I would write him a note overnight on what I felt they needed and what we could offer. I was beginning to think it might be a bad idea actually to go out there, partly because of home, partly because it would be seized on as a big bad story, but most importantly because it did not feel like what the military call a permissive environment.

TB and I had a cup of tea out on the terrace. There was a rumour around that the *Mail* had some big Carole story they were saving up to do damage either during a euro campaign or the next election. TB said he continued to believe she was basically straight and didn't want to harm them. Sally sensed he was more worried about it than he was letting on to us. GB was now causing grief on the Olympics.

He said to TB 'Do it anyway, you've already made up your mind.' I saw Les Hinton [News International chairman] and without being absolutely explicit, told him I was thinking about leaving. He started to go over the sorts of things they might ask me to do, columns in the *Sun* and *The Times*, books, speeches, etc. He was the first person outside the immediate circle that I had raised it with, albeit obliquely. The only thing really holding me back was a basic loyalty to TB, my fear that he would be weakened, and GB emboldened if I went.

Friday, May 16

On the one hand, the papers came out fine for TB with a sense that he was back in control of the process and that the Cabinet was being used to shift to a more pro-euro position. On the other, there was still the sense, e.g. *The Times* and the *Guardian*, that GB was clearly set against a referendum in this parliament. TB called an EMU meeting for 11, just before he left for Chequers. He said we had to correct the impression, by the weekend, that GB was against a referendum in this parliament. I said that was easy enough for me to say to people but I couldn't deliver what GB said. I suggested that I try to negotiate an agreed statement with Ed. I discussed it with him and with Jeremy and then drafted something. There was a risk of course that it would be seen as protesting too much. I felt we should get TB to echo their usual line – not dogmatic and emphasise the tests – whilst GB should echo ours, namely that he would fight for a yes vote if the tests were met and it was not the case that in principle he was against a referendum in this parliament.

It took an hour or so. When I read it to TB, he was fine. GB came back with a couple of changes that were relatively insignificant, there basically just to clutter it up, but we kept the basic thrust, i.e. unity and a position more subtle than was being ascribed to both. Phil Webster [*Times*], who was usually my first yardstick port of call on tricky issues like this, thought it did the job well. [Trevor] Kavanagh's response was that it showed GB had seen off TB, a bit odd given that I had written it, and in the end it was probably not one of my greatest triumphs, but further evidence of the dysfunctional nature of their relationship.

I got a message to call TB. He asked 'Are you on a landline?' I said yes. 'I think there may be a case for moving him come what may. It's just not tenable like this. He is impossible to deal with at the moment.' The press as a whole were not totally convinced by the statement but at least they knew we were trying to keep the act together. I was also dealing with getting more of our people into Baghdad by Monday.

Saturday, May 17

Conference call with JP before the *Today* programme. The euro was tricky but he was fine. TB felt the statement we had done went well. I felt that it had given the press the chance to take the piss in saying we were protesting too much. We did however get up the message for the party and the rest of the government that we were trying our best to be united on this. I had been a little bit troubled by something Matthew Freud [PR] had told me last night, namely that there was talk around I was thinking of leaving and that I would be absolutely mad and I had the best job in the world for anyone interested in politics and the media, and nothing I ever did afterwards would replace it. Fiona was pressing for a kind of 'road map' re my leaving, but it felt like we were going round in circles a bit. I wanted out, but I felt bad and guilty about it. Philip was strongly of the view that GB would feel it would be easier to go for TB if I wasn't there. But then again, after nine years, surely it was time to get a life back, and get things with Fiona back on track long before the kids move away.

We also had another Leo [Blair] episode to deal with. Some of the papers were doing stuff on the school they expected him to go to. During the day, he fell over [at Chequers], banged his head, so they called NHS Direct who suggested he go to Stoke Mandeville Hospital [Buckinghamshire]. He got the all-clear very quickly but we were back into another potential PCC situation.[1] TB felt we shouldn't push it, while CB told Fiona she felt we should. TB called me as his guests for dinner at Chequers were arriving, including Chris Meyer [former UK ambassador to Washington], Peter Hain, Ben Kingsley [actor], Richard and Judy [Madeley and Finnegan, TV presenters]. Chris Meyer was being touted as the leader of the Olympic bid, presumably by himself as he was very busily not denying it.

Sunday, May 18

Watched GB on *Frost*. The reality was that he was not very warm on EMU. He said he would fight in a referendum as hard as TB if there was one, but the constant emphasis was on the tests. It was an odd performance all round. He was very but-but, his legs stuck together making him look tight and unrelaxed, and he had this odd habit of putting both hands on the arm of the sofa. He was also

[1] The Press Complaints Commission editors' code calls for respect for private and family life, including health.

dropping in references to Raith Rovers [Scottish football club] in an obvious attempt to give himself a touch of man-of-the-peopleness. When I briefed TB on it afterwards, he said it sounded like a real wasted opportunity. He felt the problem was that whatever the issue, GB was obsessed with idea of winning or losing. He can't just be part of a team making the right decisions. He has to win, and be seen to win, in the decision-making process.

Fiona spoke to Peter M re CB. Fiona felt Cherie was in something of a state of denial. She just didn't want to live a normal life really. Peter was broadly sympathetic to Cherie, but the cumulative effect was negative. He also said *en passant* that he thought GB got the best of me in the joint euro statement because it still meant he had the lock on the process through the tests, which in the end were not scientific but a mix of economic and political. He sounded pretty down about his life, said in terms that he had another busy but ultimately meaningless week ahead of him.

Monday, May 19

The euro was pretty much back where we had started a few days earlier with GB 'reasserting control' via the economic tests. The issues were conflating in the Eurosceptic papers which was deeply irritating. We weren't really motoring on public services either. Also unhelpfully, someone had briefed Colin Brown [*Independent*] yesterday that TB would do a press conference on Thursday on better asylum figures, and the right-wing press were gearing up to undermine all that in advance. On the euro, we had the first round of Cabinet trilaterals and that plus the IGC was the main news of the day. We were not in the right place on the IGC. And on the euro, there was still a lack of unity.

At the party meeting with Hilary A, Ian McC and David Triesman, TB was very open. He said that on Europe and on the public services, the party felt division. 'If GB and I were united on this, there would not be a problem. We have to sort it.' Ian McCartney said the party was feeling more and more remote, partly from TB but also from the whole government. It was partly about Iraq but it was also about the way we spoke and the claims that we made and the way we made them. The values didn't come through powerfully enough. TB kept telling me that the EMU stuff was moving our way but there was very little sign of that from GB and his lot.

Jeremy sat in on all the trilaterals. Hilary was clear they could be read either way. So was Ian, who said that on the basis of what he had read, he certainly wouldn't rule it out. JR was more sceptical, Patricia and Charles more pro and Jeremy said that on a number of specific detailed points, Patricia got the better of GB. Giscard [d'Estaing, chairman of the Convention on the Future of Europe] was due in for dinner with TB to discuss the Convention, but Danny Pruce [press officer, foreign affairs] and I proposed against drawing attention to it. Europe was suddenly right back at the top of the agenda again and I didn't feel we had a proper strategy for it. Even though he was mainly focused on the euro, in the chats we had in between, he was banging on about reform again. 'I know I'm right about this.' If we don't take on reform the Tories will rebuild around it, and win their way back by promising to do things that we should be doing. It was just crazy to stand in the way of reform. Wrong for the country, wrong for the party.

Sally having told me he was in denial about me leaving, I wrote him a note setting out why I was going. Also, Godric was going to announce at the four o'clock that he was moving on. Then just before, bizarrely, Ari Fleischer announced he was leaving. I had David Hill in for a chat, and asked him, if I moved on, whether he would take on my job. He said he feared he was too old at fifty-five. He had got himself into a nice position [in commercial public relations] and didn't know if he had the energy to get up for another massive job. He was clearly tempted, said he felt it was probably a no, but he would think about it.

Tuesday, May 20

In for a meeting on the Convention [on the Future of Europe], trying to get a grip on overall strategy and message. We were not in a good place on the euro, or on Europe more generally. Ian McCartney came to see me, said he was really worried about the party, that the sense of division had definitely driven through. TB said the euro trilateral with Andrew Smith [Work and Pensions Secretary] in particular, and to a lesser extent with Alistair Darling, was comical because they were totally on the Balls script. Most of the others were pro. Some in particular were clear that if the judgement was not now, we had to be clear we would be going in before too long. TB was convinced GB was moving a bit, but his CBI speech was pretty sceptic, and was emphasising all the obstacles.

Then we heard that Peter M had done a lunch with the women's lobby and had said, off the record, that TB had been outmanoeuvred by a 24-hour political obsessive, and that because GB had won that battle, we were in danger of making the wrong decision for the country and the government on EMU.[1] Of course the chances of it staying off the record were zero as Peter must surely have known, and for once it gave GB the moral high ground. Even though nobody seriously believed we would have put Peter up to do it, it allowed GB to present himself as victim. TB was furious at Peter's stupidity. He said it also made it much more difficult to bring him back.

Wednesday, May 21

Peter M all over the press. TB up the wall about it. GB was on to him, Ed was on to me, saying that unless we denounced and disowned Peter, people would think TB supported what he said. TB was up in the flat on his own working on PMQs. He was looking more isolated, or maybe that was just my guilt at the thought of leaving. PMQs was clearly going to be EMU division and/or the latest education fuck-up, namely schools sending kids home because of lack of funds.[2]

Peter M was not in a mood to back down. He said he believed in the euro, he intended to carry on fighting for it, and as he was a backbencher, he should be allowed to behave like one. He did not believe there was any chance of him coming back to government and he therefore intended to speak out more freely. He said he did believe we were making the wrong decision and it was because TB had been outmanoeuvred. Then in his ultra-haughty voice, he said he was about to do a doorstep for ITN and then sit down to write an article for the *Guardian*. TB just shook his head and rolled his eyes when I told him.

PMQs was OK-ish but we didn't have a good answer to the question 'why not a referendum?' and we needed one fast. TB didn't really dump on Peter M or defend GB so afterwards GB came in, TB called me in and said Gordon felt he had not been firm enough. I had to agree. GB said unless you put him down he will do this every day, day after day, because it's a campaign to divide and undermine the government and it has to stop. It was of course an exact mirror of

[1] Mandelson was quoted as saying 'Gordon Brown is a politician right down to his fingerprints, twenty-four hours a day, seven days a week. Tony is not. If he was as obsessed with politics he would not have let himself be outmanoeuvred by [his] Chancellor in the way that he potentially has.'

[2] Edenham High School in Croydon, South London, had unilaterally decided to send 720 pupils home because wages for temporary staff could not be paid. Changes to schools funding from government had been cited as the reason for sudden budget deficits in some schools.

what Peter, and from time to time we, said about him. TB was pretty meek about it. Jonathan said that the trilaterals he had been at had been OK, but then when the two of them were together, there was a rhythm of low murmuring followed by explosions. 'It's like watching a marriage fall apart.'

I had lunch with Phil Stephens to discuss his book on TB [*Tony Blair: The Making of a World Leader*, published 2004]. He told me he had extensive notes of all my previous lunches with him. I was trying to tell him that TB was basically the same person. He seemed almost as interested in Cherie as TB, which for someone from the *FT* was a bit odd. [David] Bradshaw and I were working on a script for TB's press gallery [bicentenary] dinner, which was annoyingly at the same time as Celtic's UEFA Cup Final tonight. David and I went to discuss it with him, and afterwards I said to him 'You do understand that I'm leaving don't you?' I could see he realised I was serious. I went through some of the arguments – that I had lost enthusiasm, that my relations with the media were bad and I didn't much care, too many groundhog days, too much pressure that I felt others ought by now to be taking. He was very nice about it, I think finally realised it was going to happen, said he agreed that if I wasn't really motivated I couldn't really do it. He said he still wasn't sure if he would fight another election. I said if he didn't, maybe all the more reason why I should go now, and if he did, I could come back.

I wasn't the only one feeling down about things. Peter M came to see me, said he was planning to move to the country, that he really wanted out of the [Westminster] village. I told him about my intentions, and reasons, and he said I would be mad to go. Life outside is not that great. What I do now matters. In the end the media doesn't matter that much. And also there's the question of duty. [Major General] Tim Cross came in for a chat re ORHA and I got TB to come round to see him too. He felt there was a lot we could do to grip it if they let us. I was quite impressed by Cross. I liked the fact that he said he couldn't do *Frost* because he said he had to go to church. He was very clipped, smart. He said that if he ever heard anyone say the Americans were involved in a conspiracy he wouldn't believe it, because they weren't capable of organising a conspiracy. We were at a bit of a disadvantage though. The Americans were a bit worried about us taking over. There was still something holding me back from sending TB the note setting out fully my reasons for departure, but I was eighty-five per cent there. I didn't much enjoy the press gallery dinner. In a way it was our two lives coming together, and though I stayed in for TB's speech,[1] I sneaked out to a bar in the [Hilton London Metropole] hotel to watch Celtic's extra-time defeat against Porto [Porto 3, Celtic 2].

Thursday, May 22

TB was very worried about the *Times* stuff on schools based on an NAHT [National Association of Head Teachers] survey on teacher sackings. Overnight, the *New Statesman* broke the story of the Attorney General's advice, which we assumed was leaked by Clare. At Cabinet, JP asked Jack to say who had received it, so he read out the list of copy addressees which ended 'Secretary of State for International Development', at which point JP just said 'Next business.' Asylum was running fine, with much better than expected figures, but TB was keen to press home the advantage by saying there would be further legislation to deal with other abuses.

After Cabinet TB saw Charles and warned him to be careful that we didn't simply sort out schools funding at a technical level but still had schools laying off teachers around the country. Cabinet was mainly Iraq. There was a hilarious moment when Gareth [Lord Williams, Leader of the Lords] was going through Lords business and said they had all been up till 2.25am on sexual offences. 'They love it in there!' roared Blunkett, who said people ought to read their Hansard, especially when they were recommending 'delete genitalia and insert penis'. TB did fine on the euro, then GB presented a short paper on the benefits and the possible steps we need to take to get there, and he was a bit warmer than usual. TB said some ministers had been honest enough to admit they hadn't read all the documents before their trilateral meetings with him and GB. What was clear was that everyone was in favour of setting a direction towards entry, and he urged them all to ignore what he called 'noises off'.

Patricia [Hewitt] spoke first after GB and was very good, said there had to be part of the assessment which set out the costs of staying out which she believed were growing, in terms of falling share of foreign investment, possible loss of trade. She felt the longer we stayed out, the higher the economic price. JP said he felt much clearer about the economics, JR that there had been a coming together of the political and the economic. Nearly all of the speeches had been in favour. TB summed up by saying he felt a clear strategy as reflected by the

[1] Blair described making his maiden speech in the Commons with a single reporter in the gallery. Afterwards, he recalled, 'I saw her later in the corridor and asked her what she thought of the speech. She said: "I'm a Hansard reporter. I just transcribe speeches. I don't listen to them."'

discussion would release energy within the party and elsewhere to start making and winning the case. The press conference was fine, TB very confident, pushing back hard on Europe, and strong on asylum. On the euro, the question that worried me most was whether the Cabinet could change the assessment but he didn't really get pressed on it. I had a meeting with Ian McCartney and Douglas [Alexander]. Douglas felt we needed a strategy for reconnection with the party along the lines of the one we did for TB last summer.

Friday, May 23

I went in for TB's meeting with John Sawers. TB wanted a note of all the things he would need to get Bush to deliver on. He popped round to my office later and said that on Europe, it would be a total disaster if we turned our backs, that he was glad the right wing was out there campaigning on the referendum and the IGC because he felt we were going to have to take on the whole argument. Alistair Darling called me about a piece in the *FT* saying that Number 10 were not impressed with him. 'If it's what Tony thinks, I'd rather know and I can go and do something else.' He said he had seen this happen to other ministers and it wasn't going to happen to him. I said I could honestly say that neither TB nor I had ever expressed such a view. I told TB who said he would speak to him. It was pretty clear they were all getting a bit jittery pre-reshuffle.

Saturday, May 24

Geoffrey Levy and Gordon Rayner had a big piece in the *Mail*, 'Carole the Conqueror', saying that Fiona was going to leave and it was a victory for Carole [Caplin]. Fiona called Cherie and said to her she was worried that CB was 'sleepwalking to disaster'. I told TB it was perfectly clear she had a link into the *Mail* and the paper was just toying with her, building her up, in the hope of using her to create a huge splash later. TB called ostensibly re Europe – again – and his continuing worries on education funding, and then raised Carole. She does Cherie's clothes and personal training. So what? He said he had seen her five times since Christmas. I said the problem was that he didn't think there was a problem, and I did. Relations between CB and Fiona had effectively broken down and it was too late to sort it out. He said it was vital that we do not let this kind of stuff take over the agenda. I said we haven't, they had. I had been warning about Carole for years and neither of you have listened. The whole thing was demeaning and belittling.

He called me again later, said he hadn't been able to speak freely because he had been in a car, but I had to understand Carole was barely involved at all any more. I said I just didn't believe it, and nor did Fiona. He said if we left now, people would think it was about this, which was belittling for everyone. Fiona spoke to Cherie a couple of times during the day but the lack of trust was pretty obvious. She asked Cherie outright if she had told Carole about her leaving. 'She said no, but I didn't believe her.' I took Rory to the South of England Championships up at Watford, and got in an hour-long run myself.

Sunday, May 25

Big pieces in the Sundays on Fiona to quit. TB called and said we had to put a lid on this. He said it was becoming dreadful for Cherie because the coverage was making her look crazy. I said it was bad for all of us. He said we had to make clear it was nonsense. I said there was no way we could deny Fiona was leaving, because she is. He was now very irritated by the whole thing, and when he was irritated with this kind of issue, he could become very irritating. It was as if this was all terrible for him when in fact they had created this madness by allowing her in so close. I gave the press office a line that Fiona had not left and that it was absurd to see this as some kind of power struggle with Carole, the usual flimflam. The problem was a number of journalists now already knew she was leaving. Philip was in the States and Georgia [Gould] needed a lift to the QPR vs Cardiff play-off finals at the Millennium Stadium, so I went down with her and Calum. She was a bit upset when they [QPR] lost, and we could see [Cardiff supporter] Neil [Kinnock] going crazy in the directors' box. The Israeli Cabinet endorsed the road map, which dominated the news. TB said he found that even at weekends now, he was working pretty much all the time, and it never stopped.

Monday, May 26

The latest Giscard [d'Estaing] draft [European constitution] appeared to the usual insane cacophony from the sceptic press. Work-wise, it was a fairly typical quiet bank holiday. I made a few phone calls whilst watching Calum play tennis, trying to get some of them off the ceiling about Giscard. We went out for dinner with David and Louise Miliband who had decided to adopt a baby and had us down as referees. David felt we were drifting politically. I agreed but somehow I lacked the energy to respond to it in a way that I would have done a while back. Meanwhile, the situation re Fiona was being made to look like the end of the Camelot show, and she was starting to get hit in the press unfairly.

Peter M called me later and said that he felt I would know for sure when I wanted to go. So did I, and it wasn't quite yet but it wasn't far off. Fiona felt TB and I worked so closely, and ninety-five per cent of the time in a pretty good spirit, so that by now I was in many ways TB's closest friend and he mine, and she understood why that made it harder to leave, because I felt I was letting him down. There was something in that, but I also felt I was letting him and myself down in not being up for the job in the way that I used to be. I had a dreadful cold but went out for a run in the afternoon and got a phone call to say that Mark Gault [close friend from university] had dropped down dead. I was pole-axed. I tried to call Susie [his wife], eventually got hold of her and she was pretty much inconsolable. He had literally just conked out sitting in a chair.

Tuesday, May 27

TB was at Chequers and I was supposed to go down for a meeting but in the end didn't as I was dealing with the fallout from Mark's death. Peter Hain gave us a problem by appearing to say that European elections would be seen as a [euro] referendum, so we had to weigh in on that a bit. I got Jack Straw to do a *Times* article on the Tories fighting old battles. GB, unbeknown to us, was doing something in the *Wall Street Journal*. It almost looked co-ordinated, but the truth was that, as so often, we had no idea what GB was up to. His piece was mainly to emphasise his European economic reform credentials for the US audience and Murdoch in particular. TB saw Adams and McGuinness and told them he thought it might be time for him to meet the IRA guys that they kept going back to see. Adams seemed keener than McGuinness. TB felt they had to give something. I took a couple of meetings on Europe. The Europe coverage showed once more the need for better rebuttal and proactive communications. As ever, the press was setting the agenda for the broadcasters.

Wednesday, May 28

The car came at 7.15 to take me to the airport, where we waited for TB. We sat down to work on his speech for Poland on Friday. He was up for a big pro-European message. He had not really read the papers so I briefed him on just how mad the *Sun/Mail/Telegraph* had been. He said they were going to have to be confronted on this. The heavy thing to do would be to say that this was a campaign headed by three people – Murdoch, an Australian living in America, [Conrad] Black, a Canadian [*Telegraph* proprietor], and [Paul] Dacre [*Mail* editor], an extreme right-winger. They thought it was fantastic that he faced down public opinion over Iraq, but terrible that he could possibly disagree over this. I was worried that we had missed the time at which it might have been possible. But he seemed up for it and was very firm when we went down the plane to see the press. After a good run around the block on Iraq, he engaged with Cabinet on Europe in a pretty robust way.

Rumsfeld had not helped set up the visit to Iraq with a statement that we may never find WMD, or that he may never have had them, which was a pretty dreadful backdrop to the visit. But TB was pretty firm, strong on both Iraq and Europe. We had breakfast together on the plane to Kuwait and as we were just chatting away over his current list of concerns – Europe and the IGC, the assessment, GB, the press, whatever – it was very hard to imagine not being on these kinds of trips, having these kinds of conversations in future. Despite everything, he was still very engaging, very funny and hadn't fundamentally changed at all. We always had a laugh on these trips, which was good for us, but also I think helped build a sense of team with everyone else, from the cops to the policy wonks.

In Kuwait we were almost in hysterics when the deputy prime minister [Sheikh Sabah al-Ahmed al-Sabah, also foreign minister] started lambasting us over our asylum and immigration policies, saying we were too soft on the Kurds and we gave too many benefits to asylum seekers. It was a pretty bizarre event, a bilateral where none of us could hear the conversation, so we sat muttering amongst ourselves while just looking over at the line of princes sitting playing with their worry beads. TB and I kept exchanging looks and we just stayed on the right side of laughter.

The news was leading on TB and Rumsfeld. What a clot. The cuttings came through to the residence where I once played the bagpipes with my namesake [Colonel Alastair Campbell, defence and military attaché]. Linda Lee-Potter [columnist] had a ghastly piece about me and Fiona in the *Mail*, obviously written to order. While TB had a bath, Kate [Garvey] and I went over what pictures we wanted from the visit to Iraq, then out to a pretty sumptuous dinner at one of the palaces. Chirac's people came on with an interesting suggestion. He wanted to do a joint article about Africa with TB and Schroeder. Schroeder was less keen than we were. TB was saying again that he found the workload really heavy at the moment.

Thursday, May 29

Up at 5, UK time. The press was dominated by WMD and Rumsfeld's comments, which was really irritating. When I thought of what we could do to fuck them up in the same way. We then heard, though we couldn't get it substantiated, that Paul Wolfowitz had said that WMD had been a bureaucratic convenience to get us into the war. Some of the top British military told us that the American top brass loathed Rumsfeld, found him impulsive, interfering, making the wrong decisions for the wrong reasons. The local Kuwaiti paper had a picture of TB and a group of sheikhs all in traditional headgear, with the caption helpfully pointing out that TB was 'second right'. I was working on a political strategy paper and planning upcoming events.

We boarded the Hercules flight to Basra. TB was up in the jump seat, David Manning and I behind. We flew over Umm Qasr, burnt-out tanks all over the place. It was very hot and arid, and a few oil wells were burning. We landed at Basra airfield to be met by [Paul] Bremer and [John] Sawers. TB afterwards was very clear that we really had to press the US to get better engaged. It was just not moving in the way it should be. I had a meeting with Bremer. He had read my earlier note and said he basically agreed with it, yet was still waiting for a replacement for [Margaret] Tutwiler. He was falling into this classic US thing of waiting for these mythical figures who were never quite delivered. He asked if I could provide someone, and I agreed to provide John Buck [FCO] to help draw up a plan. He also agreed to the idea of more of our people going out there if we got a plan in place. So it was useful but I could sense he was feeling pretty overwhelmed by the whole thing.

John Sawers was as tiggerish and enthusiastic as ever in his light suit and white shirt looking every inch 'our man in a hot country' and revelling in the machine gun-toting close protection squad. We then drove off to a visit to a school. Nice kids, lovely reception. He did a little speech in the playground while I talked to General [James] Conway [Marine Expeditionary Force], who said how impressed he was by how light we travelled compared to GWB. I told him about Rumsfeld's WMD comments and he didn't seem too surprised.

Our military had accommodated brilliantly to what was going on. The recurring theme though was that the Americans were not quite getting it right. TB had a fairly long briefing on how Basra was won, and then on to the speech to the troops. It was by a river under an awning, hot, but with a breeze, and his words were OK without being brilliant. He was full of praise for the troops, said it was a defining moment for the country, which the press felt was OTT. But he said afterwards he really believed it changed the way people in the region thought about the future, as was clear from the discussion with the

Kuwaitis last night. I hung round talking to the press about a ghastly Gilligan story [aired that morning on the *Today* programme] claiming that the spooks were not happy with the dossier, which was clearly a repeat of the stories at the time.[1] We left for the flight to Umm Qasr by Chinook [helicopter], then down to see the army and navy in a very well-organised session. Several soldiers asked me my marathon time. Some of them had been following the *Times* column but hadn't seen the result. They were a nice crowd. One came over and said he had never been much of a fan of TB or the government but both had grown on him and he felt that went for a lot of them. We went on to the minehunter, [HMS] *Ramsey*, where he did a Forces Radio interview.

TB clearly got a charge from the positive response, though earlier there had been no applause for his speech, which was a surprise, but then it was pointed out to me they had been told to be quiet. On the way back to the chopper, the Number 2 in the base said they had just heard that someone who worked in a photo shop had sent the police pictures of soldiers maltreating Iraqi PoWs. Bad. The reception he got was warm all day but General [Peter] Wall [1st UK Armoured Division, responsible for security in Basra] said that at night there was a lot of criminality. On the dockside, bizarrely, given I was spending so much time thinking about my own future, one of General Wall's protection team asked me whether I had a lot of pressure. I said yes. You wouldn't miss it for the world, he said. I'm not sure about that, I said. 'You just hang in there.' Odd. He was from Stirling.

We flew back to Kuwait and the relief of a cool, air-conditioned place. TB had to get changed into a suit for the official send-off and called me in for a chat. He said he found our troops really terrific, easily the best, and he was glad that we came. On the plane, we both worked on the Poland speech. He felt he needed a harder political strategy based on public service reform, Europe and the poverty agenda. He felt that post EMU, what we needed most was Number 10 and Number 11 working far more closely together on policy. I said I didn't think it was possible. He felt GB allowed himself to be influenced too much by his in her circle. He thought Balls was clever but got too many backs up, which would not help him once he entered Parliament. There were two things that might shift GB to be more

[1] Andrew Gilligan, had alleged on the *Today* programme that Downing Street ordered the transformation of the September 2002 dossier on WMD in the week before it was published. He claimed it had been 'sexed up', including via the insertion of information Downing Street 'knew to be untrue' and against the wishes of the intelligence agencies.

co-operative. The first was that he now genuinely believed TB might move him. 'He's already said to me if I try to move him to Foreign Secretary, he will go on the back benches.' Second, he was very worried about being portrayed as anti reform. He said that though DFID offered the most extreme picture of GB influence over minister and department, there were other parts of departments where things only happened if he said so. The Civil Service often talked of ministers being lazy. In truth, often they were just doing what they were told, or not doing what they were told not to do. TB said the real nightmare is that he is head and shoulders above the rest, which is why it is always better to try to work with him. He said he had always been sincere in saying to him that he wanted to hand over to him at some point, but he made it very difficult.

I was keen to get to Mark's [Gault] funeral in New York, and mentioned it to TB, who said he would prefer it if I stayed for the whole trip but would understand if I didn't. Over dinner on the plane TB, AC, DM, Tom Kelly. Serious stuff on Iraq. TB said it reminded him of FMD [foot and mouth disease] before we gripped it and the military sorted it. People knew what problems needed to be solved, but nobody was gripping it. Paul Bremer was impressive but looked like he was overwhelmed. David and I explained to him that the problem was the US. His critics looked at Bush, said he'd won his war and now seemed less interested. Rumsfeld fired off orders the whole time. The State Department was marginalised. Bremer spoke to Rumsfeld and the Security Council were out of the loop. There was not much we could do to make it better.

Alarmingly, TB said what he felt it needed was for me to go out there and be his person totally gripping it, alongside someone who was GWB's person. I said I was not keen, but he clearly was. He said he would speak to GWB, Russia and France and make them realise it could go belly up. I felt that the US had an electoral strategy that meant they just kept moving on to the next bold thing. He said we shouldn't see it as a conspiracy, it's just that they had a bigger and more difficult bureaucracy.

Overnight we had a telegram about the US warning that there could be two Brits among those at Guantanamo Bay that could end up being executed. I said to TB it would be dreadful and it couldn't be allowed to happen. He said he didn't think they would go through with some of this tribunal stuff, but I wasn't so sure. He then turned to Chirac. Giscard [d'Estaing] had said to him that Chirac was a man of strong but changing emotions. TB said he only really understood strength. Since we turned on him over Iraq he had become much nicer and treated TB with much more respect. TB believed Chirac would try hard to get back onside with Bush, but another telegram was saying that Bush was only in the mood to tolerate, not to forgive. David M suggested we try to get Jeremy Greenstock to go to Baghdad.

TB was worried about [visiting] St Petersburg [EU–Russia Summit]. He wanted to be low-profile and felt it would be a disaster for Putin if the whole thing was over the top because people would think he was suffering real *folie de grandeur* and possibly becoming corrupt. We had a nice enough dinner on the plane and I was in a reasonably good mood, which ended as we approached Warsaw [tour taking in Warsaw, St Petersburg and the G8 summit in Evian, France]. I gave him the note I had done setting out a plan for my departure. He read it, gave me a quizzical look and then said 'Keep it, don't put it in my box, don't copy it round.' Meanwhile Fiona had told her staff she was going, so it was all going to be a bit messy. Part of me felt I couldn't let Fiona down but part of me felt I would be a real loss to him. I had grown very friendly with David Manning, who I liked, for his seriousness and commitment. He said he felt TB would be bereft and I should probably fix on the general election and make clear I would be going then. We arrived at the hotel in Warsaw and TB was pretty much doing the speech himself now. I went for a run then tried to work out how I could get to Mark's funeral.

Friday, May 30

WMD firestorm was getting worse. I told TB the papers were really pretty grim as he woke up, and he was worried that the spooks would be pissed off with us. He felt that in part the attacks coming now were about Europe. 'It's another attack to go to the heart of my integrity,' he said. We decided we would have to hit back at the press conference even though it would take away from the Europe speech. He said he was happy with the speech. He was a bit jumpy about the spooks [September dossier] stuff and said we had to get him all the facts on it. I said the facts were that it was the work of the agencies and the idea that we would make these things up was absurd. I spoke to Julian Miller [Cabinet Office intelligence and security official] in the car, and then to John Scarlett during TB's meeting with the Polish PM [Leszek Miller].

John S said he was emphatic in saying to people that it was not true that we pressured them, and they were saying that. But he stopped short of agreeing to do a letter about it. He was very much up for helping us but only so far. As TB's meeting went on, I did a very strong line of rebuttal and when the press conference came up, he hit back hard on it. The meeting with the Poles was excellent. Though the prime minister and the president [Aleksander Kwasniewski] were different sorts of people from different parties, they were on the same agenda. They were pro NATO, anti Chirac, determined to protect the transatlantic alliance. The president was really concerned about the neocons in the States and TB didn't go that far to placate, though he did say he sometimes felt the analysis was right but the way they secured their objectives was all wrong.

On the Polish referendum [on entry into the EU], the president said the Pope [John Paul II, a Pole] had helped in saying vote yes, but a lot of the priests were saying vote no. He said turnout was a problem and they really wanted TB to do a big vote-yes pitch, which he did. They also asked him to offer support to Ukraine and to get Russia to be nicer to former satellites. The press conference was a bit of a shambles and I rather childishly enjoyed the sight of two burly Polish women manhandling Trevor Kavanagh and others out of sight. We went for a break at [UK ambassador] Michael Pakenham's residence and sat out in the blazing sunshine. TB's speech [at the Royal Castle] had gone down well.[1]

I eventually decided to go to the funeral, and arranged to meet Jeremy Greenstock while I was out there to put the idea of him going to Baghdad. Cherie joined us on the plane for the flight to St Petersburg, which whizzed by with lunch and a bit of work. They had the papers from the last couple of days. TB had a rare look at the *Mail* and said it's not just vile, it's evil. On my future, he said don't do anything yet, you must distance it from all the Carole stuff. I said fine, so long as he understands we are serious about leaving. He said he understood that but it required careful handling.

We arrived and were driven to a specially built complex of so-called cottages for the leaders attending the anniversary celebrations [300 years since the foundation of St Petersburg]. The cottages were grand, ornate identical homes built for the purpose of this event. It underlined TB's worries about *folie de grandeur*. Marble of dubious quality all over the place. Huge en suite bathrooms, lavish but rather tacky furniture, gyms and pools. Yet the overall effect was pretty horrible and the people working there were not much less surly than during the Communist days. TB went off for a ceremony and then we went to the Mariinsky Theatre concert to join the leaders. I had been

[1] Blair said 'For Britain and Poland the lesson is the same: accept the European Union as a modern reality, join it wholeheartedly, fight to make it, economically and politically, an instrument of future strength and prosperity for the nations within it.'

dreading it but actually quite enjoyed it. Chirac, TB and wives were seated together. The body language was OK. By the time I got back to the cottage, I was trying to work out what I had really added today. I had sorted our response on the [September] dossier, helped out re the funeral, done a note on forward strategy, talked to Fiona a few times but that was about it.

Saturday, May 31

TB away at a stack of different events and ceremonies. I met up with him at the EU–Russia summit. He said they were all wondering why they were there. Lots of the other leaders had been rolling their eyes around at the nature of the event. He said Chirac had been very warm to him and had sent him a note thanking him for what he said about France in the Warsaw speech. He was being very fulsome with TB in front of all the others. Chirac asked me if I enjoyed the concert. He said it was too long, and that music events should never be longer than forty-five minutes.

At the summit, TB was taken into the leaders' room while the rest of us were taken to what must once have been a dungeon. I had a long chat with Bela Anda [Schroeder's spokesman]. He said Schroeder was getting fed up with all the stuff coming out of Condi Rice's mouth and might fight back at some point. TB came back to the cottage after what he said was the most extraordinary fireworks spectacle he had ever seen. Both he and Bush said neither of them could have got away with something like it. He had obviously been talking to some of them about the nature of opinion in Britain. He said we had to do something about the press on Europe, and we may have to take them on properly. I said I have been saying that for years. He said I know, but you have to pick your moment and your issue, and you may be right, but this is it. He said it may be that we have to do it even if we lose because ultimately we should do the right thing.

He was also musing on the 'prophet in his own land' phenomenon. You didn't have to be at an event like this for long to see how the other leaders, particularly those from the accession countries, saw the UK as perhaps the best place imaginable, and TB in the very top league. Even the French and the Germans were clear that Bush would not be moving in the way he was on the Middle East without TB's influence, but all we got from our media was total shit. GB sent through a forward strategy note for TB that happily was similar to mine in the way he saw the dividing lines. I did a long run with Rod Lyne [UK ambassador] out on a trail near the sea. We had a bilateral with [Atal Bihari] Vajpayee [Indian Prime Minister]. Kashmir, Iraq,

MEPP, Nepal, Peter Bleach.[1] He was more fluid and talkative than usual, but very frail. He walked very slowly now and his hearing aids were clearly very powerful. We were still being hit hard on WMD and the Sundays were going to be doing it even bigger with a lot of the focus on me.

Sunday, June 1

With DM to the airport, had a readout of the papers, pretty grim. On the plane I told TB and he was a bit down about it all. Also, he and Cherie seemed to have had a row and she was really lip-quivering. TB went down the plane to see the press, again pushing back on WMD. He was fine but the WMD issue was now digging into us. TB kept saying 'What are the allegations?' I said it's that we made them do something they didn't want to do. But it's ridiculous, he said, and so it went on. At Geneva, he left for Evian and I stayed on the plane to come back with Cherie, Alison etc. The Sunday papers were on there, and were even worse than media monitoring had said. The *Sunday Times* had a story about an email showing I'd discussed the dossier with John Scarlett and there was a suggestion that I had tried to get JS to write a conclusion. In fact John had drafted one and I'd said I didn't think that it worked. There was an account in the *Observer* of meetings with TB, JS, C, Jack Straw and complained it wasn't right. There would be grains of truth in all this but it was just crap. Indeed I'd bent over backwards not least because I was fearful this kind of thing could happen.

Gilligan had a big piece in the *Mail on Sunday* having a go at me from the alleged source that he had, with descriptions of meetings there had never been and things I was said to have done that I never did.[2] But it was grim, and grim for me, and also for TB with huge stuff about trust. It was definitely time to get out. I called John Scarlett when I got back and he remained, at least to me, very supportive, said he'd always been happy to do the dossier, had always insisted it was his work, and would only release it if happy with it. Maybe there were some people lower down who were not happy at the idea

[1] Bleach, a British-born mercenary, was serving a life sentence for involvement in the Purulia arms-drop case. In 1995, a large consignment of unauthorised weapons had been dropped by aircraft in West Bengal. He would be pardoned by the Indian government in 2004.

[2] Gilligan had written 'I asked him [Gilligan's then unidentified source] how this transformation happened. The answer was a single word. "Campbell." What? Campbell made it up? "No, it was real information. But it was included against our wishes because it wasn't reliable."'

of a dossier because of the need to preserve secrecy and because of the fear it would be politicised, but that was not the case for the people at the top. He was emphatic that the agencies were pushing back and denying all this, but there was precious little sign of that in the Sundays.

He said he was minded to set everything out in a note to ministers, which they could then draw on themselves. He said we were being made to accord to our stereotypes – you are the brutal political hatchet man and I am the dry intelligence officer. It's not very nice but I can assure you this is not coming from people at the top. He was clear I had never asked him to do anything he was unhappy with. I said before long, once the left was bored with WMD they would be on to the idea that we were victims of what security services have always done to Labour governments. TB didn't believe in that stuff but he was clear that there was something going on here. John S recalled the various stages of the dossier process; how we said we would present the evidence, then how we retreated last Easter because we feared it would raise the stakes too high and it was not a great document. Then how more and more intelligence came in, then how we agreed to go for it at the time we did. Then on to the production through Julian Miller. I said it was really bad, all this stuff.

Monday, June 2

In early, WMD still raging and it was going to be the big build-up to Wednesday, PMQs and the G8 statement, then hopefully some kind of catharsis. TB was still in 'it's ridiculous' mode and getting more and more irritated by what was essentially a media-driven thing. The main problem of course was that there were no WMD discoveries beyond the two labs, and no matter how much we said that there were other priorities now, the public were being told as a matter of fact that we had done wrong. We had Clare S, Robin C and a lot of backbenchers on the rampage now. So it was difficult. I did the morning meeting which essentially I used to get together the briefing for Wednesday. Meeting with Jonathan to try to get a sense of where to go on the WMD story. ISC [Commons Intelligence and Security Committee] inquiry or a letter from John S to TB saying there was no improper interference in the process. [Andrew] Marr was back from holiday and decided to peddle the line that AC would be the scalp the Commons was looking for. So here we go again, Black Rod, Cheriegate, all over again.

On the flight out to New York, I did a bit of work and then read [Harold Wilson's former press secretary] Joe Haines' book [*Glimmers of Twilight: Harold Wilson in Decline*]. Pretty grim reading and the problems with Marcia [Falkender, Wilson's former political secretary] worse than anything we had. His section on the BBC of today was brilliant. I was met by Jeremy Greenstock's driver Gary and his Bentley and taken to the residence. I did a bit of paperwork, then out to meet friends from university who were over for the funeral. Rebekah Wade [*Sun* editor] was over for a News Corp meeting and I had a drink with her and Sarah Murdoch [wife of Lachlan, Rupert Murdoch's elder son] at Soho House and gave her a hard time over their coverage of Europe, and made-up stories.

Later I sat down with Jeremy [Greenstock] and explained that TB was looking for someone to go to Iraq effectively to be his man, and we would be urging Bush to do the same. Jeremy wasn't keen. He said he was an Arabist not far from retirement and desperate for a break and not sure he really wanted to keep doing government work. He also felt that unless and until the Defense Department moved over and let the whole bigger operation take over, it was not going to work. He really admired David M for the way he worked with Condi but said he found it quite alarming that what was basically happening was that David was almost tutoring the American president and his team. He felt TB had much more influence over Middle East policy than on Iraq and he was clear TB had to stay close to GWB. But he felt sometimes they just didn't care sufficiently either about the way things blew back on us or actually, whether things got better or not.

The impression was almost of a country-by-country war strategy and they were far less focused on what happened after the fighting stopped. It was brought home to me later when Rebekah and Les Hinton dragged me out to Langan's [restaurant] and the *New York Post* editor [Colin Allan] said 'WMD just isn't an issue here. Nobody cares.' So we had to be careful. I said to Jeremy G I was worried that TB was setting himself up for too much of the blame if it went wrong. He said that Bush didn't really grip these guys at all, but Rumsfeld was off the leash and out of control. He said the other reason why he was hesitant was because the American system knew that he thought very little of Rumsfeld.

Tuesday, June 3

Godric called just before his briefing, said the frenzy was going apace and was obviously going to keep going up to Wednesday. I spoke to Jonathan and we agreed a way forward was for the ISC to trail an inquiry before TB formally announced it and John S to make clear nothing improper took place. I wrote a long note for TB re what we should try to do in rebuttal of the continuing WMD allegations. Defensive and offensive, give context and explanation, inquiry, defend ourselves re agency interference nonsense, and also hit back in that the people who were saying there would be no WMD were the people saying this other stuff too. Five pages or so, culminating in MEPP and they said we would never do that either but we are, GWB is there etc. We had to fight back but also put over a more subtle message. But there was no doubt we were in trouble on it, and the trust thing was back, which was partly about trying to undermine him on the euro. I felt it was an OK piece of work though and hoped it helped him. He was going to be feeling the heat on it, although the Beeb would try to deflect it to me.

I finished my speech for the funeral and then dictated a long note to TB by telephone. I guess the main point was that he needed to give a sense of process, show understanding of the concerns but also make clear we did the right thing because of the better things now happening. Met up with some old friends in a bar before the funeral, then up to the church. I read my speech over the phone to Fiona and was worried I wouldn't be able to hold it together. Susie [Mark Gault's widow] was in a bad way and the boys just looked out of it. The speeches were fine. His brothers [Philip and Hugh], me, two good friends and a McCann-Erickson [advertising company] executive. I just about got through without breaking down. The worst bit was when the boys told me that Mark was still their best friend.

The event afterwards was pretty dreadful. A series of corporate speeches, one of which seemed to be saying that what he would want was for the company to use this to go out and pitch for business. It really was the worst of corporate America. I got a lot of nice plaudits for the speech, certainly got the most laughs. Mark's dad [Jim Gault] said he didn't get the impression that some of the people speaking at the wake really knew him at all. WMD still raging at home. I spoke to TB, who said it was grotesque. There was no story here at all, but it was being driven by the BBC as a huge crisis for us. He said he liked my note. I got on the plane and slept all the way back with the help of a sleeping pill.

Wednesday, June 4

I arrived back and the big story was John Reid saying rogue elements in the security services were out to get us. By the time I landed, Switch[board] called me to say that C, John Scarlett and [Sir] David Omand [permanent secretary and security intelligence co-ordinator, Cabinet Office] had all called for me. I called Richard [Dearlove, C] who said there would be a bad effect on the staff if they felt ministers couldn't trust them. I said I'm sure Reid would not have meant to attack them as a whole but clearly someone was stirring it. I said TB would be very supportive at PMQs. Scarlett said he was pushing back the attacks on me and my integrity. I'd asked for all my notes to be dug out on the dossier and I was provenly in the clear. I'd done a long three-page process note on Sept 9 last year making clear it must be one hundred per cent their product and there must be nothing in it they're not happy with. And there was also a long note I made with detailed drafting suggestions.

I went to a TB meeting re what to say about it all with Omand, Scarlett, David Manning, Sally M, Clare Sumner [private secretary], Jonathan. Scarlett was fine re what we were going to say, namely we did not override them. TB was pretty cool with me and the truth was he wasn't taking much advice. I had a chat with Bruce [Grocott, Lords chief whip] about my future and he said he was worried the operation would fall apart if I went. Then a better than usual meeting with Balls and Mike Ellam [head of communications, Treasury] to lay the ground for a euro statement. It was all about the body language. We really had to go out of our way to show a united front. Peter Hyman was trying to push towards a referendum in this parliament, or a change of gear to the next steps, but Ed was not having any of it. It was an OK meeting but I suspect they felt they had got their way. Fiona was really fed up with Cherie. It transpired she hadn't sorted the finances of the Bermuda trip. Fiona also discovered CB had agreed to a *Harper's Bazaar* [fashion magazine] interview.

Thursday, June 5

The main focus of the day was the euro Cabinet. TB and GB had had literally dozens of meetings and TB remained convinced that something had moved in GB, that he wanted to be in a pro position but he also wanted to keep the anti press on board. Ed Balls had revealed that yesterday when I said the best way to signal a gear change was for the *Sun* and the *Mail* to say this was getting serious and there was a real fight on and Ed said yes, but we don't want the *Sun* to go for us next week. WMD still raging on and I sent a long letter of complaint to the BBC re Gilligan, pointing out factual inaccuracies e.g. the fact that he said the JIC [Joint Intelligence Committee] was a Number 10 committee.

TB seemed pretty clear with me that he was thinking of standing down before the election, but I couldn't be sure that he wasn't just stringing me along a bit. He had made no mention of the note I showed him last week about my departure, and was clearly hoping it would just go away. The euro Cabinet started with TB making quite a long exposition of where we were, then GB, as usual in rather more dense form but not too bad. The discussion was OK, though nobody openly said what I suspected most of them thought, namely that the assessment was more negative than the earlier discussions had led them to believe. GB was pleased with the process, as were we all, as there had been no real leaks on this for weeks, ever since we took the decision to involve them all. Patricia H and Charles C were both very strong on the costs of staying out. Peter Hain was very pro, Margaret Beckett far more pro than I thought she would be. Helen [Liddell] and Tessa [Jowell] were very pro. JR, DB and Jack S a little bit more sceptical, Darling and Andrew Smith more so. But it was a good discussion and the mood was definitely 'yes but' rather than 'no but', with a lot of focus on the steps to get there.

The discussion ended with a barnstorming JP performance in which he said that when TB and GB were united, and the Cabinet involved properly, there was nothing we couldn't do. So the mood was good. But then GB went out in the street and did his usual 'nothing to harm the national economic interest', so we ended up with the usual headlines, facing both ways. We had also agreed a joint TB/GB letter which I drafted and sent over but it came back with lots of changes that made it more dense and Brownish. Even the little things were difficult with them. We were going right up to the statement knowing that it would all be in the body language and the briefing.

Reid's comments had upset the spooks and Jack said to me they should have been told straight away about what he had said. But at the same time, there was some stirring going on somewhere and they needed to grip it, surely. I left for the ballet with Fiona and David and Janice Blackburn [friends]. I didn't like ballet at the best of times, and these weren't the best of times. I have never been so stared at in my life. I felt like I was an exhibit in a zoo. It was a mix of 'He doesn't look too evil' and 'What on EARTH is he doing here?' I wondered myself.

Friday, June 6

Iraq meeting with ministers and officials, TB wanting to get fully briefed on how bad it was, for example reconstruction work going too slowly, what the military really thought. He was due to speak to Bush later. Jack was scathing re Rumsfeld, said 'Let's be honest Tony, he has no affection for you or the government and couldn't care if we survive. He just wants his troops home.' TB was looking pretty fed up with this. He realised that WMD was one thing but if we didn't grip this it would give us problems for the future. [General Sir] Michael Walker [new Chief of the Defence Staff, succeeding Admiral Sir Michael Boyce] was much less friendly than [CDS preceding Boyce, now General Lord] Guthrie.

The Bush call began with lots of congratulations re the MEPP summit. GWB was sympathetic re the way we were getting hit on Iraq and WMD which was still running today because Blix had criticised our intelligence. There was a fair bit of the usual friendly banter but TB was getting a little exasperated at the Pentagon's seeming lack of grip. At the office meeting, we had yet another discussion on strategic message. TB and GB had been discussing it and they wanted to go for a message based around 'choice and equity'. I didn't like it at all. I also felt we needed less new policy and more focus on seeing existing policy through, and with far greater drive on message. There was a lot of reshuffle talk in the press. Derry [Irvine] was in a terrible state because of all the talk of him being for the chop. DB was fretting on all the suggestions that he would lose out [as Home Secretary] with the creation of a new Ministry of Justice.

TB wanted Ann Taylor [chair of ISC] to do a quick investigation into the 45-minutes stuff.[1] TB was telling us that we had to get back on domestic politics but then also saying he wanted to make more speeches on Europe, wanted better rebuttal on Afghanistan and more of our people into Iraq. I can't say I blamed him wanting to avoid domestic because it was such hard work dealing with GB at the moment.

Saturday, June 7

Lots of pick-up on yesterday's *Guardian* splash on a briefing note Peter M did re TB and GB during the '94 leadership contest, on which GB had scribbled 'change'. It was not much of a document but such was the media interest in TB/GB chemistry that it was reproduced in most papers with various interpretations. Peter M was adamant he wasn't responsible and if there was a gainer out of this, it was GB,

[1] Taylor would chair the Commons Intelligence and Security Committee Inquiry into the published intelligence assessments of Iraqi WMD capacity, including the claim made in the September 2002 dossier that WMD could be launched within forty-five minutes. The committee's eventual report would describe the 45-minute claim as 'unhelpful', lacking context and assessment. Though the ISC would conclude editorial changes had been made within Number 10, Campbell would be exonerated from Gilligan's charge of having 'sexed up' the document.

because it showed him both as Mr Fairness and Mr 'I'm in charge'. TB was worried about the euro and I briefed the *Observer*, based on TB, JP and GB interventions at Cabinet, to the effect that the idea of a referendum in this parliament was still on the agenda. I told Neil [Kinnock] that the line would be 'yes but not yet' and he was happy enough with that. I also told him about leaving, and he said I should leave if I wanted, but he was worried about it.

WMD was still rumbling on with the BBC driving it as hard as they could and we were bracing for more Sunday stuff, a lot of which basically directed at me, e.g. David Clark [former special adviser to Robin Cook] in the *Mail on Sunday*, AC must go. The *Sunday Times* went back to the old dossier and why we didn't publish it. The *Sunday Telegraph* led on a so-called apology from me to Richard Dearlove re the [February 2003] dodgy dossier, the *Indy* talked of the spies recording all the pressure put on them, and so it went on. I felt I was being royally set up for a fall.

The Sundays arrived, ghastly, full of absolute shit about me, which would keep the story going. Also I'd been invited by FAC [Foreign Affairs Committee] and ISC to give evidence so it was going to be a grim few weeks. I worked out a line with Danny Pruce re the *Sunday Telegraph* – it was not the case at all about an apology, but that I had made clear to those who produced the [February 2003] dossier they should have acknowledged the author of the article [Ibrahim al-Marashi] and I assured agencies that greater care would be taken about anything that impacted on them or their work or their reputation. Of course, the BBC just took that as a green light to say that we had said that we had abused the intelligence.

Sunday, June 8

Ludicrously, my 'apology' to SIS was leading the news and being conflated into a sense that it was an apology over the main [September 2002] WMD dossier rather than – the reality – that it was about the so-called dodgy dossier [February 2003] about which I'd accepted mistakes were made, sent a letter to the system about it, and on which Omand suggested new procedures. But it was an outrage the way the BBC was twisting this. Anyone listening to their bulletins would think I'd apologised – all I had done was give assurances – and that I'd admitted we abused intelligence material – I didn't. We were going through a totally mad phase.

The first call of the day was from GB who wanted to know what to say on *Frost* and we agreed it was best to get on to the bigger theme of WMD and why we did the right thing. I explained the line and the fact that this was the second dossier they were talking about. In the event there was very little about it, mainly Europe and the euro, he was pretty good, very strong and confident, pushing a pro-European line and the effect was pretty good. I called Richard Dearlove on the way to Calum's tennis match, said I was really dismayed that our exchanges were leaked and twisted in the *Sunday Telegraph*. He was in Cornwall, said he could not recall an apology, not at least a letter, felt there may have been something verbal. Then he said that he may have told the ISC he had had an apology. I also told him that some of the papers said he and Eliza [Manningham-Buller, director general of the Security Service, MI5] had threatened to resign. He said that was totally untrue. He was actually more concerned at news that he was going to be Master at Pembroke College [Cambridge] was going to break. I agreed with Richard that he would deny the resignation story and re the apology we just had to put out the line that we had not had major rows but that somebody was stirring it.

JR, Hilary A and Tessa all called during the day, just to say they would do anything they could to help. Hilary said Dennis Skinner [Labour MP] had called offering support but also saying 'Don't trust spies, they're treacherous.' JR said whenever ministers got into trouble, I would organise operations to help them, and did I want him to get one organised for me? Hilary said much the same. Then a call from Margaret Beckett who was doing media in the afternoon and who said that it was an accolade that they kept coming at me, and it was because I did the job well that they went for me. I said I had been interested to see how pro EMU she had been, far more positive than she used to be. She said it was partly the views developed at the DTI. She felt the assessment was more negative than the tests.

The *Mail on Sunday* had done a story that CB was going for an Olympics job and TB wanted her to go to the PCC. The trouble was there was something in it. He put her on to me, and she was very defensive, just said 'What's the problem?' I said we just needed to know, because we were asked about it. We agreed to say she was not interested in running the bid but others had been keen that she would help as appropriate.

Monday, June 9

Most of the papers were reasonably low-key on the AC 'apology', apart from the *Mail* which splashed on it and was its usual vile self. Blunkett said on *The Politics Show* [BBC] yesterday that we shouldn't have done the second dossier and called for an apology. I was reasonably curt, said it was obvious he had to find a use for some

Sheffield steel. Hilary A and Sally said the PLP were virtually solid for me and that Dennis Skinner had been going round the place saying 'Who do you trust? AC or a spy? He is one of ours.' The euro was obviously leading the news and we had set it up OK. The *FT* had done 'GB sells advantages of the euro'. Mike White [*Guardian*] talked of a change of gear.

The statement was still a bit ambiguous though and the Q&A revealed the tensions between them. TB felt the statement had come along but he was still worried. He called Jonathan and me up there at 8, both of us in running or cycling gear. Jonathan was his usual jovial self. 'Surprised you are still here,' he said. TB said he was not yet sure GB was going to go for this. Jonathan said how do you guarantee he won't just do the same thing again next year? TB said he would know in a matter of weeks if this was serious or not, and if it wasn't, he would have to move him. We talked a bit about the reshuffle and TB was dreading having to sack Derry, who he was sure would take it very badly. I was working with Ed, Jeremy and Peter H on a Q&A and material for the press conference tomorrow.

I saw Jonathan to tell him I was definitely leaving now. He said TB had mentioned it, so maybe he had accepted it. Jonathan felt sure I would regret it. He said he knew that he would. He reckoned I would have a long period of decompression and he was sure the business appointments people would be very difficult. He said he had always felt I was like an extra battery for TB, and he would lose extra power. I spoke to David Omand who, like everyone else, was feeling that DIS [Defence Intelligence Staff] were probably responsible for the briefings. I said to him the only thing that could be seen as an apology were my exchanges with him re the handling of intelligence post the dodgy dossier.

C called later to say he had been through all the correspondence and there was no apology. He was glad he had denied the resignation story. I was of course not sure who would be at it, but somebody was. I went over to the Commons for the GB statement on the euro, which was OK-ish but the Tories seemed to unsettle him and he wasn't clear. [Shadow Chancellor Michael] Howard was strong. TB called me straight away and asked me what I thought. I said it didn't work. No, he said, it didn't. He just wasn't clear. He was pointing both ways and people picked up the tension. The pro columnists and commentators were very dismissive. Ed Balls and I agreed it hadn't gone terribly well. It had been a big day, but we had not really taken the big step forward that we planned. IDS wrote to TB saying that I should appear before the ISC and the FAC, underlining that this was now a political campaign. Sally felt the more obvious that was, the more support I would get.

Tuesday, June 10

Press pretty grim. The pro press were very disappointed, the *FT* scathing, while the antis remained aggressive. As GB said, we don't have a single newspaper supporting us on the position we set out yesterday. I ran in, up to see TB and Jonathan in the flat. TB was in shorts and a T-shirt, making toast, though at least with marmalade rather than the usual olive oil. He said the problem was lack of clarity. It just wasn't clear where we were going [on EMU policy] so people felt we were saying the same as in '97 or '99. GB was also throwing in all this stuff about the housing market and TB couldn't see how it was going to be possible to move on it before an election. We went through likely difficult questions. I said what do you say to the question – 'how long will it take to remove the obstacles to the euro?' 'The best way would be to get out a gun, shoot the obstacle and then have a reshuffle,' he said. He was no longer in any doubt that GB was still slowing it down deliberately. 'It's the dead hand, the paralysis of progress.'

We discussed the requests from the FAC and the ISC for TB and me to go to their inquiries into WMD. TB was clear that I shouldn't go, and that he should only go to the [select committee chairs] Liaison Committee. Then a chat with him and GB on the euro. You could tell from his confident body language that GB was where he wanted to be. He was also making clear that if we wanted to make the necessary housing-market changes, that could include a tax on housing, and lots of other things that would not be palatable. TB was sitting behind his desk asking perfectly reasonable questions and GB suddenly got up and stood over him. 'We have to stick to the language of the statement.'

I was saying that we, i.e. Number 10, had got too focused on 'referendum possible this parliament' and had therefore set ourselves up for defeat in the eyes of the media. GB was saying we should get back on to a message about Europe as a whole. I said the day after a statement on the euro, that would be seen as a retreat. GB was being very warm to me which meant he felt confident and at the press conference he was much more relaxed than TB who was twiddling with his pen too much, though afterwards he felt it was worth doing. *The Times* came in for lunch and Sally and I were passing each other notes about how bored we were.

TB spoke to Jeremy Greenstock who agreed to do the Iraq job, despite his reservations. News broke that Manchester United were prepared to sell [David] Beckham to Barcelona.[1] Alex [Ferguson] called later from the south of France and said he had definitely played his last game, and that his people had been in negotiation with Real Madrid for months. As far as he was concerned, the sooner they got the money for new players the better. He said even in France, he was picking up how much they were throwing at me at the moment. He said the one thing you and I both appreciate is pressure and it looks to me like they want to go for you till they've got you. He said the important thing was still to stay in control over when and how I went. I watched the news for once and Andy Marr was basically a television columnist now.

Wednesday, June 11

Things just hadn't worked on the euro and TB was pretty fed up when we went up for the PMQs pre-meeting. He was confident though we could get into the Tories on 'in or out' of Europe. But in terms of a gear change, it hadn't worked, and the judgement was settling that GB had basically thwarted him. TB feared we were making the wrong decision for the wrong reasons. He thought the Tories would come at us today on trust/WMD and/or trust/division/euro. We discussed the reshuffle. Alan Milburn had been to see TB on Monday and told him that he was going to leave. He had spoken to Sally first, who also told him I was thinking of leaving and during the day I had various conversations with him. He said I may think he was the last person to say this, but he really thought I shouldn't go. He said everyone knew the stuff about me was bollocks but he really didn't think I should go at a time I was under pressure. He had told very few people about his own situation and asked me what I thought he should say. I said that he should say that he faced a choice between career and family and chose family, that it was not political but personal. He said he was sad but convinced it was the right thing. Alan's decision was going to be a big talking point and it would be presented as a blow to TB. Alan said he felt wretched doing it now but he felt he had no choice. TB said he felt it made it a bit more difficult for me to go straight away. I suggested Hilary A for the job.

I decided to go for a letter of apology from the *Sunday Telegraph* over the 'apology' story at the weekend. John Scarlett said it had been a real eye-opener to him how newspapers could write whatever they

[1] Though the two clubs announced a possible deal, Beckham subsequently went to Real Madrid for a transfer fee of £25 million.

wanted. PMQs was fine, and TB/GB did OK at the PLP, with people feeling they were up for it, though Peter M seemingly embarrassed himself by doing a long apology to GB re his recent comments. TB said afterwards it was a real lapse of judgement. Greenstock said yes to TB to go to Iraq after John Sawers. TB went off to Paris for dinner with Chirac.

Thursday, June 12

TB reckoned the Chirac dinner last night went well. He had found him much warmer than usual, wanting to put Iraq behind them and work together closely. TB felt it should be possible to reshape Britain's future in the EU but we had to seize it. Jonathan, Sally, David Hanson, Hilary A and I were going through the list pre reshuffle. Through the day we had all the usual stuff. Sorting out the big changes first, then going through the list, endless discussion. Messages coming through, for example, about [junior minister in the Lord Chancellor's Department] Yvette Cooper's very high expectations for herself. For health, we had been thinking of Hain – Simon Stevens and Alan both opposed. Hewitt – Hilary A opposed. Reid – but the problem was his Scottishness [health being a devolved matter in Scotland]. TB though felt that wasn't insurmountable, and he wanted a Blairite moderniser in there. The changes at the Lord Chancellor's Department, not least to the courts, took up a lot of discussion, and I knew TB was dreading the Derry discussions.

TB saw JP who told us he had just been with GB who was pushing for a big job for Douglas [Alexander] and also for Michael Wills [junior Home Office minister], though not in the Treasury. TB then saw GB, who was pretty thunderous about the whole thing. After he had left, TB said that despite everything, he was still prepared to help him become leader, but he had to work with him on the euro and public services. If he didn't, he would fight another election and eventually put him out. He didn't really want to fight another election, and as things stood, only GB could make him.

I spent part of the day drafting resignation letters. Cabinet was pretty surreal because everyone knew there was going to be a reshuffle. Several people now knew about Alan, pretty much everyone knew about Derry and yet on they went with a discussion about Europe, the Middle East, Congo, Iraq. TB said the UK European Convention team had done a brilliant job. *Le Monde* had been running the line that we had pretty much bulldozed our way to getting everything we wanted. Afterwards, Alan came to my office and we finalised the letter. I said there would be all manner of conspiracy theories, political, financial, sexual, you name it. He said it was none of that, he would be full of regrets but it was the right thing to do. He had another go at persuading me not to leave. I had actually been thinking about whether to do my own announcement today. I discussed it with Sally and she seemed upset about it. We got the Milburn announcement out for the lunchtimes. He did interviews while we had another session on the reshuffle.

TB saw Derry. He and I had a perfectly amicable discussion re families before he went in. Previously, TB had argued he needed to shake things up and put an elected MP in charge of the new department, so when he told Derry it would be Charlie F [Lord Falconer], he was particularly pissed off. 'You are getting rid of me and putting in another peer, that's not exactly what I expected.' As he left, he looked pretty miserable.

He then saw Helen Liddell, then Reid who was not immediately too keen on health, wanted to think about it. These reshuffles were always awful. During a break, I asked TB why we didn't announce my departure at the same time. We were out on the terrace. He asked why I was so sure I wanted to go. I said I wasn't really working as hard or as well as usual. Most days I woke up feeling depressed and didn't think it would improve. For ten minutes or so, he seemed almost up for it. Then he said it wasn't a sensible day to do it, because it would give another boost to GB. He was also not convinced that I was one hundred per cent sure, and said he thought I would get a second wind before long. He sacked [Michael] Meacher [environment minister] by phone, who made clear he would be difficult. He didn't do Nick Brown [minister for work] because he was on *Question Time* tonight. We finished by 7.30, with another day of it ahead tomorrow. Eight-mile run.

Friday, June 13

The Milburn announcement seemed to be taken at face value. Despite all the crony attacks, the Charlie appointment seemed to be OK. But there was a sense of things being a bit of a mess re Scotland and Wales.[1] I was in for eight then out on the terrace with the others to go through the list again. We needed a few more sackings to make room – Lewis Moonie [defence], Barbara Roche [social exclusion and equality]. Tessa Blackstone [higher education] as well. TB wanted to

[1] The offices of Secretary of State for Scotland and Wales were combined with other portfolios, Alistair Darling taking Scotland and transport, and Peter Hain taking Wales and Leader of the House of Commons

promote Kim Howells [culture, moving to higher education] and wanted Des Browne [junior Northern Ireland minister] to do asylum but Blunkett came in and argued for Bev Hughes [Home Office minister] to stay with him. David could be very difficult and egotistical at these reshuffle times.

GB, who for years had been a nightmare at reshuffles, was relatively quiet. His attempts to protect Nick Brown were pretty half-hearted. He did his usual appeal for Douglas to go into the Cabinet – 'Don't be ridiculous,' said JP – and he was of course arguing for the promotion of Michael Wills. Hilary A and Sally were regaling us with stories of how Michael would not even sit with his officials on the same part of a train. TB said to GB 'If he's so good why not take him to the Treasury?'

GB said it was 'Not appropriate I'm afraid.' We spent most of the morning going through the lists again and again, making sure there were no glaring mistakes, Jonathan keeping tabs on the numbers. We finally got Estelle who said she would think about the arts minister job. We had a hiccup with [Baroness] Patricia Scotland who wasn't sure about the job [minister for the criminal justice system] with Charlie but he persuaded her. Lewis Moonie was difficult. Meacher made a few threatening noises. Barbara Roche very unhappy.

We shifted Yvette [Cooper] to ODPM [Office of the Deputy Prime Minister] and she had learned from last year, in that she didn't complain. He sacked Nick Brown by phone. Nick said he would 'continue to support him and the government' – joke. Then getting people with new jobs to come through the door – Margaret Hodge [minister for children], Malcolm Wicks [minister for work and pensions], Chris Pond [junior work and pensions minister], Hazel Blears [Minister of State, Home Office] – all fine, real freshness and enthusiasm. Hilary A was an absolute brick throughout all this, softening people up when she knew they were on their way out, keeping in touch with all the Cabinet ministers about who they did and didn't want. Sally also had a real toughness about her in these situations. Then another hiccup re Tommy McAvoy [government pairing whip] threatening to walk re Bob Ainsworth [Home Office minister] being made deputy chief whip. Then Melanie Johnson [moving from minister for competition and consumers to public health] wanted a long conversation with him about this and that concern, and he was starting to get frazzled, asking if they all thought he had nothing to do but listen to their outpourings.

By the time we started doing the bulk of appointments by phone, he had got it down to a very curt 'I'd like you to join the government as X. You should call Y minister and get the drill. There you are, well done.' The Tories went on a line that he was a dictator because there had been no consultation about changes at the Lord Chancellor's Department. They felt they were on to something with it being a bit of a constitutional mess, while we were trying to get it pitched as a dividing line of privilege vs modernisation and change. I had a bad phone call with Dominic Lawson [*Sunday Telegraph* editor] who was refusing to apologise over the spooks story. Then talking to various incoming and outgoing ministers. I felt Alan Johnson to universities [minister for higher education, having left school at fifteen] was the best move. Brian Wilson [former energy minister] was very down. 'What do you need to do? Do you have to creep and cause trouble like some?' He said he had always been supportive. I said I think TB would admit man management was not his forte. Brian was also of the view that until TB sacked GB, he would never get the government he wanted.

Saturday, June 14

It was now pretty much a given in the media at least that the reshuffle had been 'botched'. Ian McCartney was out and about defending it but the general feeling was we had fucked up. TB called, clearly pissed off. The truth was the press was in total kicking mode. There was no debate about whether the reform of the LCD was a good thing or a bad thing, it was all about the handling. TB said of course if Alan [Milburn] had not gone we wouldn't have needed the other changes, but we hadn't remotely prepared the ground. I was feeling ground down and fucked off. I tried my best with the Sundays but they had written us off on it. I asked TB if he wanted me to work on Tuesday's [Fabian Society] speech to try to get things back on an even keel and he said no, they'll just say it's all spin. We now had a press who could only operate at the level of hyperbole, frenzy and venom. Every story had to be bigger than the last one.

Neil and Glenys were round for lunch. I walked in and Fiona said 'bad news'. She said did I remember a couple of years ago when she had sent an email to the wrong address, and the *Mail on Sunday* seemed to have it. We tracked it down and in it, she was absolutely vile about Anji [Hunter], her influence, her undermining of Fiona and Sally. Judging from what the *Mail* were putting to us, my impression was they didn't have the email as such, but knew of the content, but it was another piece of soap opera we could do without. Anji was pretty upset about it when I told her. Dealing with it meant I didn't really have a proper chat with Neil and Glenys.

Neil said he thought I should be the next European commissioner, which I thought was pretty crazy. He felt I would do it better than any of the other names being touted, but I felt it was a non-starter. Glenys felt the problem with the reshuffle was that it felt like we weren't gripping things in the way we used to, and she thought that was because I was fed up with it. Peter M called, said much the same and added that the problem was not just the presentation but the substance of the reshuffle and he blamed 'Baroness Morgan of Huyton' [Sally Morgan]. He said her main talent was to undermine and she had poisoned TB against his return and got others to do so. I said TB had been thinking of bringing him back but he felt that both his speech to the women's lobby and his 'apology' at the PLP made it very difficult. I suggested to him he still had a judgement problem about himself.

Charlie Falconer was on *Frost* tomorrow. We agreed things had not been well handled but we had to get it back on to some proper dividing lines. The Sundays were on to the theme that the reshuffle shifted the balance to GB but it overlooked the fact that Clare had gone. Charlie asked me what my own intentions were. He said he was very worried that if I left, there would be a new template created by the media for the government, namely TB fucks up after AC's gone, and creates more space for GB.

Sunday, June 15

Charlie fine on *Frost*. TB was pretty down though, felt the media was vile at the moment. It was just one of those periods of malaise and we had to get through it. Jack Straw called re the dossier Q&A for the FAC, which was going to be the next big dumping on me. There was a lot of shit coming my way again. George Pascoe-Watson [*Sun*] called and asked me outright if I was planning to leave in the next few months. I dodged it. I had decided I was just going to pick a day soon, and go for it. The consensus in the Sundays was that the wheels were starting to come off a bit. TB said 'They'll go into total hysteria when they know you're going.' Maybe.

Monday, June 16

The reshuffle was still rumbling on. GB's people were briefing that he had secured positions for Scotland and Wales in Cabinet. Hoon, Hewitt and Tessa were all saying to Sally that it was a dreadful mess, but she took that to mean they had all wanted health. But the truth was that we hadn't really thought it through and now we had problems of definition. We also had the PLP getting a bit jumpy re competence. Whatever else they said about the centre, at least they thought we usually ran a pretty efficient operation. TB seemed a bit down at his morning meeting and was asking what he could have done differently. Anyway, it was done and now Charlie F had to make the thing work, and Reid [replacing Milburn as Health Secretary] had to establish himself for competence and leadership.

What we had really lacked was political narrative and momentum which was why I was arguing for a proper political speech [to the Fabian Society] tomorrow. Peter H and Patrick Diamond [policy adviser] had done what everyone thought was an excellent draft. Everyone, that is apart from TB, who felt it risked sparking a reaction similar to the [September 1999] forces of conservatism speech. He felt it was too simplistic about left and right. We argued about it on and off through the day, using a draft of my speech-briefing note. It started with us talking about closing the progressive deficit and ended with a top line that he was holding firm to reform, which was kind of heard-it-all-before territory. He never wanted to go for the right in isolation. Through the afternoon, the draft went backwards. Peter and Patrick had based it on the progress made on the themes of his '94, leadership acceptance speech, but he wanted the basic argument to be all about commitment to future reform.

As I was about to leave for home, I bumped into TB who had just seen a group of MPs. We went into his office. He said he was really worried about the reshuffle because we had mishandled it and it was really unsettling the troops. I felt he was overdoing it, and exaggerating how bad it was. He said he was feeling very discombobulated, about me going, about Peter M – they had dinner last night – and by the constant feuding with GB. He felt tired and couldn't get focused. Tessa had also warned him that there was a feeling he didn't really look after his own in a way that GB looked after his people, the same point Brian Wilson had made. He looked pretty ground down. I felt really bad now about leaving, but I still knew it was the right thing to do.

Tuesday, June 17

We had managed to get TB's Fabian [Society conference] speech up as a lead story but inevitably they were seeing it as a post-botched reshuffle attempt to get back on the front foot, and with Robin and Clare giving evidence to the select committee we were never going to get an easy run at it. I kept trying to assure TB that it was all a bit of a frenzy that would pass, but he seemed really worried. The PLP was definitely edgy. Hilary [Armstrong] told him that if he didn't bring back the Hunting Bill for a third reading soon we would not have a hope in hell of winning the foundation hospital vote. TB said sane people just will not understand how we can put at risk our whole public service agenda over hunting. Hilary said he had to understand that hunting went deep, and was symbolic, also that even with it we couldn't be sure of winning on foundation hospitals. She was very straightforward with him, and a very solid citizen. She was one of the few people I knew who seemed able to combine being close to the end of her tether with total niceness. Even Jack Cunningham [former Cabinet minister], who called me for some briefing for interviews, said we looked really ragged, that it felt like 'the opposite of the Midas touch'. He said we had to get a grip pretty damn quick. Mark Mardell [BBC] even talked on the news about 'a whiff of decay'.

TB said he wasn't clear about a way forward at the moment. The atmosphere was about as bad as it could be for the speech he was making. Rory got his first byline doing work experience at *The Times* on a story about Gaddafi's son and was enjoying winding them all up about the fact he had known in advance Milburn was leaving. I had a flare-up with Rebekah [Wade] because Trevor Kavanagh, absurdly, was trying to run the line that the speech was a warning about future tax rises.

We set off for the speech. 'I suppose "Blair relaunch backfires" will be the headline,' TB said. Probably. I watched the speech but I could tell it was going to get a bad press. The most important thing now was that we get IDS on the floor tomorrow, paint them as the people who resist all change that benefits the many. TB was very down, and hinting again it was because of me going. He called again later. Even if we had fucked up the reshuffle, the reaction was totally overblown. He said the press has become a real drag on the country, but I'm not sure what we do about it. It sometimes feels like living in the reverse of a police state. Anything the government does it automatically bad, anyone who attacks us automatically good. Tomorrow was going to be tough. He had to wipe the floor with IDS or we could be in a bit of trouble.

Wednesday, June 18

The speech coverage was pretty crap, tax being the line in several papers, ludicrously. TB was pretty fed up with it all. We all pretty much accepted the reshuffle had been fucked up and we now needed to get into a good old-fashioned tribal war with the Tories about it. He looked pretty nervy before we went over [for PMQs, then a statement on changes to government functions caused by the reshuffle] but he did fine. IDS was dreadful so the focus was on him in the end. I had a bizarre email exchange with Richard Desmond [*Express* proprietor]. I complained about the *Express* splash on the speech – Blair knifes the middle class – and sent him the speech, asked him to read it, and tell me how they get that headline out of it. He sent an email saying he totally agreed and signed it off 'Fuck editors, fuck Brown, yes to Tony and Alastair.' I had a meeting then with David Hill, Hilary C [Hill's partner] and Fiona to discuss whether he would do my job.

Then up for a meeting with TB. Peter M was there, and said when you boiled all our problems down, they went to the TB/GB fault line. TB said you either had to manage it or use the nuclear option but we had to realise the nuclear option had the potential to be disastrous for all of us. He felt in the end he had to manage him, get him to agree to his strategy. He certainly felt the ground had shifted a bit and that the Cabinet was different post reshuffle. Peter also felt we had to separate out the total oppositionalists from the malcontents. Above all, Blairites had to get a sense he still had energy and policy worth fighting for. Peter felt there was a lack of project, a lack of politics, a lack of communication strategy. Party and government were too much in silos. He was right, and what I felt in myself was that I lacked the energy to do it all again. Got home in time to see the news on GB's Mansion House speech. Back to square one re the euro.

Thursday, June 19

TB got a fairly good press out of yesterday's reshuffle statement but there was no doubt there was something of a sea change going on. TB set off [for Greece, EU summit at Porto Carras], pissed off that neither I, nor Sally, nor Jonathan, who was in Belfast, was going with him. The morning meeting was focused on Greece and the coverage of Beckham was massive after his transfer to Real Madrid. Just before Cabinet, David Hanson told me that his intelligence was that the FAC were looking to clear TB and Jack but have a go at me, particularly over the dodgy dossier. He said he feared an all-party whack at me would be really bad news. I had a bad feeling about it, sensed they were really going to go for me.

I talked to Neil [Kinnock], said I was ready to go and felt instinctively that I had to do it soon. He said I should ride it out. But when I told him my worries about the FAC, he changed his tune, said maybe do it sooner because 'with our ridiculous media they will treat it like a mini Nagasaki near the Thames' and it will wipe everything else out. He said if he was TB, he would be shitting himself. He said his feeling was always that I should have been doing Jonathan's job and overseeing somebody else doing mine. He felt me leaving was bad for TB but right for me. 'You're taking too much shit and you don't need it or deserve it.'

Cabinet was dull and short. We were facing difficulties putting legislation through because of the Lords. Gareth Williams kicked off by saying 'I bring you greetings from the men in tights.' But GB wasn't in the mood for joking, as he was still raging at them trying to get more powers over his taxation. Jack briefed on the European Council issues. He described [Romano] Prodi as 'a rampant federalist' who seemingly had said 'I want to kill myself' when he saw the draft Convention, because it wasn't federalist enough. There was quite an interesting discussion about how we counter, via patriotism, their attempt to use Euroscepticism to hit the patriotic buttons.

I had a good long meeting with Peter M and we agreed an outline plan based on the policy ideas coming forward. He felt TB had slightly lost the values part of our big arguments. Andy Marr called to warn me the Sundays were doing a story that I was planning to leave. I said nothing. Then he called me again later and said he had been told by a member of the government that I was definitely going to go. I said nothing had been finally decided. Meanwhile the FAC, because some Labour MPs were missing, voted to summon me because Gilligan said he'd seen documents showing that I'd asked for changes, and also re the second dossier. I called Tom Kelly who was with TB in Greece. TB said to hold firm, get Andrew Turnbull to reply to the committee and say that I should not go. TB said we should co-operate with the ISC and that was that. I meanwhile had done a note to Jack S re how to handle the dossier issue. I told TB of the rumours doing the rounds that I was going to go in July or September. He said 'Why can't you deny it?' I said that's difficult and clearly people are talking. Very curtly, pretty cool, he said 'I'm afraid that's what happens.' Both Fiona and Godric were of the view that some of us were being bugged by someone flogging stuff to the media, or by the media per se. It was extraordinary how many private conversations were getting out.

Friday, June 20

Just when we thought things might be calming down a bit, I woke to the radio news leading on Peter Hain saying that we should look to raising the top rate of tax. He had briefed the *Mirror* in advance of his Bevan lecture and they had splashed with 'tax the rich'. He had also briefed the *FT* on his continuing support for PR [proportional representation]. Why do we fucking bother? If there is one thing we didn't need right now, it was disarray, on an unnecessary debate about tax. I called Hain, who was still in bed and I said this thing was raging, leading the news and [Michael] Howard was out saying it showed Labour red in tooth and claw. He sounded a bit detached from it all, said he was just trying to get up a debate about inequality and he was amazed it was going so big. I said we should call *Today* and offer to go on, make absolutely clear we are not going back to tax and spend and this is all part of the problem of a political debate conducted constantly in the media at the level of frenzy and hyperbole.

He went on and pretty much regurgitated the same message. The problem was he was relying on the offending paragraphs that had been pre-briefed and I told him we would have to rewrite the speech making clear no minister can undermine HMG tax policy in this way. I agreed with Balls and Austin that we would have to turn it into a story about process and discipline. I spoke to TB who was about to do a doorstep. He was not happy. Our top line was a clear commitment not to raise the top rate, and TB said he had not spent ten years changing the Labour Party to go back now. The problem was it just looked like another dent in TB's authority. Then the frenzy got worse when Charles Clarke seemed to say – though in fact he didn't – the same thing. Pat McF's view was that Hain never said anything without thinking it through whereas Peter M was more of the view that it was stupidity.

I did a long note for TB setting out what we needed to do in the next few weeks up to conference. He was aware of how bad things were but clear that he could see a way forward. Philip's view was that we had lost any sense of political project and that the party was getting silly and complacent because there was no sense the Tories could get anywhere near us. By the time we had finished with Hain's speech, all of the difficult stuff on tax and PR was out. There was a bit of talk around that he was trying to position himself as a possible future leadership challenger from the left. I was pleased with the note, eight pages, emphasis on values, the need to reimpose strategic themes, tying in existing and future policy and events. TB got back late, though he left the summit before it finished. The Europe stuff had gone well but Hain gave us a problem we could have done without. For once the phone was going infrequently, though the Sundays were still chasing me re departure.

Saturday, June 21

I hadn't slept well. I was avoiding answering the phone other than to the office because by now all the broadcasters and half the Sundays were trying to ask me if I was going. Now was probably not the right time. It would be seen as bad for TB and bad for me if I went under a cloud. The *Independent on Sunday* had a story with quotes from Eric Illsley [Labour MP on FAC] that they were going to go for me personally re the Iraq dossier and I felt the best thing for me to do was to go to give evidence and get my retaliation in first. I was sure of my ground, so why not? I did a note to Jack saying that when he gave evidence, there were two central points that needed to get over re the dodgy dossier. One, I was unaware of the plagiarism. Two, that it had nothing to do with the people named in the email about it, like Alison [Blackshaw]. We desperately needed to reposition on this and I was thinking the best way was for me to surprise them by saying I positively wanted to give evidence.

Sunday, June 22

I did the Hampstead 10k in forty-six minutes. Tough, but really enjoyed it. I had been up early to do a note to Jack S on the *Independent on Sunday*, and called re the same. I spoke to TB, first re the general scene, on which he felt we had been here before and we could get out of it. I said we had to keep going on the long term and ignore the media. I also said I was worried about the FAC and thought I should go. I sent him a note explaining why, and copied it to Jack. I said to TB I feared none of the questions and that we had to get to a point where they accepted we did nothing wrong regarding the first dossier, made mistakes re the second. I said I was confident, really felt I should take the heat on it and get it into a better place. If not, the report would come out the day before the Liaison Committee and that would be a real problem for him as well as me. I thought the best thing to do was a note to TB, which I did, giving the reasons why we should break the convention and then give it to Donald Anderson [Labour MP, FAC chairman] as a letter. Jack S agreed with me I should appear because it was clear that a lot of the evidence given so far related to communications issues. TB was persuaded first by me and then by Jack that it was the right thing to do. Jack spoke to Donald Anderson and we agreed a process, that he'd write to Donald, and I subsequently gave him a memo.

TB sensed that me going to the FAC would go very big, but I was in no doubt I had to do it, try to get my reputation in a better place and I felt more confident if I could do that myself. Melanne Verveer [Hillary Clinton aide] came round for tea, advising Fiona she should get out because Cherie had made her position untenable, advising me to get out and get going on memoirs. She thought I could do well on the US speaking circuit. She said Bush was still getting away with murder because he had brilliantly hijacked the security issue and the Democrats didn't really know how to handle it. Clinton's view was that Bush was a far better politician than people gave him credit for. There was an intruder at Prince William's twenty-first birthday bash which gave us a massive news sponge.[1]

Monday, June 23

The William situation was still the main attraction but by the time of the eleven o'clock, it was clear I would be a strong second. I had redone a memo and Jack's letter to the FAC. At the office meeting, TB looked dreadful and there were long pauses as he went through his weekend note, the usual list of the usual subjects, the usual hits on departments. He was getting more and more frustrated at what he called the lack of radical policy direction in the public services. Andrew Adonis would say that we were doing this, trying that, pushing on this, but TB was irritated. Geoff Mulgan [policy adviser] had meanwhile done an excellent note, which was a brutal assessment of our lack of long-term strategy on policy. He said we had lost authority at the centre, that Number 10 had got bigger but less effective, and that our overall narrative was no longer clear. He gave lessons from other midterm governments around the world, and said that they sometimes got renewal through brutal changes of personnel.

As I read it, eight pages of pretty good stuff, I noted Jonathan could hardly keep his eyes open, I was moving on in my mind already, and the contributions around the table were pretty rambling and anecdotal. It was pretty dispiriting. Towards the end I said to TB 'For God's sake try not to look so miserable. It's not as bad as all that. When we have an agenda and we just get on with it and ignore the press, we are always strong.' But he just kept asking if the overall plan was OK. Pat and I were arguing that we needed a clearer message – it was not about choice but about our values. Then I said: are you OK for us to announce me going to the FAC and he said he was not so sure any more. Someone had got at him, but I enlisted Andrew Turnbull, who persuaded him it was the way to avoid the Liaison Committee being about me/WMD/trust.

So Jack and I then finished the letter to Donald Anderson and got it in time for the eleven o'clock briefing. TK briefed on it, and it ran

[1] The intruder, Aaron Barschak, self-styled 'comedy terrorist', had gained easy access to Prince William's twenty-first birthday party, dressed as Osama Bin Laden in a ball gown.

for most of the day. We had a party meeting, TB again casting around for support and Hilary A being very clear about problems in the PLP. I was now totally focused on FAC, reading lots. Clare Sumner and Catherine Rimmer [Number 10 Research and Information Unit] were doing lots of work for me. Then to a meeting with Michael Jay and Dickie Stagg [FCO official] to go through what MJ would say tomorrow when he appeared with Jack, then back to see John S, Clare Summer, Tom and Godric to begin to go through the difficult questions.

Alison [Blackshaw] was back from holiday and getting me out all the files and I was beginning to work out all the answers to the difficult questions, for example [Ibrahim] al-Marashi's claim [as the plagiarised source for the February 2003 dossier] that his life had been put in danger. Hilary A said some of our members on the committee were worried. They felt I could easily deal with Gilligan, but al-Marashi was not so easy. Clare had established who in the CIC was responsible for not telling people where it all came from, but we agreed I would take responsibility at the FAC.

Tuesday, June 24

Fairly big coverage of me going to the committee. Vile in the *Mail* needless to say but not bad overall. I spent most of the day with Clare and Catherine, who were terrific. Clare had got to the bottom of the whole [February 2003 dossier] thing. I spent several hours going over and over again the text of my memo which we eventually got to the FAC by 6.15pm. Jack S was keen that I apologise upfront. I agreed, but later came to the view that I should not and said it was because I was worried it would leak. My strategy was to apologise to Dr al-Marashi for the mistake and then demand an apology from the BBC not just for me but for the PM, etc. John Scarlett was getting my memo put through the agencies.

I saw TB, whose main interest seemed to be how the FAC would impinge on him. He gave little advice at all. At least Jack was suggesting changes and improvements. Jack also came over, very friendly, said the most important thing was that I was nice and polite and didn't go for them. Then to a series of TB meetings on political strategy. He was infuriating me going on about our lack of plan, and I could tell he was as infuriated with me as I was with him, because I was constantly banging on about values, saying he was too technocratic on reform. TB said we had alienated the left on Iraq, the right on Europe, the party on public service reform. Yet he felt on all three we were in the right. Our problem was we weren't explaining it properly – blah – we didn't have a proper communications plan for it – blah – so on and so forth, blah blah blah. I was pretty heavy with him, and he with me. Peter M was very good at seeing all the points where actually we agreed and by the end we kind of knew what needed to be done, by way of changing the draft plan from the weekend.

I then spent four hours with John Scarlett and Dickie Stagg to go over all the questions, etc. Meanwhile, six UK RMPs [Royal Military Policemen] were killed, which was really grim. I discussed with Neil [Kinnock], with Fraser Kemp [Labour MP] and a few others how to approach it. They all felt go for the BBC but be clinical and be forensic. John S was keen that I didn't include the agencies in any general attack on the BBC. Jack's evidence didn't go brilliantly. He said I had commissioned the paper, and the BBC said that undermined me before my appearance. But I felt confident.

Wednesday, June 25

Jack had set me up badly by saying that I had commissioned the dodgy dossier and it was 'a complete Horlicks'. He called me while I was preparing for the committee with Clare and Catherine. I said I didn't want to speak to him but I would see him at the House before PMQs. There was quiet a lot of build-up in the news, full of the usual agenda stuff. TB asked me up to the flat. He said he really wanted me to stay calm at all times and treat the committee with respect. We had worked out the right strategy, concede the apology to Dr al-Marashi, be as detailed and as full as possible, go on the BBC, broaden it, demand an apology and get up the big-picture message about the cynicism of people who say that the prime minister would go to war on the basis of this. TB and I agreed that the media were a real democratic problem, but he didn't really want to do anything.

It was an odd feeling to go out from Number 10 with lots of good wishes and with the media there for me, not TB. PMQs was pretty low-key. Afterwards TB had another private word. He said look, this is the reverse of the usual. I am telling you that you have to be calm and not get peevish. Clare S and Catherine R were brilliant in preparing me, going through the difficult questions again and again. Meeting with John Scarlett, Godric, Tom, etc. Over at the House, feeling not bad, long walk to Boothroyd Room, there were crowds outside the room, and I had to wait around the corner. I got in, slow start with [Sir] John Stanley [Conservative MP] before a break for a vote at 4. Three hours in total. I picked up after a while. I got most of my lines in, and it went pretty well. I thought the Labour MPs were reasonably helpful, I think they were glad I apologised and they went for the BBC thing pretty well. I cut my hand on the sharp object in my palm (a paper clip). It was gruelling, and I walked back exhausted, followed back by cameras, but there was a nice round of applause when I got back. I felt a lot better. Flank opened on the BBC.

Then to the Leukaemia Research reception and we got the cameras in, partly to get coverage for the charity, partly to give fresh pictures of me looking a bit more normal and less wound up than I was at the committee. The kids were brilliant. I did a good speech, and they gave me a great cartoon as a present for having raised so much. David Davis [Shadow Deputy Prime Minister] came, which was nice of him. By the time I got home, I was totally shagged out. There was loads on the news. It had been live on the news channels plus CNN. I felt the tactic of going myself had worked. TB called late, said 'Everyone was saying you did superbly, which you did. There is no Cabinet minister who could do that as well.' Audrey [Millar, Fiona's mother] called, said she liked [LBC radio talk show presenter] Nick Ferrari's line, that I don't pick fights I can't win.

Thursday, 26 June

Huge coverage in the papers and some great cartoons. Generally I was thought to have done well, though the BBC were still focusing on dissent and opposition to me. During the morning we put together a letter following [BBC director of news, Richard] Sambrook's interview in which he made further contradictory statements. I put together a letter, and got Clive Soley [Labour MP] to do a letter saying that the source should speak to Donald Anderson and, if not, Gilligan should be recalled. We were on a roll, all right yesterday and today, we had good messages of support coming through. I was up at 5 to work on the letter that I was to send to the committee to deal with their extra requests. It took hours and hours and hours. I went through all the different exchanges of correspondence with John Scarlett. It took hours for me, John, Clare and Catherine to get it sorted. I also wrote to [Greg] Dyke [BBC director general] and to Sambrook and put the Sambrook letter out to the press. I was going to nail Gilligan completely, and then the *Mail*.

Pre Cabinet, Jack S came up to me and I was very short with him and did not engage. Later I told Michael Jay I took it very personally, felt betrayed, that the FCO had basically been interested only in protecting JS and the FCO. TB called me in before Cabinet. 'You did brilliantly.' 'No help from ministers,' I said. 'You have to understand these guys are not as used to pressure as we are,' he said. 'They panic.'

I said I'd taken a lot of shit for these people and got very little back. I'd thought JS was a bit different.

At Cabinet, I was working on my supplementary letter to the FAC. They were mainly discussing Iraq and TB talking about the general situation. Ian McCartney did me proud, said that yesterday I had shown passion, values, conviction and humility and an awful lot of ministers could learn from that. He said he had watched it on the news and he hoped every party member had seen it because it showed that we believed in something. JR said something similar and then had a real whack at Peter Hain for 'launching a debate' on tax. Putin was in for lunch, which was OK as was the press conference, though it didn't really fly. The media were still obsessing about me the whole time, though we were doing pretty well. The BBC letter went well though and I felt it was turning our way a bit. TB's demeanour about the whole thing had changed. I had never had so much coverage as in the last few days but TB said it was the right thing to do, I'd have been hung out to dry if I hadn't done it. We had a farewell dinner for David Manning [moving on to be UK ambassador to Washington]. I had a nice chat with John Scarlett and his wife. Condi was over, which was quite a tribute to David. He was such a nice guy, and TB rightly paid him a very warm tribute.

Friday, June 27

Ran in, thirty-one minutes. I had been going through the FAC memo until late last night. Early in to go through it again. John Scarlett had a lot of cuts and a few changes and he was really good. We had a long discussion about whether we should be specific that I had previously pointed out an inconsistency between the text and executive summary of the 45-minute description. I decided to put in a general line in relation to the ironing out of inconsistencies. I had to leave for a speech meeting with TB, at which Peter H and I were trying again to tilt the balance towards values and away from the technocratic side of reform. TB was keen to get back on public services but we had to cut short the meeting because Derry arrived to see TB. They had bumped into each other at a state banquet recently, where Derry completely blanked him. He looked totally forlorn as he waited outside and I chatted to him for a minute or two before he went in.

Clive Soley and Phil Woolas [Deputy Leader of the Commons] were doing media defending me. There weren't that many ministers out but I don't think that meant they weren't behind me. Audrey [Millar] did however remind me of the observation that if you want a friend in politics, get a dog. I did the final memo with the last changes then sent it to Clare Sumner to get ready to send while I went with Calum and Charlie [Calum's friend] to Wimbledon. I lost my rag in the morning watching Jack's live evidence, where he was umming and aahing and when asked whether the 45-minute claim was in the first dossier, looked shifty. He did not just say yes. I had even talked to him about that point in the morning when I spoke to him at the request of John Scarlett to let him know that I HAD probably made a point to John S re forty-five minutes but it was not a request. So what the fuck was going on?

I suggested to Danny Pruce to get a note to Ed Owen [Straw's special adviser] saying that the answer was yes, and why didn't he say that? I said that I felt badly let down and this was what happened when a department cared about itself, not the government. John Williams [FCO] left a hurt message on my mobile saying it was not deliberate, though I was not so sure. But I sent him a softer message back. At Wimbledon, C called me to say he thought I'd done brilliantly at the FAC, that I'd moved the debate on and people in the agencies felt I'd done well. He said we had to win this because it was so unfair and wrong. We went for lunch at Wimbledon. Julie Kirkbride [Conservative MP] was at our table. She said she was totally supportive of me re the BBC and she agreed with pretty much everything that TB said. I said I was determined to get an apology. We watched Andy Roddick and Venus Williams [US tennis players], but I was constantly being called out.

Jack S called me after his private session at the FAC, said it went well. He asked me to understand that he'd not done it deliberately. We went in for tea when news came through that Sambrook had replied. It was real sophistry. Their line now was that it was OK to report a source even if you didn't know what he said was true. He said I had a vendetta against Gilligan and that I was intimidating the BBC. He also had a line that they would express regret if story turned out to be false. So they were both blustering and on the run. I wrote a very angry response, probably too angry. 'Weasel words, BBC standards debased beyond belief,' I really went for it. Once it was drafted, we had a conference call to discuss it.

We drove back and I listened to the BBC *Six O'Clock News* in the car. It was a total PR job on the BBC letter, and a straight hit at me. I got in to the office and Jon Snow [news anchor] had asked me to go on *Channel 4 News*. Hilary C had said no but I was tempted because I knew the story inside out. The office was split, half in favour, half against. Jonathan feared it would make me the story even more. I spoke to TB, who said do you really want to do it or don't you? I said I do. OK, be calm and be careful. The important thing is you do what is appropriate and don't go over the top. I got into the car and headed there gathering my thoughts. I was taken straight to the studio. Snow seemed not to be expecting me, but there I was. I felt I won it re the words and was able to pick him up on fact a couple of times, but I did get a bit too angry. The clips used in later bulletins were good though.

Lots of calls of support came in, including John Reid, Neil and Glenys, Philip. The office was OK, but TB said he felt I was too angry and Fiona was livid I'd done it at all. She did one of her 'you never listen, never acknowledge anyone else's views' numbers. Peter M called and said get a strategy for the weekend, keep calm, get friends and don't lose it. The Tory line on *Newsnight* [BBC] was that I'd flipped my lid and was a liability. But we kept going and I was sure we were going to win. I had the idea of calming it down by saying that we would go to the BBC Complaints Unit. Tom Kelly said it would suit their purposes, not ours.

Saturday, June 28

I was up at 5.50 and did a note to Fiona apologising that I had sent the kids home on their own and gone on. I felt it was the right thing to do, but if she thought it was a mistake, please understand the pressures, and the need I feel to be vindicated, and understand that I'll get out as soon as we are through this. I listened to Ben Bradshaw [fisheries minister, former BBC journalist] on the *Today* programme who was excellent. [John] Humphrys [presenter] was getting very childish and petulant and Ben got him to say that Gilligan DID check it with MoD. The MoD press office told us that he didn't, that all he had said to them was that he was on talking about an interview with [Adam] Ingram [Armed Forces minister] re cluster bombs, said he had a WMD story but it would not bother them. So we got Ben Bradshaw to put out a statement plus a letter to Sambrook, which was running later and kept them on the back foot.

I got some very supportive phone calls through the day. Rory answered the phone to Nick Soames [Conservative MP], who before realising it wasn't me went off on one – 'You sex god, you Adonis, you the greatest of all great men' – before Rory said 'I'm his son.' Soames was totally supportive, said keep going, these people are total shits. He said in part we had created this monster, seen it as a beast and we fed it well. But it was now out of control and we had to get the control back. He said bad journalism is like pornography. Every time you fail to check it, it gets closer to being the norm. 'Do you think my grandfather [Winston Churchill] had a spin doctor? Course he fucking did.' He said we had to win but he would be happy to speak up for me at any point. He was in great form. 'Tell the prime minister that the next time I'm called at PMQs I intend to say "What is a lifestyle guru and do I need one?"' He said he had once said that the Royal Family was like a great tree and if you hack at the roots hard enough eventually the tree will die. That is what's happening to politics thanks to our wretched media. Keep going, because they don't like it up 'em.

I spoke to Robin Oakley [CNN European political editor, formerly BBC] who said the same, that he had always considered I was straight and what was happening was wrong. Geoff Hoon called saying he wanted to be out there supporting me. John S called to say he was a bit worried about my interview. He felt I'd done so well on Wednesday, maybe I should have quit while ahead, but he also said he had spoken to C and they were all really pleased they had such a loud champion of the spooks. I told him of the extraordinary moment yesterday, like something out of a film, when I was dictating my response to Sambrook from the marquee at Wimbledon and who should walk by but a spook I recognised.

I felt we were in a much better position. I did the Sunday broadsheets. I spoke to Neil [Kinnock] and got some nice words out from him, also Alex F, Soames and Oakley. John Reid called, keen to do something, ditto Bruce Grocott. Letter from Blunkett saying don't quit. Ben Bradshaw was brilliant on the media and I told him so. He said he felt it really strongly and we really had to make this stick. TB said keep going hard for another day or two, then we leave it to the committee.

Gilligan called the MoD press office in a bit of a flap to say that the call to the press office of May 28 was indeed the only one he made. We had media outside the house the whole time but I decided to go out for a run anyway. Home for dinner with the Goulds and the Kinnocks. Neil was in one of his wonderfully over-the-top, often comic rages – at the BBC over me, at Glenys over Iraq. His big rage was at the idea of Peter M going to Brussels. The papers came. They were mixed. Some of them had MPs saying I would be cleared, others that Gilligan intended to sue. Fiona seemed a lot happier. I felt very lucky that I had friends like Neil and Glenys, Philip and Gail [Rebuck], Alex, the handful of others who were calling the whole time to help me through. I did a conference call for the Sunday broadcasts with John Reid, Margaret B, Douglas, Valerie Amos, Geoff H. JR did most of the talking. The agreed top line – one month in, one question remains, is the story true? This was getting clearer.

Sunday, June 29

TB wanted to work out an exit strategy. John Birt [former BBC director general] had suggested that I put it in the hands of the FAC and say I'll do nothing until after that, which was probably the right thing to do. He said it was important that I didn't let my emotion come into this too much. Birt drafted my letter to Sambrook, which we got out by 4pm. By then Sambrook digging in deeper by saying that they never said TB lied – what the fuck do they think saying something whilst knowing it to be untrue means? Sambrook said we'd acknowledged their source was right (!) and that the real question was where are the weapons. They were beginning to look silly and defensive.

Monday, June 30

The BBC were trying to move the goalposts to the 'dodgy dossier'. Peter M said [Greg] Dyke was personally masterminding it and had written parts of Sambrook's letter to me himself. Peter said they'd got themselves on a hook, whereby they felt their independence was under attack but they'd parked on very weak ground. I went up to see TB who said he didn't want it going beyond next week. His rationale was that he didn't want every single media organisation against him. I said we had to get it absolutely proven that we were right and use that to force a rethink of the political journalism culture. I could see he was up for suing for peace. He/Peter M wanted to get it stitched up in advance.

TB wanted desperately for us to get back on the domestic agenda. At the office meeting we had a decent enough discussion of the plan I put forward. The message he felt most comfortable with was that we were doing things that would make us unpopular in the short term but deliver results in the long term. I still felt we were too short on values. I did a revised version on the next four weeks and resubmitted it later. I talked to a few editors and commentators to try to explain this was about BBC journalism not WMD. Dennis Skinner called on his first day back in Parliament after his illness. He said keep at it. He thought I was brilliant on Channel 4, the MPs were totally behind me and 'I'll tell [Andrew] MacKinlay [Labour MP on FAC] he has to back you because TB needs you. I'll tell him he's worth ninety-nine Roger Liddles [special adviser] and TB is surrounded by twats whereas AC is fine and probably against the war anyway.'

[Peter] Kilfoyle was the only Labour voice apart from [Bob]

Marshall-Andrews, who I didn't count as Labour, to be offside. I spent the rest of the day with Clare S, Catherine R and David Bradshaw trying to agree lines re next steps. The BBC guidelines were shot to pieces by this story. Gilligan issued his threat to sue. I had been quoted as saying: If that guy sues, I'm a banana. Tony Parsons [columnist] had a supportive column in the *Mirror*, attacking the Beeb. Ben Bradshaw was piling it on to Sambrook and did a letter to the BBC governors about where guidelines were broken. I had a sense of it motoring. I hoped that Scarlett might send a letter of support to the FAC, or maybe C. The jury still out on Channel 4. I got some good feedback, but both [John] Birt and Scarlett thought it had been a bad idea. Mum phoned and said she had lost half a stone in the last few weeks. A friend from Ayrshire had called her to say the vicar yesterday had said a special prayer for me because I was standing up for truth against lies. Seven-mile run.

Tuesday, July 1

Hunting was the main story after the government had to bow to MPs' pressure and the story was that we were heading for a total ban. Gay marriages [proposed same-sex civil partnerships] were going big. I got good feedback from Peter M, Philip and Jonathan who all felt the forward-plan note I had done was strong. *The Times* had stuff on Dyke being in charge. The *Guardian* said the BBC would offer an apology for what was inaccurate if it was accepted they were justified in the broader context. The *Telegraph* had an Alan Cochrane [Scottish editor] piece pro me, a leader [column] on the fence. There was a vile piece from Hugo Young [*Guardian*] who said the BBC had behaved impeccably. Defending the indefensible.

I sent a letter to Charles Moore [*Telegraph* editor] re his leader. Lots of letters were coming in in support of what I was doing. Nice one from Joe Ashton [Labour MP]. Letter to Dyke re his letter to TB that 'if we make mistakes we will admit we were wrong and apologise'. The intelligence from the BBC was that they were going to fudge the two dossiers in their response to the FAC report, and say there was sufficient concern re abuse of intelligence to justify the story. Meeting with TB. He asked where it was going. I said Birt told us yesterday – a defeat for BBC. I put to him a plan to use this to isolate small parts of the BBC and the *Mail* as the real cancers in our media. 'How are we going to get back on to domestic politics?' TB asked. I said this was part of the answer. We had to change the media dynamic and this was part of it. Get back to honest public service broadcasting, etc. He was not totally against it.

I gave him a plan which I thought would help him get into a better place. One, we get through the FAC. Two, we brief that TB has asked AC to put together a new A team of fresh blood including a new policy head and a replacement for me before I work myself out of the job. Three, I leave but we say I will come back for the election in a different position. He seemed up for that. I said to him that I sometimes felt he hadn't really defended me properly and I had to do a lot of this myself. Yes, he said, and I've let you! He said 'You're motoring again, which is good.' I was clear though I was still going. He said he felt there were two problems with the media and GB, but they were better problems to have than a recession or a national crisis. Re the BBC, Peter M was asking me not to get too heavy with Greg Dyke. Rebekah Wade came to see me and said Murdoch had asked why the *Sun* wasn't doing the story properly. Research [and Information Unit] was going through the worldwide coverage of it all so that we could show just how far the original story had gone round the world. I had a meeting with David Omand. He said he was worried re Gilligan saying the source was clearly someone fairly high up.

Wednesday, July 2

The BBC row was lower in temperature. Then news came from Westminster of a very bloody meeting of the FAC yesterday, the Tories going very political, Richard Ottaway [Conservative MP] saying he wouldn't endorse anything that exonerates me, [Sir John] Stanley putting down lots of amendments and saying they may do a minority report. It was clear it was going to go line by line and was difficult. Also I didn't realise Ottaway had replaced [Sir] Patrick Cormack [Conservative MP] who was much more with us on this.

At the PMQs meeting, TB was clearly unhappy with our position on hunting. The PLP really wanted the ban, but TB didn't. It was tough though. Meeting with John Scarlett and Clare Sumner. John S had agreed with Jack S that Jack would send a note, also cleared by C, that made clear the intelligence for the second dossier was cleared. I argued strongly that it would also help if they said the attacks on me were an attack on their integrity too because it suggested they connived and colluded with me. John was worried, felt that really was him moving the JIC tanks out in front of me. John was being helpful but didn't want to be political support. Ditto C, who put his name in support of a Straw letter that introduced the thought that if the allegations persisted they were also aimed at the agencies. The MoD were putting out a letter of complaint re Gilligan claims that he had checked his story with the MoD press office. We were still on top but if the committee split on party lines it was going to be very difficult for us. This was taking up too much of my time.

PMQs was OK. IDS hopeless, [Charles] Kennedy did a bit on me – crap – and then back for a meeting of the Iraq Communications Group. The guy from the DIS was just back from Iraq and said things were getting worse not better. Gerard Russell [Islamic Media Unit, FCO] was really worried about the Arab media operation. I had a meeting with Gavin [Millar, QC, Fiona's brother]. He said the BBC had broadcast a libel but that I wasn't named at first. It was the *Mail on Sunday* that did the libel. I could sue the BBC for aggravated libel because of all the other media who supported the story. He felt I could go for Gilligan but though the BBC would not want to litigate he felt the *Mail on Sunday* probably would. He undertook to read all the papers, felt it would be OK but I had to be clear what I was getting into. They could mount a wider defence. On balance he felt probably don't do it, but the most important thing was to be cleared by the inquiry.

Meeting with Peter M. He was worried it would be really bad for TB/trust if I did not get vindicated. It was not going to be easy and everyone said it was getting tribal. I spoke to [Nicholas] Soames, who said he would defend me and attack the Tories for undermining the intelligence agencies. Peter M felt that we had to get some kind of deal with the BBC, but Gavyn Davies [BBC chairman] had gone into his shell and would do nothing to – allegedly – undermine BBC journalism! Peter M felt I had to get victory without humiliation for the BBC.

Thursday, July 3

The *Guardian* splashed on my memo to the FAC. They did it dead straight, quite helpful to me. Greg Pope [Labour MP, FAC member] decided to confess that he leaked it. I had no idea he was doing it. I thought it was a disaster but Hilary A and Bruce [Grocott] said it would be fine and not to worry. Soames had called me late last night to say he had run into C and asked him straight out if the story against me was true. C said no, and Soames said can I say so? Yes, said C. He was a bit pissed when he phoned and basically said he would do anything to help me, adding 'Especially if you stop TB using the Parliament Act on hunting.' He wanted to go on the media, called the *Today* programme and seemingly told them 'You are dozy, dishonest cunts and I am coming on your programme to say so.' He was, though, serious that he wanted to go on and make the point that this was an attack on the intelligence agencies as well as on me.

[Andrew] Marr did the interview and was now redefining the allegations as us having given 'undue prominence' to the 45-minute point. Total bollocks. C called me after the interview to say he was surprised Soames had gone public, that he thought he meant he was going to speak to Tory MPs on the committee. But he added 'Secretly, I'm pleased that I've been outed.' I said 'We will keep your pleasure secret, C.'

Then to a strategy meeting with TB, GB, JP, Douglas Alexander, Ian McCartney and David Triesman. TB said he would give the Cabinet next week a political sitrep and then have a polling and political discussion. JP said we needed a lot more than that, and there followed a positive and good discussion. JP's main point was that we didn't do enough to promote what we had done and talk about our values. The party felt itself on the defensive because that's how we came across to them. GB said we had to think forward to the election, the issues, big choices and values dividing lines, and then think back, then plan from here to then. He felt there was so much focus on reform that we were losing sight of values, that the messages were too technocratic. It was exactly what I had been saying. But TB was worried it was a bit of a JP/GB stitch-up to block some of the reforms. He said if we didn't have reform we would not be New Labour. We would look like we were running out of steam.

I said I still felt we could put together a clear single strategy based on the establishment of delivery, motivation of the party through values and dividing lines, then the next steps on future reform. What is the point of suddenly launching ID cards or LEAs [local education authorities] reform on an unsuspecting world? The ground work has to be about the values. GB made the point that the stuff running today on Lottery reform was fine, OK on its own, but not remotely strategic. Jonathan felt afterwards it was a hopeless meeting but I felt it gave us the right parameters of a better strategic approach.

Then Cabinet, during which I was only half listening because I was rewriting Pat McF's draft of TB's speech for tomorrow [in Liverpool, on public service reform], trying to reassert values and politics. I got a call from Hilary A around 12 to say the committee had agreed the report, with some amendments from [John] Maples [Conservative MP], but [Sir John] Stanley had been seen off. She felt it would be OK on the BBC issue, and that I could say that I was in the right, even if they didn't want to say that the BBC were in the wrong. So it felt fine and I felt we were back on top. But the BBC reporting then moved either on to the second dossier or whether the select committee system could be fair as it was run by the parties, etc.

Long chat with Peter M re strategy. He felt we should not reveal tactics, keep our powder dry and see what happened. The BBC was panicking according to everyone now. JP came to see me for about an hour, first re politics, saying TB had to stop dropping massive reforms on us that we hadn't had a chance to think through. He really felt we should get rid of some of his policy people. He also wanted to discuss the plan for him and Pauline [his wife] to come out with Pauline's child from way back.[1] He was a bit nervous but I assured him it was the right thing to do and agreed the plan he had worked up with his kids and Pauline.

TB called a couple of times from the North-West where he was doing a Granada TV special on the NHS. We were mulling over the debate on how to respond to the FAC. Jack S wanted to do a Commons statement, which I didn't think was very clever. I felt we had to get it all pinned on the BBC story and go for that and that meant it could be better that I did the media on the day. There was of course a worry that if I did it, the story would become me/spin rather than HMG.

Off to [broadcaster] David Frost's party, people generally supportive, including Frost. I avoided Dyke and Davies. I had a good chat with [General Sir] Mike Jackson who wanted me to kill Gilligan. At the Hillary Clinton book launch at the Orangery [Kensington Palace], Jim Naughtie [BBC *Today* programme presenter] was urging me not to do a big attack on the BBC generally, saying it was not the majority view that we were anti war, etc. I said I had a very good case in having a go at them. Chatted with Bill and Hillary Clinton a bit, both still very supportive. It was a nice enough evening but I was getting very down at Fiona's constant portrayal of me as having brought all these problems on myself. Peter M called to say BBC were trying to shift the terms of the story in all their reports and we had to lodge that.

Friday, July 4

Got Ben Bradshaw to do another letter to Sambrook pointing out how they were changing their story, and at the 11 Godric did the same, also pointing out that Hoon had been refused an appearance on the *Today* programme. I spoke to Robert Jackson [Conservative MP who later defected to Labour] who had called saying he wanted to help. We eventually agreed he would do an article for the *Sunday Telegraph*, getting out the line that I was not totally opposed to the BBC but to this strain of reporting that was anti politics and anti public life. I had a series of long chats through the day with TB and Jack re how

[1] At the age of sixteen, Pauline had given birth to a son. The boy, given up for adoption, had been identified as Lieutenant Colonel Timothy Paul Watton OBE.

to handle Monday. JS wanted a Commons statement. I said it was crazy because it put the onus on the Tories rather than us. I said we had to get it all on to the BBC/forty-five minutes.

I spoke to Hoon who said that a man had come forward who felt he was possibly Gilligan's source. He had come forward and was being interviewed today. GH said his initial instinct was to throw the book at him, but in fact there was a case for trying to get some kind of plea bargain – say that that he'd come forward and he was saying yes to speaking to Gilligan, yes he said intelligence went in late, but he never said the other stuff. It was double-edged but GH and I agreed it would fuck Gilligan if that was his source. He said he was an expert rather than a spy or full-time MoD official. GH and I agreed to talk tomorrow.

I was meanwhile doing my letters re BBC behaviour as well as a bit for TB. TB [public service reform] speech went OK but low-key. I was talking to TB, Peter M, Ben Bradshaw and later John Scarlett. We needed to work out our strategy for Monday. Godric said there was a case for us simply saying we had been cleared, the ball was now in the BBC court, and wait for their response before further action. Peter said we should be nice about the BBC and get ready to go for them on Monday. TB wanted closure. Peter M was being extremely helpful at the moment, and I was grateful that he was turning his mind to it. Ben Bradshaw ditto. Soames was in a bit of a panic after his interview and saying nobody must know that I helped him set it up, because I was such a bête noire for the Tory Party. Meeting on EMU, in which I was falling asleep the whole time.

Saturday, July 5

The BBC story seemed to be moving our way. The governors were to meet tomorrow to discuss it. The BBC started briefing aggressively that they would stand by their story and warn the governors it would be the end of BBC independence if they backed down. I spoke to TB and we agreed I should send a fairly emollient letter to the governors, and a file, to set out our side of the story vis-à-vis the BBC, and say it was not about attacking independence, or a broader attack, but dealing with one specific set of allegations.

Jack called a couple of times to say he felt he should do the bulk of Monday's media, and I should be low profile. I was not so sure. He later called to say the FAC was going to be in Rome on Monday, so no point in a Commons statement, but we had to work out a line. I agreed with Jack that it had to be about the BBC story because that was where the focus was. There was a case for saying nothing and going up to do discussion stuff, e.g. do we do a phone-in or discussion with BBC. Catherine Rimmer went into the office to put together the file for the governors. Meanwhile I was dealing with the car, which had been broken into, then took the boys to various sports events, then saw Gavin [Millar] again, who having read through everything felt I had an open-and-shut case for libel but that we should wait and see what the BBC said on Monday.

I was out running when Martin Sheehan [press officer] called to say the *Sunday Telegraph* were doing Dyke presenting new evidence to the governors to justify the story, the *Observer* saying that C met [John] Humphrys and [Kevin] Marsh [editor of *Today*] shortly before the *Today* programme story. I organised a conference call with C and a colleague of his. C said – and I knew this – that he met them a few weeks before this story, but when Humphrys recently said in his interview with John Reid that he had sources too, C's colleague got on to Humphrys to be assured he did not mean C. We agreed that they call the Press Association and BBC – or get the FCO to – and say they discussed nothing that would add to Gilligan's story and they should stop digging. It was a big So What. C agreed we should say it added nothing to the story. It looked like the last desperate throes, but it was possible the governors would go for it and back Dyke. C wanted to get Humphrys to deny the story.

I ran home, exhausted, and got the papers. They were pretty tricky. It was also still not clear whether the FAC would clear me or not, or had split on party lines. Alex F called from the women's final at Wimbledon, said he had been at the same table as Gavyn Davies, who seemed pretty out of sorts. Later I did a conference call with Tessa and Ben Bradshaw to go over their interviews tomorrow. Tessa called later to say she had really tried to speak to me but I never returned calls or messages. It was true that I was to a large extent trying to rely on my own resources.

Sunday, July 6

Ben Bradshaw did well on *GMTV*. I called Hillary Clinton before she did *Frost*, so that she had the full picture. TB's *Observer* words on the BBC and me were leading the news.[1] I spent much of the weekend

[1] In an interview, Blair had told the *Observer* 'The idea that I or anyone else in my position frankly would start altering intelligence evidence or saying to the intelligence services "I am going to insert this", is absurd. There couldn't be a more serious charge, that I ordered our troops into conflict on the basis of intelligence evidence that I falsified. You could not make a more serious charge against a prime minister. The charge happens to be wrong. I think everyone now accepts that that charge is wrong.'

talking to TB and Geoff H re the 'source', the man who felt he was the source because his colleagues said he sounded like what Gilligan was saying. He had come forward earlier in the week to confide that he'd seen Gilligan in a hotel, that he'd made some of these comments, but not others, for example about me. GH, like me, wanted to get it out that the source had broken cover to claim Gilligan had misrepresented him. TB and I had a long chat about it and TB was worried, felt that he or GH ought to tell the FAC about this. His worry was that it could lead to them reopening the inquiry. I wanted, as GH did, to get it to the BBC governors that we may know who the source was, that he was not a spy, not involved in the WMD dossier and was a WMD expert who advised departments. TB was fine about that but backed off after speaking to Omand, who felt the guy had to be treated properly and interviewed again. GH and I felt we were missing a trick.

I suggested to GH to speak to TB to try to persuade him we should do this and maybe GH should speak to Sambrook and tell him that he was a nobody re the dossier. GH said he was almost as steamed up as I was. TB said he didn't want to push the system too far. But my worry was that I wanted a clear win not a messy draw and if they presented it as a draw that was not good enough for us. We were getting the files to the BBC and when the governors arrived, the BBC put out a line that they never said we lied, so we hit back on that. Michael Howard on Sky said I was the most malevolent influence ever. TB felt that we should not push [MoD permanent secretary] Kevin Tebbit/David Omand too hard, and could maybe bring it out tomorrow if we needed it. TB was also feeling that we had to have something for the ISC to go for and that could be this. Jack – who'd spoken to Donald Anderson – said that the Tories had not supported the report so it was going to be split on party lines, and unclear and very messy.

As the governors met, it was clear we were heading for a bad day tomorrow. TB said we had to get it on to the issue of the UK media culture. 'It is a disgrace the BBC are behaving like this, it really is.' He said to me how are you feeling about it? I said fed up about the whole thing. He said don't be fed up. It's important and we have to keep to it. All this media stuff is really important and we had to stick to it. I was suddenly feeling stressed, exhausted, deflated. Tom Kelly was briefing and said the press were bored with the story. The problem was I'd felt we were going to win and it was going to be a messy draw at the FAC.

Source idea went nowhere as he had to be interviewed again by Martin Howard [deputy chief of Defence Intelligence], DIS and

Personnel. TB called to tell me not to worry. Martin Sheehan called after the BBC governors broke up and I listened to Gavyn Davies' statement. Dyke had got them on to the same line, defending the story, extending it to general issue of coverage. It was pretty poor, but clear they were all going along with the BBC line, if not defending the story. TB and I agreed the line that would put the focus on the claim that they never said we were lying, and we made clear what the central allegations still were.

Monday, July 7

There was a demo outside the house. I slept badly. Endless FAC blurb on the radio. I spoke to Peter M before going out, and did a good clip before getting into the cab. I felt it could go any way really. I was feeling a bit under siege, and very tired. Up to see TB. We were not clear what it was going to say, but he said we should make clear that we were not going for BBC independence, but they had to correct the story. TB's feeling was that we had to press ahead with it and be robust, but also look for a way out with the BBC. We met in my office – Jack, his officials, Clare Sumner, Godric, John S – to wait for the [FAC] document to arrive. A first reading seemed fine for me but less brilliant for the government as a whole re WMD. It was pretty clear-cut re me, but with Tory amendments. But even those did not support the BBC story. I did a quick skim read, some good, some bad.

Then round with Jack and John S to see TB who was meeting Kevin Tebbit, Omand and others re 'the source'. He was an ex-inspector, who advised the government, was aware of information going into the dossier but not involved in drawing it up. He'd once sat next to Jack as an expert at a select committee. Kevin said the guy claimed he never mentioned me. He was a bit of a show-off though. Felt that maybe Gilligan just put in the stuff about me. It was agreed he should be interviewed again, and then we should get it out that the source was not in the intelligence community, not involved in drawing up the dossier. Agreed we should be saying the source was misrepresented by Gilligan. TB was keen for Tebbit and Omand to be in control of the process. I watched the FAC press conference. Donald Anderson very clear re me. [Sir John] Stanley said I was a sideshow, Bill Olner and Gisela Stuart [Labour MPs and FAC members] were supportive. Tories and Andrew MacKinlay not too bad for me, and overall the impact was pretty positive.

TB said we have to be forensic about getting up the main points about the BBC allegations. Just before Jack [Straw] was due to go out in the street, John Stanley said the BBC was 'wrong' re the central allegations against me, so we put that into Jack's clip and he added that they must apologise. Sambrook was up defending the BBC, saying the report justified the decision to broadcast the story as the parties were split, etc. Everyone at our end said he came across as pathetic, but the problem was that the public probably believed them. TB was wanting to calm things down. For example, I wanted to do a discussion programme with Sambrook, but TB said do a letter instead. Then, when I did the letter, I got good advice from John Birt, who said claim victory and don't rejoice. He said the BBC would not apologise and therefore there was no point pushing it. I should be magnanimous. He said they look ridiculous, they can't answer the question if it's true or not. Birt said he knew what it was like to be on the receiving end of injustice, which is what this was, but you have to live with it. He said the biggest worry was where these wretched weapons were. TB rewrote my statement to be a bit more emollient. It was not strong enough for me or the team. Hours of coverage all day. I felt it was OK for me but others thought it was too muddy.

Several chats with MoD, Pam Teare [MoD director of news], then Geoff H re the source. I felt we should get it out through the papers, then have a line to respond and let TB take it on at the Liaison Committee. TB felt we had to leave it to Omand/Tebbit judgement and they didn't want to do it. We had to go for natural justice. GH said there was a problem that the source once gave evidence alongside Jack Straw. We were briefing that the BBC would eventually apologise. Wall to wall all day, source issue not moving. More calls for public inquiries. All went fine for me, but there were lots of difficult questions for the government as a whole. Jack was at home with food poisoning. Tessa good, Margaret B good on the media. The story was moving from me to WMD issue generally, on which not so good for us. TB was working up for the Liaison Committee tomorrow. I called my mum to tell her it was all going fine. She said she had not watched or listened to any of the news all day.

I was beginning to think I should say I'm going soon, maybe even this week. Source going better but not necessarily him. We were OK. John Scarlett was a bit worried that people felt I was running intelligence meetings. The agencies didn't come out great. Lots of unanswered questions. The problem for TB was the Iraq WMD were not found. GH wanted to get up the source, Tom and Godric felt it was best to wait until tomorrow, we had to do it right. The story on the FAC report was the whole of *The World at One*, ten to fifteen minutes on news, thirty minutes on *Newsnight* – Donald Anderson was strong.

Tuesday, July 8

The papers were disgraceful. Even for me, though cleared, they managed to muddy the waters, e.g. the *Telegraph* saying they would constantly call for my resignation. *Mail* vile, and left press not that great. It was even worse for TB, and of course the issue was moving quickly on to WMD rather than BBC. Up to see TB in the flat who was preparing for the Liaison Committee. He said the papers were unbelievable, 'It is truly Orwellian the world that we live in, I just don't know what to do with this constant rewriting of history and moving of goalposts.' Meeting with TB, JS, Scarlett, DM, etc. to go over the Liaison Committee. It was still not clear how we were going to handle the case of the MoD official.

Halfway through the TB evidence, I called Geoff Hoon. He was not remotely on top of the case. He said he had not checked out where we were on it. Also admitted he'd been crap on *Today* programme when asked who wrote the dossier and he hadn't seemed to know it was John Scarlett. Said he should get going on the source issue, TB clear that we should leave the bureaucracy to deal with it. Scarlett on good form as ever. TB off to the House, did pretty well. Gave no quarter on Iraq/WMD/kitchen Cabinet. He was a bit dozy on the issue of Europe, didn't push on the euro, OK on the reshuffle, overall a bit tired but OK. He came back and continued to try to sort the source issue. He met Scarlett and Omand and agreed to try to resolve it through a letter to Ann Taylor [ISC chair]. Word then came back she didn't want a letter on it. That meant do it as a press release.

Jonathan, AC, Tom and Godric, John S and Kevin Tebbit went to Godric's room and wrote a press release. Tebbit drafted a letter from GH to Gavyn Davies offering to give him the name of the source. Martin Howard had interviewed [Dr] David Kelly [government scientist and weapons expert], and was pretty convinced that he was the source, though of course we could not be sure. Tebbit took the draft away to the MoD and had to clear it with David Kelly, who was on a motorway. Then out by 6 and briefing mainly on the fact that the BBC put out a non-denial denial within two hours.

I told TB I still wanted to leave and why not now? Said he was really against it, it was the last thing he needed, and at the moment there would be meltdown in Parliament and that we should wait until Commons was not sitting. I said but I've only got two weeks left. Political strategy meeting with TB, GB, JP etc. PG presented the latest poll, which was bad. TB felt we had to get up delivery, get an acceptance of progress made. But he was tired and unfocused and GB's response was pretty brutal. He said we had no strategy to deal with the right-wing press, no clear plan for the election, no decision on election dividing lines. TB then asked him to circulate the strategy paper he had sent to TB, which he said he agreed with. GB said he wouldn't circulate it until he had the raw polling – to which he always had access anyway if he wanted it. It was one of those meetings in which whatever TB said, GB then said something slightly different. JP pitched in with a warning about putting too much new policy out there. It meandered on for about half an hour but got nowhere.

Wednesday, July 9

The BBC story was going away because they were refusing to take on the source idea. There was a big conspiracy at work really. The biggest thing needed was the source out. We agreed that we should not do it ourselves, so didn't, but later in the day the *FT*, *Guardian*, and after a while Mike Evans [defence corrrespondent of *The Times*] got the name. It was going to be difficult to keep it going and of course the politicians really wanted out of it. The story was moving away and as the source row grew, I felt I'd lost. Brendan Foster [former Olympic runner] came to see me, and he said TB was still the best there was. He said he would be amazed if I ever left the job until TB went because there couldn't be a better job and in many ways he was right.

TB went to the PLP and everyone said he did well. Then PMQs. I wanted him to turn the heat on the BBC but he wasn't really up for it and IDS and he ended up with some pretty vicious exchanges about WMD. Strategy meeting. Stan [Greenberg] went through the polling detail and though we were still ahead, it was a gloomy picture. Peter M, Philip and I put forward our tired responses and it all felt a bit jaded. TB felt WMD/Iraq was hurting him personally very badly and of course it was. Re GB, he said there was no point pretending that we would ever get back to being one big happy family, so we had to work around him as best we can.

By the time I got home, I felt really tired. Heat, pressure and stress, the problem of knowing when to leave, it was all pretty grim really. TB was not really engaging with me re my departure. Andy Marr led the news, massively ramped across all channels, with a story about senior sources saying we were unlikely ever to find WMD. It transpired the source was Jack Straw. JS apologised to me later saying he thought he was just chatting for background, not that Marr was going to do a big story. It was an outrage the way the BBC was now using its reporters and outlets to promote its line on the issue.

Thursday, July 10

Marr WMD story still going big. [Robin] Cook on *Today*, John Major at 8.10. TB said the BBC coverage was actually a scandal. It was like dealing with the *Mail* on this, not the BBC. It was like Orwell's *Nineteen Eighty-Four* and all that. I got Ben Bradshaw on to TV re the WMD story saying this was a BBC diversionary tactic re the source. The FAC met and agreed publicly to call Dr Kelly [to the committee] and privately they were writing to Gilligan, so this was still moving in an uncertain direction. Geoff Hoon got a letter of apology from Sambrook about the claim they'd put the allegations to us.

Political Cabinet at 3. TB did an OK introduction but once Philip's polling was done they had what Douglas [Alexander] called 'a meeting of government by anecdote' designed to promote views we already knew they had. Alistair Darling on the Libs, Andrew Smith on local campaigning methods, Pat H on targets, DB wanting more ASBOs, Charles Clarke on green issues, Hain on the need at least to think about tax. Not a good discussion. JR was the only one who really said anything worth taking on board. GH also spoke quite well, echoing John in the line that we needed to keep on with reform as a way of holding the middle ground but do it according to our values. GB was not as impressive as usual, started well with his line about working back from the election, then seemed to run out of steam a bit. JP was very passionate, defended TB saying that he alone must not take the blame for Iraq, because it was a decision we all took and we all had to stand by it.

TB spoke better summing up and he was very open about the conundrum – that we needed reform to make change but the individual changes could always be unpopular till they got through and made an impact. It was a tired Cabinet and a tired meeting and we were going to have to raise our game. TB looked tired. Both JP and GB had big bags under their eyes. There was no real drive or energy in there. TB felt the coming fight would be a very traditional left/right one. Asylum, immigration, Europe, tax and spend. We have to get to acceptance of a minimum basis of delivery. But we have to show we have the only viable long-term strategy for the future. We must not concede the intellectual and political dominance we have in the political debate. But the values must be clearer. On the issue of trust, WMD – lack of – is obviously a problem. But trust is best addressed by reconnecting with people on the issues they really feel strongly about – crime, antisocial behaviour, health, education. It is through the values that we get the dividing lines and through detailed policy that we highlight them.

Charles C agreed with the analysis, but said the party as a family feels ill at ease with us and we have to make the party feel more involved. Alistair Darling was on his usual worry re the Libs, said he would relish a traditional left/right fight but we needed to be clear about how to handle the Lib Dems within that. In Scotland tactical voting was now common. We must not underestimate the Lib Dem threat in some areas. The argument has to be that they are not risk-free. Jack S felt the position was more difficult than PG's polling suggested. He felt we were kidding ourselves if we thought trust was just policy-based. We are delivering a huge amount of what we promised, but a lot of people don't like us. Part of the problem was that too often we defined ourselves against the party. We alienated our own people. We sometimes win the vote without being clear about winning the argument. He said he was all in favour of being at our best when at our boldest, but there was no point picking fights for the sake of it. Jack was being pretty tricksy at the moment and TB was very deliberately raising his eyebrows and making sure people clocked his reaction. Andrew Smith said people on the [social housing] estates felt we were pursuing Middle England at their expense. Pat H said values not management were the key. It goes deeper than the language we use. All people hear is targets, efficiency, all fine but limited. They need to hear values. Talking about users of public services like they were customers was also alienating. There were too many confusing initiatives, too many targets, not enough willingness to listen and engage. GH was clearly worried about the general drift. He said it would be a disaster if we in any way abandoned the middle ground. Both the traditional working class and the middle classes are better off and 'I'm worried that if we listen too closely to party and unions, we get pushed to making a false choice.' TB nodding.

Bruce [Grocott] said the party was not so much rebellious as moribund and he felt that was worrying. Peter Hain – music to my ears – said we had to generate a bigger debate about the future of politics and the dire impact of the modern media. Hilary A was cogent and intelligent as ever. She said to TB 'You warned the PLP that division was the death of all previous Labour governments. But you have to realise they feel the only way they get listened to is by being difficult, including voting against the government.' She was worried it was becoming habit-forming. She said to be fair TB spent a lot of time every week talking to backbenchers and he is the busiest of all of them. Yet a lot of ministers just don't bother.

There was a coffee break and TB was not terribly happy at the general tone and tenor, felt they were all conceding too much and also in some cases coming up with the wrong answers. JR spoke first, and said though TB 'took the trust issue on your own shoulders' it was about all of us and they had to do more as a group to address it. He spoke well, if for too long, about the need for themes rather than policy initiatives to drive our politics. He felt the strategic audit should force us to agree the overall priorities, and we should not just be fighting our own departmental corners. He also said we should not get too despondent. We were six years into government with a massive poll lead. We had made mistakes but we were basically seen as competent and delivering. Nor should we be amazed at the forces ranged against us – the right-wing media hate us because we're in power. The ultra left hate us because we're moderate and sensible. Sacked ministers have their own grievances. We have to build the alliances to defeat them in argument.

GB agreed, said it was an amazing success story that we had stayed dominant for six years. We know how we did it and we have to carry on with the same rigour and discipline. He felt the Tories were following a Bush strategy – try to shut down debate on the traditional right-wing issues. Try to get people to forget the Tory past. Try to get the economy taken for granted. They want to spread disillusion in public services and then move to tax cuts and privatisation. He felt we had to work back from the next election, agree the themes and dividing lines and then plan back. He felt on the economy it should be stability and enterprise. We need a strong public services dividing line. Another on the nature of progressive change. Families. The state of Britain and national identity.

JP did his usual speaking up for TB. Through some of the contributions TB had been drumming his fingers. JP seemed pretty irritated too, maybe not because of the content but the lack of balls being shown by a fair few of them. He said TB had 'done a very noble thing' in accepting responsibility for the trust issue. But it was not just his problem. Trust was the responsibility of the whole Cabinet. He felt Iraq would, long term, be seen to be the right thing to do. 300,000 people in mass graves – never let people forget it. He said in the PLP we had nearly fifty people there permanently trying to poison fifty more, plus they could always call on the Lords, lots of our own people included, to damage us. We had ex-ministers feeding it all the time. We have to fight back harder, get into the kind of mode we're in for elections. It was good rousing stuff and lifted the mood.

TB said he had listened carefully. He said that being in government did not fit easily with the party's culture, which prefers to campaign than to govern. We have done a lot but we are not the government of the party's dreams. No government ever will be. But they need to know if we divide, if we go back to the ways of the past, we will be out again. Also if we lose the capacity for renewal, we will go out. New Labour is not a finite thing. It means a Labour Party constantly renewing to meet the challenges of a world of change. He said '97 to '01 was all about establishing credibility to govern. We did some terrific things – but a national minimum wage does not transform the country. We did the basics well. But in a second term we are challenged more. The country and the party want more. But in meeting the party's demands we must not yield up the middle ground because that is where the country is. It is not just about what Middle England wants, but the challenges of today are best met in the middle ground. There are some policy solutions that neither party nor government will like. But we have to do what we think is right for the long term.

He said the unspoken message from some – and he was looking at GB – was to go easy on reform because it would anger people. GB said 'I'm not saying that,' but TB ploughed on – 'There is no division in my mind between the need to reform and staying true to our values. It is not inconsistent. We are being true to our values in making the reforms needed to improve life for the people we represent.' He said he wanted people to think over the summer about how that applied to their departments. Think long term. We could avoid a bit of political pain by opting out of difficult policy decisions. But it would be a mistake for the long term. I was left thinking he was the only one there who could speak like that. JP had warmed it up well but the bulk of the contributions had been either tired or timid and distinctly lacking in leadership.

Douglas [Alexander] was good on the new politics. If he didn't look so boyish, he would make so much more of an impact because he talked a lot of sense. But listening to them, I did feel that a lot of our problems about lack of strategic capacity were caused by the fact that for a while now I had not been fully engaged. Also on policy, as Bruce G pointed out, most of the good things we had done were from the first term. Dan Bartlett called me later from Air Force One, said his sense was we were winning.

Friday, July 11

Still a lot of focus on Iraq and intelligence and whether it was poor, or wrong. Fiona and I went to the unveiling by [Nelson] Mandela [former President of South Africa] of a blue plaque at [South African politician] Joe Slovo's old house in Lime Street in Camden. The Milibands were there and I had a nice chat with Ed about how much he enjoyed his time out in America. I shared a car with him to the office and he agreed there was very little direction and strategy.

To the Ritz where I was having lunch with Clinton, with Peter M and Philip. Mary McCartney [photographer] was taking some pictures. BC had had just two hours' sleep after getting in from Greece. He was dressed in golf-type clothes. He was a lot thinner than the last time I had seen him. Doug Band [Clinton aide] had organised lunch, which seemed to be a succession of different meals, and Clinton was eating a lot of them. First a plate of eggs, then bacon, then hamburgers. First we talked about Bush. We talked a bit about the US scene. I asked why he never stayed in embassies when he travelled. He said Bush had some mean people round him. 'I could, but I'm not sure about the welcome.' He said he was not much for having things named after him but there had been a Clinton Fellowship for Israeli and Palestinian students and at first the Bush administration changed the name and then they took away the money. 'These are ruthless people you are dealing with.' On Marc Rich [indicted in 1983 for illegal oil deals with Iran and tax evasion] and the controversial pardon [by Clinton on his last day in office], he said that Cheney's chief of staff [Lewis 'Scooter' Libby] had testified for the guy. 'You have to understand that what they care about is power. They control the press, they control the agenda and they hoard power ruthlessly.' They were changing the law to allow the White House to be more secretive. He said the view in DC was Bush had put all his [Texas] governor papers into his father's presidential library because that meant they couldn't be got at.

He said Bush liked TB because he stayed with him but if somebody came along they thought would help them more, they would go for them. He was speaking very slowly, calmly, matter-of-factly, probably conscious that we were on the lookout for signs of bitterness, but there was precious little of that and it was pretty compelling. He felt Bush had lost an election and having 'won' it he was now behaving as if he had walked it. But they were clever, and so was Bush. He was good at dealing with opponents. I asked him what Bush would do with the BBC. 'If he could kill the governors, he would. But he can't, so he would do a deal.'

On Iraq, he said the Bush lot had never been keen on Blix. He said Powell was the one who really wanted to let the inspectors work, and now it was looking bad for them, but because they still had control of the media, Bush was not yet under pressure. September 11 had changed the American people's psychology. Bush understood that and the Democrats had not worked out how to respond, how to fight it. He was angry about Bush, philosophical about the campaign [Al] Gore fought, hopeful for Hillary.

Peter M had to leave to do an interview. Philip, BC and I went over to the sofas and out poured something of a masterclass in political strategy. He followed our politics closely, and I asked him what his remedy would be for our problems. He said he was touched that we trusted him so much that we could openly lay out the problems we had. He said first, you have a weak Opposition. Keep them weak by coming up with the forward policy positions and push them where you want them. Second, TB is about as good as they get. Keep reminding everyone of that. Third, on the press, he said you need a strategy to get back credibility. He said he'd followed my troubles and was sympathetic. He said that I'd always been the number two target after TB and that I'd taken a lot. I'd been right to fight for myself and I did a great job, but now move on. Don't keep digging the hole. Let others do it. Go back to the media and say I didn't lie, but maybe I missed something. I always strove to tell the truth but I've thought deeply about it all. I've got a job to do and so have you, and it's best if we can do it without regarding each other as subhuman. He said the problem was they felt it was a pattern of behaviour – manipulation and bullying – and that I had to show them I was real again. He said they don't like me in part because I was one of them and now I'm not.

Next, a strategy for the PLP. Understand their lives and reach out to them. They have shitty lives. You guys go to DC. You have real power. They get a weekend in their constituency. Give them some romance. They think you guys have gone Hollywood and they want more local. It's about their psychology. It's the same with the press. Some you will never win but others you will if you are nice to them, involve them. Your MPs know TB is better than them but that doesn't mean they are nothing. Fifth, you have to reconnect. People are falling out of love with Tony because they think he has fallen out of love with them. He's a statesman and that's great but their world is here and now and they are paying him to sort out their world, here and now. They know he has to do this other stuff but they want to know he cares about them, here and now. Sixth, the Third Way is fine, but it has to be a third way with liberal values. Don't just push a reform message. He has to have good old-fashioned left causes too, for the poor, whatever. It's about values not reform.

It was the same argument I had been having with TB. I said so, and he said yes, but maybe he thinks you are just beating up on him. It's all about balance. He has to balance the Third Way message for his new coalition with the liberal message for the party. You have to balance frank advice with real support. On TB himself, he said he had to rediscover his joy in politics. He needed new stimuli without throwing everything out. He had to keep change with continuity. He came to the point about me not beating up on Tony. He could see for example why I thought Carole [Caplin] was a problem, but other people's emotions and psychology are not always the same. 'My brother was a cocaine addict and the word to remember for addicts is HALT. Yes, it means stop. But it also means I'm Hungry, I'm Angry, Lonely and Tired. You usually find the reason in one of those.' Clearly talking now about Monica Lewinsky [White House intern with whom he had had an affair], he said 'I wasn't hungry but I was angry, lonely and tired. I was being beaten up by everyone. Ken Starr [Independent Counsel, prosecutor] was trying to put me in jail. Friends were leaving me and enemies were killing me. Hillary was angry with me. This ball of fire came at me as I felt H, A, L, T.'

He said he sometimes thought Tony wanted a blue ribbon and a gold badge for the work he does, 'but the ribbon and the badge are the JOB. It's a privilege. It's a great job he's got and yes it's tough but who says it shouldn't be? Get his juices flowing again.' So he summed up. Keep the Tories weak. Get back credibility with the press, remembering that you are the best and that's why they judge you so harshly. It's the same with Tony. You've got to show you're real. Get your troops back in shape by loving them a bit. Reconnect with the public by showing it's about them. Get TB to rediscover his joy in politics. He told a story about the first woman he ever loved, how he left her and drove her into the arms of a friend and she ended up hating both of them and it always bugged him. Years later when he was president he made contact with her and they talked it over, and he felt happy that he had resolved an important thread in his life. Another story about a friend he fell out with but then when he became president they rediscovered that friendship. So keep your friends, get some joy back into your politics, get a left liberal cause.

Philip then asked him what he thought I should do, whether he thought I should leave the job. Again, he was terrific on the analysis. A long pause, then said these are the factors: 1. Is it hurting you more than you're getting out of it, especially for Fiona and the family? 2. Is it hurting Tony more than you are putting in? 3. Can anyone else do it? 4. If you stay can you deliver a new strategy? Only you know, but remember it's a great job and I don't like to think what could have happened if you had not been there. He also thought in some ways Fiona would blame herself for having let Carole take Cherie over, but she shouldn't. Really warm and friendly. He took me to the door and said 'Hang in. There are three centres of power in your politics. You guys, the Tories, the press. You have an affirmative programme. The others don't. Their job is to stop you doing your job. Don't let them. Raise your eyes above them, and stay with it.'

As we left, both Philip and I observed that he was about as near to being a political strategic genius as we knew. Philip asked if it made me want to stay and it did but I wondered if TB was up for the change needed. I told TB later what Bill's analysis had been and he agreed with most of it, apart from some of the liberal stuff. We finished the [Third Way conference] speech and then headed for the Metropole [hotel]. Lynn Forester [Lady de Rothschild] told me she had been at a dinner recently where C had really stuck up for me during a row with Lord Carrington [former Conservative Foreign Secretary]. Bill C said he had really enjoyed our lunch, hoped he had helped, but on my own situation, he said only I could know.

TB's speech was OK without being brilliant. He told a very funny story about an early experience canvassing and asking a woman in Hackney what she thought about getting rid of nuclear weapons and she said 'I don't have nuclear weapons, I have rats and I want to get rid of them first.' Bill gave a terrific speech, very hard on the Republicans, strong on why our values were right for today and said that we had to fight the resurgent right. Think. Feel. Fight. We had to understand that there was indeed a Fourth Way, namely aggressive conservatism. These people want real change and we should be the ones resisting it, winning the argument for our own agenda for change. They want more power for people at the top. They want America and her allies to dominate everything. He told about how they ran smears against people who even asked questions of e.g. their policy in Afghanistan. He said the Third Way worked and we had to stick with it and fight for it.

It was a really good speech, easily the best I had heard for a while. I don't know why TB was so reluctant at the moment to do the values. I loved Bill's line about the Fourth Way. He was also very funny in parts, like when he told of how he had to cut into a meeting with [Viktor] Chernomyrdin [former Prime Minister of Russia] on nuclear arms control because Turkey and Greece were about to go to war over an island with 200 sheep on it. In the car later, TB said he agreed with Bill's analysis in many ways and on some of it we should act. Re me, and the four questions BC had posed, TB said three answered themselves. He said his one worry was about whether he could get a real replacement.

Saturday, July 12

The *Guardian* ran a piece on the front about me maybe leaving. There was also a lot of coverage on the theme that TB's position was becoming perilous. Clare Short did a pre-record for *GMTV* saying TB should go. There was a lot of noise from the unions digging away at the Third Way conference. We also had the bizarre resignation of Michael Wills, who resigned in interviews without actually telling TB or anyone at Number 10.[1] The BBC row was weakening but would come back on Tuesday with the FAC.

Sunday, July 13

TB called a couple of times. He had spent a fair bit of time with Bill C who had given him pretty much the same analysis.

Monday, July 14

WMD was still going big. The BBC were operating a news blackout on the source issue. The *Scotsman* had a page 1 story about GB preparing to take over. The drums were definitely beating. GB was getting marked up the whole time, and TB marked down. GB was making clear he wanted to visit Murdoch in the States during the holiday. TB press conference in Surrey went OK, but it showed up further evidence of the BBC simply driving their own agenda. They cut away from initial questions and instead ran a commentary alongside saying all the UK media was interested in was WMD/Iraq. Guto Harri [BBC] was claiming that TB didn't answer the question about whether he backed the intelligence. He did. I got John Sawers to call Trevor Kavanagh who was doing a two-page spread on Iraq being better than everyone says.

TB came back, and had a meeting with John Scarlett, DM, Clare Sumner, Jonathan re his upcoming session with the ISC. Then to the den to discuss what TB would say at the reception for [former Labour leader] Michael Foot's ninetieth birthday. I said to him that I felt he needed at some point to make clear what his plans were for himself in the future because people were making assumptions about him going, and were therefore starting to peel off and take licence. Michael Foot arrived around 6 and although physically he wasn't in great shape, mentally he was all there, and determined to have a good time. Speeches were fine. I had an interesting chat with John Cole [former

[1] Wills resigned as a junior minister (for information technology in the criminal justice system), vowing to campaign for the abolition of the EU Common Agricultural Policy. He claimed every UK family paid £70 per year to support Europe's cattle.

BBC political editor] about the BBC. He felt BBC journalism was not in good shape, but didn't really want to get involved.

Tuesday, July 15

Ran in, forty-five minutes. We were looking forward to [David] Kelly giving evidence to the FAC, but Godric, Catherine Rimmer and I all predicted it would be a disaster and so it proved. Despite MoD assurances he was well schooled, a mix of the MPs' malice – Tory – and uselessness – our people – was going to give us a bit of a headache. By the end of the day, we were down as usual. I tried to have another discussion re a successor with TB. We had both spoken to David Hill again and it was clear he would come. There was a slight problem in that a lot of people were urging me to stay, but I had pretty much decided. Gerard Russell showed me a two-page spread on me in an Arab newspaper. There was even stuff in the press today about my haircut, so it was getting more not less ridiculous.

There was a good atmosphere at the office summer garden party, where I played the bagpipes on the balcony, much to the amusement of GB and the people he was entertaining at Number 11, including John Edmonds [GMB general secretary]. The FAC, despite a big row on the committee today, were saying that Kelly was probably not the source, thereby spectacularly missing the point. I had an hour or so with John Scarlett and Clare Sumner to go over ISC inquiry issues. TB did it this morning and all was fine, but Clare was a bit worried because TB said that he wrote the foreword [to the dossier] when in fact I did the draft.

Wednesday, July 16

I got a cab in and the driver had also done the marathon, so we chatted away about that. We thought the Tories would do a mix of FAC and NHS and TB/trust at PMQs but when it came to it IDS went for me, as did one of their backbenchers. IDS quoted the *Mail on Sunday* made-up story of me saying TB couldn't cope without me. I bumped into Rod Gilchrist [deputy editor, *Mail on Sunday*] at a party for Michael [Foot] later, and thoroughly enjoyed telling him he was scum.[1]

TB was pretty down today. PG, Sally, Pat McF, Peter M and I had

[1] The next Sunday, Gilchrist wrote of the encounter: 'Campbell, his newly cropped convict haircut – which gives him all the charm of Magwitch – on public display for the first time, thrust his face within an inch of mine and declared: "You're scum." I said I wasn't, but why did he think I was? His response came quickly. "And your paper's scum, too."'

a long meeting specifically to discuss TB and how to get him back in shape. We were all a bit tired and the whole operation needed a blood transfusion, new energy. I did a note based on the discussion and later saw TB in the flat. It was ragingly hot. He looked a bit ridiculous in a sleeveless grey vest, matching shorts and flip-flops with 'Bermuda' emblazoned on them. Unlike me, though, he loved the heat.

PMQs had been fine, but he agreed the whole operation was a bit tired. He felt on policy, on media strategy, and on systems for reaching out to the party, we had to improve. GB was motoring in the party and there was a danger that we were leaving the field to him. We had a pretty tired meeting with Ian McCartney and the party people. We went round in circles. We were pressing TB to focus more on progressive causes, but he felt he really had to be the one constantly emphasising the hard edge of New Labour.

I had a long chat with Dan B who said Bush was finally taking a bit of a hit on Iraq. He had picked up on the fact that the Tories were calling for my head and said Bush was unimpressed at the way the Tories had behaved. At Michael's ninetieth at the Gay Hussar, which Fiona had pretty much organised, there were a lot of the Old Labour people urging me to stay. Bostock [AC's GP] had said earlier he was worried I would crack up again if I suddenly went from all-out activity to doing nothing.

Thursday, July 17

In for a meeting with Clare Sumner and John Scarlett, before my ISC appearance. Clare discovered that I'd said to the FAC that I did see JIC assessments so we had to agree a line on that. John was concerned I had to make clear that I was not chairing intelligence meetings. I was due to give evidence from 8.30 to 9.45. I went over with Clare and Catherine Rimmer. I went in with Ann Taylor [chair], who joked that I had two minders, whereas TB had only had one. It was more relaxed than the FAC. I got them laughing telling them the story about how John Sergeant didn't want the PM to come down the plane to see the press because he was watching a film.

Michael Mates [Conservative MP] was very friendly, made a joke about a bet we once had and also said he had no doubt I did not put the 45-minute point in the dossier and he hoped the committee would say so. Gavin Strang [Labour MP] was interested in whether we should use intelligence publicly at all. Ditto others, but I felt it went OK. Mates put to me that C had said that no intelligence should be used with other material but I was not aware of that and said so as it didn't accord with my memory. It was over in just an hour. The clerk asked me via Ann T if I thought Gilligan should go to jail. I said don't get me going.

We then left for the airport, and on the plane [to America], TB was working on his speech [to Congress, where he was being awarded the Congressional Gold Medal]. He was very keen for it to be a pro-US as well as pro-EU speech. We didn't bother seeing the press on the way out. We flew over Guantanamo Bay, and agreed it was best to play it low profile but argue for change. The speech was strong and between us we made it stronger.

Cherie was in friendlier than usual form but meanwhile back home John Burton [Blair's constituency agent] had got a tip that 'enemies of CB' were going to meet at the Hilton Olympia in Kensington, and Fiona asked Mark Bennett [Labour press officer] to check it out covertly. It turned out to be a meeting in the bar between Ian Monk [PR] and Paul Dacre. Mark somehow got close enough to hear them, make notes and he reported back a lot of detail re their discussion about Carole [Caplin]. I did a note to TB which also included the fact that Monk sent a statement to PA re Cherie's clothes in Washington. I felt bad that I was going to be leaving him when things were getting tougher not easier. Also GB was really motoring now.

We landed and straight away I had a rash of messages re Gilligan's evidence to the FAC. Basically Donald Anderson went out with John Stanley and Andrew MacKinlay and then said that Gilligan was an unsatisfactory witness, that he had changed his story re me, and there was a danger of unfairness to me. So we were pretty happy about that. We had a discussion about whether I should say something. Godric and I thought maybe but TB felt it was better that I stay out. We went up to Congress, where we had a discussion and then a conference call about it. It was clearly the best news we'd had for ages, and Tom K in London said it was running very much for us and against Gilligan and I should stay out. TB got an amazing reception at Congress. It was interesting to watch which parts of the speech went down particularly well with Democrats, and which with Republicans. It was a good speech though. Our press were obsessing about his line 'if we are wrong' re the WMD/terrorism link, and saying it was moving the goalposts.[1]

Then up to the White House. As we walked into the Oval Office, Bush was very friendly, said 'Hey, congratulations, you took on the

[1] Blair said, 'Can we be sure that terrorism and weapons of mass destruction will join together? Let us say one thing: if we are wrong, we will have destroyed a threat that at its least is responsible for inhuman carnage and suffering. That is something I am confident history will forgive.'

bastards, and you did great.' He said he had seen some of my testimony and that Dan [Bartlett] had kept him informed. 'You did great. You showed that if you are in the right, if you believe it, and you give no quarter, you can prevail.' He kept coming back to it during the meeting, almost embarrassingly so. Cheney was as impassive as ever, [Colin] Powell was chirpy but looking tired, while Condi was more subdued than usual. At the press conference Adam Boulton gave TB a full toss on the BBC but TB didn't really hit it to the boundary.

We went out for a drink on the balcony overlooking the lawns. The mood was pretty relaxed. They did a bit of substance on Iraq, but not much. They agreed that [Paul] Bremer needed a lot more help. On the [Guantanamo] detainees, Bush said his big worry was that one day one of them got out and killed someone. TB at one point asked him about Libya and it was clear from the answer that Bush thought he meant Liberia. GWB was now smoking a massive cigar and producing huge amounts of smoke. I was also struck by his shoes, which looked phenomenally expensive. At the dinner, I was seated between Powell and Dan. Apart from a fairly interesting discussion on Africa, it was mainly small talk. I had enjoyed the trip, but was also glad that I was now heading home rather than going on with TB to the Far East. I headed to the airport with Sally and Alison, who had a selection of very good cuttings about Gilligan from the first editions. There was a Tory MEP at the airport who said he was proud to be British listening to TB's speech to Congress.

Friday, July 18

We landed at Heathrow about 9am, and we sat there for ages. I turned on the phone, and got a message from media monitoring that Kelly had disappeared. Then a message to call the Number 10 duty clerk, very urgent. I was told Kelly had gone for a walk yesterday and his wife [Janice] had reported him missing this morning. I felt sick. I called Tom. It took ages to get off the plane and when we did I felt dreadful. I told Sally and Alison, who were both shocked. I could sense a juggernaut moving my way. Terry [Rayner, Number 10 driver] drove me home. I spoke to Hoon who said [Kevin] Tebbit would handle it initially but he would go up on the media if needed. He said he felt it had to be properly handled from the start. I then spoke to JP in Cyprus. He said he felt he should come back, and I was grateful. In part it was about himself. He said he was worried that with TB out of the country, they'd come looking for him on a beach, and he also said he could be back to steady things. He felt GH and

JS were a bit too close to it all and I should stay out of it. I said what will Pauline think about it, and he said don't worry, I'll sort it.

Then Tom told me that a body had been found. This was getting more and more grim. Tom did the eleven o'clock. Then TB came on from the plane. I said I'd really had enough. He said we should announce a judicial inquiry now. I said I really wanted to go and felt I should do it now. I had been determined to clear my name, I was always going to go now, it may not seem the time to do it, but it's exactly the time to do it because I was clear it had all gone too far and we needed to step back and think. Philip came round to the house and was in two minds. He felt wait until tomorrow. TB said it would be a disaster for me if I did that. Charlie Falconer [Lord Chancellor], who called me re the inquiry, said I would be mad to do it. All people would remember is Dr Kelly killed himself and AC went. They would not hear your arguments and they'd think you were making it about you. TB called a couple of times and said we have to be really strong about this. I said I'm fed up being strong, I want to get a life back. There was a mass of photographers outside by now.

I called Neil [Kinnock] who clearly didn't know about Kelly and was telling me that Gilligan was done for. I told him re Kelly and he said Jesus H. Christ. I said what to do. He said hold tight, be strong and don't let the bastards take you as a scalp. He said he would support me whatever but felt I had to do that. Peter M came on, said I must not go, now or in the future, because that was what they all wanted. You must hang in. John Scarlett called and we had a long chat about the whole thing. He was very supportive, said that even though he'd had a bit of flak, he felt fine. Charlie F said I'd be mad if I quit, Peter M said I'd regret it, TB thought it would be really bad for me, Godric that it would look like my fault.

Jonathan called from the US, said he felt physically sick, and should he come back to help? I said no, he said don't do anything rash. Rebekah [Wade] sent me a nice message, you've done nothing wrong, told the truth, more principles than these other people. Just hang in and don't give them the satisfaction. Piers [Morgan] was not totally unsympathetic but felt there was no escape for me or for Tony. He felt the mood had just turned, and people would keep going on it. I was the story and that was that even though it was unfair. Fiona was desperate for me to go. So was I now. But I wanted some honour and dignity. Things quietened down but then I wept because of the pressures I was under, and the sadness I felt for Kelly's family. JP called after his return and said he would be around to help if needed. The rolling news was relentless and really grim. Everyone feeling grim about it all. I said to journalists who got through on the phone that I was shocked and felt dreadful, it was about our media culture, but I had done nothing wrong.

Saturday, July 19

The papers, as expected, were totally grim, the *Mail* needless to say the worst, pictures of TB, Hoon and me and 'Proud Of Yourselves?' Lots re me and suggestions that I would get the blame. The *Mail* was disgusting, the *Telegraph* less so. The only person who came out well was Kelly. There was not nearly enough directed towards the BBC. Cameras started gathering outside at 6 and by 9 there were four or five film crews and a dozen or so photographers. We had to go through the elaborate charade of getting the kids and Fiona out first and then being driven to meet them. I got Mel [Cooke, a neighbour] to drive me away, and she said she had always had a fantasy about being a getaway driver. The mood of the hacks was reasonably sombre but they still asked if I planned to resign, and later that cunt Jonathan Oliver [*Mail on Sunday* reporter] asked TB if he had blood on his hands.

During the day, lots of people called with messages of support. John Reid, who said his secretary was really angry and hang in. Kim Howells – don't let the bastards get you down, because lots of our people love you. Margaret Beckett said she was really angry the media could blame me when this was about the media. Blunkett – solidarity and support. Bruce Grocott of course, Syd Young [former *Mirror* journalist], Richard Stott, [Roy] Greenslade [both former *Mirror* editors] who all said this was about the curse of modern journalism.

But the most important conversation was with JP. He'd come back yesterday and did a little doorstep at the Policy Forum. I asked him what he thought I should do. He said I hope you stay because you're a vital part of the team and I think TB still needs you. But everyone will be giving you advice because of what THEY want, not what's best for you. You've been under massive pressure for years, paid a big price and so has Fiona, who has lost her sparkle. I've noticed you've been a bit detached and so has she and you should do what you think is right for you. I asked if he thought I could go before the inquiries were completed and he said no. But then as with David Mills [husband of Tessa Jowell], he came round to it being possible. Everyone I spoke to felt I was in the right, but maybe that was because of the kind of people who phoned me. JP and I also discussed TB/

GB and he said it was bad on both sides. He was pissed off that TB wanted Douglas and Hazel Blears on the NEC rather than GB. TB had complained GB had not even discussed it with him, but JP felt they were as bad as each other. TB did the press conference in Tokyo and looked dreadful.

Clive Hollick [Labour peer and media businessman] called me, said he'd been to a BBC do last night and they were all very bullish, behaving arrogantly like it was their duty to bring down the government. He said Dyke was defensive and non-apologetic, but did say they were thinking of making clear Gilligan's only source was Kelly, and they wanted to know what we would do about it. I said we would not make any comment, and TB later said we must not cause them any mischief. TB was looking haggard and unshaven as they arrived in Japan.

The body was formally identified, Clare Sumner was checking out what kind of an inquiry it would be. She spoke to the secretary [to the Hutton Inquiry, Lee Hughes] who said it would be MoD people first, then the BBC. I said it was important we send them our side of the story and try to get the facts clear early. I was feeling very down by now. Much of the press gunned at me. Brendan Foster called and said he felt TB should do more, be more human and emotional, make clear nobody wanted this to happen. He told me the story of a journalist who killed himself, and at the time a colleague got the blame but in fact it turned out the guy's wife had left him with their four children. He said the point is that people who kill themselves are disturbed, and they say things in suicide notes and final conversations that can haunt other people forever. He felt strongly that I should not do anything rash and hang in for now.

Philip said Peter M was spooked about me going because of something GB said to him once, namely that TB was a weak person with two strong people – me and Peter – propping him up. He felt that once we were gone, TB was gone too. The Kelly family issued a statement which basically said everyone should think deeply about the fact his life had been made intolerable. This would obviously be a hard time. TB called. It was 5am there. He said he couldn't sleep, he felt grim and was about to do an interview with [Adam] Boulton, which he didn't want to do. He said I had to stay and we had to fight this through.

Sunday, July 20

I didn't read the papers but by all accounts they were pretty grim. The main focus was on the Kelly family statement, alongside lots of commentary about us, very little of it nice. I went for a run and felt myself moving towards saying something about it. I went through my argument and the various scenarios. I had a long chat with JP. He said he was glad he came back, said he'd thought about my position. He felt I'd done my bit for TB and the government and should be allowed to decide the next part for myself. I said maybe long term it was the right thing for Tony because he'd be able to reorder things for the future. JP said you've obviously decided to go. I think you deserve to do what you want. We discussed the call from Clare Sumner a few moments earlier that the BBC were about to make a statement that Kelly was the source. JP agreed I had a window and should seize it and go for it if I felt it was the right thing to do. The BBC statement went out. Sky really going for the BBC, but the BBC's own coverage was like *Pravda*.

I spoke to Godric on the flight from Korea to China to tell him I wanted to make clear publicly that I was going to go very soon, say that it was agreed with TB ages ago, and the family had had enough. I said to GS that I would quite like to do it tomorrow, with the BBC on the back foot. TB called from Shanghai on the way from the airport to the hotel, and said it was a mad idea. I said it was not. It was a good thing for me and a good thing for him. He said don't do it. I know what you're worried about, you're worried that it's not going to happen, that you'll go at a time not of your choosing, with them hounding you out. But it's a big moment this, and if you don't do it properly, it will be a real problem. It's just mad. They're on the defensive, let the stuff about the BBC sink in and then do it when I get back. If you do it when I'm out of the country it will be even worse. It will look like I was not involved and you bounced me. If you want to do it, fine, but I promise you it's not a good idea. I said I really had to know I was getting out on my terms. I said I was confident about the inquiries but I was also confident about FAC and a fat lot of good that did me. He said don't forget that in the end we're all in this together and we have to help each other. He said 'When you leave I want to be able to say that there are two ACs, the one parts of the media portray and the one I know who is a great person.' He said it was better we do that at the end of the week or after you go on holiday. I said OK but I wanted a guarantee. Sky was really going for the BBC though Boulton was still being a total cunt, e.g. in saying I was not totally exonerated because I was chairing intelligence meetings, etc. ITN was OK, but the BBC was like a house magazine. Geoff H called, said he was determined to go to the [British] Grand Prix because he was not having his life dictated by the worst excesses of the British media. Quite right. Once the dust settled I would have to deal with the BBC etc. and I would have no stomach for it all. I hated these people. The BBC/*Mail* link was now beyond the pale.

We went for dinner at the Goulds', joined by Charlie and Marianna [Falconer] and Peter M. Charlie felt I now had a window to go. Marianna was not sure I really wanted to go and said I should just take a holiday to think about it. Peter felt I was the one person in Number 10 who gave TB muscular advice which he listened to. I still felt I could do a fair bit from the outside. Peter M was unconvinced. He said three things will happen: 1. the media will rejoice; 2. champagne will flow in Number 11; 3. there will be panic in the PLP and ministers will become even more useless. I found it hard to see how I could stay in a position related to the media when I had such total contempt not just for a few of them, but for most of them, and certainly for the media culture and prevailing style. Charlie was clear that once I went, though I would still be able to help, I would not be able to pull the levers and that was a problem for TB, though he completely understood why I wanted to go. What was important was that we gave TB good replacements quickly.

Monday, July 21

The papers were finally turning to the BBC, but the *Mail* was vile and Robert Harris [author, former journalist] had a vicious piece in the *Telegraph*. I had to fight my way through a [media] scrum to get into the cab. I was feeling shit and keen to go. I had a nice cabbie who was basically onside, and felt the thing was moving towards the Beeb. Bruce, who had been persuaded that my leaving was the right thing to do, came back and said don't do it because 1. you are TB's last line of defence, and 2. they'd say it was an admission of guilt. [David] Bradshaw, Peter H were saying much the same thing. Jonathan came back from the States and he, Sally and I met discuss how to do it and what I would say. Jonathan said he probably agreed it was the right thing, but we needed a replacement sorted first.

The day was largely taken up with going through the Clare Sumner/Catherine Rimmer file. [Lord] Hutton was announcing his plans at 10.30 and it was clear he would go as wide as he wanted and do most of it in public.[1] He looked far too Tory for me, though as Fiona said, that might mean he was pro war whereas a left-wing

[1] Lord Hutton, former Lord Chief Justice of Northern Ireland, would chair what was formally known as the 'Inquiry into the Circumstances Surrounding the Death of Dr David Kelly CMG'.

judge almost certainly would not be. Peter M was terrific on *Today*, skewering Humphrys on what he said on May 29 about the Gilligan story and Humphrys was very defensive. Clare Short came on with her usual whine. Geoff Hoon was page 1 of the *Mail* for being at the Grand Prix. He said to me last night he didn't really want to do the job if his family had to live life according to the morals of the immoral *Daily Mail*.

The first big meeting of the day was with Jeremy and Jonathan, Sally, Catherine Rimmer – Clare now away – and John S to go through chronology. It was very hard to remember all the comings and goings and toings and froings about the whole thing. CR had dug up all the emails and the ones that caused possible problems, one from Jonathan asking me or Sally to speak to Ann Taylor. Also one from me that the ISC should delve into the source, Gilligan and me. But it was OK really.

Omand came over at 3 for another meeting at which he was much more formal and said Hutton would want us to send a consolidated account but each person would have to give evidence on their own account. There was a real possibility of this going in any direction and of course the BBC were clearly now going to suggest that Kelly did say all these things. Clive Hollick called to say would it be sensible for me to see Greg Dyke for a private chat. I felt probably not. The press was trying to put the focus on who put the name in the public domain and going for the fact that the MoD said they would confirm the name if it was put to them.

Tom Kelly did the eleven o'clock with a fairly straight bat. Meetings for two hours or so. Omand setting up a little team to work full-time on the inquiry while we were on holiday. It was going to be tough. The BBC were trying to maintain that the Susan Watts [BBC *Newsnight* journalist] story was the same as the Gilligan story. It wasn't. It was a softer version. Ditto Gavin Hewitt [BBC journalist]. I had a long chat with Graeme [AC's brother] in Poland who said that every time he turned on a TV channel, I seemed to be on it, whatever the country.

Tuesday, July 22

Fiona has a real downer on me at the moment. I said surely you can understand the pressure I'm under at the moment. She said a lot of it was of my own making because I went from one obsession to the next and she feared I would never change. She was ducking out of the decision re timing of departure though. Neil, Sally, Charles Clarke, Mum, Godric, lots of others I spoke to, pretty much all felt that if I went on Friday it would be taken as an admission of guilt of some sort. Neil said I should wait till September, maybe go after the ISC.

Godric called me after TB's Q&A in Shanghai. TB was not happy with the positioning of the media on the inquiry after Tom's briefing which was being taken as a hit on GH. TB said we had set up the inquiry and now had to shut down on all this, stop commenting, stop engaging with the media on it. But then, later in the day, he went down the plane to talk to the hacks, despite me warning Godric no good would come of it. And he said he did not authorise the leaking of the name. He had been caught on a classic 'When did you stop beating your wife?' type question and rose to it. But it meant more pressure on me and Geoff Hoon. I could not believe he had done that. I was pissed off with him, and with the people with him for letting him talk to the hacks. There was just no point in the current atmosphere. He should do the formal press events and nothing else.

I also felt it would make it much harder for me to leave on Friday. JP called. He said he had been thinking about my situation. It was obviously a case of when not if I was leaving now and he just wanted to say I should make that judgement in my own interests. He said I had given a phenomenal amount to the government and the party and I was owed that at least. I should decide how and when to depart, and he would be around to speak up for me whenever that was. He also called Fiona with the same message. I called GH, said I couldn't believe TB had dropped us in it like that. I don't think he meant to, but they were all taking his statement as HE didn't authorise it but someone else – GH or AC – did. I saw Bob Phillis [chief executive, Guardian Media Group] and told him I would be leaving. His view was that it was good for me, a tragedy for TB.

Later came news that Uday and Qusai [Saddam's sons] were dead. Charles Clarke called. He said you should not leave. There is a lot of respect for you out there, even among the people who attack you, and I think you will regret going. I set off for King's Cross then off to Retford. Mum looked really bad. She had lost half a stone in the last few weeks and was clearly worrying herself silly about me. I said I'm not losing sleep or losing weight so there's no need for anyone else to. But she was finding it tough. She said every time she turned on the telly news or the radio, someone was having a dig. She said she wouldn't be happy till I was out of it. She wouldn't have that long to wait. TB called from Hong Kong. 'Well, you dropped a bollock today,' I said. He said I know, I should never have gone down the plane. Paul Eastham [*Daily Mail*] had said 'Why did you authorise the leaking of the name?' And he got provoked.

It was leading the news, a great frenzy unleashed around it. The atmospherics meant it was terrible if anyone ever suggested the name should have been out there. Truth was there was a case for it being said – what WAS Kelly doing talking to journalists? Did he in fact say more? TB said the whole thing felt Dreyfusian. I felt it was a cross between Kafka and Orwell. He couldn't work out what the public really made of it. It wasn't good but he felt they would know there was something wrong about the media reporting of it all. He agreed it was impossible for me to resign on Friday now. He felt at the end of the holiday, or around publication of the ISC report, or maybe announce in August, and go at conference because I was still popular in the party.

He intended to go ahead with the public service delivery press conference on Wednesday. He felt it was important the public saw we were still focused on the business of governing. He had spoken to Charles Powell [former adviser to Margaret Thatcher, brother of Jonathan] recently who told him of the day they told Thatcher the Tories had slipped to third in the polls during the Westland helicopter scandal. You just have to keep going. I put him on to Mum and they had a nice little chat. He said people underestimated the toll on families when someone was going through the media mill. She said she had lost half a stone with worry but he was doing a great job and keep going. It cheered her up a bit and she was telling everyone that he'd been talking to her. It was an odd irony that Paul Eastham had inadvertently postponed my departure. Shame I couldn't let the silly fucker know.

Wednesday, July 23

Had a really bad night because Grace was up with asthma and hay fever. Mum seemed better and Dad was looking stronger too but they were both worried about everything. I read some of the papers and now everything was being recalibrated away from the notion that it was inevitable Kelly's identity would become public, to the sense that anyone who spoke about him to anyone else was effectively responsible for killing him. It was all part of the new hysteria. I did a note setting out the need to reframe the debate by getting people to see events through the eyes of then not now. I talked to Charlie F who said he felt it was very hard for a judge not to be influenced by the one-sided nature of the media debate. He said that even he, after TB's ridiculous outburst on the plane, assumed it meant that what he was saying was that HE hadn't authorised leaking the name, but Geoff or I had via a strategy put together without TB's knowledge.

I was genuinely shocked. I said 'Christ, Charlie, don't tell me you actually believe it?' He said what he knew was that we were losing the PR battle. That was because the media framed the debate the whole time to suit the BBC line. It was also because we had announced the inquiry and then vacated the field, whereas the BBC were at it the whole time. He felt we should be explaining the broader context – Kelly's fear it would come out, his worry about a cover-up, suicide not something anyone ever imagined would happen. Jonathan said there was no way Tebbit would do that kind of statement. He felt we just had to trust the judge. He felt there was a chance the judge would be getting irritated because it was so obvious what the media were up to.

I was worrying about whether me having told *The Times* that the other papers had the name would become a problem, whether it would be thought to contribute to the outing. I knew I'd done nothing wrong but in the frenzied atmosphere it could so easily be misinterpreted. The BBC briefed that Susan Watts had Kelly on tape and we were able to say we thought that would be good for us because her story had been very different to Gilligan's even though the BBC spin machine was trying to make out something different.

It was all getting nasty though. Fiona was getting letters saying what's it like sleeping with a murderer. Liz [Naish, AC's sister] was getting abusive phone calls. I was getting letters with fake blood on the envelopes. And they wonder why I get angry. I was working on the overall narrative note Catherine Rimmer was co-ordinating. Geoff Hoon visiting Mrs Kelly was the main story. The media were on autopilot, presenting it as her having a go at him over the way the MoD handled him. He called me later and said they had had a really good chat, she was very friendly and very strong. He said she wanted to get a message to me that the way I was being hounded by the press was an outrage. I was really touched by that. I thought again about writing to her but worried about how she would feel about that now the inquiry was on its way. Geoff said he found the meeting really moving. She was friendly, the family was nice and he left feeling a lot better than when he went in. Not that that would remotely be reflected.

Thursday, July 24

In to finish my various notes to send to the Hutton Inquiry. Catherine R had put together a huge folder and was working away. TB called me up to the flat and said he felt pretty chirpy, that apart from the press they had a good trip. He was in two minds about whether I should go now or a bit later. He was clear it had to be planned properly, and seen to be as much about the nature of the media as about us. He said what the media had managed to do was define me as the epitome of a political culture that they represent and which I had spent my career fighting – distorting, manipulating, lying, spinning control freaks. He felt they had to be challenged on that basis.

Both he and Godric felt that once I had gone there was a chance of getting the debate on to that basis. TB said his and my interests on this were convergent – I wanted to be able to go in a position where people felt I had something to say that was significant, and he wanted me to be able to do that too, and give him the space to make change and challenge the culture. He said to me later that there was a part of him that felt I WAS being driven out by the media, or at least by the state of my relations with them. He was a bit gobsmacked at how offside Fiona was. He was perfectly nice but a part of him was obviously calculating how to use my departure while at the same time keeping me on board should he want to call on me. He said he would be very surprised if we didn't end up speaking most days, and most weeks that he would hope I would put something down on paper. He saw Geoff H, told him he had no worries about his future, that we would tough this out.

Geoff came to see me afterwards and I told him I had agreed with TB back in April I would go and nothing had happened since that made me want to change my mind. He said if I went, he felt it would be a disaster. TB was great, so were lots of people around him, but 'one thing that people know about you is that you give good advice and you're never afraid to say what he doesn't want to hear'. He felt TB was becoming a bit remote and he was worried if I wasn't there everyone else would be telling him he was the emperor and one day he'd be left standing with no clothes. I said that my mind was made up and I was telling him because I knew the media would try to up the pressure on him without me there. He was pretty much a total Blairite, a decent bloke. I felt I was dropping him in it a bit.

On Kelly though, he said he was absolutely confident of the outcome of the inquiry. I then did a ring-round of the people in the know to get their views on us doing this tomorrow. Fiona said yes, Tony said yes. I called Neil, who said everything in him said no. I called in Godric and Tom. They said no, that it would be seen as an admission of guilt to go right now. I had a chat with Phil Webster [*Times*], who felt the same. Then to a TB meeting with Omand, Scarlett, Jonathan, Jeremy, Matthew Rycroft [private secretary, foreign affairs], Catherine R, Tom and Godric.

There were mixed reports of what Hutton was like. Jonathan said [Gerry] Adams and [David] Trimble were united for once – in saying he was dreadful. Scarlett said he was an Ulster puritan, but nobody knew if that helped or hindered. He was a conservative with a small c. It was a fairly sober meeting, because the truth was none of us knew where or how this would end, and it was fraught with risk. We went over all the background material we would need, and the areas we would need to prepare on. I called Ann Taylor as she was about to board a ferry in Newhaven and told her in confidence I was going to leave. I was thinking about when, and felt that if the ISC report was going to clear me, that might be the time to do it. She said she was hoping to publish during the two weeks in September when Parliament was sitting. She couldn't go into content but we could speak nearer the time.

Dennis Skinner called to tell me that the NEC had turned on Tony Robinson [TV actor and NEC member] who had said we should be nice to the BBC. Skinner said they had to support AC 'because he's probably against the war anyway' and the party should support him against all the lies and distortions against us. He'd also had a pop at Mark Seddon [editor of *Tribune* and NEC member] for writing for the *Mail*. 'I'm not listening to anyone who writes for the fuckin' enemy.' My own mailbag was running around 6 to 1 in my favour though there were some pretty unpleasant ones among the antis. I knew Mum would be getting upset, called her and she said she'd been losing weight again. Truth be told she didn't have that much to lose. She said she wouldn't sleep well again until I was out of there. She said every time she turned on the radio or the TV someone seemed to be having a go. I said it was fine, that I was doing fine and in in any event it is not going to go on for ever. Joe Ashton [Labour MP] called, said the PLP was strong for me. He said it pissed him off how the papers liked to say the party was against me. He said the party knows you do a great job for Tony, and they know that your enemies are your enemies because you do their job better than they do theirs – and that goes for Tory MPs having a pop as well as all the journalists doing the same. I got a similar message from Dale Campbell-Savours [Labour MP]. He said he was sure I could convince myself that I actually wanted to leave, but I needed to think about who would be happiest about that – our enemies.

Bruce [Grocott] popped in for a chat, and said something similar. He said he didn't know what my plans were, and he knew he couldn't believe the papers, who were probably speculating about me going because that's where they wanted the story to go, but he really hoped I stayed. He said it must be hard at the moment, but it has always been hard, and you can get through this. He said he knew I could convince myself that actually it was in my interest to go, but it wasn't. He said it was what our enemies want and they would be the happy ones if it happened, not me. Bruce had always been such a strong support and I felt like I was letting him down, as well as Tony, in even thinking about going right now. He said he had seen day in day out how much TB relied on me, how much the whole operation did. He said there are going to be real storms ahead and I needed to be there to help him through them. 'You are strong. I can see how horrible this is but just don't give your enemies any satisfaction at all.' I said I thought I was too far gone. The family was very clear they'd had enough and after all they had done for me, I owed them this. My relations with the media were also now pretty poisonous and I felt there had been times when I had done TB harm as well as good. He said that was nonsense – which is pretty much what TB had said, saying we conceded too much on the whole fuss about spin. He said I think it will be bad for TB and the government if you leave, and therefore bad for the country. 'These people going on at you don't think about things like that. I'm the last person to try to persuade you not to listen to arguments from your family, but if you go, it is a victory for people who actually don't care too much about the country, but about the next story or the next attack.' I said it meant a lot to me that he said all this, but I had pretty much made my mind up about it. I confessed it had felt pretty lonely and brutalising at times but it helped to have people like him giving such strong support.

The FAC put out a statement saying that at Gilligan's request they would not be publishing a transcript of his evidence in the private session but sending a copy to Hutton. I bumped into Gisela Stuart. She said it would be terrible to publish it now because it showed both Gilligan and Kelly had got it wrong, though Gilligan was worse. I got home and Fiona was walking down the stairs as I walked through the door. 'I've been fired,' she said. 'What?' She said CB had called and said she felt she ought to leave soon. She accused Fiona of briefing against her, which Fiona said was ridiculous though she accepted there had been a breakdown of trust between them. Fiona said she did believe Carole was a menace but it was not true that she had ever briefed against her, let alone against Cherie. She was really upset that CB could think as she did. She was due to go out to the ballet and I said just try not to worry about it, Cherie will regret what she said. I watched the [BBC] *Ten O'Clock News*, and Marr opining that a world without me – i.e. post spin – would be the best thing for both the media and Number 10. Not a word about the Gilligan transcript. Marr had become a PR man for the Beeb, nothing else. So the news was basically GH not commenting, followed by a tendentious two-way about me.

Philip called and said don't fight it any more, you know you are going so just think of that, and don't fight. Get out ASAP. I was being inundated with nice messages, ninety per cent from party people, a small number from hacks. JR and DB called, saying don't go. Darren Murphy [special adviser] said don't give the *Mail* and GB the pleasure. He said I was the ONLY person GB feared – and that included TB and JP – and he would rejoice at this.

Friday, July 25

As part of their continuing obsession, *Today* led on the story that I was planning to leave. We had the 'wishful thinking' line in the mix but it was clearly true and though they got details wrong – e.g. saying I would not go till Hutton reported – I was baffled as to how they got hold of it. Peter M called. I asked whether he thought I should do a clip on the way out. He thought not. Audrey [Fiona's mother] was staying with us, said don't give them any satisfaction at all. I walked out, said simply 'Dream on' and went on my way. I went up to Les Hinton's house. Though I didn't go into timings I told him I would not be there much longer. We discussed a few options with News International. I was most interested in doing something on sport for a bit. He of course was most interested in books and political columns.

I went in and told TB about CB's call and said it was unforgivable that she spoke to Fiona like that after all she'd done for her. He said people were too fraught at the moment and Cherie was feeling under pressure. I said she needed to apologise, otherwise there would be badness between them that helped nobody. He said the problem at the moment is that the public will begin to wonder whether we are governing the country. All they hear is all this stuff about personalities, process and the rest and they start to wonder if that's all we do. There was a case for me going right now, but I was tired and I needed a holiday to marshal the arguments and get things in a better place first. He said he was still finding it hard to imagine life without me being around the whole time. I said I would be available to help, but in a different way. He once thought he needed Peter around the whole time, but he didn't, provided he could call on him. It would be the same with me.

Peter M joined us and he and I were chatting away while TB was just looking out of the window, a bit vacant. After a while, he said 'I can't see the way to rebuilding trust unless we find WMD. And at the moment I don't see how we regain momentum.' Peter and I said things would look very different after a break, also that he needed to get focused on conference, where we always seemed to get things back on an even keel. We agreed that for Wednesday's press conference he should say the focus was public services and anything at all re Iraq he should just say wait for Hutton. Peter M was being very helpful and supportive, albeit in his usual spiky way. He said it was poignantly ironic that he should be helping me plan my departure when I had so spectacularly been responsible for his 'defenestration'. It was to his credit though that apart from the odd joke, he'd never really shown bitterness at his second resignation, and still helped when I was the one needing support.

I drafted an email to put round the building telling people what was going on but TB, Charlie F and Jonathan talked me out of sending it. They felt it might leak and thought it best just to let the media say what they want but not fuel it. Catherine R was doing a great job getting the materials together for Hutton. David Omand seemed a bit too laid-back, saying everyone should go away and have a good holiday. The BBC were still spinning away madly and of course would carry on using their output to help shape their case. It would take a very strong mind not to be influenced. Dyke wrote to TB claiming a Cabinet minister had told Marr there would be 'revenge'. TB drafted a pretty rough reply which Peter felt we shouldn't send.

Peter M asked if I was going to conference. I hope not, I said. 'Who will write your speech?' he asked TB. 'Alastair and I will,' he said. 'He'll have more time if he's not doing everything else.' TB went off to Chequers and I called in all my staff. I said that they'd all have been hearing and reading all this stuff. I wanted them to know I was going to use the holiday to decide what to do. I said whatever decision I took, I was proud of the team I had built and grateful for the phenomenal support they gave me, but ultimately a decision like this had to be for me and the family, and a holiday was the right place to make it. I could tell that they knew where it was heading.

[David] Bradshaw came to see me later, and seemed close to tears. He said people in here would be devastated if I went, that I underestimated how much of what they all did they did for me, because I made it a great place to work, and I took all the hits for them, and let them take risks. He said nobody ever understood how I managed to do the job the way I did, but he was worried if I stopped doing it, the place would collapse. Gone was his usual mickey-taking Scouse humour, and in its place an impassioned plea to stay. But I think he knew it would fall on deaf ears, though I was really touched by his warmth and trust.

We went for dinner at the Blackburns' [David and Janice]. Peter M there too and we were really going for a couple of people there who were close friends of Tom Bower and Veronica Wadley [husband and wife, *Mail* journalist and *Evening Standard* editor]. They seemed shocked by the strength of our hatred of Dacre. I said your friend Wadley works for the most poisonous influence in British life. He and his papers are evil. They add nothing of good to the world whatever. I was confident of being cleared by Hutton but wish he'd had the *Mail on Sunday* in there too. They hid behind the BBC. David Blackburn got the plot re the BBC, had followed it closely and could see all the holes in their arguments. He said he felt it was possible that I would be vindicated but also that Gilligan would not be condemned. I felt relieved it was more out in the open that I would be going. Catherine MacLeod [*Herald*] had done a piece making clear I had agreed with TB on May 28 that I would go. I felt I would be free to do lots of different things but also stay involved in a different kind of way, less intense, less demanding, with less contact with the media.

Wednesday, July 30 (holiday, Puyméras, Provence)

Writing by Philip and Gail's pool. Everyone has gone to Vaison to get bikes. Feeling a pretty big sense of foreboding. Catherine Rimmer just texted me to say the first question at TB's press conference was about me and my future. No doubt they're going to try to keep me as a big issue for him. JP very nice about me on the *Today* programme apparently. Michael Barber [head of the Prime Minister's delivery Unit] did his delivery slides presentation at the press conference, and did it well by all accounts, but it was unlikely to get much coverage. They couldn't give two tosses about the public service agenda. CR said the public services slide show had been excellent punishment for the hacks. The other major soap event was Carole C who had done a big picture spread in *Hello!* magazine, which the press were going big on. Sally called me, said she had been to see TB yesterday and told him 'that woman' is going to destroy you if you do not sort it out. She said TB went mad at her, saying it was ridiculous how we were all against Carole. I think TB just liked her, and liked the fact she had been a help to CB, but there wasn't one of us who didn't find it a bit odd. I was feeling fairly detached. I was moving on psychologically and there were plenty of options to consider. News International were pressing pretty hard. I wrote I was keen to do sport before politics and based on a few chats with the boys I started to work up an idea for a series on how to decide who the greatest sportsmen of all time were.

TB called me the day I left but then we had radio silence for a while. Peter M called for a few chats, not least re the *Sunday Telegraph* when Gavyn Davies wrote a piece on how we were allegedly threatening BBC independence. This followed the letter from Dyke to TB claiming Marr had received a call from a Cabinet minister warning that we planned to get revenge. Marr's behaviour in all this had been disgraceful, and he had just become part of the BBC's lobbying and PR operation, which was going on relentlessly. I spoke to Tessa [Jowell] before she did *The World at One* and also did a note saying we had to make clear there was no link between the row and [BBC] Charter review.

Meanwhile there was more coming out about Kelly and his contacts with the press. The BBC were successful in keeping things focused on how Kelly's name came out, and pretty much ignoring other more relevant issues. On the drive down through France I'd had a worried call from David Hill. He said someone was getting to TB over the Order in Council issue [the ruling allowing AC and Jonathan Powell to direct civil servants]. It was probably a mix of senior civil servants, who would be keen to use my departure to rein back, and Peter M who was keen to use it – for the right reasons – to give a sense of a post spin era. Bruce Anderson [*Independent*] was already on to the theme that we were now spinning non-spin as the new spin. But I was worried a change would weaken DH in the job. I told him I felt it was imperative that he keep it, particularly as the [Bob] Phillis [review] team was split on the issue and Bob needed support.

PG meanwhile was worried we were nearing a tipping point re TB. He had just been to the US with Ian McCartney, Pat McF, Douglas and Alice [Cartner-Morley, pollster] and came back both awestruck by the professionalism and ruthlessness of the Republican operation, but also alarmed at how people had started to talk of TB almost in the past tense, and focusing more on legacy than forward agenda. We drove down via a stopover in Paris to see John and Penny Holmes [UK ambassador to France and his wife]. Penny was very alarmed at the CB/Carole situation. John [Blair's former foreign policy adviser] said of TB. 'You must do something to try to distance himself from Bush. Nobody here believes Tony will do anything that Bush doesn't want and he is seen as even more right wing and unpopular here than he is in the UK.' He felt TB gave Bush very strong support early on and Bush has exploited it. He does not get enough back in return and his European policy is paying a price. He felt the two GBs were Tony's big problems – his foreign policy was foundering on his closeness to Bush. His domestic policy was stalling because GB kept his foot on the brake the whole time. Also, he said the thing I managed to give him – grip and good presentation – was now likely to weaken. He felt TB didn't grasp the scale of the challenge at the moment. He had let things drift – never tackled Gordon properly, never really worked out a proper euro strategy, never dealt with Carole and the lifestyle image issues. He was paying the price and there were the beginnings of a feeling of decay. Philip felt the same.

We had a more or less painless journey down and the kids were on good form. I had meanwhile decided that I would pretty much leave as soon as we got back from holiday, the reasons as per the note I had done earlier. I felt I could continue to advise from outside on strategy and maybe do election planning. I would make speeches to make a living, write on sport and politics after a while, also do more on the leukaemia fund-raising front and motivational stuff for the party. I had a vague notion of getting involved with the ad agency. Maybe do a chat show but it might be difficult because part of the public argument I intend to make is how awful modern TV has become. I was thinking a lot about the media culture and its impact on the health of democracy. The balance had gone from being a good check-balance to just creating a culture of negativity.

I spoke to Richard Desmond in Majorca at one point. He said 'You can't go because Tony needs you too much.' I said people always underestimated Tony. I told him I might do a film on Dacre and [Lord] Rothermere and he was very up for it. 'How much do you want? We'll do it.' I was not going to be short of offers but I had decided no to the consultancy and lobbying route. Just not my thing. PG felt I needed to strike while the iron was hot re the US speaking scene. Nice call from Jonathan Prince [Democrat strategist], who was working for [Senator John] Edwards [Democrat presidential hopeful]. He said there was a fair bit of coverage of my travails in the States. 'Just hang in there. They only hate you because you're too good for them.' I was getting a lot of 'hang in' messages, but my mind was set. I was clear I had to go.

On the Saturday I had a long chat with Alex F who was out in the States, raving about the Nike training centre. I told him I was definitely leaving now. 'Give my congratulations to Fiona,' he said. 'Maybe I gave you the wrong advice. Maybe you should have left when you first thought of it, but the one thing nobody can ever take from you is that you know you've done a great job, and you should now do what is right for you and the family. You've given enough.' Fiona was still detoxing on the CB stuff, still angry about Carole but the more there was about her in the press in a way the better it was for Fiona as she tried to shape a new professional future too. Catherine Rimmer was keeping me in touch with the Hutton team. It now seemed Hutton would read himself in, then take witnesses from the 11th to the 18th, first the MoD, then the BBC, then others, then reflect, maybe re-interview, report maybe in October. So it was definitely going to be another interrupted holiday. Also the whole conference season would have Hutton as the backdrop.

I was now reaching a settled feeling about leaving – I felt excited at the prospect of new and different things to do. It would be nice for the family as a whole that I travelled less, saw them more, and could earn decent money. I sometimes felt I had been pressured by Fiona, but equally I knew she had my interests as well as her own at heart. But I also knew I would need to stay involved in some way, not least because I still felt at my best I was the best, and could make a contribution. It's just that I hadn't been at my best for a while. I also felt sad at the thought my team would break up. As I whirred things round in my mind it was clear for the first time I was thinking more about my own future than TB's. I would help if I could but he would have to help himself.

The weather was beautiful and I was pretty much running every day, including a couple of big ones. We didn't see that many papers. Philip felt the combination of no WMD plus Carole would get the party unnerved. I was getting into my stride on the sports series and by the weekend had written four or five articles. The *Mail* were still going at me hell for leather according to Catherine R. Sad fuckers.

Thursday, July 31

Catherine Rimmer kept the faxes coming thick and fast. Matthew Lewin [journalist neighbour] did a piece for the *Press Gazette* about the press in the street outside the house and general BBC standards. Bill Hagerty [editor, *British Journalism Review*] did a piece attacking the BBC. The Hutton hype was winding down in advance of him saying tomorrow how he intended to proceed. I had a long chat with Jonathan who said TB had finally seen the light re Carole. 'I know we've heard it before but *Hello!* was the last goodbye.' After the call

Catherine R called again to say that Hutton wanted to see me and Jonathan on August 21.

I had been hoping to be able to see out the holiday but no luck. We now had to work out how best to get myself fully briefed and also properly psyched up. It put a real dampener on things and Fiona was even more pissed off now. Ross [Kemp, actor] and Rebekah [Wade] came over and we had a nice enough time with them. They, along with Gail and PG, felt I was on strong ground but I felt Hutton would feel he had to make some criticism of everyone. Philip felt TB had panicked in calling an inquiry. Kelly killed himself because he killed himself and we should have held our nerve. He was pretty down on TB at the moment.

Ditto Rebekah who felt public services were going backwards, though as I kept telling the News International lot, they tended not to use them. She and I discussed a number of News International options going from occasional columns up to a deal across titles. TB felt the *Sunday Times* was the paper to do a column in. PG felt the *Sun*. The Hutton traffic was fairly steady, with people calling regularly. Tom K and Catherine both felt the order of witnesses was good for us – MoD, then BBC, then us, then TB, then Geoff H and then John Scarlett who I felt sure would be a very strong witness.

Friday, August 1

Catherine R called again re flights as we felt there may be a case for her coming out to brief me. She was very happy with *The Times* which did a big number, and the *Guardian* had the Gilligan [FAC hearing] transcript which did not do him much good and suggested he was backing off the central allegations against me. John Stanley and Eric Illsley [FAC MPs] gave him a very hard time on it. Rachel Kinnock was due out so I was getting a new package of briefing material to come out with her. Truth was the holiday was pretty much going down the Swanee but hopefully it would be the last to be like this. Also I was pretty desperate to be cleared and so I had to keep my focus the whole time. I needed to be at my best when I reached the witness stand and a lot of the preparation had to be done now.

Hutton was doing his stuff at 11 and it would dominate the media all day, plus everyone was saying it was important I stay hidden away on the day of the funeral. I was finding it easy, and quite therapeutic, to do the sports series and had done the concept and the first few drafts in a matter of days. But I was not plugged into the political scene apart from re Hutton though I suppose that was about the only politics going at the moment. Neil was hilarious on the sports greats idea. I told him about the idea over dinner on the evening they arrived and for pretty much every sport he had a Welsh name to suggest. He was adamant John Charles [Wales and Leeds United striker] was better than Pelé or Maradona. He had a Welsh boxer better than Muhammad Ali.

By now I had a huge Hutton file to read. Hutton did his opening statement which seemed to be pointing heavily towards the BBC but it was also clear the manner in which Kelly's name came out was going to be a big part of it. I felt the weight of it all building again. Catherine felt the statement would worry the BBC more than us. PG felt Hutton came across as clear and strong and it was important I came over as being clear and strong. Later I spoke to Omand and Charlie F. CF said he felt there was no need to be too nervous but Hutton was not someone to be pushed around. Omand felt GH was the one who might be in difficulty and said they were all getting a bit jumpy at the MoD. I'd felt the name should come out and that Kelly should appear before the FAC and ISC and that it was important we knew what was what. I felt comfortable in that position but it may be others would see it very differently. I told Neil I was very nervous about it all. He said there was no need because if I told the truth it would be fine. He felt Hutton would just want facts.

Saturday, August 2

Neil was being very supportive, though he was also in a rage re a few EU situations. I was working on a witness statement which meant going over the whole thing again and again. I wasn't sleeping well. I called Joe Haines [Harold Wilson's former press secretary] for a chat. He felt I had to maintain control of my own exit, don't go under a cloud or looking like I've been harassed out. He said what had happened was awful, that Gilligan should be ashamed. The coverage of the Hutton statement was OK but there was still an awful lot being pointed at me.

Sunday, August 3

I read the Kelly MoD interviews, which were pretty good for our case. I had had another night waking up, tossing and turning. I then just lay there waiting for the church bells to ring, and every time came the thought that they'd toll for me. Fiona was being very supportive and keeping the kids' spirits up but it was like we had a big dark cloud over us the whole time.

Tuesday, August 5

Peter M in the *Sunday Mirror* had said TB was clear we would be OK. I sent a message round the system saying we should all just shut up. The *Indy* yesterday splashed on Number 10 describing Kelly as a Walter Mitty character.[1] I told the office we had to disown it very forcibly at the eleven o'clock, which Anne Shevas, who hated doing the briefings, duly did. But it emerged that it was Tom who had said it, when chatting to Paul Waugh [*Independent*]. He had been going over the questions Hutton would want to look at, had not remotely intended it to run as a story and now it was the latest frenzy. I said he should apologise and drop a line both to Mrs Kelly and to Hutton. PG and Gail thought it was a bad idea to involve the widow because we had no clue as to how she would react. I had earlier drafted a letter to Mrs Kelly myself and discussed with JP whether he thought I should send it. He felt the sentiments were fine but you could never tell how people in grief and shock would react. He said he would take it to the funeral and make a judgement then as to whether to give it to her. There was no other major story around at the moment so several of the papers splashed on Tom on the Tuesday. He was feeling wretched and I called him to say not to worry too much about it. I got a message through to TB to call him too.

Jamie Rubin [former US State Department chief spokeman] called to offer support. He said he assumed that I knew the BBC were in the wrong but they got into a 'won't back down to him' situation and it all got out of hand. Pretty much. Even out on holiday, Philip was doing notes for me. He was seeing and reading more of the media than I was, I having pretty much given up on reading the papers. He felt that what came through, even in the ones who hated me, was a sense of really deep commitment and professionalism and work ethic and it was important that side of me was what came over to the judge. He felt I should strive to de-personalise, de-emotionalise my own role. Be focused and professional.

The office sent through my ISC evidence which I had to sign off. Again I felt confident in the facts. Neil could tell though how nervous I was. He said I could not bottle up something like this and if I wanted to talk to him at any time, he was there. He was very warm and supportive and also lifting a lot of the pressure on the family too. Even though Fiona and the kids were still doing all the things we do on holiday they were clearly feeling the tension a fair bit. Philip felt

[1] From a 1939 story by James Thurber, *The Secret Life of Walter Mitty*, dealing with the imagined adventures of a mild-mannered dreamer.

the problem was that the media were effectively running this as the government on trial. The press were helping the BBC to reframe the debate in their favour, without vacating the field, so that they were both player but also 'neutral' spectator. Not. JP went to Kelly's funeral and called me afterwards. He said Mrs Kelly had been fine with him, had not been seeking to blame the government for his death, which made me feel a lot better. I was starting to work on my own statement. I was not impressed with the advice we were getting from the Cabinet Office about lawyers.

Thursday, August 7

We had dinner in Malaucene with Ian and Andrea Kennedy [personal friends]. I was looking forward to getting some hard-headed and objective advice from Ian about how to approach it. His chairing of the Bristol babies inquiry [into baby heart deaths at Bristol Royal Infirmary, begun in 1998] had been seen as pretty good, and he was always very good on problem solving generally. He felt, based on what he had read in the press, that I was fine on the substance. But he was amazed that I did not already have my own lawyer, and he was really pressing me to get my act together, or get the Cabinet Office to get theirs together. He said he had advised everyone involved in Bristol to have their own lawyer.

What would happen, he asked, if the nub came down to a difference of opinion between, say, me and Geoff Hoon, or me and John Scarlett? Was I really saying there would just be one government lawyer representing everyone? He thought it was ridiculous. I was already feeling pretty sick, having heard from the inquiry team that the judge wanted me to give him my diaries, or at least any relevant extracts. The request came as a real shock. Sandra Powell [secretary] had called me to read through all the various areas he wished to ask me about, and as she ran through them, I felt absolutely fine. It was only when she faxed through the letter that I noted at the end this request to see anything from my diaries. Ian thought it was probably just a fishing expedition but now not only was I worried – as I said to Fiona, Christ knows what I've written in there – but I was also beginning to panic a little about what Ian had said re the need for my own lawyer. I was very pleased Ian would be around.

Friday, August 8

Ian got hold of Alan Maclean, who had been one of his legal team for the Bristol inquiry, and made arrangements for him to come out next week. I called the Cabinet Office and asked for a list of lawyers to choose from. Rosemary Jeffreys [Treasury Solicitor's Department] gave me a list but of course what we didn't know was who was available and this was the worst time imaginable to be trying to find one. I put a call into James Goudie [QC] for his advice, also Charlie F and Derry, and TB. Charlie in particular thought I would not get on with Jonathan Sumption [QC], who was the one Alan Maclean and Ian were recommending. The general view was that he was right wing, a bit quirky and someone who would want things done his way. Charlie felt we were both strong characters who would get on each other's nerves. Ian was strongly of the view that if Alan was saying he was the best, and also as his reputation was so strong, we should try to get him.

Alan got on to his clerk. It transpired Sumption was staying at his place in France, and had indicated immediately he was keen to do it. I was also trying to sort the shipping out of my diary for this year. The summer holiday is the one time of the year where I don't take it with me, and instead just scribble a few notes every now and then when I feel like it. Poor old Audrey had to get into the house, root around under the bed and then get the book to Number 10. Originally the plan was to get it shipped out with books that were being sent out for Gail but her stuff was coming out late so Number 10 had to sort it out. I was now finding it really hard to sleep. The request for my diaries felt like a hostile act to me. I suspected I was the only one being asked to do this. And why – because the papers had said I kept a diary. Why isn't everyone asked if they keep a personal diary, and to provide any relevant bits?

Sunday, August 10

I had received the request for my diary on Thursday and now, finally, this year's was being flown out by Peter Howes [duty clerk]. As I left the house, and said goodbye to Fiona, I did actually wonder momentarily whether it would be the last time I saw her, whether what I discovered on reading my own diary would be so awful that I would want to top myself. It was only a passing thought, but it was there, and it came back several times as I drove down to Marseilles. I knew I had done nothing wrong, but in this climate, things had gone beyond reason, it was like a drama or a novel, and nobody had control of events. I tried not to be in a panic on the drive down, but I was. I couldn't remember what I wrote in my diary the minute I wrote it. On the few occasions I ever looked back, I was always surprised at things that happened, things I said, things other people had said. I just didn't know.

I met Simon Lever [UK Consul General in Marseilles] as we waited for Peter to come through. I managed to hide any nerves I had from Peter, who was dressed like he was just having a nice day trip to an airport on an aeroplane. But inside I was feeling sick. He handed me the package and I set off back to the car. I put it on the passenger seat, thought about opening it there and then but the car was hot and I wanted to get away from the airport. I drove for maybe half an hour and then pulled into a service station. It was now unbelievably hot. I opened the envelope slowly and then pulled out the diary, put it down again and just stared at it. What I had written in there, or so I felt, had the capacity to deliver vindication or destruction. One bad word, and who knows, for me, for Tony, for the whole bloody government.

When I thought of some of the things I've said in there about ministers, about colleagues, about the press, about the BBC. By the time I finally started flicking through it, I was sweating. It was now so hot that even in the shade of a few trees, the sweat was falling down my face. I found the various sections on the dossier. At first glance, it seemed fine, and I started to feel a bit better. There was certainly nothing I could see that would mean I would have to resign straight away. A few bad bits, a bit too colourful in parts, but overall manageable. The best thing was that in terms of all the facts in there, they supported what we had been saying about events.

It then suddenly dawned on me I had made a terrible mistake. I had been so focused on Kelly's death, which was after all the subject of the inquiry, that I had only got this year's diary sent out when of course it was last year that the dossier was put together and it was clear from the inquiry team's letter that was absolutely central. I felt sick all over again. What an idiotic thing to do. As I sat there, feeling a mixture of relief that my cursory flick through had revealed nothing terrible, and anger at my own stupidity in not getting both diaries sent out, the phone went.

It was Number 10 with Godric. When I told him what I was doing, he was horrified. He said he thought it was unbelievable that he [Lord Hutton] was asking for my diaries. Like me he saw it as a hostile act. Maybe, he says, it shows he basically buys into the media line on us. Godric was so principled and proper, and a believer in playing fair, that he seemed if anything even more shocked and upset than I was. He made the same point I had – why hasn't everyone been asked if they keep a diary? But anyway, we were beyond that. He then got more and more anxious as I told him what I was organising on the legal front. He said that he had heard nothing from the Cabinet Office other than the fact he would have to give evidence. He had had the same conversation I had had with Omand on the day Hutton set out his terms, namely take a bit of a break and see what happens. It was, as Charlie F had also observed, a bit Heath Robinson.

Godric was asking whether I thought he should go back straight away. I could tell that I had ruined his holiday, if it wasn't already ruined. I got home, and we went out to Villedieu for the evening. Ian [Kennedy] said he really thought I should put my fate in the hands of a good team of lawyers now, stop trying to make all the decisions myself, stop relying on the government or the Cabinet Office. He said Alan was terrific. Sumption was now on board and he described him as having 'a brain the size of a planet'. I also now had Adam Chapman from the Treasury Solicitor's Department. After Fiona and the kids had gone to bed, I went back through the diary, read it all more slowly and in more detail. The thought of it all being put before the inquiry did not exactly fill me with joy, but it wasn't the disaster I feared. I was kicking myself though re not getting 2002 sent out. I wasn't even sure where it was, so poor old Audrey was going to have to look around the house and we'd have to go through the whole process again.

Wednesday, August 13

Ian had really acted as a fantastic catalyst in getting a proper legal team together. Alan Maclean was staying with the Kennedys at Faucon and I met him briefly last night. He said he, Sumption and Adam Chapman had read the papers on the train from Toulouse to Avignon, where the other two were staying overnight. He said they had concluded that there were only two fundamental questions for me: 1. did I play around with the dossier on the 45-minute point, and 2. did I play a part in a conspiracy re Kelly? He said they all three of them felt, based on all the material they had read, that the answer was no to both. He said Sumption was very clear about it. 'He has pretty much decided that you are the cowboys and the BBC are the Indians.' He said Sumption was reflecting overnight on how we handle the issue of the diary request. I went over to the Kennedys' this morning. Alan and Andrea were getting the printouts on the inquiry from the Internet.

We were into the third day and the BBC case appeared to be falling apart. Gilligan by all accounts a poor witness, Susan Watts to her credit refusing to toe their line and so making things worse for the BBC. The MoD seemed to be doing OK in stressing that they did what they could for Kelly. Sumption and Adam Chapman arrived a bit late. He was not at all what I expected. I'd expected someone rather overbearing, tall, smooth. He seemed a bit shy and nervy, as though a comfortable holiday home was not really the place for this kind of thing. He had a mass of all-over-the-place grey hair. His clothes didn't quite hang together. He was carrying a biography of [John Maynard] Keynes [economist]. We got down to business straight away and I took to him fairly easily, despite all the warnings. He was sharp, to the point, and very clear. He repeated the view Adam had expressed, about the two main questions, and said matter-of-factly 'I don't think you have to worry about that.'

He was also very direct about my diary. He said the prime minister has established an inquiry, Lord Hutton has been appointed, the PM has said he and his staff will co-operate fully, and this is an example of the judge asking for full co-operation. He felt it would be a very bad move to refuse to provide it, or to seek to frame an argument as to why I should. He said the judge would not appreciate it, so I should just accept I would have to do it, and take whatever heat came from it. It was what I had been expecting to hear, and in any event I had already gone through the pain barrier on that one.

On the draft statement I had done, he felt it was fine, in that all the relevant facts were in there, but both he and Ian felt it was too personal and too emotional. All the judge would want is fact. Adam and Alan worked on my statement while Jonathan S and I sat at the dining room table and went through my diary. He felt that he would have to be the judge of what Lord Hutton would deem to be relevant to the inquiry. In terms of what went in, and what stayed out, even though we did not know what Hutton intended to do with this stuff, and even before Sumption knew what I had written, he was at the broader end of the margin. I was sort of hoping that his attitude would be 'when in doubt, keep it out'. It was the opposite. He clearly felt that the more open we were, the fairer the judge would be. I read through page after page, putting pencil marks through the bits he felt were irrelevant, but also making notes in the margins of the vague subject matter to show he had been through it.

Occasionally he would have a doubt but would usually say 'No harm including it.' Some days there was nothing relevant at all, on other days a line or two. At other times, virtually everything would go in. Obviously TB, other departments and the agencies were going to have to see this, and that would maybe have its own problems, but I had now pretty much decided that I was going to take Ian's advice to take this guy's advice, unless it clashed with TB's interests, and as the day wore on, that seemed less and less likely. I found the whole experience really stressful though, going over all the same ground again, not just Iraq, but the other big policy nightmares, TB/GB, Cherie and Carole, also some of the rows with Fiona, some of the guilt at not being there enough, some of the other political stuff, the hatred of some of the media, the pressure, the agonising at my own situation.

When the kids came round later in the day, I also felt a growing sense of injustice that I was the only witness having to do this, when I wanted to be having a normal holiday with the family, and after they went down to the pool, I just started sobbing. 'I'm sorry,' I said to Sumption, whose expression didn't really change. 'It's all right,' he said. 'I totally understand why this is difficult.' I said I don't understand why this is happening to me. He said 'If I were you, I would feel that too. It is dreadful that you are being asked to bare your soul when in my view you have done nothing wrong. But the prime minister set up the inquiry and you have to co-operate with the judge when he asks for this. If he thinks your diary may contain something which helps him, he is entitled to ask for it, warts and all.' I composed myself pretty quickly, and we went back to the task in hand.

It took five or so hours, and I felt totally drained at the end. 'So how was that voyage of discovery for you?' I asked him. 'It was certainly a discovery. I have read so much about you. Now I think I know you. In fact I don't think I've ever learned so much about someone so quickly.' He writes books on medieval history and he said 'I wish there had been people keeping records like this in those days. It would make my life so much easier.' He felt there was something 'wonderfully Victorian about it'.[1] He said it would one day be an amazing service to historians, 'but I can see why that does not hold much appeal to you right now'. It was an odd experience, to have sat down with a total stranger, and gone through so much detail of my own life and work, and at the end of it to be talking as though we had known each other for ages. I noticed he hadn't shaved properly, and as the day wore on his clothes seemed to get scruffier, but I felt by the end of the day that I was with someone who knew what he was doing.

In the ensuing days, first Jeremy [Heywood] – on TB's behalf – and then TB himself came on to say they didn't agree with Sumption's

[1] Sumption's vast multi-volume *The Hundred Years War between England and France* would be described by journalist Allan Massie as 'an enterprise on a truly Victorian scale'.

strategy re the diaries. They felt it was unfair, but also wrong, to ask someone to submit a private diary to a public inquiry. I could tell TB was really worried about it, not least by the number of times he told me not to worry. But Sumption resisted the pressure. TB's argument was that we should fight harder for me not to have to do this. Sumption was adamant that would backfire badly with the judge – on me, but also on the government. Although he did not articulate it in this way, I saw his strategy was maximum openness for minimum disclosure.

We now had to work out process. I was thinking I should probably go home, but Alan felt I should stay here for as long as possible, that if I went back, I would be miserable without the family, would follow the inquiry the whole time, which at the moment I was managing to avoid, and he felt I would do better on the stand if I stayed here than if I went back. I called Alison [Blackshaw] and asked her to come out and join us, so that I could get the diary extracts properly typed up. She arranged to come out tomorrow. We went for dinner at the Goulds' and I felt so much better. Sumption went off again. I don't know if it was a joke or not but according to the others he 'owned a village' somewhere in the south-west of France. As he left he said I could call him at any time, but he really believed I had nothing to worry about on the substance. I was really worried about the fact I had told *The Times* two other papers had the name but on my first meeting with Sumption, he said it didn't matter.

Though I felt more at ease with the process, and more confident now I knew I had some decent lawyers involved, I was still not sleeping well, and was feeling real stress not just about the obvious, but also the idea that Fiona and the kids weren't really having much of a holiday with all this going on around them. Every morning now, I was waking up at 4 or 5, waiting for the next ringing of the bells at the village church, and from time to time the old 'ask not for whom the bell tolls . . .' lodged in there. It was impossible not to imagine the worst. The kids kept me going really – the thought that eventually we would get a proper family life back again, and the knowledge that no matter how bad it was, apart from the occasional fleeting moment, I did not think of doing what Kelly had done.

Thursday, August 14 – Friday/Saturday, August 15/16

TB was calling regularly now, and was clearly getting more and more anxious re my diaries. At first he had been dismissive, saying it was a fuss about nothing, but I sensed that was him trying to make sure I didn't get too worried. Now he was getting more agitated and angry, and strongly disagreed with the Sumption strategy. He felt we should be fighting harder for non-disclosure. I explained Sumption's strategy as I saw it – maximum openness for minimum disclosure and on the substance he thinks on balance that, whilst there are difficulties in there, it helps our case. Yes, said TB, but you are dealing with lawyers and we are politicians in a political situation. I said yes, and part of the politics is that he set up an independent inquiry and promised full co-operation and we cannot now be seen not to co-operate. What is more, if we refuse and it becomes known, then all hell will break loose again and a lot of it around me. I said I was confident that Sumption's strategy was right and I thought we had no choice. He asked me several times 'What's in these things?' I explained that I was getting Alison out to help me transcribe, but that in Sumption's view there was nothing catastrophic. There was a fair bit of bad language. 'How much?' A fair bit. 'Fuck?' Yes. 'Cunt?' Probably, can't remember. 'Bloody hell, Alastair.' He asked if there was anything disparaging about him, or about ministers. Nothing too bad re him. Lots of criticism of Clare [Short], yes, one or two others. Bits and bobs re him and GB. Me thinking of leaving. Fiona and Cherie. 'What?' Yes, but Sumption did not think any of that needed to be put in. We ended up swapping notes on the extent to which our respective holidays had been ruined. He also said I shouldn't worry, that the diaries sounded more embarrassing than damaging, though by now he was back in 'let's keep AC calm' mode.

He called every few hours now, chatting over various things, and eventually I said please let me get on and finish the transcription, and then we can make a judgement as to how bad or not it all is. But he was generally reassuring in these circumstances. He said it was horrible for me, and horrible for all of us, but I should take strength from the fact I had done nothing wrong, and he was confident we would come through this. He said 'What is the worst thing that can be said against you – that you went over the top? But you had every right to, because these were allegations made directly against you, not just me, and you had every right to defend yourself.' He felt that there was a chance Hutton would decide this was as much a story about our rotten media culture as the nature of government.

The inquiry was certainly not going well for the BBC, no matter how hard the media tried to spin it their way. But none of us could really gauge which way Hutton was going. We just had to get on and make our case as best we could. Alison arrived, bringing with her my 2002 diary, and a quick flick through that also reassured me, in that it showed how much care we had put into the September dossier, and it showed in terms how I tried to ensure the agencies were happy with every word and every part of the process. Alison and I started to go through the stuff I had gone over with Sumption. It was not as bad as I feared, though there were one or two points where she winced, usually when I was swearing or saying something derogatory about someone, though it was all stuff she had heard before.

We set up in the dining room/lounge bit of the house and worked on it most of Thursday night, all day Friday, when the lawyers went back to London, most of Saturday, as Alison and I travelled back to England by train, and I finally got a full typed version to Sumption at his house in France by Sunday pm, well ahead of the Monday 5pm deadline, though a lot of people would want to see them before then. He had initially secured a delay to my deadline because of the work required transcribing the diaries but then they came back and said no, the original timetable stood, so we had been working flat out to get through it. Thousands of words and he was trying to reach a deal with the inquiry that it would not be submitted as evidence as such, which would then have to be published along with everything else, but as a supplementary statement.

Fiona and the kids had adapted pretty well considering, and were just carrying on doing everything around us, while I was trying to grab a half-hour here, a half-hour there. It was great having Alison out at the house. The kids liked her and once we got going, I realised it was not going to take quite as long as I feared. When I left for home, and my appearance at the inquiry, Fiona was pretty cold with me, said good luck, but with a 'if you'd listened to me, you wouldn't be in this mess' look on her face. 'Sorry for ruining the holiday,' I said. She smiled, shrugged and just said do your best and get back as soon as you can. She was understandably angry that the holiday was being so disrupted. Grace was crying, and later apparently asked the boys if I could go to jail. Rory went off on a bike ride, I guess to avoid saying goodbye, though he and I had had a good chat earlier. Calum was putting on a brave face and playing the hard man. 'Never forget you're a Campbell, and nobody messes with our family.'

On the train, we had a table to ourselves and so were able to carry on with the transcription, but it meant me whispering into Alison's ear as I dictated and I am sure there were people on there who thought I was at it with her. Then some creep from the *Daily Telegraph*, who I don't think could believe his luck that I was on the train, came up and started to make small talk, pretending to be an ordinary passenger. He was not very convincing. 'Which paper are you from?' Er, the *Telegraph*, I wondered if I could do an interview about your coming appearance at the inquiry, blah blah. 'I'm busy.' Alison had typed for hours and hours on end, God knows how many. Her view was that it wasn't great – particularly the language – but that it did show the kind of pressures we were under and also that we were most of the time just trying to do our best. I had not been seeing the papers at all, had been binning the media briefs, but the impression I got from Philip, who was following it more closely via the Internet, was that it wasn't going well for the BBC. Ian K emphasised to me again and again that I should trust Sumption, who would be focusing on one thing only – the judge. I had decided to do just that, and though Sumption was happy to argue over a point, and accept my view on things, equally I was happy to listen to him and trust his judgement.

I arrived home and decided to go in through the Farthings' [Michael and Alison, neighbours] back garden so that the press in the street didn't know I was there. Audrey was looking after me, and had been reading every word. She felt it was not going well for the BBC. But they were really gearing up for me, and they were desperate for me to fail. Peter M called, and said did I have any idea how much the media wanted me to be a disaster in the witness box? TB was calling more regularly from Barbados now. Before the diaries got out to him, he kept asking me the same questions re content. All I could do was give him Sumption's view. He felt they were neither good nor bad. But on the positive side, they underlined our side of the story. They showed I did nothing wrong re the dossier. They showed I got very angry re the BBC, and made very clear why. They did show I wanted to put out Kelly's name, but didn't and instead did as I was told by him. As for the bad language and the loose language, Sumption's view was that the judge would not take it amiss. This was a private diary and he would understand.

The point of substance I was worried about related to where it looked like Geoff Hoon was suggesting a kind of 'plea bargain' [see July 4]. It was becoming clear to me that my lawyers were very much trying to get me to think of myself rather than the government as a whole, and particularly GH. If he had said that, and I recorded it, and it was a problem, it was a problem for him, not me. But I found it hard to think like that. I saw this still as the government under attack, me included, but also the government as a whole. They felt GH could use a 'cut-throat defence', and go for me, and therefore it was better I go for him, but I was not comfortable with that.

I called him on the Thursday or Friday, not sure which, and warned him about the line in my diary that they were calling the 'plea bargain point'. He was in the States on holiday and said he felt a lot better having gone away, despite the advice to stay. I felt he was under similar family pressures to my own. He said he had indeed been intending to throw the book at Kelly when it became clear he was Gilligan's source, but then calmed down and felt his honesty was to be commended and even rewarded in some way. He said he was grateful for my call and did not give me the impression he was worried about his own position. The only journalist I was talking to at all really was Phil Webster. *The Times* were about the only paper left covering the story from all sides so far as I could see. Most of them were totally with the BBC, but my sense was their case was falling apart.

Sunday, August 17

I was into the office early to go through a mass of material prepared for me by Clare [Sumner] and Catherine [Rimmer], who were both absolutely brilliant. They were so on top of the detail, and so driven by a belief that we were in the right. The diary extracts were circulated internally and also to a few in other departments. TB thought they were fine, though was worried about one or two observations made re him. Jeremy was still passionately of the view that it was just wrong that I had to do this, and we should have fought harder to stop it happening, but things had really moved on from that. I was trying to avoid adding to the big build-up to Tuesday at the inquiry, so I got back home via the neighbours' garden network again. I guessed if they had no new pictures they would give less space.

Had they had a camera in the garden they would have got a nice shot of me ripping my trousers, and cutting my leg, on the Farthings' trellis fence. I decided as well that tomorrow I would stay in Number 10, let the press continue to think I was at home, in a hotel, or wherever, just avoid being seen until I have to be. I had a nice dinner with Audrey, just chatting away about the whole thing, what Bob [Millar, Fiona's father] would have made of it, the effect it was all having on my mum and dad. Audrey was a hundred per cent full-on supporter, didn't believe a word against me, hated the BBC for what they'd done, and was not that sympathetic to Kelly, felt he should never have got involved with Gilligan in the first place.

Monday, August 18

I felt OK but reckoned I had now averaged three hours' sleep a night since I got that wretched letter re my diaries. I was going to have to rely on a mix of real preparation, nerve and adrenaline to get me through. TB was working on his own witness statement and remained confident. Catherine R had collated all the various comments from departments about the diaries, and the requests for further redactions from some, including TB. She and I then did a conference call with Sumption, and went through them all. Some he accepted but the bulk he didn't, and he was absolutely clear he was not taking something out just because the prime minister wanted it. Jonathan [Powell] was back to give evidence, and I got the feeling he had very deliberately not allowed it to ruin his holiday. The downside meant he was not terribly well prepared and I was worried he was a bit cavalier.

He had also grown his usual summer holiday beard and I was urging him to shave it off as it looked a bit ragged. Hutton did not strike me as a beard man. But Jonathan was adamant he was not changing anything just because he had been dragged back for this. He was nervous though, as was I. I noticed at one point a slight shake in his hand, and when the two of us were alone, without the lawyers and researchers around, he let the front down a bit and seemed really quite anxious. He went off and by all accounts did fine, though he rather dropped Tom Baldwin [*Times*] in it by indicating that Baldwin was the one who briefed me re the Sambrook lunch. I said I would have to find a way of rebutting when I gave evidence tomorrow.

Stephen Parkinson [government lawyer] came back with Jonathan and then sat down with me for a really helpful, but quite gruelling, Q&A session. I felt by now that I had every word and every argument just about right, and there were no questions I absolutely dreaded. I felt on top of the facts. It was still not clear how the judge or the QC [James Dingemans, senior counsel to the inquiry] intended to use my diaries which was still a bit of a worry. But there too, I felt confident I could defend myself, even though there was the odd embarrassment or difficulty in there. I was getting a lot of Good Luck messages coming through, and there was definitely the sense on the media that after TB, I was the one they were really waiting for. In fact for some of them, I was a tastier target than he is, because the thing was coming over now as being about government vs media. I was impressed by Parkinson, very calm, very clear, tested my answers well.

I was getting lots of advice, not least from TB, re how to deport myself. Always answer the question, not the question you want to answer. Make your answers short answers. Do not waffle or lecture. Don't be worried about pausing, or asking for time to reflect. If you cannot remember, say so. Call him 'My Lord' regularly. Look at him even if he is not looking at you. Be polite to all the lawyers. Above all, do not get riled. I remembered him saying the same thing before the [Rupert] Allason trial. 'And you won,' said TB. Yes, but not before the fucking judge gave me a sideswipe.[1] I called John Scarlett and made sure he was OK about the various references to him. He said he was fine. It must be dreadful for someone whose entire life has been about secrets, and dependent on staying low profile, now to be so out there in the public domain. He said he wouldn't have wanted it that way but he was sure we had done nothing wrong and it was important we were vindicated. He wished me luck. I said when the lawyer or whoever first uttered the words 'your diary', the press would get out their todgers and have a great collective wank. I went out for a quiet dinner with Gavin [Fiona's brother], Alan Maclean, Clare and Catherine. By the end we were the only people in the restaurant and we had a good laugh, but I was now as nervous as hell. The Number 10 staff had made me up a bed in John Birt's old office. It was fine, but slightly surreal. I got a message that there were people queuing outside the court [Royal Courts of Justice] overnight to try to get in. The thing had become a bloody circus.

Tuesday, August 19

I woke up to the sound of Big Ben. I heard four chimes but looked at my watch, and saw it was 5. I knew I wouldn't get back to sleep. It was so quiet now. I thought of Fiona and the kids asleep in Puyméras. I thought of Mum and Dad, and wondered whether Dad would see out the year. I thought of all the people who had been such a help in recent weeks. I thought about Mrs Kelly, really wished I knew what she really thought about all this. I was nervous but I had gone over everything fully, I was confident there wasn't a single difficult question we hadn't thought of, and I was confident my answers would withstand questioning. I scribbled a few thoughts – push hard on the dossier, express depth of anger at the BBC without getting angry, admit I wanted Kelly's name out, but emphasise I did nothing to make it happen.

I got up and went to TB's gym for a run on the treadmill. I just wanted to work up a sweat, without getting too tired, so ran for twenty minutes. I went down to the press office. The TVs were on and on both news channels there were people outside my house

[1] Campbell had been sued by Allason for malicious falsehood in 1996. Mr Justice Drake, the judge in the trial, said of Campbell 'He did not impress me as a witness in whom I could feel one hundred per cent confidence', had not been 'wholly convincing or satisfactory' and had been 'less than completely open and frank'. The comments were resurrected by the media in advance of Campbell's Hutton Inquiry appearance.

saying they were expecting me to leave any minute. I called Audrey, who was so proud of herself that we'd managed to go through the whole three days without any of them seeing me. There were snappers covering every exit from Number 10. I had a shower and got dressed in the office and as I came out the first person I bumped into was Bill [Wells] the messenger, who had also been the first person to wish me luck on the day of my FAC appearance. There was something wonderfully Dickensian about Bill. The conspiratorial wink, the little smile that was always there, the walk that wasn't so much a walk as a shuffle. He said to me 'Whatever happens, whatever anyone says about you, you're a good man and that's a fact.' I found it very comforting. I felt almost that it was a positive omen of some sort, he having lodged in my mind from the FAC day too. Everyone was supportive. Bill making tea, Felicity [Hatfield, secretary] making toast, Alison sorting my flight to Marseilles, Catherine R and Clare S coming in, their arms as ever full of huge, perfectly ordered files and folders, just going over the same old Q&A material.

Adam Chapman and Alan Maclean arrived. Alan had unsettled me a little at dinner when he said that my diary extract re 'we didn't do it ourselves' ['We agreed that we should not do it ourselves', July 9], could be read as saying we got others to do it. We went over how to deal with that. He knew it was innocently meant but said it was the one part he would zone in on if he was looking for a bit of a forensic challenge. Finally we left. Dave Borritt [Number 10 driver] drove us down there. I didn't want to arrive with an entourage so CR, CS and Alan got out early and went ahead. I drove up as close as we could get to the court entrance.

The demos were far bigger than we had been led to believe but I was glad we had turned down the chance of going in the back. I walked straight through. They were shouting and screaming, some through loudhailers, but I had got the blinkers on, got into my best Roy Keane mode and just walked on, Adam at my side. There was a bank of cameras to the right, and I ignored them too. I caught sight of the odd placard, one saying 'Ban the Campbell, ban the bomb'. I reached the door and CR looked like she was crying. I was taken by the cops and an usher to a little room upstairs. Within seconds, text messages were coming in. It had clearly gone out live. 'Entrance the stuff of legend' from Martin Sheehan. The court official said she had never known anything like it. People had been queuing since 1 to get into the marquee. She said there were journalists in there from all over the world. I bumped into Harry Arnold [ex-*Mirror* colleague] on the stairs. Another lucky omen. I looked out of the window and saw a group of journalists I knew. It dawned on me that the little group was made up of people I actually liked. Another one.

I was feeling OK. I was pacing up and down this tiny little room, making a few black-humour jokes about executions, drinking tea, when someone from James Dingemans' team came to see me. He said that Dingemans intended to refer to my diaries but not read from them. He would refer to them in questioning and if I wanted to read from them, I could, or I could paraphrase. I was fine with that. I was taken through by the usher, who was really looking after me. There were dozens of hacks around and I made a point of not looking at any of them, not letting any of them catch my eye, just talking to the usher and getting to my seat. Once I was there, I looked around at the lawyers, all chatting away to each other, and the people in front of the judge's bench, including a beautiful young woman just a few feet from me. She smiled really warmly and I smiled back and decided whenever I felt my hackles rise I would just look at her.

Hutton came in, everyone stood until he had settled himself, and away we went. Dingemans went through things very carefully and methodically. After the first couple of answers, I felt I was OK and that I just had to relax now and rely on my knowledge of the detail of everything. Listen to the question. Answer it. I had the file in front of me but I was really relying on the short list of points I had made to myself, and also the witness statement. We focused on the dossier right up to lunchtime. Hutton came in at several points and it took me a while to work out that didn't necessarily mean he was probing or trying to catch me out. On the contrary, on one occasion it finally dawned on me that if I looked at my diary extracts I would see the answer I was searching for. Dingemans was very clear and polite and helped my nerves settle quickly. I later thanked him for handling the diaries so sensitively. There were a few lighter moments, e.g. when I said [press officer] Danny Pruce's comments were above his pay grade, or that I didn't always respond to Jonathan's emails, and when I said at one point TB's comments were not taken on board. But I felt totally confident on the dossier and the overall impression was surely one of very good working co-operation with the spooks.

On the BBC again I felt Dingemans was fair in the way he took me through the correspondence with Sambrook. Here I think it helped that Hutton had my diaries because he had the full picture about the reasons for my rising anger and frustration. It was also clear that this was not some rampage for myself but for TB and the government. On Kelly, I felt comfortable with what I was saying. I was clear and straightforward, said it would have been much better if we had been clearer at the start rather than put in place a process that allowed the press to control when he was identified. I said in a way I was pushed to the margins of that decision and so did not really say, in the way I normally would perhaps, what I thought, because others involved may think I had a clear vested interest. Hutton was interested in why we didn't just batten down the hatches, why did he have to appear at the committee, to which I said it was inevitable and it would have been better if we had all faced up to that at the start.

By the time we broke for lunch I felt I was in good shape. The lawyers and CR/CS came to see me and said the tone was spot on, just keep going as you are. I had a coffee and a sandwich with CR and CS and was now worrying that my evidence would take us into another day. But we whizzed through the second half of my statement and the second session wound up fairly quickly and I could head back to France. There was an interesting moment when Dingemans, referring to a point in the diary where I said Gilligan would be fucked [July 4], where I answered in a way designed to convey the meaning without using the word, and I could see a little smile at the corner of Hutton's mouth. So he didn't mind the occasional in-joke. I felt that he and Dingemans had both been fair. However, they hadn't raised the admission I had thought about briefing the press (re Kelly's name) before TB appeared at the Liaison Committee. That meant when Godric got in there tomorrow, it was a problem for us. At least it was there in my statement, so it would not be news to the judge, but it would be new to the media. I felt it went OK and that was what all the talking heads seemed to be saying by the time I got back to the office.

There was a very warm reception as I got back in. I felt pretty tired and was desperate to get back to the family. I saw Tom and Godric before I left for Gatwick. I think my doing well had given them a bit of confidence too. I said the most important thing was to remember it is not a lobby briefing. They are not out to get you. Unlike the lobby, they actually want the truth. The only dramatic moment had been when they showed me an email that Gilligan had sent to David Chidgey [Liberal Democrat MP] re Kelly which I said was 'unbelievable'.[1] Dingemans said 'Don't make a speech on that,' but the fact the BBC had not disclosed this meant Gilligan was in big trouble now.

[1] Gilligan's email named David Kelly as Susan Watts' source for a BBC *Newsnight* story.

When I was on the train, TB called. He said everyone seemed to think I had been the perfect witness. He said that after the initial panic – in which I had shared in spades – the diaries had actually worked in our favour. He said he had said a prayer for me this morning. So had Cherie, who sent me a note saying well done, and how sad she felt that she and Fiona had fallen out, and was there anything she could do? TB said he felt confident re the outcome. He also felt Geoff Hoon would be OK too. He had been reading up more of the background from the inquiry so far. Hutton would not be impressed by the way the BBC handled it all. He would probably also think Kelly was a bit at fault – something I had picked up from the judge as well. TB had felt throughout that the fact I lost it at times was OK, in that the judge would see why, because he would understand the seriousness of the allegations against me, when maybe those who made them did not. I had lost count of how many times TB had called in recent days, particularly about the diaries and his worries about Sumption's strategy. He now accepted it had been the right strategy. I had been totally open. Sumption had redacted parts he thought irrelevant to the inquiry. But when we had finally handed them in on Monday at 5pm, nobody could say we were not being open. They had been gentle with me in the way they questioned me on them. There had been no reference to my bad language and only the phrase 'plea bargain' was specifically picked out.

I called Sumption from Gatwick, as I sat in the departure lounge bar, with the news blaring away, endless coverage of my evidence. He said he had been following it on the website all day and I did well. He sounded genuinely pleased. I thanked him, said I could not have had better advice and support. He said the next part of his plan was not to push for lots of cross-examination of the other witnesses. It was tempting to want to tie the BBC people in knots, but he reckoned Hutton would have probably made up his mind by now. I said it seems an age away that I was sitting crying my eyes out at Ian and Andrea's dining room table, going through the last days of July in my diary. I watched ITN and *Channel 4 News* in the first-class lounge. The general view was I did fine. It had been a pretty extraordinary holiday so far. The first few days great. Then starting to get stressed as I worked on my witness statement. Then the dire sinking feeling when that letter came through with the list of areas to cover – fine – and then the bombshell request for my diaries, and suddenly feeling like I was in some awful Kafkaesque nightmare. Neil trying to assure me it wasn't a hostile act. Then Sumption and the lawyers coming on the scene. His legal advice clashing with TBs political instincts, and me backing the lawyer. Then Alison coming out, then home for the final preparations, and now all done, and on a plane back to France.

Wednesday, August 20

I finally got to Puyméras at midnight. It was fantastic to see the kids, and Fiona and I seemed to get on for the first time in ages. I was trying to switch off now but the message coming from London was that both the broadcasters and the press were overwhelmingly positive. As expected we had a problem when Godric went through his evidence and he was asked about the idea I had had for briefing before TB went to the Liaison Committee that someone had come forward and even though it was in my witness statement, I had not been asked about it yesterday; he was, and so the media went off on one about me having misled the inquiry. Of course Hutton knew that was balls but it meant more crap in the press. The Tories were also on to me re what they claimed was a discrepancy re forty-five minutes in my evidence to the FAC, and now this. Also, the Chidgey email was going big as a problem for Gilligan, but Catherine R was worried because she had done research for the whips. The BBC case having been poor, and us having so far thought to have done well, they were now working up the line that Kelly was caught in a mincer between the two of us. Philip had a load of the cuttings sent out and I did seem to have done OK. Even the *Mirror* and the *Independent* were not that bad. I had prepared better than for the FAC, partly because more was at stake. Also, I was more nervous and that had helped. On the diaries, Dingemans had been particularly kind in that he gave the impression I had volunteered them. I went to see the Kennedys to thank them for all their help, then sent a stack of thank-you letters. PG was worried that Peter M was moving in to fill the vacuum that would be there when I left. He felt it would kill stone dead any chance of using my departure to put spin to rest as a problem.

Thursday, August 21

I called Geoff H in the States. He had read my evidence online, felt I did well and accepted that contrary to what some of the media tried to say, I did not drop him in it. He felt able to deal with the 'plea bargain' point. I was somewhat suprised to hear Kevin Tebbit had said he couldn't recall saying that Kelly didn't want to be named in the first wave of publicity. He also apparently gave a little soliloquy at the end which people didn't think was very clever.

Friday, August 22

David Hill called me, said TB now seemed seized of the need to get rid of the Order in Council. Clearly people were getting at him. I was pretty sure Peter M was on that track. I felt very strongly that it was a mistake, that my departure would be enough to signal some change, but that he should not allow his central operation to be further depoliticised. PG was increasingly of the view that TB was a bit out of touch and remote.

Saturday, August 23

I was struggling to pack a whole holiday into a few days, and failing. TB called. He said he had read the transcripts of everyone's evidence to the inquiry. He thought I had been 'brilliant'. He said he honestly felt it was word-perfect and he was sure the judge would have been impressed. 'I think you just put it so much clearer than everyone else.' My worry was that Hutton, based on some of the interventions he had been making, seemed to think it would have been possible for Kelly's name not to come out, and we didn't. TB said he was going to have to use his own evidence to be clear with him the nature of the media world we have to deal with. His worry was that Hutton may in the end just feel he has to have a balance of blame, rather than just state the truth, which is the whole thing stemmed from the *Today* programme broadcasting what they did and then refusing to back down. Though I was still getting an OK press for my own evidence, the focus re me had moved to what Godric said. It was irritating, though if Hutton was reading the press, it would give him another example of how they worked. Some of them were saying he looked amazed to hear what GS said re me. It had been in my own bloody statement.

TB and I discussed when was the best time for me to leave. He said if I was totally decided, it was probably better to go sooner rather than later. We discussed the Order in Council. He said he was not sure it mattered as much as my note suggested. In the end people in the system would know David Hill was his person. Yes, but the Order in Council makes explicit that he can instruct them. This weakens him from the start and that therefore weakens you. It was an important symbol and symbols should not be underestimated. He said he felt he had to signal change. I said my leaving would be the change. Yes but though David may not be you, he is still a Labour spin doctor.

He said he hoped I would continue to advise him informally, and that we would be able to speak regularly and go over things. He said there were not many people who were both good at strategy and good at tactics. Re conference he now accepted Hutton would overshadow it but he still felt we had to get back on to the domestic agenda. Philip felt he had to explain Iraq better than we had so far because that was the source of most of the negativity about him. I felt he had to make the affirmative case for progressive politics. He said he had had a good meeting on holiday with Murdoch, Elisabeth [Murdoch], Les [Hinton] and Irwin Stelzer [Murdoch adviser]. He said he knew most of us had had a crap holiday but he had enjoyed himself despite everything and felt rested. But he knew the knives were sharpening for him and once I was gone he would have lost his main lightning conductor.

Tuesday, August 26

I had managed to get in a couple of nice and reasonably relaxing days, Fiona and I getting on well, but it was still on balance a pretty grim holiday. I had hoped to have time to think through what to do after I left, but the Hutton business really put paid to that. We set off for Troyes today to break the journey back. TB called when I was in the hotel gym. He was now back in the UK. He felt that whereas my evidence was good, Jonathan's was a bit loose in parts. John Scarlett was up today and I had called him last night. He was very calm, very proper, focused but anxious. He said he was sure he had done nothing wrong and would be fine. He felt we had a good story to tell but he would rather that he didn't have to be there to tell it. His evidence, needless to say, went well. So did Omand's.

TB felt having looked at all the interventions by the judge that he was closer to our arguments than the BBC, whose evidence had been poor. He felt if there was one area where Hutton may have problems with the government it was over whether the MoD took sufficient care of Kelly. He was moving towards a line on Thursday of saying he accepted responsibility for everything as PM. He really hoped Hutton would draw a line and we would regain the space to get back focused on the domestic agenda. It was far from certain that would happen. PG told me the groups done recently were dreadful. I'm not sure TB got the scale of how bad public opinion was in parts. Philip and Peter H were both worried now that Peter M was TB's main influence re strategy and communications, and also responsible for reorganisation of the office. TB felt I should get a column, make money speaking and basically keep helping him but in a different way. There was big coverage of the memo I wrote him from New York [June 3]. It was actually a good piece of work, but they were using it to show I was pulling the strings etc.

Wednesday, August 27

Scarlett got a terrific press. Hoon did badly, gave the sense he was trying to blame everyone but himself. We got home about 6 so that Rory could watch Man U vs Wolves [1–0]. I spoke to Alex [Ferguson] who said he was now sure it was the right thing for me to leave. He had followed the whole thing and felt I would be fine. TB was being briefed by the lawyers and seemed fine. He felt he should go big on the seriousness of the allegations and how those making them failed to see that and make sure he took responsibility for difficult decisions.

Thursday, August 28

Geoff H got a dreadful press; now it was TB's turn to take the stand. I missed his first briefing meeting, felt it far better he see the lawyers first and then work out what if any thought we needed to give re the media. He asked me what the desired headline would be. It was somewhere in the area of TB taking responsibility (which GH had not done) whilst defending the decisions we took. It was also an opportunity to lay out what it is like making some of the decisions he has to. People felt GH did very badly, and gave himself some real problems. We had done well so far because everyone had been clear about the facts, even where they were difficult. But Geoff had opened us up. I felt he had ensured that more of us would be called to the second phase of evidence-taking than might otherwise have been the case. John Scarlett and I were already pretty much settled to the notion that we would certainly be called back. David Omand then said he thought I did really well. Re the diaries he said 'I hope you have all your diaries safely locked up somewhere – otherwise the men in black might come looking for them.' I was not entirely sure whether he was joking or not. Probably not.

TB set off and everyone, including the media, said he did well. He said on his return he had felt totally robust, and the facts didn't frighten him on this. No doubt his legal experience helped a bit too, and he felt that even though the inquiry team were in the driving seat, they were conscious of the fact that he was, when all was said and done, the prime minister. There were no attention-seeking histrionics, just more of the same fairly painstaking probing. He was clearly pleased it had not gone badly. I said that my evidence had gone well, his evidence had gone well, and I felt I should go tomorrow. It is the right moment. He looked really taken aback, but when I said we had agreed it would happen soon, why not now? Everybody is expecting it soon, but nobody is expecting it this soon, so why not? I was keen, within the limited room I had, to maintain an element of surprise which would help me shape the mood around it. He then started to warm to it. He said I should use it to get up a big argument about the nature of the media. I felt not yet, that I should just do it, be very nice about him and the government, make the case for progressive politics, but then be pretty low-key until Hutton was over. I had agreed with Jeremy Heywood that when Fiona and I left we would have five weeks' notice to work out. I told very few people what was happening – Godric, Tom, Anne, Alison – who all seemed both shocked and not shocked. My real desire was to keep it all quiet till tomorrow.

We had a meeting with Sumption and team in the Cabinet Room to go over the plan for the next stages, and in particular Sumption's note re what we should aim to get from the inquiry. Again, he made an interesting strategic call. He did not think we should press for lots of cross-examination. Nor did he think we should be saying to Hutton that the BBC should be criticised. All we would ask for was an acceptance that the story was wrong and that we were justified in challenging it. Also on Kelly, he obviously thought it would be wrong to attack him, but equally he hoped to steer the judge towards accepting that Kelly did wrong. TB was as near to deferential towards Sumption as I had seen him with anyone for ages. He knew his reputation for being very clever if a bit awkward, and we had all been saying how good he had been so far. It was interesting how much the legal side of this was actually about presentation too. A lot of the points made by the lawyers were tactical presentational points, but with the audience the judge, not the press or public. What I liked about Sumption most was that he didn't seem to care what the press or public were thinking about all this. He was totally focused on the judge.

Friday, August 29

I slept in a bit, having had a bit of asthma through the night. In to finalise my statement. TB didn't want any sense in there that he kept persuading me to stay. He thought it would be weakening. He wanted to write his own words about me, that there are two ACs, the one he knows and the one the media likes to portray. I left him to it, put changes into my own statement and then made a few calls. I told JP, who was very supportive, thanked me for everything and said he would like to do the media on it once we'd made the announcement. I called Margaret B, DB, JR, Tessa, Charles C, Ian McC, Pat H, GH and a few others. I decided not to call GB because I didn't trust his operation not to get it out ahead of me. Later – once it was out there and loads of messages were coming in – there it was on a long list typed up by Alison. 'The Chancellor's secretary called to say he wanted to thank you for everything you'd done for the party.' He couldn't even bring himself to call.

MB was very nice, said she really valued the way we had always worked together, that I had done a great job but there was a limit to what anyone could take. JR said he had been at a party meeting at the weekend and when he did a big defence of me, he got a great response. Ian McC put out some really nice words. So did Robin C. JP said his main line on the telly would be that I had decided I wanted a change, spend more time at home, that I was steeped in Labour and would be badly missed. I got a message to Hutton as I didn't want him to hear it on the media first. I told Dan [Bartlett], who said Bush would be disappointed because he was 'one of your biggest supporters', and I told Clinton and thanked him for his recent advice.

Once I finished my statement I got Alison to send out a message that I wanted to see all my team and anyone else in the building who was around. They knew what was coming so they weren't exactly shocked, but there was a lot of sadness in there. I said they knew I had been thinking about going and today was the day. I had had a great time and it had been an amazing privilege and one of the things that meant most to me was the team I had built up. I could not have done any of it without them and certainly in recent weeks I could not have asked for more by way of support. I said everyone was replacable, I would leave with nothing but good memories of them, but Fiona and I desperately wanted to get a life back for ourselves and the children.

I suppose I knew it would go quite big but it was ludicrous just how big it went. Someone told me PA gave it the same Priority tag as a royal death or prime ministerial resignation. For several hours, once they did the breaking news Whoosh, they did literally nothing else. They had some so-called intelligence expert in the studio when it broke and they had him blathering away without knowing what on earth he was talking about. Matthew Doyle and Mark Bennett [Labour press officers] organised JP in Leeds, JR for later bulletins and some good backbenchers. The Tories put up Ann Widdecombe [former minister], Theresa May [Conservative Party chair] and eventually IDS. They looked shrill and ridiculous, trying to make it a disaster day for TB.

I gathered my thoughts again before doing a round of interviews with the broadcast political editors. They came in one by one and I used pretty much the same messages – great privilege, downside all taken by family, big on values, make the case for politics. It was also going big in the States and across Europe. Graeme [AC's brother] said he had been channel-hopping in Poland and found me simultaneously on Russian, Polish, French and Portuguese telly. The news channels were going with it hell for leather in the outer office and the endless two-way blather reminded me why I had got fed up dealing with them all. They just went on and on and on until another talking head was found. It underlined how out of hand the whole thing about me had got.

TB said even he was surprised how big it was going. He said I was a big personality and even though some of them hated me, they knew it was a big personality leaving the centre of the stage. Some of the hacks were trying to build it as a huge blow to him – could he cope blah? – which must have been a bit galling. Peter H was now also talking of leaving. He was worried Peter M was moving into the gap and it would not help us. My worry was more that there would be a concerted Civil Service retrenchment effort. All in all, things went fine today. Lots of nice messages, most media people saying I did well, even if I had become a problem.

The announcement re Fiona was in there though buried in all the avalanche of coverage re my leaving. It was a real sadness to me that she was leaving on bad terms with CB and with Tony too. But she was clearly happy we were on the way, and maybe surprised I had brought it to a head so quickly. They were straight on to what would I do in the future, and making assumptions I would make a fortune. The truth was I didn't really have a clue what I would do. I didn't speak to many journos. It was all kind of on autopilot. Boulton was pretty sour as ever, Marr OK, [Nick] Robinson [ITN] a jerk. Andy Bell [Channel 5] and Gary Gibbon [Channel 4] pretty straight. After a while they started to cover the coverage – the fact that it was so big abroad, that so many foreign hacks came into the street when the statement went out, the Trevor McDonald [ITV] special, US network websites doing it as number one or two and Boulton et al. saying they couldn't think of any official who would ever have sparked this kind of interest by announcing his departure. Catherine Colonna [Chirac's spokeswoman] called and said '*Tu es un star mondial, tu sais. Il faut saisir le moment*.' [You are a global star, you know. Seize the moment.] She said the president '*te salue*' [salutes you]. It was all a bit weird. Twenty minutes on ITN news, fifteen on the BBC, hours on Sky, the Sundays preparing to do pages and pages on it.

I cleared my desk. Went on a last walk round the building to say a few thank-yous and goodbyes, met Fiona and then we walked out together. I didn't look at the hacks and I didn't bother to listen, let alone answer. I just wanted to get out, and get home. There was a horde of media waiting in the street when we got home, more than I think we'd ever had. We parked at the top of the road, then walked down and we were swarmed as we tried to walk down the pavement.

Fiona got left behind a bit and I kept looking back and she had virtually disappeared. I stopped and yelled at a few of them and she caught up for a bit. The live reporters were describing what was going on, others shouting, snappers falling over each other. Ridiculous.

We got it and Audrey was very upset I had gone. She felt it was the right job for me and I should have stayed with Tony to the end. I was cheered by a message from Hutton. I had earlier asked Clare Sumner to tell Lee Hughes [secretary to the inquiry] what was going on and that I was keen he understood I would be doing interviews but would not talk about anything being investigated by him. The message came back now that he was very touched that I took the trouble to tell him in advance. I was probably reading too much into it but I had felt giving evidence that he felt I was an OK personality and I felt the same from the tone of his message today. I also thought that if he had watched any of the coverage, he would see once more what a nightmare culture we dealt with. I had a hunch that the diaries will have had a similar effect. TB felt the same, that the diaries gave an insight into what it was like trying to handle these big decisions surrounded by the 24-hour media trying to trip you the whole time.

Neil, Glenys, Rachel [Kinnock] and the Goulds came round for dinner and I think shared some of the relief. Rachel had been one of the first suggesting I leave ages ago, feeling it was time I stopped taking hits for others. Neil and PG were ambivalent but agreed it was the right time for me. TB called a couple of times. He had seen some of the news and couldn't believe how much coverage it was getting. He felt it was partly about the size of my personality but was also a reflection of their obsession with themselves. Philip had been following it all day and said I should get the tapes of the live coverage. 'You'd have thought the Pope had died.' We had a nice evening and Fiona was definitely more relaxed and I sensed the kids, though annoyed at all the bollocks in the street every time they came and went, were feeling a change for the better was happening. My asthma was bad though, partly the air, partly the current stress, also maybe a bit of anxiety about the total lack of certainty about what I would now do with myself. People were telling me I could make a fortune on the lecture circuit, but I can't say it held that much appeal. The most important thing was to try to get things at home on a better keel, rest, and then take stock. As I left, TB had said 'You do realise I will phone you every day, don't you?' I said yes, and I hope you realise sometimes I won't be there.

To be continued . . .

Index

Illustration Acknowledgements

Picture research: Amanda Russell

p. v Picture of Philip Gould by Adrian Steirn

Section 1

p. 1 top: Marty Lederhandler/Press Association Images; centre, left: Getty Images; centre, right: Chris Ison/Press Association Images; below: Getty Images

p. 2 top: Getty Images; centre: Getty Images; below, left: Getty Images; below, right: Sipa Press/Rex Features

p. 3 below, left: Getty Images; below, right: Getty Images

p. 4 top: Getty Images; inset: © Chris Ridell, New Statesman, 12 Nov 2001/British Cartoon Archive, University of Kent, www.cartoons.ac.uk; below: Press Association Images

p. 5 top, left: Fiona Hanson/Press Association Images; top, right: Richard Gardner/Rex Features; below: Getty Images/Terry O'Neill

p. 6 top: Press Association Images; below, left: Rex Features; below, right: Getty Images

p. 7 top, left: Antony Jones/Press Association Images; top, right: Stefan Rousseau/Press Association Images; below: Author's private collection

p. 8 top: Nick Danziger/nbpictures; centre: Nick Danziger/nbpictures; below: Sipa Press/Rex Features

Section 2

p. 1 top: Nick Danziger/nbpictures; centre: Nick Danziger/nbpictures; below: Nick Danziger/nbpictures

p. 2 main: Rex Features; inset, above: Press Association Images; inset, below: Rex Features

p. 3 top, left: Author's private collection; top, right: Author's private collection; below: © Jonathan Pugh

p. 4 top: Sipa Press/Rex Features; below: Stephan Rousseau/Press Association Images

p. 5 top: Author's private collection; below: Morten Morland/NI Syndication

p. 6 top, left: Getty Images; top, right: Press Association Images; below, left: Rex Features; below, right: Press Association Images

p. 7 top, left: Topfoto.co.uk; top, right: Stefan Rousseau/Press Association Images; below: Topfoto.co.uk; inset: Priscilla Coleman/Topfoto.co.uk

p. 8 main: Rex Features; inset: Reproduced by kind permission of PRIVATE EYE magazine www.private-eye.co.uk

KT-210-436

THE ULTIMATE BOOK OF THE

HORSE AND RIDER

THE ULTIMATE BOOK OF THE HORSE AND RIDER

JUDITH DRAPER, DEBBY SLY AND SARAH MUIR

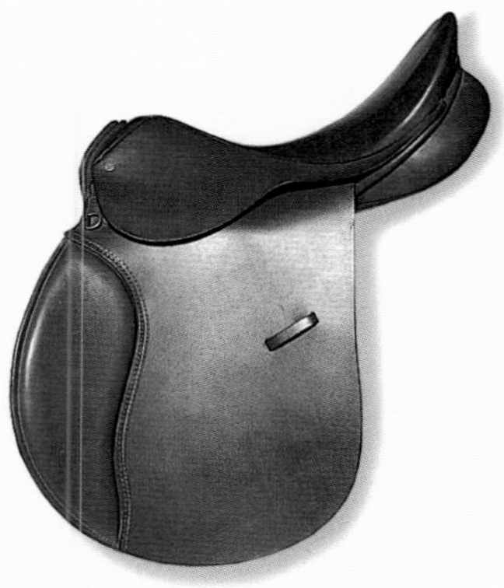

LORENZ BOOKS

First published in 1999 by Lorenz Books

Lorenz Books is an imprint of
Anness Publishing Limited
Hermes House
88–89 Blackfriars Road
London SE1 8HA

ISBN 0 7548 0085 7

A CIP catalogue record for this book
is available from the British Library

Publisher Joanna Lorenz
Project Editor Felicity Forster
Designer Michael Morey
Jacket Design Mabel Chan
Illustrator Rodney Paull
Indexer Dawn Butcher
Editorial Reader Kate Henderson
Production Controllers Jessica Arendt and Ben Worley

Previously published as separate volumes, *The Book of Horses and Horse Care*, *The Practical Rider's Handbook* and *Saddlery and Horse Equipment*

Printed and bound in Germany

1 3 5 7 9 10 8 6 4 2

Contents

INTRODUCTION

BREEDS OF THE WORLD

HORSE AND PONY CARE

LEARNING TO RIDE

WORLD OF THE HORSE

SADDLERY AND EQUIPMENT

Introduction

The World of the Horse and Rider

The horse is one of the most beautiful and complex animals, and has fascinated mankind for many thousands of years. The purpose of this book is to capture some of the magic associated with horses – why so many have devoted their lives to them. It also aims, on a more practical level, to provide invaluable information for anyone with an equestrian interest, whether you ride for pleasure or competition, are planning on buying your first horse or pony, or just love horses.

Your Horse and You

This book starts by tracing the history of the horse, from its prehistoric ancestor – the Eohippus – to the modern *Equus caballus*, that we know as today's horse.

Breeds of the World is a comprehensive pictorial guide to the diverse variety of breeds and types of horse and pony around the world, from Appaloosas to Welsh Cobs, and from hacks to polo ponies. Each breed and type is described in detail, including its main characteristics, how the breed has developed and its uses.

Buying your own horse is a major step which most people who ride will want to do at some point. The section **Buying a Horse** provides a detailed guide to the subject, from how to choose the right horse or pony to suit you and your needs, to where to look for a horse, trying it and getting it vetted.

BELOW
The Shagya, a Syrian-bred Arab horse with a dished face, large wide-set eyes, a short back and high-set tail.

BOTTOM
Choosing the right horse is never easy – there are so many different breeds with different temperaments and characteristics. You need to find an animal that suits you.

RIGHT
Owning a horse brings with it a huge responsibility; you should not consider it without making sure you are fully aware of the commitment involved in feeding, grooming, general stable management and first aid.

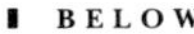

BELOW
There are a number of different types of bedding to consider for your stable. This horse is lying down on shredded paper, which provides a dust-free bed, especially good for horses with allergies to straw or respiratory problems.

BELOW RIGHT
The amount of feed your horse needs depends on many variables, such as how much exercise he has and how much time he spends outside grazing. When providing a haynet like this one, make sure it is tied high enough to prevent the horse from catching a foot in it.

Once you have bought your new horse or pony, this is where the fun – and hard work – begins. As the owner, you are responsible for your horse's health and welfare. With this in mind, **Keeping a Horse** provides useful information on the day-to-day management of horses and ponies, whether they live in a field or are stabled, including practical information about feeding, bedding and field management.

The **Daily Care** of the horse looks at how to keep your horse healthy and ensure that he has enough exercise to keep him fit, as well as how to recognize when he may be unwell. There is a useful guide to common ailments and how they should be treated. The horse's feet are also thoroughly discussed, including the anatomy of the hooves and the typical ailments which affect them.

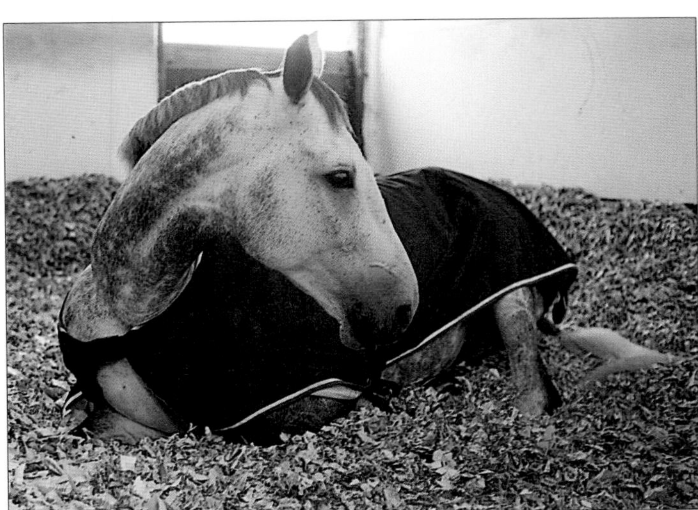

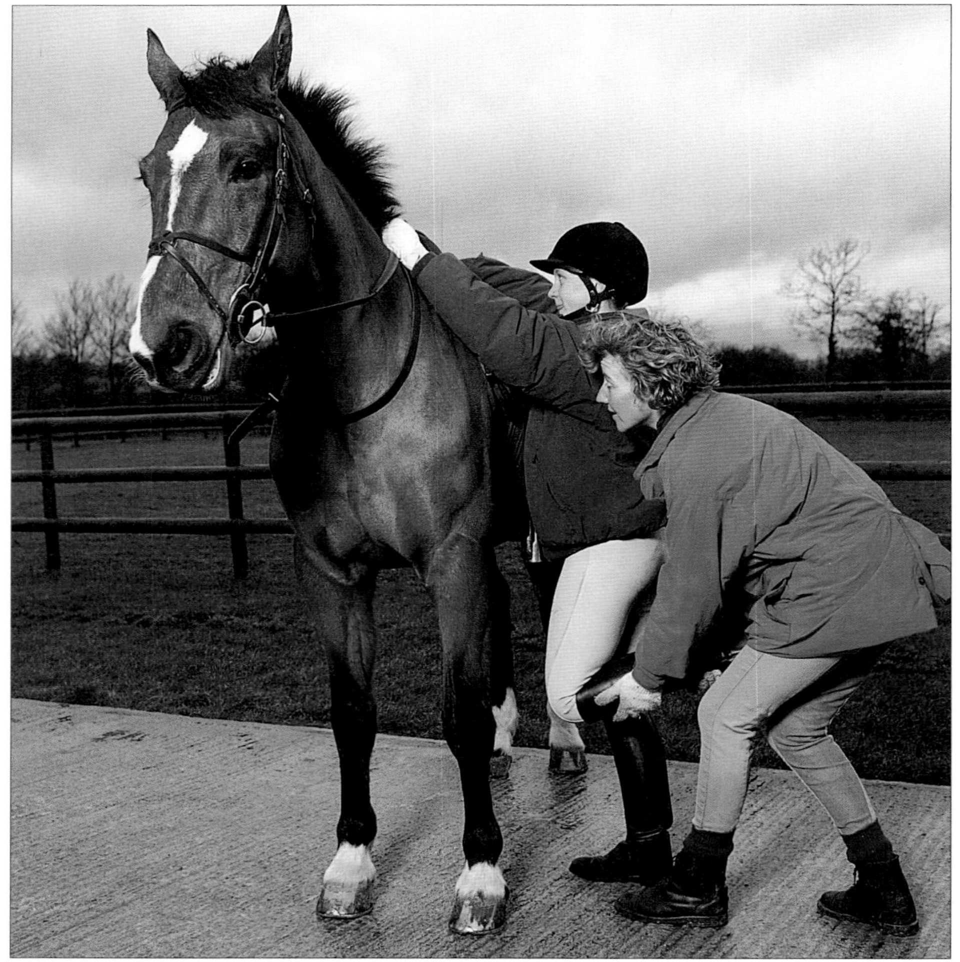

LEFT
Once your horse is tacked up and ready, it's time to climb aboard. It's much easier to mount a horse with a helper to give you a leg-up to support you. This method is a good way to learn how to mount, and it is also far less stressful on the horse's back.

BELOW LEFT
Position the stirrup iron so that your foot can go into it easily. For the near-side foot (left foot), turn the stirrup leather in an anticlockwise direction before placing your foot into the iron.

BELOW RIGHT
Learning to ride requires patience and practice. Each pace – walk, trot, canter and gallop – gives you a different sense of speed and motion.

Riding horses is a demanding yet ultimately fulfilling pastime which has brought a great deal of pleasure and fun to many (although it is not without its many disappointments, as any rider will tell you!). It is important to remember that whatever your ambition, whether it be to compete at the highest level or to go on a gentle hack through beautiful countryside, riding should be enjoyable for you and your horse. The relationship between the rider and his or her mount should always be a partnership.

Learning the art of horsemanship requires dedication and patience on the part of the pupil – the rider never stops learning. Horses, like humans,

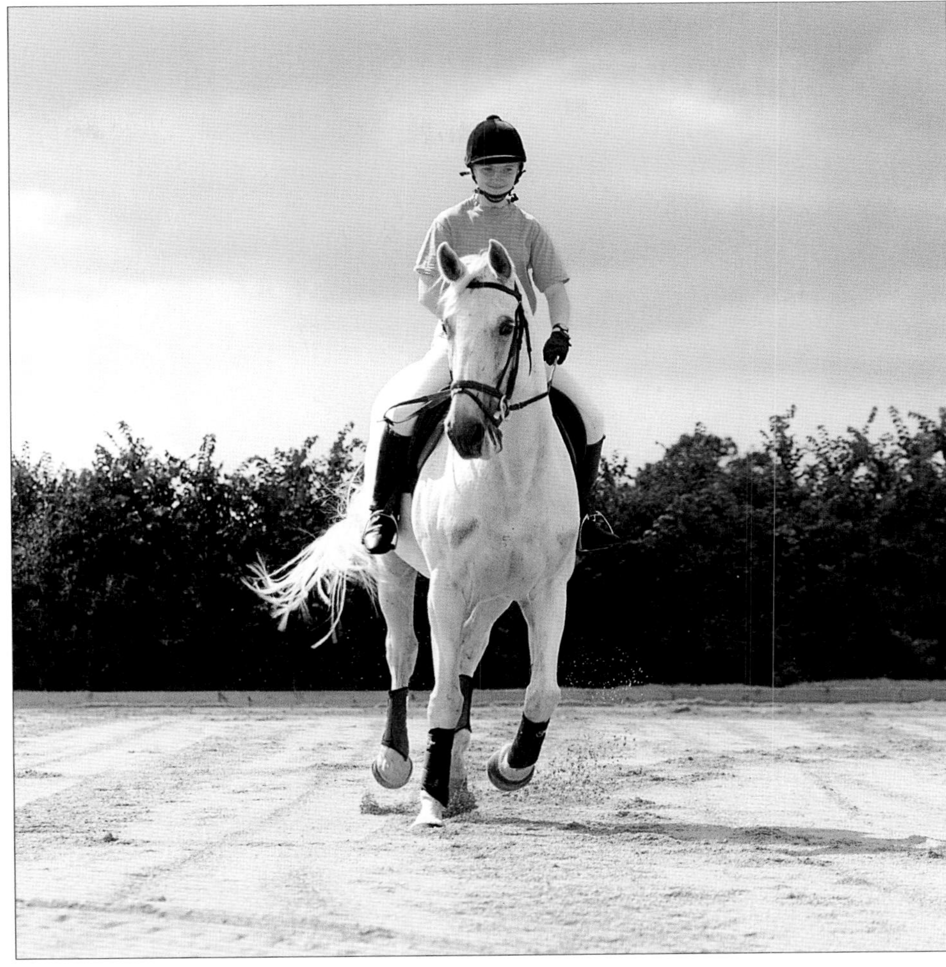

RIGHT
Cantering brings with it an exhilarating feeling of speed and power, combined with a wonderful sense of freedom. The horse and rider should appear to be moving as one.

BELOW
The bridle is one of the first pieces of riding equipment you will learn to use. When putting on the bridle, you should hold the horse's nose with your left hand, hold the bridle in your right hand, bring it in front of the horse's face and then gently lift it into his mouth.

are individuals, and we can learn as much from them as they can from us.

The section **Learning to Ride** will prove invaluable to anyone with an interest in riding, including first-time riders, those returning to riding after a period of time, or anyone who feels they need to do a little "revision". We look at where to learn, the basic clothing and equipment the rider needs, how to prepare the horse for riding, and how the rider communicates with his or her horse.

Although there is no substitute for actually being on a horse, when you are learning to ride the time spent in the saddle is often relatively little (it may be only an hour a week), so it is useful for the budding equestrian to be able to read and learn more about horsemanship. Such knowledge will hopefully be able to be put into practice the next time you ride.

In **Mastering the Paces** we look at how the horse moves, showing the four paces – walk, trot, canter and gallop – in detail, as well as the transitions between these paces. As the rider gains confidence and balance and learns how to coordinate himself, he

RIGHT
Show jumping is an Olympic sport, combining technical ability, athleticism and balance. Competition riding can bring out the best in horse and rider.

BELOW
Most horses can be trained to jump. This horse has jumped too high for these fences, but with practice will be able to negotiate different distances and heights.

can then develop his skills and learn more about influencing his horse – for example, the half-halt, lateral work, variations within paces and the counter canter – creating and building upon the all-important rider-horse partnership.

Preparing for Take-off is a useful section on learning how to jump. Starting with simple exercises over trot poles and low fences in the arena, we progress to the exhilaration of riding around a cross-country course, how to cope with difficult terrain and preparing for the unexpected.

As your riding skills develop further you may want to take part in competitions, so in **The Competition World** we describe the wide variety of equestrian sports which exist, and how to choose one that suits you and your horse's temperament. From the pleasure and excitement of jumping or mounted games, the grace of dressage or vaulting, to the special demands of endurance riding or the thrill of taking part in a race, there's something for every rider in this section – along with the idea that the main aim of competing should be to have fun.

ABOVE
Learning to jump requires practice. This horse is jumping smoothly over a fence; the horse is collected and the rider well-positioned.

LEFT
Riders with good overall horsemanship skills can put themselves to the test by competing in horse trials or eventing.

BELOW
Taking part in a dressage competition is the perfect opportunity to show off your horse. Dressage is a very popular sport and is as enjoyable to watch as it is to partake in.

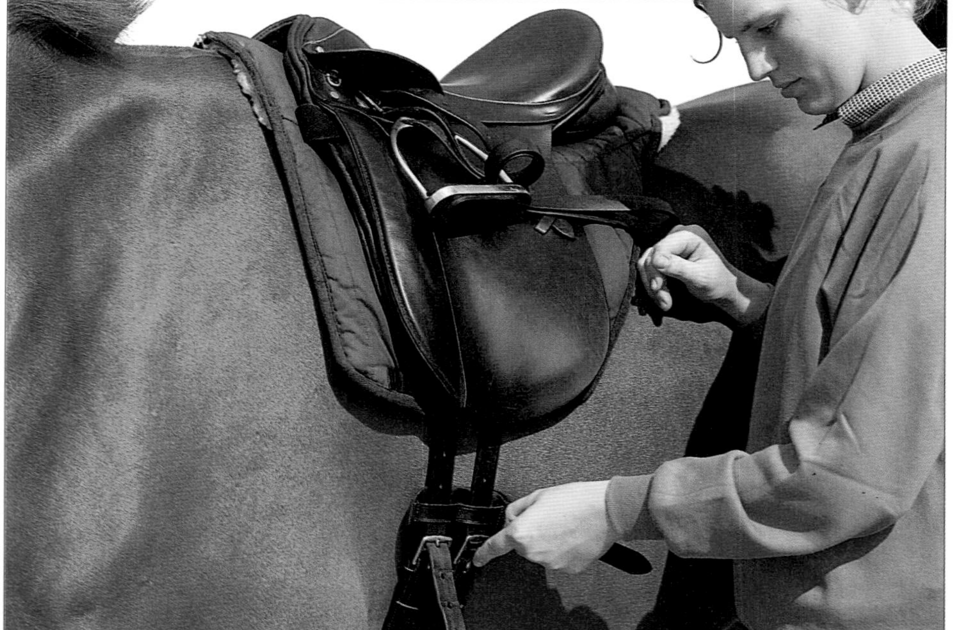

LEFT
The saddle is one of the most important pieces of equipment you will need to buy, and because of the skill and craftsmanship involved in producing a saddle, it is usually the most expensive. Take good care of your saddle and you will enjoy it for many years.

BELOW
It is advisable to seek professional help when choosing a new saddle, to ensure that it fits the horse correctly and is suitable for your riding needs.

Riding, like skiing, sailing and many other activities, requires specialist clothing and equipment. A visit to your local saddlery or tack shop will confirm the bewildering array of tack and equipment on sale – not all of it necessarily essential. With this in mind we have provided a detailed guide to **Saddlery and Equipment**, focusing on the everyday saddle and bridle, as well as explaining how and why many of the more unusual items of equipment are used.

The Saddle is an essential piece of riding equipment and one of the most expensive items the owner has to buy for his or her horse. There are saddles designed to suit every style of riding, so we explain which is the best for you and your chosen type

▮ BELOW
Choosing the right bridle and bit can be a daunting task – they come in a huge variety of shapes and sizes. The traditional bridle is made of leather.

▮ BOTTOM
Combined with the rider's legs, voice and body position, the bridle and bit provide the communication which allows the rider to control the horse.

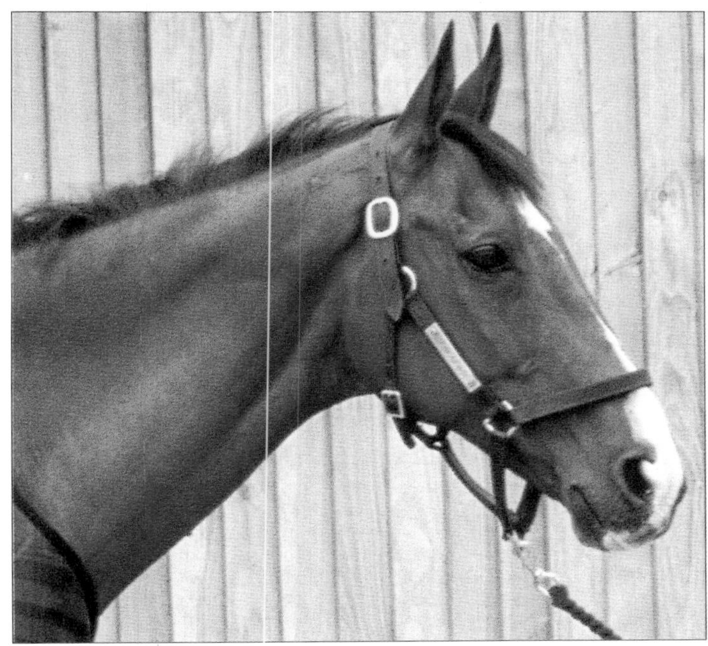

of riding. There is also a section on essential saddle accessories including girths, stirrups, breastplates and saddle cloths, as well as a guide to saddle care.

The bridle is an equally important piece of equipment, and like the saddle should be chosen carefully, with the comfort of the horse and the safety of the rider firmly in mind. The subject of **Bridles and Bits** is a complex one and it is important to choose the right combination of tack to suit the horse and the rider – too mild a bit and you could be left with an unstoppable horse, too strong and you could unwittingly inflict pain on the horse. We explain the different types of bridle and noseband, and look in detail at bits and bitting, describing the various bit groups and the different actions they have on the horse.

RIGHT
A dressage whip may be used when schooling a horse – this long whip can be used to give a gentle flick without the rider having to let go of the reins.

BELOW
Not only is grooming essential for the health of your horse – removing dust, dead skin and hair, and providing massage for improving muscle tone – it also makes your horse look absolutely spectacular for competitions.

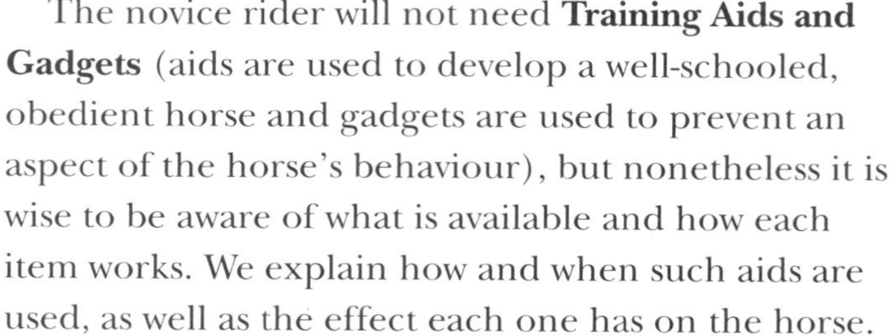

The novice rider will not need **Training Aids and Gadgets** (aids are used to develop a well-schooled, obedient horse and gadgets are used to prevent an aspect of the horse's behaviour), but nonetheless it is wise to be aware of what is available and how each item works. We explain how and when such aids are used, as well as the effect each one has on the horse.

Grooming is an essential part of the daily care of your horse, important for his health as well as his appearance. In **Grooming Equipment** we show the basic kit you will need and explain in detail how to groom your horse, from picking his feet out and daily brushing, to clipping the horse and the finishing touches required for a competition.

BELOW
This horse is dressed for travelling, with a poll guard for the head, rugs to keep him warm, hock and knee boots to protect his legs, and a bandage to protect his tail.

BOTTOM RIGHT
Stable bandages provide warmth and protection. They should always be used with padding underneath, otherwise pressure sores may form.

The horse in the wild has evolved to withstand the rigours of outdoor life, but many riding horses lead an "unnatural" life. As we place greater demands on the horse, expecting improvements in athletic performance and transporting horses to and from competitions, the need for special **Horse Clothing and Equipment** has increased. From boots and bandages to protect your horse's legs, to rugs and blankets which keep the horse warm and dry, the range of horse clothing is enormous. We guide you through the maze of clothing and equipment available, as well as providing an invaluable, step-by-step guide to putting on boots, bandages and rugs, so your horse will be protected from head to tail.

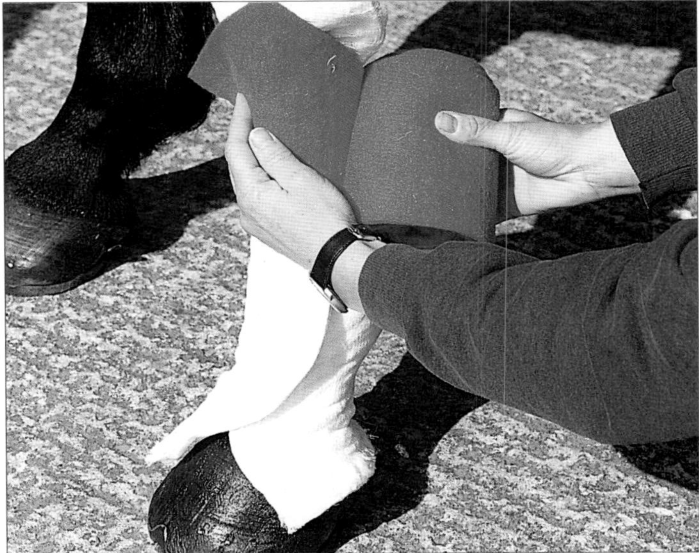

Finally, we come to **The Rider's Clothes**. Like the horse the rider needs special clothing and equipment for his or her chosen discipline. Much of today's riding clothing – especially competition attire – is influenced by tradition. For instance, the jacket worn by the show rider is based on the traditional coat worn by a huntsman.

This is not to say that fashion does not have an influence. As sports such as endurance riding become more popular, so new fabrics and colours are introduced to update the rider's wardrobe.

The most important considerations for any rider are comfort in the saddle and safety. Clothing for riding has developed to meet both these requirements. This section looks at the basic items that every rider needs: a protective hat, sensible footwear, and jodhpurs or breeches, and explains the correct dress for competitive riding. We also look at artificial aids (whips and spurs) explaining how and when they should be used by the rider.

We hope that you enjoy *The Ultimate Book of the Horse and Rider* and that it will prove to be an invaluable source of information for horse riders and horse lovers alike. Whatever your equestrian ambitions might be, never forget the great pleasure and satisfaction that being involved with horses can give, and that ultimately the most successful relationships between horses and people are based on mutual respect – a true partnership.

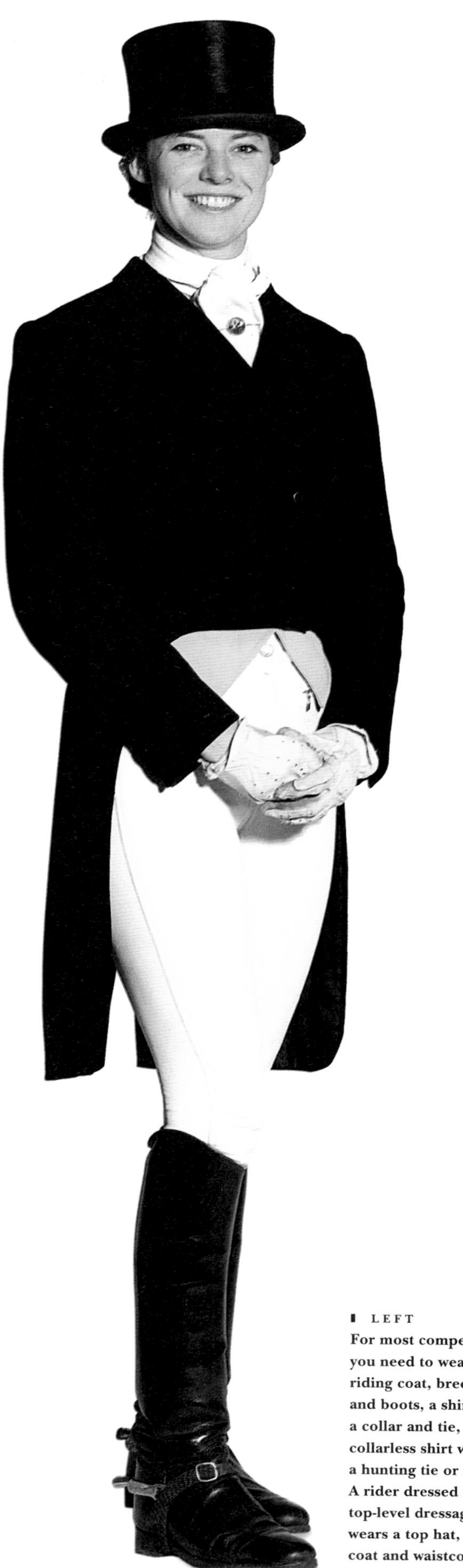

LEFT
For most competitions you need to wear a riding coat, breeches and boots, a shirt with a collar and tie, or a collarless shirt with a hunting tie or stock. A rider dressed for top-level dressage wears a top hat, tail coat and waistcoat.

RIGHT
For more ordinary, everyday riding, choose clothes that are neat and safe. Tall leather boots will provide protection and keep your feet and lower legs dry, gloves will give you a good grip on the reins, and a hard hat provides essential protection for your head.

Breeds of the World

Introduction

The lives of humans and horses have been bound together for many thousands of years. Appreciated first as just another source of food, the predecessors of the modern horse were hunted like any other wild animal. In time there came a steady process of domestication as nomadic peoples began to herd horses in the same way as they did goats and other animals. Ultimately, however, it was as a means of swift transport that the horse really came into his own. Men learnt to ride. Their whole lives were transformed. Horses became their chief means of transportation, remaining so until well into the twentieth century. Domestication, coupled with a gradual increase in human population, signalled the end of the truly wild horse. Today, even those horses which live in herds on the few remaining extensive areas of suitable grassland are not truly wild, for they are all "managed" by humans to one degree or another. Nevertheless horses retain much of the instinctive behaviour which enabled them to exist without man's intervention and it is necessary to understand what makes them "tick" if we are to enjoy our continuing association with them.

The History of the Horse

The modern horse, *Equus caballus*, belongs to the family *Equidae*, which also includes asses and zebras. *Equidae* are placed in the order Perissodactyla, to which tapirs and rhinoceroses belong and which descended from the Condylarthra, a group of primitive, long extinct mammals which were the ancestors of all hoofed mammals.

Fossil remains have made it possible to trace at least some aspects of the evolution of the modern horse over a period of some sixty million years, indicating how it gradually adapted to changes in its environment. The known history of the modern horse starts with Eohippus, also called the Dawn Horse, which is known to have lived in North America during the Eocene epoch (fifty-four to thirty-eight million years ago). An animal no larger than a small dog, Eohippus was designed for life as a forest browser moving around on soft soil. It had four toes on its forefeet, three on its back feet and pads similar to a dog's. Its small, low-crowned teeth were suited to eating leaves and other low, soft vegetation. It would probably have had a camouflage colouring to help it to escape predators. During the Oligocene epoch (thirty-seven to twenty-six million years ago) first Mesohippus then Merychippus, showed distinct changes: the legs became longer, the back straighter (Eohippus had an arched back) and the whole animal larger. One toe disappeared on the forefoot, leaving three toes on both fore and hindfeet. The teeth also showed signs of change, the pre-molars becoming more like true molars.

In this slow process of evolution, the most significant change of all occurred during the Miocene epoch (twenty-five to seven million years ago) when forests gave

PREVIOUS PAGE OPPOSITE
A Cleveland Bay.

PREVIOUS PAGE
A Furioso.

LEFT
The zebra is one of the small group of animals belonging to the family *Equidae*.

BELOW LEFT
The Highland Pony probably resembles Pony Type 2 of pre-domestication times.

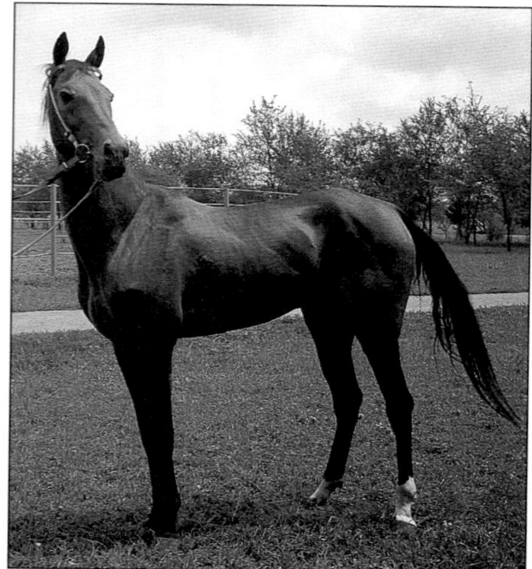

BELOW RIGHT
The wiry Akhal-Teke is thought to approximate to Horse Type 3.

RIGHT
Horse Type 4 resembled this refined little Caspian Pony. The Caspian was "re-discovered" in 1965.

BELOW RIGHT
Pony Type 1 lived in north-west Europe and looked like the present-day Exmoor Pony.

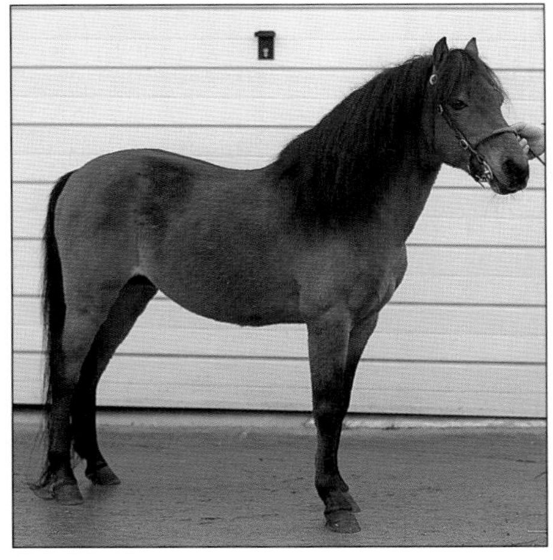

way to grassland and the horse's ancestors became plains dwellers. This significant change in environment called for teeth designed for grazing, as opposed to browsing, a longer neck to make grazing easier, longer legs to facilitate flight from predators and feet suitable for harder terrain. During this time the single toe, or hoof, began to evolve: the outer toes no longer touched the ground and the central toe became larger and stronger.

Then the history of the horse family becomes somewhat more complex, with various sub-families developing. Eventually, however, these became extinct and it was Pliohippus which provided the link in the chain from Eohippus to the modern Equus. Pliohippus evolved some ten to five million years ago and had long legs with a single hoof on each. Its direct successor, Equus, the genus of modern horse, finally emerged a million years ago.

During the Ice Ages of the Pleistocene epoch, Equus migrated via the land bridges which then existed to Europe, Asia and Africa. However, the disappearance of these land bridges (e.g. across what are now the Strait of Gibraltar and the Bering Strait) when the ice receded about 10,000 years ago meant that if an animal had become extinct in one continent, that continent could not be repopulated – at least not without the help of man. This is exactly what happened in America: for some unexplained reason the horse disappeared. It was not seen again until European colonists reintroduced it thousands of years later.

All members of the modern *Equidae* family are swift runners with only one functional toe on each foot (the modern horse's ergot – the horny growth at the back of the fetlock – is believed to be the vestiges of the pad of its ancestor, Eohippus). All live in herds and all have cheek teeth designed to grind plant-food.

Present-day horses and ponies are said to trace back to three distinct types, produced by variations in their natural environment. Northern Europe provided a slow-moving, heavy horse *(Equus silvaticus)* from which the world's heavy horse breeds are derived. Then there was the primitive Asiatic Wild Horse, survivors of which were found still living wild as late as 1881 (and called the Przewalski Horse); and finally the rather more refined Tarpan, from eastern Europe.

Later on, by the time that man began domesticating the horse, four sub-species had evolved: two pony types and two horse types. Pony Type 1 inhabited the north-west of Europe and resembled the modern Exmoor Pony. Pony Type 2, which was bigger and more heavily built, lived in northern Eurasia. The Highland Pony is probably the nearest modern-day equivalent. Horse Type 3 was a little bigger still, but much more lightweight in build and suited to hot climates. Its nearest equivalent is thought to be the Akhal-Teke. Horse Type 4, found in western Asia, was the smallest but the most refined and was the forerunner of the Caspian Pony.

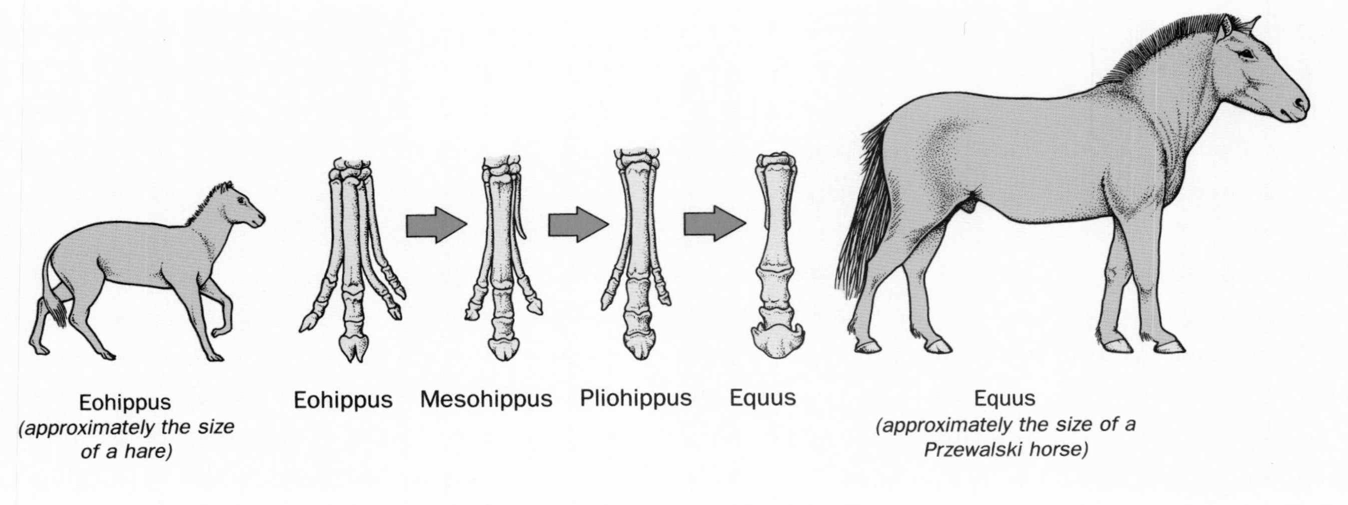

Horses in the Wild

LEFT
This Dartmoor Pony is typical of a number of breeds which, although they have been domesticated for a very long time, have retained the ability to thrive in semi-wild conditions.

The horse is a herbivore, that is, an eater of plants. Like all herbivores horses are basically grass eaters. In the wild the horse is a nomadic grazer and spends up to twenty hours out of every twenty-four grazing. When food is plentiful a wild horse thrives and puts on weight; when it is scarce, and weather conditions harsh, he loses condition. Nature, as usual, has arranged for foals to be born in the spring when the weather is mild and the grass lush – thus ensuring that the mares have a plentiful supply of food, which in turn ensures ample milk for the foals. Mares come into season every twenty-one days during the spring and summer, until around September or October, and the gestation period is approximately eleven months.

Horses are by nature herd animals. In the wild they live in social groups within a larger group (the herd), each small group comprising a stallion, some mares, their foals and yearlings and perhaps one or two two-year-olds. Depending on the power of the stallion, the total size of the group is usually in the region of a dozen. Young, timid stallions and old ones who no longer have any mares often live in bachelor groups – horses do not like to be alone. Just as family life is important to them, so is friendship. Horses indulge in mutual grooming with their teeth, they play together and relax and doze together. A stallion will groom a favourite mare even when she is not in season (grooming is also used to stimulate a mare sexually) and will play with the foals – though eventually he will drive out the more mature colts who must then either join a bachelor group or begin to collect their own band of mares.

Horses communicate with each other by a number of means, both vocal and physical. Their "vocabulary" includes neighing, nickering, squealing and, more rarely, roaring. A loud neigh enables a horse to make contact with another from whom it has been separated; a quieter, lower nicker may be used by a stallion to a mare, a mare to her foal or between friends as a greeting; squeals are signs of excitement and are used when horses are in close contact, particularly sexual contact; horses may emit loud roars and

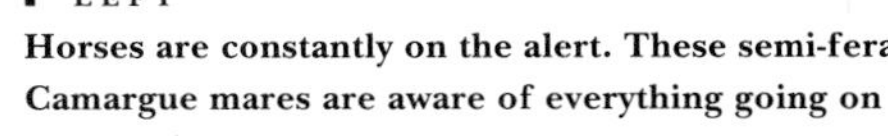

▮ LEFT
Horses are constantly on the alert. These semi-feral Camargue mares are aware of everything going on around them.

screams during a fight that has serious intentions, as opposed to the sort of play-fighting indulged in by young colts, and a mare may well scream her disapproval at a stallion who pesters her when she is not ready to be mated.

Body posture is another means of communication. A relaxed horse looks relaxed: a hind foot resting, head lowered, eyes partly closed, lower lip drooping. An excited stallion prances around, head tucked in, tail raised, his whole outline saying "look at me". A startled horse looks tense and alert, signs which indicate to its companions that there is cause for alarm.

Smell is also important to horses. Mares and foals recognize each other by smell. When meeting, horses will put their noses close together, often blowing down their nostrils, before deciding whether or not to be friends. Smell also plays a part in sexual communication – a stallion smells the vulva and urine of an in-season mare and can tell the difference between the dung of another stallion and that of a mare (he will urinate over a mare's dung but add his own dung to that left by a stallion).

A horse's ears, too, being tremendously mobile, say a good deal about what he is thinking – where his attention is focused, what mood he is in. Drooping ears indicate that the horse is in a dozy state, alert ones that something has caught his attention; ears that are turned back may show that the horse's attention is focused behind him or they may indicate submission or fear; ears laid flat denote anger or fear.

Having eyes set on the sides of his head, the horse can see almost all round him, the only blind spots being immediately behind and a little way in front of his head – he can keep an approaching object in focus merely by turning his head slightly. The horse's sense of touch is enhanced by the whiskers on his muzzle which enable him to judge how far an object is from the end of his nose and may also be useful for assessing texture, for example when he is grazing.

The horse's long legs enable him to travel at speed, essential for an animal whose natural form of defence is to run away. Since he is not equipped to fight predators such as wolves, lions and snakes, his chief means of survival is flight. This helps to explain why domesticated horses often prefer to shelter from bad weather by standing by a hedge or wall rather than making use of a specially provided man-made building: horses feel safer in the open air where they can easily gallop off if anything frightens them.

▮ LEFT
All horses and ponies are by nature herd animals, living in small social groups comprising a stallion, his mares and various offspring.

▮ RIGHT
Nature has equipped the Shetland Pony to withstand harsh winter weather. The thick coat ensures that the pony stays warm and the skin never gets wet.

Conformation

Conformation, or the horse's overall make and shape, varies a good deal from breed to breed. What constitutes "ideal" conformation varies according to the work which the horse is required to perform. In spite of these necessary variations, however, certain guidelines can be followed when looking for desirable conformation. They relate to proportion: if a horse is correctly proportioned he will be better balanced, less prone to unsoundness and more able to perform his allotted tasks than a horse with less harmonious proportions. Indeed, many a horse with conformational defects has been condemned as "difficult" when it is simply his shape which prevents him from carrying out what his master requires.

A horse is deemed to have "correct" proportions when certain measurements are equal. For example: the length of the head, the depth of the body at the girth, the distance from the point of the hock to the ground, the distance from the chestnut on the foreleg to the ground, the distance from the croup to the fold of the stifle and from the fold of the stifle to the point of the hock should all be the same.

The domesticated horse is required to work, which means that certain features of his conformation are of particular importance. If a horse is deep through the girth, that is from the top of the wither to below the elbow, then his lungs will have plenty of room to expand – essential for any working horse. The length of his back is also important, particularly for the ridden horse. Too long, and it will be inclined to weakness; too short, and it may restrict the action.

Starting at the front, it is important that the horse's head is in proportion to his overall size. An over-large, heavy head will upset the overall balance, putting extra weight on the forehand, which already carries 60 per cent of the horse's total weight. Too small a head will also affect the balance. The upper and lower jaws should meet evenly at the front – if they do not this will inhibit the horse's ability to bite food such as grass. The nostrils should be large and wide, and large eyes are preferable to small ones, which experience has shown often denote a less than generous temperament. The set of the head is also important. If there is not sufficient clearance between the mandible (the lower jaw) and the atlas (the top bone in the neck), the horse will have difficulty in flexing at the poll, a requirement in the more collected gaits. There should be room for two fingers' width when the horse's head is raised.

In the riding horse the neck should be fairly long and curved. There should be no tendency to fleshiness around the

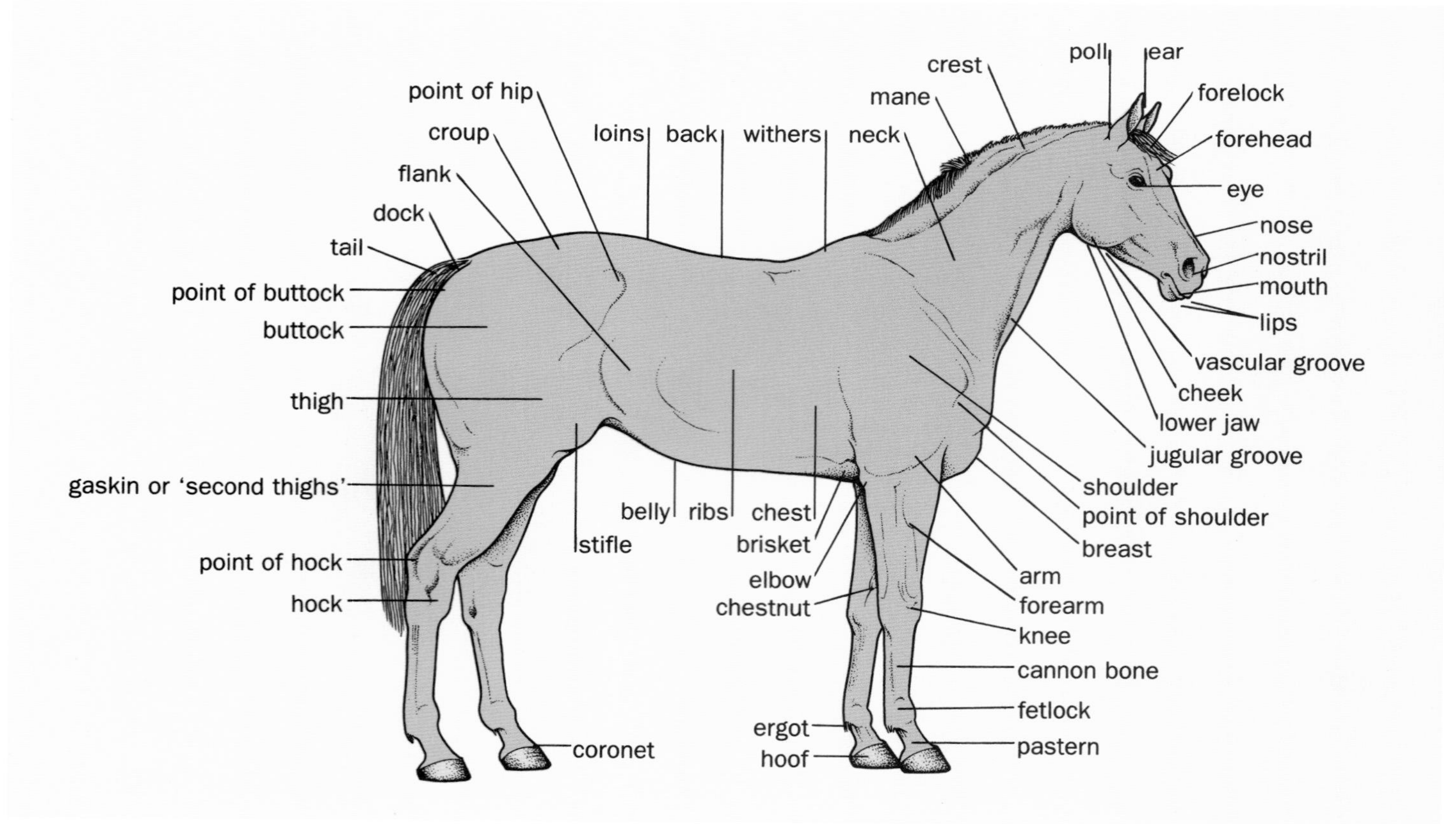

LEFT
The long neck and sloping shoulder of the Thoroughbred are associated with speed. Depth through the girth ensures plenty of room for the lungs to expand.

throat, which again would restrict the flexion of the head. This is particularly important in the riding horse. A long neck is associated with speed, a shorter one with strength. Hence the heavy draught breeds lack the length of neck seen, for instance, in the Thoroughbred. The shoulder should be well sloped (the angle of the scapula gives the slope). Such conformation enables the horse to take longer strides than a straight shoulder, which results in short, restricted action. A straight shoulder may produce jarring, which can be detrimental to the forelimb. Horses with straight shoulders tend to give an uncomfortable ride, too. The shoulder should be muscular but not "loaded", i.e. too heavy. The withers should be of a good height and well defined. If they are too high, it may be difficult to fit a saddle. If they are poorly defined, it may be difficult to keep a saddle in place. With the draught horse, which must wear a collar and for whom pulling power is more important than extended paces, a slightly straighter shoulder is acceptable.

The chest and body should be reasonably broad, but not excessively so, otherwise the horse's movement will be affected. Narrowness in the chest, giving the forelegs the appearance of "coming out of one hole" is a serious fault, causing the foreleg joints to brush against each other. The back should rise slightly to the croup, and be well muscled. Short, well-muscled loins are essential: the lumbar vertebrae have no support from the ribs, yet it is the loins which transfer the thrust from the engine (the hindquarters) to the body. The croup of the fully grown horse should be the same height as the withers and should not be too sloping, a feature which, combined with a low-set tail, is usually a sign of weakness. Croup-high horses throw extra weight on to the forehand, thus putting more strain on the forelimbs.

The horse's engine is in the back, that is in the hindquarters. They should therefore be strong and muscular. When standing still the hindlegs should not be stretched out behind him or tucked under him – a line dropped vertically from the point of the buttock to the ground should touch the hock and run down the rear of the cannon bone.

The forelegs should be straight and strong, with long, muscular forearms and large, flat knees. Short cannons indicate strength and there should be a good measurement of bone (the measurement being taken around the cannon below the knee). The amount of bone determines the weight-carrying ability of the horse. The amount of bone varies with the type of horse but as a rough guide a lightweight riding horse standing 16.2hh should have a minimum of 8 inches (20cm) of bone, a heavyweight horse of the same height at least 9 inches (23cm).

The pasterns should be of medium length and slope. The forefeet should be rounded and look like a matching pair. "Boxy" upright feet are prone to jarring. Large, flat feet may be more prone to bruising of the sole and to corns. The hindfeet, which bear less of the horse's overall weight when he is stationary, should be more oval in shape than the forefeet. Viewed from the side the slope of both fore and hindfeet should be a continuation of the slope of the pastern. The feet should point directly forwards.

COMMON CONFORMATIONAL DEFECTS

Back at the knee – where the knees, when viewed from the side, tend to extend backwards.

Calf knees – knees which are shallow from front to back.

Cow hocks – hocks which, when viewed from behind, turn inwards, as in a cow.

Ewe neck – where the top line of the neck is concave and the lower line convex.

Herring-gutted – where the horse has an upward slope from front to back on the underside of the belly.

Over at the knee – where the knees protrude forwards.

Pigeon toes – toes which turn inwards.

Roach back – where the spine has an exaggerated upward curve.

Sickle hocks – hocks which when viewed from the side have a concave line in front of the hocks and a slanting cannon bone.

Slab-sided – where the ribs are flat as opposed to "well-sprung".

Splay-footed – where the toes turn outwards.

Sway back – where the back has an exaggerated hollow.

Tied in below the knee – where the measurement of bone just below the knee is less than that farther down the cannon bone.

Colours and Markings

Equine coat colouring is controlled by numerous genes acting in combination to produce a multitude of variations in pigmentation. These genes, which are inherited, are located on paired structures known as chromosomes: the modern horse has 64 chromosomes, half of which are inherited from the sire and the other half from the dam. Some genes are dominant, others are recessive. For example, in horses chestnut is recessive to all other colours, bay is dominant to black, and grey is dominant to bay and black. The dominant greying gene can result in horses which are born with a dark coat turning progressively more grey as they

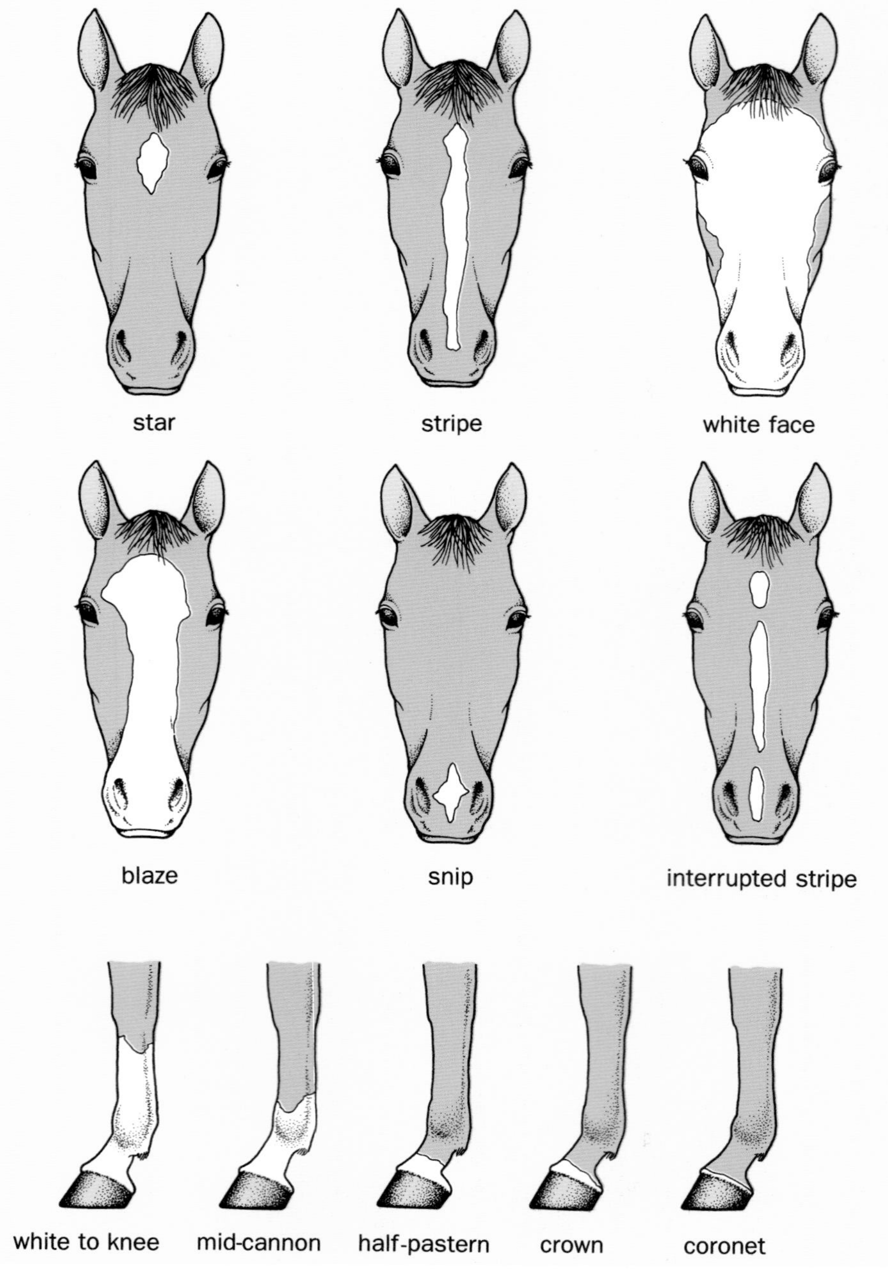

FACIAL MARKINGS

These include: Star, stripe and interrupted stripe, snip, blaze, white face, white muzzle

LEG MARKINGS

For registration purposes leg markings are described in detail, using points of the anatomy: e.g. white to fetlock, white to knee, white to hock, etc.

Two less specific terms are also in popular use: sock (white colouring from the coronet up to the knee), stocking (white colouring from the coronet up to and over the knee or hock).

HOOF COLOURS

The horn of the hoofs can vary from blue or black to white and may be marked with dark stripes.

grow older. This is especially noticeable in the Lipizzaner, whose foals are born dark and, with rare exceptions, turn grey as they mature. Albinos occur where there is a congenital deficiency of colouring pigment. The hair is white, the skin pink and eyes often blue.

A horse is always described by its coat colouring, followed by other distinguishing features, where applicable, such as white markings and the colour of the mane and tail.

Some horses have more than one clearly defined coat colour. Broken or part-coloured horses such as piebalds and skewbalds (known as Pintos or Paint Horses in America) have irregular patches of two different colours while Spotted Horses show a variety of spotted markings. Black legs go with bay body colouring.

Horses' eyes are normally dark, although blue eyes also occur.

EQUINE COLOURS

Grey A mixture of black and white hairs throughout. The coat varies from light to iron (very dark). The skin is black.

Fleabitten Grey Grey coat flecked with brown specks.

Dappled Grey Light grey base coat with dark grey rings.

Bay Reddish coat with black mane, tail and "points" (i.e. limbs). The coat colour may vary from red to brown or yellowish.

Black All black except for occasional white marks on the legs and/or head.

Chestnut Varies from a pale golden colour to a rich, red gold. The mane and tail may be lighter or darker than the coat colour.

Liver Chestnut The darkest of the chestnut shades.

Sorrel A light-red chesnut.

Brown A mixture of black and brown hairs, with black limbs, mane and tail. A very dark brown horse may appear almost black.

Roan A body colour with white hairs interspersed, which lightens the overall effect.

Strawberry Roan Chestnut body colour with white hair giving a pinkish-red tinge.

Blue Roan Black or brown body colour with white hair giving a blue tinge.

Dun Light sandy-coloured coat with black mane and tail, often accompanied by a dark, dorsal eel-stripe extending from the line of the neck to the tail, and sometimes by "zebra markings" (stripes) on the withers and legs – the vestiges of a primitive form of camouflage. Dun can vary from yellow to "mouse", depending on the diffusion of pigment. The skin is black.

Palomino Gold coat with white mane and tail.

Spotted Small, more or less circular patches of hair of a different colour from the main body colour and distributed over various areas of the body.

Piebald Large, irregular patches of black and white.

Skewbald Large, irregular patches of white and any other colour except black.

Cream Cream-coloured coat with unpigmented skin (also known as cremello).

White Markings White markings on the face and legs and, occasionally, on the body, are a valuable means of distinguishing one horse from another and are therefore noted in detail on veterinary certificates and registration papers.

Brindle Brown or grey streaked or patched with a darker colour.

OPPOSITE ABOVE
The predominant coat colour of the Lipizzaner is grey, but foals are born dark and it takes several years for the coat to change to the typical "white" colouring associated with the breed.

RIGHT
Spotted coat patterns have existed – and often been highly prized – throughout man's long relationship with the horse. Spotted horses are particularly associated with the Nez Percé Indians of North America.

Horses

There are more than 150 different breeds and types of horses in the world. The development of each of them has been influenced by man. Domestication resulted in selective breeding and, in many instances, more nutritious feeding, both of which led to an increase in the size or the quality (or both) of the horse. However, the biggest influencing factor was the work which humans required their particular horses to perform. Those who needed to move heavy loads bred for strength, while others in need of fast transportation bred for speed. The terms coldblood and warmblood (which have nothing to do with temperature) are used to describe horses. Coldblood refers to the heavy draught breeds which are believed to be descended from the prehistoric horse of northern Europe. Warmblood refers to the lighter, riding type of horse. Nowadays the term "warmblood" is used in connection with the horses being bred for competition riding. The breeds in this book are organized by continent, then subdivided into countries within each continent.

"Wild" Horses

PRZEWALSKI HORSE

The horse no longer exists as a truly wild animal, although the Asiatic Wild Horse, believed to be one of the precursors of the domesticated horse, can still be seen in zoos in various parts of the world. The Asiatic Wild Horse *(Equus przewalskii przewalskii Poliakoff)* was "discovered" – or rather a small herd was – as recently as 1881 in the Tachin Schara Nuru Mountains on the edge of the Gobi desert by the Russian explorer Colonel N.M. Przewalski. Before that it was believed to have been extinct, over-hunted for its meat by Mongolian tribesmen. The Przewalski Horse, as it is widely known, differs genetically from the domesticated horse, having 66 chromosomes instead of 64. In appearance it has several "primitive" features: a large head, with the eyes set high up rather than to the side of the head as in the case of the modern horse; long ears; thick neck; heavy body with a dark dorsal strip and zebra markings on the legs. The Przewalski stands about 12–13hh and is always yellowish dun with a light-coloured nose and dark mane and

ABOVE
These Kaimanawa horses live in feral herds in New Zealand's North Island. Like the Brumbies of Australia they are unpopular with stockmen because they compete for food with domestic animals

PREVIOUS PAGE OPPOSITE
A Mustang.

PREVIOUS PAGE
A Trakehner.

LEFT
The Asiatic Wild Horse or Przewalski Horse is the only surviving race of the species from which domestic horses are descended. Its chromosome count differs from that of the domesticated horse.

INTERESTING FACTS

Free-ranging horses and ponies exist in several parts of the world. In North America there are the Mustangs and also two types of island-based pony, the Sable Island, which lives in small numbers on the windswept island of that name off the coast of Nova Scotia, and the Assateague, whose home is off the coast of Maryland and Virginia. The Sable Island Ponies, thought to be descended from horses turned loose more than 200 years ago, are not managed, but the Assateague Ponies are rounded up annually and receive veterinary care. The population is controlled as necessary. In Europe, the Camargue horses lead a semi-wild existence in southern France and several of Britain's mountain and moorland pony breeds lead, to a certain extent, free-ranging lives, as do some of the horses bred in the former USSR.

tail. The mane, which grows upright, is shed each spring and there is no forelock. Intractable by nature – it cannot be trained for riding – the Przewalski can survive on a minimum of food and endure extremes of heat and cold.

TARPAN

Eastern Europe and European Russia were the home of the Tarpan, another horse widely believed to have been an ancestor of the modern horse. It survived in the wild until the nineteenth century. One authority claims that the last true Tarpan in captivity died in 1919, in which case the Tarpan which exists today, running semi-wild in reserves in Poland, must be a "reconstruction", almost certainly bred from the Konik, which it strongly resembled. Experiments with crossing Przewalski stallions and Konik mares have also produced an animal which looks very like the original Tarpan. The Tarpan was (and is) more lightly built than the Przewalski, standing about 13hh and with a brown or mouse dun coat, dark mane and tail and, frequently, primitive dorsal stripe and zebra markings.

BRUMBY

Australia's "wild" horse, the Brumby, is not a true wild horse, equine animals having been unknown in Australasia until the arrival of European settlers a few hundred years ago (the assumption being that because there were no land bridges linking the Americas with Australia, Eohippus and its descendants had no means of migrating there). The Brumbies which live in feral herds in the Northern Territory and, to a lesser extent, in central Australia, are descended from settlers' horses who wandered off into the bush, producing offspring that grew up under wild conditions. When rounded up and broken in some Brumbies have, over the years, been useful to man but today they are generally regarded as a pest and are culled because they compete for food with domestic animals.

See also Camargue, Mustang, Sorraia.

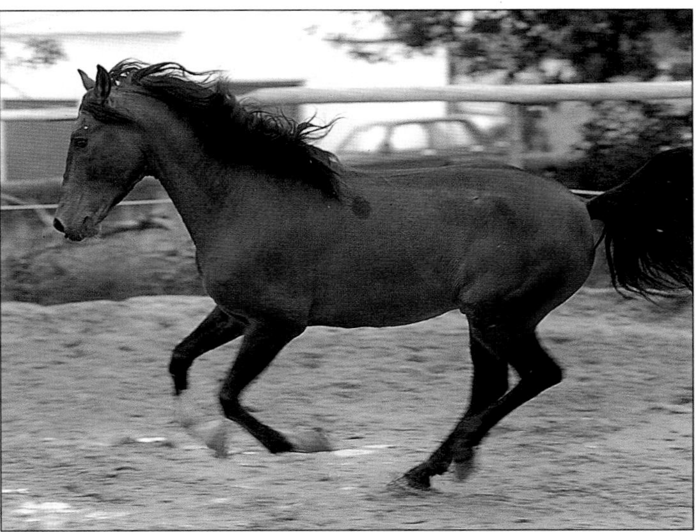

ABOVE LEFT
The primitive looking Konik pony is found in Poland and is a descendant of the Tarpan. Crossed with Przewalski stallions, Konik mares produce Tarpan "look-alikes".

LEFT
The Sorraia pony, which can be found living in semi-feral conditions in Portugal, is believed to be of ancient origin.

Arab

The oldest and purest of all horse breeds, the Arab is considered by many people to be the most beautiful equine animal in the world. With its refined head and dished profile, expressive eyes, high spirits and unique, floating action, it is undoubtedly one of the most exquisite of creatures. Although it has certainly been bred with great care for many centuries, its exact origins are unclear. Depictions of horses in ancient art suggest that horses of Arab type lived in the Arabian peninsula as long ago as 2 ,000 – 3,000BC. Like the desert tribes with whom they have lived for so long, Arab horses became superbly well adapted to life in a harsh environment, having extreme powers of endurance, tremendous soundness and the ability to thrive on the most meagre of rations.

More than any other horse, it is the Arab which has influenced the development of equine

INTERESTING FACTS

The unique outline of the Arab is determined by the formation of its skeleton, which differs from other equine breeds in several respects. The Arab has 17 ribs (other horses have 18); five lumbar vertebrae (other horses have six), and 16 tail vertebrae (other horses have 18).

BREED DESCRIPTION

Height 14.2 – 15hh.

Colour Predominantly chestnut, grey, bay and black.

Conformation Small head with broad forehead, fine muzzle, concave profile, wide nostrils and small ears; deep, clearly defined jowl with the throat set into it in a distinctly arched curve; graceful, curving neck; long, sloping shoulders with well-defined withers; deep, roomy body with broad, deep chest and short, level back; high-set tail; hard, clean limbs with well-defined tendons and dense, fine bone; hard, well-shaped feet; fine, silky mane and tail.

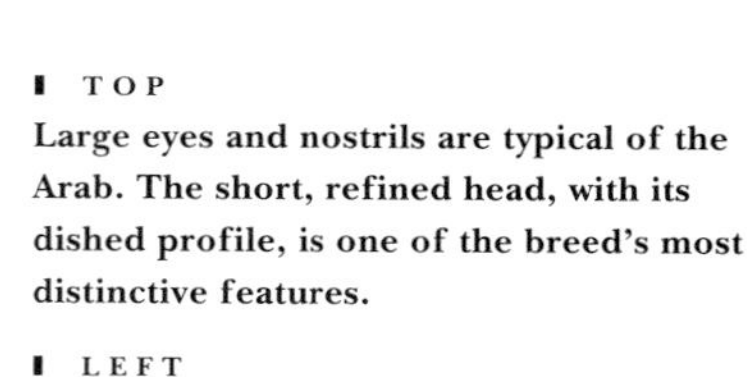

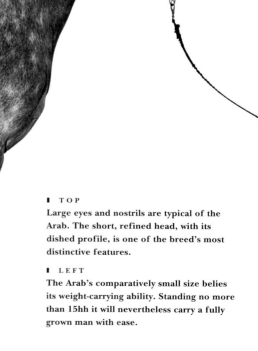

TOP
Large eyes and nostrils are typical of the Arab. The short, refined head, with its dished profile, is one of the breed's most distinctive features.

LEFT
The Arab's comparatively small size belies its weight-carrying ability. Standing no more than 15hh it will nevertheless carry a fully grown man with ease.

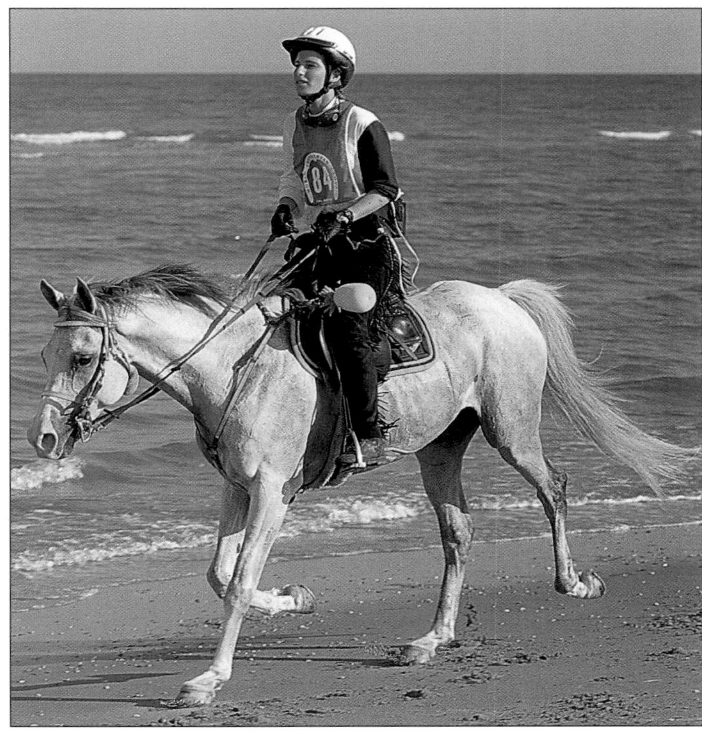

breeds throughout the world. This Arabian influence was initiated in the seventh and early eighth centuries AD when the followers of Islam spread across North Africa and into Spain. The horses they took with them were greatly superior to the native stock of other lands and so began a process of upgrading, through the introduction of Arab blood, that was to go on for many centuries and, indeed, still goes on today.

Pure-bred Arabian horses are now bred throughout the world. As well as appearing in the show ring, they are particularly suited to the sport of endurance riding. In recent times, too, there has been a resurgence of interest in Arab racing.

ABOVE LEFT
The Arab horse often appears to float over the ground. This remarkable action, coupled with a gentle temperament, makes it a popular riding horse throughout the world.

ABOVE RIGHT
The breed's legendary stamina makes it the perfect choice for endurance riding which at the top level involves covering a distance of 100 miles (161km) in a day.

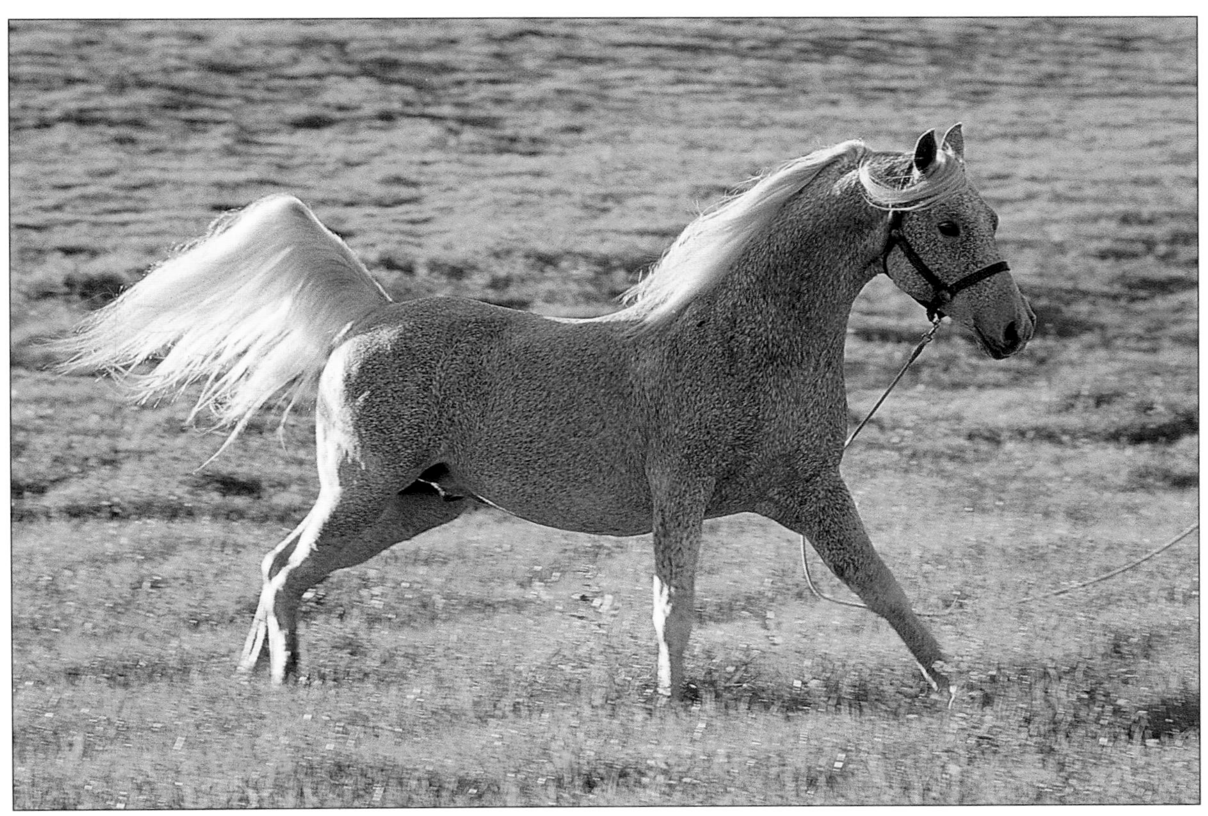

LEFT
With its elegance, spirit and exceptional looks, it is easy to see why the Arab is often considered to be the world's most beautiful horse.

Barb

The Barb comes from Morocco, Algeria and Tunisia – the coastal regions of these North African countries were formerly known as the Barbary Coast, "Barbary" meaning foreign or, more specifically, non-Christian lands. Opinions differ as to the Barb's origins, lack of documentary evidence making it impossible to do more than hazard an educated guess. According to one school of thought, the Barb may trace back to an isolated group of wild horses which survived the Ice Age. If that were true, it would make the Barb an even older breed than the Arab. Another theory links the Barb to the Akhal-Teke, the horse of the Turkmens.

Although it is unlikely that the breed's true origins will ever be revealed, what is certain is that the Barb has had more influence on the development of equine breeds throughout the world than any other horse except the Arab. As with the Arab, it was the spread of Islam which led to the forerunners of today's Barbs reaching Europe from the early eighth century onwards (the first Muslim army, seven thousand strong, landed in Spain in the spring of 711). Once established on the Iberian peninsula the Barb horse played a major role in the development of the Andalusian, which subsequently became one of the major influences in horse breeding all over the world. Among the many historical references to "Barbary" horses perhaps the most famous is Roan Barbary, belonging to the English king, Richard II (1367–1400). During the sixteenth century Henry VIII imported a number of Barbary horses into England and a century later the Barb played an important part in the evolution of the Thoroughbred. Elsewhere the influence of the Barb is still evident in the Argentinian Criollo and the American Mustang.

BELOW
The Barb lacks the refinement and elegance of the Arab but is equally tough and enduring.

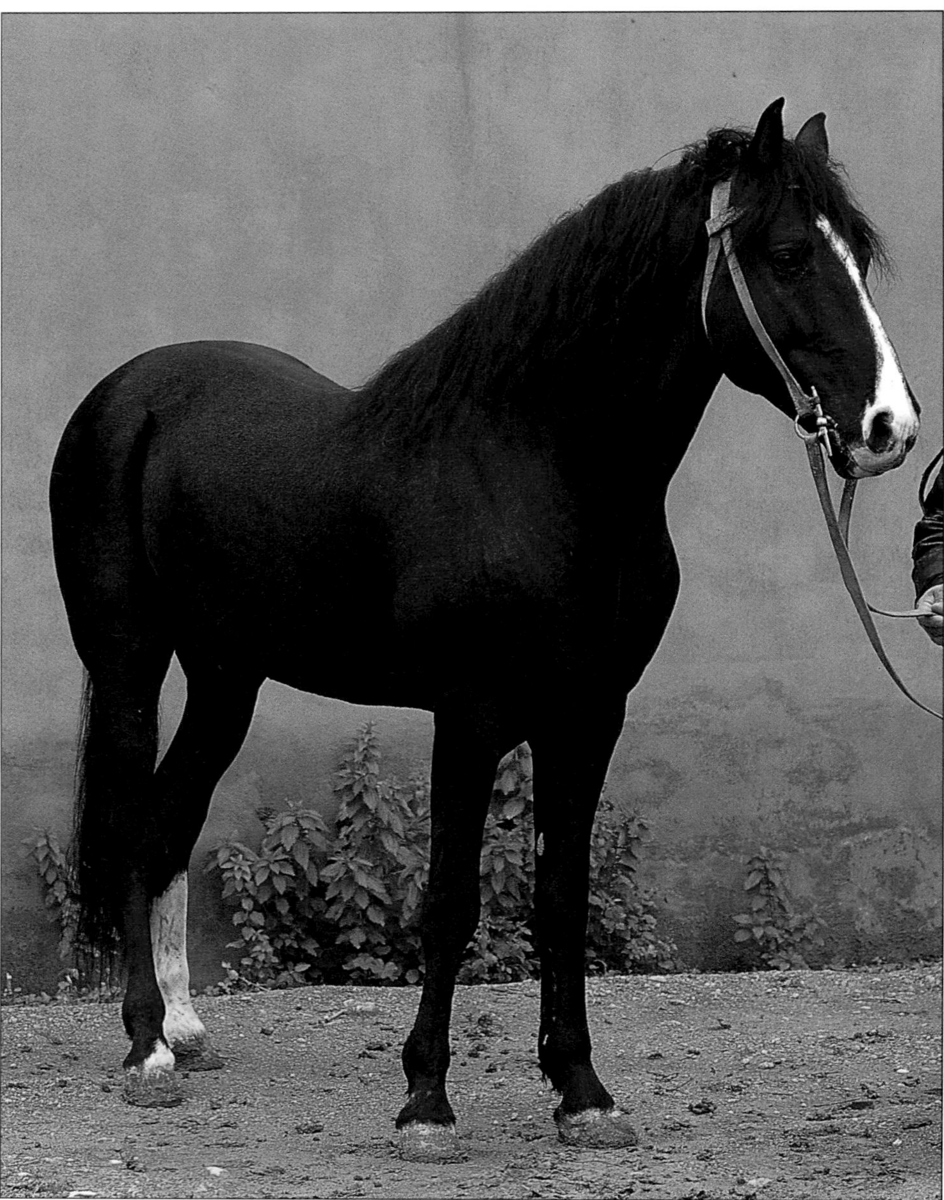

Despite its importance as a progenitor of other breeds, the Barb has achieved less widespread renown than the Arab, no doubt because it lacks the Arab's unique visual appeal, being much less refined and generally less impressive in appearance. Nevertheless it has the same boundless stamina and endurance, the same ability to thrive on meagre rations, the same sure-footedness – and an impressive turn of speed over short distances.

BREED DESCRIPTION

Height Around 14.2 – 15.2hh.

Colour Predominantly grey, bay, brown and black.

Conformation Narrow head with convex profile; arched neck; flat shoulders with well-defined withers; short, strong body; sloping hindquarters with fairly low-set tail; rather slender, but strong, limbs; narrow, but hard, feet.

BELOW
Dressed in ceremonial attire, Barb horses and their Moroccan riders are a colourful sight at a modern "Fantasia".

INTERESTING FACTS

The most well-known Barb horses of modern times were those ridden by the Spahis, men of the Algerian and Tunisian cavalry regiments in the French army. The Spahis originally came from Turkey but were incorporated into their army by the French when the latter occupied Algiers and Tunis. Barb horses still feature in the exciting present-day North African festivals recalling these countries' military pasts.

BELOW
In the dramatic rifle-firing charge seen at North African festivals, Barb horses demonstrate their impressive speed over a short distance.

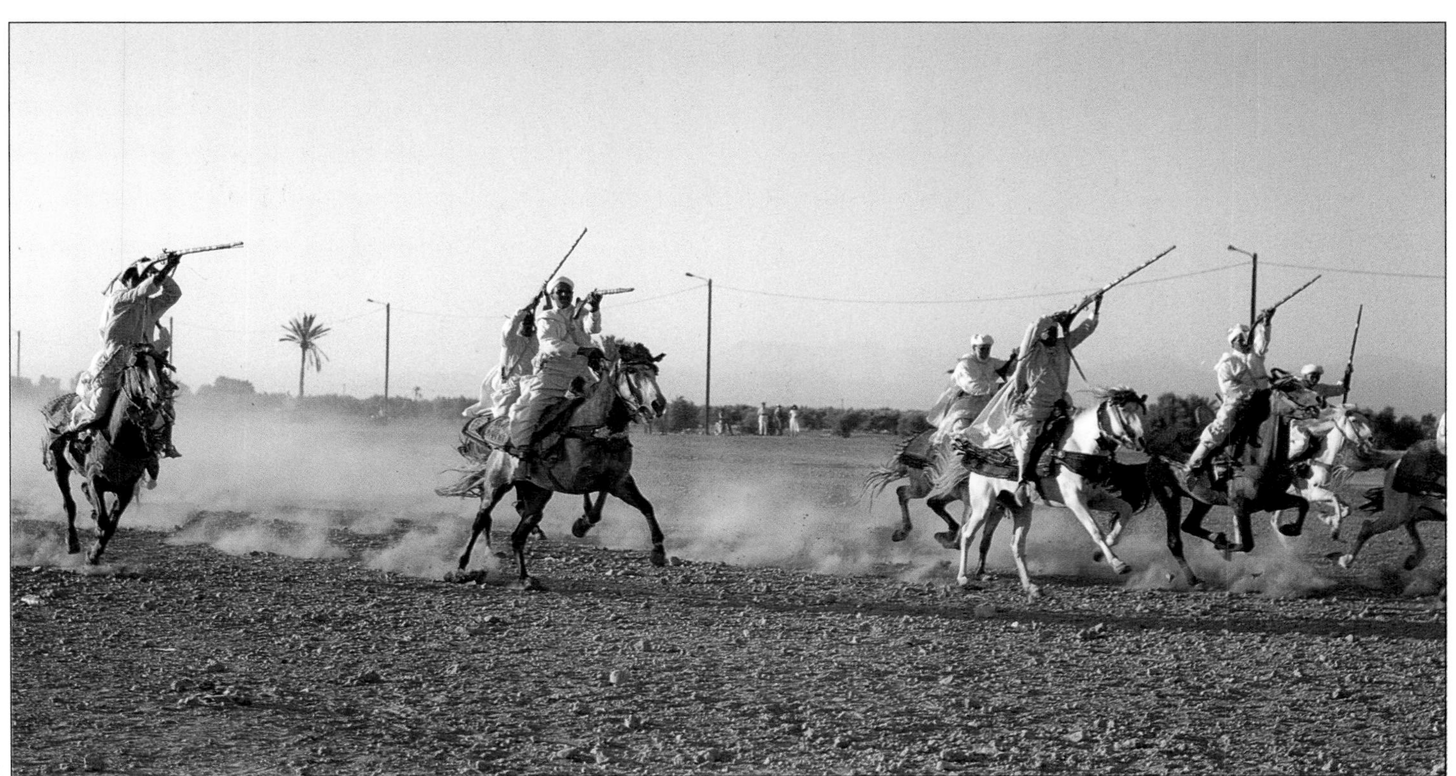

Andalusian

As its name suggests, the Andalusian comes from the sun-baked region of southern Spain which is close to North Africa. While it is without doubt an ancient breed, its origins are uncertain. Whatever native horses existed in Spain when the Muslim invaders arrived in 711 – they may well have resembled the primitive Sorraian Pony still found today in Portugal – must surely have been crossed subsequently with the invaders' Barb horses, which were imported in such great numbers.

After the last Muslim state, Granada, had fallen to the Christians in 1492, Spain began to assume a new importance in the western world and so, too, did her horses. Taken to the Americas by the sixteenth-century Conquistadores, Spanish horses provided the foundation stock for the majority of new breeds developed by the settlers. In Europe, meanwhile, the Spanish horse became the preferred mount of monarchs and of the great riding masters, including the Englishman, William Cavendish, Duke of Newcastle, who in the seventeenth century wrote that: "If well chosen it is the noblest horse in the world; the most beautiful that can be. He is of great spirit and of great courage and docile; has the proudest walk, the proudest trot...the loftiest gallop and is the lovingest and gentlest horse and fittest of all for a king in Day of Triumph." The Lipizzaner is a direct descendant of the Andalusian, while other famous European breeds influenced by Spanish blood include the Frederiksborg, the Friesian (which in turn

LEFT
The Andalusian's handsome head, a more refined version of the Barb, is as eye-catching and as distinctive in its own way as that of the Arab.

RIGHT
The Andalusian is not particularly tall but its compact, muscular frame is indicative of great strength.

BREED DESCRIPTION

Height 15 – 15.2hh.

Colour Predominantly grey (including "mulberry" – a dappled, purplish grey) and bay.

Conformation Handsome head with broad forehead and large, kind eyes; fairly long, thick but elegant neck; long, well-sloped shoulders with well-defined withers; short, strong body with broad chest and well-sprung ribs; very broad, strong, rounded hindquarters with rather low-set tail; medium length limbs, clean cut and elegant but strong; long and very luxuriant mane and tail.

LEFT
On point duty in present-day Barcelona. Thanks to its excellent temperament and willing nature, the Andalusian is an ideal all-purpose riding horse.

BELOW
Grey is one of the predominant Andalusian colours, along with bay. Spotted strains were once popular and were responsible for the founding of the Appaloosa breed in America.

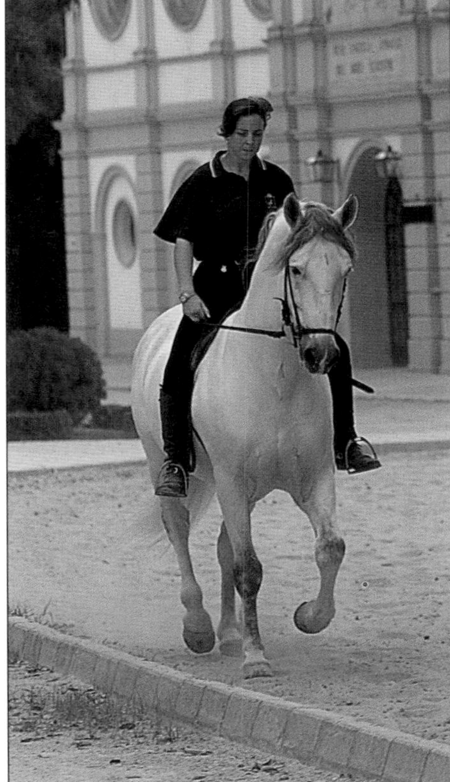

INTERESTING FACTS

The Andalusian horse's survival down the centuries, which included some pretty turbulent times, was aided by the monastic orders, particularly the Carthusians, who became especially skilful at horse breeding. In times of danger, horses were moved from the great studs to remote monasteries for safe keeping. The Carthusians were instrumental in maintaining purity of line and produced animals of consistently high quality.

influenced the Oldenburg), the Holstein and the Connemara.

The Andalusian is one of the most elegant of horses. Possessing tremendous presence, lofty paces, agility and a gentle, willing nature, it makes an excellent all-round riding horse and is particularly well suited to the movements of the *haute école* (high school). It can also be seen to great effect taking part in the colourful annual *ferias*, or fairs, of its native Andalusia.

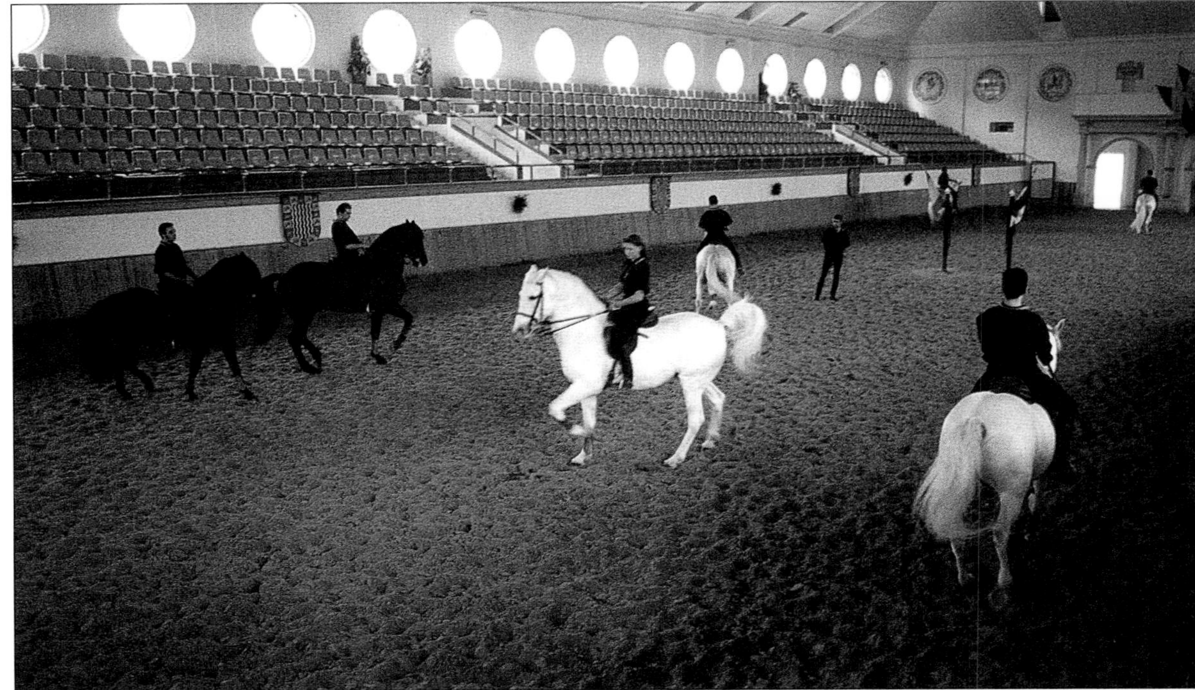

RIGHT
The breed's proud bearing and lofty action lend themselves perfectly to the movements of the *haute école*, or high school.

Thoroughbred

The life of man has been inextricably interwoven with that of the horse for more than 4,000 years but in all that time no achievement has excelled the "invention" of the Thoroughbred. Quite apart from being the world's supreme racehorse, the Thoroughbred has played a vital part in the upgrading of numerous old horse and pony breeds and in establishing as many new ones.

Henry VIII set the process in motion during the sixteenth century when he founded the famous Royal Paddocks at Hampton Court. His daughter, Elizabeth I, founded another stud at Tutbury, in Staffordshire. Both monarchs imported horses from Spain and Italy to cross with native stock. Under subsequent monarchs – James I, Charles I and Charles II – horse breeding and racing gained impetus. By the beginning of the seventeenth century regular race meetings were being staged at Newmarket, Chester, Doncaster and Lincoln. Many noblemen took up the

BREED DESCRIPTION

Height Variable. May be as small as 14.2hh or over 17hh. Average 16 – 16.2hh.

Colour All solid colours, the most common being bay, chestnut and brown. Also grey, black and roan. White markings are permissible.

Conformation Variable, but the best specimens have excellent conformation characterized by a refined, intelligent head; elegant neck; well-sloped shoulders; short, strong body with great depth through the girth; strong, muscular hindquarters with well -set tail; clean, hard legs with well let-down hocks and a minimum of 8 inches (20cm) of bone below the knee.

ABOVE RIGHT
The head of the Thoroughbred is typically refined, with large eyes and nostrils. The dished profile so characteristic of its Arabian forebears is not found in the Thoroughbred.

RIGHT
With its well-sloped shoulders, powerful hindquarters and long limbs, the Thoroughbred is the ultimate "racing machine". The deep girth ensures plenty of room for the heart and lungs.

RIGHT
The bigger, slower developing stamp of Thoroughbred often makes a first-rate steeplechaser. Chasing calls for courage, stamina and speed, qualities for which the Thoroughbred is renowned.

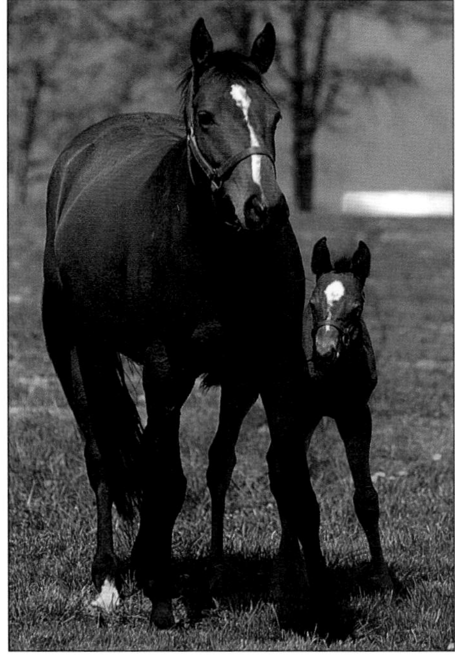

BELOW RIGHT
Thanks to carefully kept records (in the *General Stud Book*) dating back some two centuries, it is possible to trace the pedigree of this foal to one of the breed's handful of foundation sires.

breeding of horses for racing, sending agents overseas to seek out good stallions. Records of the time repeatedly refer to Barb, Barbary, Arabian, Hobby and Galloway horses (the Irish Hobby and Scottish Galloway were famous "running" horses of the day) – and it is on this blood that the modern Thoroughbred was founded.

The exact breeding of the Thoroughbred's forebears will never be known since horses often changed names when they changed hands and the terms "Arabian", "Barb" and "Turk", were frequently used inaccurately. However, what is certain is that during the last quarter of the seventeenth century and the first quarter of the eighteenth, Englishmen or their agents bought a number of eastern stallions, crossed them with English mares of mixed pedigree and started a dynasty of great racehorses. The most famous of these stallions were the Byerley Turk, the Darley Arabian and the Godolphin Arabian, who are recognized as the founding fathers of the Thoroughbred. In 1791 *An Introduction to a General Stud Book* appeared and following the publication of several more preliminary editions, there came, in 1808, Volume I of the *General Stud Book.* A horse is classed as Thoroughbred if both its parents are entered in the *General Stud Book* (or in the equivalent official Thoroughbred stud books in other countries).

The Thoroughbred is a handsome horse, alert, spirited and full of presence. It has an easy, ground-covering stride at the gallop and possesses boundless courage and immense stamina, qualities which stand it in good stead on the racecourse, in the hunting field and in three-day eventing.

INTERESTING FACTS

The Byerley Turk was captured by Captain Byerley at Buda in the 1680s, ridden by him at the Battle of the Boyne and sent to England to stand at stud. His great-grandson Tartar sired Herod, one of the most important sires in Thoroughbred history. The Darley Arabian, foaled in 1700, was acquired by Thomas Darley and sent to England from the Syrian port of Aleppo. He was responsible for founding the Eclipse line – Eclipse was one of the greatest racehorses of all time. The Godolphin Arabian was foaled in the Yemen in 1724, exported to Tunis via Syria and later given by the Bey of Tunis to the King of France, who subsequently sold him to Edward Coke, from Derbyshire. He was eventually acquired by Lord Godolphin and was responsible for founding the Matchem line. The Herod, Eclipse and Matchem lines, plus the Highflyer (Highflyer was a son of Herod) are the four principal tail-male lines of the modern Thoroughbred.

BOTTOM
Thoroughbreds hurdling at speed at Cheltenham, spiritual home of the sport of jump racing. The Thoroughbred's athletic prowess makes it equally suitable for sports such as hunting and three-day eventing.

Anglo-Arab

A more substantial horse than the pure-bred Arab, the Anglo-Arab is produced by mixing Arab and Thoroughbred blood. The Anglo-Arab can result from a first cross between a Thoroughbred stallion and an Arab mare or vice versa. It can also be produced by breeding Thoroughbred to Anglo-Arab or Arab to Anglo-Arab, or Anglo-Arab to Anglo-Arab. As a result of these different permutations, the amount of Arab blood varies a good deal. So, too, does the size and appearance of the horse. The biggest horses are often produced by using an Arab stallion on a Thoroughbred mare and the best examples of the Anglo-Arab will inherit the endurance and stamina of the Arab and the speed and scope of the Thoroughbred, but not the latter's rather high-strung temperament.

France has been a notable producer of Anglo-Arabs since the first half of the nineteenth century. The French Anglo-Arab traces back to two eastern stallions, Massoud (an Arab) and Aslam (which is said to be of Turkish origin). They were imported from Syria and crossed with three imported English Thoroughbred

BREED DESCRIPTION

Height Around 15.3 – 16.3hh.

Colour Usually chestnut, bay or brown.

Conformation Variable, but the best specimens tend towards good Thoroughbred conformation: intelligent head with straight profile, expressive eyes and alert ears; long neck with more prominent withers than the Arab; sloping shoulders; short, strong body – rather more sturdy than the Thoroughbred – with deep chest; somewhat long hindquarters; good, sound limbs; strong, well-shaped feet.

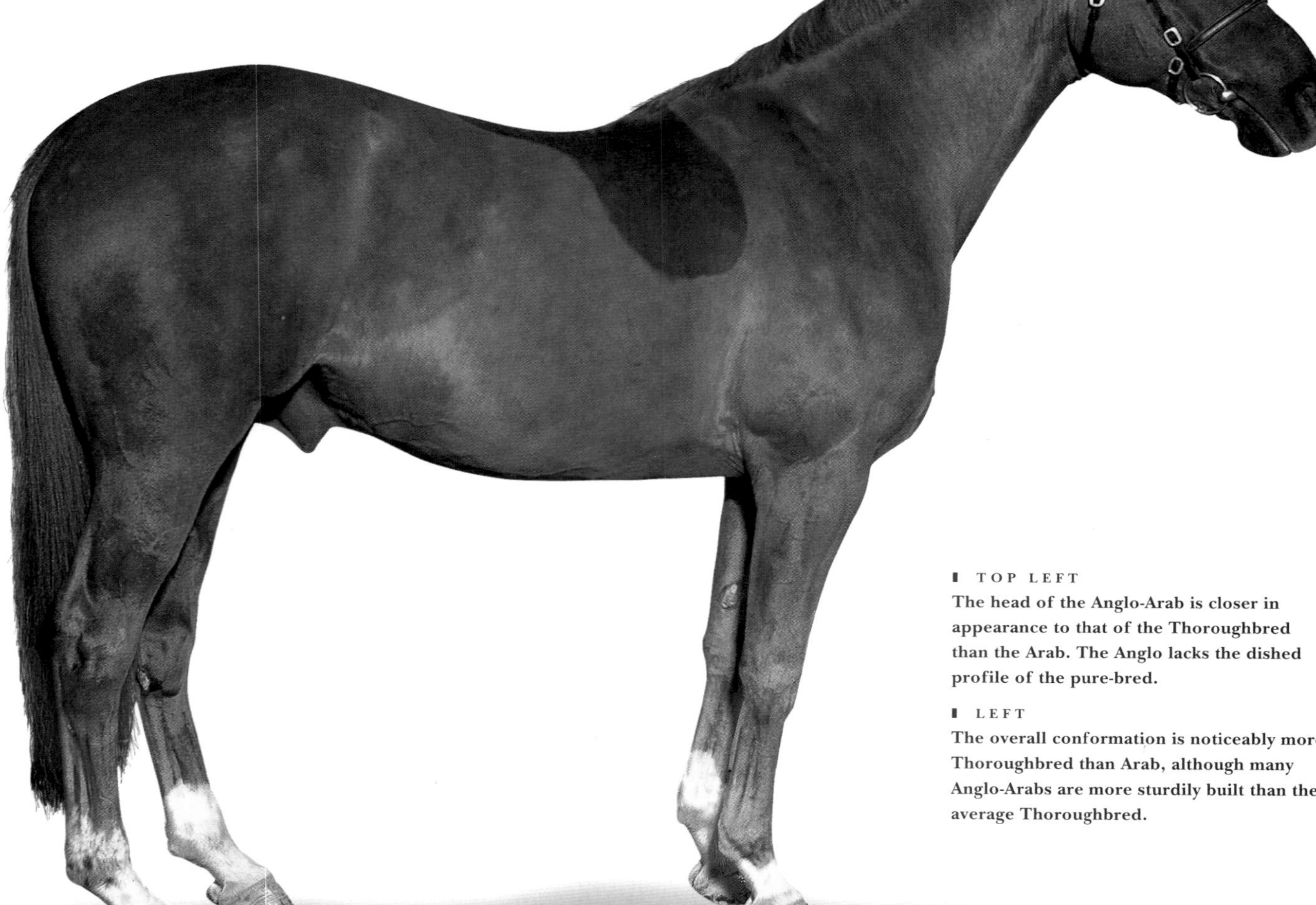

TOP LEFT
The head of the Anglo-Arab is closer in appearance to that of the Thoroughbred than the Arab. The Anglo lacks the dished profile of the pure-bred.

LEFT
The overall conformation is noticeably more Thoroughbred than Arab, although many Anglo-Arabs are more sturdily built than the average Thoroughbred.

LEFT
The crossing of Thoroughbred with Arab blood has produced some outstanding competition horses in the Olympic disciplines, including dressage.

mares, Daer, Comus Mare and Selim Mare. Their three daughters, Delphine, Clovis and Danaë became the foundation stock of France's first breed of sports horse. At one time the Anglo-Arab was much used in France by the military and as a general riding and competition horse. More recently it has been an influential factor in the development of the modern sports horse, the Selle Français.

BELOW
In recent years French Anglo-Arabs such as this one have achieved great success in top-level three-day eventing, holding their own against the best of the Thoroughbreds and Warmbloods.

INTERESTING FACTS

Before the development of the Selle Français, the French Anglo-Arab was highly successful in the competitive disciplines, particularly show jumping. Many of the horses ridden by the dual Olympic champion Pierre Jonquères d'Oriola were Anglo-Arabs, the most famous being the little gelding Marquis III (a very successful Grand Prix and Nations' Cup horse) and Ali-Baba, on whom d'Oriola won his first Olympic title at Helsinki in 1952. More recently French Anglo-Arabs have been successful performers with the French three-day event team. They include Twist la Beige (winner of the European Championship in 1993) and Newport and Newlot (both European team silver medallists).

Noriker

Bred and developed over several thousand years in the mountain regions of Austria, the Noriker is an attractive looking light draught horse. Strong and hardy, this horse is noted particularly for its calm temperament, sound limbs and sure-footedness. These characteristics make it an ideal all-round work horse over difficult mountainous terrain.

As with most horses, despite its ancient origins there was no formal breeding programme until fairly recent times. The Prince-Archbishop of Salzburg is credited with forming a stud book some 400 years ago. It was then that standards were drawn up, for both mares and stallions, and stud farms established.

Because of its toughness and capacity for hard work the Noriker became popular throughout Europe. Different strains evolved, including the Bavarian, now known as the South German Coldblood and found in Upper and Lower Bavaria. Various colour lines, tracing back to Andalusian and Neapolitan horses, also had an influence on today's breed and were responsible for the dappled and brindle colourings.

BREED DESCRIPTION

Height Stallions 16 – 17hh. Mares 15.3 – 17hh.

Colour Brown, chestnut, black, grey and brindle. White body markings are not acceptable. Too many or too large white markings on the head and limbs are not desirable.

Conformation Straight profile, wide nostrils, medium-sized eyes; medium-length neck with thick, curly mane; good sloping shoulders; broad, deep chest; medium-length, well-muscled back; long limbs with powerful forearms, large clean joints, well-muscled second thigh and good, sound feet.

INTERESTING FACTS

The breed takes its name from the ancient state of Noricum (during the Roman Empire Noricum was roughly approximate to present-day Austria). However, the Noriker can be traced back to pre-Roman times, when a heavy war horse was developed in Thessalonica. Horses of this type were taken to Noricum by the Romans. In due course they were crossed with other coldblooded horses of the region and became admirably adapted to the harsh conditions of their new environment.

ABOVE
Most Norikers are brown but the breed embraces a wide range of coat colours, including this attractive dark chestnut with flaxen mane.

LEFT
The Noriker's sturdy build and good limbs and feet make it an ideal work horse in mountainous regions. Like most mountain breeds, it is a good mover, with a particularly active trot.

Belgian Draught

One of the world's finest and historically most important heavy horses, the Belgian Draught is an ancient breed, closely connected to the Ardennais. The Flanders Horse, as the breed was known during the Middle Ages, had an influence on the development of several other renowned "heavies", including the Shire, the Suffolk Punch and particularly the Clydesdale. Nowadays the Belgian Draught is also known as the Brabant, after its main breeding area in central Belgium.

ABOVE
The Belgian Draught is an impressive horse, combining great strength with a gentle temperament and willingness to work. Despite its size, it is economical to keep.

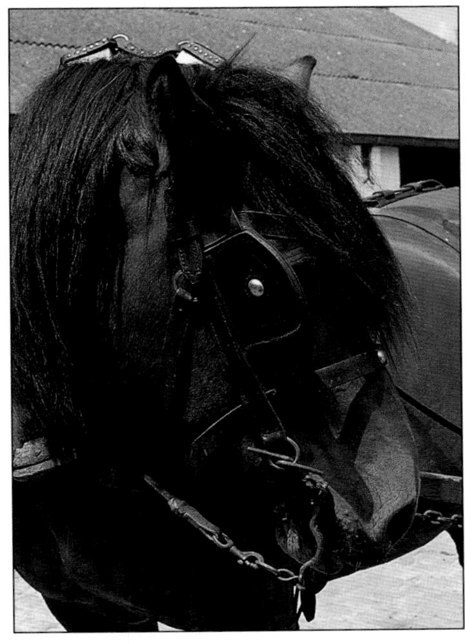

ABOVE LEFT
The head is rather plain but the eyes have the kindly expression associated with so many of the heavy breeds.

Despite widespread mechanization, this gentle giant of a horse, known for its kind nature and willingness to work, can still be found in modest numbers in many areas of Belgium and is also much appreciated in North America.

Over the years breeders have managed to maintain the excellence of these horses by a policy of strict selection and some inbreeding. The result is a handsome individual – its short neck, strong shoulders, short limbs, deep-girthed body and huge hindquarters, coupled with the most amenable of temperaments, make it the ideal draught horse for work on the land and there is no finer sight in the equestrian world than a team of these magnificent animals hitched to a smart brewers' dray.

BREED DESCRIPTION

Height 16.2 – 17hh.

Colour Predominantly red-roan with black points, chestnut and sorrel. Bay, dun and grey also occur.

Conformation Small, rather plain head but with intelligent expression; short, muscular neck; massive shoulders; short, deep, compact body; rounded, powerful hindquarters; short, strong limbs with plenty of feather and well-shaped, medium-sized feet.

INTERESTING FACTS

Towards the end of the last century there were three recognized types of Brabant horse, each based on a different bloodline. Those from the celebrated stallion Orange I, known as the Gros de la Dendre line, were mainly bay in colour. A stallion called Bayard founded the Gris du Hainaut line, with its greys, red-roans and sorrels. A third line, the Colosses de la Méhaigne, descended from the bay stallion Jean I. Today the descendants of these bloodlines all come under the general title of Belgian Draught or Brabant.

LEFT
Massive hindquarters are typical of the breed. These horses have docked tails.

Frederiksborg

The stud after which the Frederiksborg is named was founded by King Frederick II during the 1560s and was famous as a provider of quality horses to the courts of Europe. The stud's foundation stock came from Spain and was subsequently crossed with the Spanish horse's close relative, the Neapolitan. The horses thus produced were both elegant and spirited and well suited to the dual requirements of the day: as a mount for work in the manège and as a charger for the cavalry.

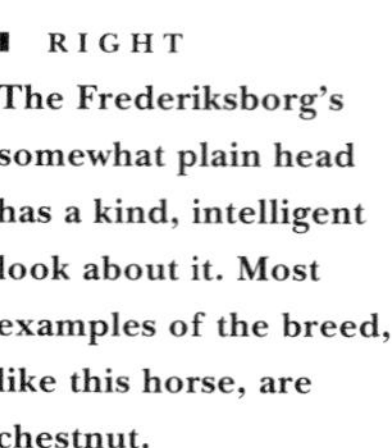

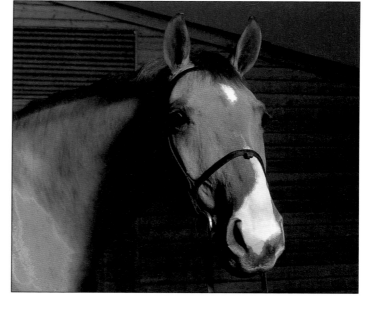

RIGHT
The Frederiksborg's somewhat plain head has a kind, intelligent look about it. Most examples of the breed, like this horse, are chestnut.

BREED DESCRIPTION

Height 15.3 – 16hh.

Colour Chestnut.

Conformation Intelligent, if somewhat plain, head; short, upright neck; strong but rather upright shoulders; strong back that tends to be long; high-set tail; good, strong feet.

The breed continued to develop through the introduction of eastern and British half-bred stallions and for several centuries the Frederiksborg was one of the most sought-after horses in Europe. Eventually, so numerous were the exports of the Frederiksborg from Denmark that stock became seriously depleted, with the result that during the first half of the nineteenth century the stud turned instead to Thoroughbred breeding. This venture was not a success and in 1871 the stud was dispersed. Fortunately, however, Frederiksborgs did not disappear altogether: private breeders went on producing them, mainly for use as light harness horses.

Frederiksborgs are still bred in Denmark, although recent demands for an outstanding sports horse have led to the development of a new horse, the Danish Warmblood, based mainly on Swedish, German and Polish stallions. Frederiksborg blood does occasionally appear in today's Danish Warmblood pedigrees, chiefly through the female line.

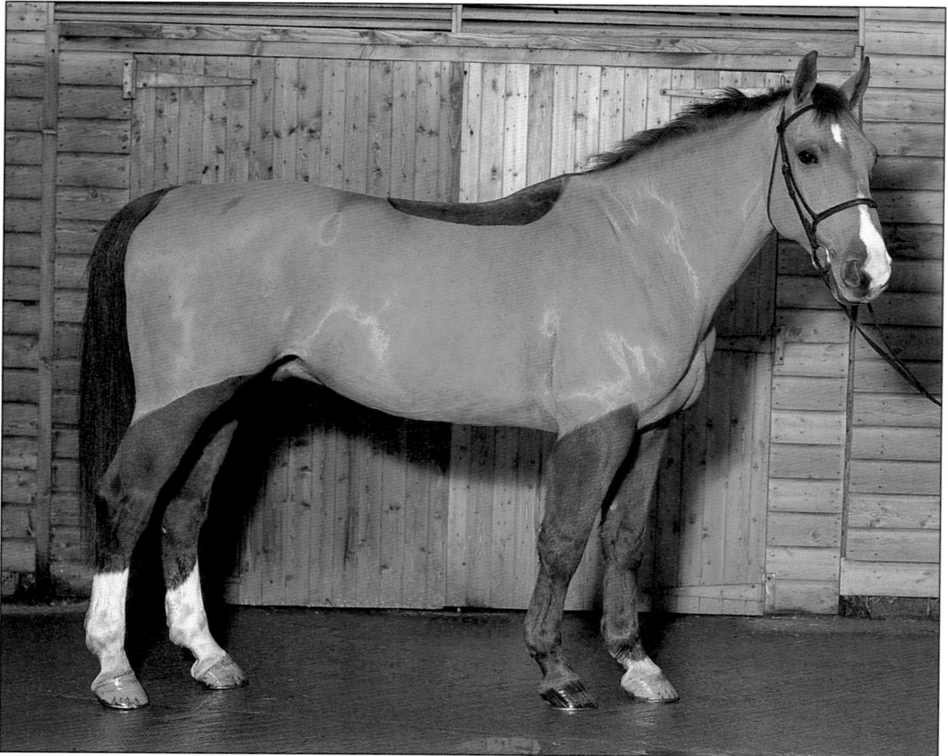

INTERESTING FACTS

The Frederiksborg played a significant part in the development of a much more well-known breed, the Lipizzaner, famous for its association with the Spanish Riding School in Vienna. The white stallion Pluto, from the Royal Danish Court Stud, was one of the six stallions on which the Lipizzaner breed is based. Pluto was foaled in 1765, the earliest of the six. More than two centuries later his descendants are still performing at the Spanish Riding School where they can be identified by the "Pluto" prefix to their names.

LEFT
The rather long back, short neck and upright shoulders are more typical of the light harness horse than the riding horse.

Jutland

Except for the feathering of its lower legs, Denmark's heavy horse bears an uncanny resemblance to the British breed, the Suffolk Punch. This resemblance is perhaps not so surprising, because the present-day Jutland was greatly influenced by the Suffolk blood introduced via the English stallion Oppenheim LXII, who stood at stud in Denmark during the 1860s.

The breed goes back much further than that, however. Heavy horses have been bred on the Jutland Peninsula for many centuries, certainly as far back as the twelfth century, when they were in great demand as war horses. Combining enormous strength with the most willing of natures, the Jutland horse made the ideal mount for the heavily armoured knights of the Middle Ages. Cleveland Bay and Yorkshire Coach Horse blood is said to have been used in the development of the Jutland, but it is unquestionably the Suffolk which has been the dominant factor, even to its chestnut colouring.

Mechanization has reduced the numbers of these attractive horses but some can still be seen, either at shows or pulling drays in the cities or, occasionally, working the land.

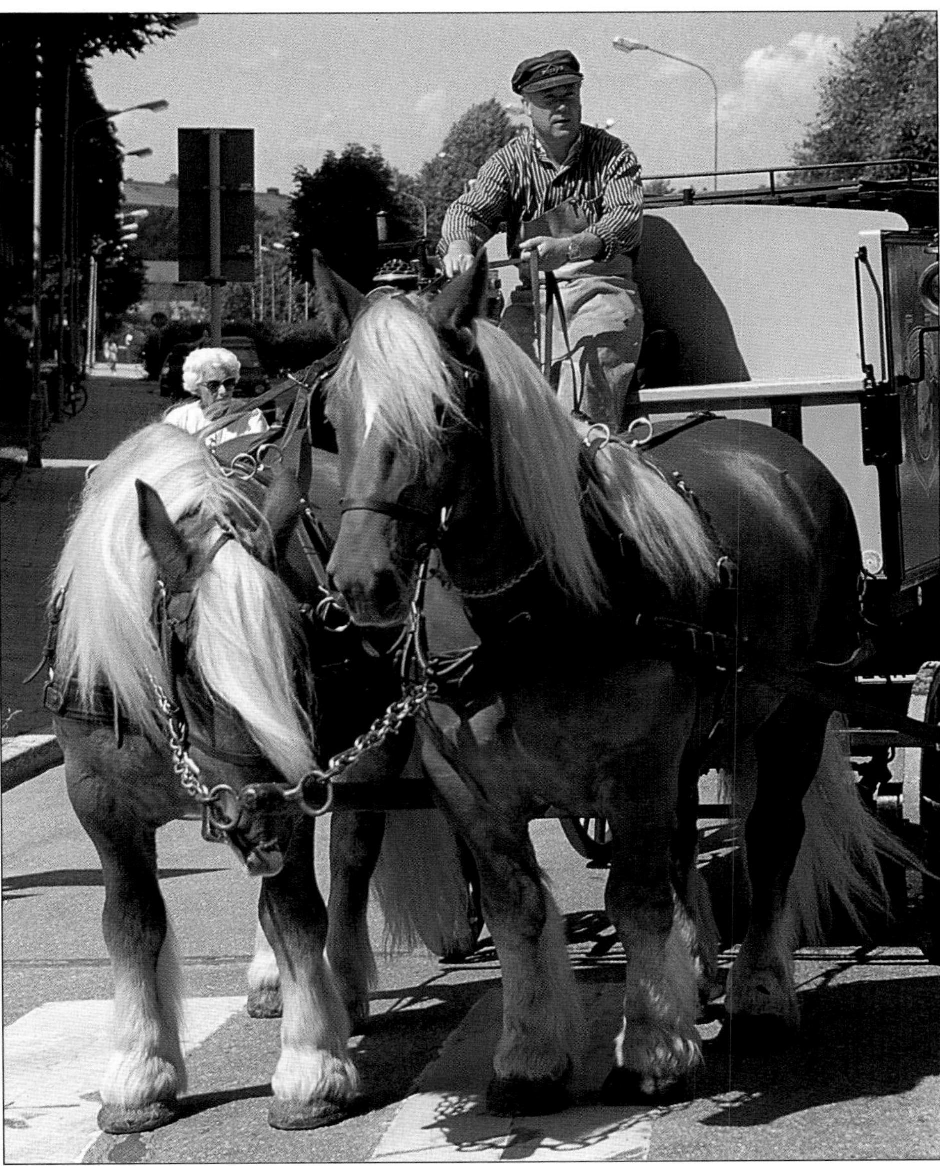

ABOVE
In common with all heavy breeds, the handsome Jutland has been the victim of mechanization but a few are still working.

LEFT
The Jutland is usually chestnut, a colour inherited through the Suffolk Punch element in its ancestry.

BREED DESCRIPTION

Height 15 – 16hh.

Colour Predominantly dark chestnut with light mane and tail.

Conformation Heavy, rather plain head, but with kind expression; short, thick neck; strong, muscular shoulders; exceptionally deep body with broad chest; round, muscular hindquarters; short limbs with plenty of bone.

INTERESTING FACTS

The Jutland was an influential factor in the development of the Schleswig, a draught horse which takes its name from the northernmost region of Germany and which towards the end of the nineteenth century was in demand for pulling trams and buses. Infusions of Jutland blood from neighbouring Denmark were being used by German breeders well into this century. The Schleswig closely resembles the Jutland and the Suffolk, both in build and colour. However, the use of carefully selected Boulonnais and Breton stallions from France has led to the appearance of some greys and bays.

Danish Warmblood

The Danish Warmblood is one of a number of horses specifically developed for use in modern equestrian pursuits, particularly the competitive disciplines of dressage, show jumping and three-day eventing.

The Danes have a long tradition as horse breeders: their first organized studs date from the fourteenth century. However, the market for horses has changed enormously this century, and especially during the last few decades. In many countries the relentless march of mechanization has transformed the horse from an essential means of transport to a "leisure" animal. In the wake of this transformation the Danes found that their native breeds – the Frederiksborg and its cousin, the spotted Knabstrup (a popular circus horse) – were not going to measure up as competitive sports horses.

To remedy this deficiency, a breeding programme was set up in 1962 to produce a new type of Danish riding horse.

BREED DESCRIPTION

Height 15.3 – 16.3hh.

Colour All colours occur.

Conformation Quality head; long, well set-on neck; good shoulders with prominent withers; muscular back and loins; long croup; strong limbs with long forearms, well-defined joints and good bone.

RIGHT
The Danish Warmblood shows the typical conformation of the modern sports horse: well-sloped shoulders, strong back and quarters, and good, sound limbs and feet.

ABOVE RIGHT
Like many other warmblood horses, the Danish Warmblood bears a distinctive brand mark on its hindquarters for identification purposes.

INTERESTING FACTS

Danish Warmbloods often excel at dressage, and none more so than the attractive black stallion Matador, who enchanted everyone with his panache and exuberant personality. Placed fifth in the Seoul Olympic Games in 1988, Matador was out of action for the whole of the following season after a serious operation for a life-threatening bout of colic. In a spectacular comeback at the 1990 World Equestrian Games he finished runner-up to the then reigning Olympic champion, Rembrandt, making his rider Kyra Kyrklund the first Finn to win a medal in any equestrian sport at senior championship level.

ABOVE
Warmblood horses have been specifically developed for use in competitive sports such as show jumping.

ABOVE RIGHT
A good deal of German blood has been used in the development of the Danish Warmblood. This is reflected in its quality head.

RIGHT
Perhaps the most famous of all Danish Warmbloods is the dressage stallion Matador, winner of the silver medal at the 1990 World Equestrian Games.

Carefully selected stallions, chiefly Swedish, Trakehner, Hanoverian, Holstein and Polish, were crossed with the various local-bred mares to improve the basic stamp of horse. Stringent grading was introduced for both stallions and mares to ensure that only the best were granted entry to the stud books. The breeding programme has been a tremendous success. The resultant Danish Warmblood is a handsome individual, well proportioned and possessed of excellent paces. It combines courage with a good temperament and makes an outstanding dressage horse.

Ariègeois

The Ariègeois, which lives in the Pyrenean mountains in the south-west of France, is a breed of great antiquity. It closely resembles the horses of southern Gaul described in Caesar's commentaries on the Gallic Wars. Its home is the high valley of the Ariège river, from which it takes its name. Well adapted to the worst excesses of its mountain environment, it is impervious to cold and outstandingly sure-footed – ice-covered mountain trails hold no terrors for the little Ariègeois.

A versatile, hardy creature, the Ariègeois has for centuries been used as a packhorse, though it can just as easily function as a small riding horse or work the land on the steepest of hill farms, where modern machinery cannot venture.

BREED DESCRIPTION

Height 13.1 – 14.3hh (the latter is rarely attained in its native habitat, although it may be on richer, lowland grazing).

Colour Solid black. Normally no white stockings or markings on the head, although the flank may be lightly flecked with white.

Conformation Light-boned, expressive head with flat forehead, straight profile, fairly short, hairy ears and bright, alert eyes with a gentle expression; fairly short, straight neck; rather straight shoulders; long but strong back and broad chest; round hindquarters with sloping croup; short, fairly slender limbs with a tendency to cow hocks; good, strong feet..

INTERESTING FACTS

The coat of the Ariègeois acquires a distinctive reddish tinge in winter. It is fine in texture, unlike the mane and tail, which are harsh to the touch and extremely thick – nature's way of offering much-needed protection from the worst of the winter weather. The Ariègeois is less well suited to heat. In summer it will seek shelter from the sun during the hottest part of the day and come out to graze at night.

TOP
Like all mountain breeds, the Ariègeois has very active paces. It has exceptionally strong hooves and is noted for its sure-footedness.

LEFT
The Ariègeois has a fairly long, but nevertheless strong, back, a powerfully built neck and deep girth. The sloping croup and low-set tail are characteristic.

Norman Cob

The Norman Cob is a light draught horse, still in use on small farms in the La Manche region of Normandy. Normandy has long been famed for its horse breeding, notably at the historic studs of Le Pin (founded as a royal stud in the mid-seventeenth century) and Saint-Lô, where the ancestors of the modern Cob were bred.

Stocky and compact, like the English Cob after which it was named, the Norman Cob was developed as a distinct breed at the beginning of this century. It was at that time that the breeders of half-bred horses first began to distinguish between those animals suitable for use as riding horses, particularly for the army, and those of less quality and sturdier build, more suited to light draught work.

The Norman Cob, as the heavier type was subsequently named, became a popular workhorse, especially in the La Manche region – even the powerful Percheron failed to supplant it there.

Over the years there has been a tendency for the Norman Cob to become heavier, to cope with the work required of it, but although it is undoubtedly sturdy and muscular, it lacks the massive stature of the true heavy horse and has never lost the energetic action, particularly at trot, characteristic of the half-bred horse.

RIGHT
The Norman Cob has always been noted for its energetic action. The lively, free-moving trot is characteristic of the breed.

BELOW
The Norman Cob has the same kindly expression as the English Cob after which it is named.

BREED DESCRIPTION

Height 15.3 – 16.3hh.

Colour Chestnut, bay or bay-brown; occasionally red-roan or grey.

Conformation Overall strong, stocky build with short, well-proportioned limbs.

INTERESTING FACTS

The tail of the Norman Cob is still traditionally docked. Down the centuries this mutilation of horses' tails has been carried out for a variety of reasons: fashion, to prevent the tail becoming entangled with harness and equipment and, in ancient times, probably to serve some ritual purpose. It used to be the fashion to dock the tail of the English Cob, but the practice became illegal in Great Britain under the Docking and Nicking Act, 1948. Quite apart from the trauma of the operation, docking deprives the horse of a vital means of protection against flies.

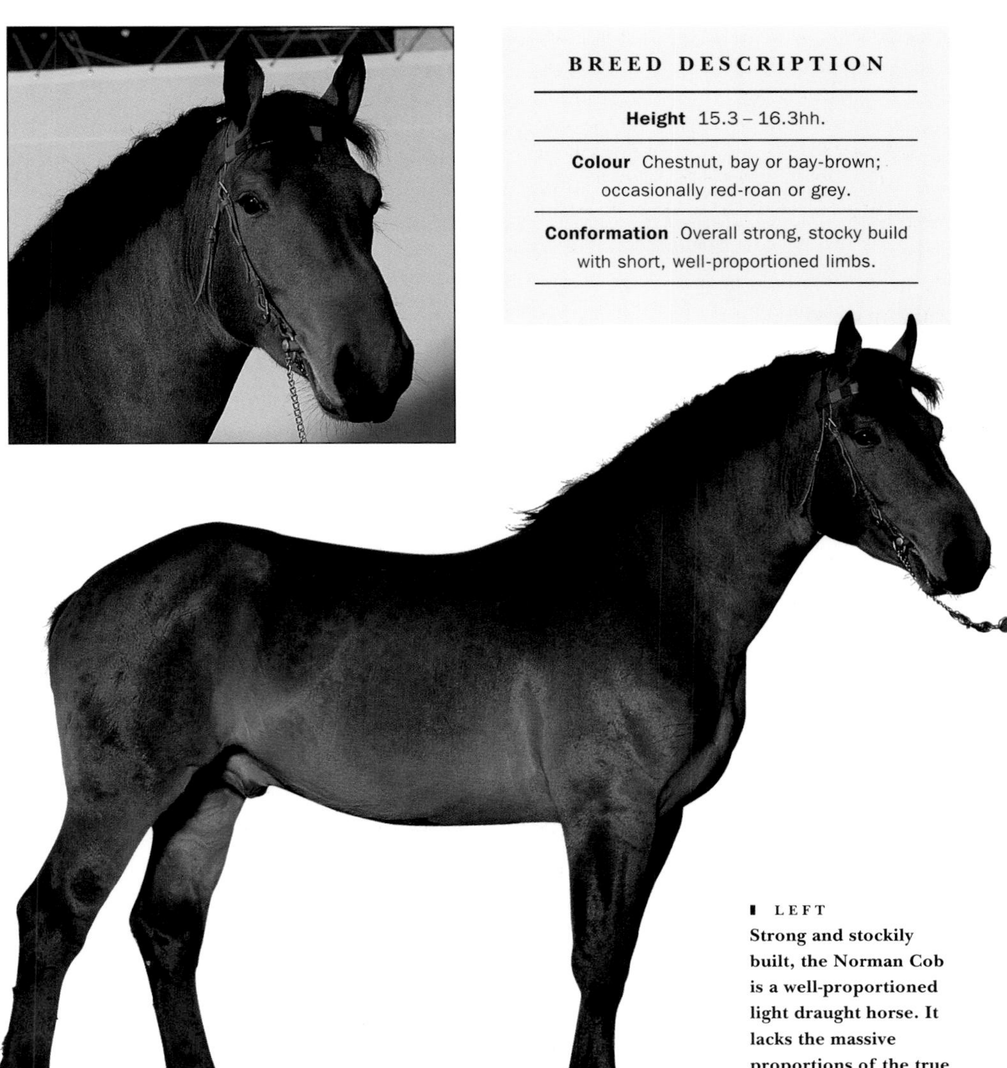

LEFT
Strong and stockily built, the Norman Cob is a well-proportioned light draught horse. It lacks the massive proportions of the true heavy horse.

Camargue

The tough little Camargue, the native horse of the inhospitable wastes of the Rhône delta in southern France, was not recognized as a breed until January 1968 yet it is almost certainly of ancient origin. It bears a strong resemblance to the horses depicted in the cave paintings of Lascaux, dating from 15,000 BC. Moreover, the even older horse skeletons unearthed at Solutré in south-east France in the nineteenth century could well be those of the breed's forebears.

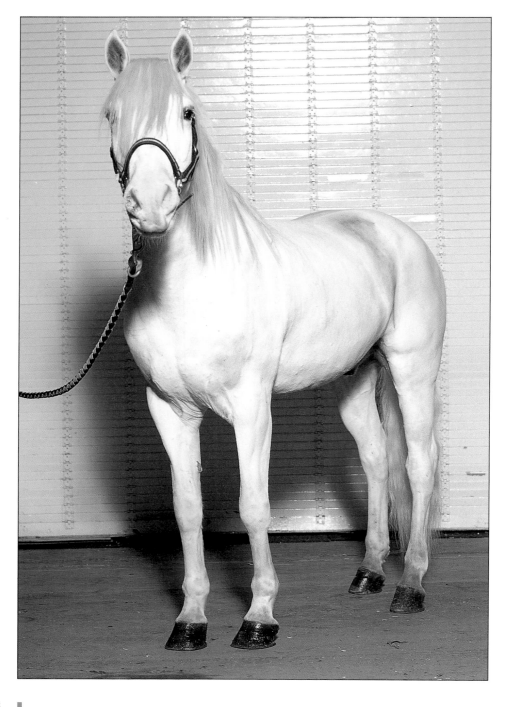

During its long occupation of the marshlands, the indigenous horse must have been influenced by influxes of North African blood, but it has retained certain characteristics of the primitive horse, particularly in its rather heavy, square head.

BELOW LEFT
Small, strong and always grey, the Camargue has been an inspiration for artists and poets down the centuries.

BELOW
The breed's ancient origins can be detected in the somewhat heavy, square head, which is reminiscent of that of the primitive horse.

The horses have always played an integral part in the everyday life of the Camargue, providing the guardians, or herdsmen, with strong, sure-footed mounts for their work with the herds of fighting bulls traditionally raised in the area. Despite its relatively small size, the Camargue horse has the strength and courage to carry a grown man safely over the most treacherous wetland terrain.

The herds, or *manades*, of Camargue horses, each with its own stallion, enjoy a semi-wild existence, being rounded up annually for inspection, branding of young stock, selection of suitable breeding stock and gelding of non-breeding males. Although the practice of fencing off pastureland and draining large areas for the cultivation of crops has, over the years, reduced the need for herdsmen, the horses are still very much a feature of the area. They have taken on a new role as mounts for the increasing number of tourists to the Camargue, which is famed for its wealth of wildlife.

BREED DESCRIPTION

Height 13.1 – 14.1hh.

Colour Grey.

Conformation Rather large, square head with short, wide-set ears; short neck; short, upright shoulders; fairly short back and deep chest; muscular hindquarters with short, sloping croup and long, bushy tail; strong, well-formed limbs with big knees and very hard, sound feet.

▮ BELOW LEFT
Despite their semi-wild existence Camargue horses are perfectly amenable to training, as this French trick-riding expert demonstrates.

▮ BELOW
The inhospitable wastes of the Rhône delta have produced a breed renowned for its toughness, strength and sure-footedness.

▮ BOTTOM
Herding the fighting bulls reared in the region is the breed's traditional role. Despite its small size, the Camargue horse will carry a herdsman with great ease.

INTERESTING FACTS

The half-wild Camargue horses have long held a romantic fascination for artists and writers. In his poem "Horses on the Camargue", Roy Campbell penned these typically evocative lines:

...in a shroud of silence like the dead,
I heard a sudden harmony of hooves,
And, turning, saw afar
A hundred snowy horses unconfined,
The silver runaways of Neptune's car
Racing, spray-curled, like waves before the wind.
Sons of the Mistral, fleet
As him with whose strong gusts they love to flee,
Who shod the flying thunders of their feet
And plumed them with the snortings of the sea.

Ardennais

One of the world's premier heavy horses, the powerful but exceptionally docile Ardennais is of ancient origin and is named after its mountainous homeland region on the French–Belgian border.

The Ardennais used to be less massive – as late as the nineteenth century it was used not only for draught work but also for riding. Arab blood was introduced around 1810 and infusions of Thoroughbred, Percheron and Boulonnais were added later. These attempts to improve the breed were not a great success and were abandoned, but the Ardennais nevertheless continued to be a most useful animal. Its energy and stamina made it invaluable to the military during the Revolution, at the time of Empire and particularly during the ill-fated Russian campaign. During World

BREED DESCRIPTION

Height 15 – 16hh.

Colour Roan, red-roan, iron grey, dark or liver chestnut and bay are the preferred colours. Bay-brown, light chestnut and palomino are admissible. Black, dappled grey and all other colours are inadmissible.

Conformation Straight profile with slightly prominent eye sockets, low, flat forehead, large expressive eyes, pricked ears and wide, open nostrils; medium-length neck, well set-on and generally arched; very strong shoulders; medium-heavy body with deep chest, rather short back and muscular loins; wide, rounded hindquarters; fairly short, strong and muscular limbs.

BELOW
Massively built, but extremely docile, the bigger type of Ardennais makes the perfect partner for heavy agricultural work.

War I the Ardennais was in great demand as an artillery horse.

It was the requirements of agriculture and other heavy draught work which led to the development of a heavier stamp of horse and today, in addition to the original small Ardennais, two other types are recognized: a larger version of the Ardennais, known as the Auxois and the heavier, larger framed Ardennais du Nord (formerly known as the Trait du Nord), the result of using outcrosses to the Belgian Draught.

▮ ABOVE

The Ardennais can still be found working on the land. Its ability to thrive on a minimum of feed makes it an economical proposition for the farmers of small holdings.

▮ BELOW

Roan is a very typical coat colouring of the breed. The eyes are invariably large, with an intelligent, gentle expression.

INTERESTING FACTS

In their writings some 2,000 years ago both the Greek historian Herodotus and the Roman emperor Julius Caesar made particular mention of the horses of north-eastern France, then known as northern Gaul, extolling their stamina and toughness. Skeletons unearthed in the region suggest that these horses stood 15hh – the height of the smaller type of Ardennais still seen today. These were the ancestors of the modern Ardennais.

Selle Français

France has been well to the fore in the development of a modern sports horse, the Cheval de Selle Français (French Saddle Horse) being one of the great warmblood breeding success stories of the twentieth century. The term Selle Français came into use in December 1958 and the first stud book was published in 1965.

The French, with their great tradition of horse breeding, laid the foundations for their modern, quality riding horse as far back as the early nineteenth century, when many regions of the country began to import English Thoroughbred and half-

BREED DESCRIPTION

Height: Medium weight small, 15.3hh and under; medium, 15.3 – 16.1hh; large, over 16.1hh.

Height: Heavyweight small, under 16hh; large, 16hh and over. (The classification "medium" or "heavy" is based on the horse's weight-carrying ability, judged on conformation.)

Colour Predominantly chestnut, though all colours are permissible.

Conformation Refined head; long, elegant neck; sloping shoulders; strong body with well-sprung ribs; broad, powerful hindquarters; strong limbs with particularly powerful forearms, pronounced joints and good bone.

ABOVE
A quality head, set on a long, elegant neck, is typical of the Selle Français. The breed is one of the world's most successful competition horses.

RIGHT
English Thoroughbred and French Trotter blood provided the base for the Selle Français. Its harmonious proportions and overall appearance are very reminiscent of the Thoroughbred.

BELOW
Some Selle Français horses such as The Fellow (in the red colours) have the speed to take on, and beat, full Thoroughbreds on the racecourse.

BOTTOM LEFT
The breed excels at show jumping. This attractive bay mare, Miss, won team and individual silver medals at the 1994 World Equestrian Games.

bred stallions to cross with their local, less refined, mares (the chief exceptions were the Limousin and south-west regions which specialized in breeding Anglo-Arabs). In Normandy, always a stronghold of horse breeding, two important horses evolved: a fast trotter, later to become the French Trotter (many of the half-breds imported from England came from Norfolk Roadster stock) and the Anglo-Norman. The vast majority of today's Selle Français horses trace back to the Anglo-Norman.

French Warmblood breeding differs from that in neighbouring countries, where the grading system is all-important. Success in competition by stallions, mares and their progeny or relatives forms the basis for selection in France. It is a system which, in a comparatively short space of time, has produced a highly successful competition horse, in appearance reminiscent of the Thoroughbred (which provided its most famous foundation sires) and possessing the necessary spirit to survive the cut and thrust of modern competitive sports. The Selle Français shines, above all, at show jumping where its claims to fame include Jappeloup (1987 European and 1988 Olympic Champion), Quito de Baussy (1990 World Champion), I Love You (1983 World Cup winner) and Galoubet (1982 world team gold medallist).

INTERESTING FACTS

Although the most important influence on the Selle Français has undoubtedly been the Thoroughbred, the French Trotter has also been a factor, not least in the pedigrees of the famous show jumpers Galoubet and Jappeloup. Galoubet has trotter blood on his dam's side, albeit a couple of generations back. But the spring-heeled little Jappeloup, whose brilliant show-jumping career culminated with success in the individual championship at the 1988 Olympic Games in Seoul and a team gold medal in the 1990 World Equestrian Games, was actually by a trotter, Tyrol II, out of a Thoroughbred mare, Vénérable.

Interestingly, Jappeloup lacked the harmonious paces usually associated with the Selle Français. He was notoriously clumsy (many a human had their feet trodden on in his company) and a far from comfortable ride. This was almost certainly the result of his powerful hindquarters – he stood higher behind the saddle than in front, typical trotter conformation.

BELOW
Thanks to the Thoroughbred blood in their veins, Selle Français horses have the speed and stamina to succeed in three-day eventing.

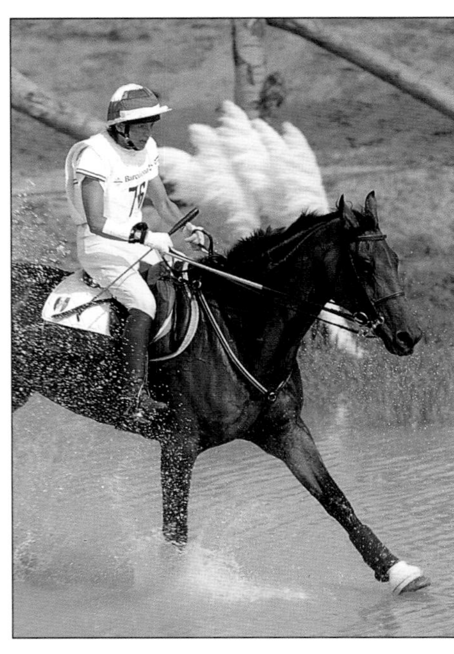

French Trotter

France – the country with the greatest tradition of trotting racing outside the United States – developed its own strain of trotter by crossing English Thoroughbreds, half-breds and Norfolk Roadsters with robust Norman mares. The process began in the early nineteenth century. The first French trotting races, which were ridden, not driven, took place in 1806 on the Champ de Mars in Paris. As the sport began to increase in popularity, purpose-built race tracks were opened, the first being at Cherbourg in the 1830s, and the breed developed and improved. In 1861 an Imperial decree gave official encouragement to the sport, leading to the formation of its first governing body.

The Anglo-Norman developed into a fine trotter and five important bloodlines became established: Conquérant, Normand, Lavater, Phaeton and Fuchsia.

BREED DESCRIPTION

Height Average about 16.2hh. The larger horses tend to make the best ridden trotters.

Colour All colours admissible. Chestnut, bay and brown are predominant with some roan. Grey is rare.

Conformation Well-sloped shoulders, giving good ground-covering action; short, strong body; immensely powerful, often sloping, hindquarters.

TOP RIGHT
The French Trotter has much of the Thoroughbred about its general appearance, although it is more sturdily built and rather less refined.

RIGHT
Racing under saddle, as well as in harness, has ensured the continued quality of this old-established breed, which has played an important part in the development of the Selle Français.

INTERESTING FACTS

The premier driven trotting race in France is the Prix d'Amérique. Its ridden equivalent is the Prix de Cornulier. Both are run over 1 mile 5 furlongs (2,650m) at the leading French track, the Hippodrome de Vincennes which, with its downhill start and testing uphill finish, is unique among raceways, which are usually flat. The Prix d'Amérique is the driven equivalent of flat racing's all-age international championship of Europe, the Prix de l'Arc de Triomphe. The Prix de Cornulier is the world's richest ridden trotting race. Very occasionally outstanding horses appear which are equally brilliant in harness and under saddle. Venutar, Masina, Tidalium Pelo and Bellino II all share the distinction of having won both the Prix d'Amérique and the Prix de Cornulier.

LEFT
French Trotters are sometimes used in the sport of skijoring, in which the horse pulls its human partner on skis.

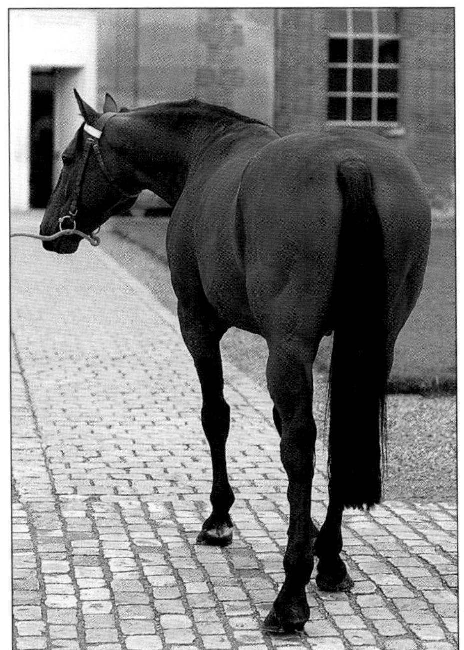

Conquérant and Normand were both by the English half-bred Young Rattler. This son of the Thoroughbred Rattler is sometimes called "the French Messenger" (Messenger being the foundation sire of the Standardbred) because of the enormous influence he has had on trotter breeding in France. Lavater was another example of the English connection, being by a Norfolk Roadster. The most prepotent of all the early stallions was Fuchsia. Foaled in 1883 he sired nearly 400 trotters and more than 100 of his sons produced winners. Some Standardbred blood was introduced over the years to give the breed more speed but the Trotteur Français Stud Book was closed to non-French-bred horses in 1937 and has only been opened a fraction in recent years to allow a very limited number of carefully selected French/Standardbred crosses to be admitted.

The French have never totally given up ridden racing. Some ten per cent of today's trotting races staged in France are under saddle and they have an important effect on breeding. Because ridden trotters race under comparatively heavy weights they must accordingly be well built horses with good balance and level action. These quality horses have played a large part in maintaining the overall standard of the French Trotter.

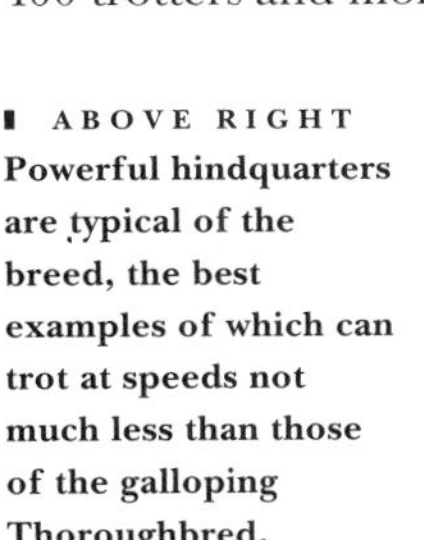

ABOVE RIGHT
Powerful hindquarters are typical of the breed, the best examples of which can trot at speeds not much less than those of the galloping Thoroughbred.

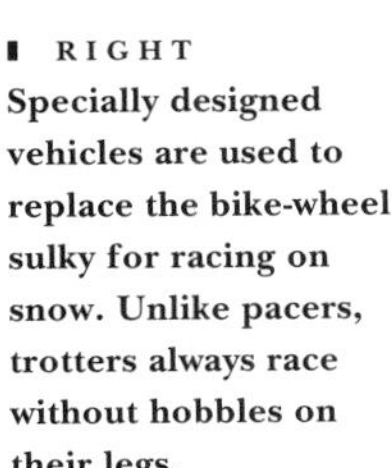

RIGHT
Specially designed vehicles are used to replace the bike-wheel sulky for racing on snow. Unlike pacers, trotters always race without hobbles on their legs.

Percheron

The elegant, free-moving Percheron originated in La Perche, in the south of Normandy. Its ancestors were Arabian horses brought to Europe by the Moors. The oriental influence is believed to have begun following the defeat of the Moors by Charles Martel near Poitiers in AD 732, and was continued after the First Crusade in 1099, when Robert, Comte de Rotrou, imported more Arab horses into France. Much later, during the eighteenth century, Arab stallions at the Royal Stud at Le Pin were made available to breeders of Percherons to upgrade their stock. The eastern influence continued until relatively recent times, one of the most important early Percheron stallions, Jean le Blanc (foaled in about 1830), being the son of the Arab stallion Gallipoly. The Percheron's great strength and courage, coupled with its sound limbs and

LEFT
The Percheron has a fine head with prominent, alert eyes and wide, open nostrils.

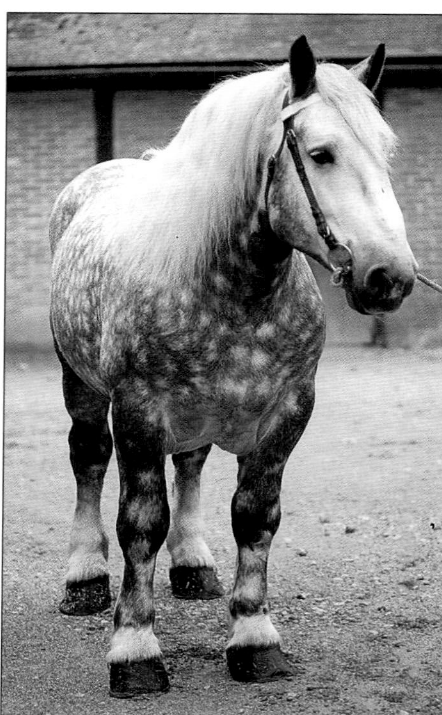

ABOVE RIGHT
The breed is noted for its broad, deep chest, powerful forearms and excellent feet.

RIGHT
Well-proportioned and clean-limbed (that is, without feather on the lower legs), the Percheron is an elegant horse possessed of surprisingly free-moving paces considering its great size.

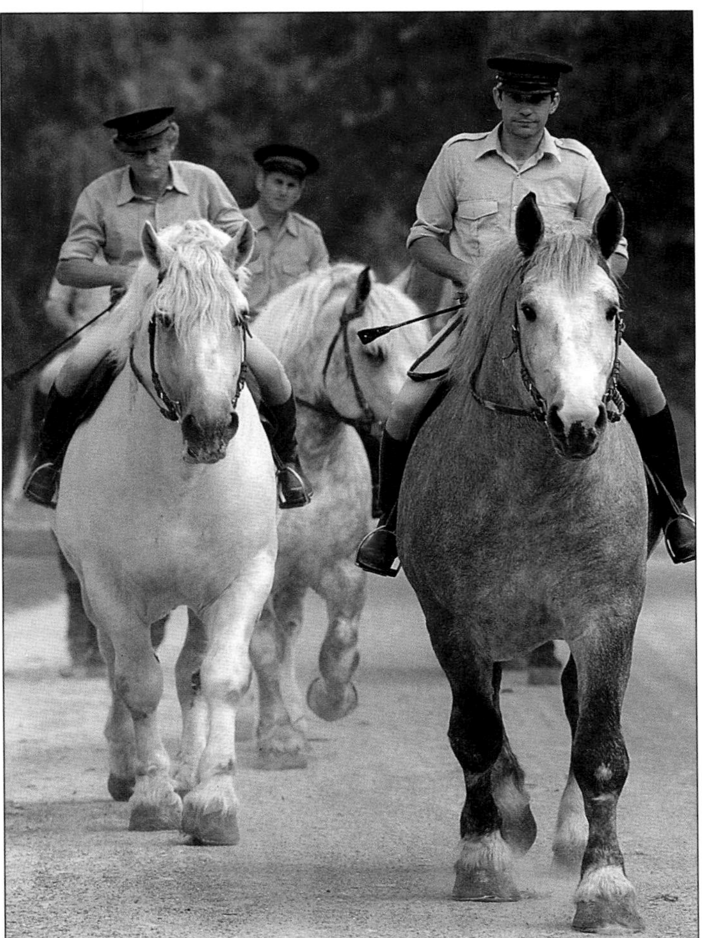

INTERESTING FACTS

One of the tallest horses on record was a Percheron named Dr Le Gear. Foaled in 1902, he stood 21hh or 7 feet (213.4m) at the withers and weighed just under 27cwt (1,370kg).

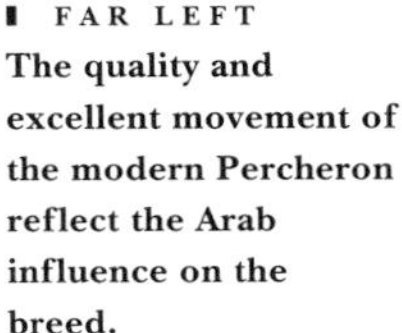

FAR LEFT
The quality and excellent movement of the modern Percheron reflect the Arab influence on the breed.

LEFT
Pause for a snack for a working horse. Percherons are so docile that they can be trained to work in a very short time.

BELOW
Thanks to its good action and amenable temperament, the Percheron goes equally well under saddle and in harness.

longevity, made it tremendously popular in various fields: as a war horse, as a carriage horse and on the land. For some four decades during the late nineteenth and early twentieth centuries it was in great demand world wide, both for work purposes and as an improver of other heavy breeds. French breeders exported a great number of Percherons, which proved to be the most adaptable of horses whatever the climate. Many went to England, some to Australia (the Percheron is said to be the first heavy horse to be taken there) and South America, and the breed became particularly popular in North America, where the black coat colouring was preferred to the grey. American buyers also favoured a heavyweight horse which, together with the need elsewhere for big horses to work on the railways, encouraged the breeding of more massive animals. Despite its great size, however, the modern Percheron is very much a quality animal, retaining the long, low action of its ancestors.

BREED DESCRIPTION

Height 15.2 – 17hh. Average 16.1hh.

Colour Grey or black.

Conformation Fine head, with broad, square forehead, fine, long ears, prominent, alert eyes, straight profile and flat nose with wide, open nostrils; long, arched neck with fairly thick mane; sloping shoulders with prominent withers; broad, deep chest with fairly prominent sternum, short, straight back and loins with great depth through the girth and well-sprung ribs; long, sloping hindquarters; clean, sound limbs with prominent, powerful forearms and long, muscular thighs, large knees and hocks, small, strong fetlock joints and good, strong feet.

Breton

Short-legged and heavily built, the Breton is a surprisingly active heavy horse, with an especially lively trot: characteristics that testify to its Norfolk Roadster and, even further back, Arab ancestry. Like so many southern European horse breeders, those in Brittany used horses brought back from the Middle East by the Crusaders to cross with their more plebeian native stock adding, in more recent times, infusions of blood from England and a number of continental countries – the latter not always with successful results.

Down the centuries there has always been more than one type of Breton horse. Two were identified in the Middle Ages, the Sommier and the Roussin. The Sommier was descended from stock bred mainly in the north of Brittany and was used for pack and agricultural work. The Roussin, a much lighter stamp of animal, was found in the south and some central parts of the region and was a popular saddle horse, noted for its comfortable, ambling gait.

Although the Breton is no longer thought of as a saddle horse, it does still come in different types – a large and small draught, and a coach-horse type known as the Postier, which is built on less massive lines than the draught horse. The Postier owes its lighter conformation and brilliant paces to infusions of Norfolk Roadster blood from England during the nineteenth century.

An early-maturing animal, the Breton is highly regarded in the French meat trade for the high yield and quality of meat it produces. However, it is still also valued as a draught animal and some Bretons can still be seen working on the land, particularly in the vineyards.

LEFT
Although the Breton is prized in the French meat trade, some examples of these attractive horses can still be seen at work as draught animals.

BELOW
Chestnut is the most usual colour for the Breton. The beautiful, kind eyes are set in a wide, somewhat square head.

RIGHT
Stocky and short-legged, the Breton is nevertheless a very active mover and has been used over the years as a warhorse, draught horse, pack-horse, coach horse – and even a riding horse.

INTERESTING FACTS

The Breton is a hardy, adaptable animal and a most willing worker. Because of its ability to work in hot climates, it has been used for upgrading purposes by breeders in Italy, Spain and even as far afield as Japan.

BREED DESCRIPTION

Height 15 – 16.1hh.

Colour Mainly chesnut; some red roan, bay and grey; black rarely occurs.

Conformation Squarish head with straight profile, open nostrils, bright eyes and small, fairly low-set ears; short, strong and slightly arched neck; rather short but sloping shoulders; short, broad and strong body with well-sprung ribs; very powerful hindquarters; short, strong limbs with very muscular thighs and forearms.

Boulonnais

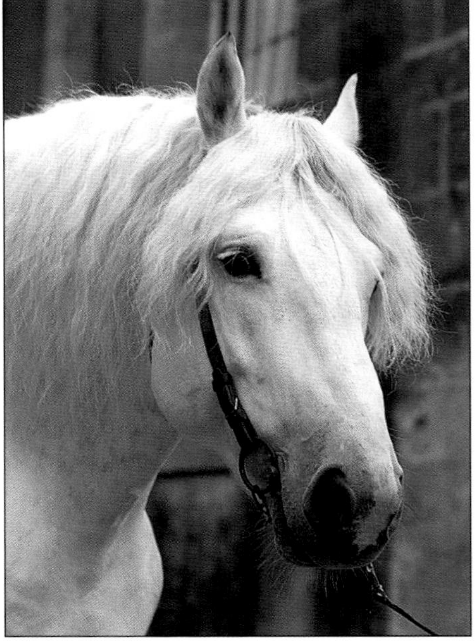

LEFT
Famous for its gentle nature, the Boulonnais is the most elegant of the heavy horse breeds.

The gentle Boulonnais, the most elegant of all the heavy horse breeds, traces back to Roman times. It is a native of north-west France and, like the Percheron, was greatly influenced by oriental blood. The Arab influence occurred more than once. First there was the arrival of the Roman armies, with their horses of eastern origin, who massed on the French coast before invading Britain. Then there were the Crusaders, who brought more eastern horses back with them. Two great noblemen in particular, Robert, Comte d'Artois and Eustache, Comte de Boulogne, are credited with importing Arab horses for use in their stables at this time. There was a slight change of direction during the fourteenth century, when Mecklenburg blood from Germany was introduced in order to breed a sturdier animal capable of carrying knights with their new, plated armour.

The term Boulonnais dates from the seventeenth century and reflects the main breeding region of that name on the north French coast. Sadly, the number of Boulonnais horses was seriously depleted during World War I because their chief breeding grounds were right at the heart of the battle zone. World War II had a second serious impact on the breed just as it was recovering. These two setbacks, plus the rapid spread of mechanization following World War II all but signalled the death blow of this fine horse. Fortunately it did survive, thanks to the efforts of a few dedicated enthusiasts, and although the meat trade features as one of the prime outlets for breeders, some Boulonnais horses may still be seen working small farms, where they can prove more effective and economical than tractors. Despite its size and substantial build, it is still possible to detect traces of the breed's Arab ancestry both in the small, refined head, with its large, expressive eyes, and in its outgoing nature.

BREED DESCRIPTION

Height 15.3 – 16.3hh.

Colour All shades of grey.

Conformation Elegant head, short and broad overall, with straight profile, wide forehead, slightly prominent eye sockets, strong, rounded, widely spaced jowls, large, bright eyes, small, erect ears, open nostrils and small mouth (in mares the head is slightly longer and less heavy); thick, often arched, neck with thick mane; muscular shoulders with fairly prominent withers; broad, straight back, broad chest and well-sprung ribs; round, muscular hindquarters with fairly high-set, thick tail; strong limbs with very prominent muscular projections in the forearms and thighs, short, thick cannons, large, flat joints and no feather.

INTERESTING FACTS

Two types of Boulonnais evolved: a large, heavy version for use in agriculture and industry, and a smaller, lighter horse suitable for less strenuous work on small-holdings and in light draught work. At one time the small type was known as the *maréeur* or *mareyeur* (fish merchant) because it was used for the transportation of fish from Boulogne to Paris. Nowadays the small type is used in agriculture, the meat trade favouring the larger animal.

BELOW
Boulonnais horses are branded with an anchor on the neck, reflecting their maritime homeland.

Trakehner

Of all the warmbloods, the Trakehner is the closest in appearance to the Thoroughbred. Organized breeding of this attractive riding horse began in 1732, when Friedrich Wilhelm I of Prussia established the Royal Trakehner Stud Administration in East Prussia (now part of Poland). A great deal of Thoroughbred and Arab blood was used to upgrade the local horses. These were descendants of the tough little Schweiken breed known to the Teutonic knights who colonized the region during the early thirteenth century. The Schweiken was a descendant of the Konik pony, which traces back to the primitive Tarpan.

Towards the end of the eighteenth century a determined effort was made to improve the Trakehner, or East Prussian, as it was also known. Inferior breeding stock at the Royal Stud was drastically weeded out, a process which led to the swift development of the Trakehner. It was soon much in demand, first as a carriage horse and subsequently as an army remount.

Renowned for its twin qualities of elegance and toughness, the Trakehner flourished for nearly two centuries – until the disastrous upheaval of World War II. During the autumn and winter of 1944 the breed suffered catastrophic losses as desperate efforts were made to evacuate the horses before the arrival of the advancing Russian troops. Of the thousands of Trakehners, many of them mares with foals at foot, who set off on the 900 mile (1,450km) journey west across Europe, few survived. Before their flight there were more than 25,000 horses registered in the East Prussian stud book. A mere 1,200 or so made it to the West

ABOVE RIGHT
The Trakehner is noted for its refined head. Large eyes and a small, tapered muzzle enhance the overall impression of quality.

RIGHT
The Trakehner's elegant outline owes much to the Thoroughbred influence. The Trakehner, in its turn, has been used in the development of the Dutch, Danish and Swedish Warmbloods.

BREED DESCRIPTION

Height Average 16 – 16.2hh.

Colour Any solid colour.

Conformation Refined head with large eyes and small muzzle; elegant, tapering neck; well-sloped shoulders; strong, medium-length body, well ribbed-up; well-rounded hindquarters; hard limbs with short cannons and excellent, sound feet.

INTERESTING FACTS

One of the most famous examples of the Trakehner is the show jumper Abdullah, a handsome grey stallion who competed for the United States. Ridden by Conrad Homfeld, he won a team gold medal and the individual silver at the 1984 Olympic Games and was victorious in the World Cup the following year. Abdullah was originally exported *in utero* to Canada and was foaled in 1970. After his retirement from competition he was used for breeding in many countries, thanks to the use of frozen semen.

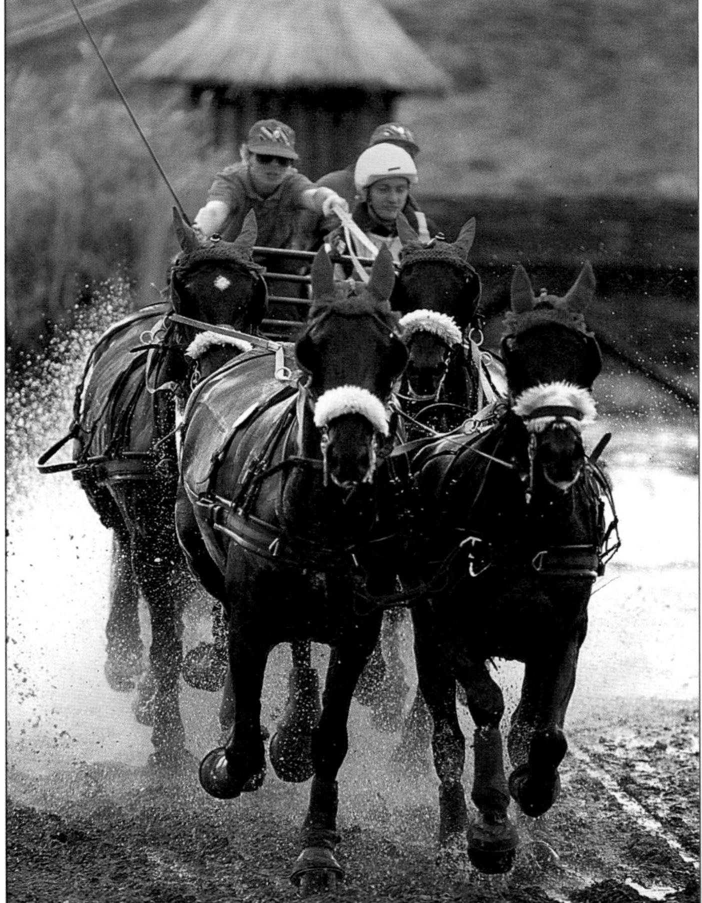

LEFT
Like the Thoroughbred, the Trakehner is possessed of courage and stamina, qualities which make it suitable for tough sports such as carriage driving.

BELOW LEFT
The powers of endurance which helped the breed survive the harsh times of World War II stand the breed in good stead in the modern sport of eventing.

BELOW
The show-jumping stallion Abdullah demonstrated the breed's fine qualities to great advantage when winning a team gold medal at the 1984 Olympic Games.

and many of these failed to survive in the very harsh economic conditions of post-war Germany.

Incredibly, thanks to the dedicated efforts of the keepers of the original stud book, the Trakehner did not die out. The surviving equine evacuees were tracked down and re-registered in West Germany and, as breeding resumed and numbers increased, the Trakehner began to take its place in the modern equestrian world. Valued for its good conformation and action, its spirited temperament and its endurance, it has found favour both as a competition horse and as an improver of other warmbloods.

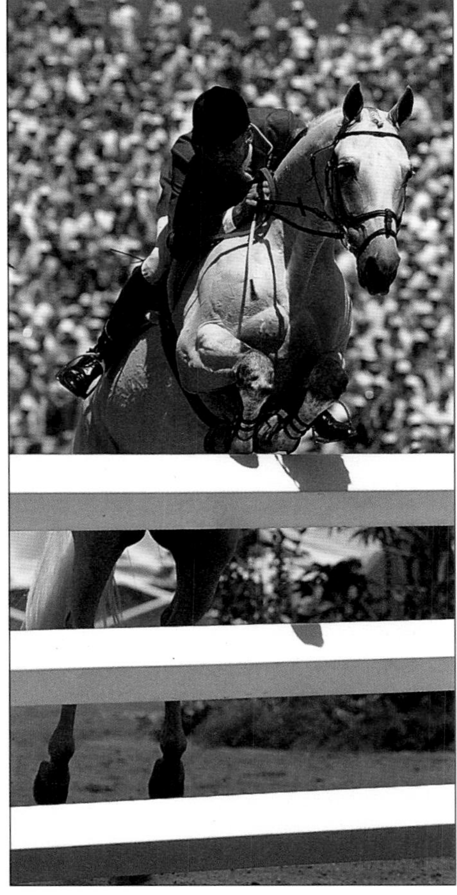

Hanoverian

George II, Elector of Hanover and King of England, was instrumental in the establishment of this famous German warmblood, thanks to the foundation of the state stud at Celle in 1735. The aim was to provide local people with the services of good quality stallions at nominal fees, the original horses being Holsteins of predominantly Andalusian and Neapolitan blood. Thanks to the later

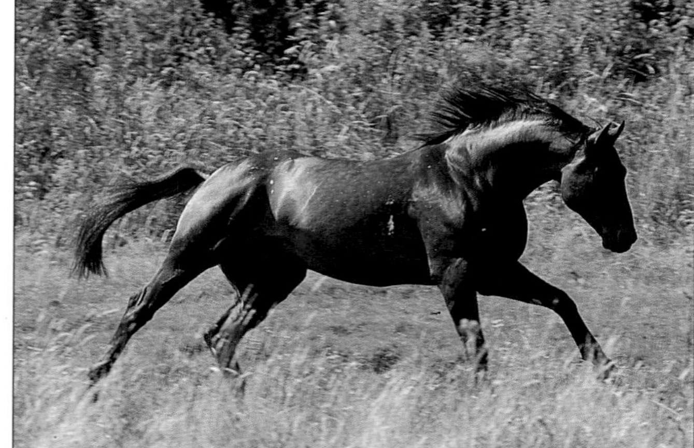

LEFT
Previously bred as an all-purpose work horse, the modern Hanoverian has been refined for use in equestrian sports.

BREED DESCRIPTION

Height 15.3 – 16.2hh.

Colour All solid colours.

Conformation Medium-sized head, clean cut and expressive, with large, lively eyes and good free cheek bones; long, fine neck; large, sloping shoulders with pronounced withers; strong, deep body; muscular hindquarters with well set-on tail; well-muscled limbs with large, pronounced joints and well-formed, hard hooves.

ABOVE RIGHT
Thoroughbreds and Trakehners were used in the development of the present-day Hanoverian. Their influence can be seen in the breed's clean-cut head.

RIGHT
The Hanoverian is noted more for its strength than its speed, hence the many successes of its representatives in dressage and show jumping.

INTERESTING FACTS

A great many Hanoverians have become household names as show jumpers, among them Dollar Girl (1995 World Cup winner with Nick Skelton), Top Gun (1992 Olympic team gold medallist with Jan Tops), Walzerkönig (1988 Olympic team gold medallist with Franke Sloothaak), Deister (three times European Champion with Paul Schockemöhle), Tigre (1978 world team gold medallist with Caroline Bradley), Simona (1974 World Champion with Hartwig Steenken) and Ferdl (1960 Olympic team gold medallist ridden by Paul Schockemöhle's brother, Alwin).

importation of English horses, including Thoroughbreds, the Hanoverian gradually began to show more quality, the aim being to produce a good all-purpose animal that was capable of working on the land but also suitable for ridden work and for use as a light carriage horse.

In common with so many other horse-breeding enterprises, the development of the Hanoverian at Celle was adversely affected by war. By the end of the eighteenth century the stud had over 100 stallions, but by 1816, after the Napoleonic wars, a mere thirty remained. To help make up for these losses, more outside blood was brought in, especially Thoroughbred. But the time came when the breed was tending to become too light for the work required of it and this influence was accordingly reduced.

After World War II, however, the Hanoverian had to be adapted to a new way of life if the breed was to survive and Thoroughbred blood was again introduced, along with Trakehner, to produce a warmblood suited to the demands of the leisure-horse market.

The modern Hanoverian is lighter and less coarse than of old and is noted for its good, honest temperament. In common with other German warmbloods, stallions are only licensed if they pass the required veterinary inspection and, after licensing, must pass ridden performance tests. Hanoverians are among the world's most sought-after sports horses, their strength and athleticism making them especially suitable for dressage and show jumping.

LEFT
Hanoverians have found favour throughout the world as show jumpers. Amadeus Z, bred in Belgium, is seen competing for Holland at the 1994 World Equestrian Games.

LEFT
Dressage is the other sport at which the Hanoverian excels. With its great strength and true, energetic action, it is well suited to this demanding discipline.

Holstein

The Holstein is probably the oldest of the German warmbloods, dating back several centuries. As early as the seventeenth century horses bred in the region were much in demand in France, Denmark and Italy. The old Holstein horses contained mixed blood, including German, Neapolitan, Spanish and oriental. During the nineteenth century they were crossed with Yorkshire Coach Horses, a policy which helped give the breed a distinctive high knee action, great presence and an exceptionally tractable nature. Holsteins became renowned for being tough but handsome carriage horses and subsequently as army remounts.

The Traventhall Stud, founded by the Prussians in 1867 in Schleswig-Holstein, is considered the modern Holstein's birthplace. However, this stud is no longer in operation and the breeds main base is now at Elmshorn.

To produce a stamp of horse suitable for today's requirements, some Thoroughbred blood was used in the period after World War II, which resulted in a lighter type of horse with less high, "carriage-horse" action and a better shoulder. Although the infusions of Thoroughbred blood may have made the Holstein rather more excitable than it was

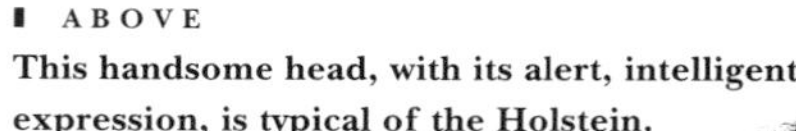

ABOVE
This handsome head, with its alert, intelligent expression, is typical of the Holstein.

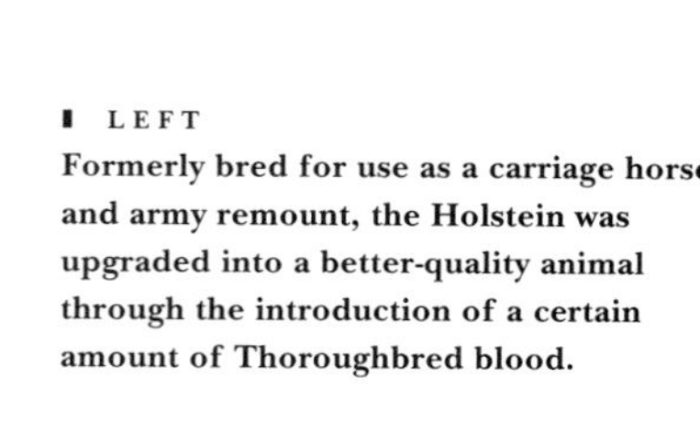

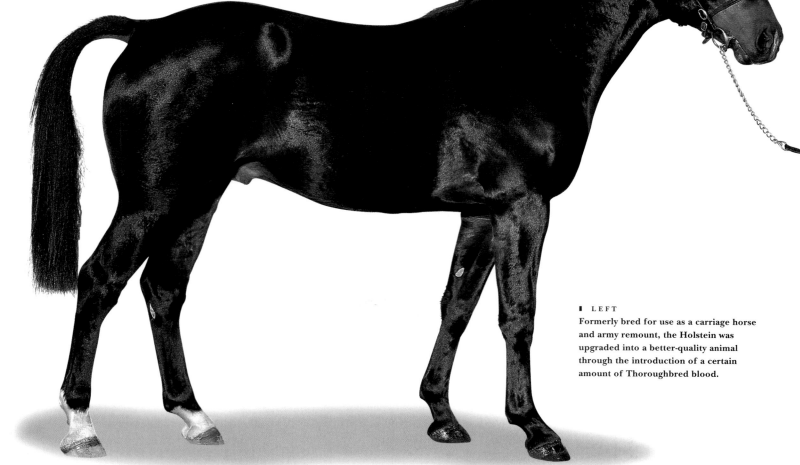

LEFT
Formerly bred for use as a carriage horse and army remount, the Holstein was upgraded into a better-quality animal through the introduction of a certain amount of Thoroughbred blood.

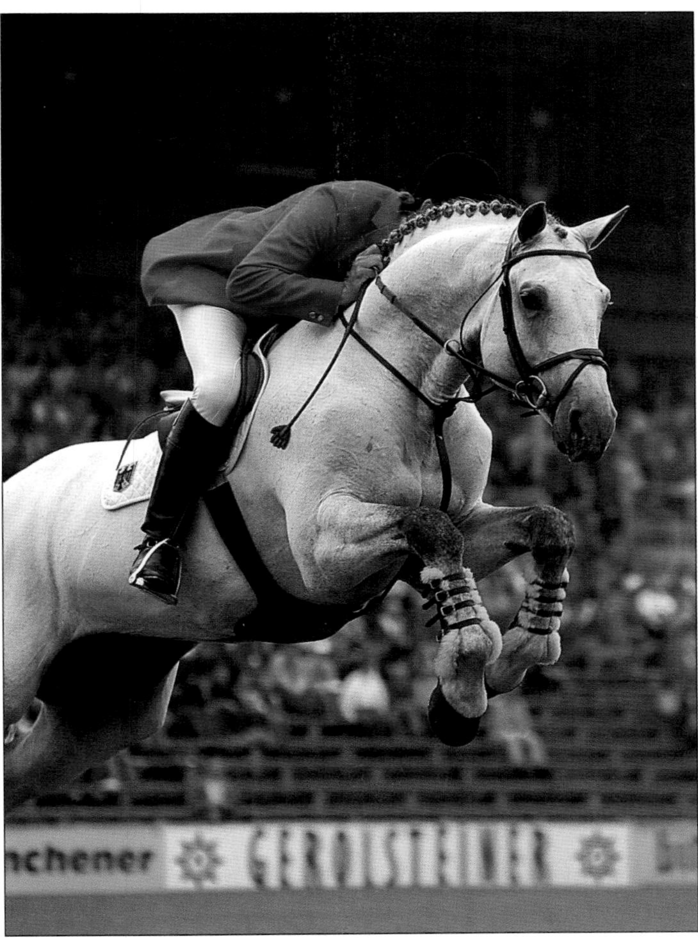

INTERESTING FACTS

One of the most celebrated Holstein horses of all time was the big bay gelding Meteor, the only show jumper to have won a medal at three Olympic Games. Foaled in 1943, he won the individual bronze medal at the 1952 Games and four years later helped Germany win the team gold in Stockholm, where he finished fourth individually. In Rome in 1960, at the age of 17, he won a second team gold medal and finished sixth in the individual contest. Ridden by Fritz Thiedemann, an exceptionally talented all-round horseman, Meteor was an outstanding ambassador for the Holstein breed. He died in 1966 and is buried at Elmshorn, the breed's headquarters.

FAR LEFT
Show jumping is a sport at which the Holstein, with its intelligent and bold character, has excelled for many years.

BELOW
The breed is noted for its powerful action, which is used to good effect in Grand Prix dressage.

of old, it has, generally speaking, retained its good temperament. Its intelligence and boldness make it a first-rate mount for top-level dressage and show jumping.

Holstein horses are not bred in such quantity as some other warmbloods nor is their breeding area particularly large. Possibly as a result, there is less variation in overall type.

BELOW
Originally prized as tough, active carriage horses, Holsteins can still be seen in harness in the competitive discipline of four-in-hand driving.

BREED DESCRIPTION

Height Approximately 16 – 17hh.

Colour All colours permissible. Bay with black points and brown predominate. Grey is quite common, chestnut less so.

Conformation Expressive head, well set-on and in proportion to the size of the horse, with big, bright eyes; long, muscular and slightly arched neck; long, sloping shoulders; strong back, deep, wide chest and muscular loins; strong, muscular hindquarters with well-muscled thighs, stifles and gaskins; short, strong cannon bones, flat knees, big, clean hocks, medium-length pasterns and good, hard feet.

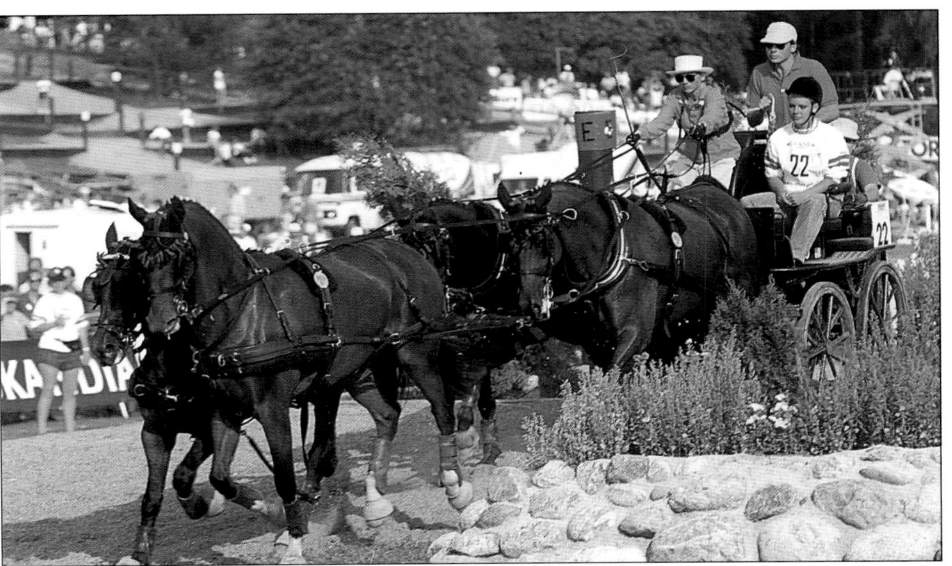

Oldenburg

The Oldenburg, Germany's heaviest type of warmblood, was originally developed as a coach horse and was based on the old Friesian horses bred in the region between the River Weser and the Netherlands. The breed takes its name from Count Anton Gunther von Oldenburg (1603–67), who played a leading part in its development, crossing stallions from Italy and Spain with the native stock. Later breeders introduced Thoroughbred, Cleveland Bay, Hanoverian and Norman blood. The result was a big upstanding horse, measuring a good 17hh, and fairly heavily built. Unlike most large animals, however, it matured early which undoubtedly popularized it as a work horse.

LEFT
The Oldenburg was originally bred as a coach horse. It is the heaviest of the German Warmbloods.

BREED DESCRIPTION

Height Approximately 16 – 17hh.

Colour Predominantly brown, black and bay.

Conformation Rather plain head, occasionally with a Roman nose; fairly long, very strong neck; sloping, muscular shoulders; powerfully built body with deep chest; strong hindquarters with high-set tail; fairly short limbs with large joints and plenty of bone.

LEFT
Careful breeding has helped eradicate coach-horse characteristics such as upright shoulders and a long back, though some modern Oldenburgs retain the rather high knee action of their forebears.

LEFT
The German rider Franke Sloothaak on his way to becoming World Show Jumping Champion in 1994. His mount is the Oldenburg mare, Weihaiwej.

As coach horses gave way to motorized transport in the early twentieth century, breeders had of necessity to change the type of the Oldenburg and look more to the production of a general-purpose farm horse. More recently, further infusions of Thoroughbred blood, and some Selle Français, have produced a horse which is considerably finer than its coaching ancestors and well able to hold its own in the competitive sports, working equally well under saddle or in harness. The Oldenburg still tends to be a big individual compared with other warmbloods but many of the coach-horse characteristics, such as an upright shoulder and long back, have been eliminated. The knee action still tends to be a little on the high side.

Oldenburg horses are exported to many countries and have proved particularly popular in the United States.

BELOW
From coach horse to dressage horse: refinement of the breed has been brought about through the introduction of Thoroughbred and Selle Français blood, making the present-day Oldenburg an outstanding sports horse.

INTERESTING FACTS

Olympic Bonfire, an Oldenburg gelding foaled in 1983, won the World Dressage Freestyle to Music Championship in 1994 when ridden by the leading Dutch rider, Anky van Grunsven.

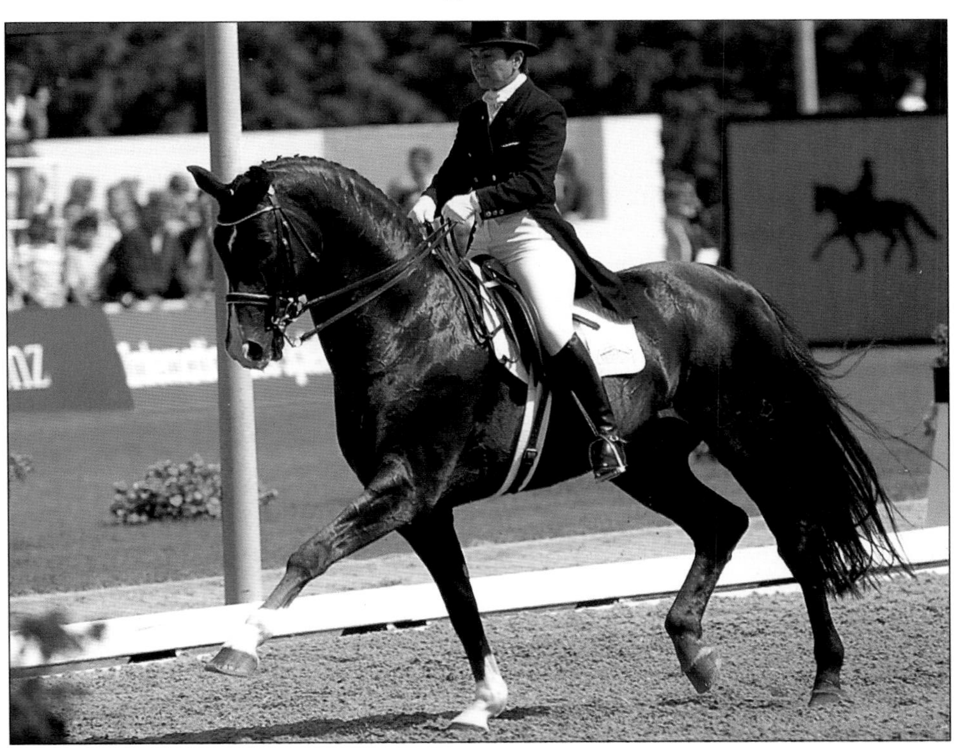

Westphalian

Closely related to the Hanoverian, the Westphalian is bred in the region of Nordrhein-Westfalen, in the north-west of Germany. Its main breeding centre, Warendorf, is famous for being the home of German equestrianism (the National Federation is based there). The area has a long tradition of horse breeding. It is known that in the early nineteenth century East Prussian stallions were made available to local mare owners to enable them to upgrade their stock. Over the years various outcrosses were made, involving Oldenburg, Hanoverian, Friesian, Anglo-Norman and trotter blood and it was not until this century that breeders finally settled for just one influence: the Hanoverian. Today's Westphalian shares the bloodlines of the present-day Hanoverian, although there are also several important ones which have developed specifically in the Westphalia region.

BREED DESCRIPTION

Height 15.3 – 16.2hh.

Colour All solid colours.

Conformation Intelligent head with good width between the eyes; well-shaped neck; deep, broad body; powerful hindquarters, although they can be a little flat.

ABOVE
The Westphalian has the same clean-cut good looks as the Hanoverian, with whom it shares a common ancestry.

RIGHT
The conformation is typical of that of the modern sports horse: a good length of neck, deep body and powerful hindquarters. It tends to be a little longer in the leg than the Hanoverian.

INTERESTING FACTS

Famous Westphalian horses include Rembrandt (Olympic dressage champion in 1988 and 1992, ridden by Nicole Uphoff-Becker); Ahlerich (Olympic dressage champion in 1984, ridden by Reiner Klimke); Fire (winner of the World Show Jumping Championship in 1982, ridden by Norbert Koof) and Roman (winner of the World Show Jumping Championship in 1978, ridden by Gerd Wiltfang). Rembrandt, one of the most handsome representatives of the breed, was the first horse in the history of the Olympic Games to win two individual gold medals for dressage. He was European champion in 1989 and also took the individual title at the first World Equestrian Games, held in Stockholm in 1990.

ABOVE RIGHT
Two Step is a Westphalian who has found fame as a show jumper. Originally named Polydektes, he is by Polydor, one of the breed's most successful sires of competition horses.

RIGHT
Ahlerich was one of the breed's most outstanding performers in the world of dressage. He crowned a gloriously successful Grand Prix career with victory at the 1984 Olympic Games in Los Angeles.

Schleswig

BELOW
The head is rather plain but the expression is kindly.

BOTTOM
The Schleswig is generally chestnut in colour.

A sturdy, compact heavy horse, the Schleswig comes from the northernmost region of Germany, Schleswig-Holstein, which borders on to Denmark and which was, indeed, at various times actually part of that country. It is not surprising, therefore, that the Schleswig bears a marked resemblance to the Jutland, the Danish heavy breed to which it is closely related. The Schleswig was developed during the second half of the nineteenth century as a medium-sized draught horse. Infusions of lighter blood, including Yorkshire Coach Horse and Thoroughbred, were made towards the end of the century but these had no lasting effect on the breed. Popular as a tram and bus horse, and for use on the land and in forestry, the breed survived World War I (during which its homeland was under Danish rule) although it was seriously depleted in both numbers and quality. The subsequent introduction of Breton and Boulonnais blood from France proved highly successful. The Schleswig recovered and flourished in large numbers until the years immediately following World War II. In time, however, mechanization took its usual toll, and numbers dwindled drastically. In recent years some of the surviving Schleswigs have been bred back to Jutlands, in order to increase the breed's size.

BREED DESCRIPTION

Height 15.2 – 16hh.

Colour Predominantly chestnut, occasionally bay or grey.

Conformation Large, rather plain head, but with a kind eye; short, crested neck; very powerful shoulders; rather long body, though with good depth through the girth; well-muscled hindquarters; short, strong limbs with some feather.

INTERESTING FACTS

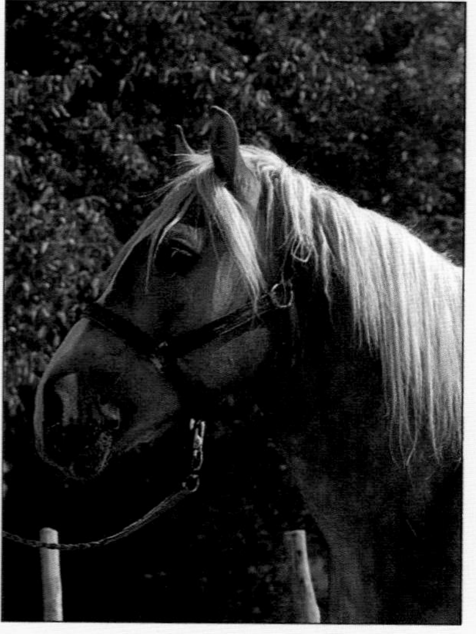

The attractive Schleswig horse, which often has a flaxen mane and tail, is extremely powerfully built and weighs in the region of 1,766lb (800kg).

South German

BELOW
The South German Coldblood has a large head and, typically, a docile expression.

BOTTOM
The South German resembles the Noriker but is a little smaller.

This strong and agile heavy horse is descended from the Austrian Noriker, which was introduced into Bavaria, in southern Germany, towards the end of the nineteenth century. With a view to improving and developing their own stamp of horse, breeders in Upper Bavaria added some Holstein and Oldenburg blood, while those in Lower Bavaria experimented with an extraordinary variety of outcrosses, from Oldenburg and Cleveland Bay to Clydesdale and Belgian Draught. In time, however, German breeders reverted to using the original Noriker blood for upgrading purposes. Originally called the Pinzgauer Noriker, after the region in Salzburg province from which that particular strain of the Austrian heavy horse came, the German version of the breed became known as the South German Heavy Horse. Today it is bred mainly in Bavaria and Baden Wurtemburg. It still resembles the Noriker, although it is inclined to stand a little less tall. It is a well-proportioned horse, with a calm, docile temperament, and can be seen in parades and at shows as well as, occasionally, at work in agriculture.

INTERESTING FACTS

The South German heavy horse is a popular attraction at shows. As well as being used by trick riders, it takes part in races – which it clearly enjoys!

BREED DESCRIPTION

Height Around 15.3hh.

Colour Brown, bay and chestnut.

Conformation Rather large head, with kind eye; short, strong neck; powerful shoulders; strong back with deep girth; good limbs with a little feather.

Cleveland Bay

A race of bay-coloured horses was being bred, primarily for pack work, in the north east of England as far back as mediaeval times. It was the preferred means of transport of the chapmen, or travelling salesmen of the day, and was accordingly known as the Chapman Horse. Taking the Chapman Horse as their base, seventeenth-century breeders used some of the Andalusian and Barb stallions that were being brought into the country at that time to produce a fine coach horse, renowned for its active paces and great stamina. This became known as the Cleveland Bay after the area where it was chiefly bred. As roads improved, and a faster type of coach horse became necessary, some Thoroughbred blood was introduced, usually by means of putting half-bred stallions to Cleveland mares. This lighter, faster version of the Cleveland Bay was called the Yorkshire Coach Horse. It had its own breed society, founded in 1886, and stud book. But the coming of motorized transport signalled the demise of coach horses everywhere and the Yorkshire breed was no exception.

ABOVE
The Cleveland Bay is the descendant of a race of bay-coloured horses bred in north-eastern England since medieval times.

LEFT
A handsome, upstanding stamp of horse, the Cleveland Bay produces excellent hunters when crossed with the Thoroughbred.

LEFT AND FAR LEFT
Cleveland Bay horses at the Royal Mews in London testify to the interest taken in the preservation of this historic breed by Queen Elizabeth II.

Its stud book was finally closed in 1936, by which time the breed had virtually died out. Fortunately the Cleveland Bay survived, albeit in small numbers. Crossed with the Thoroughbred, the breed produces fine upstanding heavyweight hunters and excellent carriage horses. The Cleveland Bay has a true, straight and free action (high action is not characteristic of the breed), moves freely from the shoulder and covers the ground well. As well as making an excellent hunter and carriage horse, the Cleveland Bay, when crossed with the Thoroughbred, has also produced some first-rate show jumpers.

BREED DESCRIPTION

Height 16 – 16.2hh, though height does not disqualify an otherwise good animal.

Colour Bay with black points.

Conformation Bold head, not too small, with large, well-set, kind eyes and large, fine ears; long, lean neck; deep, sloping, muscular shoulders; deep, wide body, with muscular loins, powerful hindquarters and well set-on tail; clean limbs (without feather), with muscular forearms, thighs and second thighs, large knees and hocks, and strong, sloping pasterns; good, sound feet.

INTERESTING FACTS

The survival of the Cleveland Bay was aided in no small measure by Queen Elizabeth II. A colt named Mulgrave Supreme, due to be sent to the United States, was bought by the Queen, subsequently broken to saddle and to harness and then made available to breeders of Cleveland Bays, both pure- and part-bred, throughout Britain. This tremendously successful promotional exercise sparked off renewed enthusiasm among breeders. Prince Philip further enhanced the breed's profile by driving, for many years, teams of pure- and part-bred Cleveland Bays at international level.

RIGHT
For many years HRH The Duke of Edinburgh drove a team of Cleveland Bays in international four-in-hand events. They have excellent ground-covering action, well suited to work both in harness and under saddle.

Hackney

The Hackney, with its high-stepping action, is a native of England though it is prized the world over as a carriage horse, especially in the show ring. The Hackney horse originated in the late seventeenth and early eighteenth centuries and is a descendant of the famous English trotting horses of the time, the Yorkshire Trotter and the Norfolk Roadster. These horses had a common ancestor, a horse known as the Original Shales, who was foaled in 1755 and was by the Thoroughbred Blaze out of a mare described as a "hackney". Blaze was by Flying Childers, generally recognized as being the first great racehorse. Blaze and his progeny, notably his two sons, Driver and Scot Shales, had a considerable influence on the development of the trotters of eastern England. Despite their shared ancestry, the horses bred in Yorkshire and Norfolk developed somewhat different characteristics – those of Yorkshire origin tended to have more quality than those from Norfolk, which were more cob-like in appearance – but these regional

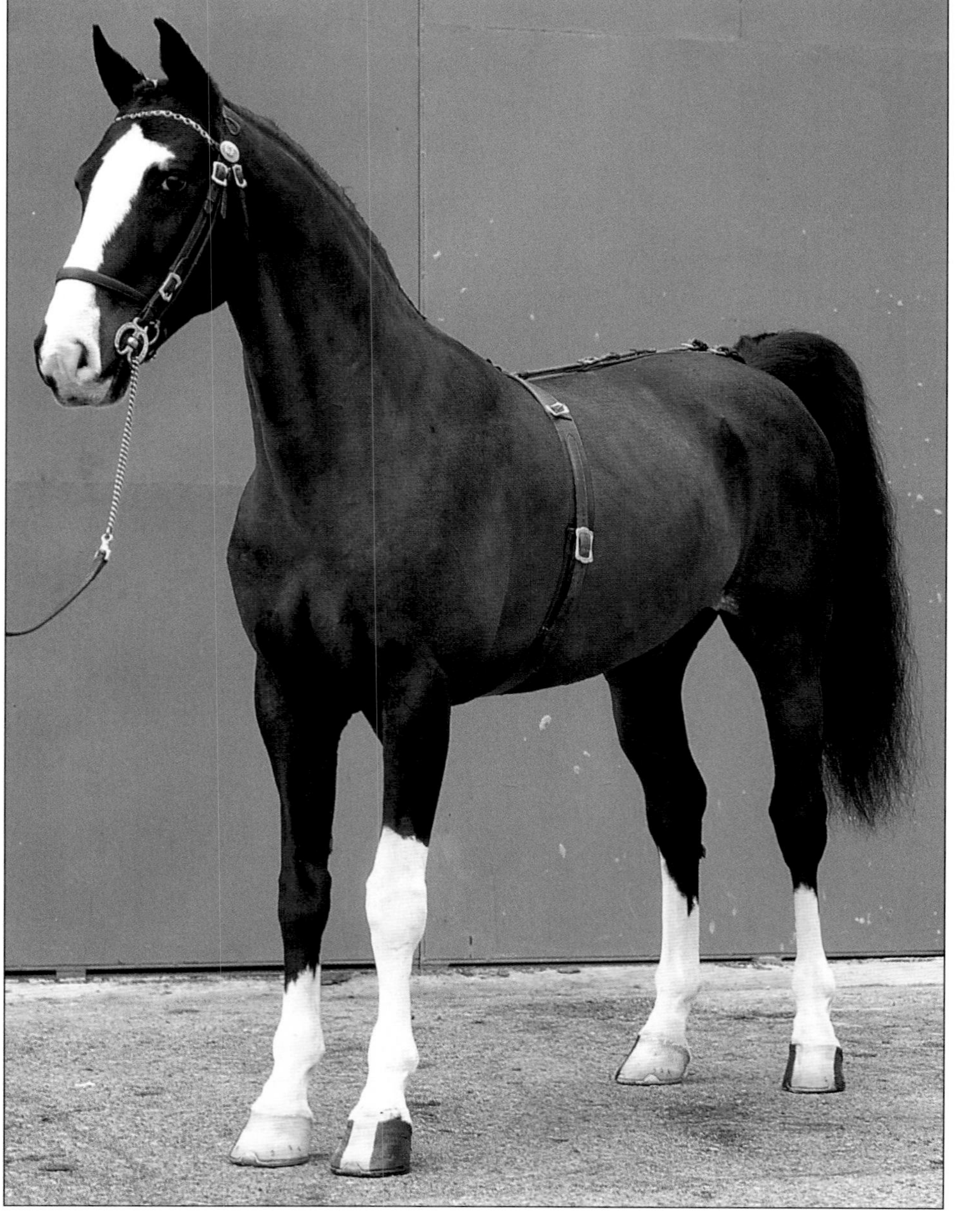

BREED DESCRIPTION

Height Hackney pony not exceeding 14hh. Hackney horse 15 – 15.3hh.

Colour Usually dark brown, black, bay or chestnut.

Conformation Small, convex head with small muzzle, large eyes and small ears; fairly long, well-formed neck; powerful shoulders and low withers; compact body, with great depth of chest; short legs with strong, well let-down hocks and well-shaped feet.

INTERESTING FACTS

The derivation of the word hackney is doubtful but it is thought to come from the Old French *haquenée*, "an ambling horse or mare, especially for ladies to ride on", and may be related to the Old Spanish and Portuguese *facanea* and Spanish *hacanea*. In the fourteenth century the word was latinized in England as *hakeneius*.

LEFT
Hackneys are popular in show rings throughout the world. Here they are being driven in an unusual three-horse combination known as a unicorn, comprising two wheelers and a leader.

distinctions later disappeared.

The Hackney pony was developed during the second half of the eighteenth century – earlier use of the term "Hackney ponies" almost certainly referred to small part-bred Hackney horses. It was the very enterprising Westmorland breeder, Christopher Wyndham Wilson, a remarkable man whose achievements included inventing the silo to store winter feed for farm animals, who was largely responsible for the development of the true Hackney pony. Wilson used a variety of pony breeds, especially the Fell, as his foundation mares, crossing them with a good-looking Hackney horse named Sir George, who was sired in 1866 and stood less than 14hh. His policy of inbreeding to the prepotent Sir George enabled Wilson to achieve his aim of developing a Hackney with real pony characteristics and in due course other breeders followed his lead. The original height limit for ponies, as recommended by the Hackney Horse Society, was 14.2hh but this was subsequently reduced to 14hh. The high-stepping action for which the Hackney is renowned was not developed until the second half of the nineteenth century, when it became the fashion to drive elegant, showy carriage horses. It is partly inherited, partly taught and can be enhanced by training.

RIGHT
In classes for single turnouts the Hackney is harnessed to a lightweight vehicle with pneumatic tyres.

OPPOSITE
The Hackney has a compact body, powerful shoulders and a deep chest. The limbs are strong and the feet invariably well formed.

Shire

England's most magnificent looking heavy horse is descended from the mediaeval warhorse known as the Great Horse, which was later given the name of the English Black. It was developed by crossing imported Flanders and Friesian horses with native stock to produce first a military mount and subsequently a farm and general draught horse. The introduction of the term "blacks" for these heavy horses is attributed to Oliver Cromwell, and was probably used originally to describe the imported Friesians, which are always black in colour. The main breeding areas of the

BREED DESCRIPTION

Height Stallions 16.2 – 17.2hh. Mares 16 – 17hh.

Colour Black, brown, bay or grey.

Conformation Lean head (neither too large nor too small), wide between the eyes, slightly Roman nose, large, prominent eyes with docile expression, and long, lean, sharp, sensitive ears; fairly long, slightly arched neck; deep, oblique shoulders, wide enough to support a collar; short, strong, muscular back, broad chest and wide, sweeping, muscular hindquarters with well let-down thighs; clean, hard limbs with 11–12 inches (28–30cm) of bone and broad, deep, flat hocks, set at the correct angle for leverage; fine, straight, silky feather; deep, solid feet with thick walls and open coronets.

ABOVE RIGHT
The Roman nose, long, sharp ears, large eyes and docile expression are typical of the Shire, the archetypal "gentle giant".

RIGHT
The magnificent Shire is descended from the medieval warhorse known as the Great Horse. It weighs in excess of 20cwt (1,016kg).

RIGHT
A team of twenty Shires makes a magnificent sight at an English horse show, admirably displaying the breed's tractable nature.

BELOW
A foal dozes in the summer sun. While Shires will never be seen in the same numbers as in olden times, the breed has enough enthusiasts to ensure its future.

INTERESTING FACTS

One of the earliest records of a Shire stallion standing at stud is of the horse known as the Packington Blind Horse. He was named after the village of Packington, near Ashby-de-la-Zouche, where he lived between 1755 and 1770. This horse, and horses said to be his progeny, had a significant influence on the breed during its formative years.

English Black were the Fen country and the Midland shires of Leicestershire, Lincolnshire, Derbyshire and Staffordshire, from which the breed eventually took its name. In the early days the breed displayed regional variations, horses bred in the Fens tending to be bigger, heavier and somewhat coarser than those from the "Shires". Those from Derbyshire and Leicestershire were predominantly black, while Staffordshire horses were more often brown.

It was not until the late nineteenth century that the breeding of these horses became formalized, as a result of the publication of the first stud book. In 1878 a breed society was set up under the title of the Old English Cart Horse Society. The name was changed in 1884 to the Shire Horse Society and the breed has been known as the Shire ever since.

Following the formation of the breed society, the Shire went from strength to strength, competing with great success in the leading agricultural shows of the time and attracting the interest of foreign buyers. Shire horses were soon being exported as far afield as North and South America, Russia and Australia. They also became an indispensable part of daily life in Britain. With their qualities of strength, stamina, soundness and good temperament, these gentle giants could be seen ploughing the land, hauling timber and pulling farm wagons, railway vans, brewers' drays and coal carts. Although mechanization took its customary toll, a Shire "revival" began in the 1960s and today these wonderful horses can again be seen at shows, ploughing the land and, not least, pulling brewers' drays on short-haul routes in cities.

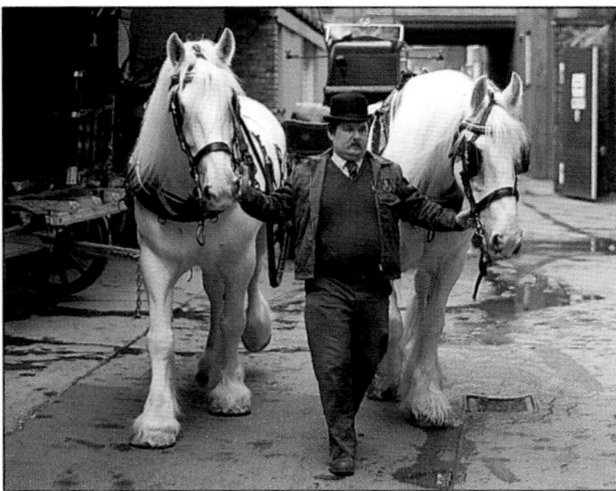

LEFT AND ABOVE
Shires hitched to brewers' drays are a popular sight at many British horse and agricultural shows. Some are still used for short-haul work in inner cities, where they are more economical than motorized transport.

Suffolk

Britain's oldest heavy breed, the Suffolk or Suffolk Punch, is named after the East Anglian county where it has been bred since the sixteenth century. Little is known of its origins, but as far back as 1506 there is an historical reference to a distinctive type of Suffolk horse. The Suffolk was developed as a farm horse and with its tremendously strong shoulders and clean legs (i.e. free of feather) it is ideally suited to working on the very heavy clay soils of East Anglia.

The breed is unique in that all Suffolks trace back to a single stallion, known as Crisp's Horse of Ufford, foaled in 1760. This purity is manifested in the fact that it always breeds true to colour: all Suffolks are "chesnut" (traditionally spelt without the first "t"). Quite apart from its coat colour, the Suffolk is quite unmistakable in appearance, having a heavy body set on comparatively short legs.

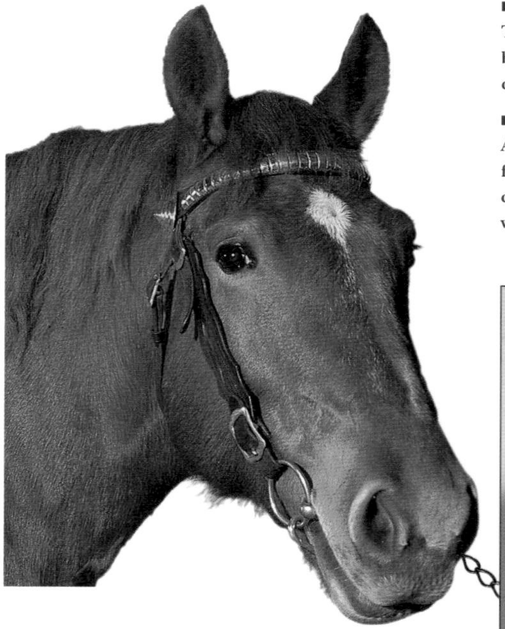

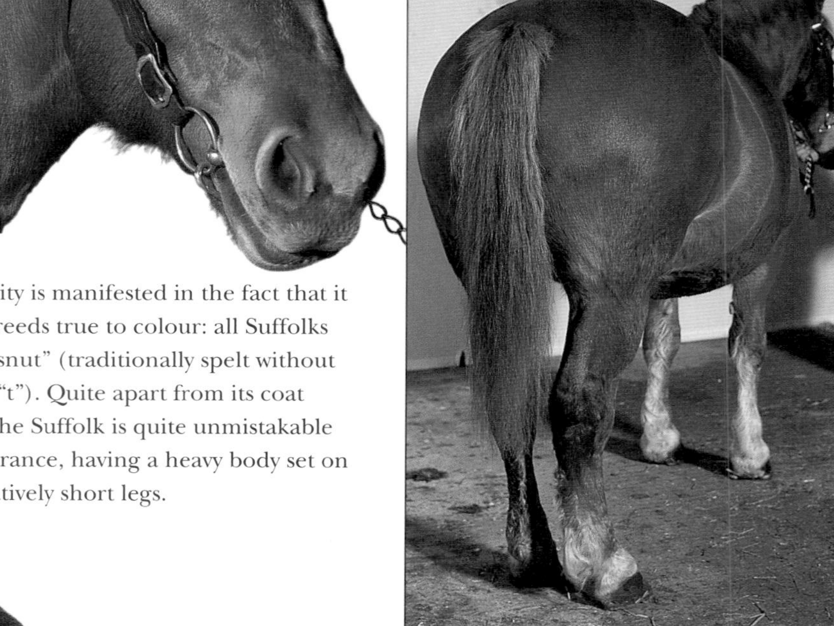

LEFT
This mare shows the typical broad forehead and full, bright eyes of the Suffolk. All Suffolks are chesnut in colour – traditionally spelt without the middle "t".

BELOW
Although there is plenty of width between the forelegs, the hindfeet are set close together. Such conformation prevents the horse damaging crops when working in the fields.

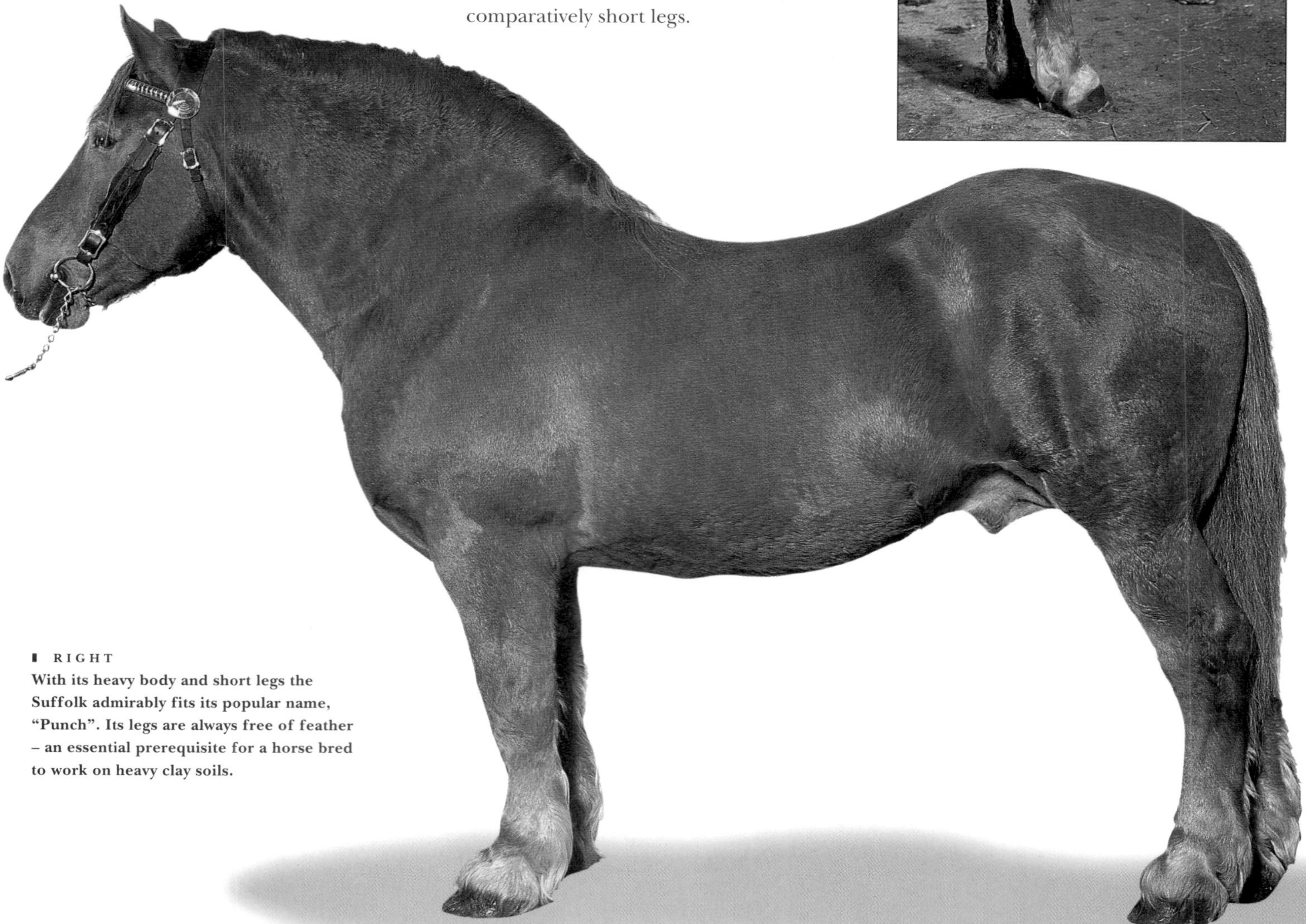

RIGHT
With its heavy body and short legs the Suffolk admirably fits its popular name, "Punch". Its legs are always free of feather – an essential prerequisite for a horse bred to work on heavy clay soils.

BREED DESCRIPTION

Height 16 – 16.3hh.

Colour Always "chesnut", of which seven shades are recognized, ranging from a pale mealy tone to a very dark, almost brown, shade. The most common is a bright reddish shade. A little white may occur on the face and the mane and tail are sometimes pale in colour.

Conformation Quite large head, with broad forehead; deep, tapering neck; long, muscular shoulders; deep, well-rounded body with strong quarters and well-set tail; fairly short, straight limbs with plenty of bone, sloping pasterns and no coarse hair; hard, sound, medium-sized feet.

INTERESTING FACTS

The ability of the Suffolk to thrive on less rations than other working heavy horses is well illustrated by the experiences of one farmer who, during the early part of this century, compared the feed requirements of two dozen cross-bred farm horses which he used for several years on one farm, and those of twenty-five Suffolks which he used for a similar period on another. While all the horses ate the same quantities of bulk food – hay, mangolds and chaff – the cross-breds each required 75lb (34kg) of corn per week, increasing by some 14–21lbs (6.4-9.5kg) per week as they grew older, while the Suffolks, even the older ones, kept their condition on a regular 50lb (22.7kg) per week.

Despite its size the Suffolk is a remarkably economical horse to keep, thriving and working on comparatively small rations. It matures early – Suffolks can be put to light work at two years of age and go into full work at three. It has an exceptionally amenable temperament and it is noted for its great soundness and longevity – it is common for horses to be in use and mares to be producing foals into their late teens and Suffolks often live until they are nearly thirty. The Suffolk's remarkable qualities combined to make it one of the most popular agricultural and draught horses of all time and, not surprisingly, its popularity spread abroad. There have been Suffolks in the United States for many years and representatives of the breed have also been exported to Australia, Africa, Russia and Pakistan (where they were used to produce army horses). Like the Shire, the Suffolk survived the coming of mechanization and can still be seen occasionally working the land, pulling drays and at shows, principally in eastern England.

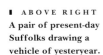

ABOVE RIGHT
A pair of present-day Suffolks drawing a vehicle of yesteryear.

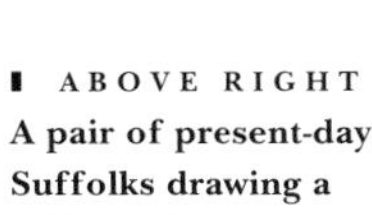

RIGHT
Suffolks can still be seen at their traditional work, ploughing. Early maturing, sound, long-lived and economical to feed, the breed possesses all the attributes so vital in a draught horse in the days before mechanization.

Clydesdale

Scotland's breed of heavy horse, as its name suggests, originated in that area of Lanarkshire through which the Clyde river runs. Today's Clydesdale, which developed more recently than the other British heavy breeds, began to evolve during the second half of the eighteenth century when imported Flemish stallions were used to improve the stock, descended from pack animals, of local farmers. Before that, during the early part of the century, a breeder named Paterson of Lochlyoch had begun to produce horses which, by all accounts, bore a distinct resemblance to the modern Clydesdale, certainly as far as colour was concerned. The stallion Glancer, to whom many Clydesdales can be traced back, was out of a mare known as Lampit's Mare, who was believed to be a

BREED DESCRIPTION

Height Stallions 17.1 – 18hh. Mares 16.3 – 17.2hh

Colour Bay, brown or black. Chestnut is rare. Often with a good deal of white on the face and legs, which may run up on to the body, particularly as flashes on the stomach.

Conformation Strong, intelligent head, with broad forehead, wide muzzle, large nostrils, bright, clear eyes and big ears; long, well-arched neck; sloping shoulders with high withers; short back with well-sprung ribs and muscular hindquarters; straight limbs with forelegs set well under the shoulders, long pasterns and a fair amount of fine feather; round, open feet.

OPPOSITE PAGE
The brisk, ground-covering paces of the Clydesdale make it eminently suitable for both agricultural and heavy haulage work.

ABOVE
Large, kind eyes and big ears give these Clydesdales the gentle, sensible expression typical of the breed. Unlike the Shire, the Clydesdale never has a Roman nose.

LEFT
Although the Clydesdale is closely related to the Shire, it has a number of distinguishing features, the most readily discernible of which is the large amount of white often seen on the limbs and extending up to the lower parts of the body.

BELOW
Wearing traditional Scottish harness decorations, the Clydesdale makes a fine sight in the show ring.

INTERESTING FACTS

One of the most famous and influential stallions in the development of the Clydesdale was a dark brown horse named Prince of Wales, foaled in Ayrshire in 1866. He was a mixture of English and Scottish blood and had outstanding action. His stud fee of £40, by no means a small sum for those days, was well worth paying – young horses sired by him fetched anywhere from £2,000 to £3,000.

descendant of the Lochlyoch horses.

Shire blood was used in the breed's development – indeed the two leading Clydesdale breeders during the second half of the nineteenth century, Lawrence Drew and David Riddell, believed the Clydesdale and the Shire to be of the same origin, and regularly interbred the two.

The Clydesdale Horse Society was formed in 1877 and the first stud book was published the following year. By this time interest in the breed had spread to other countries and Clydesdales were soon being exported, often in large numbers, to work the vast wheatlands of North America; others went to Australia, South America and Russia. It was, without doubt, the Clydesdale's docile nature combined with elegance and great activity that endeared it to heavy horse enthusiasts all over the world. Describing his action, the breed society says that the inside of every shoe should be made visible to anyone walking behind.The Clydesdale is an exceptionally sound horse, great emphasis having always been placed on good limbs and feet.

RIGHT
Many Clydesdales were exported to North America to work in agriculture. Their descendants can still be seen, though in rather different roles. This team is being used to haul the starting stalls at Santa Anita Racetrack.

Furioso

Hungary has long enjoyed a world-wide reputation as a horse-breeding country and as a producer of fine horsemen. The famous stud farm at Mezöhegyes, founded in 1784 by the Emperor Josef II, quickly became established as one of the great breeding centres of Europe. One of the most important breeds developed there was the Furioso, which was produced by crossing Thoroughbreds with mainly Hungarian mares. The chief influences were the English Thoroughbred stallion, Furioso, after whom the breed was named and who was acquired by Mezöhegyes in 1841, and another English horse, North Star, who was imported during the 1850s. Using these two bloodlines Mezöhegyes began producing quality carriage horses and good, heavyweight riding horses. For a time these two bloodlines were kept separate, with North Star proving a particularly successful sire of harness racehorses. He was descended from the 1793 Derby winner, Waxy (a grandson of the great Eclipse), and is said to trace back to Norfolk Roadster blood, which could account for his progeny's success in harness. Towards the end of the nineteenth century the North Star and Furioso strains were merged, after which the Furioso became the dominant force.

BREED DESCRIPTION

Height About 16hh.

Colour Any solid colour.

Conformation Fine head (denoting its Thoroughbred ancestry); well-sloped shoulders; strong back; good strong limbs and feet.

INTERESTING FACTS

The Csikos horse herders of Hungary are renowned for their trick-riding skills. Their breathtaking displays, often performed with Furioso horses, are famous all over the world.

TOP
The present-day Furioso is a quality all-purpose riding horse, built on somewhat heavier lines than its Thoroughbred ancestors.

LEFT
Large herds of horses, including the Furioso, have traditionally been raised on the grasslands of Hungary.

Nonius

Like the Furioso, the more heavily built Nonius evolved at the Mezöhegyes stud farm founded by the Emperor Josef II. The breed's foundation sire was an Anglo-Norman horse by the name of Nonius Senior. He was foaled in 1810, captured in France by the Austrians in 1814 and installed at Mezöhegyes in 1816. Nonius was said to be by a half-bred English stallion out of a Norman mare and almost certainly had Norfolk Roadster blood in him. He was by all accounts not the most prepossessing individual and would have won no prizes for conformation, but during his sixteen years at stud he became a tremendously successful sire. Mated with mares of various breeds, including Arab, Lipizzaner, Spanish and Turkish, as well as Hungarian, he produced good quality horses, the best of which were mated back to him. In this way a distinctive type emerged – to be known as the Nonius.

During the 1860s, infusions of Thoroughbred blood were made, a policy which led to the development of two different types of Nonius: one, a large horse suited to light agricultural work and as a carriage horse, the other, a smaller, finer animal suitable for riding. In more recent times, as the need for farm horses diminished, the larger type of Nonius was used mainly for driving, a skill at which Hungarian horsemen have long excelled. Both types of Nonius combine active paces with a calm, willing temperament.

BREED DESCRIPTION

Height Large type 15.3 – 16.2hh. Small type 14.3 – 15.3hh.

Colour Predominantly bay, with some black, brown and chestnut.

Conformation Attractive, honest head; sloping shoulders; broad, strong back; strong hindquarters; sound limbs.

BELOW
The head, though lacking refinement, reflects the breed's kind, tractable nature.

BELOW
Thoroughbred, Norman and Norfolk Roadster blood all played a part in the development of the Nonius. Today's sturdily built individuals make good all-round riding and driving horses.

INTERESTING FACTS

There are two distinct types of harness used for driving purposes. These Nonius horses are wearing breast harness. For pulling heavy loads horses wear collars to enable them to use the full strength of their shoulders.

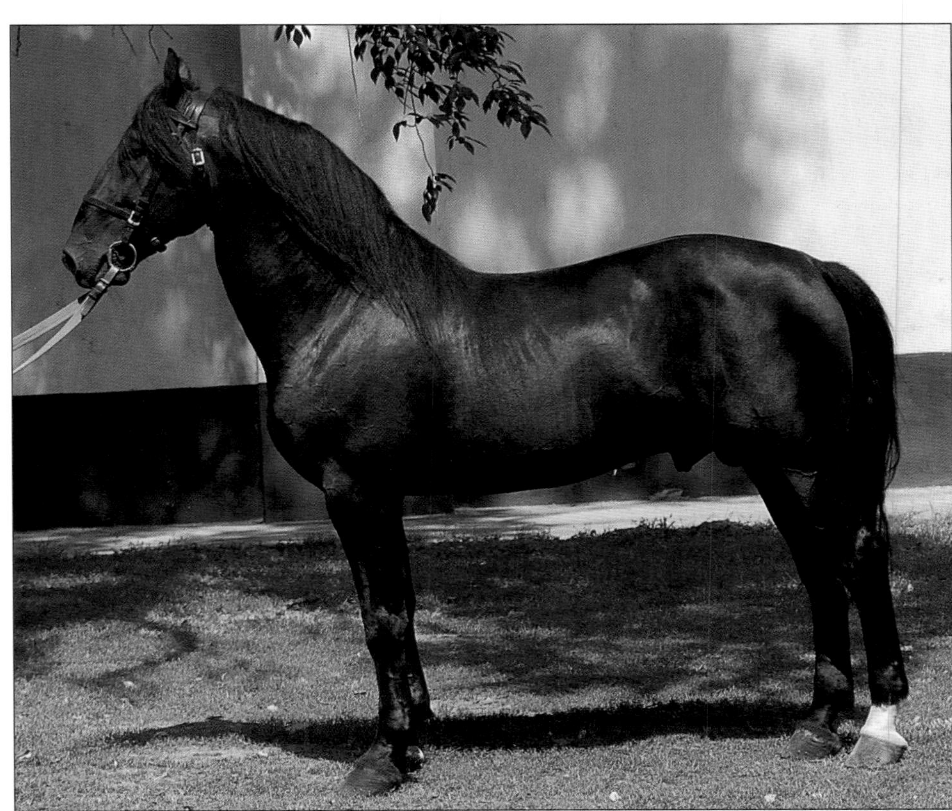

Hungarian Half-bred

The Hungarians began producing leisure and sports horses during the 1960s, continuing their tradition of breeding fine horses. They imported Hanoverians and Holsteins to cross with the Furioso and the Gidran in order to develop an animal suited to modern requirements. The Gidran, which to all intents and purposes is the Hungarian Anglo-Arab, can be traced back to an Arabian stallion known as Gidran Senior, imported into Hungary in 1816. Gidran's son, Gidran II, bred from a Spanish mare, became the foundation sire of the type which bears his name.

Initially a variety of mares were used, but later Thoroughbred blood was introduced and, subsequently, more Arab blood. This breeding policy

BREED DESCRIPTION

Height 15.3 – 16hh.

Colour Any solid colour.

Conformation Variable, but usually well proportioned with good, sloping shoulders and strong hindquarters.

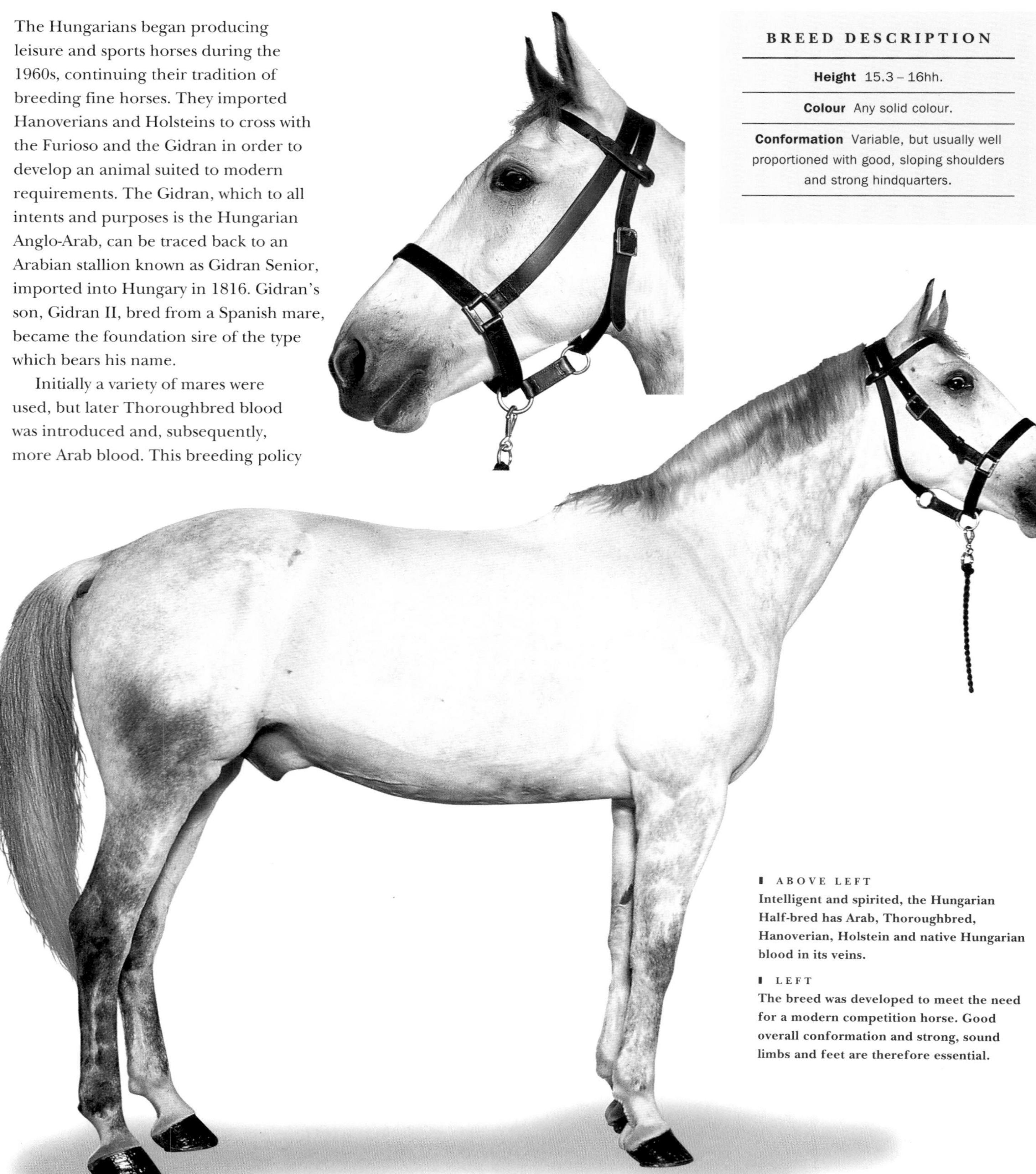

ABOVE LEFT
Intelligent and spirited, the Hungarian Half-bred has Arab, Thoroughbred, Hanoverian, Holstein and native Hungarian blood in its veins.

LEFT
The breed was developed to meet the need for a modern competition horse. Good overall conformation and strong, sound limbs and feet are therefore essential.

INTERESTING FACTS

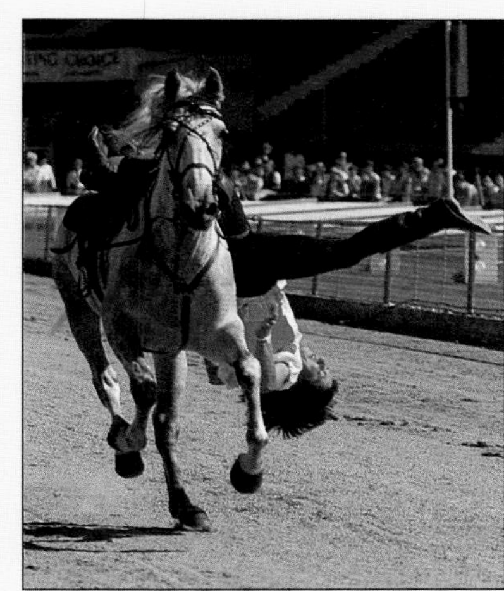

The Hungarian Half-bred has a good temperament which lends itself to training for a wide variety of activities – as this daring trick riding display proves.

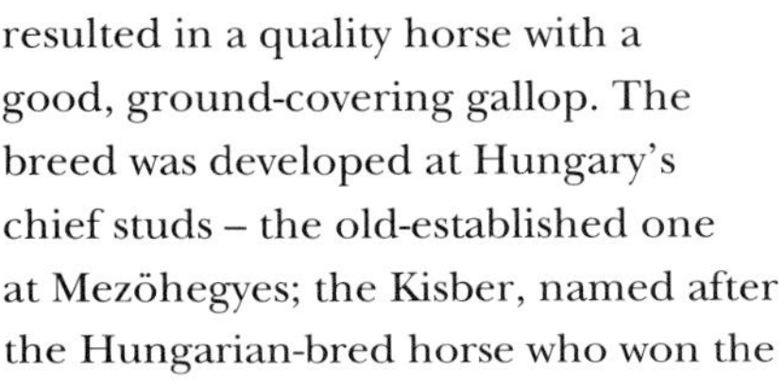

LEFT
Speed, stamina and a ground-covering stride make the half-bred a suitable partner for the tough sport of three-day eventing.

BELOW
Hungarian Half-breds have achieved their greatest competition successes in the gruelling sport of four-in-hand driving. They have been exported to many countries for this purpose.

resulted in a quality horse with a good, ground-covering gallop. The breed was developed at Hungary's chief studs – the old-established one at Mezöhegyes; the Kisber, named after the Hungarian-bred horse who won the British Derby in 1876, and the Kecskemet, which is famous for its cross-bred driving horses, based on Lipizzaner and trotter blood.

Hungarian Half-breds have achieved outstanding success in the sport of international four-in-hand driving, where they have competed not just in the hands of the traditionally dashing and skilful Hungarian drivers but also for a number of other European nations, notably Switzerland and Britain.

Shagya

The Shagya is a strain of Arabian horse bred in Hungary and descended from a stallion of the same name. Shagya was a Syrian-bred horse, foaled in 1830 and imported to the Hungarian stud at Babolna some six years later. Shagya was used to cover quality mares which, although they were of mixed blood (including Hungarian, Thoroughbred and Spanish, as well as Arabian) were distinctly "eastern" in overall appearance. By employing the practice of inbreeding, the Babolna Stud produced the distinctive type of Arab horse seen today. The Shagya is rather taller and has a noticeably bigger frame than other Arabs (Shagya himself

ABOVE LEFT
The wide-set eyes and tapered muzzle, with its large nostrils, are typical of the Shagya.

LEFT
The Shagya tends to have a rather more substantial frame than the pure-bred Arab, though its overall outline is very similar.

INTERESTING FACTS

The Babolna Stud, home of the Shagya Arab, was founded in 1789 by the Emperor Joseph II. Hungary has one of the oldest traditions of organized horse breeding in the world, its first recorded stud (founded by Prince Arpad, who died in 907) dating back more than 1,000 years. During the mid-eighteenth century horse breeding began to slip into a gradual decline and it was Joseph II who was largely responsible for revitalizing it. He founded the Veterinary College in Budapest, decreed the building of the famous Mezöhegyes stud farm in 1785 and subsequently Babolna, thus paving the way for the golden age that Hungarian horses enjoyed during the nineteenth century.

BREED DESCRIPTION

Height 14 – 15hh.

Colour Predominantly grey but all other Arab colours occur.

Conformation Refined head, with dished profile, small, tapered muzzle and large eyes; elegant, curved neck; sloping shoulders; short, slightly concave back with strong loins, level croup and high-set tail; good, strong limbs with especially good, well-formed feet.

was a little taller than normal for an Arab, standing over 15.2hh). But the overall appearance, with its beautiful, dished face, large eyes, short back and high-set tail, are all characteristic of the pure-bred Arab. Combining toughness with elegance, the Shagya was bred as a riding horse and found favour as a cavalry mount in the days before mechanization. Nowadays it is bred for leisure riding and is exported to a number of countries.

ABOVE
Mares and foals at the Babolna Stud in Hungary, home of the Shagya Arab. Babolna was founded by Royal decree more than 200 years ago.

BELOW
Grey is the breed's predominant colour, although all other Arab colours also occur. Shagya Arabs often stand a little taller than their pure-bred relatives.

Icelandic

BELOW
The tremendously thick mane and forelock give much needed protection against the severe weather conditions of the northern winters.

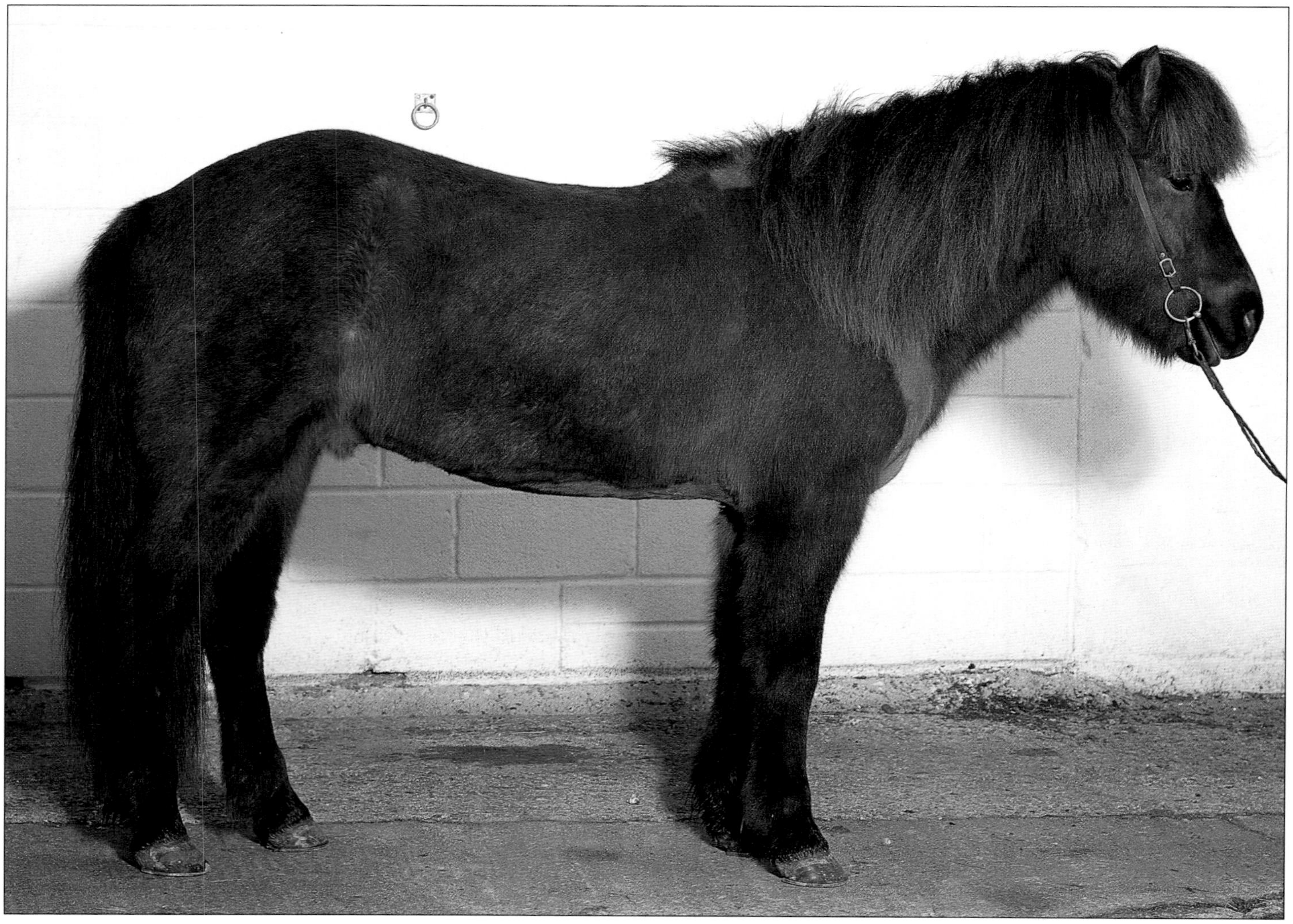

BOTTOM
Stocky and compact, with short, strong limbs and notably hard, sound feet, the Icelandic horse is perfectly adapted to its harsh environment.

The little Icelandic horse is probably the purest horse breed in the world. Its ancestors were taken to Iceland by ninth-century settlers, travelling from western Norway and the north of Britain. They were small, sturdy horses who adapted well to the rigorous Icelandic climate. Later some imports were made of eastern horses, but these had such a detrimental effect upon the original stock that in AD 930 the Althing (parliament) passed a law forbidding the import of further horses. Although this law seems to have been flouted occasionally, for the last 800 years there have been no infusions of outside blood. As a result the Icelandic horse has changed little since the age of the Vikings.

It is an outstandingly tough, weather-resistant little horse (although it stands no more than 13.2hh it is always referred to by the Icelanders as a horse, not a pony). A strong swimmer – there were no bridges over Iceland's numerous turbulent rivers until the beginning of this century – it is also remarkably sure-footed. It can be seen carrying a full-grown man at speed, with ease and safety, over mountainous terrain during the traditional autumn sheep round-ups.

Some Icelandic horses are noted for their keen sense of direction and

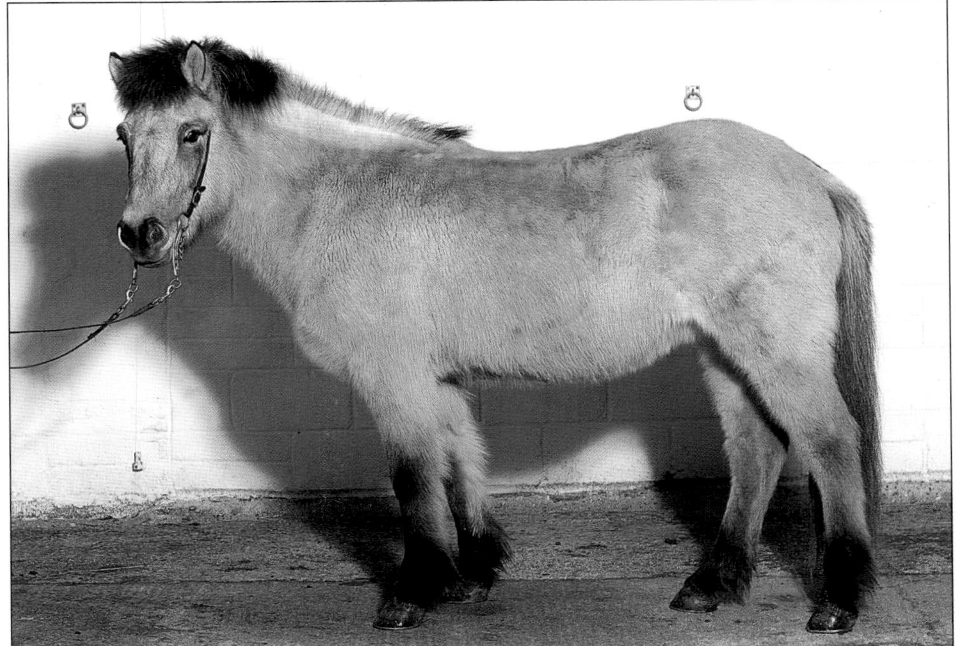

LEFT
Icelandic Horses, which have changed little since Viking times, come in a wide range of attractive coat colours, including dun, palomino, piebald and skewbald.

BREED DESCRIPTION

Height 12.3 – 13.2hh.

Colour Any.

Conformation Fairly heavy head; short, well-carried neck; compact body with short back and deep girth; sloping, wedge-shaped, very strong, muscular hindquarters; strong limbs with short cannons and strong hocks; strong, well-shaped feet.

extraordinary homing instinct. After the annual round-up, while sheep are penned and sorted into each farmer's flock, horses are often turned loose and will set off alone down the valleys to their homes. There are also many recorded instances of horses that have been sold to another part of the country travelling for weeks to return to their original homes.

While some local selection of breeding stock probably took place from time to time, it was not until 1879 that Iceland undertook a practical selective breeding programme. It was begun in Skagafjördur, the country's most famous horse-breeding area. Conformation is naturally taken into account, but it is the quality of the horse's gaits which is of prime importance. These are: the fetgangur (walk), the brökk (trot – used when crossing rough country), the stökk (gallop), the skeid (lateral pace – used to cover short distances at high speed) and the tölt (a running walk used to cover broken ground).The tölt is a gait of four equal beats – the sequence being near hind, near fore, off hind, off fore – with which the horse achieves great speed.

INTERESTING FACTS

In days gone by horse fights were a popular form of entertainment in Iceland. Playing on the natural instinct of stallions to fight each other for possession of a mare, Icelanders would set two specially trained stallions against one another, using goads to urge them on. This pastime was so dangerous that it was a common occurrence for handlers to be injured or even killed.

BELOW
Notwithstanding its diminutive size, the breed is immensely strong and fast. It is a popular all-round riding horse in many countries outside its native Iceland.

Irish Draught

Irish horses are renowned for being the best hunters in the world and none more so than those produced by crossing the Thoroughbred with the versatile Irish Draught. Although there are no early formal records or stud books, Ireland's light draught horse is known to trace back many centuries, to the time when Norman horses were introduced to Ireland and crossed with the native animals, which at that time were small of stature. Later infusions of Andalusian – and, probably, eastern – blood helped improve the overall quality (and height) of the Irish horses. The result was very much an all-round horse, totally suited to the Irish country way of life: capable of working on the small Irish farms but active enough to be harnessed to a trap or to carry a rider safely across country. The modern Irish Draught is generally accepted to have evolved from the crossing of imported Thoroughbred stallions with the best of these country-bred mares. The numbers of these splendid horses declined in Ireland following the famine of 1847 and some heavy horses were introduced from Britain, but this tended to lead to a coarsening of the Irish Draught. To save the best of the remaining stock, in the early years of this century a scheme of subsidies was introduced by the government, for approved stallions of Irish Draught and hunter type. As a result the active, clean-legged general-purpose

LEFT
A typically handsome, intelligent Irish Draught head. The breed is renowned for its innate good sense, coupled with boldness and athleticism.

RIGHT
Substance and plenty of bone are the hallmarks of the modern Irish Draught. The conformation should incorporate all the features of the correctly built riding horse.

BREED DESCRIPTION

Height Stallions 16hh and over. Mares 15.2hh and over.

Colour All solid colours.

Conformation Small, intelligent head; sloping shoulders; strong body with deep chest and oval rib cage; powerful hindquarters; strong limbs with plenty of flat bone and no feather.

LEFT
As a safe conveyance across the most testing of hunting countries, there is nothing to beat the Irish Draught and the Irish Draught/ Thoroughbred cross.

BELOW LEFT
The international show jumper Mill Pearl: a good example of the Irish Draught cross with the ability to perform at the highest level.

BELOW
The breed possesses good, natural balance and the action is straight and true.

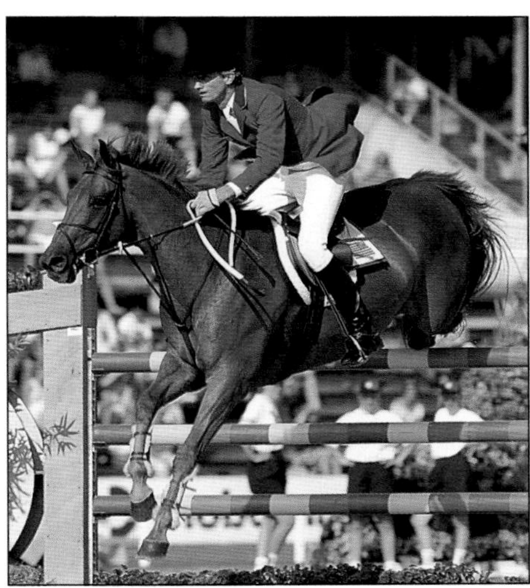

Irish Draught horse survived and in 1917 the Department of Agriculture introduced "a scheme to establish a Book for Horses of the Irish Draught type", in which 375 mares and 44 stallions were entered as being suitable and sound. The Irish Draught Horse Society was formed in 1976.

The excellence of Irish-bred horses owes much to the limestone pastures on which they are raised. The mineral-rich land contributes to the growth of strong bone and the production of good, upstanding animals. Today's Irish Draught has plenty of substance but is also an attractive looking, well-balanced, quality horse, with straight, athletic action. It is noted for its intelligence and kind temperament. It has an inherent ability to cross the most testing of hunting country with total assurance and because of its jumping prowess is a successful producer of top-level show jumpers.

INTERESTING FACTS

Since World War II many of the world's leading show-jumping horses have been Irish bred, with a fair percentage being by registered Irish Draught stallions. One of the most famous names in show-jumping breeding is King of Diamonds, an Irish Draught who sired many famous horses, including Special Envoy – who has jumped with great success for Brazil, ridden first by Nelson Pessoa then by his son Rodrigo – and Mill Pearl, ridden by the United States Olympic champion Joe Fargis.

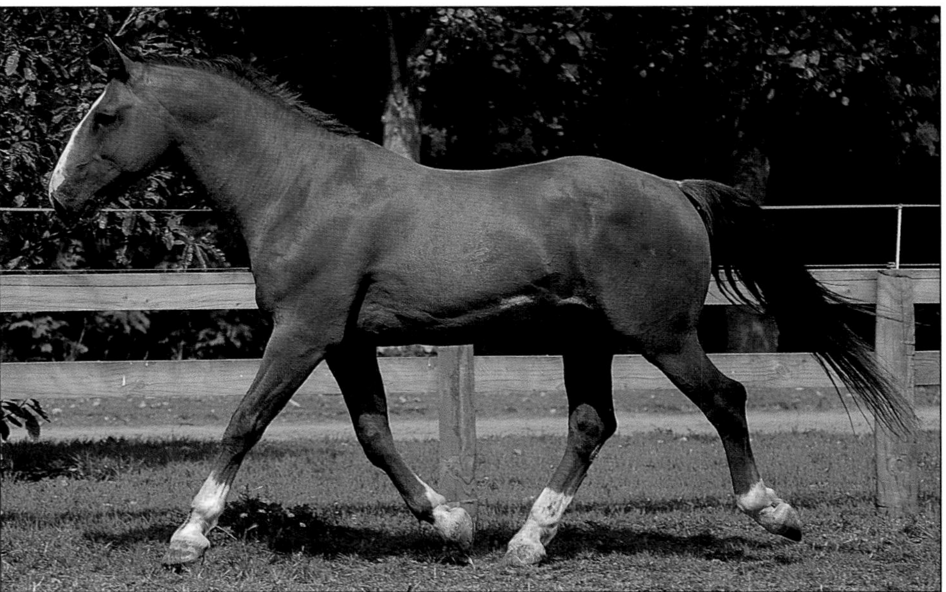

Maremmano

Maremmano horses are bred in Tuscany and are the traditional mounts of the *butteri*, or cattlemen. Maremma, a coastal tract on the Tyrrhenian Sea extending from Piombino to Orbetello, is a former marshland which was drained in ancient times but later reverted to being an unhealthy wasteland. Drainage was reintroduced earlier this century and the area is now used as pastureland.

The origins of the Maremmano horses are obscure but it is likely that they are descended from the Neapolitan horses (founded on Arab, Barb and Spanish blood) made famous in the sixteenth century by Federico Grisone. Grisone was the founder of the Neapolitan riding academy and regarded as the first of the great classical riding masters after the Greek, Xenophon (c. 430–350 BC). A good deal of outcrossing took place later – some involving imported English horses, including the Norfolk Roadster – so that the horses which became known as the

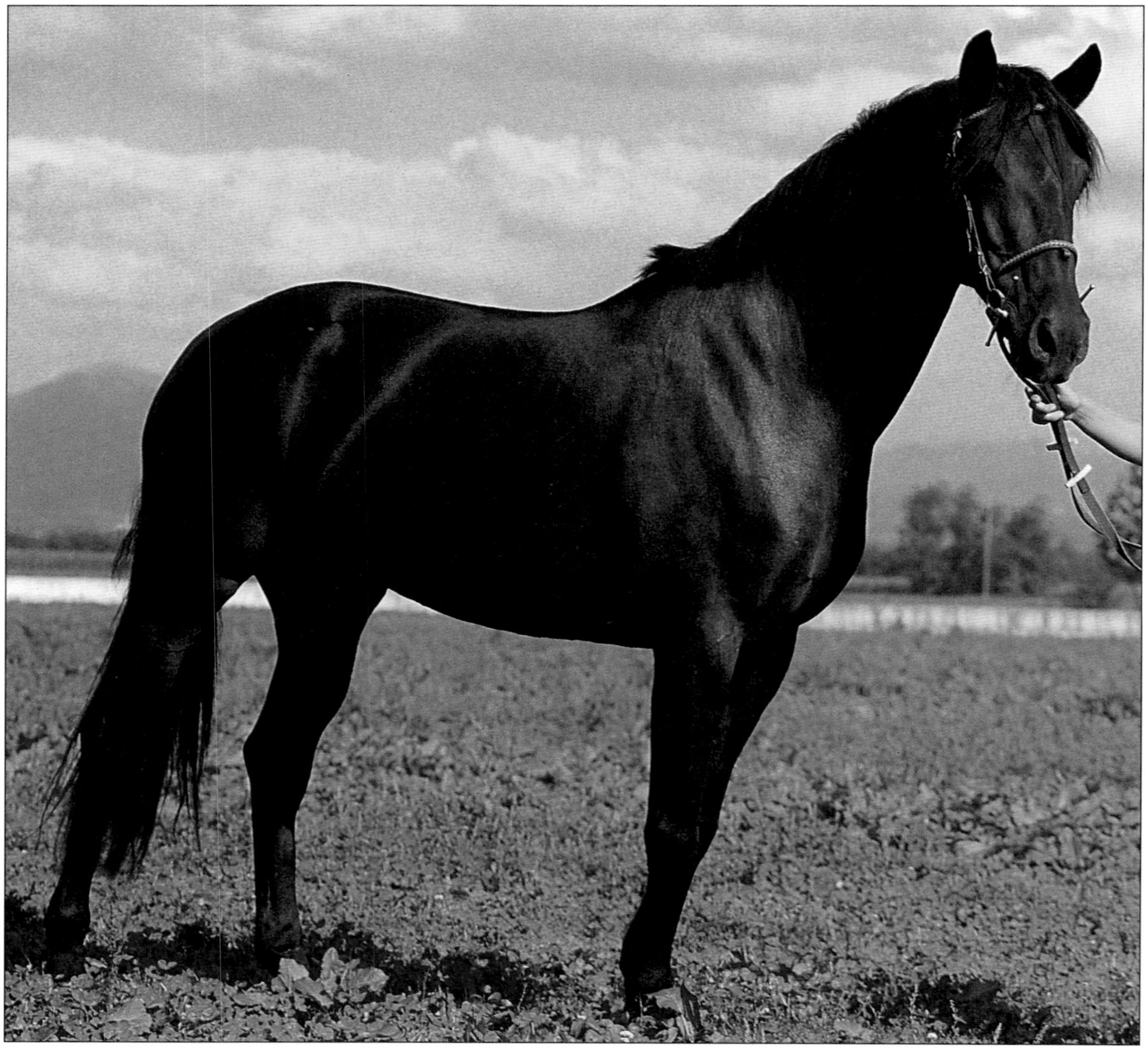

RIGHT
The Maremmano is a strong horse possessed of a quiet temperament, and although not particularly speedy it makes a useful all-round riding horse.

LEFT
Maremmano horses vary a good deal in type and conformation. This horse is much more refined than many examples of the breed, with an especially elegant head.

BELOW
A Maremmano wearing the traditional tack of the *buttero*, or Italian cowboy. Its toughness and reliability make the breed an ideal mount for working with cattle.

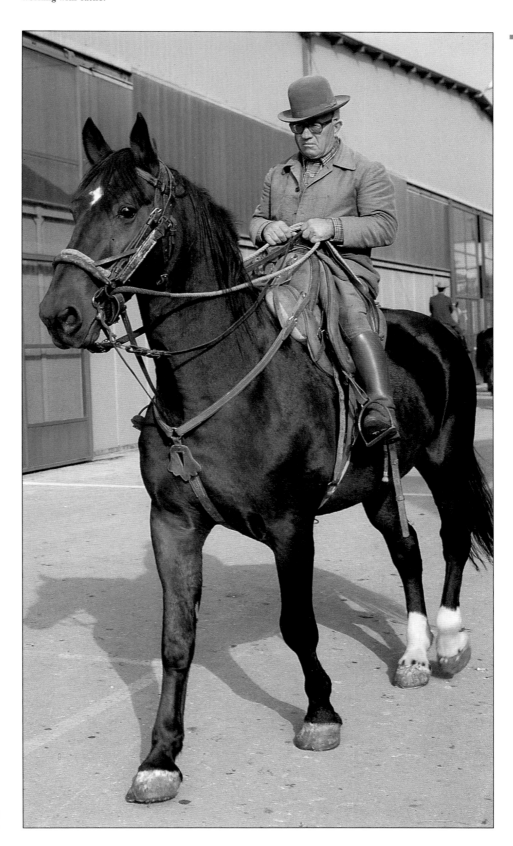

BREED DESCRIPTION

Height Variable, usually around 15.3hh.

Colour Any solid colour.

Conformation Variable. Overall appearance somewhat coarse, with rather upright shoulders, flat withers and low-set tail, though conformational improvements are being made through the introduction of Thoroughbred blood.

Maremmano were something of a mixture and of no fixed type. By no means the most beautiful looking of horses, nor the speediest, they are nevertheless good, honest workers, combining strength and toughness with a calm temperament. Amenable by nature and economical to feed, they have proved useful as army and police horses, as well as in agriculture – they are strong enough to perform light draught work – and cattle herding.

INTERESTING FACTS

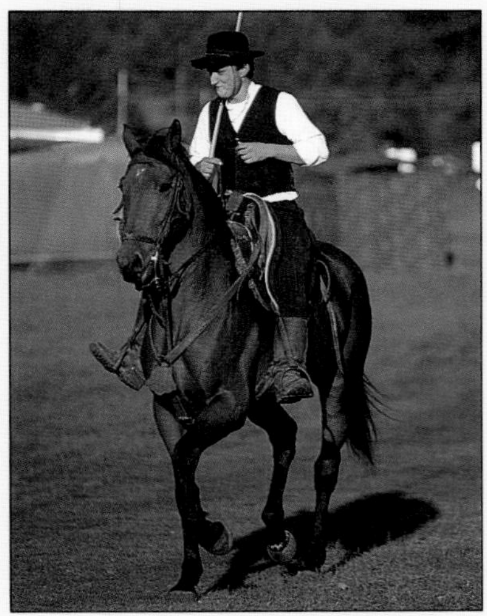

During the seventeenth century Italy became one of the world leaders for horse breeding. Most famous of all was the Neapolitan, of which the Maremmano is possibly a descendant.

Murgese

Originating from the Orfano plain and the hill districts near Gravina, the original Murgese horse can be traced back at least 500 years. During the late fifteenth and early sixteenth centuries the governor of the port of Monopoli, which for some years belonged to the Venetian Republic, kept a stock of Murgese stallions and several hundred brood mares in order to provide remounts for the cavalry. However, somewhere down the years the breed died out and the modern version dates only from the 1920s.

The Murgese is basically a light draught horse, though inferior in quality to the Irish Draught and showing no great uniformity of type. It can be ridden, but a better stamp of riding horse is produced by putting a Murgese mare to a Thoroughbred or warmblood stallion, the latter giving the progeny more quality, and paces better suited to a saddle horse.

INTERESTING FACTS

The breeding of warmblood horses for present-day leisure and sport use is less advanced in Italy than in some other European countries, but an Italian Saddle Horse is gradually being evolved by crossing the best stock from the country's existing saddle breeds and types and crossing them with imported warmbloods and Thoroughbreds. Horses being merged in this way include the Salerno, which traces back to Neapolitan stock, and which also has Andalusian, Arab and Thoroughbred blood in its veins, and the Sardinian and Sicilian Anglo-Arabs.

BREED DESCRIPTION

Height 15 – 16hh.

Colour Usually chestnut, though other solid colours occur.

Conformation Variable. Overall appearance suggests a light draught horse. The head tends to be plain, though with an honest expression, and the hindquarters rather poor, with a low-set tail.

ABOVE
Although basically best suited to light draught work, the Murgese can make a useful riding horse. This example of the breed has been fully trained as a police horse.

TOP LEFT
Although the predominant coat colouring is chestnut, some dark colours do occur.

LEFT
The Murgese is Italy's breed of light draught horse. However, it lacks definitive type and the overall quality of the light draught horse of Ireland.

▮ BOTTOM LEFT
The head is small with a straight profile. The eyes are large and bright, the ears small and mobile.

▮ BELOW
Chestnut coat colouring with a flaxen mane and tail is typical of this attractive breed. It has inherited the active paces of the Breton, which had an important influence on its development.

Italian Heavy Draught

Italy's premier heavy horse, the Italian Heavy Draught – also known as the Agricultural Heavy Horse – bears a distinct resemblance to the handsome Breton, which has had an important influence upon its development. The Italian Heavy Draught originated at Ferrara in the north of the country during the second half of the nineteenth century, when Neapolitan blood was crossed with Arab and Hackney

BREED DESCRIPTION

Height Stallions 15 – 16hh. Mares 14 – 15hh.

Colour Predominantly chestnut with flaxen mane and tail. Occasionally dark bay.

Conformation Square head with broad forehead, large eyes and nostrils and small, mobile ears; muscular, slightly arched neck; well-sloped shoulders; deep chest, short, strong back with broad, slightly sloping croup; short strong limbs with muscular forearms and large joints, short pasterns and large, well-shaped feet.

to produce an active, lightweight workhorse. In due course the need arose both for a heavier agricultural animal and a heavy artillery horse, and breeders accordingly began introducing new blood, notably Boulonnais. Then, in the 1920s, pure-bred Breton stallions were used to establish the stamp of horse now known as the Italian Heavy Draught.

An attractive looking horse, stocky and muscular in build, the Italian Heavy Draught is noted for its conformation and active paces. It is capable of maintaining a good speed even when pulling heavy loads. The limbs are short and very strong with well-developed muscles and large joints. Although the need for draught horses has decreased in Italy, as elsewhere, the Italian Heavy Draught can still be seen at work on some of the smaller farms, and is also used for meat production.

INTERESTING FACTS

A stud book for Italian Draught Horses was opened in 1961. Horses accepted for registration are branded on the nearside of the hindquarters with the breed mark, a five-runged ladder within a shield.

Friesian

The Friesian is one of Europe's oldest horses and down the centuries it has had an influence on a number of other breeds, notably the Oldenburg in Germany and Britain's Fell and Dales ponies. The breed's homeland is Friesland, in the north of the Netherlands. The remains of an ancient coldblood type of heavy horse have been unearthed there, from which the modern Friesian is believed to be descended. Eastern blood, introduced into the Netherlands during the time of

LEFT
The Friesian's friendly disposition is evident in its kind but alert expression. The rather long head is set on a well-arched neck.

BREED DESCRIPTION

Height 15 – 16hh.

Colour Always black.

Conformation Rather long head, with short ears and alert expression; elegant, arched neck with long, flowing mane; powerful shoulders; strong, compact body with strong, sloping hindquarters and rather low-set, very full, tail; short, strong limbs with good bone and a fair amount of feather.

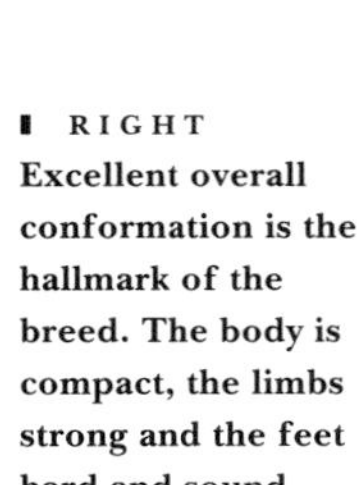

RIGHT
Excellent overall conformation is the hallmark of the breed. The body is compact, the limbs strong and the feet hard and sound.

LEFT
An attractive turnout much appreciated throughout its native land: a Friesian driven to a traditional high-wheeled gig.

INTERESTING FACTS

The Friesians' noble bearing makes them ideal for ceremonial occasions. These horses were part of a six-strong team pulling the Dutch Royal Carriage at the opening ceremony of the 1994 World Equestrian Games in The Hague.

the Crusades, had an influence on the development of the Friesian, as did the Andalusian during the Eighty Years' War, when the Netherlands were occupied by the Spanish. The Friesian horse which thus developed was an active all-rounder, suitable for work on the land but, because of its ability to trot at speed, also useful as a harness horse and for riding.

During the nineteenth century, when trotting became extremely popular, breeders sought to improve the Friesian's already active, high-stepping trot, by outcrossing to trotters. This led to the Friesian becoming lighter in build and less useful as a farm horse. By the beginning of World War I its numbers were seriously depleted and the decline continued between the wars. However, lack of fuel during World War II led to a revival in the breed's fortunes as farmers once again turned to it for draught work.

During the second half of this century there has been a resurgence of interest in the breed and it is now very popular as a carriage horse. A well-balanced horse with proud bearing, the Friesian looks exceptionally attractive when pulling a traditional high-wheeled Friesian gig. The breed is noted for its kind temperament.

BELOW
Appreciation of Friesians is not restricted to Holland. This handsome team was pictured in a busy London street.

Gelderland

A number of different breeds went into the making of the Gelderland, which comes from the region of the same name in the central Netherlands and was developed during the nineteenth century. Native mares were crossed with, among others, English, French, German, Hungarian and Polish stallions to produce a good stamp of dual-purpose horse, one that was big and strong enough to do farm work or pull a carriage but not so heavy that it could not be used for riding. Hackney blood was also used in a breeding programme that was noted for its well-founded principles of selection, only horses that had proved themselves to be good, sound workers being used at stud. As mechanization spread, and horses were needed less for use on the land, breeders introduced Thoroughbred blood to lighten the Gelderland.

A typical carriage type of horse, the modern Gelderland, with its excellent shoulders and good, free action, has been used successfully in the sport of four-in-hand driving and has also provided one of the main bases for the production of the Netherlands' sports horse, the Dutch Warmblood.

LEFT
Strong and active, the Gelderland makes an excellent carriage horse and has also played a part in the development of Holland's remarkably successful competition horse, the Dutch Warmblood.

INTERESTING FACTS

The Gelderland is one of two types of all-purpose horse developed in the Netherlands, the other being its northern neighbour, the Gröningen. The Gröningen is somewhat heavier than the Gelderland. It has Friesian and Oldenburg blood in its ancestry, as well as some Suffolk Punch. Like the Gelderland, it has played an important part in the development of the Dutch Warmblood.

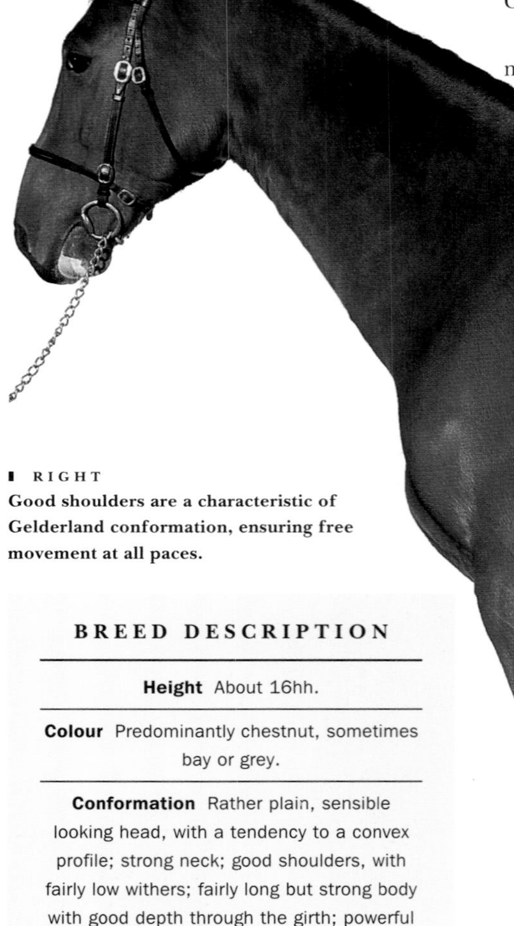

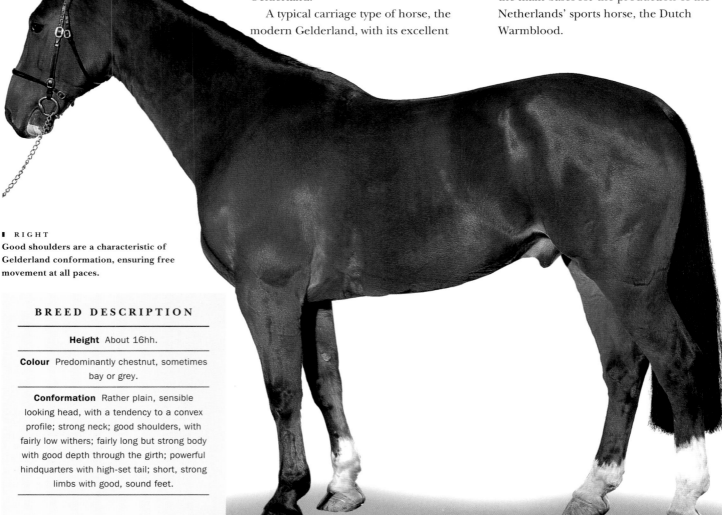

RIGHT
Good shoulders are a characteristic of Gelderland conformation, ensuring free movement at all paces.

BREED DESCRIPTION

Height About 16hh.

Colour Predominantly chestnut, sometimes bay or grey.

Conformation Rather plain, sensible looking head, with a tendency to a convex profile; strong neck; good shoulders, with fairly low withers; fairly long but strong body with good depth through the girth; powerful hindquarters with high-set tail; short, strong limbs with good, sound feet.

Dutch Warmblood

The production of the Netherlands' highly successful leisure and competition horse began with the selection of the best Gelderland and Gröningen mares, who were then mated with Thoroughbred stallions. The latter, also carefully selected, were imported from all over the world, including Britain, Ireland, France and the United States. Many of these came from the best racing lines, a fact which was to prove highly beneficial: as time went on Dutch breeders found that the stallions who produced the best warmbloods had themselves enjoyed successful racing careers. In addition to Thoroughbreds, some Trakehner stallions were used in the early years, and a number of Holstein mares were imported and put to Gelderland or Gröningen stallions. Later on warmbloods of the type which the Dutch breeders were seeking to develop, such as the Holstein and Selle Français, were introduced into the breeding programme, and a dash of Hanoverian and Westphalian blood was added. At the same time there was a gradual decrease in the amount of Gelderland and Gröningen blood used. The result is a riding horse of harmonious proportions, with straight, true action, an easy, ground-covering stride at all paces and a good temperament.

BREED DESCRIPTION

Height 16 – 17hh.

Colour Any solid colour, with bay and brown the most usual.

Conformation Quality head, with alert, intelligent expression; good, sloping shoulders with pronounced withers; strong back and hindquarters; good, sound limbs, with plenty of bone and short cannons; good, sound feet.

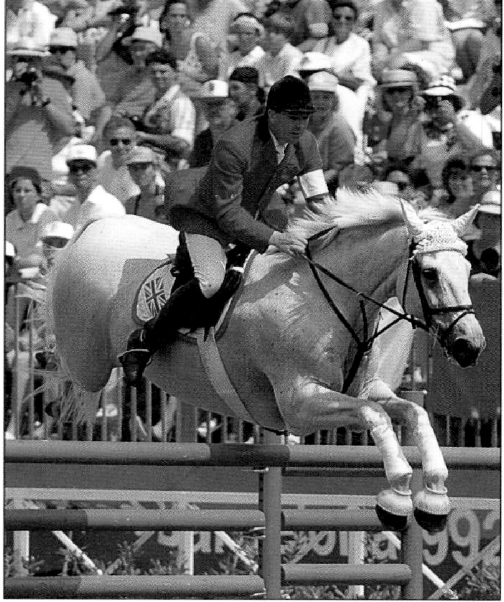

LEFT
Milton is a grandson of the Trakehner Marco Polo, one of the most influential Dutch Warmblood stallions.

INTERESTING FACTS

One of the most important stallions in the breeding of Dutch Warmbloods was the Trakehner Marco Polo (1965–1976). By the Thoroughbred Poet, he was only small but he produced some top-class show jumpers. They included Marius, who was ridden with great international success by Britain's Caroline Bradley. In Britain Marius combined his competitive career with stud duties and had the distinction of siring Milton, the world's most successful show jumper.

Dutch breeders use a highly efficient, performance-based selection system to produce their horses and, despite its relative newness, the Dutch Warmblood has already demonstrated the correctness of their approach by achieving success at top international level in dressage, show jumping and carriage driving. Dutch Warmbloods have been used in the establishment of other warmblood strains, too, notably in Britain, the United States, Australia and New Zealand.

LEFT
The Dutch Warmblood is a quality horse possessed of a good temperament. The correct proportions of its conformation result in excellent action, thus ensuring its suitability for modern competitive sports.

Lusitano

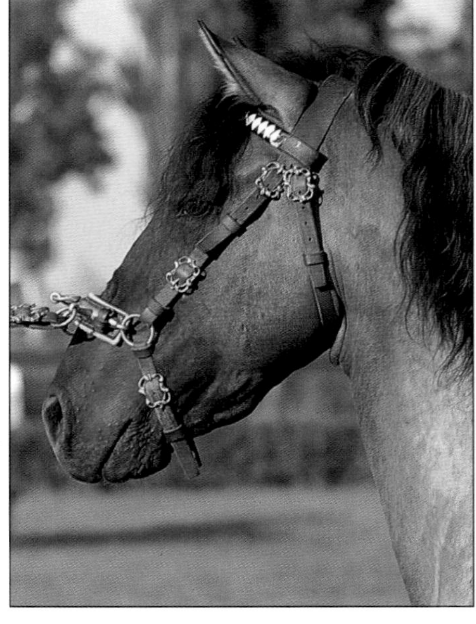

BREED DESCRIPTION

Height Generally 15.1 – 15.3hh. Some horses reach over 16hh.

Colour Often grey or bay, but any true colour is found, including dun and chestnut.

Conformation Long, noble head, typically with a convex profile, finely curved nose and large, generous eyes; powerful, arched neck, deep at the base and set at a slightly wide angle to the shoulders, giving the impression of being fairly upright; powerful shoulders; short-coupled body with deep rib cage, broad, powerful loins, gently sloping croup and rather low-set tail; fine, clean legs with excellent dense bone; abundant silky mane and tail.

As its appearance suggests, the Portuguese Lusitano is a close relative of the Andalusian in neighbouring Spain. Indeed, until quite recent times the horses bred on the Iberian peninsula were regarded as being one and the same. It was not until the early years of the twentieth century that the two countries decided to establish independent stud books.

Since opening their own stud book the Portuguese have made great strides in monitoring and improving their breeding programme. They have been diligent in preserving the Lusitano's greatly admired qualities of strength and courage. These attributes led to the breed being very highly esteemed as a warhorse (the best Iberian horses have always been bred along the long frontier between Portugal and Spain where endless battles were fought).

These same qualities also make the Lusitano an ideal mount for the demanding sport of mounted bullfighting. In Portugal, where it is considered a disgrace for a horse to be injured during a bullfight, the horses are extremely well trained, using their inherent powers of acceleration and manoeuvrability to evade the bull.

As they have proved down the centuries, Lusitano horses are most amenable to training. Intelligent, gentle and affectionate, they work hard and enthusiastically. Possessed of good natural

ABOVE LEFT
This noble head and powerful, arched neck are characteristic of the Lusitano. The breed is also noted for its silky mane and tail.

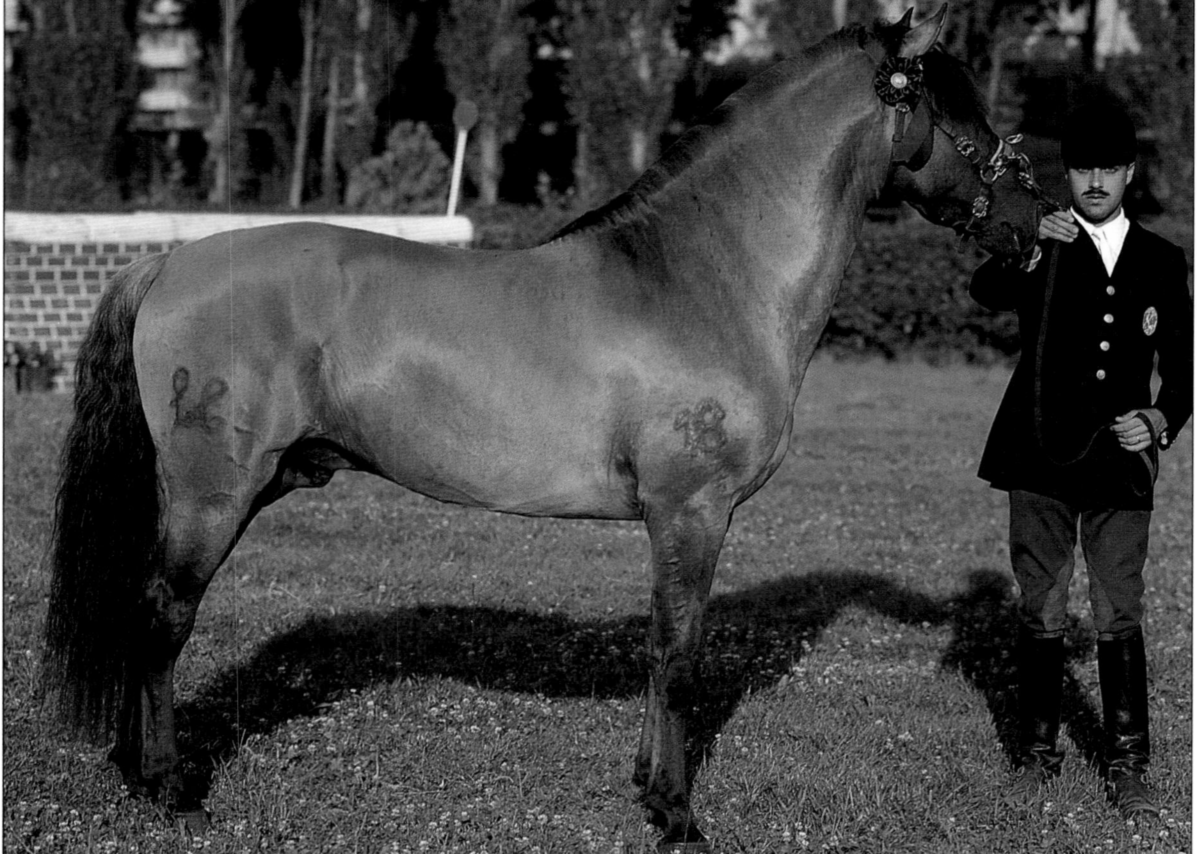

LEFT
The overall outline of the Lusitano is virtually the same as that of its close relative, the Andalusian.

INTERESTING FACTS

The Lusitano horse gives an exceptionally smooth, comfortable ride. Agile and intelligent, it makes the ideal mount for the mounted bullfighter.

balance and with agile, elevated paces, they give a smooth comfortable ride. With their proud bearing and tremendous joie de vivre they have, not surprisingly, always excelled at high school work. However, it is not only in the manège that the breed excels. More and more Lusitanos are proving themselves well suited to modern sports such as show jumping and carriage driving. People who work with them testify to the great understanding which quickly develops between horse and human.

ALTER REAL

The Alter Real is not a distinct breed but an offshoot of the Lusitano. It takes its name from the town of Alter do Chão, in the Portuguese province of Alentejo, the world "real" meaning royal in Portuguese. The royal stud founded at Alter supplied the royal manège in Lisbon with high-school and carriage horses. The stud flourished for many years, producing a fine line of horses which were valued not only in Portugal but all over the Peninsula. However, the stud's progress suffered serious interruption on a number of occasions, notably during the Peninsular War, and the Alter Real horses went into decline. Attempts to resurrect the strain towards the end of the nineteenth century by importing English, Norman and German blood were not successful, nor was a subsequent attempt, using Arab horses. Through the introduction of Andalusian blood at the end of the century, the Alter Real Lusitanos were finally re-established but after the fall of the monarchy in the early twentieth century, many horses were sold or destroyed. The Alter Real line would have died out but for the efforts of the d'Andrade family, who during the early 1940s saved two stallions and a handful of mares and instigated a breeding programme. Today the Alter Stud is state run and again produces horses for high school work. The Alter Real is essentially a Lusitano, although it is always bay, brown or black in colour.

BELOW
The bay colouring of this mare at the Alter Stud is typical of the Alter Real Lusitanos.

BOTTOM
Portugal's horses are renowned for their muscular strength, great impulsion and elevated paces.

Bashkir

The small Bashkir horse comes from the southern foothills of the Ural mountains, taking its name from the region of Bashkirsky where it is kept in herds. It goes equally well in harness and under saddle and for centuries has been used as a pack and general work horse as well as a supplier of meat and milk. Stockily built, with a thick coat, mane and tail, it can survive in the open in temperatures as low as -22° to -40° Fahrenheit (-30° to -40° C). It is able to withstand ferocious blizzard conditions and will dig through snow a metre deep to find food. Furthermore, its tremendously hard feet enable it to work without being shod. The Bashkir is undoubtedly one of the hardiest breeds of horse or pony in the world.

A type of Bashkir also exists in the north-west of the United States, prompting the theory that these horses' ancestors travelled over the former land-bridge between Asia and North America (now the Bering Strait). The horse, however, is generally believed to have become extinct on the North American continent as long ago as the Ice Age and was not reintroduced until Spanish explorers of the modern era "discovered" the land. It is therefore much more likely that the Bashkir was introduced from Russia in fairly recent times.

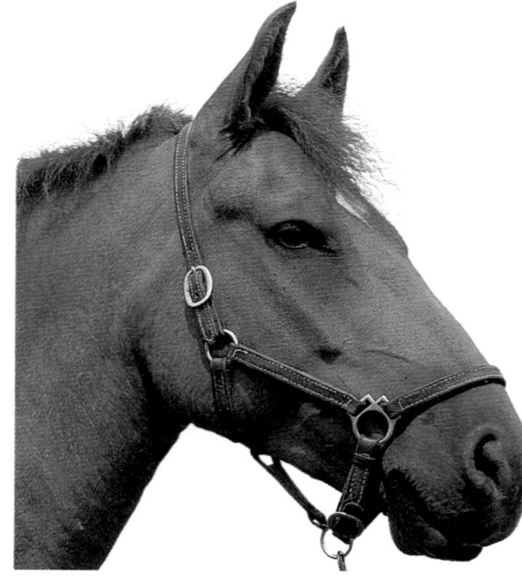

INTERESTING FACTS

Bashkir mares are renowned for their milk yields. During the lactation period of some seven to eight months, a mare will produce upwards of 330 gallons (1,500 litres). In a number of areas of the former USSR horses are still run in herds and their milk is used to produce the fermented liquor known as kumis, which is both drunk by the local herdsmen and bottled on a large scale for consumption elsewhere.

BREED DESCRIPTION

Height 13.3 – 14hh.

Colour Predominantly bay, chestnut and brown.

Conformation Massive head; short, fleshy neck; low withers; wide, deep body with broad, straight back; comparatively short legs with substantial bone; good, hard feet.

ABOVE LEFT
The Bashkir's head is heavily built and set on a short, fleshy neck. The chest is broad.

LEFT
With its stocky build, short strong limbs and exceptionally hard feet, the Bashkir is well equipped for life in a harsh environment – though, as this picture shows, it also thrives in less rigorous surroundings.

Don

Don horses were made famous by the Don Cossacks, who between 1812 and 1814 helped drive Napoleon's invading troops from Russia. The Cossacks' horses were descended from those of the nomadic steppe people and were of mixed blood. Early influences would have included the Nagai from Mongolia, the Karabakh (a type of light riding horse), the Turkmen and the Persian Arab. During the nineteenth century infusions of Orlov and Thoroughbred blood were made and outcrosses were also made to the part-bred Arab horses produced at the Strelets Stud in the Ukraine. All these crosses, used to upgrade the old Cossack strain, ceased at the beginning of this century, since when no more outside blood has been used in the breeding of Don horses.

Like most Russian breeds, the Don was traditionally reared in herds on the vast expanses of the steppes, and accordingly developed into a tough individual, capable of thriving with minimal help from humans. It was ideally suited to its original role as an army remount while nowadays it is used for general riding purposes. Various inherent conformational defects tend to limit the quality of its paces but its strong constitution makes it a suitable mount for endurance riding.

INTERESTING FACTS

The Don Cossacks were famous for their dashing horsemanship. Riding with short stirrups (a style not adopted in western Europe until much later), they would surprise their foes through the sheer rapidity of their movements. The French General Morand described how they "spring from a state of rest to the full gallop, and at that gallop they make a dead halt: their horses second their skill and seem only part of themselves." They operated in swarms, harassing the enemy rather than charging them, and were particularly skilled in picking off stragglers. With their equally agile horses, they were especially useful for reconnaissance and raiding work.

TOP
Don horses are predominantly chestnut. Calm and willing workers, they go equally well in harness and under saddle and have great endurance.

ABOVE
The Don tends to lack good riding horse conformation: straight shoulders and rather upright pasterns are common faults.

BREED DESCRIPTION

Height 15.3 – 16.2hh.

Colour Predominantly chestnut and brown, often with a golden sheen.

Conformation Medium-sized head with wide forehead; average length neck; strong body with broad, straight back and loins and rounded croup; rather sloping hindquarters; straight limbs with well-muscled forearms and second thighs, but a tendency to calf knees (an inward curve below the knee), sickle hocks and upright pasterns; short, thin mane and tail.

Budenny

A breed of relatively recent origin, the Budenny was created by crossing Don and Chernomor mares with Thoroughbred stallions (the Chernomor was the horse used by Cossacks who settled in the Kuban during the eighteenth century and was similar to the Don, though somewhat smaller and lighter in build). The chief purpose was to produce a good army remount, possessed of great endurance. Breeding was centred in the Rostov region, using a process of careful selection. The best mares were bred to the

INTERESTING FACTS

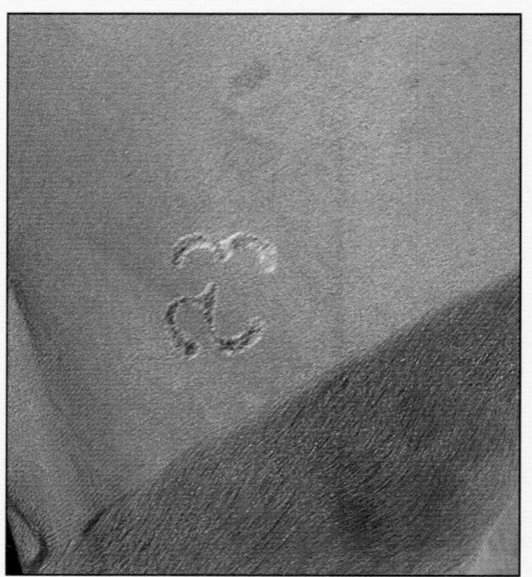

Russian horses are often hot branded as an aid to identification. The chestnut horse on the facing page has also been freeze-branded on the saddle patch. This is a valuable form of individual identity marking which helps to deter horse thieves because the owner can easily be traced.

ABOVE RIGHT
The Thoroughbred influence on the present-day Budenny is particularly noticeable in the refinement of head, with its lean good looks, bright, intelligent eyes and alert ears.

RIGHT
The overall conformation, while showing good depth through the girth and a reasonably well-sloped shoulder, lacks the harmonious proportions of the Thoroughbred, notably in the hind limbs, which are inclined to be a bit weak.

best Anglo-Don stallions. The brood mares were both well fed and, unusually in Russian horse breeding at the time, stabled during the worst of the winter weather, thus ensuring that they produced better, healthier foals than they might otherwise have done if forced to burn up their resources merely on keeping themselves warm. The young stock were tested on the racecourse between two and four years of age.

The robust constitution of the Don horse and the excellent action of the Thoroughbred proved to be a good combination and as a result the Rostov military stud farm was soon turning out an upstanding horse, with a tractable nature, which proved suitable for both riding and light draught work. Named the Budenny, it was officially recognized as a breed in 1949.

As the need for army remounts ceased and interest turned to pleasure riding and sport, more Thoroughbred was added to improve the Budenny. Although the Thoroughbred influence is quite evident in the overall light build, the Budenny has a noticeably heavier body while the legs tend to be a bit light on bone. Today the breed is used as a general purpose riding horse, especially in the sports of show jumping, dressage and steeplechasing.

BREED DESCRIPTION

Height 16hh.

Colour Predominantly chestnut, some bay and brown. The coats of some Budenny horses have a golden sheen (a throwback to the Chernomor and Don horses).

Conformation Well-proportioned head with straight or slightly concave profile; long, straight neck; reasonably well-sloped shoulders with high withers; comparatively heavy body with short, straight back and long croup; fine, straight limbs, though with a tendency to small joints and rather weak hindlegs; usually well-shaped feet.

RIGHT
The predominant Budenny coat colouring is chestnut. Some horses have a striking golden sheen.

Kabardin

Sure-footedness and a well-developed sense of self-preservation are the hallmarks of the Kabardin and little wonder, for its home is the northern Caucasus, where it has for centuries been accustomed to carrying men over the toughest mountain terrain. It traces back to the sixteenth century and is derived from the horses of the steppe tribes who were crossed with Turkmen, Persian and Karabakh horses. Originally the Kabardin was itself fairly small. Raised in herds, which were (and still are) grazed on the high pastures during the summer and in the foothills during the winter, it developed into a typical mountain breed: tough, sturdy and possessing great endurance.

The numbers of Kabardin horses were seriously depleted as a result of the Revolution and it was during the 1920s, when efforts were made to re-establish the breed, that a bigger stamp of horse began to be produced, one suitable as an army remount and for agricultural work. The Malokarachaev and Malkin Studs became the producers of the best modern Kabardin horses, which are used to improve stock in neighbouring areas as well as for general riding and driving purposes.

INTERESTING FACTS

The Kabardin's prowess at carrying a rider safely over mountainous terrain is legendary. It will pick its way unerringly over narrow, rocky mountain tracks with all the assurance of a mountain goat and has an uncanny ability to find its way in the mist or dark. Its typical mountain-horse conformation may not be conducive to speed, but its paces are nevertheless cadenced, light and smooth.

BREED DESCRIPTION

Height 15 – 15.2hh.

Colour Predominantly bay, dark bay and black, usually without distinguishing markings.

Conformation Long head, often with Roman-nosed profile, with sharp, mobile ears; well-muscled, medium-long neck; fairly straight shoulders and low withers; strong body, with short, straight back and short, often concave loins; strong limbs, with generally good joints, good bone and short, strong cannons, although the hindlegs tend to be sickle-shaped; good, strong feet; usually long, full mane and tail.

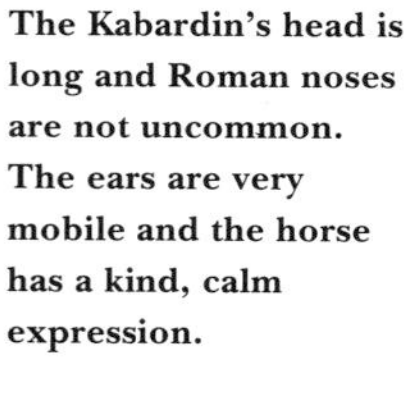

ABOVE
The Kabardin's head is long and Roman noses are not uncommon. The ears are very mobile and the horse has a kind, calm expression.

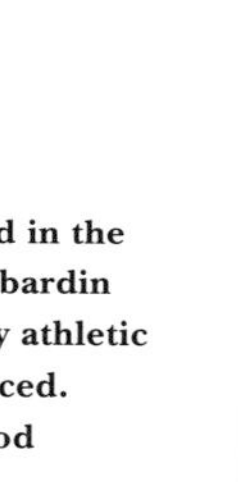

RIGHT
Having evolved in the mountains, Kabardin horses are very athletic and well balanced. They make good jumpers.

RIGHT
Despite rather straight shoulders, Kabardins make good all-round riding horses. They are agile and sure-footed.

Tersk

Like the Kabardin, the Tersk comes from the northern Caucasus, though it is a breed of more recent origin, having been developed from 1921 onwards at the Tersk and Stavropol Studs.

The Tersk is based on Strelets horses, the part-bred Arabs which were formerly bred at the Strelets Stud in the Ukraine. The Strelets was produced by crossing pure-bred Arabs with, among others, high quality Orlovs and Anglo-Arabs (some Thoroughbred blood was also used, though this was not a dominant factor). The result was a horse with a distinctly Arabian look about it but one which was bigger built than the pure-breds.

By the 1920s there were very few Strelets in existence. The few that did remain, including two stallions, were taken to the Tersk Stud in an attempt to increase their numbers. The mares were put to pure-bred Arab stallions; and various cross-bred mares, including Strelets x Kabardin and Arab x Don, were covered by the Strelets stallions. After some thirty years the new type, known as the Tersk, became fixed. It has inherited the general appearance of the Arab, though it stands a little taller, and also its elegant paces. A handsome horse, usually grey in colour, it combines a kind temperament with tremendous energy, attributes which have made it a favourite in circuses and also as a sports horse.

BELOW
Tersk horses are invariably refined and elegant. Their predominantly light grey colouring adds to their attraction.

BOTTOM
The breed shows unmistakable signs of its Arab ancestry though it is usually a little taller than the pure-bred Arab.

BREED DESCRIPTION

Height Stallions 15hh. Mares 14.3hh.

Colour Predominantly light grey or "white" with a silvery sheen.

Conformation Fine head with large, expressive eyes and medium-length, mobile ears; medium-length neck set high on well-sloped shoulders; strong body with deep chest, wide back and muscular loins; fine legs with well-defined tendons; fine mane and tail.

INTERESTING FACTS

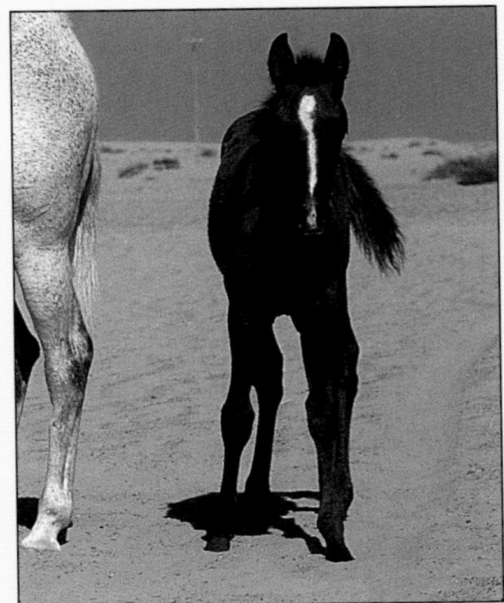

Nowadays most of the world's Tersk horses are produced at the Stavropol Stud. Stavropol is in the northern Caucasus between the Black Sea and the Caspian Sea.

Orlov Trotter

The Orlov shares with the Standardbred and the French Trotter the distinction of being one of the world's foremost breeds of trotting horse. Indeed, before the development of the Standardbred it was probably the most famous of all trotters. Although the Orlov is less well known now outside its native land than the other two members of the triumvirate, it nevertheless plays an important role both in Russian harness racing and in the upgrading of other Russian breeds.

The Orlov takes its name from Count Alexis Orlov (1737–1809), founder of the Orlov Stud near Moscow. The Count imported from Greece a grey Arab stallion called Smetanka. Despite Smetanka's short stud career, he was to prove highly influential in the development of this popular breed. Smetanka's grey son Polkan, bred out of a Danish mare and foaled in 1784, produced Bars I, who became the foundation sire of the Orlov Trotter.

The breed was developed by Count Orlov and his stud manager V.I. Shishkin at the then newly founded Khrenov Stud in the province of Voronezh

LEFT
The head of the Orlov Trotter is inclined to be coarse and rather small.

BREED DESCRIPTION

Height Stallions 16hh. Mares 15.3hh.

Colour Predominantly grey. Bay and black are commonly found. Chestnut is rare.

Conformation Small, often somewhat coarse head; long, often swan-shaped, neck set high on the withers; long, straight back with muscular loins and broad, powerful croup; fine, squarely set legs with a minimum of 8 inches (20cm) of bone below the knee.

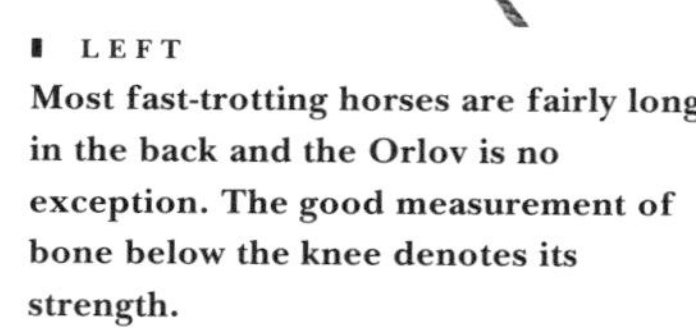

LEFT
Most fast-trotting horses are fairly long in the back and the Orlov is no exception. The good measurement of bone below the knee denotes its strength.

INTERESTING FACTS

Count Alexis Orlov, the breed's founder, was a soldier famous for his courage and audacity. In 1762 he played a part in the assassination of Peter III. The Count's older brother, Grigorei, who distinguished himself during the Seven Years' War, had attracted the attention of Peter's wife, soon to become Catherine II. However, having helped place her on the throne, Grigorei found himself ousted from the Empress's favour by his fellow conspirator, the handsome Prince Potemkin. Alexis is reputed to have knocked out Potemkin's eye – and turned to horse breeding as a diversion from affairs at court!

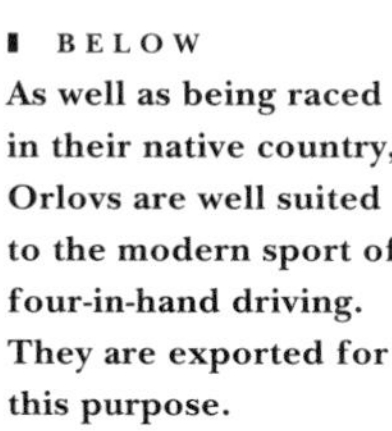

RIGHT
The Russian Trotter is part Orlov, part Standardbred. It is faster on the racetrack than the Orlov.

to which the stock from the Moscow stud was transferred in 1788. Bars I was used to breed from Arab, Dutch and Danish mares as well as half-breds imported from England. Inbreeding back to Bars I was practised extensively. During the early part of the nineteenth century the breed continued to improve thanks to the systematic training and racing of trotters in Russia.

Later, as the Standardbred began to demonstrate its supremacy on the racetrack, the Russians started importing horses from America to cross with the Orlov. The resultant half-breed, subsequently known as the Russian Trotter, proved faster than the Orlov. Imports of Standardbreds ceased at the outbreak of World War I but in recent times the traffic has resumed to maintain the speed of the Russian Trotter.

BELOW
As well as being raced in their native country, Orlovs are well suited to the modern sport of four-in-hand driving. They are exported for this purpose.

BELOW
This horse, hitched to a training vehicle, demonstrates the Orlov's tremendously powerful action.

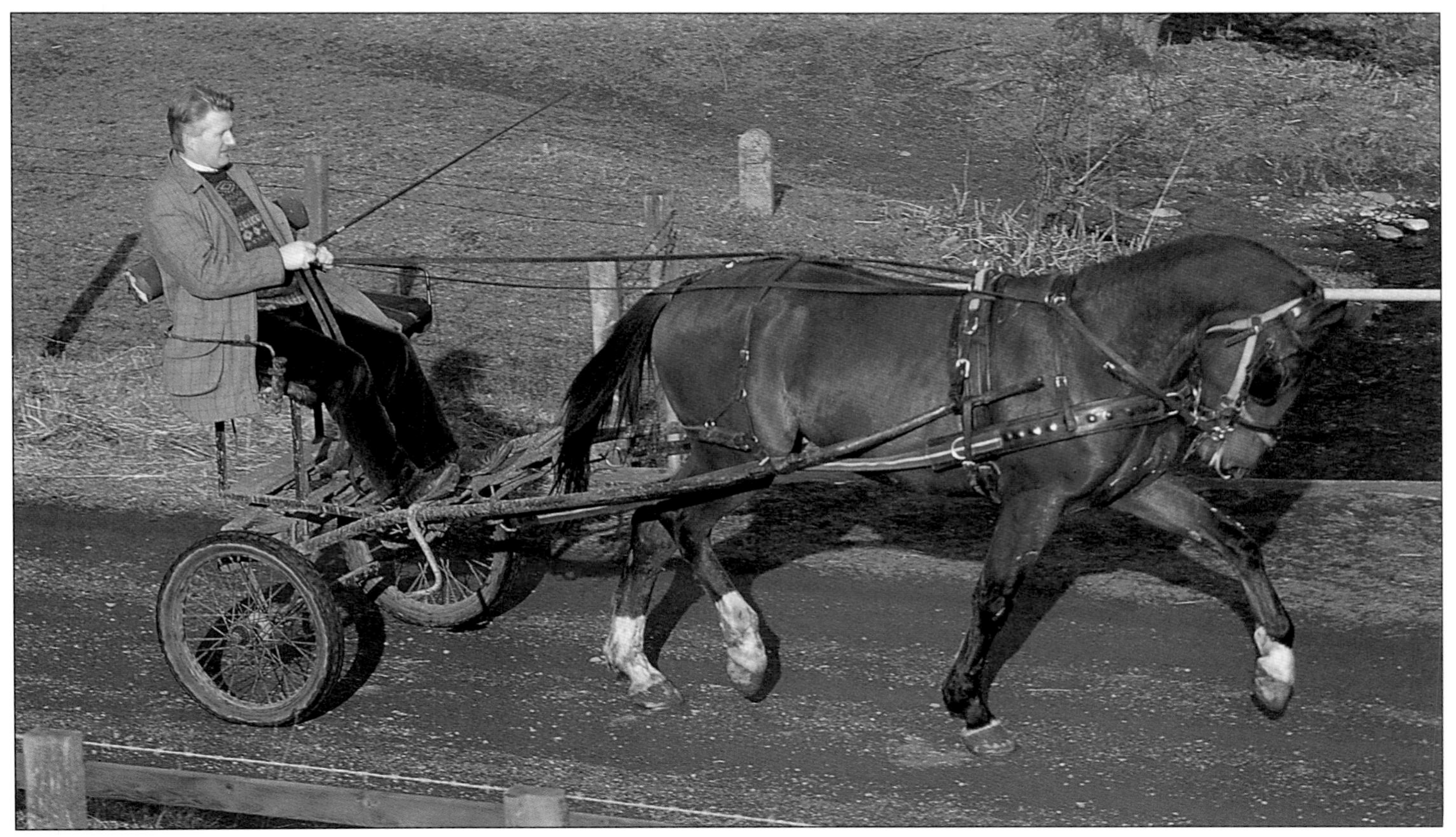

Vladimir Heavy Draught

The Clydesdale played a significant part in the development of the Vladimir, a heavy draught horse created in the provinces of Vladimir and Ivanovo, to the north-east of Moscow. During the early years of this century stallions of various heavy breeds were imported from Britain and France to cross with the local mares of the region in order to produce a good-quality heavy work horse. Among the most influential of the foundation stallions were the Clydesdales Lord James, Border Brand, both imported in 1910, and Glen Albin (1923). Shire stallions were also used, though to a lesser extent, and some Cleveland Bay, Suffolk, Ardennais and

Percheron blood is also said to have been introduced. The experiment met with success, the result being a powerfully built heavy horse, well suited to all types of heavy agricultural and draught work. Named the Vladimir Heavy Draught, it was recognized as a breed in 1946.

Its docile nature makes it easy to handle, while its active paces – no doubt inherited from its Clydesdale forebears – mean that despite its massive build it can be used to pull the famous Russian troikas. Another bonus is its early maturity: the Vladimir is so well developed by the age of three that it can start work and also be used at stud, where the stallions are noted

OPPOSITE ABOVE
The Vladimir Heavy Draught combines great strength with the most docile of natures – note this horse's kindly expression.

OPPOSITE BELOW
Clydesdale blood was used with great success in the development of this breed, which is renowned for its powerful build and active paces.

BREED DESCRIPTION

Height Stallions 16.1hh. Mares 15.3hh.

Colour Predominantly bay, also black and chestnut with white markings on head and legs.

Conformation Large, long head with convex profile; long, muscular neck; pronounced withers; wide chest, rather long, broad back and long, broad, sloping croup; long limbs; some horses carry feather.

for their good fertility rate. Minus points include, in some horses, a rather long back, which is not conducive to strength, and a flat-sided rib cage (the reverse of "well sprung" or rounded ribs, which enable the lungs to work to maximum efficiency). The Vladimir is the largest of the Russian heavy breeds. Stallions have a girth of some 6 feet 9 inches (207cm) and weigh in the region of 1,688lb (758kg). Mares are only a little smaller, with a girth of 6 feet 5 inches (196cm) and a weight of 1,507lb (685kg).

INTERESTING FACTS

Other heavy horses in the former USSR include the Russian Heavy Draught, founded a century or so ago, and based largely on the Ardennais, and the Soviet Heavy Draught, which was founded by crossing Belgian Heavy Draught stallions with local harness-type mares. Both were registered as breeds in 1952. The Russian Heavy Draught is quick to mature and remarkably long lived. It was formerly known as the "Russian Ardennes".

LATVIAN

The Latvian is a powerfully built harness horse renowned for its weight-pulling ability. It is of recent origin, dating only from the early 1920s when local mares were crossed with German, English and French horses to produce an all-round worker possessed of strength, stamina and good, active paces. There are two distinct types of Latvian horse: a heavy harness type which is based largely on Oldenburg, Norfolk Roadster and Anglo-Norman outcrosses and a lighter version which has a preponderance of Hanoverian blood.

Latvian horses have good overall conformation and great freedom of movement. Stallions stand up to 16.2hh, mares up to 16hh. Black is the predominant colour of the heavier type, while most of the lighter weight horses are chestnut.

The Latvian harness horse was recognized as a breed in 1952 and although some outcrosses to Oldenburg and Hanoverian horses have been made since, these have been on a fairly limited scale. The breed is especially noted for its placid temperament which, together with its strength and energy, make it a popular working animal.

North Swedish

Forestry is the chief area of employment for the North Swedish horse, a small, compact, agile draught horse ideally suited to moving timber in confined spaces, over difficult terrain and often in inclement weather conditions.

The breed is descended from the ancient native work horse of Sweden which was influenced by the Døle horses from neighbouring Norway. At some time during the nineteenth century, outcrosses were made to horses of lighter build from outside Scandinavia but towards the end of the century there was a move to produce a heavier stamp of horse, more suited to pulling the heavier types of machinery which were then becoming available. Consequently stallions from larger breeds, such as the Clydesdale, were imported.

BREED DESCRIPTION

Height Stallions around 15.2hh. Mares around 15hh.

Colour Any solid colour.

Conformation Fairly large head with longish ears; short, crested neck; strong, sloping shoulders; rather long, but deep, strong back; rounded hindquarters with sloping croup; short, strong limbs with good bone; the mane and tail are usually very abundant.

The possibility of the old Swedish horse dying out altogether as a result of these crosses prompted interested parties to form an association to save it, the aim being to breed from the old-type stock still found in the remoter parts of the north of the country, using Døle stallions. Government support during the early years of the twentieth century aided this aim and during the 1920s performance testing was introduced as a means of selection, something which is still used today. Horses are tested for their draught aptitude as well as draught efficiency. The former test involves pulling a sled laden with logs, the judges awarding points according to the horse's performance and its condition after the work. For the efficiency test the horse is hitched to a wagon and its actual pulling power is measured by a dynamometer.

Lumbering is an area where heavy horses can prove more efficient and more cost effective than mechanized transport, and the North Swedish Horse continues to thrive in its traditional environment.

LEFT
Small and compact, the North Swedish horse is particularly strong through the neck and shoulders. Its short limbs have plenty of bone.

INTERESTING FACTS

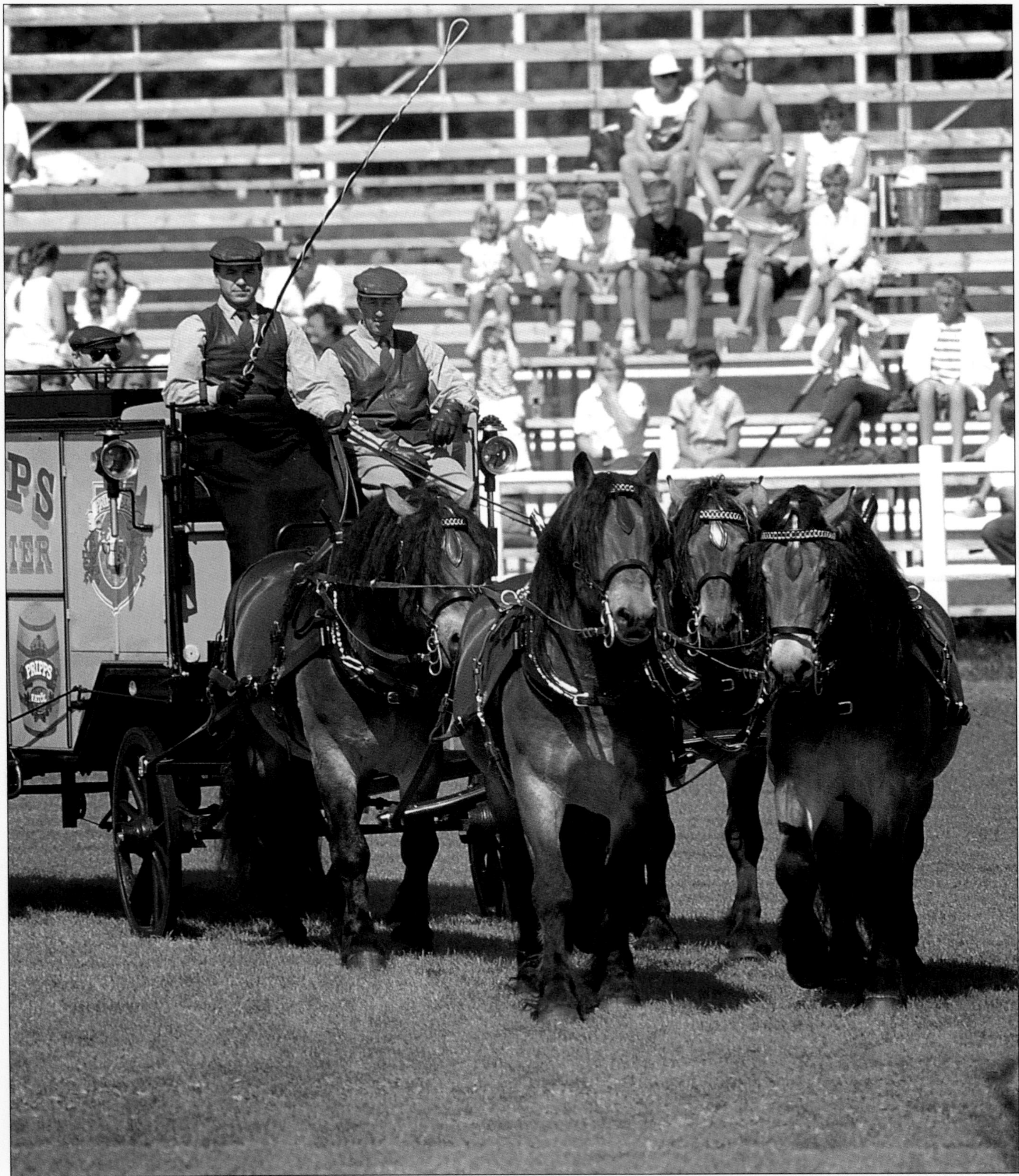

North Swedish horses make good all-round draught animals. They are, however, most often associated with agricultural work and, more especially, forestry. They begin work as three-year-olds and within a couple of years are sufficiently mature to be capable of working an eight-hour day. Stallions weigh anything from 1,440 to 1,655lb (650–750kg) and mares 1,200 to 1,545lb (550–700kg).

Swedish Warmblood

LEFT
This handsome head is typical of the Swedish Warmblood, which is noted for its intelligence and pleasant disposition.

BOTTOM
Although overall conformation varies, most examples of the breed have a long, elegant neck and well-proportioned limbs and hindquarters.

Sweden has been renowned for its fine riding and carriage horses for many centuries, so it is not surprising that the Swedish Warmblood should have had such an impact on present-day competitive sports, particularly top-level dressage.

The Skåne province of what is now southern Sweden (the area had previously been under Danish rule) was noted for its horse breeding as long ago as the twelfth century, when Archbishop Absalon raised remounts there for his cavalry. Then in the mid-seventeenth century, Charles X of Sweden founded the Royal Stud at Flyinge, to the north-east of Malmo, to supply horses for the royal stables and the army. Down the years horses from a wide variety of breeds were used at the stud to produce a quality cavalry horse. They included Holsteins, Hanoverians, East Prussians, Frederiksborgs, Arabs, Thoroughbreds and Oldenburgs, with the East Prussian and Hanoverian blood being particularly influential.

Officers of the Swedish cavalry mounted on Swedish horses enjoyed tremendous success in all three equestrian disciplines (dressage, show jumping and three-day eventing) at Olympic level both before and after World War I. The Swiss army bought many Swedish horses after World War II, a number of whom found fame in the dressage world. When mechanization signalled the demise of the cavalry horse it was a natural progression for the Swedes to channel their horse-breeding efforts towards leisure and

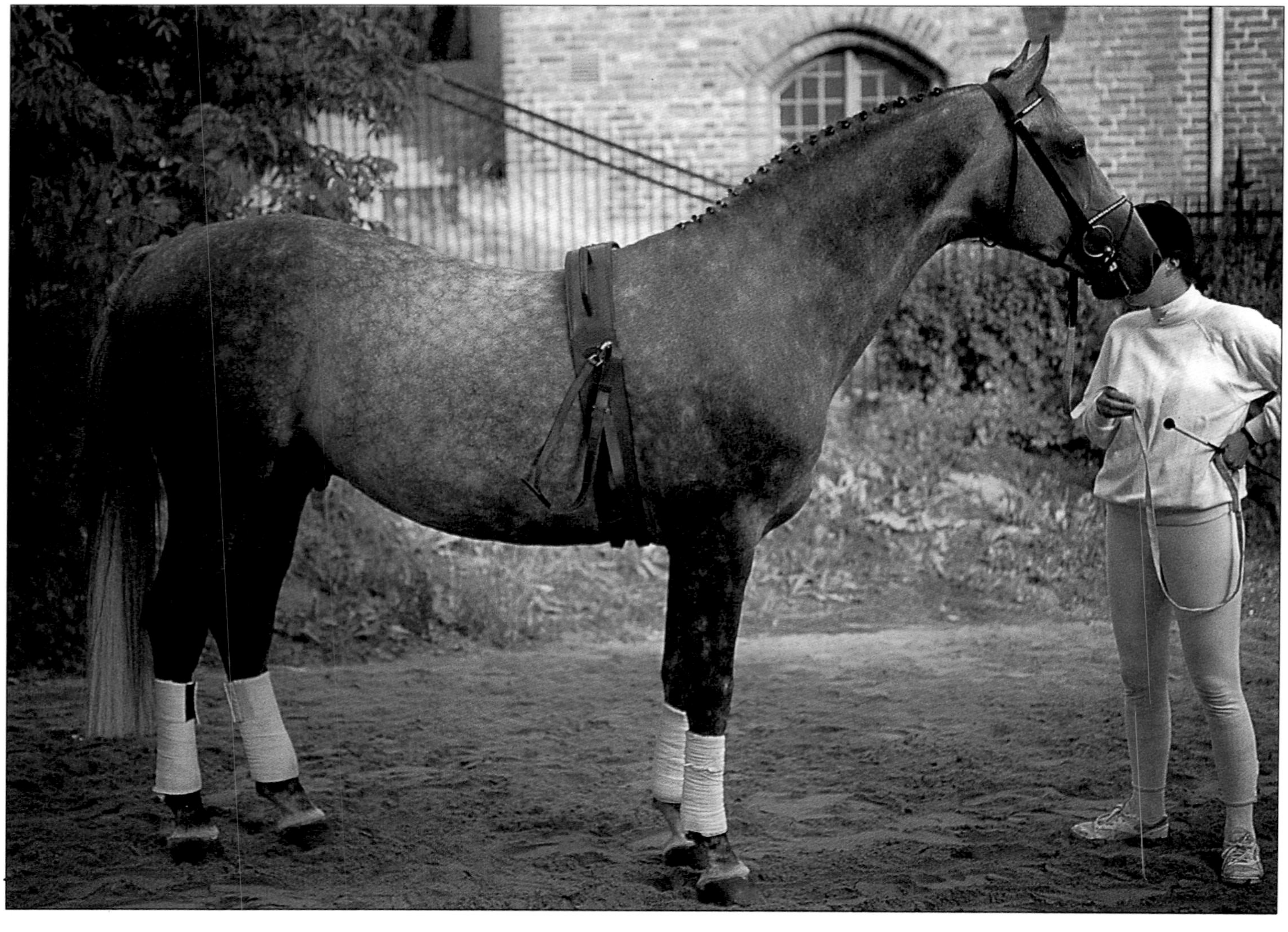

RIGHT
Warmblood mares with their foals put on a fine show to an appreciative crowd during the 1990 World Equestrian Games in Stockholm.

BOTTOM LEFT
Thanks to infusions of outside blood, including Thoroughbred, the breed has become a good all-round sports horse.

BOTTOM RIGHT
Swedish Warmbloods have traditionally excelled at the demanding discipline of Grand Prix dressage.

BREED DESCRIPTION

Height 15 – 17hh.

Colour Any solid colour.

Conformation Variable, but usually a handsome head, with wide forehead and kind, intelligent eyes; long neck; shoulders sometimes tend to be rather straight, depending on the bloodline; well-proportioned body, hindquarters and limbs.

INTERESTING FACTS

Swedish-bred dressage horses which have found fame at the Olympic Games include Piaff, winner of the individual gold medal in Munich in 1972, when ridden by the West German, Liselott Linsenhoff. Piaff's sire was Gaspari, who competed for Sweden in the 1960 Games in Rome, where another Swedish horse, Wald, won the individual silver medal in the hands of the Swiss rider, Gustav Fischer. In Tokyo in 1964 Fischer's compatriot, Henri Chammartin, was the individual gold medallist on yet another Swedish horse, Woermann. Also Swedish bred was Gauguin de Lully, winner of the individual bronze medal at the Seoul Games in 1988, again competing for Switzerland.

competition. There was no doubting the Swedish Warmblood's prowess as a dressage horse and in recent times top jumping blood has been introduced from France, Germany and Holland. Carefully selected Thoroughbred stallions have also been used on warmblood mares.

To maintain the excellence of the breed, in terms of both conformation and temperament, Swedish Warmblood stallions are graded and must pass a performance test, veterinary examination and assessment of type, conformation and action. There is also a system of progeny testing, the results of which are available to mare owners seeking a suitable stallion.

Akhal-Teke

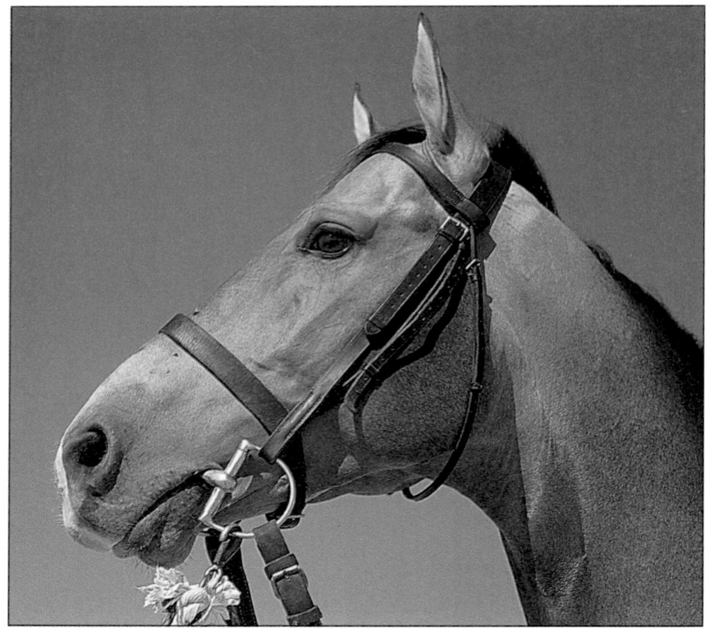

LEFT
The Akhal-Teke's head is always very fine, with large expressive eyes and beautifully shaped ears.

One of the most striking looking horses anywhere in the world, the Akhal-Teke, or Turkmen, has been bred for some 3,000 years in the desert oases of Turkmenistan, a region to the north of Iran and to the east of the Caspian Sea. Although the Turkmen people probably introduced a certain amount of Arabian and Persian blood at some stage, its isolated homeland has kept the Akhal-Teke freer from outside influences than many riding

BELOW
The luminous sheen on the coat of this horse is typical of the breed, as is the lean overall appearance.

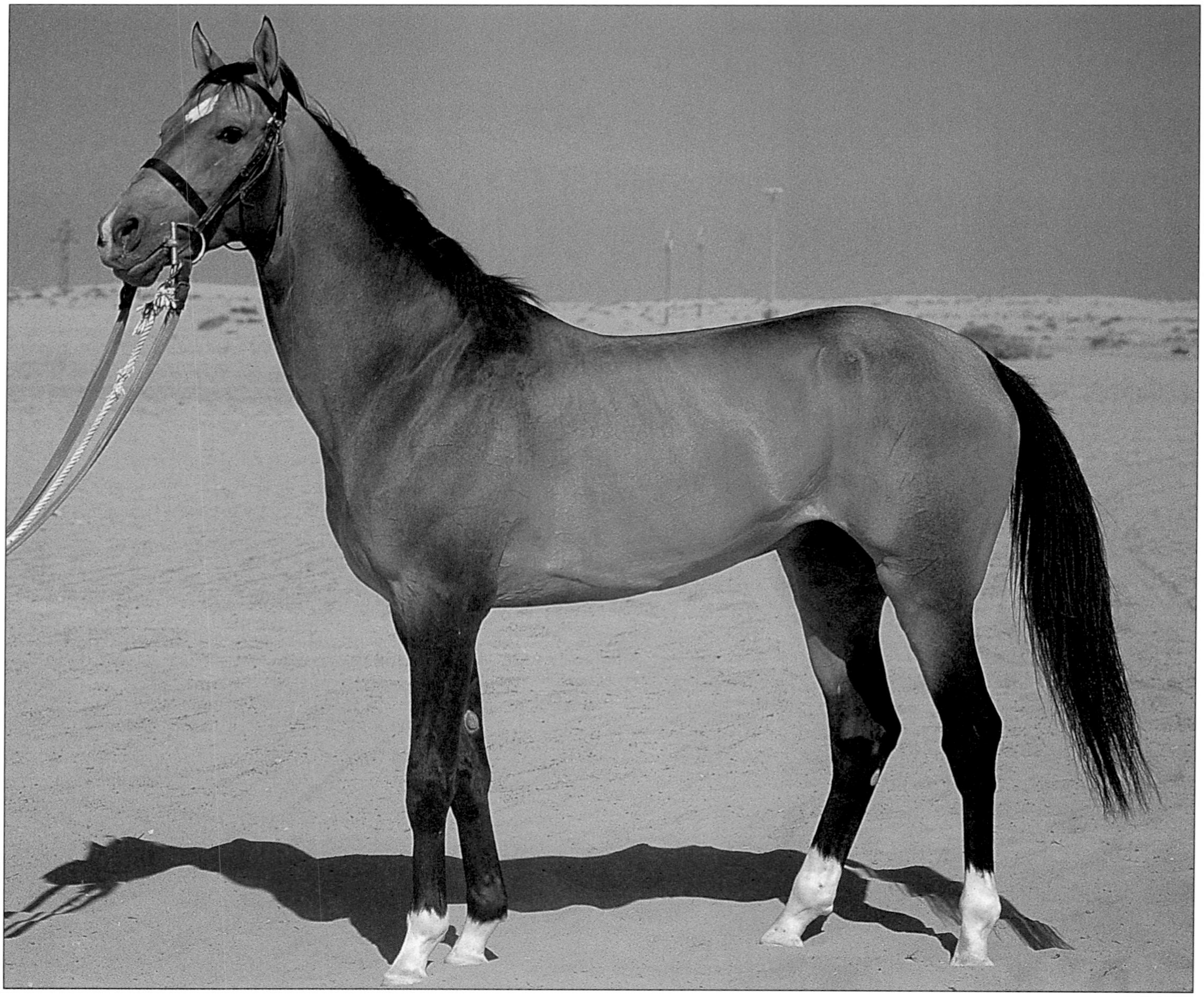

RIGHT
Akhal-Tekes make good all-round riding horses, their legendary stamina making them excellent mounts for competitive endurance riding.

BOTTOM RIGHT
Despite being raised for centuries in desert conditions, the breed adapts perfectly well to life in the much less rigorous climate of western Europe.

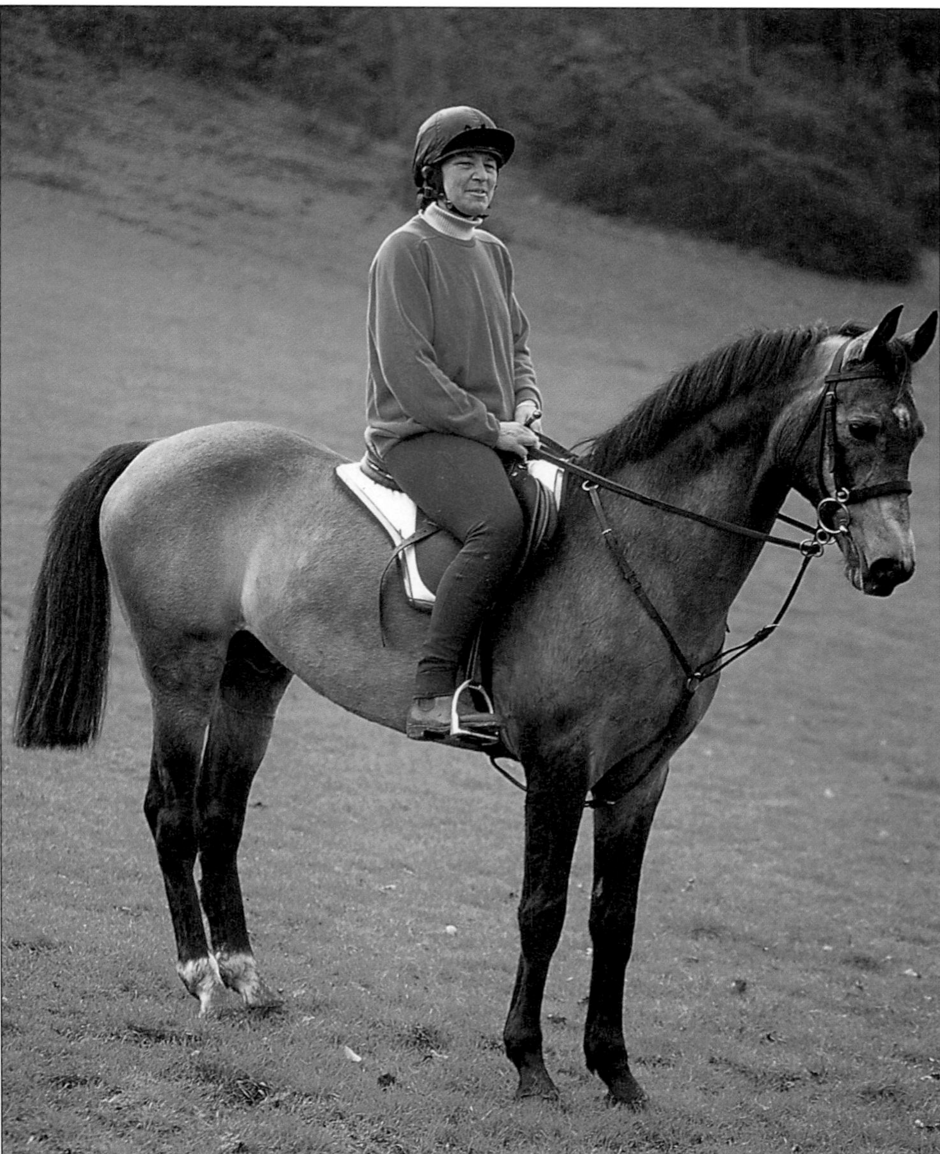

BREED DESCRIPTION

Height 15.1 – 15.2hh.

Colour Bay and chestnut, often with a remarkable golden sheen; also grey and black.

Conformation Very fine head with wide nostrils, large, expressive eyes and long, beautifully shaped ears; long, straight and often thin neck set high on the shoulders; sloping shoulder with high withers; long, often weak back, shallow rib cage and a tendency to poor loins, lacking in muscle; narrow hindquarters but with muscular croup and long, muscular thighs; strong, straight forelegs with long forearm, and long hindlegs which tend to be sickle shaped with cow hocks; small but hard feet; sparse mane and tail; thin skin.

horses. Raised to withstand the extreme conditions of the desert – fiercely hot days alternating with cold nights – the Akhal-Teke developed into a tough, lean horse, whose undoubted conformational defects are offset by its fast paces, stamina and tremendous hardiness. This hardiness owes much to the rigorous lifestyle imposed upon it over many centuries. The traditional Turkmen method of horse management did not included stabling. The animals were wrapped in felt, with only their heads uncovered, and kept on tethers. Their diet included meagre amounts of dry lucerne, barley and some mutton fat. Foals were weaned very young and the horses raced as yearlings. Nowadays Akhal-Tekes are kept along more modern lines, out at grass by day and stabled by night. They are still raced, though not until they are two- or three-year-olds, as is the custom in the Thoroughbred racing world.

Spirited and athletic, they are used for general riding purposes, including show jumping and dressage, and at stud in the development of other riding horse breeds. Their phenomenal stamina also makes them the ideal mount for endurance rides, since they are capable of covering great distances, in extremes of temperature, on the most modest of rations. One of the most celebrated of all endurance rides took place in 1935, when Akhal-Teke horses travelled from Ashkabad to Moscow (their journey included crossing the Karakum desert), completing a distance of 2,580 miles (4,152km) in 84 days.

INTERESTING FACTS

The Akhal-Teke used to be renowned for its devotion to its rider – which is not surprising if one tale told about the Turkmen training techniques is true. According to this story, a young horse would be kept alone in a pit or enclosure. Stones would be thrown at it by everyone but the owner. Only he would treat it kindly and offer it food. Thus the horse learnt to trust only one man and to fear all others. This could account for the breed's sometimes difficult temperament.

Morgan

LEFT
The head of the Morgan is expressive, with large, prominent eyes and shapely ears set rather wide apart. Mares may have slightly longer ears than stallions.

The American Morgan horse is highly unusual in that it can be traced back to just one stallion, the extraordinary little Justin Morgan, who stood a mere 14hh but who excelled in weight-pulling contests and races, both under saddle and in harness.

Justin Morgan was probably foaled in 1789 and was originally named Figure, later taking the name of his first recorded owner, Thomas Justin Morgan, who came from farming stock in Vermont but who was also a music teacher and church composer. How Justin Morgan was bred has never been satisfactorily resolved because of the lack of recorded evidence. Plausible claims have been made for Thoroughbred, Arab, Welsh Cob and Dutch ancestry. What is beyond dispute is that despite his small stature – he weighed no more than 850lb (386kg) – Justin Morgan proved himself a remarkably strong work horse, and he undoubtedly worked extremely hard for a succession of owners. He was used for ploughing, as a harness horse and in woodland clearance and was never beaten in log-hauling matches against rivals weighing nearly half as much again.

He was, moreover, a wonderfully prepotent sire, passing on to his progeny all his own remarkable attributes of strength, endurance, speed and, not least, his gentle temperament. Three of his sons were to have a particular influence on the development of the breed of which he was the founder: Sherman Morgan, foaled around 1808, Woodbury Morgan (1816) and Bulrush Morgan (1812). The Sherman Morgan line was noted for its excellent harness horses and had an important influence on the foundation of other breeds in the US: the Quarter Horse, Saddlebred, Standardbred and Tennessee Walker. The Woodbury Morgans were much in demand as saddle and parade

LEFT
The top line of the Morgan is distinctive. The gentle curve from the poll to the back gives the impression of the neck sitting on top of the withers rather than in front of them.

BREED DESCRIPTION

Height 14.1 – 15.2hh with some individuals over or under.

Colour Bay, chestnut, brown or black. No white markings permitted above the knee or hock, except on the face.

Conformation Expressive head, with straight or slightly dished profile, broad forehead, large eyes and short, alert ears; slightly arched neck; sloping shoulders and well-defined withers; compact, deep body, with short back, well-sprung ribs, broad loins and deep flank; well-muscled hindquarters with high-set tail; straight, sound legs, with short cannons, flat bone and sufficiently long, sloping pasterns to provide light, springy step; good, sound feet with dense horn; full, soft mane and tail.

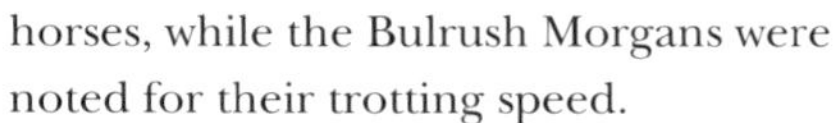

horses, while the Bulrush Morgans were noted for their trotting speed.

Like so many other breeds, the Morgan horse went into decline with the coming of motorized transport, but thanks to the efforts of enthusiastic members of the Morgan Horse Club, founded in 1909, the breed survived. Today there is a thriving population of Morgan horses in the United States plus recognized breed clubs in Canada, Britain, Australia, Spain, New Zealand, Germany, Italy and Sweden. The Morgan is kept as a show horse and is also to be seen competing in a variety of spheres, such as cutting horse, stock horse and reining horse classes, hunter-jumper division, dressage and roadster and carriage driving competitions.

INTERESTING FACTS

A Morgan horse named Comanche, the mount of Captain Myles Keogh, was the only non-Indian survivor of the Battle of the Little Big Horn in 1876. He recovered from his many wounds and lived to the ripe old age of 29.

ABOVE
The versatile Morgan horse is equally at home in harness and under saddle.

LEFT
Morgan horses are well up to carrying the weight of adult riders. The action is straight and springy.

Quarter Horse

The Quarter Horse, as its name implies, excels at racing over a short distance – a quarter of a mile to be precise. It traces back to the horses taken to America by the Spanish Conquistadores. During the seventeenth and eighteenth centuries the waves of English settlers in the eastern states used the local Spanish-based stock to cross with their own, imported horses to produce a good, all-round work horse, suitable for every type of ridden work, for tilling the land and for work in harness. Tough and stocky, these horses became the settlers' "right-hand men". Spreading westward, they became indispensable during the great days of cattle herding when the chief requirement was for a totally dependable mount, one which was athletic and fearless working among cattle. In time these horses developed an innate "cow sense" and could anticipate the movements of a steer, stopping and turning at breakneck speed.

It was the Englishman's growing enthusiasm for racing which led to these all-purpose horses being raced in impromptu contests: on the road, in a clearing, anywhere where a couple of

ABOVE LEFT
The head of the Quarter Horse is short and wide with large, intelligent eyes, alert ears and a small muzzle.

ABOVE RIGHT
The chest is broad and deep, and the forelegs wide set. The muscling on the insides of the forearms gives the appearance of a well-defined inverted V.

RIGHT
The breed is noted for its strong, close-coupled back and deep girth. Well-muscled hindquarters and strong, low-set hocks give the horse its tremendous acceleration.

BREED DESCRIPTION

Height 14.3 – 16hh for mature stallions and mares.

Colour Any solid colour.

Conformation Short, wide head, with small muzzle, large, wide-set, intelligent eyes and medium-length, alert ears; fairly long, flexible neck; sloping shoulders and well-defined withers; compact body with broad chest, deep girth, short back, well-sprung ribs and powerful loins; broad, deep, heavy and well-muscled hindquarters with long, gently sloped croup; good limbs, with short cannons, broad, flat, low-set hocks, muscular thighs and gaskins and medium-length pasterns; oblong feet with deep, open heels.

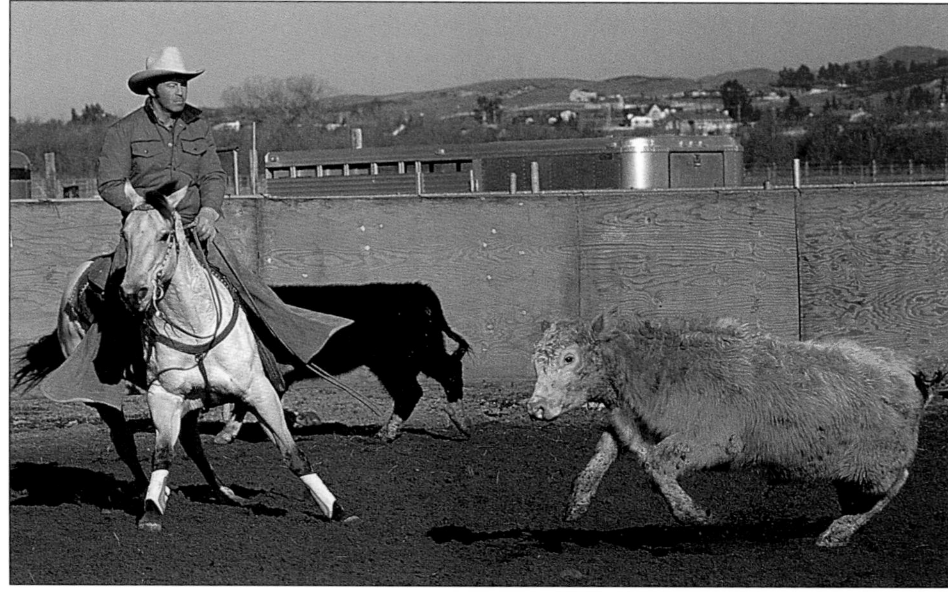

horses could be galloped upsides for a few hundred yards. The Quarter Horse, as it was dubbed, developed immensely powerful hindquarters, which could propel it into a flat-out gallop virtually from a standing start, and the speed to sprint over short distances. Eventually, however, as Thoroughbred racing became established, interest in Quarter Horse racing dwindled. Still later, when mechanization brought about a lessening of the horse's importance in ranching, the Quarter Horse, in common with riding horses all over the world, became a leisure riding horse.

Today the Quarter Horse enjoys great popularity in Western-style competitions such as barrel racing, in rodeos and, once again, in racing over short distances. Thanks to a revival of interest in the latter sport, Quarter Horses now compete on proper tracks for big purses.

INTERESTING FACTS

The American Quarter Horse Association was formed in 1940. Its registry is now the largest of any breed in the world, with more than two million horses listed.

ABOVE
Quarter Horses have an innate "cow sense" and are able to anticipate the movements of a steer.

BELOW LEFT
The Quarter Horse makes an ideal mount for traditional Western sports.

BELOW RIGHT
The breed is well known for its pleasant disposition and gentleness and as a result is used in a wide variety of activities.

Saddlebred

Formerly known as the Kentucky Saddler, the elegant Saddlebred was developed by the early nineteenth-century settlers in the southern states of North America. To meet their requirements for a quality utility horse, the plantation owners interbred horses of various kinds, including the Narragansett Pacer (a speedy strain of pacing horse from Rhode Island) and the Thoroughbred. The end result was a good-looking animal who gave an exceptionally comfortable ride – essential for long hours spent in the saddle on crop-inspection tours – but was equally well suited to pulling a carriage. In 1891 a group of leading breeders established the American Saddle Horse Breeders' Association and a Saddle Horse Registry was set up.

Blessed with the most amiable disposition, intelligence, speed and natural balance, the Saddlebred could (and still can) be used for all manner of different purposes, including working with cattle. Not surprisingly it has made the transition from work horse to pleasure

BREED DESCRIPTION

Height 15 – 17hh; average about 15.3hh.

Colour Usually chestnut, bay, brown, black or grey; also palomino, spotted and occasionally roan.

Conformation Well-shaped head with large eyes set well apart, small, alert ears and wide nostrils; long, arched neck; sloping shoulders with sharp withers; short, strong back; well-muscled hindquarters with level croup and high-set tail; straight, strong limbs with long, sloping pasterns; good, sound hooves, open at the heels.

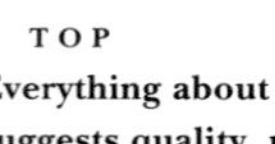

TOP
Everything about the Saddlebred's head suggests quality, refinement and intelligence. The neck is always long and elegantly arched.

LEFT
The Saddlebred's top line is distinctive: the croup is long and level, the back short and the well-defined withers higher than in most other light breeds.

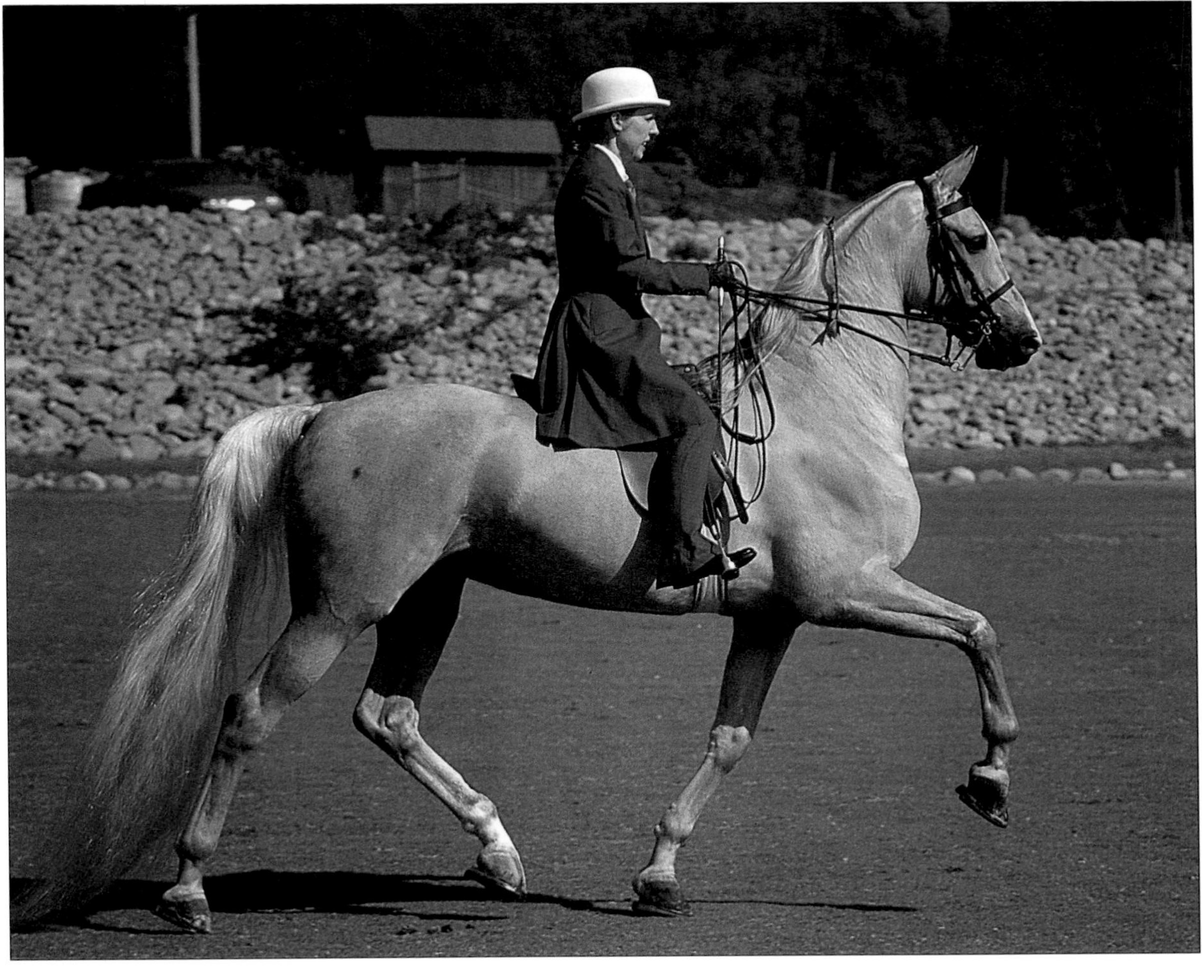

LEFT
Long, well-sloped pasterns contribute to the comfortable paces for which the breed is famous.

BELOW
As well as being popular riding horses, Saddlebreds go equally well in harness. The peculiar tail carriage is not natural, being achieved through an operation and maintained by keeping the tail in a device known as a tail set when the horse is stabled.

horse with no difficulty whatsoever and can be seen today competing in show classes under saddle and in harness.

In the show ring, ridden Saddlebreds are classified either as three-gaited or five-gaited. The three-gaited horses are shown at walk, trot and canter. The walk is springy, the trot has high action and the canter is slow, smooth and rhythmic. The five-gaited horses show these three paces plus two others: the slow gait and the rack. The slow gait is a high-stepping, four-beat gait executed in a slow, restrained manner. The rack is a fast, flashy, four-beat gait in which each foot strikes the ground at equal intervals and which is free from any lateral movement or pacing. The practice of growing the feet unnaturally long (to enhance the action), and operating on the tail to make it unnaturally high set, developed for the show ring.

Outside the artificial confines of the show ring, in its handsome natural state, the Saddlebred makes an excellent all-round riding horse – easy to train, fast, possessing great stamina and having a good jump, too.

INTERESTING FACTS

In their natural state the Saddlebred's strong hooves are well formed. For showing purposes they are grown to an unnatural length and shod with heavy shoes.

Standardbred

The American Standardbred is to harness racing what the English Thoroughbred is to flat racing and steeplechasing. During the past century or more, every country where harness racing flourishes has imported Standardbred horses to upgrade its own trotters and pacers.

BREED DESCRIPTION

Height 14 – 16hh.

Colour All solid colours, predominantly bay, brown, black and chestnut.

Conformation The Standardbred is a powerfully built horse, of rather less quality and refinement than the Thoroughbred and somewhat longer in the body and shorter in the leg. The shoulders are long and sloping and the croup invariably high.

OPPOSITE PAGE
The gaits are so inherent that Standardbreds often show a marked preference for the trot (shown here) or the pace over the gallop, even when they are at liberty.

Strangely enough the foundation sire of the Standardbred was a horse who only ever raced at the gallop: the English Thoroughbred, Messenger. A grey tracing back to the Darley Arabian, Messenger was foaled in 1780 and raced on the flat for three seasons, winning eight of his fourteen starts. Exported to Philadelphia in May 1788, he stood at stud in America for twenty years, covering mainly Thoroughbred mares to start with then, after racing was suppressed in New York, all types of non-Thoroughbreds. Some of his descendants became fine flat

ABOVE
The head of the Standardbred is not exactly refined but the overall aspect is workmanlike and the expression sensible.

LEFT
In comparison with that other great racehorse, the Thoroughbred, the breed is rather long in the back and short in the leg. The shoulders are invariably long and well sloped, giving the horse the necessary freedom of movement.

INTERESTING FACTS

One of the greatest Standardbred trotters of all time, and the horse who did much to revive waning interest in harness racing in the 1930s, was the flying grey, Greyhound, who in 1938 trotted the mile in 1:55.25, a record that stood for 31 years. The mobile starting gate, introduced in 1946, eliminated time-wasting starts and together with greatly improved racing surfaces has contributed to the recording of increasingly faster times by both trotters and pacers.

racehorses but it was his ability to throw good trotting stock (not so much his immediate progeny as their descendants) that earned him lasting fame. His great grandson, Hambletonian, became a prolific sire of trotters and Hambletonian's four sons, George Wilkes, Dictator, Happy Medium and Electioneer, founded the sire lines responsible for virtually all harness racehorses in the USA today. Hambletonian was out of the Charles Kent Mare, who was inbred to Messenger, and descended, through her sire, Bellfounder, from the famous Norfolk Trotter, Old Shales.

In addition to the dominant Messenger line, two other important influences on the early development of the Standardbred were the Clays (descendants of a Barb stallion imported from Tripoli in 1820) and the Morgan horse. Neither produced important families within the breed but both are believed to have helped establish its characteristic gait.

The first register of trotters was published in 1871 and the term "Standardbred" was introduced eight years later when a set of qualifications was drawn up for the admission of horses into the register. The original "standard", from which the breed takes its name, was judged to be the ability of a horse to cover a mile (1.6km) in 2 minutes 30 seconds (as trotters and pacers improved, this time had to be reduced). Standardbreds race either at the pace (a lateral gait) or the trot (a diagonal pace). Up until the last couple of decades of the nineteenth century, trotters were more popular than the marginally faster pacers, but this is not so today.

ABOVE
Although the pace is one of the breed's natural gaits it is usual for pacing racehorses to wear hobbles to encourage them to maintain the lateral movement.

LEFT
Racing harness includes many items not generally seen in other horse sports. The shadow rolls on this horse's bridle are designed to prevent him from seeing and taking fright at shadows or "foreign objects" on the ground.

Missouri Fox Trotter

Although a stud book for the Missouri Fox Trotting Horse was not opened until 1948, the breed began to evolve in the early part of the nineteenth century. Settlers travelling westwards across the Mississippi river from Kentucky, Tennessee and Virginia took with them a variety of horses, including Thoroughbreds, eastern-bred stock and Morgans, and then interbred them to produce a horse suited to the conditions of their new home in the Ozark Hills region of Missouri.

The chief requirement, especially of doctors, sheriffs, stock raisers and the like, was for a horse that could be ridden for long periods, often over rough terrain, with a minimum of fatigue either to horse or rider. The answer was found in the gait known as the fox trot, in which the horse walks with its forelegs but trots behind. The Fox Trotter does not put its hindfeet down with the jarring action characteristic of the

BREED DESCRIPTION

Height 14 – 16hh.

Colour Any. Most commonly sorrel and chestnut sorrel with white markings.

Conformation Neat, clean, intelligent head with pointed, well-shaped ears, large, bright eyes and a tapered muzzle; graceful neck, in proportion to length of body; well-sloped, muscular shoulders; deep, strong body with deep, full chest and short, strong back; strong, muscular limbs; strong, well-made feet.

ABOVE
This neat, intelligent looking head, with its bright eyes and well-shaped ears, is typical of the Missouri Fox Trotter.

RIGHT
The body is deep, the back short and the overall impression one of compactness. Well-sloped shoulders ensure good riding action.

LEFT
The legendary comfort experienced when riding a Fox Trotter comes from the unusual action of the hindfeet, which slide forward under the horse as he puts them down, rather than hitting the ground with a jarring action.

INTERESTING FACTS

In the fox trot the horse's hindfeet disfigure the tracks of the forefeet, that is the hindfeet touch the front tracks and slide forward. The horse should travel in a collected manner, with animation, rhythm and style. The horse's tail is slightly elevated and moves in a bobbing rhythm with the gait. The flat-foot walk should also be performed with style and animation. It is an animated four-beat gait in which the horse overstrides its front track with the hindfeet. The typical canter of the Fox Trotter is collected, with the head and tail slightly elevated.

normal trot, but slides them along under him. The result is a smooth, comfortable gait at which the horse can travel for extended periods without tiring. The ability to walk in front and trot behind is inherited but it can also be enhanced with training. The overall quality of the Fox Trotter was improved over the years through infusions of Saddlebred and Tennessee Walker blood and today the breed is noted for its compact, muscular build and its sure-footedness.

Having become obsolete as a means of transport, the Fox Trotter is now used as a pleasure horse, being ideally suited to trail (long-distance) riding. It is also ridden in show classes in which it is judged 40 per cent for the fox trot, 20 per cent for the flat foot walk, 20 per cent for the canter and 20 per cent for conformation, the only exceptions being two-year-olds, who are judged 50 per cent for fox trot, 25 per cent for walk and 25 per cent for conformation.

BELOW LEFT
Originally bred as a means of transport, the present-day Fox Trotter is well suited to modern leisure riding. It is renowned for its sure-footedness.

BELOW
Unlike the Saddlebred and the Tennessee Walking Horse, the Missouri Fox Trotter is shown with normal-length feet. Artificial appliances such as weights and tail sets are forbidden.

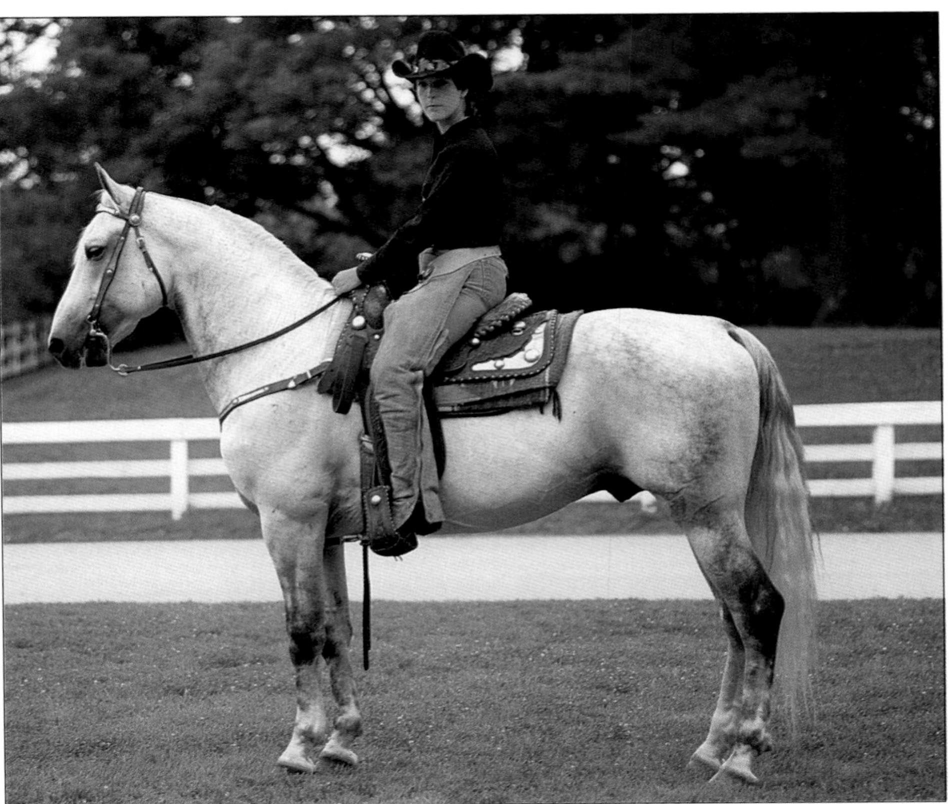

Tennessee Walking Horse

The Tennessee Walking Horse traces back to the Narragansett Pacer and, like the Saddlebred and the Missouri Fox Trotter, it was developed as an exceptionally comfortable riding horse with gaits not found in other breeds. Originally known as the Southern Plantation Walking Horse or Tennessee Pacer, it was an invaluable mode of transport for planters carrying out crop inspections, being fast, robust, comfortable under saddle and having a most tractable temperament.

The foundation sire was a horse named Black Allan, who arrived in Tennessee in 1903. Black Allan's sire came from a line of Standardbred trotters, while his dam was a Morgan. Black Allan was crossed with the Tennessee Pacers of the time to produce the forerunners of the modern Walking Horse. Saddlebred blood was also introduced, the most important influence being that of Giovanni, who in 1914 was brought from Kentucky to stand at stud in Tennessee. By adding Saddlebred blood, breeders succeeded in producing a better quality, more refined, animal. Today's Walking Horse, which might be decribed as a somewhat more powerful version of

LEFT
The Tennessee Walking Horse is customarily ridden in a plain bit with long shanks and on a single rein which is held with a light hand and flexed wrist.

BELOW
The Walking Horse has the substance of the Standardbred and the style of the Saddlebred which are two of the breeds on which it is based.

BREED DESCRIPTION

Height Average 15 .2hh.

Colour Any. Black and solid colours are most popular.

Conformation Intelligent but rather plain head; strong, arched neck; well-sloped shoulders; powerful body with broad chest; strong hindquarters; clean, hard limbs.

the Saddlebred, is therefore an amalgam of Thoroughbred, Standardbred, Morgan and Saddlebred blood. The Tennessee Walking Horse Breeders' Association was formed in Lewisburg, Tennessee, in 1935 and the Walking Horse was finally recognized as a breed in 1947.

Walking horses are fine all-round riding horses, their inherently kind nature making them especially suitable for novice riders. They are also popular horses in the show ring.

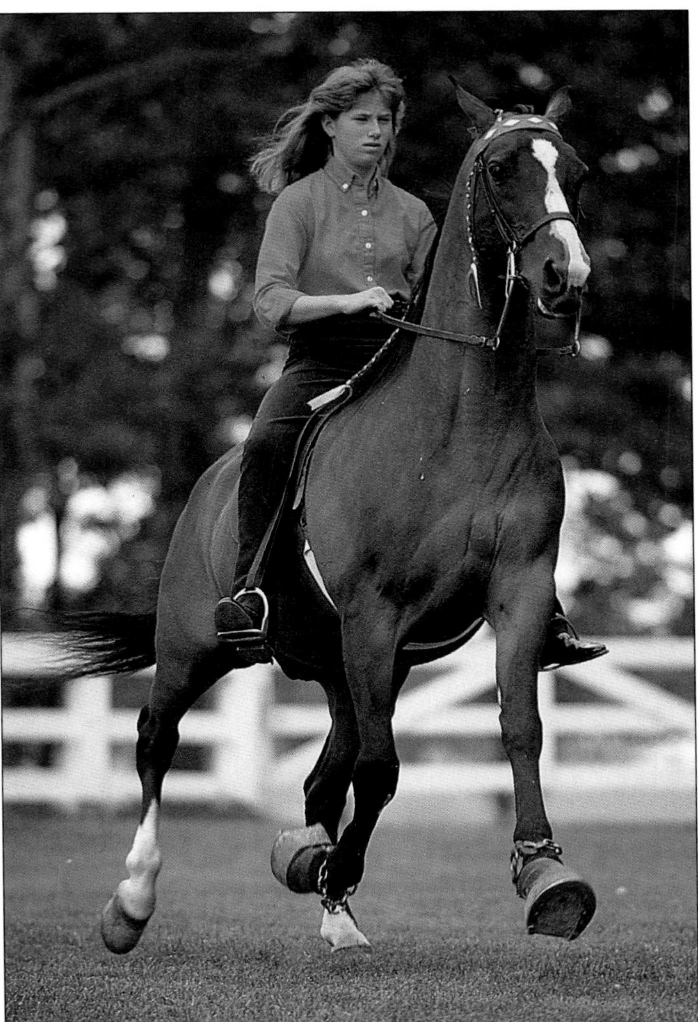

LEFT
The breed's unique gaits are inherited – young foals are seen to "walk" alongside their mothers with the ease of older horses – but are encouraged with artificial aids applied to the forefeet.

FAR LEFT
An impressive collection of Walking Horse trophies won in America, where the breed is a popular show-ring attraction.

BELOW
The exaggerated outline of the show horse is produced in part by the extra-long forefeet. The rider sits way behind the normal saddle position (on what is generally held to be the weakest part of the horse's back).

INTERESTING FACTS

The Tennessee Walking Horse's distinctive gaits – the flat-foot walk, the running walk and the canter – are inherited. Small foals can be seen performing the running walk beside their dams. Both walks are a loose, four-beat gait, with high action in front. As it moves, the horse nods its head in rhythm with the rise and fall of the hoofs, and the hindfeet overstride the tracks left by the front feet. The flat-foot walk should be loose, bold and square with plenty of shoulder motion. There should be a noticeable difference in the tempo between the two walks. The canter has a distinctive "rocking chair" motion.

Mustang

Mustangs, the "wild" horses of North America, are descended from the horses taken to the New World by the sixteenth-century Conquistadores. As Spanish colonizers began moving north from Mexico into what is now Texas, so the Indian tribes with whom they came into contact began to have their first experience of horses. Initially, the Indians were inclined to kill and eat any horses they captured from the settlers. In time, however, as they began to realize the value of the horse as a means of transport, they learnt how to handle and ride them.

By the second half of the seventeenth century, some tribes were taking horses from the Spaniards and using them in mounted raids against the newcomers – during which they would acquire more horses. So began the gradual spread of the horse to other tribes (either by trading or by theft) and the movement of the horse northwards. Many of the horses who subsequently ran "wild" would have done so after getting loose during skirmishes between Indians and Spaniards. Others, perhaps those who were lame or needed resting, were probably turned loose, their owners intending to round them up later. Some domestic horses put out to graze on the range simply wandered off. Gradually these horses joined together to form feral herds, which flourished in the wide open spaces of the Great Plains. By the late eighteenth and early nineteenth centuries there were huge numbers of "wild" horses grazing the plains – one authority estimates the number to have been as high as two million.

The turning point for the Mustang, as these feral horses became known, was the westward spread of civilization. Many were

LEFT
This Mustang shows unmistakable signs of its Spanish ancestry in its attractive head and luxurious growth of silky mane.

BREED DESCRIPTION

Height 13.2 – 15hh.

Colour Any.

Conformation Because of its mixed ancestry (the original Spanish stock was progressively diluted as a wide variety of settlers' horses, who either became lost or were abandoned, joined and interbred with the wild herds) there is a good deal of variation. The best are sturdily built with strong, clean limbs and feet.

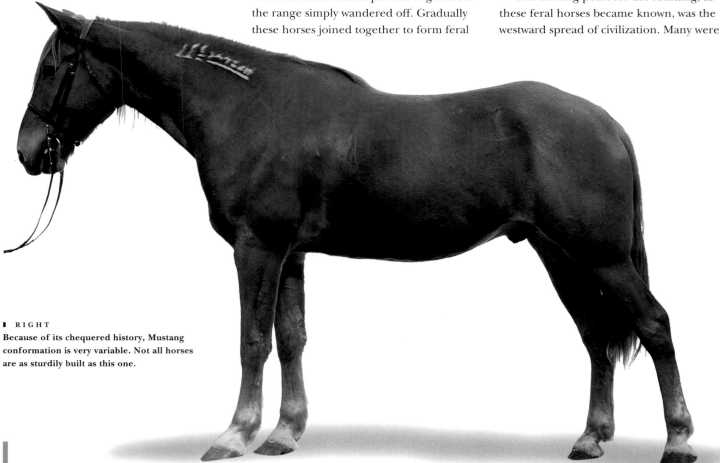

RIGHT
Because of its chequered history, Mustang conformation is very variable. Not all horses are as sturdily built as this one.

LEFT
Centuries of living in a feral state led to the development of a tough, enduring type of animal.

killed, others were rounded up for use as draught animals, some were used for cross-breeding. Large numbers were used as army remounts in the Boer War. During the twentieth century still more have been killed for the meat and pet food trades.

Public pressure led to the introduction, in 1971, of an act giving protection to wild horses in the United States and there are several ranges where they still live, albeit in much reduced numbers. Domesticated Mustangs often make good riding horses. Because of their inherent toughness, they are well suited to endurance rides.

LEFT
A fine stamp of Mustang which looks well under saddle. The majority of domesticated Mustangs make good all-round riding horses.

INTERESTING FACTS

The term mustang probably comes from the Spanish word *mesteno*, from *mesta*, meaning an association of graziers or stock raisers. In thirteenth-century Spain *mestas* were organizations of sheep owners. Stray sheep were called *mestenos*, meaning "belonging to the *mesta*". Some etymologists think that mustang comes from the word *mestengo*, a later form of *mostrenco*, from the verb *mostrar*, to show or exhibit. Stray sheep, sometimes referred to as *mostrencos*, were shown in public to give the owner the chance to claim them. But according to the wild-horse authority J. Frank Dobie, English-speaking people in the American south-west did not know the word *mostrenco*. Dobie dates the introduction of the term Mustang to the early nineteenth century.

RIGHT
Decorated in traditional style, these horses reflect their links with the Indian tribes who came to rely on the horses first introduced into America by the Conquistadores.

Australian Stock Horse

Horses were not indigenous to Australia and the modern Stock Horse is descended from the first imported animals, shipped over in small numbers from South Africa during the latter part of the eighteenth century. The precise breeding of these early imports is not known but they were probably of mainly Arab and Barb blood. It was not long before regular voyages began between Europe and Australia, each ship with its quota of horses aboard, and so Australia's equine population steadily grew.

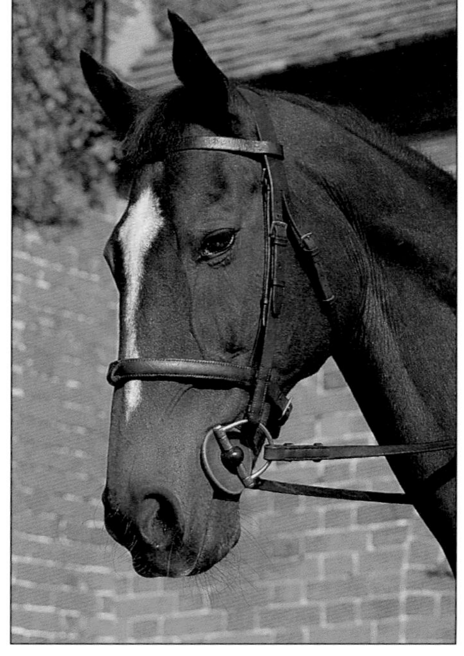

BREED DESCRIPTION

Height 15 – 16.3hh.

Colour Any solid colour.

Conformation There is considerable variation, but the best types are similar to the Thoroughbred, with particularly good sound limbs and feet.

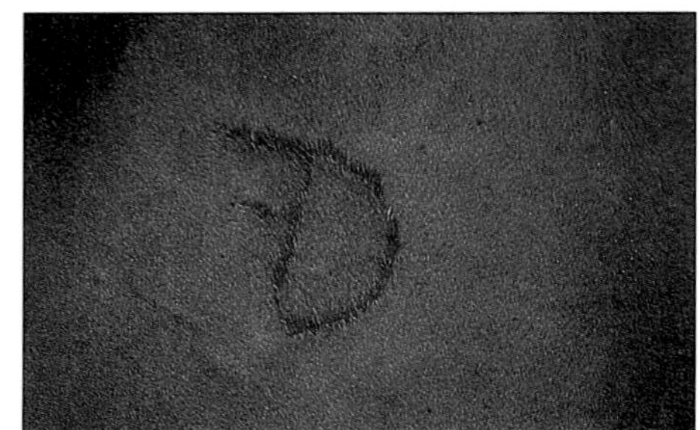

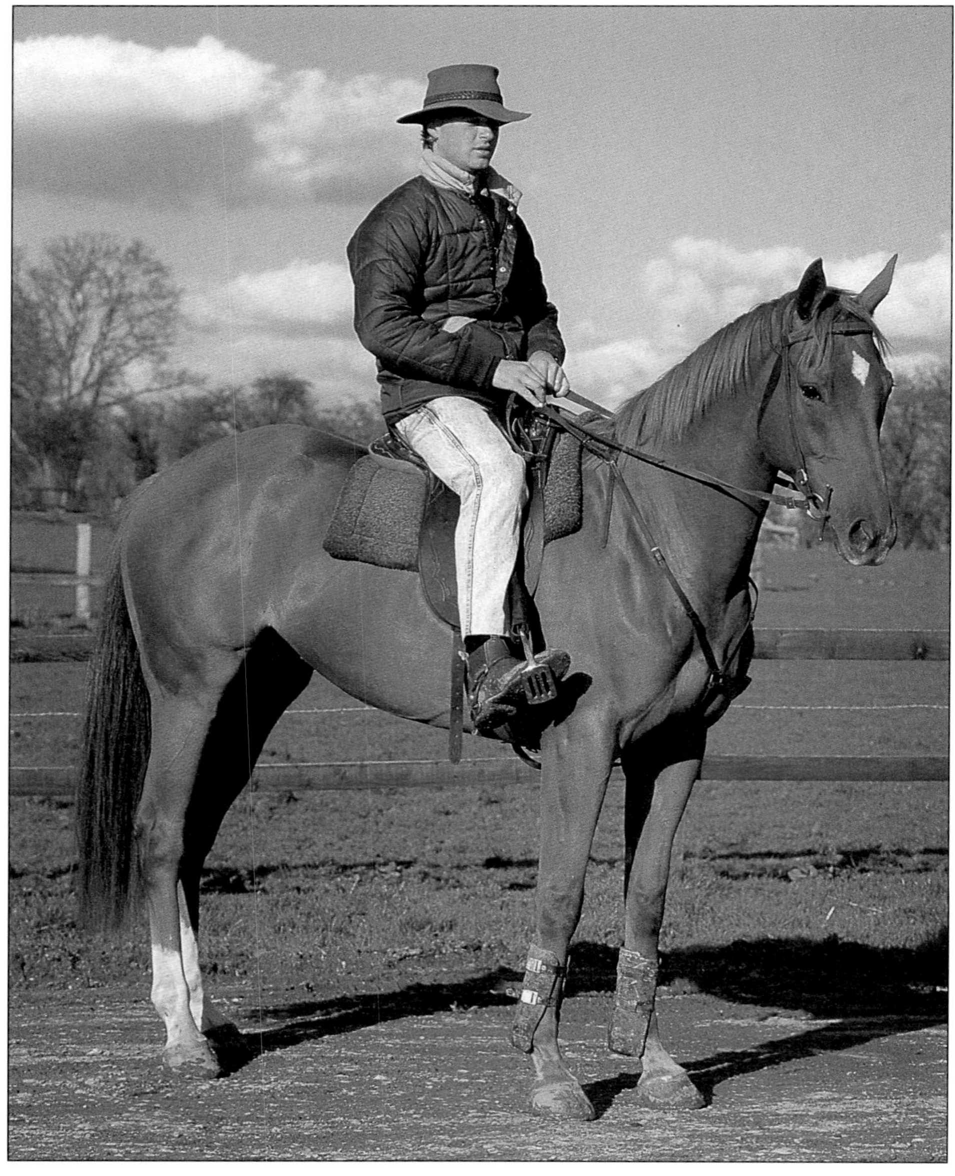

Tough horses were needed to help settlers explore their rugged new home and, not surprisingly, Thoroughbreds and Arabs were the most popular imports. Thoroughbreds were required, too, to satisfy the growing interest of the settlers in racing, a sport which rapidly gained popularity from the early years of the nineteenth century onwards.

The horse which evolved for everyday use was a tough all-rounder: hardy, reliable, of good temperament, able to work in harness or under saddle, to plough the land, clear timber, and herd cattle and sheep. Until 1971, when the term Stock Horse was introduced, it was known as the "Waler" (after New South Wales). Walers were renowned for their stamina, courage and soundness and were accordingly highly prized by the cavalry.

The present-day Stock Horse is the descendant of the Waler. It has almost certainly been influenced by a number of breeds other than the Thoroughbred and Arab – Quarter Horses, various ponies and heavy breeds such as the Clydesdale and Suffolk Punch were all imported into Australia over the years and some out-crosses would have been made – but the Stock Horse is essentially a quality riding horse. Still in demand for cattle herding, at which it excels, it can also be seen taking part in rodeos and is suitable for general riding purposes, including competitive sports.

▮ LEFT
There is as yet no set type within the breed. This striking-looking horse shows unmistakable signs of his eastern ancestry.

▮ BELOW
The breed was and still is a cattle-herding horse par excellence: tough, enduring, sound and good-natured.

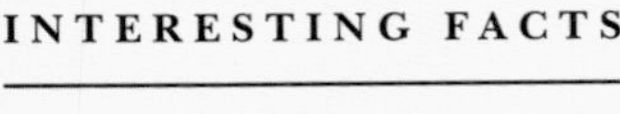

INTERESTING FACTS

Regal Realm is one of a long line of Australian Stock Horses to compete successfully at the highest level. Ridden by Lucinda Green he won the individual gold medal at the World Three-Day Event Championships in 1982, helping Britain to take the team title. The following year he was runner-up in the European Championships, winning a team silver medal. At the Los Angeles Olympic Games in 1984 he won another team silver and finished in sixth place individually. A year later he was a member of the victorious British team in the European Championships. When he retired from international competition he returned to his native land.

▮ OPPOSITE ABOVE LEFT
The head resembles that of the Thoroughbred, which is one of the major influences in the development of the Australian Stock Horse.

▮ OPPOSITE ABOVE RIGHT
It is usual to brand Stock Horses for identification purposes. This brand is on the horse's shoulder.

▮ OPPOSITE BELOW
Many Stock Horses show the refinement and good overall conformation of the Thoroughbred. They have as a result produced some good sports horses.

Criollo

BELOW
Originally the mount of the gauchos, or cowboys, of South America, the Criollo has achieved world-wide fame in the world of polo.

BOTTOM
The sturdy, compact Criollo is one of the world's toughest horses, with strong short limbs, plenty of bone below the knee and exceptionally sound feet.

A descendant of the horses taken to South America by the sixteenth-century Spanish Conquistadores, the Criollo comes from Argentina and is one of the toughest breeds of horse in the world. Its hardiness is the result of many years of natural selection. Some of the Spanish horses and their descendants formed feral herds on the pampas, where the extremes of climate – intensely dry, hot summers and severe winters – would have proved intolerable to all but the sturdiest individuals. Those that survived adapted to their harsh environment remarkably well, no doubt helped by the fact that they were descended from Andalusian and Barb horses, both breeds noted for their endurance. The Criollo, as it became known, even developed a coat colour – Criollos are predominantly dun – which helped render it inconspicuous against the dry pastureland of its habitat.

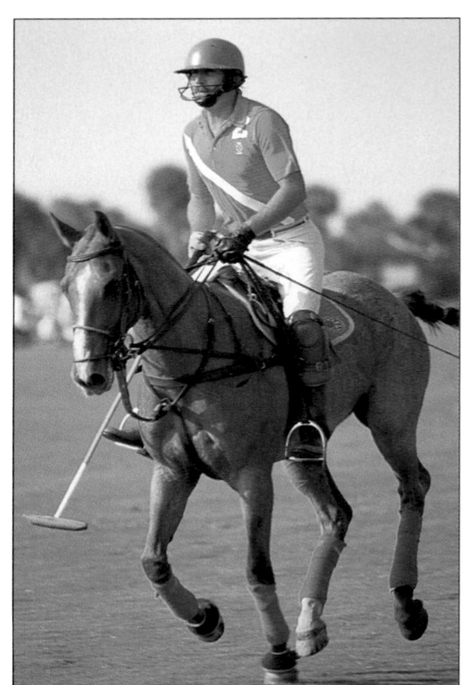

BREED DESCRIPTION

Height Around 14 – 15hh.

Colour Usually dun with dark points and often with a dorsal stripe.

Conformation Medium-sized head, with wide-set eyes and alert ears; muscular neck; short, deep body with well-sprung ribs; short, strong limbs with plenty of bone and good, sound feet.

The Criollo became the favoured mount of the gauchos, the cowboys of the pampas, and an indispensable riding and packhorse for settlers in the huge and frequently inhospitable countries of South America. It can be found throughout the continent and although there are some variations, the result of adaptation to differences in habitat and climate, wherever it is bred it retains its basic qualities of stamina and soundness. Crossed with the Thoroughbred, the Criollo produces a fine polo pony, the Thoroughbred blood providing the extra speed required in the modern game.

INTERESTING FACTS

The most famous example of the Criollo's extraordinary powers of endurance was "Tschiffely's Ride", a journey undertaken by the Swiss-born traveller and writer Aimé Felix Tschiffely (1895–1954). In 1925, together with two Criollos – the 16-year-old Mancha, and the 15-year-old Gata – Tschiffely set off from Buenos Aires to ride to Washington D.C. in the United States. Alternately riding one horse and leading the other as a packhorse, he completed the journey, over some of the most arduous terrain in the world, in two and a half years. The horses were then shipped back to South America, where they spent their retirement, Gata living to the age of 36 and Mancha to 40.

Peruvian Paso

The Paso (meaning "step") is another breed which owes its origins to the Barb and Andalusian horses introduced to South America by the Spaniards. The first horses to arrive in Peru were taken there in 1532 by Francisco Pizarro (c.1478–1541).

The Paso's characteristic lateral gait is thought to have been inherited from the Spanish "jennet", which was a riding horse akin to the old English ambler. The lateral movement has been preserved down the centuries; the Paso usually demonstrates a preference for it over the canter. The paso is unlike any other lateral gait in that the horse's forelegs arc out to the side as he moves. With his hindlegs he takes long, straight strides, carrying his hindquarters low, with his hocks well under him. This combination of flowing foreleg movement and powerfully driving hindlegs gives a particularly smooth ride. The Paso is said to be able to reach speeds of up to 15mph (24kph) and to maintain the lateral gait over rough terrain for extended periods without tiring.

Fairly small and stockily built, the Paso is noted for its sure-footedness, its ability to thrive on meagre rations and its kind nature. It makes an ideal ranch and long-distance riding horse.

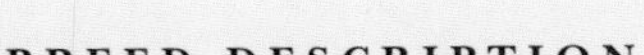

BREED DESCRIPTION

Height 14 – 15.2hh.

Colour Any, but predominantly bay and chestnut.

Conformation Intelligent looking head; fairly short, muscular neck; strong shoulders; strong body with broad, deep chest; strong, rounded hindquarters; short, strong limbs and excellent feet.

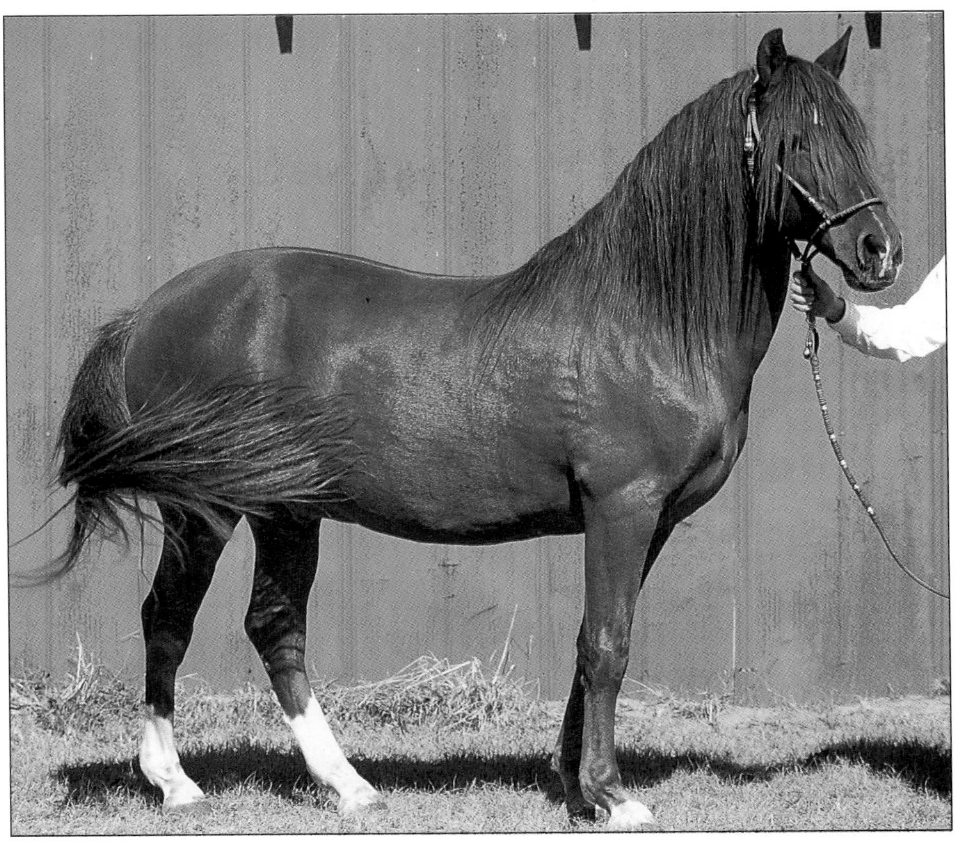

ABOVE
Compact and well-muscled, with powerful hindquarters and short, strong limbs, the Peruvian Paso is a tremendously strong individual.

LEFT
The Paso's long silky mane (and tail) is reminiscent of that of its Spanish ancestors, introduced into South America during the sixteenth century.

RIGHT
Horse and rider make an attractive, workmanlike picture in their traditional Peruvian tack and costume. The Paso is up to carrying a good deal of weight.

INTERESTING FACTS

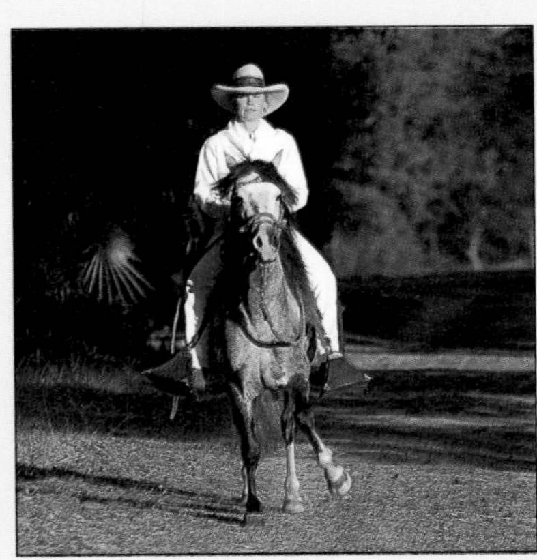

The Peruvian Paso is not the only horse to show a natural preference for a lateral gait but the curious outward arcing of the forelegs, which move rather like the arms of a swimmer, is unique to the breed.

Ponies

Broadly speaking a pony is a small horse, "small" usually meaning no higher at the withers than about 14.2hh (a hand is 4 inches). However, not all small horses can be classified as ponies. Arab horses, for example, often stand below 15hh but they are very much horses, with the proportions and characteristics of the horse. An unusually small Thoroughbred is certainly not a pony and the remarkable little Caspian, although it is classified as a pony, actually resembles a miniature horse.

True ponies have very distinct pony characteristics, which include a proportionately short length of leg in relationship to the depth of the body. True ponies are perhaps best exemplified by the Mountain and Moorland breeds of Britain and Ireland, remarkable animals which have existed in the comparative isolation of their island home for thousands of years. These ponies, which are now divided into nine distinct breeds, are possessed of extraordinary strength in relation to their size. Fashioned by a harsh environment, they are tough, sure-footed, able to exist on minimum rations and have an inherent sagacity often lacking in their larger cousins.

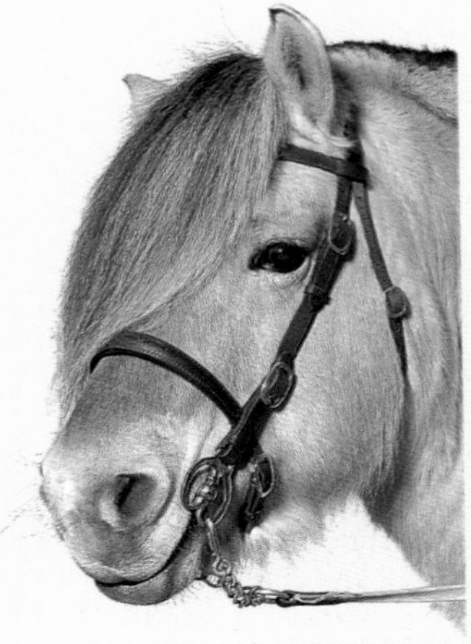

Haflinger

Austria's attractive Haflinger pony is named after the village of Hafling in the southern Tirol, the region where it was first bred hundreds of years ago. Its ancestors were indigenous mountain horses and ponies which were upgraded with Arabian blood. All modern Haflingers trace back to a half-bred horse named El Bedavi XXII – who was bred in Austria and was a great grandson of the Arabian stallion, El Bedavi – and to El Bedavi XXII's son, Folie.

Over the years inbreeding has resulted in a pony of very definite type: small, but powerfully built, always chestnut in colour, hardy and sure-footed as befits a mountain pony, and with the active paces of its Arab forebears.

With its amenable nature, the Haflinger makes an excellent all-round riding and driving pony. Before mechanization it was in great demand for agricultural work and as a pack-pony. Nowadays many Haflingers are used for leisure riding. The breed has been exported to a number of countries, and is especially popular in Germany and Switzerland. It is noted for its longevity.

BREED DESCRIPTION

Height Around 14hh.

Colour Chestnut with flaxen mane and tail.

Conformation Intelligent looking head, with large eyes, small ears and slightly dished profile; sloping shoulders; strong, deep body with fairly long back and muscular loins; powerful hindquarters; strong limbs and excellent feet.

PREVIOUS PAGE OPPOSITE Exmoor ponies.

PREVIOUS PAGE A Norwegian Fjord pony.

LEFT The "Hungarian Post" – Haflinger style! The breed combines strength with very active paces and can be trained to perform in a wide range of equestrian activities.

BELOW LEFT Haflingers are true all-rounders, equally adept at work in harness and under saddle. This handsome team was photographed in Switzerland.

BELOW The Haflinger's good temperament is easily discerned in this attractive head, with its large, kind eyes and alert expression.

INTERESTING FACTS

Haflingers which are entered in the breed's stud book are traditionally branded. The brand mark is the alpine flower, the edelweiss, at the centre of which is placed the letter "H".

Sorraia

Formerly used for farm work and general riding purposes, the primitive looking Sorraia survives today mainly in small feral groups. Its homeland is in Portugal in the region between the rivers Sor and Raia, tributaries of the Sorraia, which flows into the Tagus estuary from the south.

The Sorraia pony is believed to be descended from the Asian Wild Horse and the Tarpan. It bears a remarkable likeness to the latter, with its small stature and large head. The Sorraia's colouring, predominantly dun, often with an eel-stripe and zebra markings on the legs, is also typical of the primitive equine type.

The Sorraia does not have the best conformation in the world. It is, however, an extremely tough individual, able to exist on poor forage and to withstand extremes of climate. The shoulders tend to be upright, the hindquarters weak and the limbs rather long and lacking in bone, though the feet are hard and sound.

LEFT
Dun is the predominant colour of the Sorraia, Portugal's small, semi-feral pony. The breed is of ancient origin and is exceptionally hardy.

BELOW
In build and overall outline the Sorraia is not unlike the primitive Tarpan. Some selective breeding is carried out in order to preserve the original form.

BREED DESCRIPTION

Height 12 – 13hh.

Colour Predominantly dun, with black eel-stripe down the centre of the back and frequently with zebra markings on the legs and occasionally on the body; also grey.

Conformation Large, primitive looking head with convex profile; straight shoulders; poor hindquarters with low-set tail; long limbs, lacking in bone.

INTERESTING FACTS

The Sorraia is believed to be related to the Garrano, the pony of northern Portugal. The Garrano shows more quality than the Sorraia, the result of infusions of Arab blood. Although small, the Garrano is inherently hardy, and has been used for all types of farm work, as a pack-pony and for hauling timber.

Exmoor

The Exmoor is the oldest of Britain's Mountain and Moorland breeds and one of the oldest equine breeds in the world. This attractive pony has inhabited the wild moorland area of west Somerset and north Devon in the south-west of England for many centuries. Ponies of Exmoor type were certainly known during Roman times and may well have existed as far back as the Bronze Age, when they would have been used for pulling chariots. Mention is made of Exmoor ponies and their owners in the Domesday Book of 1085.

The remoteness of its habitat has meant that the Exmoor pony has been subjected to very little in the way of "improvement" through the introduction of outside blood. The rigours of life on the moor have produced a tremendously hardy pony, strong enough to carry an adult rider in spite of the fact that the ponies stand no higher than 12.3hh.

The Exmoor Pony Society was founded in 1921 to improve and encourage the breeding of Exmoor ponies of the traditional moorland type. By carrying out rigorous inspections, it ensures that no pony lacking true Exmoor type is registered as a pure-bred. When ponies are passed for registration, they are branded on the shoulder with the

BREED DESCRIPTION

Height Stallions and geldings not exceeding 12.3hh. Mares not exceeding 12.2hh.

Colour Bay, brown or dun with black points. No white markings anywhere.

Conformation Clean-cut face with wide forehead, large, prominent eyes, wide nostrils and clean throat; good length of rein; well laid-back shoulders; strong body with deep, wide chest, well-sprung ribs and broad, level back; clean, short limbs and neat, hard feet.

TOP
The Exmoor's attractive head, notable for its large eyes, small, mobile ears and intelligent expression, is full of true pony character.

RIGHT
The Exmoor is a fine stamp of pony: hard and strong, vigorous, alert and symmetrical in appearance. Its general poise indicates its good natural balance.

LEFT
An Exmoor foal in his native habitat. Ponies have inhabited the moor for many centuries and are totally adapted to life in a tough environment.

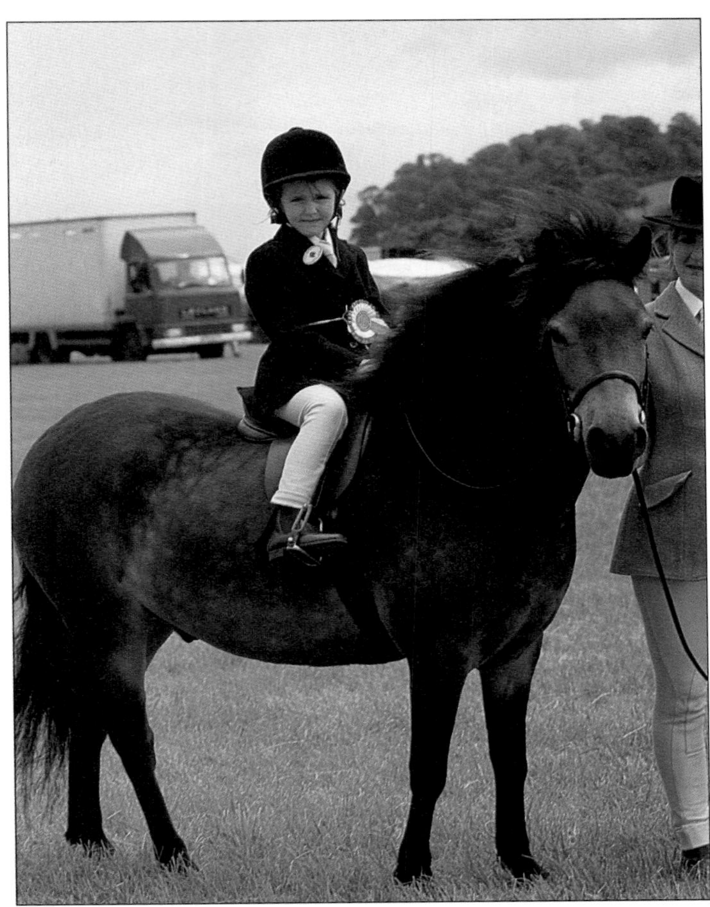

ABOVE
Correctly handled and schooled, the Exmoor, for all its great strength, makes a good riding pony for a small child.

Society's star brand. Beneath this the pony's herd number appears, while on the nearside hindquarter there is the pony's own number within that herd.

Herds of ponies still run "wild" on the moor, although they are rounded up annually for inspection. The Exmoor's robust build and constitution make it an excellent riding pony and they are also used in the sport of driving.

INTERESTING FACTS

The most instantly recognizable features of the Exmoor are its mealy coloured muzzle and its large, prominent eyes. The latter are termed "toad" eyes because of their heavy top lids. The eyebrows are surrounded by light, buff-coloured hair.

LEFT
The breed's inherent athleticism makes it a good all-round performance pony for an older child.

Dartmoor

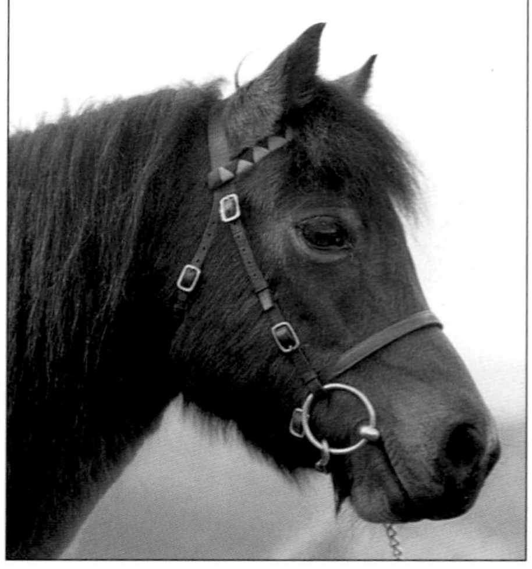

BREED DESCRIPTION

Height Not exceeding 12.2hh.

Colour Bay, black or brown preferred, but no colours are barred except skewbald and piebald. Excessive white markings discouraged.

Conformation Small, well set-on head with small, alert ears; strong, medium length neck, not too heavy, stallions to have a moderate crest; strong back and loins; strong, muscular hindquarters with full, high-set tail; hard, well-shaped feet.

Unlike its neighbour, the Exmoor, the Dartmoor Pony has been influenced by a number of breeds over the many centuries during which ponies have run free on the high moorland of Devon, in south-west England. Ponies are thought to have lived on the moor during Saxon times. Later the important trade route which existed between Exeter and Plymouth would have been travelled by horses of many different types, some of which would almost certainly have had an influence on the native stock. Arabs and Barbs, brought back by Crusaders, are also believed to have found their way onto the moor.

Climate and the hardships of existing in such a wild region would have ensured that the animals roaming the moors achieved a certain degree of uniformity, particularly with regard to size. During the Industrial Revolution the requirements of the mining industry prompted a new development: the crossing of Dartmoor Ponies with the much smaller Shetland, in order to produce animals suited to working underground. This proved to be a highly retrograde step as far as the Dartmoor Pony was concerned. The type of riding-quality pony that had evolved began to deteriorate. In order to set matters right, new blood had to be introduced, including Welsh Mountain Pony, Polo Pony and Hackney.

The first stud book for Dartmoors was opened in 1899 and the height limits for

▮ LEFT
Strength and active paces make the Dartmoor a good harness pony.

INTERESTING FACTS

There was a steady decline in the numbers of ponies of true Dartmoor type after World War II and many of those found on the moor were only poor quality cross-breds. However, in 1988 the Dartmoor Pony Society Moor Scheme was set up in order to encourage farmers with unregistered pure-bred type ponies to offer them for registration and to provide them with the services of pedigree stallions. The aim is to establish a pool of pure-bred ponies – hardy enough to thrive on the moor – to which breeders can then go for true native pony characteristics. Suitable mares from the moor are put in large enclosed areas known as newtakes together with a pedigree stallion. Their female progeny are inspected and those which pass muster are entered in a supplementary register of the stud book. In due course these ponies will also be mated to a fully registered stallion, and so on until their descendants, on inspection, can be admitted to the full stud book.

▮ RIGHT
Dartmoors have a calm temperament and make good mounts for children.

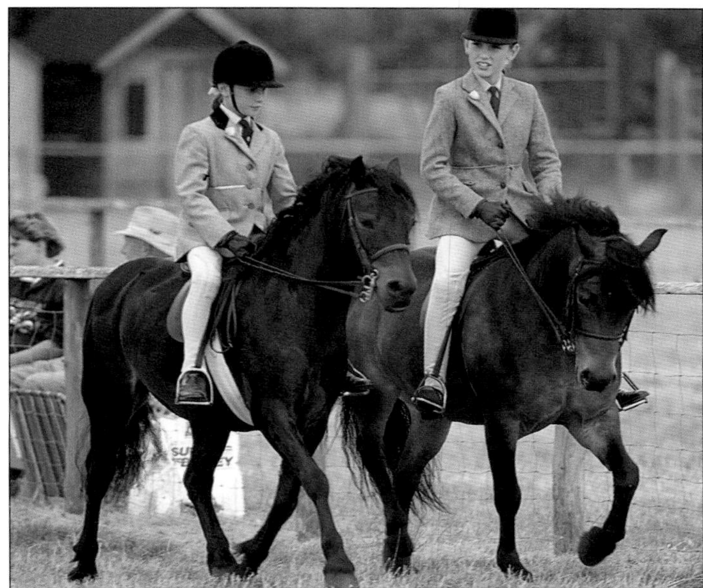

▮ OPPOSITE TOP
The Dartmoor's neat, well set-on head with its small, alert ears, shows true native pony character.

▮ OPPOSITE BOTTOM
The best examples of the breed combine quality with great hardiness.

▮ BELOW
Although Dartmoor ponies declined in number and quality after World War II, in recent times measures have been introduced to ensure the preservation of a pool of hardy pure-breds.

stallions was given as 14hh and for mares 13.2hh. It was more than twenty years before this was reduced to the present 12.2hh. Hackney blood was prominent in a number of the foundation stallions. However, the most influential sire of those early years was undoubtedly The Leat, who was by a pure-bred Arab (Dwarka, who stood 14.1hh) out of a Dartmoor mare. Standing 12.2hh, The Leat was a beautiful looking pony with excellent conformation. During his short stud career only a handful of his progeny were registered, but many of the best present-day ponies trace back to him.

At its best the Dartmoor is a hardy, quality riding pony with smooth, low, free action. Its sound constitution, intelligence and excellent, calm temperament, make it an ideal pony for a child.

Welsh Mountain

The rugged landscape of Wales is home to four distinct equine breeds: two ponies, designated Section A and Section B in the Welsh Pony and Cob Society Stud Book, and two cobs, designated Section C and Section D.

At the base of all Welsh breeding is the beautiful Welsh Mountain Pony, Section A, which has thrived for many centuries in the tough environment of its native land and is considered by many people to be the most beautiful of all ponies. The development of the breed is obscure, but it goes back at least to the times of the Romans, who crossed horses of eastern origin with the native Welsh stock. In more recent times, particularly during the eighteenth century, some Thoroughbred, Arab and Barb blood was introduced.

The modern Welsh Mountain Pony is courageous and spirited, yet kindly, and makes a superb child's riding pony. It is also an outstanding performer in the increasingly popular sport of carriage driving. It has evolved as a supremely hardy individual, able to endure harsh weather conditions and to thrive on sparse rations. It has been used to improve other breeds, including the New Forest, and also in the development of the British Riding Pony. The Welsh Mountain Pony is popular in many countries outside its native Wales. It has been exported to Europe, the United States, New Zealand and Australia.

BREED DESCRIPTION

Height Not exceeding 12hh.

Colour Predominantly grey, though bay, chestnut and palomino occur and any solid colour is permitted.

Conformation Small, clean-cut head, tapering to the muzzle, with bold eyes, small, pointed ears and prominent, open nostrils; lengthy, well-carried neck; long, sloping shoulders; strong, muscular back with deep girth, well-sprung ribs and strong loins; lengthy, fine hindquarters with tail well set on and carried gaily; good, strong limbs, with long, strong forearm, well-developed knee, large, flat hocks and well-shaped feet, of dense, hard horn.

ABOVE
The eastern influence is clearly visible in the beautiful head, with its big eyes, wide nostrils and dished profile.

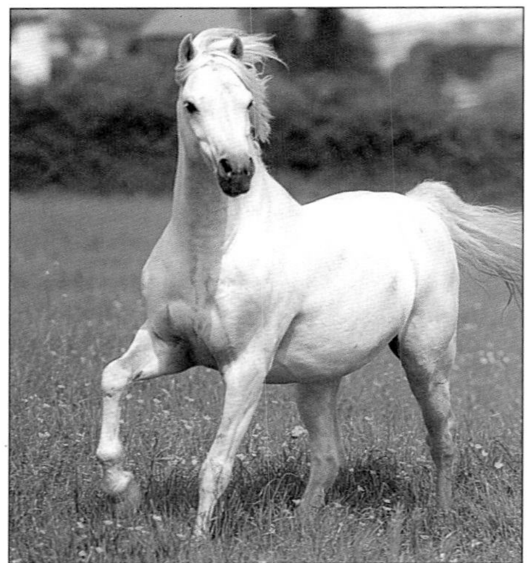

LEFT
The Section B is larger than the Welsh Mountain Pony but the best examples have the same true pony character. The action is straight, quick and free.

BELOW
Section A ponies like this one were used in the development of the Australian Pony, which is based on Welsh and Arab blood.

INTERESTING FACTS

The Welsh Pony (Section B) is larger than the Mountain Pony, though it retains the true pony characteristics. Arab, small Thoroughbred and small Welsh Cob stallions were crossed with Mountain Pony mares to develop this quality riding pony, which stands up to 13.2hh. Formerly used for shepherding and hunting, Welsh Ponies are now much in demand as children's riding ponies.

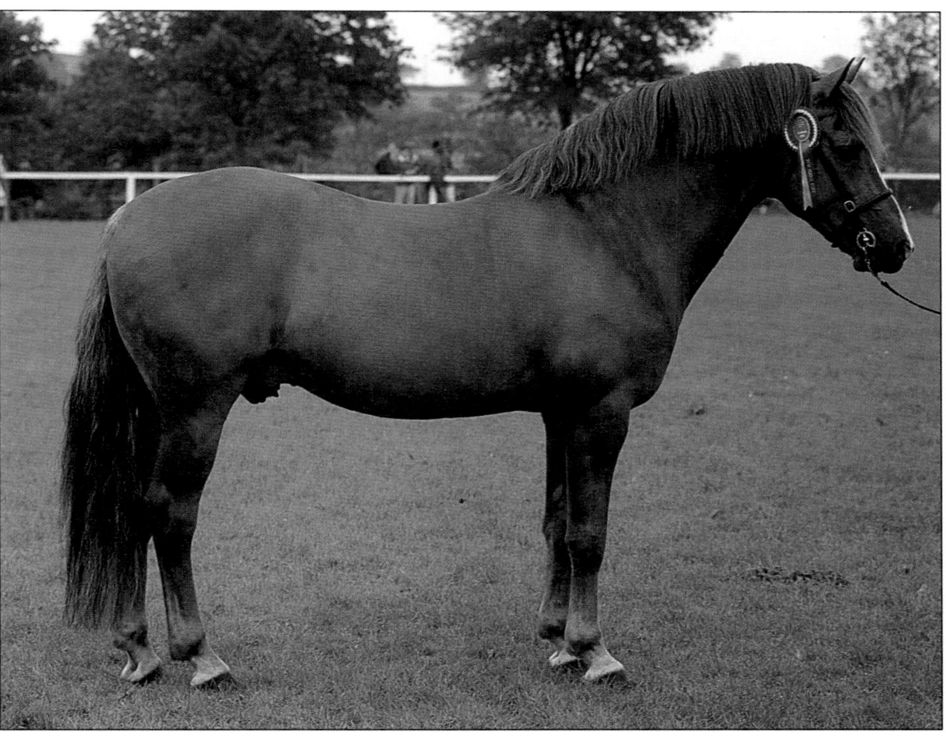

New Forest

Wild horses are known to have existed in the New Forest, in southern England, as far back as the time of Canute (c. 995–1035). The exact origins of today's New Forest Pony are, however, unknown although it has certainly been influenced down the years by a variety of other breeds. During the eighteenth century the Thoroughbred stallion Marske, the sire of the great racehorse Eclipse, was used for a time to serve New Forest mares and in the mid-nineteenth century an Arab stallion belonging to Queen Victoria was allowed to run with the herds. Hackney blood was also introduced. While these infusions of outside blood added to the pony's size, they were detrimental when it came to the preservation of true pony substance and to rectify the situation, outcrosses were made to stallions of other native breeds, including Dales, Dartmoor, Exmoor, Fell, Highland and, later, Welsh Mountain.

Today's New Forest Ponies, like many Exmoor and Welsh Mountain Ponies, still roam freely in their native habitat. Life in the Forest can be hard, the food supply often meagre and low in quality. This tough environment has produced a hardy, sure-footed animal. The pony's action is free, active and straight and its good temperament makes it easy to train. As a result they make excellent all-round riding and driving ponies. They are popular not only in their native country but also in mainland Europe, North America, Australia and New Zealand.

BREED DESCRIPTION

Height 13.3 – 14.2hh.

Colour Any colour except skewbald, piebald, or blue-eyed cream.

Conformation Rather large head; fairly short neck; well-sloped shoulders; deep body; strong hindquarters; straight limbs with plenty of bone and good hard, round feet.

INTERESTING FACTS

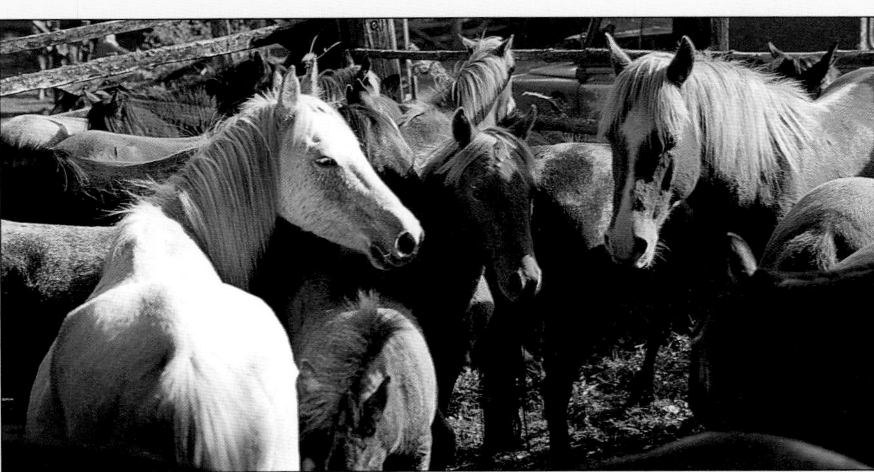

The ponies are owned by the New Forest Commoners, who carry out an annual "drift" or round-up in order to select those which are to be sold. The remaining breeding stock is then returned to the Forest.

TOP
The best type of New Forest Pony is strongly built and possesses good, well-sloped riding shoulders, powerful hindquarters and strong, sound limbs

ABOVE LEFT
The New Forest's head indicates the breed's typically calm, tractable temperament.

Welsh Cob

The Welsh Cob (designated Section D in the Welsh Pony and Cob Society Stud Book) is derived from the Welsh Mountain Pony, of which it is, in essence, a larger version. It traces back at least to the twelfth century when eastern-type horses were brought back by the Crusaders and crossed with the local ponies. Subsequently infusions of Yorkshire Coach Horse, Norfolk Roadster and Arab blood were made.

Tough, sound, spirited and courageous, yet with an amenable temperament, the

ABOVE
The action is straight, free and forceful. The whole foreleg is extended from the shoulders and as far forward as possible in all paces, with the hocks well flexed, producing powerful leverage.

RIGHT
The Welsh Cob Section D is described by the breed society as the embodiment of strength and hardiness.

BREED DESCRIPTION

Height Above 13.2hh – usually 14.2 – 15.2hh.

Colour Any, except piebald and skewbald.

Conformation Quality, pony head with bold, widely set eyes and neat, well-set ears; long, well-carried neck; strong, well laid-back shoulders; strong, deep, muscular body; muscular hindquarters; short, powerful limbs with long, strong forearms, strong, muscular second thighs, large, flat joints and well-shaped feet.

INTERESTING FACTS

By crossing Welsh Mountain Pony mares with small Welsh Cobs breeders produced the Welsh Pony of Cob Type (Section C in the Stud Book), a smaller version of the Cob and a marvellous all-round riding and driving pony. It shares all the characteristics of its larger cousin, but does not stand over 13.2hh. Like the Cob, it was formerly much used by hill farmers and also to transport slate from the mines of North Wales. After World War II it was in danger of becoming extinct, but its numbers have since recovered and nowadays it enjoys popularity as a trekking pony, a small hunter and as a driving pony.

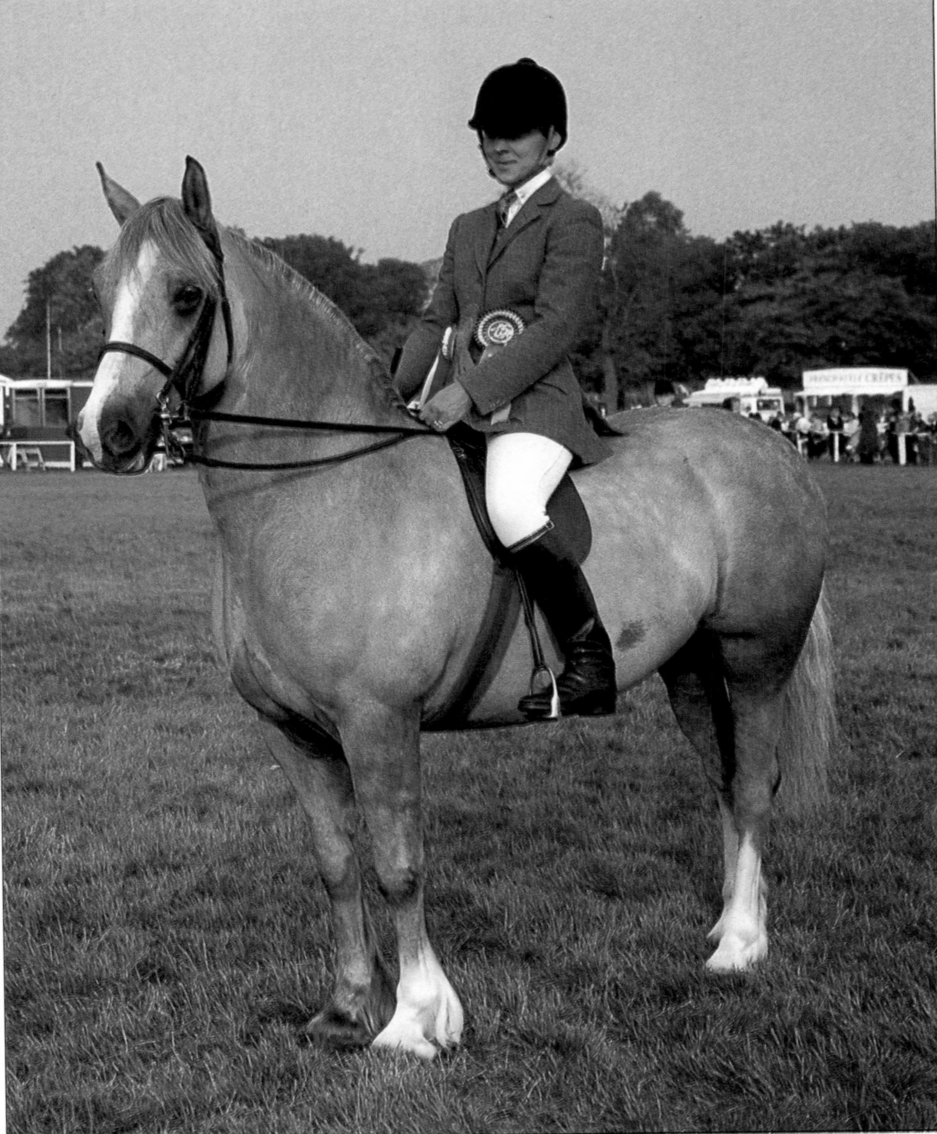

RIGHT
A popular attraction in the show ring, the Welsh Cob is also a good hunter and a marvellous all-round performer in competitive sports.

Welsh Cob was traditionally used for all manner of heavy work on the hill farms, being equally at home in harness and under saddle. It was also formerly much in demand by the army, particularly for

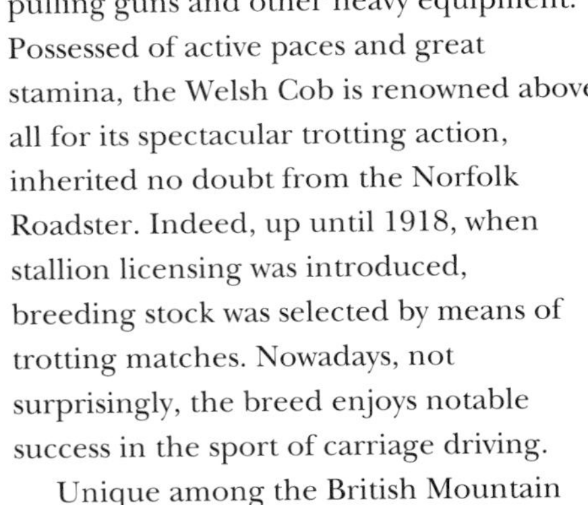

pulling guns and other heavy equipment. Possessed of active paces and great stamina, the Welsh Cob is renowned above all for its spectacular trotting action, inherited no doubt from the Norfolk Roadster. Indeed, up until 1918, when stallion licensing was introduced, breeding stock was selected by means of trotting matches. Nowadays, not surprisingly, the breed enjoys notable success in the sport of carriage driving.

Unique among the British Mountain and Moorland breeds, the Cob has no upper height limit, but whatever its size it should retain true pony characteristics – its quality head testifying to its Welsh Mountain Pony ancestry. When crossed with the Thoroughbred (particularly the second cross) the Welsh Cob produces excellent competition horses.

RIGHT
A quality head, depth through the girth and strong limbs, with an abundance of flat bone, are prerequisites of this sturdy breed.

Highland

One of the strongest and heaviest of Britain's Mountain and Moorland breeds, the Highland Pony comes from the Highlands of Scotland and the islands off the west coast. Ponies are believed to have inhabited the region many thousands of years ago. The modern Highland Pony, sure-footed, hardy and long-lived, evolved as a result of various outcrosses, particularly Arab and Clydesdale. The Dukes of Atholl, influential breeders of Highland Ponies for several centuries, almost certainly introduced eastern blood as early as the sixteenth century.

Until fairly recently the breed was divided into two types: a more substantial mainland type, which stood up to 14.2hh, and the lighter, somewhat smaller Western Isles type. Although the Highland Pony Society, founded in 1923, no longer recognizes these distinctions, differences in type can still be discerned to some extent.

BREED DESCRIPTION

Height 13 – 14.2hh.

Colour Various shades of dun, also grey, brown, black and occasionally bay and liver chestnut with silver mane and tail.

Conformation Well-carried head with broad forehead, alert, kindly eyes and wide nostrils; strong, arched neck with clean throat; well laid-back shoulders; compact body with deep chest and well-sprung ribs; powerful hindquarters with strong, well-developed thigh and second thigh; strong limbs with short cannons, flat, hard bone and well-shaped, hard, dark hooves; silky feather, not over-heavy and ending in a prominent tuft at the fetlock; long, silky, flowing mane and tail.

The Highland is a strong, sturdily built pony, a real all-round worker which in its time has carried men to war, been the mount of shepherds, worked in harness, hauled timber, taken deer-stalkers into the hills and carried the shot stags – weighing

LEFT
The Highland Pony is a willing worker. It is still used on Scottish estates to carry game panniers and to cart shot stags.

ABOVE
Highland Ponies are noted for the beauty of their coat colouring – including the whole range of duns – and for the silky texture of their abundant manes and tails.

upwards of 16 stone (224lb/101kg) – back down. It is much used for pony trekking and makes a fine general-purpose riding pony, well able to carry an adult. Pure-breds can be seen taking part successfully in a number of competitive sports, including driving and dressage. Crossed with the Thoroughbred the Highland makes an excellent hunter and more than one successful three-day event horse has had Highland blood in its veins.

INTERESTING FACTS

One of the most striking features of the Highland is its colouring, particularly the various shades of dun: yellow, golden, mouse, cream and fox (yellow dun is believed to have been the breed's original colour). Most ponies show at least one of the characteristics of the primitive horse, i.e. a dorsal eel-stripe and zebra markings on the legs. These markings testify to the antiquity of the breed.

BELOW
Versatility is one of the most valuable characteristics of the breed, which will haul timber as easily as it will carry a rider to hounds or go in harness.

OPPOSITE TOP
The Highland Pony's head is broad between the eyes, short from eyes to muzzle and well-carried on a strong, arched neck. The eyes have a kind expression.

OPPOSITE
Moulded by its harsh natural environment, the breed is strong, hardy, long lived and economical to feed. It is eminently sure-footed over the most treacherous terrain.

Shetland

Named after the remote group of islands situated to the far north-east of mainland Scotland and in the same northern latitude as south Greenland, the Shetland Pony is the smallest of the British native breeds. Its origins are uncertain but there have certainly been ponies in the Shetlands for many centuries and it may well trace back to far more distant times.

Small of stature, it is nevertheless immensely strong – one of the strongest equine animals, in relation to size, in the world. Wonderfully well adapted to the vagaries of the islands' northern climate and the poor quality grazing, the Shetland is inherently hardy. Its action is free and straight, with a characteristic lift to its joints – the result of centuries of traversing rough, rocky or heather-covered terrain. An integral part of the lives of the islanders, the ponies have traditionally been used both under saddle and as pack animals, carrying everything from grain to peat for fuel. They were formerly much in demand for coal mining, their small size and great strength making them perfect for work underground. Breeding flourished, though there was little attempt at selective breeding before the middle of the nineteenth century.

The Shetland has also found favour far from its native islands as a children's riding pony. It can be strong-willed but it is intelligent and responds to correct handling. With its active paces and manoeuvrability, it makes a particularly good driving pony and can be seen competing right up to international level.

BREED DESCRIPTION

Height Not exceeding 40 inches (102cm) at three years or under. Not exceeding 42 inches (107cm) at four years or over.

Colour Any colour except spotted.

Conformation Small, well-carried head with broad forehead, bold, dark, intelligent eyes, small, erect ears and broad muzzle with wide open nostrils; strong, deep body with short back and muscular loins; broad, strong hindquarters; strong limbs, with good, flat bone and short cannons; tough, round, well-shaped feet.

LEFT
The Shetland's profuse growth of mane and tail afford valuable protection from the severe weather of its northern homeland.

LEFT
Short-legged and stocky, the breed is noted for its great strength in relation to its diminutive size.

LEFT
Shetlands are very active little ponies and take part with great enthusiasm in Shetland "Grand Nationals", which raise money for charity.

BELOW
In spring the Shetland begins to shed its thick winter coat, designed to keep out extremes of wet and cold.

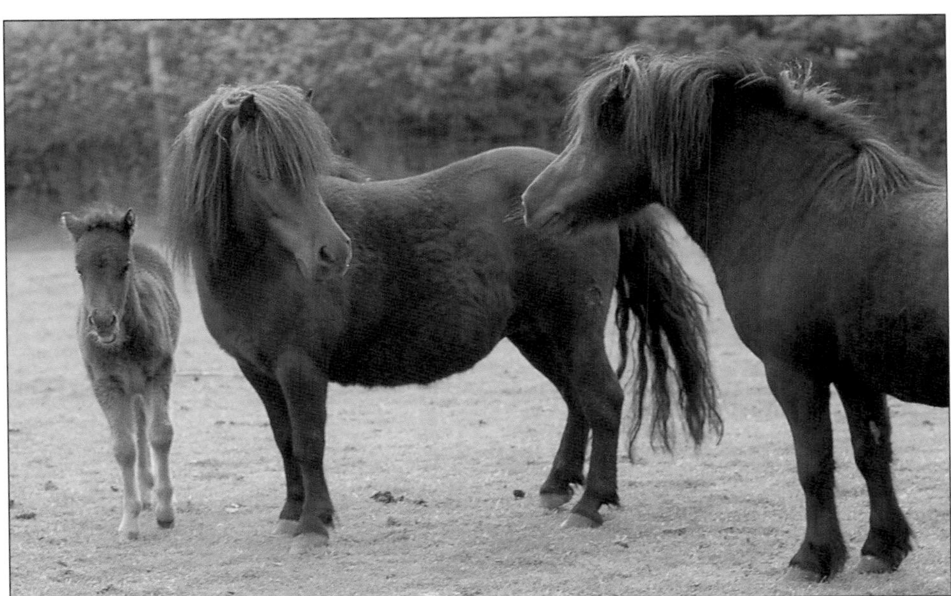

ABOVE
Shetland Ponies can be wilful, but in the hands of a competent child they make good riding ponies.

RIGHT
Centuries of living on rough, rock-strewn terrain have made the ponies both active and sure-footed. Their feet are well-shaped and extremely hard.

INTERESTING FACTS

In winter the Shetland Pony grows a double coat as protection against the inclement climate of its native home. The coat has "guard hairs", which shed rain and keep the pony's skin completely dry, however severe the weather. The mane and tail are profuse.

Dales

The Dales Pony comes from the Upper Dales (river valleys) of the eastern side of the Pennine Hills in northern England. It shares the same ancestors as its slightly larger neighbour, the Fell Pony, whose traditional home is on the western side of the Pennines. These ponies are believed to be descended from horses of the Roman period, when Friesians were introduced into northern England – this could have been the source of the Dales' predominantly black colouring. In more recent times various outcrosses are said to have been made, Norfolk Roadster among them. Some Welsh Cob blood was used during the nineteenth century and also Clydesdale. Despite the introduction of the latter, the Dales has retained its pony character, as can be seen in its neat head with its small, mobile ears.

The Dales is noted for its tremendously active paces and its great strength in relation to its size. At one time it played a vital part in lead mining, working both under- and overground, carrying loads of lead ore to the sea ports. It was also much used by the army. Stamina, courage and a docile temperament, coupled with its great strength and energy make the Dales a first-rate all-round riding and driving pony. It jumps, is intelligent, has a sensible, calm temperament and can carry an adult with ease.

BREED DESCRIPTION

Height Not exceeding 14.2hh.

Colour Predominantly black, also bay, brown and, occasionally, grey.

Conformation Small, neat head, with wide forehead, bright eyes and small, erect ears; well-sloped shoulders; strong, deep body with short back, well-sprung ribs and strong loins; well-developed hindquarters; strong limbs with short straight cannons, good, clean joints and broad, very hard, well-shaped feet; fine, silky feather at the heel.

INTERESTING FACTS

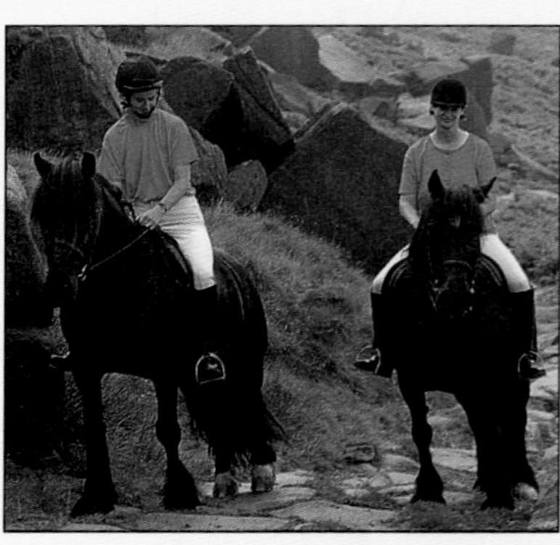

Dales Ponies are inherently sure-footed. Their forebears are said to have been used by the Romans when constructing Hadrian's Wall in the inhospitable tract of country between the mouth of the River Tyne and the marshes of the Solway Firth in northern England.

TOP
There have been native ponies on either side of the Pennines and in the Scottish borders for many centuries. They trace back in part to the Scottish Galloway although the Dales' black colouring probably comes from the influence of Friesian blood.

LEFT
The breed is particularly renowned for its strong limbs, good bone and excellent feet.

Fell

Like its relative, the Dales, the Fell Pony is believed to be descended from the Friesian which was brought to northern England during Roman times. Down the centuries it, too, was almost certainly influenced by the now extinct Galloway, the mount of border reivers (raiders, particularly cattle thieves) who needed a strong, fast, sure-footed horse for their nefarious purposes.

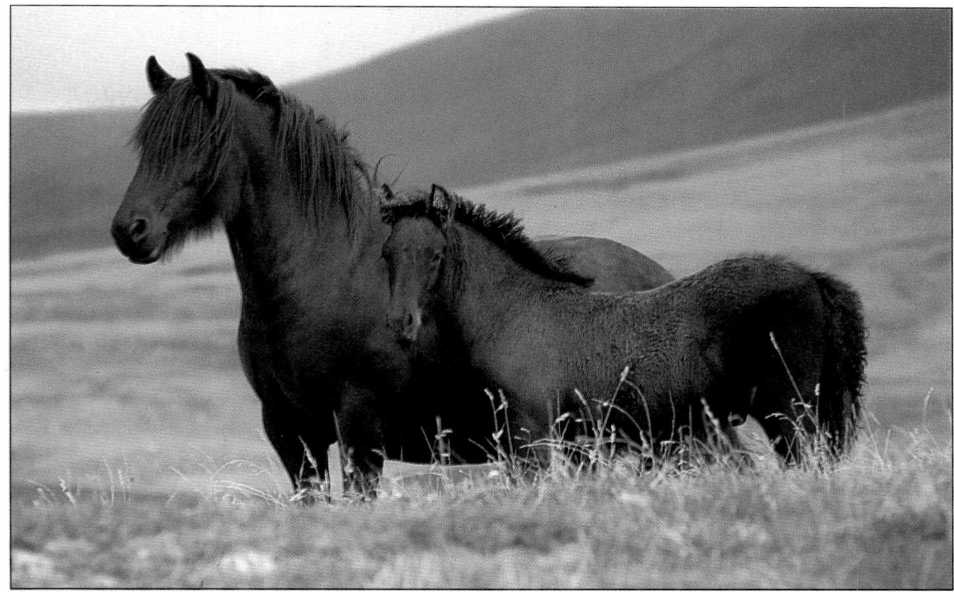

BREED DESCRIPTION

Height Not exceeding 14hh.

Colour Black, brown, bay and grey, preferably with no white markings, though a star or a little white on the foot is allowed.

Conformation Small, well set-on head with broad forehead, bright, prominent eye, small, neat ears, large nostrils and fine throat and jaws; strong neck but not too heavy, giving a good length of rein; good, sloping shoulders; strong, deep body with muscular loins; strong hindquarters with well set-on tail; strong limbs with plenty of good flat bone below the knee and well-formed feet with characteristic blue horn.

The Fell has evolved as a somewhat smaller, lighter pony than the Dales (official recognition of a distinction between the two did not come until 1916, when the Dales Pony Improvement Society and the Fell Pony Society were formed). The Fell is, nevertheless, enormously strong and, like the Dales, was used as a pack-pony. During the eighteenth century it transported lead, coal and iron ore to the coast, carrying up to 16 stone (224lb/101kg) at a time in panniers. Some were used in pack-trains to carry produce such as wool as far as London.

The Fell is noted for its good paces, having a fast, active walk and a swift trot. Now that it is no longer in demand for pack work, shepherding and general farm work, it has become a popular all-round pleasure pony. It makes an excellent mount for trekking, goes superbly across country, both under saddle and in harness, and has the paces to do well in pure dressage.

ABOVE
Fell ponies are native to the western side of the Pennines. They are slightly smaller than their near neighbours, the Dales, but have the same inherent toughness and active paces.

BELOW
The Fell makes a first-class riding pony. These ponies, pictured at a breed performance show, were competing in show jumping and mounted games as well as in show classes.

INTERESTING FACTS

HRH The Duke of Edinburgh competes in trials with a team of HM The Queen's Fell Ponies. With their lively trot and great stamina they are well suited to the marathon phase, run over a distance of 16 miles.

Connemara

Elegant, hardy, intelligent, possessed of tremendous agility and jumping prowess, the Connemara is arguably the best performance pony in the world. It is Ireland's only indigenous breed; it takes its name from the wild, rocky region on the western seaboard of Ireland where ponies have existed, in one form or another, since ancient times.

How this paragon among ponies developed is unclear. One theory is that it is descended from Barb and Spanish horses introduced into the west of Ireland as early as the sixth century BC, when the Celts overran the whole of Europe. These horses would then have been crossed with the indigenous stock. Also, during subsequent centuries of trade between the west coast of Ireland and the Iberian peninsula it is highly likely that quantities of horses would have been imported. The breed undoubtedly does show signs of Spanish and eastern blood to this day. The suggestion that the Connemara is descended from horses of the Spanish Armada that swam ashore after being shipwrecked in 1588 is nowadays dismissed by most experts as mere fancy!

LEFT
The Connemara's beautiful head possesses great refinement. Grey is the breed's predominant colour.

Arab stallions are known to have been imported by landowners during the middle of the nineteenth century, but it is impossible to say what influence, if any, they had on the Connemara. During the latter part of the century, however, Welsh

BREED DESCRIPTION

Height Not exceeding 14.2hh.

Colour Predominantly grey but also brown, dun, black and occasionally chestnut and roan.

Conformation Short head, often with slightly dished profile, with broad forehead, dark, full eyes, small ears; long, arched neck giving good length of rein; well-sloped shoulders; deep, compact body; strong hindquarters with high-set tail; good strong limbs with short cannons and plenty of bone below the knee; strong, sound feet.

RIGHT
Excellent conformation - notably the well-sloped shoulders - make the Connemara a superb riding pony, possessed of strength, free-going movement and superb balance.

INTERESTING FACTS

Little Model was one of many part-bred Connemaras who have achieved great success in the competitive disciplines. By a Thoroughbred stallion out of a Connemara mare, Little Model, a grey, was originally trained for circus work. The British dressage rider Mrs V.D.S. Williams spent a good deal of time persuading him to "unlearn" various tricks before he could concentrate on Grand Prix work. Together they competed in the 1960 Olympics, finishing in a very creditable eleventh place. The following year they were third in the European Championships – Britain's first placing in a dressage championship. Sadly, because he was such a bad traveller, Little Model never competed abroad again although he enjoyed many successes at home.

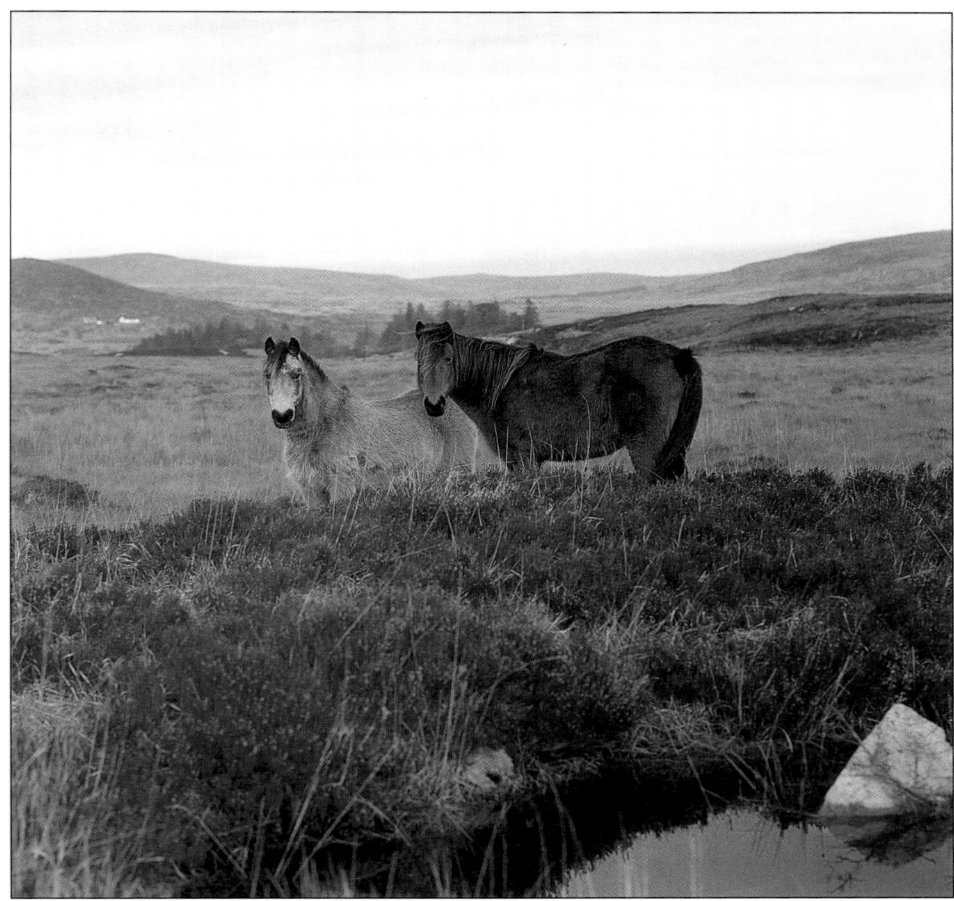

ABOVE
Connemaras in their natural habitat of western Ireland.

blood was certainly introduced and did play a part: one of the Welsh stallions, Prince Llewellyn, sired Dynamite out of a native mare. Dynamite in turn sired Cannon Ball (foaled in 1904), who is the first stallion listed in the Connemara Stud Book. Other attempts to "improve" the breed included the use of Thoroughbred, Hackney and Clydesdale blood.

Finally, in 1923, the Connemara Pony Breeders' Society was founded in Galway. It had the backing of the Department of Agriculture and the intention was to improve the breed from within, by seeking out the best type of mare and an appropriate number of similar quality stallions to use as foundation stock. The result of these efforts is an outstanding, quality pony of fixed type, courageous but sensible, able to excel in virtually all sports, from show jumping and three-day eventing to dressage and driving. When crossed with the Thoroughbred it produces a top-class performance horse.

BELOW
Traditional pony power: carting seaweed in Galway.

ABOVE
As a ridden pony the Connemara cannot be bettered. Spirited but sensible, courageous but kind, it is an ideal mount for children and adults alike.

Fjord

Norway's unusual looking Fjord Pony is believed to have inhabited Norway and probably other parts of Scandinavia since prehistoric times. At a quick glance it is not unlike the Przewalski's Horse (the Asiatic Wild Horse) in appearance, though the head is much less heavy and "primitive", being more pony-like in size and shape. Ponies resembling the Fjord are depicted in Viking art. They can be seen fighting, a pastime which was also popular in Iceland and which may have been engaged in for sport, as a form of performance testing or, probably, a combination of both.

Hundreds if not thousands of years spent in a mountainous habitat have produced a pony that is perfectly adapted to its environment. Sturdy and muscular, the Fjord has short, strong legs with good joints and hard, sound feet. Down the centuries its inherent sure-footedness, strength, soundness and tremendous stamina have made it an invaluable helpmate to farmers. Used to coping with severe weather conditions and undaunted by the most rugged terrain, it also proved the perfect pack-pony for use on mountain trails.

Nowadays the Fjord Pony can be found in a number of countries outside Scandinavia, including Germany, Denmark and England. It makes a good general-purpose riding pony and also goes well in harness.

BREED DESCRIPTION

Height 13 – 14hh.

Colour Most shades of dun with a black dorsal eel-stripe and, often, zebra markings on the legs.

Conformation Pony-type head with broad forehead and small ears; muscular neck; strong, deep body; fairly low-set tail; short, strong limbs with good joints, short cannons and plenty of bone; hard, sound feet.

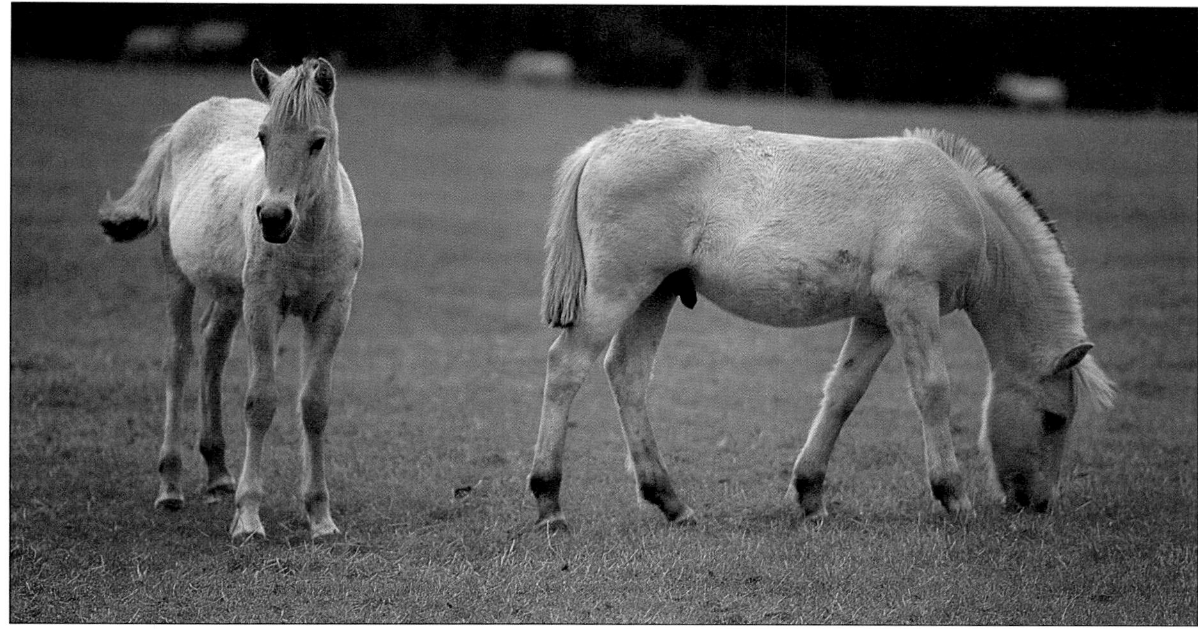

▮ LEFT
Although its natural environment is the mountains, the adaptable Fjord can be found in many other types of country, where it is valued both for its attractive appearance and its performance ability.

▮ OPPOSITE TOP
The Fjord has a true pony head, with small ears, large, wide-set eyes and a small muzzle which is lighter in colour than the rest of the coat.

▮ OPPOSITE
The pony's stocky build testifies to its great strength. Deep through the girth and with a particularly muscular neck and strong legs, it is a great little worker in areas not accessible to machines.

▮ LEFT
The striking colouring of the mane and tail, with their black and silver hair, is unique to the Fjord Pony.

▮ RIGHT
Fjords make excellent driving ponies. They have a kind, willing temperament but are active movers and, like all mountain breeds, exceptionally sure-footed.

INTERESTING FACTS

One of the most distinctive features of the Fjord Pony is its unusual mane and tail colouring. Both mane and tail have black hairs in the centre, with silver on the outside. The stiff mane is traditionally cut in a curve with the dark inner hair standing higher than the outer silver hair.

Caspian

In 1965 an exciting discovery was made in northern Iran, in a remote, mountainous region not far from the Caspian Sea. Some three dozen miniature horses, no taller than a small pony but with the outward characteristics of a diminutive horse, were found. Detailed scientific examination revealed that these little horses had certain physical characteristics that did not match those of other horses: an extra full-sized molar on each side of the upper jaw; a scapula that was a different shape from that usually found in equine animals, and a slightly different formation of the three parietal bones in the head.

The Caspian Pony, as it has become known, is believed to be the direct descendant of the earliest equine animals that roamed the region around 3,000 BC. Bones have been excavated in Iran that point to the existence in the area of a very similar small horse at that period, a seal in the British Museum shows King Darius riding in a chariot drawn by horses of Caspian type, and other artefacts of the period exist depicting similar small horses. It is thought possible that the Caspian is a far-off ancestor of the Arabian.

For many centuries the Caspian was mysteriously "lost". After its re-discovery a careful breeding programme was set up at studs in order to safeguard its future. Caspian Ponies can now be found in a number of European countries as well as Australia, New Zealand and the United States.

BREED DESCRIPTION

Height 10 – 12hh.

Colour Bay, grey and chestnut, with occasional white markings on head and legs.

Conformation Short, fine head with large eyes, vaulted forehead, fine tapering muzzle with large, low-set nostrils and very short ears; graceful neck; sloping shoulders; slim body with straight back and high-set tail; slim limbs but with dense, strong bone and little or no feathering at the fetlock; neat, oval, unusually strong hoofs.

The Caspian is extremely hardy, and possesses great speed and endurance as well as a kind temperament. It has dense bone and exceptionally hard, tough feet, which do not require shoeing. It makes a good riding pony and despite its small size has remarkable jumping ability.

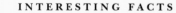

INTERESTING FACTS

Despite its lack of height, the Caspian has wonderful natural action; it can keep up with a horse at walk, trot and canter. Even at this early age the foal shows tremendous length of stride.

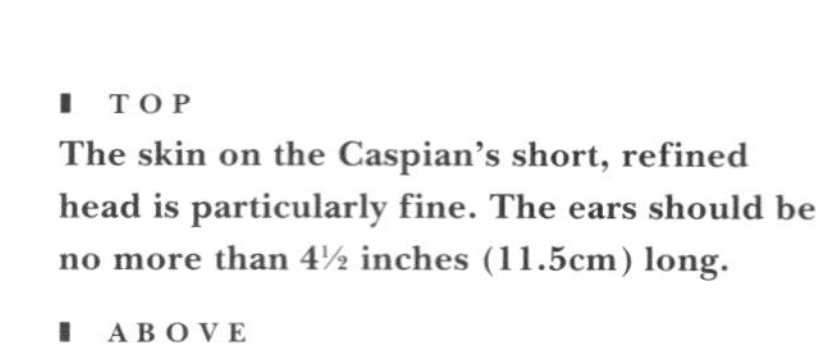

TOP
The skin on the Caspian's short, refined head is particularly fine. The ears should be no more than 4½ inches (11.5cm) long.

ABOVE
On account of its small size the breed is described as a pony, although it has all the attributes of a miniature horse.

Riding Pony

▮ BELOW
The Riding Pony looks like a miniature Thoroughbred but should have the characteristics of a pony, not a horse. A good length of neck and well-sloped shoulders ensure the required freedom of movement.

Any pony which can be ridden is, technically, a "riding pony" but the Riding Pony which has been developed in Britain for showing purposes has evolved into a very definite type. It is essentially a child's hack, the equivalent of the adult rider's Thoroughbred show hack. It is not, therefore, surprising that small Thoroughbreds have been used in its development. Together with the Arab, the Thoroughbred was crossed with native ponies, particularly the Welsh and the Dartmoor, to produce ponies of great quality and excellent conformation. The best examples, while resembling the Thoroughbred in miniature, will not have lost the bone and substance of the native ponies and should certainly look like ponies, not small horses.

Since it is by definition a child's mount, the Riding Pony must have a sensible nature and be safe for children to ride; but since it is also a show pony, it must have presence and the long, low, graceful action of the Thoroughbred. The perfect combination of these elements, together with the retention of true pony character, is the challenge faced by all breeders of Riding Ponies. Riding Ponies may be entered in the National Pony Society Stud Book.

BREED DESCRIPTION

Height Show class divisions – up to 12.2hh, 12.2 – 13.2hh and 13.2 – 14.2hh.

Colour Any whole colour; white markings are permissible.

Conformation Fine, quality head, with large, well-spaced eyes and small ears; fairly long neck; good sloping shoulders with clearly defined withers; medium length back, deep through the girth; well-muscled hindquarters with well set-on tail; clean, hard limbs with flat joints, short cannons and well let-down hocks; good, sound feet of equal size; no feather.

INTERESTING FACTS

In the show ring, as well as the height divisions there are classes for ponies ridden side-saddle, for pairs of ponies and for novice ponies. Ponies are judged on their paces, conformation and manners but are not required to jump.

Pony of the Americas

This breed of spotted pony originated in the 1950s, the foundation sire, Black Hand, being the result of a mating between a Shetland pony stallion and an Appaloosa mare. Black Hand was the equivalent of a miniature Appaloosa. Interest in this concept of a spotted pony soon spread and the Pony of the Americas, as it became known, is now a popular all-round riding pony throughout the United States and also in Canada. It has its own breed society and stud book.

The Pony of the Americas stands no more than 13.2hh and must have one of the recognized Appaloosa colourings. It should be well proportioned, with substance, style and refinement – something like a miniature cross between a Quarter Horse and an Arabian. The pony's paces should be smooth and the action straight and free. The Pony of the Americas is a versatile performer. It is shown in Western pleasure and performance classes, as well as under English saddles and in harness. It has a kind nature and makes an ideal all-round riding pony for children.

ABOVE
The head is clean cut and the pony has a kind eye, which reflects its docile, friendly nature.

BELOW
In overall appearance the Pony of the Americas is not unlike the Quarter Horse, but with more refinement.

INTERESTING FACTS

Leslie Boomhower, of Mason City, Iowa, was responsible for the mating of Shetland to Appaloosa which produced the breed's foundation sire.

BREED DESCRIPTION

Height 11.2–13.2hh.

Colour Normal Appaloosa markings – leopard, snowflake, blanket, frost, marble.

Conformation Clean-cut head, sometimes with slightly dished profile, with large, kind, prominent eyes and medium-sized, alert ears; slightly arched neck; deep, sloping shoulders with prominent withers; round, full-ribbed, heavily muscled body with well-sprung ribs and short back and loins; muscular hindquarters with long, level croup; strong limbs, with good clean joints; wide, well-shaped feet.

American Shetland

BREED DESCRIPTION

Height Up to around 42 inches (103cm).

Colour Any.

Conformation Fairly long head with straight or slightly dished profile; long, graceful neck with pronounced withers; sloping shoulders; short, strong body and hindquarters; fairly long limbs.

Shetland Ponies were first imported into America during the 1880s and quickly became popular. In 1890, when the American Shetland Pony Club was formed, there were over two hundred listed American breeders – Buffalo Bill Cody featuring prominently among them. Today there are large numbers of American Shetlands but, although they retain the name "Shetland", they do not bear a great deal of resemblance to the native "Sheltie" of Britain's Shetland Isles.

The American Shetland is the result of crossing pure-bred Shetlands with Hackney Ponies, with the addition of a little Arab and Thoroughbred blood. In appearance it is more like a Hackney than a British native pony. It is more refined than the true Shetland, being somewhat narrower and longer in the body and with longer, more slender limbs. The head, too, has lost the true pony character. Its high, extravagant action, which testifies to the infusion of Hackney blood, makes the American Shetland a popular harness pony.

LEFT
The American Shetland usually stands a couple of inches (5cm) taller than the true Shetland. The same range of colours occurs as in the original Scottish breed.

ABOVE
Due to the addition of Hackney, Arab and Thoroughbred blood, the American Shetland has lost, in varying degrees, the true native pony character of its British ancestors.

INTERESTING FACTS

The high-stepping action produced through the infusions of Hackney blood, has resulted in a pony well suited to harness classes. As with the American gaited horses, the action is enhanced by means of growing the feet longer than normal. Shetlands compete in classes for singles, pairs and tandems as well as in draught harness and under saddle.

Types

Horses and ponies with unusual or exotic coat colours and patterns have occurred throughout history and have usually been highly prized by man, regardless of their breeding. In recent times registers or stud books have been opened in some countries for the most popular of these colour types – in fact some now qualify for the title "breeds". The term "breed" is used to describe horses who have been bred selectively over a period of time and who have, as a result, developed fixed characteristics. Horses belonging to a particular breed have their pedigrees recorded in a stud book. The term "type" describes a horse bred for a particular purpose, such as hunting. Any number of permutations can be (and are) used to produce a horse suitable for riding to hounds and hunters cannot therefore be described as a breed. Horse and pony types, although few in number compared with the established breeds, nevertheless have an important role to play in the world of leisure riding.

Palomino

Throughout history man has prized horses with golden-coloured coats. Horse's with this striking colouring are depicted in works of art, often dating back many centuries, from Asia, Japan and a number of European countries. Golden horses are referred to in Homer's *The Iliad* and in Norse legend. In Spain Queen Isabella, sponsor of Columbus, encouraged their breeding, as a result of which they are often referred to in that country as "Isabellas".

There are various suggestions as to the derivation of the word Palomino, now used to describe golden horses. The most likely is that it comes from Juan de Palomino, who received a horse of this colouring from Cortès. Other theories are that it comes from the name of a Spanish grape or from the word *paloma,* meaning dove. Palomino colouring features in a number of breeds, therefore the term Palomino refers to a colour type, not a specific breed.

BREED DESCRIPTION

Height The registry of the Palomino Horse Breeders of America (PHBA) admits horses standing between 14 and 17hh.

Colour Body colour of a newly minted gold coin, with variations from light to dark. The skin is usually grey, black, brown or motley, without underlying pink skin or spots except on the face or legs. Black, hazel or brown eyes. White mane and tail with not more than 15 per cent dark, sorrel or chestnut hairs. Dorsal stripe and zebra stripes not permitted.

Conformation To be eligible for registration with the PHBA a Palomino must show refinement of head, bone, and general structure appropriate to the breeds recognized by the PHBA and be suitable for carrying Western or English equipment. It must show no pony or draught horse characteristics.

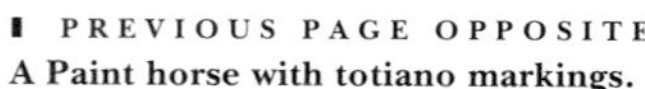

PREVIOUS PAGE OPPOSITE
A Paint horse with totiano markings.

PREVIOUS PAGE
Typical Palomino colouring.

ABOVE
Palominos always have a white mane and tail. For registration purposes the head must be of true riding horse proportions, with no pony or draught characteristics.

LEFT
This Quarter Horse is an admirable example of the requirements of the PHBA, which call for a body colour "of a newly minted gold coin".

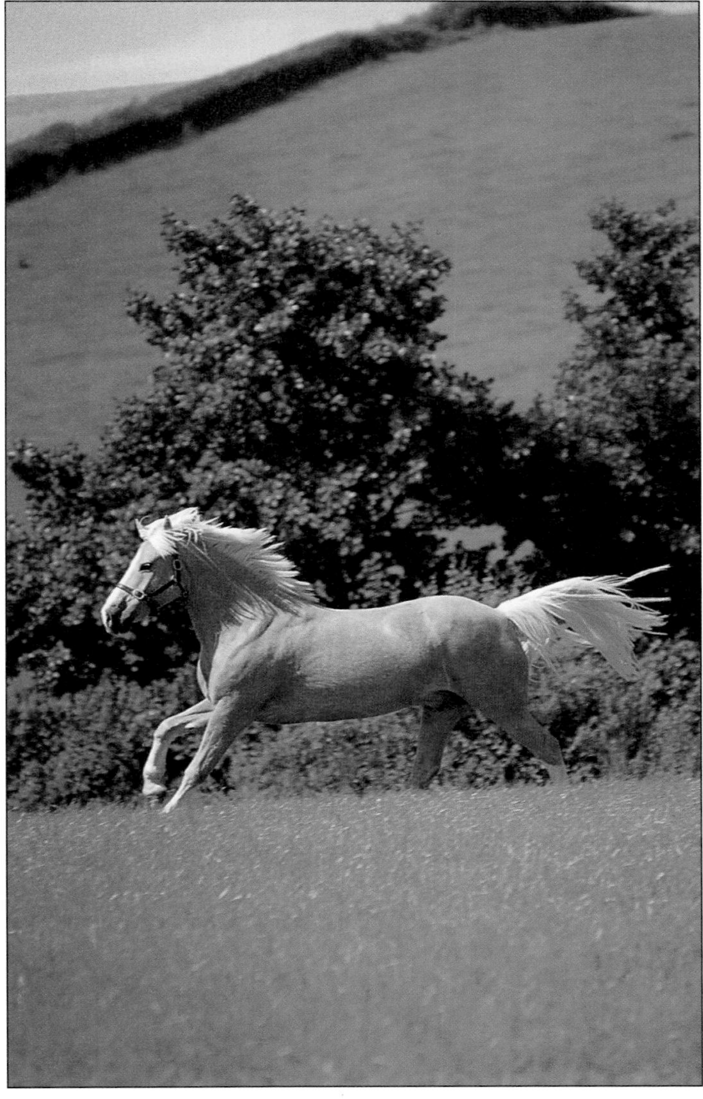

RIGHT
Palominos, like this English pony, are found all over the world and do not have to be of any particular breed to qualify for registration as such.

BELOW RIGHT
Golden-coloured horses have been prized throughout history and in all parts of the world. These two were photographed in France.

INTERESTING FACTS

Palomino colouring occurs in a number of breeds. In the United States they include the Morgan Horse, the Quarter Horse, the Saddlebred and the Tennessee Walking Horse, while in Britain there are some striking looking Palominos among the Welsh Ponies and Cobs.

They may occur in many parts of the world, but Palomino horses are particularly associated with North America, where they were introduced by the Spanish Conquistadores. The origin of this type of colouring is uncertain but it is thought to have come from the Arab – though it is not found nowadays in the pure-bred Arabian horse. One of the intriguing, if frustrating, aspects of Palomino horses is that they do not "breed true", in other words there is no sure-fire way of ensuring Palomino colouring in a foal. It is all a question of genetics and the genetics of equine coat colouring is a complicated subject, involving dominant and recessive genes. Put simply, mate a Palomino to a Palomino and there is only a 50 per cent chance of a Palomino foal. There is a 25 per cent chance that the foal will be sorrel (a bright chestnut) and the same chance of the result being a pseudo-albino, known as a cremello. Cross a Palomino with a sorrel and the chances are still only 50 per cent – and any Palomino colouring that is achieved may be too poor to be eligible for most Palomino societies. Cross a Palomino with any other colour and the chances of producing a Palomino foal diminish.

Despite the uncertainties involved in breeding for colour, Palomino horses retain their age-old appeal. Being good all-round riding horses – conformation should never be sacrificed for the sake of colour – they can be seen taking part in all kinds of activities, from cutting horse events to trail riding.

Appaloosa

The spotted coat colouring of the American Appaloosa traces back to stock imported by the Spanish Conquistadores. Spotted horses became particularly prized by the Nez Percé Indian tribe who lived in the region that is now northern Idaho, north-east Oregon and south-east Washington. The word Appaloosa is derived from Palouse country, an area named after the Palouse river.

The Nez Percé are said to be the first Indian tribe to have practised systematic breeding of horses. Following the defeat of the Indians by the US army during the latter half of the nineteenth century, the horses which escaped slaughter became scattered. It was not until the 1920s that efforts were made to re-establish the Appaloosa horse, using the descendants of those which survived as a basis. In 1938 the Appaloosa Horse Club was founded in Oregon. Its objectives were to collect records and historical data relating to the origin of the Appaloosa, to preserve, improve and standardize the breed and to set up a register for approved animals.

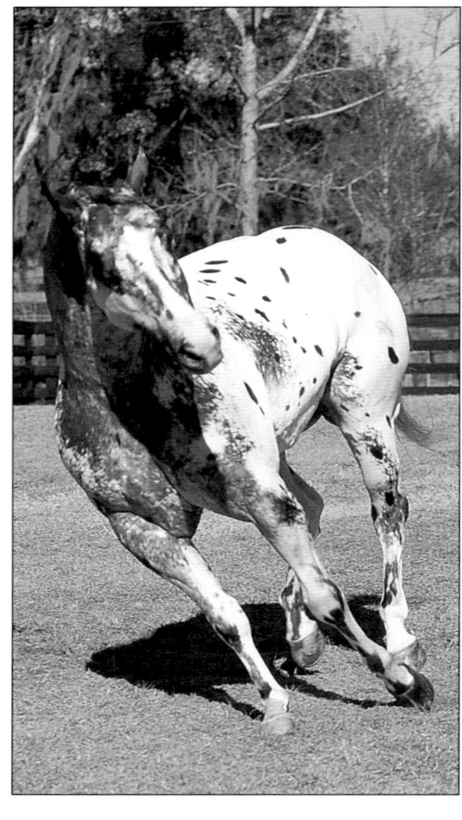

LEFT
The eye-catching markings of the American Appaloosa are derived from Spanish stock imported by the Conquistadores.

BELOW LEFT
The Appaloosa is a compact, muscular stamp of horse. The sparse mane and tail hair are characteristic of the breed.

The re-establishment of the Appaloosa has been a great success and today the breed is widely used in all types of Western riding, for endurance riding and in the show ring in both hunter and jumper classes. Appaloosas are mainly associated

BREED DESCRIPTION

Height Around 14.2 – 15.2hh.

Colour Spotted. The skin is mottled (especially noticeable around the nostrils and genitalia).

Conformation The Appaloosa is a compact stamp of horse with a well-shaped neck, short, strong back, powerful hindquarters and strong limbs with extremely good, hard feet.

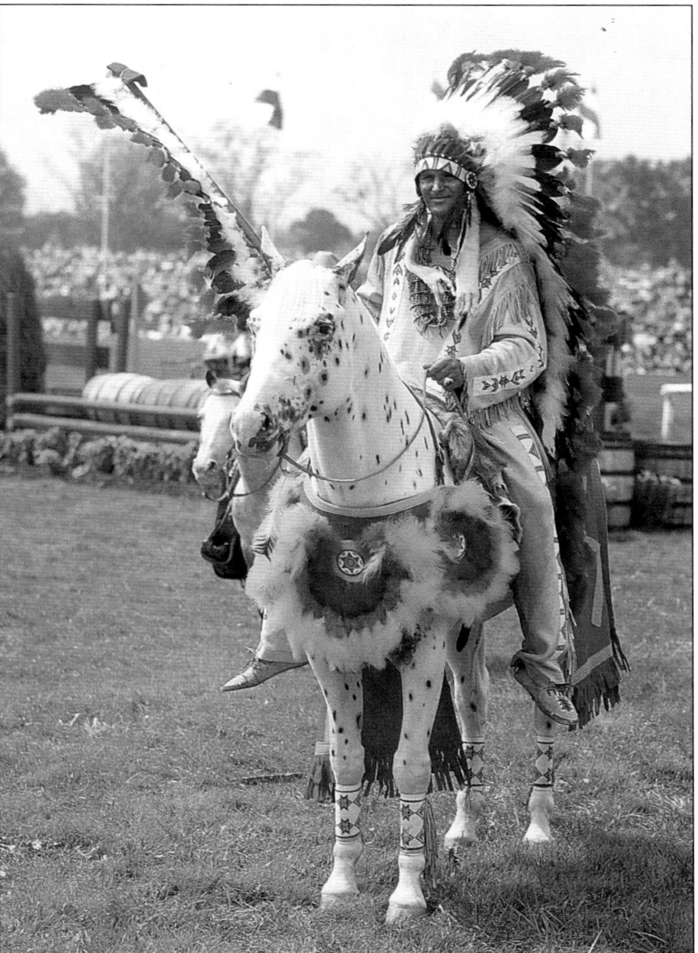

LEFT
This horse and rider, decked out in traditional style, recall the time when spotted horses were the preferred mounts of the Nez Percé Indians.

FAR LEFT
Spotted horses are popular in many countries outside the United States. There is a thriving Appaloosa society in Britain – this horse was photographed at the Royal Windsor Horse Show.

with the United States but they are also found in many other countries.

There are five main Appaloosa coat patterns: leopard – white colouring over the loins and hips with dark, round or egg-shaped spots; snowflake – dark spots all over a white body but usually dominant over the hips; blanket – white area over the hips without dark spots in the white; marble – mottled all over the body; frost – white specks with a dark background. Other distinguishing features include white sclera round the eyes and, often, vertical black and white stripes on the hooves. The mane and tail tend to be quite sparse.

INTERESTING FACTS

In America gaited spotted horses, that is those who show the ability to perform an intermediate gait other than the trot (such as the rack, foxtrot, running walk or pace) are termed Walkaloosas. To qualify for registration with the Walkaloosa Horse Association, which was founded in 1983, a horse must meet one of three criteria: either be the progeny of a registered Walkaloosa stallion and mare, or show Appaloosa colouring and demonstrate an intermediate gait other than trot, or be the product of verifiable Appaloosa (colour) and Paso, Foxtrotter or Tennessee Walker blood. The Walkaloosa's colouring is typical of that found in the Appaloosa, including white sclera round the eyes. Coat patterns include, but are not limited to, leopard, blanket and snowflake. The Walkaloosa, like the Appaloosa, is noted for its kind, sensible nature and makes an outstanding pleasure and trail horse.

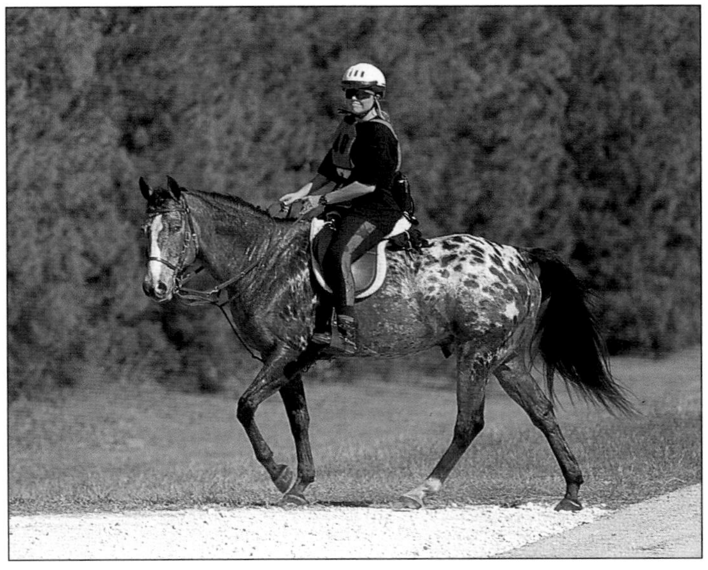

LEFT
Noted for its strong limbs and the excellence of its feet, the Appaloosa makes a good endurance riding horse.

Paint Horse

BREED DESCRIPTION

Because horses of various breeds are eligible for registration as Paint Horses, there is accordingly a degree of variation in the height and overall size. However, all American Paint Horses have distinct stock-type conformation. This may be generally defined as an animal whose bone and muscle construction make it highly adaptable to ranch work. It will be both versatile and athletic.

Horses with broken coloured coats (also known as piebalds and skewbalds) are found all over the world, though they are particularly associated with the North American Indian.

In America a horse with this type of colouring may be registered either as a Paint Horse or as a Pinto, depending on the horse meeting certain criteria. The American Paint Horse Association was founded in 1962 to provide a register for horses with individual, colourful patterns of contrasting light and dark hair and skin, and distinctive stock-type conformation. To qualify for registration with the APHA horses must be bred from registered American Paint Horses, registered American Quarter Horses or registered Thoroughbreds and must meet a minimum colour requirement. A horse with a predominantly solid-coloured coat must have a definite "natural" Paint marking, which is defined as an area of solid white hair with some underlying, unpigmented skin. A horse with a mainly white hair coat must have a contrasting area of colour with some underlying, pigmented skin. The contrasting areas should be visible at the time the foal is born and at the time of registration.

The APHA maintains two registries, the Regular and the Breeding Stock. To be eligible for inclusion in the Regular

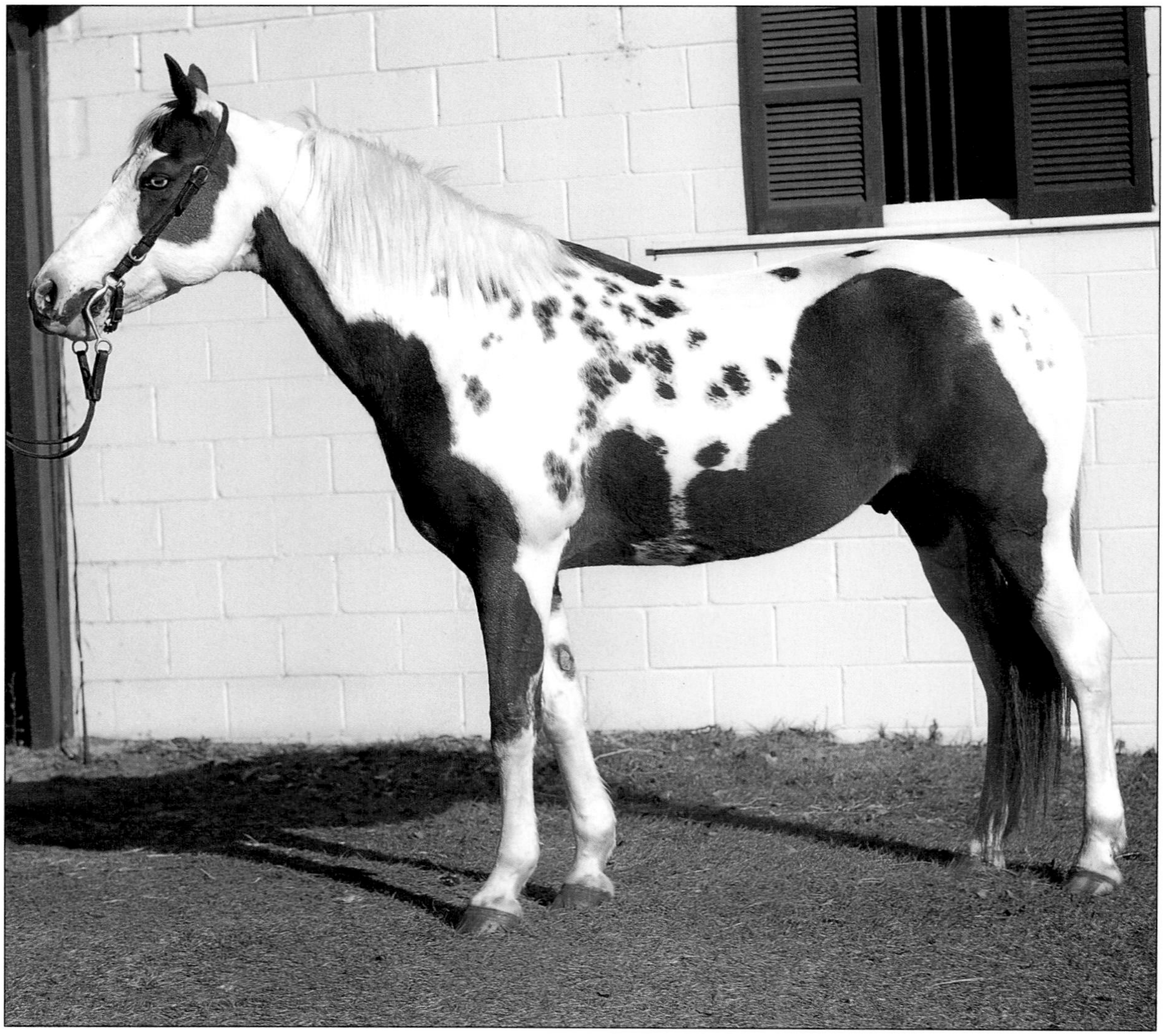

TOP LEFT
This Paint horse has tobiano markings: dark colouring on the flanks, a "shield" down the neck and chest and white legs.

OPPOSITE
Paint horses have always been associated with the American West. The horse on the left is an overo with a bald face.

LEFT
The characteristic shape and build of the Paint horse is that of the stock horse: good overall riding horse conformation and a sturdy, compact appearance.

Registry the foal must have at least one "natural" Paint marking which is a minimum of 2 inches (5cm) in diameter. If a horse does not meet the required colour requirement but meets the other registration requirements (for example a solid-coloured foal resulting from a mating between two registered American Paint Horses), it may be entered in the Breeding Stock Registry.

The spectrum of coat colours in the Paint Horse encompasses all of the tones known in the horse world. The patterns range from almost total colour with a minimal amount of white to almost total white with minimal colour. The patterns are distinguished by the location of colour on the horse, the two major ones being overo and tobiano.

Overo horses have the following characteristics: the white usually will not cross the back of the horse between the withers and the tail; generally at least one and often all four legs will be dark; generally the white is irregular, rather scattered or splashy, and is often referred to as calico; head markings are often bald-faced, apron-faced or bonnet-faced; the tail is usually one colour.

Tobiano horses have the following characteristics: the dark colour will usually cover one or both flanks; generally all four legs will be white, at least below the hocks and knees; generally the spots are regular and distinct as ovals or round patterns which extend down over the neck and chest, giving the appearance of a shield; head markings are like those of a solid-coloured horse – solid colour or with a blaze, stripe, star or snip; the tail usually displays two colours.

Horses with overo and tobiano characteristics are called toveros.

BELOW

Like the Paint horse, the Pinto has overo or tobiano colouring (this horse is a tobiano). For registration purposes, Pintos are divided by conformation type.

INTERESTING FACTS

The Pinto Horse Association of America was founded in 1947 to provide a registry for horses and ponies with the same overo and tobiano colour patterns found in the Paint Horse. Pintos come in all sizes. from miniature to full-size horses. They are divided by type – stock, hunter, pleasure and saddle – the type being based on conformation.

Stock Type Horse – of predominantly Quarter Horse breeding and conformation (horses which are double registered as Paint generally fall into this category). Conformation is that generally associated with a Western breed of horse. Pony – Western type, displaying conformation similar to the Quarter Horse.

Hunter Type Horse – of predominantly Thoroughbred/Jockey Club breeding (a few Paint Horses fit this category). Conformation is that generally associated with an English riding horse. Pony – reflects conformation associated with the Thoroughbred horse and Connemara pony.

Pleasure Type Horse – of predominantly Arabian or Morgan breeding. Pony – reflects carriage and conformation associated with the Arabian, Morgan or Welsh Pony.

Saddle Type Horse – of predominantly Saddlebred or Tennessee Walking Horse breeding, displaying the high head carriage and animation. Pony – reflects conformation and action of the American Shetland and Hackney Pony.

For registration in the Colour Division a Pinto must have noticeable white markings on the body, not including the head and legs. Those areas must be large enough to show Pinto breeding and colour pattern. A dark cheek or cap, or spotted face on a white horse, is a marking common to the Pinto. An all-white horse with a coloured area on the head and on the body is a Pinto, as is a solid coloured animal with a spot on the body; but the amount of colour, its location, the bloodlines of the parents and the sex and age of the animal determine whether it may be registered in the Colour Division or in the Breeding Stock Division.

Knabstrup

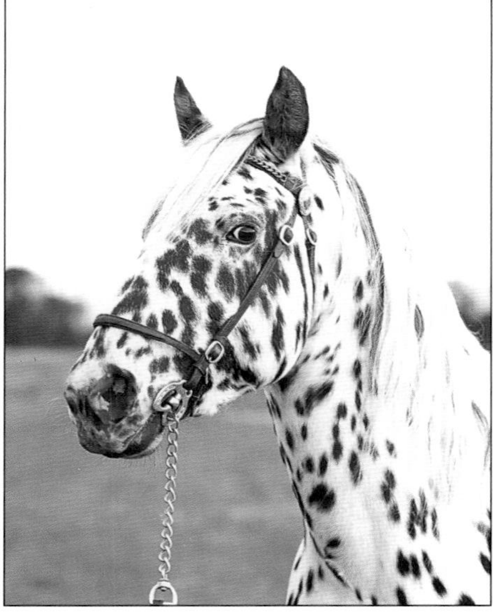

Spotted horses have been known – and have often been highly prized – since ancient times. They can be seen in early Chinese art and there were spotted strains of the Noriker (Austria's old-established light draught breed) and the Spanish horses which were so influential in the development of many of the world's modern breeds. Denmark's once-famous Knabstrup is of Spanish ancestry and dates back to the time of the Napoleonic Wars. At that time a spotted mare named Flaebehoppen was acquired by a butcher called Flaebe (hence her name). Flaebehoppen, an exceptionally fast mare possessed of great endurance, was bred by her next owner, Judge Lunn, to Frederiksborg horses and founded a line of spotted horses. Named the Knabstrup, after Lunn's estate, this strain was rather less substantial than the Frederiksborg but was tough and sound and, because of its attractive markings, became popular as a circus horse. Subsequent crossings back to the Frederiksborg reduced the number of pure-bred Knabstrup horses but examples of the breed are still to be found, though not in anywhere near the numbers of the American Appaloosa.

BREED DESCRIPTION

Height Around 15.2 – 16hh.

Colour Mainly white, with brown or black spots of varying size over the body, head and legs.

Conformation Variable, but the best examples have reasonably good overall conformation, with a kind, intelligent head. The mane and tail are usually sparse, as in the majority of spotted horses.

INTERESTING FACTS

The breed's remarkable talents as a circus horse were demonstrated in America not so long ago when a centre-ring attraction consisted of a large Bengal tiger riding a Knabstrup horse. The horse wore protective harness – in case the big cat slipped and decided to hang on with his claws!

TOP LEFT
The mottled skin colouring of the lips and muzzle, so typical of all spotted horses, can be clearly seen on this Knabstrup.

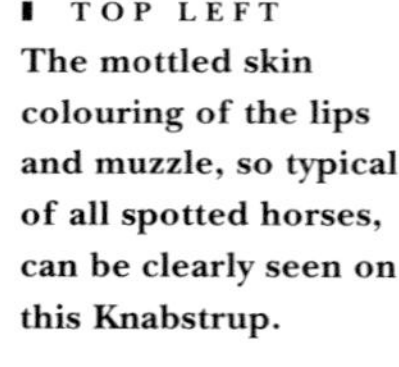

LEFT
The characteristic white body hair with all-over dark spots, together with its intelligent, kind nature, made the Knabstrup a popular circus horse.

Spotted Pony

Spotted Ponies are known to have existed in Britain, and especially in Wales and the West Country, for many centuries. The Romans are said to have brought spotted horses into the country and some of the ancestors of today's Spotted Ponies would have been imported Spanish horses. The creation of a breed society for these striking looking animals is, however, of very recent origin. A British register for spotted horses and ponies was created in 1947 and then in 1976 the organizing society was split, with ponies up to 14.2hh coming under the aegis of the British Spotted Pony Society and larger animals being entered in the British Appaloosa registers.

To qualify for registration ponies must display some of the following features: white sclera round the eye; mottled skin – this part-dark, part-pink skin is usually most evident around the genitals, lips, muzzle, eyes and inside the ears; and striped hooves. If ponies are of solid colour but have proven spotted breeding, they are eligible for entry in a separate register but they should preferably show some breed characteristics. Piebald and skewbald ponies are not eligible, nor are their progeny.

Spotted Ponies may be of small, riding or cob type, but all should show true pony character and must have bone, substance and active paces. They make good all-round performance ponies, both under saddle and in harness, and there is growing interest in ridden and in-hand show classes. British Spotted Ponies have been exported to Australia, North America and several European countries, including France, Germany and Holland. Indeed, the demand from overseas has led to so many good mares and stallions being exported that the breed society has now introduced performance and sire-rating awards in order to encourage breeders to keep more of the best stock at home.

BREED DESCRIPTION

Height Not exceeding 14.2hh.

Colour Leopard (spots of any colour on white or light background); few spot leopard (white base coat with few spots); snowflake (white spots on dark base coat); blanket (area of white over hips and hindquarters, with or without spots, any base colour).

Conformation Quality pony head with big, bold eyes set well apart, small, neat, well-placed ears, prominent, open nostrils and clean, well-defined throat; good length of neck, moderately lean in mares, inclined to be more cresty in stallions (slightly heavier neck allowed in cob type); good, strong, sloping shoulders, well laid back, with well-defined withers; strong, muscular body with deep girth and well-sprung ribs; lengthy, strong, well-muscled hindquarters with well set-on tail (slightly finer hindquarters in riding type); good limbs, with long, strong forearms, well-developed knee, well let-down hocks, short cannons; well-shaped, dense hooves.

INTERESTING FACTS

As with all colour types, breeding for spots is a question of genetics. Some ponies which have spotted coats when young may lose their spots as they grow older. They are known as "faders". Fading is caused by the dominant grey gene. Raised spots, that is ones that stand out above the rest of the pony's coat, rarely fade. The colour of the foal's coat cannot be used as a guide to the adult pony's colouring, since the colour often changes with the first change of coat.

TOP LEFT
The British Spotted Pony has the large, expressive eyes, neat, mobile ears and open nostrils that are characteristic of all good types of pony.

LEFT
Versatile and strong, the British Spotted Pony makes a good all-round riding pony and has also been used with great success in four-in-hand driving.

Hunter

As its name implies, a hunter is a horse used for riding to hounds. It is a type, not a breed, and there is no fixed "recipe" for producing a hunter. It is, however, generally accepted that the finest hunters are bred in Ireland, Britain and, to some extent, the United States.

The type of horse required for hunting varies according to the nature of the country hunted – a big, quality Thoroughbred type may be perfect for galloping and jumping over the grassland of the English "shires", but will be less than ideal for areas of heavy plough or trappy hill country, where boldness and speed are less important than steadiness and sure-footedness. Whatever the exact type of horse required, however, a hunter must have correct conformation, without which he is unlikely to stand up to the hard work required of him. He must be well balanced and give a comfortable ride. He needs to be agile and fearless but also well mannered and controllable. He must have the necessary speed to keep up with hounds and the stamina to see him through a long day of physical exertion, often twice a week during the hunting season. He must also have jumping ability, the exact degree depending on the type of country hunted.

The Irish hunter is often produced by crossing the Thoroughbred with the Irish Draught, while many of the best British hunters have an element of native pony blood, again laced with Thoroughbred. There is no fixed height and in hunter showing classes in Britain and Ireland the horses are divided according to their weight-carrying ability.

INTERESTING FACTS

In British show classes a lightweight hunter is a horse capable of carrying up to 12st 7lb (175lb/79.37kg); a middleweight is capable of carrying between 12st 7lb and 14st (175–196lb/79–89kg) and a heavyweight over 14st (196lb/89kg). Horses are judged on conformation, action, soundness, ride and manners. There are also classes for ladies' hunters (ridden side-saddle) and small hunters (14.2 – 15.2hh). In working hunter classes horses are required to jump a course of natural looking obstacles.

ABOVE LEFT
In the show hunter, the judge is looking for as near perfect conformation as possible. The horse must also give a good ride and be well mannered.

LEFT
Depth through the girth is essential to allow for expansion of the lungs. Well-sloped shoulders ensure free-going action. The horse's weight-carrying ability is determined by its overall build and the amount of bone (measured round the cannon, below the knee).

BREED DESCRIPTION

Height From 14.2hh upwards.

Colour Any.

Conformation Well set-on head and neck, giving good length of rein; well-sloped shoulders; strong, shortish back with well-sprung ribs and great depth through the girth; strong loins; powerful hindquarters; strong limbs with large joints and plenty of bone; strong, well-shaped feet.

Cob

The cob is a short-legged "stuffy" type of small horse, stocky in appearance and capable of carrying a heavyweight rider. Its kind, unflappable, willing nature and impeccable manners, coupled with its weight-carrying ability, make it an ideal mount for a heavyweight elderly rider – or indeed for anyone who is not particularly athletic.

As with the hunter, there is no set formula for breeding a cob. Many of the best are produced by chance, although Irish Draught blood is often used with great success, particularly when mixed with Thoroughbred. The cob's sturdy, muscular proportions are not designed for great speed, but it should none the less have active paces and be able to gallop and to jump well.

At one time the cob was used as an all-purpose horse, performing equally well in harness and under saddle. Nowadays it is most often seen as a riding horse – the best make excellent hunters. Under British Show Hack and Cob Association rules, cobs are exhibited in two weight classes: as lightweights, capable of carrying up to 14 stone (196lb/89kg) and as heavyweights, capable of carrying over 14 stone. There are also working cob classes, in which the horses must jump a working hunter-type course of fences.

The cob's mane is traditionally hogged (cut short). It used to be the custom to dock the tail of cobs but this cruel practice was made illegal in Britain under the Docking and Nicking Act, 1948.

INTERESTING FACTS

In the show ring cobs are judged like hunters and are expected to show that they can gallop. The judge rides each exhibit in turn to assess the quality of ride they give.

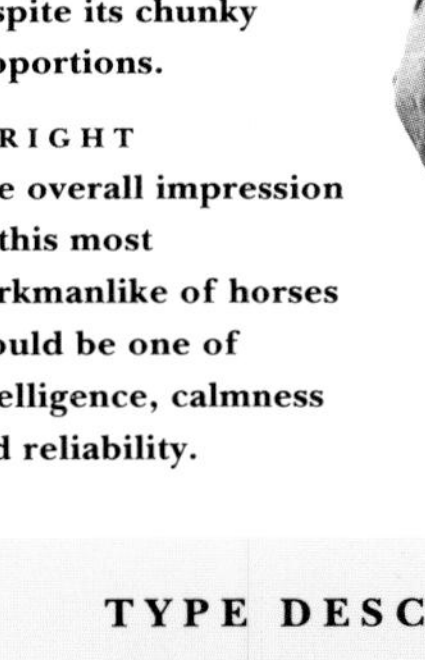

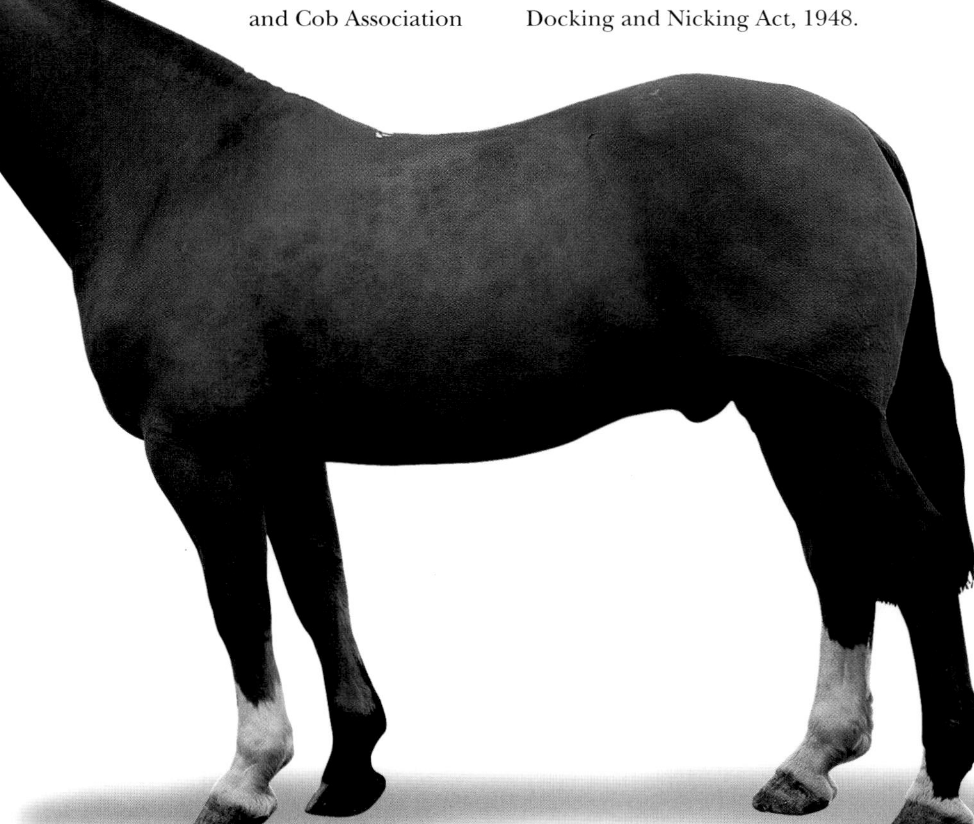

ABOVE RIGHT
Good conformation ensures that the cob possesses tremendous freedom of movement despite its chunky proportions.

RIGHT
The overall impression of this most workmanlike of horses should be one of intelligence, calmness and reliability.

TYPE DESCRIPTION

Height Up to about 15.3hh (in show classes not over 15.1hh).

Colour Any.

Conformation Intelligent-looking head, with no suggestion of coarseness; fairly short, arched neck; strong, sloping shoulders; broad, deep body with short back and powerful loins; strong, well-muscled hindquarters; short, strong limbs with plenty of bone; broad, open feet.

Hack

ABOVE
Gaiety and lightness of movement are essential attributes of the show hack.

In Britain the hack is a supremely elegant, refined type of show horse – although the word "hack" is also used to describe any horse suitable for general riding purposes (as opposed to competitive sports, such as eventing or hunting).

The term hack goes back to the days before the motorization of transport, when "park hacks" were used by the most fashionable people of the day for leisure riding, notably in London's Rotten Row, in Hyde Park. In appearance and manners the park hack was impeccable, thus complementing its elegant, well turned-out rider. In the hunting world riders formerly made use of the "covert hack", a quality horse with less substance than a hunter, to take them to the meet – their grooms having ridden the hunters on beforehand at a leisurely pace to conserve their energy for the day ahead.

Today's show hack is nearer to the park hack and is usually Thoroughbred, or near Thoroughbred. It is judged on conformation, presence, action, training, ride and manners – it should give a comfortable ride and its manners should be faultless. During judging, horses are usually required to give a solo show, designed to demonstrate the horse's correct training and obedience. It should include walk, trot and canter on both reins and a good halt, with the horse standing still on a loose rein.

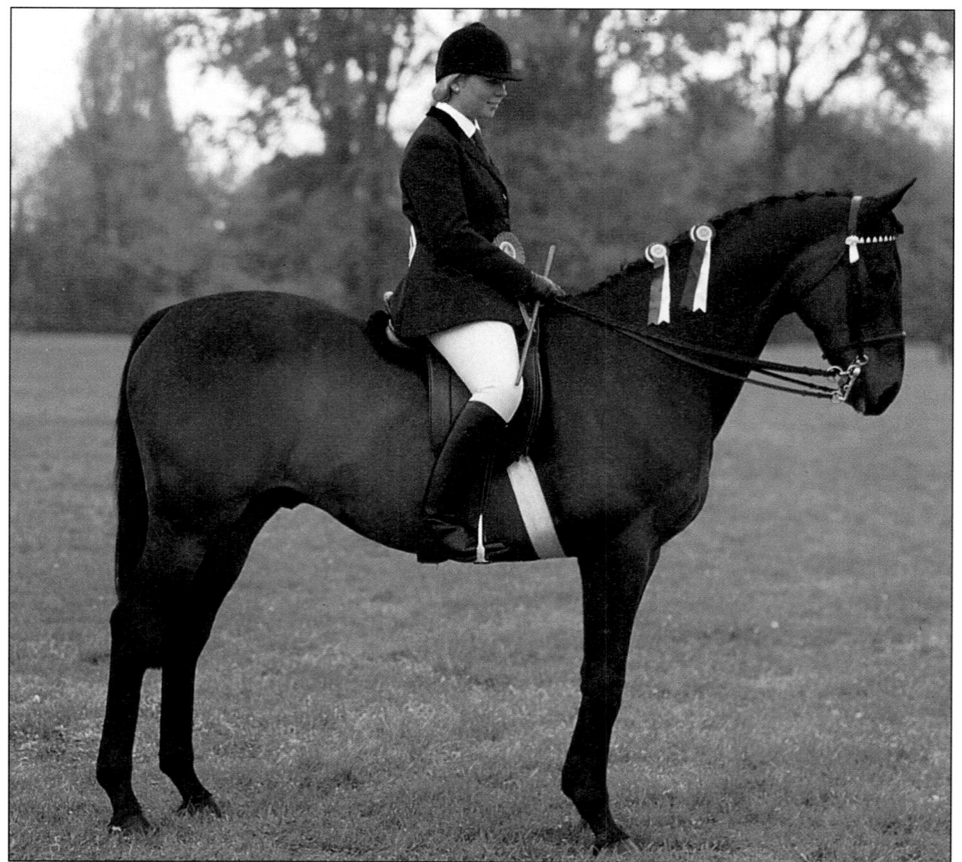

TYPE DESCRIPTION

Height 14.2 – 15.3hh.

Colour Any solid colour.

Conformation Small, quality head; elegant neck; well-sloped shoulders with prominent withers; strong body with deep girth and well-sprung ribs; well-rounded hindquarters; good, sound limbs with at least 8 inches (20cm) of bone; good, sound feet.

INTERESTING FACTS

Hacks are shown in two height classes: small hack, for horses exceeding 14.2hh but not exceeding 15hh, and large hack, for horses exceeding 15hh but not exceeding 15.3hh. There are also classes for ladies' hacks (14.2 – 15.3hh) in which horses are shown under side-saddle.

LEFT
The hack has the overall refinement of the Thoroughbred. It must give a smooth, comfortable ride and have perfect manners.

Polo Pony

The ancient game of polo is believed to have originated in Persia some 2,500 years ago. It was subsequently played in India, the Far East and Tibet, reaching the western world – England and then North and South America – during the nineteenth century. Any pony used in the game is technically a polo pony but the modern polo pony has evolved as a definite type. Many of the best animals are bred in Argentina or at least are descended from Argentinian stock.

By the beginning of the twentieth century the sport was well established in Argentina, where breeders produced suitable mounts by crossing their Criollo horses with imported Welsh ponies. After the 14.2hh height limit for polo ponies was abolished in 1919 the Argentinians began introducing English Thoroughbred blood, which produced animals of greater quality and with more speed.

The polo pony must be capable of short bursts of speed but does not require the long stride of a racehorse. Far more important is a smooth action, which makes the rider's job of hitting the ball easier, the ability to accelerate and decelerate quickly, and to make fast turns. The essential qualities of the polo pony are courage, stamina and natural balance.

FOLLOWING PAGE
Mares and foals at grass in Kentucky.

LEFT
A typically intelligent looking Argentinian polo pony. It is customary to hog the mane to prevent the hair obstructing the player's stick.

TYPE DESCRIPTION

Height Around 15.1hh.

Colour Any.

Conformation Variable, the chief requirements being: fairly long, well-muscled neck; sloping shoulders with well-defined withers; strong, deep body with fairly short back and well-sprung ribs; well-rounded, muscular hindquarters; strong limbs with short cannons, good joints and plenty of bone; well-shaped, round feet.

RIGHT
Whatever their height, polo ponies are always referred to as "ponies", not horses.

INTERESTING FACTS

Between the two World Wars some of the best polo players were to be found in India, where the game was popular both with members of the native aristocracy and in the Indian army. The game there was immortalized by Rudyard Kipling (1865–1936) in *The Maltese Cat*, the story of an inter-regimental match seen through the eyes of the equine participants. A flea-bitten grey, brilliantly quick on his feet, "The Cat" knows more about "playing the game" than most humans!

Horse and Pony Care

Buying a Horse

Everyone who takes part in sport on a regular basis reaches the stage when they want their own equipment. Whether it is a tennis racquet, a fencing foil, a pair of skis or a yacht, owning rather than hiring makes life easier on two counts: the equipment will be available whenever it is required and, most importantly, the owner's performance will almost certainly improve because that equipment will have been selected with their skills and limitations in mind. Riders, however, are faced with a problem not encountered by other sportsmen: their most important piece of equipment is not a man-made object which, to varying degrees, can be tailored to fit individual needs. The horse is a living creature, with a mind, will and personality of his own. He is an expensive animal both to buy and to keep. Choosing the right one is not always easy; choosing the wrong one can be disastrous, both for an owner's bank balance and for his or her confidence. The prospective horse owner should proceed with caution and the rewards will be great.

Choosing the Right Horse

Before you buy a horse make an honest assessment of your riding ability, bearing in mind that most people tend to over-estimate their skill. Talented, experienced riders get the best from all sorts of horses, even those with difficult temperaments. They can school and bring on the young horse, improve the poorly educated older one and ensure that the well-trained performer is used to the best effect. A novice rider, who has only just mastered the basics of horsemanship, can do none of these things and should choose a mount accordingly. The novice needs a correctly schooled, well-mannered mount with a kind disposition, one who will look after his rider. The term "schoolmaster" is aptly used to describe these equine paragons.

For the majority of people cost is one of the most important factors and the purchase price will be determined by a number of things: the type, size and conformation of the horse or pony; its age; its temperament and manners; its performance capabilities (either proven or potential) and its level of schooling.

PREVIOUS PAGE OPPOSITE
A Dartmoor pony: a suitable ride for a child.

PREVIOUS PAGE
A Karbardin horse: ideal for endurance riding.

LEFT
With the right horse, the experience of ownership will be enjoyable and rewarding for both horse and rider.

Generally speaking, an unbroken two- or three-year-old will be cheaper than a four- or five-year-old which has already received some schooling; after that the horse gradually increases in value until it reaches the age of about ten. Once into its teens, it will tend to decrease in value.

Apart from price, your choice of horse or pony will be determined by your size and weight; your riding ability; your stabling/grazing facilities; the amount of time you have to look after it, and the use to which you intend to put it. For example, there is no point in spending a lot of money on a flighty Thoroughbred if you are a nervous rider who wants to do no more than go for quiet hacks; similarly, a pure-bred Arab is not going to take you to the top in the show-jumping world. As to size, much depends on your own build – someone with long legs will certainly be more comfortable on a big horse than someone with short legs and vice versa, and it is usually easier to ride well if you are neither under- nor over-horsed. Temperament and manners are a vital consideration, too. Nervous riders need placid (though not lazy) mounts if they are not to be frightened and put off riding altogether, while a bolder rider will be able to cope with, and enjoy, a more spirited ride.

RIGHT
The majority of warmbloods, specifically developed as sports horses, make fine show jumpers. This horse is a Holstein.

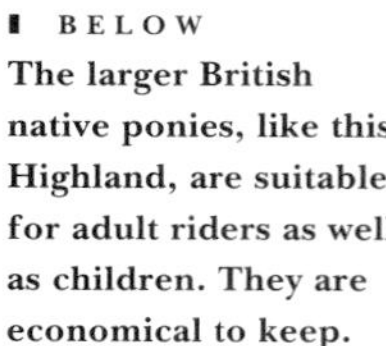

BELOW
The larger British native ponies, like this Highland, are suitable for adult riders as well as children. They are economical to keep.

BELOW
If quiet hacks out are your aim, make sure you don't choose the horse who is too spirited.

RIGHT
For endurance riding, choose a horse with proven stamina. Arabs and part-bred Arabs are particularly suited to the higher levels of this sport.

BOTTOM
Experienced riders will be able to school young horses, but novice riders should learn on a more experienced horse.

Unless you are planning to become involved in an activity which requires a specific breed – such as a particular category of showing – you will have a wide variety of breeds and types to choose from. Always bear in mind, however, your intended use for the horse: for endurance riding he will need great stamina; for eventing, stamina plus speed; for dressage, excellent movement. While stallions often excel in the last named discipline and are increasingly seen in other types of equine competition as well, they do require more expert handling than geldings and mares, and are not suitable for the novice horse owner. Mares can be more moody and take rather more understanding than geldings (very often, though, a good competition mare is very good indeed). They do, of course, come into season regularly during the summer months and this can be a problem.

If you have good stabling and grazing facilities, you can keep any type or breed without a problem. Lack of stabling will tend to determine what you can or cannot buy, particularly if you live in a region where the winters are cold and wet and/or the summers excessively hot. A British native pony will do perfectly well living out all year round, provided supplementary feed is given in winter, as necessary. A thin-skinned Thoroughbred, on the other hand, may not thrive unless he has the shelter of a stable, at least at night. If you wish to keep your horse at peak fitness for competition work or hunting, you will certainly need the use of a stable.

Then there is the question of how much time you can devote to looking after your horse. If you have a full-time job, and limited time for weekday exercising, life will be easier for you and your horse if he can live out or at least be turned out during the day.

If you are not planning to do a lot of strenuous competition work, then age need not be too much of a factor, though of course the older the animal the more work he is likely to have done and the more wear and tear there will have been on his legs and body by the time you buy him. However, for general riding purposes horses and ponies often go on well into their late teens and even early twenties. A young horse will, of course, have many more useful years ahead of him and will be easier to sell on for a good price. However, young horses are not suitable for the novice rider, who will be unable to give them the necessary schooling.

Where to Buy

LEFT
There are plenty of horses available from private vendors. Be sure to find out as much as possible about the horse.

There are various ways to buy a horse. These include at a public sale, through a dealer, from a private vendor advertising in the equestrian or local press, or perhaps from the riding school where you have been taking lessons.

The novice rider is generally advised not to buy at a public sale. The problem is not that all sales are conducted by less than reputable people – that is certainly not the case – but that everything takes place so quickly and there may not be sufficient opportunity for the purchaser to ride the horse. Buying in this way calls for an expert, practised eye and it is incumbent upon the purchaser to be observant. For instance, if a horse offered for sale has an obvious physical defect, the onus is on the purchaser to see it – a subsequent plea of ignorance will not be accepted. On the other hand the horse must correspond to its description – a horse described as a show jumper must be able to jump – and the buyer is entitled to return it if this proves not to be the case (or, if necessary, to sue for damages).

Dealers are businessmen with a reputation to maintain and are unlikely to try to sell you a bad lot. Your local riding school may be able to put you in touch with one or, failing that, you may see them advertising in the equestrian press. The advantages of buying through a dealer are that you will almost certainly have the choice of several horses and there should be plenty of opportunity to see them being handled and to ride them yourself. Some dealers may also allow you to try the horse at home and, if you have a horse to sell, may offer part-exchange terms.

Buying from a private vendor – and there are always a great many advertising in the equestrian and farming press as well as in local newspapers – may seem the simplest way of acquiring a horse but it is not necessarily the safest. Here the rule is *caveat emptor* (let the buyer beware), a common law maxim warning you that you cannot claim that your purchase is defective if you have not obtained express guarantees from the vendor. Many of the horses and ponies described in the "For Sale" columns are up for sale for perfectly genuine reasons but others may not be. It is easy to compose an advertisement praising their good points but omitting their shortcomings. Just because a horse is good to box and shoe does not mean that he is quiet to clip or sensible in traffic. The brilliant jumper may refuse to go into a horsebox or trailer. The otherwise perfect equine specimen may, when you get him home, persist in jumping out of his paddock, refuse to be caught, or chew his stable, his rugs, his bandages – or all three. Often it is not so much what the advertisement does say but what it omits to say, so you must be prepared to ask the right questions.

If you have been attending a good riding school, the proprietor should be able to advise on the purchase of a horse or pony and may well have one on the premises which would suit you. The advantage here is that the instructor will have a good knowledge of your skills and limitations as a rider.

LEFT
Buying horses from sales is best left to the experts because everything happens so quickly.

Trying a Horse

▌ BELOW
When trying a horse, ride him at different paces and have a jump if you wish.

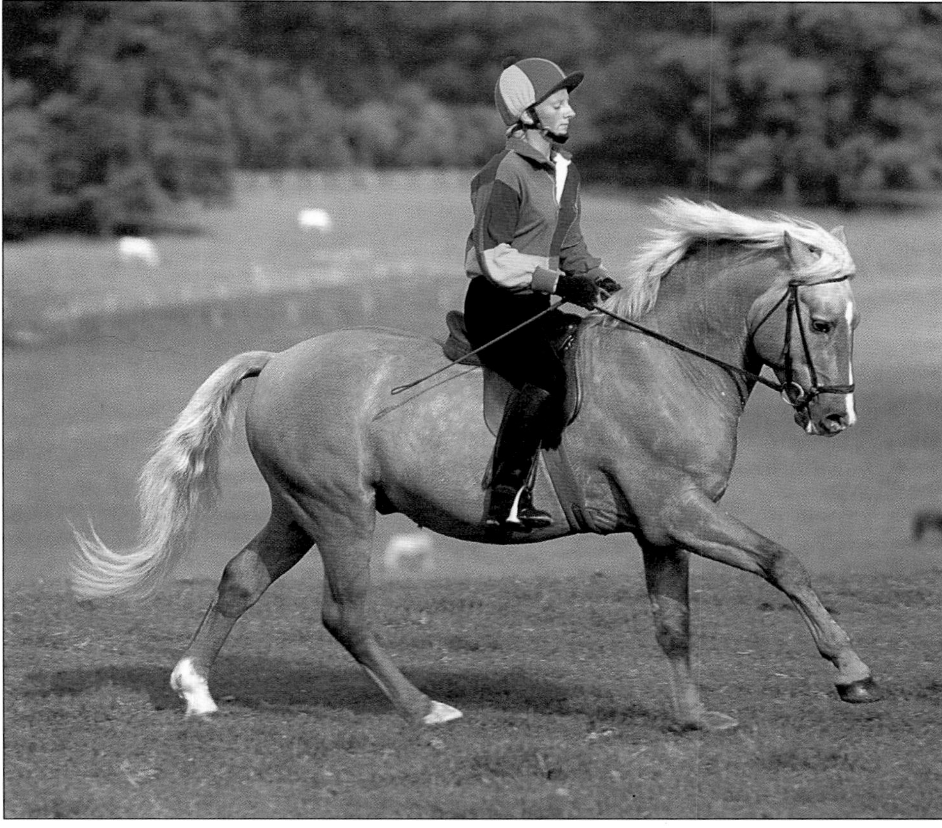

When you learn of a horse which you think may suit your purpose, the first step is to make an appointment to see it and try it. Always take a more knowledgeable person along with you both to offer expert advice and to act as a witness to any sale. If you have no one who will do this as a friend, it is worth paying for an expert opinion.

Explain to the vendor exactly what you want to use the horse for and ask specific questions: is the horse good to box, clip, shoe, catch, in traffic, etc. Ask to see the horse led up outside and pay close attention to how he behaves while he is having his rugs removed and his bridle put on. Note the bit which is being used. Cast an eye around the inside of the stable and the door for signs of kick marks or chewing. It may be that this is not the horse's usual box but if it is, such signs could indicate a behavioural problem. Ask to see the horse stood up outside and view him from both sides to assess his conformation before having him walked and trotted up. Make sure that he is trotted up on a loose rein both away from you and towards you (leading a horse on a short rein can help to cover up defective action).

Before you ride him, watch the vendor put him through his paces to see how he goes with a familiar rider. Then ask your expert adviser to try him. If the vendor failed to ask the horse to do certain things, such as strike off on a particular leg at canter, it may be that there is a problem, and your adviser (who should have noticed even if you have not) can look into the matter. Finally, ride the horse yourself. Does he feel right for you: not too big, not too wide, not too narrow? Is there a good length of rein? Put him through his paces, have a jump if you wish, take him out on the road to make sure he is safe in traffic and generally try to get the feel of him.

It is not easy in a relatively short time to assess whether this is the horse you really want to have on a long-term basis, so if possible arrange to have him at home on trial, say for a week. This will enable you to get to know his character, to ride him in more relaxed circumstances and also to get to know more about his general behaviour: is he well mannered in the stable, is he good in the company of other horses, will he willingly go away from other horses, is he safe in the company of dogs and in all traffic (not just cars) and so on. However well he suits you from the riding point of view, it is important that you should actually like him, too.

If you do decide to have a horse on trial, make sure that the arrangements are agreed and set down in writing – you will be responsible for feed, vet's bills and so on and will be liable for negligence.

Horses sold at public sales usually come with a warranty or warranties. A warranty is a statement of fact made before or during a transaction – for example a horse may be "warranted sound". Privately sold horses do not always come with a warranty and if you ask the vendor for one and he or she declines, then you may have grounds for suspicion (on the other hand, in these days of increasing litigation, the vendor may simply be being extra cautious). When in doubt, consult your expert equestrian adviser and, if necessary, a solicitor. The law does give some protection to buyers of horses, as in the case of other merchandise, the big difference being that the horse is a living creature and therefore far less predictable than, say, a television or a refrigerator or a motor car.

When you do find the horse of your dreams and decide to purchase, buy him "subject to a veterinary certificate" and ask your own veterinary surgeon (not the vendor's) to carry out the inspection.

Vetting

If possible, you should be present when your veterinary surgeon carries out his examination of your proposed purchase so that he can discuss the horse with you.

The examination will begin with a preliminary visual inspection. The vet can deduce a good deal from the general attitude of the horse when approached: his stance might show signs of lameness; the condition of his stable could indicate behavioural problems such as box-walking (constant pacing round and round the stable), assuming that the vendor has not switched the horse to another box to hide the evidence; his head carriage can indicate problems of balance or vision; how he reacts to being handled will be indicative of his temperament.

The vet will take in the horse's general state of health, noting any discharges from the nose or eyes, the condition of the skin; and the presence of lesions, or heat in a

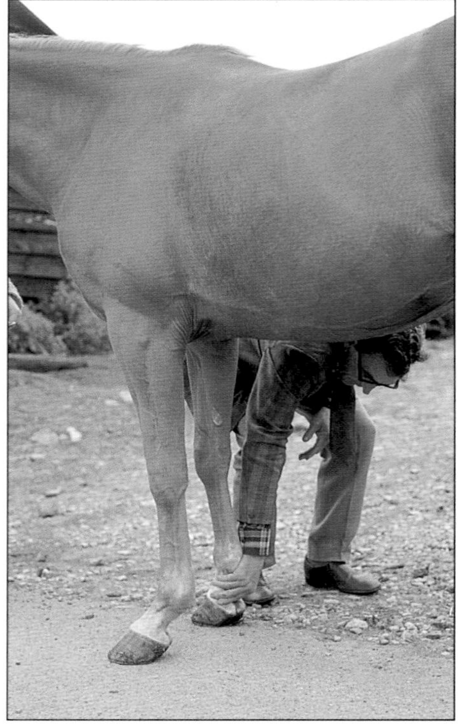

tendon or joint. He will also examine the eyes and heart.

Once outside his stable, the horse will be stood up squarely on flat ground while the vet makes a detailed appraisal of his conformation. This is followed by a manual examination of the entire horse:

OPTIONAL EXTRAS

For an additional charge various optional extra tests can be carried out. Blood tests may be used to detect anti-inflammatory drugs, designed to mask lameness. X-rays may be used where there is a suspicion of unsoundness (such as navicular disease) in the foot. Mares may be given a rectal examination if this is specifically requested.

the head, including the mouth and teeth, the neck, ribs, sternum, back, abdomen and the limbs. Once the horse has been examined at rest he will be walked and then trotted in hand both away from the vet and towards him to enable him to detect any signs of lameness. Turning the horse to either side on a tight circle, backing him for a few strides and lungeing him at trot on a hard, flat surface are other tests which may reveal problems of unsoundness.

Flexion tests may be carried out on the limbs, particularly if there is a suspicion of lameness. However, opinion differs on these flexion tests, as they can actually induce lameness if they are used with sufficient force.

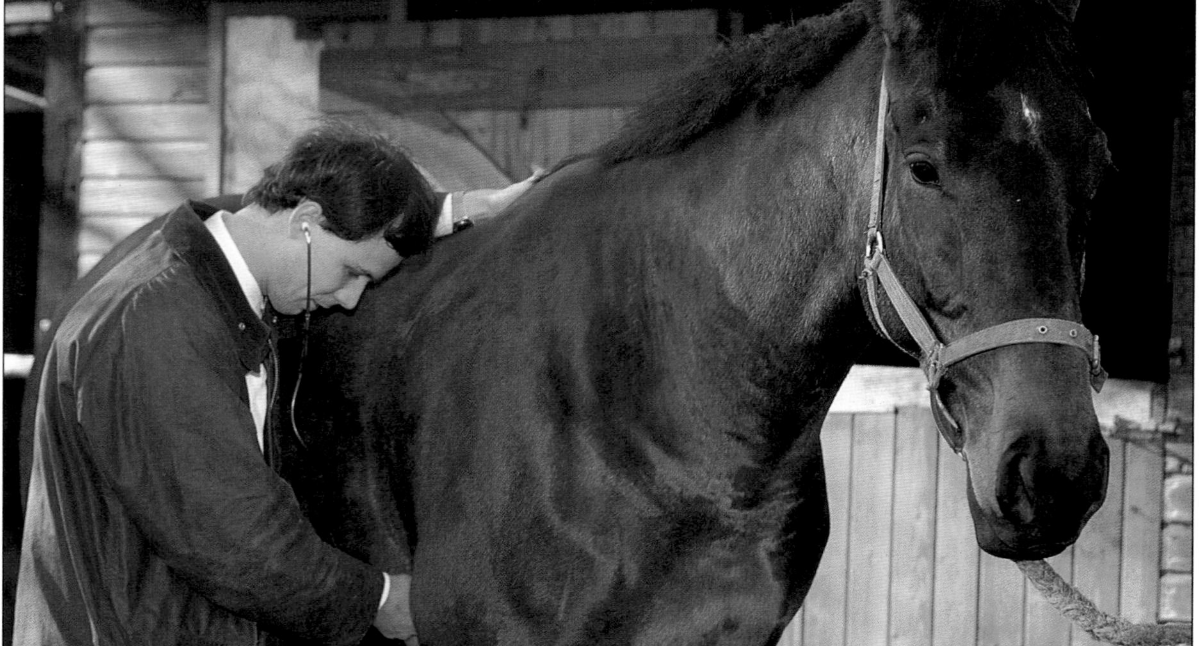

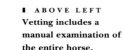

ABOVE LEFT Vetting includes a manual examination of the entire horse.

LEFT The vet will check the horse's heart and respiratory rates both at rest and after exercise.

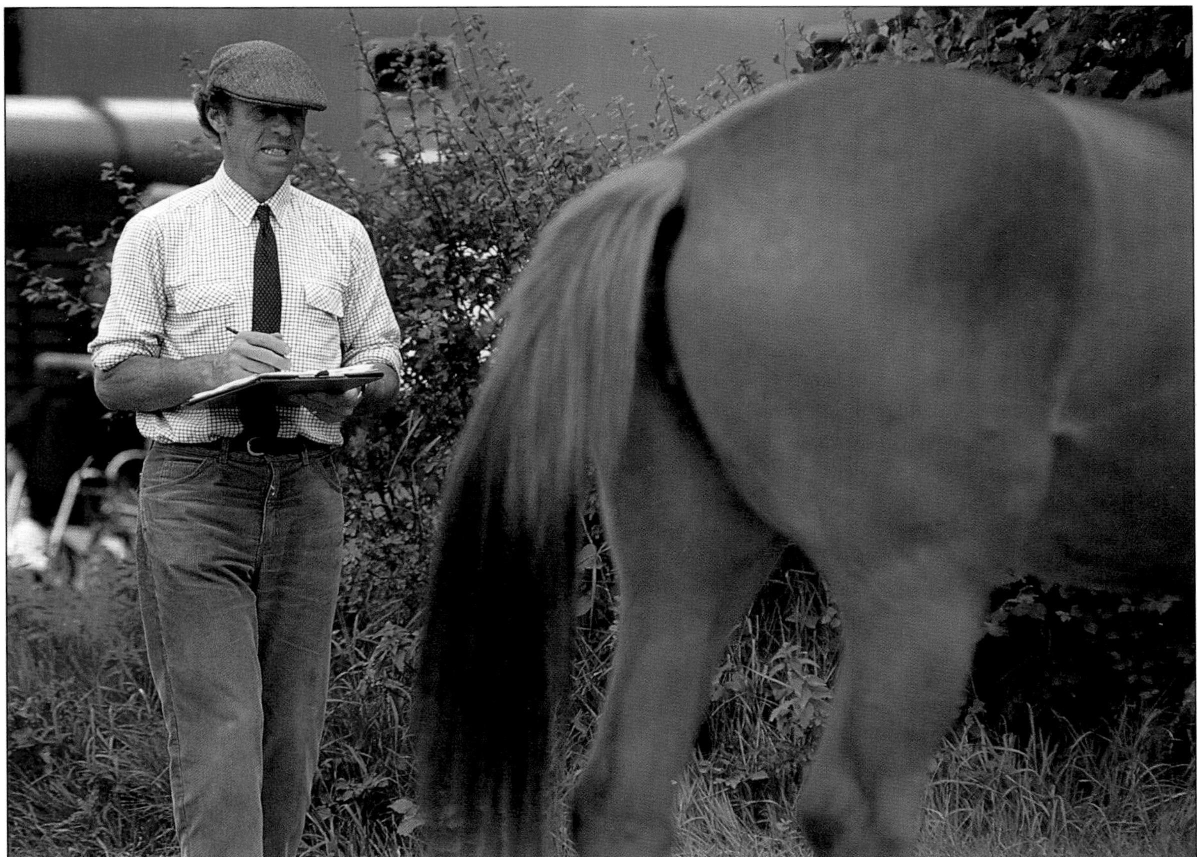

LEFT
The horse is stood up outside the stable while a detailed appraisal is made of his conformation.

BELOW
During the vetting procedure the horse will be warmed up under saddle, then given a gallop. Fast work sometimes produces signs of an old lameness problem.

To test the horse's wind and heart he is tacked up, warmed up gently at walk, trot and canter and then given a gallop. The vet will note whether the horse dips its back when the saddle is put on and the rider mounts. Some horses habitually do this, in others it may be a sign of back problems. After exercise the vet will listen to the lungs for any signs of abnormal respiration and to the heart for any irregularity. After the horse has been cooled off he will be rested for half an hour, after which he will be trotted out again in hand. If the horse is suffering from muscular or arthritic problems, which might disappear while the horse is warm, they may well reappear after this period of rest. Signs of old lameness might also appear after fast exercise. A further examination of the heart and respiration may also be made. The vet will then complete the certificate.

The certificate includes a detailed identification of the horse, the vet's report and his opinion as to its suitability for purchase, bearing in mind the use for which it is required. It is important to remember that the certificate is not a guarantee, but an opinion expressed by a qualified person. The certificate means that the horse has been found to be free of certain disorders at the time of examination. It does not and cannot mean that the horse is and will remain completely free from disease – vets are certainly not clairvoyant. Nor does the certificate guarantee that the horse is free from so-called stable "vices" such as crib-biting or weaving. If you would like a written warranty to this effect, you must obtain it from the vendor.

FEED ROOM

Keeping a Horse

Horse ownership is a big responsibility and should not be entered into lightly. Certainly no one should consider it unless they have the necessary facilities and have first mastered the rudiments of horse care. These include a knowledge of feeding, grooming, general stable management and basic first aid. All horses and ponies need safe accommodation and daily attention – they cannot be set aside on a Sunday afternoon and forgotten about until the following weekend. Unlike small domesticated animals, who share their owners' home, they need large facilities of their own, maintenance of which takes time and money. Depending on the work required of them and their breed or type, horses can either be kept at grass or stabled, or a combination of the two (known as the combined system). The owner will therefore need access to grazing, a stable, a weatherproof storage area for feed, bedding and tools and somewhere secure to keep tack and other equipment.

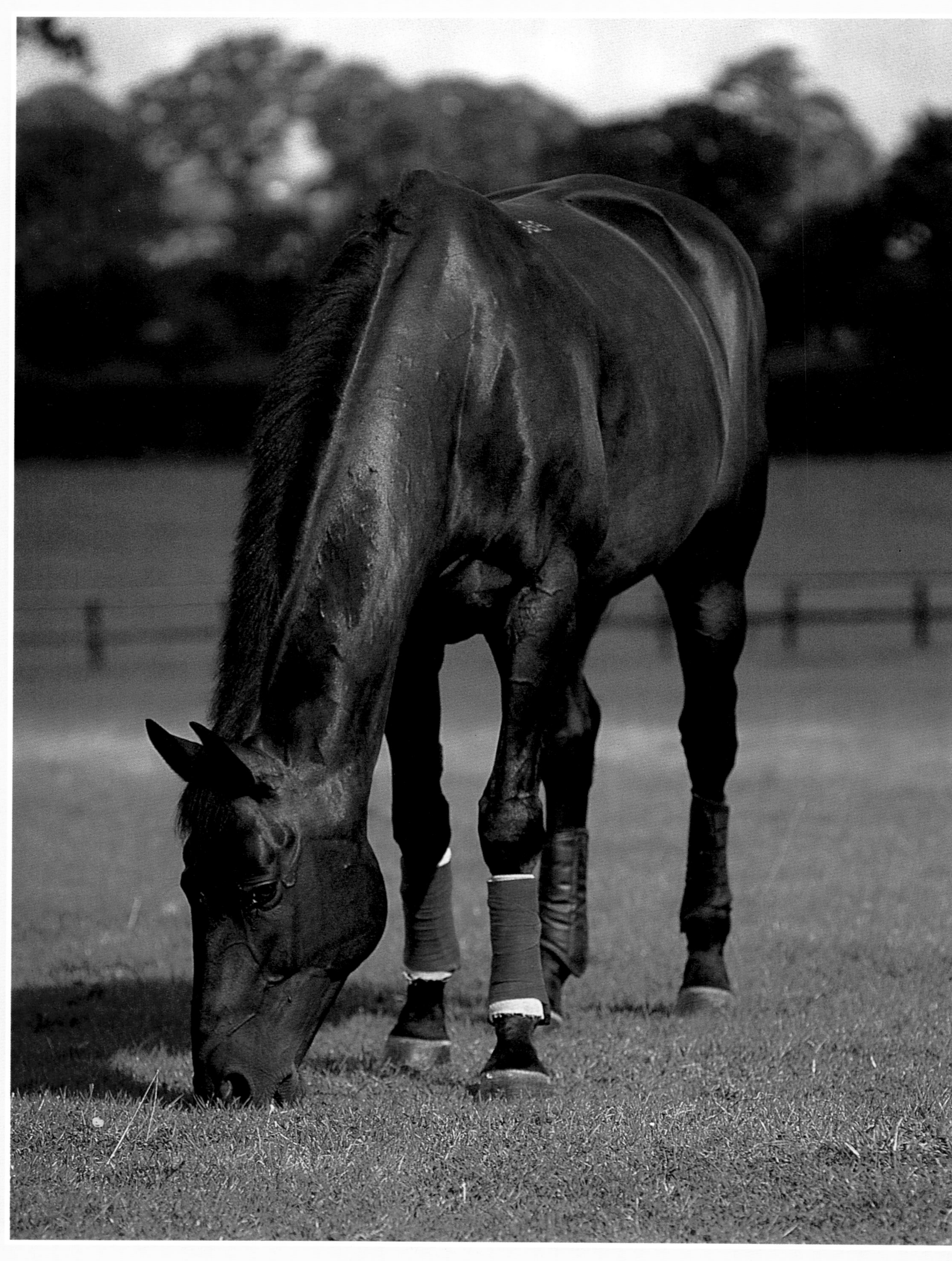

THE HORSE AT GRASS

The horse is by nature a nomadic, grazing animal, so it is far more natural – and less stressful – to keep him in a paddock than in a stable. However, a fenced paddock, no matter how large, is still an unnatural environment for a horse and certain precautions must be taken if the horse is to be safe and secure.

PREVIOUS PAGE OPPOSITE Stabled horses need constant care and attention.
PREVIOUS PAGE Most small ponies are quite hardy and can live outside all year round.
OPPOSITE Fit horses who spend part of the day at grass should wear bandages and boots to guard against injury.
ABOVE Brood mares grazing in a well-fenced paddock.

Fencing

All fields used for grazing horses must be securely and safely fenced. Since it is the horse's nature to roam, if he sees a gap he will certainly go for it. Similarly, if there is anything on which the horse can injure himself, he will find it – the domesticated horse is notoriously accident prone.

Undoubtedly the most effective (but unfortunately also the most expensive) fencing is good **wooden post and rail**. It is sturdy, long lasting and looks attractive. The wooden support posts, which should be 4 inches (10cm) square, must be driven well into the ground since horses like to rub against fencing, particularly when they are changing their coats. For a 4 foot (1.2m) fence the posts should be no less than 6 feet 6 inches (2m) in length. The fence should be constructed of good-quality wood and treated with non-toxic preservative to give protection against the weather and to discourage horses from chewing it. The top rail should be level with the top of the posts, which should be cut on a slope to allow rain to run off. Where possible the rails should be attached to the inner side of the posts. This prevents the horse banging into the

LEFT
Provided they are sufficiently high to deter the horse from jumping out, well-maintained stone walls are effective barriers.

BELOW LEFT
Fixing the rails to the insides of the support posts prevents horses pushing them off when rubbing against them.

SAFETY CHECKLIST

- Make regular checks of all field boundaries.
- Repair any broken sections of boundary immediately.
- Keep wire fencing taut at all times.
- Set the lowest strand of a wire fence 18 inches (46cm) above the ground.
- Block off gaps in hedges with stout fencing – never use loose strands of wire.
- Never use pig or sheep netting – horses tend to put their feet through the squares of wire and can become caught up.
- Never use sheep posts, with sharp, upward pointing ends.
- Fence off potential danger areas, such as treacherous ground or ditches.
- When using electric fencing, ensure that it is visible – to humans as well as horses – by tying strips of strong plastic (for example, from feed or fertilizer bags) at intervals along the wire.
- Avoid metal or concrete fence posts – they will do far more damage than wooden ones should a horse collide with them.

OPPOSITE TOP
Good-quality wooden post and rail fencing makes the perfect horse-proof boundary and looks attractive.

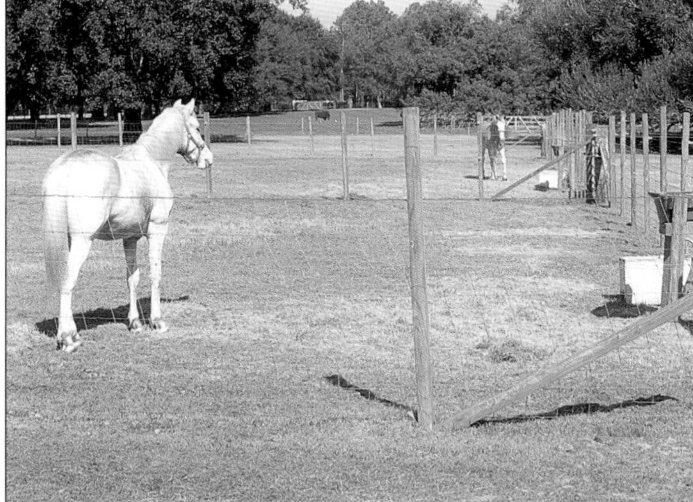

LEFT
Electric fencing can be very useful, especially for dividing paddocks into smaller sections. Horses quickly learn to respect it.

BOTTOM
Curved fencing with no right-angled corners is safest for horses.

BELOW RIGHT
Rusty metal, barbed wire and concrete posts are potentially lethal to horses. Sections of poor fencing like this should be replaced.

posts when galloping about and also prevents him from pushing a rail off if he leans or rubs against it.

A tall, thick **hedge,** provided it is without poisonous trees or shrubs, can also make a good boundary. Beech and hazel are particularly suitable since horses will not eat them. Unlike a fence, a hedge provides horses with shelter in bad weather. It will, however, require regular trimming to keep it in good order – if gaps begin to appear they must be fenced off.

Probably the best boundary of all is a combination of the two: a good dense hedge with a post and rail fence running immediately in front of it.

Cheaper, less attractive but equally effective fencing can be constructed with **wire mesh**. The mesh must have small, V-shaped openings so that there is no possibility of a horse catching his foot in the holes. Mesh fencing needs to be erected professionally to prevent sagging. It is also likely to stretch when leant on.

Plain wire fencing will provide a good horseproof barrier so long as it is well constructed. It should consist of four or five strands of wire attached to stout wooden posts, with strainers at the corners to keep them taut. An alternative, and one which makes the fence more easily visible to the horse, is to use a wooden rail in place of the top strand of wire. The strands of wire should be some 12 inches (30cm) apart and the placing of the lowest strand is particularly important. It should be about 18 inches (46cm) above the ground. Any lower and the horse may put a leg through the strands and become caught up; any higher and he may be tempted to put his head underneath. Plain wire is more suitable than barbed wire. If the latter cannot be avoided, it must be kept absolutely taut – loose barbed wire can cause dreadful injuries if any part of the horse becomes caught up in it. Horses can also cut themselves if they rub against the barbs.

Electric fencing has its uses, especially for temporarily dividing one area of a field from another, for example when resting one section of grazing.

Stone walls will also contain horses very well, provided they are sturdy and high enough – all boundaries should be a minimum of 4 feet (1.2m) high, otherwise horses might try to jump out. Like a hedge, a wall will afford some protection against the weather.

Modern **plastic fencing**, which comes in a variety of colours, may not look as "natural" as wood but it does have certain advantages: horses do not chew it, it does not rot and it will absorb impact without causing injury. Like wire, it should be correctly strained on strong, wooden posts.

Whatever the fencing used, right-angled or sharp corners should be avoided in paddocks where horses are kept. Rounding the corners of the field makes it less likely for a horse to injure himself when galloping about, either by coming to an abrupt halt (with the possibility of jarring the legs) or actually crashing into the boundary. Acute corners can also be traps for a timid horse who might find himself literally "cornered" by a more aggressive companion.

Gates

Good access to fields is most important. Gateways must be wide enough to allow not only horses to pass through safely but also large machinery (such as a tractor and harrow) which will be required from time to time to keep the pasture in good condition. For safety's sake it is better for gates to be situated away from busy roads. Wooden and metal gates are both suitable for horse paddocks. All gates should have cross bars for added strength.

It is best to have a gate hung by an expert to ensure that it does not sag, drag on the ground or swing. Gates must open easily otherwise a horse could try to push his way out while you are still struggling to open it. The safest way to hang a gate is so that it opens inwards into the field. This will prevent a horse pushing it open as soon as you unfasten the catch. A wooden gate should be heavy and solidly built and, like fencing, should be treated with preservative. Galvanized metal gates will require regular painting. Gateposts need to be very strong and should be set about 3 feet (90cm) into the ground with concrete to keep them firm. They will require strong hinges and a horse-proof catch, that is one that the horse cannot unfasten with his teeth. All catches should be easy for a person to open with one hand. There should be no protruding hooks or other fastenings on which the horse could injure himself.

Horse stealing is not uncommon and so it is vital to secure all gates. Use heavy-duty chain with a strong padlock and fit one to BOTH ends of the gate so that would-be thieves cannot simply lift the gate off its hinges. Avoid climbing over gates as it tends to weaken them. If you must, always climb over the hinge end and do it quickly.

During wet weather the ground in gateways quickly becomes poached by horses being taken in and out on a daily basis or simply pacing up and down waiting to be fed. If possible, gates should be situated on well-drained ground, and not in a muddy hollow.

SAFETY CHECKLIST

- Make regular checks of all gates.
- Replace/repair worn or damaged catches/hinges immediately.
- Keep gates securely fastened, using chains and padlocks at BOTH ends.
- Never fasten gates with bits of rope or string – horses can bite through them and they are easily removed by thieves.
- Avoid gates less than 6 feet (1.8m) wide – horses can easily bang themselves, especially their hips, as they go through.
- Avoid gates that open directly on to a main road – it is dangerous leading a horse straight out into traffic and will also make theft easier.
- Never use flimsy metal gates – they are too easily bent and broken.
- Avoid rusty metal gates – horses can easily injure themselves.
- Avoid straining gates by climbing over them.
- Avoid feeding horses close to the gateway – the ground will quickly become poached in winter.

BELOW
Gate posts must be strong. Gates should be securely fastened at both ends with sturdy chains and padlocks.

BOTTOM
This broken gate is totally unsuitable for a paddock. Rusty metal may cause serious injuries and flimsy barriers encourage horses to escape.

Shelters

In the wild, horses make use of natural shelter such as trees, banks or rocks for protection from extremes of wind, wet or heat or to escape from flies. For horses kept in the confines of a paddock it is essential to provide an equivalent form of protection. Most domesticated horses retain their natural instinct to shelter beside a good, thick hedge or under a tree rather than going inside a confining man-made structure. But not all paddocks have hedges and trees and so a wooden shelter may be the only alternative.

Since horses are happiest when kept in company with others of their kind, a field shelter needs to be large enough to accommodate the number of horses that graze together, without risk of squabbling and overcrowding. It should be positioned on well-drained ground. If this is not possible, the floor and the area around the shelter may need a hard surface, such as concrete. The shelter should be built with its back to the prevailing wind. It must be strongly constructed and treated with preservative. The roof must be sufficiently high to give horses plenty of head room (thus avoiding possible injury) and should slope towards the back so that rainwater runs away from the entrance. Open-fronted shelters are the safest, because it is easy for a horse to escape should he be bullied by a companion. Any fixtures and fittings, such as mangers, hay racks, etc., must be strongly made and fitted at a good height from the ground, again to prevent injury. They should be checked regularly and repaired as necessary, as should the whole shelter.

Some types of smaller field shelter are designed with a bottom door which, when closed, converts the shelter into a stable. This can be very useful if you have no other stabling but sometimes need to keep your horse or pony inside. It can also be used as an isolation box in the event of the horse contracting a contagious illness.

A less costly type of shelter may be provided by means of a wooden screen, erected in conjunction with the fencing. Windbreak screens need to be about 6 feet 6 inches (2m) high and can either be straight or double-sided, using a corner of the field. Multi-angled screens, affording protection from different directions, can be built free-standing in the open away from the fencing.

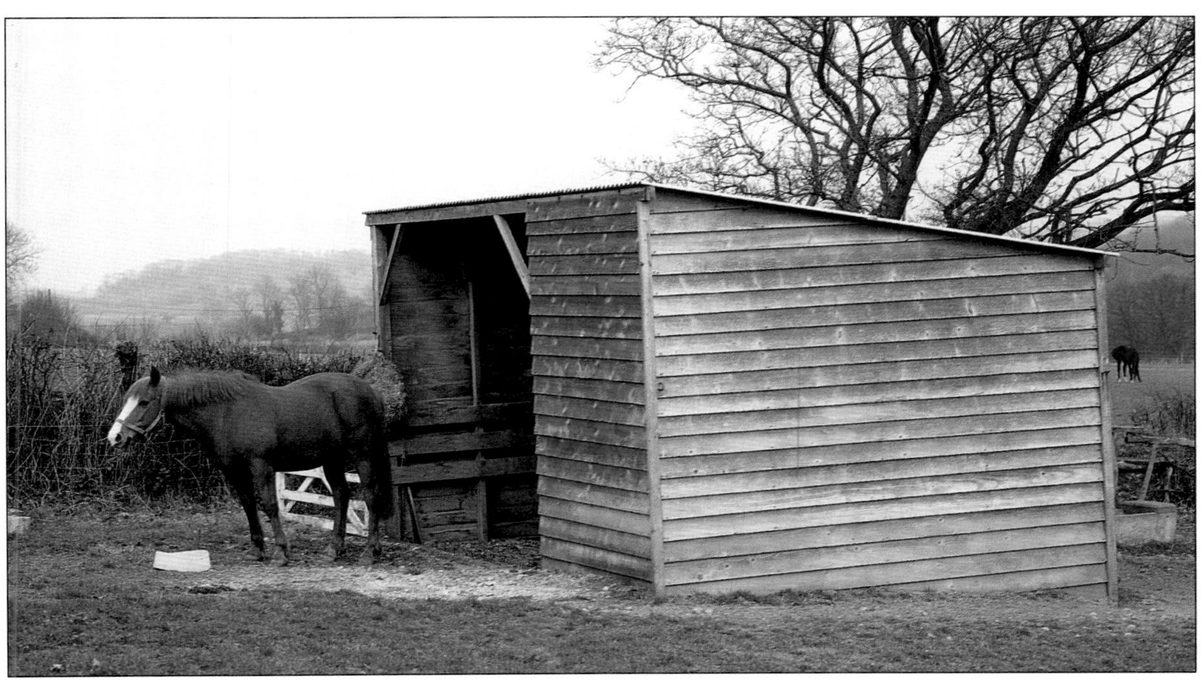

TOP
A well-designed wooden field shelter with high, sloping roof, wide front opening and strong kicking boards.

LEFT
This small shelter, with its narrow opening, is suitable for a single horse. With the addition of a door it could convert into a stable for emergency use if necessary.

Poisonous Plants, Shrubs and Trees

There are a good many plants, shrubs and trees which are poisonous to horses and ponies. Some, such as the **buttercup**, which are poisonous if eaten in large quantities when fresh, are not particularly palatable. On the other hand horses will readily eat yew, all parts of which are lethal. A quantity as small as 1lb (0.5kg) can kill a horse. All paddocks should be rigorously checked for dangerous plants before horses are put out to graze and regularly checked thereafter – remember that however well you tend your own grazing it can still be contaminated by seeds blowing from neighbouring land.

One of the most dangerous plants of all is **ragwort**, which is tall and easily recognized by its bright yellow flowers. Ragwort contains alkaloids which poison the liver and the effects are cumulative: small doses eaten over a long period of time are just as lethal as a large amount eaten in a short time. There is no specific treatment for ragwort poisoning and the effects are usually fatal.

Ragwort can be eliminated by spraying – the best time is between late April and late May, before the flower shoots develop and while young plants are just becoming established. Or it can be dug up, though this can be hard work. All the roots must

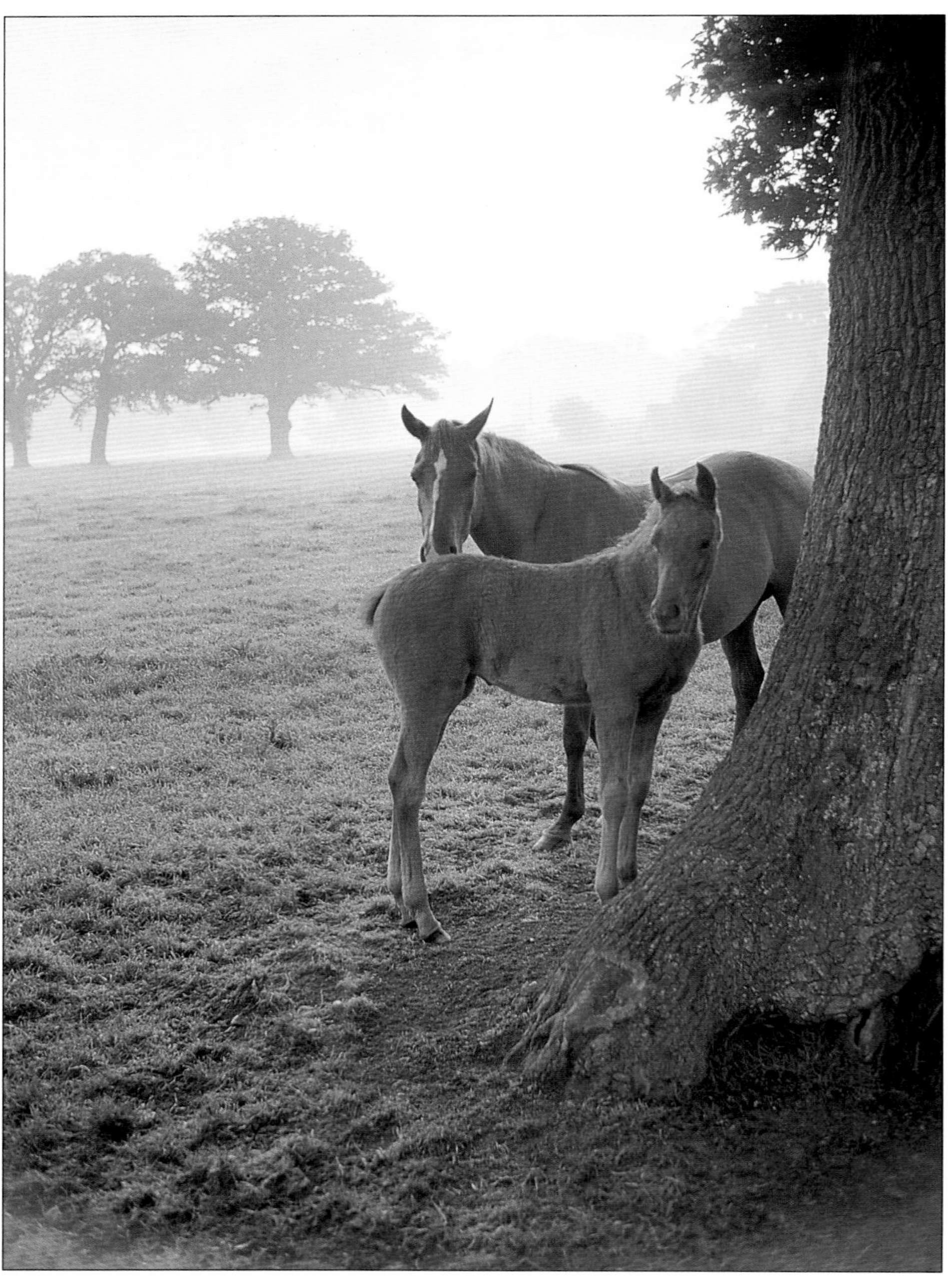

BELOW LEFT
Horses appreciate the shelter afforded by mature trees such as this oak. But acorns, if eaten in large quantities, can be poisonous so they should be removed.

SAFETY CHECKLIST

- Learn to recognize poisonous plants and trees.
- Before putting a horse in a new paddock, make a thorough check of grassland and hedges for signs of poisonous vegetation.
- Dig up and burn poisonous plants.
- Fence off any poisonous trees which cannot be removed – make sure they are well out of reach of horses or ponies.
- Make regular checks of all paddocks and hedges – remember that poisonous plants can spread from neighbouring land.
- Never leave poisonous plants which have been dug up lying about in the paddock – many plants, notably ragwort, are far more palatable to horses when wilted or dead.
- Practise good pasture management: a good, dense sward of grass helps prevent poisonous plants from seeding.
- If there are poisonous trees in the vicinity, keep an eye open for fallen twigs or branches – particularly during windy weather.
- If paddocks adjoin gardens, make regular checks for cuttings dumped over the fence by their owners – they may contain poisonous plants.
- After using chemical weedkillers keep horses off the grass for several weeks and at least until there has been a good downpour of rain.

CLOCKWISE FROM RIGHT
Ragwort, yew, laurel, rhododendron and privet: all are highly dangerous to horses. Ragwort must be eradicated from horse pasture; the trees and shrubs must either be removed or fenced off out of reach.

be removed from the ground and the flower heads should be burnt. Attempting to control ragwort by cutting it when it is in flower to prevent the production of seeds is unlikely to solve the problem since the plants will often grow more vigorously the following year. If a paddock is really badly infested with the plant, the best solution is to plough the land and reseed it. The better the grassland management the less opportunity there will be for ragwort to become established. The denser the sward of grass the less likely ragwort is to seed.

Foxgloves, which like ragwort become more palatable when they are dried in hay than when fresh, are also lethal to horses. As little as ¼lb (100g) may prove fatal. Symptoms of foxglove poisoning include convulsions and difficulty in breathing. A horse will die in a matter of hours.

Hemlock has a similarly disastrous effect though it takes larger quantities (around 5–10lb or 2.5–5kg) to cause death. All members of the **nightshade** family are poisonous, as is **monkshood**. **Horsetails**, commonly found growing in boggy conditions, are very dangerous if eaten in large quantities in hay. Horses do not usually eat the growing stems.

Shrubs and trees to be avoided at all cost include **rhododendron** (small quantities cause death through failure of the respiratory system), **oleander**, **laburnum** (especially the seeds), **box**, **privet** and **laurel**. All parts of **yew**, living or dead, are lethal in small quantities – again there is no known antidote. **Meadow saffron** contains a poison which may take time to build up in the system, by which time the horse is beyond help, and the poisons present in **bracken** also have a cumulative effect which causes poor growth, lack of co-ordination and general loss of condition. Care should be taken if there are oak trees in or around a horse's paddock. The crop of **acorns** varies from year to year. If they are eaten in large quantities, they can be harmful. They should be raked up and removed.

Plants, shrubs and trees which are poisonous to horses include:
Bracken, buttercup, flax, foxglove, hemlock, horsetail, lupin, meadow saffron, nightshade, purple milk vetch, ragwort, St John's wort, yellow star thistle
Box, laurel, oleander, privet, rhododendron
Buckthorn, laburnum, magnolia, yew
Acorns

Water

Horses and ponies kept at grass must have constant access to a clean supply of water. A natural supply of running water, such as a stream or river, is ideal but nowadays it is all too likely that it may be polluted. If it is not, then horses and ponies may be allowed free access provided the bottom is gravel (if it is sandy the horse may ingest sand with the water).

The approach to the drinking area must be clean, fairly flat and safe. Steep banks are not suitable since the horses will slip and slide down and the bank will eventually collapse. If the stream is narrow, this could arrest the flow of water. Any fencing that crosses the stream or river must be checked regularly to ensure that horses cannot escape from their paddock by wandering off along the waterway. Streams which are not free flowing in summer are not suitable, since the water will tend to become stagnant. Horses should never be allowed access to polluted rivers, stagnant ponds or boggy areas: these should be securely fenced off.

The alternative to running water is a man-made container. A galvanized water trough, purpose-built, fed by mains water and controlled by a ballcock provides an efficient water supply, although there is always the problem of pipes freezing in winter. The feed pipe needs to be buried to a suitable depth and the length of pipe which is above ground will need to be well lagged. It is essential that the ballcock is enclosed so that horses cannot damage it.

If mains water is not available, troughs can be filled by hosepipe or, if convenient, by bucket. Troughs such as this with static water will require baling out every week and refilling. Smaller containers, such as old stone sinks, plastic tubs and buckets can also be used but they will need more frequent filling. The advantage of small, lightweight containers is that they are easy to clean and they can be moved about to different areas of the field to prevent wear and tear on the ground. The disadvantage is that they are easily knocked over. Standing a bucket or tub in an old car tyre is one solution to this problem.

Water troughs are best positioned parallel to a fence. Horses drink a lot so the approach to a trough will be in constant use. It should be hard – it may be necessary to lay concrete or hard core.

LEFT
A natural supply of running water is ideal provided it is pollution free.

BELOW
A galvanized trough makes a suitable alternative.

BOTTOM LEFT
All water containers must be well filled and cleaned regularly.

SAFETY CHECKLIST

- Check your horse's water supply every day.
- Bale out and clean all water containers regularly.
- During severe weather be prepared to break ice on water two or three times a day.
- Fence off all sources of stagnant water.
- Never place a water trough in the corner of a field where a horse may be trapped by one of its companions.
- Never place a water trough under deciduous trees or near a hedge where leaves, twigs and seeds can foul it.
- Avoid placing troughs in the middle of fields where they can become a source of injury.
- Recess water troughs into the line of the fence to minimize projections and the risk of injury.
- Never place a water trough slightly in front of a fence so that a horse could trap his leg between it and the fence.
- Avoid using containers such as old baths that have rough edges or dangerous projections.

Grass Management

▮ BELOW
Grazing cattle with horses, or in rotation, helps control worms and weeds.

▮ BELOW LEFT
Droppings must not be allowed to accumulate in the paddock. If they cannot be picked up regularly, they should be harrowed.

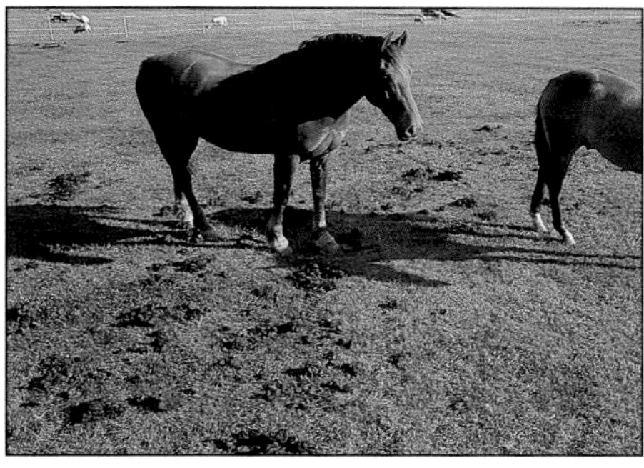

Careful management is required if a paddock is to withstand the horse's close-biting method of grazing and the constant wear and tear inflicted by his feet. Poor quality grazing quickly becomes "horse sick" – barren areas alternate with patches of intrusive, unpalatable weeds such as nettles, docks and thistles – and without a good grass sward it will also become badly poached in wet weather. Even good quality grazing will deteriorate if it is not given the right attention.

The ideal pasture is one that has been sown with seed selected and mixed specifically with horses in mind. A good basic mixture would contain 50 per cent of perennial rye grass, 25 per cent of creeping red fescue and 25 per cent of a mixture including crested dog's tail, meadow grass and a little wild white clover. Timothy should also be included if you intend to take hay from the paddock.

Rye grass grows well in most conditions although on poor, light soils it will decline after a few years if it is not fertilized. Two different types should be included in the mix. Creeping red fescue is particularly useful in difficult conditions (it is often used on sports grounds) and again two different types should be included. Smooth-stalked meadow grass will grow in dry, sandy soils while the rough-stalked variety, which horses find very palatable, thrives in moist, rich soils. Its dense, low growth helps prevent the intrusion of weeds and poisonous plants. Clover is useful because its root nodules contain nitrogen-producing bacteria. Its inclusion in the mix will help reduce the need for fertilizing. It is important to choose wild clover rather than one of the farm varieties, which grow very aggressively and can take over an entire paddock.

Even with the right basic mixture of grasses, the amount and quality of grazing produced will vary according to a number of natural factors. These include soil type, rainfall, wind and altitude. Soil should be tested for its suitability to sustain grass. For example, if it is acidic it will need to be treated with lime (horses must be kept off the grazing until the lime has been washed in by rain).

The best grazing is produced on well-drained land. The installation of underground drainage is expensive but it may be essential where ground is so badly drained that it is both unproductive and easily poached by a horse's feet. Where drainage exists it is important to maintain it. Check ditches regularly, and remove any blockages which prevent water from running away freely (remember that blocked ditches on neighbouring land can prevent the free run of water from your paddock). Check all pipes leading into and out of ditches and repair as necessary.

Ideally the horses' droppings should be removed frequently as this will help to control worm infestation. Where removal is not practical, for example on large acreages, the droppings should be harrowed regularly. This should be done during warm, dry weather (which will spread out the droppings and kill the larvae). Another aid to worm control is the grazing of cattle either with the horses or in rotation. The larvae will be destroyed in the cattle's digestive system. Cattle and sheep will also help keep paddocks tidy by eating the rougher herbage. Sheep do less damage to wet ground than cattle.

Harrowing in the spring helps to pull out dead growth and make room for new, and a field should always be harrowed before the application of fertilizer. Rolling will help to firm the soil and repair poached areas. Weed control is also best carried out in spring as soon as new shoots appear. Persistent weeds should be dug out and burnt before they seed.

Pasture needs to be rested periodically. If you have nowhere else to put your horse, divide off the paddock into two or more sections. Rest one portion, graze horses in another and, if possible, graze cattle or sheep in a third.

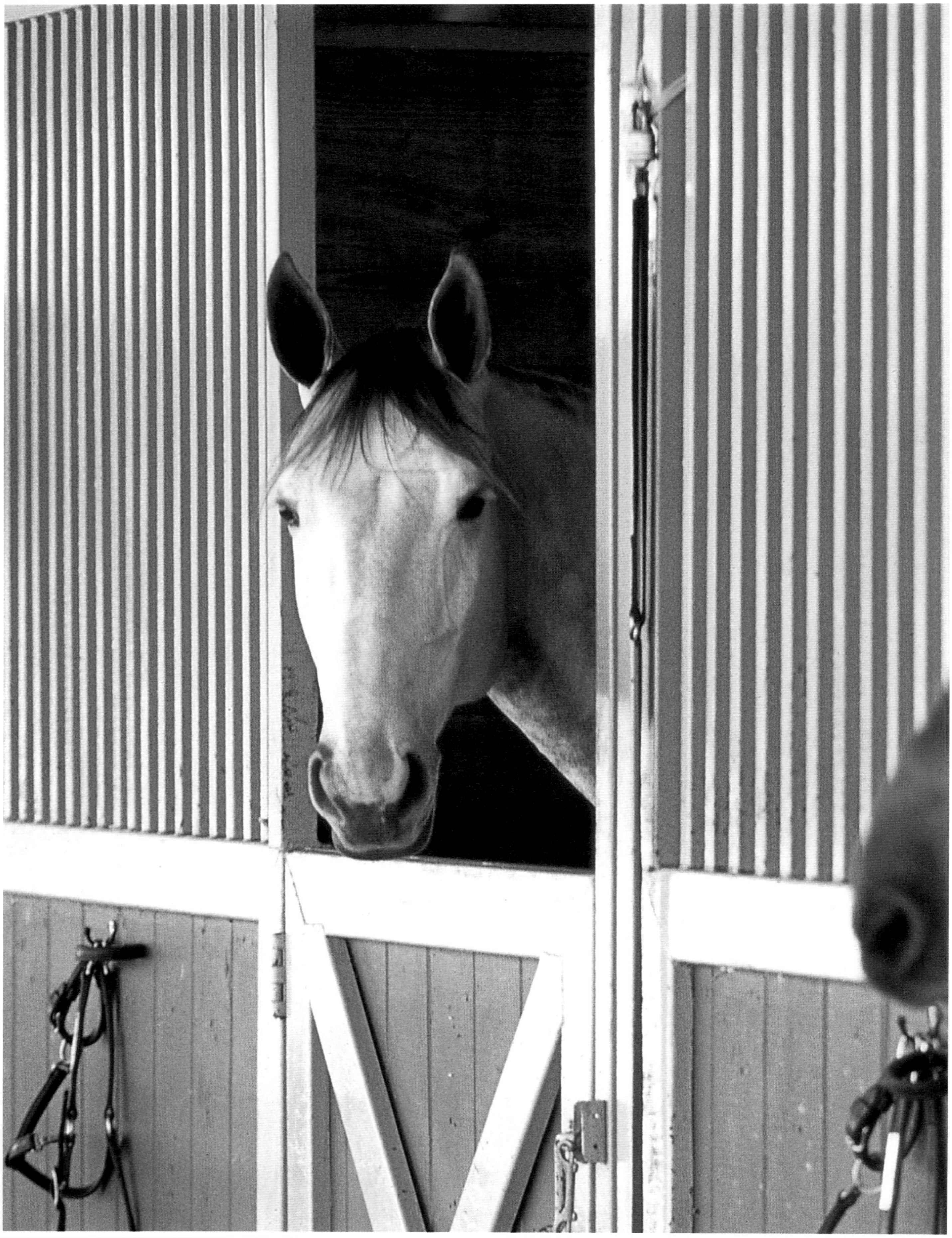

THE STABLED HORSE

Well-designed stabling is vitally important to the horse's health and safety, whether the horse lives in most of the time, whether he is kept on the combined system (that is part stabled, part out at grass) or whether he is stabled only occasionally.

OPPOSITE All stables should have horse-proof fastenings on the outside of the doors.

ABOVE Roughened concrete provides a suitable surface for a busy stableyard.

Stables

Care must be taken with the positioning and construction of stables. This applies equally to a single stable and to a large yard. Stables should be sited so that cold north and east winds cannot blow in and should be positioned on well-drained ground. When planning new stabling, various factors should be taken into consideration. These include the supply of water and electricity as well as vehicular access. It is preferable, too, to build stables near a house, in order to deter thieves.

The most popular type of stable is the loosebox, or box stall. These are usually made of wood, concrete blocks or brick and may be roofed with wood (protected by waterproof felt), tiles, slates or heavy-duty corrugated plastic. Metal should never be used for stabling because it is hot in summer and cold in winter; it is also likely to cause injuries to the horse. A loosebox must be large enough for the occupant to be able to move about, roll, lie down flat and get up again in comfort and absolute safety. A horse standing 16hh and over needs a loosebox measuring at least 12 feet x 14 feet (3.7m x 4.3m); a horse up to 16hh, 12 feet x 12 feet (3.7m x 3.7m), and a 14hh pony, 10 feet x 12 feet (3m x 3.7m). A stable of 8 feet x 8 feet (2.4m x 2.4m) is adequate for small ponies.

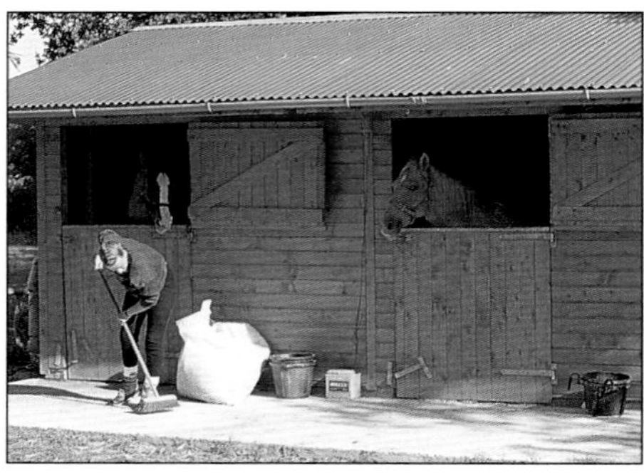

BELOW
Good airy barn stabling provides a suitable alternative to looseboxes, especially in a hot or very cold climate. The disadvantages are the ease with which disease can spread and the fire risk.

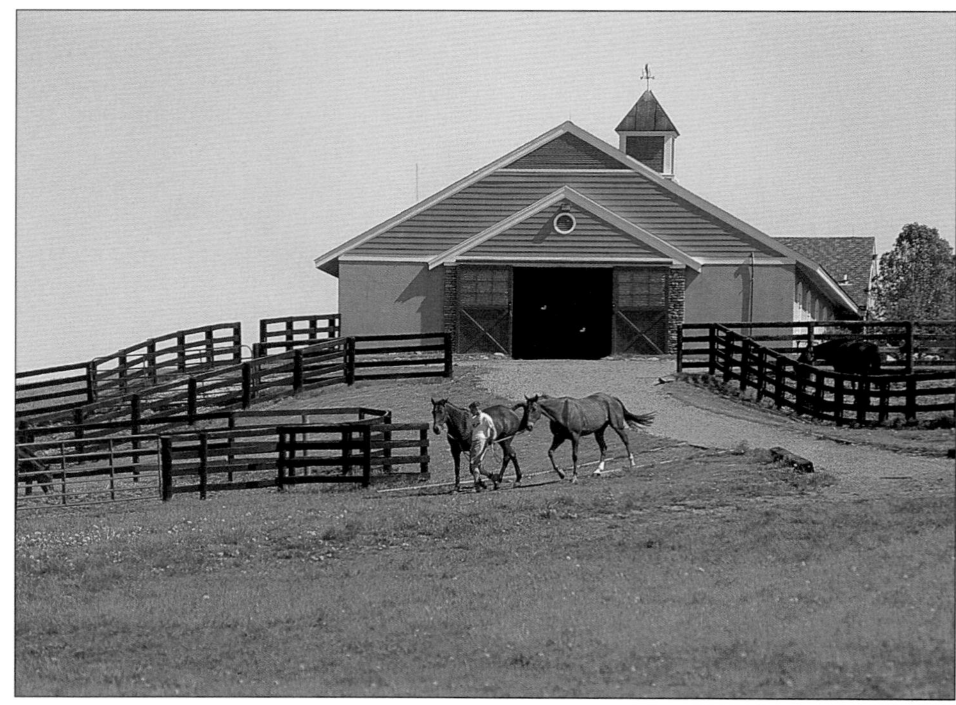

The roof should be sloped and fitted with effective guttering and downpipes. A high ceiling or roof is essential to prevent the horse hitting its head. If the stable has a ridge roof, the eaves should be no less than 7 feet 6 inches (2.25m) above the ground and the top of the roof should be from 12–15 feet (3.7–4.5m) high. The lowest point of a single-planed roof should be no less than 10 feet (3m) high.

Wooden kicking boards, to a height of at least 4 feet (1.2m), provide added strength and security. The stable floor should slope slightly towards the rear of the box (to aid drainage) and the surface must be hard-wearing and non-slippery. Roughened concrete is most often used. It may be covered with a special rubber material to give better purchase. Drains inside the stable are best avoided as they tend to become blocked with bedding and can also trap a horse's hoof.

For safety, the stable door must give plenty of clearance – it should be at least 4 feet (1.2m) wide and 7 feet (2.1m) high for a horse. It should be made in two halves, opening outwards, and the top half should fasten back securely for the free circulation of air and to enable the horse to see out. Only rarely is the weather so severe that it is necessary to close both halves of a stable door. The top edge of

OPPOSITE TOP
A well-built block of brick stables. The overhang gives extra protection to horses and humans from extremes of weather.

OPPOSITE MIDDLE
Note the protective strip on the top of the doors and the kick-over bolts at the bottom.

BELOW
The inside of a barn complex. With kit and equipment conveniently to hand, this type of stabling is popular with humans though it can be a boring environment for horses.

BELOW
A converted container makes a poor and potentially dangerous home for a horse. Metal is cold in winter and hot in summer and the horse could easily injure himself on the makeshift door.

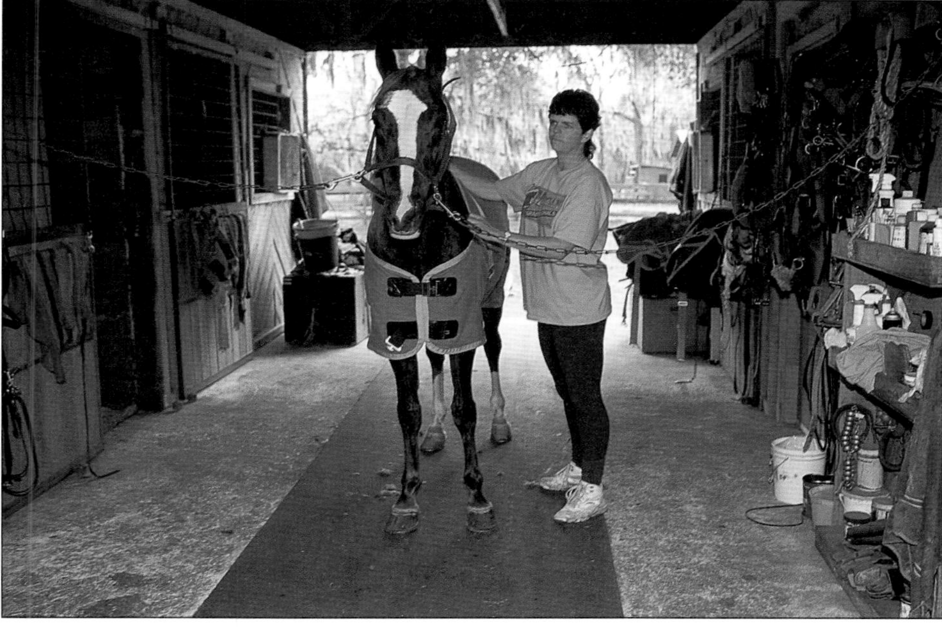

SAFETY CHECKLIST

- Provide adequate fire extinguishers (water and foam)/fire hose/sand buckets in the stable area – your local fire prevention officer will advise on suitable precautions. Have fire extinguishers serviced regularly.
- Ensure that all electrical wiring is protected with suitable conduits to prevent interference by horses and rodents.
- Ensure that all light fittings are out of reach of the horse.
- Fit waterproof switches, well out of reach of the horse.
- Keep stable fixtures and fittings to a minimum: two rings, one to tie up the horse, one (if required) for a haynet; water bucket or automatic waterbowl; manger.
- Make regular checks for protruding nails, screws, splinters etc.
- Make regular checks of all door bolts and hinges and keep them oiled.
- Fit protective grilles to all windows.
- Keep all drains clean.
- Cover open drains in the stable yard area with strong grids.

the bottom door should be securely fitted with a protective strip of metal to prevent the horse chewing the wood, and the door should have a horse-proof bolt at the top and a kick-over bolt at the bottom.

The stabled horse needs a constant supply of fresh air, so good ventilation is essential. The open top door and high roof help provide this. What the horse does not need is a draughty environment. Windows, which help ventilate and light the stable, are usually positioned on the same side of the box as the door to prevent draughts. If they are to provide maximum air and light, they should not be obscured by the top door, which tends to be the case with some stabling. Windows must be fitted with protective grilles. Additional ventilation can be provided by means of ventilation cowls in the roof, or louvre boards in the eaves. Additional light may be provided by a window in the wall opposite the door. If this is also used for ventilation, it must be above the height of the horse's head to prevent cross-draughts.

Internal stabling, where lines of looseboxes are contained within a larger building (which can be an existing barn or purpose built), is popular in some countries and is particularly useful in areas which experience extremes of heat or cold. Correctly constructed, such stabling will be warm in winter and cool in summer, but care must be taken to provide good ventilation – infectious diseases are more likely to spread in this type of stabling arrangement. Doorways and centre aisles must be wide enough to enable horses to move about without banging themselves – sliding stable doors are often the best in this situation as they do not protrude into the gangways when open. The running channels must always be kept clean.

Another way of keeping horses under cover is the yard system, where a number of horses are given the run of a large barn or a partially covered area. The yard system is labour saving, since the horses can be kept on deep litter; and horses enjoy being together with the freedom to wander about. Care must be taken, however, to choose horses who get on with each other, otherwise biting and kicking will occur.

Bedding

BELOW
Wheat straw is less palatable than oat or barley straw and is therefore the most suitable for horses.

BELOW LEFT
Deep straw, well banked up the sides of the stable, provides the horse with a safe, comfortable bed.

An ample supply of bedding encourages the horse to lie down to rest, thus taking unnecessary strain off the legs and feet; it reduces the likelihood of injuries such as capped hocks when the horse does lie down; it allows the horse to roll in comfort and protects him from injury when he does so; it reduces the jarring effect on the legs and feet that may result from standing for long periods on hard flooring; it prevents the horse from slipping up; it encourages him to stale (male horses, particularly, are usually very reluctant to stale on a bare floor); it provides warmth and insulation from draughts and it helps to keep the horse and his rugs clean.

There are a number of types of suitable bedding, all of which have pros and cons. **Straw** has traditionally been the most popular – and economical – and many people still prefer it since it makes arguably the warmest, most comfortable bed and allows free drainage. It is normally easily available though it may become scarce in wet years. Wheat straw is the best for horses, being less palatable than barley or oat straw, both of which are also likely to contain awns which can get into a horse's eyes or irritate the skin.

Straw has the advantage of being much easier to dispose of than some other forms of bedding: it can be burnt (in a safe place, well away from stabling, hay stores, etc) or contractors may collect it for use as mushroom compost. The main drawback of straw is that it may be dusty or contain fungal spores, which can cause an allergic reaction in some horses, leading to respiratory problems. This in turn can affect the horse's work performance because he will not be able to take in enough oxygen. Coughing is often the first sign of problems in this respect.

It can sometimes be difficult finding a supply of small straw bales, too,

BELOW
Good-quality wood shavings are a useful alternative to straw though they provide a rather less warm bed. They are also more difficult to dispose of.

particularly if you live in an area where there are few horse owners and therefore not much demand for the old type of bale. Straw is best bought in small bales because they are easier to handle. The large ones, weighing half a tonne or more, are difficult to manoeuvre and often present storage difficulties, especially for someone keeping horses on a small scale. It will take about four small bales to put down a good, thick straw bed in an average sized loosebox and upwards of half a bale a day to maintain the bed, the exact quantity depending on the amount of time that the box is occupied.

Aside from straw, **wood shavings** are probably the most popular form of bedding nowadays. Correctly managed, they provide a clean, hygienic bed which will not be eaten by the horse. Shavings do not have spores and, provided they are dust free (having been passed through a dust extractor by the suppliers), they can be a good alternative to straw for horses with any sort of respiratory problem.

They are packed in strong plastic bags and it is therefore possible to store shavings outside, provided there has been no damage to the wrappings in transit. Shavings do have their share of disadvantages, however. They are difficult to dispose of – being slow rotting they cannot be spread on the land – and bales are fairly heavy to handle. Shavings are also much heavier to handle when wet than straw. There is also the possibility of foreign bodies, such as sharp fragments of wood or nails, being present – though this should not be a problem with good-quality shavings. Some horses' skin may be irritated if the shavings are from wood which has been treated with chemicals and foot problems sometimes occur.

Unlike straw, which traps pockets of air, shavings pack down closely. A bed of shavings is therefore less warm than a straw bed and rather less comfortable to lie on, particularly as it is less stable than straw and more prone to exposing bare patches of floor. A shavings bed will use approximately three bales per week.

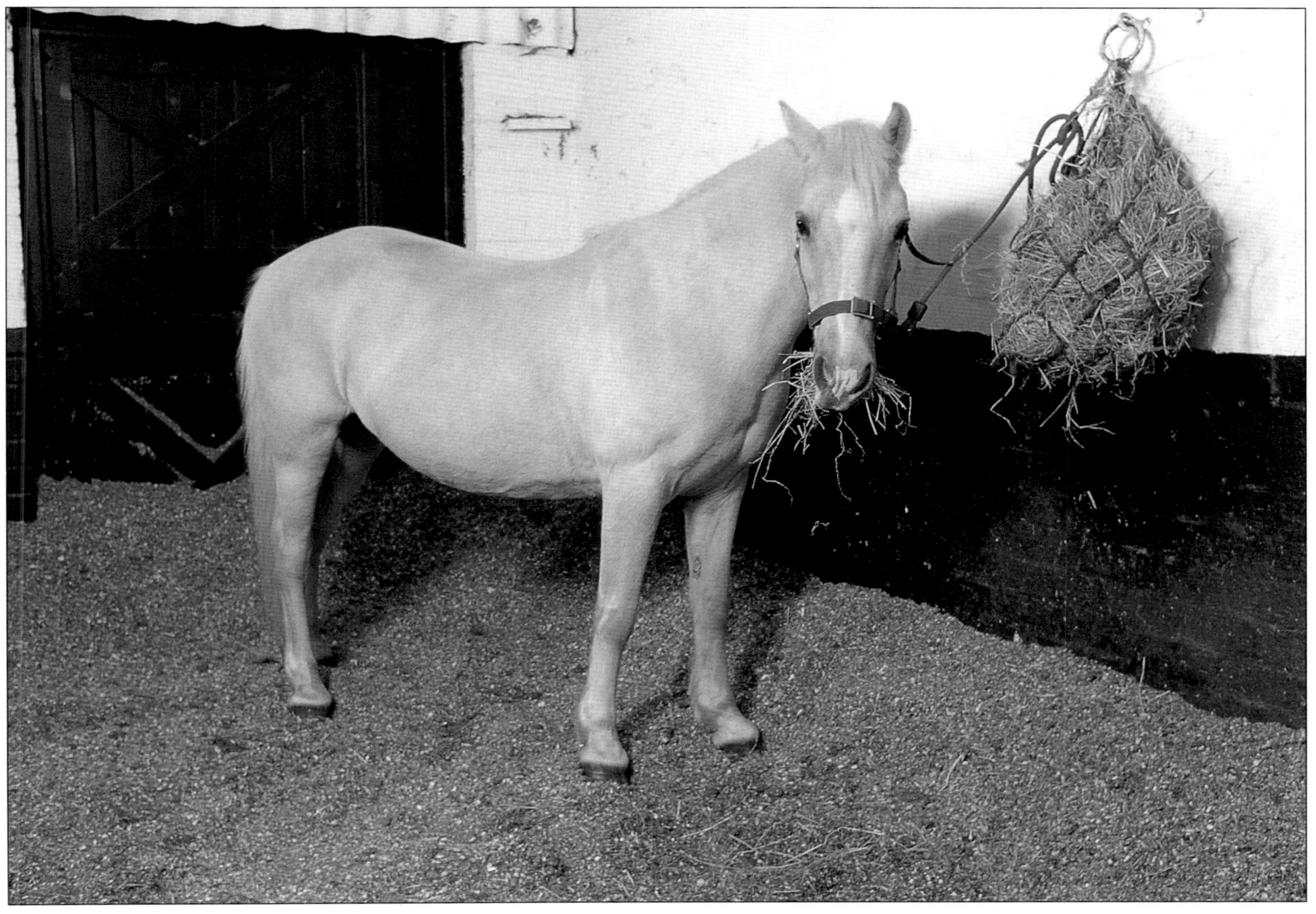

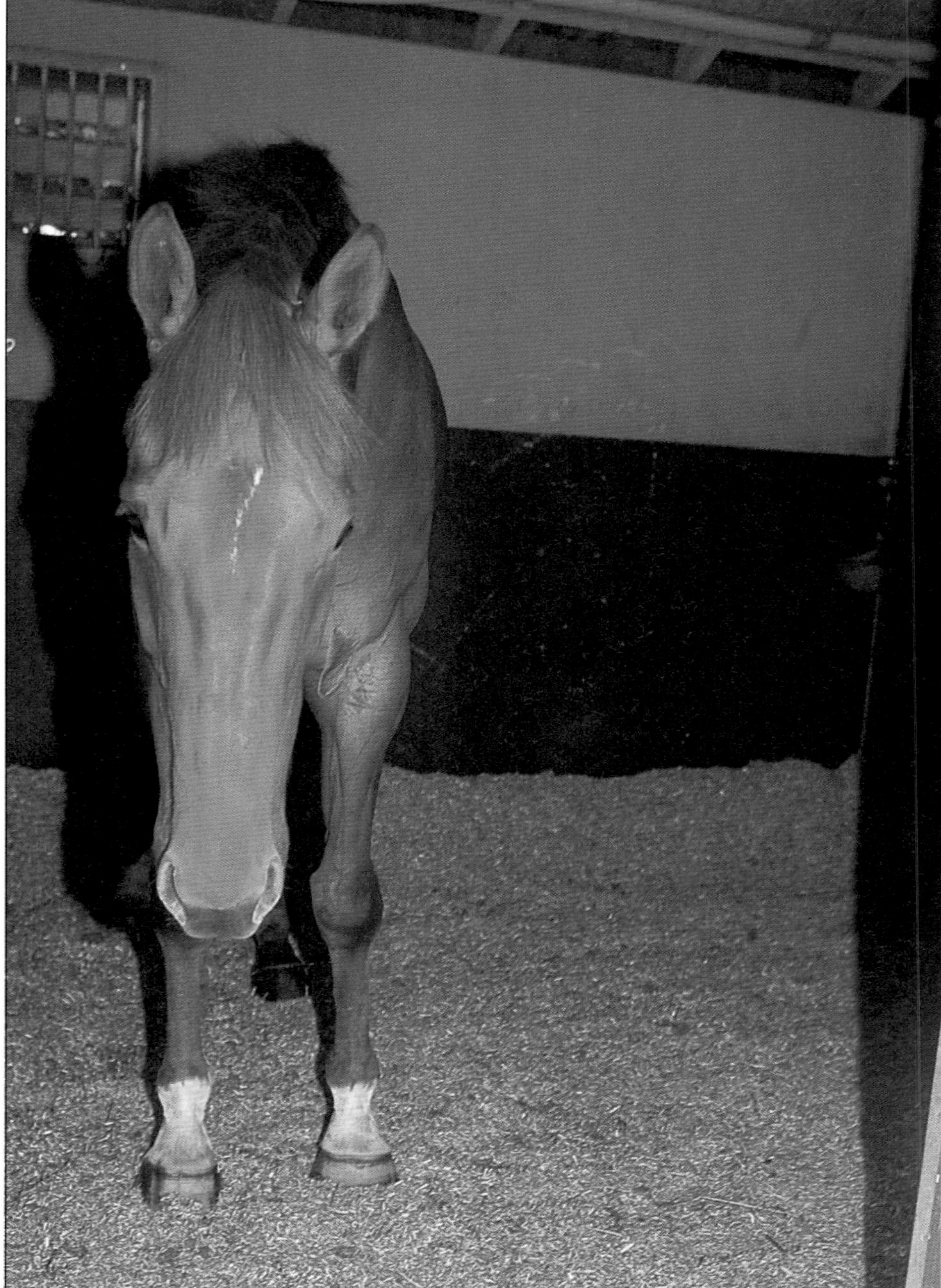

Aubiose is a fairly new and entirely natural product made from the hemp plant. It is proving particularly beneficial for horses with dust allergies and has the advantage of being exceptionally absorbent: four times more absorbent than wood shavings and twelve times more than straw. The bed is more expensive than other forms of bedding to put down initially, an average stable requiring some eight bales, but thereafter it is economical to maintain as it requires only half to one bale a week. When the bed is first laid it needs dampening with a hose or watering can to help it settle and activate its sponge-like properties.

Aubiose works by soaking up liquids in a small area at the base of the bed, in much the same way as cat litter. The top layers of the bed remain dry. It is a labour-saving form of bedding since mucking out consists simply of frequent removal of droppings and a light raking over to keep it level. It is recommended that the saturated bedding should be removed every five to ten days, depending on the horse. It is also suitable for use with the deep litter system.

Another big plus for Aubiose is the fact that it rots down to a valuable compost within five to six weeks and is therefore easy to dispose of. Its only disadvantage, apart from the initial cost, is that it is very free flowing (the particles are smaller and softer than shavings) and so it is not so easy to bank up the sides of the bed.

Shredded paper provides the most dust-free bed of all and is, as a result, often used for horses with allergies to straw or respiratory problems. It is also increasingly used for high-performance horses, such as eventers or racehorses, whose lungs need to be kept as free as possible of dust. Paper is cheaper to buy than shavings but on the other hand a deeper bed is required because it becomes saturated more quickly than either shavings or straw. On the plus side, it is light and easy to handle and provides a really warm bed. On the minus side it is often made from printed paper and this may cause staining of the horse's coat, particularly with greys, which causes extra work for the owner or groom. It is also difficult to control a paper-bed muck heap when it is windy. Again the bed will need around three bales per week.

Peat moss may be used for bedding in areas where it is easily available . Like shavings, it is usually sold in plastic-covered bales. It, too, has its good points and its bad points. It provides a comfortable bed, is not palatable and should be reasonably easy to dispose of. However, its main advantage over other forms of bedding is one of safety: it will not burst into flames in the event of a fire. On the other hand it is expensive, heavy to handle, needs frequent mucking out and forking over to prevent it becoming soggy and compacted and is so dark in colour that it is difficult to identify the wet areas.

Rubber matting can be used for bedding purposes but, apart from the fact that it is totally dust free when used on its own, it has more minus points than plus ones. It certainly does not look very attractive and, more important, provides

OPPOSITE
Hemp is a relatively new type of bedding for horses. It is exceptionally absorbent. Rather expensive initially, it is economical (and easy) to manage thereafter.

BELOW
Rubber matting is dust free, long lasting and labour saving but affords little comfort unless other bedding is used on top.

BOTTOM
Paper, being dust free and warm, is ideal for bedding down horses with respiratory problems. Printed paper can cause coat stains, especially on grey horses.

little warmth or protection from draughts. It does not absorb wet and if it is used without a covering of other bedding material, the droppings will be scattered about by the horse, who will then lie in them and, as a result, tend always to be dirty. There is little to prevent a horse becoming cast (the banked-up sides of conventional beds help in this respect). When used on its own its chief advantage, apart from being dust free, is its low-cost maintenance: after the initial outlay there is no more bedding to purchase and the matting should last for a number of years. Mucking out can be done by hosepipe, and is both quick and easy.

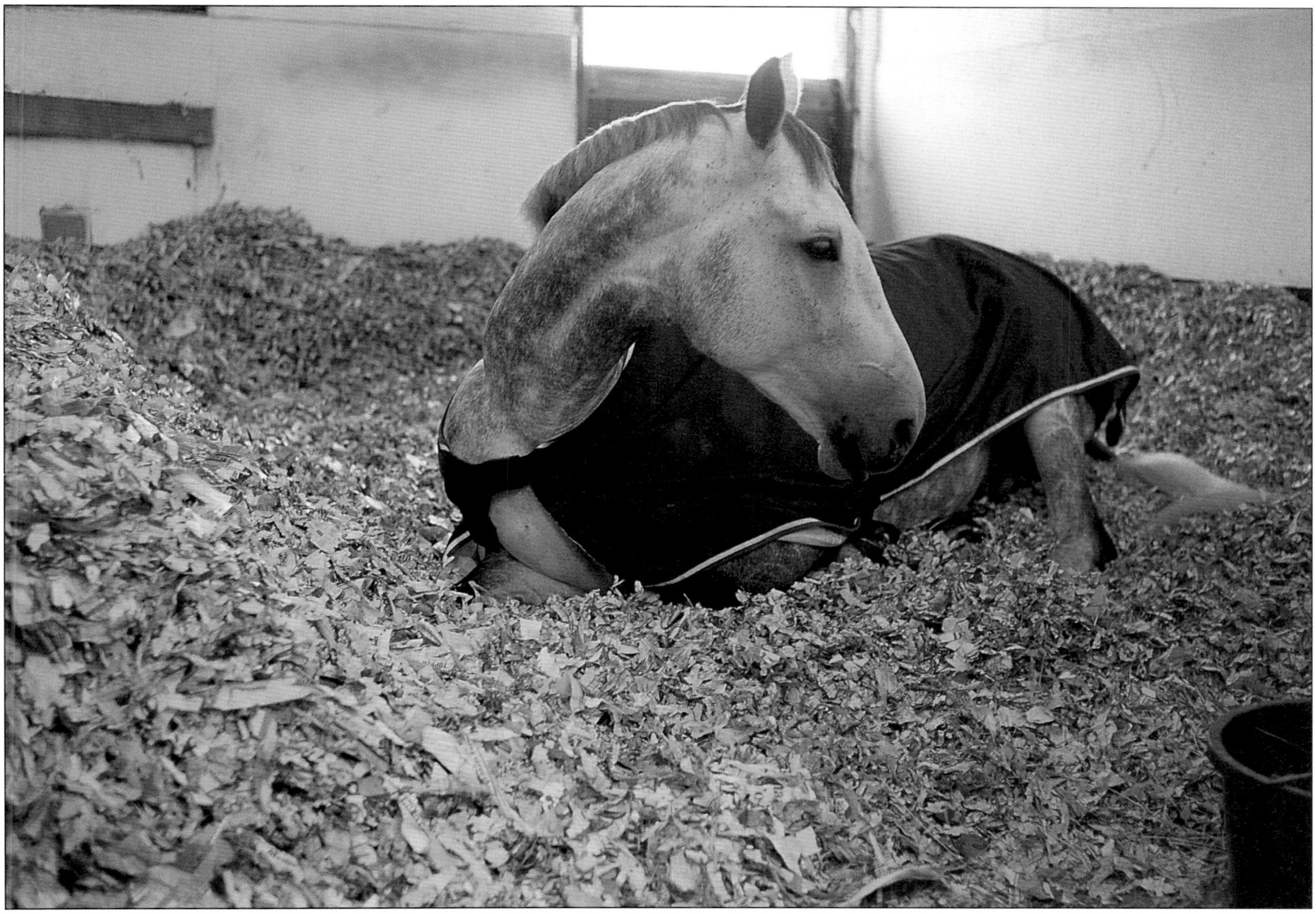

Management of Beds

Good management of beds is essential to keep the horse's environment healthy and to keep both the horse and his rugs as clean as possible. Stables can either be mucked out every day or you can adopt the deep litter or semi-deep litter system. The horse should be tied up during mucking out or, preferably, removed from the stable altogether. This protects him from any dust which may be disturbed while the bedding is being moved about and also makes the job easier.

Daily mucking out entails the removal of all droppings and soiled bedding. The best system is to take up the bed completely to allow the floor to dry while the horse is out. This is less of a chore with lightweight bedding materials such as straw and paper than with something heavier such as shavings.

You will need a wheelbarrow or a muck sheet, a fork and a strong yard broom with hard bristles. For mucking out a straw bed many people use a four-pronged fork for lifting droppings, but the same job can be accomplished with a three- or even a two-pronged fork. Much depends upon the skill of the wielder – the fewer prongs, the lighter the fork, the less tiring the job and the faster you can work. For mucking out shavings you will need a shavings fork, which has more prongs set closer together. The advantage of using a muck sheet is that you do not normally need a shovel. Most of the soiled litter can be forked or swept on to it and any remnants can be hand lifted, provided you wear protective gloves. When a shovel is required, it should be large and lightweight.

The muck sheet or wheelbarrow is positioned across the doorway and visible droppings collected and placed on/in it. The bedding is cleared away from one corner of the box (usually the one on the same side as the door and furthest from where the horse is tied up, though if the box is large enough the other corners may be used in rotation to ensure that all corners of the floor are dried out regularly). The floor in that corner is then swept clean. The corner is used to stack all the clean bedding – the squarer and neater the better since it will take up less room. All the droppings and wet straw are placed in the wheelbarrow or on the muck sheet and the entire floor is swept clean. Finally, a thin layer of the clean bedding is scattered across the box as standing litter. This will prevent the horse from slipping but will facilitate the drying of the floor. Assuming that the horse will stay tied up to be groomed and then exercised, the box can be left with the bed up for some time, which will help ensure that the floor – the sides as well as the centre – dries out before the bed is put down again.

An alternative, though not quite so satisfactory, method is to clear the bed completely from one wall of the box each day, thus ensuring that each bank of bedding is turned on a regular basis.

When putting down the bed again the existing bedding should be used to provide a good, deep covering to the entire floor area (right up to the door, to prevent draughts) and new bedding used to bank up the sides (with a straw bed if a

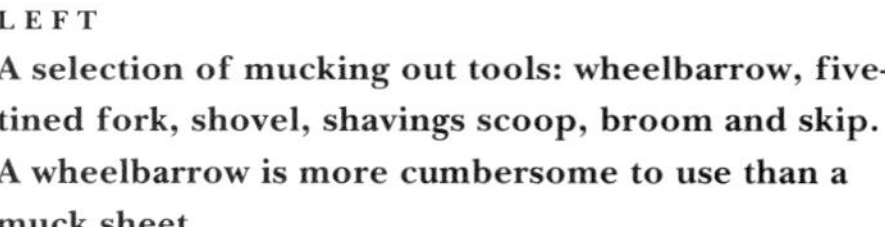

LEFT
A selection of mucking out tools: wheelbarrow, five-tined fork, shovel, shavings scoop, broom and skip. A wheelbarrow is more cumbersome to use than a muck sheet.

ABOVE
The horse should be tied up during mucking out and setting fair. (Note that, for safety, coats should be fastened while you are working with horses.)

▮ RIGHT
A muck heap sited in a three-sided bunker is easier to manage and to keep tidy than a free-standing one.

▮ BELOW
Position the muck heap where there is good drainage and easy access – for large vehicles as well as wheelbarrows.

horse has a tendency to eat it, new straw should be covered with a layer of the used bedding which will be less palatable). Banked sides keep out draughts, help protect the horse from injury when he is rolling or lying down and may help prevent a horse becoming cast (that is stuck with his legs in such a position that he cannot get up again).

To keep the bed as clean as possible, droppings should be picked up regularly throughout the day in a container known as a skip or skep, which may be made of metal, plastic or rubber. At evening stables the bed should be set fair, that is straightened out and put tidy for the night, care being taken to bank the sides well and ensure that the entire floor area is evenly covered.

To keep a horse on deep litter the stable needs to be large (in a small one the bed will quickly become sodden) and well ventilated. This system saves time as it involves the daily removal of the droppings only, not the wet bedding underneath. The old bed is left undisturbed and covered with fresh bedding each day. This type of bed needs careful management and is better suited to horses who are out by day as this enables the bedding to dry out more. A deep litter bed is warm in winter and may stay down for as long as six months. However, if it begins to build up too high or to smell it must be completely removed. The box should be thoroughly dried out before a new bed is started. Woodwork will tend to deteriorate more quickly with this type of bed because of the dampness in the lower layers.

A good compromise is the semi-deep litter system, whereby the droppings and the worst of the wet bedding are removed daily and the whole box given a complete muck out once a week or once every few weeks. This works well with shavings beds. With any deep-litter system, frequent removal of droppings is essential.

Management of the muck heap is also important. For convenience it should be sited reasonably close to the stables, with a dry, level approach and easy access for large vehicles. It should be downwind of the stables. A muck heap can be free-standing or contained in a three-sided bunker – breeze blocks are particularly suitable for this purpose – which makes it easier to keep the heap tidy. Make sure that there is adequate drainage away from any paths or driveways.

During mucking out the entire stable floor should be swept clean and, if possible, allowed to dry before the bed is put down again.

The sides of the bed should be banked well up the stable walls to help keep out draughts and to prevent injury when the horse lies down.

A skip is used for the periodic removal of droppings during the day. Skips may be made of plastic, metal or rubber.

Feeds

The horse is a herbivore, that is an eater of plants and especially grass and herbs. Left to live a totally natural life, the horse will spend some twenty hours out of every twenty-four grazing, slowly moving from place to place in his search for satisfying food. Horses are what are known as trickle feeders: they have comparatively small stomachs in relation to the size of their large intestines and need to top up with food at regular intervals. In the wild they put on condition when food is plentiful and lose it when it is not. The unnatural conditions imposed upon horses by man – the lack of constant access to grass and the need to burn up energy by working – mean that they must be fed suitable alternatives to grass if they are to thrive. Feeding horses is a complex subject. Like humans, horses are individuals and vary a good deal in the type and quantity of food they need to maintain health and fitness. Basically, however, the domesticated horse's diet consists of roughage, or bulk food, and concentrates.

ROUGHAGE

The usual way to feed roughage is in the form of hay, which is simply dried grass. There are two types of hay: seed hay and meadow hay. **Seed hay** is suitable for horses in hard work, because it is usually more nutritious than meadow hay. It is taken from grasses specifically sown as an annual crop, which will include top-quality plants such as rye grass and timothy. **Meadow hay** is cut from permanent pasture and is softer to the touch and often greener in colour than seed hay. It contains a greater variety of plants than seed hay (some of which may be of inferior quality) and is usually less nutritious and therefore more suitable for animals in light work.

A newer way of feeding bulk is in the form of **haylage**, which is grass sealed in plastic bags. It comes in different nutritional levels and is particularly suitable for horses with respiratory problems. Haylage may be mixed with hay or replace it altogether as the horse's bulk feed.

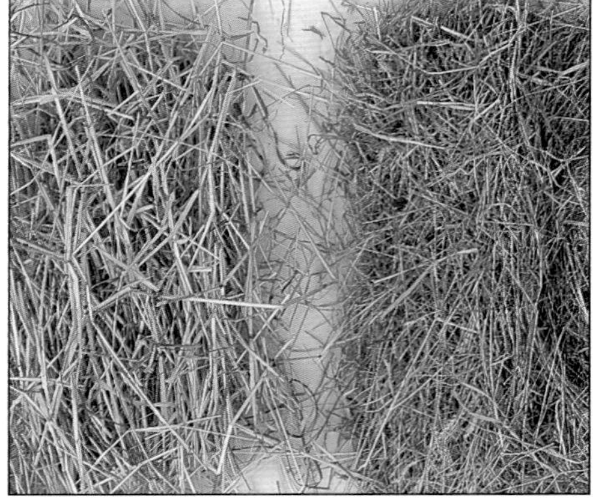

Seed hay (left) and meadow hay (right)

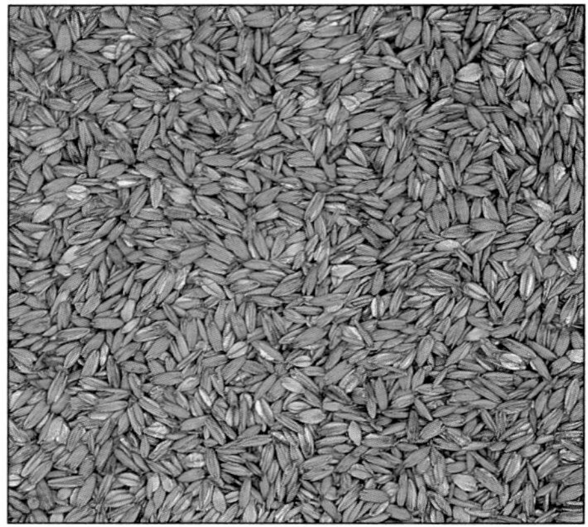

Crushed oats

Bruised barley

Flaked maize

Chaff or **chop** is hay, either alone or mixed with one-third proportion of oat straw, which has been chopped into small pieces by passing it through a chaff cutter. It may be added to concentrates to encourage mastication and aid digestion.

CONCENTRATES

Food such as oats and barley are known as concentrates. These are the energy-giving foods which, when fed in the correct balance with the roughage, enable the horse to perform the work required of him without losing condition.

Oats have always been considered the ideal cereal for feeding to horses. The fibrous husk covering the rich seed encourages chewing and helps prevent the horse from eating too quickly, which can seriously disrupt his digestive system. The one drawback is that oats have a low calcium-to-phosphorus ratio and the horse's diet should therefore contain a calcium supplement to balance the minerals in the roughage. Oats may not be suitable for feeding to all equine animals, however, as they can have a heating effect, making them difficult to control. Oats should be lightly rolled and used within two or three weeks thereafter, otherwise they lose nutritional value.

Barley has a higher energy value than oats but is lower in fibre. It may be fed cracked, rolled, flaked (heat treated) or micronized. It may also be fed as a mash, which is prepared by pouring boiling water over flaked barley and allowing it to cool before feeding. Whole barley should never be fed unless it has first been cooked to soften it, otherwise it is too indigestible. It should be covered with boiling water and allowed to simmer for several hours until the grain has split, swollen and become soft.

Bran

Linseed (which must be boiled before feeding)

Soaked sugar beet

Molassed chop

Horse and pony nuts

Coarse mix

Maize is high in starch but low in protein and fibre. It is usually fed flaked or micronized. It can be very heating and should be fed only in small amounts.

Bran, a by-product of wheat, is high in fibre and often fed to horses who are off work or on a low-protein diet. It may be fed dry in small quantities, mixed with the horse's other feed, or as a mash. This is made by putting the bran, together with a handful of salt, in a bucket, pouring boiling water over it (not so much that the mash is sloppy), covering and allowing it to steam and cool.

Linseed, the seed of the flax plant, is rich in oil and often fed to improve the condition of the horse's coat. It is poisonous (it contains prussic acid) if not first boiled. The linseed is covered with cold water and soaked overnight. The following day more water is added (about 4 pints/2 litres to 2–3oz/110g of linseed) and the mixture is brought to the boil and simmered for several hours. When the resultant jelly has cooled it may be added to a bran mash or to the horse's ordinary feed.

Sugar beet is a highly digestible source of energy and fibre. It has a good calcium-to-phosphorus ratio and may be used to correct the imbalance of those elements in cereals. Sugar beet pulp (the remains of the root vegetable after the sugar has been extracted) comes in cube form or shredded. Before feeding it is essential to soak it for at least twelve hours using at least double the amount of water to pulp. Cubes may require soaking for longer in more water. If it is not adequately soaked, it will swell up in the horse's stomach, with potentially fatal results.

Molasses is a by-product of sugar. Dark and sticky in appearance and very palatable, it may be added in small quantities to the feed to supply energy, improve the condition of the coat and to tempt fussy feeders.

Concentrates which come in cube form or as coarse mixes are known as **compound feeds**. They are made from a variety of ingredients and are scientifically prepared to provide a balanced diet. Specially formulated compound feeds are available for foals, brood mares, competition horses, and so on. They are particularly useful for the novice horseman as a good-quality compound feed takes much of the guesswork out of feeding.

Feeding

LEFT
Feedstuffs should be kept in a clean feed room, in dry, rodent-proof containers. All feeds should be carefully measured.

To work out a suitable feed ration for your horse you must take into consideration his size, his age, his type and the amount and nature of the work he is doing. Feeding is both a science and an art. Science tells us much about the principles of feeding and the nutritive value of the various feedstuffs but horses are all individuals and ultimately the proof of the pudding is in their appearance and performance. You can learn to judge the correct, healthy condition for a horse of a particular breed, age, size and build doing a particular job of work by studying similar animals to your own which are being used for similar purposes (perhaps at your riding school or in local competitions).

The ratio of bulk feed to concentrates will vary according to the nature and amount of work the horse is required to do. A horse in light work does not require a great deal of energy-giving feed (it will merely serve to make him a "hot" ride). On the other hand a horse such as a hunter or an eventer needs more energy-giving feed and less bulk. For a horse in light work (doing up to about six hours a week hacking and light schooling) and for

The following is an approximate guide to total food requirements based on height (but bear in mind that it is only approximate, since horses vary a good deal in build and a finely made animal may require less food than a heavyweight doing the same amount of work):

Height	Daily feed requirement
Under 12hh	14 – 16lb (6.3 – 7.2kg)
12 – 13hh	16 – 18lb (7.2 – 8kg)
13 – 14hh	20 – 22lb (9 – 10kg)
14 – 15hh	22 – 24lb (10 – 11kg)
15 – 16hh	24 – 26lb (11 – 12kg)
over 16hh	26 – 28lb (12 – 12.5kg)

To find a more accurate yardstick it is customary to measure feed requirements against the horse's body weight (the horse requires a total daily intake of about 2-2.5 per cent of its body weight). The best way to check his weight is to use a weighbridge. Failing that you can estimate his weight by using the following formula:

$$\frac{\text{Girth}^2 \times \text{length (in inches)}}{300} = \text{weight in lbs}$$

NB Measure the girth round the largest part of the barrel at the moment when the horse has breathed out; measure the length from the point of the shoulder to the point of the buttock.

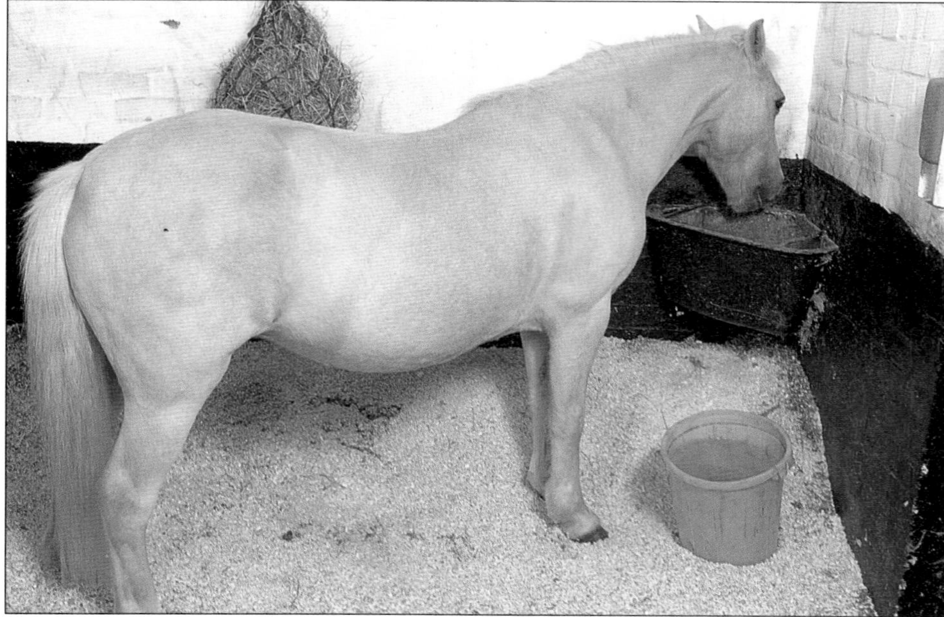

TOP LEFT
Some barn-type stabling incorporates swinging feed bowls. They are labour saving in large yards with a lot of horses to feed.

ABOVE LEFT
Hook-on plastic mangers are useful for feeding horses kept at grass.

LEFT
A large corner manger is a suitable way to feed the stabled horse. Mangers must be cleaned out regularly.

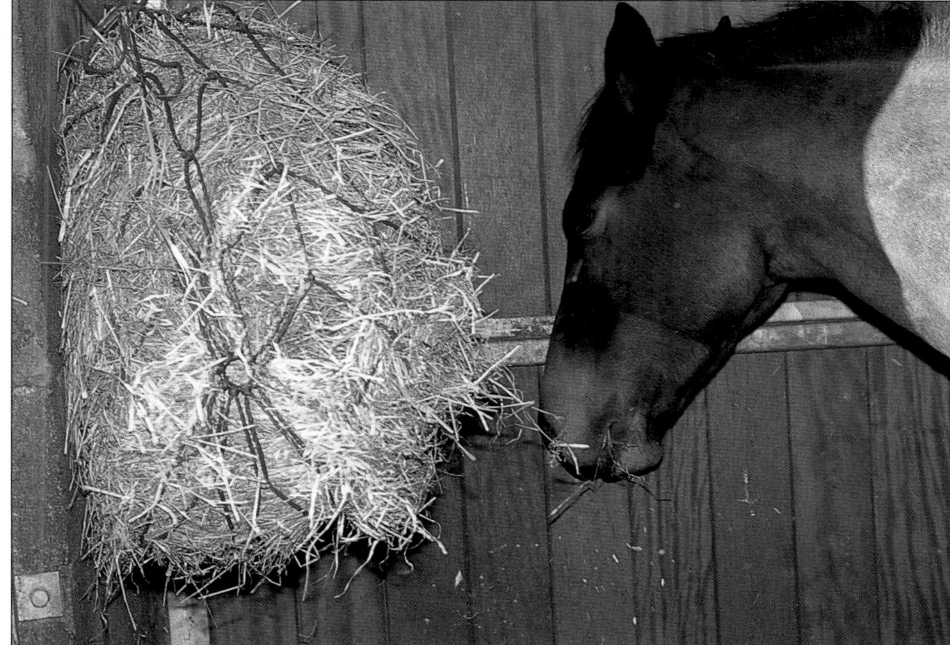

most ponies the ratio should be 30 per cent concentrates to 70 per cent bulk. For a horse in medium work (doing up to ten hours work a week, including up to two hours schooling a day, some dressage, show jumping and hacking) the ratio should be 50 per cent concentrates to 50 per cent bulk. For a horse in hard work (more than ten hours a week, or including fast work such as hunting, eventing or endurance riding) the ratio should be 70 per cent concentrates to 30 per cent bulk. These are general guidelines and all horses are different, but however hard he is working the horse should never receive less than 25 per cent bulk by weight.

Horses and ponies living out at grass during the winter require the same amount of food as stabled horses in order to maintain their health and condition during bad weather. During the spring and summer (assuming that the weather is fine) good-quality grazing should provide enough nutrition for ponies and coldblooded horses doing no more than an hour or two of light work, though it is best to check their weight regularly to make sure. During the winter, grazing will do no more than provide maintenance. In severe weather it will not even do that and the horse will lose condition if he does not receive supplementary feeding.

GOLDEN RULES OF FEEDING

- Feed nature's way: little and often – the horse has a small stomach in relation to its size.
- Divide the concentrate ration (preferably mixed with chaff or other small roughage) into three or four feeds a day – never give more than 4lb (1.8kg) of concentrates in one feed.
- Feed at the same times each day.
- Wash mangers regularly with clean water.
- Never leave uneaten feed in the manger – if your horse regularly fails to eat up, either you are overfeeding or there is something wrong with him or the feed.
- Never feed directly before exercise – allow up to two hours for digestion.
- Never feed immediately after work – allow an hour for the horse to recover.
- Never make sudden changes to a horse's diet – introduce new feedstuffs gradually over a period of at least a week.
- Feed hay after concentrates and give the bulk of the hay at night.
- Never leave a horse for longer than eight hours without food.
- Always ensure that the horse has clean, fresh water available.
- Have the horse's teeth checked regularly – sharp edges must be rasped down to enable him to chew his food efficiently.
- Worm the horse regularly.
- Keep feed in clean, dry, rodent-proof bins, and hay in a waterproof feed shed, protected from damp ground.
- Add variety to the feed by giving succulents such as sliced apples and carrots (sliced lengthways to prevent choking), especially if the horse is a shy feeder.

TOP LEFT
Haynets must be tied securely and high enough to prevent the horse from catching a foot in them. Feeding hay on the ground is safer and more natural.

LEFT
Horses should have access to salt, to counteract any deficiency in their diet. A salt lick is a convenient way of providing it.

FAR LEFT
Soaking hay in clean water for a few hours before feeding helps prevent horses inhaling mould spores.

Water

Water makes up approximately 60 per cent of an adult horse's body weight, the exact percentage depending on his age and condition. It is present in all his body fluids and is vital for the correct functioning of the blood, the digestion and the excretion process. A horse can survive for several weeks without food but only for a few days without water.

The quantity of water required by a horse on a daily basis varies according to his diet, the prevailing weather conditions, his work load and his general health. A stabled horse may drink in the region of eight gallons (37 litres) of water a day, although the amount may be as little as five gallons (20 litres) or as much as ten (40 litres). A horse at grass may drink less than a stabled horse because of the moisture content in the grazing. A horse will drink more when the weather is hot and humid or when he sweats as a result of hard work. A sick horse may be reluctant to drink.

It is vital for the stabled horse to have access to a constant supply of fresh, clean water, the only exception being before hard, fast work. Horses are extremely fussy about the water they drink and will go thirsty rather than drink dirty or tainted water.

Water for the stabled horse may be provided either in buckets or by means of an automatic water bowl. The advantage of using buckets is that you can easily check the amount of water the horse is drinking. Water buckets should be large and strong – heavy-duty rubber is the most resilient. Plastic buckets, though convenient because they are light to carry, are not the safest as they tend to split and can cause injury. Metal buckets are stronger but they, too, might cause injury to a restless horse.

Buckets should be positioned in a corner of the stable, not right by the door but not too far from it, either, so that they are easy to reach for refilling. The handle should be positioned away from the horse. Many horses can be trusted never to knock a bucket over, even when it is empty. Others get into the habit of playing with theirs. Some are just naturally clumsy and will knock a bucket over when moving about the box. Water buckets can be fixed to the wall with clips or, if the stable is roomy enough, stood in a rubber tyre.

LEFT
Heavy-duty rubber water buckets are ideal for the stabled horse. They are safer and more durable than plastic.

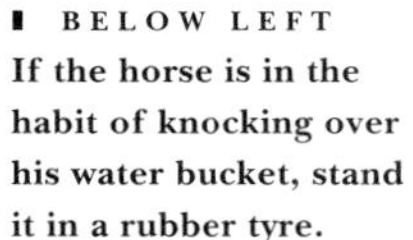

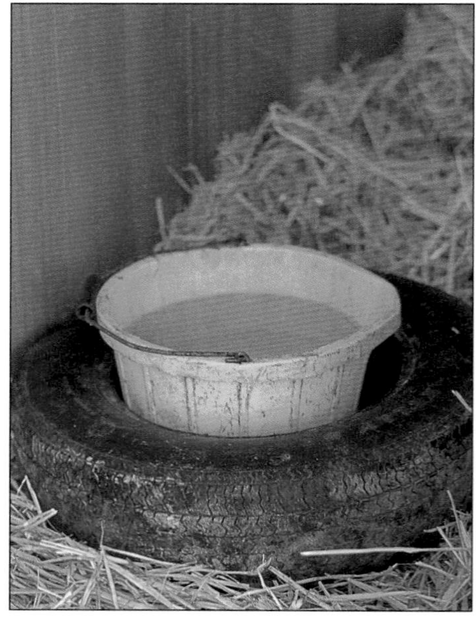

BELOW LEFT
If the horse is in the habit of knocking over his water bucket, stand it in a rubber tyre.

During the day water buckets should be checked and refilled regularly. Water should be replaced rather than topped up to ensure a fresh supply. At night a big horse will need two buckets so that there is no possibility of his going short. Buckets should be scrubbed out regularly with clean water.

Automatic drinking bowls, connected to the water supply and controlled by a small ballcock, are popular in large yards because they are labour saving. However, they do have several disadvantages. Compared with buckets they are quite small and may not permit a horse to enjoy a deep drink. Unless they are fitted with a plug (which should be recessed into the bottom out of the way of the horse's teeth) they are difficult to clean. Also, it is not possible to judge at a glance how much a horse is drinking. Since water consumption, like food consumption, is an indication of the horse's state of health, this is not ideal. It is, however,

BELOW
An automatic drinking bowl provides an alternative to buckets. The bowl must be checked frequently to ensure that the water supply is operating correctly.

BELOW
The stabled horse must have constant access to clean water. A large horse will need two buckets.

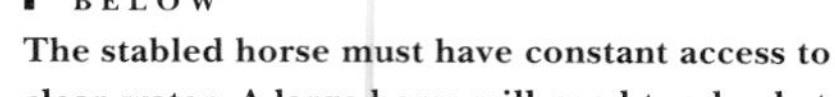

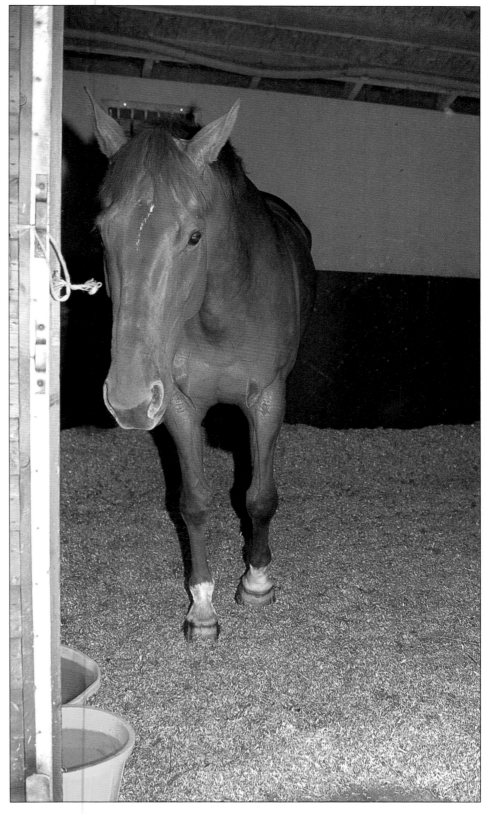

GOLDEN RULES OF WATERING

- Always provide the stabled horse with a constant supply of clean water.
- Always water before feeding.
- Never work a horse hard immediately after a long drink.
- After hard work (such as hunting or cross-country) give a horse a small quantity of water – about half a gallon (2.5 litres) every quarter of an hour until he is satisfied.
- When giving electrolytes (minerals to replace those lost during strenuous exercise) always offer plain water as well.
- Keep all water utensils clean.
- Check automatic water bowls every day.

possible to install drinkers fitted with a meter which overcomes this problem. All projecting fixtures in a stable are a potential source of injury to the horse and a water bowl is no exception. Conversely, there is every possibility of a bowl being damaged by the horse. Drinking bowls must be rigorously checked every day – a blocked supply will cause the horse great distress while an overflowing bowl with swamp his bedding. Precautions must be taken when fitting pipes so that they cannot freeze in winter.

Daily Care

Horses must be kept fit and healthy if they are to perform the work required of them. Keeping them that way requires daily care and attention. It is the responsibility of the owner to ensure that the horse has sufficient regular exercise of the right type and to learn how to recognize the signs of ill-health. Every horse, whether he is kept stabled or at grass, should be checked over carefully every day to ensure that he is well, sound and has no injuries or fresh lumps or bumps. Horses are creatures of habit. They thrive on a regular routine and therefore should be visited, fed, exercised and so on, at the same times each day. Some common equine ailments and minor injuries can be dealt with by the competent horseman, others will need veterinary attention. The owner must judge when to seek expert advice, bearing in mind that the sooner treatment begins, the better the chance of a cure. Regular visits from the farrier are also an essential part of horse care. There was never a truer maxim than "no foot, no horse".

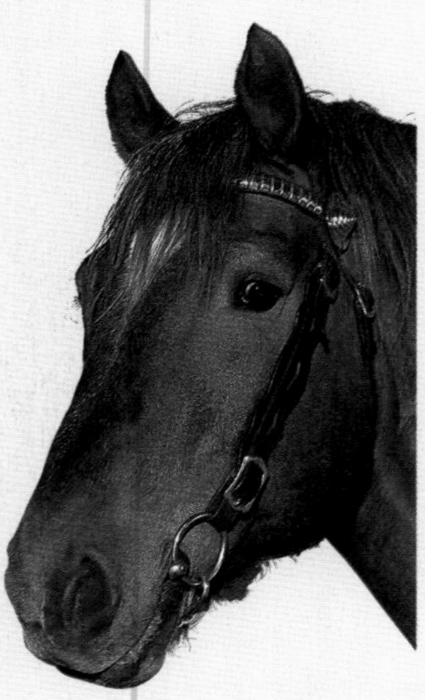

Exercise

The horse needs daily exercise for the maintenance of health and, like all athletes, when he is in work he needs additional exercise to build up and maintain condition.

Where fitness of the horse is concerned exercise is always linked to feed. A horse who is kept at grass, provided the paddock is not very small, has the opportunity to take all the gentle exercise he needs to stay healthy. Space and the freedom to move around at will are an intrinsic part of the horse's everyday life in the natural state so the bigger his paddock the nearer it is to his natural environment and the more contented he will be.

STABLE "VICES"

Being cooped up in a stable for some twenty-two hours out of every twenty-four is unnatural and boring and may lead to a horse developing bad habits, or stable "vices". These include wood chewing, box-walking (aimless walking round and round the stable), crib-biting (in which the horse takes hold of the manger or the top of the door or some other convenient object with his teeth and swallows air) or weaving (in which he stands, usually with his head over the door, and sways from side to side). Virtually all stable vices can do harm to the horse in one way or another. All can be avoided if the horse is not allowed to become bored and frustrated.

LEFT
The stabled horse requires regular daily exercise to keep him healthy. Hacking out helps to get him fit and enables him to relax after work.

OPPOSITE
For racehorses, and other horses in hard work, a carefully planned exercise programme is essential.

PREVIOUS PAGE OPPOSITE
Most ponies, like this Haflinger, thrive when kept at grass.

PREVIOUS PAGE
Despite its size, the Suffolk Punch is an economical breed to keep.

BELOW LEFT
In their natural state, horses and ponies such as this Exmoor mare and foal have all the exercise they need.

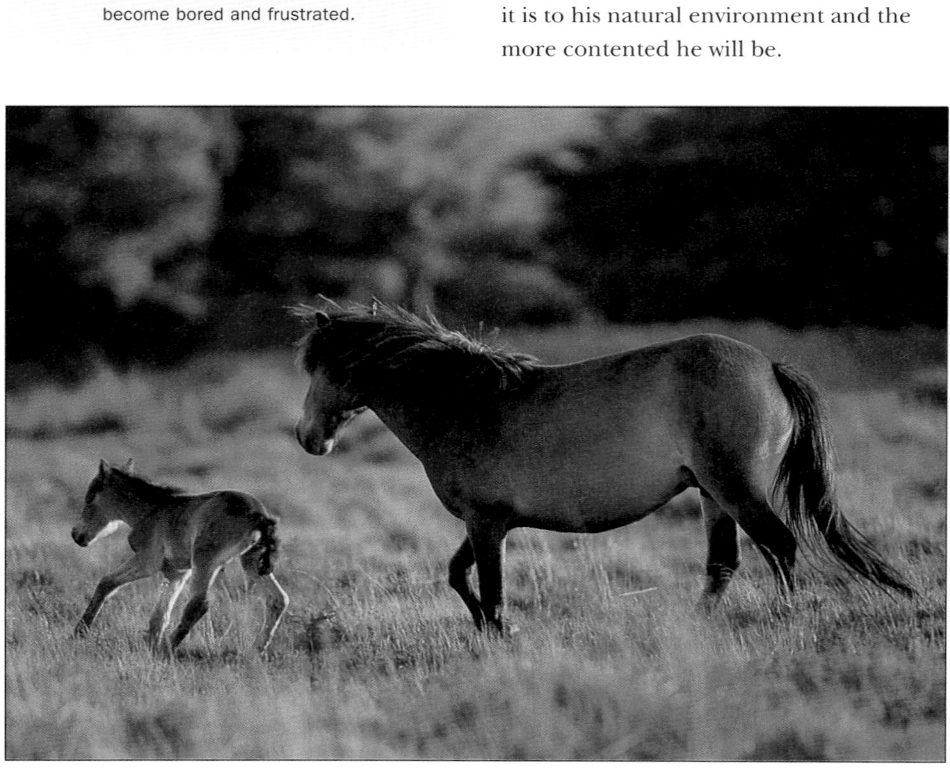

However, the totally grass-fed horse will not be fit to do anything other than light work in summer. By keeping the horse in a stable it is possible to monitor his food intake and gradually build up his physical fitness to enable him to carry out the work required of him. But because the stabled horse is deprived of his freedom for part, if not all, of the day a good exercise regime is essential if he is to be happy and healthy and not become unmanageable.

If possible, all stabled horses should spend part of the day turned out at grass in addition to their normal work routine. There is a danger of fit horses doing themselves harm when turned out, so it is essential to have safely fenced paddocks and to fit protective boots to guard against accidents. If for some reason it is not possible to give the stabled horse his usual exercise (for example in bad weather when it may be impossible to ride on the roads), he should be turned out for a time each day or at the very least led out and allowed to eat some grass. Another alternative to ridden exercise is to work the horse on the lunge.

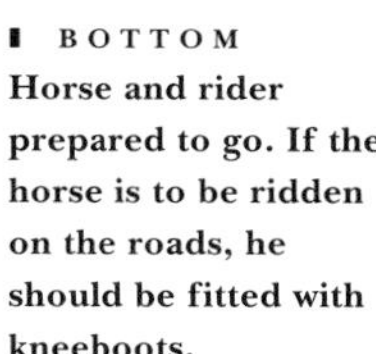

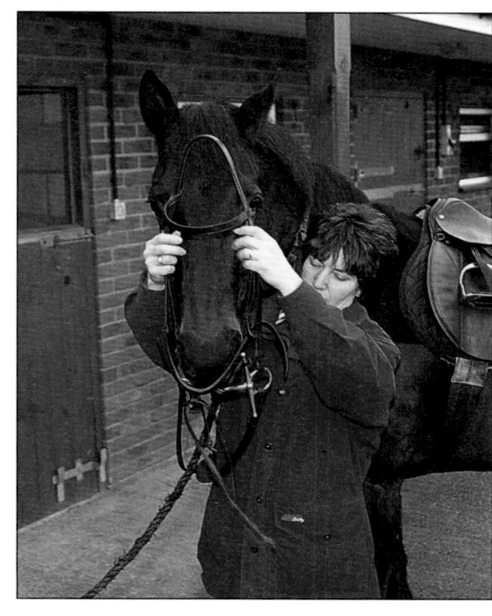

RIGHT
For exercise purposes a simple snaffle bridle and general purpose saddle are usually adequate.

BOTTOM
Horse and rider prepared to go. If the horse is to be ridden on the roads, he should be fitted with kneeboots.

Before being exercised or worked the horse should be given a quick grooming to make him neat and tidy. Stable stains should be sponged off and all remnants of bedding removed from his mane and tail. His feet should be picked out and his shoes checked.

An all-purpose saddle is suitable for general hacking out and roadwork. A numnah will protect the saddle from grease and dirt from the horse's coat and will also be more comfortable for his back.

Keeping a bridle for everyday use will minimize the wear and tear on the bridle you use for "best", e.g. for showing or competing. The bitting and bridling arrangement will depend on the horse. Most can be hacked out safely in a snaffle with a cavesson noseband. If you do need a little more control, you may prefer to fit a Grakle or flash noseband. Whether or not you use a martingale will again depend on the horse and how difficult or otherwise he is to control.

When exercising on the roads it is advisable to fit the horse with kneeboots – fitted correctly they will not impede his action. It is all too easy for a horse to slip up on tarmac and injure his knees, yet it is surprising how few people take this simple precaution. Brushing boots are another useful means of protecting the horse's legs.

A clipped horse in winter will need an exercise sheet to keep his loins warm. This is placed under the saddle to prevent it slipping back. It should be fitted with a fillet string, which passes under the tail to prevent it blowing up in the wind.

You can exercise two horses at the same time by riding one and leading one, in which case the led horse should wear a bridle and you should lead him either by the reins or on a leather lead rein run from one bit ring, through the other and into your hand. Never lead a horse on a lunge rein which could easily become tangled, and never wind a lead rein or reins round your hand. The ridden horse must always be between the led horse and the traffic and you should always ride on the same side of the road as the direction of the traffic. Avoid riding and leading on roads where there is anything but light traffic and never ride and lead unless the horses are traffic-proof and well behaved. For maximum control the led horse's head should be at or just behind the ridden horse's shoulder.

For more serious work – schooling, dressage, jumping and so on – the horse should wear the saddle and bridle most suited to that activity and protective boots or bandages. For jumping, fit his shoes with appropriate studs to prevent slipping.

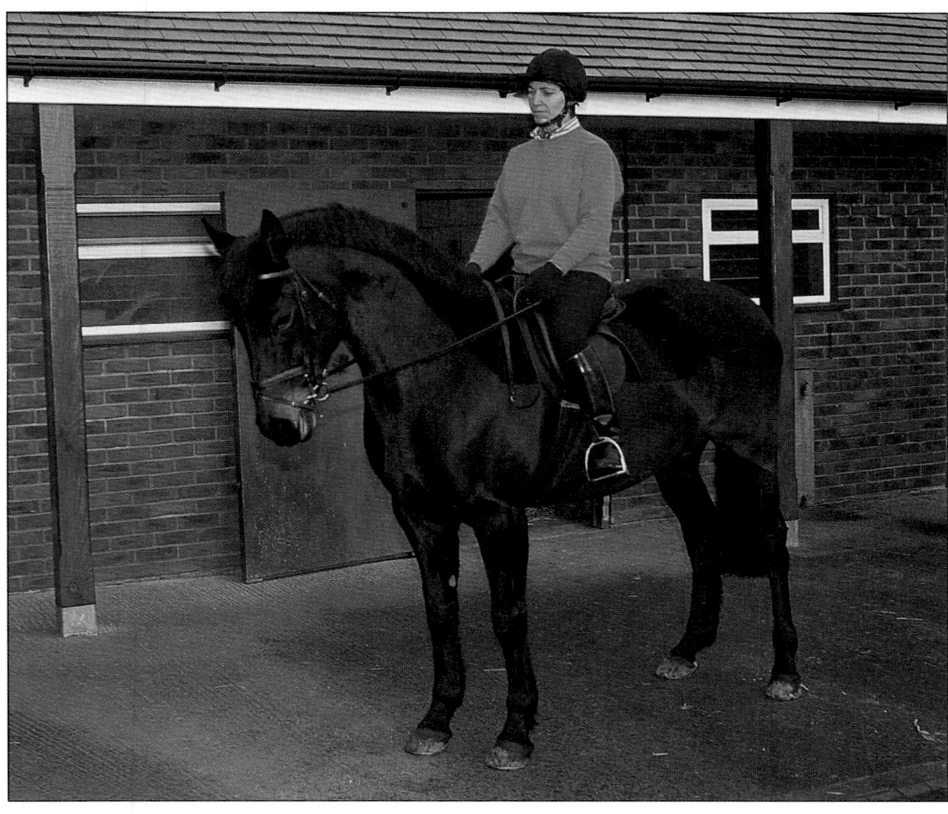

Fitness

LEFT
Hillwork builds up muscle, particularly in the hindquarters, and improves the horse's lung and heart capacity.

BOTTOM
Hacking out makes a welcome break from school work for both horse and rider.

Broadly speaking the fitness training of the horse can be divided into three distinct stages. First, there is a period of slow work designed to strengthen him up in readiness for more serious work. Second, there is the build up designed to bring him to the necessary fitness for most everyday riding activities. And third, there is the fine tuning required to bring him to a peak for physically demanding pastimes such as regular hunting, show jumping, eventing or racing.

FIRST STAGE

The period of slow work is vital and should never be rushed. The tried and tested way to make horses fit, and to prevent strains and sprains when they begin serious work, is roadwork. When the horse is first ridden after a period of rest, he must have walking exercise only. Three-quarters of an hour a day is sufficient to begin with if the horse has been out at grass. Gradually, over a period of **two or three weeks** (preferably longer if the horse is ultimately going to be asked to do a lot of hard, fast work), this can be increased to an hour and a half to two hours a day.

Although this is slow work, the horse must not be allowed to slop along any old how. He should be kept going forward, straight and in a good rhythm in order to start the process of building up muscles in the right places. The exercise route should be varied as much as possible to keep the horse alert and interested and he should have a day off each week to allow him to relax.

Trotting can begin during weeks **three to four**. To begin with the horse should walk for about thirty minutes before starting to trot. This will give his muscles time to warm up. His exercise period

▪ LEFT
By week five the horse should be fit enough to start a little gymnastic jumping.

▪ BELOW LEFT
Serious schooling can begin when the horse has been in work for about six weeks.

should also finish at walk, in order to cool him off. The trot should be controlled and rhythmic and in the early stages the periods of trot should be short and interspersed with longer periods of walk. As the days progress and the horse begins to feel fitter, the periods of trot can be made longer. The pace must always be controlled: trotting flat out on the roads (or any other hard surface) jars the horse's legs and can lead to injury. Uphill trotting is better than trotting on the flat because it reduces the strain placed on the front legs. At all times when trotting the rider should change the diagonal regularly and, when trotting uphill, keep the weight forward.

During **week four** some periods of schooling on the flat can be introduced. They should be no longer than about twenty minutes and cantering should be kept to a minimum. To encourage the horse to relax and to continue the building-up process, he should be taken for a hack afterwards.

Week five can see the introduction of a little hillwork, one of the finest ways of building up muscle. Hacking and flatwork should continue.

By **week six** he should be ready for a canter work-out, in which he should be allowed to stride on but without going into a wild gallop. As with trotting, uphill cantering is the most beneficial.

SECOND STAGE

Once the first stage in the fitness programme is completed the horse will be in a fit state to begin more serious work. Work on the flat, incorporating suppling exercises such as serpentines and circles, should be introduced. The schooling sessions should be kept short to begin with but may be gradually increased in length as the horse becomes more toned up. Gymnastic jumping exercises over grids and on circles and elements of circles will all help to improve his athleticism.

THIRD STAGE

The type of fitness required in a particular horse is always governed by the type of work required of him. For example a show jumper needs the muscular power to clear big fences but is never required to gallop flat out for a prolonged period. On the other hand the three-day eventer needs great stamina and endurance to be able to cope with the demands placed on him.

Getting the horse fit for sports which require speed and endurance involves longer periods of canter work. Canter work must be introduced gradually and should always be carried out on good ground to reduce the risk of injury. Short periods of canter are sufficient to begin with. Later, periods of long, steady cantering may be used to bring the horse to a high degree of fitness. Only rarely is the occasional really fast galloping necessary, as for instance with the fine tuning of a racehorse or three-day event horse. The main thing to remember is that the faster the pace the more chance there is of injury occurring.

Even when the horse reaches peak fitness for the activity required of him, he should be allowed regular periods of relaxation if he is not to become sour – hacks in the countryside or spells at liberty in the paddock. During a rest day after strenuous work the horse will appreciate being led out for a bite of grass.

The Healthy and the Unhealthy Horse

Recognizing signs of ill-health in the horse is all part of good horse management. The experienced horseman can tell at a glance when something is not quite right with an animal in his or her care. Learning to recognize the warning signs means an early diagnosis which, in turn, means a better chance of successful treatment.

A change in the horse's eating habits is often the first indication of something being amiss with his health: if a normally good feeder loses his appetite, be suspicious. A change in behaviour is also a reliable early-warning signal. For instance, if a normally bright, alert horse suddenly becomes listless, it may well be the first sign of a health problem. Any form of nasal discharge, coughing or a dull "staring" coat are also indications of ill-health. A change in the consistency and frequency of the horse's droppings may also mean that all is not well.

All owners should learn to check their horse's temperature, pulse rate and respiratory rate so as to know when to call for veterinary help.

The normal temperature of the healthy horse is around 101.5° Fahrenheit (38°C). You should learn to take your horse's temperature by practising while he is healthy so that you will be capable of making a fast, accurate reading should the need arise. The temperature is taken with a clinical thermometer which is inserted into the rectum and held there for about one minute. It is best to hold the horse's tail steady to prevent him swishing it and possibly dislodging the thermometer.

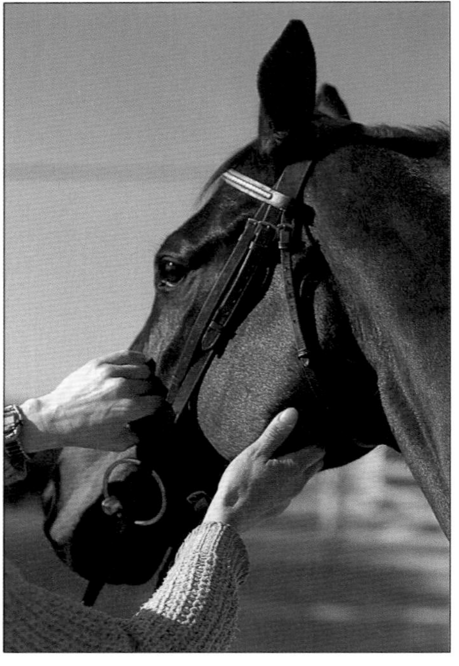

The horse's pulse is to be found along the edge of the lower jaw. In the healthy horse the heart rate is about 40 per minute.

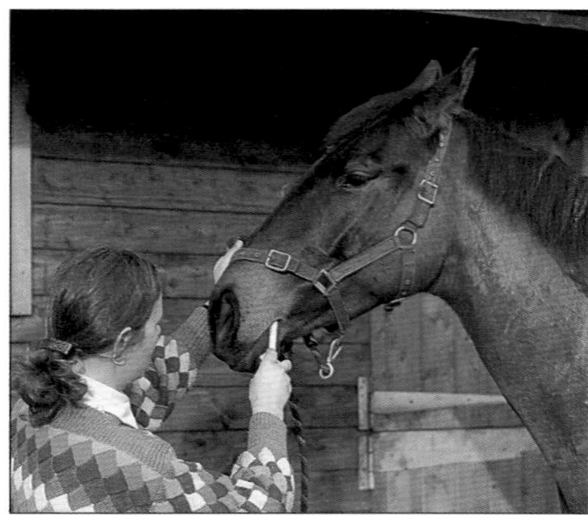

All horses carry a worm burden and require regular worming. The usual method of worming is to administer an oral paste.

At rest the healthy horse has a heart rate of about 40 per minute. If the heart rate exceeds 60 per minute, there is definitely something wrong with the horse. To count the heart rate you need a stethoscope but failing that it is possible to count the horse's pulse rate by resting a finger over the artery situated about halfway along the bottom edge of the lower jaw. Locating the pulse will take a certain amount of practice.

In the healthy horse at rest the respiratory rate can vary from about eight to sixteen breaths a minute. To count the respiratory rate watch the horse's flanks.

Like humans, some horses have heart murmurs or faulty heart rhythms. If a heart abnormality is only present when the horse is resting and disappears when he begins to work, there is usually no cause for alarm.

Problems with the limbs manifest themselves in various ways. Often the slightest suspicion of heat or a tiny swelling may be an indication of a serious tendon problem. Actual lameness can be detected by watching the horse as he is trotted both away from you and towards you. Watch for a sinking of the hindquarters or a nod of the head as one foot hits the ground (it will be the other limb which is causing the pain). When acquiring a new horse take note of any scars or bony enlargements so that you can distinguish new problems from old conditions or injuries.

All horses carry a worm burden which must be controlled by regular worming if it is not to cause serious damage to their health. Your veterinary surgeon will advise on a suitable worming programme.

In young horses a raised temperature and cold-like symptoms such as a nasal discharge may indicate an infestation of ascarids. These are quite large worms which can cause colic. In the adult horse the main danger comes from the large red worm, or *Strongylus vulgaris*, whose immature larvae burrow into the small arteries in the intestinal wall. The damage

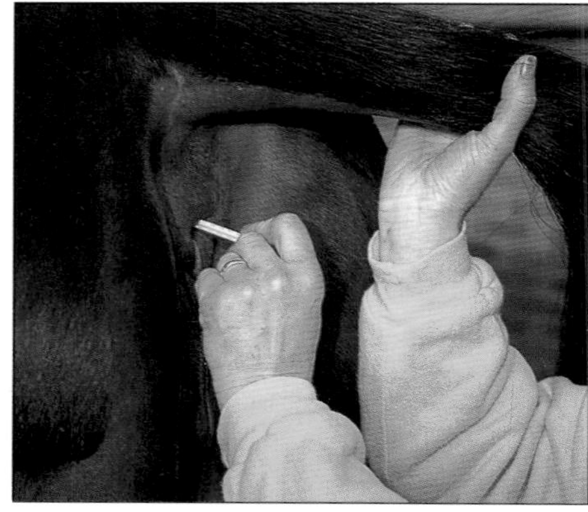

The horse's temperature is taken by inserting a thermometer into the rectum. The normal temperature is about 101.5° Fahrenheit (38°C)

▮ LEFT AND BELOW
To detect lameness, watch the horse trotting towards you and away from you. Look for a nod of the head or sinking of the hindquarters.

they cause to the walls of the blood vessels may result in a blood clot. An infestation of *Strongylus vulgaris* can cause colic and anaemia. It may also disrupt the normal movement of the bowels.

If the horse is seen rubbing his tail, he may be suffering from pin worms, which inhabit the rectum.

Cream-coloured eggs attached to the horse's hair, particularly on the legs, during summer are the eggs of the horse bot, a fly whose larvae are able to penetrate the skin and migrate to the horse's stomach. If the infestation is severe, bots can produce ulceration of the stomach wall and may affect digestion.

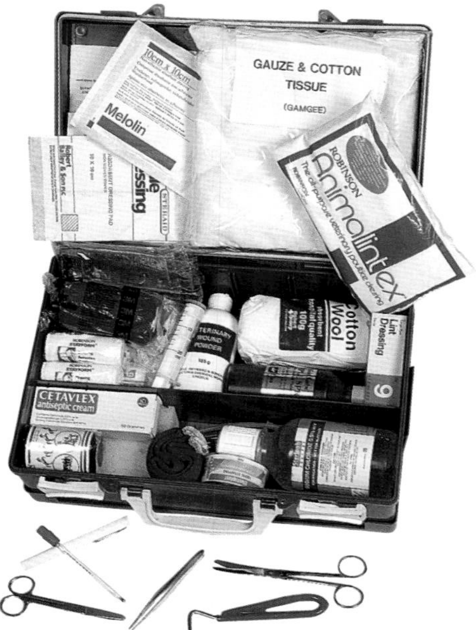

Every horse owner should have a well-stocked equine first-aid kit readily available at all times.

▮ BELOW
Mud fever usually affects the lower legs. This horse also has capped hocks and windgalls (painless fluid-filled swellings just above the fetlock joints).

▮ BOTTOM LEFT
The irritation caused by sweet itch often results in the horse rubbing the mane and tail hair at the affected areas.

Common Ailments

Azoturia, also known as set fast or tying-up, is a stiffening up of the large muscles of the back and hindquarters. It results from the accumulation of large amounts of lactic acid. It is not always possible to determine the reason, though too much food combined with too little exercise is a common cause. The horse begins to sweat up and has difficulty in moving forwards. The muscles feel hard to the touch and the horse will clearly be in pain. Dark, red-coloured urine may be passed. The horse should be rugged up and not moved. The veterinary surgeon should be called. He or she may prescribe drugs to relieve the pain and inflammation.

In **chronic obstructive pulmonary disease** (COPD) the airways to the horse's lungs become, as the name suggests, chronically obstructed. COPD is the result of an allergic reaction to fungal spores, for instance in the horse's hay or bedding. Symptoms include a nasal discharge followed by a cough. The horse's ability to perform hard work diminishes and in time his respiratory rate at rest increases. Treatment includes rest, fresh air, antibiotics and clean stabling with dust-free bedding and spore-free feed.

Equine influenza occurs in two main strains with numerous subtypes; a serious respiratory disease, it can prove fatal. Symptoms include a horse going off his feed, a raised temperature and general cold-type symptoms. Antibiotics may help and the horse must be rested. Horses can be vaccinated, very effectively, against many strains of flu – indeed vaccination is mandatory for most competition horses.

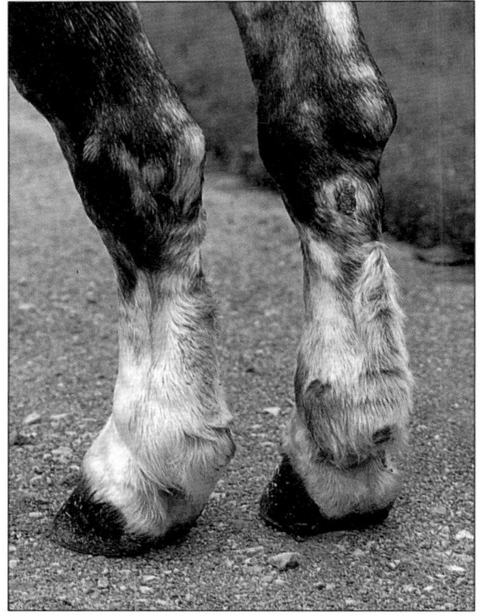

Grass sickness is a painful and fatal disease affecting the horse's nervous system. It is typified by loss of condition, muscle twitching, difficulty in swallowing and a green nasal discharge. In an acute case the horse may die in a few days. Others linger for weeks or months. Its cause is uncertain and it is more common in some regions than others.

Mud fever is a bacterial infection of the skin which affects the legs and/or lower body. It is most often seen on the lower legs. Raw areas develop which ooze serum and then form scabs. At the back of the pasterns and heels cracks often develop in the skin. The condition is most often seen in skin exposed to very muddy or very dry, dusty conditions. Skin with white hair is most susceptible. The best way of preventing mud fever and cracked heels is to protect the skin, when dry, with a barrier cream. Treatment involves clipping the hair from the affected area, regular washing (with antiseptic shampoo) and removal of scabs, careful drying and the use of antibiotic ointment.

COLIC

Colic is abdominal pain which may occur for a number of reasons, such as a sudden change in diet, migrating worm larvae, impaction of the intestines or, in rarer cases, a twisted gut. Signs of colic include the horse standing and looking round at, or trying to kick, its flank, sweating and/or repeated lying down and rolling.

The horse should be put in a stable on a deep bed to guard against injury if he wants to lie down and roll and the vet should be called. He or she may administer pain-relieving or relaxant drugs and/or a lubricant, depending on the type of colic. If a twisted gut is diagnosed, immediate surgery is essential to save the horse's life. Potentially life-threatening attacks of colic are accompanied by a high temperature (above 103° Fahrenheit/39°C) and raised pulse rate (above 60 per minute).

Rain scald is a skin infection caused by the same bacterium as mud fever. It occurs on the upper surfaces of the body. Like mud fever it is treated with antiseptic shampoos and the removal of the scabs which harbour the bacteria.

Ringworm is a fungal infection of the skin and hair. It occurs as small crusty, hairless patches and is infectious. An affected horse should, therefore, be isolated. Ringworm is treated with special antibiotic skin washes which should also be used on the horse's tack to kill off all traces of the infection. The stable should also be treated. Careful control is required as ringworm can affect humans, too.

Strangles is an infection of the lymph glands under the jaw caused by the bacterium *Streptococcus equi.* Affected horses have difficulty in swallowing and the glands under the jaw become swollen. The temperature may rise to as high as 106° Fahrenheit (41°C) and there is a nasal discharge. Infected horses must be kept warm and given soft food. Antibiotics may help. The abscesses in the glands should be treated with hot fomentations – once they burst the horse's condition usually improves. The pus from burst abscesses is highly contagious and horses affected by the infection should be isolated. A policy of strict hygiene must be adopted to prevent the spread of the infection on clothing and equipment. Abscesses which burst internally are very serious since they can cause pneumonia.

Sweet itch is a skin irritation caused by hypersensitivity to the bites of midges and is therefore found chiefly during the spring and summer. It usually occurs along the mane and the base of the tail, which become inflamed and sore. The irritation is such that the horse will often rub out all the mane and tail hairs at the affected places, making the skin raw. A susceptible horse or pony will suffer from sweet itch annually and must be protected from midge bites by being stabled at dusk and dawn when the insects are most active. Benzyl benzoate is used to sooth the sore areas and helps to repel the midges. Fly repellents will also help and mosquito netting should be fitted over open windows and doors while the horse is stabled. Special sheets that cover the entire neck and body give useful protection.

All horses should be vaccinated against **tetanus** and given a booster injection every other year. Tetanus is caused by a bacterium found in the soil and may enter the horse's system via a wound, especially a deep puncture wound. Typical symptoms are stiffness of the muscles, twitching, the horse standing in a stretched-out manner and, as the disease progresses, overreaction to sudden noises or movements. Eventually the horse is unable to stand and death occurs when the breathing muscles become affected. Some horses do recover from tetanus since the infection can be halted by the use of antibiotics and antitoxin. Early diagnosis is essential and the horse will need to rest in a quiet, dark stable.

Common Injuries

Back injuries, either to the bones or muscles of the back, are often the result of falls. Treatment involves rest and the use of anti-inflammatory drugs. Faradism (stimulation of the muscles by electricity), massage and laser therapy may also help.

A **capped elbow** – the term used for a bursal enlargement at the point of the elbow – is usually caused by the horse's shoe striking the elbow when he is lying down. The swelling is soft and is hot and painful when it first appears. A **capped hock** is a similar injury, caused by the horse striking his hock against something hard like the wall of his stable (perhaps through the use of too little bedding) or the partition in a horsebox (hock boots should be fitted to guard against this, particularly if the horse is a bad traveller). Unless the condition causes lameness or there is an infection, it will not require treatment. In the case of a capped elbow the horse should be fitted with a "sausage boot" (a protective ring) on the pastern. This protects the elbow while it is healing.

An **overreach** is an injury to the heel or the back of the tendon of the front legs caused by the horse striking itself with the toe of its own hindfoot. Overreaches should be carefully cleaned. An antibiotic dressing will help guard against infection. Overreaches can be serious – there is often extensive bruising – and are often slow to heal.

Splints are bony swellings found between the splint bones and the cannon bones. Although splints are most commonly found on the inner side of the forelegs, they can occur on either side of the leg and on the hindlegs. Splints often appear when a young horse first begins work. Conformation is a contributing factor. In many cases splints are associated

LEFT
Wounds must be thoroughly cleaned and then treated with ointment or powder. Leg wounds tend to heal less well than wounds to the body where the skin is looser.

FIRST-AID KIT

The horse owner's first-aid kit should include:

- Disinfectant – for washing wounds.
- Skin swabs – small swabs impregnated with disinfectant for cleaning wounds where there is no clean water supply.
- Wound cleansing cream or liquid.
- Wound ointment or powder.
- Wound dressings.
- Crêpe bandages.
- Adhesive bandages.
- Gamgee tissue.
- Cotton wool.
- Cold packs.
- Poultices.
- Thermometer.
- Scissors (sharp, but with rounded ends for safety).
- Fly repellent.

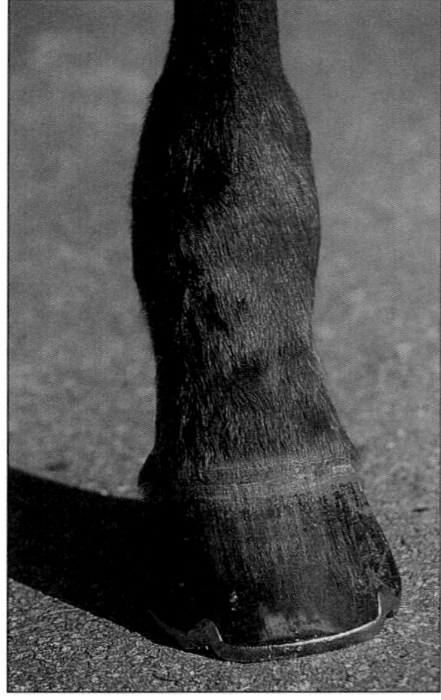

Swollen joints can be the result of injury, infection or a dietary problem.

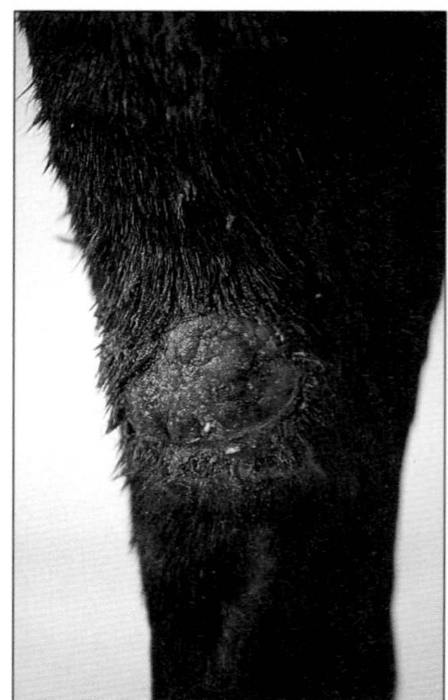

Fibrous tissue known as proud flesh may form a permanent blemish which will require surgical removal.

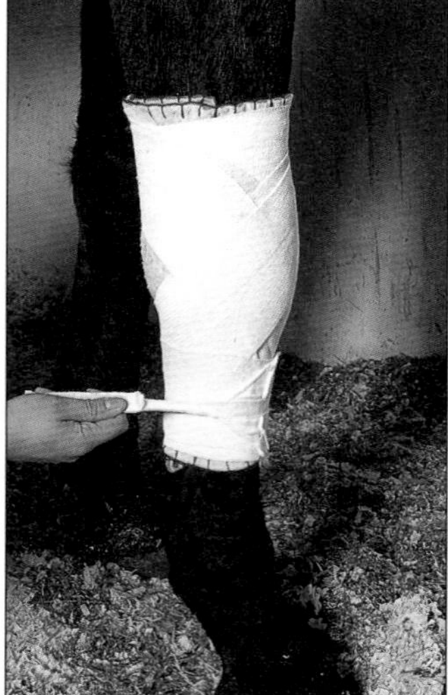

When bandaging a knee, cotton wool or Gamgee tissue should be used under the bandage.

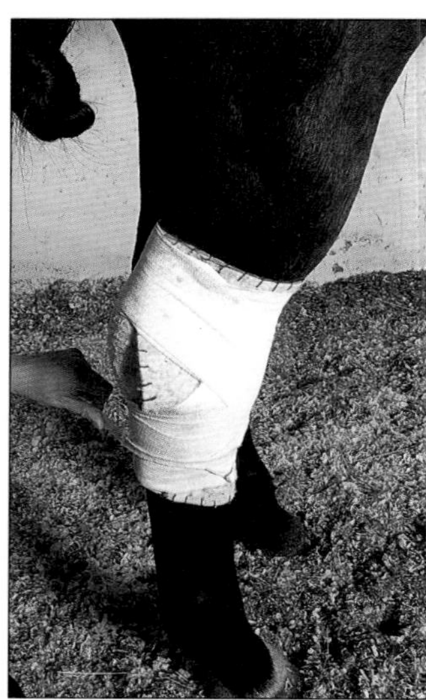

The correct way to bandage a hock.

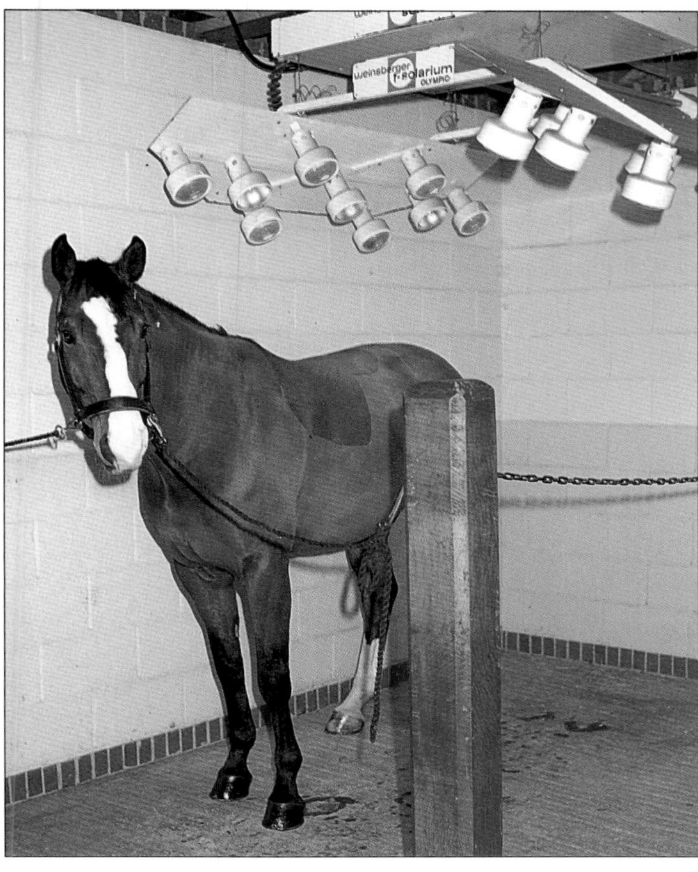

LEFT
Infra-red helps to relax muscles and soothe pain. This horse is enjoying a spell in a solarium.

BELOW LEFT AND RIGHT
Eye injuries, such as cuts and bruises, can be dangerous and require professional attention.

BOTTOM
Stimulation of the muscles by electricity (Faradism) is useful in the treatment of back injuries.

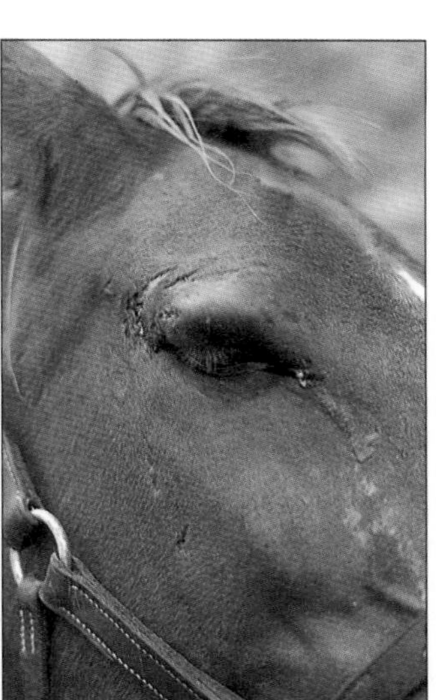

with poor foot and limb balance, in which case corrective shoeing often helps. Lameness may result, in varying degrees, while the splint is forming but often the pain associated with splints disappears in time. In the case of persistent lameness, the leg should be X-rayed to eliminate any possibility of a fracture.

Because of the strain put on the legs when galloping and jumping, **tendon injuries** are all too common in horses, particularly in the forelegs. The superficial and deep flexor tendons, which run down the back of the cannon bones, the suspensory ligament, which is immediately behind the lower part of the cannon bone, and the check ligament, situated below the knee, are all at risk. Tendon and ligament injuries are the result of sudden stress, which causes the fibres to tear. The injury causes pain, followed by heat and swelling. Cold is the most important part of the treatment: ice packs or, in an emergency, a pack of frozen peas, should be applied to the site of the injury as quickly as possible. Ice packs should be replaced frequently and the limb should be bandaged firmly, though not too tightly, for support. Laser treatment may help to reduce the swelling. The oldest – and best – treatment for all strains and

sprains is rest. A leg which has suffered a serious tendon injury is more likely to stand up to future work if the horse is given a period of twelve to eighteen months off. The veterinary surgeon can determine, by using a scanner, when a tendon injury has healed.

Horses suffer all types of **wounds** as a result of falls, accidents in the field and stable, and bites and kicks from other horses. Some, such as grazes, heal quickly provided they are kept clean and dry. Others can cause serious problems. **Puncture wounds** are often the most dangerous since bacteria may be carried deep into the wound. Although it is impossible not to notice a large, jagged laceration accompanied by a copious flow of blood, it is easy to overlook a deep puncture wound simply because the wound to the skin is small and insignificant looking. It is important to ensure that such wounds heal from the inside out – poulticing may be necessary to draw out infection.

All wounds should be cleaned, if possible, with cold water though it should be remembered that continuous washing will not stop a wound from bleeding. The application of a pressure pad (such as a clean handkerchief) will help control the flow of blood while you are waiting for veterinary help. Large wounds may need stitching. If there is any doubt about the horse's vaccination status, he must be given a tetanus injection. If a wound needs covering to keep it clean, medicated gauze should be used as it will not stick to the wound. Wounds on the body, where the skin is loose, heal better than leg wounds which tend to develop proud flesh as they heal. Proud flesh is fibrous tissue, projecting beyond the level of the skin surrounding the wound and often forming a permanent blemish. The veterinary surgeon may advise using caustic preparations to arrest its development or it may need to be removed surgically.

Poulticing and Cold Treatments

The application of heat by means of a poultice helps to repair injury by stimulating the blood supply to the affected area. Heat also has a "drawing" effect, and will help to bring any pus to the surface.

Poultices may be made with kaolin, or specially impregnated padding can be bought. To make a hot kaolin poultice the tin of kaolin, with the lid loosened, is placed in a pan of boiling water for several minutes. When the kaolin is hot (no hotter than can be borne on the back of your hand) it is spread over a piece of lint, covered with gauze and applied to the injured area. To keep the heat in, polythene or aluminium foil is then wrapped over the gauze, followed by a piece of Gamgee tissue and the poultice is held in place with a bandage.

The poultice should be changed at least twice a day. All the kaolin must be removed from the wound before a new poultice is applied, otherwise the drawing effect of the new poultice will be lost. The main drawback of kaolin is that it is messy to put on and remove. This problem can be overcome if you use ready-made poultices consisting of kaolin enclosed in a thin envelope of polythene.

Gamgee-type tissue impregnated with chemicals with drawing properties is also available. This must be activated by soaking in warm water. Like the envelope type of kaolin poultice it is easy to apply though it does leave a residue on the skin which must be cleaned off before another poultice is applied.

Bran may be used to poultice the horse's foot in the case of problems such as a septic foot or corns. Boiling water is poured on to one or two scoops of bran to form a crumbly, not excessively wet, mixture. Test the bran for heat on the palm of the hand before applying it to the foot. The bran may be applied in a foot poultice boot, which is strapped on to the foot, or it may be placed in polythene and sacking and secured in place with a bandage. Horses sometimes try to eat bran poultices so it is advisable to add a little disinfectant to the boiling water to act as a deterrent. The poultice should be left on for twelve hours.

Tubbing is used for some foot wounds, which may require more regular applications of heat. Hand-hot water is placed in a non-metal bucket or tub and the horse's foot placed in it. Horses who are unwilling to cooperate by immersing their foot should be encouraged by having hot water gently splashed on their leg.

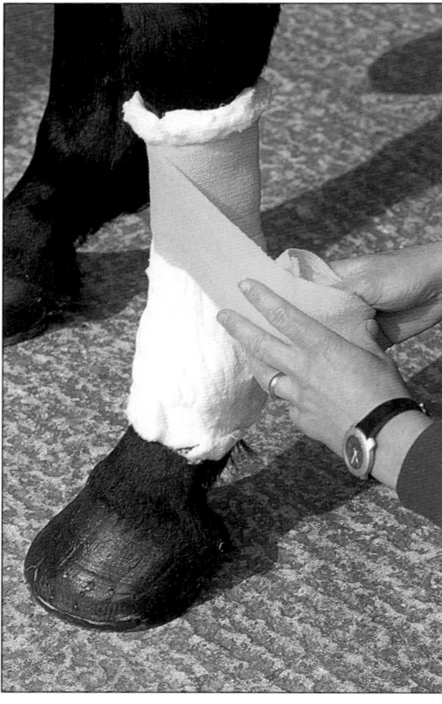

TOP
Three types of equine boot designed to keep dressings in place on the horse's foot. Alternatively sacking, secured by a bandage, may be used.

FAR LEFT
Gamgee-type tissue, impregnated with chemicals, makes an effective poultice. It is soaked in warm water before application.

LEFT
Poultices should be removed at least twice a day. Any residue must be cleaned off the horse's skin before re-poulticing.

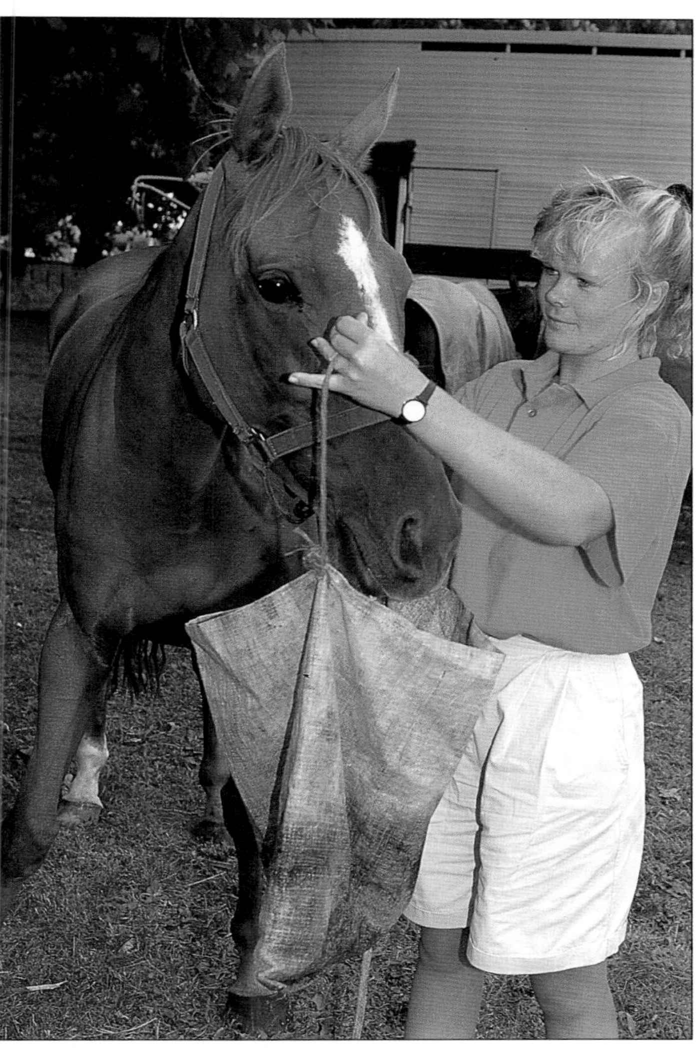

LEFT
Inhalants are sometimes used when horses have respiratory tract problems. The bag containing the inhalant is fitted like a nosebag.

BELOW
Hosing with cold water helps to reduce the swelling and heat which accompany most leg injuries.

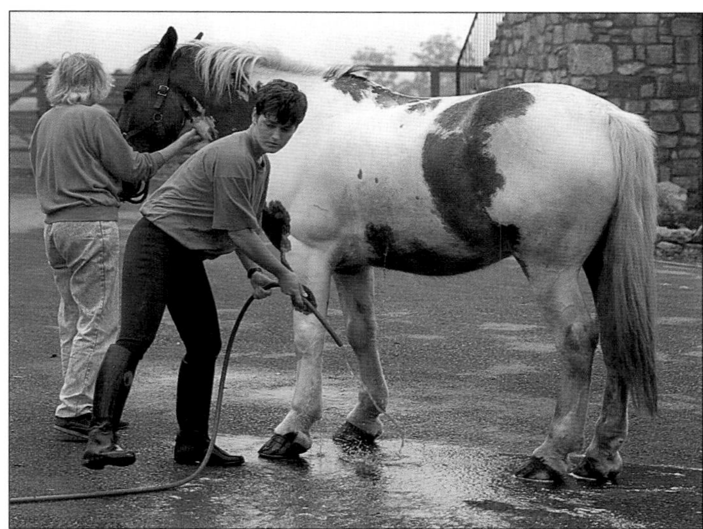

BELOW LEFT
Another effective method of applying cold treatment: a hosepipe attached to a "hose boot".

BELOW RIGHT
Hot or cold tubbing can be carried out by standing the horse's foot in a bucket – always providing he cooperates!

Epsom salts and antiseptic may be added to the water. Tubbing lasts for about twenty minutes and should be carried out at least twice a day.

Where cold treatment is required as opposed to heat, there are various methods. Cold water may be applied with a hose for regular periods of about ten minutes. The horse should be accustomed to the feel of the water by starting at ground level and then gradually working it up the foot and leg. The legs should be bandaged between hosing sessions. Where suitable facilities are available the hose can be bandaged to the horse's leg. He should be given a haynet to keep him occupied. Walking or standing a horse in a river or in the sea is equally beneficial.

Specially designed flexible packs, which retain their cool temperature for quite a long time, can be obtained. They are cooled in a freezer and bandaged into place. Special bandages are available, too. These are designed to absorb water and are flexible enough to be applied even when the water is frozen. Another way to apply cold to a leg is to soak bandages in cold water (care must be taken to remove them before they start to dry out as they might shrink). Crushed ice in a polythene bag or, in an emergency, a packet of frozen peas may be bandaged round a leg. A thin layer of Gamgee should be placed over the leg first.

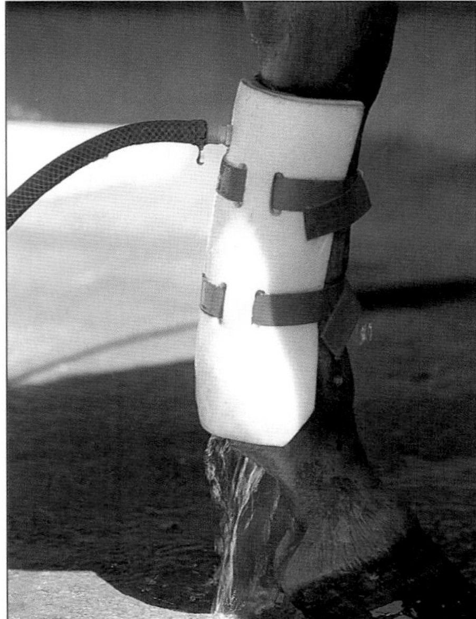

Anatomy of the Foot

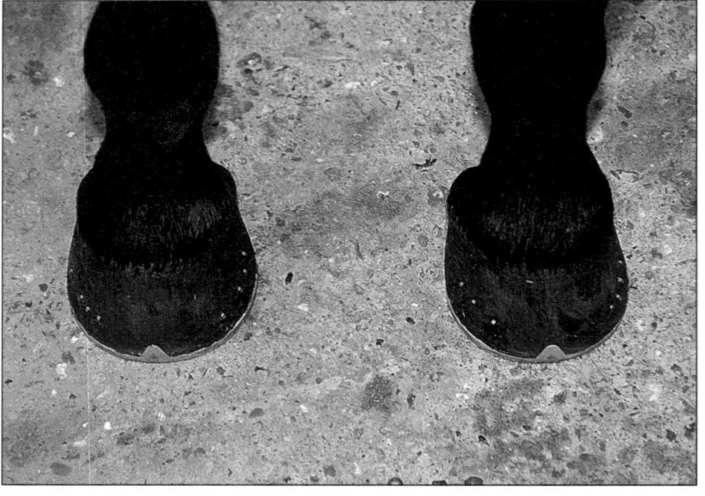

LEFT
A well-matched pair of forefeet. The toe clips steady the shoes while the nails are driven in and help to ensure an accurate fit.

Lameness in horses occurs far more often in the foot than in any other part of the limbs. This is not surprising considering the amount of strain put upon the feet of domesticated horses required to pull heavy loads or carry a rider, particularly at fast speeds or over jumps.

The term foot is used to describe the hoof – the dense horny covering – and all the structures contained inside it. The external, insensitive part of the hoof comprises the wall (the outer, protective layer of the foot); the sole (a plate of hard horn just under an inch (2cm) thick; the frog (a wedge-shaped mass of soft elastic horn), and the periople (a thin layer of epidermis between the hoof wall and the skin).

The function of the sole is to give protection to the sensitive inner structures and to help support weight. The frog performs the same functions as the sole as well as providing grip and acting as a shock absorber. The periople controls evaporation from the underlying horn.

The internal part of the hoof comprises the sensitive laminae, the sensitive sole, the sensitive frog, the perioplic corium and the coronary corium.

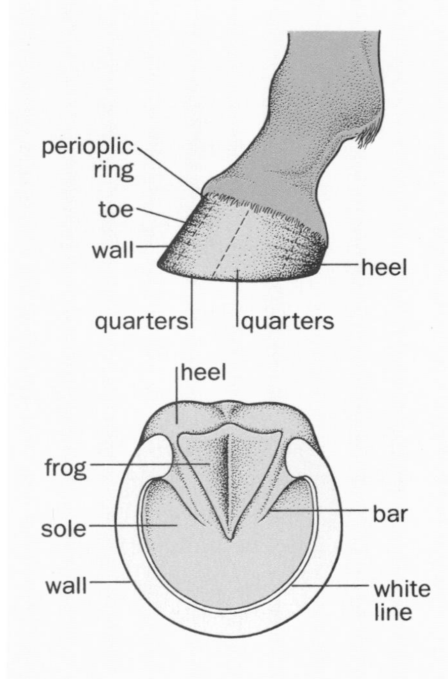

Laminae are interlocking leaf-like structures which attach the hoof to the pedal bone. Hundreds of sensitive (or primary) laminae dovetail with thousands of horny (secondary) laminae which grow outwards from the interior of the wall of the hoof.

The sensitive sole, which is attached securely to the lower surface of the pedal bone, is a thin layer of tissue which corresponds to the horny sole and supplies it with nutrition.

The sensitive frog supplies nutrition to the digital cushion on which it is moulded. This cushion is a wedge-shaped fibro-elastic pad situated in the hollow behind the heels. It has an important part to play in reducing concussion by expanding when the foot takes weight.

The perioplic corium or ring situated just above the coronary corium (coronary body) supplies nutrition to the periople. The coronary corium, a thick structure situated above the sensitive laminae, lies in the coronary groove and supplies nutrition to the wall of the hoof.

On the ground surface of the sole, where the sole meets the wall, is a narrow band of soft plastic horn known as the white line. This white line is of great importance to the farrier because it indicates the position of the sensitive structures of the foot and the thickness of the wall, thus helping determine where nails can be driven into the wall to hold shoes in place without encroaching on the sensitive areas.

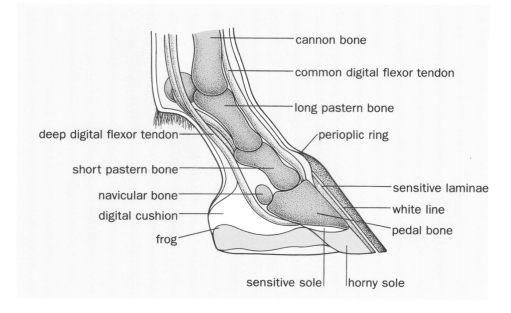

The Role of the Farrier

Horses have been shod with metal shoes for over two thousand years and although it is impossible to say for certain who first had the temerity to try nailing a shoe to the horse's hoof, it is widely assumed to have been the Celts and the Gauls.

The need to protect the feet arose when man began to use the horse as a beast of burden and for riding. The unnatural wear and tear inflicted upon the feet of the domesticated horse results in the hooves being worn down more quickly than they are renewed – this would not occur in the horse's natural state. The damage caused to the hoof is worse when travelling over hard, rough ground or in a wet environment. The latter leads to the growth of softer horn, which wears away more quickly. This explains why horses in dry, hot climates, which promote the growth of hard horn, can often do a considerable amount of work unshod without any ill effects.

The role of the farrier is of vital importance, since the horse cannot work adequately if his feet are painful. It is the farrier's job to ensure that the horse's feet are not only well and securely shod but are also correctly trimmed. The horn of the hoof is constantly growing and fitting a metal shoe to the hoof prevents excess growth being worn down naturally, as is the case with the unshod horse. The average monthly growth of horn is around ¼–⅜ inch (5–9mm) and the horse needs to have his feet trimmed about every four or five weeks, depending on the rate of growth. If his old shoes are not worn, they may be refitted – these are known as "removes".

Shoes may be fitted either hot or cold. The advantage of hot shoeing is that it ensures a better fit because the shoe can be finely adjusted to fit the foot (the shoe must always be altered to fit the foot, not vice versa). The shoe is heated in the furnace and held against the prepared hoof (which is insensitive) for a short time. The imprint it leaves indicates to the farrier any necessary adjustments required. Once these have been made the shoe is plunged in cold water before being nailed on to the foot.

It is important to remember that horses who are unshod, perhaps because they are resting, still need regular attention from the farrier. Being confined in a paddock is not the same as being free to roam in search of food, and the horse's hooves will not wear down as they would in the wild.

The farrier's work is very skilful. He must be able to trim the hoof, and drive nails into the insensitive part of the hoof wall, with great precision. One slip, and the result will be a lame horse. Nor is farriery simply about the routine trimming and re-shoeing of horses. It also involves skilled remedial shoeing, which calls for a detailed knowledge of the anatomy of the horse's limbs, including the bones, the joints, the muscles, the vascular system and the nervous system. Defective action, caused by less than perfect conformation or injury, can be greatly improved by expert trimming of the foot and the fitting of specially designed shoes. In these cases, the farrier will work in conjunction with the veterinary surgeon.

At one time it was the practice for the horse to be taken to the farrier for shoeing, which meant that the farrier had all the facilities of a permanent forge on hand. Nowadays it is usually the farrier who has to travel to the horse with a mobile forge, so the onus is on the horse owner to provide him with a suitable working area.

A dry, level surface for the horse to stand on is essential, as is good lighting. In summer, when flies are a nuisance, the horse should be in a shady area, either in a building or under a tree, and it is advisable to have some fly repellent handy.

The horse's feet should be cleaned and dried beforehand and it is the owner's responsibility to ensure that the horse is as well behaved as possible. Most horses will stand quietly. But remember that feeding or moving other horses about while a horse is being shod can make him extremely restive – and the farrier's job that much more difficult.

LEFT
In order to make horseshoes, the farrier must be skilled in bending, turning and shaping metal. He uses an anvil specially designed for the purpose.

The Farrier's Tools

The farrier's tools are divided into two categories: forge tools, that is those used while making shoes, and shoeing tools, that is those used while preparing the foot and nailing on the shoe.

Forge tools include the anvil, on which the metal is shaped; various hammers and tongs; the stamp, used for making nail holes in the shoes; the fullering iron, used to make a groove round the edge of the ground surface of the shoe and the pritchel, a steel punch used to finish off the nail holes and also for carrying hot shoes to the horse's foot for fitting.

Shoeing tools include hammer, pincers, trimmer and rasp. The farrier's shoeing hammer, which has a short, curved claw, is used to drive in the nails, to twist off the points of the nails and form the clenches, and to pull out nails.

When removing shoes the farrier uses a buffer (or clench cutter) to cut off the clenches or knock them up before withdrawing the nails.

Pincers are used for raising and levering off shoes and for withdrawing nails. They are also used to turn the clenches. For trimming, a hoof trimmer, cutter or parer is used. This is a tool with a pincer-like head, one side being sharp and the other flat. To remove the overgrown wall of the hoof the flat side is placed on the outside of the wall and the sharp cutting side on the inside.

When removing ragged pieces of frog or loose flakes of sole a drawing knife is used. The searcher, a similar tool but with a thinner blade, is designed for use when cutting out corns or paring away the horn round puncture wounds.

The farrier's rasp is partly coarse, partly smooth (file cut) and has serrated edges. The farrier uses the coarse side to remove excess hoof wall and for the final levelling of the bearing surface of the foot. The coarse side is also used to finish off the clenches. The file cut surface is used to finish off the shoe and to shape the clenches. Using the serrated edges the farrier removes the sharp edge of the wall (to prevent it splitting) after the shoe has been nailed on.

STUDS

Although shoes help to give the horse added grip on grass it is often essential to fit studs in the shoes as well. Studs may be permanent or of the screw-in type (in which case the shoes are provided with screw holes by the farrier). Screw-in studs

1 Having cut off or knocked up the clenches (the turned-over points of the nails), the farrier uses pincers to lever off the old shoe.

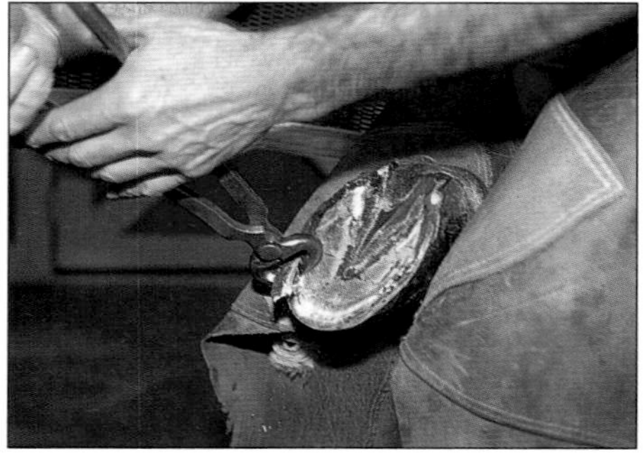

2 Excess growth of hoof is removed with a trimmer, which has one flat and one sharp side.

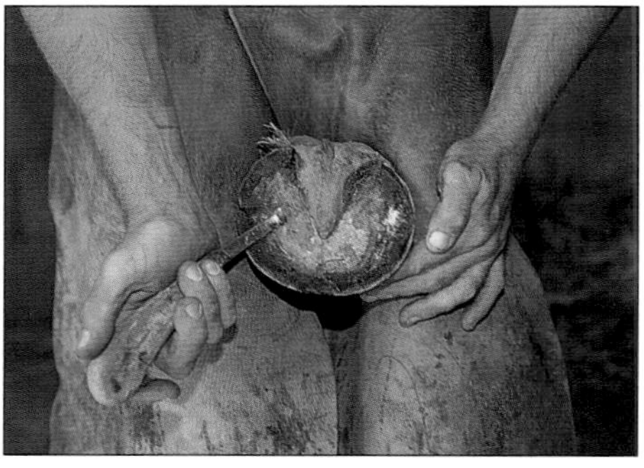

3 A drawing knife is used to lower the hoof wall and remove loose flakes of sole.

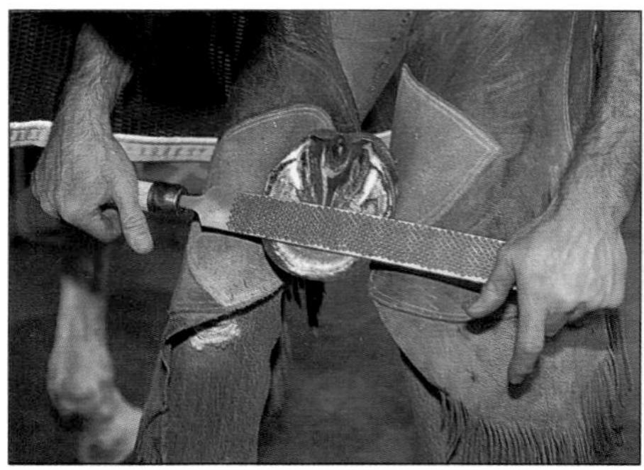

4 The bearing surface of the foot is levelled with a rasp before the shoe is fitted.

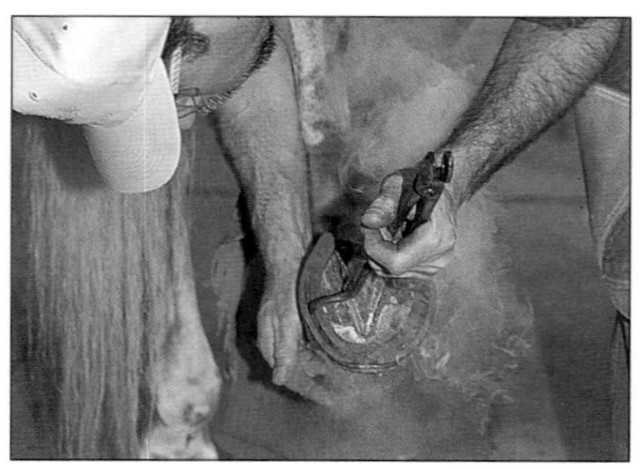

5 Hot shoeing ensures a better fit than cold shoeing and causes the horse no pain.

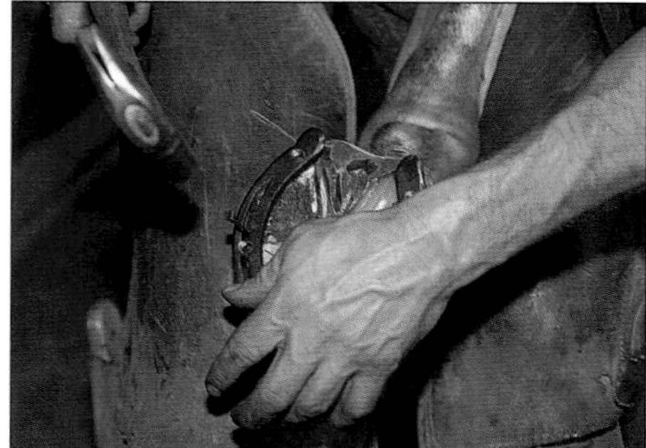

6 Nails are driven into the insensitive wall of the foot to hold the shoes in place.

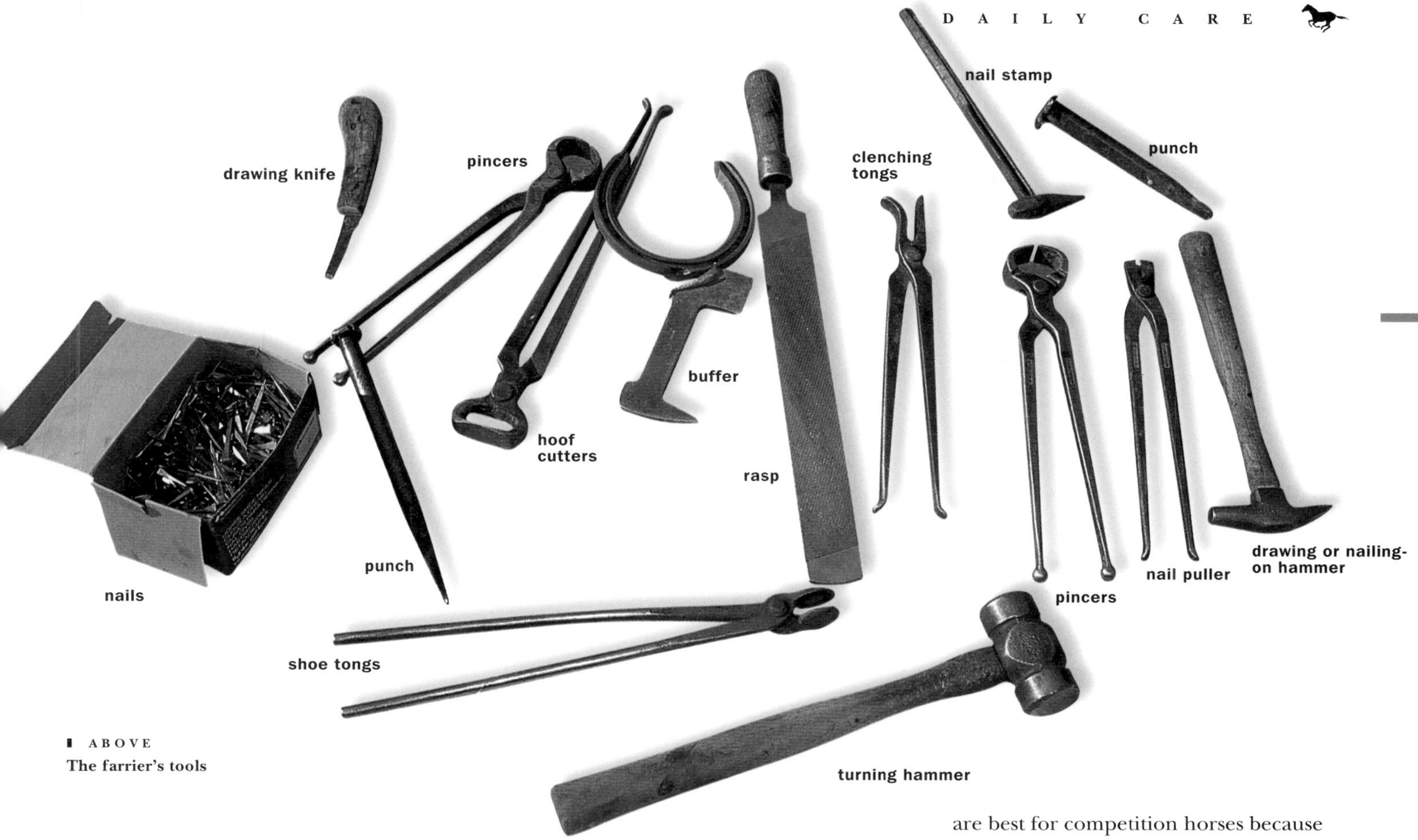

drawing knife
pincers
nail stamp
punch
clenching tongs
buffer
hoof cutters
rasp
nails
punch
shoe tongs
pincers
nail puller
drawing or nailing-on hammer
turning hammer

ABOVE
The farrier's tools

are best for competition horses because they require different types of studs according to the work they are doing and the state of the ground.

There is a wide range of studs available, varying from small ones for everyday hacking and road work (these are usually made with a tungsten core and are very hard wearing) to large round or square ones suitable for use in soft going and pointed ones which enhance the grip on very firm ground. There are two schools of thought about the fitting of studs: some people fit only one stud on the outside of each shoe. Others believe that this may throw the foot out of balance and so fit one on either side of the shoe.

RIGHT
Screw-in studs are essential for the competition horse. After use they are removed and the holes plugged to protect the threads. A T-tap (centre) is used to clean out the screw holes before inserting the studs.

The farrier uses the rasp to smooth the horn and shape the clenches.

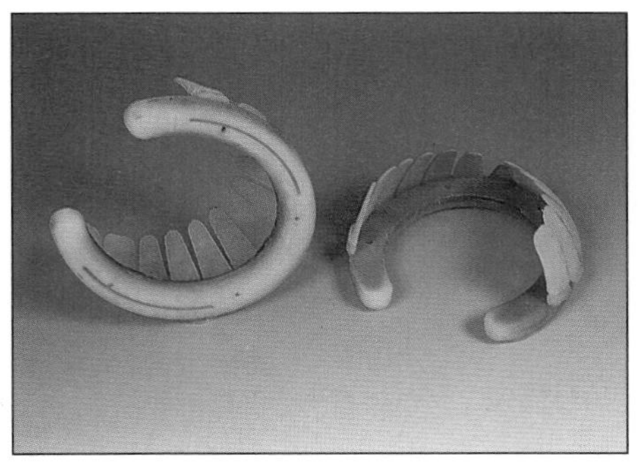

Lightweight plastic shoes are a modern alternative to metal ones. They are attached to the hoof with glue.

Studs are screwed into place shortly before the horse competes. The size and shape depends on the ground conditions.

Common Foot Problems

Corns occur most often in the front feet. A corn is a bruise of the sole in the angle between the wall of the foot and the bar (known as the "seat of corn"). Corns are caused by pressure and can be the result of a stone becoming wedged, faulty shoeing or shoes having been left on too long. The shoe should be removed and the discoloured horn pared away. The condition can be complicated by the presence of infection, in which case poulticing will be necessary. Pressure can be relieved from the area by fitting a shoe on which the ground surface of the heel is lowered so that it does not make contact with the ground.

Laminitis (also known as "founder") is a painful condition resulting from inflammation of the laminae. The feet become hot and the horse adopts a typical leaning back stance in order to take the weight off the front of the forefeet. Although the pathological cause is not yet completely understood, laminitis is associated with excessive concussion and the presence of inflammatory toxins which damage the blood vessels, particularly those in the feet. It is often the result of faulty diet (over-fat ponies, with overlong feet, kept on too rich pasture are the classic example) although it can also be caused by retention of the afterbirth in the broodmare.

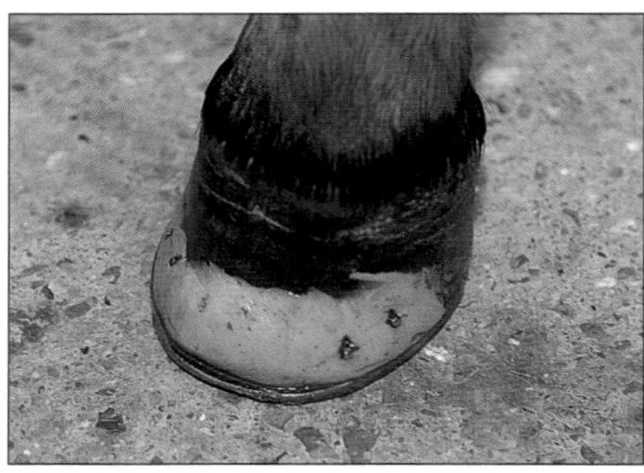

An example of the farrier's skill: this defective hoof has been artificially lengthened.

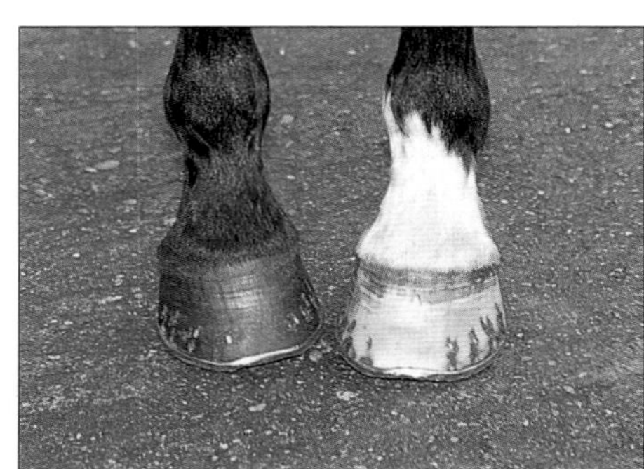

Pigeon toes (those which turn inwards) cause uneven wear on the shoes.

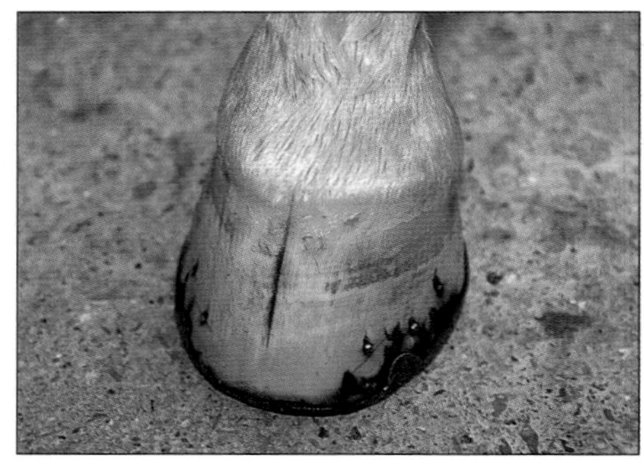

A sandcrack may produce lameness if the sensitive part of the foot is affected.

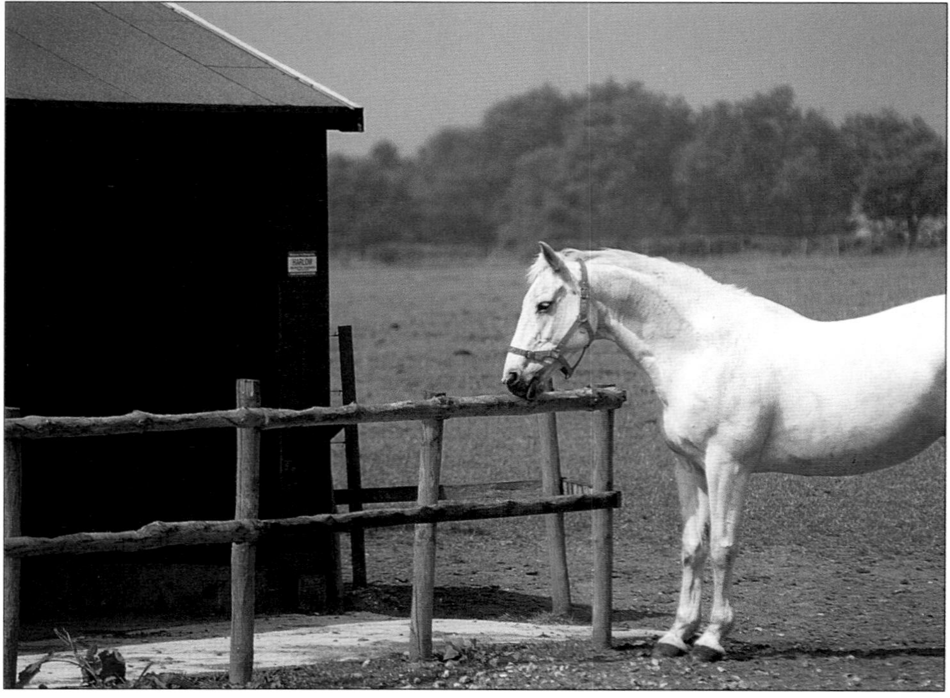

This leaning back stance is typical of a horse suffering from laminitis. He takes the weight on his heels to relieve the pain. Laminitis is one of the major causes of equine lameness, particularly in ponies.

Veterinary treatment is essential. If diet is the cause, the vet may advise a purgative. The horse should be stabled (standing the horse on sand is said to reduce the pain because it provides support to the feet). The vet may prescribe drugs (including pain killers) and if the horse or pony is overweight, he will advise on a suitable diet.

One of the dangers of laminitis is the possibility of pedal bone rotation. Except in the mildest cases, therefore, when the horse may be gently led out in hand, the horse must be given box rest.

Good foot care is vital. Corrective trimming will help restore the structures of the foot to their normal alignment and will limit the rotation of the pedal bone. Special shoes can also be fitted.

Navicular disease is believed to be the result of poor foot conformation and/or concussion, caused by hard work. Bony changes occur in the navicular bone, a small, shuttle-shaped bone which acts as a fulcrum for the deep flexor tendon before the tendon attaches to the under side of the pedal bone. In most cases both forefeet are affected.

A horse with navicular disease will put his foot on the ground toe-first as he attempts to avoid pressure on the affected area. In the early stages, lameness wears off during exercise but as the condition progresses the periods of lameness both increase and become more prolonged. As time goes on, the horse may become prone to stumbling.

Although the condition is incurable, various treatments are employed to help relieve the pain. Corrective shoeing is used to raise the heels and reduce concussion to the navicular area. The horse may be given anticoagulants or anti-inflammatory drugs. Laser and ultrasound treatment may also be beneficial.

Pedal osteitis is inflammation of the pedal bone. It is often the result of jarring but can also develop after an attack of laminitis or following puncture injuries to the sole of the foot. It usually affects both forefeet and the horse will tend to shuffle when he moves. The demineralization of the bone is visible on X-ray. Careful shoeing can bring relief to what is usually an irreversible condition. Laser and ultrasound therapy may be beneficial.

Ringbone is an abnormal bony growth which occurs either at the centre of the pastern (high ringbone) or around the coronet (low ringbone). It is usually caused by injury. There is heat and swelling and the horse may have a shortened stride and tend to be more lame when turned sharply. Rest may help give relief in less serious cases. Where more serious injury is involved the horse may not become fully sound again, although some horses continue to work if given anti-inflammatory drugs.

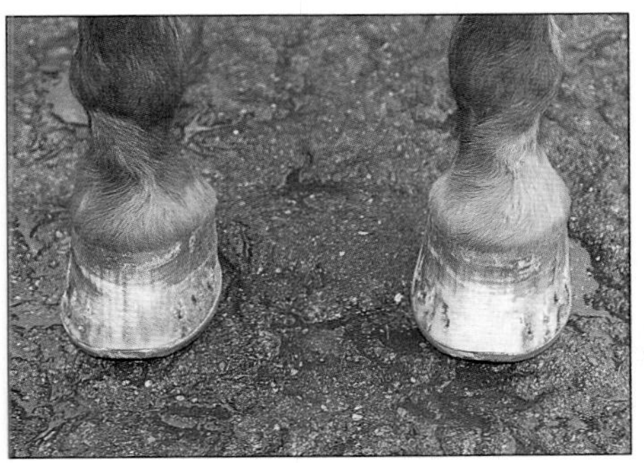

"Boxy" feet have an angle of more than 55° and are associated with upright pasterns.

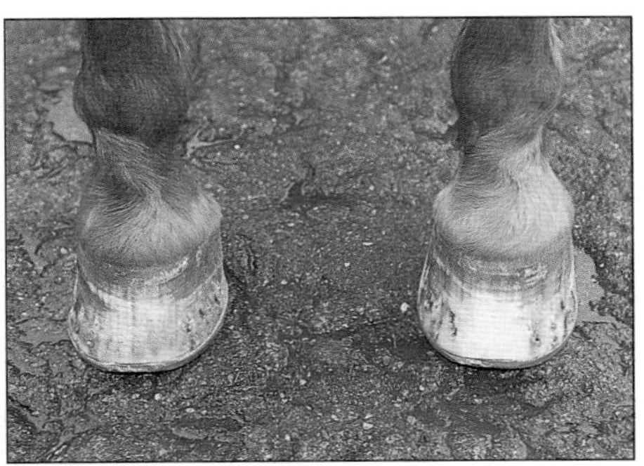

Shoes with rolled toes reduce strain on the tendons and the navicular bone.

A **sandcrack** is a break in the wall of the hoof and may occur anywhere between the coronet and the ground surface of the foot. Sandcracks may be the result of injury, poor nutrition, an overdrying of the hoof (for instance in very dry weather), too much rasping during the shoeing process or neglect, for example lack of regular trimming by the farrier. Lameness may result if the crack is serious.

The farrier may be able to arrest the progress of a sandcrack by making grooves in the hoof wall to isolate the crack. Metal clips may also be used or, in the case of a deep crack, it may be necessary to fill it with a special bonding substance. Because the crack opens when weight is put on the foot as it is placed on the ground, a shoe with clips may be fitted.

Seedy toe is a condition in which the wall of the foot parts company with the sole at the white line. It may be the result of bruising of the toe area or pressure from the toe clip of a shoe. Sometimes it follows laminitis. Treatment involves cleaning out the cavity and filling it with tow. The farrier will be able to trim the foot and shoe it in such a way that further damage is avoided during movement.

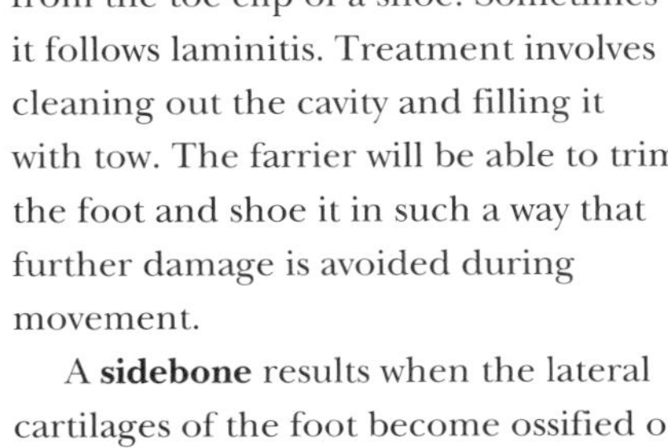

A **sidebone** results when the lateral cartilages of the foot become ossified or converted into bone. The ossified cartilages can be felt at the junction of the hair and the hoof in the area of the quarter of the foot. Sidebones are usually caused by concussion. Heavy or common-bred horses are the most susceptible. The horse may be lame while the cartilage is ossifying and sometimes lameness persists once the sidebones have developed because of pressure on the wall of the foot. The condition does not normally require treatment other than short-term rest but if lameness persists the farrier may be able to relieve the pressure with corrective shoeing and grooving of the hoof to allow expansion.

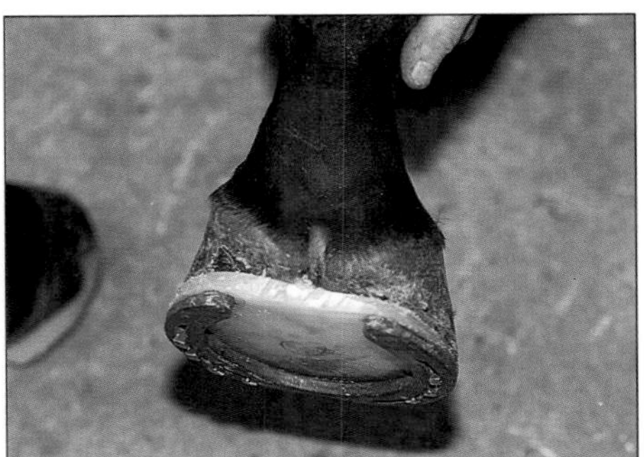

A plastic wedge raises the heel of a hoof which slopes too much.

Thrush is caused by bad stable management (dirty bedding and failure to pick out the feet regularly). It is easily detected by the evil smell coming from the frog, which is moist and may have a black discharge. The affected area of the frog must be opened out to expose it to the air and treated with antiseptics.

Learning to Ride

Before Climbing Aboard

There are few more enviable sights in the world than a horse and rider enjoying a happy, trusting partnership. To be able to harness the spirit and beauty of an animal as majestic as the horse so that he is happy to work with you, and willing to do all that you ask of him, has to be one of life's greatest pleasures. A horse and rider in harmony appear to move by magic, but whilst the spectator may appreciate the words of Robert Surtees – "there is no closer secret than that between a rider and his horse" – anyone who has experienced some of the setbacks that can occur whilst trying to acquire the art of horsemanship may wonder whether these words were spoken with admiration, envy or in sheer frustration!

For some, horse riding is an occasional pastime, for others it is a lifelong passion – either way it should be a pleasure for both horse and rider. Learning to ride involves two living creatures – the rider is reliant on the horse's generosity and co-operation; the horse, in return, deserves fair and sensitive treatment from his rider.

If You Have Never Sat on a Horse...

If you have never so much as sat on a horse or pony, there will be a great deal to take in to start with. It will help to have an overall idea in your mind of what it is you are trying to achieve.

Once you have mounted, the means of communication with the horse are through the use of the legs, seat, hands and voice. Anything that you ask the horse to do – from simply walking forwards to performing an intricate dressage movement to jumping a huge fence – is achieved by using a combination of leg, seat, hand and, sometimes, the voice. The art of riding lies in learning to feel what the horse is doing underneath you, and understanding how to influence what he does and how well he performs by mastering this subtle combination of leg, seat and hand. These means of communicating with the horse are called aids. Leg, hand and seat aids, as well as your voice, are called natural aids and they can be backed up by the artificial aids, which are the spur and whip. The spur is a short stump of blunt metal which is worn over the rider's boot just above the heel; the whip is either a short stick or a longer schooling whip.

Ultimately, riding a horse should have the same smooth feeling of power and control as driving a high-performance sports car or a speed boat. Just as a powerful car responds instantly to a light touch on the accelerator pedal, a horse should move forwards the instant he feels a light squeeze from the rider's leg. The feeling of lightness and control which power steering in a car gives you is the same feeling that a well-schooled horse should give you through the reins. Just an inclination of your hand to guide the horse in one direction or another, or a slight squeeze and hold of the rein to help gather up all his energy and power, is all that should be needed. It takes a long period of careful training for a horse to become as responsive as this, and it takes time and practice for a rider to get to the stage of being able to provide that training.

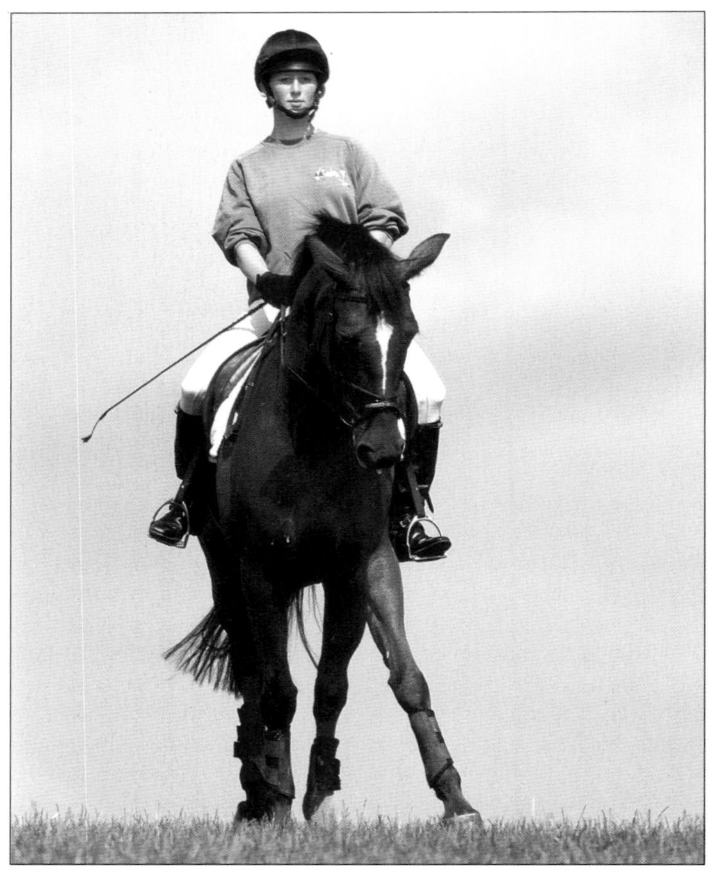

LEFT When performing the half-pass you may have to do something different with each hand and leg, which is why attaining an independent seat should be the aim of all riders.

In the beginning, as a general rule of thumb, the novice rider should appreciate that it is the legs that are used first and foremost to instruct the horse to do something. The legs create the power, while the hands gently guide the horse in the right direction.

As a beginner, you will usually find yourself riding in a circle around an instructor. The hand and leg on the inside of the circle, i.e. the hand and leg nearest the instructor, are referred to as the inside hand and leg. The hand and leg on the outside of the circle are known as the outside hand and leg. If your inside hand is your left hand, i.e. you are going in an anti-clockwise direction, you are said to be riding on the left rein. If you are told to change the rein, this involves turning the horse around and circling in the opposite direction, so that the inside hand is now your right hand, which means you are now riding on the right rein.

Your arms and hands are linked via the reins to the bit in the horse's mouth. This line of contact is all part of your communication with the horse, and to make life comfortable for him you must aim to relax your arms, so that as the horse's head and neck move you follow that movement. Ideally this is done whilst still maintaining a consistent but soft contact with the horse's mouth. The idea is not to let the reins keep going slack and then tight, but to relax your arms enough to follow what the horse's head and neck are doing whilst keeping a constant feel on the reins. The feel that you have down the reins to the horse's mouth is known as the contact, and the ultimate aim is to ride

AN INDEPENDENT SEAT

The key to all successful riding is to attain what is commonly known as "an independent seat". The means of communication with the horse are through your seat, legs, hands and voice – that is six different things and on some occasions you may have to do something different with each of them at the same time! To do this you must be able to sit securely and centrally in the saddle, whilst leaving your legs and hands free to communicate with the horse. This means being able to keep your balance without gripping with your legs, or hanging on by the reins, in all paces. Only then can your legs, seat and hands be used independently of each other to ask the horse to perform some of the more elaborate and enjoyable movements that he can offer you.

In an ideal world, any would-be horseman would first gain this independent seat by riding a horse or pony that is being lunged. To begin with you might hold on to the front of the saddle or to a neck strap to help you keep your balance, but as your body and muscles gradually become used to the movement of the horse underneath you, it becomes easier to remain relaxed and balanced. Various exercises without reins or stirrups will help to reinforce the balance and security of your seat until you have attained true independence of hands, seat and legs at all paces. Lungeing can be a tiring and time-consuming operation, besides which, most potential riders are in a rush to enjoy more of the thrill and excitement of horse riding. But if you really want to master the art of riding, it is time well spent, and this will be repaid when you discover how much more effective and sensitive a rider you are when you do progress to more exciting things. Remember – patience and practice are the keys to becoming a successful rider.

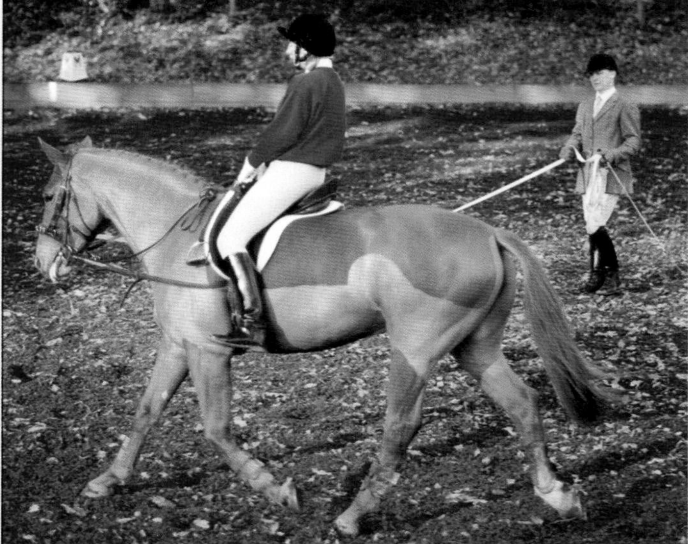

LEFT
Learning to ride on the lunge is one of the best ways to acquire the feel and balance that are needed to develop an independent seat. Once this is achieved, you can start to ride properly and really influence the horse.

with a very light contact. It sometimes helps to imagine that the rein is an extension of your arm and that your hands are attached directly to the bit in the horse's mouth. As the horse's head moves your arms will have to move with him.

However ambitious or otherwise you may be, by persevering and mastering the correct techniques of horse riding, your satisfaction and enjoyment of your hobby or sport will be greatly enhanced. You may have no desire to reach the dizzy heights of the competition world – perhaps a simple hack through the countryside is your idea of paradise – but either way, life will be more enjoyable for both you and your horse if you at least attempt to master the art of horsemanship.

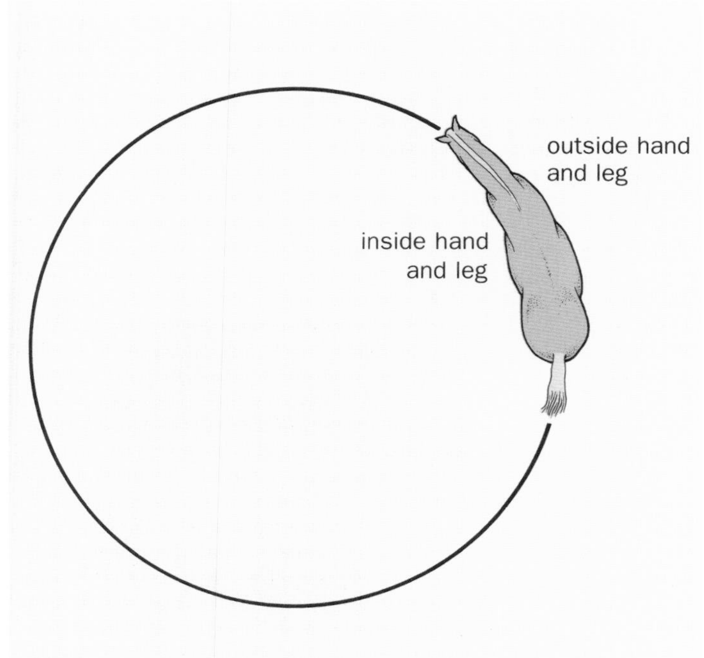

Riding on the left rein.

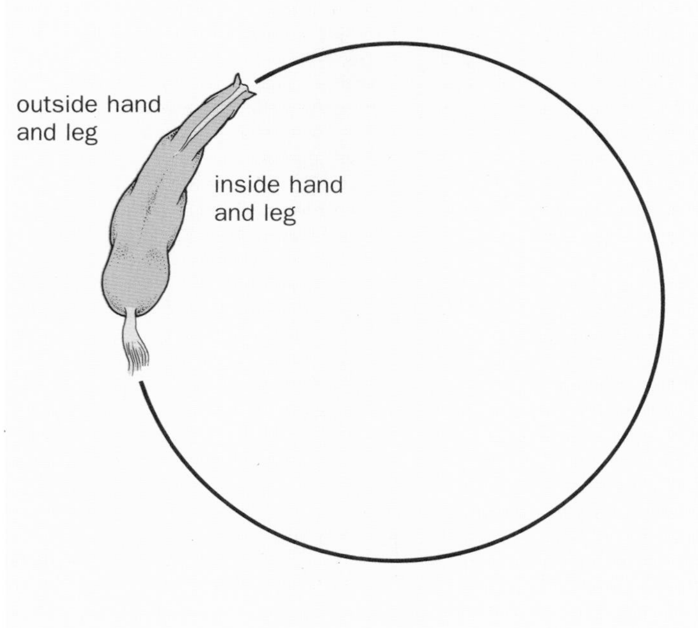

Riding on the right rein.

Understanding Horses and Ponies

The first thing that any would-be rider must appreciate is the sheer strength and bulk that a horse or pony represents. Common sense should tell even the most inexperienced person that the relationship between horse and rider cannot possibly be based on force – if it were, the horse would win every time. As a rider, you are totally dependent on the horse's co-operation, and so the partnership between horse and rider is one of mutual respect.

Much of the secret behind the successful handling of a horse or pony either from the ground or from the saddle is based on the human being in the partnership appearing both calm and confident. So before considering actually riding a horse or pony, it is well worth spending time just getting used to working with them. Most riding establishments would be more than happy to accept an offer of help around the yard and this is a good opportunity to learn how to feel comfortable around horses.

Spending time helping to care for and handle horses helps beginners to feel at ease with them.

Spending time grooming and preparing the horse you are going to ride is all part of building up a good partnership.

A horse is happiest if he is handled confidently and positively. He is far more likely to become nervous and unsure if his handler is jittery and tentative. A horse or pony should always be handled firmly, but fairly, so that he learns what is expected of him. It is the rider's job to teach the horse what is acceptable and what is not. The training of a horse has the same basis as the training of any other animal – when the horse does what is required he is rewarded, when he does not he is quietly reprimanded. It is vital that the handler is consistent in what he or she asks. It is not fair to drape yourself around your pony's neck, hugging and kissing him, only to turn round and wallop him when he shifts his position and accidentally steps on your toe! It is wrong to punish the horse when it was you, the handler, who put yourself in a position where you could get hurt. Although you may think it at the time, the horse would not step on you on purpose if he could avoid doing so!

Your voice is the most valuable form of communication you can have with a horse or pony. He will know from the tone of your voice whether you are pleased with him or otherwise. So it is your voice which should be used to tell the horse when he is behaving well and when he isn't. Your commands should be kept clear and simple – if the horse does something wrong, then a stern "No" is often all it takes to let him know. A long, angry tirade will only confuse him, and wear you out. Keep it simple – "No" when he is wrong, and "Good boy" or "Good girl" when things are going well. Far too many people forget to tell the horse when they are pleased with him.

Horses, like people, have different temperaments and characters, and not every horse will get on in the same way with every person. A very sharp, nervy horse probably won't feel comfortable with an equally bolshie person – he is more likely to respond to a quieter character. An extrovert person can sometimes inspire confidence and coax a little more effort out of a horse with a more laid-back character.

NEAR SIDE, OFF SIDE

Some of the first things to learn in order to avoid confusion all round are the terms used to describe each side of the horse. If you stand facing in the same direction as the horse, his left-hand side is known as the near side, and his right-hand side is known as the off side. The horse is led from the near side; you mount and dismount from the near side. The same terms are used to describe each of the horse's limbs – if a horse is said to be lame on his off fore, this refers to the front leg on the right-hand side.

Where to Learn

Some children are lucky enough to be put on a pony before they can even walk – long before they are in a position to control their ponies off the leading rein, they will have developed a natural seat. This is because someone else has been in charge of the pony – all the rider has had to worry about is staying on board. It is the same principle as being lunged.

For those who haven't had that lucky start, if time and money allow, the best investment is in a course of lunge lessons at an equestrian centre with a good reputation. The advantages of this are that you will be receiving individual attention and, most importantly, you will start to acquire a deep, balanced but relaxed seat in the saddle. Lungeing will also give you the opportunity to concentrate on trying to feel how the horse is actually moving underneath you.

There is the danger of the first riding lesson being a miserable experience. Avoid any establishment where novices are put on badly schooled, bored mounts and stuck in a class with any number of other potential riders, and where inexperienced or simply incompetent instructors swagger around bawling instructions or criticism. The poor riders are expected to master the correct riding position, keep their balance in the saddle, and manoeuvre unresponsive creatures around the arena. These new riders will either give up or become aggressive jockeys, oblivious to the reality of true horsemanship.

All too often a lack of communication and understanding between horse and rider leads to a lack of co-operation.

Lunge lessons will help the rider to develop a good seat, from which he or she will be able to communicate effectively with the horse. For any rider unable to enjoy such an opportunity, the next best thing is to opt for individual lessons, rather than group lessons. Once some of the basics have been mastered, riding in a group can be a positive and enjoyable experience, but if learning from scratch there is nothing to beat individual attention right at the beginning. This may either be at a commercial riding school or equestrian centre, or with a private individual who may give lessons using their own horses and facilities.

Always ensure that the instructor of your choice has a good reputation both for teaching ability and for being safe and responsible. In most countries there is some form of recognized teaching body and a structured system of examinations for instructors; if you have nobody to advise you, always opt for a registered and approved instructor. But if someone is highly recommended to you by more experienced riders, do not be afraid to try them even if teaching is not their profession – some people are naturally gifted teachers.

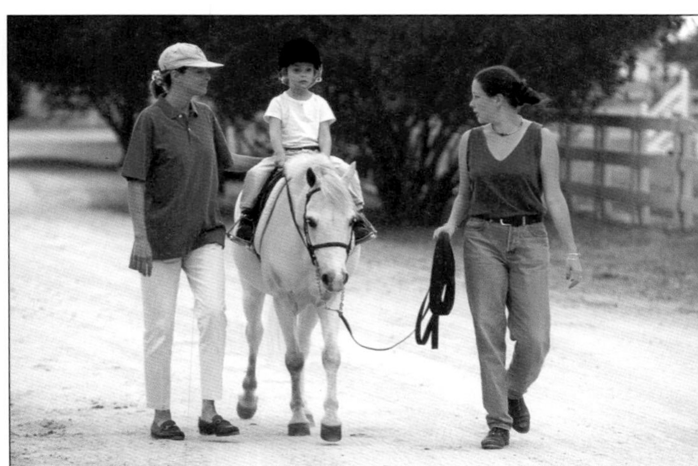

With a willing helper to lead the way, the world is yours to explore. It is a great advantage to learn to ride at such an early age. There are classes for young riders on lead reins at most local gymkhanas.

Group riding lessons are beneficial and fun once the potential rider has had a chance to master some of the basics.

Clothing and Equipment

HARD HAT

One vital item that the rider must have is a hard riding hat, also known as a crash hat or skull cap, which conforms to a recognized safety standard. Any romantic notions about feeling the wind blowing through your hair, or galloping across the prairie in your designer stetson should be dismissed – it is only fair to yourself, and to those who will have to pick up the pieces if you have an accident, that you wear the correct headgear. The design and effectiveness of riding hats has improved dramatically. A riding hat must always be worn with a safety harness to hold it in place; a traditional hard hat with an elastic chin strap is next to useless.

Hard hats come in various designs – looking like the traditional velvet hat with a built-in peak, or like a crash hat or skull cap as worn by racing jockeys and cross-country riders. The latter are more bulbous looking than the traditional type. Some of the newest styles, popularized in America, are very lightweight, vented helmets which protect the head whilst allowing the rider to stay surprisingly cool.

Whatever your standard of riding, and no matter how little or often you ride, your first priority should be to wear equipment of the highest safety standards. The highest current safety standards are the European PAS 015 and the American ASTM/SEIF 1163.

The majority of approved riding or training centres insist that their clients wear protective headgear and, similarly, whenever a rider competes he or she will generally be required to wear a proper hat. A riding hat should always be replaced once it has suffered a hard blow, either through the rider falling, or through being dropped accidentally.

RIDING BOOTS

The second most important item of clothing, from a safety point of view, is footwear. Long or short boots of some kind should be worn; it is important that they are not so wide that there is any risk of them being caught in the stirrup in the

The jockey-style crash hat or skull cap can be worn on its own, or you can fit a "silk" to it – dark blue or black for dressage and show jumping, and a colour to match your outfit for cross-country riding.

The velvet riding hat is styled on the hunting cap and looks quite formal. It is particularly suitable for show-ring riding, dressage and show jumping. A stock, which is a kind of scarf or neck tie, should always be worn for cross-country riding as it does give some support to the neck in the case of a fall.

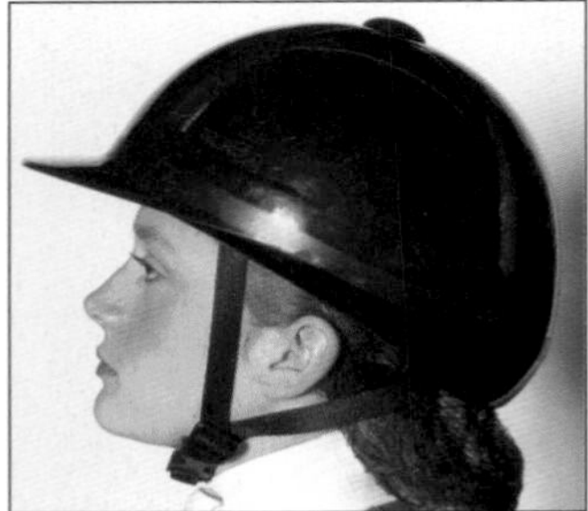

The lightweight vented helmet is fast becoming a popular choice. If it is made to the ASTM/SEIF 1163 standard, it is just as safe as any other hat made to an accepted safety standard such as the European PAS 015. In fact, the ASTM standard hats are stronger in terms of their impact resistance.

Jodhpurs are usually made of a stretchy material and are designed to be worn with short boots.

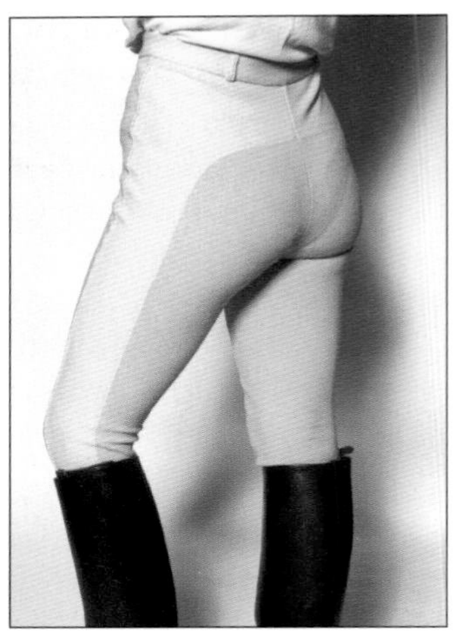

Breeches are designed to be worn with long riding boots.

Short leather jodhpur boots can be worn with jodhpurs or with a pair of "half-chaps" to protect the rider's lower leg.

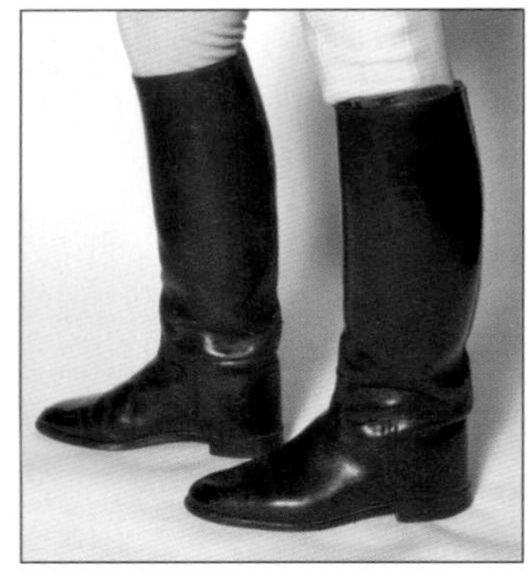

Long riding boots can be made of either rubber or leather.

OPPOSITE
It is advisable to carry a stick of some sort even if you think you are unlikely to need it. It is too late if you go out without one and your horse decides on that particular day to ignore your leg aids. From top to bottom: schooling whip, two types of riding sticks, and a hunting whip.

RIGHT
Whatever type of gloves you choose, make sure that they have non-slip palms; otherwise the reins will slip through your fingers.

event of a fall, and they should only have a small heel – again so that there is no risk of the rider's foot becoming trapped.

There is a good range of casual and affordable boots designed for leisure riding, although they would not usually be acceptable in the competition world. For any form of competition riding, the correct turnout is long boots (ideally leather rather than rubber) or short, leather riding boots such as jodhpur boots.

GLOVES
Most riders like to wear gloves. These should have non-slip palms.

TROUSERS
For the sake of comfort, wear trousers designed specifically for riding. Any garment with a thick seam will chafe against your skin, and anything too thin or flimsy will simply wear through. Jodhpurs or breeches come in a huge variety of styles and colours, and can be purchased as either competition or casual garments.

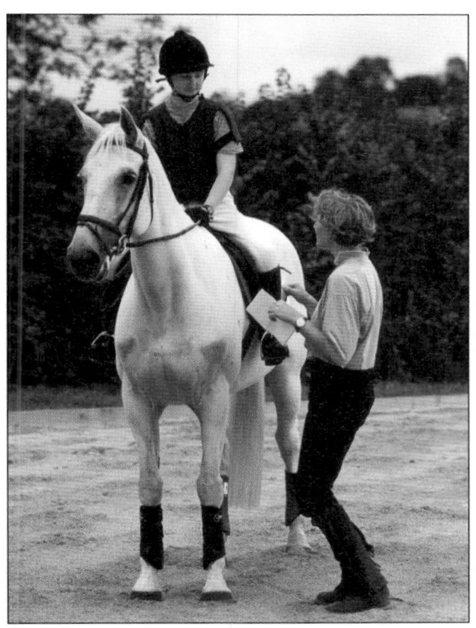

Protective clothing is important for both horse and rider. This rider is wearing a jockey-style crash helmet with safety harness, a body protector and long leather riding boots. Her horse is wearing protective leg boots to reduce the risk of injury through knocking into himself, or being scratched or cut by anything whilst being ridden.

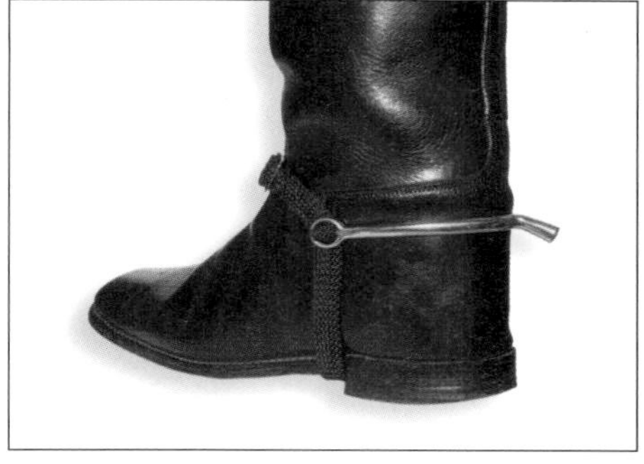

If spurs have to be worn they should be as short as possible and must have a rounded or blunt end. They should never be worn by a beginner. In fact, they should not be worn until you have good control of your lower leg; otherwise you will be spurring your horse unnecessarily.

A neck strap can prove invaluable as an aid to staying in the saddle if the horse plays up or jumps awkwardly. Hold on to the strap with one hand to help keep your weight deep in the saddle, making it harder for you to be thrown off. It can also be used as an aid to help slow the horse down.

CHAPS
If short boots are to be worn, it is also advisable to wear what are known as chaps or half-chaps, which are shaped leggings made from leather, suede or waterproof material. Half-chaps are worn below the knee and protect the lower leg. They are usually fastened by either Velcro or a zip, and prevent the stirrup leather rubbing against the rider's calf. Full chaps are just like the ones cowboys wear; they cover the whole leg and are fastened with a belt around the waist. As well as offering some protection to the leg, they have the advantage of keeping the rider warm.

BODY PROTECTOR
These are padded, vest-like garments and are mandatory in most countries for sports such as horse racing and the cross-country phase of horse trials. With lightweight breatheable materials of ever-better quality appearing on the market each year, they are nothing like as cumbersome and hot as they used to be. They can be worn either over your usual riding top, or underneath your clothes. The ones worn over the top tend to be the most convenient and are available in an array of colours and designs. In an ideal world they would be worn whenever you rode, not just when you intended to jump or compete.

NECK STRAP
A final, small piece of equipment that also adds to the rider's safety is a neck strap, which is worn by the horse. This is a leather strap (an old stirrup leather makes an ideal neck strap) worn loosely around the horse's neck. It sits just above the withers and is well positioned for you to grab hold of if you lose your balance. Neck straps can make the difference between staying aboard and hitting the deck when jumping, and have saved many a rider from being thrown off; they also prevent a horse from being "jabbed" in the mouth.

Sitting Comfortably

Before you even get as far as sitting on a horse there is quite a lot of groundwork to master, such as tacking up and mounting. Riding schools vary in their approach to tacking up for beginners. Some have the horse ready and waiting for his rider, others feel that tacking up is all part of the learning process and that it will give you a few minutes of unpressurized time in which to start to get to know your horse. If a friend is teaching you, it is all part of the fun to help get the horse ready.

Tacking Up

The order in which the horse is tacked up varies, but any form of boots should be put on first, once the horse's legs have been checked for signs of heat or swelling. This should have been done while the horse was being groomed, but it is good practice to double check when putting on the boots – there is no point tacking up and then finding that the horse is lame!

Whether the saddle or bridle is put on next is a matter for discussion. Some riders like to put the bridle on first, so that they have better control of the horse should he pull back and break free from his headcollar. Others like to put the saddle on first so that, having removed the horse's warm rugs, the saddle goes straight on to a warm back and the horse's muscles will remain warm underneath the saddle. On a cold day, a rug should be kept over the horse's back and quarters while he is being tacked up.

PUTTING ON BOOTS

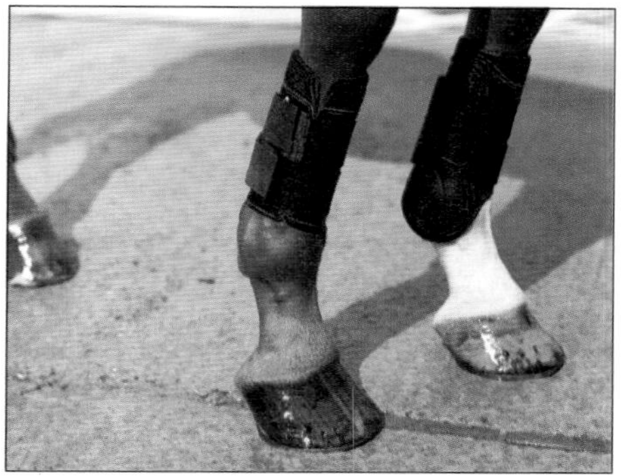

Protective boots reduce the risk of injury. Hold the boot securely in place and fasten the first strap. Then fasten the second strap firmly enough to prevent the boot slipping. Tighten the first strap if it seems looser than the second strap. These boots protect the tendon area of the legs as well as the inside of the fetlocks. Many horses are prone to knocking one leg against the inside of the opposite leg – this is called brushing – and boots prevent the horse from injuring himself as a result.

PUTTING ON THE BRIDLE

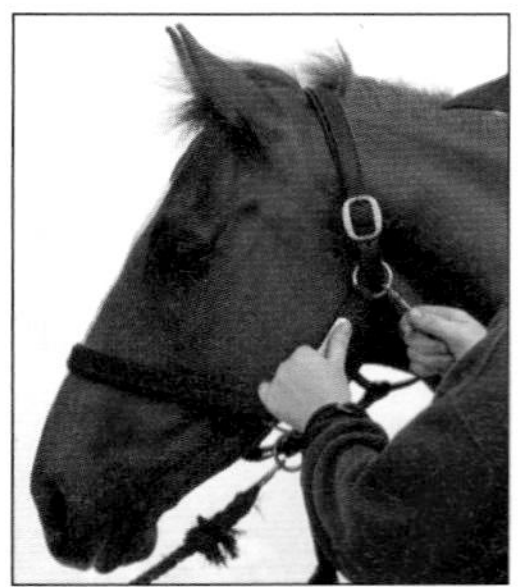

1 Whilst being tacked up or groomed, the horse is usually secured by a headcollar. Before removing the headcollar put the bridle reins over the horse's head so that you have a means of holding him.

2 Remove the headcollar by lifting the headpiece forward and then gently over the horse's ears.

3 With one hand holding the horse's nose to keep his head steady, bring the bridle up in front of his face.

4 Use your right hand to hold the bridle, lay the bit over the palm of your left hand and gently lift it up into the horse's mouth. Use your thumb to press his gum in the gap where his teeth finish which will encourage him to open his mouth.

5 Once the bit is in place, keep some tension on each side of the bridle to hold it there whilst you bring the headpiece of the bridle up and over the horse's ears. Do not allow the bit to bang against his teeth as this will make him wary next time.

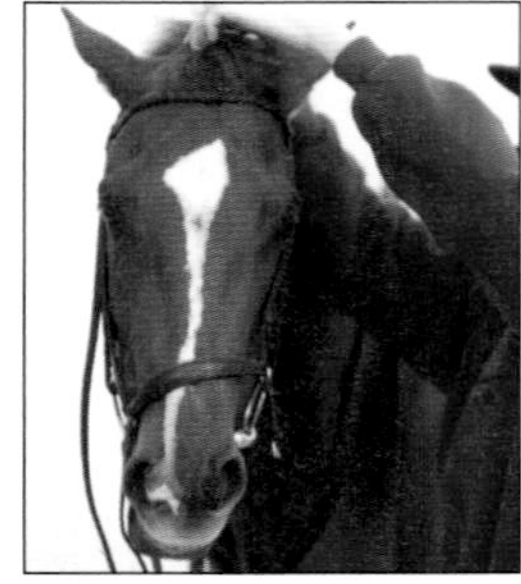

6 With the headpiece in place, separate the hair of the forelock from the rest of the mane (to let the bridle sit comfortably, cut a small section out of the mane where the headpiece sits). Bring the forelock forward and lift it clear of the browband.

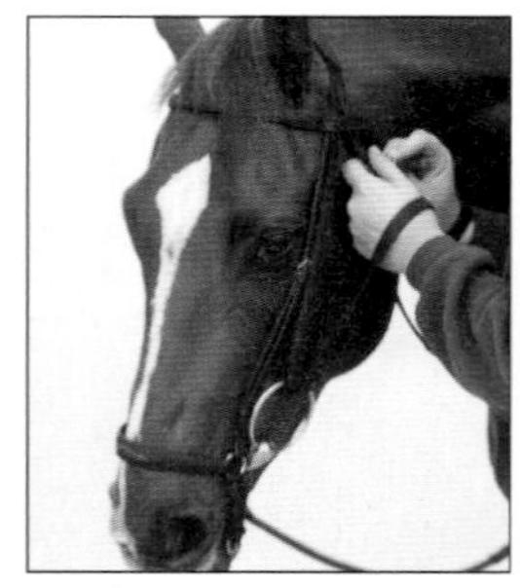

7 Keep your hand looped through the rein so that you have a contact with the horse, and therefore control over him, and then do up the throatlash.

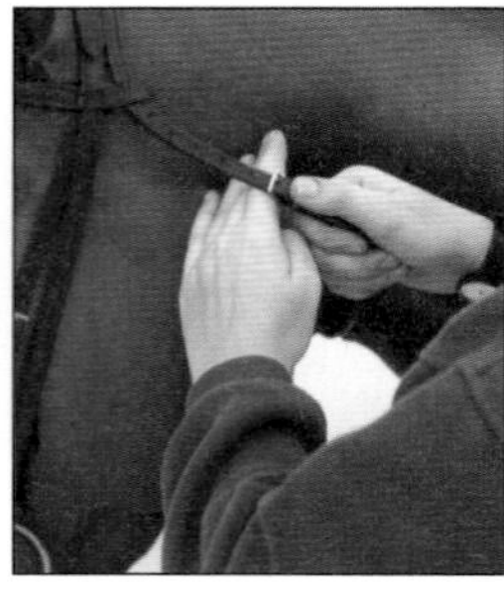

8 It should not be fastened too tightly – make sure you can still get four fingers of your hand between the horse's cheek and the throatlash.

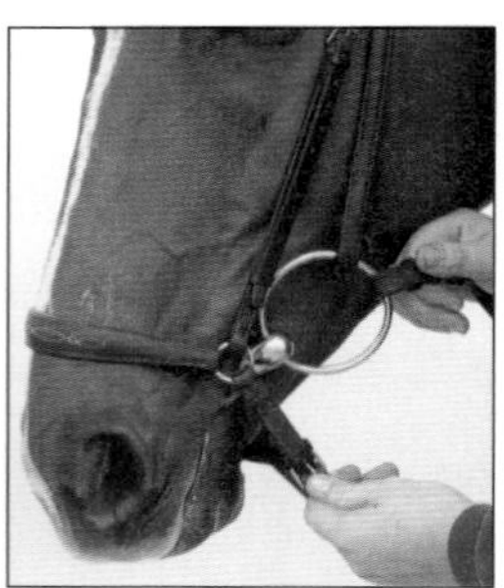

9 Fasten the noseband – in this case a drop noseband which does up below the bit rings. A cavesson noseband, used for lungeing, sits higher up the horse's nose and does up above the bit rings.

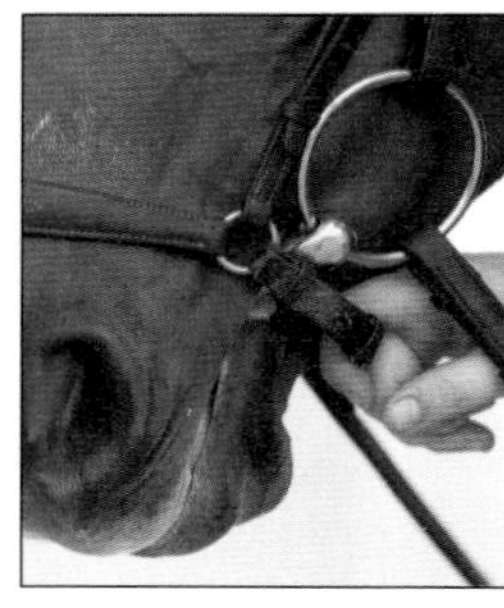

10 You should be able to place one finger between the horse's chin and the noseband.

SADDLING UP

1 Place a soft, padded numnah on the horse's back. This acts as a cushion between the horse and the saddle and can relieve pressure points and reduce the risk of rubbing. It is also a warmer layer to have against the horse's skin than the leather of the saddle.

2 Keeping the saddle well clear of the horse's back, lift it so that it is poised in the right position to be lowered on to the back. Lower the saddle into place, making sure that the saddle flap on the off side is lying flat.

3 Use your left hand to lift the numnah so that it is not pulled tight over the horse's withers. It should be tucked up to lie snugly under the pommel of the saddle, clear of the withers.

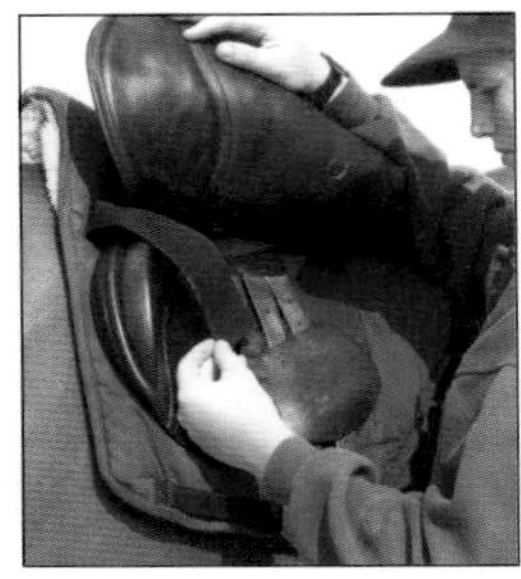

4 Most numnahs have two straps that hold them in position under the saddle. The first one is usually attached to the girth straps, so pull it over the knee roll of the saddle and put it on the strap before you do up the girth.

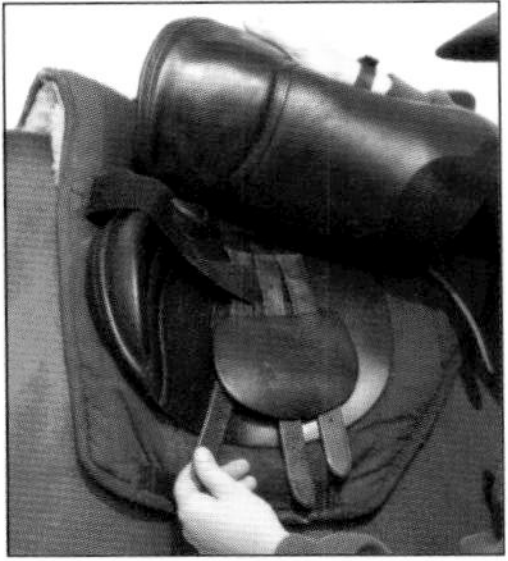

5 Position the strap above the buckle guard, otherwise you will not be able to pull this down into the correct position. Pull the girth strap out from the buckle guard, thread through the numnah strap, then put the strap back through the buckle guard.

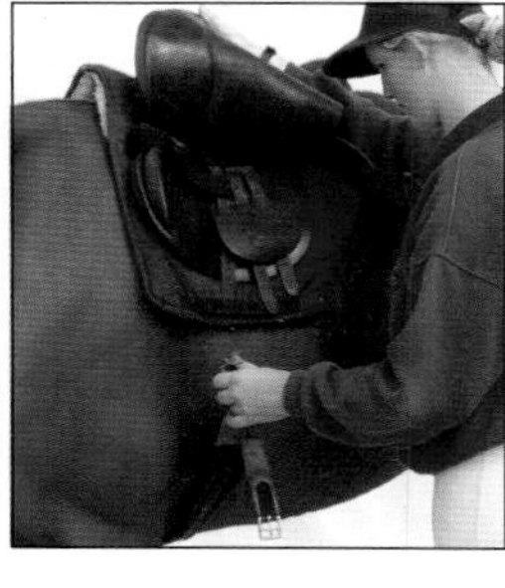

6 Buckle the girth to the saddle on the off side. Return to the near side, and reach under the horse's belly to catch the girth. Thread the girth buckles through the second securing strap of the numnah and fasten them, one at a time, to each girth strap.

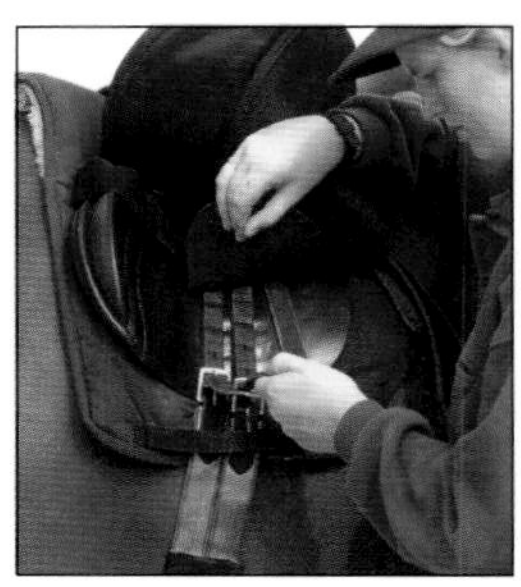

7 Gently tighten the girth, one buckle at a time, until you can just squeeze the flat of your hand between the horse's belly and the girth. Fasten the girth equally on each side.

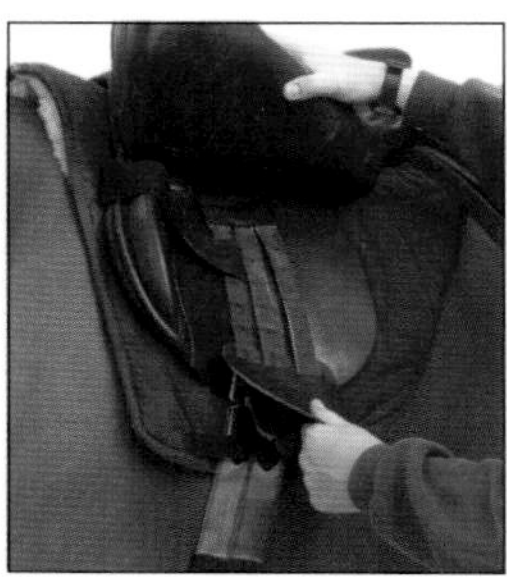

8 Pull the buckle guard down so that it covers the buckles – otherwise they will gradually wear a hole through the saddle flap.

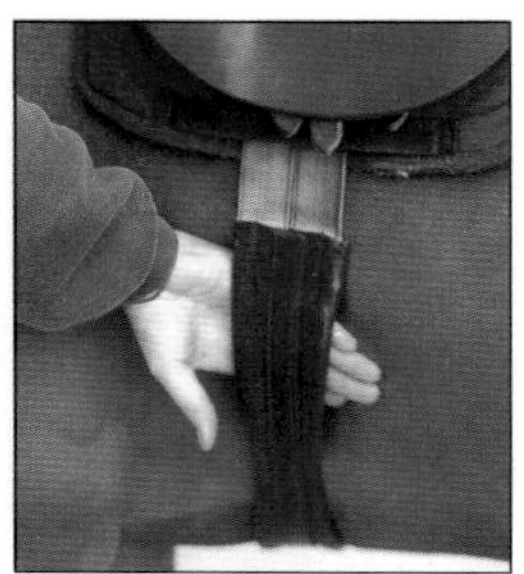

9 Smooth down under the girth so that there are no wrinkles of skin caught up which might rub. Slide your hand under the girth just clear of the saddle flap and run it down under the horse's belly, taking particular care to smooth any wrinkles in the horse's elbow area.

10 A correctly fitted jumping saddle, with the girth tightened and the stirrups run up so that they don't swing and bang against the horse's sides. A jumping saddle has forward-cut flaps and knee rolls to allow the rider to keep his or her leg on the saddle even when riding with shorter stirrups.

PUTTING ON A DRESSAGE SADDLE

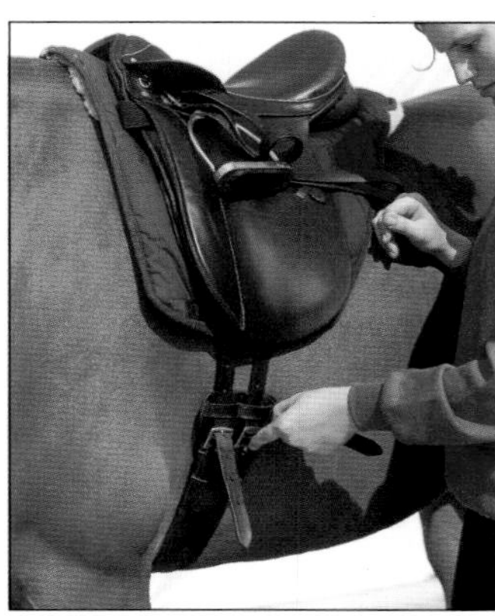

1 A dressage saddle has long girth straps which do up below the saddle flap. The girth must still be tightened gradually, one buckle at a time, and the skin and hair smoothed down underneath it.

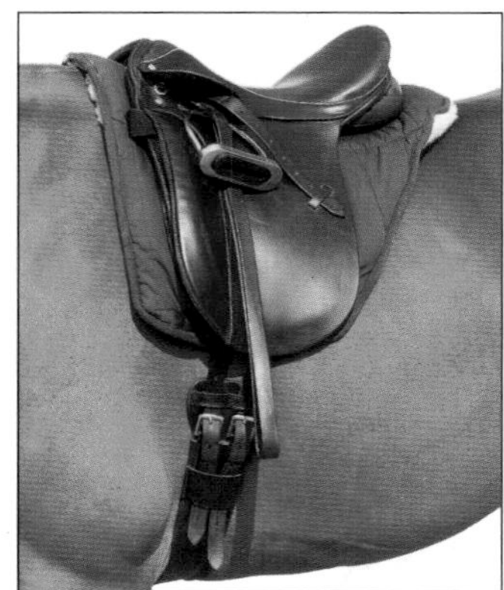

2 Dressage saddles allow your legs to hang much longer and closer to the horse's sides. This gives the best possible position for you to communicate with the horse through your legs and seat.

LEADING A TACKED-UP HORSE

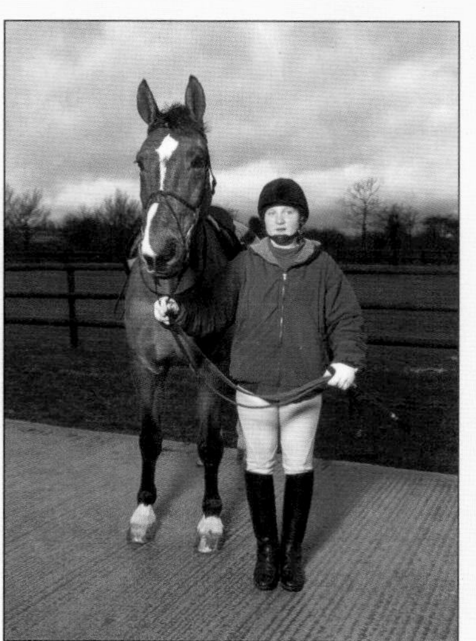

LEFT
When leading a tacked-up horse, stand on his near side and bring the reins over his head. The stirrups should be run up so that they do not swing or bang against the horse's sides. Carry the excess loop of rein and your riding stick in your left hand. Have the stick pointing backwards so that you can give the horse a tap behind the girth if he refuses to walk on. You should always wear a riding hat whenever you lead a horse.

Mounting

So now it is time to step aboard. It is essential to learn how to mount correctly from the ground but, as a general rule, it is far less stressful on the horse's back to use a mounting block or be given a leg-up. Either of these methods is also a lot safer than mounting from the ground. A great many accidents occur when riders are trying to get on their horses. If you do mount from the ground, ideally an assistant should stand on the far side of the horse and, by putting his or her hand in the stirrup iron, should use some of his or her own weight to counteract your weight swinging up from the other side. This helps to reduce the amount of twisting and pulling on the horse's spine.

Voilà! You are now mounted on your horse. Put your right foot in the stirrup and then take up a rein in each hand.

MOUNTING FROM THE GROUND

1 Before attempting to get on your horse you will need to put the reins back over his head, and to let down the stirrups.

2 As you pull the stirrup irons down, keep them away from the horse's sides so that they don't knock him. When they are fully down, place them gently back against his sides.

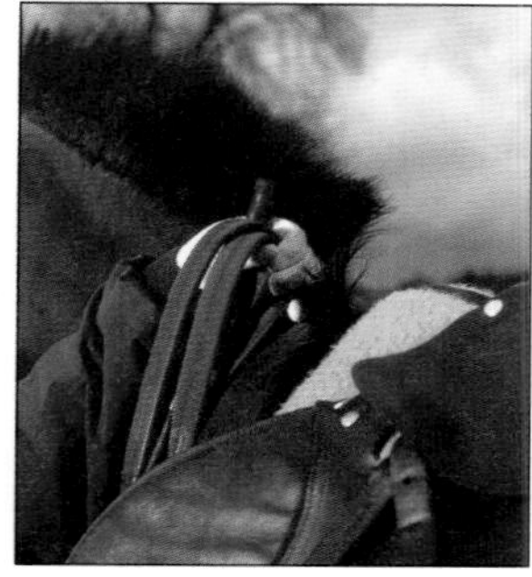

3 Stand on the near side of the horse, facing his tail, and put both reins in your left hand. It also helps to loop a finger through the neck strap and hold on to a little piece of the mane.

4 Take the stirrup iron in your right hand and turn it to face you. The stirrup should be turned clockwise, so that once you are mounted the stirrup leather lies correctly against your leg.

5 Lift your left leg and place your foot in the stirrup iron. Put your right hand on the seat of the saddle.

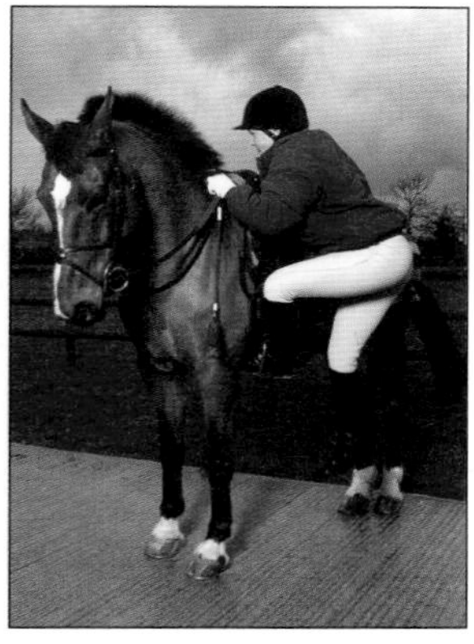

6 Push with your right leg to spring off the ground and, at the same time, reach to the far side of the saddle with your right hand.

7 Once you are high enough off the ground, you will be able to grip the far side of the saddle with your right hand and this will help you to balance. Keep bringing your right leg up until it is clear of the horse's back and hindquarters.

8 At this point start to swing your right leg over the back of the horse. Bring your right hand back to the front of the saddle and rest it on either the pommel or the horse's neck to help you support and balance your upper body.

9 As your right leg starts to come down over the off side of the horse, take your weight on your hands and arms so that you don't flop down in the saddle. Lower your seat gently into the saddle.

GETTING A LEG-UP

1 If someone is going to give you a leg-up on to your horse, you should stand on the near side facing the saddle. Take both reins and your stick in your left hand – making sure you carry the stick down over the off-side shoulder of the horse otherwise you will hit your helper in the face with it as you mount up! Rest your left hand on the horse's neck or on the pommel of the saddle, and reach up with your right hand so that it is resting near the back of the saddle.

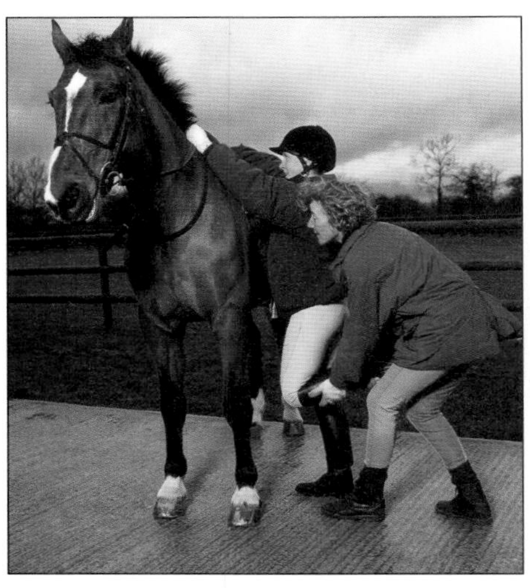

2 Bend your left leg up from the knee so that your helper can take hold of it with both hands.

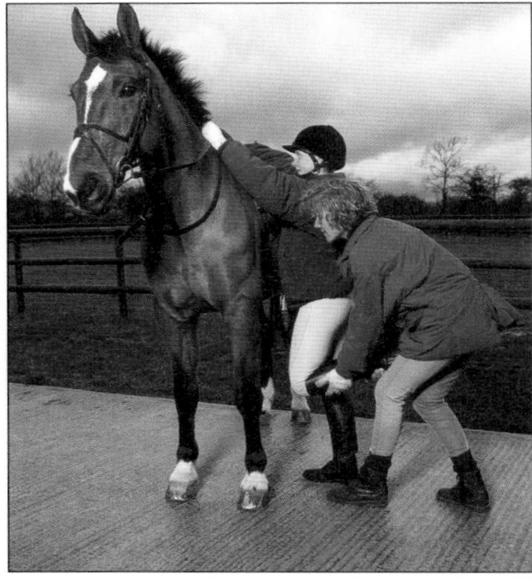

3 Sink your weight down into your right leg and when your helper gives the command be ready to spring up in the air off your right leg.

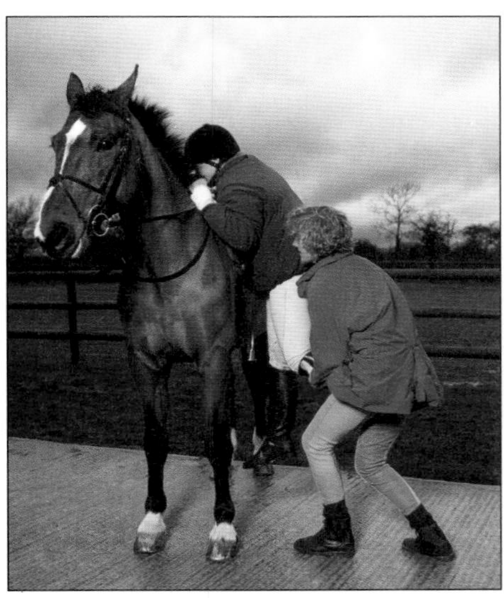

4 As you spring up off your right leg, your helper will also lift your weight by lifting your left leg up. Take your weight on your hands so that you are supporting your upper body and can control the moment when you want to swing your right leg over the horse's back.

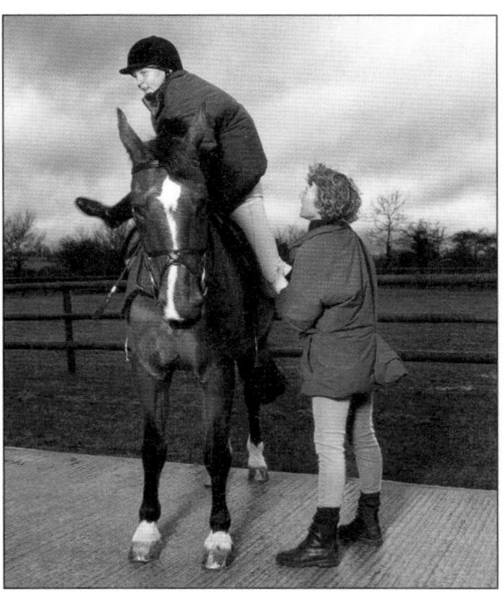

5 As you swing your right leg over the horse's back you will need to transfer your right hand from the back of the saddle to either the pommel or the top of the saddle flap on the off side. Make sure you continue to support your upper body on both your arms.

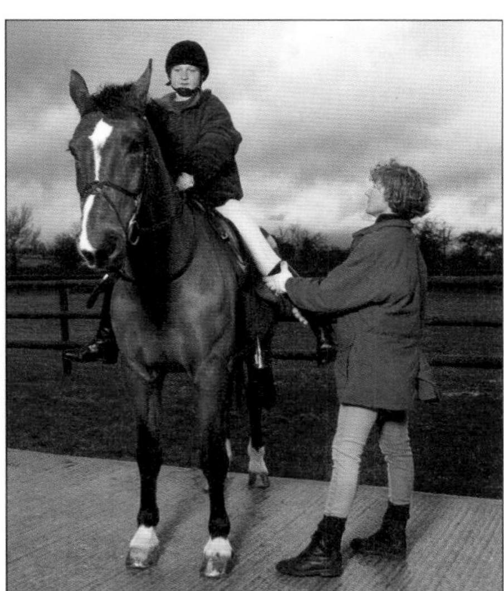

6 With your weight on your arms you can lower your seat down gently into the saddle.

USING A MOUNTING BLOCK

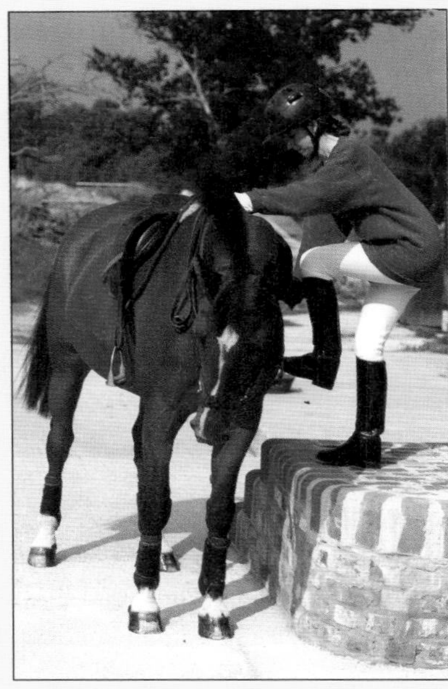

It is far less stressful for both horse and rider if you are able to get aboard by using a mounting block. The horse is led alongside the mounting block so that his near side is parallel to the block. Use the stirrup to mount in the normal way. Now that you are that much higher off the ground, there is less strain on the horse's back when you step up into the stirrup.

Adjusting Tack

Having learned how to tack up and mount your horse, there are one or two other small adjustments you will need to make once you are on board. The first thing you must do is tighten the girth. Although this is tightened from the ground before you mount, your weight pushing the saddle down on to the horse's back will cause the girth to need retightening. Also, many horses push their stomachs out against the pressure of the girth, and only relax again once their riders are in the saddle.

It is only once you are sitting on your horse that you can feel if your stirrups are set at a comfortable length for you; they may need adjusting. When you change from riding on the flat to jumping you will also want to shorten your stirrups whilst still sitting on the horse.

TIGHTENING THE GIRTH

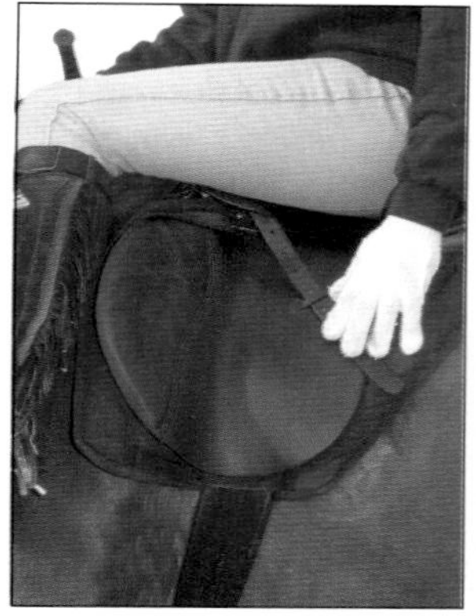

1 To retighten the girth, put both reins and your stick in your right hand and bring your left leg clear of the saddle flap.

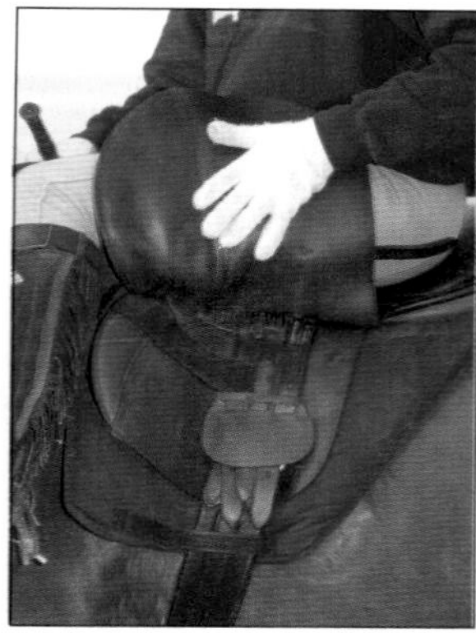

2 Reach down and lift up the saddle flap so that you have access to the girth straps.

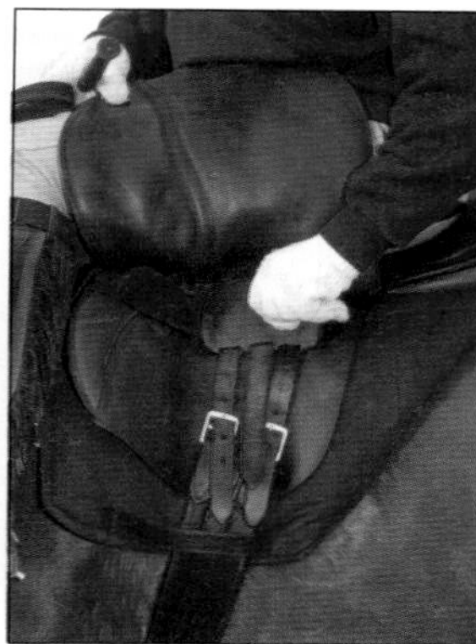

3 Hold the saddle flap out of the way with your right hand; with your left hand, pull the buckle guard up away from the girth straps and buckles.

4 Take hold of the first girth strap and pull it up gently. Use your index finger to press the spike of the buckle through the hole.

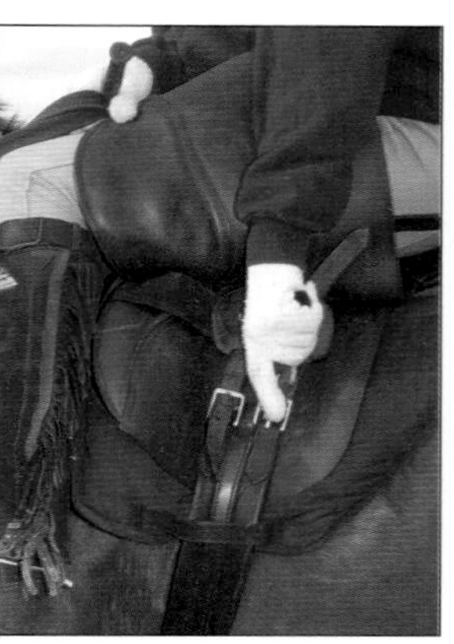

5 Do the same to the second girth strap – make sure each is tightened by the same number of holes.

6 Pull the buckle guard back down so that it sits snugly over the girth buckles. Put the saddle flap back down and return your leg to the correct position.

HOLDING THE REINS

1 Hold the reins by allowing them to lie across the palm of your hand. The end that comes from the horse's mouth passes between your third and fourth finger.

2 It rests over the top of your first finger and is held in place by closing your thumb and fingers. You can lengthen the reins by relaxing the tension in your hand and letting them slip through your fingers.

3 This picture shows you how to hold a stick as well as your reins. When your thumb and fingers close back around the rein and stick, they are held safely in place.

ADJUSTING THE STIRRUP LEATHERS

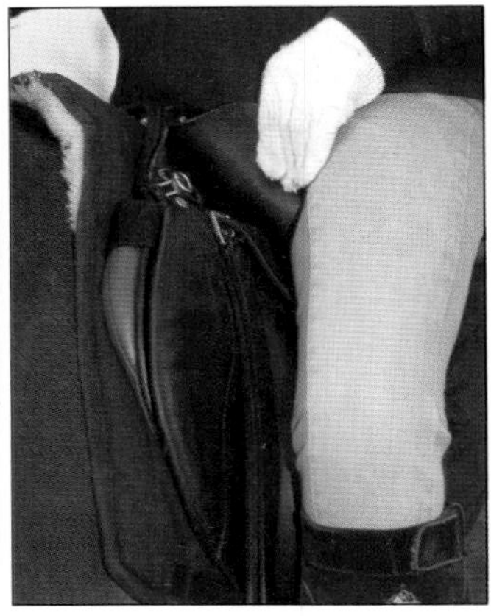

1 Once you are in the saddle you may need to adjust your stirrup leathers in order to sit comfortably and correctly. Put the reins and stick in your right hand, and use your left hand to lift the leather flap that covers the stirrup-leather buckle.

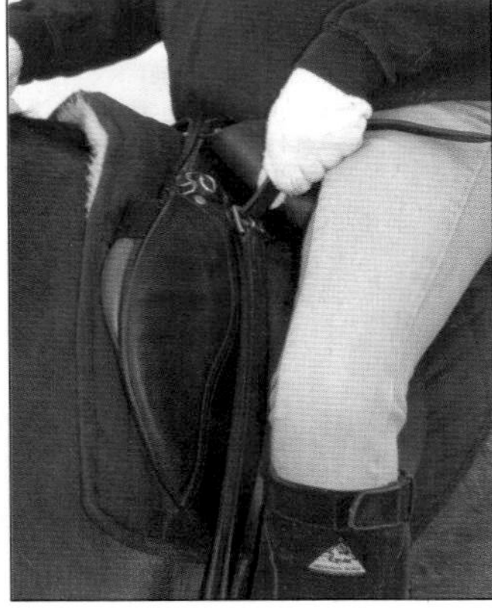

2 Pull the free end of the stirrup leather out of its keeper if necessary, and then pull it upwards so that the buckle is released.

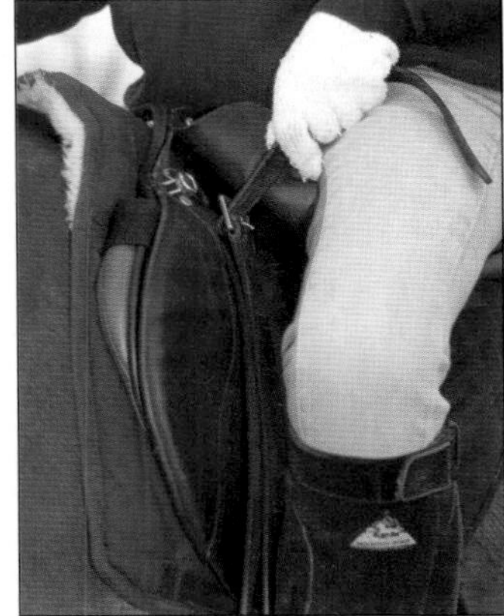

3 To shorten your stirrup, pull the stirrup leather upwards, as shown. To lengthen your stirrup, put your weight down into the stirrup iron and with your left hand allow the stirrup leather to slide back down through the stirrup bar.

4 When the stirrup is at the required length, push the buckle back through the appropriate hole.

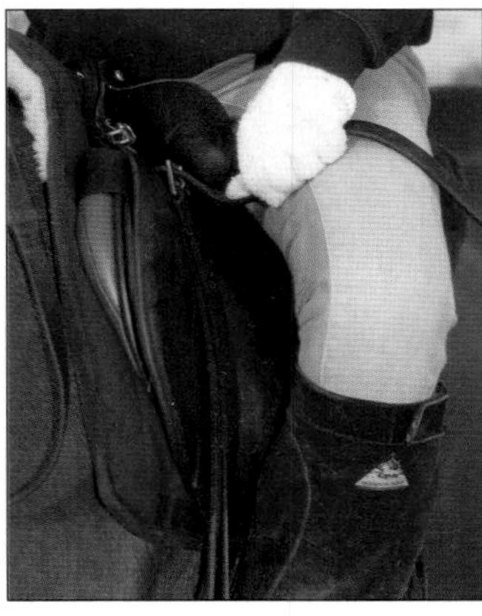

5 Make sure the stirrup-leather buckle slides back into position, hard up against the stirrup bar.

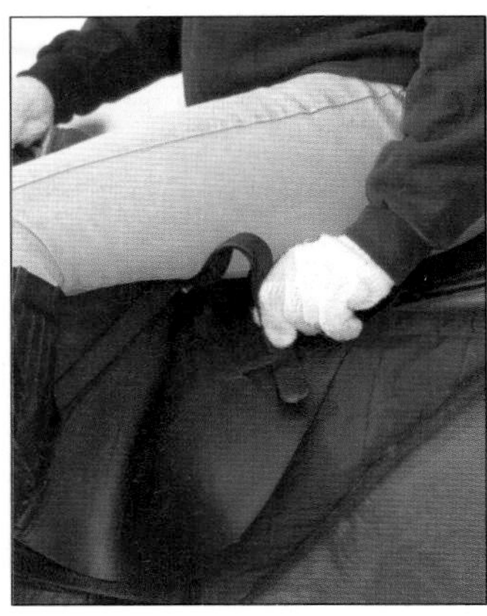

6 Push the free end of the stirrup leather back through the keeper.

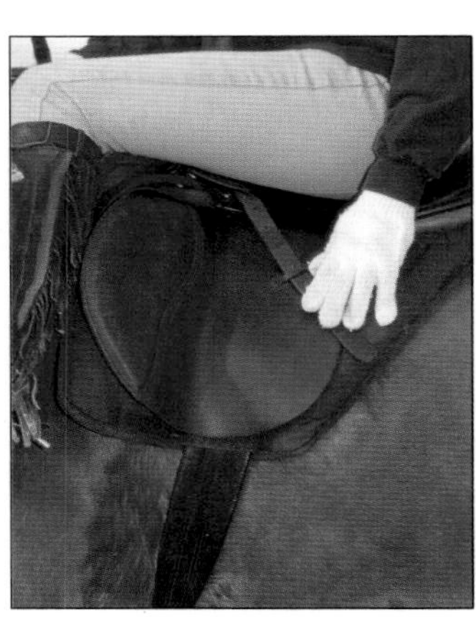

7 Ensure that the leather is lying flat before repeating the procedure for the right stirrup.

POSITIONING THE STIRRUP LEATHER

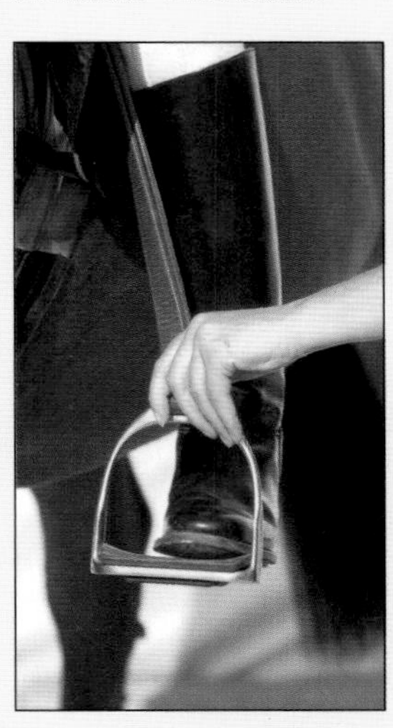

Each stirrup leather should be turned outwards, rather than inwards, in order to position the stirrup iron so that your foot can go into it. This allows the stirrup leather to curve smoothly across the inside of your leg. So to put your right foot (off-side foot) in the stirrup iron, give the leather a quarter turn in a clockwise direction. For the near-side foot (left foot), turn the stirrup leather in an anti-clockwise direction.

4 You should always hold both your hands at the same height, usually just above the withers and a few inches apart. The basic rule for hand position is that there should be a straight line running from your elbow, down your arm, through the wrist and hand, down the rein to the horse's mouth. It is this rule that dictates the exact position of your hands, which will therefore alter depending on what the horse is doing with his head carriage. This hand and arm position allows you to maintain a soft, elastic but consistent contact with the horse's mouth. (See The Hands which illustrates three different but correct positions.)

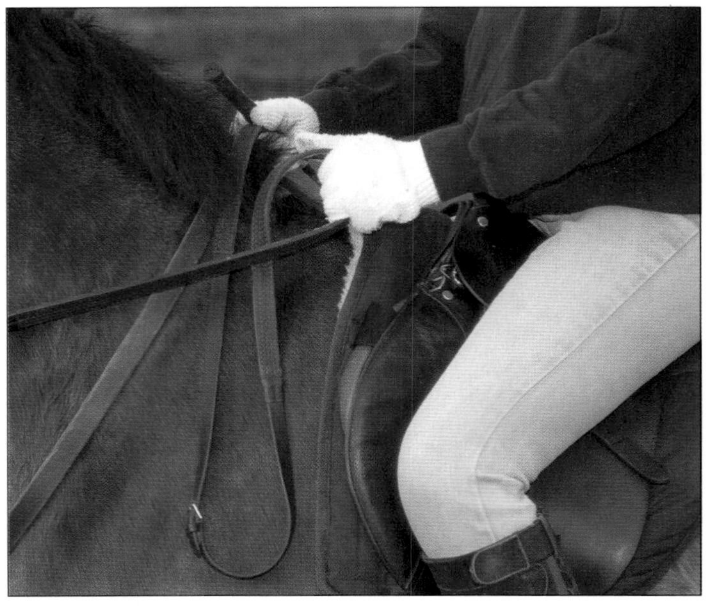

Dismounting

Dismounting from the horse should also be done correctly. Do not be tempted to follow the example of countless cowboys and Indians in Wild West movies by flinging your leg over the front of the saddle. If the horse throws his head up you will, at best, be knocked off backwards or, at worst, startle the horse so that he either jumps or bolts, leading to even more painful consequences. Always remove both feet from the stirrups, lean forward and swing your right leg up and over behind the saddle. As obvious as it may sound, always check that the ground where you are about to land is safe and free of obstacles before you dismount.

GETTING OFF

1 To prepare to dismount from your horse you should take both feet out of the stirrups and put both reins, and your stick, in your left hand.

2 Rest both hands on the pommel of the saddle or on the horse's neck. Lean your upper body forward.

3 Now swing your right leg up and over the horse's back.

4 Swing your left leg back and out slightly so that it meets your right leg which has now swung over on to the near side of the horse. Use your hands on the saddle to help support your body.

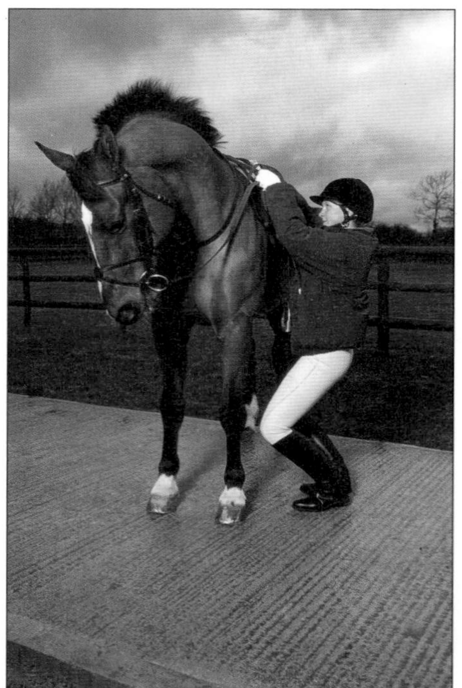

5 Allow both your legs to drop to the ground together. Bend your knees as you land to absorb the impact.

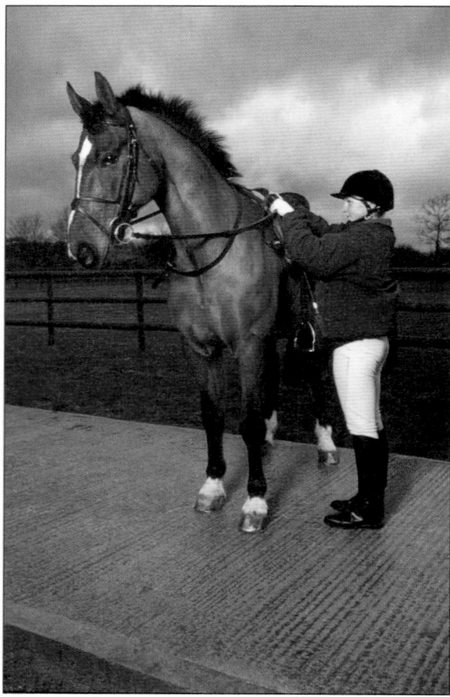

6 Straighten up and you are ready to run up your stirrups, take the reins over your horse's head, and lead him back to his stable.

The Ideal Position

Once on the horse, you should try to adopt a proud and elegant posture. The ideal, classical position is like that of a person standing with their knees slightly bent, not sitting in an armchair. Your ear, shoulder, hip and heel should all be in line, with equal weight placed on each seat bone so that you are not tipped too far forward or sitting back on your buttocks. Always remember how heavy your head is in relation to the rest of your body – if you look down, or tilt your head to the side, or push it too far forward it will affect your, and therefore the horse's, balance. Your legs should hang long and loose down the horse's sides. When your foot is balanced in the stirrup, think of allowing your weight to sink down into your heel.

Although it is often frowned upon today by many who consider it unsafe, anyone who was fortunate enough to learn to ride bareback tends to adopt a correct position automatically. Often, it is the addition of the saddle and the stirrups which compromises what was otherwise a near-perfect position.

By practising the ideal position on the ground, you can start to get a good feel of what you are aiming for, before the added complication of the movement of the horse underneath you enters the equation. Similarly, while sitting on the stationary horse you can be shown how to follow the movement of his head and neck, so that you do not restrict the horse or harm him by pulling on the reins in an attempt to keep your balance.

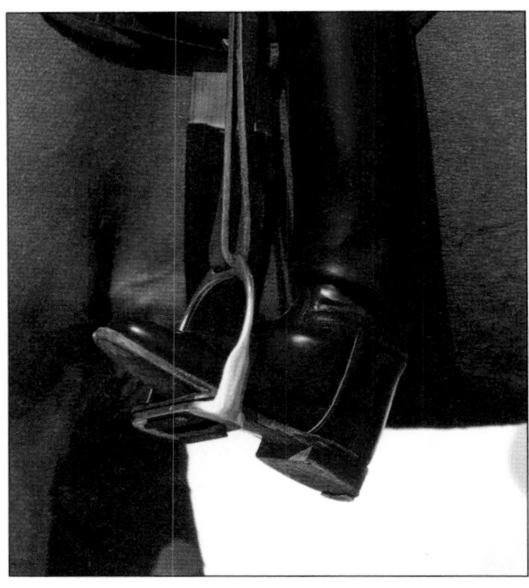

Your foot should be balanced centrally in the stirrup, with the stirrup tread positioned under the ball of your foot and your weight lowered gently down into your heel.

If you sit a child on a pony bareback, his or her leg position will automatically be long and low as required for the classical position.

As soon as a saddle is introduced, note how the child adopts an armchair seat. The best way to acquire a natural, classical seat is to learn to ride either bareback or without stirrups.

1 You can practise the classical riding position on the ground. First stand straight, with your legs about 2 feet (0.5 m) apart, and your arms bent at the elbow as if you were holding the horse's reins.

2 Keeping your whole body straight and upright, simply bend your knees slightly – now you are in the classical dressage position. For jumping you simply bend your knees more. Your position on a horse should be as if you were standing with your knees bent, rather than as if you were sitting in a chair.

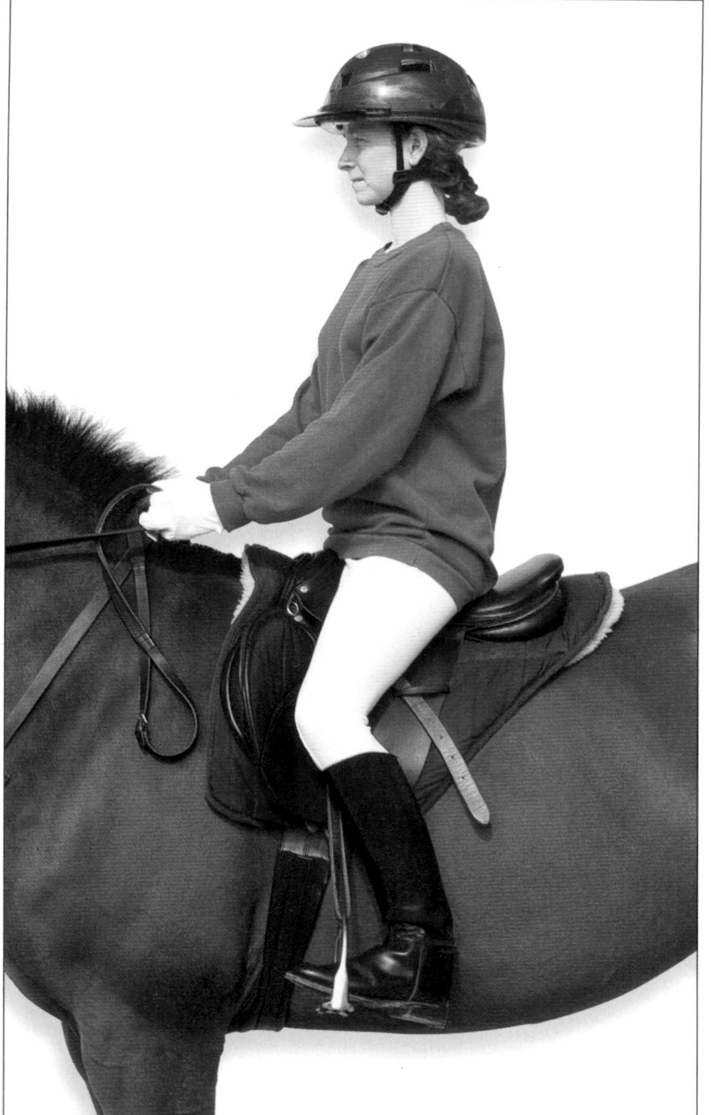

LEFT
Your position in the saddle should be exactly the same as the position you have practised on the ground. See how this rider appears to be standing with her knees bent rather than sitting on the saddle. Note how there is a straight line through the rider's ear, shoulder, hip and heel. Similarly there is another straight line running from the elbow, down through the wrist and hand to the rein and eventually to the bit.

COMMON FAULTS

How not to sit! You should not allow your weight to fall on to the back of your bottom as if you were sitting on a chair. Note how, when this happens, the rider's lower leg swings forward and becomes ineffective as a result.

You should not sit with your weight pitched forward. It prevents you from sitting properly and using your legs correctly – and it is painful! Note how this position causes the lower leg to slide back.

PRACTISING A SOFT CONTACT

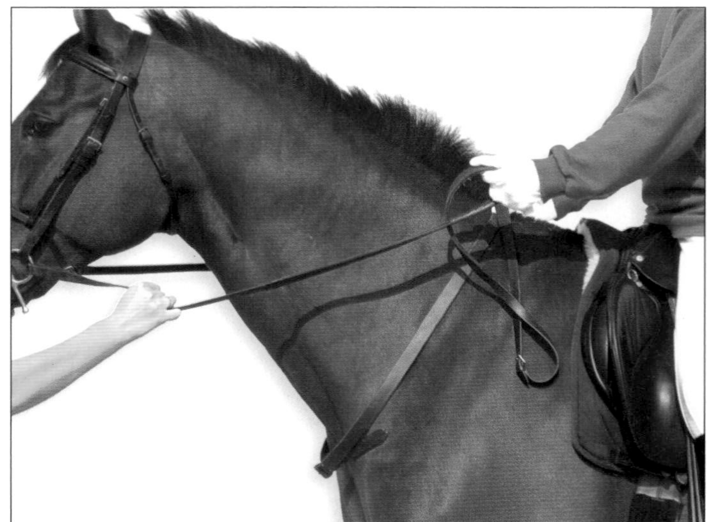

1 One of the secrets of sympathetic and effective riding is to learn how to maintain a soft but constant contact with the horse's mouth, whilst allowing him to move his head and neck freely. Take up a rein in each hand and ask a friend to hold the rein further down towards the horse's mouth.

2 Ask your friend to mimic the movement of the horse's head and neck by drawing the rein forwards and then releasing it. Concentrate on maintaining the straight line from your elbow, through your wrist and hand down the rein. Keep your elbows and wrists soft and relaxed, and allow your whole arm, from the shoulder down, to be moved by the pull on the reins.

The Hands

Never forget that your hands are attached directly via the reins to a large piece of metal in the horse's mouth. Like your own, the horse's mouth is soft and sensitive, and you must never be harsh or abusive with your hands. One of the most important ideas to grasp is that your hands belong to the horse's mouth. Although a light, consistent contact must be maintained so that you have a line of communication with the horse, that contact should be elastic. Your hands must follow the movement of the horse's head and neck. It should feel as if you are shaking hands politely with someone; there is equal pressure and movement from each party. It is not polite to clasp someone's hand roughly and shake it violently as a terrier might shake a rat! Nor is it kind to grasp the reins and swing and tug on them. An old Spanish proverb suggests that "you should ride as if with reins of silk". This can only be achieved if the whole arm stays soft and relaxed, right from the shoulder through the elbow to the hand. The elbow opens out softly to allow the hands to go forwards as the horse's head moves.

COMMON FAULTS

A common fault is to have stiff, straight arms and to turn the wrists and hands outwards. You can see from this position how harsh it all looks, and how impossible it would be to keep a sympathetic contact with the horse.

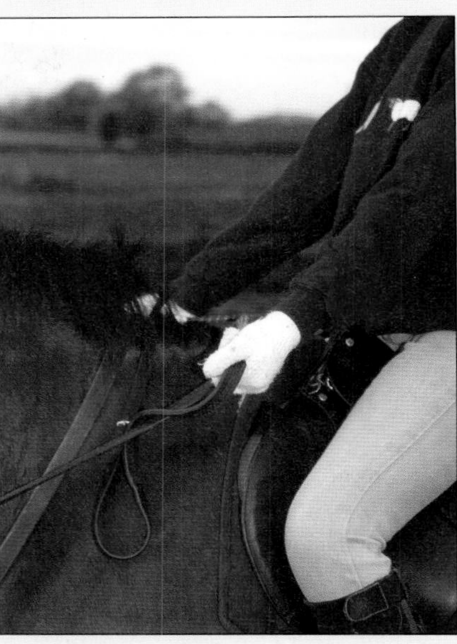

A similar error is to carry your hands so that the thumbs are pointing downwards – again this prevents you maintaining a soft, consistent contact with the horse's mouth.

The exact position of the hands, how close they are held to the withers, depends upon the horse's head carriage. There should always be a straight line from the elbow, through the wrist, down the rein to the bit; so if the horse is working with his head quite low, the hands must be carried a little lower and to either side of the withers in order to keep this straight line. When the horse is working in a rounder outline, the hands can be carried a little higher; and when you find yourself riding a highly schooled horse who carries his head and neck higher still, your hands should be carried a few inches above the withers. The rule of thumb is to be aware of keeping the straight line from the elbow, through the rein to the horse's mouth.

You must adjust your arm position, following the horse's head and neck, so that you maintain an imaginary straight line from your elbow, through your wrist and hand, down the rein to the bit. This horse is working in a good outline in trot and you can see how the straight line is maintained.

When you encourage the horse to stretch and lower his neck, you must still keep the straight line. This rider has allowed her arms and elbows to be drawn forwards and down so that the line is maintained.

Here the horse is working with more pronounced flexion and bend through his neck. In this case you should raise your lower arms and hands slightly to maintain the line.

The Legs

The most important way that you can communicate with the horse is through the legs and seat. Your legs should hang long and relaxed around the horse's sides, with no tightness in the knee joints in particular. It is the insides of the calves which squeeze against the horse to ask him to move either forwards or across to one side or the other. If you run your hand down the inside of your leg just below the knee, you should feel the slight outward bulge of your calf muscle; it is this part of the leg which is used to communicate with the horse.

Check that your stirrup length is correct by allowing each leg to hang long and loose, and free of the stirrup. You should then only need to turn your toe up slightly to find the stirrup. This is the position that you should be aiming for, although at first it is likely to produce too much pull down the back of the thigh and calf muscles. Until your muscles have toned, stretched and strengthened sufficiently, it is sensible to ride with the leg in as long a position as is still comfortable. With time, and particularly as you begin to find your balance on the horse and the beginnings of an independent seat, you will gradually find it easier to ride with the leg in a longer position.

To find the correct stirrup length that will allow you to adopt the classical position for flatwork, you should sit deep in the saddle and just allow your legs to hang long and loose without putting them in the stirrups.

This is the classical position viewed from the front. You can see how the rider's legs would completely encompass the body of the horse; it is this position that allows the leg to support the horse at all times, and from which you can communicate with the horse through your leg aids.

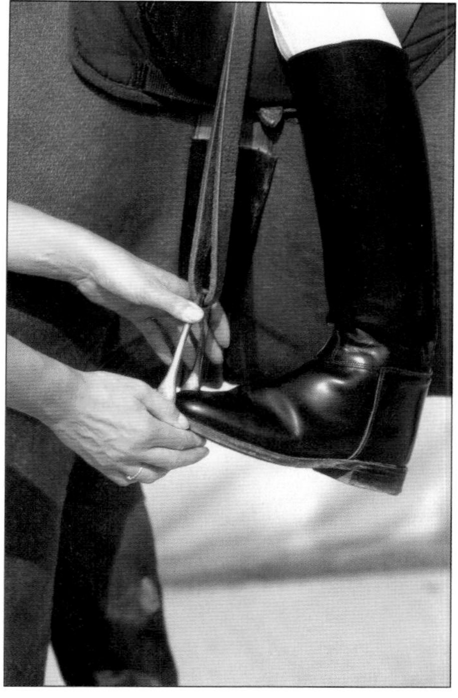

Ask a friend to adjust the stirrup leather so that you only need to turn up your toe to find the stirrup iron. It may take some time for you to be able to ride comfortably with such a long stirrup length as your muscles will need to supple up and stretch, but this is what you are aiming for.

Keep your knee joint relaxed and let it fall away from the saddle slightly, which will allow the leg to hang correctly around the horse's side. Contrary to popular belief, you should not grip with the knees as doing so will effectively push your seat up and out of the saddle. Equally, if you hold your knees tightly against the saddle, you cannot squeeze the horse's sides with your legs. The knee and the toe have to be turned slightly outwards to allow the inside of the calf to press against the horse's sides; which you will need to do to apply a leg aid correctly.

A common fault is for the lower leg to be drawn back and upwards in order to press against the horse's side, but this is an

LEFT
To apply the leg aids correctly you need to be aware of exactly what your lower leg is doing. When the horse is moving at the pace you wish him to, keep your legs gently in contact with his sides, but do not actively do anything. The lower leg and the knee joint should remain soft and relaxed.

ineffective means of communication. The lower leg must lie close to the girth; it will come into contact with the part of the horse's belly which is fractionally behind the girth. For some movements, such as turning, or when the rider wants to control the horse's hindquarters, the lower leg is used a few inches further back behind the girth. But the leg is always used in the same way – with the weight down in the heel, the knee and toe turned out slightly and with a squeeze or nudge inwards, not backwards. If you conjure up in your mind a picture of an old-fashioned, bow-legged horseman, you will have a good idea of how the rider's legs are used against the horse's sides, and why some riders end up looking bow-legged!

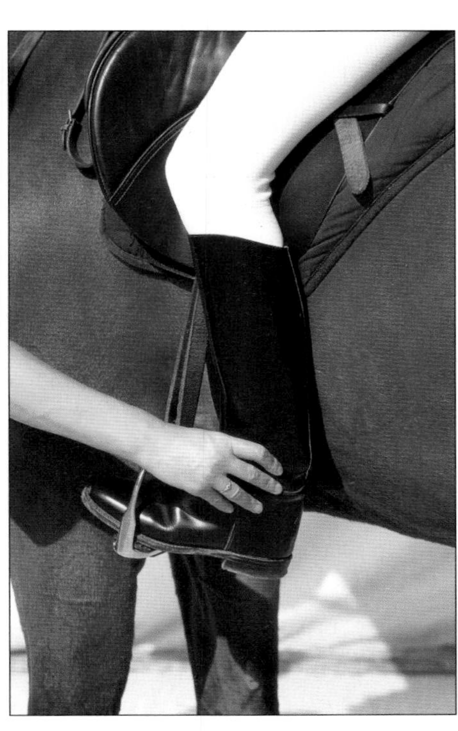

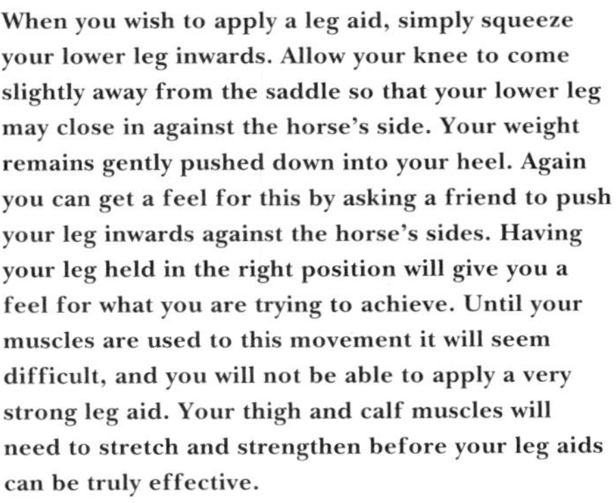

When you wish to apply a leg aid, simply squeeze your lower leg inwards. Allow your knee to come slightly away from the saddle so that your lower leg may close in against the horse's side. Your weight remains gently pushed down into your heel. Again you can get a feel for this by asking a friend to push your leg inwards against the horse's sides. Having your leg held in the right position will give you a feel for what you are trying to achieve. Until your muscles are used to this movement it will seem difficult, and you will not be able to apply a very strong leg aid. Your thigh and calf muscles will need to stretch and strengthen before your leg aids can be truly effective.

COMMON FAULTS

Picture one shows a bad leg position – see how the lower leg is pushed forward and away from the horse's sides. This is usually a result of the rider adopting an armchair seat in the saddle. It leads to the leg aids being incorrectly applied.

In picture two, instead of squeezing inwards this rider has drawn her lower leg back and, as a result, her weight has come out of her heel and her heel is higher than her toe. At this point it is very easy for the stirrup iron to slip off your foot. This type of leg aid is ineffective – the lower leg is simply being brushed backwards across the horse's side and is not being applied to the more sensitive area just behind the girth. A horse that is ridden like this will never be able to differentiate between an aid to move forwards and an aid to move his quarters, when the rider's lower leg is applied further back behind the girth.

Lungeing Exercises

LUNGE LESSONS

The handler keeps a contact with the horse via the lunge line. The lunge whip can be used behind the horse's hindquarters to encourage him to move forwards, or it can be flicked towards his shoulder to keep him out on the circle. Both rider and handler should wear a riding hat; the handler should also wear gloves.

One of the best ways to encourage an independent seat is to be lunged. When the horse is lunged, the handler on the ground can control the horse's speed and direction, leaving you free to concentrate fully on your position. Lunge lessons are given at most riding establishments. It is important that the horse you ride is calm and steady on the lunge, and that the person who is lungeing you is capable and confident in what they are doing. A lungeing cavesson should be used over the horse's usual bridle. This is like a padded headcollar with a reinforced piece on the noseband which has rings attached to it. These take the lunge line. The handler should maintain a position which allows the lunge line, the lungeing whip and the horse to form a triangle.

The voice rather than the lunge whip should be used to ask the horse to move forwards. The lunge whip should only be used to back up the voice if the horse does not respond, and then should be moved quietly so that the horse does not suddenly shoot forwards. He should be allowed to settle into a steady rhythm; this will make it easier for you to relax and find your balance. Both horse and rider should be allowed periods of rest during these exercises.

Lungeing should only ever take place on a secure surface. If you only have a field and it is hard and rutted, or deep and wet, the horse is likely to injure or strain his tendons if he is made to work on it. Lunge lessons should not last for more than 20–30 minutes, and work should be carried out in both directions. Working on a circle is tiring and stressful to the horse's limbs, and once you are tired or sore you will not be able to do anything more to improve your position. If anything, it will get worse as you tense up with effort. If you are struggling, it is much better to stop than to keep on until you reach the point of exhaustion or frustration.

RIDING WITHOUT STIRRUPS

Although work without stirrups is usually carried out on the lunge, or in an arena or *manège*, if you have the opportunity to hack out regularly, it is worth making yourself ride for a few minutes each time without stirrups. Normally, the stirrups would be crossed over in front of the saddle so that they don't bang against the horse's sides, but this is not advisable out on a hack in case you need the stirrups back in a hurry. You should only ride without stirrups on a hack at walk. At this pace they should not swing so much that they knock the horse's sides or elbows. Equally, you can quickly slip them back on if necessary. After only a few minutes of riding without stirrups, when you put your feet back in them they often feel too short – that is the time to let the stirrup leathers down a hole so that gradually you can ride at a longer length.

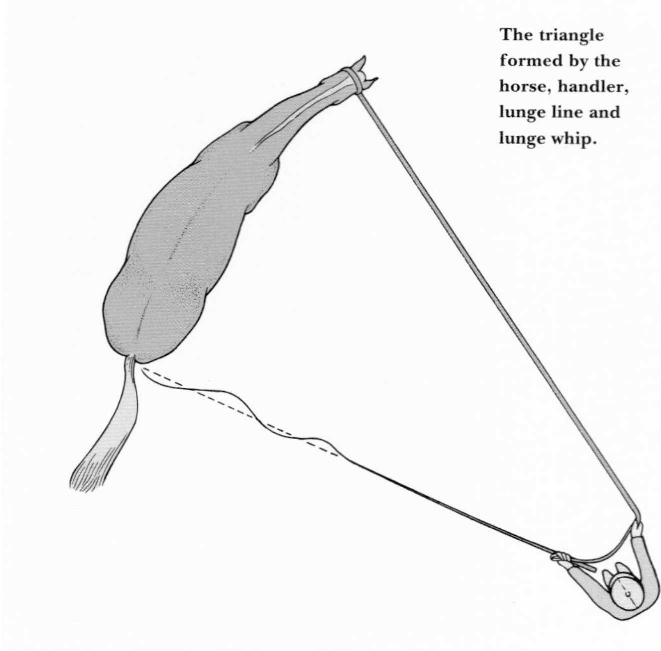

The triangle formed by the horse, handler, lunge line and lunge whip.

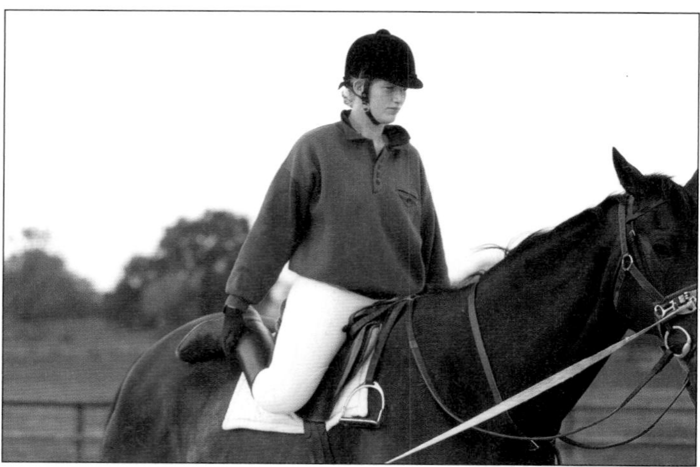

To help stretch the thigh muscles, practise this simple exercise. Bring your feet up under your bottom and hold them in position with a hand around each ankle. This has the added advantage of helping you to keep your shoulders up and straight, and it automatically puts your seat in the correct position in the saddle. When you take your stirrups back after these exercises, you may feel that you want to lengthen the stirrup leathers. This is a good sign and is the start of the path towards attaining the classical position.

STRENGTHENING EXERCISE

1 Practise riding without stirrups and, to help build up your confidence and balance, spread your arms out to either side.

2 To help strengthen and supple your upper body, twist first round to the left...

3 ... and then back to the right.

HOLDING THE LUNGE LINE

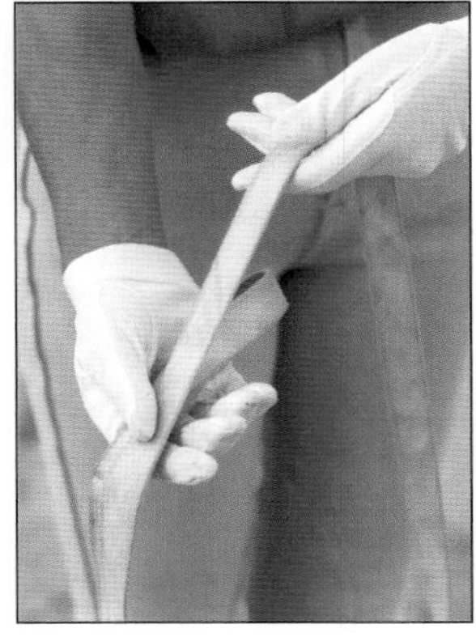

1 It is important that whoever is going to lunge you knows how to do this safely and correctly. One of the biggest risks to the handler is getting his or her hands trapped in the lunge line should the horse panic and try to run away. The safest way to hold the lunge line is not to loop it around your hand but to do the following: lay the end of the lunge line across the palm of your hand. Do not put your hand through the loop that most lunge lines have on the end.

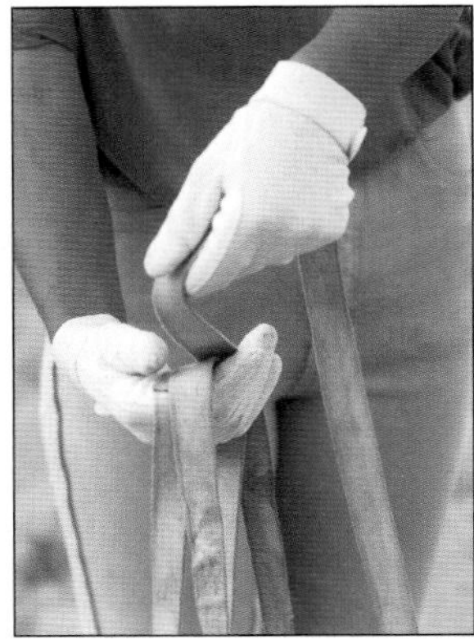

2 Lay the lunge line, in equal loops, backwards and forwards across the palm of your hand. Continue to loop the line across your palm until it is the desired length, i.e. you are the distance you want to be away from the horse.

3 Now you can close your hand around the loops and keep a contact with the horse as he moves. If you want to let more lunge line out so that the horse can work on a larger circle, just open your hand and allow one loop to fall away. If the horse did panic and pull away you could close your hand tight around the line and try to stop him. But if he has built up too much speed and is determined to get away, the lunge line will be pulled out of your hand, and you will be free of it. If it is looped around your hand and the horse bolts, the loops will tighten like a noose around your hand. You will either be dragged or have your fingers torn off. Either way the horse will escape if he is determined, so it is better to let him go if you have to and at least remain in one piece and in a position to retrieve him.

"ROUND THE WORLD" EXERCISE

LEFT
The horse or pony you learn to ride on should be a sensible and calm one. This young rider is making the most of her pony's kind nature to have some fun, whilst also increasing her confidence on horseback. Exercises such as this one – called "Round the World" – should only ever be carried out on a quiet pony and with someone on the ground to hold the pony's head.

Mastering the Paces

Having climbed aboard, it is now time to experience some forward motion! The first thing you will suddenly be aware of is just how much the horse moves underneath you. The horse has four legs to operate and, at walk, these move one at a time. As each shoulder or hindquarter swings the appropriate leg forward, you will feel it. Each pace that the horse can offer you – walk, trot, canter and gallop – will give a different sensation of speed and motion, and you must learn to absorb it, and to remain balanced on the horse at each pace, whilst still maintaining the correct, classical position. To the outside eye, horse and rider should appear to be moving as one.

Absorbing the Movement

In an attempt to follow the movement of the horse, many riders end up trying too hard and do too much with their bodies. This, instead of creating a picture of harmony, actually looks completely unco-ordinated; the horse appears to be moving to one beat, and the rider to another. It is also uncomfortable.

The first thing to bear in mind is that your seat belongs to the saddle which, in turn, belongs to the horse's back. The saddle will mimic the movement of the horse's back and you should imagine that your seat is glued to the saddle. Sit deep in the saddle, with your weight taken equally on each seat bone. When striving for a deep, balanced seat, it sometimes helps to imagine that your legs have been cut off, about half way down the thigh; therefore it is the top half of the thighs and the seat itself which embrace the saddle. By sitting up straight and keeping the shoulders balanced above the hips, your weight sinks down into the saddle. This allows the legs to hang long and loose around the horse's sides, with the foot supported softly by the stirrup. The arms follow the movement of the horse's head and neck, and this is achieved by keeping the elbows soft and relaxed with your shoulders remaining still. If your seat is glued to the saddle, and your shoulders, head and neck remain still, the only part of your body that is free to move is the area between your hips and your ribcage. So the hips and stomach are rocked gently forwards and back by the movement of the horse. It is by being soft and supple through the hips, the lower back and the stomach that you are able to move as one with the horse. Always remember that it is the horse that moves your body, and so your body must remain relaxed to allow it to be moved by the horse. You should not create any additional movement yourself – this is most likely to happen if your body is tense.

THE WALK

The walk is described as a four-time pace because the horse moves each leg individually; if you listen to his footfalls you hear four separate hoofbeats. In trot, the horse moves his legs in diagonal pairs, so this is known as a two-time pace.

The sequence of footfalls in walk is as follows: outside hind, outside fore, inside hind, inside fore. The horse should take strides of equal length and he should look energetic and purposeful. If you watch a horse walking you will see that his whole body is in action; the movement flows through the muscles of the hindquarters, up over the back, and through the shoulders and the neck. The horse should look supple, athletic and powerful. Although the walk is the horse's slowest pace, he does use his neck to quite a degree, which means you must be particularly aware of allowing your arms to follow the movement so that you do not restrict the horse.

MOVING WITH THE HORSE

At walk the rider allows his hips and stomach to be rocked gently forwards and back by the push of the horse's hindquarters beneath him. Notice how the rider is maintaining a straight line from the elbow, through the lower arm, and down the rein to the bit. A light but constant contact is kept with the horse's mouth by allowing the arms to follow the natural movement of the horse's head and neck as he walks.

Transitions

Changing pace on a horse, whether it be from halt to walk, or from trot to canter etc, is known as performing a transition. Like changing gear in a car, whether you are increasing or decreasing pace, it should appear smooth and effortless.

Transitions are achieved by a subtle balance of the use of the hand and leg. Use your lower leg to activate the horse's hindquarters, which is where his power comes from. You can then use your hands to guide that power in whichever direction you wish.

■ REFINING THE USE OF THE LEGS AND HANDS

To walk forwards, squeeze your legs against the horse's sides and allow your hands and arms to be drawn forwards. If the horse ignores you, give him a sharper nudge with your heels. If this is ignored, give him a tap with the schooling whip or stick behind your lower leg. If you have to do this, you must be very quick to keep the soft forward movement of the hands. The horse may jump forwards if he is tapped with the whip, and he must not then be punished by being pulled in the mouth. Remember to reward the horse for obeying and going forwards. With practice, he will listen to you and a squeeze with your legs will be sufficient.

To halt the horse, squeeze with the legs but do not allow your hands to be drawn forwards so much. The horse will realize that his forward movement is being blocked and will either slow down or shorten the steps he is taking. Continue to decrease the forward movement of the hands until, if necessary, they are returned to the normal halt position and do not move forwards at all. This complete blocking will halt the horse.

As with the leg aids, the long-term aim is to use as light and gentle an aid as possible. To begin with you may have to block completely with your hands but, with practice, the horse will become more attentive until only a slight reduction of the forward movement of the hands is enough to halt him.

HALT TO WALK AND WALK TO HALT

1 At halt the rider still keeps a light contact with the horse's mouth and lets the legs hang long and loose by the horse's sides. The lower leg is in contact with the horse but is not actively doing anything. Note how a straight line is maintained from the shoulder to the hip to the heel. The position would be better still if the rider kept her chin up – a common fault of many riders is the tendency to look down!

2 To go forwards to walk, the rider squeezes both legs against the horse's sides and, at the same time, allows the hands and arms to go forward to follow the forward movement of the horse's head and neck. Once the horse is walking positively forwards the rider allows her legs to relax against the horse's sides. The arms and hands are drawn gently forwards and back by the movement of the horse's head and neck. This movement is led by the horse. The rider does not pull back on the reins.

3 To prepare to return to halt, the rider squeezes her legs inwards against the horse's sides and at the same time reduces the degree to which she allows her arms to follow the movement of the horse's head and neck. On a well-schooled horse this very slight blocking of the free forward movement will be enough to halt the horse.

4 On a less responsive horse the rider will have to continue to reduce the degree to which the hands follow the horse's head and neck to the point, where they are held still, which will completely block the forward movement. As soon as the horse halts, the rider should soften the hands as much as the horse will allow whilst still remaining at halt. Until the horse halts, the rider's legs remain actively against the horse's sides, gently pushing him up into the hands. Once he has halted, the legs relax and remain gently in contact with his sides.

COMMON FAULTS

If the rider decides to do nothing with her legs and simply pulls on the reins in an effort to slow down you can see what happens – the horse resists the request to slow down and throws his head and neck in the air in order to fight the pull of the rider; this is described as the horse hollowing against the rider. The whole picture looks tense and uncomfortable. The rider must first ask with the legs and then only use as much hand as is absolutely necessary to achieve the desired result.

Changing Direction

You cannot continue in a straight line forever, so once you are confident with forward movement you must be able to change direction.

When the legs are used together either on or fractionally behind the girth, and the hands are also moving together, the horse is kept in a straight line. To go around a corner, or to turn, the horse has to bend through his body. In order to achieve this, the hands and legs must be used individually. If one leg is allowed to slide further back behind the girth this will make the horse move his hindquarters away from the leg in question, i.e. if your right leg is used behind the girth, the horse will be encouraged to move his quarters across to the left, and vice versa. So, to make the horse turn, one leg is used in the normal place to encourage him to keep moving forwards, and the other leg is used further back behind the girth to control the hindquarters.

The horse should never be turned sharply – any turn should be thought of as part of a circle, so to turn right think about circling away to the right. Then the right hand and leg are referred to as being on the inside, while the left hand and leg are now on the outside.

TURNING RIGHT

1 Horse and rider are about to turn off a straight line and away to the right. The rider has moved the right hand a few inches away from the withers, towards the right. This is called opening the hand, and it invites the horse to turn his head and neck to the right in preparation for the turn.

2 The rider's inside (right) leg is used on the girth to keep the horse moving forwards; the outside (left) leg is used behind the girth to stop his quarters swinging too far to the left. The left hand and arm soften so that the horse keeps bending to the right. The right hand stays to the right of the withers, inviting the horse to move that way.

3 As soon as the horse has turned as far round to the right as the rider requires, the hands and legs return to their normal position.

4 To turn right, the rider's inside (right) hand is moved a little to the right of the withers – opening the hand; the inside (right) leg remains on the girth, encouraging the horse to move forwards.

5 The outside hand is softened so that the horse can bend his head and neck away to the right, whilst the outside leg is used behind the girth to control the degree to which the hindquarters move.

TURNING LEFT

1 To turn left, the rider opens the inside (left) hand a few inches to the left to invite the horse to turn his head and neck in that direction.

2 The outside (right) hand is softened forwards to allow the horse to turn away to the left, while the outside leg is used back behind the girth to control the swing of the hindquarters.

3 As soon as the horse is heading in the required direction, the rider's hands and legs return to the normal position.

4 To turn left the inside (left) hand is opened out to the left to ask the horse to turn his head and neck to the left, while the inside leg is used on the girth.

5 The outside (right) hand must be allowed to soften forwards to allow the horse to turn away to the left. The outside leg is used behind the girth in order to control the hindquarters.

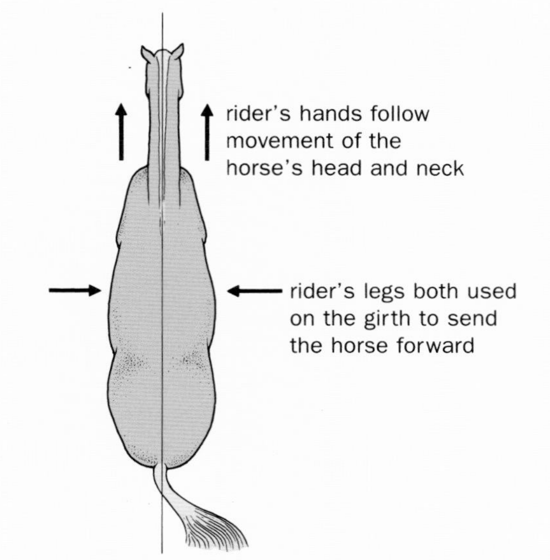
rider's hands follow movement of the horse's head and neck
rider's legs both used on the girth to send the horse forward

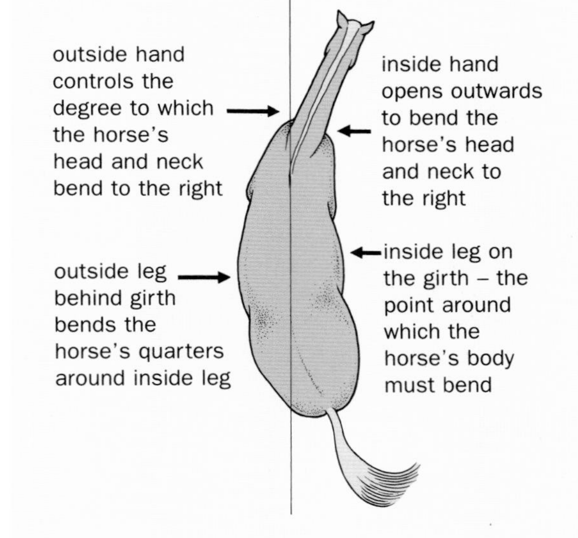
outside hand controls the degree to which the horse's head and neck bend to the right
inside hand opens outwards to bend the horse's head and neck to the right
outside leg behind girth bends the horse's quarters around inside leg
inside leg on the girth – the point around which the horse's body must bend

RIGHT
Riding forwards on a straight line.

FAR RIGHT
Bending the horse so that he can turn right.

Forwards to Trot

The trot is the next pace that the horse can offer you, and many new riders find this one of the hardest to master. When the horse trots the rider feels a far more powerful force of movement from beneath than is experienced at walk. In order to feel comfortable at this pace, you must try to keep your body relaxed so that it absorbs the movement, rather than tensing up and being bounced around by the horse.

■ THE RISING TROT

When the horse trots you can either sit deep in the saddle the whole time – which is known as the sitting trot – or you can rise out of the saddle with each stride, in time with the beat of the trot. It is far less tiring – and more comfortable – for the new rider to learn the rising trot, than it is to master the sitting trot. Once you feel at ease at this pace, and are able to stay relaxed and balanced, then is the time to practise the sitting trot.

When the horse trots, he is springing from one diagonal pair of legs to the other. To rise to the trot, allow the spring from one pair of legs going forwards to lift your seat out of the saddle. The seat returns to the saddle as the other pair of legs springs forwards. So as the horse moves each pair of legs in a one-two, one-two, one-two beat, you are sitting and rising to the same beat: up-down, up-down, up-down.

THE TROT

The trot is a two-time pace – the horse springs from one diagonal pair of legs to the other. If you listen to his hoofbeats, you only hear two footfalls within each complete stride. The outside hind and the inside foreleg move forwards together; this is followed by a brief period of suspension, and then the inside hind and outside foreleg move forwards as a pair.

PRACTISING THE RISING TROT

1 Rising to the trot can be practised when the horse is stationary. The rider sits in the normal classical position, attempting to keep the knee-joints in particular as long and relaxed as possible. Keeping the lower legs as still as possible, the rider should think of just allowing her hips and stomach to swing forwards.

2 The seat only comes out of the saddle enough to allow the seat bones to be clear of the saddle. The hips are then allowed to return lightly to the normal sitting position. The shoulders and arms remain still – the rider should think of allowing the hips and stomach to swing forwards and up towards her elbows.

■ RISING ON THE CORRECT DIAGONAL

When riding in rising trot in a circle, the rider is meant to rise in time with a particular diagonal pair of the horse's legs. The easiest way to explain what this entails is for you to look down and watch the horse's outside shoulder for a few minutes once you are in trot. You should be rising out of the saddle as the outside shoulder goes forwards. As it comes back, you should sit again.

The reason for bothering to rise on the correct diagonal will become clear later when you are concerned with improving the quality of the horse's work. The horse will find it easier to balance himself on a turn or circle if the rider is in the saddle when the inside hindleg and the outside foreleg are touching the ground. As the horse uses his legs in diagonal pairs, this is achieved by sitting as the outside shoulder comes back, and rising as it goes forwards. When you change the rein and circle in the opposite direction, it follows that you must also change the diagonal, i.e. rise as the new outside shoulder goes forwards. Changing the diagonal is achieved by sitting for an extra beat before rising again. So instead of sit-rise, sit-rise, you would sit-rise, sit-sit-rise and this will put you on the correct diagonal.

RIGHT
In sitting trot the rider retains the correct classical position, allowing her stomach and lower back to absorb the movement of the horse. Note the straight line through the shoulder, hip and heel, as well as the line from the elbow, down along the rein to the bit.

COMMON FAULTS

A common mistake in rising trot is actively to try to push the body up and down. This causes the shoulders and arms to bob up and down, which is disconcerting and uncomfortable for the horse as it is his mouth which suffers if there is excessive movement of the hands and arms.

Another common mistake in rising trot is for the rider's shoulders to tip forwards. This puts the rider off balance and means the hands are often rested on the horse's neck in an effort to regain balance. If the hands are resting on the neck, they cannot keep a soft but continuous contact with the horse's mouth. The shoulders must stay upright, just as they do when the rider is stationary; only the hips should move forwards. If the shoulders remain balanced and in line with the rider's heels, the rider will not be pushed off balance by the movement of the horse.

THE SITTING TROT

In sitting trot you should remain sitting deep in the saddle, maintaining the same classical position as when stationary and at walk. The movement of the horse is absorbed by the stomach and lower back, so that you remain deep in the saddle without being bounced up and down. As you feel the horse's legs springing forwards underneath you, try to think of allowing your ribcage to sink down towards your hips. This means that the stomach and lower back act like a concertina: as the horse springs along in trot the stomach and lower back are either contracting or expanding to absorb the movement. You must stay relaxed so that your legs can hang long and loose by the horse's sides, and your arms can still stay soft and maintain a light contact with the horse's mouth. It helps to make a conscious effort to keep breathing – you would be surprised how many riders hold their breath as soon as they concentrate too hard on something. Steady breathing helps you relax.

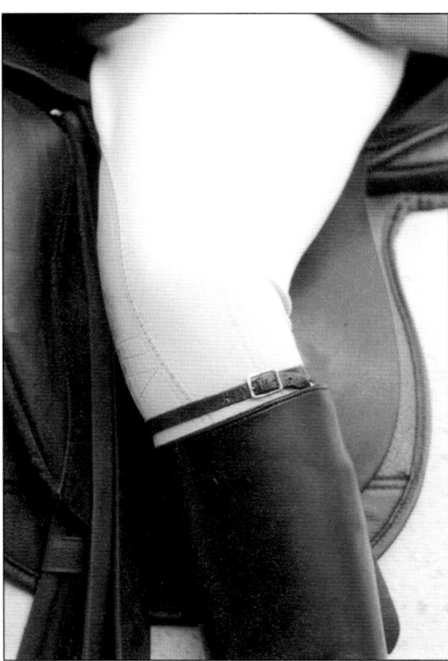

In sitting trot the knees should be long and loose.

Gripping with the knee makes your seat insecure.

COMMON FAULTS IN THE SITTING TROT

LEFT
Back to the armchair position! How not to sit – the lower leg has slipped forwards and the rider is now sitting on the back of her seat. The line from the shoulder through the hip to the heel has been lost.

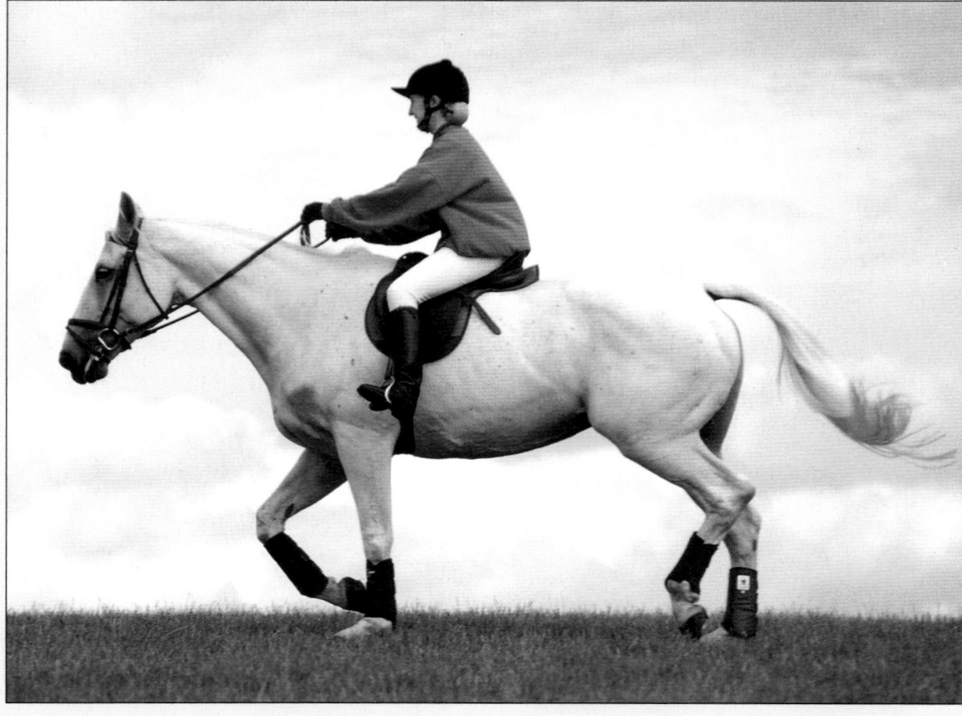

LEFT
If you fall into the armchair position your body is unable correctly to absorb the movement of the horse. You will be bumped up and down and, as a result, you will find your hands and arms bobbing up and down as well. It's uncomfortable for both horse and rider.

FROM WALK TO TROT TO WALK

1 The horse should be walking forwards actively and attentively before the rider asks for trot. See how the rider is keeping a contact with the horse's mouth without actually pulling or restricting him. The rider's legs are in contact with the horse's sides but are not being used actively. By keeping both the legs and the hands in contact with the horse in this way, you will be keeping open your lines of communication.

2 To ask for trot, the rider squeezes both legs actively against the horse's sides and softens the hands forwards so that the horse feels free to increase the pace and go forwards into trot.

3 Once the horse is settled in trot, the rider's legs and hands return to just being in contact with the horse. The leg is there to squeeze the horse forwards should he slow down, and the hand is there to guide him.

4 To return to walk the rider sits deep in the saddle and squeezes the legs against the horse's sides. (If the rider had been in rising trot, she would return to sitting trot to achieve this.)

5 Then, instead of softening the hands forwards, she keeps the hands still so that the horse's forward movement is blocked, bringing him back to walk.

6 As soon as the horse settles in walk, the hands and legs relax sufficiently to keep just a light contact.

On into Canter

It is at canter that the new rider will first experience the true exhilaration of riding a horse. The feeling of speed and power as the horse eats up the ground with each stride gives a real buzz. But despite the increased speed, the rider generally finds this a very smooth pace.

▮ LEFT
In canter, the rider sits deeply in the saddle and allows the hips to be rocked forwards and back by the movement of the horse. The arms and hands must stay soft and relaxed so that they can follow the movement of the horse's head and neck. Note once more the straight line through the ear, shoulder, hip and heel, and again from the elbow, down the rein to the bit. At all paces, the correct classical position should be maintained.

■ CANTERING ON THE CORRECT LEG

If you watch a horse cantering in a circle, he should appear to be leading each stride with his inside foreleg. In practice, the inside foreleg is actually the last leg to be moved by the horse within each canter stride, but to the observer it does appear to be leading the stride. When this is the case, the horse is said to be cantering on the correct leg, or the correct lead. So when cantering on the right rein, i.e. circling to the right, the inside (right) foreleg should appear to be leading; and, when cantering on the left rein, the inside (left) foreleg appears to be leading.

To ask the horse to canter forwards on the left lead you should use the inside leg on the girth and the outside leg behind the girth, whilst opening the left hand slightly to keep the horse bent left, and just keeping a feel on the outside rein to stop the horse simply accelerating in trot. To canter on the right lead the aids are reversed; the right leg is used on the girth, the left leg is used behind the girth, and the right hand is opened slightly to bend the horse to the right.

THE CANTER

The canter is a three-time pace, with the legs working in the following sequence: outside hind goes forwards, then the inside hind and outside fore go forwards together, followed by the inside foreleg. There is then a period of suspension when all four feet are off the ground, before the stride pattern is repeated – outside hind, inside hind and outside fore together, then inside fore.

Cantering on the correct leg. This horse and rider are circling on the left rein and you can see how the horse's inside (left) foreleg appears to be leading.

Cantering on the wrong leg. Here you can see that, although the horse is still circling to the left, it is the outside foreleg that appears to be leading the stride.

FROM TROT TO CANTER TO TROT

1 Before asking the horse to canter, the rider must go into sitting trot and be sure that the horse is working forwards actively and attentively.

2 To ask the horse to go forwards into canter on the left rein, i.e. to canter on the left lead, the rider sits deep, presses the inside (left) leg on the girth, but asks more actively with a squeeze or a nudge of the outside leg back behind the girth. This is because it is the horse's outside hindleg that starts off the stride, so the rider activates this leg by using her own outside leg behind the girth. The inside hand is opened out slightly to the left to encourage the horse to keep a bend to the left, but the outside hand may have to keep more of a feel than usual on the outside rein to prevent the horse from simply trotting faster. In this picture the outside hind is just about to take the first step of the canter stride.

3 Once the correct canter is established, with the left leg leading, the rider just keeps her outside leg in place behind the girth to encourage the outside hind to keep initiating the canter stride. The inside leg remains on the girth, so that the horse's body is bent around the rider's inside leg as they progress around the circle.

4 The arms and hands move forwards with the movement of the horse's head and neck, and the rider sits deep in the saddle, allowing her hips to be rocked by the horse's stride.

5 In order to return to trot the rider sits deep in the saddle and closes both legs against the horse's sides.

6 The rider reduces the degree to which she allows her hands and arms to move forwards with the horse's head and neck, so that the horse's forward movement is blocked. You may have to keep a slightly stronger feel in the outside hand to help bring the horse back to trot.

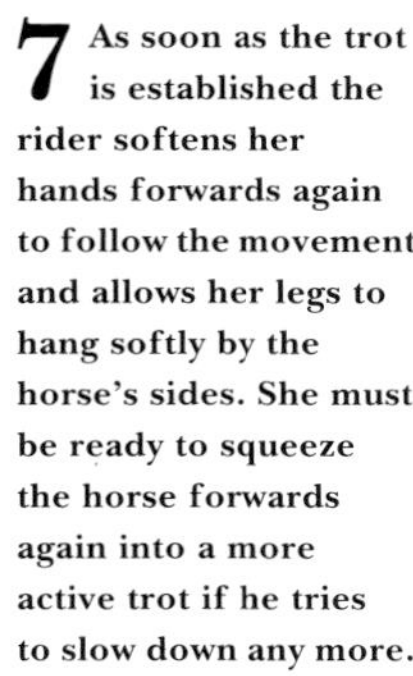

7 As soon as the trot is established the rider softens her hands forwards again to follow the movement and allows her legs to hang softly by the horse's sides. She must be ready to squeeze the horse forwards again into a more active trot if he tries to slow down any more.

COMMON FAULT

A common fault when asking the horse to canter is for the rider to tip forwards and look down over the inside shoulder. As soon as the rider's shoulders drop forwards she is pushed off balance, and then the hands tend to drop down on to the horse looking for support. The rider must stay sitting upright and use her hands and legs independently to ask for the transition to canter. Leaning forwards simply unbalances both horse and rider, and this makes the job harder.

CANTERING IN THE FORWARD SEAT

By taking the weight out of the saddle, the rider can encourage the horse to relax his back and put a little more life and swing into his paces. In canter this is often done out on a hack so that the horse is allowed to bowl along effortlessly under his rider. In a schooling session, the rider may take his weight out of the saddle to help the horse relax and use his back more. This is often done when the horse is being warmed up before he is asked to jump. It is called riding in the forward seat, and the rider simply lifts his seat bones out of the saddle and allows his weight to sink down into his heels and the stirrups. The rider will need to have gained a good sense of balance to do this, and will also need quite strong leg muscles, as it really stretches the backs of the calves. If you feel you keep tipping back in the saddle, you probably need to bring your shoulders slightly further forwards. If you feel you are tipping forwards on to the horse's neck, you need to raise your shoulders and check that your lower leg has not slipped backwards, which will in turn push your weight forwards.

Full Speed Ahead – The Gallop

Riding your horse at the gallop is an invigorating and exciting experience, but for it to be safe and enjoyable for both horse and rider you must develop a well-balanced, secure seat and feel confident about controlling your horse. Balance and security are important because if you lose balance at this pace you will either topple off, or end up hanging on to the reins. The horse will fight this pressure on his mouth and you may find yourself no longer in control. At this pace the horse is at full stretch and, to allow him to use himself fully, you should bring your weight up out of the saddle, push your seat further back and tuck your upper body in behind the horse's neck, very much like a race jockey but without quite such short stirrups.

At gallop the horse is at full stretch – he lengthens out his body and neck, and each leg is fully extended as it powers forwards over the ground. The rider tucks his upper body in behind the horse's neck so that the outline of the two is as streamlined as possible. The seat is taken out of the saddle, which means the rider's weight is dropped down into the heel and is also pushed further back to allow the rider's upper body to tuck in behind the horse's neck. The rider's arms extend forwards as the horse stretches his neck forwards within each stride. It is usual to ride with shorter stirrups when galloping as this makes it easier for the rider's weight to be lifted out of the saddle. The lower leg remains on the girth unless the stirrups are pulled up very short, in which case the lower leg is usually pushed forwards in front of the girth with the weight well down in the heel, as demonstrated by any race rider.

THE GALLOP

The gallop is a four-time pace with the legs working in the following sequence: near hind, off hind, near fore, off fore. Because the walk is also a four-time pace it is often said that if a horse has a good walk he will also be a good galloper. Watch race horses walking around at the track and you will appreciate this!

HIGH SPIRITS

Most horses enjoy a good gallop and will quite often let their riders know this by popping in a high-spirited leap or buck. If the rider is able to sit this out, it is no more than clean, harmless fun, but it becomes less amusing when it is sufficient to unseat the rider. When cantering or galloping, always keep a contact through the reins with the horse's mouth in order to help balance him. If the horse becomes playful and over-excited in his work, it is even more important to maintain this contact.

STOPPING A HARD-PULLING HORSE

It is often at the faster paces, canter and gallop, that the horse becomes over-excited to the extent that he is less responsive to his rider, particularly when it comes to slowing down again. Whilst in theory it should be possible to stop a horse at any pace by using the subtle balance of hand and leg, in practice the horse's excitement can override his desire to listen to his rider. If you find yourself struggling to slow down a galloping horse, make sure your lower leg is pushed forwards whilst still squeezing both legs against the horse's sides. The slightly forward lower leg position allows you to brace yourself against the stirrup. When a horse gets strong, it is easy to be pulled forwards out of the saddle; the lower leg slips back putting the rider in a very vulnerable position. Shorten up the reins as much as you can and put one hand, still holding the rein, tight into the horse's neck. Use the other hand

to keep a strong hold on the other rein and, by gradually giving and taking this rein, the horse will start to listen again and will slow down. If you keep a continuous pull on the rein, the horse will simply lean on the bit and become stronger still – give and take the rein to prevent him doing this. Circling the horse will also cause him to slow down.

Influencing the Horse

There is a subtle difference between learning to ride and actually influencing the horse. The new rider will spend the early period of training simply learning how to sit correctly balanced on the horse, and mastering the basic aids which will enable horse and rider to proceed at walk, trot and canter, to halt and to circle left or right. Until you achieve this balance and the resultant independent seat, you will be little more than a passenger on the horse. Once you have acquired an independent seat, you can concern yourself with how well or otherwise your horse is performing underneath you. Riding a horse should be a pleasure for both parties – the ultimate aim is to be mounted on a co-operative horse who will respond to your lightest instruction. When this is achieved, those observing you may well marvel at that closest of secrets – the one between a rider and his horse.

Control of the Horse

Use your hands and legs to control and influence the horse's shoulders, hindquarters, head and neck. When making a turn or circling, the horse's shoulders and hindquarters are controlled by the rider's use of the legs. When combined with the hands, this can be taken further still to move the horse in a number of different ways. The rider's leg can be used behind the girth to encourage the horse to move sideways (laterally) away from the leg, or to control the swing and direction of the quarters. The use of the leg on the girth encourages the horse to bend around the leg and allows the rider to control the horse's shoulder.

MOVING TO THE LEFT

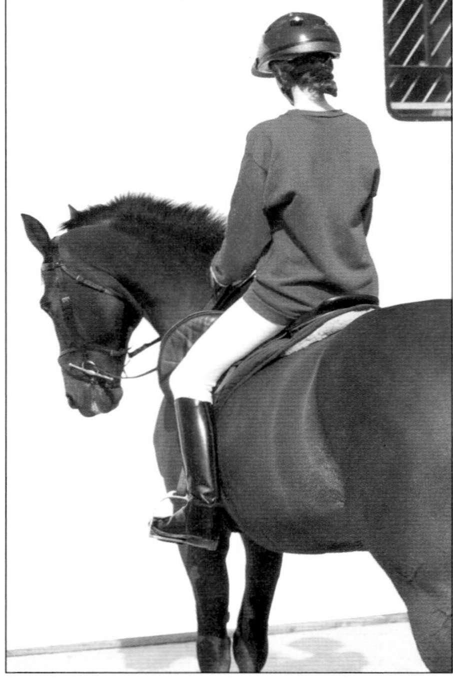

1 Whilst at halt, if the rider keeps a light feel on the outside rein (the right rein), opens out the inside rein a few inches and squeezes the horse's side with her inside leg on the girth while the outside leg remains relaxed, the horse will bend his head and neck to the left.

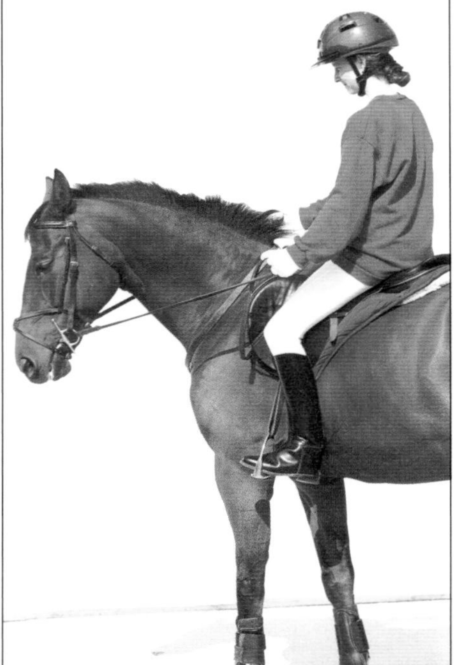

2 If the rider actively presses the outside (right) leg against the horse's side, but blocks the horse's forward movement by not softening her outside hand forwards, and just holds her inside leg against the horse's side behind the girth to keep the hindquarters still, the horse will step across to the left. His hindquarters remain still because the feel from the inside leg stops him stepping across with his hindlegs, but he will move his shoulders and forelegs across to the left. To straighten up again, the rider presses her left leg against the girth to push the horse's shoulders back over to the right. The left hand prevents the horse from stepping forwards, and the right hand is opened out to the right to invite the horse to step over to the right. The left leg stays back behind the girth to keep the horse's hindquarters still.

MOVING TO THE RIGHT

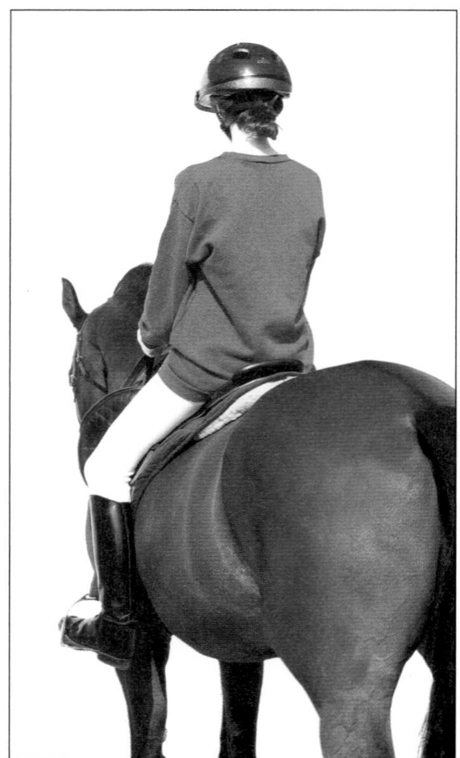

1 Similarly at halt, if the rider keeps a light feel on the outside (left) rein and opens the inside hand whilst pressing the inside leg against the girth, the horse will bend his head and neck to the right.

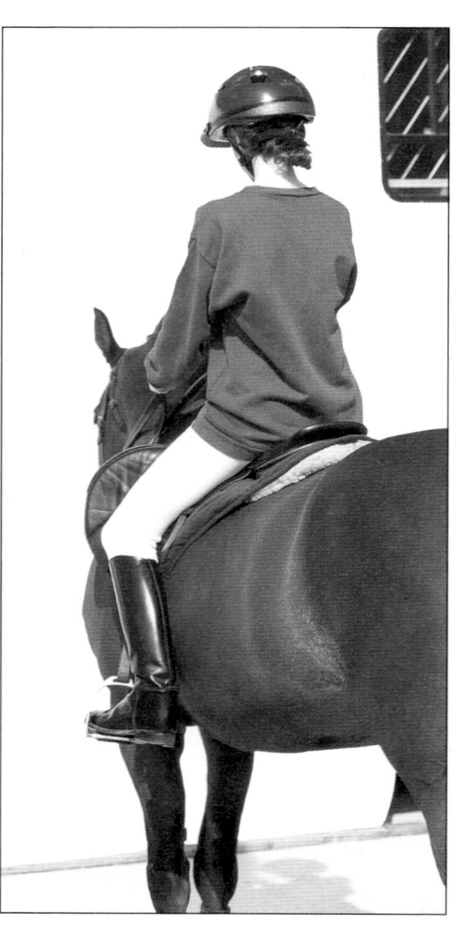

2 If the rider brings her outside (left) leg back behind the girth whilst blocking any attempt by the horse to move forwards with the outside rein, and keeps her inside (right) leg on the girth to keep the horse's shoulders stationary, then as she presses her outside leg against the horse he will swing his quarters over to the right. To straighten the horse up again the aids are then reversed – the right leg is used behind the girth to push the quarters back over to the left, whilst the right hand prevents the horse from stepping forwards. The left leg is used on the girth to make sure the shoulders remain still. Once the horse is straight again, the rider's legs and hands return to the normal position.

The Rider's Goal – To Lighten the Forehand

If you watch a horse showing off loose in a field you will see how proud and active he can look: his neck is high and arched, and he will use his hindquarters powerfully to produce round, elevated paces. As soon as a young or unschooled horse is asked to carry a rider, this picture can change dramatically: the horse's outline becomes flatter and longer, his steps lose their spring and he may lean on the bit by carrying his head and neck low, so that the rider always has a horrible, heavy feel in the hand; alternatively, he may carry his head high in an effort to evade the effect of the rider's hand on the rein and the bit. The rider has to teach the horse how to rebalance himself so that he can comfortably deal with the unbalancing effect of a rider on his back and regain his proud, elegant and light bearing.

An unbalanced horse usually takes advantage of the fact that the rider is holding the reins and will lean on the bit, so the rider is in effect helping to carry the weight of the horse. When this happens the horse is said to be on his forehand, i.e. more of the combined weight of the horse and the rider is carried on the horse's shoulders and forelegs than on the hindquarters and hindlegs. If you piled a lot of heavy weights on to the front of a car it would become heavy to handle, and similarly the horse becomes heavy in the rider's hand and is difficult to steer and control. If the weight is taken off the front of the car and loaded on to the back, suddenly the car is light and manoeuvrable in front.

The rider's aim is to encourage the horse to carry more of the weight on the hindquarters than on the forehand. In order to do this the horse has to lower his hindquarters and allow his hindlegs to step much further under his body. When he does this, his shoulders, head and neck are automatically raised and this is called lightening the forehand, or transferring the weight from the forehand to the hindquarters.

ENGAGING THE HINDQUARTERS

1 **A young or unschooled horse will carry himself in a long, low outline; see how low the head and neck appear to be, and how long and flat the overall picture is as a result.**

2 **The rider has used her legs and seat to encourage the horse to bring his hindlegs further underneath him, and just keeps enough of a contact on the rein to prevent the horse speeding up. The effect of the rider's legs pushing the horse up into the contact maintained by the hand is that the horse starts to bend and flex his hocks more, so that they can step further underneath the body. This is called engaging the hocks or hindquarters.**

3 **Various schooling exercises, combined with the horse learning to become more responsive to the leg and seat aids, gradually allow the rider to encourage the horse to use his hindquarters more.**

4 **The horse's outline is now rounder, and the forehand has been raised slightly higher than the hindquarters so that the horse is carrying more of the weight on the hindquarters and has lightened the forehand. Asking the horse to transfer the weight in this way, from the forehand to the hindquarters, is always brought about by greater use of the rider's legs, not by pulling the horse's head and neck up and in with the reins. The rein contact should remain soft and elastic, only blocking sufficiently to prevent the horse from speeding up when the leg is applied, instead of engaging the hindquarters more as is required.**

Control and Motion – Introducing Lateral Work

When first learning to ride, you are concerned primarily with being able to send the horse forwards into walk, trot, canter and gallop, and being able to halt. As your skills develop, you learn how to make the horse move sideways, either by moving his whole body or just his shoulders or hindquarters. This is known as lateral work, and is invaluable for a novice rider as it teaches him or her to feel and influence the horse's movement. For the horse, it is used as a suppling exercise and to encourage him to work more actively with his hindquarters.

Lateral movements include leg yielding, quarters-in (both described here), shoulder-in and half-pass (see Developing Lateral Work). All horses should be introduced to these exercises as part of their overall training programme. Practise them at walk and, once you have mastered control of the shoulders and hindquarters, you will realize just how manoeuvrable the horse can be.

■ LEG YIELDING

In this exercise the horse is asked to move forwards and sideways at the same time; the inside hind and foreleg cross over in front of the outside hind and foreleg.

■ QUARTERS-IN

In this exercise the horse continues walking in a straight line but he brings his quarters in to one side. If working on a sand surface, the horse's hoofprints would leave three lines of tracks: the inside line is formed by the inside hind, the middle line is made by the inside fore and the outside hind (which follow each other), and the outside line is made by the outside fore.

■ REIN BACK

The rein back is when the horse is asked, quite literally, to walk backwards. It should only ever be performed in walk although, when frightened, the horse will be quite capable of running backwards at a respectable speed!

Although the rein back is not a lateral movement, it is all part of teaching horse and rider the full extent of the control and motion they can achieve.

The horse should step backwards, in a straight line, moving his legs clearly and positively in diagonal pairs – inside fore and outside hind together, followed by outside fore and inside hind together.

LEG YIELDING

LEFT
To leg yield across to the left, as this rider is doing, she brings her right leg behind the girth which tells the horse to move sideways; her left leg remains on the girth, encouraging the horse to keep moving forwards as well as sideways. The right hand is opened a few inches which encourages the horse to keep a slight right bend through the body; the left hand keeps enough of a feel on the rein to prevent the horse bending too far to the left and, combined with the push from the right leg behind the girth, invites the horse to step sideways. To leg yield away to the right the aids are reversed – the left leg is used behind the girth, the right leg on the girth, the right rein keeps enough contact to invite the horse to step to the right, and the left rein is opened a few inches to encourage the horse to keep a slight bend through his body.

QUARTERS-IN

RIGHT
In these pictures the horse is being asked to bring his quarters into the left whilst continuing to walk forwards in a straight line. The rider uses her outside (right) leg behind the girth to move the quarters across slightly. Her inside leg stays on the girth to encourage the horse to keep moving forwards and to prevent the shoulders moving out of line. The left hand is opened slightly which, combined with the pressure from the left leg on the girth, encourages the horse to keep a bend through his whole body. The outside hand takes up enough of a feel to keep the horse's shoulder moving forwards in a straight line.

Quarters-in to the right is achieved by reversing the aids – the left leg is used behind the girth, her right leg, now the inside leg, stays on the girth, the right hand is opened slightly and the left (outside) hand takes up enough of a feel to keep the horse's shoulders moving forwards in a straight line.

REIN BACK

1 The rein back can only be successfully performed if the horse is calm and relaxed when at the halt.

2 The rider squeezes both legs against the horse's sides, but makes sure that she blocks the horse's forward movement by not allowing her hands to move forwards. Because the legs are applied actively, the horse knows he has to move somewhere. The rein contact is telling him he cannot go forwards and so he goes backwards. Some horses, as demonstrated here, understand what is required more easily if you apply both legs behind the girth, and then lift your seat bones off the saddle. This encourages the horse to step back underneath you as required.

3 Having taken one step back with one diagonal pair of legs, the horse proceeds to step back with the remaining diagonal pair. The horse should only be asked to step backwards for a limited number of steps. As a reward, allow him to walk forwards again whilst making a fuss of him.

Acceptance of Contact

Right from the start the horse has to learn to accept, without tension or resentment, the fact that the bit in his mouth is attached, via the reins, to the rider's hands, and that there will always be a light but sympathetic contact between the two. It is vital that you achieve a balanced, independent seat so that you are not tempted to hang on to the reins in an effort to balance yourself. Your priority is to learn to follow the movement of the horse's head and neck so that you are able to keep a constant but sympathetic contact with his mouth. In the early stages of training, you should not concern yourself with how the horse is carrying his head and neck, but only with learning to feel, follow and maintain the contact. Once the horse knows that the contact is constant, but kind, he will learn to accept it. Your elbows must remain soft and relaxed so that the contact can be maintained. It may be necessary to open the hands out a little wider than usual so that there is no obstruction – whatever the horse does with his head, you can follow it with your hands.

BASIC PRINCIPLES

Before you can hope to achieve a lightening of the forehand, there are a number of basic principles that you and your horse must master. These form the basis of all horses' training and progression, whether or not you are dealing with a horse who has never been properly schooled, and are as follows:

- Acceptance of the rein contact.
- Free forward movement.
- Maintaining a rhythm.
- Bend and flexion through the body.
- The use of half-halts to engage the hindquarters and rebalance the horse.

Once you have mastered these principles, you will be equipped with the means to ride your horse to the maximum of his potential.

COMMON FAULTS

How often have you seen a horse slopping along like this? The rider is not keeping a contact with the horse's mouth and, although she is actively using her legs, the horse is completely ignoring the aid and continuing to plod along in a lethargic and uninterested manner.

The horse must respond the same way in all paces. Here, in trot, we can see the result of the rider failing to keep a contact with the horse's mouth, and the horse blatantly ignoring the rider's leg aids. The rider is working hard with her legs whilst the horse is being extremely lazy with his!

FOLLOWING THE HORSE'S HEAD AND NECK

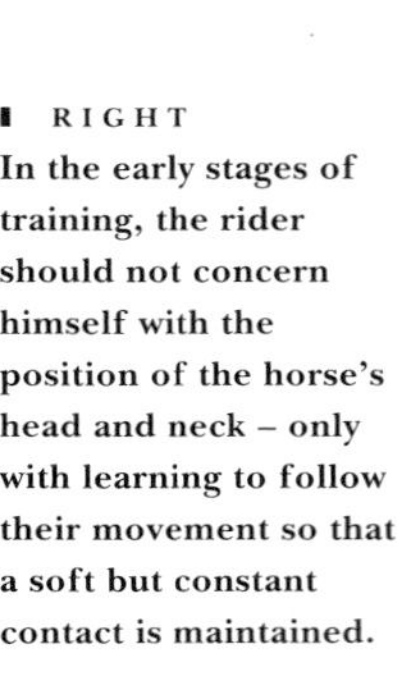

RIGHT
In the early stages of training, the rider should not concern himself with the position of the horse's head and neck – only with learning to follow their movement so that a soft but constant contact is maintained.

Free Forward Movement

The horse also has to learn to respect the rider's legs, i.e. when you use your legs against the horse's sides, he must respond by going forwards if both legs are used together or by moving away from the leg if used as a lateral (sideways) aid. The vast majority of problems experienced both on the flat and over jumps are caused by the horse ignoring, or being slow to react to, the rider's leg aids. The horse's first reaction should always be to move forwards. Once the horse respects the leg and is willing to maintain free forward movement without you continually having to reapply the leg aids, he is said to be in front of the leg and on the aids – he is attentive and ready to react to his rider's commands instantly.

In the early stages of training, you should use your voice combined with a squeeze from both legs to ask the horse to move forwards. If the horse does not respond, use your voice again, backed up with a sharp nudge with both heels against the horse's sides. If this is still ignored, squeeze your legs against the horse, use your voice to ask him to walk on and give him a tap with the schooling whip or stick behind your leg at the same time as the leg aid is applied. You must be ready to allow forward movement with the hands, particularly if the horse jumps forward when the schooling whip is used. As soon as he moves forwards, reward him by praising him verbally. You should then relax your legs against the horse's sides. As soon as he slows down again, repeat the process. Gradually the horse will learn to respond to the first light aid.

KEEPING A SOFT CONTACT

1 **Here the rider has shortened her reins sufficiently to keep a contact with the horse's mouth. She has applied the leg again and backed it up with a tap from the schooling whip. Already the picture is one of greater alertness and activity.**

2 **The rider maintains the contact and uses the leg once more to ask the horse to walk on a little more energetically.**

3 **This time the horse responds instantly; the rider's leg can relax and the horse maintains the forward movement without further nagging. Note how the horse's outline is now much rounder and shorter as he begins to lighten his forehand.**

4 **In trot, the rider takes up contact with the horse's mouth and backs up her leg aids with a tap from the schooling whip.**

5 **Immediately the horse offers much more in the way of forward impulsion. Now that he is thinking forwards, see how he lengthens his steps and voluntarily raises his head and neck into a rounder, shorter outline.**

6 **The rider can relax her legs and enjoy the free forward movement that the horse is offering her. But as soon as he drops back from this page, the rider starts the process over again.**

Maintaining a Rhythm

Now that the horse accepts the contact and moves forward willingly from your leg, both you and he need to learn to maintain an even rhythm in all your work. This rhythm must not be too slow or the work will lack impulsion and power; neither must it be too fast or the horse will tend to become unbalanced and will be pushed on to his forehand. Aim for a rhythm in each pace which gives you the feeling of free forward movement without feeling rushed. The ultimate aim is to use a light squeeze from the legs to ride the horse up into this rhythm; then to relax and enjoy the experience whilst the horse willingly maintains the rhythm, without continual nagging from either hand or leg.

Once the horse is responding quickly to the leg you are half way there. Some horses have naturally rhythmic paces and will automatically maintain the rhythm. Others will need a reminder from leg, voice and/or schooling whip to keep up to the rhythm, or they may need to be slowed down. Having got the horse thinking forwards, be careful not to dampen his goodwill by restricting him with the reins if he goes too fast. The use of a neck strap to slow the horse is a better method to use; it prevents the horse from learning how to lean on the bit or to fight you by shortening and tensing his neck.

By pulling on the neck strap instead of blocking with the reins, you can slow the horse down. Practise in the arena, first using the strap to bring the horse from walk to halt, and then from trot to walk etc. Once the horse understands its use, this method can be used to steady him within any pace. But remember that you must still use your legs and voice, if necessary, in the same way as you would do if you were going to use the rein contact to slow down.

USING THE NECK STRAP

1 **Here the rider is introducing the neck strap by using it to bring the horse back from trot to walk. She has put the reins in one hand and holds the neck strap in the other.**

2 **The rider then uses her legs with a light squeeze against the horse's sides, whilst using her voice and a firm pull on the neck strap to slow the horse down. Although the rider wants to slow down, the leg is still applied because it encourages the horse to bring his hindlegs further underneath him so that he can keep his forehand light. If the leg is not used, the horse will simply shift his weight on to the forehand and will become heavy and unbalanced in the rider's hand.**

3 The horse comes back quite happily to walk without the need to block with the rein. He is rewarded with a pat and praise from his rider.

4 When working in trot, if the horse has a tendency to speed up out of the desired rhythm the rider can just loop a finger through the neck strap and take a pull on it until the horse slows the rhythm down again.

5 When the horse responds, the neck strap is released and he is praised by his rider.

Bend and Flexion

▮ BELOW
The horse is bringing his hocks well underneath himself, the hindquarters are lowered slightly and the poll and jaw are relaxed so that the front of the face is on the vertical.

In all the horse's work, the rider is striving to ensure that the horse's hindlegs follow in the same tracks as his front legs, i.e. his quarters are not allowed to swing out or his shoulder to fall in. This is referred to as straightness in the horse, which is a term that causes some confusion. For the horse to be straight, i.e. for his hindlegs to follow in the same tracks as his forelegs, when working on a turn or a circle he has to bend through his body; his whole body must form a slight, continual curve around the rider's inside leg. So in order to be straight the horse has to bend!

The degree of bend that the horse shows through his body is dependent on the size of circle or turn you are riding. For example, to ride a 65½ foot (20 m) circle the horse shows only a slight bend through his body, but to manoeuvre himself around a 33 foot (10 m) circle there will be a greater degree of bend.

ACHIEVING BEND

1 The rider should concentrate on making sure that the outside hand is really following the horse's movement in a soft, allowing way, whilst still maintaining a light contact. This ensures that the horse's forward momentum is not stifled by a restricting outside hand. The rider then opens the inside hand, setting it in the open position by simply tensing the muscles of the arm, not by pulling back on the rein. The inside leg is used on the girth to keep the horse pushed out on to the circle, and a firmer contact is only taken up on the outside rein if the horse falls in on the circle, i.e. allows the circle to get smaller and smaller. If he does this, the rider must keep pushing the horse out with the inside leg and draw him back out on to the original circle by using the outside rein.

2 The rider should now feel the horse bending through the body and neck; if the horse resists and does not respond by offering some bend through his body, the rider simply opens the inside rein out further and sets it there – still without pulling back on it. The inside leg is kept on, and should be backed up with a tap from the schooling whip if the horse continues to fall in on the circle rather than bend through the body.

3 As soon as the horse offers the bend, i.e. when you can see a glimpse of his inside eye and nostril, use both legs against his sides to encourage him to bring his hocks further underneath him and to flex through his topline. When you feel the horse relax his poll and jaw so that the nose is lowered and his face is on the vertical, soften the inside rein and allow it to follow the movement in the same way as the outside rein. Praise the horse verbally – this is his reward for yielding to your leg and hand. The horse is now beginning to work in self-carriage, i.e. he is carrying more weight on his hindquarters and is lightening his forehand. Note that his head and neck are higher and more arched than in picture one; this is a result of the hocks being brought further under him.

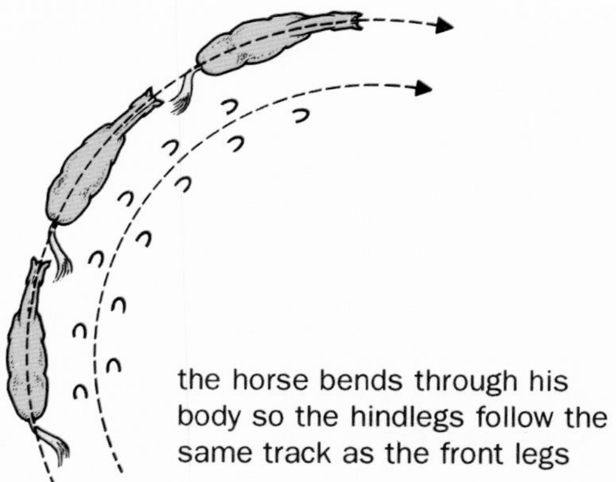

the horse bends through his body so the hindlegs follow the same track as the front legs

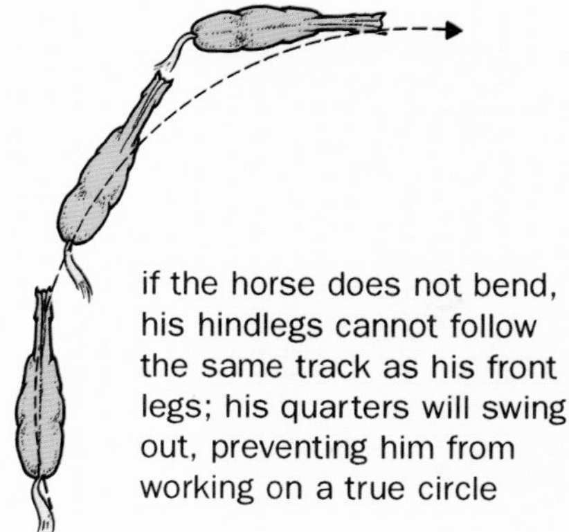

if the horse does not bend, his hindlegs cannot follow the same track as his front legs; his quarters will swing out, preventing him from working on a true circle

LEFT
How a horse goes around a corner.

The more the horse has to bend his body the more he has to use his hocks, and the inside hindleg in particular has to step much further across and under the horse's body in order to follow in the track of the inside foreleg. Having ridden simple turns and circles, you will know that the inside leg is used on the girth with an open inside hand to encourage the horse to bend around the inside leg, whilst the outside leg is used back behind the girth to prevent the quarters swinging out. The outside hand is used to prevent the horse bending his head and neck too much to the inside. On an unschooled horse the aids have to be exaggerated until he realizes what it is you are asking him to do. Once the horse is willing to offer you the bend through his whole body, you can ask him to flex right through his topline so that his whole outline becomes soft and round and he offers you no resistance whatsoever. The horse's topline describes the area from the top of the tail, over the hindquarters, back, withers and neck, and on up to the poll. When the horse flexes through his topline, his hindquarters are lowered as his hocks come further underneath him, he stays soft through his back, arches his neck and relaxes his poll and jaw so that the head is carried in a relaxed manner; the horse will lower his nose so that a vertical line could be drawn down the front of his face.

The horse should be introduced to this work in trot – it is very easy to stifle his forward momentum if it is first asked for in walk. Ride forwards into trot, bearing in mind the principles of having a horse who will respond happily to your leg and settle into a rhythm without being nagged by your leg or hand.

With time and practice, you will find that the horse will become more and more responsive to the request to bend and flex. After a while, you will not need to open the inside hand in such an exaggerated fashion; simply moving the hand over

OBTAINING THE CORRECT DEGREE OF BEND

The rider should only ask for a slight bend through the horse's body and neck, so that the outside of the horse makes a continual curve around the rider's inside leg. The rider only needs to see a glimpse of the horse's inside eye and nostril to know that the bend is correct.

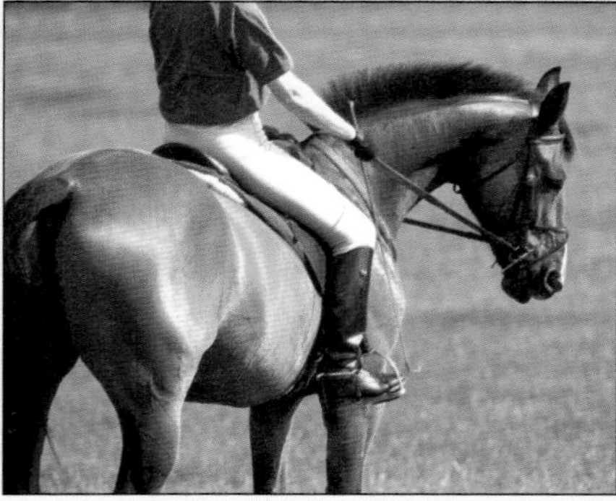

A common fault is for the horse to bend only through the neck from the withers, so that his body is still straight. In this position the horse can avoid having to step under himself more with his hindlegs, so his quarters will swing out as he goes around a corner. If his hocks are not underneath him, he can neither turn correctly nor flex through his topline when asked. The rider must use the outside rein to reduce the degree of bend in the neck, the outside leg to keep the hind-quarters from swinging out, and should reinforce the inside leg by tapping the horse with the schooling whip behind his or her lower leg.

Another fault is for the horse to tilt his head towards the inside. He is allowing the rider's inside hand to draw his nose to the inside but is ignoring the outside hand, so instead of bending through the neck and poll, the horse simply tilts his head to one side. More contact should be taken up with the outside rein to correct this.

BEND AND FLEXION – THE OVERALL PICTURE

1 The horse is ridden forwards into trot; the rider opens her inside hand and closes her inside leg on the girth to ask the horse to bend around her leg. The outside hand stays soft and allows the horse to move freely forwards, unless it has to be used to prevent him bending too much through the neck.

2 Here the horse has responded by curving his whole body around the rider's inside leg; see how the neck looks more relaxed and softer than in the first picture. This is because the horse is working willingly, without resistance.

3 Now that the rider has obtained the correct amount of bend, she closes both legs against the horse's sides to encourage him to be more active and step further under himself with his hindlegs. The horse is now flexing through his topline, i.e. his quarters are lowered and his back and neck are round and soft, which in turn raises and lightens his forehand.

4 The result is a picture of power with softness, and roundness with activity. See how the horse is bent around the rider's legs; he is also using his hindquarters actively which allows his forehand to be light and elevated. The increased power shows in the way the horse is stretching his front legs forwards, and matching this up behind by stepping under himself further with the hindlegs. His neck is carried higher and is more arched than in the first picture but he remains soft and light in the rider's hand. This is the start of self-carriage.

about an inch will be sufficient. Much further down the line in the horse's training, it will also only be necessary to take up a feel on the inside rein and to close the legs against the horse's sides to achieve bend and flexion.

Once the bend and flexion are established in trot, you can strive for the same result in both walk and canter. But the vital thing to remember with this training method is always to reward the horse by softening the inside hand the instant that he offers you even the tiniest degree of flexion and relaxation. To begin with it will be a case of working quite hard to ask the horse to bend and then to flex, followed by the reward of softening the inside hand as soon as he does so. He may only offer you the bend and flexion for a few strides before you have to repeat the process and ask again, but as he begins to understand what is wanted and his topline muscles up as a result of the work, he will offer it to you for longer periods.

Gradually you will be doing less asking and more rewarding; you will find yourself riding for longer with both hands soft so that the horse is working on a light contact. But you will need to be persistent and consistent in your training.

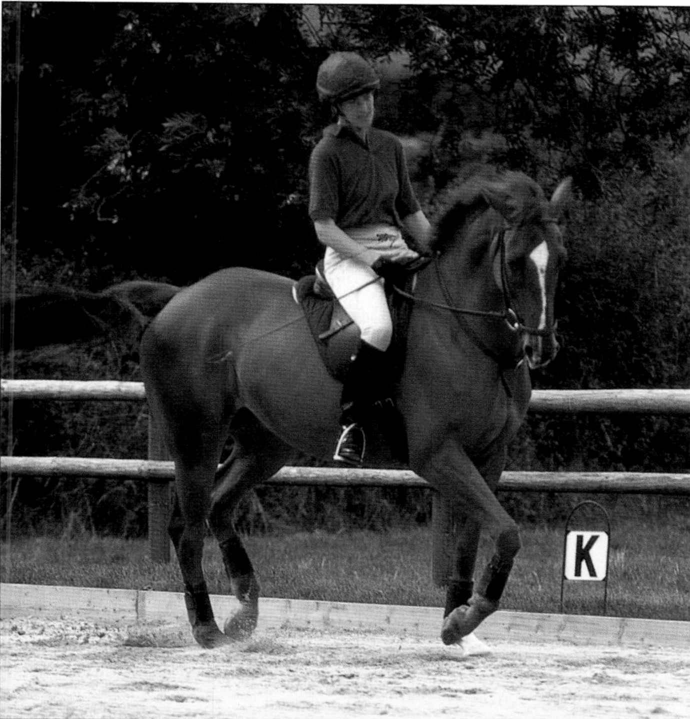

This horse has offered the rider the required degree of bend and flexion – note the arch of his neck and how his forehand appears lighter and higher than his hindquarters. You can see how he is really flexing his hock as he goes to step forwards with his hindleg and, most importantly, note how the rider has softened the inside rein so that the horse is holding this outline himself.

RIGHT
As soon as the horse responds to the rider's aids by bending through his body and then flexing through his topline, the rider must soften the inside hand and praise the horse verbally as a reward. This is the only way that the horse can know that he has responded to the aids in the right way.

RIGHT
While the inside hand is being softened, it can also be used to pat the horse's neck as further praise.

CORRECT USE OF THE INSIDE HAND

It is vital to ask the horse to bend his whole body around your inside leg by opening the inside hand and using the inside leg to keep the horse out on the circle. By using your hand and leg in this way, when the horse does respond he will produce a continuous bend through his body, neck and head. You may have to open your inside hand very wide, you may have to back up the inside-leg aid with a tap from the schooling whip, and your outside hand may have to take up more of a contact to stop the horse bending his neck too far to the inside, but, when the horse drops his resistance, relaxes and responds to these aids, he will be working correctly.

If the horse is slow to respond and refuses to offer the requested bend, it is very tempting to cheat! If you cross your inside hand over the horse's withers instead of opening the hand out and backing it up with the inside leg, the horse will instantly bend, but this bend will only be from the withers, it will not be right through the body. The crossing over of the rider's hand cuts off the horse's forward impulsion and cuts off the bend at the withers. So whilst you will be able to see the required glimpse of the inside eye and nostril, it will not be backed up by the correct use or position of the horse's hindquarters.

Crossing the inside hand over in this way is something that many riders, even at high levels of competition, are tempted to do. Some do not realize that it is a false measure and are satisfied with the false bend that the horse offers them, but their future is limited and their potential will not be fully realized. The temptation to cross the hand over is simply a sign that the horse is not respecting the rider's inside leg and/or the outside hand. So instead of giving in to the temptation, use it as a reminder to yourself to use your inside leg and outside hand correctly, even if this means not continuing with the exercise until the horse is prepared to move away from the inside leg (see Free Forward Movement). Always go back and correct the underlying fault if any training exercise is not progressing well. Never think that a short cut such as crossing the hand over or losing your temper will pay long-term dividends. Get the basics right and then you will have something permanent to build on. Be consistent, and be quick to praise your horse.

When asking the horse to bend, you must open your inside hand and use your inside leg.

If you cross your inside hand over, the horse will bend only from the wither.

Working Within Each Pace

Once both horse and rider have begun to understand the basics of a correct and acceptable way of working in each pace, the rider can take the horse's performance further. Having mastered the principles of free forward movement and obtained a degree of bend and flexion, you can further influence the horse by seeking to improve his paces. Plenty of horses have a pleasant enough way of going – they are able to maintain a round outline and a good rhythm in each pace – but this can be nurtured to produce a horse who puts real power and flair into his work. The use of half-halts and the introduction of lateral work help the horse to become more balanced and bring him nearer to working in self-carriage.

The Half-halt

The half-halt describes what happens when the rider closes his or her legs and hands momentarily against the horse. This serves to rebalance the horse in whatever pace he is working; the rider's legs push the horse's hindlegs underneath him further whilst the hand blocks any acceleration in pace which the horse might offer. The power that the legs have created is trapped by the rider's hand so that, instead of accelerating, the horse lowers his hindquarters and elevates his forehand slightly, becoming better balanced and lighter in the rider's hand. The half-halt can be used to (1) rebalance

HALF-HALT AT TROT

1 This horse is producing an active trot, and is maintaining a good outline; considering that he is only young the overall picture is soft and round. The rider is sitting quietly with the leg aid on, but only needs to maintain a light contact with the reins to the horse's mouth.

2 Now the horse is becoming unbalanced. He has probably overpowered himself with the push from his hindlegs and is poking his nose forward and starting to lean on the bit in an attempt to balance himself. The soft, round outline is disappearing.

3 To rebalance the horse, the rider uses a half-halt. She closes her legs on the horse's sides and pushes him up into her hand which, just for a second, is blocked against the horse's forward movement. In effect, the horse's body is squashed up together; his outline becomes shorter because his hindlegs are pushed further under his body so he is able to carry more weight on them, which in turn lightens and elevates his forehand.

4 The horse is rewarded by the rider relaxing the leg and softening the hand again. The softening, or giving of the rein, has been exaggerated in this picture to show that once the horse is using his hindquarters and hocks more actively he is able to carry himself and remain light in the rider's hand (self-carriage). So although the rein is completely loose, the horse is maintaining his own balance and a correct outline.

HALF-HALT AT CANTER

1 Here you can see how this horse is falling on to his forehand at canter. The impression in the picture is that the horse's weight is falling forwards and that he is leaning on the bit and, therefore, on the rider's hands for support.

2 The rider uses a half-halt to rebalance – she closes her legs against the horse's sides and blocks any forward acceleration with her hands.

3 Now the horse is balanced and light in the rider's hands. In picture one the hind-quarters appear higher than the shoulders (on the forehand). Now the shoulders are higher than the hind-quarters (the forehand is elevated and lightened).

the horse in any pace, (2) warn the horse that the rider is about to ask him to do something such as change direction and (3) build impulsion within each pace which can be stored to produce collected work, or released to produce extended work.

■ ACHIEVING THE HALF-HALT

Every horse will respond to a combination of hand and leg. You have to find out what combination is needed for your horse to obtain the desired result. Too much hand and the horse will either resist by throwing his head up, or he will simply slow down. Too much leg and the horse will try to accelerate and be pushed on to his forehand, which will unbalance him.

First, practise the half-halt at walk. At a given point, close your legs against the horse's sides and reduce the degree to which you allow your hands to follow the contact, as if you were about to halt. Just as you sense the horse is about to halt, soften your hands forward again, keeping your legs on the horse's sides so that he continues in walk. Once you get the feel of how much leg and hand is needed to produce this effect of almost but not quite halting the horse, you will have achieved a half-halt. Then practise it at trot and at canter. Each time, act as if to bring the horse back to the slower pace and, at the last second, allow him to continue in the original pace. Once you have mastered the half-halt, you can use it more subtly to forewarn the horse that he is about to be asked to do something different.

THE RIDER'S SEAT AS AN AID

The rider's body weight can be used, through the seat, to influence the horse – it can create or block the amount of impulsion that the horse is working with. If you think about using your seat as an aid too soon, there is a risk that you will simply become stiff in the body and will no longer be able to move with the horse. The use of the seat will develop naturally once you have achieved that all-important independent seat. If you think back to the use of the hands and arms, and how these stay soft and relaxed so that they follow the movement of the horse's head and neck, that is how you should think of your own body weight. Just as you can change the degree to which your hands follow the head and neck movement, for example when asking the horse to slow down or halt, your body weight can be used either to encourage the horse to use himself more actively, or to slow him down. Letting the seat move freely with the horse encourages active movement; reducing the degree to which the seat moves with the horse slows him down. The use of the body weight or seat should always be subtle and sympathetic. The feel for its correct use will come naturally once an independent seat has been achieved, and once you understand how and why you need to influence the horse.

TOO MUCH HAND

If the rider makes the mistake of using too much hand and not enough leg, the horse will soon let her know by not offering the desired response. Here the rider has tried to rebalance the canter by raising and pulling back with the hands, with no back-up from the leg. The horse responds by simply falling back into trot.

Developing Lateral Work

The shoulder-in and half-pass are the most useful lateral-work exercises in terms of encouraging the horse to use his hocks more actively and effectively underneath him. The mistake that many people make is to think of them simply as requirements of a dressage test. This is not how they should be viewed – lateral work is used to improve the horse's overall way of going. These exercises teach the horse to respond to different uses of the hand and leg, to be supple through his body, and to place his hocks further underneath him in an effort to carry more of his body weight on the hindquarters rather than on the forehand.

COMMON FAULT

A common mistake is for the rider to ask for too much angle so that the horse works on four tracks instead of three, i.e. each leg is put down in a separate track. The rider has crossed her inside hand over the horse's withers so that the horse is only bending from in front of the withers, through the neck, instead of through the body and neck. The whole point of the exercise has been lost; the horse is not supple through the body, only through the neck, and the hindlegs are not being encouraged to take any extra weight at all. To correct this mistake the rider needs to take up more contact in the outside hand to reduce the bend in the neck, use the outside leg to stop the quarters swinging round any further, and the inside leg to push the shoulders back towards the track which will reduce the angle of the horse's body until he is working correctly on three tracks.

■ SHOULDER-IN

The shoulder-in is similar to quarters-in, in that the horse moves on three tracks, but here it is the shoulders that are brought in, not the quarters, as the horse continues to move forwards. The footfalls are as follows: the inside track is made by the inside foreleg, the middle track by the outside foreleg and inside hindleg together, and the outside track is made by the outside hindleg.

It is quite difficult in shoulder-in for the new rider to keep the horse moving forwards in a straight line. The horse may try to swing his quarters out one way, or may drift sideways instead of holding the position and moving forwards in a straight line. If you are working in an arena it helps to do the following: as you bring the

SHOULDER-IN

1 It is easiest to practise lateral movement in an arena so that you have a straight edge to work along; here the rider is about to ride shoulder-in in trot down the long side of the arena. She has already ridden a 33 foot (10 m) circle in trot in the corner that she is just coming from. This circle gives the rider an idea of the correct amount of bend that the horse should hold throughout the shoulder-in. To start the shoulder-in she goes to ride another 33 foot (10 m) circle, but, as soon as the horse's front legs have left the track to start the circle, she uses the outside hand to prevent him continuing on the circle, and the inside leg to keep him moving forwards along the side of the arena.

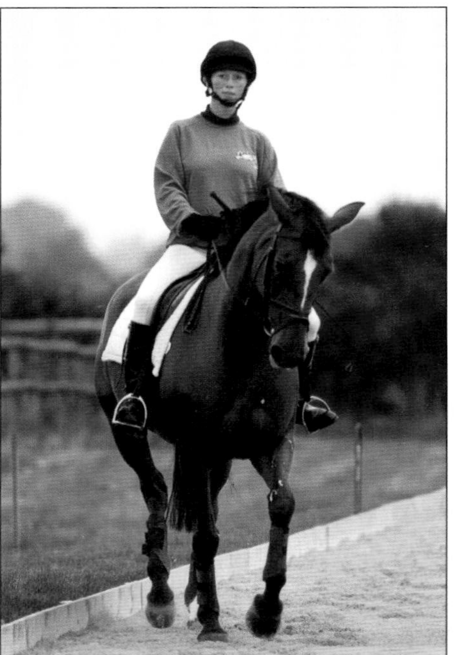

2 As the horse progresses down the long side of the arena in shoulder-in, you can clearly see how he is working on three tracks (inside fore, outside fore/inside hind, outside hind). This exercise encourages the horse to be supple as he has to maintain a bend through his body and neck; it also introduces the horse to the idea of carrying more weight on the inside hindleg. As the inside hindleg touches the ground, you can see that it is placed directly under the horse's belly and beneath the rider. So at this point the horse is carrying much of his body weight, as well as the weight of the rider, on that inside hindleg.

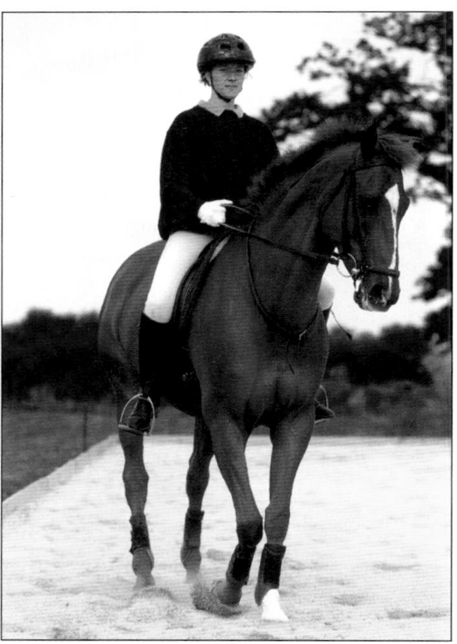

3 To help keep the horse moving forwards in a straight line whilst in shoulder-in, the rider should look straight ahead and think of her outside hip as pointing the way forwards.

HALF-PASS

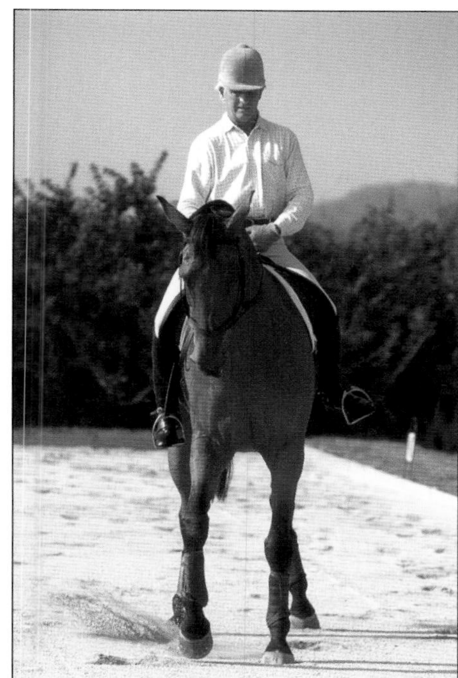

1 To ride the half-pass, shown here in walk, the rider would turn down the long side of the arena and ask the horse to go into shoulder-in. Instead of continuing in shoulder-in, he would then use the outside leg back behind the girth to push the horse's hindquarters across until they are almost directly in line with the shoulders. The outside leg stays in place telling the horse to move sideways, whilst the inside leg also keeps him moving forwards. The outside hand controls the degree of bend through the horse's body and neck whilst the inside hand remains open, inviting the horse to step forwards and sideways.

2 In half-pass the horse must remain bent around the rider's inside leg so that he is bent in the direction in which he is moving. In this picture, the rider's outside leg can clearly be seen in use behind the girth to push the horse sideways. Half-pass can be ridden in walk, trot and canter.

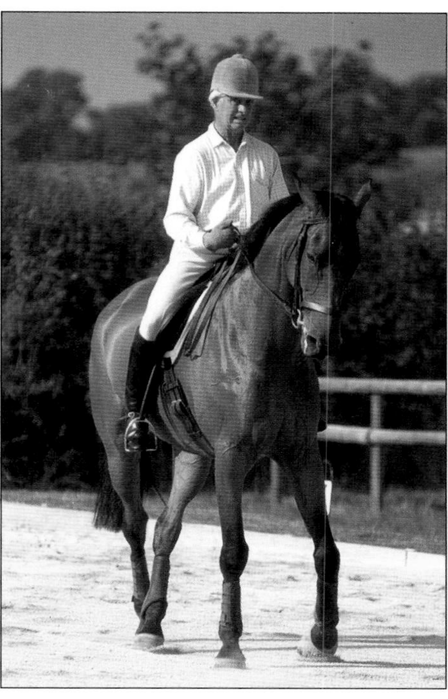

3 This picture shows how, in half-pass, it is the outside hindleg which has to come across and under the horse, thereby having to take the weight of both his own body and the rider's. The exercise also encourages the horse to be supple through his body and, in particular, through his shoulders.

horse's shoulders in off the track, make sure you are looking ahead yourself and think of your outside hip as a pointer; if you imagine keeping your hip moving forwards in a straight line, the horse's outside shoulder will move forwards on the same line. The correct position for the rider in shoulder-in is for the hips to stay parallel with the horse's shoulders, but for the shoulders to be held straight as if you are riding forwards in a straight line as normal. You should look straight ahead.

HALF-PASS

In half-pass the horse moves diagonally across the arena, taking good-sized steps forwards and sideways, and keeping his body bent in the direction in which he is moving. His shoulders are allowed to be just fractionally ahead of his hindquarters as he makes this movement. His outside hind and foreleg cross over in front of his inside hind and foreleg.

COMMON FAULT

A common mistake is for the horse to try to make life easier for himself by not **maintaining the correct bend. See how the horse is now bent to the outside which, in effect, means he is now simply leg yielding. The rider needs to ride the horse forwards in a straight line so that he knows straightaway that his response was not acceptable. Shoulder-in should be re-established, and the rider should use the outside leg to bring the quarters over and to keep the horse stepping sideways. As soon as the horse offers the wrong bend again, he must be ridden forwards in a straight line and the process repeated. The rider may need to tap the horse with the schooling whip just behind the inside leg to make sure he is listening to this leg and remains bent around it.**

Variations Within Each Pace

The horse is capable of a number of variations of each pace, e.g. in trot or canter the horse can work in a collected, working, medium or extended pace, and he can work in collected, medium or free walk. As the horse's responsiveness to his rider increases and his training progresses, he should be able to offer all of these variations smoothly and without resistance. When asking the horse for variations within each pace, think in terms of asking for more power and impulsion rather than more speed.

MEDIUM WALK

The medium walk is the pace the horse naturally offers his rider – the sort of pace that would be produced out on a hack. The horse takes long, relaxed steps and he overtracks, which means his hind feet step further forwards than the hoofprints left by the front feet.

WORKING TROT

The working trot is the pace the horse naturally offers his rider. It is an active pace with the horse maintaining a round outline whilst working in a forward-thinking rhythm. It is the sort of trot the horse would produce out hacking – relaxed but active. The same is true of the working canter.

COLLECTED TROT

In the collected paces, which can be either walk, trot or canter, the horse shortens his whole outline by lowering his hindquarters and bringing his hocks further under him, and by elevating his forehand so that his neck is raised and arched. The horse takes shorter, rounder steps, with greater elevation.

MEDIUM TROT

RIGHT
The medium paces require the horse to work with increased impulsion so that he takes longer, rounder steps than he would do in the working paces. He lengthens his whole frame slightly whilst still keeping a round outline.

EXTENDED TROT

In the extended paces the horse stretches his whole frame and takes steps of maximum length with maximum impulsion. As with all the variations in pace, the horse must still remain in balance and in a rhythm. This horse could still afford to lengthen and stretch his neck a little more forwards so that the overall picture was of a longer frame.

FREE WALK

LEFT
The free walk is often asked for in a dressage test – the rider offers the horse a long length of rein and the horse stretches his head and neck down and takes long, relaxed steps forwards, with his hind feet overtracking his front feet. Because the horse has been taught always to expect a contact between his mouth and the rider's hand, when the rider offers him a long length of rein, he stretches his head and neck down to seek out the contact he is used to feeling. To allow the horse to stretch his head and neck fully, the rider allows her arms and hands to go forwards and down so that there is still a straight line from her elbow, through the arm, down the rein to the bit.

EXTENDED CANTER

In the extended canter the horse lengthens his whole frame and fully extends his legs to take the longest possible steps whilst still remaining in balance. The horse in these pictures needs to lengthen his neck a little more and to take his nose forwards a fraction so that he is not behind the vertical.

Achieving Collection and Extension of the Paces

Producing these variations within each pace involves bringing together the techniques and principles with which you should, by now, be familiar. Whether the horse is working in the collected, medium or extended paces, he has to maintain the same rhythm in his work. In other words, you do not slow the horse down in order to achieve collection, nor should you go faster in order to extend the horse. To achieve collection, the rider uses the half-halt so that the horse's hocks are pushed further underneath him whilst the hand prevents him from accelerating. The trapping by the rider's hand of the power produced by the use of the leg causes the horse to shorten his frame and put that power into taking shorter, higher steps. Medium or extended work is achieved by first using half-halts to collect the horse and then releasing that power and energy in varying degrees by softening the hand forwards, which enables the horse to lengthen his frame and his stride. Whether the resulting pace is medium or extended depends on the degree to which the rider softens with the hand whilst continuing to ask for more power and drive from the hindquarters. To be able to produce these variations in pace, you have to develop a feel for creating and storing energy for collected work, and for directing that energy forwards into either medium or extended work.

COLLECTING AND EXTENDING THE HORSE

1 When practising collecting and extending the horse, it is easier to work within the confines of an arena. The short side of the arena which provides two corners in close proximity to each other is a good place to ask for collection, whilst the long side, or even across the diagonal, provides room for extending the paces. This rider is using half-halts to collect the horse as he progresses through the corner of the arena and begins to turn across the diagonal. A corner is a good place to start to ask for collection, as the horse has to bring his inside hindleg further underneath him in order to negotiate the turn anyway. Note the raised, arched neck and the way the hock is being raised and flexed.

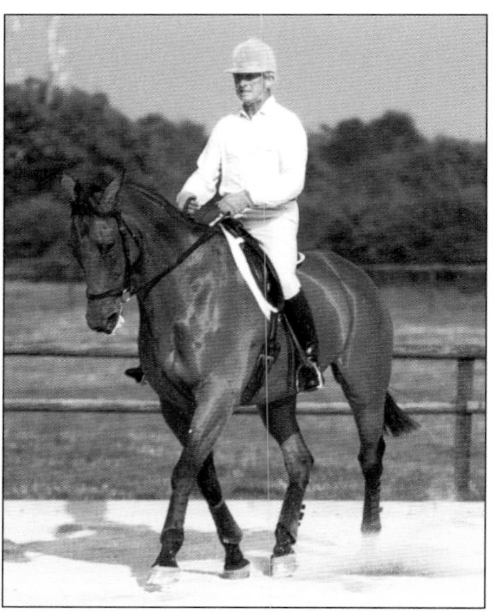

2 As the horse starts to cross the diagonal, the rider continues to collect the energy that was built up as they came through the turn. The horse's outline remains relatively high and short.

4 The outline is now lower and longer as the horse extends his limbs forwards to cover as much ground as possible with each stride.

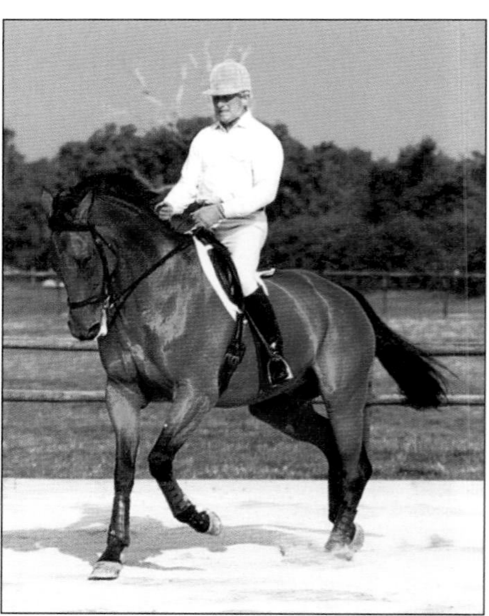

3 Once the horse is completely straight, the rider asks the horse to extend. He continues to ask for impulsion and drive from the hindquarters by keeping his legs actively on the horse's sides, but now he releases that stored power by softening the hands forwards so that the horse can lengthen his frame and strides. Note how the horse's hindquarters are still lowered, and how the first surge of released energy has really elevated his front end as the horse begins to extend his steps.

RIGHT
Teaching the horse to counter canter.

Introducing Counter Canter

Counter canter is a movement required in many dressage tests, and it demonstrates the horse's suppleness, balance and obedience. Counter canter involves the horse cantering with the left leg leading whilst being worked on the right rein, and vice versa. The horse must keep his head and neck bent over his leading foreleg, so that he is in fact bent in the opposite direction to that in which he is moving.

Counter canter is introduced by cantering on the left rein across the diagonal to the opposite track. As the horse reaches the other side and turns on to the right rein, he should be asked to maintain the canter with the left leg leading for a few strides, before being brought back to trot.

Once horse and rider are comfortable with this, shallow loops can be ridden in canter down the long side of the arena; whilst the horse is on the track he is cantering as normal, whereas whilst he is negotiating the shallow loop he is in fact in counter canter, provided he maintains the original bend of his head and neck over the leading foreleg.

COMMON FAULTS

In this picture, the horse is still cantering with the right leg leading but, instead of maintaining the bend of his head and neck to the right, he has bent to the left, i.e. he is now bent in the direction in which he is travelling. The rider must correct this by opening the right hand and closing the right leg on the girth to ask the horse to maintain the bend to the right.

Another common mistake is for the horse to bend his neck too much to the right. This causes him to lose balance and his whole body drifts back to the track instead of following the path of the 16½ foot (5 m) loop. When this happens the horse's hindlegs are not following in the same tracks as the front legs – the horse is simply falling sideways or falling out through the shoulder. If the rider now took up more contact on the outside (left) rein to straighten out the bend of the head and neck, used the left leg behind the girth to stop the quarters swinging out to the left, and opened the right hand whilst keeping the right leg on the girth to encourage the horse to bend his neck to the right, the correct counter canter would be restored.

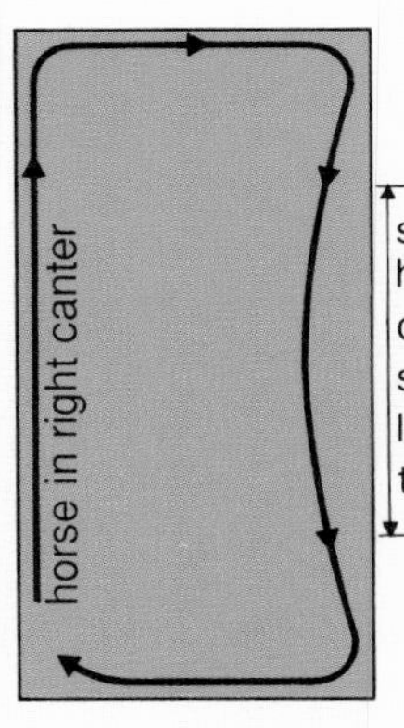

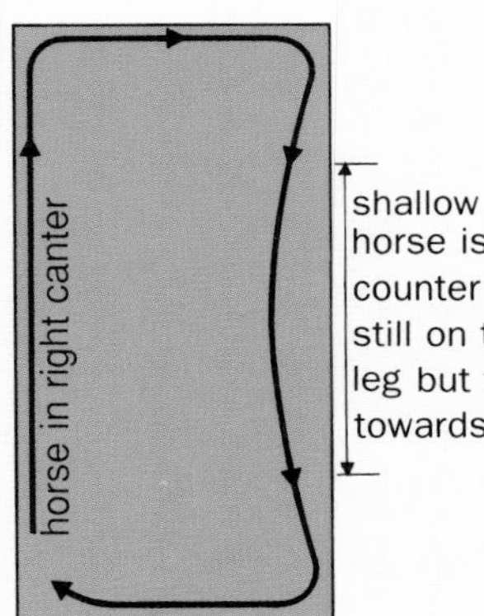

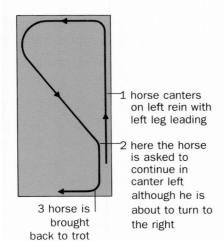

2 here the horse is asked to continue in canter left although he is about to turn to the right

RIDING A 16½ FOOT (5 M) LOOP IN COUNTER CANTER

1 **The horse canters around the arena on the right rein with the right leg leading as normal. Instead of continuing down the long side of the arena, the rider turns the horse off the track and rides a smooth 16½ foot (5 m) loop along the long side. As the horse negotiates the first curve of the loop he must continue to canter on the right leg.**

2 **With his head and neck slightly bent to the right, he starts to follow the loop around to the left. He is therefore bent away from the direction in which he is moving. The horse's body must remain straight – his hindlegs must follow in the same tracks as his forelegs, with only his head and neck showing a bend to the right.**

3 **As the horse follows the loop around to the left and back towards the track, he must still maintain the canter on the right lead, with his neck bent to the right.**

Riding a Flying Change

The flying change is when the horse changes directly from cantering with the left leg leading to cantering with the right leg leading, and vice versa. It is called for in some dressage tests and can be built upon in more advanced dressage so that the horse can literally change from one leg to the other on every stride, almost as if he were skipping! For the everyday rider, the flying change is most useful when jumping a course which requires changes of direction at canter. For example, instead of landing over a jump with the left leg leading, then having to come back to trot before picking up canter on the right lead in order to turn right to the next fence, the rider can simply land, take a few strides forwards in canter and then ask for a flying change as he turns towards the next jump.

Before the horse can be asked to perform a flying change, he must be responsive and obedient to the leg, and his canter must be balanced and able to show a degree of collection. He should willingly perform walk-to-canter transitions, be able to produce 33 foot (10 m) circles in canter, and work in counter canter before progressing to a flying change.

Some horses can tend to become excitable or nervous when they are introduced to this movement, so be sure to teach it carefully and patiently.

CHANGING THE LEAD

1 This movement is best taught by asking the horse to change from counter canter back to normal canter. This horse has been down the long side of the arena on the right rein, and has then cantered a half-circle so that he is now cantering across the diagonal with the right leg leading.

2 As the horse nears the track and the ensuing left-hand corner, the rider must indicate to the horse that he must change from right canter lead to left canter lead. The rider momentarily blocks the horse's forward momentum by closing and setting the left hand, whilst at the same time changing her leg aids from asking for right canter to asking for left canter, i.e. the rider's left leg is now applied on the girth, and the right leg used behind the girth to tell the horse to put his right hindleg down on the ground first. Remember that if the right hind starts the stride off, it is the left foreleg that appears to be leading. In this picture, you can see how the rider's left hand has blocked the horse's forward momentum so his forehand is elevated as a result.

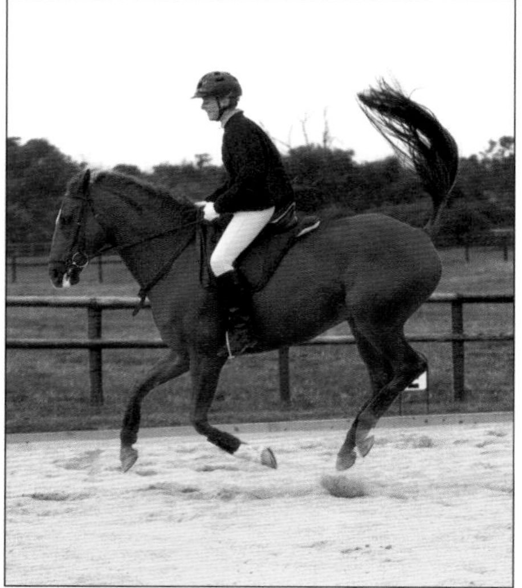

3 In this picture, the horse is in the period of suspension that follows each canter stride, and it is only at this point that he is able to perform the flying change. So the blocking of the forward movement makes the period of suspension just a fraction longer, giving the horse time to re-arrange his legs so that he lands on the opposite lead, i.e. he changes from the right lead to the left lead. This young horse has overreacted to the rider changing the position of her leg aids (bringing her left leg back on to the girth and using her right leg behind the girth). He has flicked up his back end higher than his forehand which unbalances him. As he strengthens up and becomes more relaxed about the exercise he will make a smoother flying change.

4 As a result of the rider changing her aids from asking for canter right to asking for canter left, the horse has landed on the left lead as required and can now continue to canter around the arena on the left rein.

Riding a Dressage Test

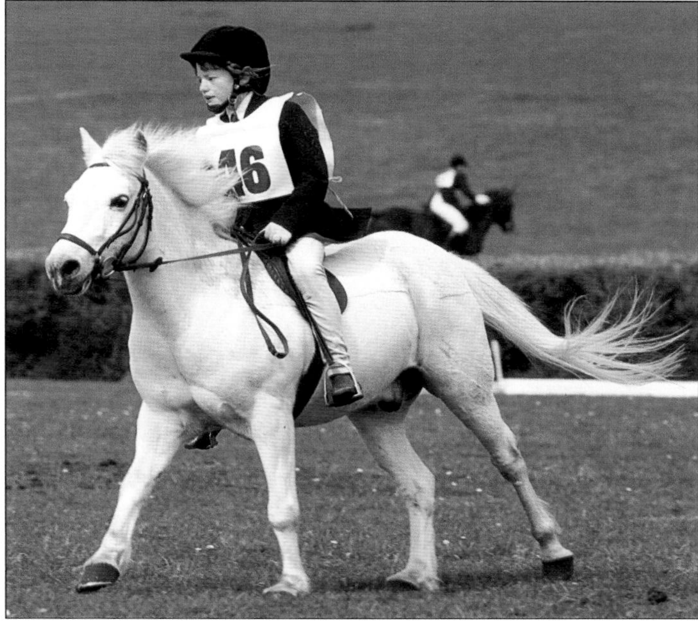

RIGHT
Notice how this young rider is looking across the arena to the marker where she has to make her next move. Keeping your head up and looking ahead to where you have to go next helps improve the accuracy and timing of the different movements you have to perform.

Once you have practised everything that has been discussed in this book so far, it will be good for both you and your horse to go out and put it all to the test by riding in some dressage competitions. These can be anything from small, local affairs to affiliated competitions.

Always make the effort to learn your dressage test off by heart, but do not practise it continually on your own horse because he will learn it himself and will start to anticipate the next movement instead of waiting for your instructions. At some competitions you are allowed to have your test read out to you, but if you are having to concentrate on instructions being read out, you cannot possibly concentrate 100 per cent on getting the best out of your horse.

Your horse should be well groomed and have his mane plaited for a dressage competition. You should wear a pair of white or beige jodhpurs or breeches, long or short riding boots, a riding jacket and a shirt and tie or stock.

All dressage tests begin with the horse and rider coming down the centre line of the arena, and all but preliminary tests require the rider to halt the horse and salute the judge. This first movement is the first impression that the judge will have of you – the only thing the judge can see from that angle is how straight your horse is as he comes down the centre line. So concentrate on riding the horse forwards in a good active pace, as it is easier to ride a straight line if the horse is moving forwards with impulsion. (Think of how a bicycle wobbles if you pedal too slowly – the same happens to a horse if he lacks impulsion.) A good straight halt will earn you good marks and put the judge in a good frame of mind for the rest of your test. Be ready with both hands and legs to correct any attempt the horse may make to drift one way or the other as you squeeze him forwards from your legs into a blocking hand and into halt.

Once the horse halts, keep a feel against his sides with your legs and down the rein with your hand. This will keep him on the aids and attentive to your next instruction. Female riders bow to the judge by putting both reins in their left hands, and bowing their heads as they drop their right hands to their sides. Male riders are usually required to remove their hats unless these are fitted with a safety harness. The reins are put in the left hand and the hat is removed with the right hand and lowered to one side as the rider bows his head. Do practise this at home, otherwise your horse is likely to shy away as you lower your hat to his side. When you are ready to ride on again, concentrate first and foremost on straightness and maintaining a constant rhythm.

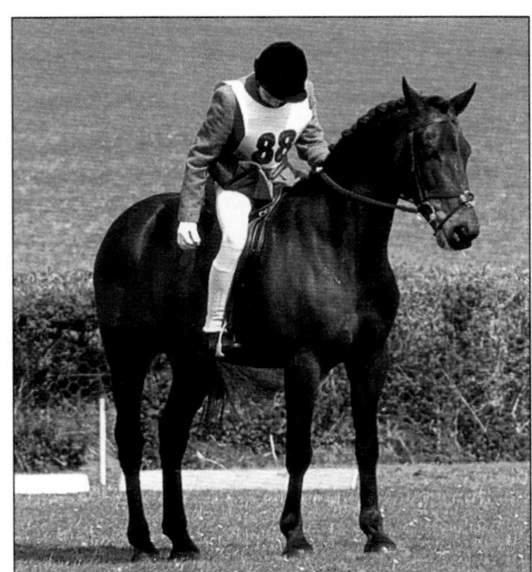

Every single dressage test includes at least one – and usually two – halts and salutes. A nice straight halt and a confident, unhurried salute create a good impression, and are aspects of the test that can be practised at home.

The various movements in a dressage test have to be carried out at the markers which are set around the arena. The correct point at which to carry out the next movement is as your shoulder is level with the marker. Always look up and think ahead to the next marker. Insist that the horse stays out on the track and uses the whole arena; do not be tempted to cut corners. If you ride the horse correctly around each corner, you will automatically be rebalancing him and asking him to use his hindlegs more actively. Remember to balance the horse during and before each new movement, with a half-halt if necessary. All tests end with another turn down the centre line and a halt and salute for the judge. No matter how well or badly the test may have gone, always perform this movement with good grace and manners. Remember that each movement in the test is marked separately, so that if you make a mistake in one movement all is not lost. If you keep your head and improve upon the mistake in the remaining movements, you will pick up marks again. Never give up – there are always more good marks to be earned. On top of all that, do make a conscious effort to smile. It will immediately fill you, and the judge, with confidence and, more importantly, it will help you to relax and to stay that way.

Preparing for Take-off

One of the best things about riding is to experience the exhilaration of riding a horse over fences. A lot of new riders are put off jumping through lack of confidence but, if you have developed any sort of feel for riding, jumping should simply be a natural and enjoyable progression.

All too often, when faced with a fence to jump, horse and rider seem to forget the basics they have been practising up until then. Balance and rhythm are abandoned as they career towards the obstacle! The secret of safe, enjoyable and successful jumping is to carry into the jumping arena the principles learnt and mastered whilst riding on the flat.

Rhythm and Balance

The two most important things for the would-be show jumper to keep in mind are rhythm and balance. If you can concentrate on keeping the horse balanced and in an even rhythm all the way to the fence, you have very little else to worry about.

You have already discovered how to encourage the horse to work in an even rhythm and to be responsive to your leg. Just because a jump appears in your path does not mean that anything changes – the horse must still be obedient enough to stay in the rhythm that you have dictated and, provided that you learn how to stay in balance with the horse throughout, clearing the fence comfortably and confidently will come naturally to both of you.

Horse and rider can practise working in a balanced rhythm by simply trotting and cantering over poles on the ground. This kind of work can be mixed in with your usual flatwork training so that the horse learns to remain calm and to apply

WORKING OVER TROT POLES

1 The horse is ridden in an active working trot through the corner and down to a line of trot poles set approximately 4 feet (1.25 m) apart, which gives the horse room to put his feet down between each pole as he takes each stride.

2 The horse must stay balanced and in the same rhythm as he approaches the line of trot poles.

3 The rider softens his hands forwards so that the horse is able to stretch his head and neck forwards as he negotiates the poles.

4 The horse should maintain exactly the same rhythm throughout the whole exercise – do not allow him to slow down at the end of the poles. Ride him through the next corner correctly, insisting he bends around your inside leg and maintains his balance and rhythm, and repeat the exercise.

WORKING THROUGH CANTER POLES

1 Exactly the same exercise should be practised in canter, except now the poles are spaced out approximately 10 feet (3 m) apart to give the horse room to canter over them.

2 The rider must keep the horse balanced and in the same rhythm through the corner and all the way up to the poles.

3 As the horse negotiates the poles, the rider simply softens the hands forwards so that the horse's head and neck are not restricted.

4 As when working over trot poles, the horse should maintain the same rhythm throughout the whole exercise.

5 As the horse completes the poles and canters on to the next corner, exactly the same rhythm and balance must be maintained throughout.

the same rules learnt on the flat to his jumping work. Far too many horses are allowed, and often encouraged, to become overexcited and go too fast when they are asked to jump. The horse should be taught to use power to clear fences, not speed.

USING POLES AND LINES OF FENCES

Trot and canter poles are often used to help introduce horse and rider to jumping. They should be spaced out in such a way that the horse can easily negotiate them, without having to stretch himself or shorten himself up. Trot poles are usually set about 4 feet (1.25 m) apart and canter poles 10 feet (3 m) apart. But if these distances do not suit your horse then, at this stage in his training, alter them to suit him. Adding lines of fences to the poles forms what is called a jumping grid. Gridwork is used to introduce the horse to the idea of jumping. Later in his training, it is used to increase his athleticism and to improve the way in which he jumps. It trains him to jump more carefully so he is less likely to injure himself or to knock fences down.

■ INSIST ON CONSISTENCY

It is only with practice and patience that you will teach the horse to carry out this exercise. Most horses thoroughly enjoy the idea of jumping but it is important to teach the horse to contain his enthusiasm so that he still remains obedient, balanced and in a rhythm.

A young horse who is being introduced to this work for the first time should have no reason to rush or get excited, provided he has been taught the basic principles throughout his flatwork training.

An older horse who already knows about jumping may get excited if he has been allowed to do so by previous riders, but practice and perseverance will teach him to keep an even rhythm.

If the horse really is inclined to rush, you should keep circling around the outside of the poles until he settles into a steady rhythm. If he still rushes as soon as he is allowed to go to the poles, simply circle him away from them again and keep repeating this exercise until he maintains the same rhythm. Alternatively, you can bring the horse back to walk and insist that he walks over the poles until he is prepared to keep the same rhythm in both trot and canter.

The opposite problem may occur with an inexperienced or nervous horse who may want to slow down on the approach to the poles until he is confident about what they are. The first few times the horse is introduced to the exercise, he should be allowed to slow down to give him time to take everything in. After that, insist that he maintains the same rhythm. It may be worth choosing a slow rhythm in trot so that the horse does not feel he is being hassled, but do insist that the horse sticks to this rhythm throughout. Once he is confident, the pace can be picked up a little and a slightly faster rhythm maintained throughout. The horse should never be rushed through these exercises – his pace should be active and yet balanced.

In jumping it is the power of the horse that is critical, not his speed. As a rider you are trying to create and store power and energy on the way to the fence so that all that power can be used by the horse to clear the fence.

Jumping Fences

It is your job to bring the horse to the fence in a balanced rhythm, to remain in balance with him over it, and to land in balance so that you can continue to the next fence.

Most riders attempt to do far too much on the approach and over a fence, which only unbalances and distracts the horse. When jumping in canter, keep a light seat on the approach to the fence. About 22–33 yards (20–30 m) away, whilst still retaining exactly the same rhythm, lower your seat deeper into the saddle and actively close your legs against the horse's sides. Keep your shoulders slightly forwards. Having closed the legs more against the horse's sides, you may have to take a slightly stronger contact in the hand to prevent the horse accelerating. As the horse takes off over the fence, remain in the same position but close your knees and lower legs tighter against the horse's sides to help you remain still in the saddle, and stretch your hands and arms forwards to allow the horse to stretch his head and neck forwards over the fence.

BASIC TECHNIQUE

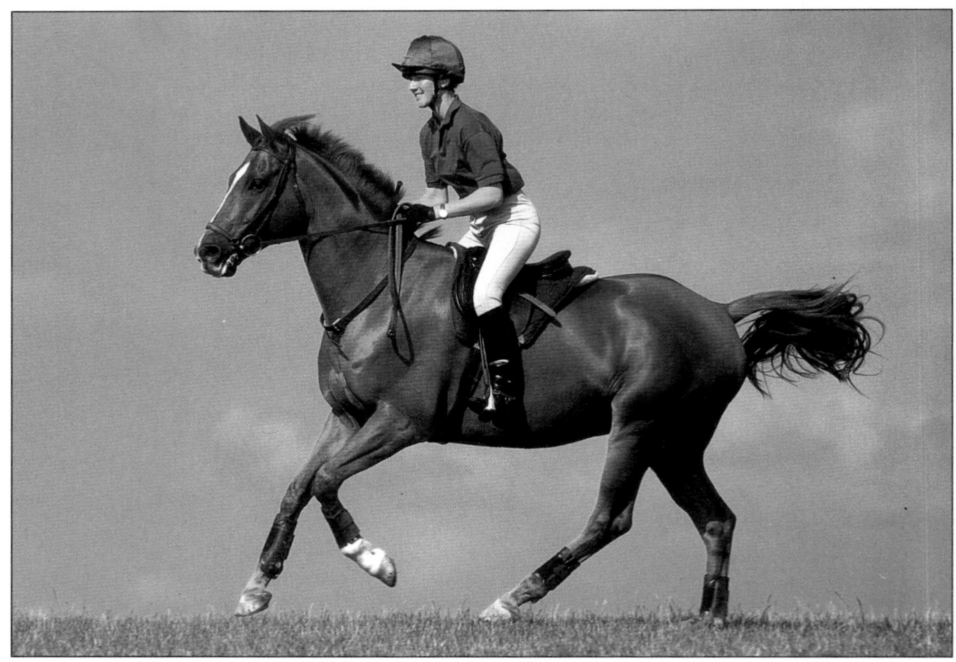

1 Here the rider is in the forward seat. Note how her seat bones are raised just off the saddle so there is less weight directly on the horse's back. This encourages the horse to remain soft through his back and to bowl along actively beneath her. The rider keeps her shoulders slightly more forward than they would be when cantering on the flat, but it is this position that allows the weight to be taken off the saddle whilst still allowing the rider to keep her balance. The lower leg is closed on the horse's sides, and the rider's weight is now taken by the stirrup iron. The horse is producing a light, active canter with his forehand nicely elevated.

2 As the rider approaches a fence, she lowers her seat into the saddle but keeps her shoulders in the forward position. The lower legs are closed more firmly against the horse's sides so that his hocks are pushed under him, but the rider's hands prevent him from accelerating. The aim is to collect the horse so that he has plenty of energy to power himself over the fence.

3 Just before the horse takes off, the rider softens her hands forwards so he can lower his head and neck to produce a supple, clean jump. The rider's seat is still deep in the saddle, her lower legs are closed against the horse's sides, her heels are pushed down and, at this point, she also allows her knees to close against the saddle to keep her body balanced as the horse jumps.

4 As the horse takes off, all the rider does is to allow her hands and arms to stretch forwards to follow the movement of the horse's head and neck. The rider remains perfectly still and balanced over the horse and, in this way, leaves the horse free to jump athletically and comfortably over the fence.

5 By adopting this technique over a fence, the rider is able to remain in balance with the horse; this means that, as they land, the two of them are still balanced and ready to face whatever comes next. If another fence were to follow immediately, they would both be in the correct position to tackle it.

6 Horse and rider look equally balanced on the approach and on landing over the fence. If horse and rider can maintain this same rhythm and balance around a whole course, they have every chance of producing a clear round, be it across country or in a show-jumping arena.

COMMON JUMPING FAULTS

GETTING IN FRONT OF THE MOVEMENT

These two pictures show one of the most common faults of which any number of riders, of all standards, are guilty. Faced with a fence, many riders seem to be overwhelmed by an irresistible desire to anticipate when the horse is going to take off and to "jump" with him! Instead of sitting quietly and maintaining their position, the rhythm and the balance, they fire their seat out of the saddle, hurl their upper body up the horse's neck and generally do about ten times more than they need to. The effect on the horse is both unbalancing and distracting. This can result in the horse hitting the fence with his front legs because the rider has loaded too much weight on to his forehand or, worse still, the horse may be tempted to put his feet back down again in front of the fence. The horse is then unable to jump at all.

You can see how easy it would be for the horse to put his front feet back down on the ground and, because the rider has come right out of the saddle and thrown all her weight forward, she would have very little chance of staying on board. In the second picture, the rider is still in a relatively weak position; her weight is balanced on her knees instead of being pushed down into the stirrups and her heels, with the result that her lower leg has slid backwards.

The rider is going to be out of balance with the horse as he lands and will not be in a very strong position to regain the balance and rhythm that they started with. If the horse stumbled as he landed, because the rider is not supporting her weight in her lower legs and heels, she would probably be thrown forwards. Again she may well fall off or at the very least she would not be able to help the horse recover as well as if she had maintained her balance.

IN TIMES OF TROUBLE!

Whilst the horse must not be allowed to rush towards his fences, it is just as important that he is not allowed to slow down to the point that he runs out of impulsion and stops. If you sense that the horse is reluctant to keep progressing forwards to a fence, you must adopt a more aggressive style of riding to encourage the horse to keep going. In this situation it is more important than ever that you keep your seat in the saddle the whole time. If you are tempted to anticipate the take-off and get in front of the movement, the reluctant jumper is presented with the ideal opportunity to stop dead!

In these pictures, the rider has pressed both legs very firmly against the horse's sides. If necessary, both heels should be used to kick the horse forwards. The seat remains deep in the saddle and the rider arches her back slightly to allow her seat as well as the legs to drive the horse forwards. The rider must not throw her hands forward at the horse as often happens – she is trying to ride the horse up into the contact so that while contact is maintained it does not actually restrict the horse's forward movement.

CHASING THE HORSE INTO THE FENCE

Another fault commonly adopted by any number of riders is to chase or rush the horse into the fence. The rider is meant to maintain the same rhythm and balance as he or she rides from fence to fence, but many people feel unable to wait for the fence. As soon as they are a few strides from it, they drive the horse forwards, immediately unbalancing the horse and pushing him on to his forehand.

This approach usually results in the horse taking off much too far away from the fence and really having to stretch to clear it. In these pictures, even the horse looks angry at this unwanted interference from his rider. If the horse is made to jump like this, he is likely to knock fences down. He is being made to use speed to clear the fences rather than power and the athleticism of his body. If he is ridden like this across country, particularly to a very upright fence, he will find it difficult to get his front legs up in the air quickly enough and risks hitting the fence; if it is a solid cross-country fence, this may well be enough to unseat his rider or, at worst, would cause the horse to fall as well.

RIGHT, TOP TO BOTTOM
In the first picture the horse's canter stride is already plenty long enough, but in the second you can see that the rider has continued to drive the horse, stretching out his frame and stride even further. Compare the look of this canter to the approach made in the first pictures in this chapter. In those pictures the canter looked light and active, and the forehand was elevated. In these pictures you can see how flat and stretched out the canter is and how all the weight is falling on the forehand.

Maintaining Balance and Position

The easiest way to learn to maintain the correct position whilst jumping is to learn how to stay in balance with the horse – and the easiest way to learn that is to remember always to maintain the same rhythm when jumping. Having already practised maintaining the rhythm, balance and your position over trot and canter poles, this exercise can be extended to include your first jump about 14 feet (4.25 m) away from the last pole. You should simply concentrate on keeping the horse trotting in a balanced, even rhythm through the trot poles and on to the fence. The horse will fit in three trot strides after the last pole and will be perfectly placed to pop over the fence.

If you find that you cannot resist the temptation to "jump" as the horse jumps, or if you feel yourself tensing up as the fence gets nearer, try the same exercise without looking at the fence at all. It's quite simple, and the horse will cope perfectly well without your eyes looking out for him, provided you do still maintain the same even rhythm.

POSITION AT TAKE-OFF

1 **Think about maintaining the correct position, keeping your seat in the saddle as you approach the trot poles but allowing the shoulders to be carried forwards a little.**

2 **Close the knees and lower legs against the horse's sides just in front of the fence, and soften the hands forwards.**

3 **As the horse takes off, allow the hands and arms to go forwards in order to follow the movement of his head and neck.**

LOOKING AWAY FROM THE FENCE

1 **Once you have lined the horse up in front of the row of cross poles, look to one side so that you cannot anticipate the fence itself.**

2 **Keep the rhythm throughout, sit deep in the saddle, allow your shoulders to move forwards a little, and close your legs and knees against the horse as he trots over the last trot pole (you will feel him do this).**

3 **As you feel him take off, just allow your hands and arms to follow forwards.**

Trotting and Cantering to a Fence

Having experienced your first jump it is now just a case of getting the feel of cantering to a fence whilst maintaining the same principles as described already. This is most easily done by extending your existing line of trot poles and small fence to include a second fence which the horse will jump from canter. This should be placed approximately 18–20 feet (5.5–6 m) from the first fence; this allows the horse to trot to the first fence, land and take one canter stride before taking off over the second fence.

Many riders at this stage feel tempted to interfere in an effort to help the horse, but the grid is set up to allow the horse to find his own way through. The biggest help you can be to your horse is to maintain the even rhythm and balance.

JUMPING TWO FENCES

1 The horse remains in trot over the cross poles and up to the first fence, just as he did in the previous exercise. The rider retains the same position and rhythm throughout.

2 Having allowed forward movement with the hands and arms over the fence, the rider now makes sure his legs are closed against the horse's sides to encourage him to canter forwards in the same rhythm. As the horse lands, the rider's hands return to the normal position.

3 Here the horse takes the one canter stride that brings him up to the second fence; the rider continues to concentrate solely on keeping his position and the same rhythm.

4 The horse clears the fence, but the rider has anticipated the jump and has allowed his lower leg to slide back a fraction and brought his seat out of the saddle. The next time he comes to this fence it would be good practice for the rider to look away so that he cannot anticipate what is going to happen!

MAINTAINING BALANCE

RIGHT
This is another horse and rider completing the same exercise. In the second picture you can see why it is so important for the rider always to soften the hands forwards on the last stride in front of the fence – see how this horse has really stretched his head and neck forwards towards the jump before taking off. This is to be encouraged as it helps the horse to produce a powerful, athletic and round jump.

In the last two pictures you can see how this rider has kept her seat in the saddle, which has allowed her to land in balance with the horse and ready for the next challenge.

1

2

3

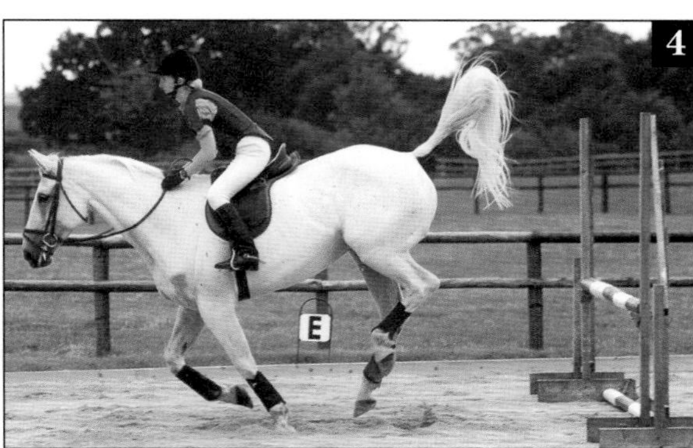

4

The Circle Exercise – Balance, Rhythm and Trust

Trotting poles and grids make it easier for the horse and rider to keep their rhythm and balance – the real test is whether or not they can maintain the same principles when cantering to a single fence. One of the best ways to ensure this is to practise this very simple exercise. Build a small jump somewhere that allows you room to canter in a large circle to it, say on a 33 yard (30 m) circle. Pick up a canter and just practise maintaining a good, even rhythm as you canter around the circle, bypassing the jump to begin with. When you feel settled enough to jump, make sure that you stick to the same rhythm – don't speed up or slow down just because you are thinking of jumping. As you come on to the last quarter of the circle before the jump, sit deep into the saddle, close your legs against the horse's sides and contain him in the same rhythm with your hand, and then look away from the jump. Maintain the rhythm and allow the horse to look after the jump. As you feel him take off, allow your hands and arms to go forwards to follow the contact. Have a friend standing in the middle of the circle to check you do not look at the jump.

Practise jumping at different speeds on the circle – the faster you go the further away from the fence the horse will take off, the slower you go the closer he will get before take-off, provided you maintain the same rhythm. This exercise will help you find the rhythm from which your horse jumps best. Once you get the idea of trusting the horse and waiting for the fence, you can go back to looking where you are going, but return to this exercise whenever you get the urge to interfere.

FINDING THE RIGHT RHYTHM

1 On the last quarter of the circle the rider sits deep in the saddle, closes the legs and hands to collect the horse whilst still maintaining the same rhythm, and then looks away from the fence.

2 The rider continues to look away from the fence, concentrating only on keeping the same rhythm and balance. Note how the horse, left undistracted by his rider, is totally focused on the fence.

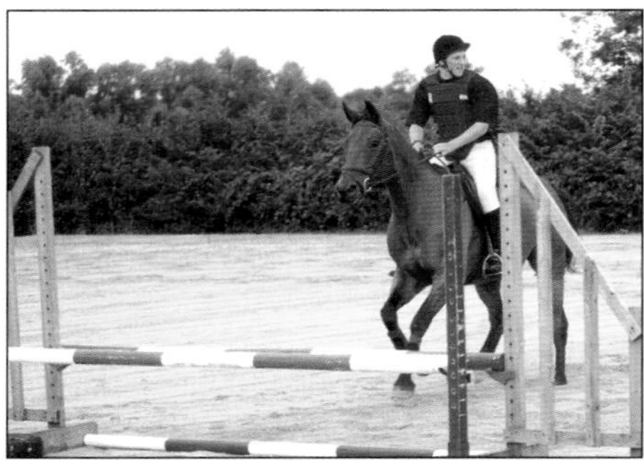

3 The horse has the fence measured up and is about to take off.

4 The rider allows his arms and hands to follow forwards whilst the horse clears the fence.

LEARNING TO TRUST THE HORSE

1 Nine times out of ten, if the rider looks at the fence at this stage he or she feels obliged to interfere by either checking or chasing the horse. This simply distracts and unbalances the horse.

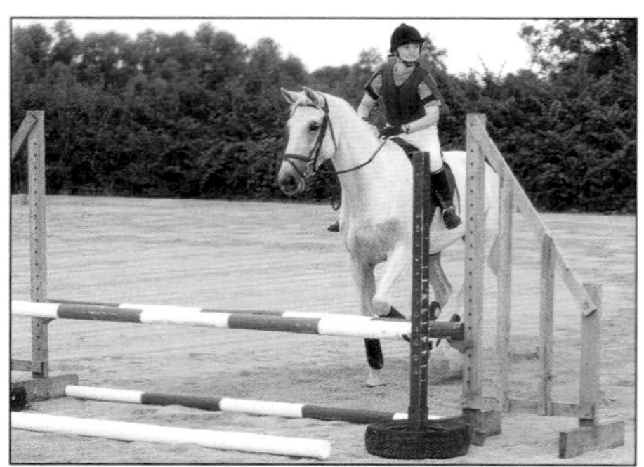

2 The rider is trusting her horse to do the job; note how the horse is fully concentrating on the task in hand and is about to clear the fence.

3 A horse can jump as big a fence as you wish in this way. Provided you keep the rhythm and balance, he will do the jumping.

Improving Horse and Rider's Jumping Ability

In the same way that, when learning to ride, the rider is more concerned about his or her own position and balance than about how well the horse is going, when learning to jump you must first master the art of keeping a balanced, rhythmic approach before worrying about trying to improve the horse's actual jumping ability.

Gridwork can be used to help in both instances – jumping the grids allows you to concentrate on improving your own balance and position, and can also be used to improve the horse's agility and ability over a fence.

Some horses are naturally more careful jumpers than others; some horses tend to throw long, flat jumps, whilst others may have a tendency to jump very high but with little scope to clear spreads. In either case, gridwork exercises can enhance the horse's performance.

■ GRIDWORK AND JUMPING DISTANCES

When gridwork is first introduced, the distances should be set to suit the horse. Once the horse is confident with the exercise, the distances can be altered – either lengthened or shortened – to improve the horse's technique. So with a horse who tends to throw a long, flat jump the distance should gradually be reduced so that he has to collect himself up and use himself more athletically, while a horse who is very short striding should be encouraged to stretch out a little by using longer distances.

You may well wonder why it is necessary to alter what the horse does naturally. The reason is that, in the competition world, show jumps and cross-country fences are built to set measurements and distances. The course designer has to build fences that can be jumped safely by different sizes and types of horse, so he has to find an average distance to use and build his fences around that. For example, an average measurement used in course designing is based on the assumption that the horse will cover 4 yards (3.65 m) with every canter stride. Extra room has to be allowed for the distance away from the fence that the horse will take off, and further distance must be allowed on the other side of the fence for the horse to land. A rule of thumb is 4 yards (3.65 m) for one canter stride, plus 2 yards (1.9 m) for take-off and 2 yards (1.9 m) for landing. If the course designer wants the horse to fit in one stride between two fences, he will place the fences 8 yards (7.35 m) apart. To fit in two strides the fences would be placed 12 yards (11 m) apart – two canter strides equal two by 4 yards (3.65 m), plus 2 yards (1.9 m) for landing over the first fence and 2 yards (1.9 m) for taking off at the second fence.

If your particular horse is to fit in the same number of strides as the course designer intended, he needs to cover the ground that the designer has based his figures on. Higher up the competition ladder, the course designer may include an extra-long or an extra-short distance, to test riders' ability to adjust the distance their horses cover. Some riders may choose to collect up their horses and fit in three strides; others may push for two.

GRIDWORK DISTANCES

As a general guide, the following distances can be used in grids:

A bounce distance (where the horse doesn't take a stride between two fences but lands and takes off again immediately)
- from trot – 3–4 yards (2.75–3.65 m)
- from canter – 4–4½ yards (3.65–4 m)

One-stride distance approached
- from trot – 6 yards (5.5 m)

One-stride distance approached
- from canter – 6–8 yards (5.5–7.35 m)

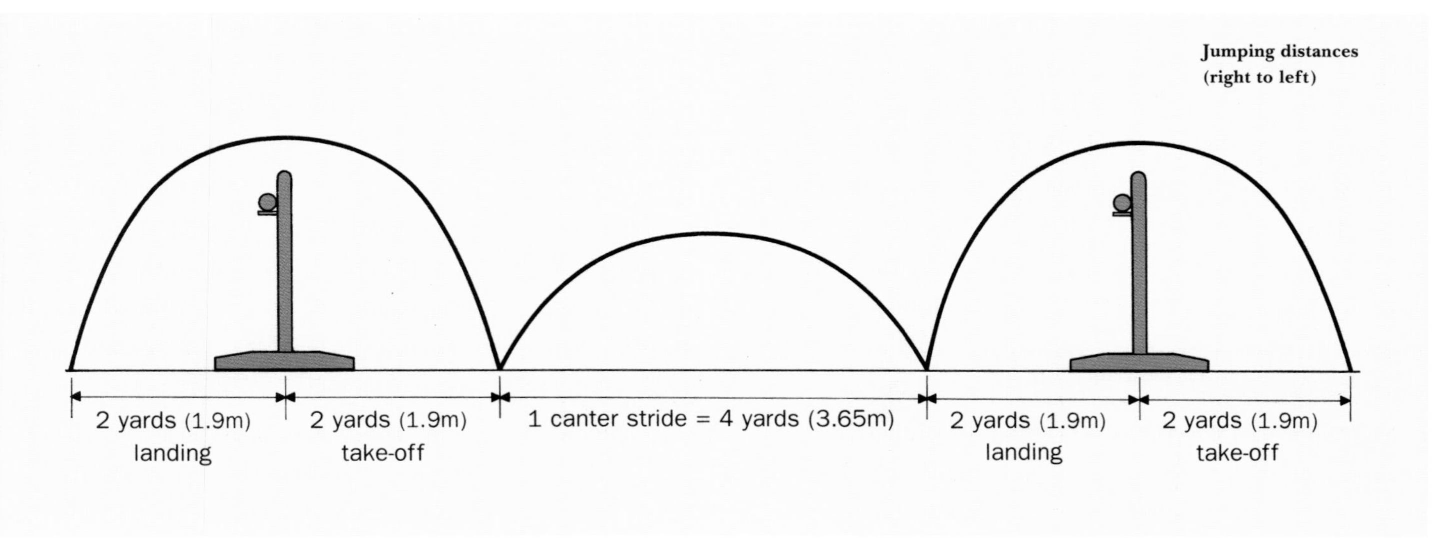

Jumping distances (right to left)

BOUNCE GRID

Gridwork Exercises

Jumping grids can be adapted and altered as much as your imagination allows, the only confines being that you use distances that are acceptable and safe for the horse. But you should always have some aim in mind when designing a grid, otherwise you may dishearten the horse or simply end up undoing with one exercise any improvement you had created with another. So don't just go blindly on – feel the difference the grid is making to the horse and change it accordingly. And if the horse throws a truly fantastic jump early on in the session, it sometimes pays to stop at that point rather than risk undoing the good work you have just created.

It is very helpful to have someone knowledgeable watching you from the ground. Sometimes they can see, better than you can feel, exactly what the horse is doing as he progresses through the grid.

1

2

3

4

5

RIGHT, TOP TO BOTTOM
The fences in this bounce grid have been set at 10 feet (3 m) intervals. The horse is introduced to the exercise by first using one bounce, i.e. two fences. This horse has approached this exercise in canter, but if the horse has never seen a bounce before you may prefer to shorten the distance and approach in trot, so that the horse has more time to work out what to do. When he is confident about tackling this, an additional fence can be added to make it a double bounce.

As you can see, a bounce distance means that the horse lands over one fence and immediately takes off over the next without taking a stride in between. It is a good exercise for improving the horse's physical and mental agility. He has to think quickly in order to organize himself correctly. Another advantage of this exercise is that it helps to make the horse confident enough to tackle lines of fences in competition. If he is used to seeing – and picking his way through – lines of poles and fences in front of him at home, he will feel more confident when faced with a complicated combination of fences in a competition.

Practising with a bounce grid also improves the rider's balance and ability to follow the movement of the horse.

■ THE COMBINATION GRID

This grid aims to improve the way the horse jumps. It starts with the horse trotting to a small cross pole, set one canter stride away from a spread or parallel fence. This is set on a distance that suits the horse's natural stride. The distance to the parallel is increased gradually, by up to 2 feet (0.5 m), and the fence is altered to become an ascending parallel, i.e. the back pole is raised higher than the front pole. Once the horse is jumping well through this, it is altered again. This time the distance is shortened gradually, up to 2 feet (0.5 m) less than the original distance, and the fence is adjusted to make it a descending parallel, i.e. the back pole is now lower than the front pole. An ascending parallel encourages the horse to be neat and careful with his hindlegs over a fence; the descending parallel teaches him to be neat and careful in front whilst still being able to stretch forwards to clear the spread.

SQUARE PARALLEL

The horse is brought to the grid in trot. The two trot poles are set 4 feet (1.25 m) apart and are, in turn, 8 feet (2.5 m) away from the small cross pole (the first jump). These serve to bring the horse into the grid balanced and straight. He takes one canter stride before jumping the parallel.

ASCENDING PARALLEL

The approach through the trot poles and the cross pole remains exactly the same. But the one-stride distance to the parallel (now ascending) has been increased. To encourage the horse to take a longer stride to help him cover the distance to the parallel, the rider simply "clicks" to the horse and closes her legs against his sides to tell him to stretch forwards. The horse responds by taking a longer stride than he did in the first grid sequence. In the last picture you can see how the horse is really using his hindquarters, and has snapped up his hindlegs to make sure he clears the back pole.

RIDER'S WEIGHT

Here the horse tackles the same grid and, from this angle, the interesting point to note is shown in the last picture. The rider has, to some degree, thrown her body weight forwards and up the horse's neck, rather than keeping her seat in the saddle. Note how she has pitched her weight to the left-hand side and look at the effect this has had on the horse's left foreleg. Because the rider's weight is loaded over the horse's left shoulder, it is harder for the horse to bring his left foreleg up as quickly and cleanly as the right foreleg. It would therefore be very easy for the horse to knock this fence down with the trailing foreleg. To avoid this, the rider's weight must stay balanced centrally in the saddle.

DESCENDING PARALLEL

The approach to this exercise is the same as before, but the one-stride distance is shortened to less than it was in the very first grid, and the parallel is now descending. The horse has to land over the cross pole, collect and shorten his stride and then be quick and neat with his front legs to clear the front pole of the descending parallel. The previous exercise will have reminded him to be really tidy with his hindlegs, so this exercise should produce his most impressive jump. Note in the last picture how very neat and tidy this horse has been with his front legs – exactly the aim of the exercise.

■ THE DOUBLE OF PARALLELS

This exercise is aimed at helping the horse who tends to throw a high, but not necessarily very wide, jump. Two parallel fences are built one stride apart, with the distance set to suit the horse's stride, i.e. approximately 8 yards (7.35 m). The horse is cantered through this once or twice and then the distance between the two fences is shortened by simply making the two parallel fences wider – the back rail of the first fence and the front rail of the second fence are moved 1 foot (30 cm) or so towards each other. This encourages the horse to throw a wider jump than usual over the first spread; he must land and shorten himself up to fit in one stride before having to throw another scopey jump over the second spread.

INTRODUCING TWO PARALLELS

The exercise is introduced by cantering the horse to two parallels, set one stride apart at a distance to suit the horse's stride. Note how soft and sympathetic the rider's hands are – allowing the horse to use himself without restriction.

ADJUSTING TO THE JUMP

Now the spreads have been made wider so that the distance between the two fences has become shorter – the two green jump wings have been moved in towards each other. In the first picture you will see that the rider has been caught out by the huge jump that the horse has thrown – she really needed to allow her arms and hands to go forwards more so as not to restrict the horse.

Having thrown such a big jump, the horse now has to shorten and balance himself quickly in order to clear the second fence. Note the improved position of the rider's hands.

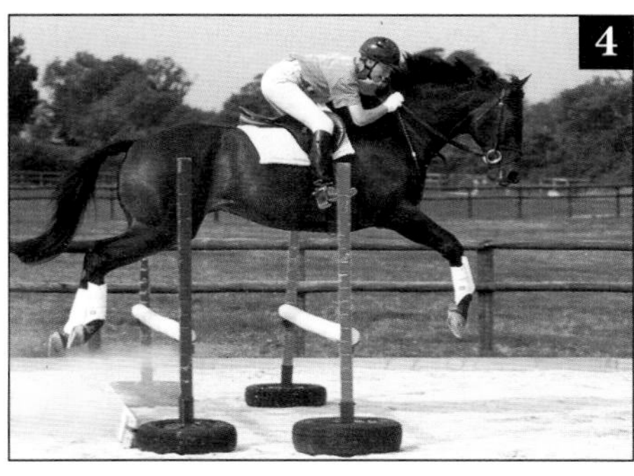

Riding Related Distances

Over a whole course of fences, two of them will often be placed on what is called a related distance. This means the designer intends the competitors to ride a set number of strides between the two. Combination fences refer to jumps which are one or two strides apart, whereas related distances refer to jumps which are anything from three to, say, six strides apart.

Gridwork exercises at home will have shown you whether or not your horse has a naturally short or long stride, and you should use this knowledge to your advantage when faced with combinations or related distances. If the horse has a naturally short stride, you will need to encourage the horse to open out his stride; you may need to ride with more pace than, say, the rider whose horse has a long, ground-covering stride. Whatever the case, when riding combinations or related distances the aim is to maintain an even stride length between the fences, not to land over the fence and then have either to check the horse or to chase him forwards towards the next element.

Watch a number of horses tackling a related distance and you will start to see how it rides best. Some riders may approach in a short, collected canter and fit in an extra stride, whilst others may let their horses jump, canter and jump out of a longer stride and fit in one stride less. If you practise the options at home you will learn which approach suits your horse, but whatever the number of strides you opt for they should be of an even length. So, to fit in the maximum number of strides, approach in a more collected canter, with a little less pace. To fit in the minimum number of strides, approach on a longer stride with more pace.

TAKING FIVE EVEN STRIDES

These two fences are set 60 feet (18.25 m) apart, and in this first exercise the rider intends to fit five strides between them. She approaches in a reasonably collected canter which encourages the horse to jump in quietly over the first fence. As she lands, the rider successfully maintains the same rhythm that she had on the approach, and this allows the horse to fit in the five even strides as required between the two fences.

TAKING FOUR EVEN STRIDES

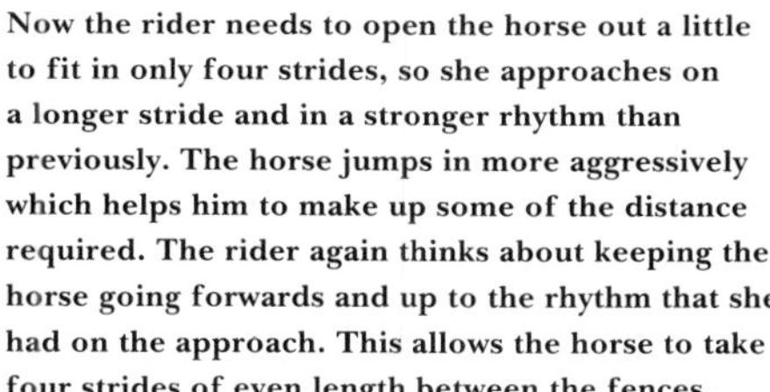

Now the rider needs to open the horse out a little to fit in only four strides, so she approaches on a longer stride and in a stronger rhythm than previously. The horse jumps in more aggressively which helps him to make up some of the distance required. The rider again thinks about keeping the horse going forwards and up to the rhythm that she had on the approach. This allows the horse to take four strides of even length between the fences.

TOO MUCH PACE

This rider, attempting the same exercise, shows how not to do it! Her plan was to fit in five strides, but instead of coming on a quieter rhythm than normal she has ridden the horse strongly into the fence so that he throws an extravagant jump. She is now going to struggle to fit in the five strides and resorts to checking the horse back, i.e. using her hands to make the horse continually shorten his stride. In the last-but-one picture, you can see how the horse is objecting to this treatment by throwing his head up and resisting the rider's hand. The horse has kindly cleared the fence for her but could easily have knocked it down, or even refused. Once the horse throws his head up, his eye is taken off the fence and he is unable to judge what he needs to do. It also makes him tense and hollow so that he cannot be as athletic. As you can see from these pictures, instead of taking five strides of even length, this horse's strides were being gradually shortened. Having made the initial mistake of coming in with too much pace, the rider may have been wiser to allow the horse to continue in the stronger rhythm and to fit in only four strides. Practising these exercises at home will give you a feel for how to get the distance right on the day and for how best to react when things go wrong.

Riding a Course of Fences

Successfully riding a course of show jumps is simply an extension of the principles practised at home – except that you need to concentrate for longer. Instead of having to keep the rhythm and balance over just one or two fences, you have to maintain them around the twists and turns of a course. But the principle is exactly the same – choose your rhythm and stick to it. Keep the horse balanced, especially on the turns, and maintain that balance and rhythm every inch of the way around the show-jumping course.

However large or small the course you are about to jump, always take the opportunity to walk it so that you can measure the distances between fences and decide the exact line that you intend to ride.

■ RIDING YOUR ROUND

As soon as you are allowed to enter the arena, pick up the canter you will be jumping from and give the horse a good canter around and in between the fences. Always be aware of being in the right position to carry on cantering around to the start markers and the first fence once the signal is given. You will be eliminated if you blatantly show your horse the fences before you start, but if there is a particularly spooky fence in the arena it is a good idea to happen to canter past it on your way to the first fence!

Once the bell sounds, stay relaxed and just concentrate on holding the rhythm and balance all the way around the route you have planned to ride.

Fences can come up on you very quickly once you are jumping in a competition arena, so look up and ahead the whole time. Look for the next fence before you have even landed over the previous one. If you have to land over a fence and then turn, say, right to the next fence, open your right hand slightly once you are in the air over the first fence, and just bring your left leg back behind the girth at the same time, to encourage the horse to land and canter away with the right leg leading. If you fail to get to the turn with the correct leg leading, either ask the horse for a flying change or bring

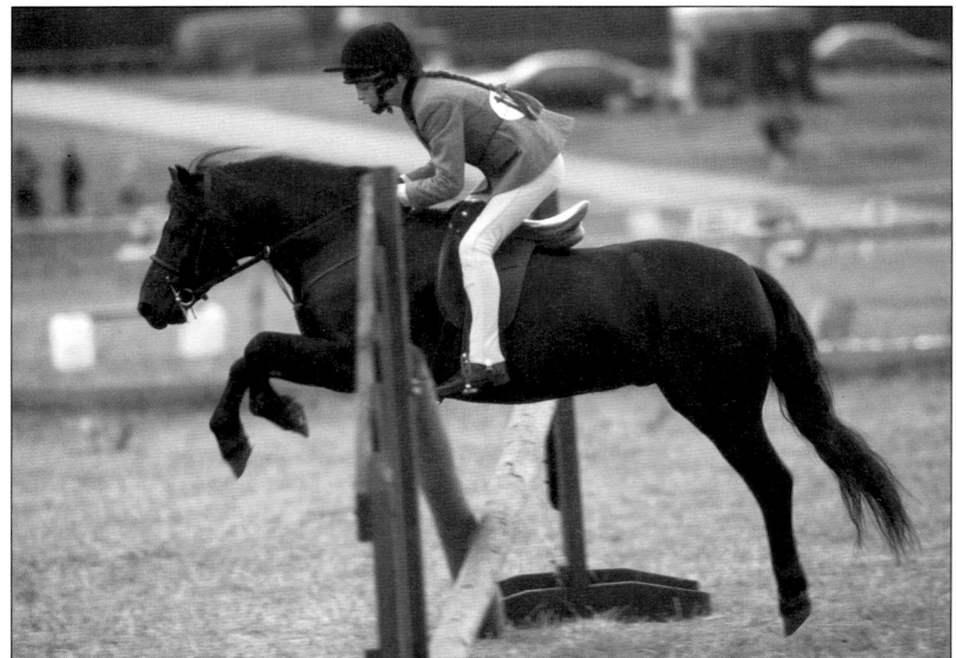

Make good use of the practice jump. Keep it very low to begin with so that you both get a confident and happy start to your warm-up. Then gradually raise it to the height of the fences in the ring. If you have an upset of any sort, put it back down and jump it a few times until you are both confident again.

WATCH THE OPPOSITION

If there is time, try to watch several other horses and riders negotiate the course. Listen out for the judges' signal to start – usually a bell, buzzer or horn – and remember that you must start within thirty seconds of hearing it.

Watch to see whether or not each of the distances between the fences is riding as you envisaged. Are the horses finding the distances long or short?

Note the turns that the other riders make to the fences and see which route appears to give the horse the best chance of clearing the jump.

RIGHT
The aim is to have a happy partnership, as well illustrated here.

WALKING THE COURSE

At all show-jumping competitions the rider is given the opportunity to walk around the course before the class starts. Make the most of this time to note the following relevant points:

- Find the start markers. You have to pass through these once the judges give you the signal to start, or you will be eliminated.
- Walk the route you intend to ride. Do not simply take the shortest line from fence to fence in order to learn the order of the course. Walk exactly where you intend to ride and memorize it.
- As you walk, note the conditions of the ground – are there any poached or slippery areas to try to avoid? Pace out the distances between any combination or related-distance fences. Remember that 8 yards (7.35 m) equals landing, one stride and take-off. Every stride after that takes 4 yards (3.65 m). So a one-stride distance between the fences is 8 yards (7.35 m), a two-stride distance is 12 yards (11 m) etc.
- As you walk any turns, ensure that you really are allowing enough room to get the horse straight and lined up for the next fence. Do not be tempted to cut corners at this stage.
- Relate the distance that you measure out to the knowledge you have of your own horse's stride length. You will know from practising at home whether your horse covers the ground easily or whether you need to open him out in order to fit in the designated number of strides.
- Note where the finish markers are. You have to pass through these once you have jumped the last fence.

him back to trot and then pick up the correct canter lead. If you simply let the horse canter on around the corner on the wrong leg he will be less balanced. There is also a risk that he will attempt to change on to the right lead but may only change his front legs, rather than the hindlegs as well. This is called cantering disunited and is very unbalancing for horse and rider.

If you have to pass the entry/exit gate during your round, just be aware that your horse may be tempted to try to rejoin his friends in the collecting ring. Keep the leg on and back it up with a tap from your stick if the horse drops back from the rhythm you asked for.

If you do have a refusal or a runout, make sure you go far enough away to give your horse a good approach on your second attempt. It is very easy to panic and just swing the horse back round and fire him at the fence again, which will only invite a second refusal. Turn him away, pick up the canter and make a good, balanced turn back to the fence. Do not be tempted to go faster and chase the horse into the fence – that will only push him on to his forehand and make it easier for him to stop again. Think of collecting him up and riding him from a strong, determined leg up into your hand. Contain the power you are creating and channel it towards the fence. Keep the rhythm consistent and do not get in front of the movement.

Make use of the turns to collect and balance the horse. Remember that to go around a corner properly he has to bring his inside hindleg further underneath himself, which in turn helps to lighten and elevate his forehand.

After jumping the last fence and passing through the finish markers, bring the horse quietly back to walk, make a fuss of him and leave the arena at walk.

If disaster strikes and you have a really bad round, remember that losing your temper is not going to improve things. Never punish the horse after his round – the time for a smack is the instant that the horse misbehaves. And never ever punish your horse with a yank at his mouth, or a jab with the spurs. If things have gone wrong, the place to put them right is back at home. Learn from what happened – analyse the mistakes and use exercises at home to correct them. Then come out another day and do it right!

Once you start jumping a course of fences, you will find that everything comes up on you very quickly. You must keep looking ahead to the next fence so that you can plan your turns accordingly.

172
Brittany Ferries
Br
Fe

Cross-country Riding

Riding across country is a true test of a horse-and-rider partnership – whether it be the genuine article when you are quite literally crossing the open countryside and jumping whatever natural hazards block your path, or the more organized version of riding a course of cross-country fences. Cross-country riding requires bravery and fitness from both horse and rider, as well as obedience and trust from the horse. Cross-country fences do not fall down, very often the horse cannot even see where he is going to land, and he cannot judge the depth of any water which he might be required to jump into. Far from being a sport for the reckless and slapdash, if the partnership is to survive it needs trust, obedience and technique.

Cross-country Jumping

BELOW
When galloping across country your weight should be kept out of the saddle, unless riding downhill or directly on the approach to a fence. This allows the horse to stretch out underneath you unhindered by your weight in the saddle.

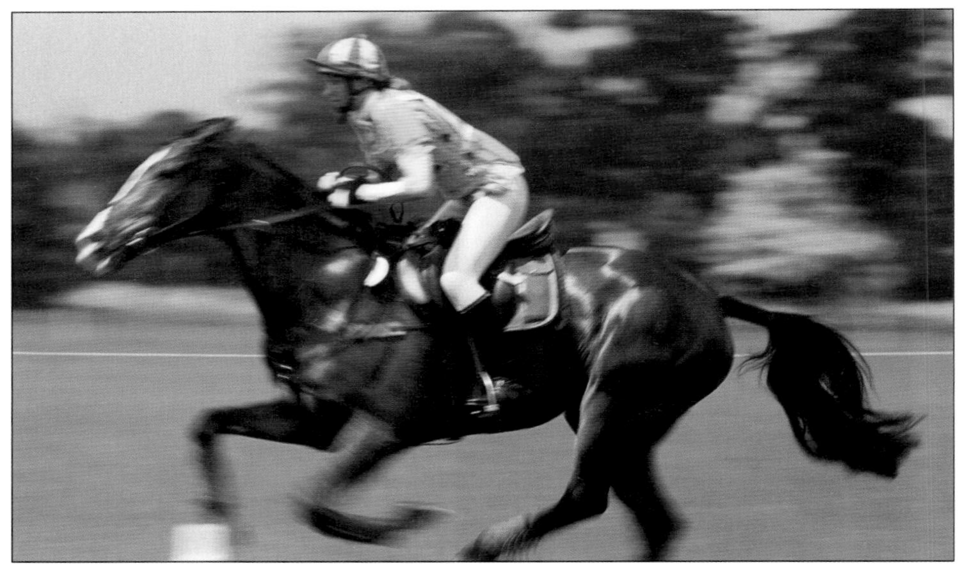

Jumping cross-country fences involves exactly the same principles of rhythm and balance that have already been discussed. The two main differences are:

■ You are generally required to ride across country at a faster pace than you would ride a course of show jumps. It is harder to balance a horse when he is travelling fast, so the rider has to work harder to achieve the same balance as when show jumping whilst travelling in the faster rhythm.

■ The terrain and the types of fence that you have to jump are far more varied than when show jumping. The cross-country course designer will use the natural terrain of the countryside to add to the questions he is asking of horse and rider. He might place a fence right on the brow of a hill, or on a hillside. He may set the course so that the rider has to cross some rougher, more undulating ground on the approach to a fence, making the job of balancing the horse harder still. If you are riding across country while out hunting, for example, you will have no idea of what kind of terrain or fences may come up next. Whatever the countryside throws at you, you have to find a way of crossing it.

SPEED ACROSS COUNTRY

When riding in a cross-country competition there is nearly always what is called an optimum time to aim for, laid down either by the appropriate rule book or by the event organizer. Anyone exceeding the optimum time will incur time penalties. This often results in riders trying to ride the course faster than they are truly capable of doing. It may be good to be competitive but it is always better for the horse, and for the rider's long-term success, for horse and rider to cross the country safely rather than fast. You should never ride faster than you can ride safely.

Remember that you will ride a better round, and probably record a faster time, if you settle in a rhythm and jump from that rhythm, than if you set off hell for leather and then have to fight for control in front of every fence. So think long term – ride your horse safely so that he learns how to deal with things properly and, just as importantly, so that his enjoyment and confidence grow. Gradually you will find you are recording good times across country without realizing you are even trying. That is how you produce a good cross-country horse.

As you approach an uphill fence you should elevate your shoulders so that you lighten the horse's forehand; this makes it easier for him to get his front end up in the air and clear of the fence.

DOWNHILL APPROACH

On the downhill approach to this fence, the rider keeps his seat well back in the saddle, and uses his legs and hands to keep the horse pushed up together so that he does not fall on to his forehand. Just in front of the fence the rider elevates his shoulders slightly to lighten the horse's forehand further and to make it easier for the horse to get his front end up and over the fence. The rider must land in balance with the horse, ready to restore the balance and rhythm immediately.

Coping with the Terrain

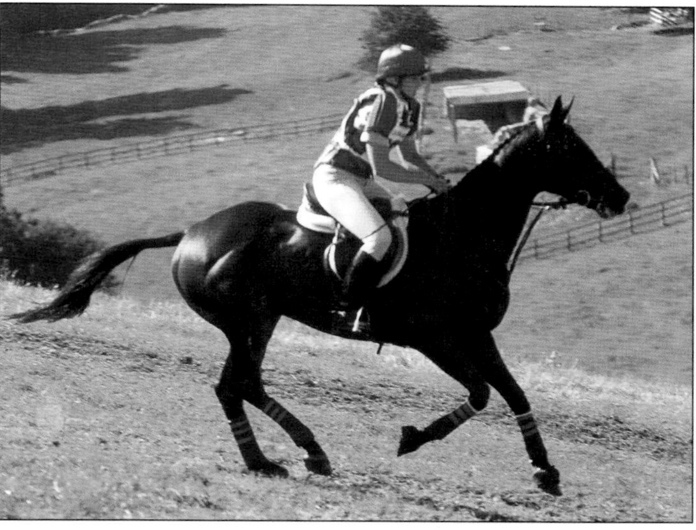

▮ LEFT
Just as when working on the flat or show jumping, the cross-country rider must keep the horse balanced between her legs and hands, over all kinds of terrain.

Keeping the horse balanced and in a rhythm across all kinds of terrain is the secret of good cross-country riding. When galloping on the flat in between fences you should adopt a forward seat, i.e. raise your seat off the saddle so that your weight is carried down through your lower legs into your heels and the stirrup irons.

In the same way that you use a combination of legs and hands when riding on the flat to keep the horse balanced and in a rhythm, do the same across country. You must be physically fit and strong to do this as you not only have to support your own weight by keeping your seat out of the saddle, but you must also continue to use your lower legs effectively to keep the horse pushed up into the hands so that he is balanced. In front of a jump, do the same as you would when show jumping – lower your seat into the saddle, close the legs and hands sufficiently to squeeze the horse up together and to keep him in the same rhythm, and then let your hands follow the horse's movement over the fence.

When galloping uphill, shift your weight further forwards so that the horse's hindquarters are free to propel him up the hill. Still adopt the forward seat, but bring your shoulders further forwards to keep your weight forwards. Although uphill fences can look imposing, they generally jump very well as the horse is already actively using his hocks. On the approach to an uphill fence, slightly elevate your own shoulders, and drop your seat down into the saddle. This has the effect of driving the horse's hocks up underneath him and lightening his forehand so that he is able to raise his front end easily to clear the fence.

Downhill fences are harder to negotiate. When running downhill the horse is more likely to fall on to his forehand, which unbalances him and usually results in him leaning on the rider's hands for support. With all his weight falling on to his forehand he may not be able to raise his shoulders and forelegs quickly and cleanly enough to clear the jump. A good number of cross-country falls occur at downhill fences simply because the rider has failed to follow the golden rule of maintaining balance and rhythm. So when riding downhill, keep your seat in the saddle, your weight well down in your heels and your lower legs pushed slightly forwards. There should be no need to lean back unless it is an exceptionally steep slope. Do not let the horse pull his head and neck down because in so doing he will pull you forward out of the saddle and then all your weight, as well as the horse's, is loaded on to the forehand. Keep your shoulders up, use your legs and seat to drive the horse's hocks under him and use a stronger contact to balance the front end. Elevate your shoulders more in front of the fence to help the horse lighten and raise his front end, and give his head and neck plenty of freedom over the fence. As you land, keep your own weight back so that you don't get pushed on to the horse's shoulders. Take up contact, close the lower legs and work on rebalancing the horse and restoring the rhythm again.

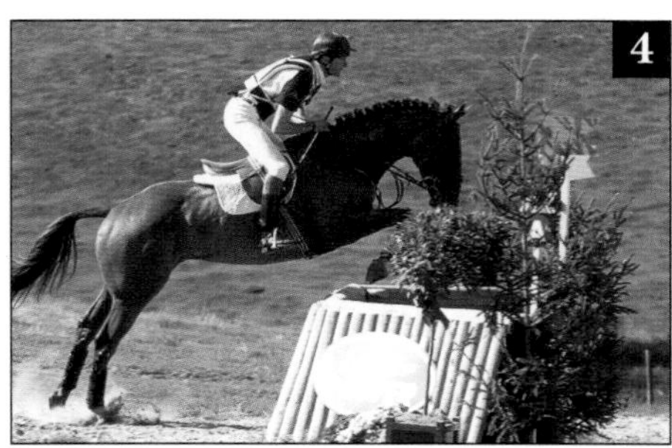

Preparing for the Unexpected

When competing at a cross-country event, the rider walks the course and is therefore familiar with the terrain and the questions that the fences ask. The horse, however, has no idea what is coming next, and it is your task to use your knowledge of the course to prepare the horse.

Having left the start box, settle the horse into a good strong canter. Any straightforward single fences are jumped out of this canter; you simply have to maintain the same rhythm and balance and allow the horse to run and jump out of his stride. But when you know a more complicated jump is coming up, you must prepare the horse for it. So if you know that after the next rail there is a ditch to be jumped just one stride from it, prepare the horse for this unexpected obstacle. On the approach to the rail, slow the horse and collect him up so that his stride is shorter but he is still in an active rhythm. Hold this strong, more collected canter all the way to the rail. An experienced horse will take this as a signal that there is more to this fence than meets the eye. It gives him time to realize that a ditch follows the rail. On an inexperienced horse, this same action will help focus the horse's attention on the fence, and will give him time to see the ditch on the other side. However, you must be prepared for the horse to be wary of the ditch, and you may need to ride more aggressively so that he keeps going and tackles both the rail and the ditch that follows.

Similarly if the next fence is followed by a step down, or involves a combination of various obstacles, always re-collect and balance the horse on the approach. If, having walked the course, you know that the distance between two fences is very tight, shorten the horse's stride on the approach and keep this new rhythm all the way to the fence so that the horse jumps it tidily and has room to take the designated number of strides. If there is a long distance between the fences, open the horse's stride out well before he gets to the jump and hold the new rhythm all the way to the fence. On landing you may need to send the horse forwards actively in order to encourage him to continue the opened-out stride on the approach to the second fence.

Landing over a drop or into water also requires some warning for the horse, and

JUMPING INTO WATER

On the approach to this log into water, the rider has shortened the horse's stride and really pushed him up together. This has elevated the horse's forehand and has helped to focus him on what is coming up. Just in front of the log, the rider is ready with a strong leg to insist that the horse keeps going now that he has spotted the water on the landing side of the fence. The rider keeps her upper-body weight back as the horse drops down into the water, and she slips the reins through her fingers to allow the horse the full use of his head and neck. Once in the water there is not enough time for the rider to shorten the reins back up; she therefore draws her elbows back behind her, which in effect takes up the slack in the reins and allows her to regain the contact and control.

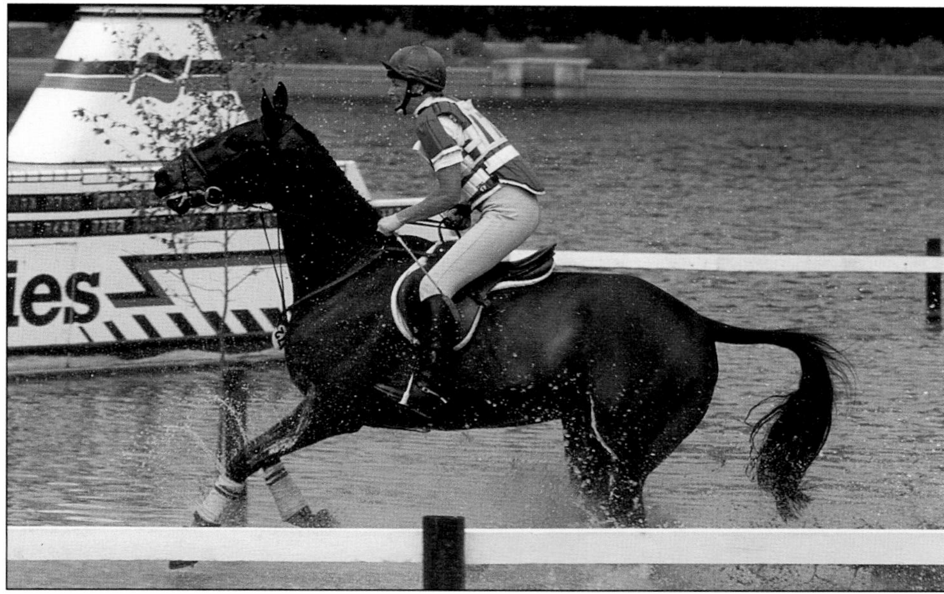

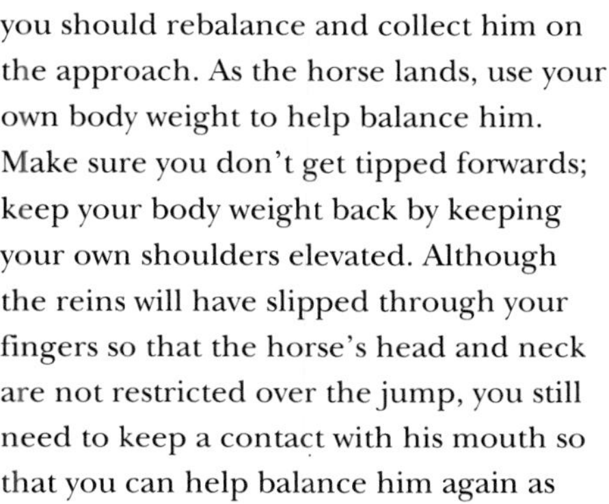

you should rebalance and collect him on the approach. As the horse lands, use your own body weight to help balance him. Make sure you don't get tipped forwards; keep your body weight back by keeping your own shoulders elevated. Although the reins will have slipped through your fingers so that the horse's head and neck are not restricted over the jump, you still need to keep a contact with his mouth so that you can help balance him again as you land. If the horse trips or stumbles as he lands, or if he is taken by surprise by the size of a drop, or by landing in water, you can use the contact through the reins to support the horse and to keep his head up slightly, and you may well be able to save him from falling. In contrast, if you have tipped forwards and let the reins go loose, if anything untoward should happen on landing both you and the horse are likely to fall.

ABOVE LEFT
When jumping into water, you must keep your weight well back. However, at the same time it is vital that you let the reins slip through your hands so that you do not restrict the horse's use of his head and neck. Note how this rider maintains a contact so that he can help to balance the horse as soon as they have landed in the water.

ABOVE RIGHT
When cantering through water the rider must keep a contact with the horse's mouth so that the horse can remain balanced and light on his forehand.

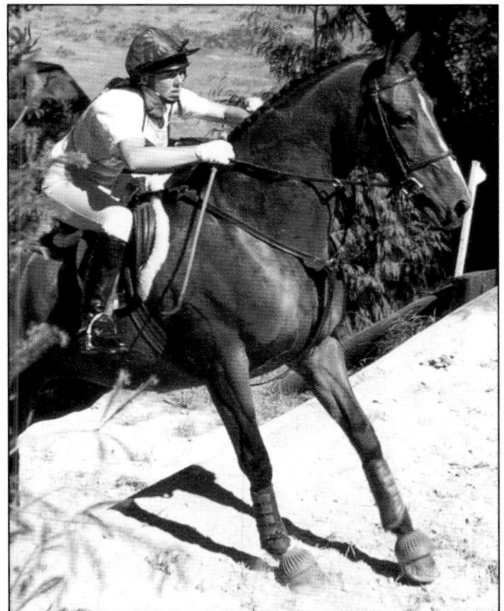

It is quite difficult to stay in balance with a horse when he jumps up on to a step or bank. The idea is to keep your seat close to the saddle, but with your weight just raised out of it so that the horse feels he can really use himself. Your upper body needs to fold forwards and your hands must also move forwards so that, once again, the horse has enough freedom of the rein to stretch and use himself as he jumps.

PATIENCE AND DETERMINATION

A lifetime can be spent mastering the art of horsemanship because, like any artist or craftsman, it is perfection that you are seeking. You may not wish to take your riding to the highest levels but you should never close your mind to the opportunity to improve. You may have no ambition to compete seriously but you should always have pride in the care and well-being of your horse. Enjoy him to whatever degree you wish but always repay him by making sure you know how to care for him. Every horse and pony, whatever his job in life, deserves to be looked after properly.

Those who do wish to strive for perfection will need patience and determination in equal measure. Patience is vital because all horses are individuals, and some will react and learn more quickly and easily than others. You must be prepared to take time to teach the horse the basics so that you have a strong foundation to build on later. A horseman should always be working for the long-term good of the horse, not for short-term gain.

Determination is needed because somehow horses always seem to create as much heartbreak as happiness. Things do go wrong – some horses simply aren't cut out for the sport for which they were bought. In the same way that not all human beings can cope with the same pressures or stresses in life, horses vary in their degree of tolerance and aptitude. Many a failed competition horse has become someone else's adored hack or hunter. So always be realistic about what you are asking of the horse. If he really isn't up to the job, it is kinder to sell him to someone who will appreciate his other talents, rather than for both of you to endure a life of frustration and misery.

Horses do go lame or become ill, often just before your main target of the season, and riders have accidents with a similar degree of bad timing! Years of work and preparation can appear to be wasted when such things go wrong, but if you have trained and prepared your horse thoroughly and carefully your chance will come.

You will never stop learning about how to get the best from your horse. Even the top riders continue to go to people more experienced than themselves for help and advice – and remember that they never stop practising their art either.

COPING WITH AN EARLY TAKE-OFF

This rider has taken quite a risk at this widespread fence by asking her horse to take off very early. On a less scopey horse there is every chance that this sort of riding will result in a fall, as the horse may be physically unable to clear the spread of the fence and will land on it. In the first picture the rider has kept the horse balanced and in an even rhythm, but in the second picture she has suddenly opened the horse out and asked him to take off. Had she maintained the rhythm and balance all the way to the fence, the horse would have been able to fit in another stride and would have taken off a little closer to the fence. As it is, having stood the horse right off, the rider has reacted in the correct way over the fence. She has kept her body weight balanced over the middle of the horse and has slipped the reins, so that he can really stretch himself out and clear the fence.

1

2

3

4

5

TACKLING TWO CORNERS – 1

1

2

3

4

5

6

This horse and rider are tackling a combination of two corners set three strides apart. See how the rider lands over the first corner and, using his knowledge of his horse's stride length, he sits quietly and lets the horse take three even strides to the second corner.

TACKLING TWO CORNERS – 2

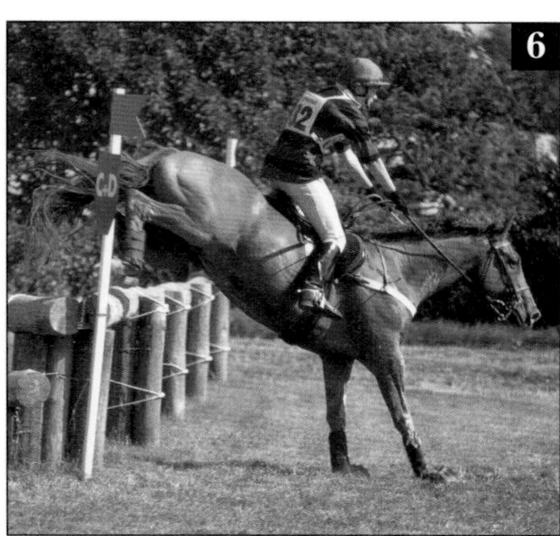

Another horse and rider tackling the same combination. Note how this rider, having landed over the first corner, knows that she has got to open her horse's stride out in order to make up the three strides to the next fence. She has sat down in the saddle and is really riding the horse forwards. Knowing her horse very well, she has even dropped the rein contact with his mouth, and thus lessened her control, to encourage him to stretch everything forwards in order to reach the fence. In this instance, it has paid off for her because she knows her horse well enough to trust him. Usually at a fence like this, which demands accuracy, you cannot afford to drop the rein contact in this way as the horse is then free to run out if he so wishes.

WHEN THINGS GO WRONG

Successful cross-country riding requires an ability to cope with the unexpected – even though you may have walked the course and know exactly how you intend riding everything, sometimes the horse has other ideas. Despite your best intentions he may jump or react differently from how you imagined. Then you need to know what to do to make the best of the situation. For example, if your horse is normally long striding you might expect him to make up the distance in a combination easily, but if there is something in that combination that makes the horse back down, such as a ditch under the jump, suddenly you may not be on the stride pattern you imagined. Experience will teach you whether it is best to shorten your horse's stride and let him fit in an extra one, or whether you are better off riding even more aggressively, forcing him to open up his stride again and to take on the fence. Some horses jump very big over ditches, or off drops, and this may alter the distance to the next fence.

Most importantly, if and when the unexpected happens, you are of most help if you can stay in balance with the horse and give him the necessary freedom of his head and neck. This all comes down to having an independent seat. If you can stay balanced without needing to hang on to the reins, and can at the same time keep thinking ahead and judging what you need to do to help the horse, you are the best asset he can have. A horse can jump out of some seemingly impossible situations, and can correct seemingly disastrous misjudgements, if his rider is not hindering him. The golden rule is to maintain rhythm and balance.

BOND TYRES

World of the Horse

The Competition World

Competing with your horse can be as low key or as serious as you wish to make it. Some riders make a living out of riding and competing with horses, others simply enjoy giving the family horse a quick wash and brush-up once a year for a local show. Whatever you opt for within that scale, there are certain things to be aware of.

Before attempting any form of horse sport you must be sure that your horse is fit and mature enough, both mentally and physically, to take part. He should be sufficiently well schooled to be obedient to your commands, and should have seen enough in his daily hacks and general training regime not to be overawed by the competition scene.

Most horses should be versatile enough to take part in any number of sports at the lower levels. But if you decide to take up a particular sport seriously, check out the requirements and skills needed to ensure that you are both suited to that sport.

Types of Competition

▮ BELOW
There are so many opportunities to compete; all abilities and tastes are catered for, from the rough and tumble of mounted games...

The wide range of horse sports that is now available means there is something to suit all types of horse and rider. From the more genteel, such as showing and dressage, to the rough and tumble of team sports such as polo and horseball, all manner of skills, both mental and physical, are tested. Some sports are judged very subjectively. Dressage and showing, for example, are reliant on the opinion of the particular judge on the day. Others are out-and-out contests of stamina and tactics, such as horse racing and endurance riding. In show jumping and cross-country-riding competitions, the skills of each horse and rider are not only pitted against their fellow competitors, but also against the questions set by the course designer. However great or small your competitive streak, there is something to suit all tastes.

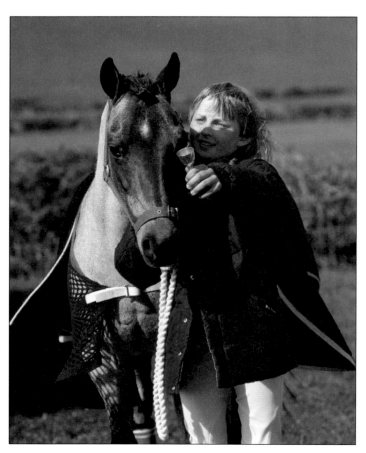

▮ LEFT
The main aim of competing at any level is that it should be fun. It is not so much the winning as the taking part – although everybody likes to win sometimes!

WELFARE REQUIREMENTS

■ All affiliated competitions will state the age at which horses or ponies are allowed to compete in that particular discipline. For example, event horses are not allowed to compete in one-day events until they are five years old. You will need to be aware of such restrictions before planning a competition season with your horse.

■ Competition horses must have an up-to-date vaccination certificate which proves that they have received their annual vaccination booster.

■ As a rider and competitor you have a responsibility to your horse and to other competitors to ensure that, if you suspect your horse is suffering from something contagious, he is kept isolated from other horses. Obviously if your horse is clinically ill you would not consider taking him to a competition but some diseases, such as ringworm or mild viruses, do not greatly affect the horse's general well-being. When this is the case you should not be tempted to hope for the best and still go – you must keep your horse at home, away from other horses, until he is fully recovered.

BELOW
...to the sheer elegance of dressage...

RIGHT
...and the test of all-round horsemanship, eventing.

AFFILIATED AND UNAFFILIATED COMPETITIONS

Most countries have a good selection of organized horse sports, and these are usually split between what are regarded as affiliated and unaffiliated competitions. The **affiliated competitions** are generally stricter and require horse and rider to be registered as members of that particular sport's governing body.

At the top end of the scale, the International Equestrian Federation (FEI) governs all international competitions involving the sports under its jurisdiction – dressage, show jumping, carriage driving, eventing, vaulting and endurance riding.

The FEI controls their rules, and approves the programme of events at regional, championship and Olympic level.

Each country's own national federation is, in turn, answerable to the FEI. They organize competitions for all levels of experience within their own country.

Unaffiliated competitions, usually run along the same lines as the affiliated competitions, are put on by individuals who are happy about taking on the organizational responsibility. To enter these you do not need to be a registered member of any governing body, but you will need to be familiar with the affiliated rules as these are often used. Many of the riders who compete in the affiliated competitions will take advantage of the more relaxed atmosphere at unaffiliated shows to introduce a young horse to the sport. The unaffiliated competitions also act as an introduction to the sport for novice riders.

RESTRICTIONS

Many sports split their competitions into classes for either different age groups of riders, or different standards or sizes of horse or pony. Pony classes are restricted either to recognized pony breeds or to any equine standing under 15hh. Showing classes are classified by size and type of horse or pony – working hunter, show hack, cob etc.

The affiliated organizations run competitions for horses of the various grades recognized by their governing body, e.g. event horses are graded from novice through to advanced, dressage horses from preliminary through to grand prix, and so on.

Local unaffiliated classes are divided up into rider age groups, size of horse or pony, or prize money or placings previously won. The novice class may be restricted to horses or ponies who have never been placed in any competitions, the next class may be limited to horses who haven't previously won a competition. The open class, as its name suggests, is open to any grade of horse or pony and is usually the most competitive of all.

To avoid disappointment and embarrassment or, worse still, elimination, do make sure you have read the rules and regulations of any competition you intend entering and comply with them.

The happy winner of a show class salutes his appreciative audience.

Choosing a Sport

It is a good idea to find out if you enjoy and have an aptitude for a particular sport by entering unaffiliated competitions before going to the expense of registering with an affiliated body.

If, for example, you decide that dressage appeals to you, start out by competing quietly against friends and neighbours at local unaffiliated shows. Having decided that this sport really is for you, register with your national federation and start to work your way up through the grades of affiliated competition. If you have the talent, dedication and time to commit to the sport, there is nothing to stop you reaching the top. If your sights really are set on the giddy heights of world championships or the Olympics, do remember that competitors at this level not only have to qualify to take part but also have to be selected by their national federation to enter as individuals or team members.

If you are lucky enough to be able to take your sport that seriously, you should investigate the opportunities that your national federation offers. Most countries that have an affiliation to the FEI also offer training to their members, as well as competitions culminating in international championships for riders of different age groups. The sports of dressage, show

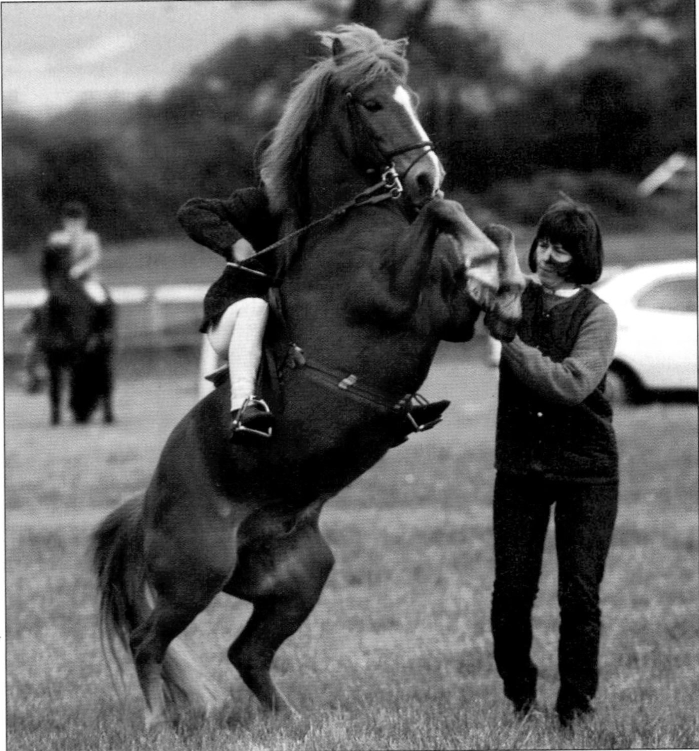

LEFT
When choosing a sport to take part in, it is important to consider the suitability of both your own and your horse's temperament. For some riders the excitement becomes too much – can you cope with this? Will it add to your fun or will it worry you?

ABOVE AND BELOW
If you wish to compete regularly then some form of transport is going to be necessary. This can be a vehicle and trailer or a horse lorry, either of which can be purchased, hired or shared. Not only will the trailer or lorry provide a safe haven for your horse in between classes, it will also tend to become the social centre of the event.

EQUIPMENT NEEDED FOR ALL EQUESTRIAN SPORTS

- You should wear a recognized safety helmet or crash hat complete with safety harness for all horse-riding activities. If you intend riding and jumping across country, you should also wear a body protector.
- Each sport has its own recognized and accepted style of dress. Dressage, show jumping and showing classes require the rider to be turned out in a riding jacket, jodhpurs or breeches, short or long riding boots and a hard hat. For cross-country riding, you can wear a sweat shirt or jumper instead of a riding jacket.

  Polo, horseball and polocrosse require breeches and long leather boots to be worn, along with a shirt instead of a riding jacket, plus protective padding such as knee pads.

  Endurance riders wear either standard jodhpurs or breeches, or more lightweight ones for hot conditions, as well as waterproofs for wet weather. They are not expected to wear riding jackets but dress according to the weather conditions.
- Your horse or pony will need a well-fitting saddle and bridle, and it is also advisable to protect his legs against strains or knocks by using boots or bandages.
- You will need water, buckets, sponges, sweat scrapers and towels so that the horse can be washed and dried off if he is hot and sweaty after competing.

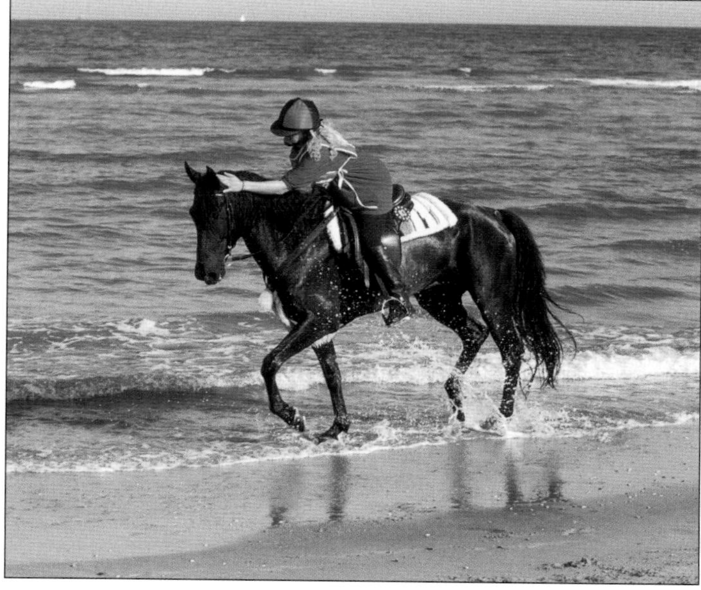

RIGHT
This competitor rewards her horse with a pat and a paddle at the World Equestrian Games Endurance competition. Endurance competitors are allowed to dress according to the weather conditions.

jumping and eventing have championships specifically for pony riders, juniors and young riders. When you reach the age of twenty-one, you have to join the senior ranks.

Within the other equestrian sports there is usually a very good choice of competition designed to cover all levels of ability and ambition. In the showing world this ranges from local shows to regional competitions, right through to national championships. For some of these classes, your horse or pony may have to be registered with a breed society or showing association; these, in turn, help to govern and organize the various competitions, local and national.

Team sports such as polo, polocrosse and horseball require greater organization and facilities, as does learning the skills of vaulting. To take part usually entails joining a local club.

BELOW
Whether you have a good or a bad day, you must always put your horse's or pony's needs first. Make sure he has time to relax and enjoy the experience as well.

BELOW
Equestrian sports involving jumping offer variety and fun. Show jumping, for example, has classes available for anyone from leading-rein contenders, through junior classes as shown here, to international senior competitions.

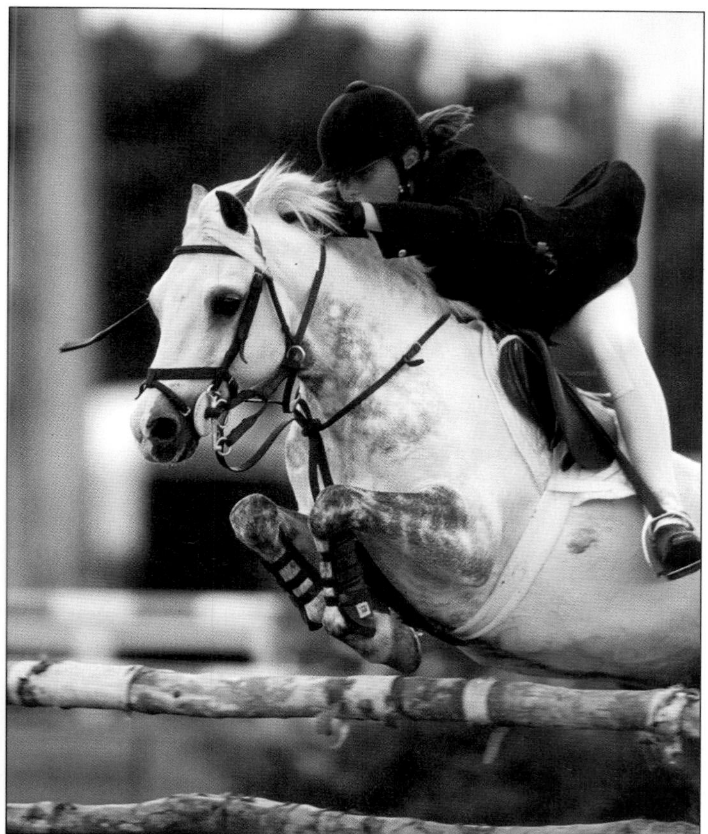

TRAVELLING EQUIPMENT

Once you decide to compete regularly, unless you are very lucky in having regular competitions held within hacking distance, you will need to transport your horse in either a horse lorry or trailer. The horse must be kept safe and comfortable when travelling.

- There should be bedding on the floor to cushion his legs and to help soak up any urine or droppings he produces.
- He should be secured with a headcollar and rope which is tied through a piece of string attached to the fixed tie ring. This is so that, should the horse fall or struggle, he will be able to free his head and neck – otherwise he may injure himself very badly.
- He will need a selection of rugs or blankets, chosen according to the weather conditions on the day, so that he becomes neither too hot nor too cold on the journey.
- He should wear protective boots or bandages on his legs, a tailguard or bandage (or both) to protect his tail from rubbing, and a poll guard to protect the top of his head.
- You should offer your horse water to drink during the journey, and a haynet, although this should be taken away at least an hour before he is due to be ridden. Take food and hay for him to eat during the day and on the journey home, and keep a check on how warm or cold he is whilst travelling.

Non-jumping Sports

Horse sports are so varied that they are difficult to categorize. For the purposes of this book, they are split into a selection of non-jumping and jumping sports. To make it to the top of any one, you need to specialize. But most riders enjoy taking part in a number of different activities, so first look at the different things you can try. Unless you have your heart set on one particular sport, it is worth experimenting to find out what really suits you and your horse. The discipline and perfectionist nature of dressage may suit your personality, or perhaps you would prefer the more light-hearted approach of mounted games. Once you have outgrown those, there are team games such as horseball, polo and polocrosse to enjoy, or perhaps Western riding appeals to you. Whoever you are, whatever your ability, there is bound to be something to which you can aspire.

Mounted Games

If you can envisage a cross between party games and a race on horseback, you will have some idea of what mounted games involve. Although adults do compete, it is primarily a sport for children – the energy, enthusiasm and agility that this sport requires ideally suit youngsters and their ponies. The beauty of these games is that there is one to suit every type and ability of pony and rider.

Mounted games can be organized for fun between a group of friends or as a serious form of competition, with regional, national and international championships provoking great rivalry between the various clubs and associations taking part. But at whatever level they are played, mounted games will help to develop your riding skills, your confidence in handling yourself and your pony and, most importantly, the realization that riding is fun.

■ HOW MOUNTED GAMES BEGAN

Surprisingly for a sport that is now dominated by children, mounted games were first played by adults. It was in India that the games we are familiar with today developed. They were then known as gymkhanas, which translated as gymnastic or athletic displays on horseback. The word gymkhana is still used in many countries today to describe the sport. The British Army, which was based in India in the late nineteenth century, adopted the games, although their mounts included donkeys, mules and camels. The games, such as "Kiss the Girl", "Tent Pegging" and "Grab the Hat", were a popular and light-hearted way not only of helping to keep horse and rider fit and supple, but also of fostering strong regimental loyalty.

When the soldiers returned to Britain, they introduced the games to their home country where they proved most popular with children, their small, nippy ponies being ideal mounts for the games. The Pony Club, which was formed in 1929 and quickly grew to become a world-wide organization with over 100,000 members, developed and spread the benefits of the games. Pony Club Mounted Games are now played in over twenty-five different countries at interbranch, interstate and international level.

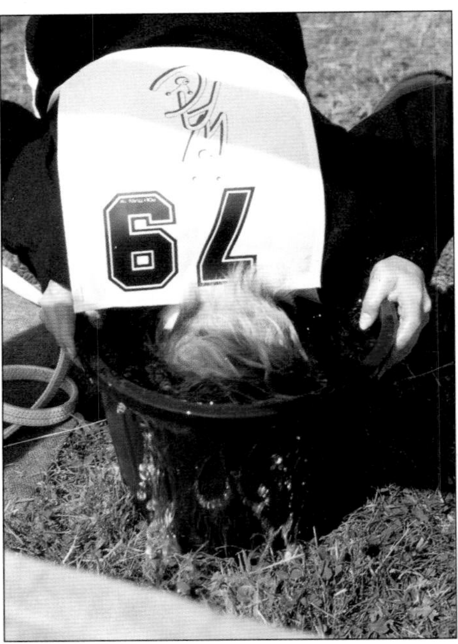

▮ BELOW
Some games rely on your pony's skills; others are down to the rider. In "Apple Bobbing" you have to retrieve an apple from a bucket of water without using your hands!

A flying start is a big advantage, whatever race you are in. Practise at home by gradually asking your pony to go straight into canter from walk, and then from halt.

For those who do not wish to lose out on the enjoyment of mounted games once they are over Pony Club age, there is the International Mounted Games Association. This holds an annual World Mounted Games Championship in a different host country each year, and membership of the Association goes up to the age of twenty-one.

Other opportunities to play mounted games are offered at local shows and gymkhanas, where there are classes for leading-rein competitors as well as for older children.

■ SKILLS REQUIRED

To enjoy mounted games for the fun and entertainment they offer requires no great skill on the part of horse or rider. But if you want to be the winner of many ribbons, or to make it on to a team and compete more seriously, certain skills are necessary.

Your pony will need to be fit, obedient, agile and unflappable – he will encounter

LEFT
Another great asset is the ability to vault on to a moving pony. It is a bit easier than it looks – if you time it properly the pony's forward motion helps propel you through the air and up on to his back.

THE RANGE OF GAMES

Each year more and more ingenious games are developed to test the pony's and rider's speed, agility, co-ordination, fitness and sense of humour!

The easiest games are designed for young riders whose ponies are being led – musical mats, musical chairs and musical statues. The children are led around on their ponies until the music stops, when they must leap off and pounce on a chair or mat. One chair or mat is taken away each time so that the rider who finds him- or herself without a chair or mat is out. In musical statues the pony, rider and leader must remain absolutely still when the music stops. The first to move is out – more often than not it is the pony who doesn't have the patience or desire to remain still.

For those who want to test their speed and agility there are the races. These can be as simple as a bending race, where horse and rider thread their way between a line of poles, or as complex and extravagant as such team races as the "Dragon Race". There are even games that include the fun of jumping. In "Chase Me Charlie", the competitors follow each other over a jump. If they clear it they stay in the game, if they knock it down they are out. The jump is raised each time until only the winner remains. "Barrel Elimination" involves jumping over a line of barrels. After each round, one barrel is removed so that the jump becomes narrower and narrower until there is only one barrel remaining to be jumped over. If the pony stops or runs out to either side, he is out of the game.

all kinds of strange objects in the varied races on offer. Most riders opt for a pony who for most other sports would be considered a touch too small for them, but a smaller pony makes it easier to reach down to deposit or retrieve objects and to mount and dismount on the move.

As a mounted-games competitor, you too will need to be fit and agile. Good co-ordination and balance are called for, as well as a good turn of speed as, in many games, the rider may be dismounted and leading the pony for much of the race. Similarly, the ability to vault on to your pony while he is cantering along is a great asset, as is the ability to dismount at speed without losing balance and falling over.

You must be able to control your pony with only one hand on the reins, as the other hand is often needed to do whatever the game entails. If the pony can be taught to neck rein, i.e. to respond to pressure on the neck from the rein rather than to a feel on the bit, controlling him with both reins in one hand will be easy.

TRAINING THE MOUNTED-GAMES PONY

Obedience in the form of fast reactions is what is required of the mounted-games pony. He must be able to start and stop quickly, turn tightly and, amidst all the excitement of the race, remain stock still while his rider carries out whatever task the game requires.

You cannot begin to improve your pony's responsiveness until he is working obediently to the basic leg and hand aids. Unless he is already at the stage where you can quietly ask him to go forwards in walk, trot and then canter, to halt, to turn left or right and to move to the side, i.e. leg yield, he is not ready to be asked to do

LEFT
It takes a tolerant pony and two agile riders to manage this feat!

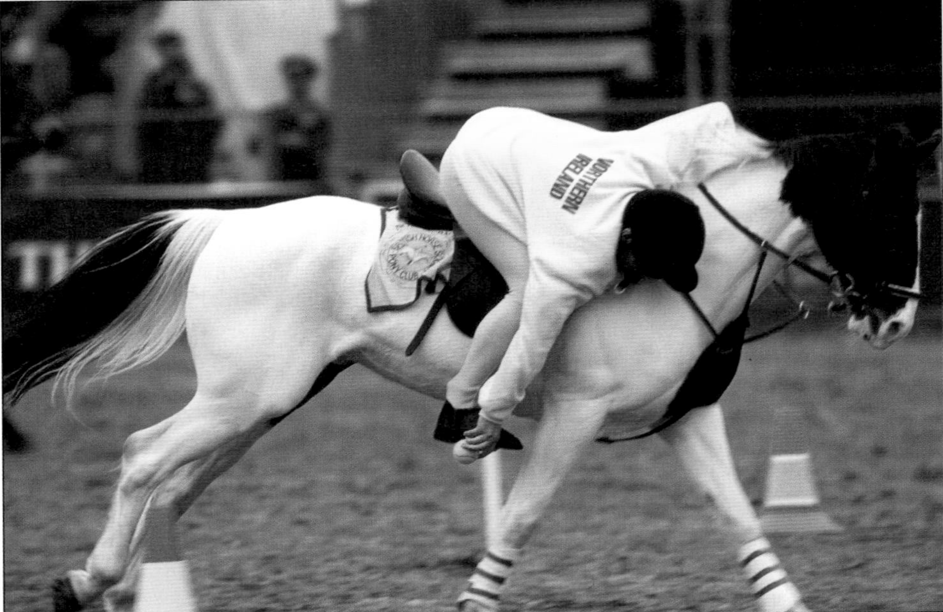

LEFT
It helps to be fit and supple and to have good co-ordination. Here the rider has to retrieve a tennis ball from the top of the cone.

anything beyond this. As in all things, establish the basics first and it will be easy to teach your pony any number of new skills.

THE QUICK START

To have any chance of winning you need to get a good start – your pony should be able to leap forwards from halt to full speed ahead. He will already know how to go up through the paces to canter; now he needs to speed up the process. You should first practise going forwards into trot from halt, and then try halt to canter. The correct aids should still be applied and they should be backed up by the voice, and, if necessary, a tap behind the leg with the schooling whip, rather than resorting to giving the pony a great thump with your heels. If you teach the pony to go forwards by kicking his sides with your heels, he will gradually become less responsive and will certainly be spoilt for any other activity. Treat this training in the same way as your flatwork – you are still looking for a quick response to a light aid.

THE QUICK STOP

Similarly, the pony must be able to come back rapidly from flat out to halt whenever required. This is not achieved by simply hauling hard on the reins. As in your flatwork training, ask the pony to halt by using your legs to drive him up into your hands which, on this occasion, do not soften or yield to him, so he is brought back to a halt. Using your voice to ask him to "Whoa" will also help him to understand and respond more quickly to the request to stop. Shift your weight slightly further back in the saddle as you ask your pony to halt. This will help push his hindquarters further under him and allow him to sit down on his hocks so that, when he halts, his forehand is still light and elevated, ready for the all-important quick getaway.

NECK REINING

In countries where horses have always been used for herding livestock, such as America, Australia, New Zealand, parts of Africa and the Far East, neck reining is commonly used. This allows the rider to carry both reins in one hand. To turn the horse to the right, the rider simply brings his left hand, which is holding the reins, over to the right-hand side of the pony's neck. The reins press against the left-hand side of the pony's neck, the pony moves away from the pressure and so turns to the right. Do the opposite to turn left.

In most European countries, ponies need to be taught to respond to neck reining. If you apply the correct leg aids before you bring the rein across the pony's neck, and at the same time incline your body weight slightly in the direction you want to go, the pony will quickly get the idea of responding to neck reining.

In the stepping-stones race the rider has to tackle the stepping stones before vaulting on to the pony and racing for the finishing line.

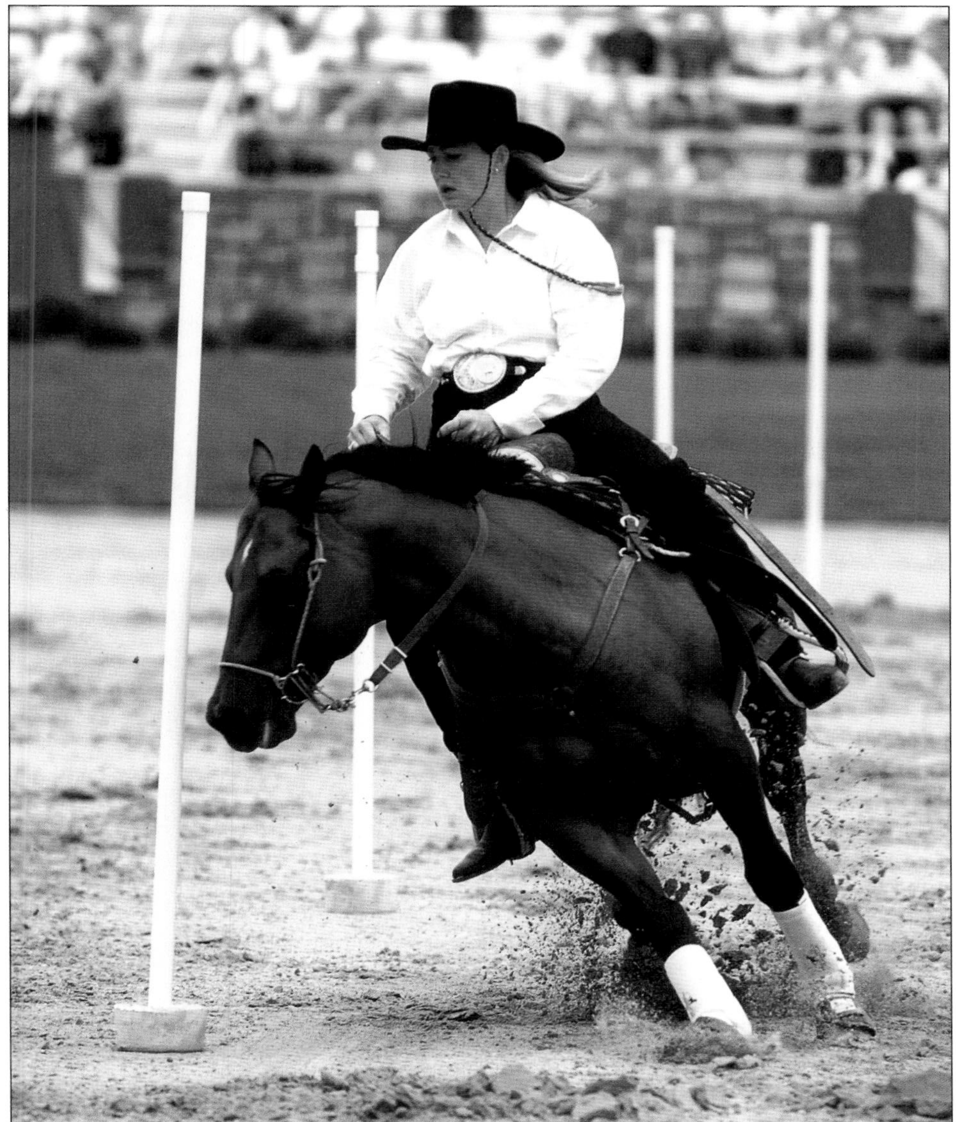

LEFT
Mounted games aren't just for children and small ponies – here an American Quarter Horse shows how good he is at bending.

pressure on the right-hand side of the pony's neck. It is sometimes helpful to use the reins slightly higher up the pony's neck when you would like him to turn particularly sharply.

GETTING USED TO THE EQUIPMENT

In a serious mounted-games competition your pony will face any number of strange objects. He must be prepared to go up to whatever the target of the game is, he may have to go under a washing-line strung with clothes, or a post hung with signboards – all manner of items have to be acceptable to him. He must allow his rider to carry flags, buckets, swords and balloons without being worried by them. He must be accustomed to noise and the general hustle and bustle, including a very noisily appreciative audience, which is all part of a mounted-games competition.

All these strange and startling things should be introduced to the pony at home. As long as you give him time to realize that none of these peculiar objects is going to

TURNING

Your pony will need to be able to turn quickly and sharply, and this can be practised at home by using a barrel as a turning point. Practise first in trot, riding up to and around the barrel, keeping your pony as tight to the barrel as you can. Remember that it is your outside hand and leg that will prevent the pony from drifting away from the barrel. Once you have mastered a tight turn in trot using both hands on the rein, try it in canter. When the pony is familiar with what is required, try it with the reins in one hand. To turn tightly to the left around the barrel, your right leg will be back behind the girth to keep the pony's quarters close to the barrel, your inside leg will be used on the girth to make the pony bend through his body and you will bring your rein hand across to the left, so that there is

The "Dragon Race" is one of the most spectacular – the riders have to kill the dragon by bursting the balloons attached to him. Then they can rescue the damsel in distress.

▮ LEFT
Mounted games are as much to do with team work as with individual ability and success.

harm him, he will soon accept them. There is no point using force – his trust has to be won and this takes time and patience. When you show your pony something new, allow him time to make up his own mind that it is harmless. Do not force him to approach this strange object too quickly. Reward and reassure him all the time that he is prepared to face it, even if he is still not very close to it. Only become stronger in your riding if he actually turns away from the object. Then you must be positive and use your legs and hands to turn him back. Once he is facing it again, reward him. Let him know you are displeased each time he tries to turn away, and gradually he will realize that you are determined that he will meet this new thing. Usually curiosity takes over and he will dare to get closer and closer. Take things slowly – go one step at a time – and this will ensure that your pony's confidence and enjoyment increase.

THE CHANGEOVER

Many races require a fast changeover of equipment – usually a baton – between two riders. This has to be practised, firstly to accustom the pony to the idea of another pony and rider bearing down on him at great speed – the last thing you want is your pony shying away. Secondly, both riders involved need to know how to hand over the item without dropping it. It should be held at arm's length so that the receiving rider has a good view of the target to be grabbed. The riders should be positioned so that the receiver can grab the baton with his or her best hand (the right hand if he or she is right-handed) and the first rider should not release the grip on the baton until he or she is positive that the second rider has taken hold of it. It is quicker to turn around and hand it over again than for the baton to be dropped and the rider to have to dismount.

■ PRACTICE FOR THE RIDER

Once you are familiar with even a small number of mounted games, you will realize that a wide range of skills is called for. All demand dexterity and agility, but some demand more specialist skills. If you are a good shot you will excel at games such as the "Hi Lo Race", where a tennis ball has to land in a high net, or the "Sharpshooters' Race", where a soft ball is thrown at a line of comic models until it succeeds in knocking their heads off. In the "Sack Race" you will need to be able to race along, leading your pony, while your feet and legs are trapped in a sack!

All these strange skills can be practised on foot at home, with simple homemade equipment. Practising the races on foot will also help to promote your overall fitness and agility, which will be all to the good when you try them out on horseback again.

VAULTING ON AND OFF

To be a truly successful mounted-games player you will need to master the art of mounting and dismounting at speed. A small pony coupled with a rider with long legs have the advantage here, although there is an art to vaulting on which makes it easier than it looks. The trick is to use the momentum created by the pony's movement to help lift you into the saddle. To begin with, practise mounting a moving pony with someone leading the pony so that he can be kept straight and at a steady speed. You should run beside the pony, who will be trotting or cantering, keeping level with the pony's shoulder. Stretch your right hand over the pony's back and take hold of the front of the saddle flap on the far side. Your left hand is holding the reins and can be rested on the pony's withers. As the pony's near-side foreleg touches the ground, spring upwards and swing your right leg over his back. If your timing is good, the pony's forward momentum will help to lift you up into the air.

To dismount from a moving pony, organize yourself so that you land facing forwards and are immediately able to run forwards so that you do not lose your balance. If you have ever stepped off a moving bus or carousel platform, you will know that unless you start running as soon as your feet touch the ground you will fall flat on your face.

Take both feet out of the stirrups, put your right hand on the pommel of the saddle and your left hand on the pony's neck. Lean forwards over the pony's neck and swing your right leg up and over his back. Use your hands to push your body clear of the pony's side and to help balance yourself as you land. Make sure you land running.

For those competing seriously, team-training sessions will be necessary, possibly even with a coach; here it is possible to see which riders and ponies are best suited to which games, and also to discuss team tactics – an important weapon on the road to victory.

The Games

As you will have gathered, any number of mounted games can be dreamed up. The Pony Club probably has the most comprehensive list, which is used for their national and international competitions. It has a good rule book, including – to avoid any breakdown in international relations – an Official International Exchange Visits rule book. Despite the fact that mounted games are meant to be fun, they can become very competitive, so it is always safest to be sure everyone is agreed on the same rules. The following is a selection of team games. Most can be adapted to suit team or individual competitions, but do not feel you have to be limited to these. Let your imagination run riot!

SACK RACE

Gallop your pony to the end of the arena where there is an empty sack. Jump off the pony, get inside the sack, and make your way back to the start, hopping, shuffling or tripping along, whilst still leading your pony. One trick is to rest an arm across the pony's withers as this will help support your weight and keep you upright. The other hand holds the sack up around you. Jump forwards, allowing the pony to take your weight and to carry you forwards a little way before landing again.

An even more amusing adaptation of this game is the "Big Sack Race". Four team members gallop to the end of the arena where a fifth team member is holding a huge sack. She takes her team-mates' ponies whilst all four of them climb into the sack and, *en masse*, wriggle their way back to the start.

GROOM'S RACE

This calls for an additional skill – the ability to control two ponies at once. You have to ride your own pony, and lead one of your team-mates' ponies, up through a line of bending poles. At the changeover point your team-mate mounts her own pony, and leads the third rider's pony back through the line of poles. And so it goes on until all the riders and ponies have had their turn and are back at the start.

LAUNDRY STAKES

One pair of riders gallops to a washing-line, carrying a basket of laundry between them. They hang out the washing and gallop back, handing the empty basket to the second two members of the team. They have to gallop to the washing-line, remove the washing, and bring it back safely to the start in the laundry basket.

BELOW
The "Basketball Race" is another favourite at the Pony Club games.

ROPE RACE

Set off at a gallop through a line of bending poles carrying a piece of rope about 3 feet (1 m) long. At the end of the arena, one of your team-mates grabs the end of the rope and you both gallop back through the bending poles together. At the other end you drop your end of the rope and a third rider picks it up; the second and third rider hold the rope and gallop through the bending poles, and so on. Be careful not to allow your pony to tread on the heels of the one in front.

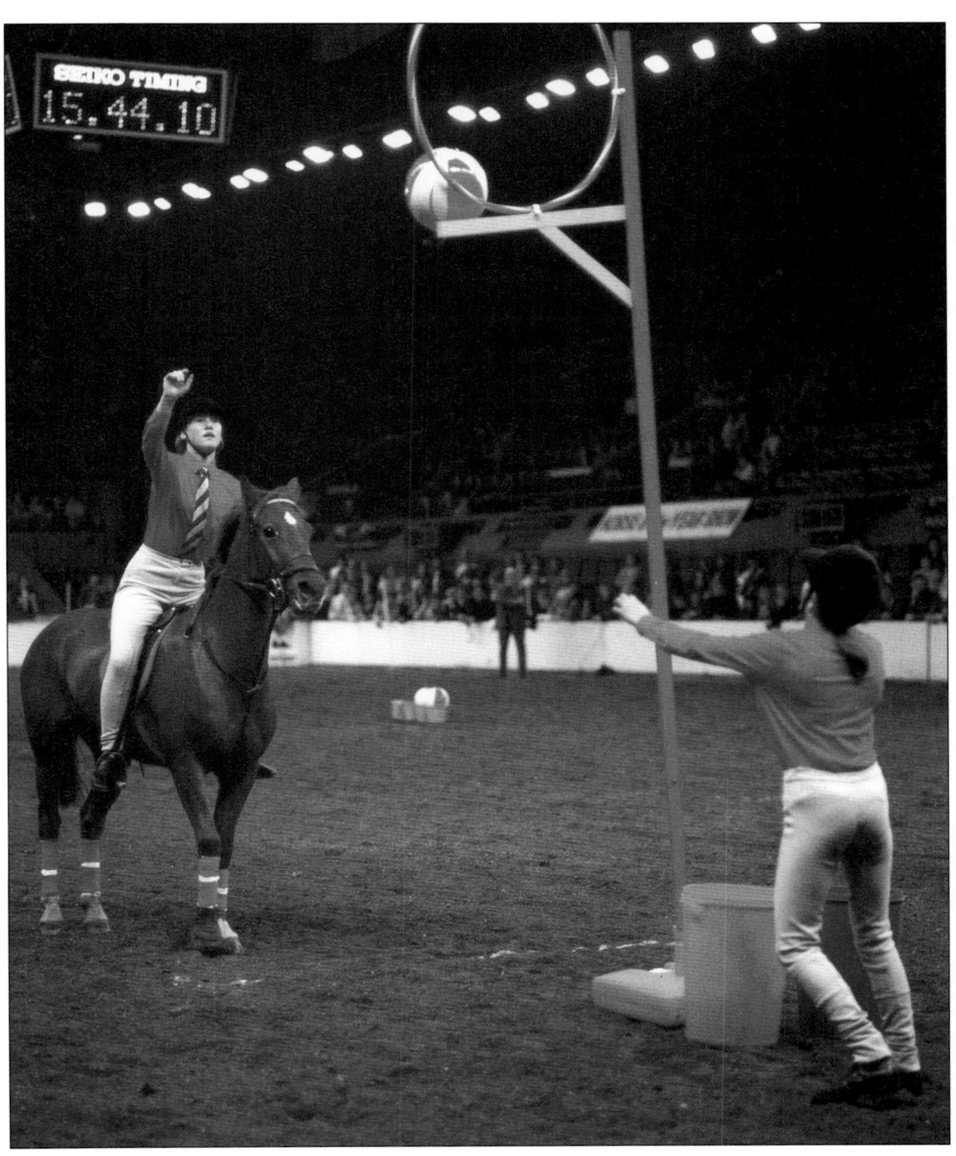

BELOW AND OPPOSITE
The greatest opportunities to play mounted games are provided by the Pony Club, which is an international youth organization. These groups of riders from many different countries are taking part in the annual Euro Camp.

BALLOON RACE
A bunch of balloons is tied to a post. Gallop to the post, collect a balloon, gallop back and pass it to your team-mate. He or she gallops with it to the post, collects a second balloon and hands both balloons to the third rider. This goes on until the last team member crosses the line with all the balloons in his or her hand.

FISHING RACE
You are given a fishing rod, which is actually a piece of wood with a hook on the end. Gallop to a bin full of wooden fish with rings in their noses, hook a fish, gallop back to the start and hang it on a peg. Your team-mate then sets off, catches a fish, brings it back, and so on until all the fish are caught.

BALL-AND-RACQUET RACE
You have to balance a tennis ball on a tennis racquet whilst riding your pony as fast as you can through a line of bending poles. You then hand the racquet and ball to your team-mate who races through the bending poles, and so on.

STEPPING STONES
Race to a line of stepping stones – usually a line of upturned buckets or similar – dismount and negotiate the stepping stones whilst leading your pony alongside. Then remount your pony before crossing the finishing line.

SHARPSHOOTERS' RACE
This race calls for another asset – a pony willing to carry two riders on his back! At the start of the race sit bareback on your pony. When the whistle goes your team-mate has to jump up behind you, and you race to the far end. Your passenger jumps off and has to throw soft balls at a row of comic figures until their heads are broken. Your passenger has to remount, and you both race for the line where the next pair of riders is ready to set off.

FIVE-FLAG RACE
Gallop with a flag in your hand to a pot at the end of the arena. Put the flag in the pot. On your way back, grab another flag from a line of pots and hand it to

your team-mate. He or she gallops to the far end and puts it in the furthest pot along with the first flag. On the way back, he or she grabs another flag from the line of pots to hand to the next rider, and so on.

DRAGON RACE

This is one of the most spectacular races to watch. It requires some quite elaborate equipment in the form of the dragon, and so it usually tends to be reserved for major championships.

The centre piece is a model dragon with balloons attached to him. For added effect he is often made to puff great clouds of smoke. One team member plays the part of the damsel in distress, captured by the fearsome dragon. Her team-mates are the knights attempting to rescue her. As a gallant knight, you race to the damsel and collect a token from her, which you tie to your lance. You then attack the dragon by bursting a balloon. When the last knight succeeds in bursting the final balloon, the damsel is rescued and led to the finish on her pony.

IMPORTANT RULES

Most competitions are run under Pony Club rules. Points to note:

- Ponies must be at least four years old, and not more than 14.2hh.
- If you weigh more than 117 lb (53 kg) when dressed for riding, your pony must be over 12.2hh.
- Your pony must wear a snaffle bridle and a conventional saddle; racing saddles are not allowed. Whips or spurs are not allowed; nor may you use the baton or your hand to encourage your pony to go faster.
- Riders must wear recognized safety helmets with a proper safety harness.
- The winner of the race is the pony who manages to get his head across the finishing line first.
- If the race involves leading the pony, the winner is the first rider across the line provided he or she still has hold of the pony. In a race involving pairs of ponies, the placing is judged from the moment that the second pony's head crosses the line.

BENDING RACE

In contrast to the "Dragon Race", this requires the minimum of equipment – just a line of flexible poles pushed into the ground at intervals. You have to ride your pony in and out of the poles, turn tightly at the end and either race for the finish or thread your way back through the poles. Barrels can be used instead of poles.

EGG-AND-SPOON RACE

Holding a spoon with a boiled egg resting in it, you have to race through a line of bending poles, out and back, without losing the egg.

These are just a sample of what is on offer if you take up mounted games. More important than the games themselves is the opportunity they provide to ignite a spark of interest in children, so that their enthusiasm for horses and riding, for fun or for sport, may continue long after they have outgrown the fun of mounted games.

Dressage

LEFT
Dressage is as much about power as it is about obedience – the horse must look as though he is moving with purpose.

BELOW LEFT
As soon as your horse is able to keep a steady rhythm in all paces, and has enough balance to trot and canter 22 yard (20 m) circles, he is ready to try some of the easier dressage tests.

The simple aim of dressage is to produce a horse who can carry his rider easily, is supple, balanced, correctly muscled, active, eager and responsive to his rider's most subtle command – yet far too many people look down on dressage as an opt-out for those who are too scared to jump!

If you wish to succeed in any horse sport, you have a far greater chance of doing so if your horse is a well-schooled and responsive ride. Whatever sport or sports you decide to take part in with your horse, you should discipline yourself to practise the art of dressage, even if you never set foot or hoof in a competitive dressage arena.

Your horse cannot perform to the best of his ability, nor be a true pleasure for you to ride, unless he has had some help and training to improve his balance and responsiveness. A horse is a far greater joy to hunt, to jump, to hack out or to compete with in any form, if he is able to balance himself so that he carries more of his weight, and that of his rider, on his hindquarters, which in turn will lighten his forehand.

THE HISTORY OF DRESSAGE

As far back as the fourth century BC, Xenophon, a Greek, wrote a book on training the riding horse. Prior to that, most interest in training lay in driving horses for chariots, rather than in riding.

From the sixteenth century onwards, a succession of excellent European horsemen laid down the foundations of classical riding and training as we know it today. The aim of these early trainers was to improve the lightness and balance of the horse. Much of the work involved training from the ground using long reins, so that the horse learnt the movements without the hindrance of a rider. Only after that was the rider taught how not to hinder the horse!

Interest in dressage fluctuated over the following centuries. In Great Britain there was far more interest in hunting and cross-country riding which, in those days, was performed very much on a wing and a prayer. The horses jumped what they were asked to jump either because they were naturally bold or because their riders were able to use enough brute force to get what they wanted. School riding or dressage was laughed at. Typically, instead of the good influencing the bad, in this particular instance the British attitude drifted across to France after the Napoleonic Wars and

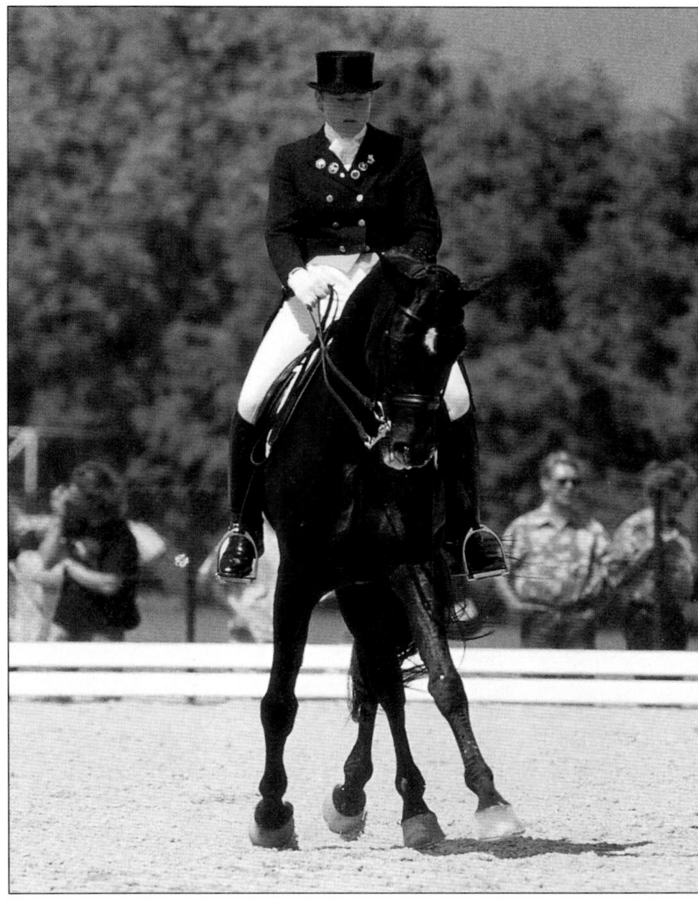

▮ LEFT
This experienced and impressive combination is performing one of the more advanced dressage movements – the half-pass.

▮ BELOW LEFT
Note how this rider is keeping a lovely soft contact whilst his horse remains in a nice outline and bent correctly in the direction in which they are going.

the interest in dressage faltered there for a while. The nineteenth century saw a revival of interest in Europe. The principles laid down centuries before were refined and adapted, but the basic requirements of free forward movement, suppleness, obedience and lightness of the forehand remained and are still the aim of dressage riders today. In many other parts of the world such as America, Argentina, Africa, New Zealand and Australia, the horse was still primarily used either as a beast of burden or as a stock animal for the herding and control of large herds of livestock. But the influence of the great riding masters, particularly those of the Spanish Riding School in Vienna and the Cadre Noir in France, spread throughout the world until dressage became a truly international sport and a passion for many riders.

■ DRESSAGE AS A COMPETITIVE SPORT

Dressage is an Olympic sport, and its governing body is the FEI. It is therefore affiliated, and there are various levels of competition for affiliated members. However, dressage is a popular and easy sport to organize which means that many unaffiliated competitions are run by various show organizers.

Dressage tests are split into the internationally recognized FEI tests and national tests, devised by each individual country. The national tests generally start with the lowest level, preliminary or novice, progressing through elementary to medium and advanced tests. Unaffiliated shows normally only offer classes up to elementary level, and may also make use of the simpler dressage tests taken from the sport of eventing. Most countries hold national and regional championships as well as participating in the international

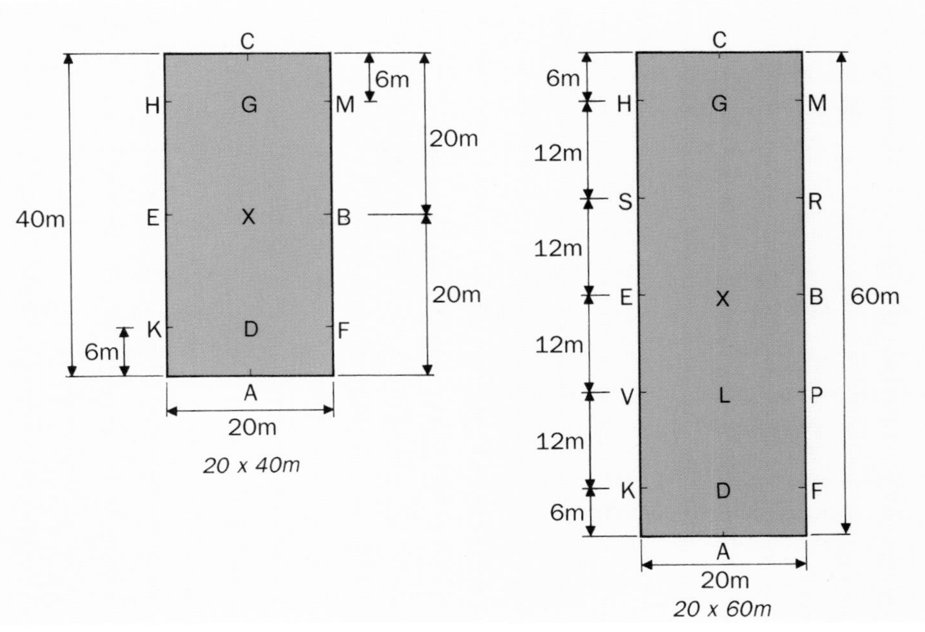

▮ BELOW RIGHT
Size and layout of the dressage arenas used for lower-level tests (left) and for advanced tests.

LEFT
As the horse progresses through the grades he is expected to show more expression in his paces. His outline should be shorter and higher, and his paces more powerful and elevated.

BELOW
Something to aim for – this combination won the gold medal at the 1988 Olympic Games. Nicole Uphoff on Rembrandt at Aachen.

FEI competitions. All tests are ridden in a dressage arena, which is a rectangle marked out by boards and letters. The letters signify where various movements should be carried out. The lower-level tests are performed in the minimum-sized arena of 22 x 43¾ yards (20 x 40 m), whereas more advanced tests are carried out in an international-sized arena of 22 x 65½ yards (20 x 60 m). The marker letters are always the same. At the Olympic Games and other FEI championships, the arena must have an all-weather surface of sand, but at other competitions it may be of grass, or may be indoors.

Lower-level tests are judged by just one person, who awards marks for each set movement in the test, plus an overall mark for the horse's way of going and the rider's performance. The judge stands behind the C marker, directly in line with the centre line of the arena. Higher-level competitions are judged by three or even five judges. Each judge sits to one side or the other of the centre-line judge and awards his or her own marks. These marks may well vary, as each judge will see the test ridden from a different angle. The final mark is taken as the average of all the judges' marks.

In all dressage competitions, you are given a precise time at which your test will start. You must work out how much loosening up and schooling work your horse needs so that he is well prepared for his test at the allotted time. Once you are sent over to the appropriate arena, you must not enter it until the judge signals you to start, usually with a bell or horn. You can ride around outside the arena, continuing to work on keeping your horse balanced, calm and attentive, until the judge's signal. Enter the arena at A, proceed down the centre line to X, the half-way point, halt and salute the judge. A female rider is required to put both reins in the left hand, bow the head, and drop the right hand to the side. A male rider is expected to remove his hat and bow likewise. After this, you can proceed down the centre line and into the first movement of the appropriate test. The test always ends with another trip down the centre line to halt and salute once more. Then proceed at a free walk, giving the horse a long rein, and leave the arena at A. After that it is a case of waiting for your mark to be put up.

FEI TESTS

- Prix St George
- Intermediare 1
- Intermediare 2
- Grand Prix
- Grand Prix Special
- Free Style Test – this is the same standard as the Grand Prix but is performed to music.

■ WHO CAN DO DRESSAGE?

Any rider can, and should, practise dressage, even if you choose not to compete. Once your horse is basically obedient, can maintain a rounded outline and can work in a reasonable rhythm in walk, trot and canter, he is equipped to perform the simpler dressage tests. The lower-level tests only require the horse to work in medium walk, working trot and canter, and may require some lengthening of the horse's stride. The horse must be able to produce a good halt, as all tests end with a halt and salute to the judge, and the vast majority of tests also start with one. A few of the very basic tests allow the

▮ RIGHT
The aim of dressage is simply to produce a fit, supple, obedient horse who is so responsive that his rider appears to be doing nothing.

▮ BOTTOM
16½ foot (5 m) loops.

horse to enter the arena and carry straight on with the test. You will need to be able to ride basic schooling movements such as 65½ or 49¼ foot (20 or 15 m) circles, and serpentines or half-circles, but none of these is outside the scope of a reasonably well-schooled horse.'

International tests have to be ridden from memory, as does the dressage test in horse trials, but lower down the scale you are allowed to have the test read out to you. It is well worth making the effort to learn the test, both out of respect for the judge who has given up a day to come and mark you, and because to ride a really good test you need to concentrate fully on getting the best out of your horse, not wondering what command is going to be called out to you next. The movements of the test should become second nature to you if you are to ride your horse to the best of your ability.

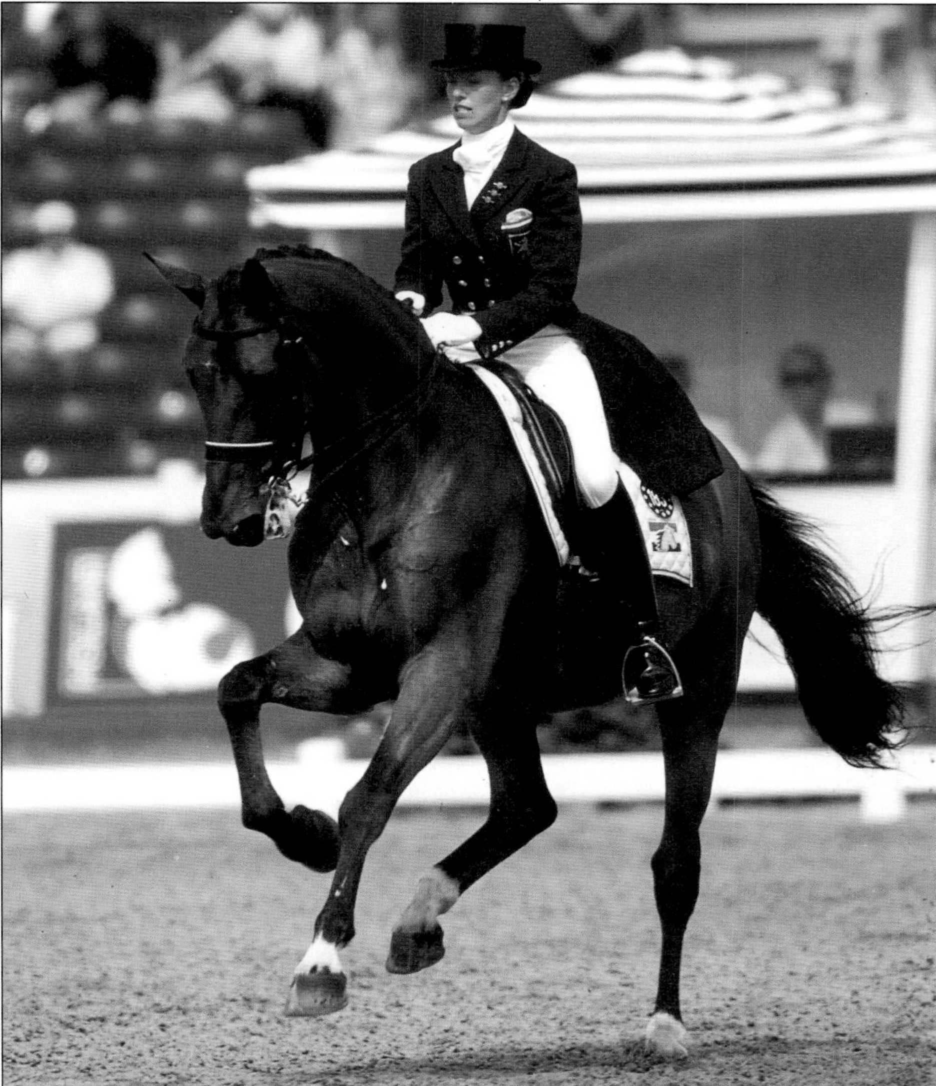

■ SKILLS REQUIRED

To be successful in any equestrian sport you need to develop a secure independent seat but, in dressage, it is equally important to develop "feel". You should be able to feel exactly what the horse is doing underneath you. Is he straight, is he giving you the correct bend, are his hocks really coming underneath him, is he relaxed enough through his neck and jaw? This feel can be developed with experience, but some riders are simply never able to accomplish it. Be patient and dedicated. The correct training of a dressage horse is a very long, careful process – there are no short cuts.

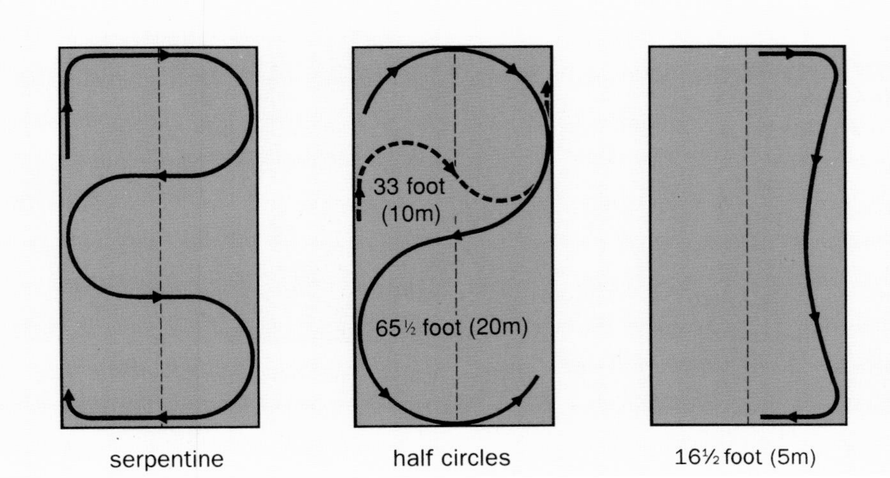

Any horse who has been correctly schooled is already doing dressage, and can therefore compete, but some horses find this discipline easier than others. A calm temperament helps, along with a willingness and quickness to learn. If the horse has good conformation and naturally good paces, he is going to find his work easier than a horse who has an awkward build and therefore struggles to move as freely. The horse should be forward thinking, and ideally he should have naturally active hocks – some horses have naturally "lazy" hocks and will find it harder to use their hindquarters. Finally the ideal dressage horse should have presence – he should make people want to stop and watch him. But don't be deterred if your horse lacks some of these qualities. Careful and consistent training can do wonders for the most unpromising candidate – it just takes more time and determination.

The World of Showing

The showing scene probably offers a wider range of opportunities for all types and abilities than any other equestrian sport. If you are the sort of person who takes pride in appearance, manners and performance – both yours and your horse's – you will enjoy exploring the showing world.

There are no Olympics or world championships for showing, but there is ample opportunity to compete. In most countries there are regional and national championships for the different categories of show horses and ponies.

If you wish to compete at the higher-level shows, you will need to register your horse with the appropriate society. Which you register with depends on the type of horse you own and which classes you wish to compete in. It usually means registering with a breed society, a show-pony society, or a hunter or hack society or association. Small, local shows do not usually require their entrants to be registered with anyone.

LEFT
Mountain and moorland ponies are shown off in a more natural state than their show-pony colleagues. Their manes and tails are left full and unplaited or braided; their legs are not trimmed either. It is probably harder to produce a well-turned-out native pony than it is to produce his show-pony counterpart who may be plaited, braided, clipped and trimmed.

Different countries vary in the interest and opportunities that are afforded to showing. In terms of expense and facilities required, it is a relatively easy sport to cater for. A grass enclosure and some respected judges are all that most classes require. Generally speaking, there are classes available to suit all ages and types of horse and rider.

IN-HAND SHOWING

Mares and foals, yearlings, and two-, three- and four-year-old horses and ponies can all be shown "in-hand", i.e. they are led by their handlers and are judged on how smartly they are turned out, their conformation, their manners and paces, and their potential suitability for adult life. As the handler, you are expected to be very smartly dressed yourself, and your horse should be sensible and obedient enough to stand in line with the rest of the class, and to walk and trot in-hand when he is required to do so by the judge.

Your horse should appear in the ring without a saddle, and with no boots or bandages of any sort. He can be led with either a headcollar or a bridle.

You can practise all the requirements at home, teaching your horse to halt squarely and to remain still, and to walk and trot calmly beside you when asked.

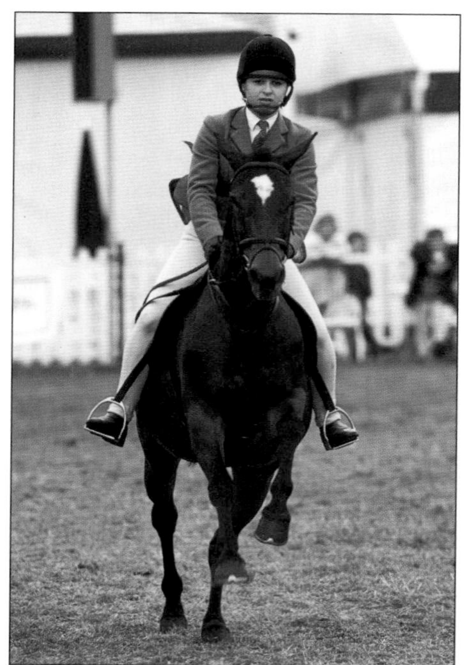

Pony and rider showing off their paces in the Working Hunter Pony class.

EQUIPMENT NEEDED

For nearly all showing classes, apart from side-saddle, you can use your normal saddle and bridle. If given the choice, a saddle which is not too forward cut is usually more appropriate. It shows off your horse's shoulders and front end rather than covering them up, and gives you more chance of impressing the judges. At higher levels of competition it may be more appropriate to wear either a top hat or a bowler hat instead of a traditional hard hat. The showing world in general strives to uphold tradition and standards, and it is worth bearing this in mind when you are buying any clothing or equipment. Keep everything clean, tidy and workmanlike and you won't go far wrong.

In many classes you have to be able to show off your horse at the gallop despite the confines of the arena. A safe, all-weather surface is provided for this show cob.

RIGHT
You may find yourself competing against "professional" showmen who will arrive with a whole string of horses or ponies to enter. This is Great Britain's Robert Oliver.

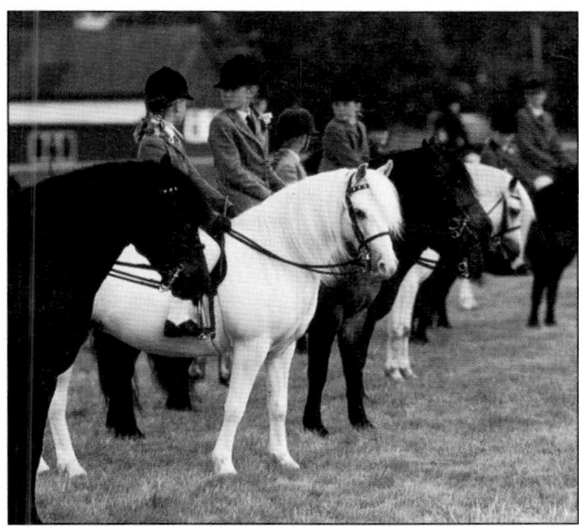

BELOW
In most showing classes all the competitors ride around together while the judge assesses them. They are then called into line, after which they may be asked to give an individual show.

SUCCESS IN THE SHOW RING

To maximize your chances of success in the show ring it is worth making use of a little ring craft. All this involves is using your common sense to ensure the judge gets the best chance to view your horse. When you are all parading in the ring together, make sure you keep some open space around your horse. If everyone is bunching up, circle away to make some more room for yourself. Do not hold your horse back and make him tense, as this will restrict his pace. Let him stay in his natural rhythm and circle away to make room.

If you are called to give an individual show, remember that the aim is simply to demonstrate your horse's paces, obedience and general way of gojng. Have something planned before you go in; do not do too much in walk as this takes up so much time, and the judge will have had plenty of opportunity to view your horse in walk already. Make sure you demonstrate trot and canter on each rein. Keep your movements simple and smooth so that your horse is able to stay in a rhythm and in balance, and to show himself off to the best of his ability. Think of it as a short but sweet dressage test, using the same degree of accuracy and concentration in the show ring as you would do in the dressage arena.

BREED CLASSES

Some classes are restricted to particular breeds so that the entrants can be judged on their trueness to type. Each breed of horse or pony should have certain characteristics which identify him as being true to type. These characteristics are listed by the appropriate breed society. Breed classes can be judged either as in-hand or as ridden classes and, once again, turnout, manners and conformation are the key criteria.

Some breeds have very specific traits which they are judged on; for example, the Tennessee Walking Horse on his walk.

If the class is ridden, you are expected to wear jodhpurs or breeches with the appropriate short or long boots, a shirt and tie or stock, and a hunting, show or

ABOVE
Many of the bigger shows are held indoors, with classes going on late into the evening. Your horse will have to become accustomed to spotlights and a far more claustrophobic atmosphere than he will have experienced at an outdoor show.

LEFT
Many classes are judged in-hand, which means that the horse is led rather than ridden.

LEFT
When showing in-hand your horse must be trained to trot quietly alongside you when required.

hacking jacket. A skull cap with a cover, or a traditional velvet hat, should be worn.

■ TYPE CLASSES

These classes are not restricted to breeds but to types of horse and pony. Within each type, the classes are usually split by height or weight. The type of horse or pony might be working hunter, show hunter, show hack, cob, riding horse, ladies' hunter etc. The hunter and cob classes will probably be further divided into lightweight, middleweight and heavyweight, whereas the working-hunter and hack classes are usually split according to height.

The classes designated "working", such as the working hunter pony, involve the competitors completing a course of fences. These are usually rustic show jumps as opposed to solid cross-country fences, but may include a stile, brush fences, a water ditch or a bank. It is usual for each competitor to jump their round, before the whole class is called into another arena where the judge will watch each one perform a short show designed to show off the horse's paces, obedience and general presence. In very competitive classes, unless you jump a clear round you may not even be called back into the second arena for further judging.

In the other showing classes the usual procedure is for the whole class to walk, trot and canter together in a large arena watched by the judge. They are then all called into a line and all, or some, may be asked to perform an individual show in front of the judge. Additionally, the judge may want to ride your horse him- or herself, and to see him, untacked, walked and trotted up in-hand. A showing class may take a long time to judge and it is on these occasions that your horse's manners and patience will be put to the test.

Breed classes are popular with many competitors. These Arab horses will be judged on their breed characteristics as well as their paces, manners and general condition.

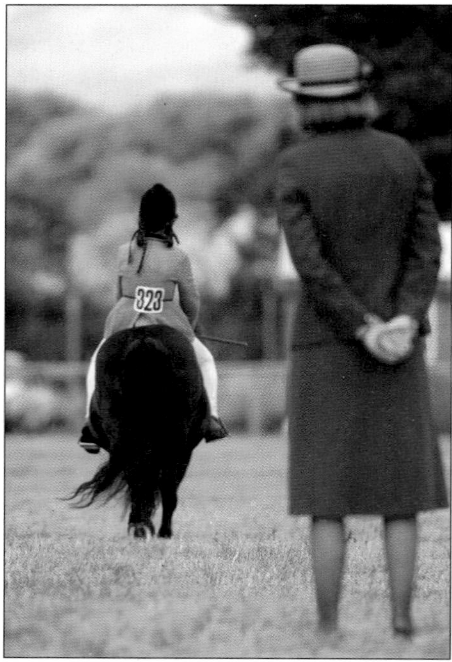

The judge may study your performance from a variety of angles.

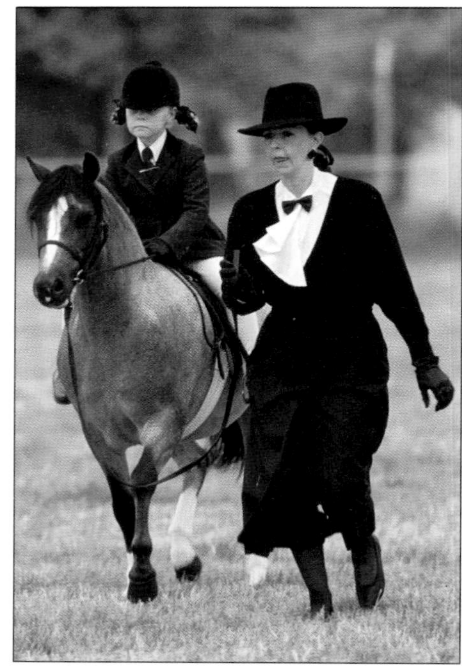

Sometimes you will find yourself eligible for several different types of class. This young rider on her Welsh mountain pony can enter the leading-rein class as well as the Welsh mountain breed class.

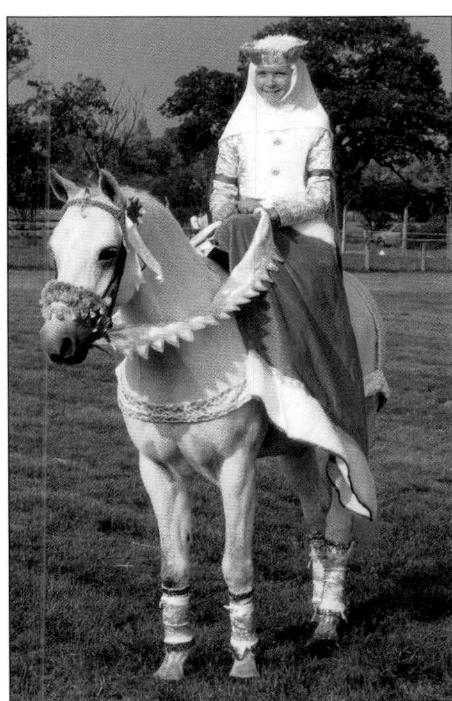

LEFT
Everybody loves to dress up – showing classes often offer the chance to compete in fancy dress.

BELOW
Side-saddle riding is growing in popularity. Here Jennie Loriston-Clarke gives a superb side-saddle dressage display.

BELOW
It takes a competent side-saddle rider to be able to jump well – note how this rider is giving her horse a good length of rein so that he is not restricted.

SIDE-SADDLE CLASSES

Riding side-saddle, as opposed to astride, used to be the only acceptable way for a lady to be seen on a horse, but, as competitive sports became more popular with both sexes, riding astride became the norm. However, the elegance and splendour of side-saddle riding have made a comeback in many countries, and shows are held specifically for side-saddle riders. Additionally, some lady riders of show hunters have enhanced their appearance and their prospects in the show ring by competing side-saddle against the majority of astride riders. Many riders take up side-saddle having ridden astride for years; others are taught to ride side-saddle in the first place – both approaches seem to be equally successful.

It is, however, an expensive sport in terms of the equipment needed – a side-saddle and riding habit will cost more than a conventional saddle and riding outfit. Second-hand equipment may prove even more expensive, as the more authentic saddles and habits are in great demand. But if you enjoy creating a real spectacle, there is nothing to beat the elegance of a well-turned-out side-saddle rider.

It takes a good horsewoman to jump successfully – too many seem unable to give their horses sufficient freedom of head and neck, but this is also true of a good many astride riders, male and female! Many ladies still hunt side-saddle although, presumably for safety reasons, riders are not allowed to compete side-saddle in horse trials.

Although much to do with side-saddle riding is judged on turnout and overall appearance, some classes are judged on equitation, i.e. on how well you ride your horse. This is a popular class with those who have taken the trouble to learn to ride well, and who have schooled their horses carefully and skilfully.

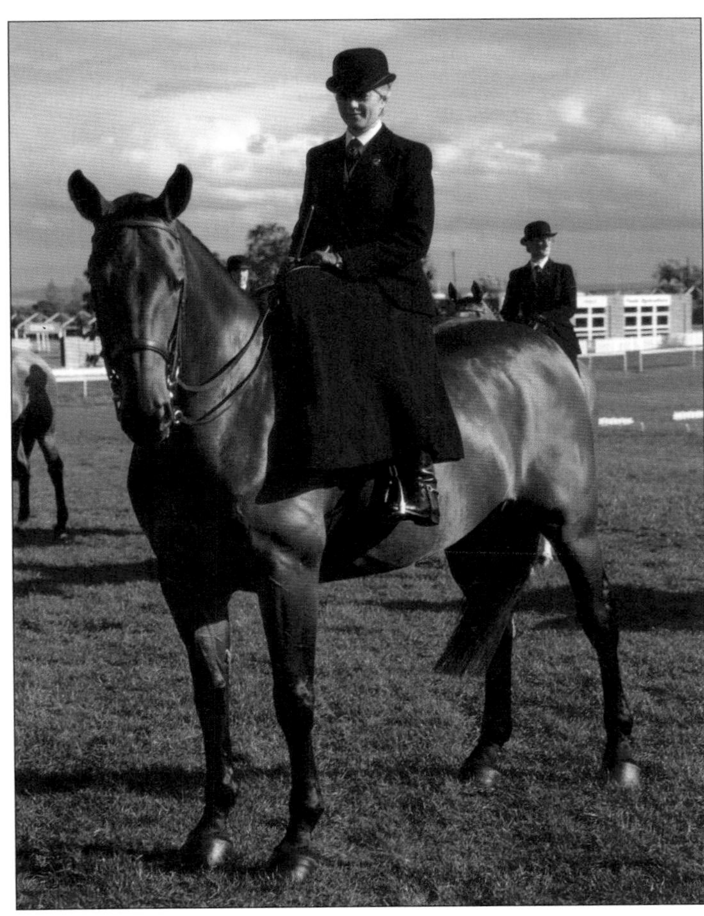

LEFT
Equitation classes are popular, as riders are judged on how well their horses perform for them rather than on how expensive or well bred they look.

Endurance or Long-distance Riding

There are two types of long-distance riding – endurance riding (which has FEI status) and trail riding. Trail riding does not involve racing – the idea is to complete the ride with your horse still in good condition. Trail rides vary from about 25 miles (40.25 km) to over 100 miles (160 km). Endurance riding does involve racing – it is a competition against the clock which tests the speed and stamina of the horse. It also tests the rider's horsemanship and judgement of pace, and of his or her horse's well-being. Each competition is split into a number of phases, each one being usually just under 25 miles (40 km) long. At the end of each phase the horse is checked by a veterinary surgeon for sores on his back or in his mouth, overreaches, and general well-being; his heart rate is monitored.

Competitions vary in length, but an international event which takes more than one day is usually over a minimum distance of 50–62 miles (80–100 km). A championship one-day competition usually covers nearly 100 miles (160 km) with a winning riding time of somewhere between ten and twelve hours.

BELOW
The horse's weight is checked at the beginning and end of the ride so that the amount of condition he has lost can be judged.

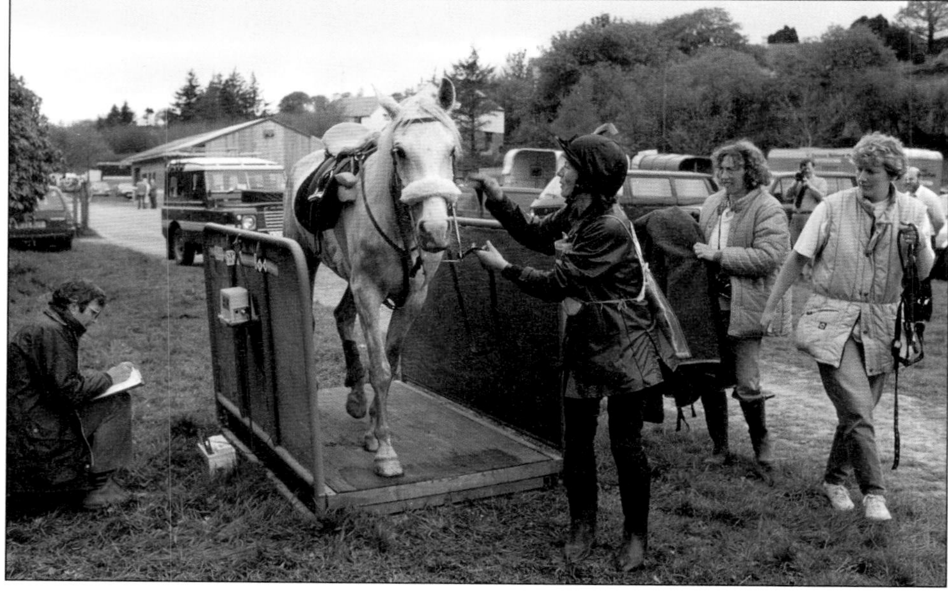

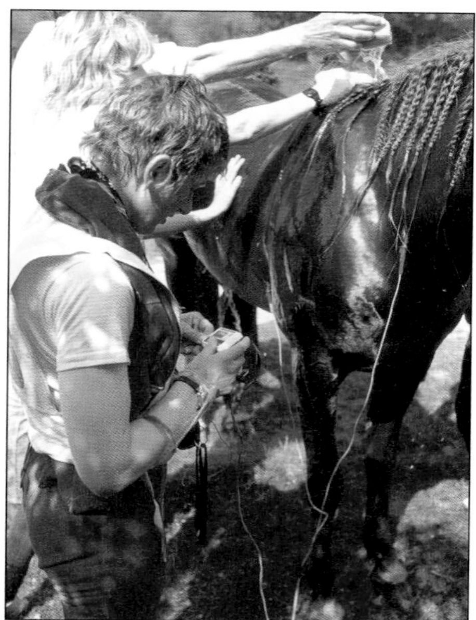

The horse's pulse rate is monitored at intervals throughout a long-distance ride; the horse has to finish in good condition.

DEVELOPMENT OF THE SPORT

For many centuries the horse has been used to transport man and his possessions over great distances. Most countries can boast feats of great endurance riding – there has always been someone who has wanted to go further than those before him on the back of a horse – but endurance riding as an organized competitive sport did not start in earnest until the 1950s.

Endurance riding today puts the horse's welfare first and foremost with strict veterinary checks. The organizers have the authority to eliminate any competitor whose horse shows signs of having had enough. Before this, some of the earliest long-distance races tested the horse's endurance to the limit, with equine contestants literally being ridden until they dropped. The care and attention lavished on today's endurance horses is some recompense for the suffering endured by the horses who gave their all in previous centuries.

Interest in competitive endurance riding spread most quickly in Europe and America. The first endurance rides were actually organized to demonstrate the suitability of different types of horses as cavalry mounts. It was in California in 1955 that competitive endurance riding started.

The endurance horse must learn to remain balanced, settled and in a rhythm, even on the lightest rein contact.

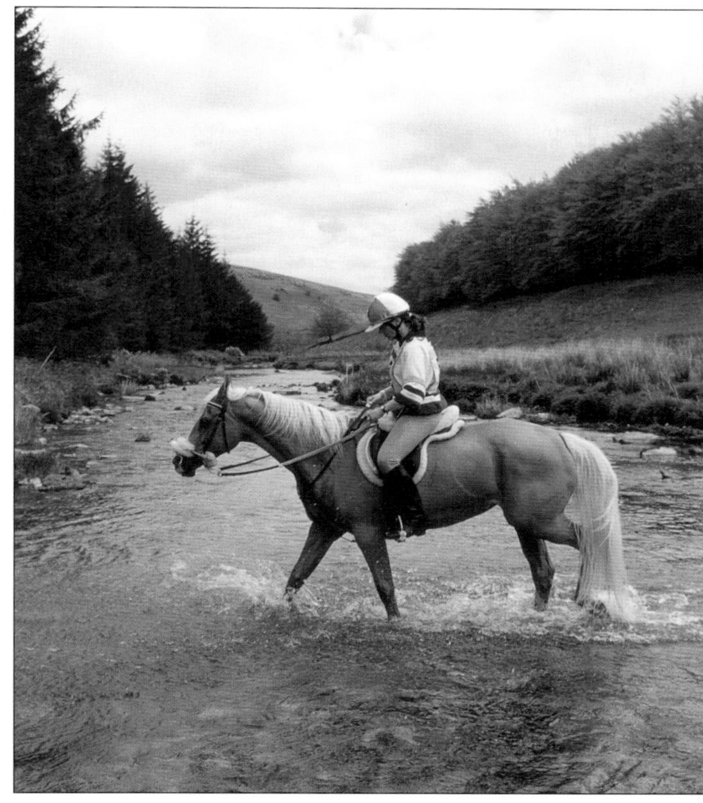

RIGHT
All kinds of natural hazards have to be tackled.

TACTICS

To succeed as an endurance rider you will need to be happy with your own company, have a good rapport with your horse and your back-up team, and an awareness of winning tactics. Who is ahead of you, who is behind you, are you keeping up with the pace, how can you avoid overtiring your horse, how can you help him if he does tire? What is your strategy at the checkpoints and the meeting points *en route* where your horse is allowed to be refreshed? Whose horse can still put in a sprint for the finish, and how far ahead of them do you need to be to make sure you sprint over the line first?

BELOW
Endurance or long-distance riding is suitable for many different types of horses.

Interest was sparked by the ride undertaken by Wendall T. Robie and a group of friends. They followed the old mining and emigrant trails over 100 miles (160 km) from Squaw Valley, through the Sierra Nevada range and on to Auburn. This trail became the world's first official endurance ride, and was named the Western States Trail Ride.

Today the popular sport of endurance riding, which has been approved as an international discipline since 1982, is governed by the FEI.

THE ENDURANCE HORSE

The main requirements of any endurance horse are that he has strong, dense bone, strong, healthy hooves, and a willingness and confidence to tackle whatever he is faced with because he will encounter all kinds of natural hazards on a long-distance ride. He should have a light, ground-covering action, and be balanced and sure-footed over all manner of terrain. He should be trained to settle into a steady trot or canter when required, and should accept a loose rein with minimal contact. A calm temperament means he will take less out of himself.

EQUIPMENT AND BACK-UP TEAM

Numnahs or gel pads are essential under saddles to reduce the risk of any rubbing or bruising, and purpose-designed endurance saddles can be purchased. Stock or Western-type saddles are popular as far as rider comfort is concerned. Many horses are ridden in hackamores (bitless bridles) to reduce the risk of sores or bruising, but these take practice and skill to use.

A good back-up team of between one and three helpers is essential during an endurance competition. They, as well as you, must be able to map read so that you all follow the same route and arrive at the same meeting points. They carry and provide everything that horse and rider may need along the way – food, water, clothing, spare tack (especially numnahs and girths as these may need changing several times during a ride), spare horseshoes, a first-aid kit, a tack-repair kit, a torch, and a grooming kit and towels.

Western Riding

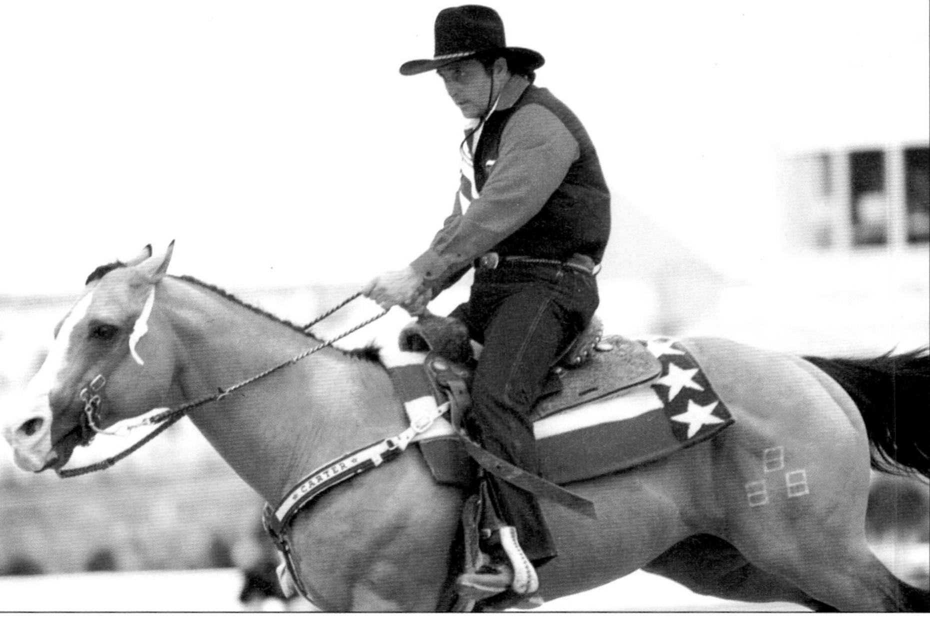

Western riding is predominant in countries where the horse is still used to work cattle, such as America, Argentina, Australia, New Zealand and parts of Africa. It also has a growing following in other countries where riders are keen to enjoy the experience of riding a light, balanced, responsive horse, along with the novelty of trying many of the Western riding skills.

■ WHAT IS WESTERN RIDING?

America is the home of Western riding, which developed directly from the needs of the early pioneers. They depended on horses for their survival – for transport, for hunting food, and later for herding and managing vast herds of cattle. They had to be able to sit comfortably, for very long hours, in the saddle. They also needed horses who were both fast and responsive and yet also calm and easy to handle. The skills that horse and rider had to learn in order to earn a living in those times form the basis of the Western-riding competitions held today.

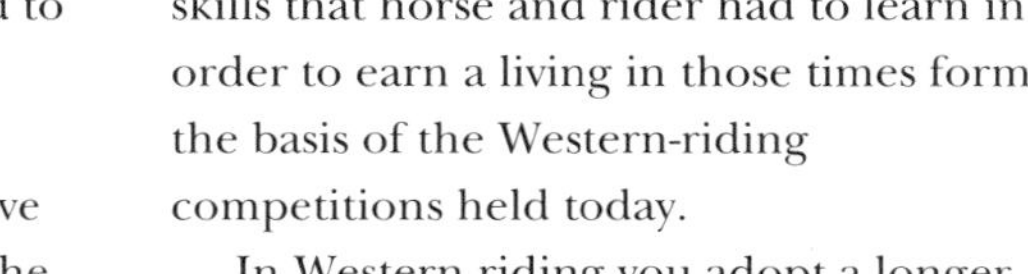

In Western riding you adopt a longer leg position than is usual for general riding. The reins are held in one hand, leaving the other free to rope cattle, fire a gun etc, and the horse is controlled mainly by the seat and weight, rather than by hand and leg. A Western horse is not ridden in an outline. He carries himself in a relaxed, but light and balanced manner, with his rider keeping the reins virtually slack. The weight of the reins is used as an aid, rather than the contact with the horse's mouth.

Western-riding competitions test everything from how the horse feels to

ABOVE
In Western riding it is the seat and weight distribution of the rider that are used to control the horse, rather than the hand and leg as is usual in English riding.

LEFT
Western tack is designed to offer comfort, practicality and security to riders spending many hours in the saddle.

EQUIPMENT NEEDED

Many riders simply enjoy riding in the Western style – hacking or long-distance riding – without going as far as competing.

A Western or stock-type saddle adds authenticity and comfort to the proceedings but is not essential during the training of horse and rider. Similarly, a standard bridle and bit can be used, rather than the simpler Western-style bridle which may or may not be bitless. But once Western tack is used, no doubt you will want to be properly kitted out too. Cowboy boots, which have a raised, supported instep and a higher heel than a standard riding boot, along with a pair of long, leather chaps are the two essentials.

RIGHT
In cattle-cutting competitions the horse has first to "cut" a selected calf out from the rest of the herd, and then to prevent the selected animal from rejoining the herd. This Quarter Horse is using his own "cattle sense" rather than his rider's instructions to keep the calf he is facing from joining the herd behind him.

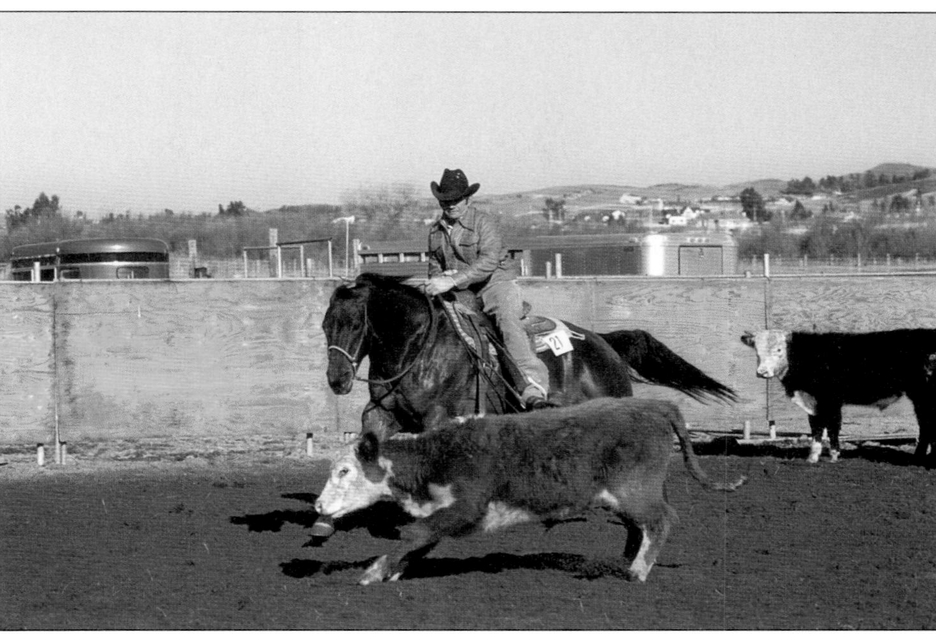

ride, his ability to perform complex reining exercises and his skill at cutting out and controlling cattle, to his ability to race through a line of barrels. There are World and European Championship titles to be won, as well as numerous regional and national events to compete in.

Many Western riders get caught up in the whole Western phenomenon. As well as learning the ridden style they may also practise other "Wild West" skills, such as trick roping, whip cracking, knife and axe throwing, as well as the fast draw and gun spinning. It is amazing what sitting in a Western saddle can do to the imagination of even the most retiring rider!

THE WESTERN RIDING HORSE

Any horse can be converted to Western riding, but not all horses will have the temperament or inherent traits for all the Western-style competitions. The American Quarter Horse is a popular and successful choice – he has the speed, stamina, agility, intelligence and in-bred "cattle sense" to succeed. Other American types, such as the Appaloosa, the Paint horse and the Pinto, also feature strongly. But any horse with natural balance and agility, who can be taught to respond to weight and seat aids rather than being held between hand and leg as is usual in English-style riding, can be taught Western skills.

SKILLS REQUIRED

As a rider you must have good balance, the patience to build a rapport with your horse which allows your commands to appear invisible to the onlooker and, if you are to become involved in cattle-handling skills, the overall fitness and

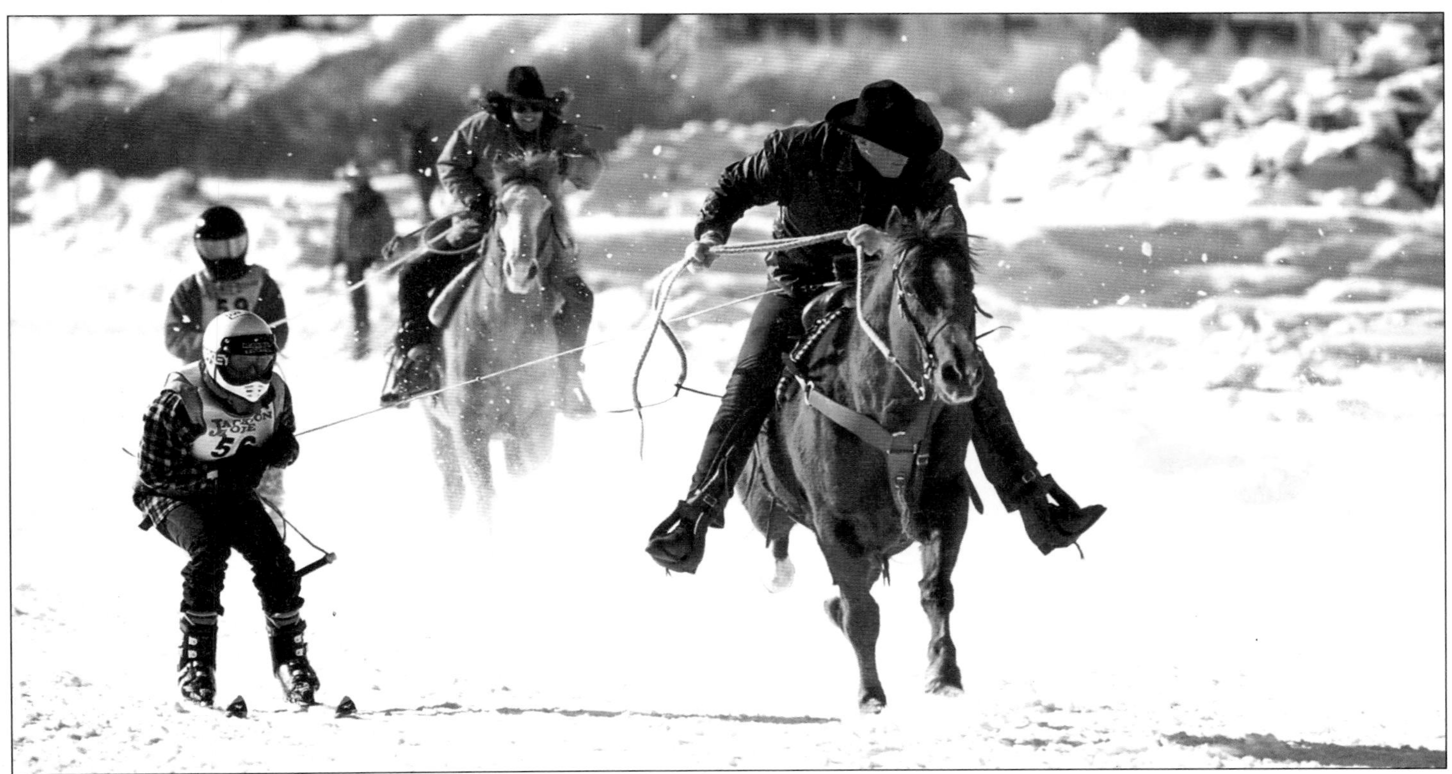

In Western riding the horse is expected to be versatile and co-operative. At the Cowboy Ski Challenge in Jackson Hole, Wyoming, the horse demonstrates his ability to carry out any number of duties, from providing the power for the skiers...

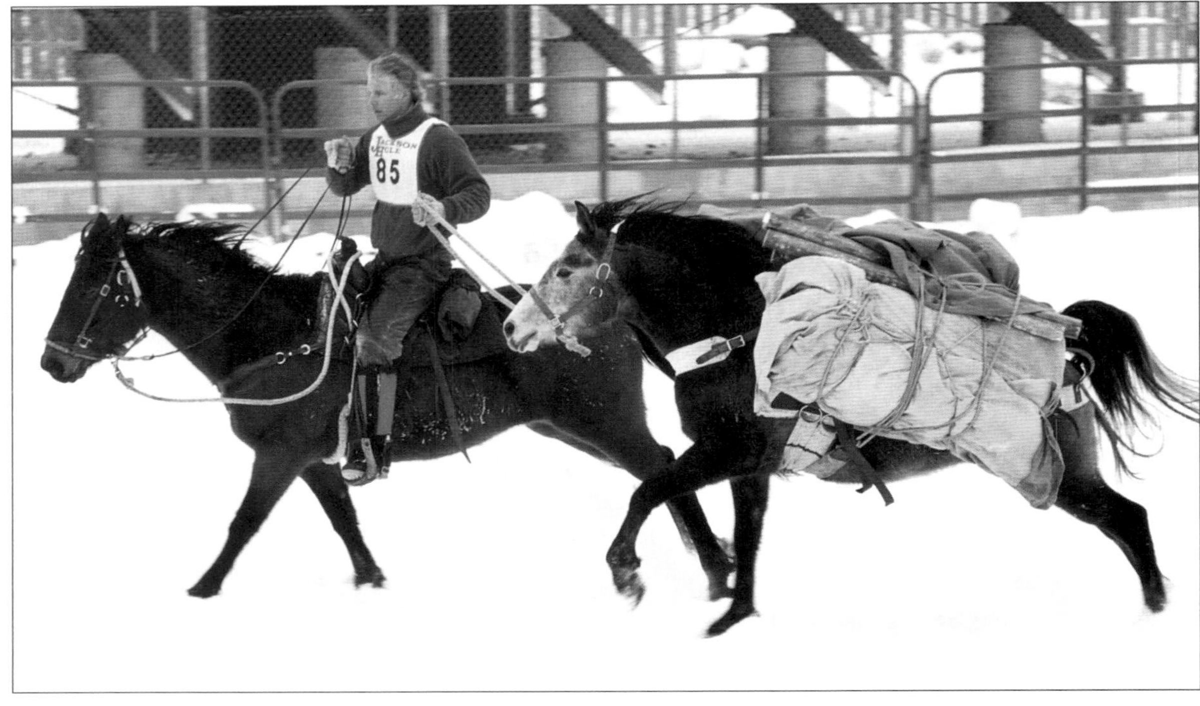

RIGHT
...to showing how essential they were to the survival of the early pioneers.

BELOW AND BELOW RIGHT
The sliding halt is one of the most dramatic Western-riding skills. The horse wears special skid boots to protect his fetlocks and to aid the slide.

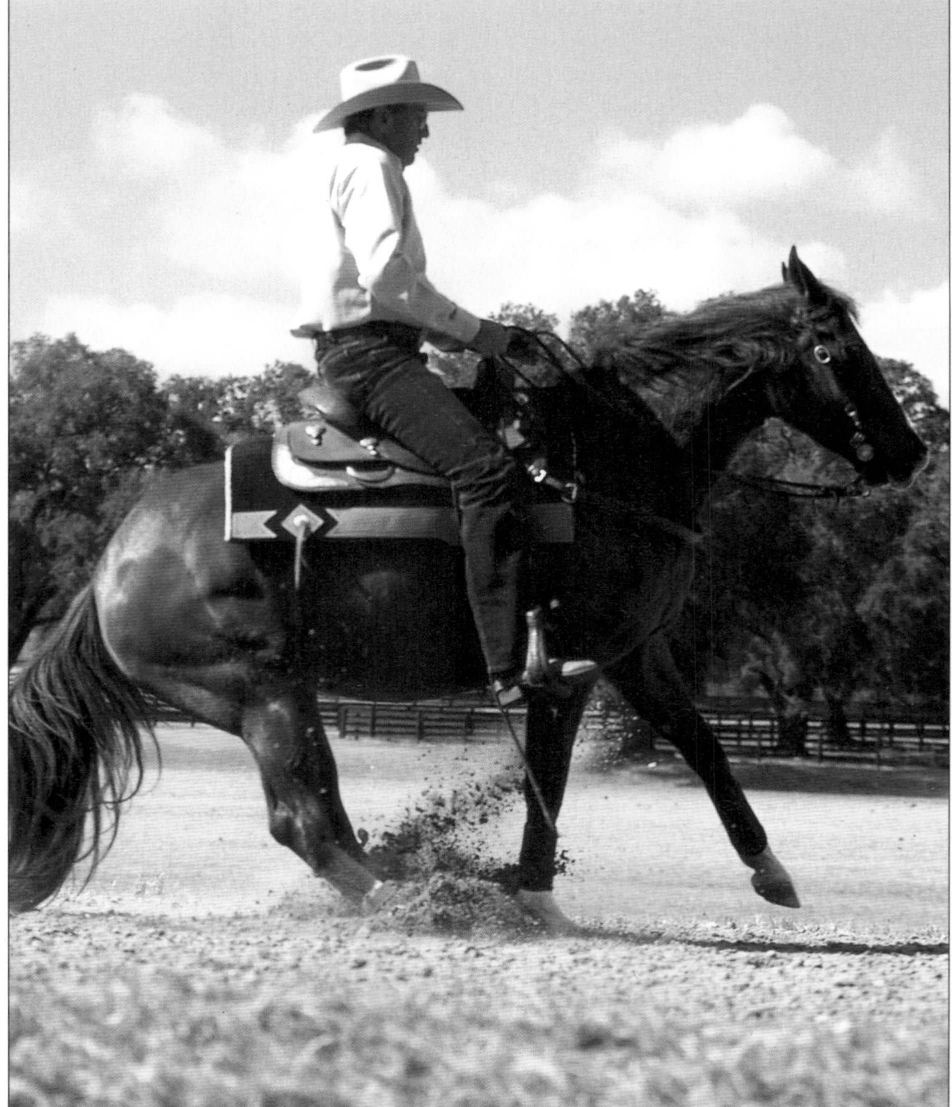

toughness which these require. For most Western showing classes, the horse has to be taught the jog and the lope – these are basically a slow, smooth trot and canter. These paces were developed for rider comfort and to reduce wear and tear on the horse's legs and joints. For most equestrian disciplines, the horse is trained to put spring and elevation into his paces, but for Western riding the paces are smooth and flat, with less knee and hock action than normal. Other classes require the horse to be taught various Western moves – the rollback which is a fast 180° turn, the spin or pirouette which is a 360° turn, the side pass (lateral work), the rein

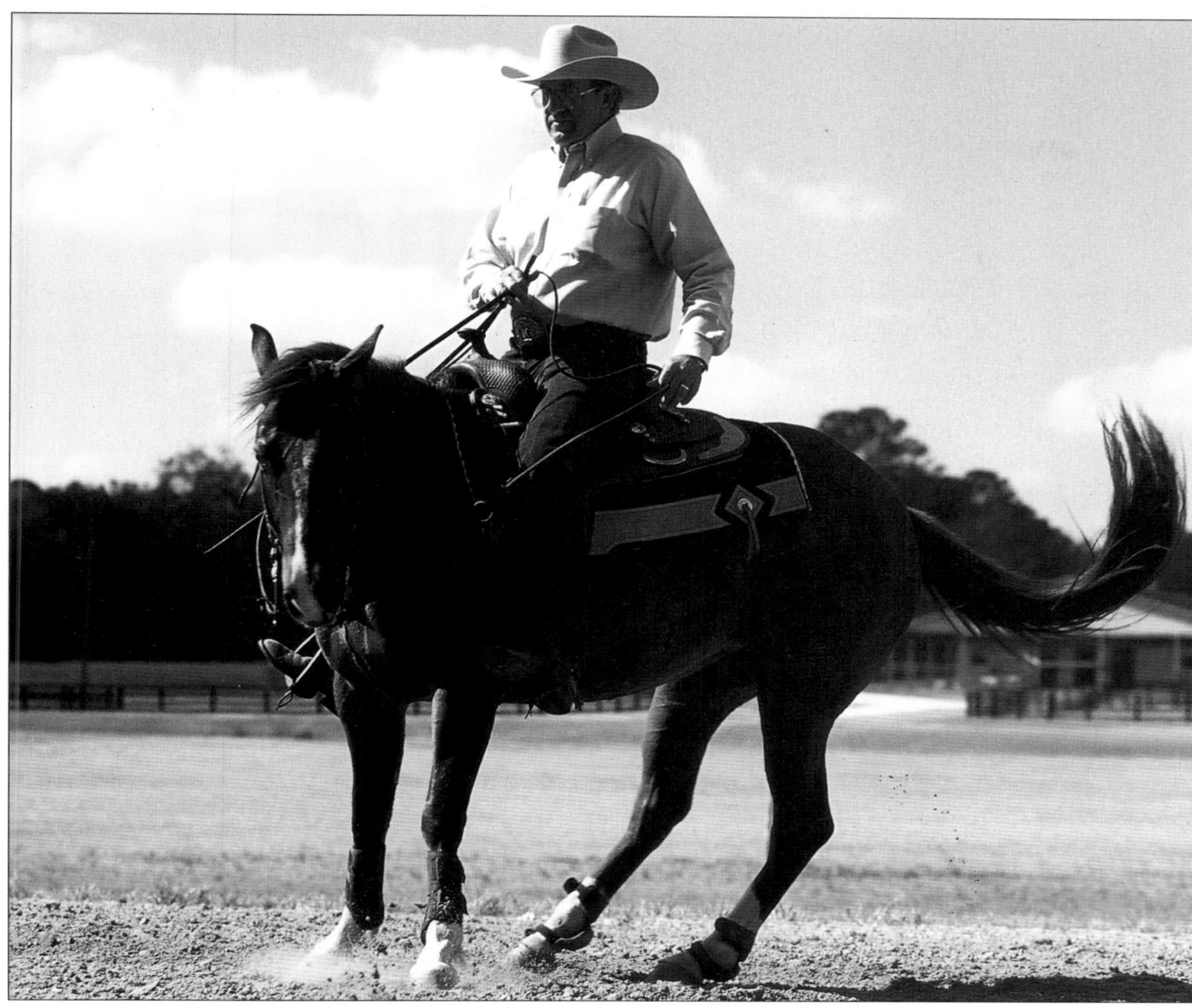

■ LEFT
The spin is one of the many Western skills that the horse has to learn.

back, the sliding halt, and the flying change.

■ **SHOWING CLASSES**

These are the easiest Western classes to train for and take part in.

■ The **Western Pleasure** class is the simplest. The horse is judged on how much of a pleasure he is to ride. He must work in all paces on both reins, with the rider keeping the reins in one hand and a minimal contact. He is judged on how smooth his paces and transitions are, and on how calm and responsive he is to his rider's commands.

■ The **Trail** class tests the horse's ability to cope calmly with the sort of hazards he might encounter when riding the trail. There are a number of tasks you and he will have to perform in the ring, such as opening and closing a gate, backing through or round an obstacle, and jumping some logs. You may have to carry an object, and your horse may have to allow himself to be hobbled (tied up) on his own.

■ The **Western Riding** class imitates some of the tasks a ranch horse might have to carry out. The horse must demonstrate a good walk, jog and lope, and may have to tackle various tasks or obstacles similar to those also found in the trail class.

■ The **Reining** class tests some of the most advanced Western-riding techniques. The horse demonstrates at speed a pattern of various Western movements – turns, circles, spins, flying changes, rollbacks and sliding halts. All of these movements are performed from the lope – the slow, smooth canter.

■ **CATTLE-HANDLING CLASSES**

These require more extensive practice, training and facilities than the Western showing classes.

■ In the **Cutting Horse** class, the rider indicates to a judge which calf he is going to separate from the herd. The calf has to be "cut out" from the herd and driven out into the arena. The rider must then adopt a loose rein and leave the job of preventing the calf from rejoining the herd to the horse. The cutting horse must be fast, athletic, brave and clever. The ability to outwit and outperform the calf is called "cow sense" and is thought by many to be an inherited trait, rather than an acquired skill.

■ The **Working Cow Horse** class is judged in two sections: first the horse performs a reining pattern which demonstrates the various Western movements, and then he has to hold, manoeuvre and control a cow within the arena, turning it several times as well as driving it along a fence line.

■ **Barrel Racing** is a fast, furious, grown-up version of that most popular of mounted games, the bending race! Horse and rider race around a course of barrels – they are allowed to touch the barrels but not to knock them over.

■ Other competitions, such as **Steer Wrestling** and **Calf Roping**, demonstrate and test the skills still required by the working cow pony and rider.

Vaulting

The sport of vaulting is probably most simply described as gymnastics on horseback. Although it is now recognized as an international sport, governed by the FEI since 1982, it developed from an early teaching method which was used to accustom novice riders to the movement of the horse, and to instil a sense of balance and confidence.

Cavalry schools in particular used vaulting exercises to teach new recruits to develop their balance whilst the horse was in motion. Vaulting also served as a good fitness and strengthening exercise for riders, as well as giving them confidence when on horseback.

■ SKILLS REQUIRED

If you wish to be a vaulter you will need to have good natural balance, be naturally athletic and have an air of grace and elegance. The sport also requires confidence – it takes a brave person to carry out many of the exercises with poise.

The horse needs to be quiet-natured, strong, unflappable and able to hold a steady, rhythmic, balanced canter on the lunge throughout the exercise.

BELOW
Vaulting teams are often called upon to give displays at various shows.

The main disadvantage of the sport is that the vaulter always requires help – someone has to be on hand to lunge the horse and, unless you are to compete only as an individual, you will need a partner or even a full team of eight to work with. Riders interested in vaulting therefore really need to join a club, although much of the actual gymnastic work can be practised on a wooden horse.

■ THE COMPETITIONS

International vaulting competitions are made up of team, individual and pair

FAR LEFT
Vaulting competitors need time to warm up in the same way as other gymnasts.

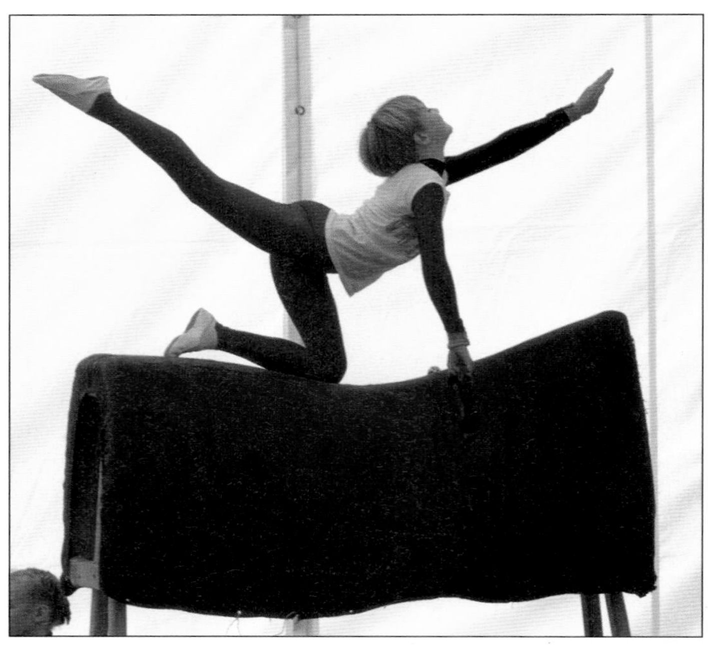

LEFT
The wooden horse is used for warming-up exercises as well as for practising set movements.

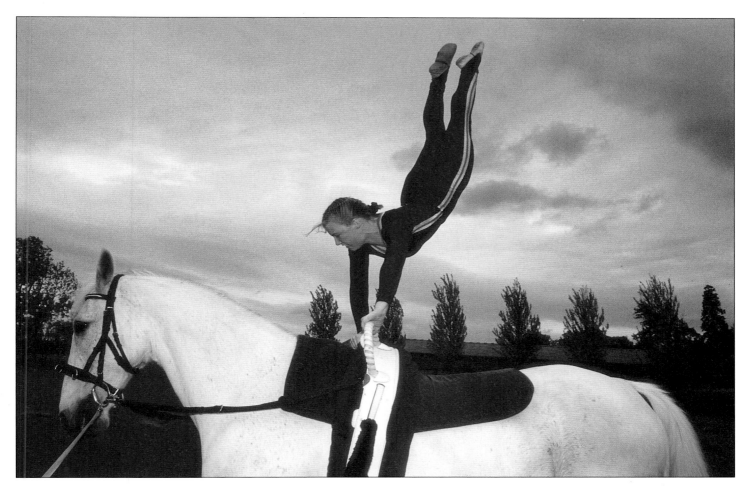

classes. The upper age limit for team vaulters is eighteen, but there is no upper age limit for individuals. A team comprises eight vaulters, one horse and one lunger, and a reserve vaulter. Both the individual and the team competitions include a compulsory and a free-style test.

The horse always works on the left rein, in canter, and must complete a circle of no less than 42½ feet (13 m) in diameter.

There are two classes of international competition – CVI one star, and CVI two star. The World Championship is held every two years, and there are also intercontinental championships, including classes for all-male, all-female and mixed teams.

DISPLAY TEAMS

As well as taking part in competitions, vaulting teams are now often called upon to provide displays at shows and exhibitions. Such demonstrations are certainly an exciting, elegant and colourful way in which to entertain a crowd of spectators.

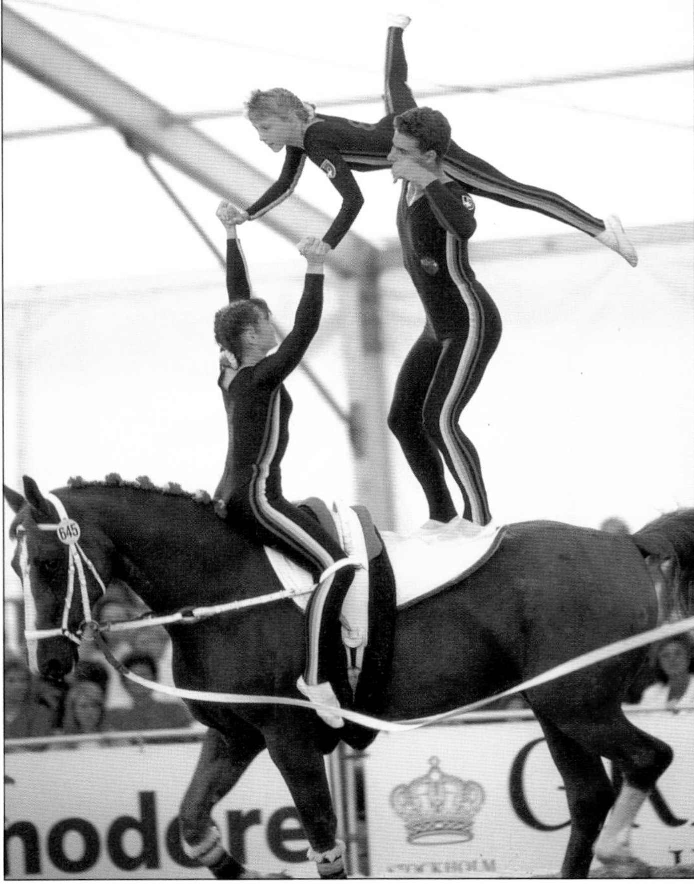

ABOVE
It takes a good athlete to maintain the grace, poise and balance of a gymnast whilst on a moving horse.

LEFT
The team horse must maintain a consistent rhythm throughout all the exercises.

Polo

Of all the team ball games played on horseback, polo is the most widely played and recognized. The sport of polo carries an unashamedly glamorous image. It has always been expensive to take part in, mainly because of the string of ponies that is needed if you are to be a professional player. Despite the growing number of polo clubs, and the opportunities for children to learn to play provided by the Pony Club, polo remains an expensive sport, the greatest opportunities being open to the wealthy or the very talented.

Polo is thought to have originated in Persia about two-and-a-half thousand years ago. Its popularity spread to China, Japan, Tibet and Manipur, where British soldiers learnt the game and wrote home about it. Soldiers in England started playing their own version based on the description they had been given, and British settlers took the game to Argentina. The late 1800s and early 1900s saw the foundation of many polo clubs, including London's Hurlingham which was the first in the Western world. Hurlingham's rules later became universal. Polo is now played all over the world.

LEFT
Polo is only too happy to flaunt its reputation for wealth and glamour. Spectators gather at the Palm Beach Polo Club.

THE GAME

Polo is played on a grass – or snow – pitch which is 901 feet (274 m) long by 600 feet (183 m) wide. Most of the pitch is framed with low boards to help keep the ball in play, and there is a goal at either end, 24½ feet (7.5 m) wide. Indoor polo is also growing in popularity.

There are four players in each team, each of whom has a specific role. The Number One is the front player; his job is to keep well up the pitch to take forward passes and to shoot at goal. When he is not in a position to score, he tries to keep the opposing team's back player (their Number Four) away from the goalmouth so that one of his team-mates may have a chance to score.

The Number Two is another front player; he is usually the most influential attacking player. He works closely with his Number One to keep moving the ball up the field to maximize their chances of taking a shot at goal.

The Number Three player is the link between the two forwards and the back. He is central in turning the play back from defence to attack and must be an extremely versatile player, able to defend, attack and score. He is usually the strongest and most experienced player in the team and is often the captain.

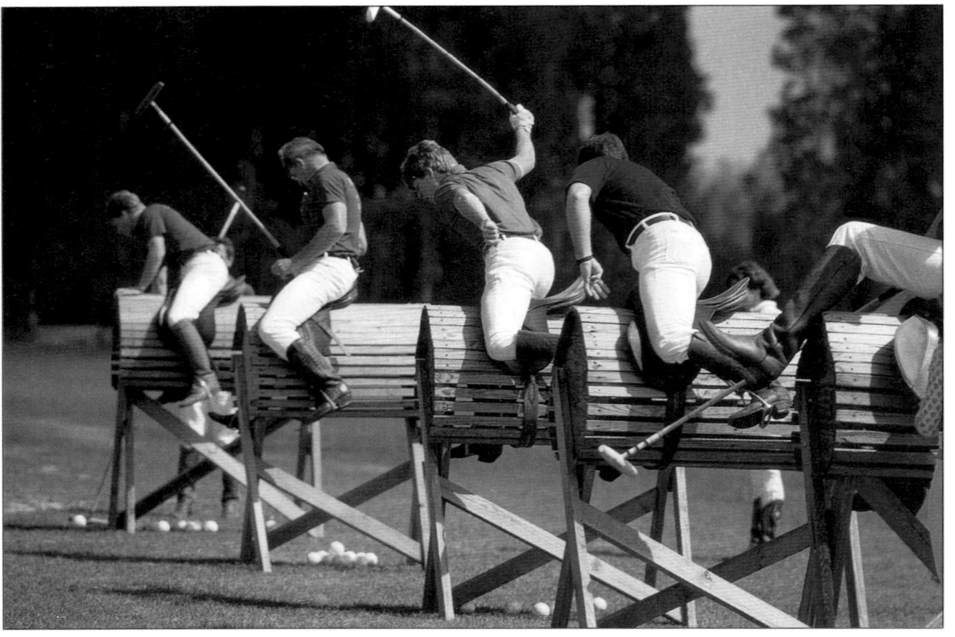

EQUIPMENT NEEDED

To play polo you must be properly dressed – breeches, long boots, helmet with optional face guard, and knee protectors. You will also need your own polo mallets.

You must have at least two ponies – there is no longer a height restriction but polo mounts are still referred to as ponies. The rules insist that ponies wear standing martingales and that they have their tails tied up so that there is no risk of them becoming caught up in anything. The polo pony needs to be brave, responsive, quick-thinking, agile, fast and tough.

LEFT
Practice makes perfect. Even the most complex shots can be practised without getting on a horse – at least not a real one.

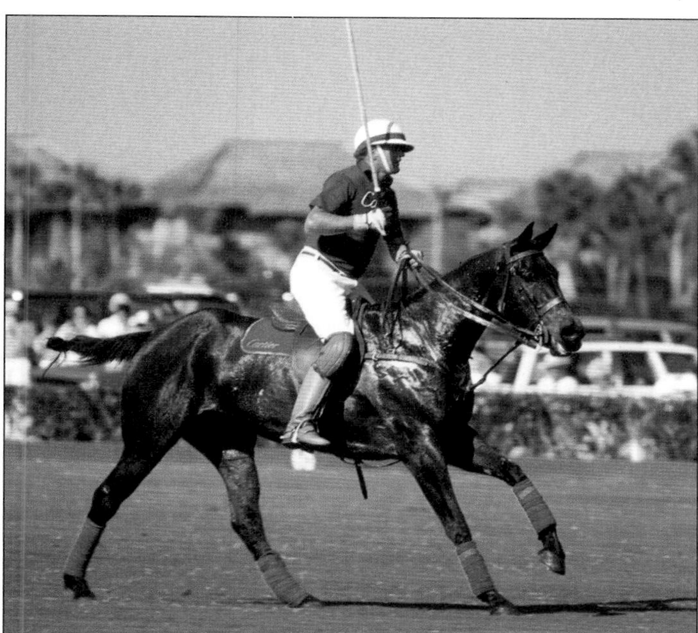

LEFT
Polo ponies need to be as alert and enthusiastic as their riders – and often quicker thinking.

BELOW
A string of polo ponies is an expensive asset, but good ponies are worth every penny to the professional player.

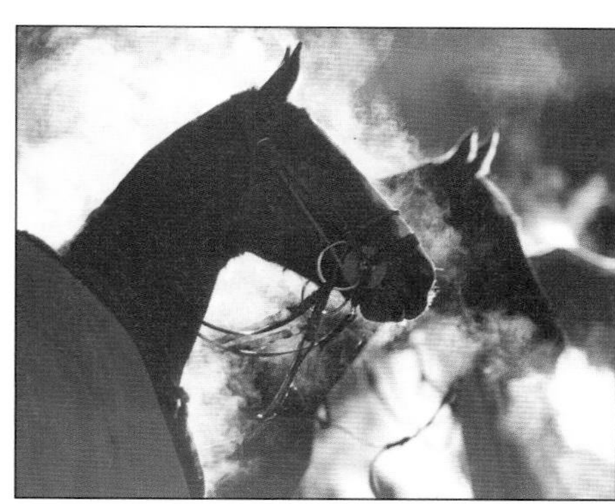

BELOW
Polo originated in far hotter climes than these, but as a winter sport continues in St Moritz.

BOTTOM
Polo ponies have their legs protected by thick bandages during play.

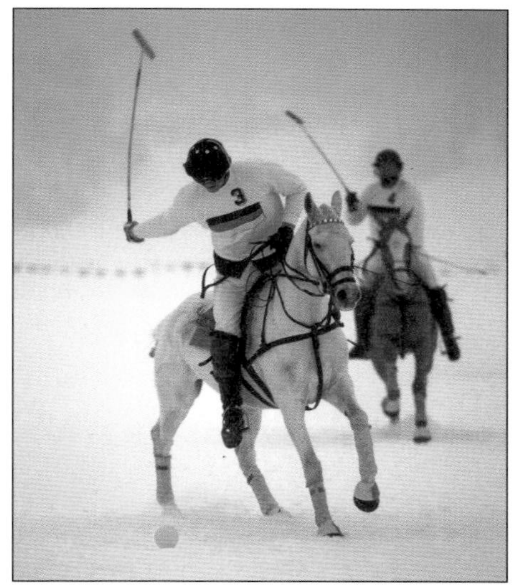

The Number Four is the back player; his main task is to defend the goal but he must also be a good hitter, able to send the ball long and hard up the field to give his forwards a chance of attacking goal.

A full polo match is divided into six seven-minute periods called chukkas. One pony should only ever be used for two chukkas per game, and should never have to play two consecutive chukkas.

Each player uses a mallet (a bamboo stick with a wooden head) to drive the ball down the pitch to the opposition's goal. The opposing team is obviously doing its utmost to prevent any progress down the pitch and to turn the ball back so it can drive for a goal of its own.

All polo players are given a handicap – this varies between -2 goals and +10 goals. The handicap indicates the player's value to the team, not the actual number of goals he has or is expected to score. Teams are given overall handicaps which dictate at which level they play – high goal, medium, intermediate or low goal.

SKILLS REQUIRED

To succeed as a polo player you should be quick-thinking, fit, have very good co-ordination and balance, be physically and mentally tough and have good anticipation of how play is going to proceed.

There are four main playing strokes to be mastered, as well as a further eight subsidiary strokes. The four main strokes are the off-side forehander, off-side backhander, near-side forehander and near-side backhander. These strokes can be practised on a wooden horse as well as on your pony. Would-be players spend many hours simply "stick and balling", i.e. cantering up and down a pitch, hitting a shot, chasing the ball and trying another stroke – up and down, round and round, gradually getting a better result every time.

The rules of polo are quite complex and the game itself is fast moving, with the direction of play changing all the time. As a player you need to have an intimate understanding of the rules, as well as a continual awareness of where everyone is in relation to the direction of play.

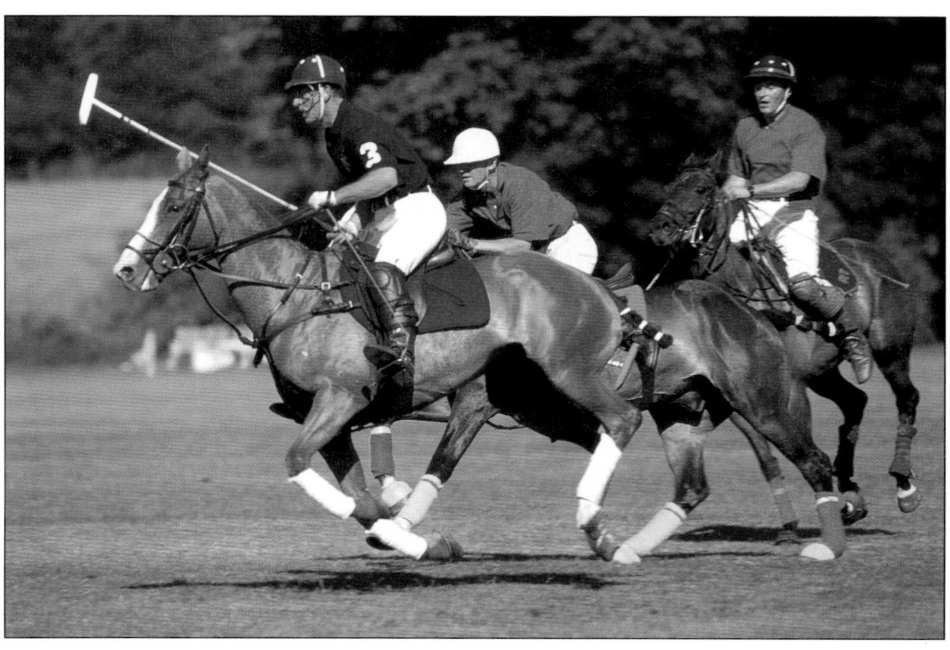

Horseball

Horseball is for those who enjoy a real contact sport – it resembles a cross between rugby football and basketball played on horseback. There are two teams of four players. The ball is about the size of a football and has leather loops sewn to it to use as handholds. The ball is thrown between the players and can be pulled from your opponents' hands, but if it drops to the ground it must be picked up without dismounting: riders have to bend down and scoop the ball up off the ground by grabbing hold of the leather loops. Whenever a rider is retrieving the ball off the ground the other riders have to keep a distance as a safety precaution; otherwise they are offside. The stirrups are tied together under the horse's belly, making it easier for the rider to reach down.

A goal is scored by throwing the ball through a suspended loop which has a net attached to it. The game is started, and restarted after a goal, by a throw-in similar to that used in rugby. The ball is tossed in the air between two riders who each strive to grab it first. The game can be played indoors or outdoors, and is a sport enjoyed by both adults and children.

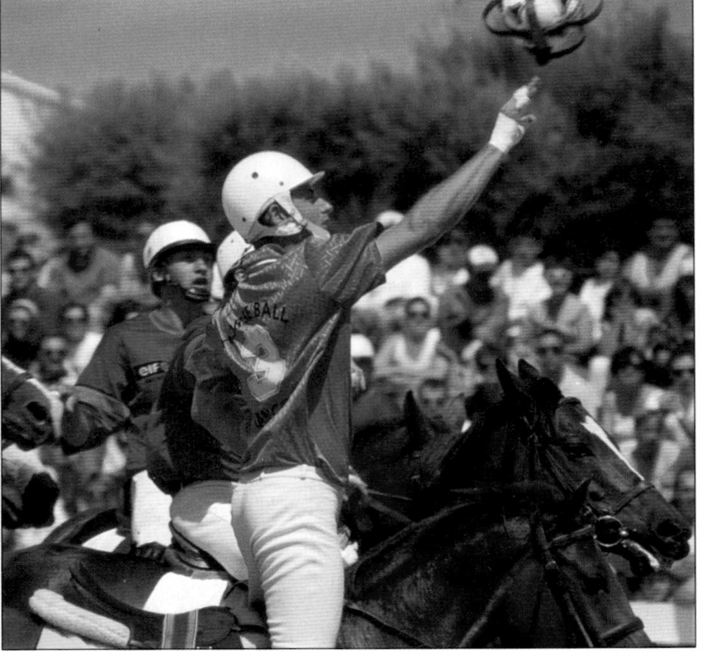

LEFT
Horseball has grown rapidly in popularity in recent years, as a game for both adults and children.

BELOW LEFT
The ball is moved rapidly down the arena towards the goal. In order to score, the ball has to be thrown through a high loop with a net attached.

EQUIPMENT NEEDED

The joy of playing horseball is that the equipment required for the sport is cheap and simple. The ball can be made by having leather loops sewn to a normal football and the goal can be made from an old netball post, using a hoop and a haynet. If you are going to play bareback, whoever sews the loops to your football can also be asked to sew handholds to a surcingle, which will hold a numnah in place on the horse's back and give you some security.

Because the ball can only travel as far and as fast as you can throw it, horseball does not require the same speed from its contestants as, say, polo. For this reason any horse or pony who is well behaved in company, i.e. can be trusted not to kick out or nip an opposing pony or rider, and who is reasonably well schooled, can be introduced to the game.

The greatest advantage of horseball is that, because the equipment is relatively cheap and easy to make, it is ideal as a fun, impromptu game for a group of friends on horseback. At the other extreme it can be played fast, furious and mean by teams with their hearts set on regional and national championship glory.

PONY CLUB HORSEBALL

The Pony Club adopted the game with enthusiasm as the organizers could see its potential as a fun way of improving riding skills and confidence. To make it additionally beneficial as a training exercise, at Pony Club level horseball is played bareback. You sit on a numnah held in place with a surcingle which has two handholds. When you have to reach down to scoop the ball off the ground, you can use the handholds to help keep your balance. To ensure that the ponies don't get pulled in the mouth, you have to drop the reins when you catch the ball.

Polocrosse

LEFT AND BELOW
Ponies and riders need to be athletic and versatile, as well as unflappable!

Polocrosse is based on the mounted game of polo and on lacrosse, a ball game that is played on foot. Whilst polo originated in the Far East and lacrosse in North America, both were introduced to Europe by returning servicemen and travellers. Polocrosse was first played in 1932 in London. It was used as an exercise to encourage better riding skills and was originally played by teams of two indoors. It quickly developed into a four-a-side outdoor game. In 1938, an Australian couple who watched the game in England took the idea back home with them to Australia, where it became the fast and exciting game that it is today. Polocrosse is played in many different countries around the world, and there are numerous inter-club championships as well as a World Championship.

EQUIPMENT AND SKILLS NEEDED

To play polocrosse you need one horse and a polocrosse racquet. The only other necessary equipment is protective boots and bandages for your horse's legs. All kinds of horses and ponies play the game, from Shetland ponies to thoroughbreds, making it a good family game. You need to have a safe and secure seat in the saddle; beyond that, it is just a case of practising your catching and throwing skills, which can be done on the ground as well as mounted.

THE GAME

Polocrosse is played between two teams of six, all of whom are equipped with a long-handled racquet which has a net on the end of it. A soft rubber ball is the object of play; it is caught in the net of the racquet and passed between players by throwing or bouncing it.

The game is split into six chukkas, each lasting for eight minutes. Each team is divided into two and they alternate for each chukka so that only three of the six team members are on the field at one time. The game is played on a large area slightly bigger than a rugby field. The pitch is divided by penalty lines over which the ball must not be carried – the player must either bounce and retrieve it, or throw it to a team-mate.

There is a goal at each end consisting of two poles 8 feet (2.5 m) apart. The ball must be thrown between these in order to score. Only the Number One player is allowed to shoot at goal. The defending Number Three player is allowed in the goalscoring area to protect the goal and to tackle the attacking Number One. The Number Two players are only allowed in the midfield area.

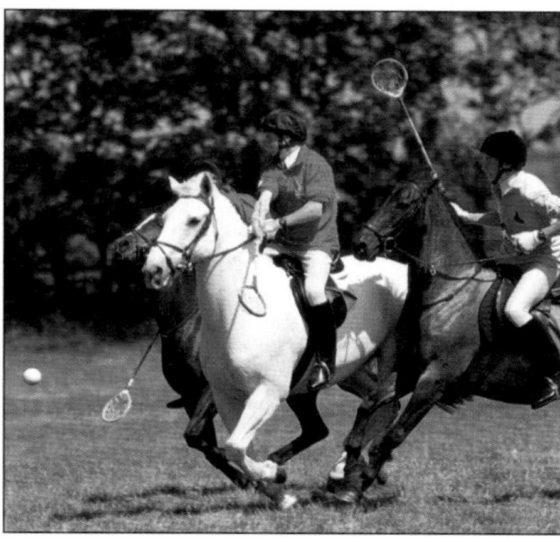

BELOW
Many younger riders are introduced to team ball games on horseback by the Pony Club. Polocrosse is a popular alternative to polo, although the Pony Club fields many high-quality polo teams as well.

Driving

Horses and ponies are well designed for the task of pulling a vehicle of some kind or other. Remember that a horse has to be taught how to re-arrange his balance and posture in order to carry a rider, whereas pulling something comes more naturally.

Driving is great fun – although many riders find it more nerve-racking than riding – and it can be undertaken in as simple or elaborate a way as desire and finances allow.

DRIVING FOR PLEASURE

Many a family pony has been converted from riding to driving once the children have outgrown him. Given a patient and common-sense approach, most horses and ponies of an equable nature will convert to driving; many even show a preference for it, though there are always exceptions.

The first stage in training a driving horse is to accustom him to wearing blinkers. He should be lunged and long reined in these, and finally hacked out in them. After that, introduce him to the rest of the harness. The next stage involves getting him to pull something safe, such as an old tyre. It is not the weight of what he is pulling that is likely to bother him, but his awareness of something following behind him and the noise it makes. Once he is comfortable with this he is well on the way to being introduced to a simple cart of some sort. Straightforward as it all sounds, experienced help should always be sought in the training process.

Driving clubs will provide a social dimension to a leisure activity which can otherwise be quite a solitary one.

ABOVE
The second phase of driving trials is the marathon, in which competitors cover a set route following various roads and tracks. This phase incorporates a hazards section where cross-country-type obstacles have to be negotiated.

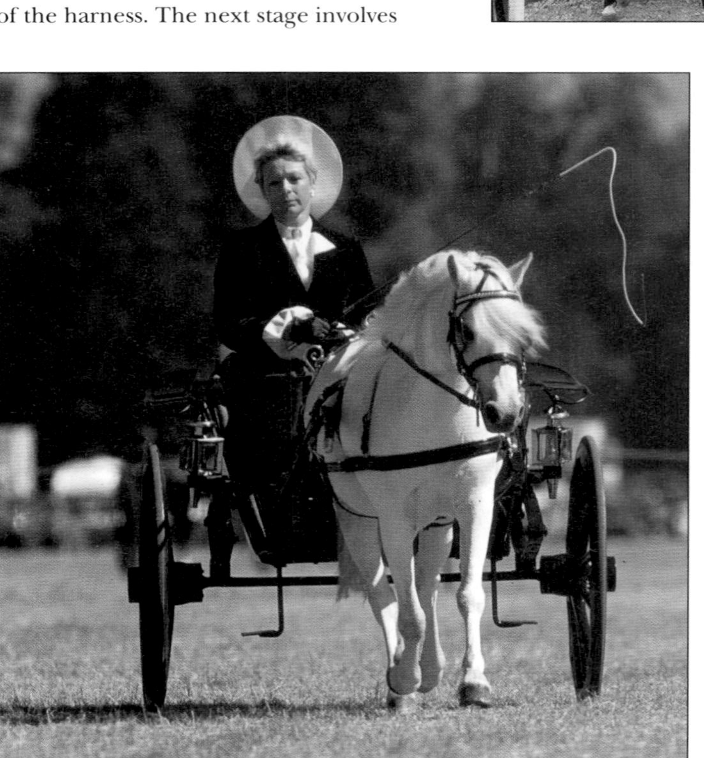

LEFT
In show-ring driving the overall turnout and performance of the competitors is judged. This smart little Welsh mountain pony is creating a good all-round impression in the ring.

COMPETITION DRIVING

The world of competition driving revolves around the show ring and driving trials. Show-ring driving follows a similar format to ridden showing classes; driving trials resemble ridden horse trials and consist of three disciplines – a dressage test, a marathon and an obstacle competition.

In show-ring driving, the full turnout of horse or pony, his harness, the cart, the furnishings and the appearance of the driver and groom are all judged, as well as the behaviour and way of going of the whole team. Competing in driving trials requires far more time, practice and equipment than show-ring driving.

Harness racing, which involves specially bred trotters or pacers pulling a lightweight racing cart, is another specialist sport which attracts a great spectator following. The horses can travel at a tremendous speed in trot, and race each other around a big circuit. The

▮ OPPOSITE
For competition purposes a team of four is about as complicated as you want to get, but horses can be driven in larger teams than this.

▮ BELOW
Driving horses and ponies, and the vehicles they pull, come in all manner of shapes and sizes, and can be driven in different ways. This pair of ponies is being driven abreast.

▮ BELOW
This pair is being driven in tandem, i.e. one behind the other.

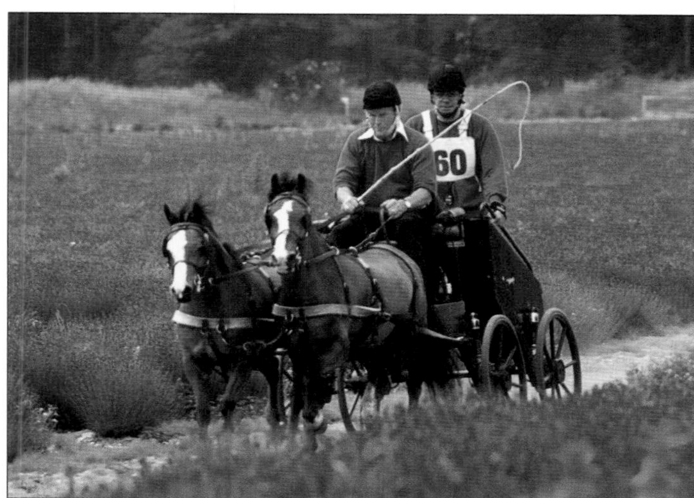

necessary equipment is relatively inexpensive as the carts are lightweight and basic in design, but it is a fiercely competitive sport.

SHOW-RING DRIVING CLASSES

▮ In **Private Driving** classes the competitors may be sent off for a drive around the surrounding roads with the judge following in a car to see how they react and behave.

▮ **Light Trade** classes are for horse-drawn vehicles which were, or still are, used for trade purposes, such as deliveries of goods. An additional requirement in these classes is for the horses to stand still unattended, which they would have to do while their goods were being unloaded.

▮ The **Concour d'Elegance** class is judged more on overall poise than on close detail.

▮ **Scurry Driving** is a popular class at many British shows. Pairs of ponies, which must be either 12hh and under, or between 12hh and 14.2hh, are harnessed to small, four-wheeled vehicles carrying a driver and groom. They race around an obstacle course marked out by cones, which involves tight turns and high speeds and a lot of noise from the spectators. Any cones knocked over are penalized by adding extra seconds to the overall race time. The groom has to play a very active role – leaning out to either side to help maintain the vehicle's balance as it swings around the corners.

▮ Additional show-ring classes include the likes of **Ride-and-Drive** competitions and **Heavy Horse** classes. There may also be the opportunity to put on a display to entertain the public.

DRIVING TRIALS

▮ For the first phase, you have to perform a simple dressage test within the confines of a large arena; this is given a mark based on the performance and on the overall presentation.

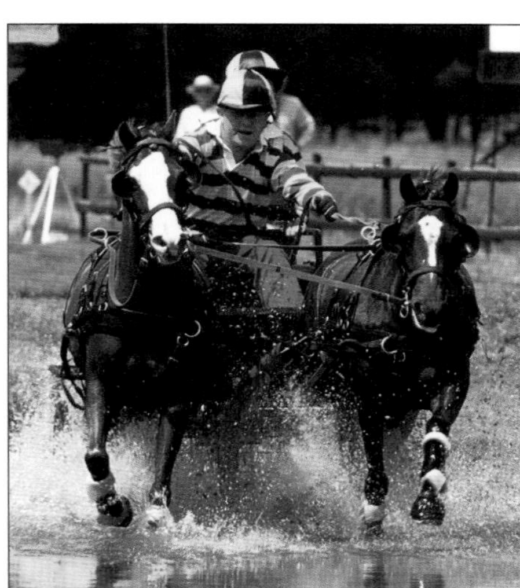

Water is a popular hazard in driving trials. This pair of ponies is negotiating a simple water crossing with great enthusiasm.

▮ The marathon, which comes next, involves covering approximately 15½ miles (25 km) in about two hours. There are five different sections and two compulsory ten-minute breaks.

– The first section can be completed at any pace, but trotting is usually sufficient to make the time.

– The second section must be performed in walk and is followed by a ten-minute rest.

– The third section usually involves a stretch of more arduous terrain and a fast trot is required to make the time; cantering is not allowed.

– The fourth section is another walk section, followed by a ten-minute break.

– With the fifth section the excitement really begins. This involves negotiating various man-made or natural hazards at speed, as this section is timed.

▮ The final phase is the obstacle or cone-driving competition. This tests the horses' obedience and the driver's ability to drive accurately between sets of cones which mark out the course. Once again, this section is timed.

▮ The overall winner is the one with the best combined score over the three different phases.

Jumping Sports

Jumping needs confidence, rhythm and balance. Once you have a fair degree of these three skills you can start to discover the world of jumping sports. Show jumping offers competitions for fun as well as for fortune seekers, and provides an excellent and safe way to practise your jumping skills and gain experience. Once you feel confident over show jumps – which fall down if you hit them – you may want to try your hand at jumping solid obstacles. Hunting and hunter trials provide you with the opportunity to do this – and when you are feeling confident enough you can progress to team chasing or eventing. For the brave and robust there is race riding – the ultimate way to jump at speed.

Hunting

There is little to beat the exhilaration of riding fast across country. You and your horse must tackle whatever is thrown in your way – balancing your horse over all kinds of terrain with the wind making your eyes stream, mud splattered in your face, encouraging him over every manner of obstacle, letting him jump out of his stride and land running, looking eagerly ahead for the next challenge.

The thrill of it usually lifts the spirits and the courage of all horsemen and women. The hedge that you sailed over effortlessly when running behind hounds may look completely unjumpable when viewed in cold blood! There is neither judge nor winner, except in the hearts and minds of those taking part. Hunting, for many, provides an opportunity to tackle much greater challenges than they might otherwise contemplate.

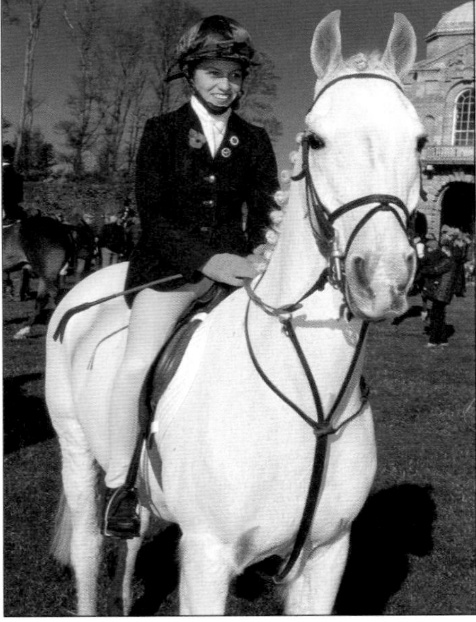

ABOVE
Hunting etiquette requires that you and your mount are smartly and tidily turned out. Your horse's or pony's mane should be plaited (braided), your tack should be gleaming, and you should be kitted out in clean jodhpurs, boots and jacket.

BELOW
The hounds are controlled by a huntsman; he is usually assisted by a whipper-in who helps to keep the hounds together as a pack.

DIFFERENT TYPES OF HUNTING

HUNTING QUARRY

Ever since man learnt to ride a horse he has used the horse's speed and agility to his advantage, including in his hunt for food. Today, hunting on horseback is a country sport rather than a means of survival. Hunting live quarry for sport is a controversial subject on which many people hold strong views. Some consider it has a valuable role to play in the conservation of the countryside and in the management of the wildlife it hunts; others think it is cruel and an outdated way to control wildlife. Hunt meets often attract protesters from various animal rights organizations and are often not publicized.

A wide variety of animals is hunted from horseback around the world. The most common ones are the fox and stag in

LEFT
You are never too young or too old to go hunting. Many children are taken out, and an abundance of youthful pensioners still hunts regularly.

England and Ireland, the wild boar in other parts of Europe, and the coyote in North America and parts of Africa. The hunting of any of these animals relies on the co-operation and permission of the landowners whose property is crossed.

Packs of hounds are bred and trained to pick up the scent and track down the hunted animal. The hounds are controlled by a huntsman and whipper-in, who are the only people actively involved in the work of the hounds. The hunt followers, or field as they are often known, are sometimes helpful in observing the whereabouts of the hounds or the direction the hunted quarry has taken, but their main role is to help pay for the upkeep of the hunt's hounds, horses and hunting country. In return for an annual subscription and a "cap" – an additional donation to hunt funds made on the day of the hunt – the hunt follower enjoys seeing hounds at work and the thrill of the chase.

In fox hunting, after a convivial half an hour or so at the meet, the huntsman heads off with the hounds to the first cover. This is usually a piece of woodland or scrubland where a fox is likely to be found. The field follow, led by the field master whose instructions you must obey at all times – and who you should avoid overtaking! The hounds are "cast" into the cover, i.e. sent in to hunt around until they find the scent of the fox. Some days are good scenting days and the hounds can easily follow the scent; other days are not so good.

Once the hounds are on the scent of their quarry, they will follow it across all manner of country. The mounted followers keep up as best they can, the bravest and most talented jumping everything in their path, the rest finding a way around the edges of fields, through gates and along tracks. A good knowledge of the local countryside helps in the task of keeping up with the hounds. If you are crossing country that has been planted with crops, only the hounds and huntsman are allowed to take the direct line after the prey. The field have to find a way round which minimizes any damage to the crops; an intimate knowledge of your surroundings makes this easier. Etiquette demands that you follow the lead of the field master, but after a good run behind hounds the field often gets split up and strung out, and it is up to you to find the hounds again.

The hounds will either succeed in catching their prey or they will lose track

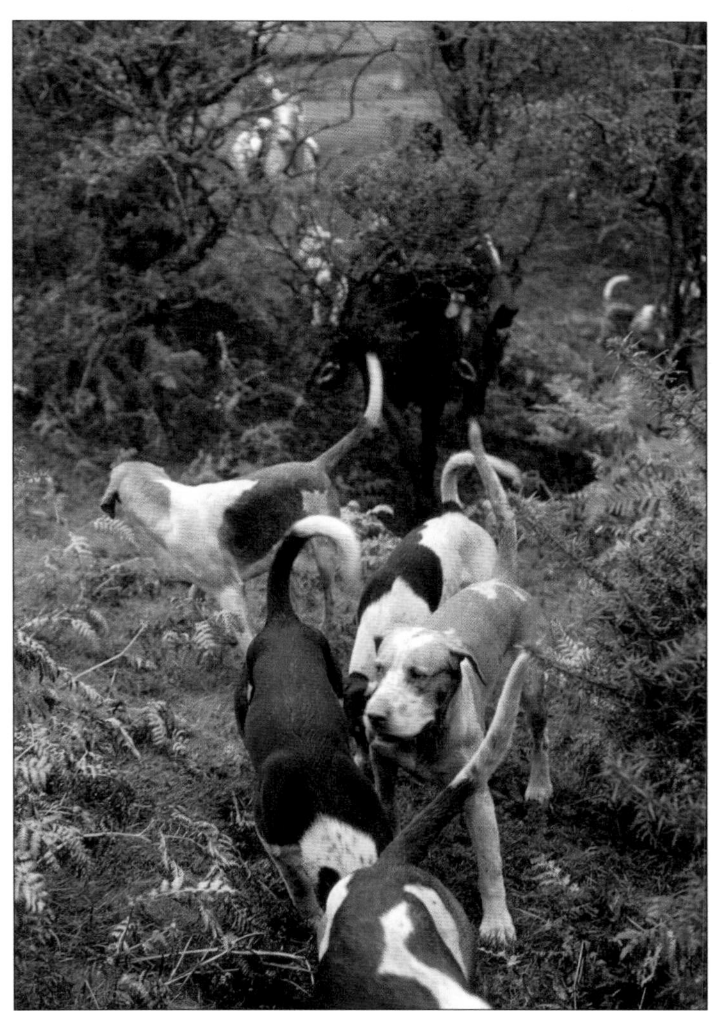

LEFT
Whether you are hunting foxes, coyote, hare, or with drag or bloodhounds, nothing very exciting happens until the hounds pick up the appropriate scent and set off.

LEFT
Out hunting there will always be those who want to jump obstacles and those who want to go around them. The choice is yours, but should be based on an appreciation of ability – yours and your mount's – rather than on pride.

of it, or may have to be called off if the fox crosses land that the hunt doesn't have permission to cross. In any case the hounds are taken to another cover to see if they can pick up the scent of another fox, and so it goes on.

Most hunt meets are organized for mid-morning, and hunting continues until late in the afternoon. At about lunchtime "second horses" are arranged. This means that the huntsman, whipper-in and master will change on to fresh horses who have been brought by lorry to a pre-arranged point. Their first horses are taken home, washed and dried off, rugged up, fed and stabled. Hunt followers may also change on to second horses if they have another horse and have been able to organize someone to deliver it for them.

Whilst hunting is a thrilling way of enjoying cross-country riding, it carries a lot of risks because there is no time to check out what you are about to jump. Many a horse and rider have fallen when, having taken off over what looks like an innocuous hedge, they see in mid-air that there is a wire or timber fence running alongside it on the far side. A scopey, quick-thinking, focused horse can usually get himself out of such a muddle, but only with experience which can be painful in the making.

DRAG HUNTING

This involves a pack of hounds and mounted followers but, instead of hunting a live quarry, the hounds follow a trail that has been laid earlier in the day by someone dragging a bag laced with a strong scent that the hounds have been taught to pick up and follow.

Drag hunting gives you the chance to ride fast across country, behind hounds. It is safer and more predictable than hunting live quarry because you are following a pre-set course. The jumps will be either safe, natural features or man-made fences. A knowledge of the country is not necessary as the course the hounds take is pre-determined. Many hunts offer days specifically for the novice or nervous, when they will make sure the jumps encountered are smaller than usual.

Subscriptions from the field help to pay for the upkeep of the hounds and kennels.

BLOODHOUNDS

Hunting with bloodhounds is another form of drag hunting. This time the hounds are following the scent of a man

EQUIPMENT NEEDED

Your horse should be well turned out with his mane plaited (braided). He will need a good, strong set of tack, as a good-quality saddle and bridle will add to your own safety. Hunting entails long hours in the saddle, often in bad weather conditions. The last thing you want is for a rein or stirrup leather to snap when you are in the middle of nowhere, riding at a flat-out gallop and heading for a large and solid post-and-rail fence!

Put an especially well-padded numnah under the saddle to make it more comfortable for the horse and to reduce the risk of him being rubbed.

Whether or not your horse wears boots to protect his legs is a matter of personal choice. Your horse's legs are at great risk of being knocked or scratched out hunting, but many boots, once they are wet and muddy and have been worn for several hours, start to rub anyway. You will need to decide which is the lesser of two evils.

As a rider you are expected to be smartly turned out. You should wear traditional-coloured breeches or jodphurs, teamed with either long riding boots or short jodhpur boots. You must wear either a hacking jacket (tweed jacket) or a plain blue or black jacket. A crash cap with blue or black velvet silk should be worn and this should have a well-fitting safety harness. If you wear a hacking jacket it is correct to wear a shirt and coloured stock (similar to a cravat or broad neck tie) held in place with a stock pin. A plain cream or white stock should be worn with a blue or black jacket.

Gloves should be worn and a stick carried. You should carry in your pockets some good, thick string, such as baling twine, and a foldaway penknife so that you can help make repairs to any gates or fences that get broken by the less able jumpers in the field. A day's hunting can end up being a very long day – find room in your pockets for a couple of sandwiches or a bar of chocolate to keep you going.

If you are going to hunt a lot, a hunting whip and a pair of wire cutters are worth buying. A hunting whip is a shaped cane with a long leather lash on the end. The cane is useful for helping you to open and shut gates, and the lash, if let down so that it hangs by your horse's legs, can be used to prevent hounds from going right underneath your horse where they are more likely to get kicked or trampled. A leather carrying pouch can be fitted to your saddle in which to put a pair of wire cutters. No matter how diligent you are, when you are crossing unknown country it is possible to get caught up in one of the hazards of agriculture – wire netting or barbed wire. A pair of wire cutters is invaluable to cut your own horse free or to help anyone else unfortunate enough to be caught out.

who sets off some time before the hunt starts. The runner will follow a previously agreed trail, making this form of hunting as safe as drag hunting. You might find the thought of a pack of bloodhounds bearing down on a fleeing man alarming, but they will not harm him when they catch him. He will most likely be smothered in wet, warm licks by his friendly canine pursuers.

SKILLS REQUIRED

Hunting suits all types of horse and pony – it seems to inspire the less cautious to be even braver, but it can also cause a great deal of over-excitement. It is important to have developed a reasonably strong and secure seat and to be able to balance your horse in order to help him tackle the varied terrain and obstacles that you will encounter. Whether you are riding around a cross-country course or are genuinely crossing the country out hunting, the approach to jumping is the same: keep the horse balanced and in a rhythm. Keep in contact with the horse with your legs, seat and hands so that you can help balance him as he negotiates the unexpected.

BELOW
Ladies traditionally only ever rode side-saddle, and the elegant picture it creates is one reason for a growing number of people returning to the habit.

Those brave and able enough to jump everything in their path will take the most direct line, following the lead of the field master. But there are plenty of others who will find their way around as best they can so as not to have to jump too much. Consider your own riding ability and the experience of your horse before deciding which party to join. When you do get the chance to jump, always give your horse room to see what it is you want him to do. Don't follow blindly behind the horse in front – your horse will not be able to judge the fence and, if the horse and rider in front fall or refuse, you will have a problem. In a crowded gateway, or if there is a queue of riders waiting to jump a narrow fence, slow your horse down well beforehand, so that you don't run into the back of everyone else. Wait your turn and give your horse room to make a good, balanced approach, and the chance to see what the fence involves.

Your horse needs to be fit, as he will be required to gallop and jump, often with little chance to rest. He should be well mannered; he must accept other horses all around him. If you have even the slightest suspicion that he may panic or kick out, keep him out of the crowd. It is your responsibility to prevent your horse from hurting anyone else. A young or inexperienced horse should be introduced quietly to the hunting field. It is often a good idea to avoid the first hour of the meet when all the horses are fresh and excited, and perhaps join the hunt later in the day. Keep the horse moving and thinking forwards but do not allow him to get caught up in the crush of the field until he is used to all the sights and sounds. It is considered an unforgiveable sin to let your horse kick a hound, so be constantly aware of where the hounds are in relation to your horse. Keep his hindquarters turned away from the hounds if they approach or pass by you.

In the excitement of the chase do not overlook your horse's well-being. At all times, keep in mind how tired he might really be – horses get very caught up in the excitement of the chase and may not appear to be tired, as their excitement and adrenalin gives them additional stamina. But this should not be abused – think of how fit your horse really is, and how much galloping and jumping he has done. Do not keep him out for too long – there will always be another day. Think responsibly about what you ask him to jump. Never be tempted to jump wire – find a gate instead. Look out too for hazards such as rabbit holes and discarded farm machinery.

BOTTOM
At the end of a long, hard day's hunting the field is greatly diminished. It is one of the most satisfying feelings in the world to be amongst the few left at the end of the day.

Hunter Trials and Team Chasing

For those who want to be judged on their cross-country-riding skills, there is the option of competing in hunter trials and team chases. In a hunter trial you may ride the course as an individual or as one of a pair. In team chasing there are four team members to motivate each other.

In hunter trials you are expected to tackle a course of cross-country fences, the height of which varies depending on the class you enter. Some competitions cater for leading-rein riders, others offer a range of classes varying from about 2 feet 6 inches to 3 feet 9 inches (0.75–1.2 m). The organizers decide upon an optimum time, which is based on horse and rider tackling the course at what is commonly described as a fair hunting pace. Within the course there is usually an additional timed section which often includes a gate that has to be opened and shut – not jumped! The winners are the horse and rider who jump clear and complete the course nearest to the optimum time – which is not revealed to the riders until after the competition. If more than one rider finishes on the optimum time, the winner is the fastest one through the timed section.

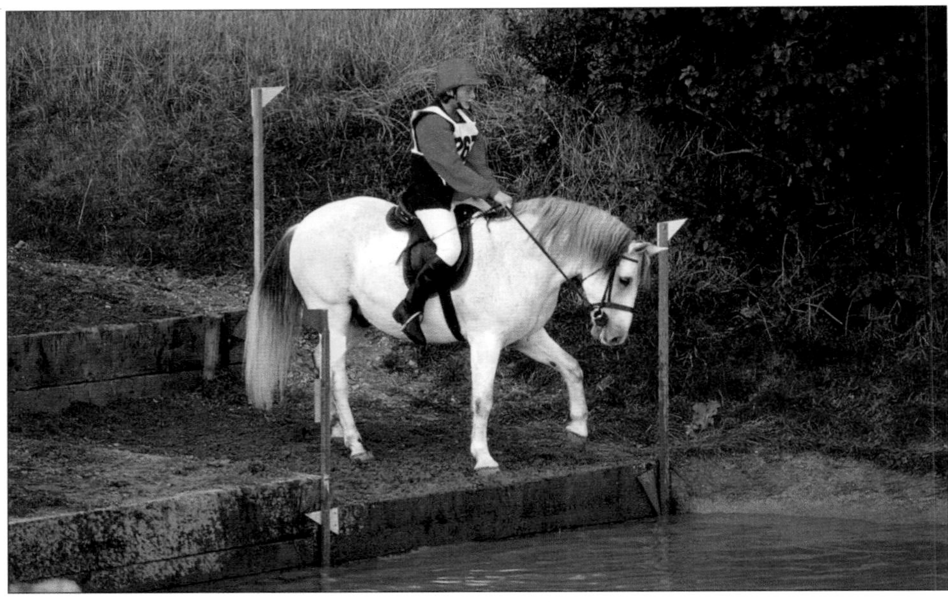

ABOVE
Water is one of the most common problems encountered at a hunter trial. There is no reason why it should be feared provided it is introduced quietly and calmly. This pony looks a bit tentative and needs to gain more confidence before he is likely to tackle water with enthusiasm.

BELOW LEFT
Hunter trials offer a huge variety of challenges for all ages and abilities. Even leading-rein riders can take part, provided their helpers are as agile as their ponies!

SKILLS REQUIRED

The main difference between hunting and competing in a hunter trial is that at a hunter trial you have to jump alone and in cold blood. You do not have the rush and excitement of hounds running and the rest of the field following to give you confidence. You and your horse have to be prepared to jump for the fun of it, although some classes are open to pairs in

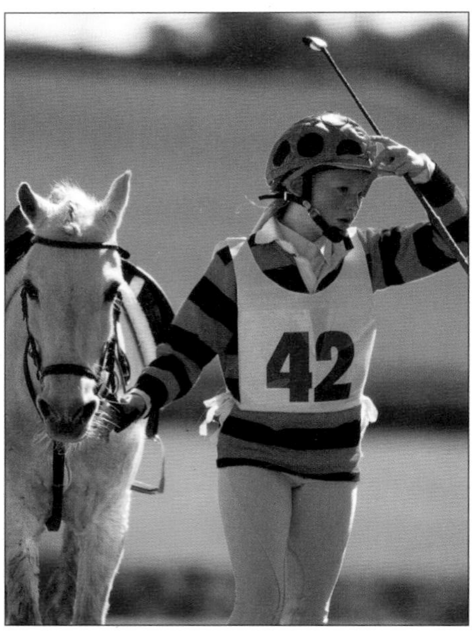

LEFT
Cross-country riding is tiring for both horse and rider, but it is always a kind and correct gesture to dismount and lead your horse or pony once you have pulled up over the finish line.

BELOW
This horse and rider have both taken a good soaking at the water hazard, but the joy of team chasing is that, provided the rest of the team got through, there is still a chance of winning. It just means there is a little consolation for the faller – his team will have galloped away into the distance!

LEFT
Competing as a pair is a good way of introducing an inexperienced or nervous horse or rider to the thrill of cross-country riding, as they can gain confidence from their partners.

which case a less confident horse can take a lead from his bolder partner. Some horses make marvellous hunters but will not jump an inch outside the hunting field. Remember to let your horse take his own line out hunting – do not just blindly follow the horse in front. If you have balanced him and helped him so that he regards hunting and cross-country jumping as fun, there is no reason why your hunter should not happily complete a hunter trial for you.

In the timed section you will have to open and shut a gate quickly without dismounting. It should be easy if your horse has learnt to listen and respond to your hand and leg aids. You just need to be sure that your horse will rein back, and move over to the right or left when you ask him, and you can practise all these skills at home.

To win the competition you will need to have a good sense of speed and timing. If you have hunted, try to think of the speed you travel at when hounds are running, and to go at that same speed on the hunter-trial course. You will know the terrain, having already walked the course. Once you are up to speed it is a case of staying in that rhythm and keeping the horse balanced.

TEAM CHASING

Team chases are held over a variety of different-sized cross-country courses. Teams of four riders set off around the course, and progress is timed from the moment a team sets off to the moment the third rider crosses the line. So if one member of your team is left behind you are still in with a chance of winning.

The winning team is the one whose first three riders complete the course in the fastest time. Penalties are not given for falls or refusals – it is all judged on speed. For this reason the number of falls can be quite high. If the lead horse falls and the others are coming too fast and too close behind, at least one other member of the team is likely to fall also. But there is never any need to give up hope – even if one of the team stops or falls, provided the team can make up time somewhere else they still have a chance of a place. Regional and national championships are held.

EQUIPMENT NEEDED

To compete in a hunter trial you need to be kitted out in your hunting attire, although most organizers allow you to wear a sweat shirt or jumper instead of a jacket. They will, however, insist that you wear a proper safety helmet and harness, as well as a body protector.

Your horse will need his usual saddle and bridle, as long as these are clean and in good condition, and his legs should be protected with either boots or bandages.

A normal riding stick or hunting whip may be carried; for hunter trials a proper hunting whip may help in opening and shutting the gate quickly in the timed section.

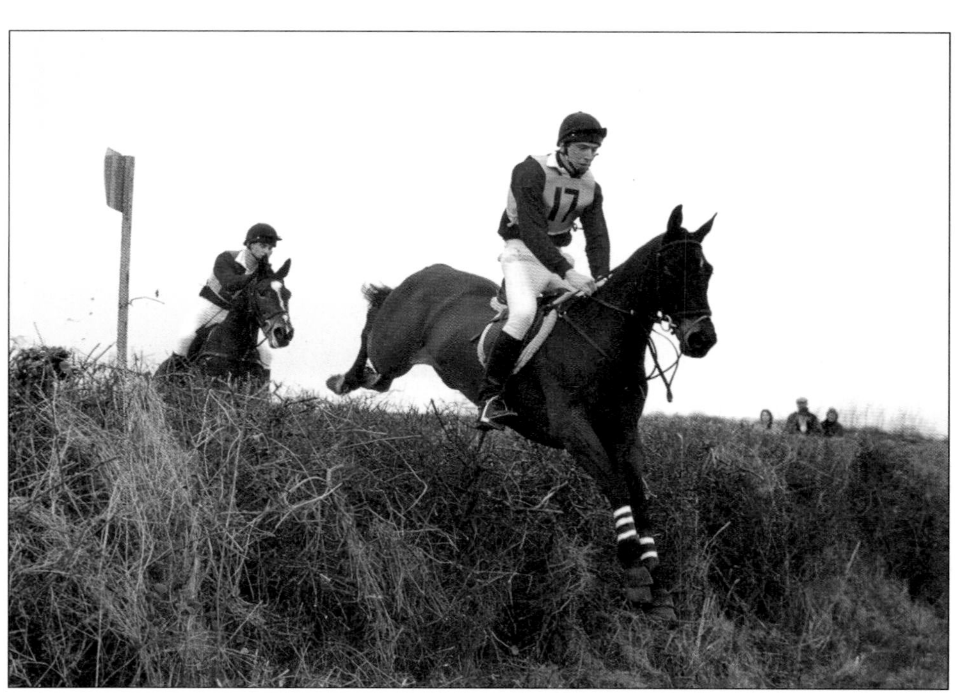

RIGHT
Team chasing involves a team of four riding fast and furiously across country. The competition is based on the time it takes for the first three team members to complete the course.

Show Jumping

LEFT
Teaching your horse to go well on the flat is as important to his success as teaching him how to jump correctly; look at the beautifully round and elevated canter that this show jumper is producing – with a canter like this, jumping the fence is almost a formality.

The sport of show jumping involves tackling a course of artificial jumps, as opposed to natural cross-country jumps. It takes place in an arena which can be grass or have an all-weather surface, indoors or outdoors. An Olympic sport governed by the FEI, it is also a popular unaffiliated sport with any number of classes being held at local shows.

Show jumping requires accuracy and care. Almost every horse or pony can jump, but they do not all have the technique or the will to clear the fences.

Show jumping developed from the "leaping competitions" which were held at various shows in Europe and America during the late nineteenth century. There were high-jump and long-jump competitions for horse and rider but the idea of jumping a course of fences was, at the time, mainly restricted to natural cross-country fences. Jumping was first included in the Olympic Games in Paris in 1900. It incorporated the high and wide competitions plus a timed competition over a course of artificial show jumps. In 1907, the first International Horse Show was held at Olympia in London, England, and the show jumping proved to be very popular. From then on competitions were organized throughout Europe and America for major trophies such as the Nations Cup. This began as a military competition open to three officers of the same nationality who had to compete in uniform. Today it is open to four riders of the same nationality, male or female, military or civilian.

BELOW LEFT AND RIGHT
If you can invest in a few jumps of your own, or team up with some friends to share them, there is much that can be practised at home. A simple thing to practise is always looking towards the next fence. This helps you to judge your turns and your approach. Once you have taken off over a fence you should be looking towards your next target; as you ride around the course you should always be looking towards where you have to go next.

SHOW-JUMPING COMPETITIONS

The simplest form of unaffiliated competition is the Clear-round Class. This is an excellent way of introducing an inexperienced horse and rider to the sport. Each rider pays a small fee to tackle a course of jumps. If you jump a clear round you win a rosette, but the real usefulness of the competition is that if you jump a fence badly you can turn around and jump it again. Most organizers of these classes are extremely tolerant and will even lower a fence for you if your horse continually refuses. In a proper competition you would be eliminated after three refusals.

RIGHT
It is important that the horse learns to jump straight, unless his rider is asking him to turn in the air. In this picture you can see that the horse is looking in the opposite direction from his rider, suggesting he has a tendency to jump crookedly. Gridwork and the use of V-poles help to teach the horse to stay straight.

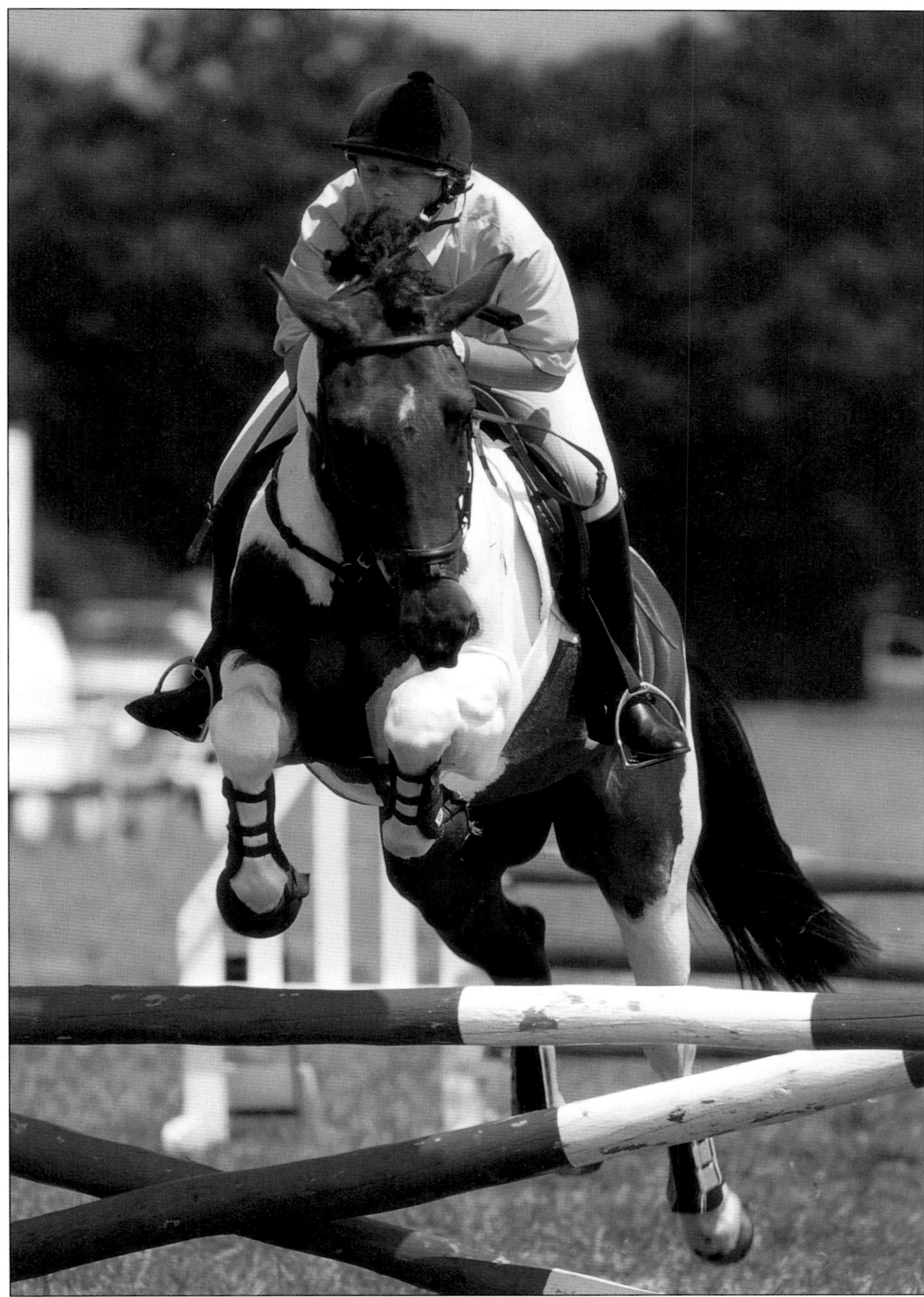

The next stage is the two-round competition. Each competitor tackles the same course of fences and if you jump a clear round you go through to the jump off. This is ridden against the clock and the fastest clear round wins.

Fences in unaffiliated classes start as low as the organizer wishes. There may even be leading-rein classes with jumps only 18 inches (45 cm) high. Fences usually go up to about 3 feet 11 inches (1.2 m). Affiliated competitions start with a novice class with fences at about 3 feet 3 inches (1 m) and continue through the grades to courses with jumps which are well over 6 feet (1.8 m) high.

There are also other types of jumping classes such as "Take your own line". This involves a course of fences which each have a different value in terms of points to be won. You jump as many fences as you can in the time allowed, in any order you like, with the aim of accumulating the maximum number of points. The *Puissance* involves jumping a short course of fences; these include a wall, which is always the highest jump. The fences are gradually raised until nobody is able to clear the wall.

Derby competitions have cross-country-type obstacles in the arena, such as banks and ditches. Some shows also hold relay competitions between teams of show jumpers, or for added entertainment they may build two identical courses side by side over which competitors race. Time faults are added for knock-downs.

One of the advantages of show jumping is that jumping a course of fences does not take as much out of a horse as, say, a day's hunting or a hunter trial, so the show jumper can compete far more frequently than many other sports horses. You could compete in a couple of different classes on the same day and, provided your horse is fit enough and enjoying his work, you might compete nearly every weekend. In

EQUIPMENT NEEDED

To develop your show-jumping skills you need to have access to at least three or four sets of show-jump wings and poles. Other than that, all that is needed is a reasonably flat surface to practise on, which can be a grass paddock when ground conditions permit, or an outdoor or indoor arena with an all-weather surface. Your horse needs only his usual saddle and bridle and should wear protective boots of some sort. Most show jumpers use open-fronted boots on the front legs so that the tendon area is protected but the horse will feel the knock if he hits a pole, and short fetlock boots behind. To compete you will need to wear breeches or jodhpurs with riding boots, and a show or hacking jacket. A shirt and tie, or stock, is worn underneath the jacket.

Whilst almost any horse or pony can be persuaded to pop around a show-jumping course, once the fences get bigger you do need a horse who is athletic and balanced. There are plenty of horses who will clatter their way around a course, gaily sending poles flying without appearing to be the least bit bothered by the experience. There is a great deal you can teach a horse but, at the end of the day, he has to want to clear the top pole.

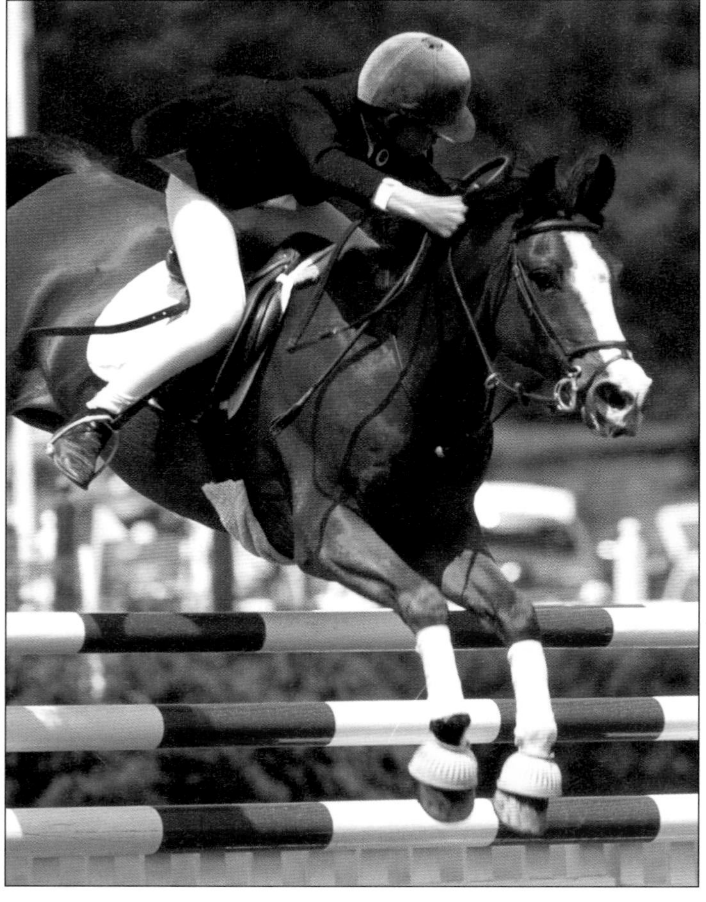

RIGHT
Riders all develop their own jumping style as they gain confidence and experience, but one of the things you must always do, no matter what your technique, is to ensure that you give your horse plenty of freedom of his head and neck. Your hands must always move forwards when the horse is jumping over the fence.

theory this offers horse and rider the chance to gain experience relatively quickly.

■ **SKILLS REQUIRED**

Flatwork training is as important to the show jumper as jump schooling. A balanced, rhythmic and elevated canter is essential if the horse is to jump successfully. Whatever it is you are jumping, your chances of clearing it safely are mainly reliant on how good an approach you give the horse to the fence. The horse must be able to negotiate corners and turns whilst still keeping his rhythm and balance, so he needs to be supple and responsive.

How much actual jump training you do depends on what suits your horse. Naturally careful horses are best not jumped too often – just enough to keep them in practice and their muscles toned up. A horse whose technique needs tidying up may be jumped up to three or four times a week.

Jump training rarely involves jumping huge fences. It concentrates on improving the horse's technique and ability over smaller fences – this reduces the risk of injury or loss of confidence. Gridwork is used to make the horse more supple, and to influence his technique and the shape he makes as he goes over a fence to maximize his chance of going clear.

The distances between fences in a grid can be shortened to encourage the horse to shorten up his stride and snap his front legs up quickly and neatly as he takes off. They can also be lengthened, which encourages the horse to stretch and to lengthen his stride and jump.

Poles can be rested on the fence or on the ground in such a way as to encourage the horse to stay straight as he jumps; many horses have a tendency to veer off to the left or right. Gridwork also gives you a chance to concentrate on tidying up your own position and to improve your balance.

The ability to lengthen or shorten your horse's stride and to react quickly when he jumps into a combination or related distance in a different way from the one that was planned, is an essential skill for the successful show jumper. Some riders have a natural eye for a stride, which means that as soon as they land over one fence they are able to gauge whether they need to alter the horse's stride length in order to meet the next fence on a good stride. Those not born with this skill can develop a good eye by practising riding different distances between fences at home, and getting a feel for the pace at which they need to approach the first

LEFT
This little pony is showing superb technique – see how tightly he has snapped up and folded his front legs, which gives him every chance to clear the fence.

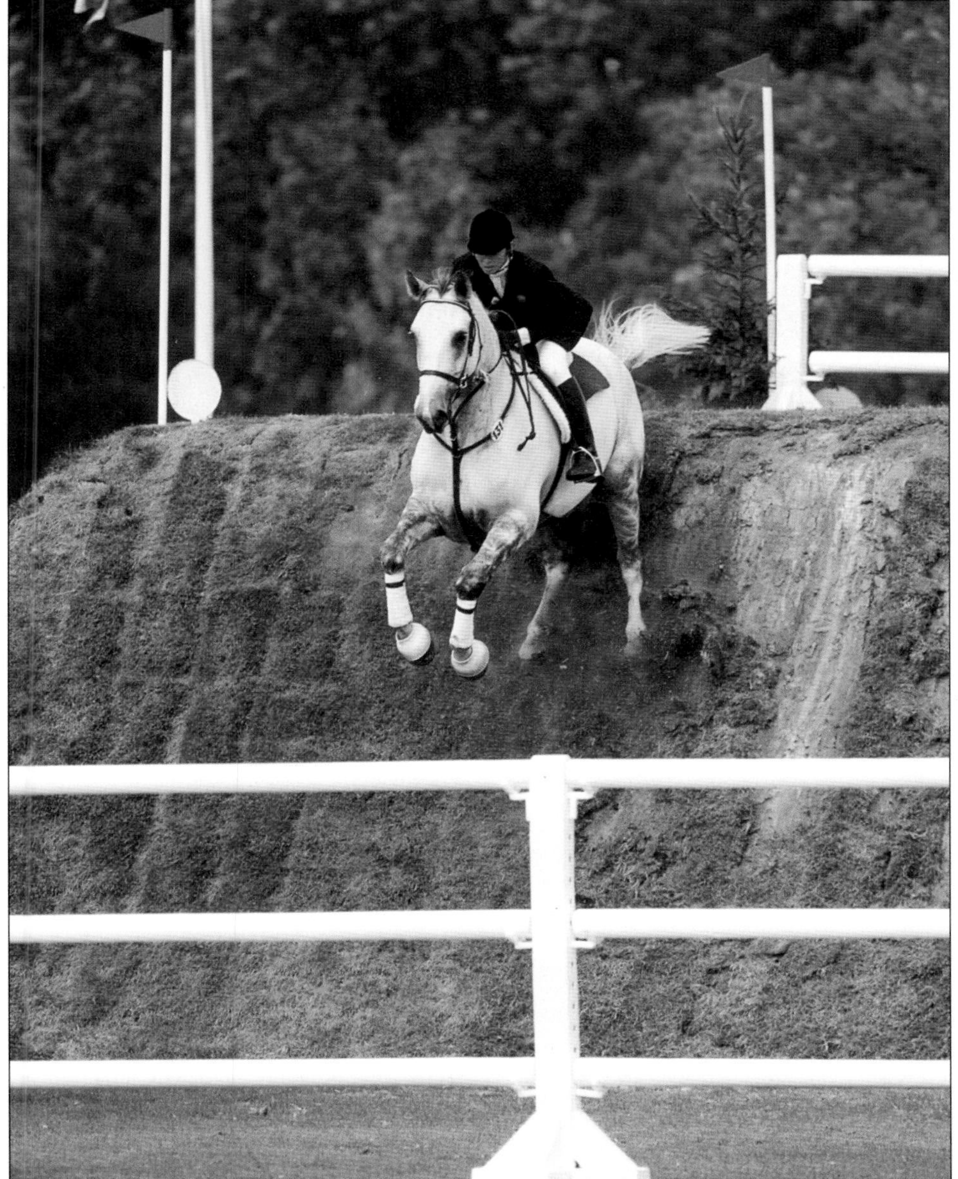

LEFT
Show-jumping competitions usually just involve jumping over fences. However, in Derby classes cross-country type obstacles are introduced; this is the world-famous Hickstead Derby bank.

horse and rider to progress through the grades. They can go as far as their ability, time and/or finances allow them.

For those looking for greater rewards, show jumping also offers very good opportunities. Through the FEI there is a training and team-selection programme for pony riders, juniors, young riders and seniors. There are also Pony Club and riding club competitions and championships. To be considered for team selection usually involves informing the appropriate selection committee of your interest and then entering a number of specified competitions where your performance will be noted by the selectors. If you are a likely candidate for a team place, you may be invited to attend various training courses – but remember that the ability to operate as part of a team is as important as being a good enough competitor to warrant selection.

BELOW
In show jumping the horse has to be taught to jump *over* water, whereas in cross-country riding you are always trying to encourage your horse to jump *into* water.

fence in order to fit in the required number of strides to the next fence.

Among the most important attributes the rider needs are patience, a cool head and confidence – if you have all three of these you will no doubt succeed in whatever sport you choose!

OPPORTUNITIES

In all sports there are those who compete purely for their own enjoyment and entertainment, and those who compete with a view to being selected for team competitions and, who knows, maybe ultimately the Olympics. Show jumping caters extremely well for both types of competitor. For the less ambitious there are no end of unaffiliated and affiliated classes and competitions which still allow

Eventing

The sport of eventing, or horse trials as it is also known, is really a complete test of all-round horsemanship on the part of the rider, and of all-round performance on the part of the horse. Horse and rider are tested on their ability to compete in the disciplines of dressage, show jumping and cross country. The dressage test demonstrates that the horse is supple, obedient and calm; the show jumping proves his agility and carefulness over fences; the cross country proves his boldness, speed and stamina. The sport is split into one-day events and three-day events. At a one-day event the order of the phases is usually dressage, show jumping and cross country. At a three-day event the cross country, combined with some additional tests of the horse's speed and endurance, is held the day after the dressage. The show jumping is held on the final day, testing whether the horse still has the necessary energy, agility, obedience and desire to clear the show jumps following the tough test of his stamina the day before on the speed and endurance phase.

■ HOW THE SPORT DEVELOPED

Eventing was started in Europe by cavalrymen, when they were not away fighting wars! The sport was originally named "The Military". It evolved as a way of testing the skills a cavalry horse would need – the dressage represented his suitability for parade duties, the cross country reflected the need to cross any terrain to seek out, confront or escape the enemy, and the show jumping showed that after the rigours of battle the horse was still fit, willing and obedient, ready to march on to the next challenge.

The first Olympic three-day event was held in 1912. Then and for some years afterwards the sport remained the domain of the military. It spread from country to country through international military competitions and, as events became more numerous, the interest of civilian riders was aroused. Now eventing is a popular sport in any number of countries around the world.

A THREE-DAY EVENT

Day one	Dressage
Day two	Speed and endurance: Phase A roads and tracks Phase B steeplechase Phase C roads and tracks Phase D cross country
Day three	Show jumping

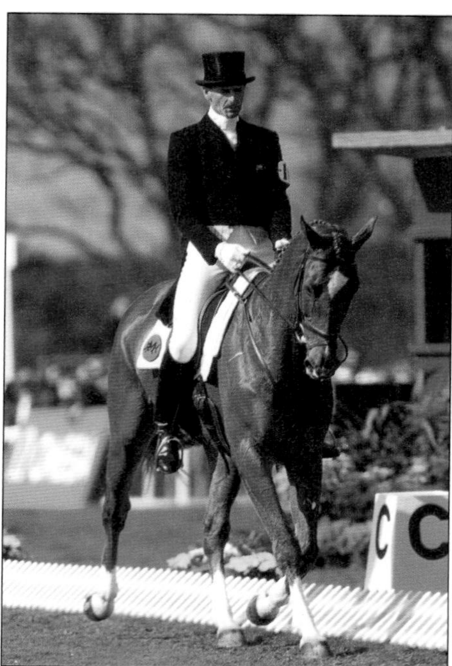

The sport of eventing involves three very different disciplines, all of which must be completed successfully in order to win. The dressage test comes first. Whilst this is simpler than a pure dressage test, it must be remembered that it is being ridden on a horse who has been prepared physically and mentally for the cross-country phase. He knows what is coming next, so it is harder for him to settle to the discipline of dressage.

■ ONE-DAY AND THREE-DAY EVENTS

At a one-day event you have to complete a dressage test, a course of show jumps and a cross-country course, all on the same day. The penalties incurred in each competition, or phase, are added together, and the winner is the rider incurring the lowest number of penalties. One-day events are an end in themselves for many riders, but their true purpose is to prepare horse and rider for the more demanding three-day event.

A three-day event can actually last for four or five days, depending on the number of entrants. All the horses are stabled together at or near the event for its duration. Before the competition begins there is a veterinary inspection, where any signs of lameness, injury or illness will result in elimination before you have started. The next one or two days are taken up with everybody completing their dressage tests.

The second part of the competition – the speed and endurance section – starts on the following day. Phase A, roads and tracks, involves completing a set route within a set time. This is usually achieved comfortably at trot, although a very short-striding horse may have to canter some of the way in order to avoid time penalties. This takes you to the start of the steeplechase, which is Phase B. All on your own

OPPOSITE
In one-day events the show-jumping phase comes after the dressage, before the cross country. At a three-day event it is the final phase, testing the horse's agility and obedience after the rigours and excitement of the cross country the day before.

you have to gallop around a circuit of steeplechase fences, again within a set time. The finish of the steeplechase takes you on to Phase C, another set of roads and tracks, which is meant to serve as a recovery period after the steeplechase. A steady trot has to be maintained for much of the way if you are to finish inside the time. You then find yourself in the ten-minute box which is a roped-off area near the start of the cross-country course. Here the horse is allowed to rest for ten minutes. He is usually washed off, has his tack re-adjusted and checked for security and comfort, and is then walked quietly around so that he does not stiffen up before the cross country, which is Phase D. In the ten-minute box, vets check the horses over and eliminate any who are already overly tired or are stressed.

After the ten-minute rest you set off on the cross-country course, which is judged in the same way as at a one-day event. There are penalties for any refusals, falls or runouts, and also for exceeding the set time. The following day there is another veterinary inspection where any horse who appears to have suffered from his exertions of the day before is withdrawn or eliminated from the competition.

This is followed by the final phase, the show jumping. This is usually run in reverse order of merit, so that the overnight leader jumps last. Any penalties incurred for refusals, knock-downs or exceeding the time are added to the dressage and to the speed and endurance penalties to give a final score. The winners of three-day events do indeed prove themselves and their horses to be successful, all-round competitors.

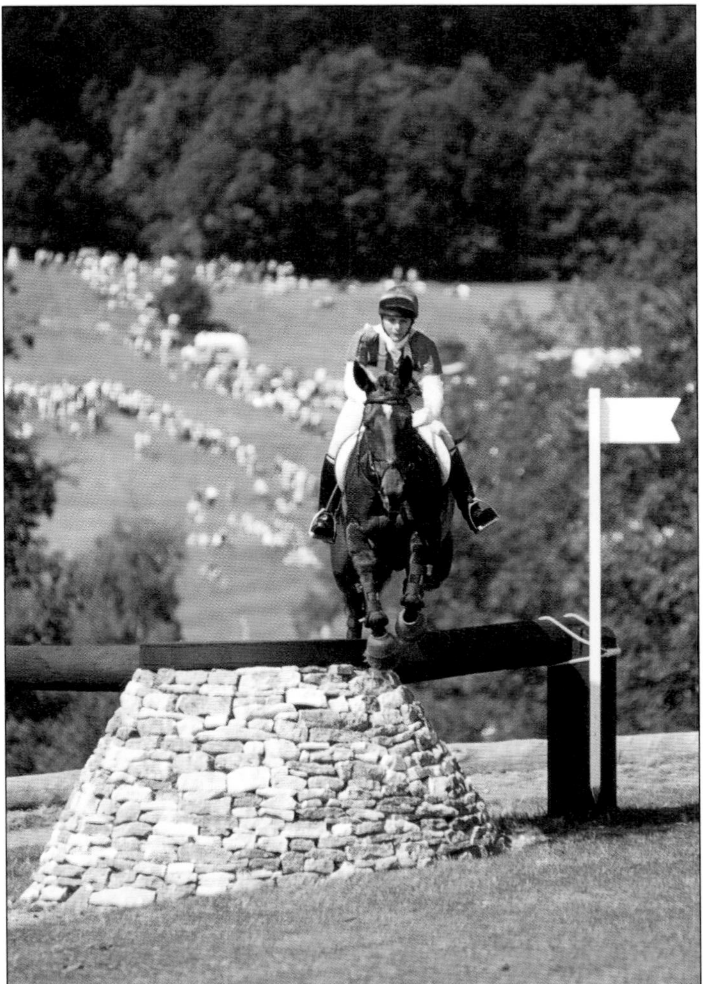

LEFT
The cross-country phase is the most important, and should be the most influential, of the three phases. For most event riders it is the favourite phase.

BELOW LEFT AND RIGHT
At a three-day event, the competitors have to tackle two roads and tracks phases, as well as a steeplechase course, before they even set out on the cross-country course. There is a ten-minute rest period between the end of the second roads and tracks and the start of the cross-country test.

LEVELS OF COMPETITION

Eventing is governed by the FEI and there are various levels of affiliated competition. There are also Pony Club, Riding Club and unaffiliated competitions although these rarely offer classes at higher than affiliated intermediate level. Affiliated one-day events are graded into different levels along such lines as novice (or below, such as preliminary or pre-novice), intermediate and advanced. These classifications or grades refer to the ability of the horse, not the rider, so in the same novice class you may find a sixteen-year-old riding in his or her first event competing against the reigning Olympic champion. For many this is all part of the charm and attraction of the sport. It is far more of an achievement to perform well against such experienced riders, even if you don't win, than it is to take first prize in a class where you knew your rivals weren't up to much anyway.

Affiliated three-day events are classified as one star (novice), two star (about intermediate level), three star (intermediate to advanced level) and four star (advanced and championship level).

In between the one-day events and the three-day events are the occasional two-day

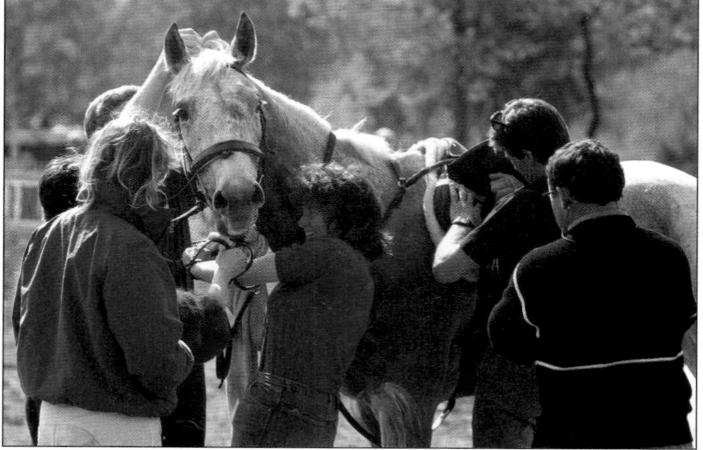

LEFT
During the ten-minute rest the horse is cooled down as much as possible by washing him off. His tack is checked over and re-adjusted if necessary.

events. These are limited in number and are usually only offered at novice level, but provide a great introduction to three-day eventing for the inexperienced rider or horse. You perform your dressage and show jumping on day one, and on day two you complete a shortened speed and endurance phase. This still consists of roads and tracks, steeplechase, roads and tracks, ten-minute halt and the cross-country course, but the speeds and distances are less than for a three-day event.

Every horse has to qualify to take part in a three-day event. For each grade there are a set number of one-, two- or less rigorous three-day events which horse and rider must have completed to a set standard. You usually need to have gone clear on the cross country, or at least have incurred only a limited number of penalties. This adds another dimension to the sport as it allows you to compete with your horse's long-term future in mind. You may well go to a one-day event and come away without a prize, but if you were able to go clear on the cross country you will have achieved a qualification towards your target of the three-day event.

■ SKILLS REQUIRED

Bearing in mind what is required for dressage, show jumping and hunter trialling will give you some idea of the myriad skills the successful event horse and rider need. But before you are put off just think of it in terms of good basic training equalling good all-round performance. If you have put some effort into schooling your horse well on the flat, and have carried through the same principles of rhythm, balance and responsiveness into your jump training, you are well on the way to producing a capable and successful event horse. Jump training, whether over show jumps or cross-country fences, requires the same technique and skills. The only difference is the speed at which you ride across country, and the fact that the natural terrain you have to cross makes it harder to maintain your rhythm and balance than when you are jumping in an arena. An

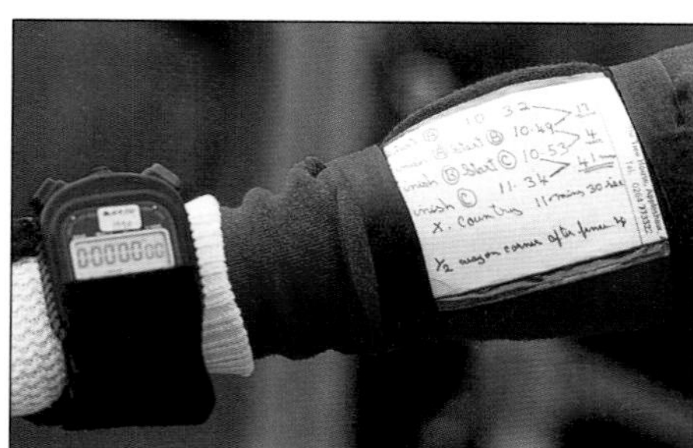

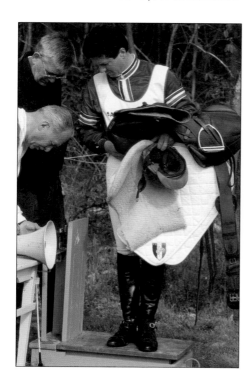

ABOVE
You have to keep note of how much time you can allow yourself on the roads and tracks phases, the steeplechase and the cross-country course. Exceeding the optimum time incurs time faults. Most riders record all their times on a card which they carry on their arm, along with a stopwatch.

LEFT
At advanced one-day events and at three-day events the horses have to carry a minimum weight of 165 lb (75 kg). This includes the rider's clothing and the horse's saddle. If you weigh in under that, you will have to carry lead weights in a weightcloth under the saddle.

EQUIPMENT NEEDED

It is possible to compete in events with a minimal amount of tack and equipment but, because of the three disciplines involved, there is a greater chance that you will need to invest in various bits and pieces. Many horses are better ridden in different tack for each phase – a horse may perform happily in a snaffle for his dressage test but may need a double bridle or a gag for the cross country. Some horses need different tack for the show jumping as well. You should use a breastplate or girth and a safety girth with your saddle for the cross-country phase. You may also want to use different types of boots or bandages for the show-jumping and cross-country phases – show-jumping boots do not offer enough protection for cross country. If you can afford it, a dressage saddle for the dressage phase will help your seat and position enormously; some riders even opt for different show-jumping and cross-country saddles although this is a little excessive. In fact, it is now possible to buy saddles with interchangeable knee rolls which allow the same saddle to be converted from a dressage model to a jumping model.

You will need jodhpurs, breeches and boots, plus a show or hacking jacket and a recognized crash hat. You must also wear a body protector on the cross-country phase. At advanced level you are expected to perform your dressage test in a top hat and tailcoat – these are expensive when new, but can often be bought secondhand.

RIGHT
This horse is about to unseat his rider, having thrown a very big but steep jump into the water at Badminton. In the circumstances, the rider has done well to keep her weight back and at the same time has slipped the reins to give the horse every chance of coping with the situation.

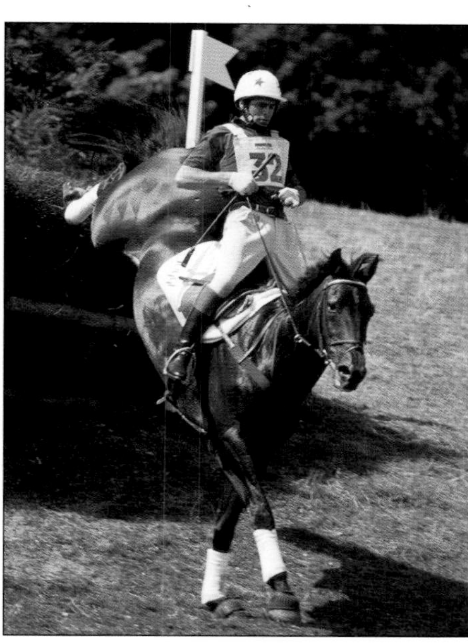

BELOW
Blyth Tait, the 1996 Olympic gold medallist, demonstrates how to slip the reins but still keep a contact so that the horse has some support to help balance him as he lands.

additional factor is the variety of fences you will meet on a cross-country course. Once your horse is familiar with show jumps he is unlikely to be fazed by anything he meets in the arena, unless you approach it badly. But the awkward obstacles that can be built into the natural terrain on a cross-country course are numerous, and each time the horse competes he may well be faced with something he has never encountered before. Cross-country training should concentrate on building up confidence and trust, and making the right decision about the approach you should take.

Water is one hazard which seems to cause more trouble than most. In the horse's early training it is important that he is never frightened in water. This means carefully choosing any water hazard you ask him to enter. Don't ask him to splash through a river unless you know it has a safe, secure bottom. If he willingly enters water for you, and then finds himself floundering in deep mud he is going to be frightened and he is not going to trust you next time you face him with water. So do not abuse his trust and willingness. Similarly do not allow the overbold or exuberant horse to frighten himself – make him approach water quietly and calmly so that he puts in a sensible jump which allows him to land in a balanced and controlled manner. If your horse is introduced to water like this, and if you take care always to be in a good position to support and balance him as he lands in water, he should never have reason to refuse to tackle a water complex.

Fitness is another necessity for both horse and rider. As long as they are regularly hacked out and given some schooling and jump training, most horses and ponies will be fit enough to complete a novice one-day event. Once you want to do more than this, special attention has to be paid to the horse's fitness and training routine. This requires knowledge and experience of how to achieve fitness without subjecting the horse's vulnerable joints and limbs to unnecessary wear and tear. You will also need to be fit, as a tired rider is of little help to a tired horse.

The event rider perhaps needs more determination and persistence than other equestrian competitors, simply because it is a lot harder to get three things to go well all on the same day than it is to get one specialist discipline to come right.

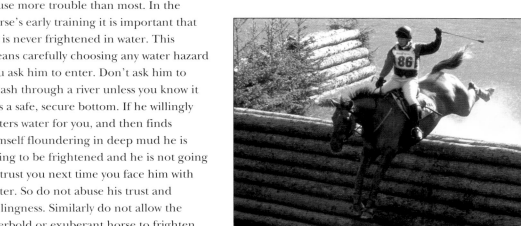

LEFT
Commonly known as "hailing a cab", this rider has thrown her arm behind her in a tactic which many riders find helps them to keep their weight back behind the horse when jumping down into water.

Race Riding

Race riding, either on the flat or over fences, offers the best opportunity to experience the full power and speed that a horse can produce. The racing industry revolves around the thoroughbred horse and, to a lesser degree, the Arab horse. Point-to-pointing, the occasional unofficial horse or pony race and the growth in Arab racing all give the amateur rider the chance to experience the thrill of race riding, and the chance to race for the fun of it. Professional jockeys are either retained or employed on a freelance basis by race-horse trainers. They often work for a big training yard in order to supplement their income, exercising and schooling the race horses, as well as racing them competitively if they are offered the ride.

LEFT
The ability to sit tight when the unexpected happens is a great asset. Note how this jockey has kept his upper body back and is still looking up and ahead, which is a great aid to keeping in balance when racing.

BELOW LEFT
Race horses have to be supreme athletes – the greatest care and attention is lavished on them to keep them in peak condition. For a change of scene, these race horses are being exercised on the beach; another day it may be over grass or all-weather gallops, or just hacking along the roads.

■ POINT-TO-POINTING

This is an amateur sport which tends to thrive wherever hunting thrives. A horse which is to go point-to-pointing has to qualify by going out hunting for a set number of days. The amateur status of the sport, and the fact that a great many who take part own just one horse which they hunt and race, all adds to its fun and social atmosphere. It is popular with spectators, even in winter when they usually end up standing around in the wet and cold, eating the traditional picnic in the car park. There are yards where the owner makes a living out of training and racing either his own or other people's point-to-pointers, and this makes some of the races very competitive.

In most point-to-points the horses jump standard brush fences which may occasionally have a ditch in front, but some courses include banks and water as well. This reflects the sport's origins when riders simply raced each other from one point, usually a church steeple, to another point somewhere in the distance. The standard of riding varies considerably; anyone who has seen the differing standards on the hunting field will know what to expect in a point-to-point race. It is for this reason that in point-to-pointing there are more falls than in professional steeplechasing or hurdling. The point-to-point course is usually an oval-shaped track marked out over an area of grassland. The fences are well spaced out around the course and, because they make use of natural terrain, some courses are much flatter than others. Competitors quickly discover which tracks suit their particular horse best.

■ ARAB RACING

This is a well-organized sport which involves flat races between Arab horses. The racing is fast and competitive, but the sport is still small enough to allow you to

EQUIPMENT NEEDED

To ride in any of these races you will need to wear an acceptable crash hat, lightweight breeches and boots, and a jumper reflecting your racing colours. In a point-to-point you are allowed to wear hunting kit. A body protector is compulsory for some types of racing, and advisable for all types. Goggles are a handy accessory, as a faceful of mud half-way around the course does little for your ability to steer your horse home. A weightcloth will also be needed. A horse can be raced in his ordinary saddle but most jockeys opt for a lightweight racing saddle.

BELOW
Despite its amateur status – which means the greatest reward is the fun to be had rather than the prize money to be won – the risks of point-to-pointing are probably greater than in either professional racing over jumps or flat racing. Falls are frequent.

train and compete your own horse with success. Races vary in length, which means horses tend to specialize in either the short, faster races, or the longer, slightly slower ones.

PONY AND HORSE RACING

There are a few pony and horse races held in most countries which give ordinary riding horses and their jockeys a chance to demonstrate their speed – or lack of it! Most of these are unofficial, although a few countries do have a national body which registers competitors and organizes races for them.

PROFESSIONAL FLAT AND JUMP RACING

The international racing scene is divided into flat races, hurdle races, steeplechase races and timber or cross-country races. Flat racing is mainly to test pure speed – many of the races are short sprints where speed rather than stamina counts most. Jump racing requires stamina, jumping ability and speed.

SKILLS REQUIRED

To race ride you need to be fit, have good balance and a feel for jumping at speed. These can all be practised at home if you intend racing just for fun. But if you want it to be more than that, the best place to learn is in a big racing yard, even if you only help out there at weekends. The more thoroughbred race horses you are able to ride, even if only on exercise, the better your fitness, position and balance will become.

Flat-race jockeys are generally quite short and also have to be lightweight. Jump jockeys, who ride with their stirrups a little longer, can be taller but need to keep their weight down so that they do not force the horse to carry more weight than he has been allocated.

ABOVE
If you fancy a career with horses, a job in a good racing yard can offer great variety, good experience and good friends.

BELOW LEFT
Dirt-track racing is common in America.

SUCCESS IS DOWN TO YOU

Competing with your horse can and should be an enjoyable experience for both of you. But if you take a look around you will see that this is not always the case – unhappy horses and riders abound at all kinds of events. Some horses are always going to be more talented than others; some will be more co-operative than others. But there will also be those who, either through lack of schooling or understanding, or simply through bad riding, do not fulfil their potential. Not everyone can afford the horse or pony of their dreams. Some think that this is exactly what they have found, only to be disappointed when things don't go to plan. A few horses, no matter how well ridden, simply lack the necessary ability or character to succeed at certain sports.

When things aren't going as well as you would like, remember too that very few talented riders are born – they have to be made. Riding has to be worked at; it doesn't just happen. You cannot be blamed for lacking a particular skill or aptitude for a specific sport – we are all made differently – but you can be blamed if you don't bother to work at your basic riding skills. So if you are going to ride, strive to ride well. GOOD LUCK!

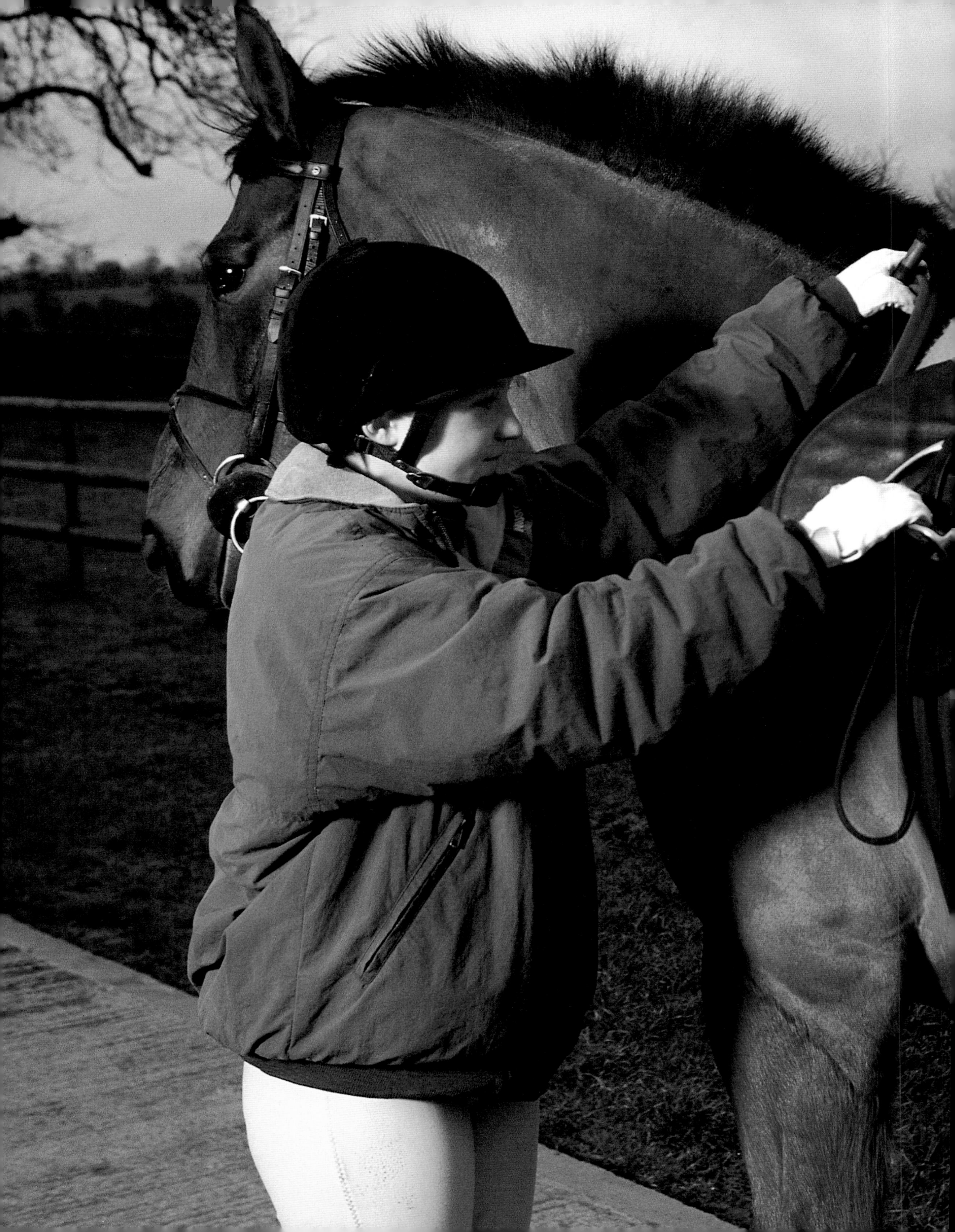

Saddlery and Equipment

The Saddle

The saddle is one of the most important pieces of equipment for the ridden horse, and, because of the skill and craftsmanship involved in producing a saddle, it is usually the most expensive.

The earliest type of saddle, first developed thousands of years ago, was nothing more than a simple blanket kept in place with breastplate and girth. The modern saddle, however, is a sophisticated piece of equipment. It has evolved as a result of the demands of modern equestrianism, whether it be the Western saddle designed to withstand the rigours of cowboy life; the dressage saddle designed to give the rider an elegant yet effective position; or the minuscule racing saddle.

The saddle's design and fit can have a tremendous effect on both the horse's performance and the rider's position. An ill-fitting saddle can cause the horse considerable discomfort and even physical damage. When choosing a new saddle, therefore, it is always advisable to seek professional help – a trained saddler will be able to ensure that the saddle fits the horse correctly.

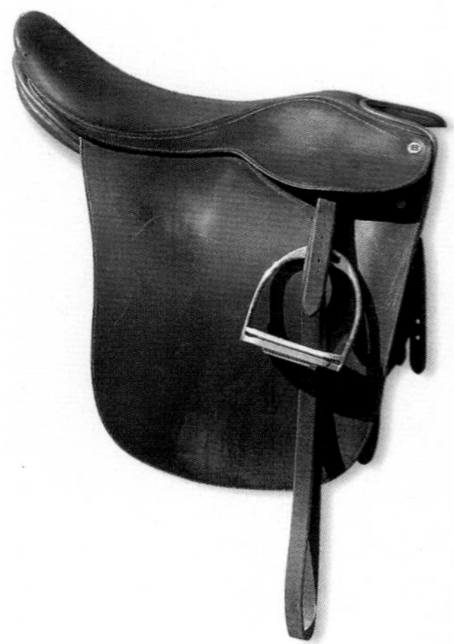

Points of the Saddle

Virtually all saddles are built upon a solid framework called a tree. This framework was traditionally made from beech wood but is now available in laminated wood, and even fibreglass and plastic. It is the shape of the tree and the placing of the metal stirrup bars riveted to the tree which determine the size and shape of the saddle. The seat of the saddle is given shape by stretching a webbing and cotton fabric over the tree. Serge or a synthetic fabric is stretched to form the seat shape and a wool or synthetic stuffing provides the padding below.

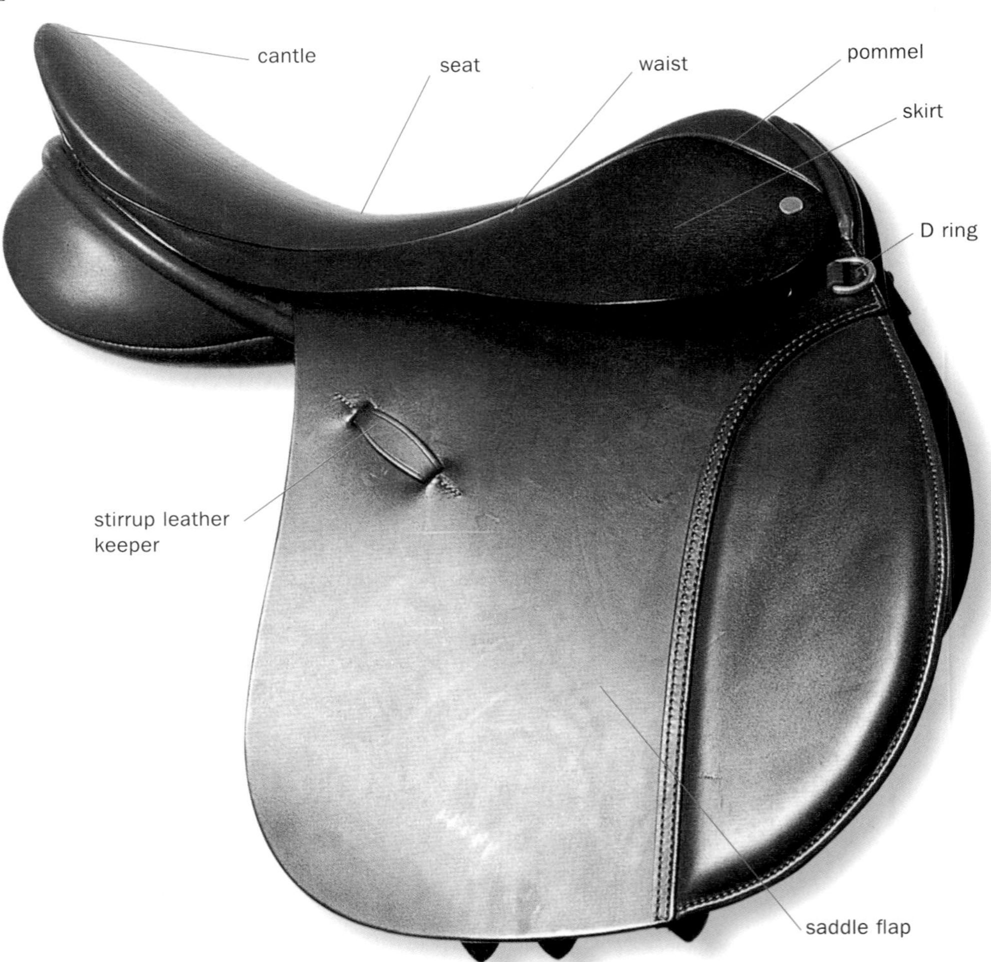

ABOVE
The general purpose saddle is the standard model for the sport. The moderate features make it suitable for all riding disciplines at a non-professional level. Specialist saddles develop individual characteristics of the general purpose saddle according to the needs of the particular discipline.

BELOW
Under the saddle flap. Most saddles have three girth straps. The first two are fixed to the web strap attached to the tree and the third is fixed independently.

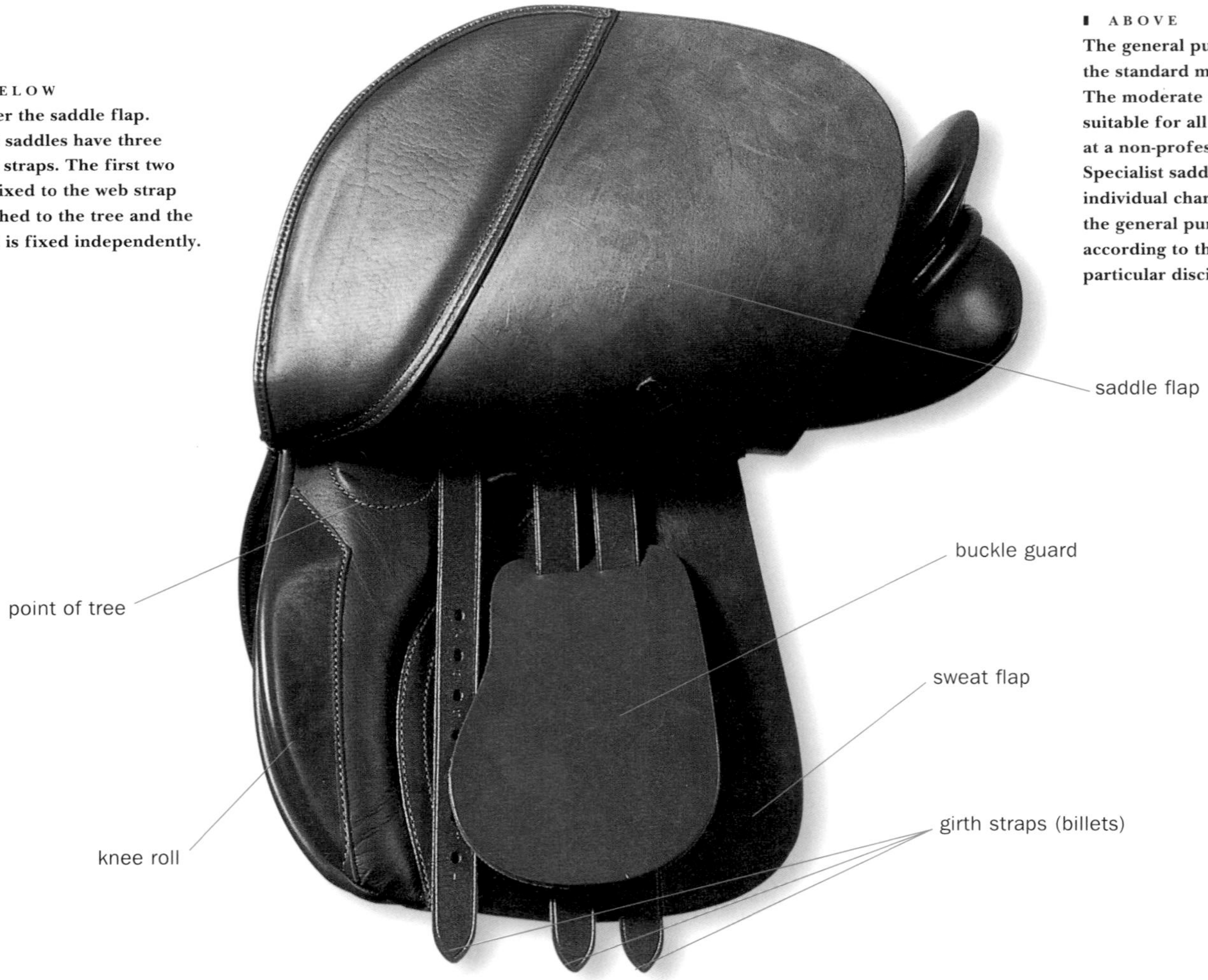

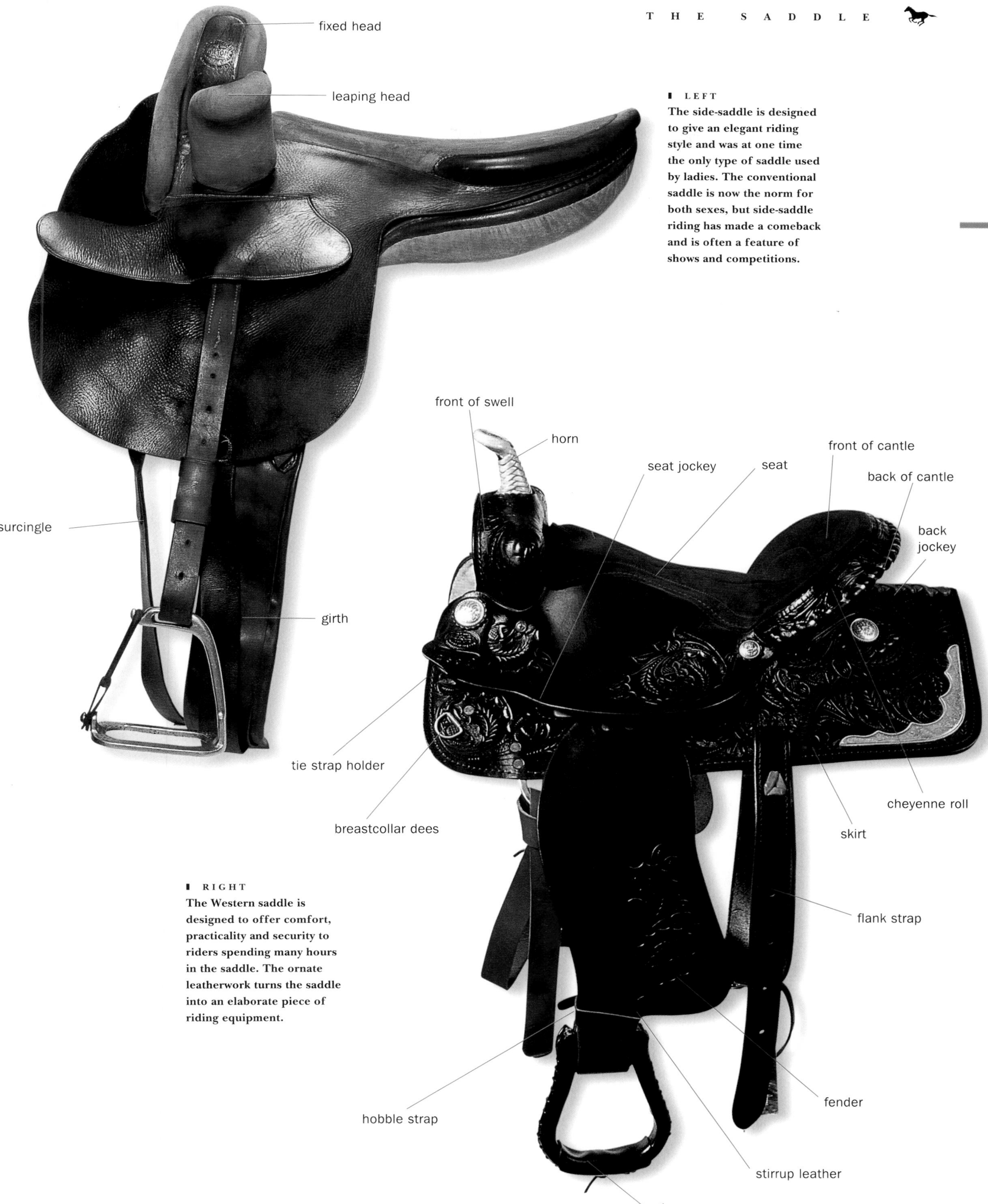

LEFT
The side-saddle is designed to give an elegant riding style and was at one time the only type of saddle used by ladies. The conventional saddle is now the norm for both sexes, but side-saddle riding has made a comeback and is often a feature of shows and competitions.

RIGHT
The Western saddle is designed to offer comfort, practicality and security to riders spending many hours in the saddle. The ornate leatherwork turns the saddle into an elaborate piece of riding equipment.

Riding and Competing Saddles

Saddles are available in a number of shapes and styles to suit the many equestrian disciplines at every level of competition from novice to professional.

The **leather general purpose (GP) saddle** is designed to be used across the board of riding activities. It is ideal for pleasure riding, hunting, novice cross-country and show jumping and basic dressage. A less expensive alternative to the leather saddle is the **synthetic general purpose saddle**, which is lighter in weight than the leather type, and easier to clean.

For most riders, the general purpose saddle is perfectly adequate for jumping. However, if you are riding at a competitive level and tackling larger fences, you may prefer the specialist design of the jumping saddle. The saddle flaps of the **Crosby close-contact jumping saddle** are more forward cut than those of the general purpose saddle. This enables you to keep your legs close to the saddle even when riding with a short stirrup length.

The **event saddle** is very similar in style to a general purpose saddle and can be used for all phases of horse trials, although some riders prefer to have an additional saddle for the dressage phase. Many famous riders have become involved in the design of saddles and the event saddle illustrated was developed by the international eventer, Mary King.

The **Albion Selecta** is a multi-purpose saddle which aims to combine the general purpose saddle with a dressage and a jumping saddle. It features easily removable knee pads which allow the saddle to be adapted for all riding disciplines from pleasure riding to jumping, dressage, cross-country and working hunter events.

The **polo saddle** has a relatively flat seat, extra-long sweat flaps and no knee and thigh rolls. It is designed specifically for the game of polo, during which the horse travels at speed and the rider needs to be able to move with ease to hit the ball.

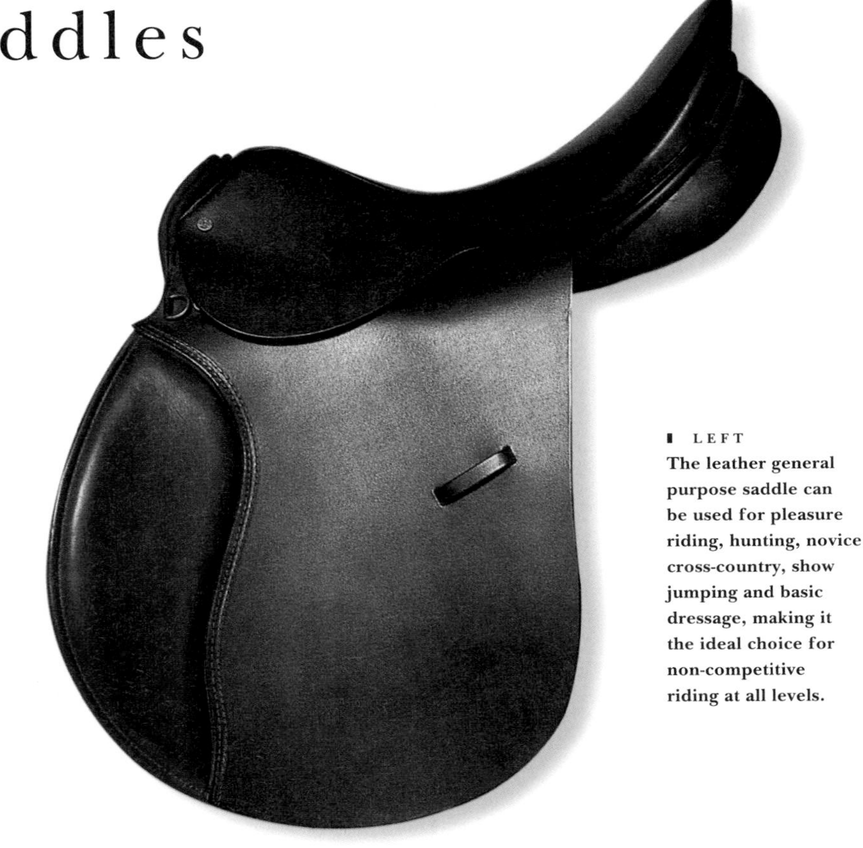

LEFT
The leather general purpose saddle can be used for pleasure riding, hunting, novice cross-country, show jumping and basic dressage, making it the ideal choice for non-competitive riding at all levels.

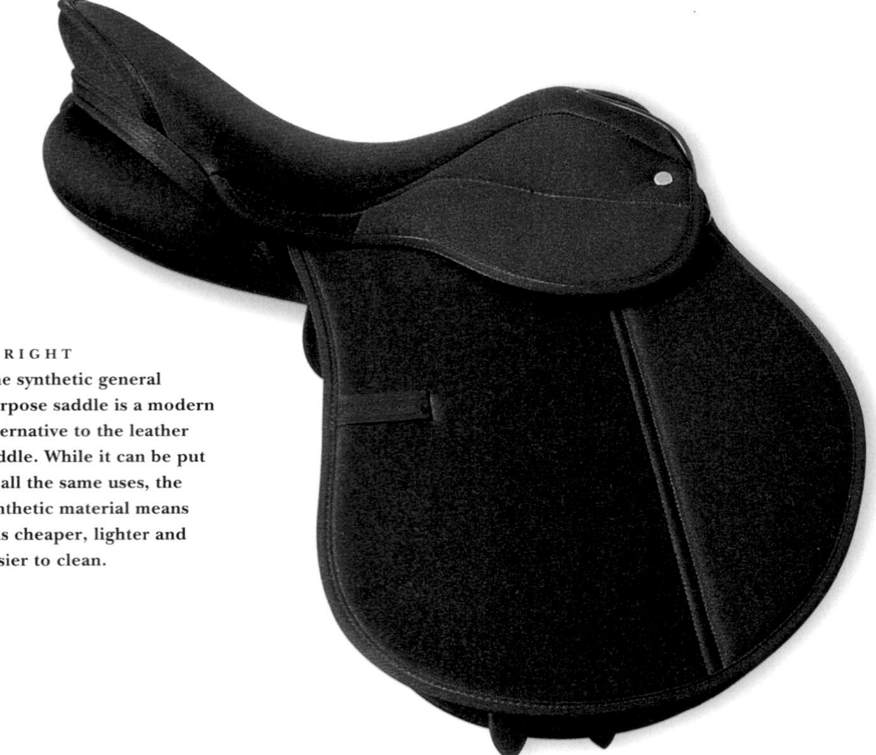

RIGHT
The synthetic general purpose saddle is a modern alternative to the leather saddle. While it can be put to all the same uses, the synthetic material means it is cheaper, lighter and easier to clean.

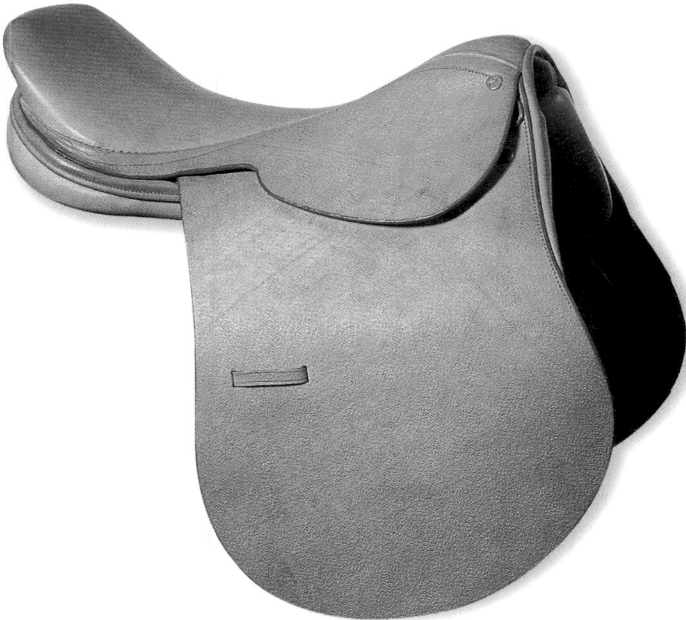

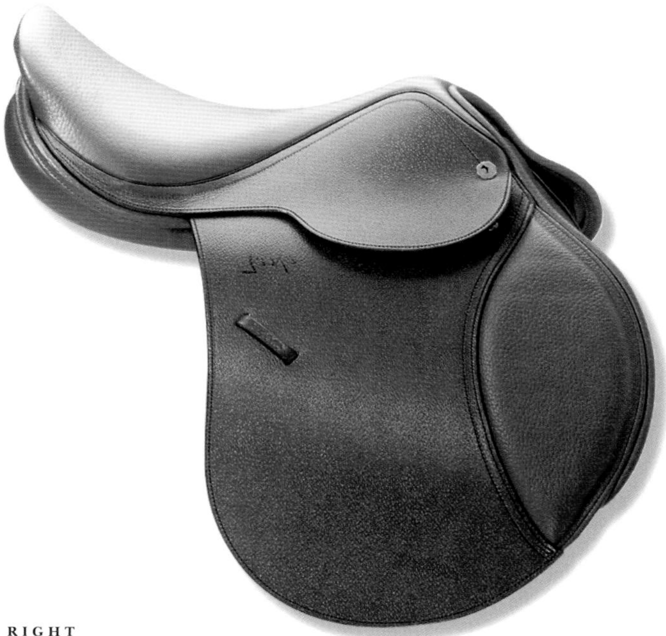

ABOVE
The polo saddle has a flat seat, extended sweat flaps and no knee or thigh rolls, all of which allow the rider freedom of movement when striking the ball.

BELOW LEFT
Event saddle. This is similar in style to the general purpose saddle and can be used for all phases of horse trials.

RIGHT
The Crosby close-contact jumping saddle. The saddle flaps are more forward cut than those of the general purpose saddle. This allows the rider to carry his legs closer to the saddle, and makes his position more secure.

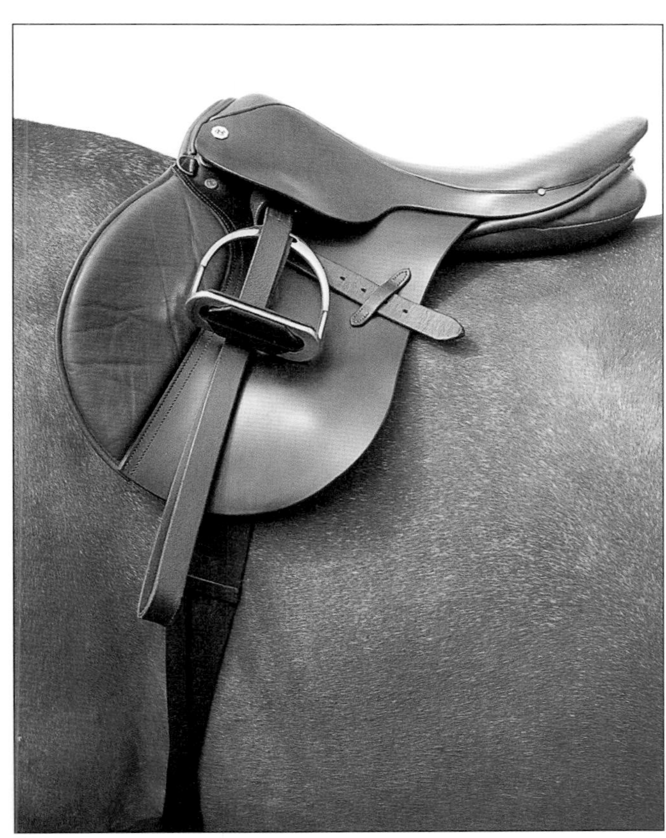

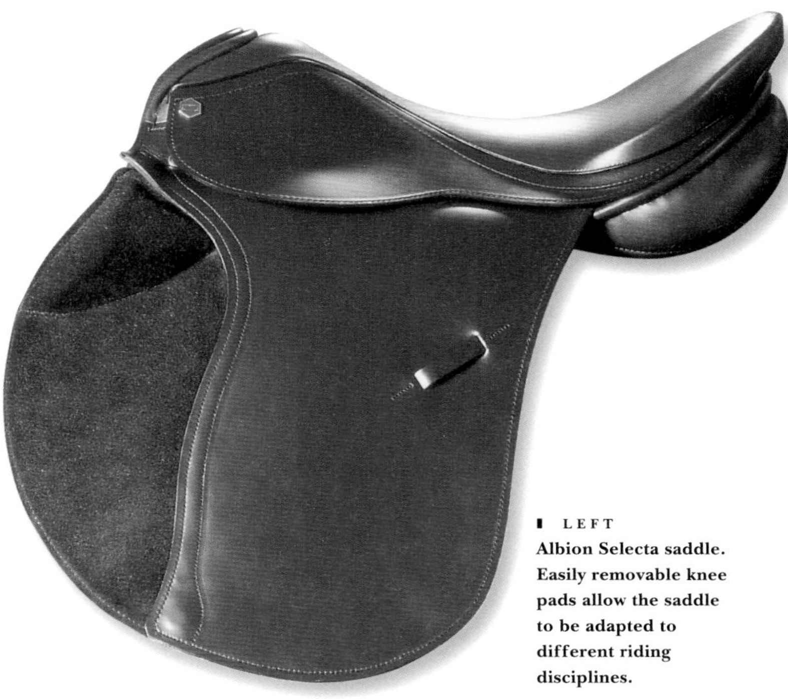

LEFT
Albion Selecta saddle. Easily removable knee pads allow the saddle to be adapted to different riding disciplines.

Showing Saddles

There are a number of saddles designed specifically to improve the horse's performance in showing competitions.

The purpose of the **showing saddle** is primarily to enhance the appearance of the show horse rather than to increase the comfort of the rider. The saddle is straight cut to show off the horse's shoulder and is simple in design, since it is the horse rather than the tack that is being judged. The showing saddle is a specialized piece of equipment and not always very comfortable; many riders prefer to use a dressage saddle for showing classes.

The **dressage saddle**, designed for riding and schooling horses on the flat rather than over jumps, has longer and straighter flaps than the general purpose saddle. This allows you to carry your legs in a longer position and closer to the horse's body. To eliminate bulk under your legs, longer girth straps (billets) are fitted and used with a short dressage girth.

The **Saddlebred saddle** is for showing American Saddlebreds and other gaited horses. It features a cut-back pommel (called a "cow-mouth") and very wide saddle flaps, which enable the rider to sit much further back in the saddle than usual.

For showing classes in which the horse is required both to jump and to be ridden on the flat, the **working hunter saddle** is ideal. The seat is deeper than the showing saddle, and padded knee rolls give a more secure seat which is helpful when jumping.

The **side-saddle,** first developed for ladies in the fourteenth century, allows the rider to carry both legs on the near (left) side of the horse, with the left foot in a stirrup and the right leg hooked over the pommel. The flat seat has a suede or doeskin cover for extra grip. Although no longer in general use, shows often feature ladies' hunter classes for side-saddle riders.

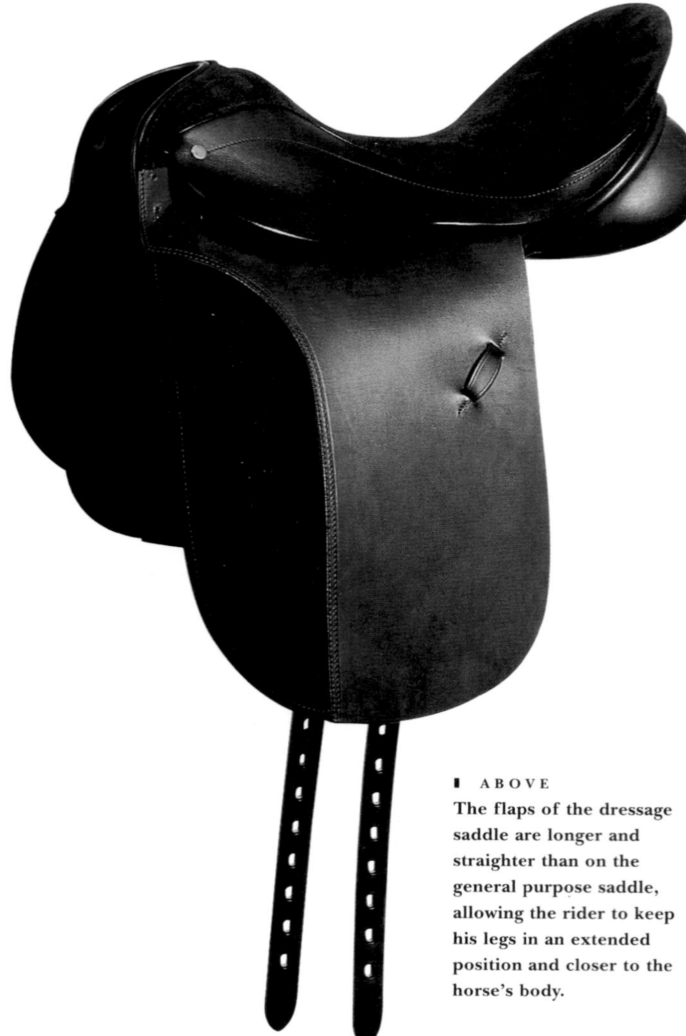

ABOVE
The flaps of the dressage saddle are longer and straighter than on the general purpose saddle, allowing the rider to keep his legs in an extended position and closer to the horse's body.

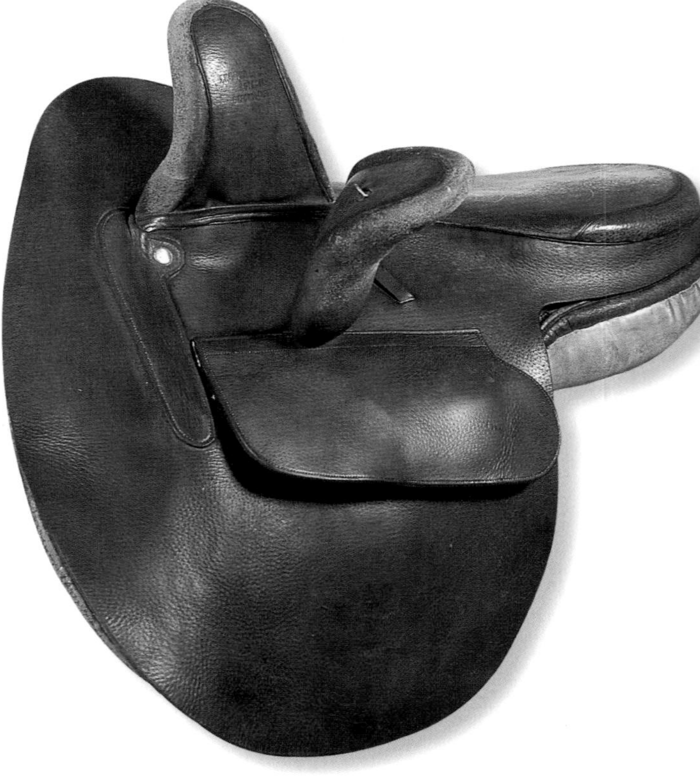

ABOVE
The shape of the side-saddle allows the rider to adopt a more elegant position, with both legs on the near (left) side of the horse.

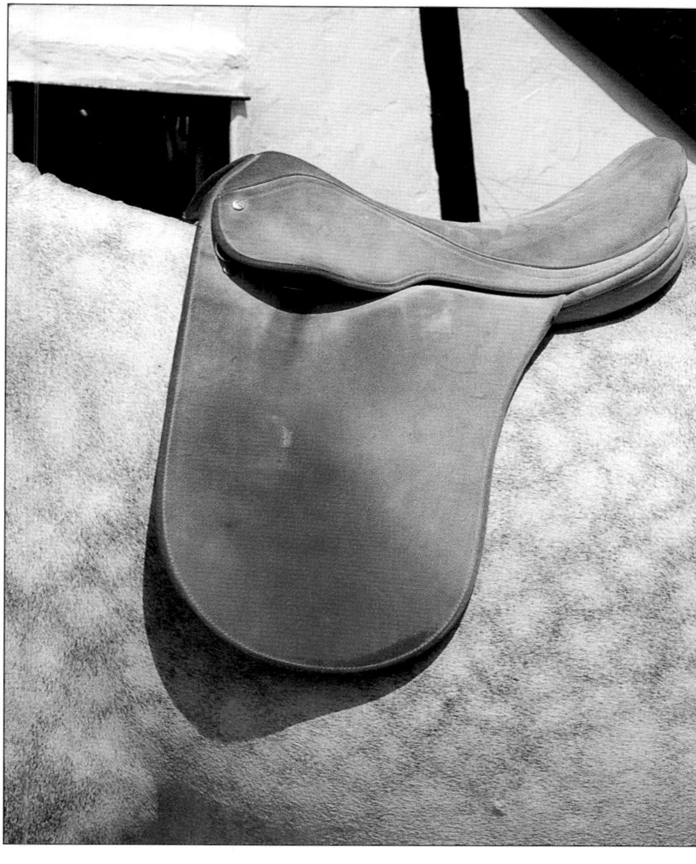

ABOVE
This showing saddle in split hide, designed by producer and rider Lynn Rusell, is specially shaped to suit larger show horses such as cobs and hunters.

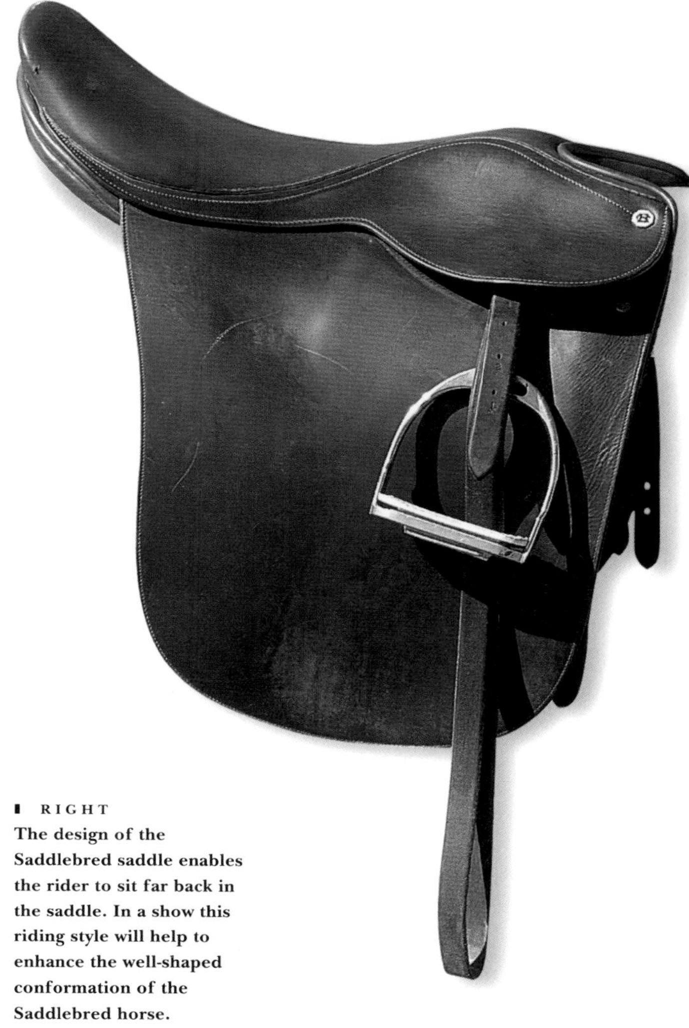

RIGHT
The design of the Saddlebred saddle enables the rider to sit far back in the saddle. In a show this riding style will help to enhance the well-shaped conformation of the Saddlebred horse.

RIGHT
The working hunter saddle is a compromise between a showing saddle and a jumping saddle.

Trail-riding and Working Saddles

Saddles which are to be ridden over long periods of time need to have an element of comfort incorporated into the design.

The **endurance saddle**, as its name suggests, is designed for long-distance rides. The seat has extra padding and the saddle panels have extra width, thereby spreading the rider's weight over a greater area and reducing the risk of localized pressure points on the horse's back. Additional D rings are fitted to the saddle so that equipment, such as lead ropes and sponges, can easily be accommodated.

The **Australian stock saddle** is a utilitarian saddle designed for the comfort of both horse and rider during the hours spent driving cattle. The weight distribution properties mean that modified versions of this saddle can also be used for endurance or trail-riding.

The **Western reining saddle** is higher in front than the standard Western saddle, preventing the rider from being thrown forward when the horse performs the characteristic sliding stop. **Western pleasure saddles** are lighter in weight than working saddles and have only one cinch attachment. Comfortable and secure, these saddles are ideal for long-distance or trail-riding.

The **parade saddle** is an ornate working saddle featuring highly intricate metal and leatherwork. These decorative saddles are specially designed for use in carnival or rodeo parades.

The **trooper** or **Cavalry saddle** is built around a steel and wood tree and is the traditional choice of the armed forces because of its strength and durability.

The **military fan saddle** is designed for working horses, such as those used by the mounted police. The saddle tree distributes the rider's weight evenly for comfort during long periods of work, often when the horse is stationary.

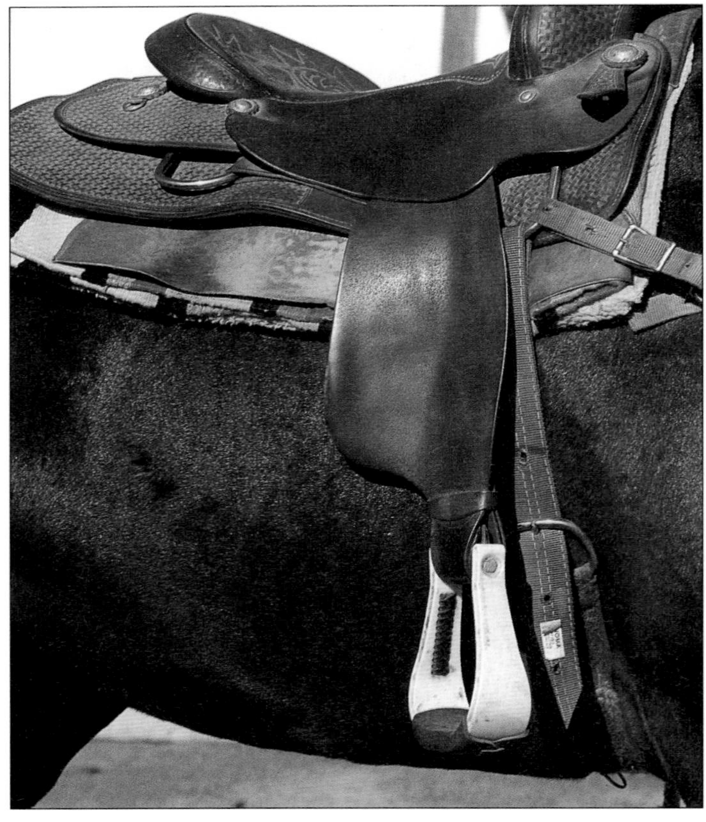

ABOVE
The Australian stock saddle is built for comfort and durability. The rider may spend several hours driving cattle on the plains, and the even spread of his weight in the saddle will become a significant factor for both horse and rider.

ABOVE
The high front of the Western reining saddle prevents the rider being thrown forward and out of the saddle when the horse performs the dramatic reining halt, which is a feature of this riding style.

ABOVE
The deep seat makes the Western pleasure saddle comfortable and secure for long-distance riding.

ABOVE
Endurance saddle. This is designed specifically for long-distance riding, with the comfort of both horse and rider in mind.

RIGHT
The elaborate parade saddle features intricately detailed leatherwork, and makes a splendid sight at carnivals and rodeos.

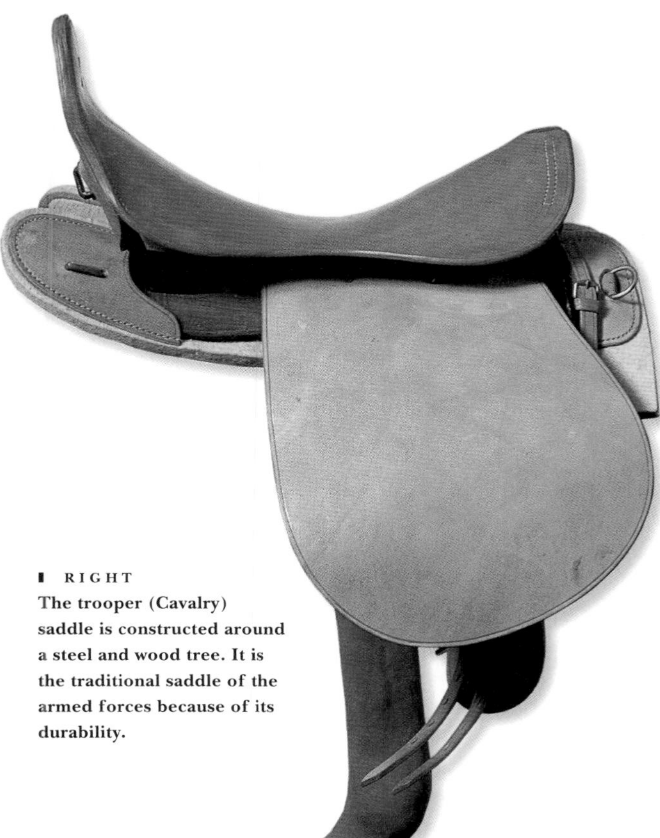

RIGHT
The trooper (Cavalry) saddle is constructed around a steel and wood tree. It is the traditional saddle of the armed forces because of its durability.

RIGHT
The military fan saddle is designed to distribute the rider's weight evenly in the saddle. This becomes an important feature when the ridden horse is motionless for long periods of time.

Racing Saddles

Horse racing, and flat racing in particular, requires a highly unusual riding style that makes specific demands on the saddle.

The saddle used in flat racing is crouched over rather than sat on, and for this reason it has a flat seat and is fitted with very short stirrup leathers. **Leather racing saddles** are necessarily light; they come in a variety of weights, starting from as little as 325g/11oz. Saddles for National Hunt racing (racing over jumps) are heavier and larger in size than the saddles used for flat racing. **Synthetic racing saddles** are becoming increasingly popular for dirt and all-weather track racing, where the sand used for the track's surface can cause damage to leather tack.

As the name implies, **race exercise saddles** are used when exercising racehorses rather than when actually racing them. Because the question of weight does not apply, the exercise saddle is usually heavier and larger than the racing saddle, and comes with a full or half-tree in leather or synthetic material. The full-tree saddle illustrated features "todsloan" saddle flaps, named after the American jockey James Todhunter Sloan, who pioneered the style of riding with shorter stirrup leathers.

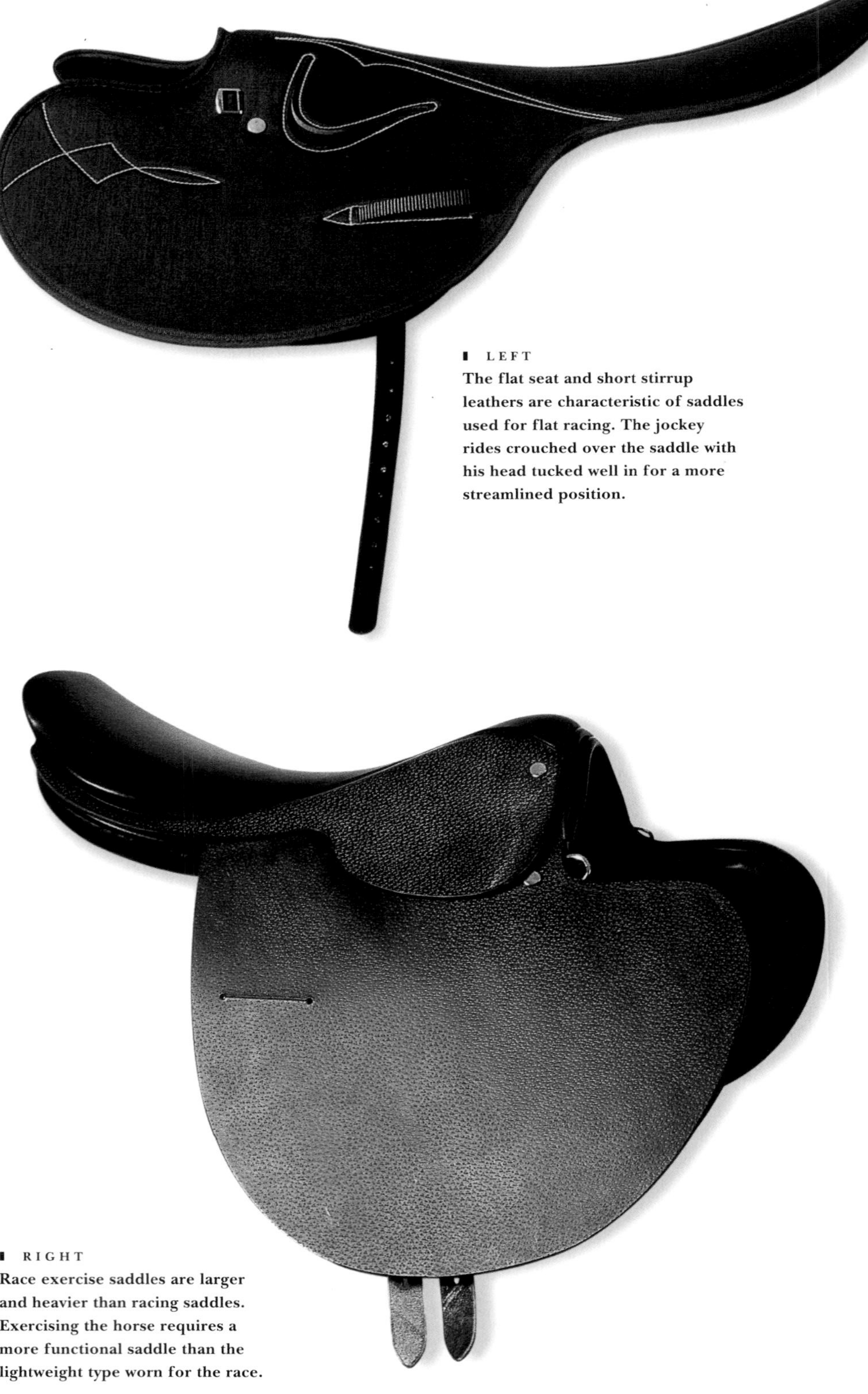

LEFT
The flat seat and short stirrup leathers are characteristic of saddles used for flat racing. The jockey rides crouched over the saddle with his head tucked well in for a more streamlined position.

RIGHT
Race exercise saddles are larger and heavier than racing saddles. Exercising the horse requires a more functional saddle than the lightweight type worn for the race.

Learner Saddles

For beginners taking their first lessons in equestrianism, a specially adapted saddle can be a huge advantage, not least because of the additional safety features which these saddles incorporate.

The **pony saddle**, designed for young children and smaller ponies, has removable panels to vary the amount by which the child is "wedged in", and a hand support for extra grip. The **felt-pad saddle** also includes the safety handle feature, and this can be very helpful for nervous children. The simple design consists of a soft felt pad with a leather covering and built-in webbing girth and stirrup bars.

The **Riding for the Disabled Association (RDA) saddle** will enable physically or mentally disabled children and adults to ride in safety. The loop fitted to the front of the saddle gives the rider something to hold on to without needing to grip and pull at the reins too tightly, thereby damaging the horse's mouth.

LEFT
The pony saddle makes an ideal choice for small children who are just learning to ride.

LEFT
The felt-pad saddle is a beginner's saddle for children. It consists of a soft felt pad with a leather covering and built-in webbing girth and stirrup bars.

RIGHT
The design of the RDA saddle enables the physically and mentally disabled to ride with safety and confidence.

Ceremonial Saddles

The Royal Mews at Buckingham Palace in London houses a large collection of saddles, bridles and harnesses belonging to the Royal Family. Much of the saddlery and equipment in this beautiful collection is of a unique historical interest.

Queen Elizabeth II's love of horses is well known and many of the gifts she receives are related to the subject of riding. The Portuguese ceremonial bridle was presented with a saddle to HM the Queen by the Portuguese government on a state visit to Portugal in 1957. The bridle has solid silver bit and fittings.

The Alamo saddle was presented as a gift to the Queen from the actor John Wayne, who directed and starred in the film *The Alamo.* The saddle had been used by the actor during the making of the film. The design of the saddle is highly ornate and features tooled fenders and decorated *tapaderos* (toe covers).

Although ladies traditionally sat to the near (left) side when riding side-saddle, it was not uncommon for young ladies learning to ride to use a saddle designed for riding on the off (right) side, as demonstrated by a pair of side-saddles belonging to Princess Mary.

Queen Victoria's side-saddle was used by the monarch in the latter half of the nineteenth century. To allow for a less restrictive riding style, the design features a pommel on either side of the saddle, so that the saddle can be ridden on either the near or the off side.

A hunting saddle used by the Prince Consort, HRH Prince Albert, during the mid-nineteenth century, is elaborately detailed in gold thread and features a holster for carrying a pair of pistols, which in those days would have been carried for the prince's personal protection.

The Kaiser's bridle, a gift from Wilhelm II of Germany, has not been used since the diamond jubilee of Queen Victoria in 1898. The lavish design features gilt trim on the bits, solid gold buckles and gold thread embellishment on the bridoon rein.

The bridle worn by Queen Elizabeth II's horse, Burmese, at the annual military ceremony, Trooping the Colour, is based on the traditional military bridle and combines a headcollar with a bridle. The detailing on the bridle is gilt and the reins are decorated with gold thread. The elaborate saddlery traditionally worn for Trooping the Colour includes gilded stirrups on the Queen's side-saddle.

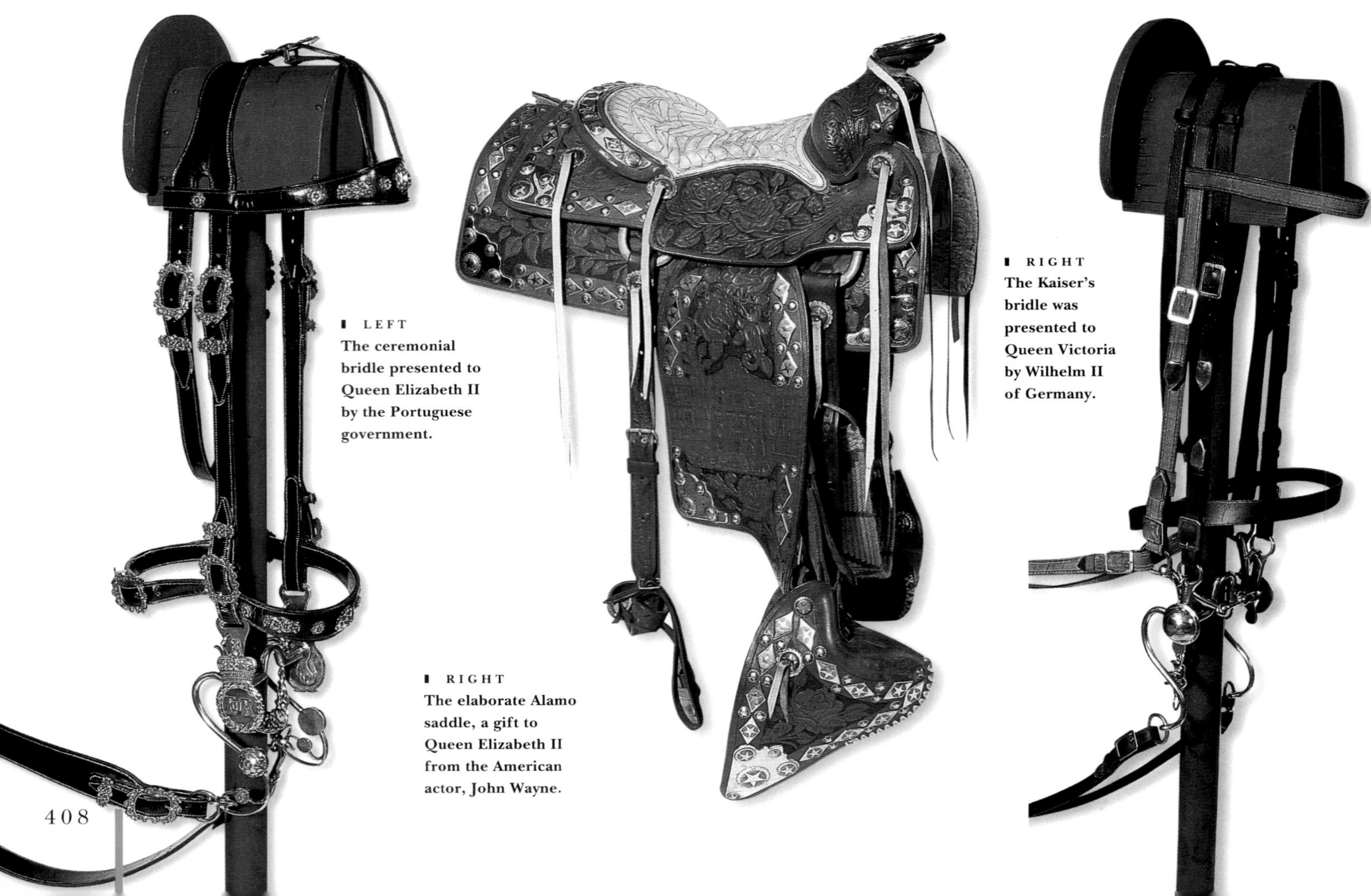

LEFT The ceremonial bridle presented to Queen Elizabeth II by the Portuguese government.

RIGHT The elaborate Alamo saddle, a gift to Queen Elizabeth II from the American actor, John Wayne.

RIGHT The Kaiser's bridle was presented to Queen Victoria by Wilhelm II of Germany.

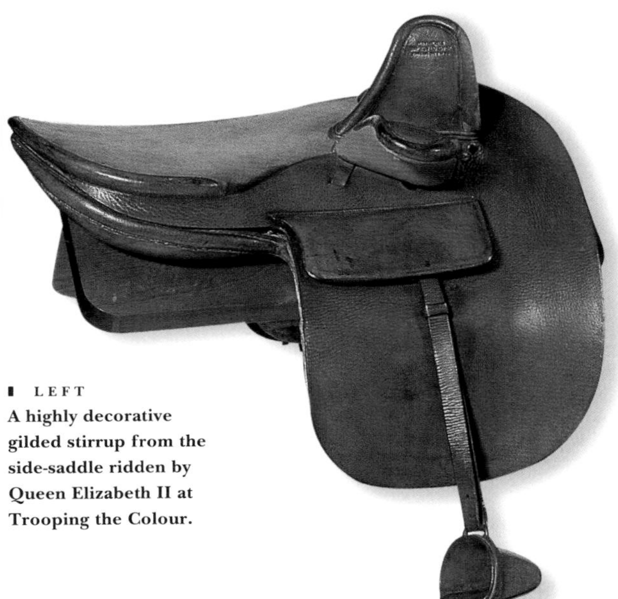

LEFT
A highly decorative gilded stirrup from the side-saddle ridden by Queen Elizabeth II at Trooping the Colour.

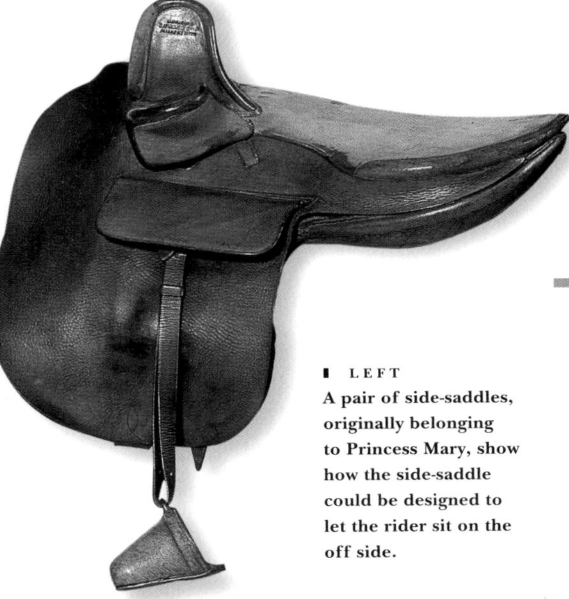

LEFT
A pair of side-saddles, originally belonging to Princess Mary, show how the side-saddle could be designed to let the rider sit on the off side.

BELOW

The military-style bridle worn by Queen Elizabeth II's horse at Trooping the Colour.

LEFT
A hunting saddle used by the Prince Consort, HRH Prince Albert, in the nineteenth century.

BELOW
Traditional detailing on a bridle worn by Queen Elizabeth II's horse at ceremonial parades.

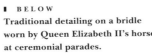

BELOW
Queen Victoria's side-saddle, with the double pommel design, allowed the Queen to ride off either side of the saddle.

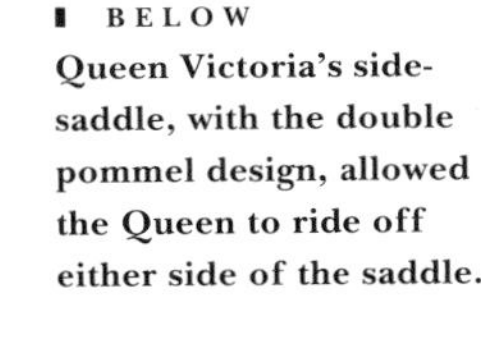

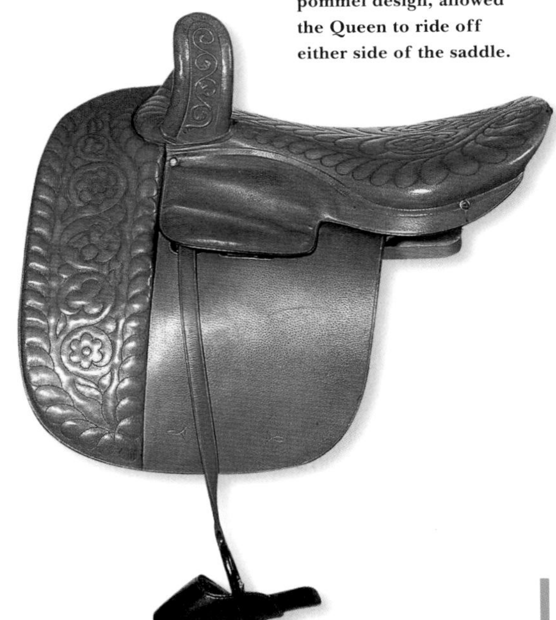

▮ ABOVE
leather Atherstone girth

▮ LEFT
Atherstone girth with elastic inserts

▮ ABOVE
Balding girth

Girths, Cinches and Surcingles

GIRTHS

Girths are used to keep the saddle in place on the horse's back. They are available in leather and synthetic materials: although expensive, leather girths are very durable if well cared for, while cotton and synthetic girths are cheaper and generally less hardwearing.

The **Atherstone girth** is padded and has a contoured shape to prevent it rubbing the horse's elbow. It is an ideal choice for general or competition use. The Atherstone is also available with strong elastic inserts at one or both ends, which allows the girth to stretch as the horse expands his ribcage when galloping. Take care not to overtighten an elasticated girth as it can still cause the horse discomfort, even though it stretches.

The **Balding girth** is made of a single piece of leather split into three. It was originally developed for polo ponies: the special shape helps to minimize chafing and girth galls.

The **three-fold leather girth** has become less common since the arrival of synthetic alternatives. It comprises a single piece of leather which is folded around a piece of oiled fabric. The girth is fitted with the open side away from the horse's elbow to prevent pinching. The oiled fabric helps to keep the leather supple.

The **Humane girth** has girth tabs which slide through special loops allowing the girth to move with the horse. The **Cottage Craft girth** is an inexpensive foam-padded, cotton girth which is both comfortable for the horse and easy to wash. **Cord girths**, made from thick cotton cords, have an open design which helps to reduce sweating while the cord strands themselves help to keep the girth in place.

Neoprene girths are available for general purpose and dressage saddles. The fabric (commonly used for wet suits) does not absorb sweat and helps to reduce rubbing. **Narrow-webbing girths** are often used on show horses and ponies, as they are less obtrusive than traditional girths. They consist of two narrow strips of webbing and a small section of textured rubber to prevent the girth slipping.

▮ RIGHT
three-fold leather girth

▮ RIGHT
Humane girth

▮ RIGHT
Cottage Craft girth

▮ RIGHT
neoprene girth

▮ RIGHT
Wintec girth

▮ RIGHT
dressage girth

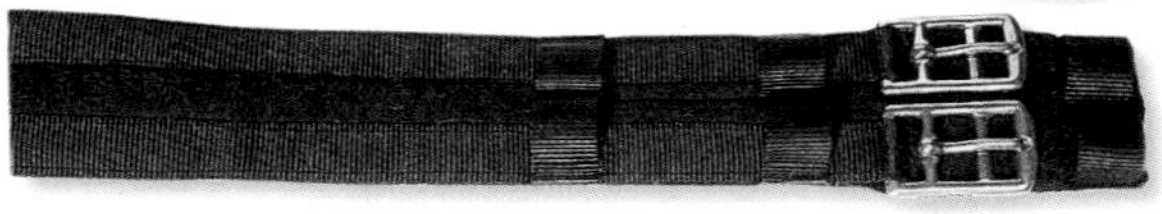

▮ RIGHT
Cottage Craft dressage girth

The **dressage girth**, also known as the **Lonsdale girth**, is shorter than a traditional girth as it is designed for use with the dressage saddle, which has longer girth tabs (billets).

The **Fitzwilliam girth**, used with a side-saddle, features an extra balance strap to prevent the saddle from slipping. The **leather stud-guard girth** is useful when competing in show-jumping events or horse trials. It is designed to prevent horses fitted with studs from injuring themselves when they snatch up their forelegs over a fence.

Racing girths are made from elastic or from webbing with elastic inserts, allowing the horse the freedom to expand his ribcage at a full gallop.

Accessories can be fitted to the girth as aids to the horse's comfort. The **fleece girth sleeve (cover)**, a soft fleece or sheepskin sleeve which slides over the girth, helps to keep the girth clean and minimize rubbing and galling. **A girth extender** is a short leather strap used to lengthen the girth. **Girth (buckle) guards** are fitted over the **girth tabs (billets)** on the saddle to prevent the girth buckles from rubbing and damaging the saddle flap. A **stud guard** is a pad of leather which is fitted to a standard girth to protect the horse when jumping, in the same way as a

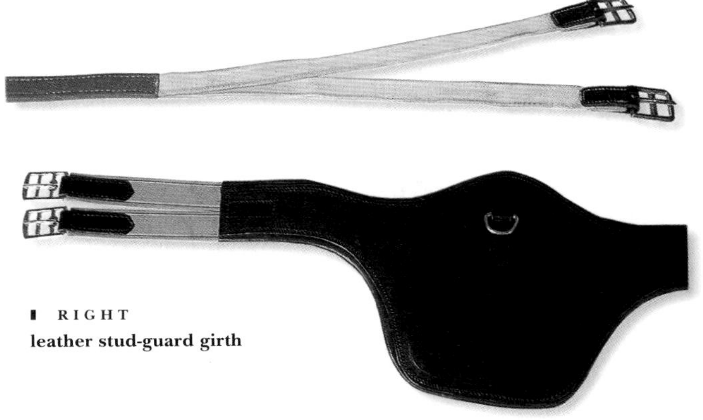

RIGHT
narrow-webbing show girth

RIGHT
leather stud-guard girth

ABOVE
A racing saddle fitted with a surcingle.

LEFT
A surcingle fitted over the saddle for cross-country riding.

RIGHT
Western fleece cinch

RIGHT
Western strand (string) cinch

RIGHT
neoprene cinch

RIGHT
all-elastic racing girth

RIGHT
racing girths

RIGHT
Fitzwilliam side saddle girth

stud-guard girth. The **sheepskin seat saver** is fitted over the saddle to make it more comfortable to ride for long periods of time – ideal for endurance or trail-riding.

CINCHES AND SURCINGLES

Western saddles are held in place with cinches rather than girths. Cinches are attached to the saddle by a large buckle at each end and are available in a range of materials: **neoprene** and **padded fleece cinches** help to reduce chafing, while **strand cinches**, made from cord or woven horse hair, prevent the horse sweating.

Racing surcingles, in elastic or webbing with an elastic insert, go over the top of the saddle. They are used in addition to a racing girth to provide extra security in the event of the racing girth breaking. For the same reason, the **overgirth** or **surcingle** is fitted over the saddle for the cross-country phase of horse trials.

LEFT
girth extender

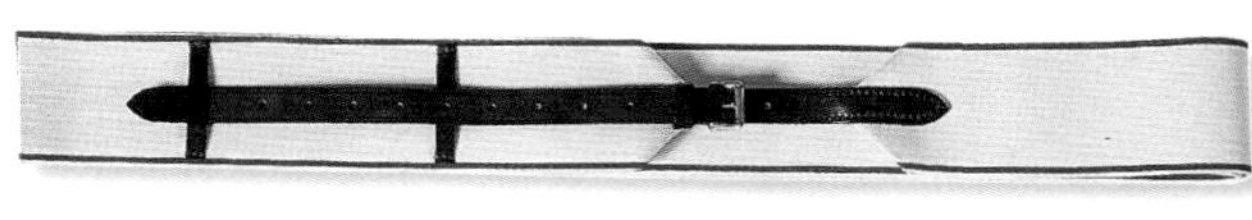

LEFT
all-elastic racing surcingle

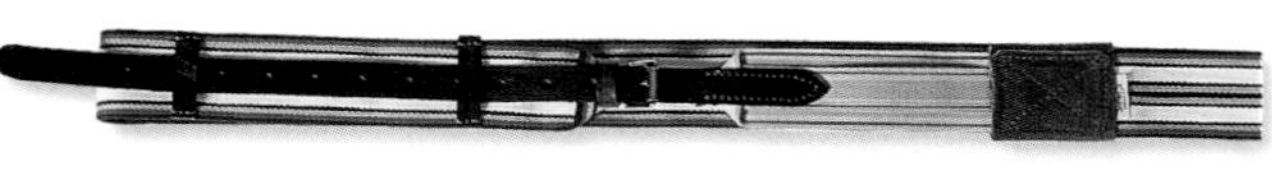

LEFT
tubular racing surcingle

ABOVE
fleece girth sleeve (cover)

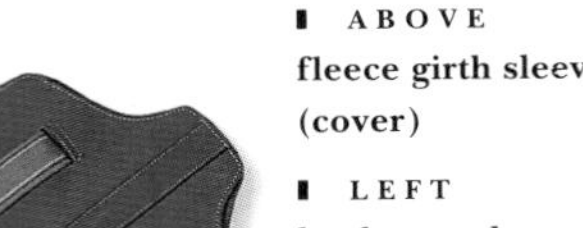

LEFT
leather stud guard

RIGHT
girth (buckle) guard

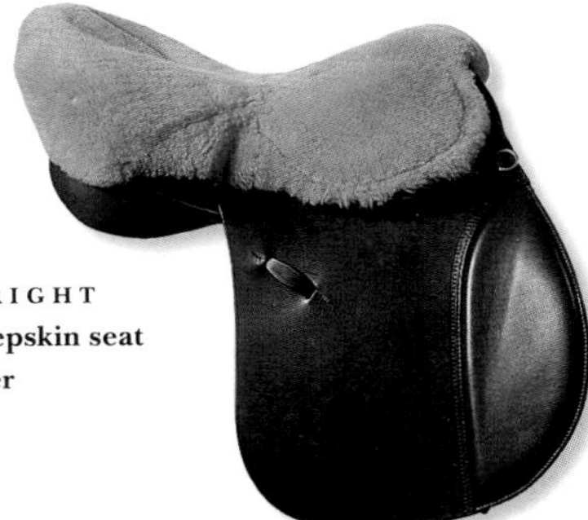

RIGHT
sheepskin seat saver

Breastplates and Cruppers

BREASTPLATES AND BREASTGIRTHS

The breastplate and breastgirth are designed to stop the saddle slipping back, and are especially useful for high impact disciplines such as galloping or jumping.

The sturdy **hunting breastplate** is made from leather or leather and elastic. Two straps are attached to the D rings on the saddle, while a strap passes through the horse's front legs and loops around the girth. A ring at the chest allows a running martingale to be fitted if necessary. The **racing breastplate** is a lightweight version of the hunting type, while the **Western breastplate**, made of tooled leather, is heavier than the English type and is used with the Western saddle only.

The breastgirth is a simple strap which is passed around the horse's chest and attached to the girth on either side of the saddle. The **leather breastgirth** is commonly used on polo ponies, while the **elasticated** or **Aintree breastgirth** allows for the movement of the horse during strenuous exercise, in particular when jumping across country. The **continental breastgirth** is similar to a normal breastgirth but is fitted to the saddle D rings rather than to the girth.

A **sheepskin sleeve (cover)** can be fitted over the chest strap of a breastgirth to prevent it from rubbing the horse.

The **neck strap** is a useful attachment for novice riders or for those training young horses. A strong leather strap, such as a stirrup leather, is fitted around the base of the horse's neck. It is useful for jumping as it gives the rider something to hold on to without pulling at the reins and risking damage to the horse's mouth.

CRUPPERS

A crupper can be fitted to prevent the saddle from slipping forward and is generally only needed on ponies. A strap is passed under the tail and attached to the back of the saddle.

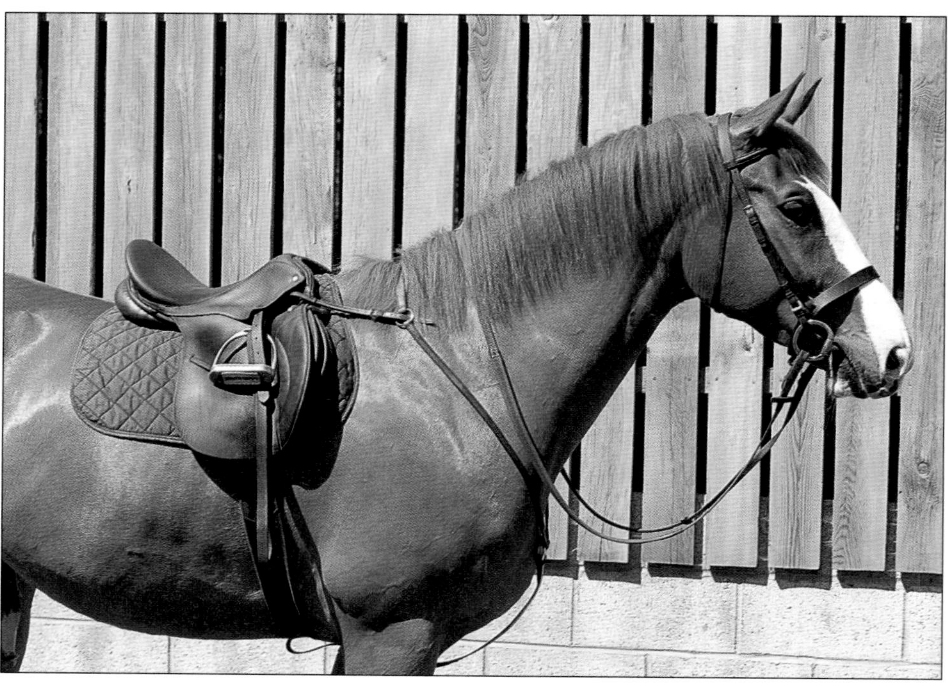

ABOVE
The hunting breastplate is used to prevent the saddle slipping back when the horse is galloping and jumping.

LEFT
The racing breastplate is a lightweight alternative to the hunting type, but it is designed to serve the same purpose.

BELOW
Western breastplate

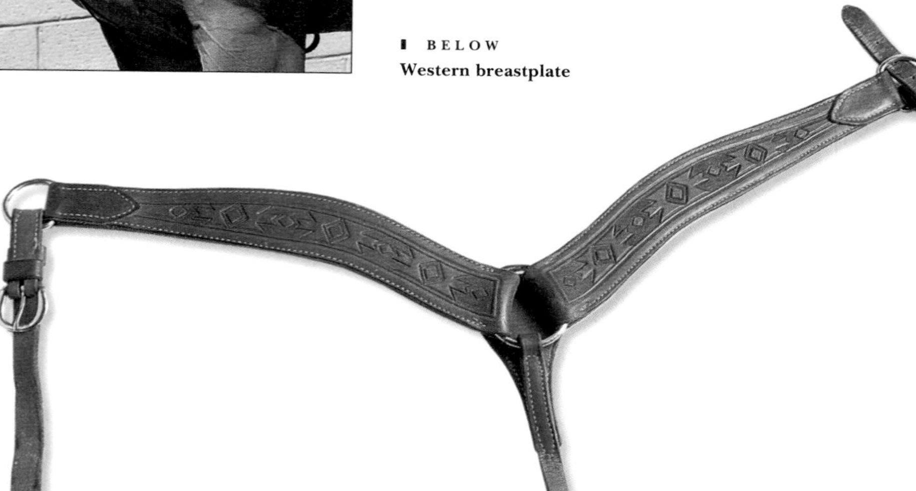

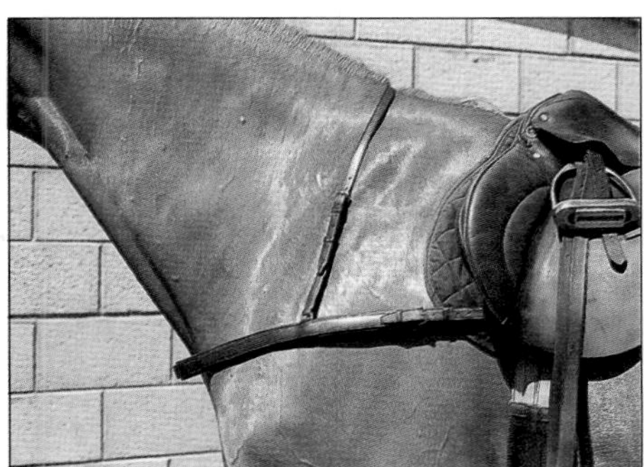

Polo ponies are often fitted with leather breastgirths.

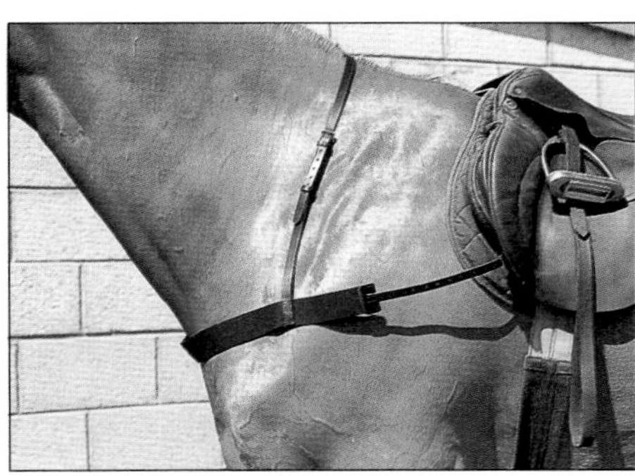

The modern elasticated breastgirth allows the horse greater freedom of movement.

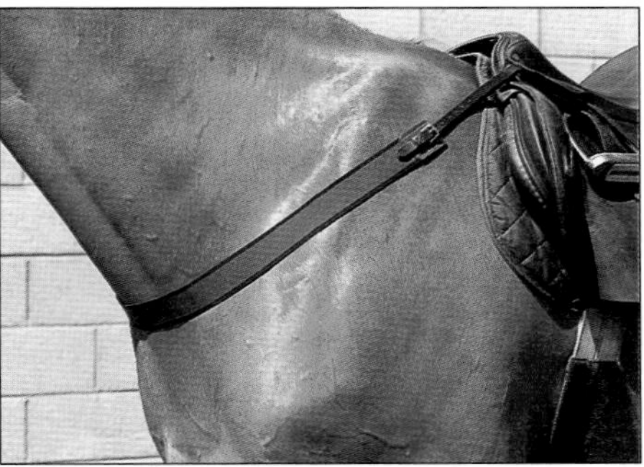

The continental breastgirth is attached to the D rings of the saddle, rather than to the girth.

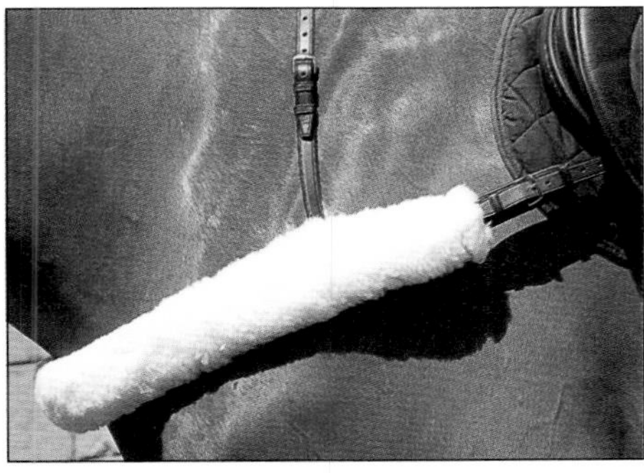

A sheepskin sleeve (cover) can be fitted over a breastgirth to prevent the strap rubbing the horse.

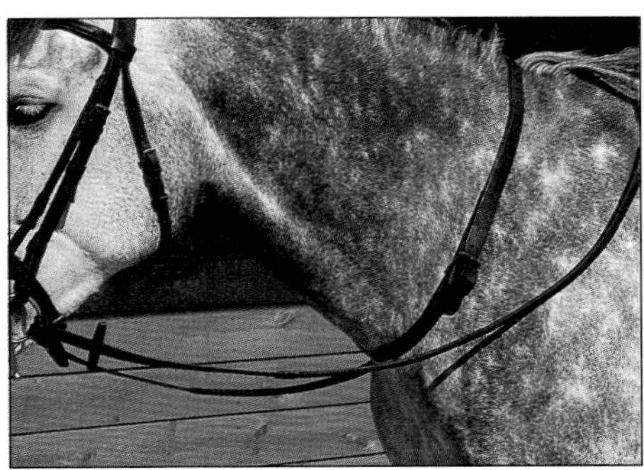

A neck strap is a useful attachment for the rider to hold on to when jumping or galloping, and can help make a nervous rider feel more secure.

HOW TO ATTACH A BREASTGIRTH

Attach the strap from the breastgirth to the girth just under the buckle, above the numnah strap to prevent it slipping down. Pass it under the first strap and round the second strap.

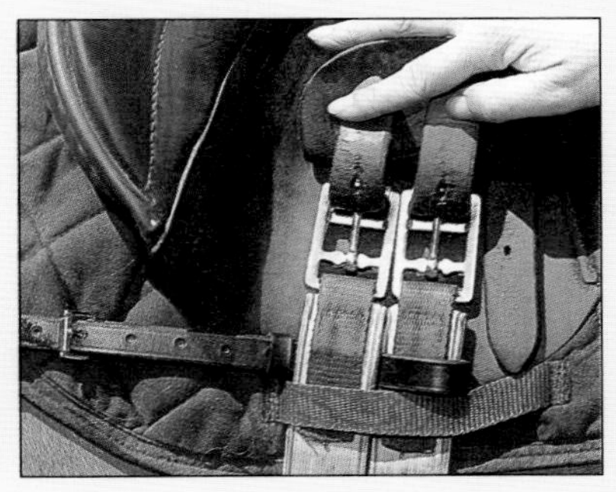

ABOVE
A crupper is often worn by ponies and smaller horses to prevent the saddle slipping forwards.

FITTING A LEATHER BREASTPLATE

1 When the breastplate is in place, check that the fit allows room for a palm's width at the chest.

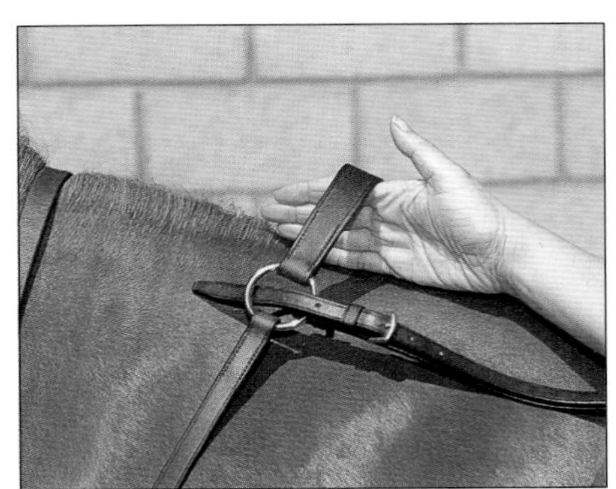

2 You should be able to fit four fingers under the strap which passes over the neck.

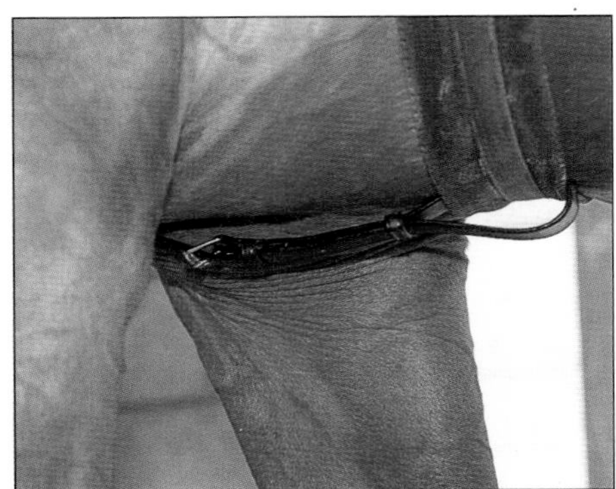

3 The breastplate keeper should be pushed tightly up to the girth so that there is no loop in which the horse could catch his foot.

Stirrups

Stirrups, also known as irons, are available in a variety of styles but are almost always made from stainless steel, which is extremely strong. For safety, the stirrup should be wide enough to allow about 1–1.5cm/½in on either side of the rider's foot to avoid the foot getting caught in the stirrup in the event of a fall.

The most common English stirrup is the **Prussian side open bottom**, also known as a **hunting iron**. Very useful for dressage and jumping are heavier models such as the **fillis stirrup**, which give the rider more balance. The **off-set fillis** is a popular choice for jumping. The eye of the stirrup is set to the inside, which encourages the knee and thigh to be pressed into the saddle for extra grip.

Alternatives to steel become necessary when weight is important. Contemporary choices include the **carbon-fibre stirrup** which is both light and strong, and features graphite treads for extra grip. **Polymer** and **Flexi-ride stirrups** are designed specifically for endurance and trail-riding. The rubberized material absorbs concussion, enhancing the rider's comfort when riding for long periods of time. **Cradle-bottom racing stirrups**, which are designed purely for racing, are made from lightweight aluminium.

Western stirrups consist of a wooden or Ralide frame covered in leather; a more decorative design is made from inlaid wood. For parades, a toe cover called a *tapadero* can be fitted to the stirrup. The **side-saddle stirrup** features a round eye through which the stirrup leather passes, allowing greater flexibility of movement for the rider's leg.

Rubber treads can be fitted into stirrups to provide extra grip for muddy boots or when riding in wet weather. The treads lie flat inside the stirrup, although angled or wedged treads are also available for dressage and jumping.

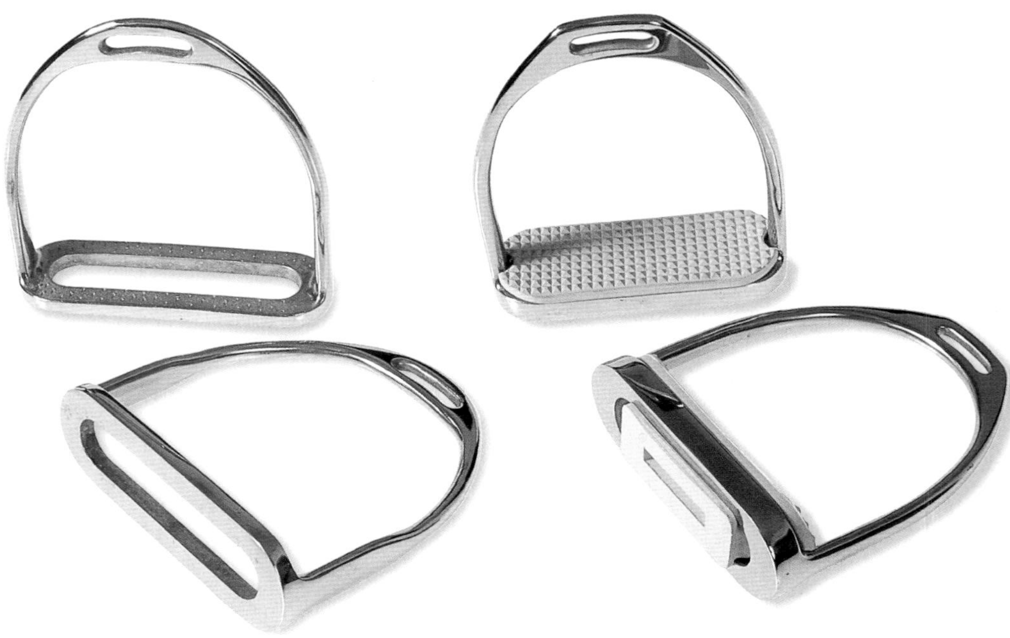

ABOVE
Prussian side open bottom stirrups are the traditional English riding stirrups.

ABOVE
Fillis stirrups are solid and heavy, and are used to help the rider balance in the saddle.

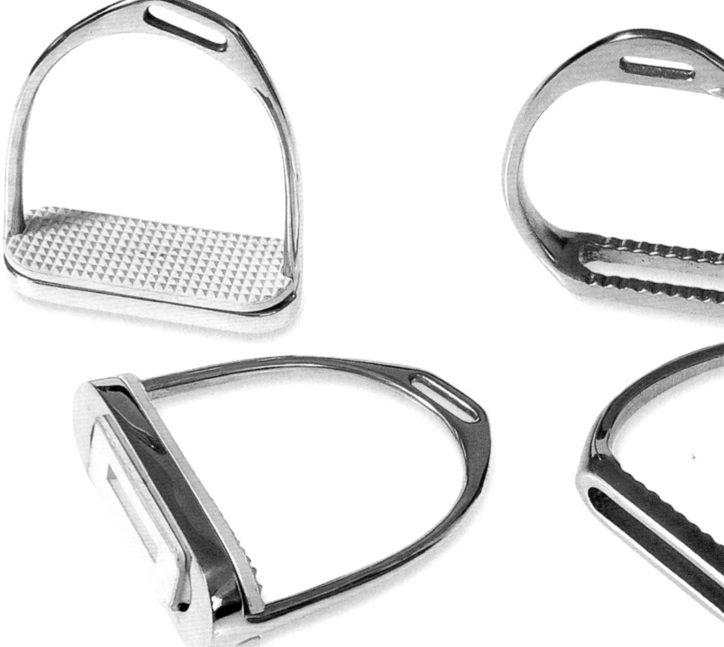

ABOVE
The eye of the off-set fillis stirrup is set to the inside, pressing the knee towards the saddle.

ABOVE
Cradle-bottom racing stirrups are made from lightweight aluminium.

ABOVE
leather-covered Western stirrup

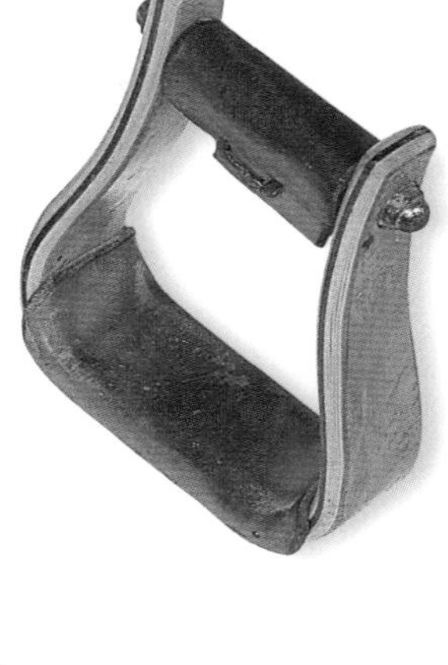

ABOVE
inlaid wood Western stirrups

ABOVE
Toe covers can be fitted to ordinary stirrups. They are commonly used in endurance and trail-riding events and will prevent the rider's foot sliding through and getting stuck in the stirrup.

ABOVE
Polymer and Flexi-ride stirrups are designed to increase foot comfort when endurance or trail-riding.

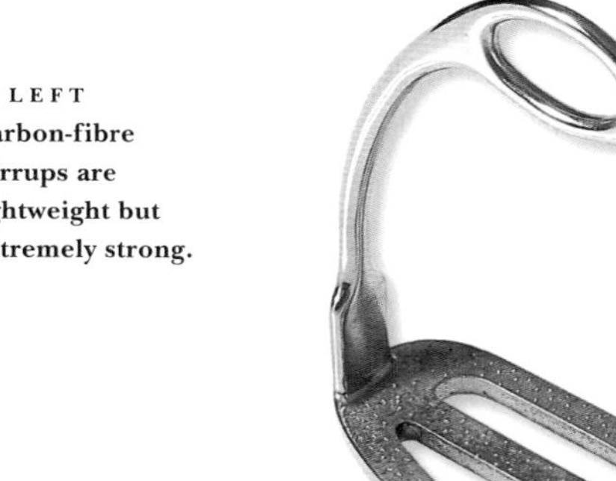

LEFT
Carbon-fibre stirrups are lightweight but extremely strong.

ABOVE
The round eye of the side-saddle stirrup allows the lower leg greater flexibility.

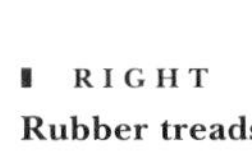

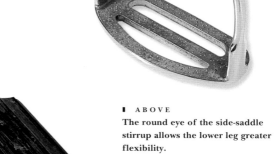

RIGHT
Rubber treads are fitted to stirrups to provide extra grip.

SAFETY STIRRUPS

In the event of a fall, the rider risks serious injury if his foot becomes caught in the stirrup. Safety stirrups are designed to prevent this by allowing the foot to be quickly released from the stirrup.

The **Australian Simplex** or **bent-leg stirrup** has a bent outer leg on the iron, encouraging the early release of the foot. The **Peacock safety stirrup** has a strong band of rubber fitted to the outside of the stirrup, which is pulled off if the foot gets caught. The **precision riding stirrup** is a new design which self-aligns to the position of your foot to increase comfort and security.

STIRRUP LEATHERS

English leathers are traditionally made from top-quality English dressed hides. **Extending leathers** have a small hook attachment which allows the stirrup to be lengthened for mounting. **Racing leathers** are lightweight and made from leather and nylon web. **Jumping** or **double-sided stirrup leathers** are reinforced with nylon to strengthen the leather and prevent it from stretching. The **side-saddle leather** has a hook adjustment to alter the length at the base, near the stirrup. **Dressage leathers** are a smart single thickness of leather with a buckle at the base, allowing the legs to be carried closer to the horse.

ABOVE
Australian Simplex safety or bent-leg stirrups. The bent leg of the iron is fitted to the outside.

ABOVE
Peacock safety stirrups. In the event of a fall, the rubber is pulled off to release the foot.

ABOVE
Precision riding stirrups self-align for safety and comfort.

RIGHT
Jumping stirrup leathers, also known as double-sided stirrup leathers, are reinforced with nylon for extra strength under extreme pressure.

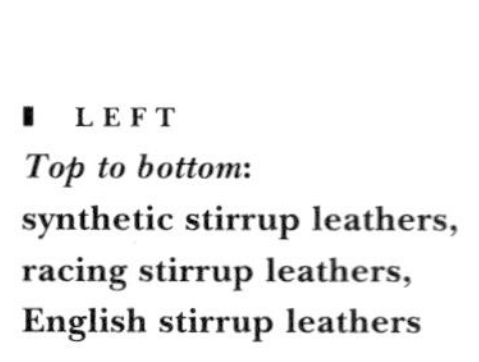

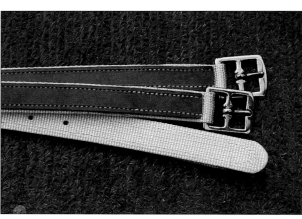

LEFT
***Top to bottom*: synthetic stirrup leathers, racing stirrup leathers, English stirrup leathers**

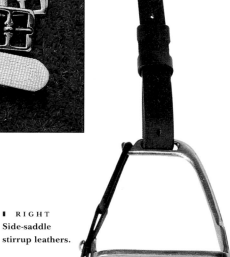

RIGHT
Side-saddle stirrup leathers.

Numnahs and Saddle Cloths

Numnahs and saddle cloths are fitted under the saddle to stop the saddle rubbing the horse's back and to absorb the concussion caused by movement. They help to keep the underside of the saddle clean by absorbing sweat and grease from the horse's body. Numnahs are saddle-shaped whereas a saddle pad or cloth is normally square or rectangular. A numnah or saddle cloth should never be used to make an ill-fitting saddle fit, and if not kept scrupulously clean they can rub the horse's back, leading to sores and even skin diseases.

Lightweight **quilted cotton numnahs** are ideal for protecting the saddle from sweat. They are held in place with straps which go round the girth and girth tabs. Available to fit general purpose and dressage saddles, they come in a variety of colours, although white is traditional for competitions.

The materials from which numnahs and saddle pads are made are chosen for their comfort-inducing properties. The **wither pad** is a small, oval pad in fleece or sheepskin which is placed between the wither and the saddle. The **pure new wool numnah**, fully washable with a cotton backing, is designed to relieve and prevent pressure sores. The **sheepskin numnah** absorbs impact and allows heat from the horse's body to pass through it. The **non-slip numnah**, made from neoprene, is designed to absorb concussion and to prevent the saddle from slipping.

Modern choices often include unique features which make them more attractive to the rider. The **Poly pad** is a thick, quilted pad which provides extra protection for the horse's back. Unlike many other numnahs or saddle cloths, it stays in place without the need for straps or loops. The **Coolback numnah** or saddle cloth features a special lining which draws sweat away from the horse's back. The **Proteq saddle pad** is a unique concept,

LEFT
A saddle cloth or numnah for a general purpose saddle.

BELOW
A Poly pad is a thick quilted pad which provides extra protection from the saddle. It is also available as a wither pad.

A quilted cotton saddle cloth and numnah for a dressage saddle.

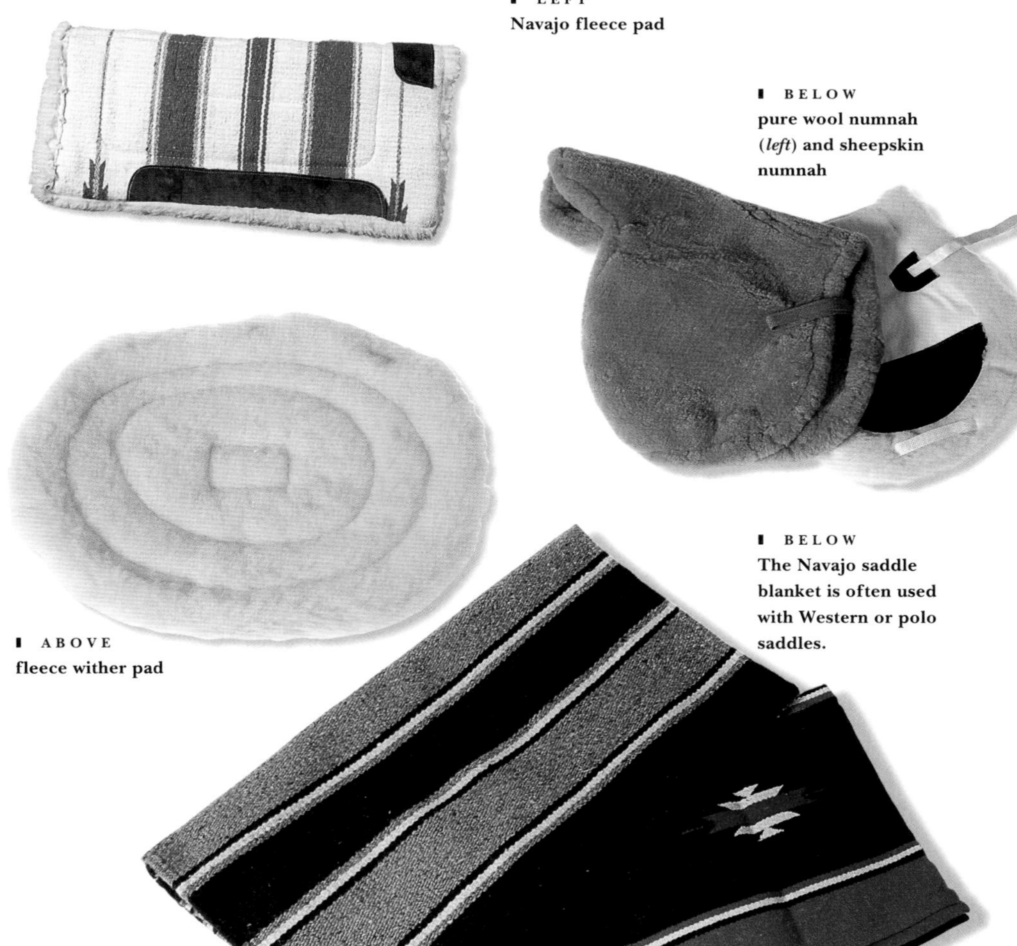

LEFT
Navajo fleece pad

BELOW
pure wool numnah (*left*) and sheepskin numnah

ABOVE
fleece wither pad

BELOW
The Navajo saddle blanket is often used with Western or polo saddles.

incorporating thousands of tiny polystyrene beads. When the saddle is in place the air is pumped out of the pad, so that the beads mould to the configuration between the saddle and the horse's back.

Western and polo saddles are traditionally fitted with the **Navajo saddle blanket**. The **Navajo fleece pad** is a Western blanket pad with a fleece lining.

The **racing weight cloth** is fitted between the numnah and the saddle. It features a series of pockets in which lead weights can be placed to ensure that the rider is carrying the correct weight for the race. Weight cloths are also used in the speed and endurance phases of horse trials.

New products designed to fit between the saddle and the numnah now make use of highly effective synthetic materials. These include the **Pro-lite relief pad**, which incorporates a visco-elastic gel and latex rubber to absorb impact, and the **gel pad**, which contains thermoplastic elastomer gel for shock absorbency. Flat or moulded **shock-absorbing pads** can be placed under the saddle to help distribute the rider's weight more evenly over the horse's back.

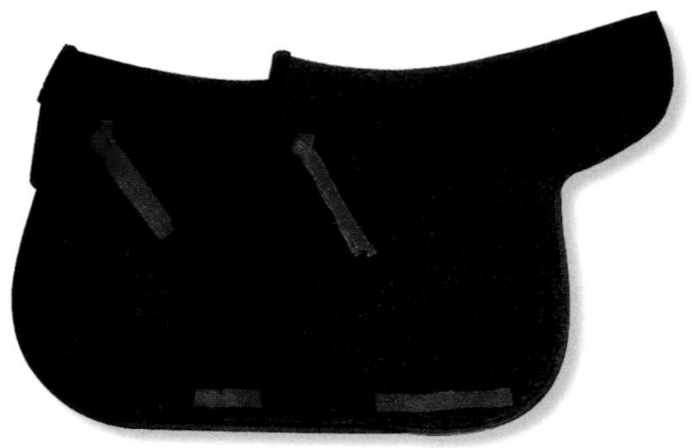

ABOVE
Aerborn Coolback numnah. This saddle cloth has a special lining which absorbs sweat from the horse's back.

ABOVE
The gel pad contains a thermoplastic elastomer gel to aid shock absorbency.

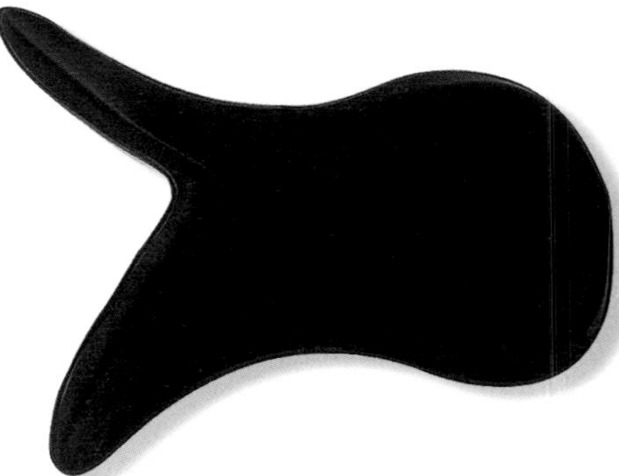

ABOVE
Placed under the saddle, the moulded shock-absorbing pad helps to distribute the rider's weight evenly.

ABOVE
The flat shock-absorbing pad is used to help distribute the rider's weight along the horse's back.

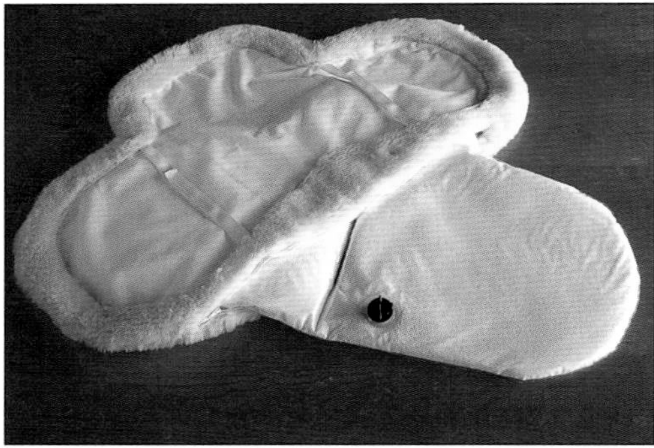

LEFT
The Proteq saddle pad incorporates thousands of tiny polystyrene beads, which help mould the pad to the horse's back.

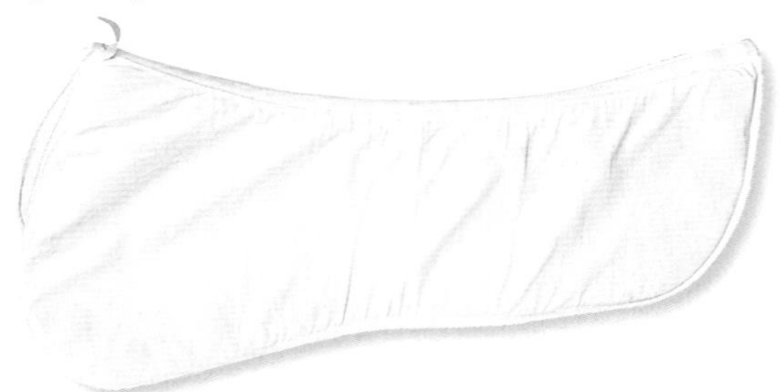

ABOVE
The Pro-lite relief pad uses visco-elastic gel and latex rubber to absorb impact and concussion.

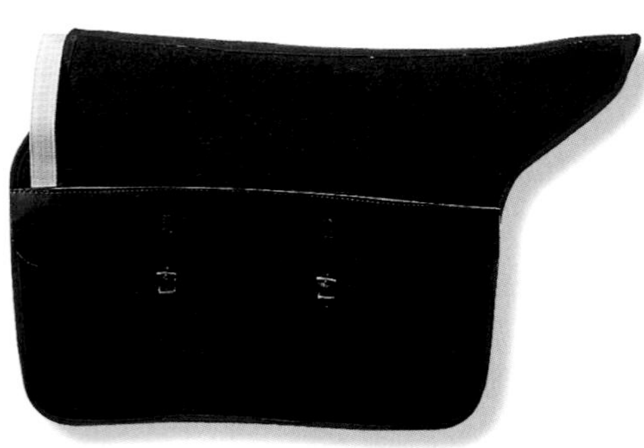

ABOVE
Lead weights can be added to the pockets of the weight cloth to ensure the jockey carries the correct weight for the race.

Saddle Bags

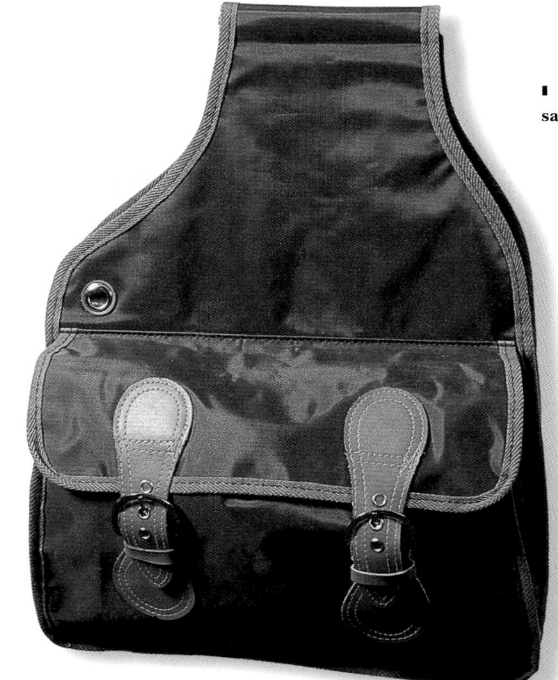

▮ LEFT
saddle pannier

Saddle bags, pouches or panniers are lightweight bags which can be fitted to the saddle, positioned behind it and hung over either side of the horse. They are functional accessories used to carry the provisions needed on rides of several hours or more.

The **trail pad**, a fleece pad incorporated into a canvas cloth with pockets, is ideal for endurance and long-distance pleasure rides. The fleece numnah sits comfortably on the horse, while the canvas overlay is suitably sturdy.

As its name suggests, the **hunting canteen** was traditionally used to carry the refreshments necessary for a day's fox hunting. The smart leather pouch is just the right size to hold a flask of warming liquor.

Argentinian saddle bags are handwoven from wool in traditional patterns. They are used by *gauchos* to carry food when riding for days at a time out on the *pampas*.

▮ BELOW
trail pad

▮ LEFT
hunting canteen

▮ ABOVE
Argentinian saddle bag

Saddle Care

A good saddle is a costly piece of equipment and it is important to look after it properly, not only because it is expensive to repair but because a damaged saddle may harm your horse's back.

HOW TO CARRY A SADDLE

LEFT
The saddle should be carried in either of the two ways shown: over the forearm with the back of the saddle nearest the elbow (*far left*), or against the side of the body with the hand holding on to the pommel (*left*).

HOW TO STORE A SADDLE

Once you have removed the saddle from the horse, it can be placed over a fence or saddle rack before being returned to the tack room. (If you leave the saddle over a stable door, the horse will most probably nudge it off.)

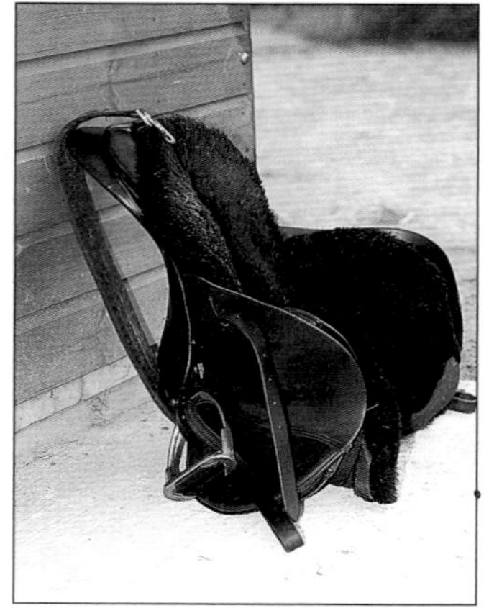

You can also put the saddle on the ground, pommel down and with the seat facing the wall. Place the girth between the pommel and the ground to protect the leather.

Saddles are best kept on saddle racks in a clean and dry tack room – damp conditions will damage the leather. Do not leave sweaty numnahs or girths attached to the saddle; remove and clean them before putting them away separately.

HOW TO CLEAN A SADDLE

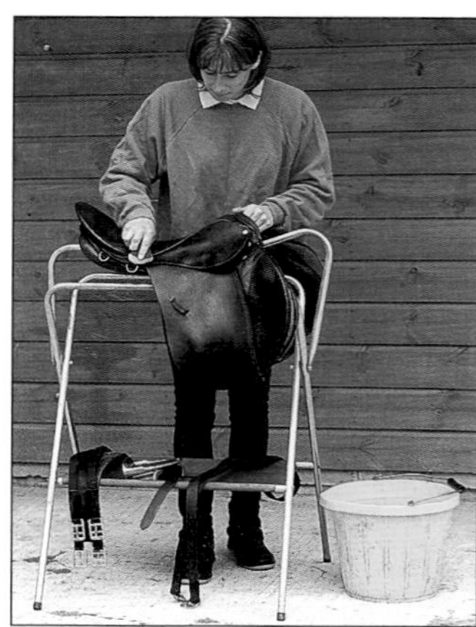

1 **Place the saddle on a stand. Remove the stirrup leathers, girth and numnah. With warm water and a dampened sponge, work all over the saddle removing any mud, sweat and general dirt. Take care not to let the leather get too wet.**

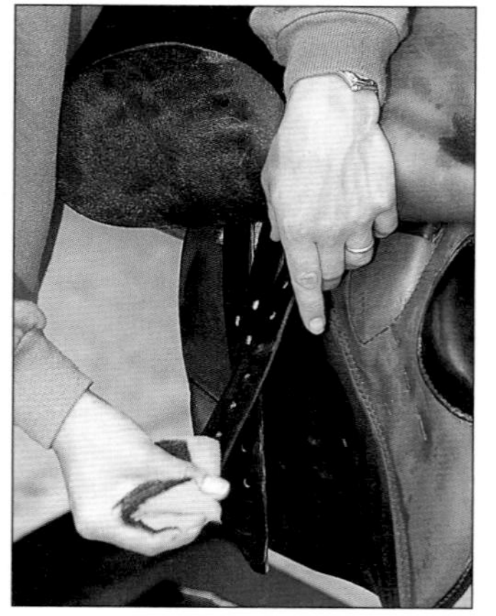

2 **Whilst cleaning, check the saddle for wear and tear. Pay particular attention to the stitching, especially where the girth tabs (billets) are joined to the saddle.**

3 **Don't forget to clean the underside of the saddle as this can get sweaty even if a numnah or saddle cloth has been used.**

4 **Allow the leather to dry slightly before applying the saddle soap. Use a fresh sponge and work the saddle soap into the leather with a circular rubbing motion. Cover the entire surface of the saddle, including under the saddle flaps.**

SADDLING UP

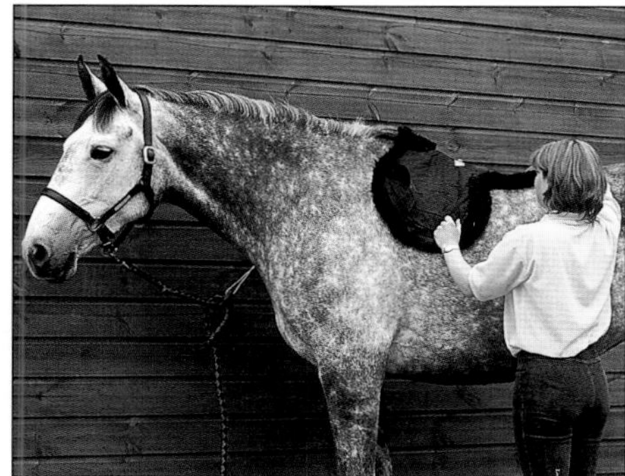

1 Place a numnah or saddle cloth on the horse's back, making sure it is positioned sufficiently high up the horse's withers.

2 Lift the saddle over the horse's back and carefully lower it into position on top of the numnah or saddle cloth. Ensure both saddle flaps are lying flat against the horse's sides.

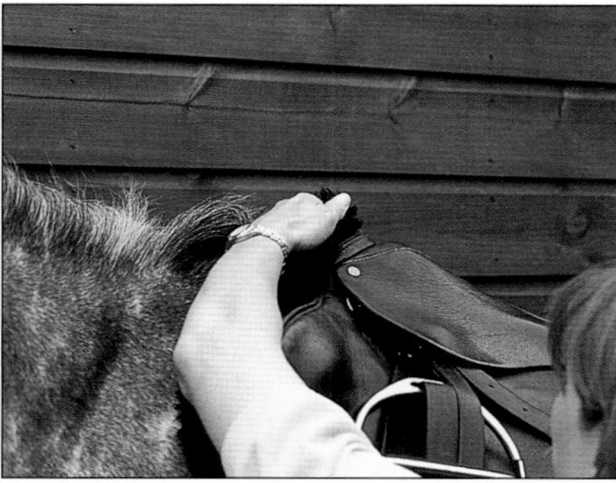

3 Pull the numnah or saddle cloth up into the gullet of the saddle so that it is clear of the horse's withers.

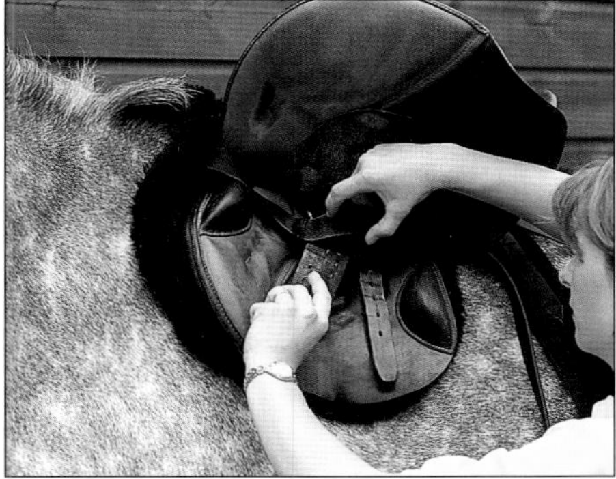

4 Numnahs usually have straps to anchor them to the saddle and stop them from slipping. Attach the top straps to the saddle's girth tabs (billets) through which the girth is fitted above the girth guard before doing up the girth.

5 Buckle the girth to the off side (right) of the saddle first and pass it through the bottom strap on the numnah. Move back to the near side (left) of the horse, reach underneath him and take hold of the girth.

6 Pass the girth through the retaining strap on the numnah before buckling to the saddle girth tabs on the near side.

5 Remove dirt and grease from the stirrup leathers with a sponge. Apply the saddle soap and check the stitching for wear. Check that the leathers have not stretched: because we mount from the near side, one leather will become longer than the other if they are not switched regularly.

7 Tighten up the girth gradually (it should be equal on both sides) until there is just room to fit the flat of your hand between the girth and the horse's side. Picking up the horse's feet, one at a time, and pulling them forward will also help you to judge if the girth is comfortable for the horse.

8 Once the girth has been tightened, slide the buckle guard down over the girth buckles to prevent them from rubbing against and damaging the saddle flaps. Slide your hand round the horse's belly under the girth to ensure that there are no wrinkles in the horse's skin.

Bridles and Bits

Along with the saddle, the bridle and bit are the most important pieces of equipment for the ridden horse. Combined with the rider's legs, voice and body position, the bridle and bit provide that important line of communication which allows you to control the horse.

Bridles are traditionally made of leather. However, synthetic bridles, which come in a choice of vivid colours, are becoming much more popular, especially in the sports of flat racing and endurance riding.

The variety of bits available can be bewildering, and choosing the right bit for a horse is almost a science in itself. To simplify matters, bits are divided into five groups which are categorized by their action, based on the area of the horse's head to which pressure is applied. The five groups are: snaffles, doubles, pelhams, gag snaffles and bitless bridles. It is important to make an accurate judgment over your choice of bit: a bit that is too weak will result in the rider having no control over the horse, while one that is too severe will encourage the horse to fight against it.

Snaffle Bridle

The snaffle bridle is a simple, basic bridle which is suitable for most types of riding. In particular it is the appropriate bridle for horses in the early stages of training. The noseband is not essential and need not be fitted; however, many horses, especially those with longer heads, tend to look better with the noseband in place. By changing the bit or fitting a different type of noseband, the action of the bridle can be made stronger, so that the rider has greater control over the horse and the way in which he carries his head.

RIGHT
The snaffle bridle is the standard type of bridle used with all single bits.

Double Bridle

The double bridle is basically the same in design as the snaffle bridle, although the addition of an extra bridoon sliphead means that two bits can be used simultaneously with two sets of reins. Unlike the snaffle bridle, which can be used with a variety of nosebands, the double bridle should only be fitted with a basic cavesson noseband so that the action of the curb is not interfered with.

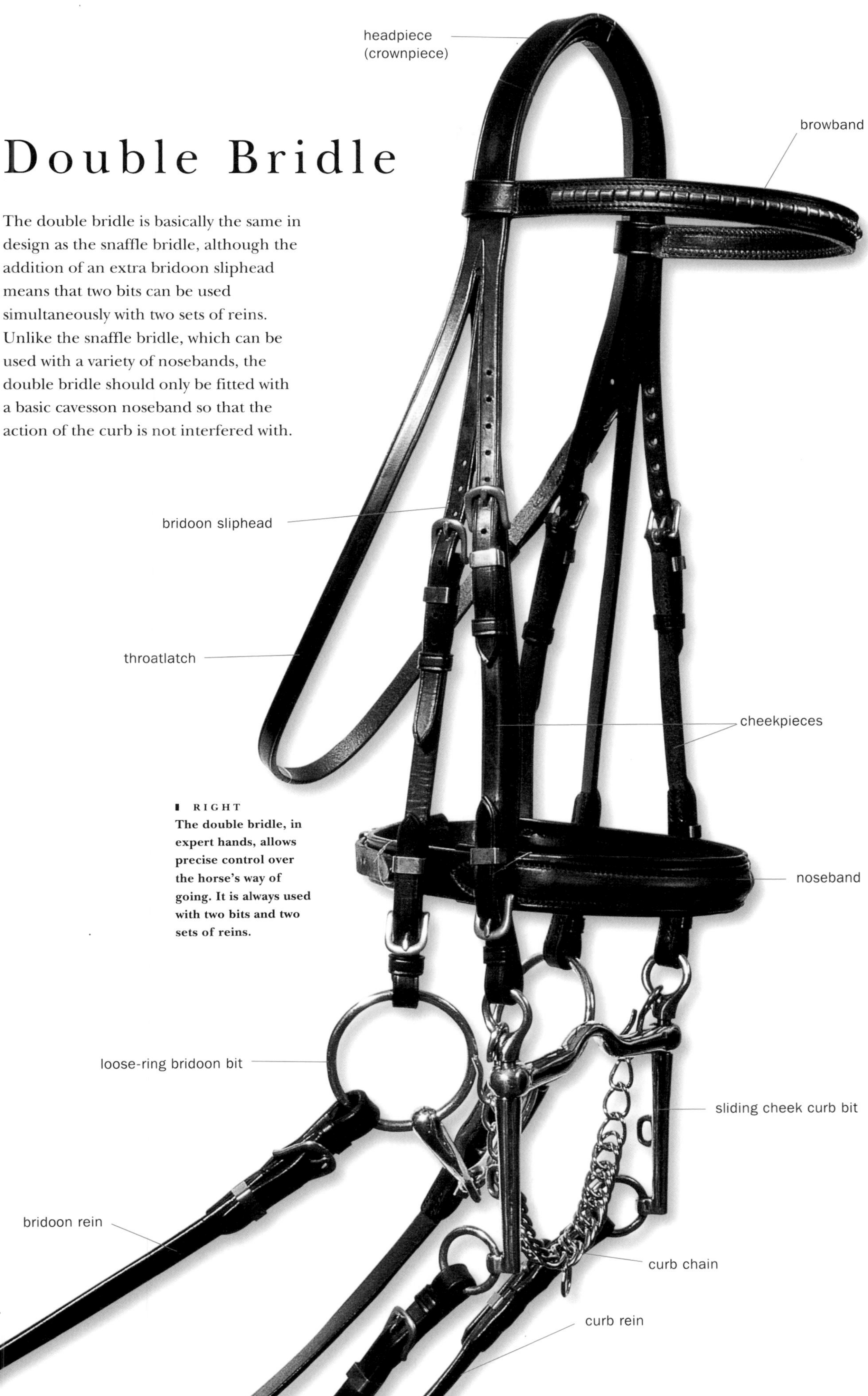

RIGHT
The double bridle, in expert hands, allows precise control over the horse's way of going. It is always used with two bits and two sets of reins.

Western Bridle

The traditional Western bridle is fastened with narrow leather thongs, which enabled the cowboy to carry out running repairs on any items of broken tack himself when he was miles from the nearest saddler. Western bridles are referred to as either "one-ear" or "split-ear". The headpiece (crownpiece) of a split-ear bridle is made from a single piece of leather which has slits cut into it to fit over each ear. This is to prevent the bridle from being pulled off accidentally. The one-ear bridle incorporates a definite loop which fits over one of the horse's ear. The reins of the Western bridle are not joined at the end. This is to avoid the risk of the horse getting a foot caught in the reins if they trail on the ground.

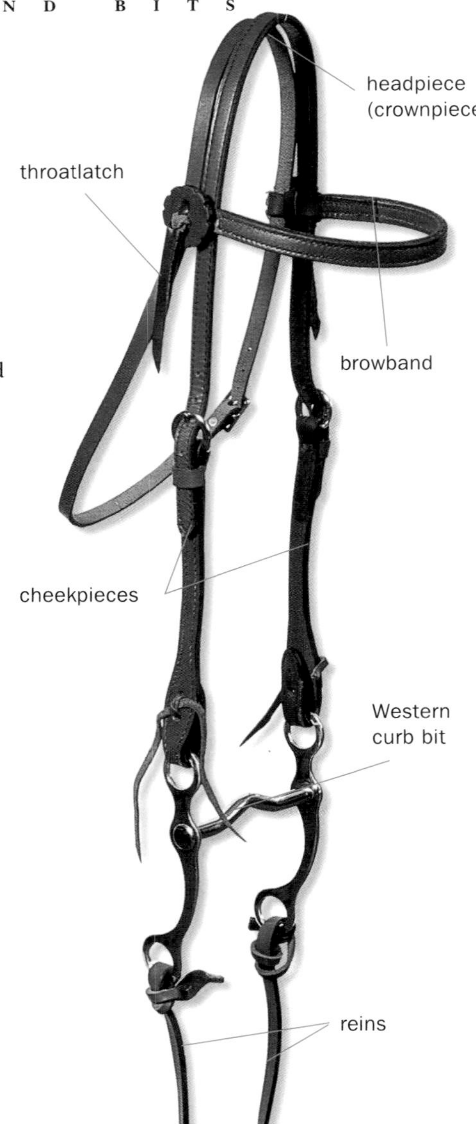

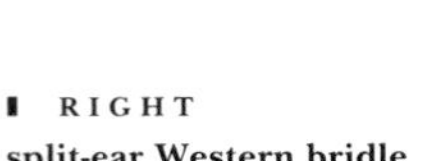
RIGHT
split-ear Western bridle

BELOW
one-ear Western bridle

Endurance 2-in-1 Bridle

The endurance bridle is a combination of a headcollar (crownpiece) and a standard bridle. The cheekpieces and reins can be quickly unclipped to leave just the headcollar in place. The headcollar can also be ridden as a Scawbrig, a type of bitless bridle, by attaching the reins to the noseband. The endurance bridle (also known as the combination bridle) has proved popular with endurance riders because of its practical design: the bit can be removed quickly to give the horse a drink during competition, while the reins very usefully double as a lead rope.

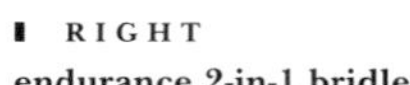
RIGHT
endurance 2-in-1 bridle

THE MAIN POINTS OF CONTROL

Bits, bitless bridles and certain types of nosebands will all act on specific parts of the horse's head.

The poll – the headpiece (crownpiece) of the bridle applies pressure here when a gag or curb bit is used.

The nose – bitless bridles and specific types of nosebands affect the nose.

The mouthcorners – snaffle bits bring pressure on the corners of the horse's mouth and lips.

Side of the face – bits with full cheeks, D rings or large racing rings affect this area.

Curb groove – the curb chain fitted with a pelham or Weymouth bit affects the curb groove.

Roof of the mouth – bits with ported mouthpieces affect this area.

Tongue – all bits apply pressure to the tongue.

Bars – all bits affect the bars, a sensitive part of the horse's mouth between the incisors and premolar teeth.

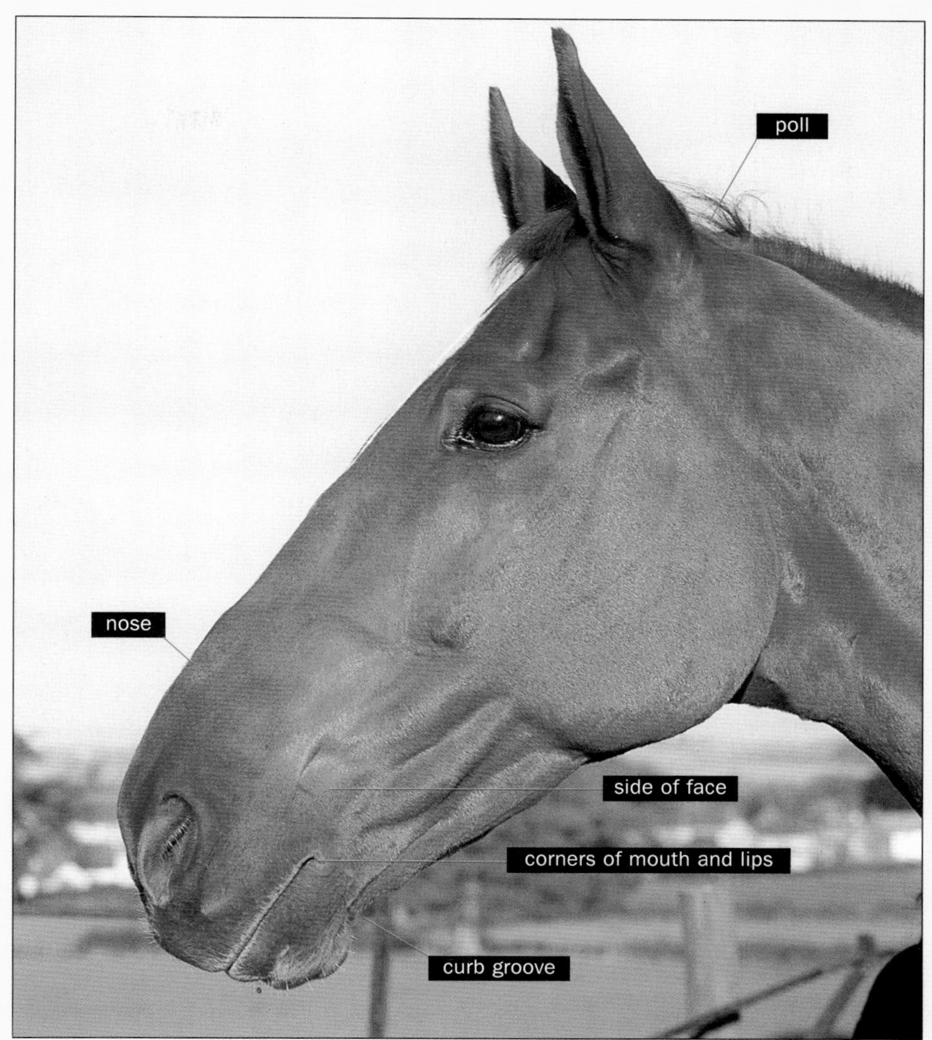

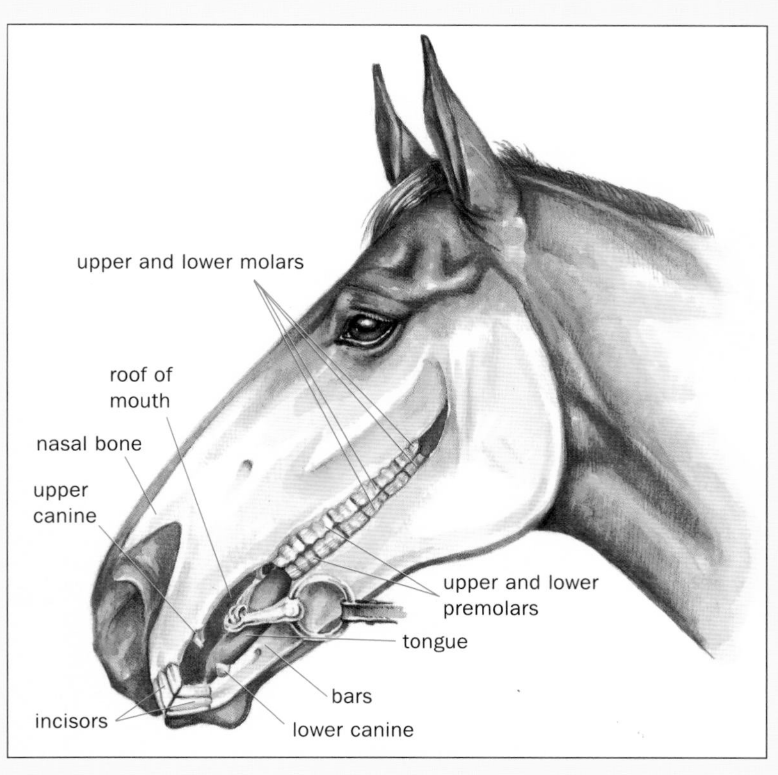

Snaffle Bits

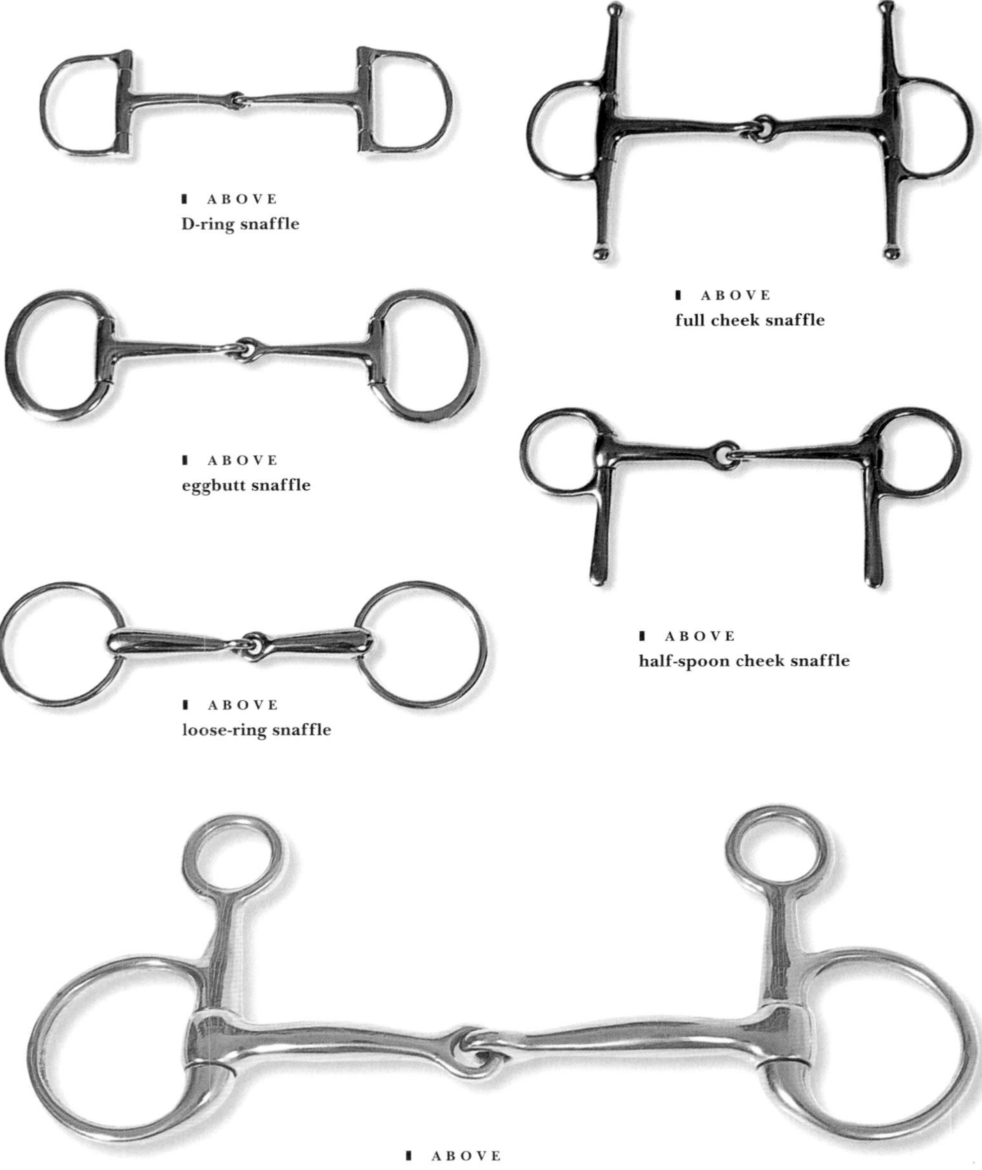

ABOVE
D-ring snaffle

ABOVE
full cheek snaffle

ABOVE
eggbutt snaffle

ABOVE
half-spoon cheek snaffle

ABOVE
loose-ring snaffle

ABOVE
Filet Baucher snaffle

The snaffle bit is the largest of the five bit groups. It contains a wide variety of different types of bit which vary in strength of action from very mild to severe. Snaffle bits act on the tongue, the bars and the corners of the mouth; some also act on the roof of the mouth. Snaffle bits encourage the horse to raise his head and bring it back towards your hands for greater control. In its basic form the snaffle is the most commonly used bit for horses in the early stages of schooling. Any well-schooled horse should go happily in a snaffle bit.

While all snaffles have the same basic action, different cheek- and mouthpieces will affect the action and severity of the bit. The single-jointed **eggbutt snaffle** has rounded edges where the rings join the mouthpiece to prevent the lips being pinched. The fixed cheek rings keep the bit relatively still in the horse's mouth.

The rings of the **loose-ring snaffle** allow the bit to move more freely in the horse's mouth, which some horses prefer. This type should be fitted slightly wider than the eggbutt snaffle, and can have rubber bit guards fitted over the rings to prevent it from pinching the horse's lips.

The **full-cheek snaffle** has extended cheekpieces which prevent the bit from sliding through the horse's mouth, and help to steer the horse by bringing pressure against the side of his face. This type of bit should be fitted with leather **fulmer keepers** attached to the cheekpieces of the bridle, to hold the bit still in the mouth and to prevent a cheekpiece from accidentally getting stuck up the horse's nostril. The **fulmer snaffle** is similar to the full-cheek but has loose, rather than fixed, bit rings.

The **half-spoon cheek snaffle** has spoon-shaped cheeks which extend downwards to put pressure on the outside of the lower jaw, helping with steering. The **D-ring snaffle** is often used on racehorses in preference to a fulmer snaffle. Like the fulmer, the shape of the cheekpieces prevents the bit being pulled through the mouth. By bringing pressure on the sides of the horse's face it can also help to steer the horse.

The **Filet Baucher** or **hanging cheek snaffle** has separate rings to which the cheekpieces of the bridle are attached so that the bit is suspended in the horse's mouth. Unlike other snaffles, the cheekpieces will exert some pressure on the horse's poll.

ABOVE
fulmer keepers

TYPES OF MOUTHPIECE

Snaffle bits come with a variety of mouthpieces which vary in the severity of their action.

The **straight bar mouthpiece** usually comes with non-riding bits such as stallion-showing bits or in-hand bits, and acts primarily on the tongue and lips.

The **mullen mouth** is a mild, simple unjointed mouthpiece, more curved than the straight bar. The mullen mouth rests on the bars of the mouth, exerting less pressure on the corners of the mouth and a more uniform pressure on the tongue.

When pressure is applied to the reins, the **single-jointed bit** squeezes the corners of the mouth in a nutcracker action, as well as applying pressure to the bars, the tongue and the roof of the mouth. Single-jointed snaffles have either a narrow, solid mouthpiece or fatter hollow mouthpiece (this latter type is known as the German snaffle). As a general rule of thumb, the fatter the mouthpiece, the milder its action.

Double-jointed mouthpieces feature a central link, which comes in different shapes and sizes. The nutcracker action is less severe than with single-jointed bits. However, these bits still act on the bars and corners of the horse's mouth.

The **French link** has a kidney-shaped link in the middle of the mouthpiece. It increases the flexibility of the bit, stops the horse from leaning and encourages him to soften his mouth.

The **Dr Bristol** incorporates a flat plate link which is much more severe in action than the French link. It is used in vigorous competition events such as jumping or cross-country. The plate applies strong pressure on the horse's tongue unless the head is carried in the position needed for the rider to control him. No small amount of pain will be inflicted on the horse if the bit is misused and it should only be used by experienced riders on particularly boisterous horses.

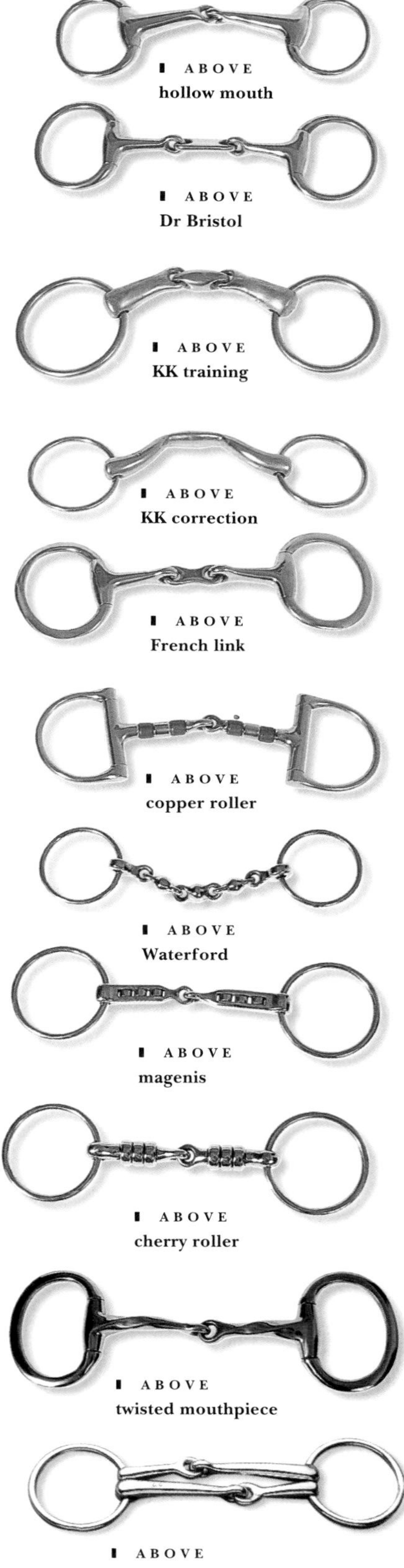

ABOVE hollow mouth

ABOVE Dr Bristol

ABOVE KK training

ABOVE KK correction

ABOVE French link

ABOVE copper roller

ABOVE Waterford

ABOVE magenis

ABOVE cherry roller

ABOVE twisted mouthpiece

ABOVE W or double mouthpiece

The **KK training bit** has a central lozenge-shaped link which is designed to shift pressure away from the lips and corners towards the centre of the horse's mouth to give a milder bit action.

The **Waterford bit** has a multi-jointed mouthpiece made up of a series of bulbous links. Because of the number of links, this mouthpiece is extremely flexible, which discourages the horse from leaning on it.

Roller mouthpieces feature a series of rollers in either steel or steel and copper. Because of the movement, these mouthpieces are used to discourage the horse from leaning on the rider's hands. There are two main types of roller mouthpieces: the **magenis** is a strong bit which features small rollers set into a squared-off mouthpiece; the **cherry roller** has rollers across the length of the mouthpiece and will encourage the horse to play with the bit, keeping his mouth relaxed. The more rounded shape of the mouthpiece means it has a kinder action than the magenis. Another roller mouthpiece, the **copper roller**, is similar to the cherry roller except that the rollers alternate between copper and steel. The copper is included to encourage the horse to salivate and relax his jaw.

The **twisted mouthpiece** is very severe, putting sharp pressure on the horse's tongue and the corners of his mouth.

Ported mouthpieces allow more room for the horse's tongue than other types of mouthpiece, while placing more contact on the bars. Bits with a high port will also act on the roof of the horse's mouth, causing the horse to raise his head.

The **KK correction bit** is a training bit made from Aurigan (a copper alloy) and is designed for strong, pulling horses.

The **W** or **double mouthpiece** has two thin, single-jointed mouthpieces attached to a set of bit rings. Strong bits like this are best left to expert riders because of the damage they can do to the horse's mouth.

Double Bits

Double bits are a combination of two bits: the **bridoon** (a snaffle bit) and a **curb bit**, also known as a **Weymouth**, which is fitted with a curb chain. The bridoon acts in exactly the same way as the snaffle, raising the horse's head, while the curb bit acts on the horse's poll and curb groove. Combining these two bits in one bridle enables you to fine tune your horse's head and neck carriage. A double bridle is used on horses who are already well schooled, particularly for dressage. It is also considered the correct bridle for the show ring. The curb bit comes with a mullen or ported mouthpiece. The length of the cheekpieces on curb bits varies but in general, the longer the cheekpieces, the greater the poll pressure.

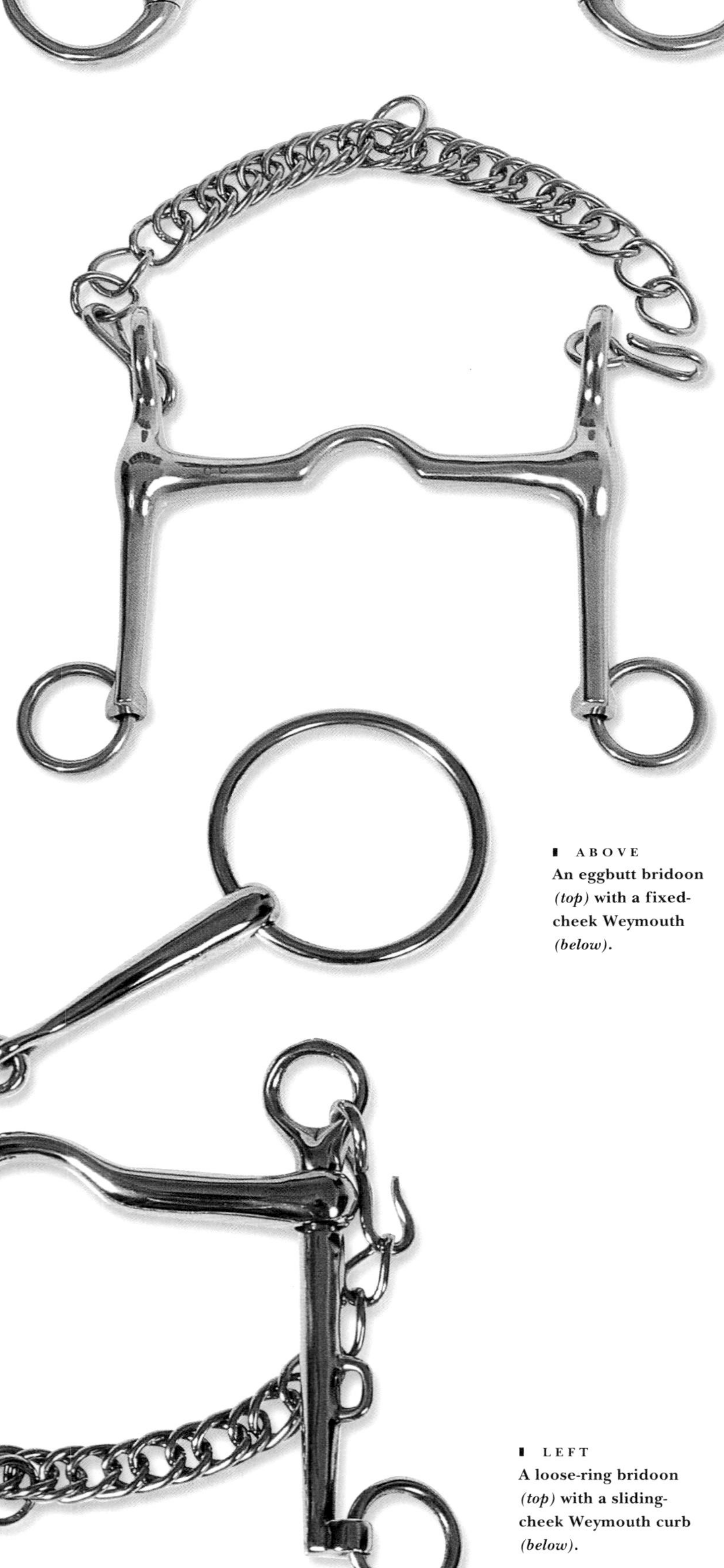

ABOVE
An eggbutt bridoon *(top)* with a fixed-cheek Weymouth *(below)*.

LEFT
A loose-ring bridoon *(top)* with a sliding-cheek Weymouth curb *(below)*.

Pelham Bits

The pelham is a compromise between a snaffle and a double bridle, combining the actions of both. As well as exerting pressure on the horse's mouth, pelhams also act on the poll and curb groove. Unlike the double bridle, it has only one mouthpiece and can be ridden with pelham roundings, the short pieces of leather linking the top and bottom rings, so that only one set of reins is needed (although it is more correct to ride with two). It is ideal for a show horse whose mouth is too small for a double bridle.

The **mullen-mouthed pelham** is the most popular pelham mouthpiece and also the mildest in action. The **jointed pelham** is very strong, the jointed mouthpiece having a direct action on the horse's tongue. The **Rugby pelham** has a loose-ring link for the bridoon rein, and as a consequence it brings greater pressure on the horse's curb and poll. The **Scamperdale pelham** is ideal for horses with fleshy lips. The mouthpiece is shaped so that it bends back at either end. This helps to keep the cheekpieces of the bit away from the horse's lips to prevent chafing. Unlike most other pelhams, the **globe pelham** is fitted with only one set of reins, which are attached to the lower rings.

The **kimblewick**, also known as the **Kimberwicke** or **Spanish jumping bit**, comes into the category of pelhams although it has less leverage action than a pelham and is ridden with only one set of reins. The **slotted-cheek kimblewick** (shown here with a hinged, copper, quarter-moon mouthpiece) enables you to choose at what height to attach the reins. The lower they are fitted, the greater the curb action of the bit. The **rounded-cheek kimblewick** has a similar action to a snaffle bit when the rider's hands are held high: lowering the hands emphasizes the curb action.

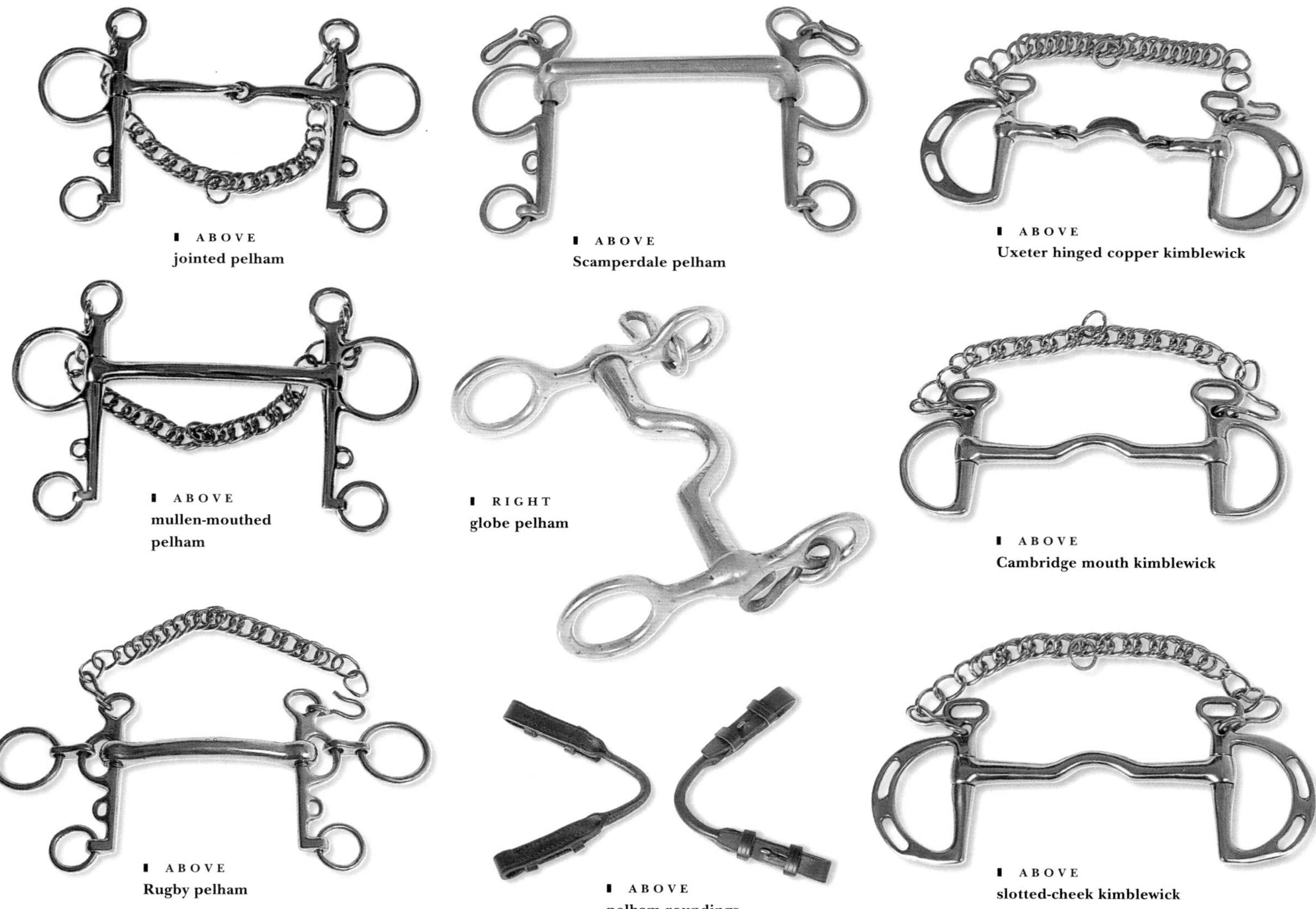

ABOVE
jointed pelham

ABOVE
Scamperdale pelham

ABOVE
Uxeter hinged copper kimblewick

ABOVE
mullen-mouthed pelham

RIGHT
globe pelham

ABOVE
Cambridge mouth kimblewick

ABOVE
Rugby pelham

ABOVE
pelham roundings

ABOVE
slotted-cheek kimblewick

Gag Snaffles

This group of bits encourages the horse to raise his head by raising the bit in his mouth, as well as acting on the corners of the mouth and the poll. Gag snaffles are popular bits for strong, fit horses ridden across country and for those who like to put their heads down and gallop off. Like the pelham, the gag snaffle should be fitted with two sets of reins (although they can be used with only one set, attached to the roundings). One set is attached to the bit ring like a snaffle, the second set to the roundings which pass from the cheekpieces through the bit rings. This enables the rider to utilize the strong gag action only when it is actually needed.

The **Balding gag** has loose-ring cheekpieces through which gag roundings pass. The **Cheltenham gag** is similar in design but features eggbutt bit rings. With both types of gag, the larger the bit ring, the more severe the bit's action.

The **half-ring**, or **Duncan gag**, is a particularly strong type of gag as it can only be used with one set of reins, which is fitted to the gag roundings.

The **Dutch gag**, also called the **continental** or **three-ring gag**, can be used with one or two sets of reins. The bridle cheekpieces are attached to the top rings to produce poll pressure. The reins can be fitted to any of the three lower rings: the lower the reins are fitted, the stronger the leverage action on the horse's mouth.

The **American gag** should also be used with two sets of reins (one set fitted to the central rings and the other fitted to the lower rings). As the gag (lower) rein is used, the mouthpiece slides up the cheekpieces, encouraging the horse to raise his head.

Gag roundings, or **running cheeks**, are leather or nylon straps which are attached to the cheekpieces of the bridle and then passed through the bit rings and attached directly to the reins. As the rider takes a contact on the reins, the bit slides up the roundings and the horse's head is raised.

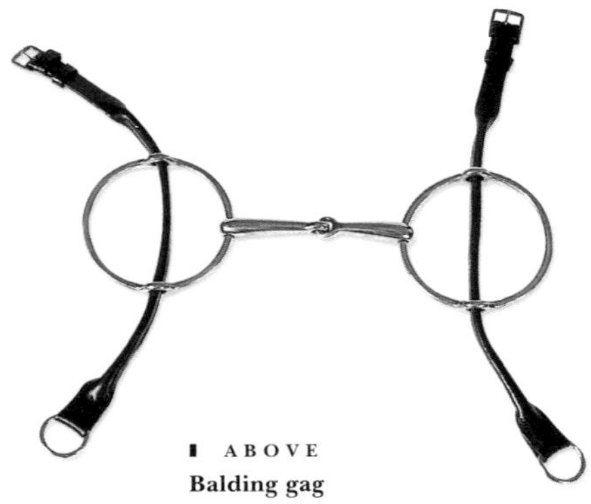

ABOVE
Balding gag

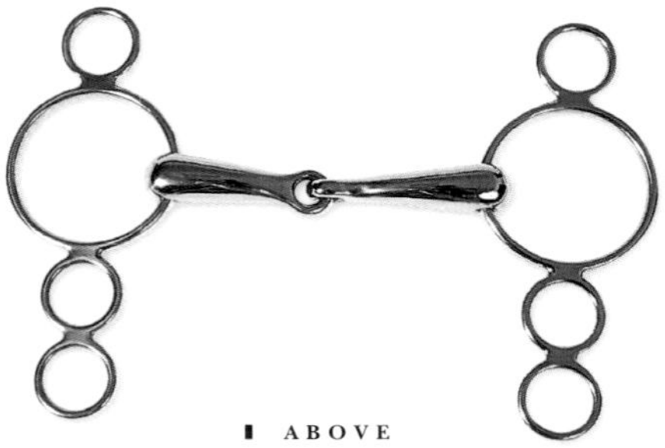

ABOVE
Dutch gag

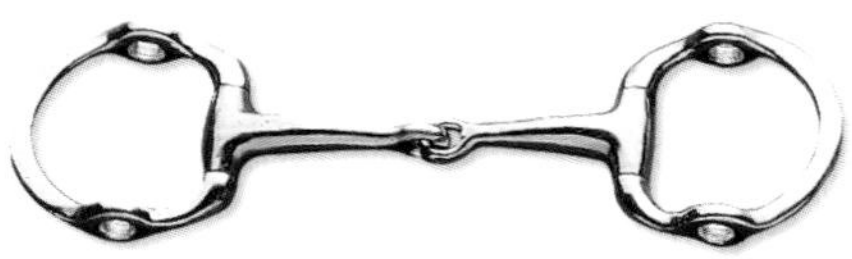

ABOVE
Cheltenham gag

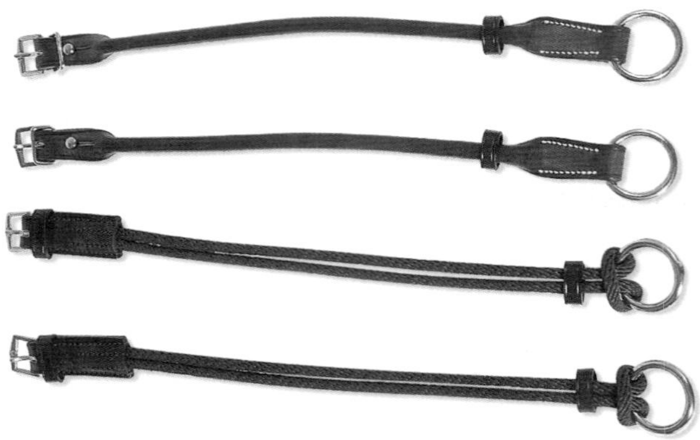

ABOVE
Gag roundings: the top two are of leather, the bottom two are nylon.

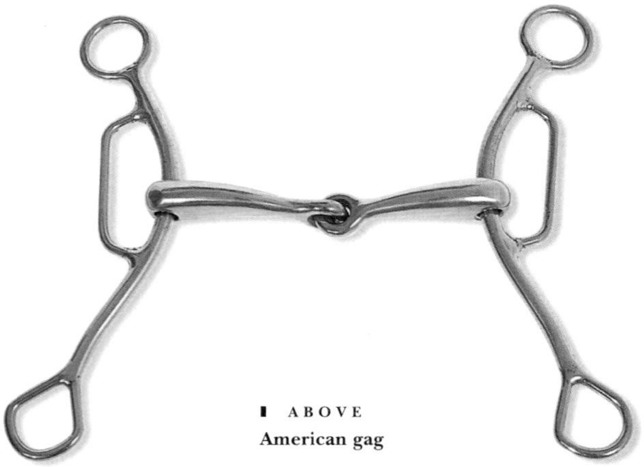

ABOVE
American gag

The Bitless Bridle

Although not a bit at all, bitless bridles, also known as hackamores, make up the fifth bit group. Instead of acting on the horse's mouth, bitless bridles apply pressure to the horse's nose as well as to the poll and curb groove. They can be used on horses who have injured their mouths but need to be kept in ridden work. Although bitless bridles have no influence on the horse's mouth, they can still be severe in inexperienced hands.

The **English pattern** or **Blair hackamore** has a padded noseband, metal cheeks and a leather curb strap (which is fitted slightly higher than a normal curb chain). Take care when fitting the English hackamore: if it is too high, the cheekpieces may rub the horse's cheeks; if it is too low, it can interfere with his breathing.

The **German hackamore** has a rubber-covered metal noseband, often worn padded with sheepskin, and a curb chain . The longer cheekpieces of the German hackamore have a stronger leverage action than the English pattern. Both types of hackamore can be used in conjunction with a bit by simply adding an extra sliphead to the bridle.

The **bosal** forms an integral part of Western training and riding. It is usually made from plaited (braided) rawhide and is used with a normal or one-ear bridle. The reins are attached directly to the "heel" knot at the back of the bridle.

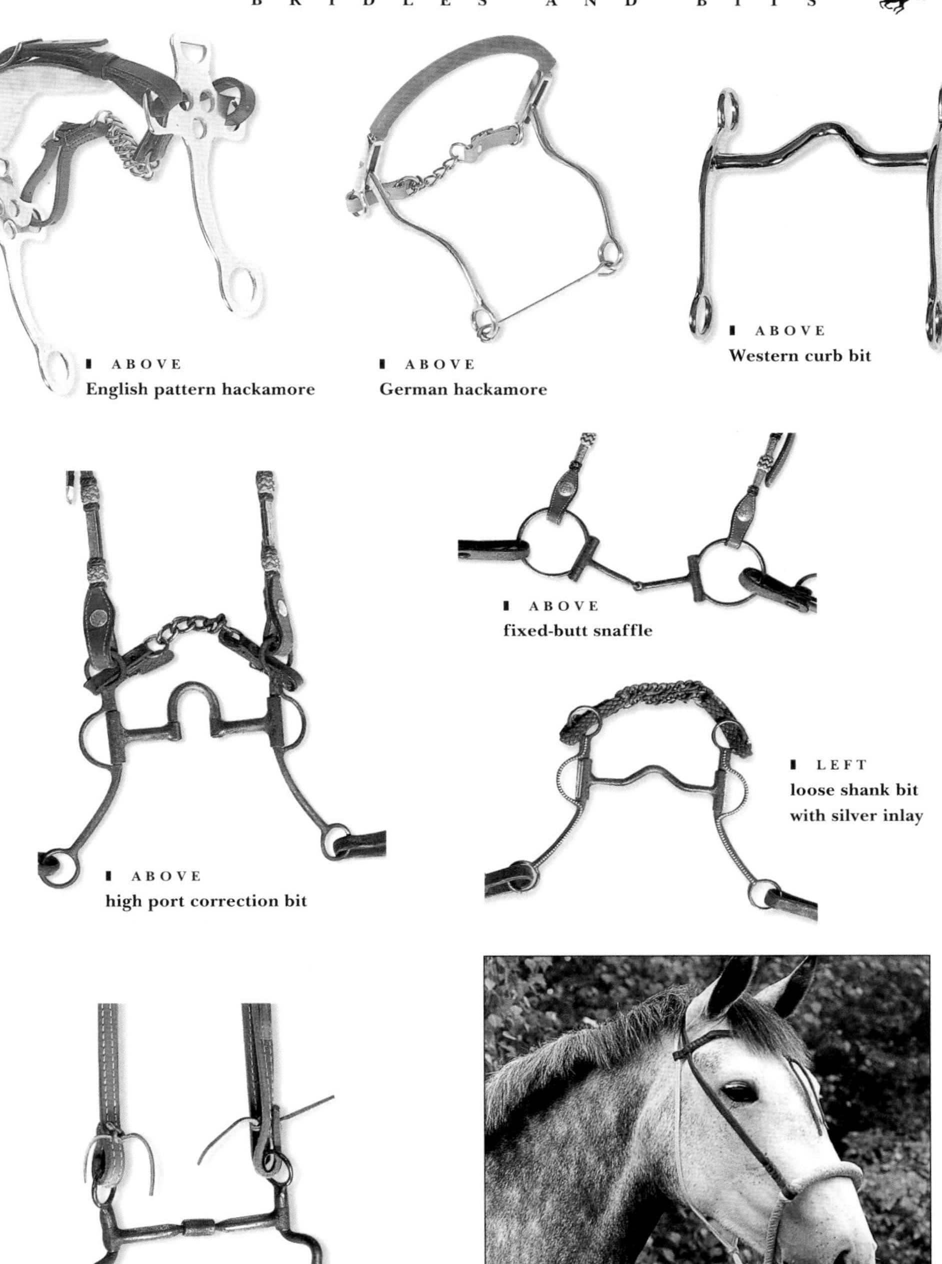

ABOVE
English pattern hackamore

ABOVE
German hackamore

ABOVE
Western curb bit

ABOVE
fixed-butt snaffle

ABOVE
high port correction bit

LEFT
loose shank bit with silver inlay

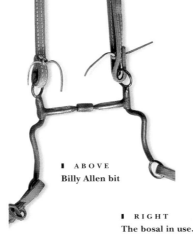

ABOVE
Billy Allen bit

RIGHT
The bosal in use.

WESTERN BITS

With their long cheekpieces and ported mouthpieces **Western curb bits** can appear severe, but in practice the Western horse is ridden with such a light contact that this is not the case. The horse is systematically trained, first using a bosal, then a combination of bosal and bit, and finally a bit alone. Western riders traditionally ride with just the weight of the rein itself maintaining the contact. Western bits are usually made out of sweet iron. This is "warmer" than stainless steel, and the rusting that naturally occurs encourages the horse to salivate.

The **high port correction bit** has loose shanks which allow the cheekpieces to swivel at the butt of the mouthpiece. The high port acts on the roof of the horse's mouth when a contact is taken.

The **low port bit** has silver inlay, a chain and a plaited (braided) nylon curb strap. The angle of the shank on the bit determines the severity of the leverage action, with a more angled shank giving a milder leverage action.

The **Billy Allen bit** has a jointed mouthpiece with a central roller, which lessens the nutcracker action of the mouthpiece. It is used as a transitional bit between the shank snaffle and a curb bit.

The **fixed-butt snaffle** is similar in action to an English eggbutt snaffle – the fixed butt keeps the bit still in the horse's mouth while the single joint has a nutcracker action on the horse's tongue.

Unusual Bits

There will always be bits that do not fit neatly into specific categories or those which have evolved with a specific sport in mind. Here are a few examples.

The **citation bit** forms part of a combination bit and bridling system called a Norton bridle. It has two mouthpieces, the thinner of which is attached directly to the noseband via the links on the bit rings. This is a highly specialized bit and bridle and is strictly for experienced hands only.

The **scourier** or **Cornish bit** has two sets of bit rings, one of which passes through holes in the mouthpiece. The inside rings are attached to the bridle while the outer rings are attached to the reins. This, combined with a grooved mouthpiece, results in a very severe bit.

The **Wilson snaffle**, like the scourier, has two pairs of bit rings. This bit is used for driving. Its action is similar to that of the scourier – pressure applied to the reins causes the bit rings to squeeze on the sides of the horse's mouth.

The **wind-sucking bridoon** or **flute bit** has a wide, hollow mouthpiece pierced with a series of small holes. It is designed to stop the horse from gulping down air when crib biting or wind-sucking.

The **tongue bit** incorporates a flat metal plate which prevents the horse from evading the bit by getting his tongue over the mouthpiece.

The **butterfly bit** is not a bit as such, but an attachment which clips on to the mouthpiece of an existing bit to increase the severity of its action.

The **loose-ring racing snaffle** has much larger bit rings than normal snaffles. The larger rings prevent the bit from being pulled through the horse's mouth. They can also help to steer the horse in a chosen direction by bringing pressure on the side of the face.

ABOVE **scourier**

ABOVE **tongue bit**

ABOVE **citation**

ABOVE **wind-sucking bridoon**

ABOVE **mouthing or breaking bit**

ABOVE **loose-ring racing snaffle**

ABOVE **Wilson snaffle**

ABOVE **butterfly bit**

Training and Showing Bits

Some bits are specifically designed for training young horses and for leading and showing horses in-hand.

The **chifney**, also known as an **anti-rearing bit**, consists of a ring which sits in the horse's mouth and is attached to a separate headstall. It is often used when leading stallions and racehorses in the parade ring.

The **Tattersall ring bit**, similar to the chifney, is useful for leading boisterous youngsters. The bit is held in place by a headstall which is attached to the two metal loops on either side. The lead rope is attached to the rear of the ring.

Mouthing or **breaking bits** are designed to encourage young horses to play with the mouthpiece. They can have a single or unjointed mouthpiece and feature small metal "keys" in the centre of the mouthpiece with which the young horse plays.

The **horseshoe stallion bridoon**, which looks similar to the **overcheck bridoon**, is designed for showing stallions in-hand.

ABOVE
A Thoroughbred yearling with a Tattersall ring bit fitted to a leather headcollar.

RIGHT
***Top to bottom:* chifney; Tattersall ring bit; horseshoe stallion bridoon; overcheck bridoon**

BIT MATERIALS

Bits are available in a wide variety of metals, alloys and synthetic materials. The following materials are listed in order of common usage.
Stainless steel is strong and easy to clean. Steel is the most popular choice of bit material. One of the disadvantages of steel is that it is a "cold" metal which does not encourage salivation.
Rubber is used to cover metal bits to soften their action. However, rubber is not particularly hardwearing and is easily chewed.
Vulcanite or vulcanized rubber is harder wearing than rubber but heavier and not as flexible.
Polyurethane and **nylon** bits are flexible if unjointed. These materials are also used to cover jointed metal bits. A mouthpiece using polyurethane or nylon can be very mild in action and often has an apple scent to make it more appealing to horses.
Copper mouthpieces warm up to the horse's body temperature more quickly than steel but are less hardwearing. They are designed to encourage horses with dry mouths to salivate.
Copper alloy bits are designed to combine the qualities of copper with the strength of stainless steel. Manufacturers claim that they improve the contact between the rider's hands and the horse.
Brass alloy bits are claimed to have the same qualities as copper. They are a combination of brass with silicon and aluminium.
Sweet iron mouthpieces rust very quickly when allowed to get wet, thereby encouraging the horse to salivate.

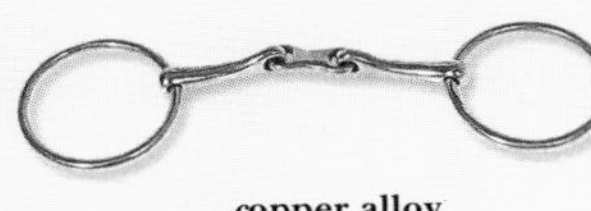

copper alloy

vulcanite

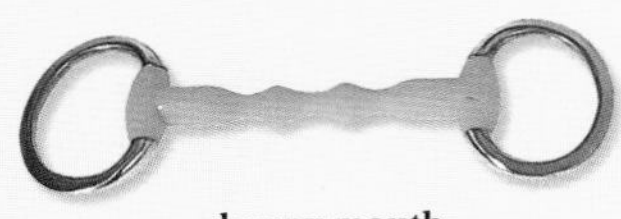

happy mouth

rubber

copper and steel

nathe

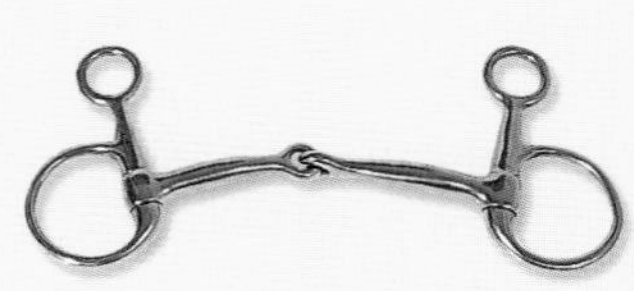

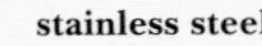

stainless steel

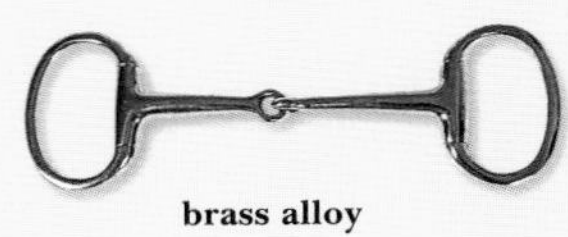

brass alloy

sweet iron

Curb Chains and Lip Straps

Curb bits and pelhams should always be fitted with a curb chain or strap. The curb chain brings pressure on the horse's curb groove. The chain or strap itself should be fitted so that it is brought into action when the shank of the curb bit is at an angle of 45 degrees.

The **Western leather curb strap** is used with a Western curb bit. The **single-link curb chain** is light in weight but, because of its design, can pinch the horse's skin; the **double-link curb chain** is preferable to the single-link type as it is less likely to do this. A **leather curb chain** is designed to be fitted to an English curb bit. The **elasticated curb chain**, like the leather curb chain, has a milder action than the metal type. The **rubber-covered chain** is more comfortable for the horse than an uncovered curb chain, and has a milder action on the curb groove.

All English curb straps or chains should be fitted with a fly ring through which a **lip strap** passes. The strap, attached to either side of the curb bit or pelham, helps to keep the curb chain in place.

Fulmer keepers are small leather straps which are fitted to the cheekpieces of a snaffle bridle. They are used to prevent the upper cheekpiece of a full-cheek snaffle from tipping forward. They also help to keep the bit raised in the horse's mouth, preventing the horse from getting his tongue over the bit.

Leather pelham roundings can be fitted to pelhams and certain types of gag bit when only one set of reins is used.

ABOVE
Western curb strap

ABOVE
double-link chain

ABOVE
single-link chain

ABOVE
leather curb chain

ABOVE
elasticated curb chain

ABOVE
rubber-covered chain

RIGHT
Lip strap fitted to a Weymouth bit.

Nosebands

Nosebands are available in a variety of designs, from those chosen purely for aesthetic reasons, to corrective nosebands which offer more control, acting in conjunction with the bit to increase the strength of the bit action or to prevent the horse evading it.

The **cavesson** is the simplest noseband design available. It is the only type of noseband to use with a double bridle and can also be used with a standing martingale. When fitted correctly, it should have little or no action on the horse's head. The cavesson should be fitted loosely enough to allow room for two fingers under the noseband.

Rope cavessons are much more severe in action than leather ones and are more commonly seen on polo ponies or strong show jumpers. The **continental** or **cinchback cavesson** is designed to be fitted

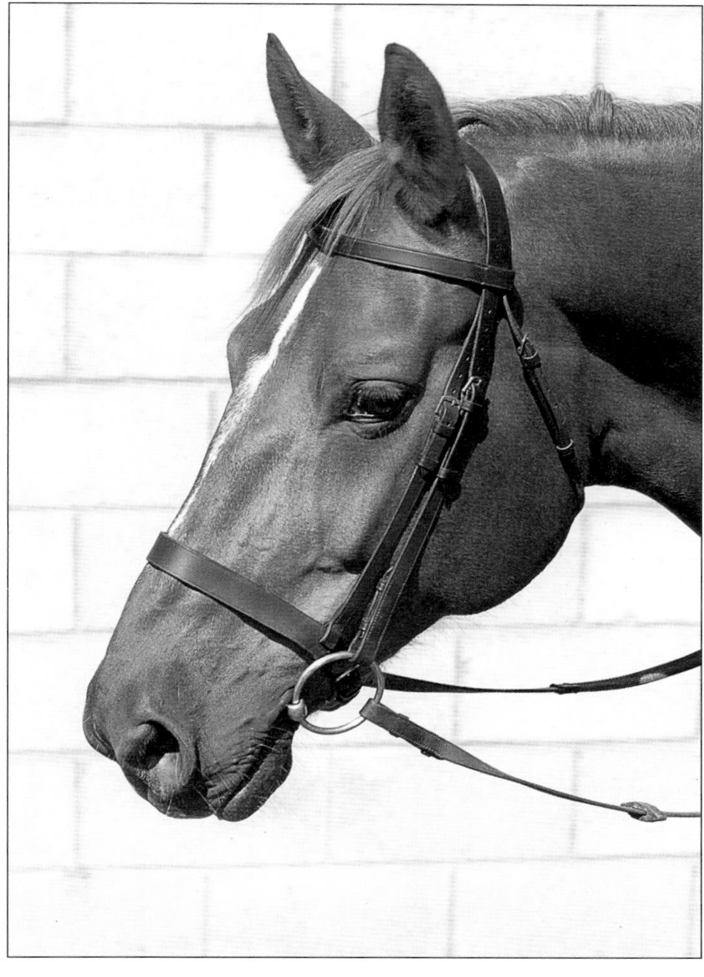

LEFT
cavesson noseband

BELOW
continental cavesson

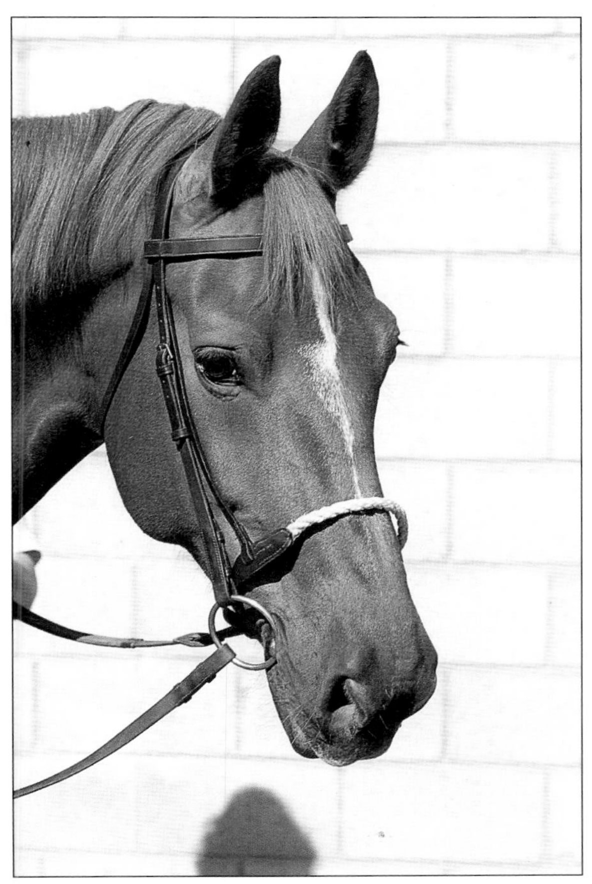

LEFT
rope cavesson noseband

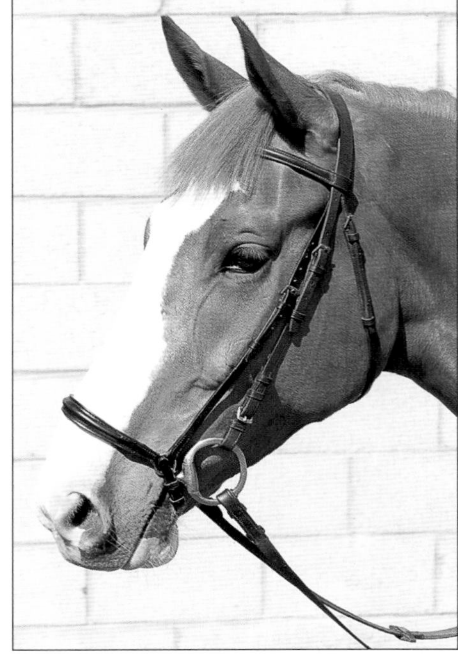

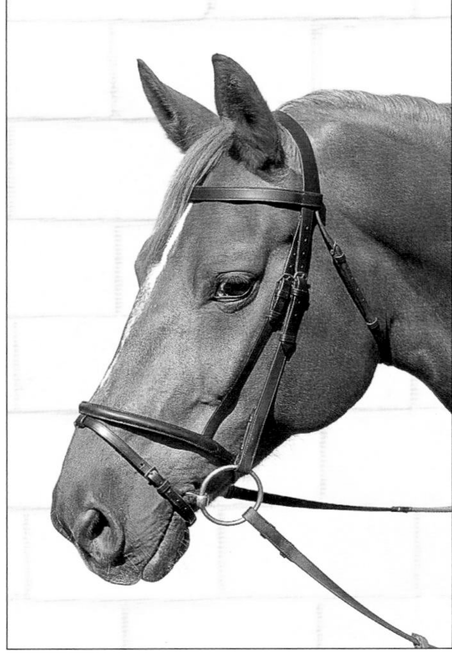

more tightly than a traditional cavesson to discourage the horse from opening his mouth. It can be used with a double bridle and for this reason is often used for dressage or showing.

The **dropped noseband** is fitted with the back strap passing below the bit. It is designed to prevent the horse from opening his mouth and evading the bit. The dropped noseband (when fitted correctly) can increase pressure on the horse's poll as well as on the nose and lower jaw. The dropped noseband should not be used if a standing martingale is fitted. Take care not to fit it below the base of the nasal bone as this can restrict the horse's breathing.

The **flash** is based on the cavesson noseband but has an additional strap which is fitted below the bit. It was originally developed for riders who wanted a noseband which closed the mouth like a dropped noseband, but which could be used alongside a standing martingale. The flash noseband is fitted slightly higher and tighter than the cavesson. Attachments are available which can transform an ordinary cavesson into a flash noseband.

The **Grakle** or **figure-of-eight** takes its name from the eponymous winner of the British 1931 Grand National steeplechase. The Grakle should be fitted snugly so that the top strap goes around the horse's jaws above the bit (resting just below the facial bone) while the lower strap passes below the bit, keeping the mouth closed. The Grakle puts pressure on the horse's nose (where the straps cross) and helps to stop the horse from crossing his jaws. Take care that the central point does not lie below the nasal bone as this will cause discomfort to the horse. There should be a short strap fitted at the back of the noseband to keep the straps in place.

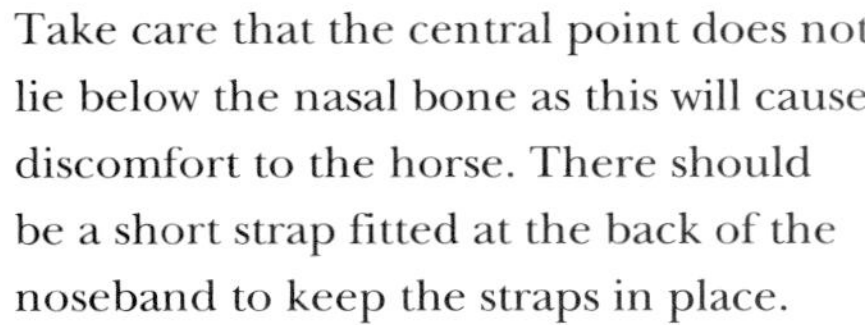

ABOVE
Left to right:
dropped noseband; flash noseband; Grakle or figure-of-eight noseband

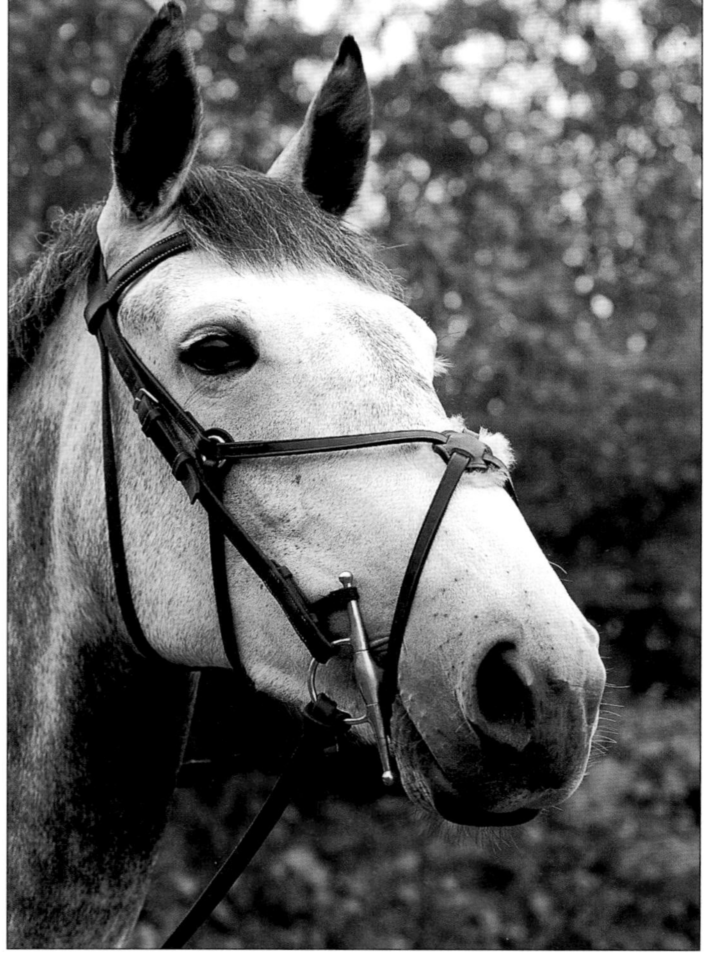

LEFT
Mexican Grakle

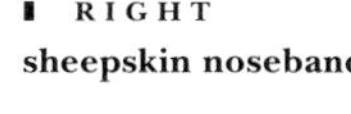

▮ BELOW
Australian cheeker

▮ RIGHT
sheepskin noseband

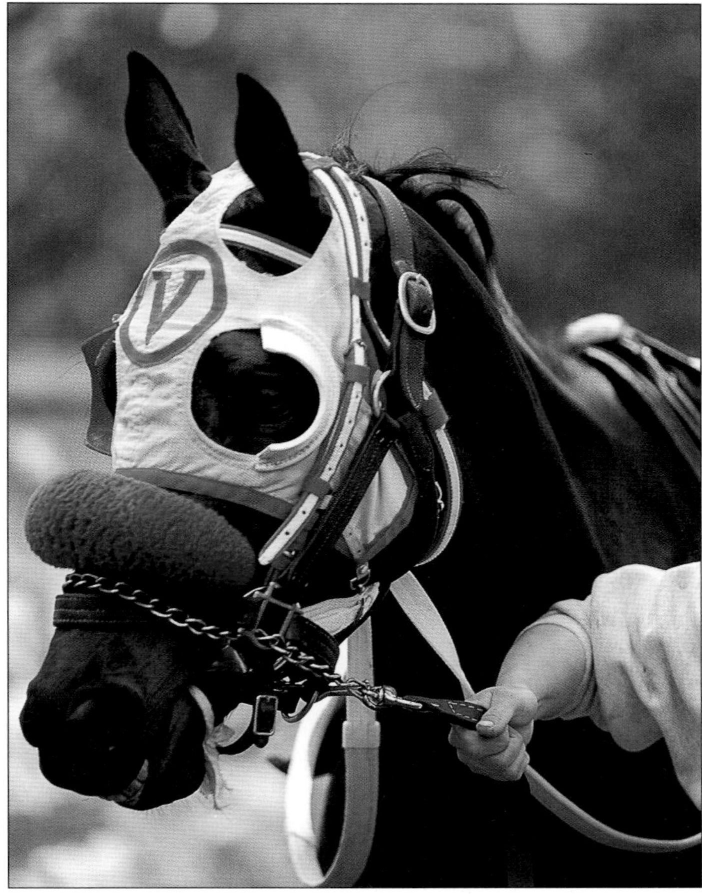

The **Mexican** or **high-ring Grakle** is fitted higher than a normal Grakle, above the cheek bones. It sits higher up the face and is thought to be more effective at preventing the horse crossing his jaws.

The **Kineton** or **Puckle noseband** is a severe noseband which derives its name from its designer, a Mr Puckle of Kineton. Metal loops pass under the bit so that when a contact is taken up, strong pressure is brought to bear on both the nose and the bit, encouraging the horse to lower his head. As with the dropped noseband, take care not to fit it too low.

The **sheepskin noseband**, often used on racehorses, is basically a cavesson noseband covered with a sheepskin sleeve. It encourages the horse to lower his head, which he must do if he is to see over the noseband.

The **Australian cheeker** is a rubber attachment which fastens to the headstall of the bridle and either side of a snaffle bit. It helps to keep the bit raised in the mouth, preventing the horse from getting his tongue over it. It is thought that being able to see the central strap encourages the horse to back off the bit.

The **controller** or **combination noseband** combines the action of a dropped and a Grakle noseband. The two straps help to keep the horse's mouth closed and discourage him from opening his mouth. The front strap is adjustable and is fitted like a dropped noseband. For very strong horses, the front strap can be reinforced with a strip of metal.

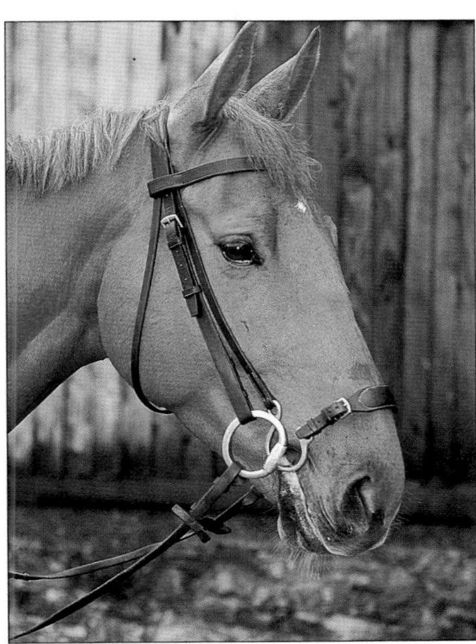

▮ BELOW LEFT
Kineton noseband

▮ BELOW RIGHT
controller noseband

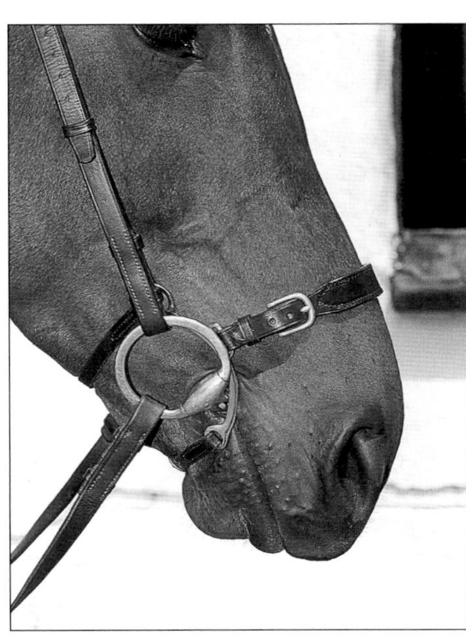

Reins

The reins provide the vital line of communication between your hands and the bit in the horse's mouth.

Plain leather reins are very smart and make an ideal choice for showing. They are often used with double bridles as they are not bulky. A thicker rein is fitted to the bridoon with a thinner rein used for the curb. A disadvantage of plain leather reins is that they can be slippery, especially if allowed to get wet. **Plain leather dressage reins** incorporate small leather "stops" which help to improve grip.

Laced leather reins have thin strips of leather laced through them to improve grip. **Plaited (braided) leather reins** are easy to grip but are more expensive than laced reins and with use they will stretch.

Rubber-covered reins are the popular choice for everyday riding because of their durability. They are very easy to grip, even when wet, and for this reason are often used for racing, eventing and general riding. **Half-rubber reins** are less slippery than plain leather ones, and are more attractive and less cumbersome than rubber-covered reins. **Continental reins** are made of webbing with leather stops to improve grip. **Rubberized webbing reins** are lightweight and incorporate rubber for improved grip.

Plaited (braided) cotton reins are light in weight and reasonably easy to grip. **Plaited (braided) nylon reins** are slightly cheaper than plaited cotton reins, but can be very slippery and will stretch easily. **Western reins** are traditionally ridden split, without being secured at the end with a buckle, to prevent the horse catching his foot if the reins trail on the ground once the rider has dismounted.

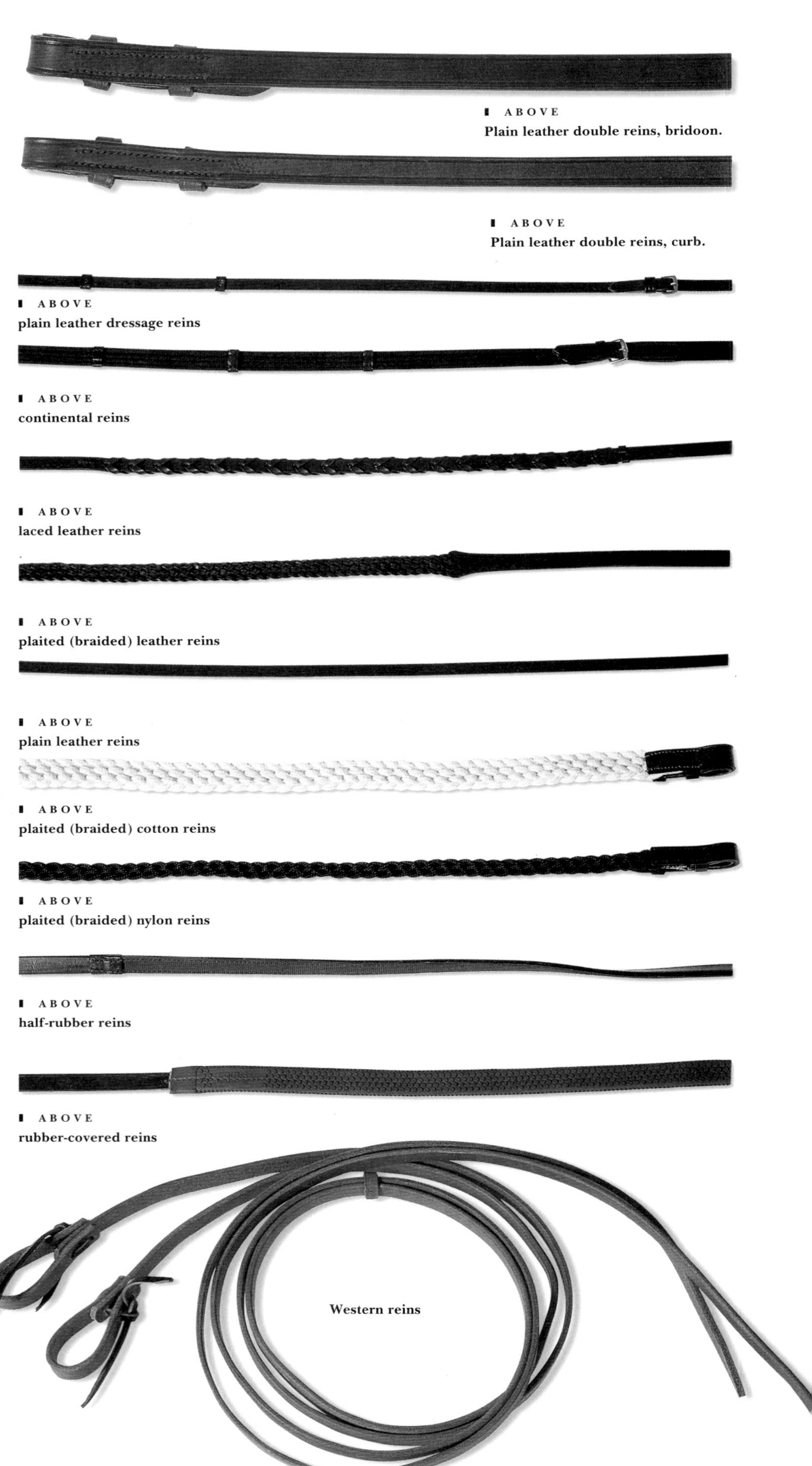

ABOVE
Plain leather double reins, bridoon.

ABOVE
Plain leather double reins, curb.

ABOVE
plain leather dressage reins

ABOVE
continental reins

ABOVE
laced leather reins

ABOVE
plaited (braided) leather reins

ABOVE
plain leather reins

ABOVE
plaited (braided) cotton reins

ABOVE
plaited (braided) nylon reins

ABOVE
half-rubber reins

ABOVE
rubber-covered reins

Western reins

Rein Attachments

There are a number of ways in which reins can be attached to the bridle, depending on the reason the horse is being tacked up. For instance in showing classes, where appearance is of the utmost importance, reins will often be stitched on to the bit. Although this makes changing the bit difficult, it does look much neater than billets (stud hooks) or buckles.

Billets are small metal hooks which fasten into a small hole in the rein to attach it to the bridle. The billet and billet hole should be checked regularly for wear and tear. **Buckles** are a secure way of attaching reins but can look bulky. Western reins are attached to the bit by **hide thongs**. **Loops** are a less secure method of fastening reins than buckles.

BELOW
Looped fastening reins

BELOW
Buckle fastening on synthetic reins.

BELOW
Western reins

BELOW
leather reins with buckle fastening

Browbands

The browband helps to keep the bridle in position on the horse's head. It is very important that the browband is fitted correctly as a browband fitted too loosely looks untidy and may not be effective in preventing the bridle from slipping back. If fitted too tightly, the browband can pinch the horse's ears, thereby forcing him to shake his head. Available in a wide range of designs, browbands are always highly decorative.

The **plain browband** is ideal for horses with heavier, coarser heads. **Padded browbands** feature a raised central section, which suits larger warmblood heads. A raised strip of coloured **plaited (braided) leather** can add contrast to an otherwise plain bridle. **Velvet-covered browbands** are available in a wide choice of colours and can be selected to match your outfit. They are popular for showing hacks and children's ponies. A delicate browband, the **plaited (braided) Arab**, is specially designed to suit the finer features of the Arab horse. **Clincher browbands** have studs (clinchers) in silver or brass. They come in all sorts of decorative designs which feature metal bobbles and small, mirrored strips. **Diamanté browbands** are popular for horses competing indoors where the light catches the stones. The **chain browband** is best suited to horses or ponies with extremely fine heads. The **bit motif browband** incorporates a gilt snaffle design. **Western browbands** can be very simple in design, with little or no ornamentation, although highly decorative browbands with silver detailing are often used for showing or parades. Not all Western bridles feature browbands: the one ear and split ear bridles do not require a browband to keep them in place.

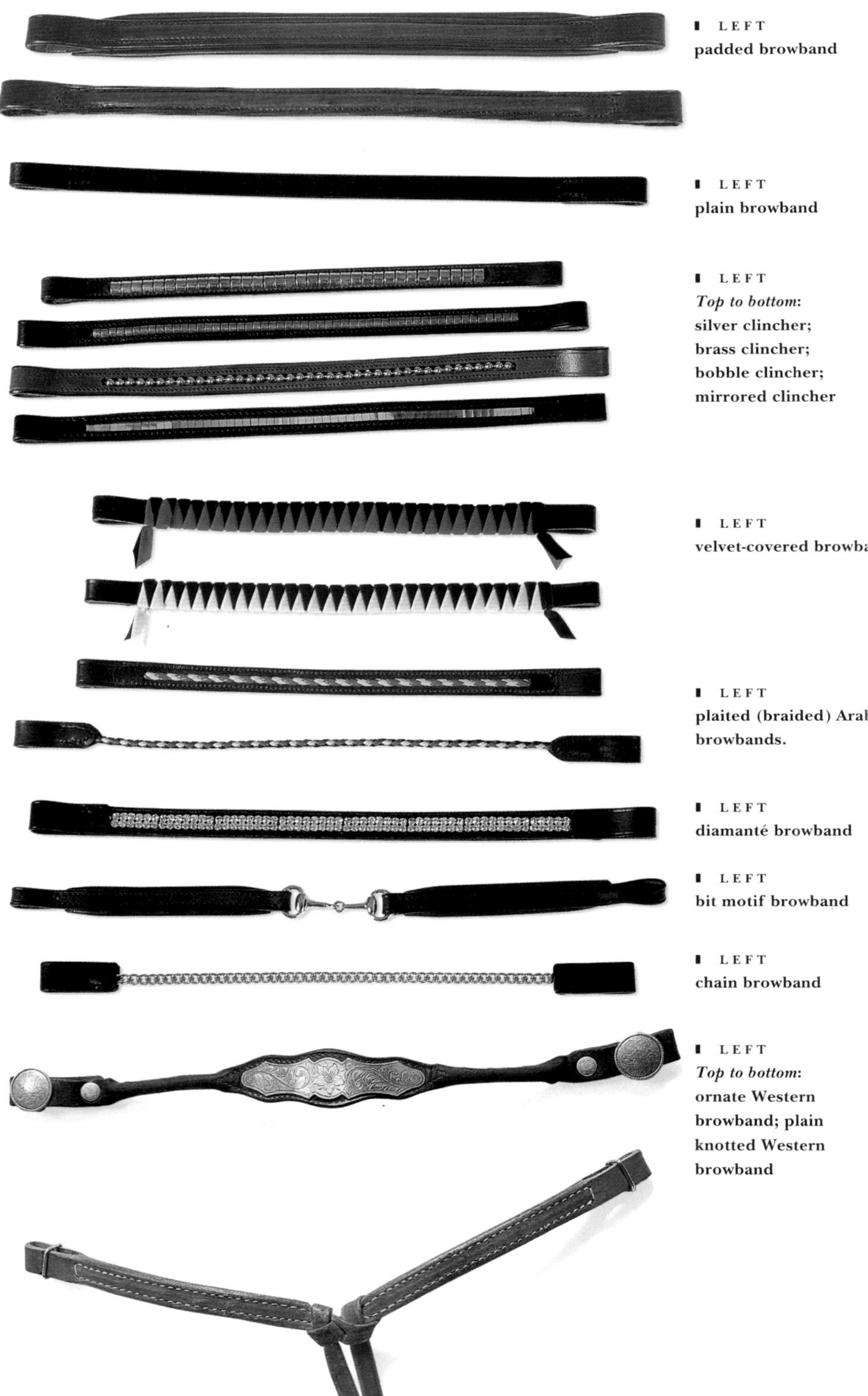

LEFT **padded browband**

LEFT **plain browband**

LEFT ***Top to bottom*: silver clincher; brass clincher; bobble clincher; mirrored clincher**

LEFT **velvet-covered browband**

LEFT **plaited (braided) Arab browbands.**

LEFT **diamanté browband**

LEFT **bit motif browband**

LEFT **chain browband**

LEFT ***Top to bottom*: ornate Western browband; plain knotted Western browband**

Bridle Accessories

There is a range of items which can be fitted to the horse's bridle or halter. Many of these pieces are corrective items designed to discourage the horse from a bad habit, while some are aids to improve his comfort.

RIGHT
Bit guards are rubber disks which can be fitted to loose-ring bits to prevent them from pinching the horse's lips. They also help to keep the bit positioned centrally in the horse's mouth.

BELOW
The pricker pad is a leather pad with sharp bristles. It is fitted to one side of the bit against the side of the horse's face to discourage the horse from leaning to one side.

ABOVE
Blinkers are mainly used on racehorses. They block the horse's view to either side, helping him to concentrate and thus improve his racing performance.

ABOVE
A face net is a fine mesh net which is fitted over the horse's head. It can help protect the horse from flies when he is turned out in the field.

ABOVE
Rein stops should always be fitted when a martingale is used. They stop the martingale rings slipping down towards the bit and getting stuck.

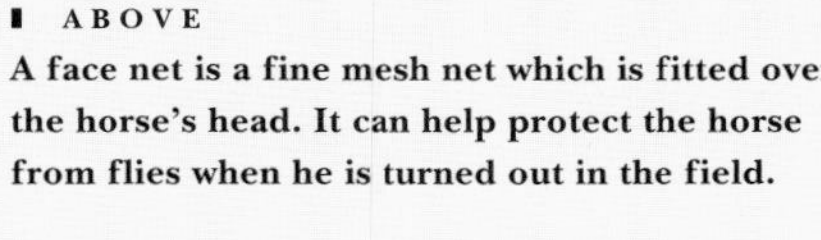

RIGHT
Martingale stops are fitted to running and standing martingales to stop the central strap slipping through the chestpiece.

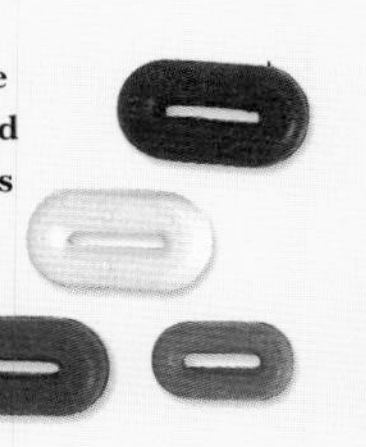

RIGHT
The tongue guard is a rubber attachment which fastens to the bit. It is used to prevent the horse getting his tongue over the bit.

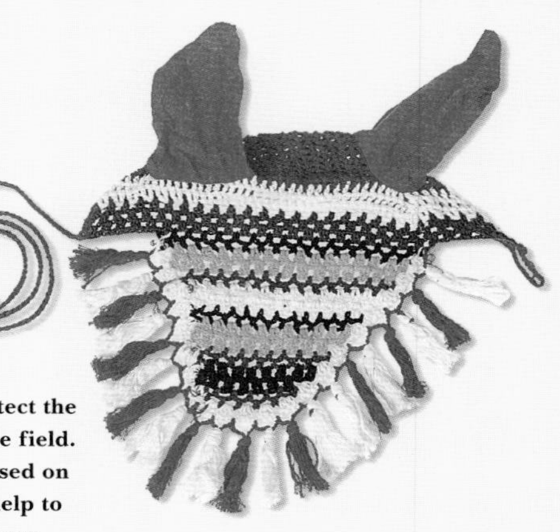

ABOVE AND RIGHT
Fly fringes are attached to the bridle to protect the horse's face from flies when ridden or in the field. The type with earpieces is also sometimes used on show jumpers competing indoors as it can help to muffle spectator noise. A simpler fly fringe can be fitted to the horse's headcollar to protect him from flies when turned out in the field.

Putting on a Bridle

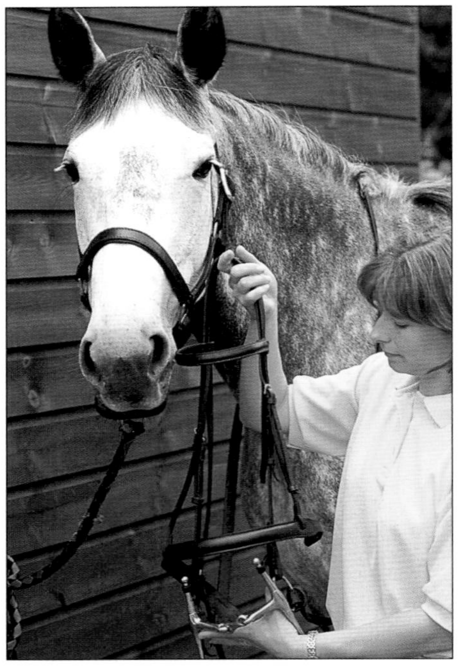

1 Stand on the near (left) side of the horse and hold the headpiece (crownpiece) of the bridle in your right hand. Place your left hand (holding the bit) under the horse's muzzle.

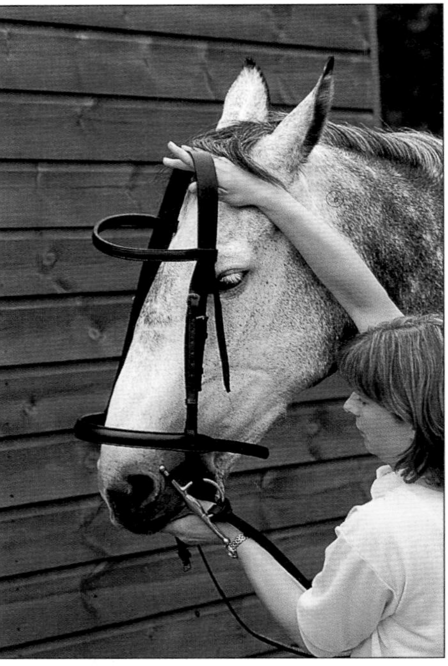

2 Press your thumb firmly but gently against the bars of the horse's mouth to encourage him to open his mouth.

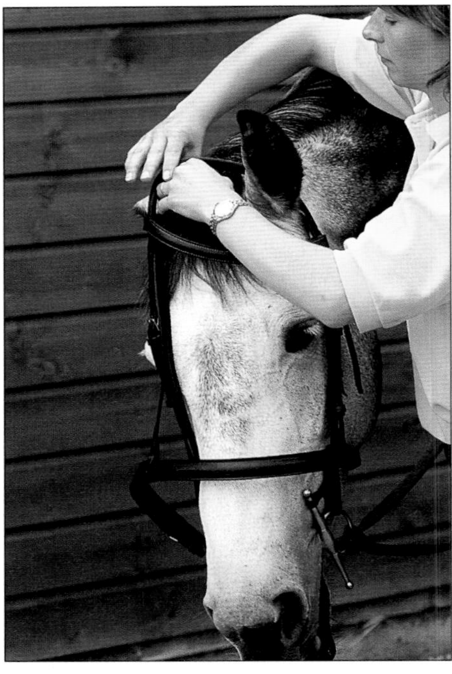

3 Guide the bit gently into the horse's mouth, taking care not to bang it against his teeth. Draw the bridle up with the right hand and, using the left hand, guide the left and then the right ear under the headpiece of the bridle.

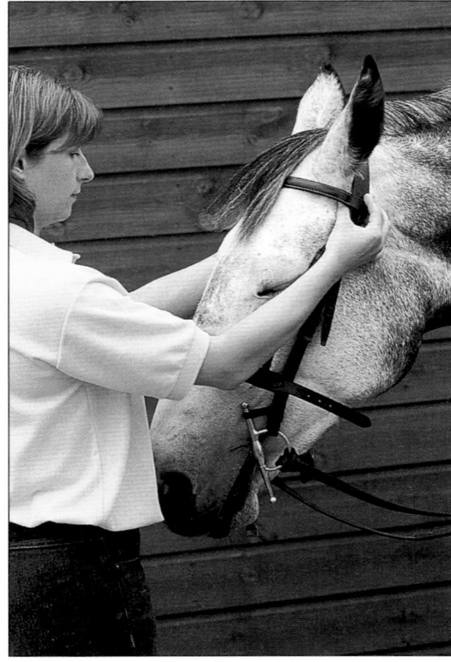

4 Separate the mane under the headpiece (a small section of mane, called a bridle path, can be clipped from this area) and bring the forelock out over the browband.

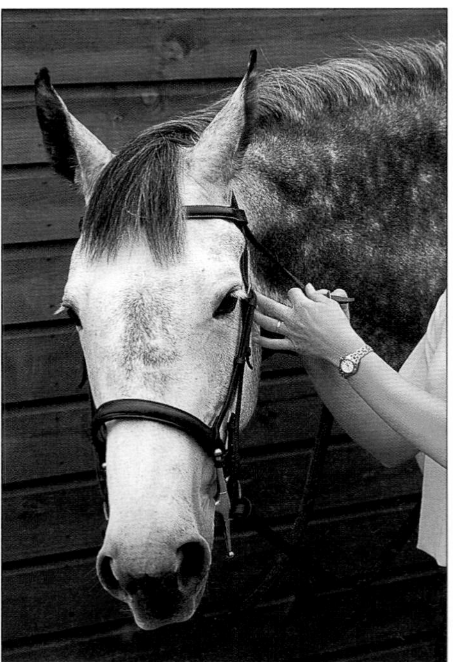

5 Fasten the throatlatch. It should be loose enough to allow you to fit four fingers between the throatlatch and the horse's cheeks.

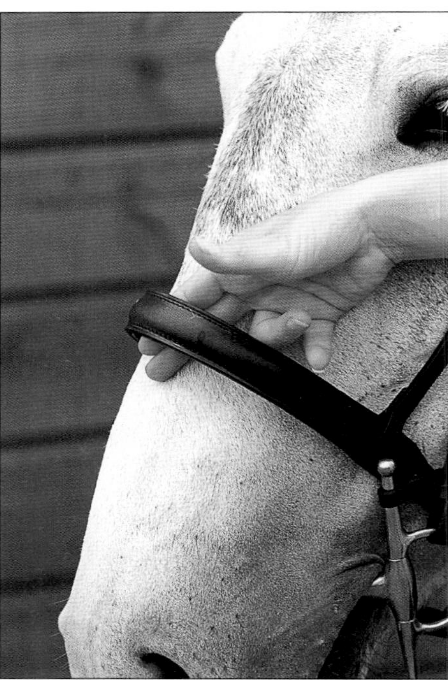

6 Fasten the noseband (in this case a cavesson) so that it passes underneath the cheekpieces of the bridle. It should be loose enough to allow you to place two fingers underneath the noseband.

Bridle Care

A leather bridle should be cleaned regularly to keep it in top condition and to prolong its life. Remove sweat and grime every time the bridle is used and once a week dismantle it completely for a thorough cleaning. A synthetic bridle can be simply wiped down with a damp cloth or immersed in water. Check the stitching and billets (stud hooks) regularly, paying particular attention to where the bit is attached to the bridle at the reins and the cheekpieces.

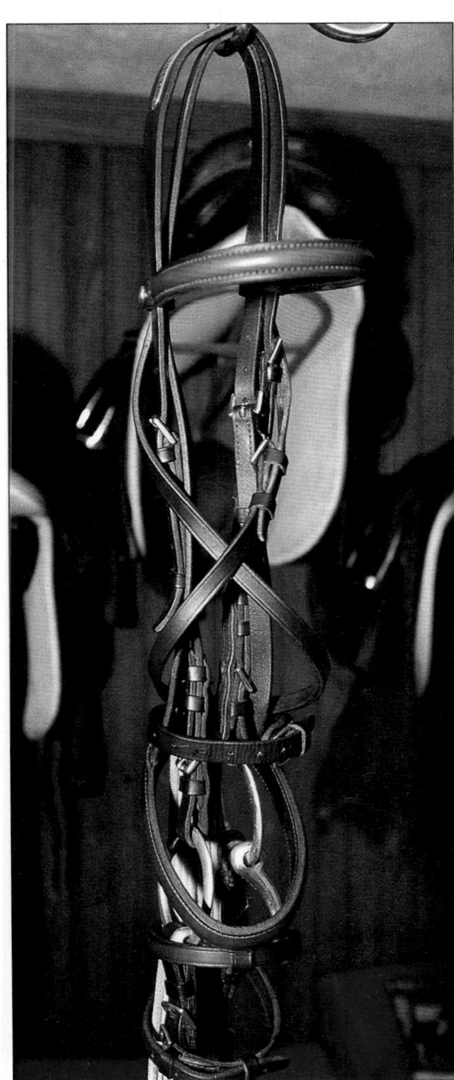

A correctly put up bridle. Cross the throatlatch over the front of the bridle, loop up the reins and fasten the noseband around it.

CLEANING THE BRIDLE

1 Hang the bridle from a suitable hook, undoing all the straps from their keepers.

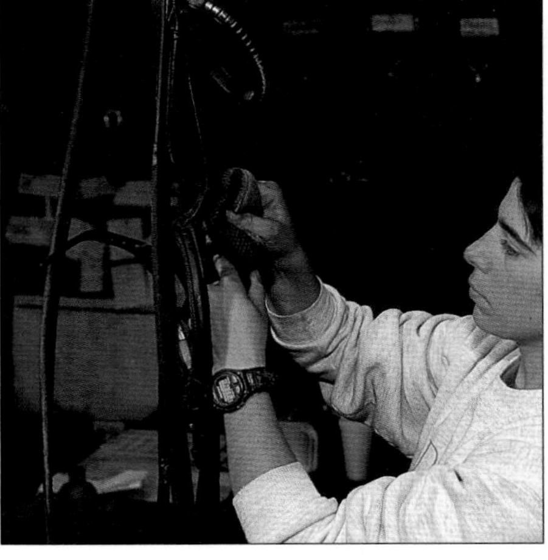

2 Wipe the bridle down with a damp sponge to remove dirt and grease.

3 Use a clean sponge to rub in lightly moistened saddle soap.

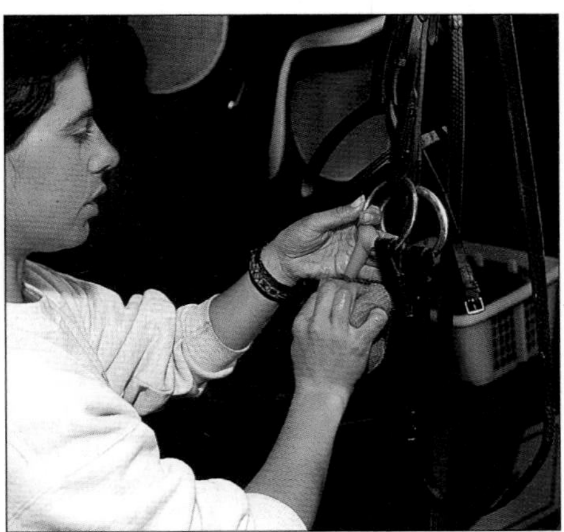

4 Wipe the bit, or rinse it under running water. Do this each time it has been used to prevent a build-up of saliva and food.

LEFT
Jockeys will often tie a knot at the end of the reins. This is a safety measure in case the buckle joining the reins were to break during the race.

Training Aids and Gadgets

There is a saying that gadgets and training aids are fine in the hands of experts but that experts have no need for them. This may apply in an ideal world but every horseman or woman, however expert, will encounter problems when schooling and training horses and may occasionally need additional help in the form of an aid or a gadget.

A training aid is a piece of equipment used to develop a well-schooled, obedient horse to improve his performance, while a gadget is a piece of equipment which prevents or restrains an aspect of the horse's behaviour which makes him dangerous or difficult to ride.

A degree of skill is required when using training aids or gadgets. The equipment must be fitted correctly, and you must be aware of its strength and severity. Only use it when it is specifically required, never as a matter of course. Training aids and gadgets in the wrong hands can damage the horse physically and psychologically.

Martingales

Martingales are designed to assist the bridle in controlling the horse. They prevent the horse from raising his head beyond the point at which the rider can control him.

The **running martingale** consists of a neck strap and a second strap which is attached to the girth and passes between the horse's front legs before dividing into two pieces. At the end of each of these straps is a small metal ring through which the reins pass. **Rein stops** should be fitted to the reins, below the bit, to prevent the martingale rings from getting caught on the bit. When the horse carries his head in the correct position no pressure is felt. However, when he raises his head above a certain point, the martingale restricts the movement of the reins which in turn causes the bit to bear down on the bars of the horse's mouth. The running martingale should be fitted so that the rings are in line with the withers to prevent it putting any pressure on the reins when the horse's head is held in the correct position. It should not be used in conjunction with a curb bit.

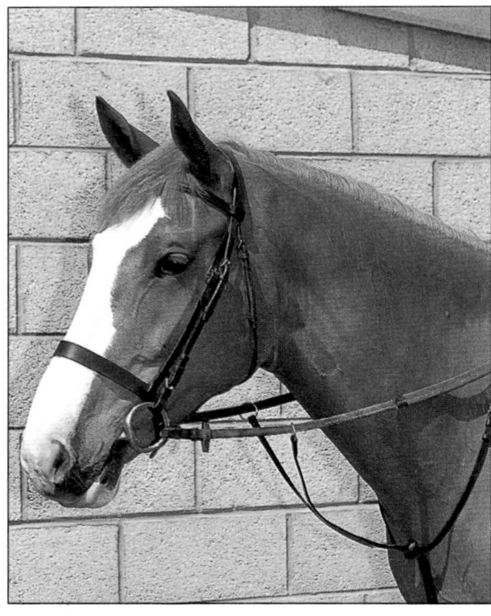

ABOVE
running martingale

BELOW LEFT
combined breastplate and martingale

BELOW RIGHT
bib martingale

The **bib martingale** is a variation on the running martingale. The two straps of the martingale are joined by a triangle of leather. This is to prevent an excitable horse from getting caught up in the straps; the design is often used on racehorses.

The **combined breastplate and martingale** is a traditional heavyweight hunting-style breastplate used to stop the saddle from slipping back. The breastplate has a central ring to which a running martingale attachment is fixed.

The **standing martingale** has a single strap which is attached to the girth, passes between the horse's front legs and is fixed to the back of the noseband (a cavesson or the cavesson part of a flash noseband). Like the running martingale, it has a neck strap. When correctly fitted it should be possible to push the martingale strap up into the horse's gullet.

LEFT
standing martingale

LEFT AND BELOW
The Irish martingale is used to prevent the reins being thrown over the horse's head in the event of a fall. It is often used on racehorses, as shown here on Desert Orchid.

A **rubber martingale stop** should always be fitted to running and standing martingales to stop the martingale from slipping through the neck strap, which could result in the horse getting a foot caught in the straps.

The **Market Harborough** consists of a leather strap attached to the girth, which passes between the horse's front legs before dividing into two straps with a clip at each end. These straps pass through the bit rings and are clipped on to one of a series of rings on the side of the reins. Like the running martingale, the Market Harborough will only put pressure on the bit (and as a consequence on the bars of the horse's mouth) if the horse brings his head up beyond a certain point. The Market Harborough should only be used with an ordinary snaffle.

The **Irish martingale**, unlike other martingales, has no direct action on the horse's head carriage. It consists of a short piece of leather with a ring at either end through which the reins pass. The Irish martingale is used to prevent the reins from being pulled over the horse's head in the event of a fall. It can also be used for horses who have a habit of suddenly tossing their heads in the air – "star gazers" – resulting in the reins being thrown over their heads.

LEFT
Market Harborough martingale

Training Reins

Training reins are used when schooling the horse to help him develop the correct musculature for ridden work, or as a corrective aid to encourage the horse to carry himself well.

Running reins, also known as **draw reins**, are long pieces of leather or webbing with a loop at each end which fit around either side of the girth; the reins pass through the bit rings (from the inside to the outside) and up to the rider's hands. Running reins encourage the horse to lower his head, bringing it towards the vertical to promote the correct development of his back muscles. Running reins should only be used with an ordinary snaffle bridle to which an independent set of reins is also attached, and the rider must be quick to release the pressure on the running reins when the horse lowers his head. It is important that the horse is ridden forwards or there is a danger that he will become over-bent (with his head held behind the vertical).

A more severe method of fitting running reins is to attach them to the girth at the chest before passing them through the front legs up to the bit and back to the rider's hands. Fitted in this way the running reins (more correctly referred to as draw reins) impart a stronger leverage action on the horse's head.

An **overcheck rein** has a centre buckle and passes over the horse's poll, through the bit rings to the rider's hands. Overcheck reins will encourage the horse to raise his head by raising the bit in his mouth, rather like a gag snaffle.

The **De Gogue schooling system** is used for ridden work or lungeing. A strap from the girth passes between the horse's legs and divides into two cord straps. A piece of leather with pulleys on either side is fixed to the headpiece of the bridle. The cord straps go over the pulleys and down to the bit. For ridden work, short reins can be attached to the straps (with a second independent set of reins also fitted). For lungeing, the cords pass through the bit rings and clip on to the chest strap.

Running reins attached to either side of the girth.

Attach running reins at the chest for more control.

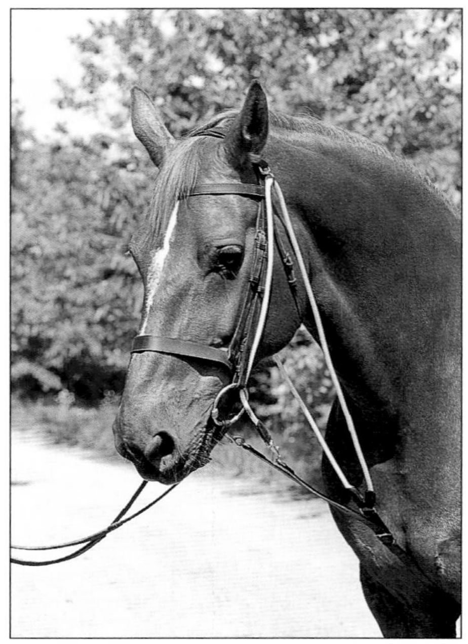
The De Gogue schooling system for lungeing or ridden work.

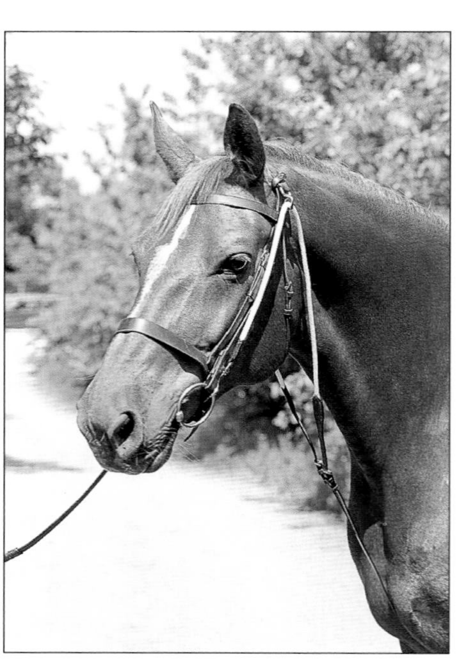
The Chambon system for lungeing or loose schooling only.

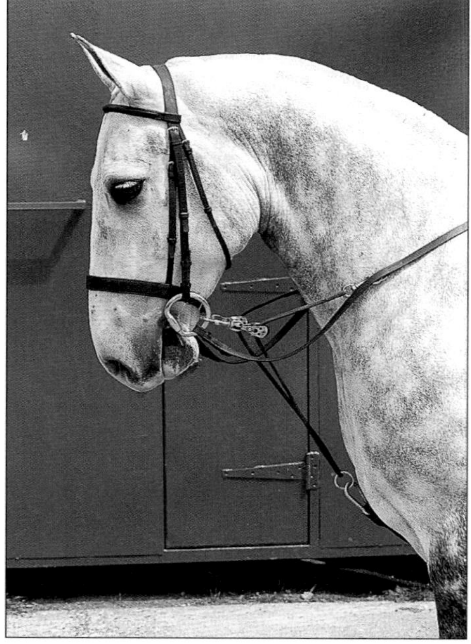
The Abbot Davies balancing rein.

▮ LEFT
Two ways of attaching the elastic training rein.

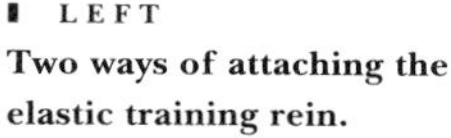

▮ BELOW
The Pessoa training system.

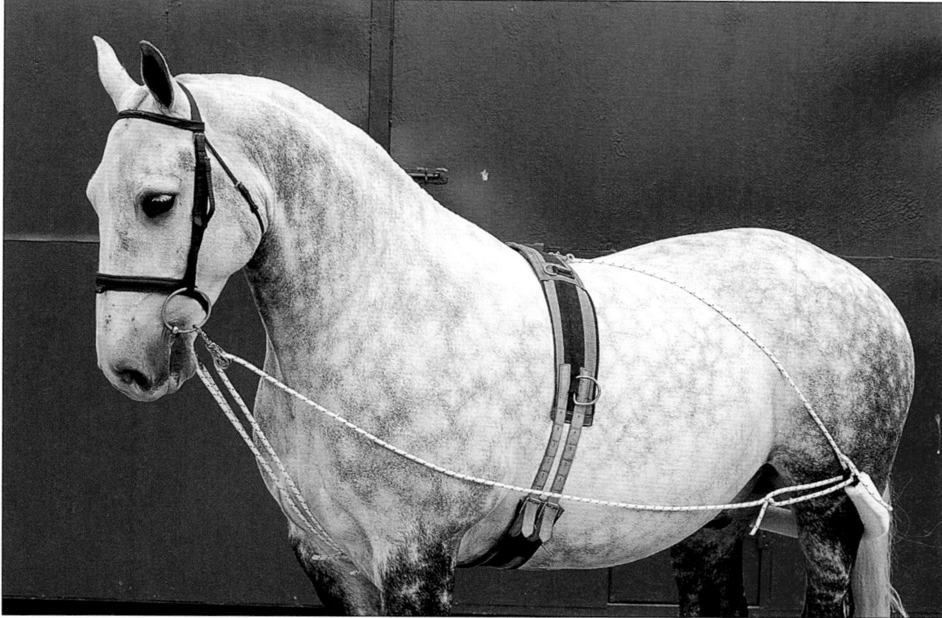

The **Chambon** is a schooling system consisting of a poll pad fitted over the top of the horse's head, to which pulleys are attached on either side. A strap is attached to the lungeing roller which passes up between the horse's front legs before dividing into two cords. The two cords fit over the pulleys and are clipped on to the bit rings. The Chambon encourages the horse to lower his head and neck and round his back, which in turn encourages engagement of the hindquarters. The Chambon can be used on horses which are being loose-schooled but is not designed to be ridden in.

The **Abbot Davies balancing rein** encourages the horse to develop the muscles of his back and hindquarters by raising his neck at its base. A combined system of pulleys and straps will prevent the horse leaning. It can be fitted from tail to mouth but more commonly, or in the latter stages of training, it is fitted from girth to mouth or mouth to ears.

The **Harbridge** aims to encourage the horse to work correctly by discouraging leaning, enhancing self-carriage and generally stimulating softness in the horse's back. It is not dissimilar in appearance to a running martingale. A strap attached to the girth passes through the horse's front legs and divides into two pieces of elastic which are clipped on to the bit rings. It should be used for flat work only, and is not suitable for schooling over jumps.

The **Schoolmasta training aid** is designed for horses which lean on the bit or have a tendency to over-bend and carry their heads behind the vertical. The system works independently of the rider's hands: straps clipped on to either side of the bit are attached to a pulley fitted to a special numnah, and this helps to correct the horse's posture.

The **elastic training rein** fits over the horse's poll, passes through the rings and clips on to the girth at the side or at the chest. The rein is designed to promote self-carriage without putting pressure on the horse's mouth.

The **Pessoa training system** aims to give the horse a rounded outline. It consists of a roller and pulleys attached from the roller to the bit rings, and to a strap passed round the hindquarters. As with all training equipment, skill and experience are needed for it to be used successfully.

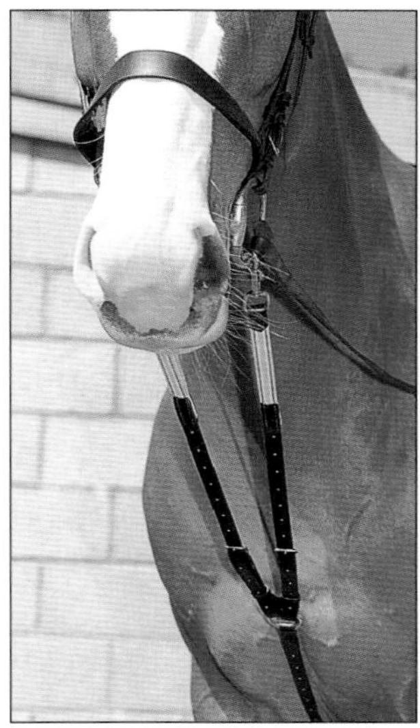

The Harbridge has two elasticated straps which clip on to the bit.

The Schoolmasta training aid is used in conjunction with a specially adapted numnah.

Lungeing and Long Reining

Lungeing is a method of exercising or training the horse from a single long rein. The horse is worked in a circle, at a distance of 20m/66ft from the handler, in both directions and in walk, trot and canter.

The **lunge cavesson** is an essential piece of lungeing equipment. It is fitted over a bridle if side reins are to be used. A lunge line is attached to the central ring on the noseband. The cavesson should fit snugly so that it does not slip when in use.

Lungeing and **breaking rollers** are necessary when side reins or long lines are used. In the examples shown here, the top roller has large rings through which long-reining lines are fitted. Side reins can be attached to the smaller D rings. A crupper prevents the roller slipping forward; a breastgirth keeps it from slipping back. Lungeing the horse with side reins fitted enables the handler to influence the horse's outline and general way of going by containing impulsion. Working the horse on long lines enables the trainer to teach the young horse to respond to the feel of reins before a rider is introduced.

The **Elwyn Hartley-Edwards breaking roller** is a webbing and leather roller designed specifically for training the young horse. It features a built-in crupper to prevent the roller from being pulled forwards as the horse is worked.

Side reins are attached to the roller and clip on to the bit rings to encourage the horse to work in a correct outline. There is some debate as to whether elasticated or non-elasticated types are better. Some trainers feel that a rein that "gives" is better than a fixed type, while others suggest that elasticated reins can encourage the horse to evade the contact of the reins.

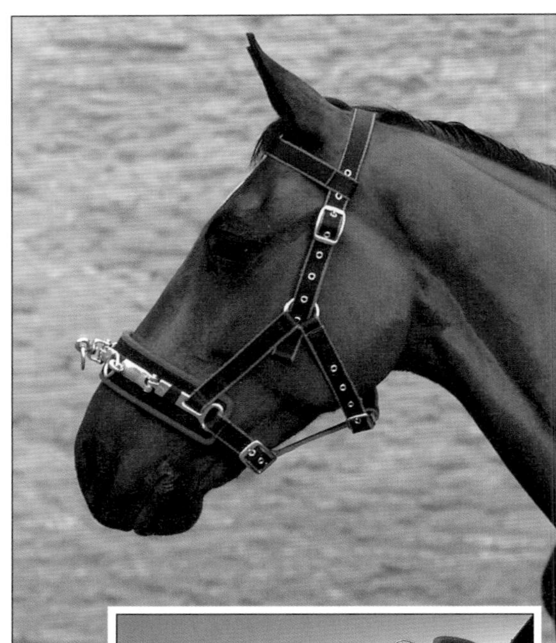

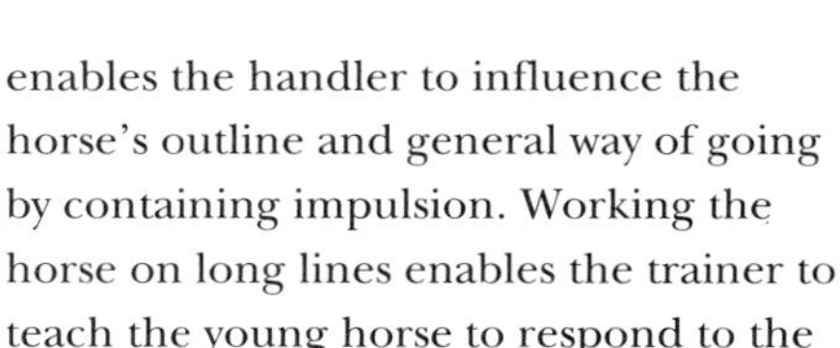

LEFT AND BELOW
Shown here are two examples of a lunge cavesson, in leather (*left*) and webbing (*below*).

BELOW
***Top to bottom*: Leather breaking roller, leather lunge roller and web lunge roller.**

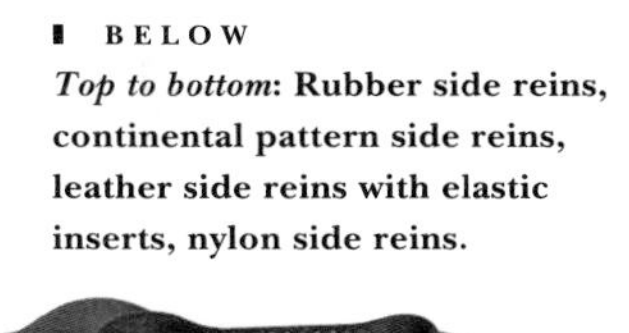

BELOW
Top to bottom: **Rubber side reins, continental pattern side reins, leather side reins with elastic inserts, nylon side reins.**

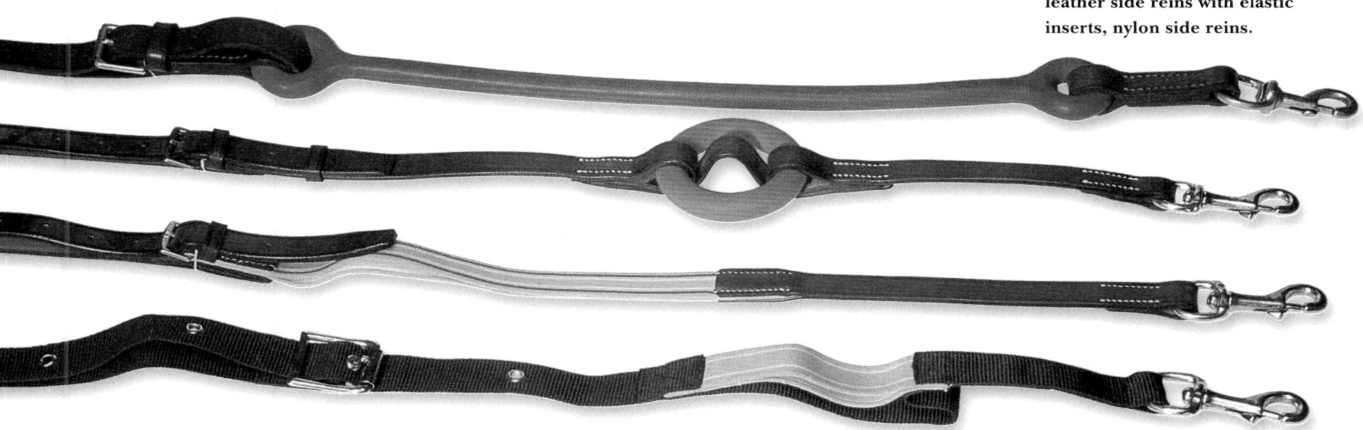

Continental pattern side reins in leather have rubber inserts which allow the reins to "give" as the horse moves. **Leather side reins** are available, many with elastic inserts. Leather side reins can be costly but if well cared for they will last longer than synthetic ones. **Nylon side reins**, with or without elastic inserts, are a cheaper alternative.

The **lunge line**, available in cord or webbing, is attached to the central ring on the lunge cavesson by means of a spring clip or a buckled strap. The lunge line enables the handler to control and guide the horse around a circle.

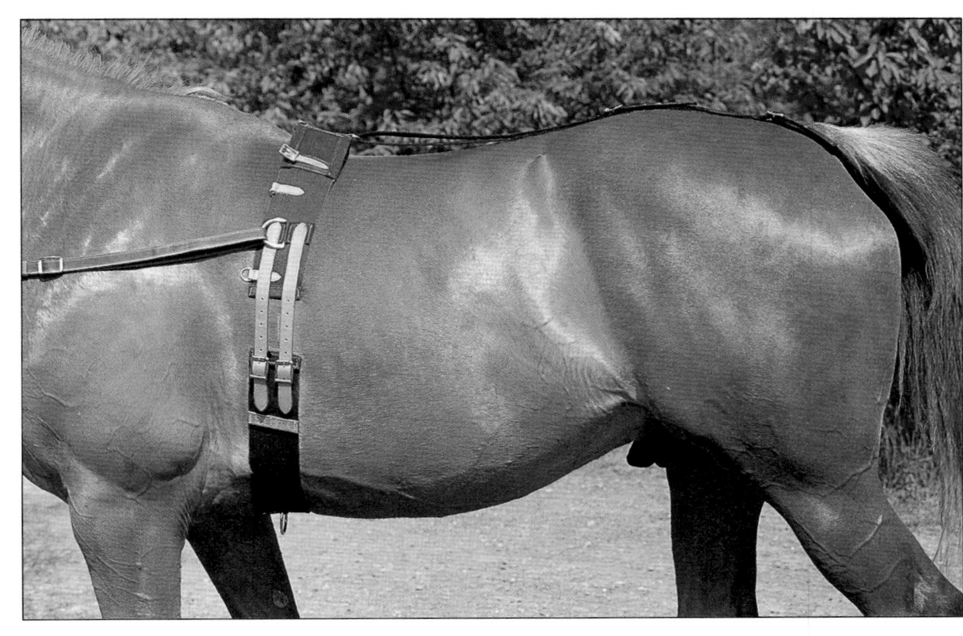

ABOVE
The Elwyn Hartley-Edwards breaking roller shown fitted with side reins and a crupper.

LEFT
lunge lines

LUNGEING CAVESSON FITTED OVER A BRIDLE

The cavesson has been fitted over a bridle with the noseband removed. The reins have been twisted and looped through the throatlatch to prevent the horse accidentally getting caught in them. The side reins are attached to the bit rings: these should only be attached when the horse is being lunged. Start with the side reins fitted loosely and adjust them as the horse warms up.

HORSE TACKED UP FOR LUNGEING

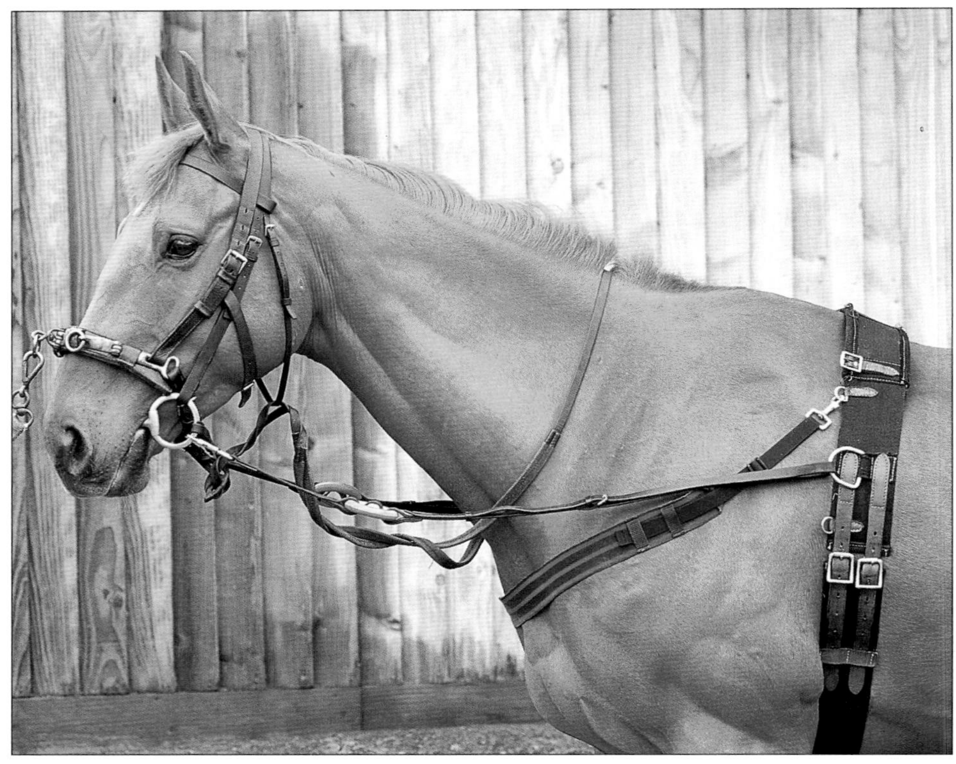

Lungeing roller fitted with a breastplate.

USING A SADDLE INSTEAD OF A ROLLER

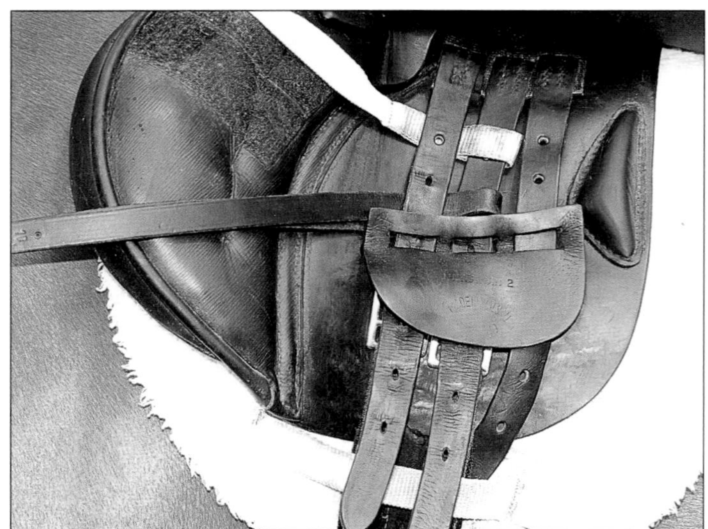

1 Side reins can be fitted to the girth straps on a saddle instead of the roller. They are useful if you plan to ride the horse after it has been lunged or if the horse is being lunged with a rider on board. The side reins pass round the second girth strap and under the first. This will prevent them from slipping down.

2 The stirrups can be removed from the saddle or, if the horse is to be ridden, they can be held securely in place by looping the stirrup leather around the stirrup and securing it with the spare end.

Lead Reins and Ropes

BELOW
plaited (braided) nylon lead rope

Lead reins and ropes are essential items of equipment when handling horses.

Lead ropes are inexpensive and sturdy, and are the practical choice for everyday use. They are clipped on to the horse's headcollar or halter so that he can be secured when travelling, or when being groomed or tacked up. Cotton and plaited (braided) nylon lead ropes come in a variety of colours: choose one to match your horse's headcollar.

When securing a horse with a lead rope, always use a quick release knot to allow the horse to be untied quickly in an emergency. Tying a horse directly to a fixed object, such as a gate or metal tie ring, can risk injuring him if he decides to pull back suddenly. Instead, attach the rope to the fixed object with a loop of bailing twine. If the horse pulls back suddenly, the twine will break and the horse will be released unhurt.

Leather and **webbing lead reins** are very smart and are commonly used for showing horses in-hand. The leather type has a double chain attachment called a **Newmarket chain**, which clips on to either bit ring and gives the handler greater control over the horse. The webbing lead rein is popular for showing and attaches directly to the headcollar or halter.

BELOW
cotton lead rope

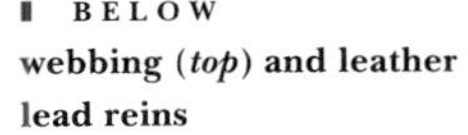

BELOW
webbing (*top*) and leather lead reins

Headcollars and Halters

Headcollars and halters are indispensable items of tack which are used to lead horses in-hand or to secure them when travelling or in the stable. Some are also designed to control or restrain horses.

The best-quality **leather headcollars** are made from English leather and, like all good-quality leather tack, they will last for years if well cared for. As an extra feature, you can attach a brass plate engraved with your horse's name.

Synthetic headcollars are ideal for everyday use. They are extremely strong, although this can be a problem – if the horse is turned out in one and gets caught on a branch, gate or fence, the synthetic headcollar will not break easily. The **synthetic rope halter** is made of strong nylon cord and fastens simply by tying. **Rope halters** are commonly used for showing young stock in-hand.

The **Controller headcollar** can be used for horses with a tendency to pull when led in-hand. The headcollar is designed to apply pressure on the nose when the horse pulls against the handler.

The **"Be-Nice"** halter, popularized by the American trainer, Monty Roberts, will train the horse to be led in-hand. The halter tightens around the horse's head and applies pressure to the poll when the horse resists being led. It should never be used to secure the horse.

The decorative **Western show halter** is made from leather with engraved silver detailing. The **in-hand bridle** is halfway between a bridle and a headcollar. It has short leather straps to which a bit is fitted and is used, as its name implies, for showing horses in-hand. The **rolled Arab slip** is a delicate halter which will enhance the fineness of the Arab head in in-hand showing classes. The **foal slip** is designed as a first headcollar for young foals. The short strap which hangs down is used instead of a separate lead rope.

A leather headcollar makes a very smart piece of equipment. A brass plate engraved with the horse's name can be fitted as an extra feature.

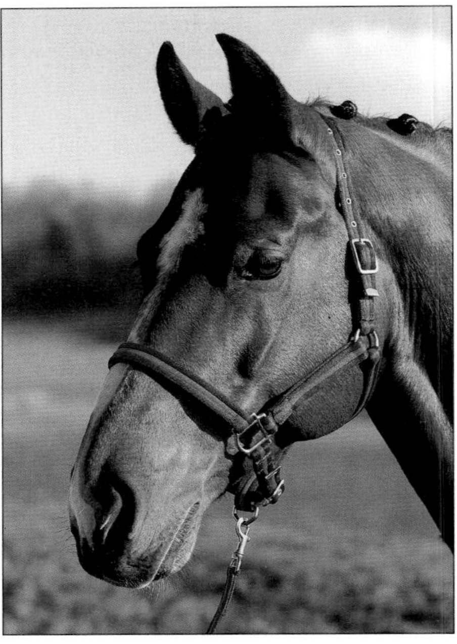

The synthetic headcollar is strong, durable and easy to care for. It is available in many colours and is a popular choice for children's ponies.

The unusual design of the synthetic rope halter means that it can be fastened without buckles.

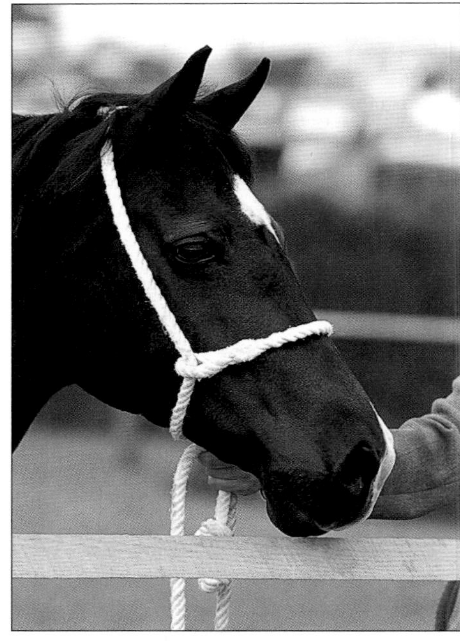

The simple rope halter is popular for showing young horses in-hand.

ABOVE LEFT
controller headcollar

ABOVE MIDDLE
"Be Nice" halter

ABOVE RIGHT
Western show halter

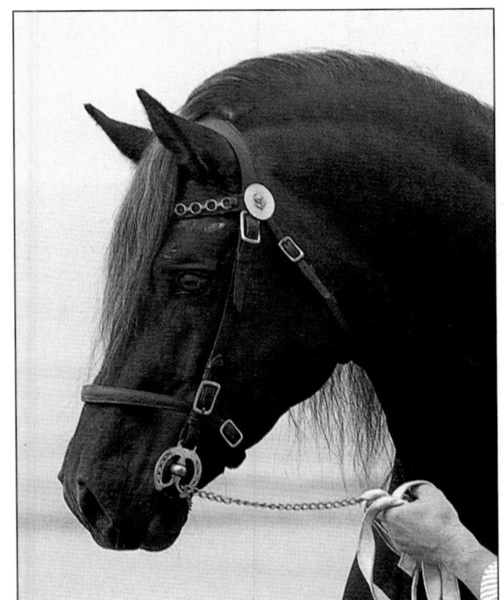

ABOVE LEFT
in-hand bridle

BELOW LEFT
rolled Arab slip

LEFT AND RIGHT
foal slip

Grooming Equipment

Regular grooming is an essential part of good horse management. It is not simply a question of making the horse look smart. Far more important is the fact that thorough brushing helps keep the horse healthy by removing accumulated dust, dead skin and hair, and helping to keep the pores open and clean. During hard work the horse's skin excretes waste matter in the form of sweat. It is important that the skin and coat are kept clean to enable this system to work efficiently. A good, strenuous grooming also serves as a massage, improving the horse's muscle tone. In addition, grooming helps to keep the horse's tack and rugs clean, which in turn prevents sores. While the stabled horse needs daily grooming both before and after exercise, the grass-kept horse requires far less attention. Although the areas under the saddle and bridle must always be cleaned before tacking up, only the worst of the mud or grease should be removed elsewhere for appearances' sake. Horses and ponies who live out need the natural grease and dirt in their coats to help keep them warm and dry, especially in winter.

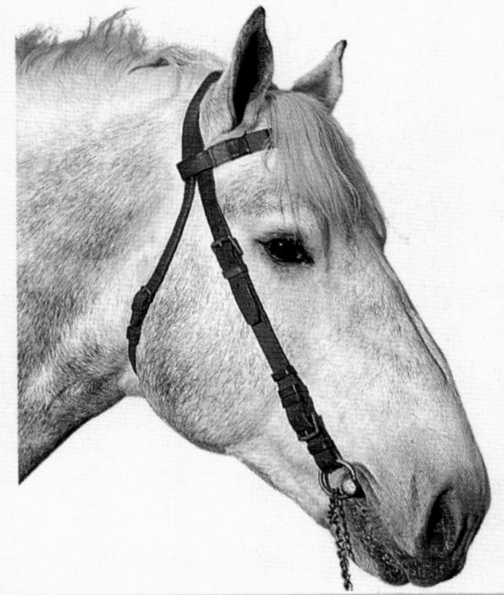

Grooming Kit

The **dandy brush** has long, stiff bristles and is used for removing dried mud and stable stains (where the horse has lain in its droppings or wet bedding) from the legs. It is too harsh to use on the horse's body or on the mane and tail.

The **body brush** has shorter, finer bristles than the dandy brush and may be used on the horse's entire body (and legs). It has a loop for the hand (leather or canvas are the most comfortable). The best body brushes have a leather back which is less likely than wood or plastic to hurt the horse if you inadvertently knock him with it while grooming. Leather, being softer and flexible, also sits more comfortably on the hand.

The body brush is cleaned after every few strokes by drawing the bristles across the teeth of the **metal curry comb**. The metal curry comb should never be used on the horse.

For dampening down the mane and tail the **water brush** is used. This usually has a wooden back and has softer bristles than the dandy brush.

Two **sponges** are required, one for cleaning the eyes and nostrils, the other for use on the dock and the gelding's sheath. The sponges should never be interchanged (having two different colours prevents them being muddled up). They should be washed out after each use.

The **hoof pick** is a vital piece of equipment, used for cleaning out the horse's feet. The end of the pick should be blunt to prevent damage to the foot. Hoof picks are easily dropped and lost in the bedding. It is a good idea to tie a piece

RIGHT
The grooming kit should include trimming scissors, thinning scissors and mane combs for use when trimming the heels, and when pulling the mane and tail.

CLOCKWISE FROM LEFT
Body brush and metal curry comb; dandy brush; water brush; rubber and plastic curry combs; 'cactus' cloth.

PREVIOUS PAGE OPPOSITE
Quarter marks put the finishing touch to a show pony.

PREVIOUS PAGE
Grey horses, like this Percheron, take more keeping clean than dark-coloured horses.

of brightly coloured twine to the handle to make it easier to locate.

A **stable rubber**, usually made of cloth, is used, slightly dampened, to give a final polish to the horse's coat. A piece of chamois leather or jute sacking is equally effective for this purpose.

A **rubber** or **plastic curry comb**, which like the body brush is fitted with a loop for the hand, may be used for removing dried mud from the coat. Care must be taken when using it on bony areas such as the legs.

A **sweat scraper** is used to remove excess water from the horse's coat after washing him down. It consists of a blade of rubber attached to a metal frame with a handle. Again care must be taken not to knock the bony parts of his body.

Also in the grooming kit will be a **metal mane comb** which is not actually required for the grooming process but for use during trimming the mane and tail. The mane comb may have thick, widely spaced teeth or thin, closer ones.

All grooming tools should be kept tidily in a container designed for the purpose. Brushes should normally be kept bristle-side up (the bristles will last longer that way). They should be kept clean by regular washing. Since hot water may soften the glue which holds bristles in place, the whole brush should be plunged into cold water after cleaning and stood bristle-side down while it dries (this is particularly important for wooden-backed brushes as the wood will deteriorate if it is left wet for long periods). All other items of grooming equipment should also be kept scrupulously clean.

For **wisping** – a form of massage involving a rhythmic thumping of the muscles of the neck, shoulders and quarters – a pad is required. Traditionally wisping was carried out with a hay wisp, made by twisting a rope of hay into a firm pad. Nowadays special pads are obtainable, often made of leather.

Sometimes the horse may need to have his mane and tail washed and occasionally his whole body. Buckets, sponges, an appropriate horse shampoo (if necessary), sweat scraper and towels will be required.

Electric groomers, which operate like a household vacuum cleaner, are useful for removing grease and dirt particularly from a horse who has not been clipped. Because of the noise horses must be introduced to them carefully and the tail should always be plaited up out of the way to avoid the possibility of the hair becoming caught up if the groomer has a rotating brush. An electric groomer is not suitable for use on the horse's head. While electric groomers are useful for removing dust and dirt, they do not provide the same massaging effect as a good hand grooming.

RIGHT
A good hoof pick is an essential item of equipment. The one on the left is fitted with a brush which is used after the pick to remove remnants of dirt from the feet.

Grooming Technique

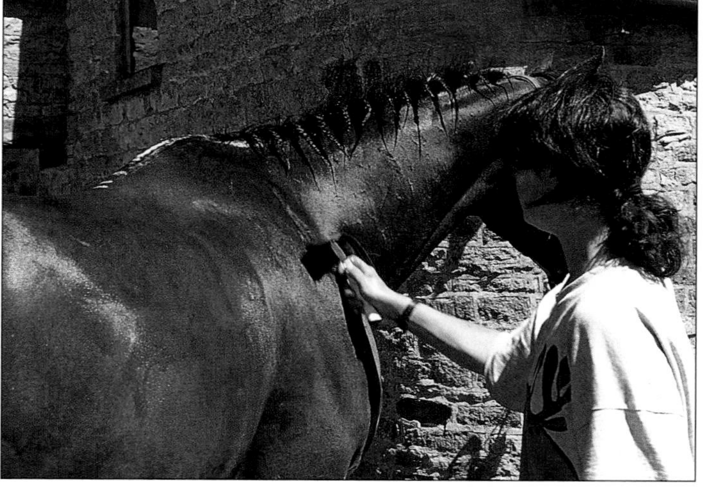

LEFT
A very sweaty or dirty horse may be washed down provided he can be dried quickly to prevent chilling. Excess water is removed with a sweat scraper.

The stabled horse needs a thorough grooming every day. This is best carried out after exercise when the horse is warm. The pores of the skin will be open and grease and dirt will be easier to remove. The horse should be tied up during grooming.

Each **foot** should be picked up and carefully cleaned out with the hoof pick. The pick should be used from the horse's heel towards the toe to avoid damaging the frog. Dirt from the feet should be placed in a skip, not in the horse's bed.

The body brush is used to clean the horse's entire **body,** starting with the neck and working down to the shoulders and the front legs, along the body, over the hindquarters and down the hindlegs. Use the brush – in the left hand for the nearside, in the right hand for the offside – with brisk, firm strokes and after every few strokes clean the bristles on the metal curry comb, which is held in the other hand. Periodically the dirt should be tapped from the curry comb. This should be done in the doorway or just outside the stable, not into the bedding. Care should be taken when grooming not to bang the horse's bony projections, for example those of the hips and legs, and the brush should not be used with too much pressure over the loins. Having completed one side, move round to the other side of the horse and repeat the process.

The body brush is also used to clean the **head,** which should be done very gently. The horse should not be tied up for this, in case he pulls back. The headcollar should be fastened round his neck, leaving his nose free.

Brush out the **mane** and **tail** with the body brush, taking care not to break the hairs. The tail should be held away from the horse's body with your free hand and

1 Grooming begins with picking out the feet. The hoof pick shold always be used from the heel towards the toe.

2 Remnants of dirt may be removed from the area round the frog with a brush.

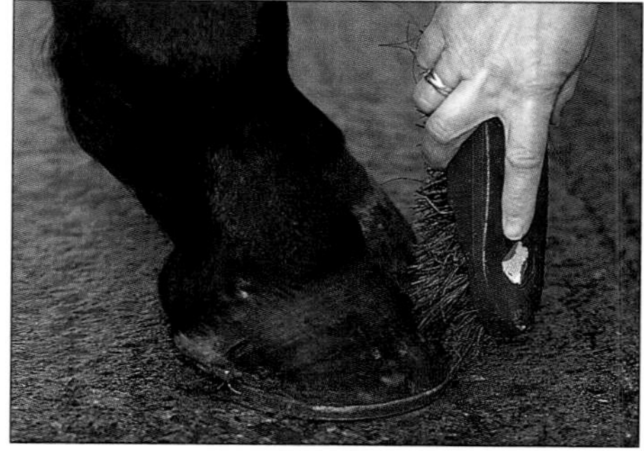

3 The hoof wall should be kept clean – a stiff brush may be used to remove mud and other forms of dirt.

1 The body brush is used to give the entire body a thorough grooming. It should be used in the direction of the lie of the coat.

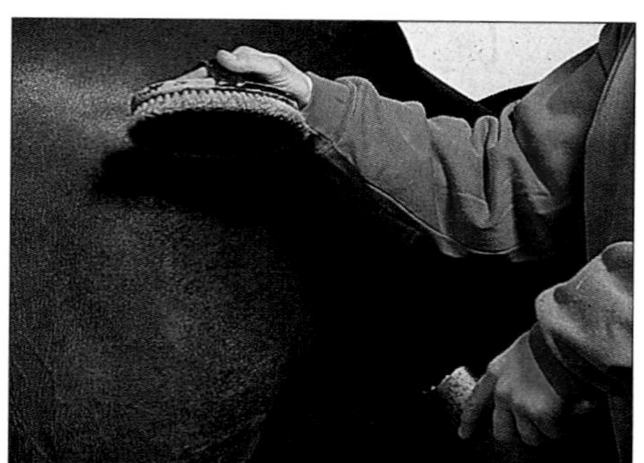

2 The curry comb is held in the spare hand and used for cleaning the body brush – never use it on the horse.

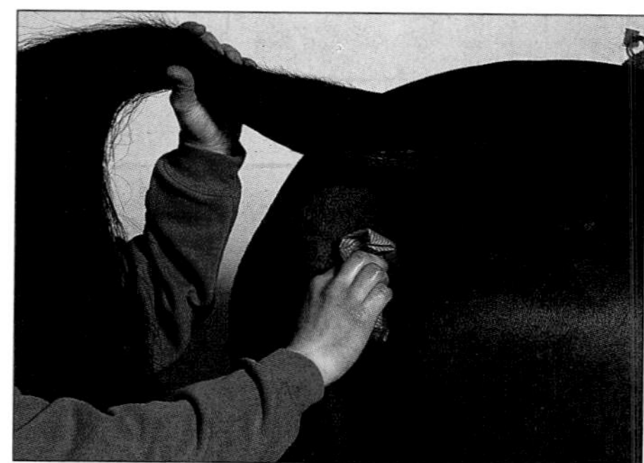

3 The dock should be sponged each time the horse is groomed. Use a different sponge from the one used for the eyes and nose.

1 Tail bandages are made of elasticated cotton and are about 3 inches (8cm) wide and 10 feet (3m) long.

2 The bandage is started high up, as near as possible to the top of the dock.

3 A loose flap is left at the top and then turned down and bandaged over. This helps prevent slipping.

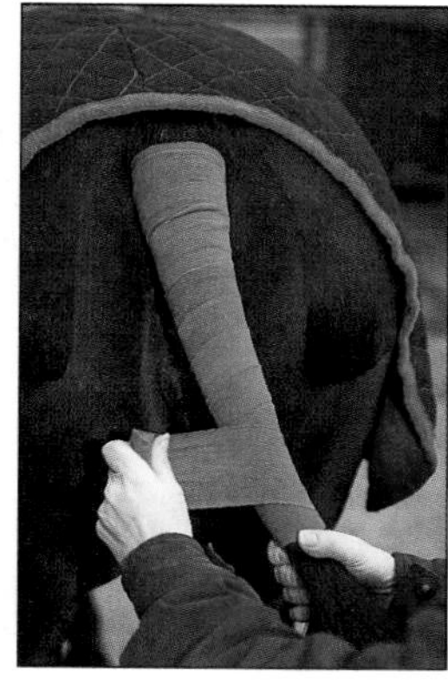

4 The bandage is applied down the length of the dock and up again. It should not be fitted too tightly

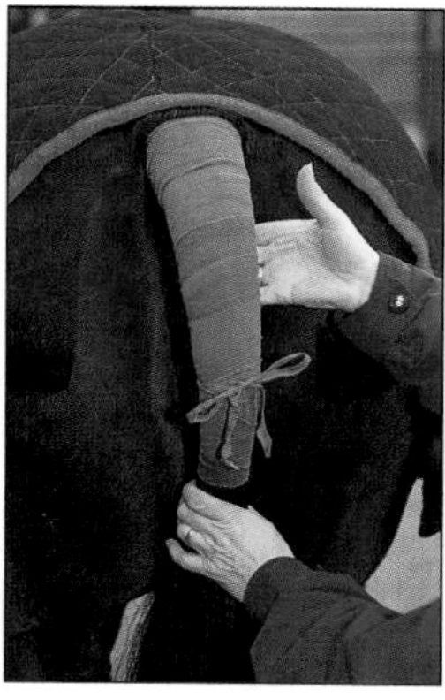

5 The bandage is secured with tapes and the dock should be eased into its natural shape.

brushed out a lock at a time. Any tangles should be teased out with the fingers. A very muddy tail will need washing. To finish off the mane and tail, dip the bristles of the water brush in clean water (not the horse's drinking water) and go lightly over the mane to "lay" it down smoothly. Do the same to the top hairs of the tail. A pulled tail should be bandaged for an hour or so afterwards to keep it tidy.

Use a damp sponge to clean the horse's **eyes** and **nostrils** and another for the **dock.** In the case of geldings the **sheath** will need sponging out once every couple of weeks or so to remove the greasy discharge which accumulates and can cause the horse discomfort. Special solutions can be obtained for this purpose or you can use a mild soap and warm water. Use the same sponge that is used for cleaning his dock. The easiest time to give him a thorough clean in this area is when he is staling. Do it carefully and gently – and beware of being kicked should the horse object. If you are unable to catch the moment when the horse is staling, clean out the sheath by gently inserting the sponge inside it and cleaning all round. Rinse the whole area several times and dry off with a towel.

The finishing touch to the whole grooming process is applied by running a damp stable rubber or other cloth over the entire coat to add a final polish. Wisping with a hay wisp or pad, when done, takes place after regular grooming since its purpose is not to clean but to **massage.** The pad or wisp is applied in much the same way as a brush, but with a firmer thump (though not too hard). It is used on the large muscular areas of the horse (the neck, shoulders and quarters). It is said to improve the circulation and muscle tone. It should never be used on the more tender areas, such as the loins, nor on the bony areas, such as the legs.

A thorough grooming will take from half to three-quarters of an hour, depending on the initial cleanliness of the horse's skin and coat – and the strength and endurance of the groom! Grooming is most effective if you stand a little away from the horse in order to put your weight behind the brush.

A less comprehensive type of grooming called **quartering** is used to prepare the horse in the morning for exercise. Its purpose is to remove any surface dirt accumulated during the night and to make the horse generally presentable. Quartering involves unfastening his rugs, turning them back over his loins and giving his front half a quick brush over, then turning his rugs forward and doing the same to his hind end. Any stains and bedding marks should be removed, if necessary by using a damp sponge or water brush. The damp areas should be dried off with a stable rubber or a towel. The mane and tail should be brushed through and all traces of bedding removed. The feet should be picked clean and the eyes, nostrils and dock sponged. Quartering takes between ten and twenty minutes, depending on the horse's size and how dirty he is.

GROOMING TIPS

- Never try to groom a sweaty horse – walk him about until he is dry.
- Never try to brush off wet mud – either hose it off or let it dry first.
- To dry off a wet horse in the stable cover him with a sheet or rug made of "breathable" material or put a layer of straw along his back and quarters with a rug over the top (this is known as "thatching").
- To remove dried mud use a dandy brush or rubber curry comb but not too roughly – it may be necessary to remove mud from sensitive areas of skin, such as inside the hindlegs, with your hand.
- In cold weather keep a clipped horse warm during grooming by turning his rugs back and forward (as when quartering) rather than removing them altogether.
- Give all rugs and blankets a thorough shaking every week – it is pointless to put dusty rugs back on to a clean horse.
- Never stand directly behind a horse.
- Never sit or kneel on the floor to reach the lower parts – always squat or bend so that you can move quickly if he does.
- Keep a watchful eye open for any skin injuries or tell-tail lumps or bumps, particularly on the legs, which could warn of impending soundness problems.
- With the grass-kept horse clean the area under the saddle and brush off the worst of the mud for appearances' sake but do not attempt regular, thorough grooming.

Types of Clip

In winter horses grow a thick coat to protect them from the weather. A horse with a thick coat who is required to do anything other than light work will sweat excessively and, as a result, be very uncomfortable, lose condition and run the risk of catching a chill if he is not carefully dried off after exercise. Clipping off the thick winter coat of the stabled horse removes these problems and also makes it easier to keep the horse clean and looking smart. A clipped horse must be kept warm with blankets and rugs. A clipped horse who spends some time out at grass will need a waterproof New Zealand rug.

There are different ways of clipping a horse or pony, depending on the work he is required to do and the type of coat he grows. A **full clip** involves removing the coat from the entire body and the legs. A thick-coated horse may be given a full clip when he is first clipped and then at subsequent clippings have his legs left unclipped. Leaving the hair on the legs affords some protection from knocks. The full clip is usually only used for horses in very fast work, such as racing, or sometimes for a show horse being prepared for early spring shows.

The most usual clip for other horses doing hard work is the **hunter clip** which involves leaving the hair on the legs and the area under the saddle. Again the reason for leaving legs and saddle patch unclipped is to provide protection. Care must be taken to dry off the saddle patch thoroughly after work.

As its name suggests the **blanket clip** involves leaving an area of the horse's back, loins and quarters unclipped (and also the legs). The hair is removed from the neck, shoulders and belly and all or part of the head. A blanket clip is suitable for a horse doing a fair amount of medium to hard work.

Horses who are kept out, and stabled horses not in hard work, may be given a low **trace clip,** which consists of removing the hair from the underside of the neck, between the forelegs, the belly and the upper part of the hind legs. Medium and high trace clips, which involve removing more of the body and neck hair are suitable for stabled horses in steady work.

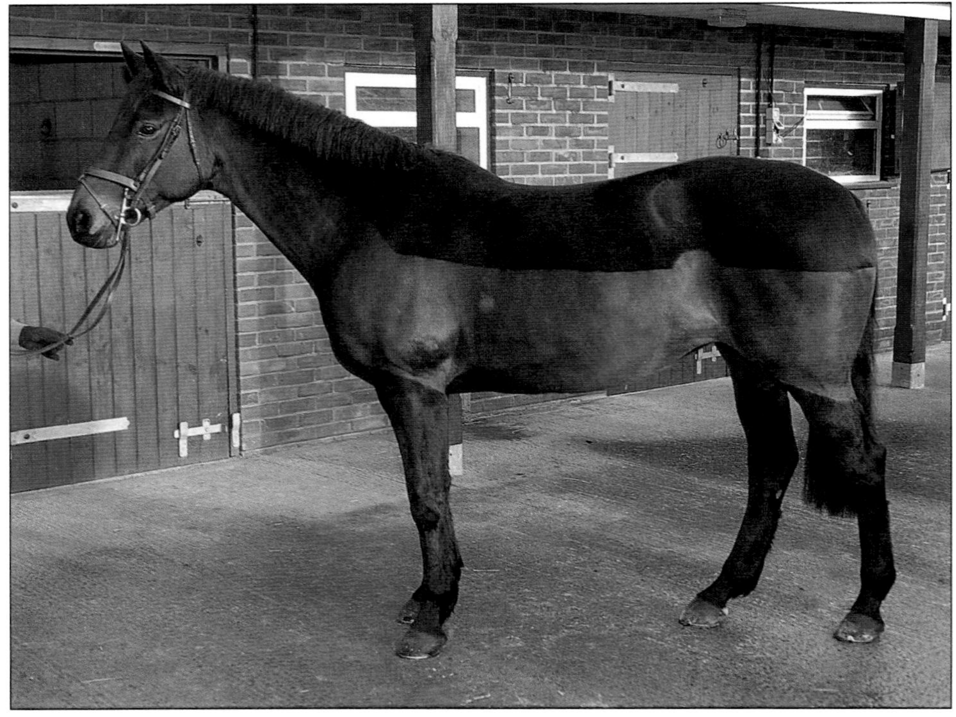

With the **chaser clip** the hair is removed from the head, the lower part of the neck, the chest, the belly and the upper part of the hindlegs. The clip finishes just behind the ears. It is often used on steeplechasers (hence its name). Many Thoroughbred horses have fine coats which may not require total removal even when they are in hard work.

There are various other partial clips suitable for the grass-kept horse used only for light work such as occasional hacking. These include the **bib clip** and the **apron clip.** In the bib clip the coat is removed only from the jowl, down the underside of the neck down to and including the front of the chest. In the apron clip an area above the forelegs and extending back under the girth area of the body is also removed. These areas, together with the flanks and the inside of the hindlegs, are usually the first to become sweaty. A tough animal, such as a native pony, could probably live out without rugs after having a bib or apron clip though in very adverse weather he might need to be rugged. When clipping the hair from the hindquarters an inverted V is left at the top of the tail. The unclipped leg hair is sloped at the top from front to back.

The horse's head is a particularly vulnerable spot because of its thin covering of skin and hair. Many people leave the head unclipped or simply clip the lower half which effectively removes the hair from the sweatiest part (i.e. the jowl) while leaving the top half with protection from the weather. Many horses dislike having their heads clipped at all. This can be caused by a number of reasons, from fear of the sound or feel of the clippers to painful conditions such as toothache or an ear infection.

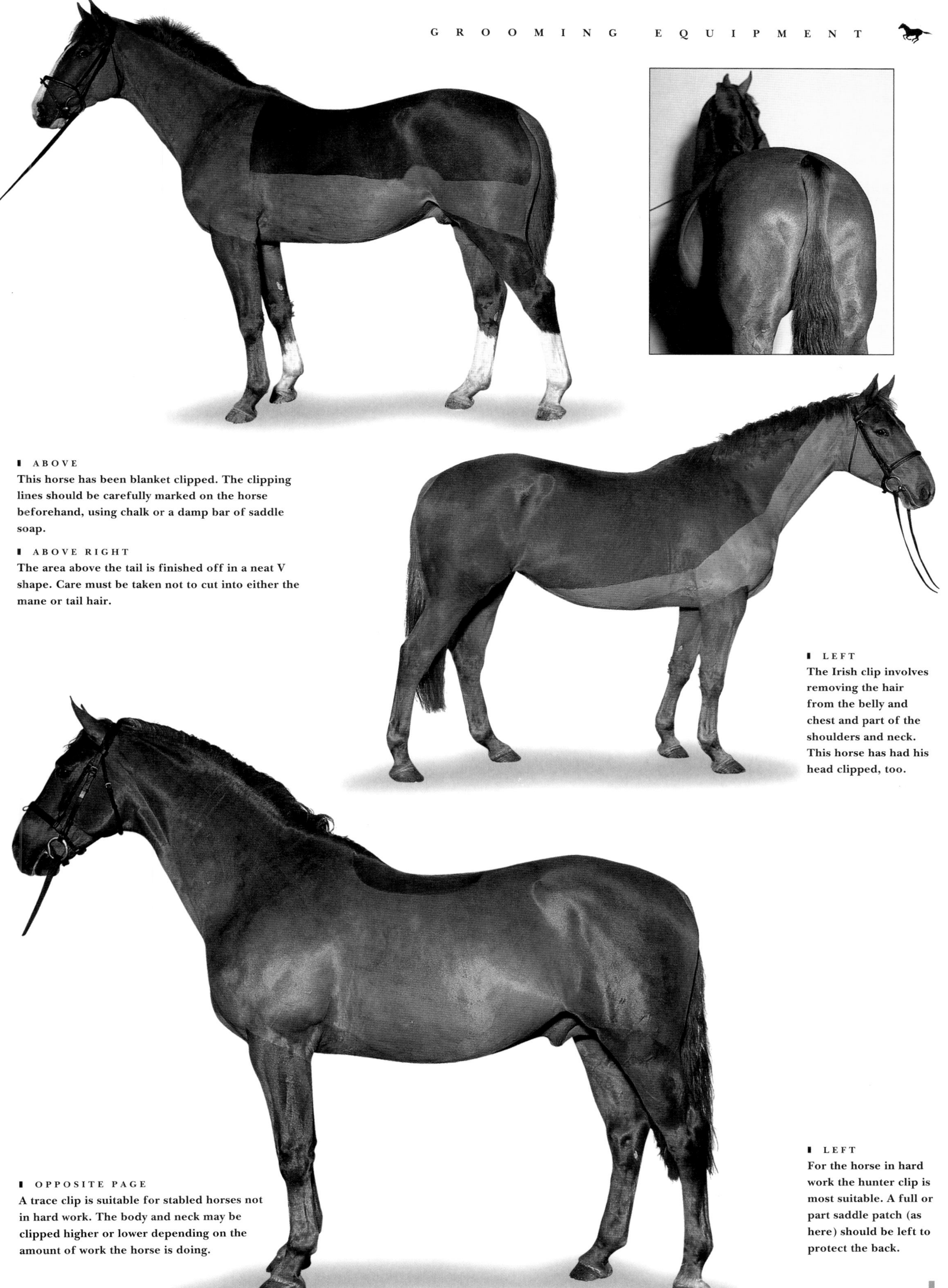

ABOVE
This horse has been blanket clipped. The clipping lines should be carefully marked on the horse beforehand, using chalk or a damp bar of saddle soap.

ABOVE RIGHT
The area above the tail is finished off in a neat V shape. Care must be taken not to cut into either the mane or tail hair.

LEFT
The Irish clip involves removing the hair from the belly and chest and part of the shoulders and neck. This horse has had his head clipped, too.

OPPOSITE PAGE
A trace clip is suitable for stabled horses not in hard work. The body and neck may be clipped higher or lower depending on the amount of work the horse is doing.

LEFT
For the horse in hard work the hunter clip is most suitable. A full or part saddle patch (as here) should be left to protect the back.

Clipping and Trimming

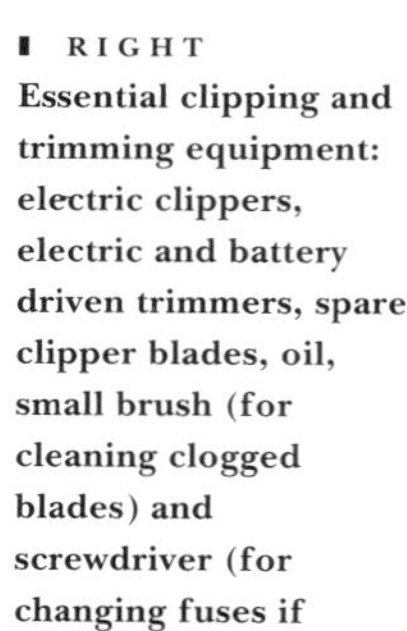

RIGHT
Essential clipping and trimming equipment: electric clippers, electric and battery driven trimmers, spare clipper blades, oil, small brush (for cleaning clogged blades) and screwdriver (for changing fuses if necessary).

Clipping horses is hard work and can be dangerous. It should never be carried out alone. The beginner should learn the techniques by watching an expert at work. If in doubt, find someone else to clip your horse, at least to begin with so that you can find out how he behaves.

Having decided on the type of clip, all lines (for example the leg lines and saddle patch) should be marked on the horse's coat with chalk or a damp piece of saddle soap. To mark the saddle patch put the horse's usual saddle on his back, without its fittings, make sure it is in the position where it lies when he is being ridden, and draw round it. It is better to make the saddle patch a little larger than it will finally need to be to make allowance for any mistakes when clipping the edges. A badly positioned saddle patch will spoil the look of the horse.

Start clipping at the front of the horse, on the neck or shoulder, and work your way backwards section by section. The clippers should be used against the lie of the coat (broadly speaking from the back of the horse towards the front) with long, sweeping strokes. Each stroke should be parallel to the one above or below it and should slightly overlap the previous one.

Take care when clipping the top line of the neck not to cut into the mane. Clip a short bridle path out of the mane just behind the ears where the headpiece of the bridle lies. This does not need to be very long: 2 inches (5cm) is adequate.

After the neck and shoulders clip the body and finally the hindquarters. Be particularly careful when clipping awkward places such as the delicate skin below the stifle and the folds between the front legs. The stifle skin should be held with your spare hand to straighten out the folds. An assistant should hold each foreleg up and forward in turn to stretch the folds of skin. Holding up a foreleg will also help prevent a horse from fidgeting or kicking. When clipping between the hindlegs be particularly watchful in case the horse does try to kick out. Keeping hold of his tail will help to prevent this.

The most difficult part of the horse to clip well is the head. If a horse is really frightened of having the clippers near his head it is far better to leave it unclipped. If the horse's head is to be clipped, first remove the headcollar. If he will not stand still without some form of restraint a halter is easier to work round with the clippers than a headcollar. Where you start will depend very much on the horse but the cheeks are probably the best place. Rest the clippers, switched off, against the cheekbone for a few moments until the horse becomes used to their presence. Then if he does not object switch on and work carefully over both cheeks, underneath from the chin to the throat, up over the front of the head and over the forehead. Because the head is so bony the clippers should be used as lightly as possible to reduce vibration. Be particularly careful when working near the eye.

Some people clip off the horse's whiskers round his muzzle but since these

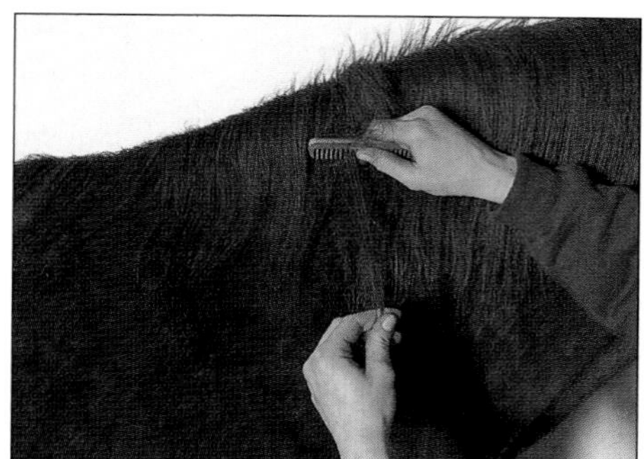

The mane is shortened and thinned by means of pulling, using a mane comb. Remove only a few hairs at a time to prevent soreness and damp the mane down afterwards.

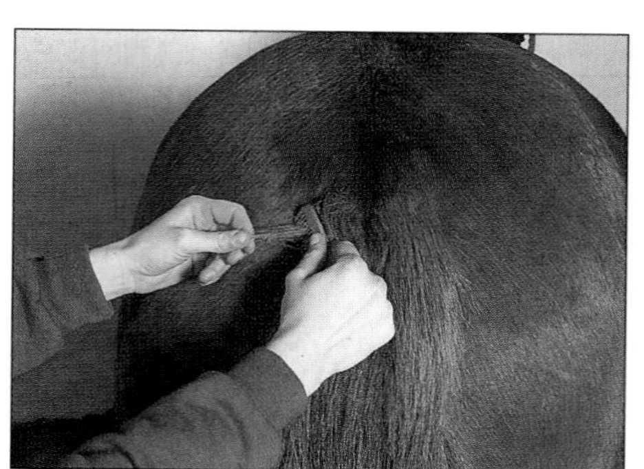

To neaten an untidy tail, pull hair from the sides and centre of the dock, preferably when the horse is warm and the pores are open.

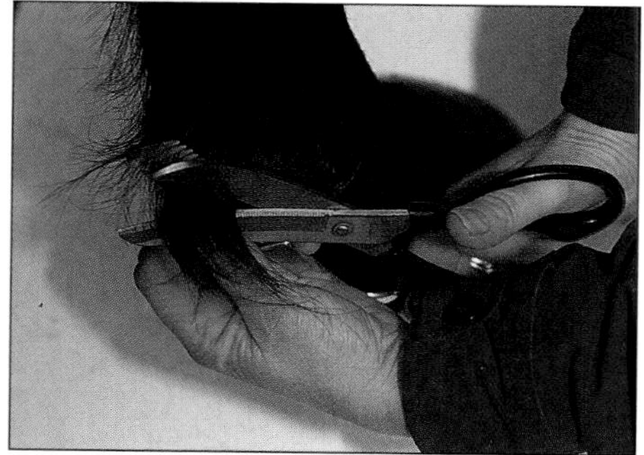

A mane comb and sharp, round-ended scissors are used to trim excess hair from the pasterns and fetlocks of unclipped legs. Take care not to leave "steps" of hair.

▮ RIGHT
Holding up a foreleg smooths out skin creases and also stops the horse fidgeting.

▮ MIDDLE RIGHT

Proceed carefully and gently when clipping the head.

▮ BOTTOM RIGHT

Holding the tail helps prevent a horse from kicking. The tail is bandaged to keep it clear of the clipper blades.

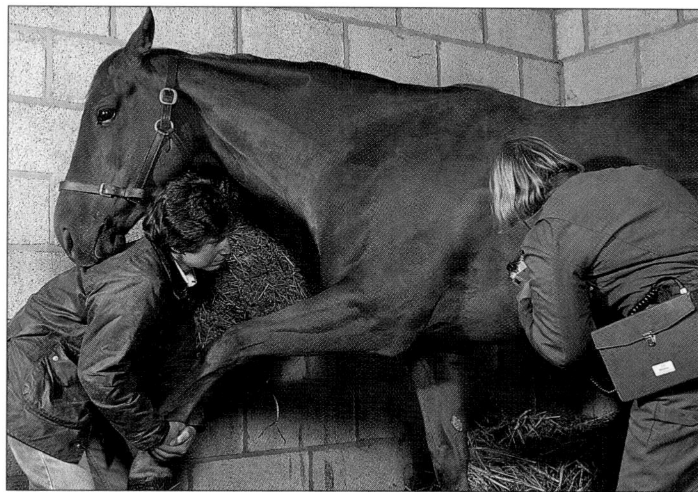

are used as sensors it is preferable, and kinder, to leave them alone.

To trim the ears, hold each one in turn and run the clippers along the outside edge only. Never try to clip the hair from inside the ear as the horse needs this as protection from insects and dirt. Never clip the eyelashes. Be careful when clipping the top of the head not to cut into the forelock.

If the horse's legs are left unclipped it will probably be necessary to trim his fetlocks and pasterns to make him look tidy. Use a mane comb and scissors (with rounded ends for safety) to remove excess feather, taking care not to create "steps" of hair but to leave a smooth line. Trim any thick hair from around the coronet.

If the horse's head is left unclipped, long hairs around the jaw may also be removed with scissors and comb. Scissors may be used to trim the long hairs from the edge of the ears.

Manes are kept neat by means of pulling, which involves plucking out strands of hair until the mane is the desired length and thickness. If the horse finds this too uncomfortable, it is possible to tidy up the mane with a thinning comb but never be tempted to use scissors which will give a very unsatisfactory result. Pulling can usually be achieved if you take your time and do only a small section of the mane at a time, spreading the whole job over a number of days.

An untidy tail can also be improved by pulling out some of the hairs from the top of the dock. Hair should be removed from the sides and, to a lesser extent, from the centre. As with the mane, it is best to remove a few hairs each day to prevent soreness. After pulling, the tail should be dampened with a water brush and bandaged to make the hair lie flat (do not leave the bandage on overnight). A pulled tail will need regular pulling if it is to keep its neat shape. A horse who lives out during the winter should not have his tail pulled – the hair at the top of the dock is there to protect him from rain and snow. To trim the bottom of the tail, raise the horse's dock to the position where he carries it when he is on the move. With your other hand hold the hair at the bottom of the tail and then cut off the hair to the required length. The end of the tail should be parallel to the ground when the horse is moving.

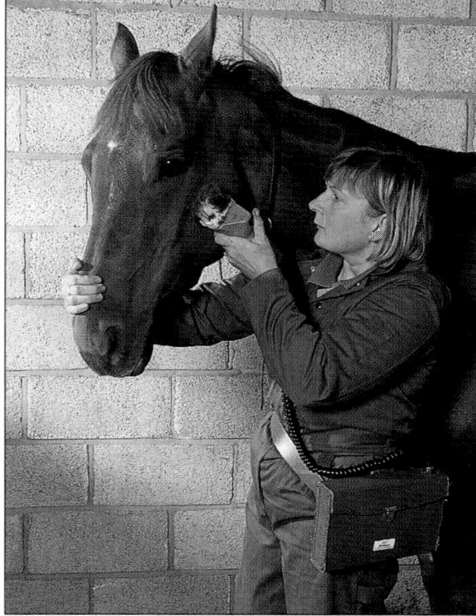

CLIPPING AND TRIMMING TIPS

- During clipping feel the underside of the blades every few minutes – if they are becoming hot, switch off and allow them to cool down before continuing.
- During clipping clean and oil the blades every ten to fifteen minutes.
- During clipping keep the horse warm by throwing a rug over the clipped areas – a cold horse will fidget more than a warm one.
- Always clip in good light conditions – start in the morning.
- Never try to clip a sweaty or dirty horse.
- For the best results do not clip until the horse's winter coat has "set" (i.e. is fully grown) – usually mid-autumn.
- To gauge the correct position and angle of leg lines measure one hand's width from where the foreleg joins the chest (for the V) and two hands' widths below the elbow; measure four hands' widths below the top of the stifle on the hindleg and two hands' widths above the point of the hock.
- Accustom a nervous horse to the feel of clippers by running hand clippers (i.e. non-motorized ones) over him.
- Have clippers serviced, and the blades reground, regularly.
- Ask your veterinary surgeon to administer a sedative to a horse who is really dangerous to clip.
- Pull manes and tails when the horse is warm, either on a hot day or after exercise – the hair will come out more easily while the pores are open, which is easier for you and more comfortable for the horse.
- Pull hair, whenever possible, from the underside of the mane – this will encourage it to lie flat.

Final Touches for Turnout

Plaiting, or **braiding, the mane** makes the horse or pony look smart, particularly if he has an untidy mane and is to appear in public. In some showing classes it is expected that the horse will be plaited. In others, such as those for Mountain and Moorland ponies and Arabs, the mane is never plaited. It is easier to plait a mane that has been pulled – a very thick, uneven mane will result in ugly, untidy plaits.

The mane hair is divided into equal bunches, each of which is dampened and then plaited, turned under and secured close to the crest of the neck, either by sewing with thread or with rubber bands. Sewn plaits are the most secure and are therefore more suitable for the horse engaged in lengthy periods of work such as hunting or eventing. Rubber bands are suitable for sports such as show jumping, where the mane does not need to remain plaited for long.

The plaits need to be fairly tight to look tidy and stay put, but beware of plaiting too tightly. If you do, it can cause the horse discomfort, particularly if he is required to stretch his neck a lot, for example when he is doing fast work or jumping.

A horse's appearance may be greatly improved by clever plaiting: making the plaits in the dip of the neck bigger than the others will help disguise a ewe neck; a small number of plaits will make a long neck seem shorter; conversely, a short neck will look longer if the mane has lots of small plaits. The appearance of a horse with a very untidy mane can be improved if the mane is hogged, or clipped off altogether. A hogged mane looks best on a horse of fairly heavy build, such as a cob – in Britain cobs are always shown with a hogged mane. Manes grow quickly and will need re-hogging every few weeks.

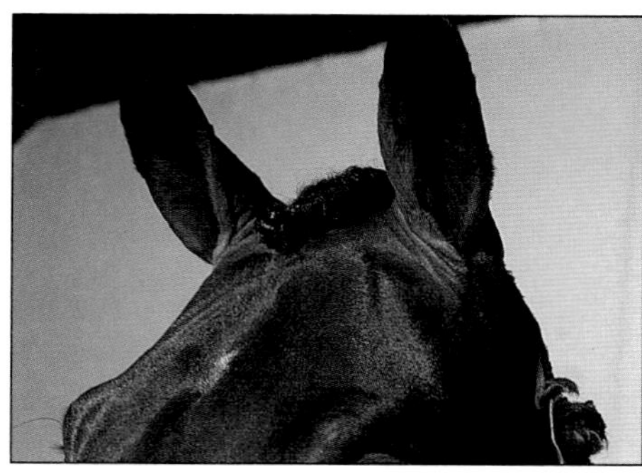

A plaited forelock gives the head a neat appearance. Plaits should be tight enough to prevent them dropping out but not so tight that they cause the horse discomfort.

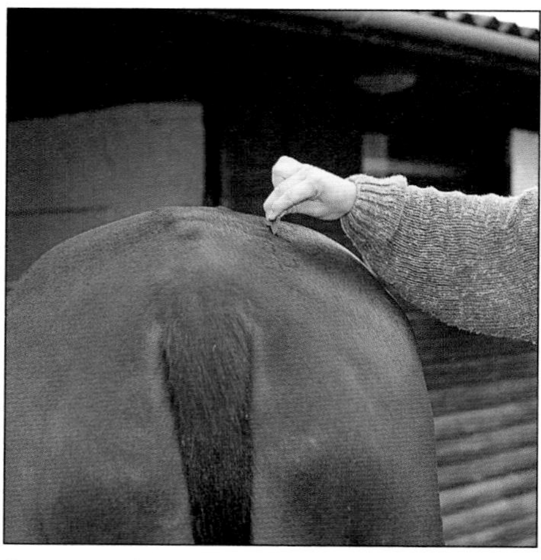

Quarter marks add the finishing touches to a well-groomed horse or pony. A chequered pattern may be made with a mane comb and stencil.

Plaiting, or **braiding, a tail** looks complicated but is not too difficult once you have had a little practice. For successful plaiting the tail must have long hair at the top – it is not possible to plait a pulled tail. The hair must be clean, well brushed and dampened before plaiting begins. When the plait is complete it should be carefully dampened with a sponge and then protected with a tail bandage. To avoid damaging the plait the tail bandage must be removed by unwinding, not by sliding it down.

In very muddy conditions, for instance when riding across country in wet weather, it may be more comfortable for the horse to have his tail put up so that it cannot become clogged with mud. To put up a tail, start plaiting from the top in the usual way. When you reach the end of the dock,

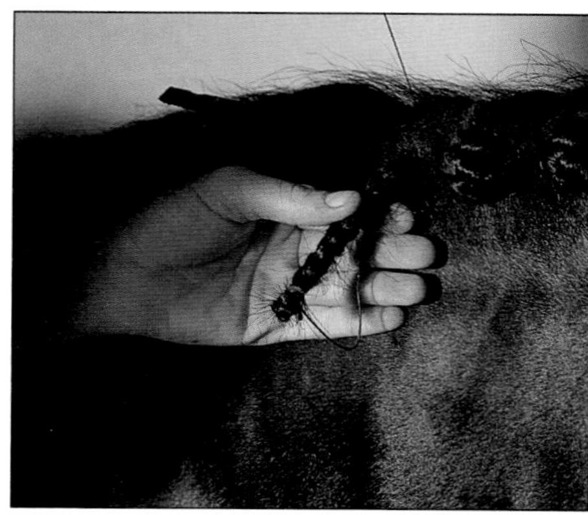

1 Plaiting a mane using needle and thread: the end of each plait is secured with thread.

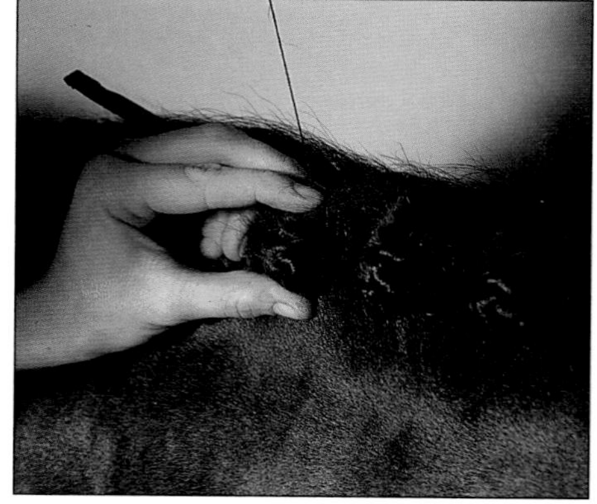

2 The plait is folded or rolled up until it is close to the crest and stitched firmly.

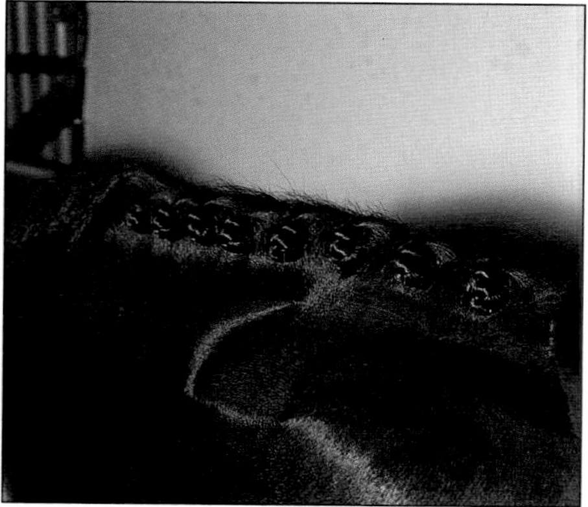

3 Finished plaits should be the same size. Using larger or smaller plaits can help disguise a poorly shaped neck.

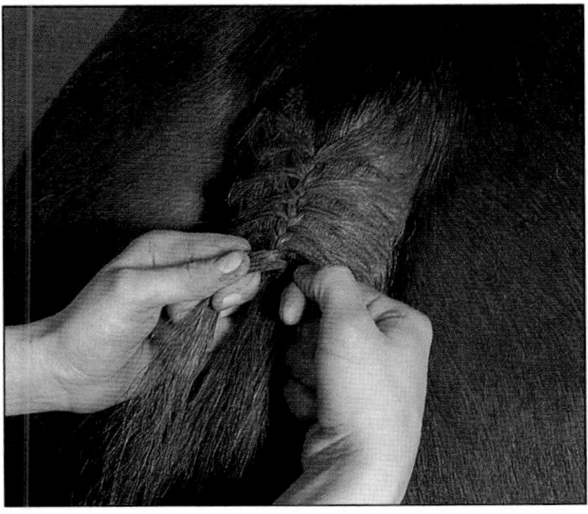

1 To plait a tail begin high up, using one bunch of hair from each side and one from the centre.

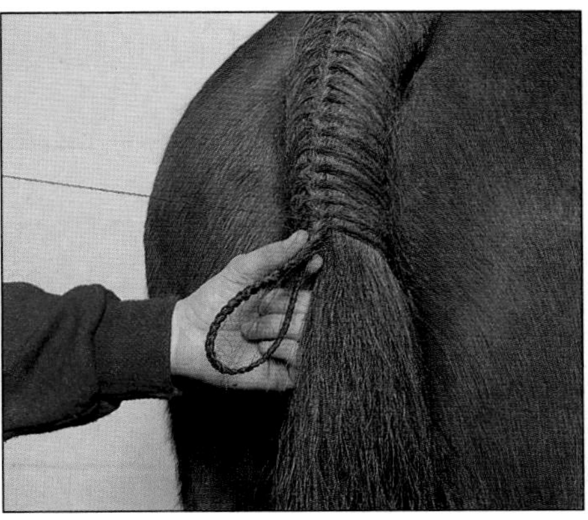

2 Plait down to the end of the dock, using thin bunches of hair from alternate sides.

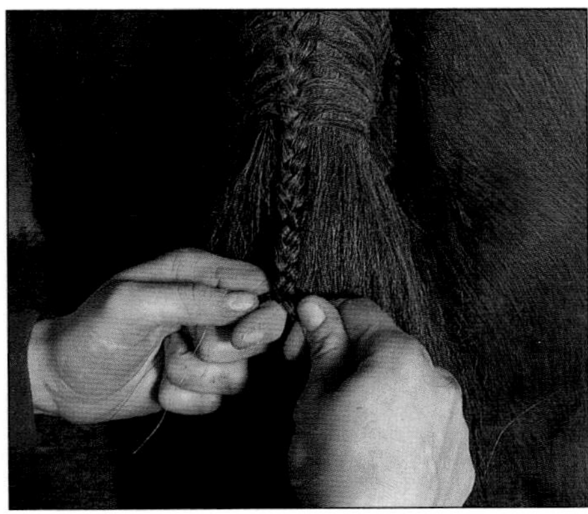

3 At the end of the dock, stop adding side bunches and continue plaiting the long hair.

divide the rest of the tail into three and continue plaiting to the end of the long tail hairs. The bottom of the plait should be secured with a thick rubber band or needle and thread. The plaited tail is rolled up under the dock and carefully sewn to hold it in place.

For smart occasions, such as showing and racing, the horse's coat may be decorated with **quarter marks.** These are applied on the hindquarters and may be drawn in with a comb, a brush, or by means of brushing over a plastic stencil. All three methods involve producing a pattern by brushing patches of the coat in different directions.

There are various other "tricks of the trade" which will enhance the appearance of a show horse. Chalk may be brushed into white leg markings. It is also useful for disguising any dirty marks on a grey coat, particularly those acquired during travelling, when there is no time to wash and dry the horse before his class. A little baby oil or Vaseline may be rubbed around the eyes and nostrils – this will accentuate the quality of the head. Human hairspray may be used to help control an unruly mane. The horse's coat may be given a final polish with coat gloss, which is specially made for the purpose.

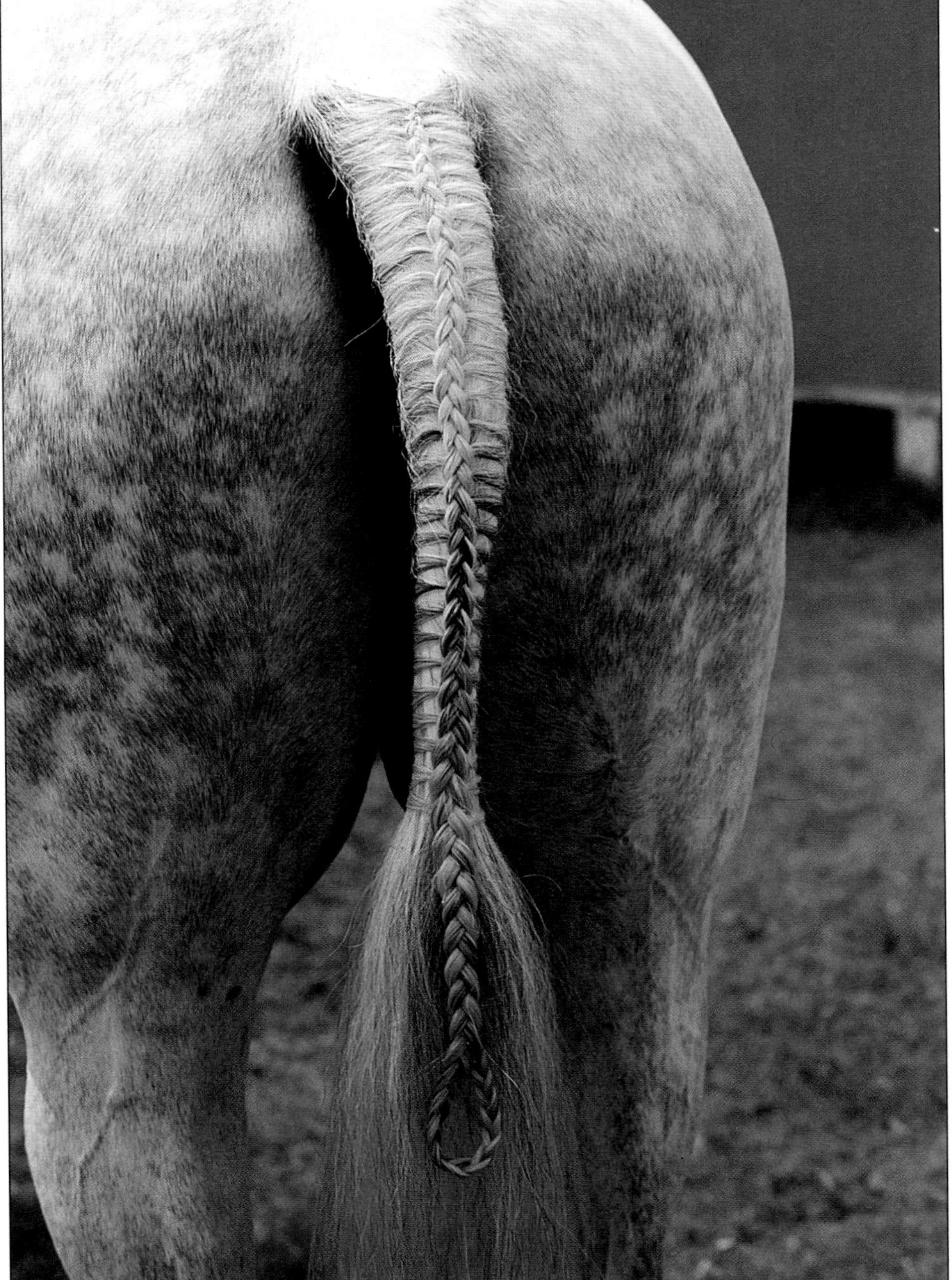

RIGHT
The end of the plait is secured with needle and thread, tucked under and sewn in place to give a smart appearance.

Horse Clothing and Equipment

The ridden horse needs a variety of clothing and equipment to keep him warm, clean and dry, and to protect him from injury.

Rugs are a necessity for clipped horses and for fine-skinned, hot-blooded types such as Thoroughbreds. Modern rugs are lighter in weight than their predecessors, making them more comfortable for horses to wear and easier to clean. They are also more effective at keeping the horse warm, dry, cool or clean.

There is always a risk that a horse may be injured during exercise or when he is competing or travelling to and from shows. To minimize the risk there is a range of equipment and clothing available to protect him literally from head to tail.

Turnout and Stable Rugs

TURNOUT RUGS

Turnout rugs are used to keep the horse warm and dry when turned out in the field. Turnout rugs are made from tough synthetic fabrics. Modern turnout rugs incorporate state-of-the-art breathable materials which are highly water- and windproof but still allow moisture to pass from the horse's body through the rug, preventing the horse from getting overheated.

The **New Zealand turnout rug** is a heavyweight canvas turnout rug, so-called because it was first developed in New Zealand. The self-righting type has breast and leg straps which help the rug to stay in place, whatever the horse gets up to.

The **Wug** and **Gladiator turnout rugs** are made from synthetic material. Both feature an extended neck which helps to keep the horse warm and dry.

LEFT
The Wug turnout rug, with its extended neck, is made from a tough yet lightweight material.

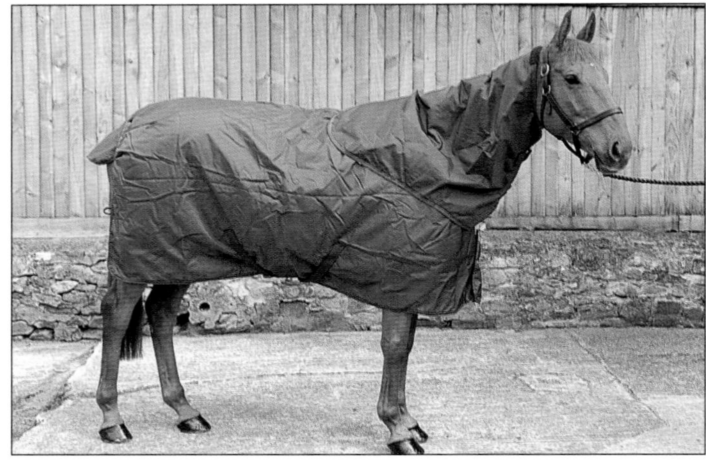

LEFT
The Gladiator turnout rug features a useful neck cover.

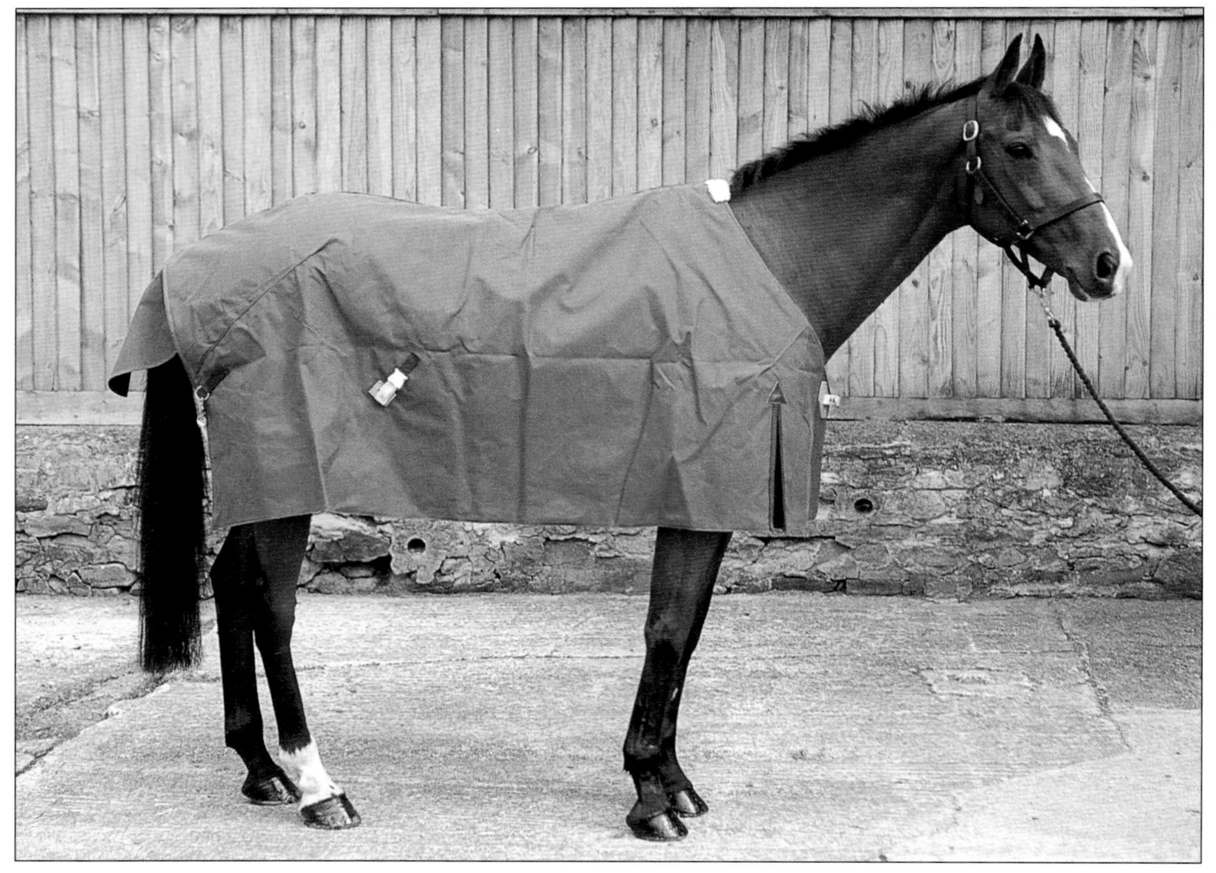

LEFT
The New Zealand rug is a heavyweight proofed canvas turnout rug.

BELOW
The stable synthetic rug can be used as a day or night rug.

RIGHT
quilted foal rug

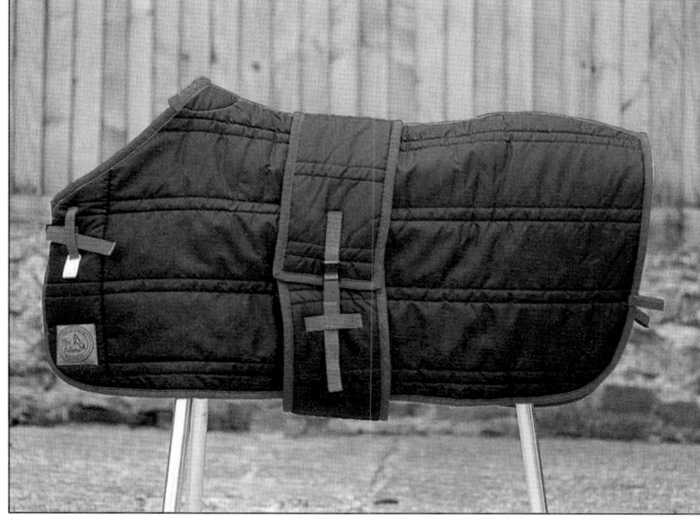

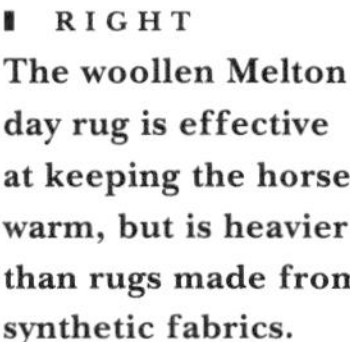

RIGHT
The woollen Melton day rug is effective at keeping the horse warm, but is heavier than rugs made from synthetic fabrics.

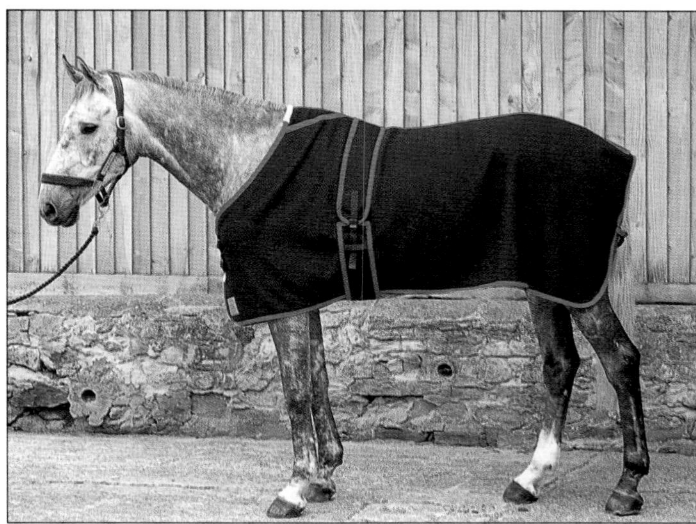

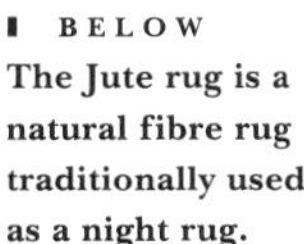

BELOW
The Jute rug is a natural fibre rug traditionally used as a night rug.

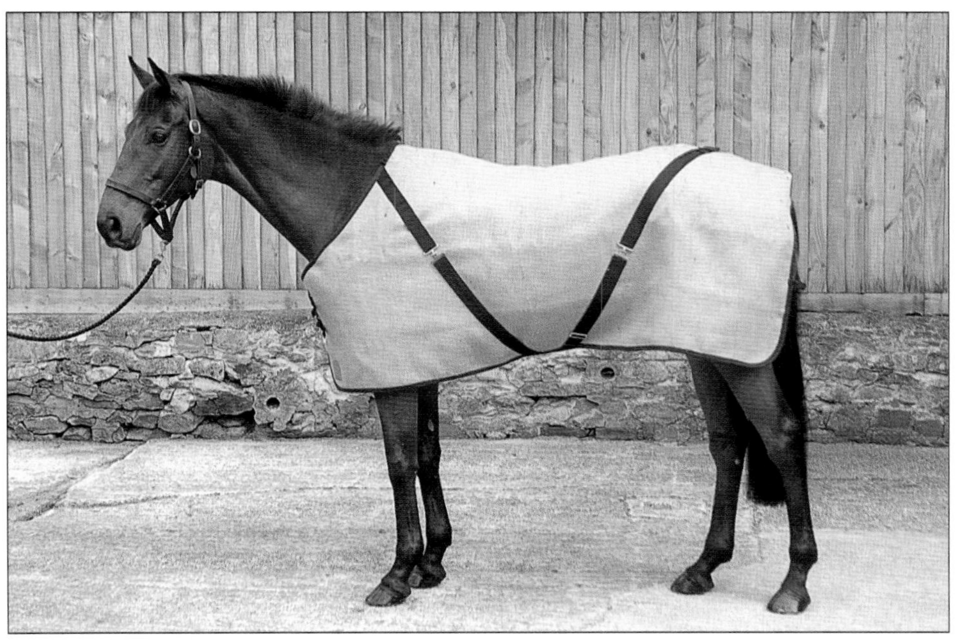

STABLE RUGS

Stable rugs keep the horse clean and warm in the stable. The models available range from lightweight cotton rugs for summer to thick quilted rugs for winter.

Melton day rugs are made of wool and are available in a range of colours. A woollen rug will keep the horse warm but it can be heavy and less breathable than modern fabrics, and is more difficult to clean. Woollen rugs can be personalized with the owner's initials or a sponsor's logo.

The **synthetic stable rug** is a modern alternative to the traditional woollen rug. New fabric technology means that stable rugs can be both lightweight and warm, allowing any sweat from the horse's body to pass through the fabric. Because they are easy to wash, synthetic stable rugs also work well as night rugs.

Under rugs (blanket liners), available in different thicknesses, are designed to be fitted under a horse's stable rug to provide extra warmth during the cold winter months. Extra warmth may also be provided by a **horse blanket** fitted under a stable or night rug.

Jute rugs, traditionally used as night rugs, have a natural fibre outer layer and a blanket lining. Their main disadvantage is that they are very heavy.

Sheets and Coolers

▮ BELOW
A linen summer (stable) sheet can be used to keep the stabled horse clean during warmer weather.

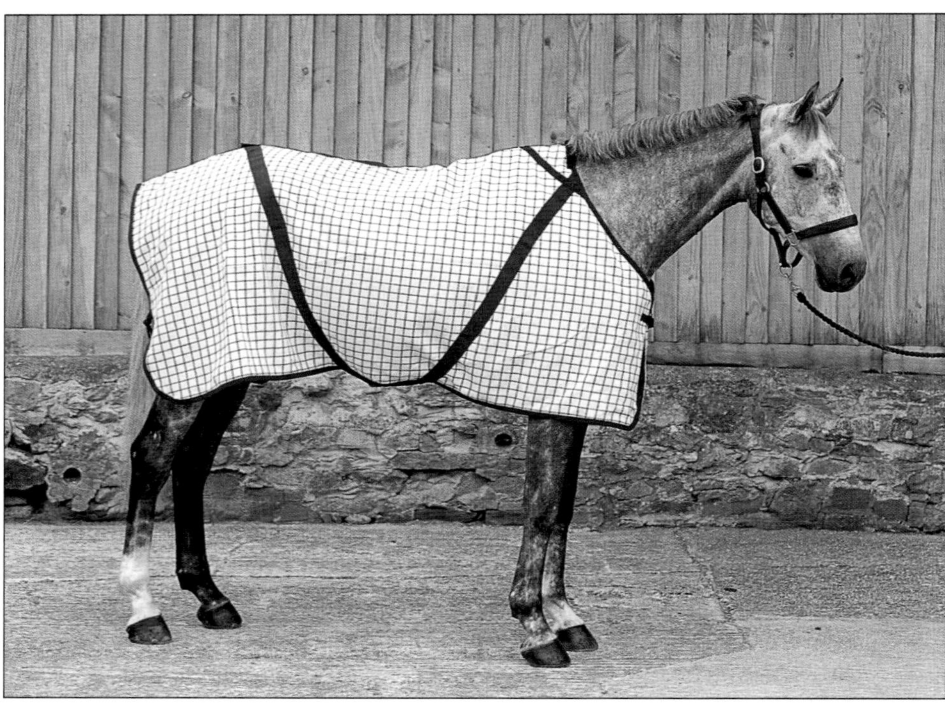

SHEETS

Sheets are made from lighter materials than turnout or stable rugs. A sheet can be used either in the summer months when the temperatures are higher, or immediately before or after exercise.

Summer (stable) sheets, made from linen or cotton, are lightweight rugs used to help keep the stabled horse clean.

Paddock sheets are shaped rugs in cotton or wool, so-called because they are used to keep racehorses warm while being paraded in the paddock before the race. The paddock rug is held in place with a surcingle and breastgirth. It can double as an exercise sheet, also called a half-sheet or quarter-sheet, to keep the racehorse's hindquarters warm during early morning exercise on the gallops.

Many exercise sheets are designed to keep the horse warm and dry while active, and are particularly useful for clipped horses. The synthetic polypropylene fabric used for the **wicking exercise sheet** will only allow moisture to pass through if the horse begins to sweat. This type of exercise sheet is worn under the saddle.

▮ BELOW
paddock sheet

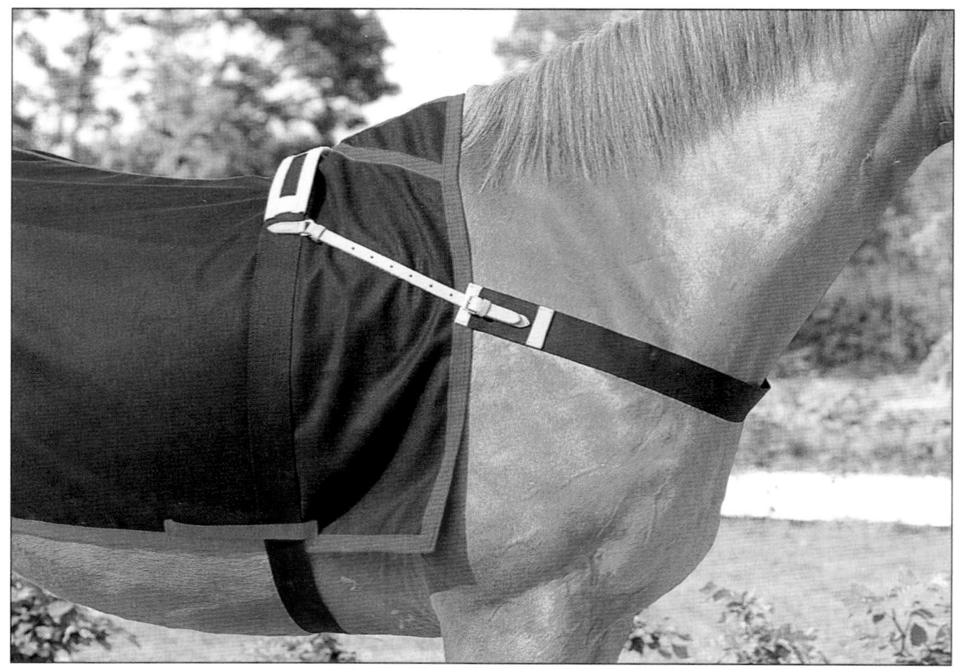

COOLERS

Coolers are multi-purpose rugs, often incorporating the latest developments in fabric technology. They allow the horse to dry off quickly after exercise or bathing without the risk of catching a chill because of a wicking effect which allows moisture to pass from the horse's body through the fabric. Cooler rugs are ideal for those horses with a tendency to sweat profusely when travelling.

The non-absorbent breathable fabric of the **Coolmasta rug** makes it suitable for use as an anti-sweat rug, a travelling rug or a stable rug. The polypropylene fabric of the **Universal wicking rug** allows dampness from the horse's body to pass through the rug to prevent chills, as does the **fleece rug**. The **Combi sweat (anti-sweat) rug and fly sheet (scrim)** is a fine-mesh rug. The knit of the cotton fabric creates air pockets which help the horse to dry off quickly. These rugs can be used on a stabled horse under a lightweight summer sheet to speed up the drying process after exercise.

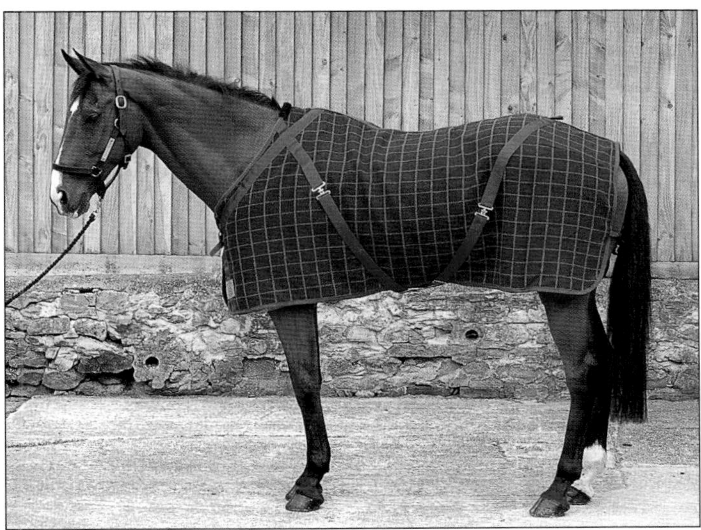

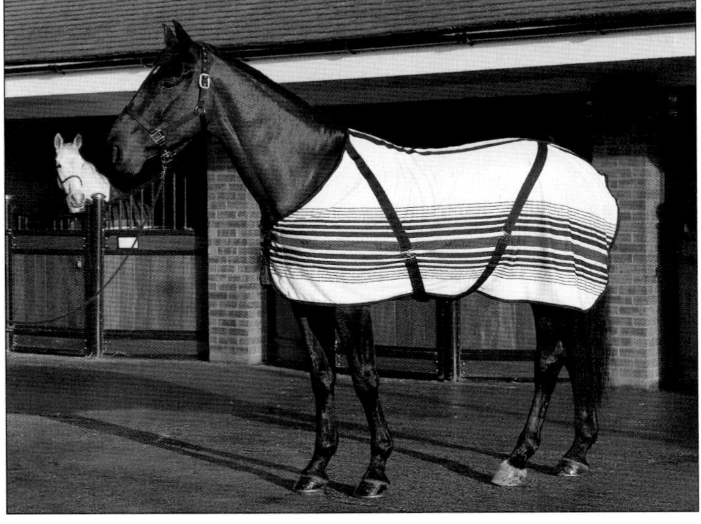

ABOVE LEFT
Universal wicking rug. A multi-purpose rug which lets body moisture through the fabric to prevent the horse catching a chill.

ABOVE RIGHT
Coolmasta synthetic rug. A cooler which is versatile enough to be used as summer (stable) sheet, anti-sweat rug, travel or day rug.

RIGHT
Fleece rug. While moisture evaporates away through the rug, the fleece fabric ensures that the horse's body temperature does not drop.

BELOW
Combi sweat (anti-sweat) rug and fly sheet (scrim). A fine mesh rug which can be used under a summer sheet to speed up drying.

BELOW RIGHT
Rain sheet. This waterproof rug (cover) will keep the horse dry at shows and competitions.

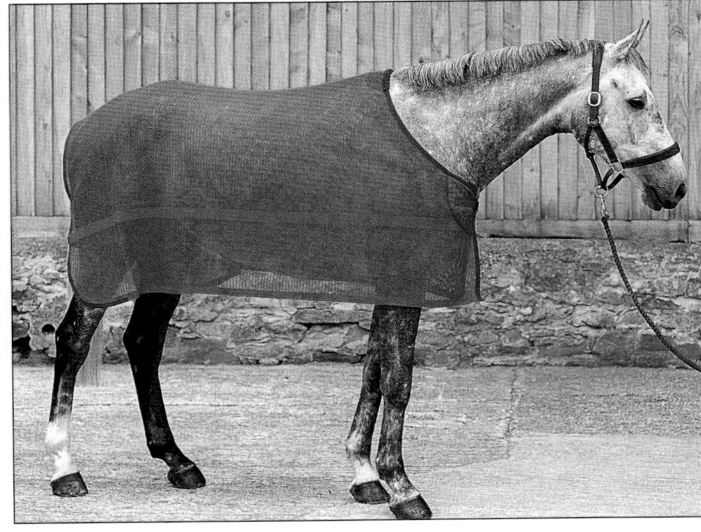

Specialist Sheets and Rugs

Besides the basic types of rug, an increasing number of rug products are available for more specific needs.

Exercise sheets will keep thin-skinned horses warm and dry during exercise sessions. The **continental waterproof exercise sheet** has a lightweight outer shell with a twill lining and can be fitted over the saddle in wet weather. The **fluorescent exercise sheet** ensures that both horse and rider are easily seen by other road users, and is especially useful for anyone who has to ride on roads at times of poor visibility.

The **rain sheet** is a lightweight synthetic sheet which covers the horse from ears to tail. The sheet will keep the horse dry at competitions and shows but should not be used on horses turned out in the field.

New-born foals do not normally require rugs. However, the **quilted foal rug** can be very useful in helping to keep a sickly foal warm in the stable.

The **rug bib (blanket bib)** is fitted under the rug to prevent it from rubbing the horse's shoulders, leading to sores and bare patches in his coat.

Hoods can be fitted to rugs to provide extra warmth and to help keep the horse clean. The **outdoor hood**, made from a synthetic material, can be fitted to a turnout rug. The **lycra hood** is used in the stable to keep the horse clean.

Chest extenders are panels of fabric with straps which can be buckled on to the horse's existing rug to provide a better fit.

BELOW
Continental waterproof exercise sheet

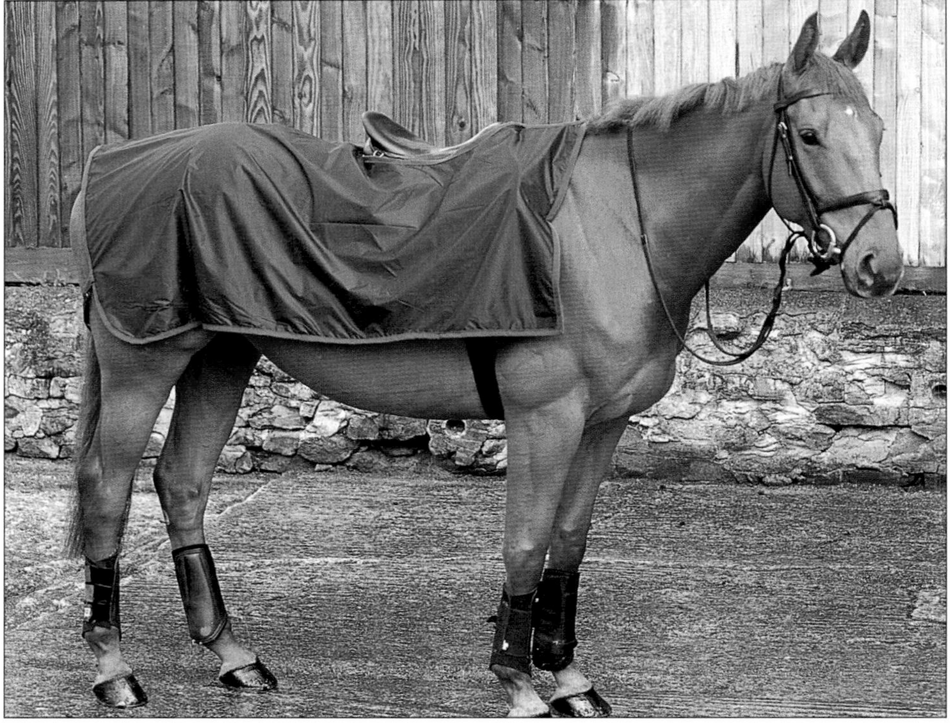

BELOW LEFT
fluorescent exercise sheet

BELOW RIGHT
wicking exercise sheet

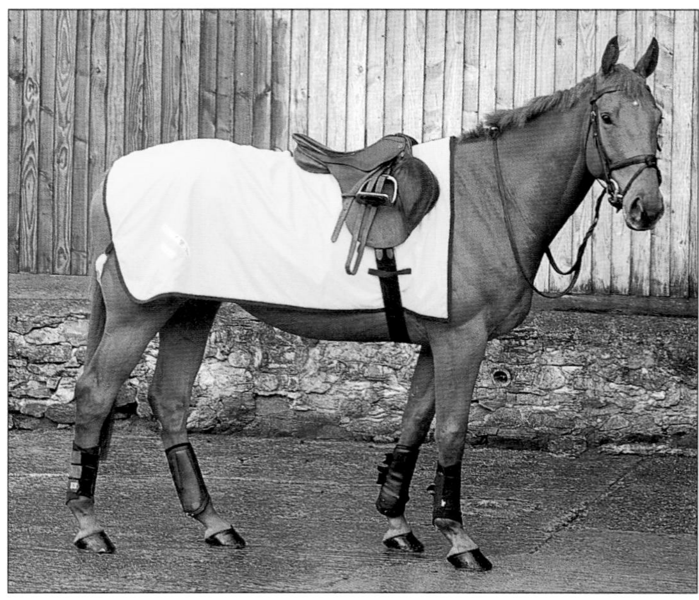

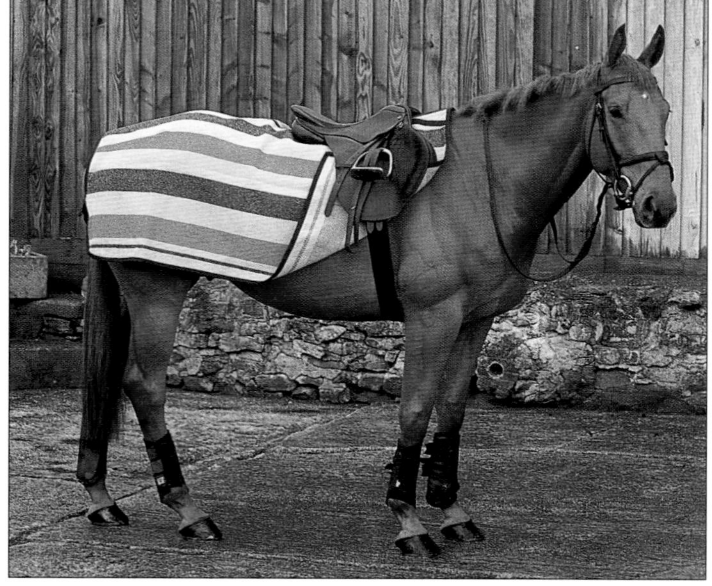

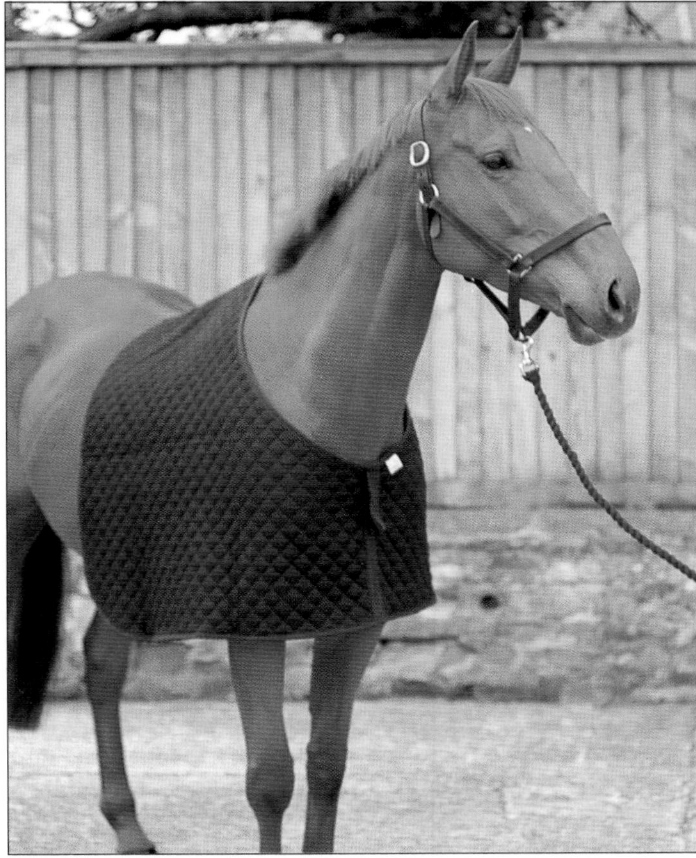

ABOVE
A rug bib is fitted under the rug to prevent the rug from rubbing.

ABOVE
golden stripe horse blanket

BELOW
lycra hood

BELOW
under rug

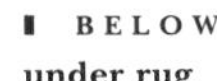

Fitting a Rug

Whatever type of rug you use, it is important that it is fitted correctly. Rugs are often left on for long periods of time and an ill-fitting rug can cause rubbing and discomfort. Rugs are sized according to their length, with the measurement based on the length of the horse taken from the centre of the chest to the tail.

HOW TO PUT ON A RUG

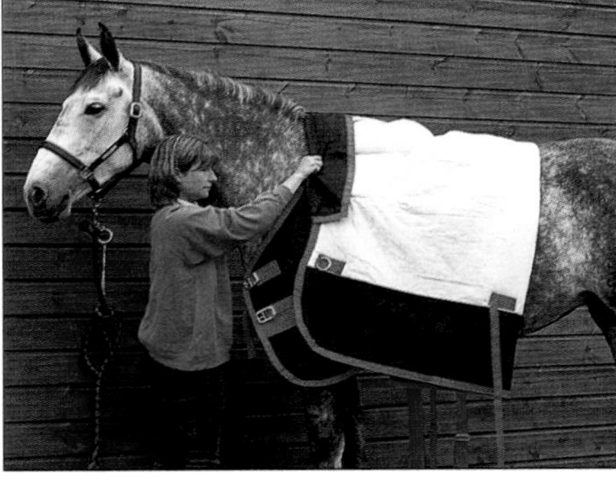

1 Stand on the near (left) side of the horse. Fold the blanket in half widthways and place it over the horse's neck. Fold the rug back over the horse's hindquarters.

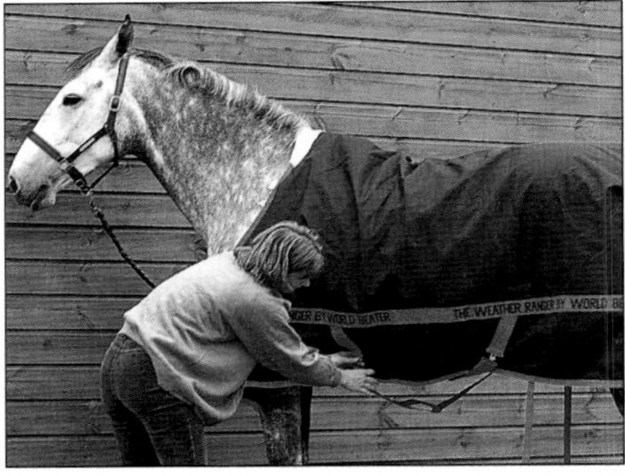

2 Fasten the cross surcingles, but not too tightly: there should be room for the width of a hand between the horse's belly and the straps. These straps should be fastened first so that there is no risk of the rug ending up hanging around the horse's neck, or worse still, his legs.

HOW TO REMOVE A RUG

To remove the rug, undo the leg straps first, then the chest straps and finally the cross surcingles. Fold the front of the rug over the horse's hindquarters and slide off carefully.

3 Next fasten the chest straps: there should be room for a hand's width at the chest.

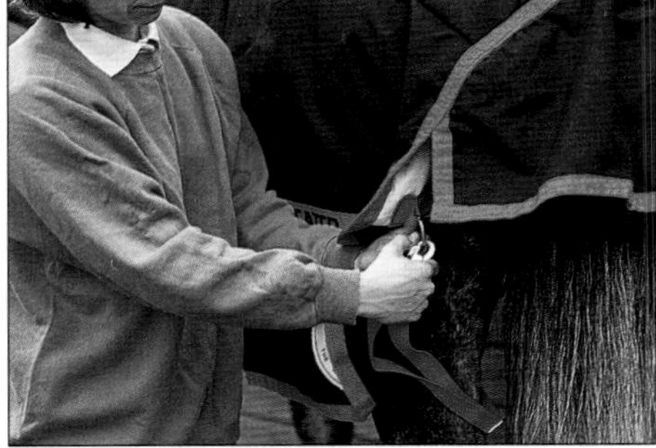

4 Finally, fasten the leg straps. Fitted correctly, the straps should hang clear of the horse's legs so that they do not rub, but should not be loose enough for the horse to get his leg caught.

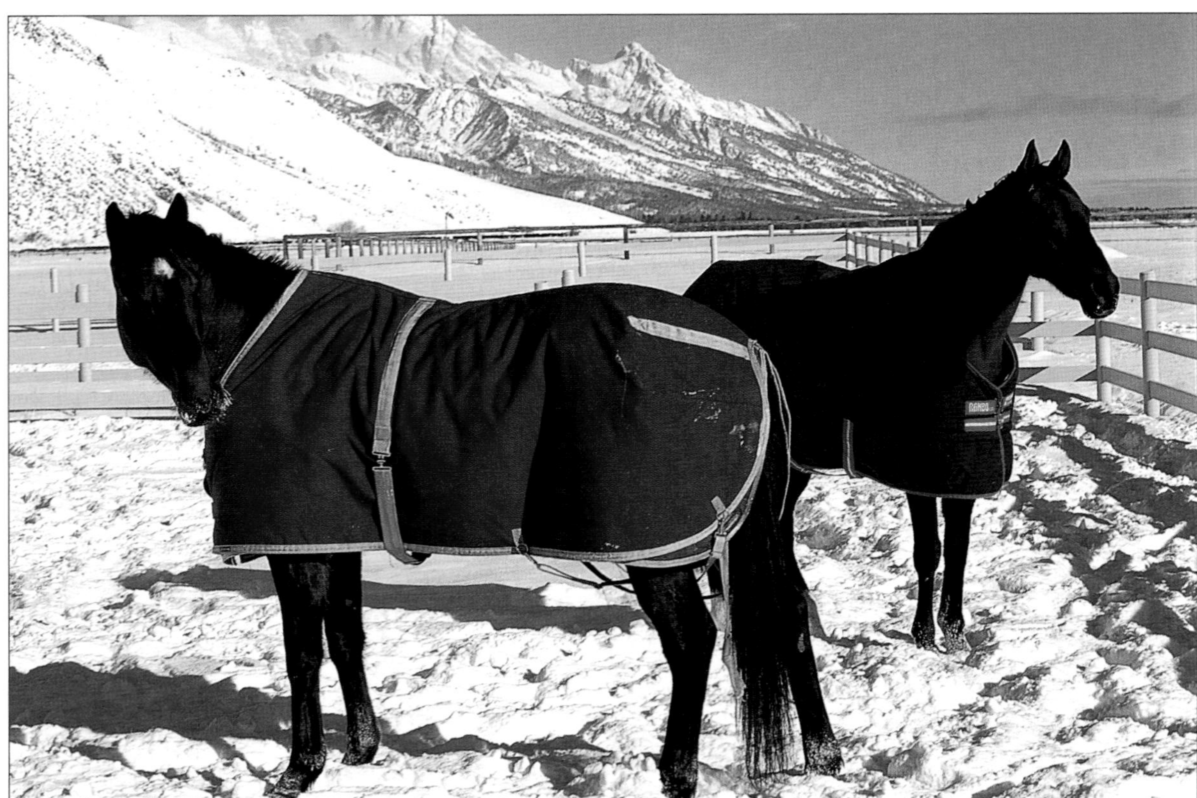

RIGHT
Modern turnout rugs allow horses to spend time out in their field whatever the weather. It is important to remember that turned out horses should have their rugs checked at least once a day, as the rug can slip and become uncomfortable for the horse.

Rug Rollers and Surcingles

Most modern stable rugs have surcingles already fitted but separate rollers and surcingles can be used to keep in place those rugs which do not incorporate their own. A separate roller or surcingle is also necessary when more than one rug at a time is worn, to keep them both in place.

Rollers and surcingles should be fitted snugly enough to secure the rug, but they should not be so tight as to be uncomfortable for the horse after long periods of time. Correctly tightened, there should be just enough room to allow four fingers between the roller or surcingle and the rug.

Surcingles used to secure rugs differ significantly from surcingles used to secure saddles, since the needs of the turned out horse and the ridden horse are not the same. The **rug surcingle** is designed for comfort. It is wrapped in protective padding and replaces the buckles and clasps of the saddle surcingle with thick rounded straps, to allow the horse the freedom to sit or roll.

The **elasticated surcingle** fits around the horse's girth. If you are using one of these, it is a good idea to fit a pad over the withers to prevent pressure sores. The **elasticated roller** has padding built in to the area in contact with the withers, as does the **jute surcingle**, which fastens with strong leather straps.

The **anti-cast roller**, made from webbing and leather, has a large metal hoop on the top which prevents the horse from getting cast or wedged when rolling in his stable (stall).

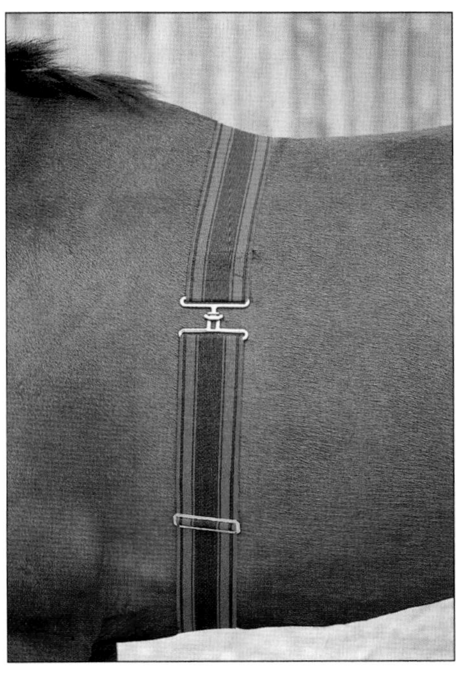

Elasticated surcingle. This type should be used with a pad over the withers to prevent pressure sores.

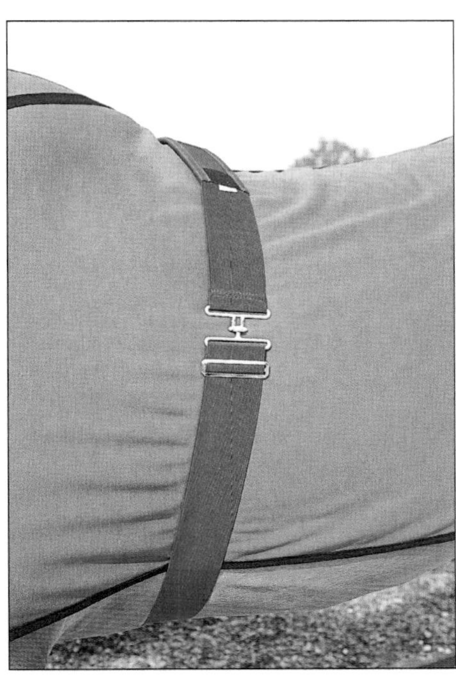

Elasticated roller. This type has padding built in to protect the withers.

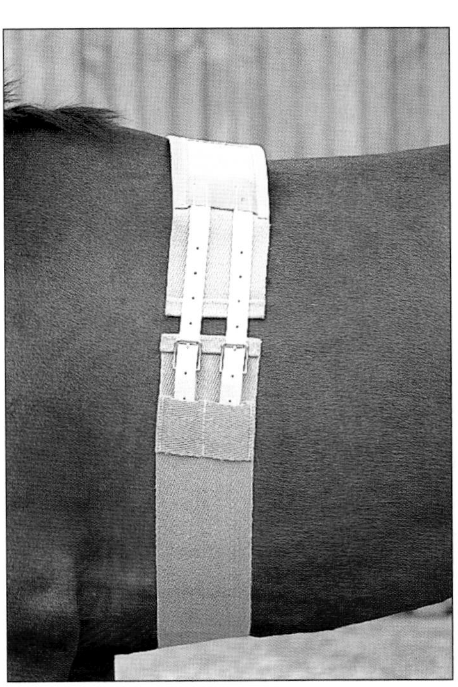

Jute surcingle. This type has built-in padding and fastens with strong leather straps.

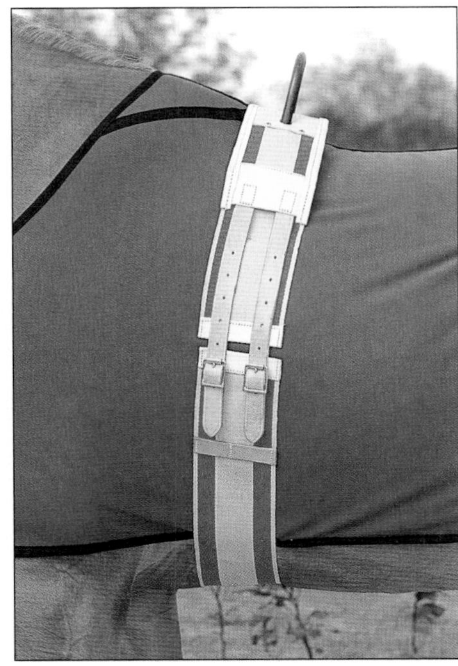

Webbing anti-cast roller. The large metal hoop on the top prevents the horse from getting cast.

Boots

Boots are designed to protect the horse's legs when travelling, turned out or being ridden, and a wide choice is available. Many equestrian activities place extreme demands on the horse's legs and protection is needed to prevent injury. Some horses are also predisposed conformationally to striking themselves accidentally while being exercised.

Brushing boots, also referred to as **splint boots**, have a reinforced pad along the inside of the boot to prevent injuries caused when one leg knocks against the other. The boot should start just below the knee and finish just below the fetlock (or ankle) joint. **Hind brushing boots** are longer than **fore brushing boots** to protect the hind cannon bone. **Leather brushing boots** have buckle and strap fastenings. They are tougher than synthetic boots but must be looked after to maintain their condition. **Synthetic brushing boots** are held in place with Velcro straps. They are lightweight and easily washed.

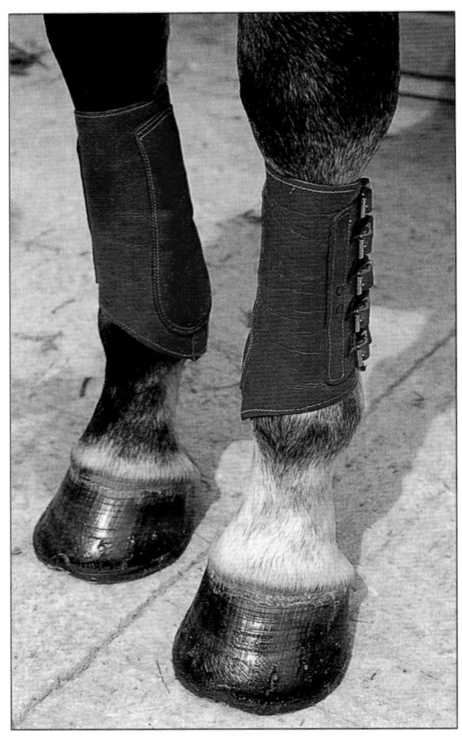

Leather brushing boots. These are used to prevent injuries inflicted as the horse is being brushed.

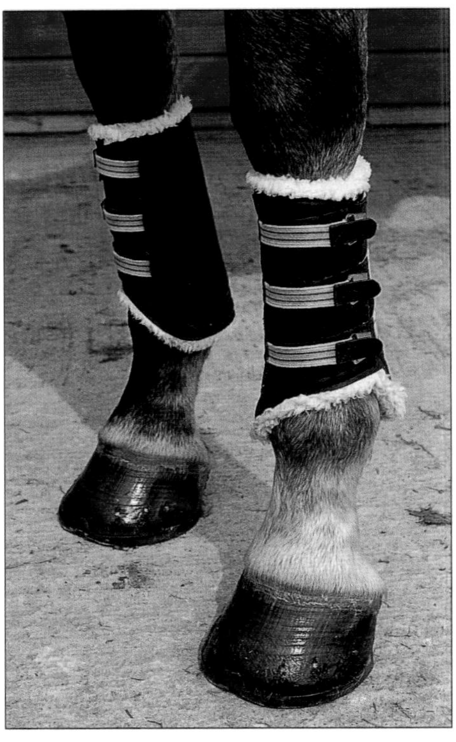

Synthetic brushing boots. These particular boots are fleece lined to prevent rubbing.

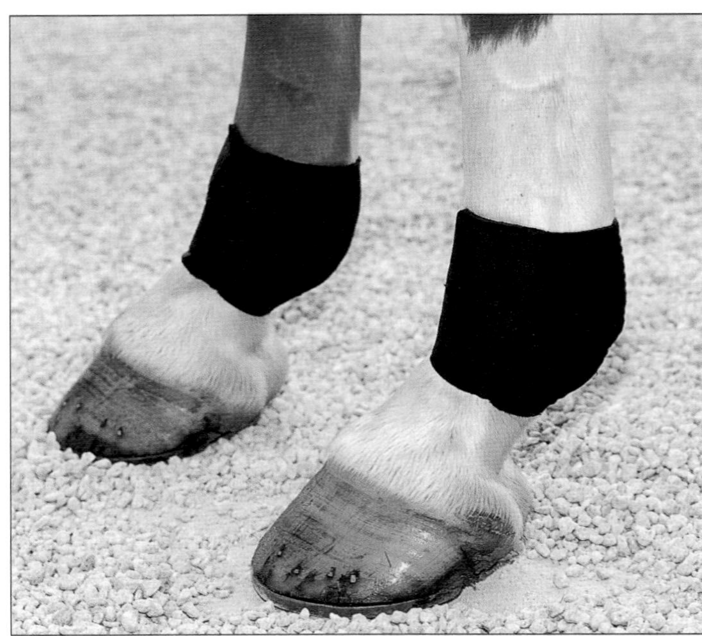

Sesamoid boots. These boots protect the base of the horse's fetlock.

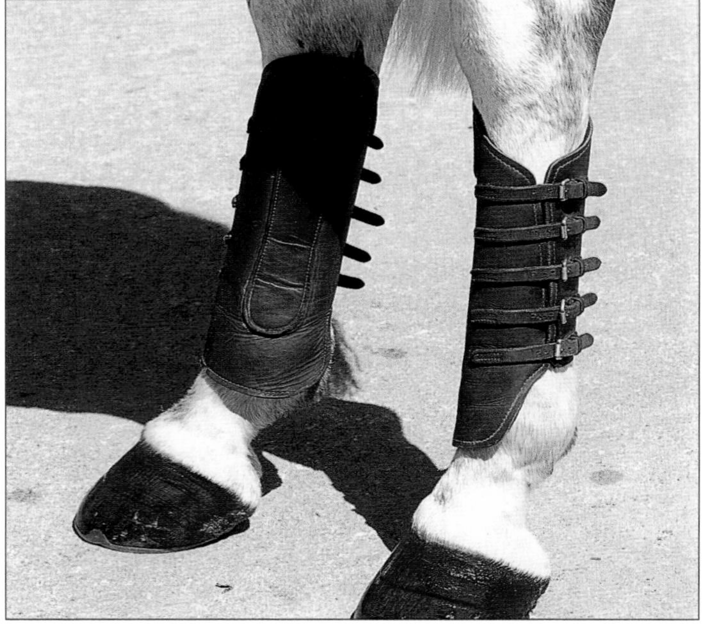

Speedicut boots. These are fitted to the hind legs to prevent injuries if the horse were to accidentally kick himself while galloping.

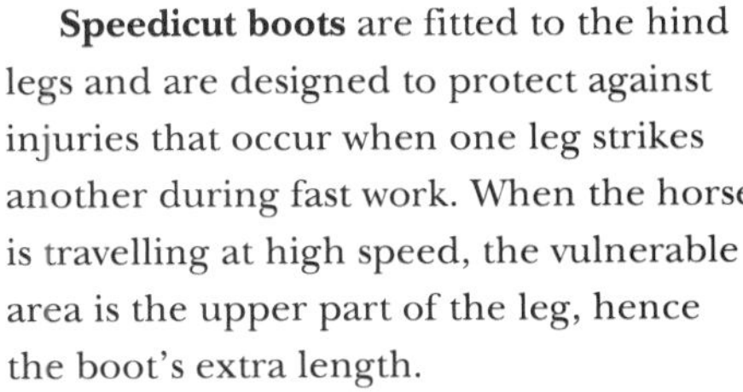

Speedicut boots are fitted to the hind legs and are designed to protect against injuries that occur when one leg strikes another during fast work. When the horse is travelling at high speed, the vulnerable area is the upper part of the leg, hence the boot's extra length.

Tendon boots are designed to protect the tendons which run down the back of the horse's lower foreleg, so are normally open-fronted. The boots should start high enough to protect the tendon and extend low enough to protect the fetlock joint. **Leather tendon boots** have buckle and strap fastenings and may be lined with sheepskin to prevent rubbing. **Synthetic tendon boots** usually have strap and clip fastenings.

Open-fronted boots are popular with show jumpers because they protect the vulnerable part of the horse's leg while still allowing him to feel the poles of the jump.

Sesamoid boots protect the base of the fetlock joint and are often used on racehorses that are trained or run on all-weather or dirt tracks. The base of the fetlock would be damaged if unprotected as it touches the ground as the result of the forces exerted when galloping.

BELOW
Leather tendon boots protect the tendons which run down the back of the horse's leg.

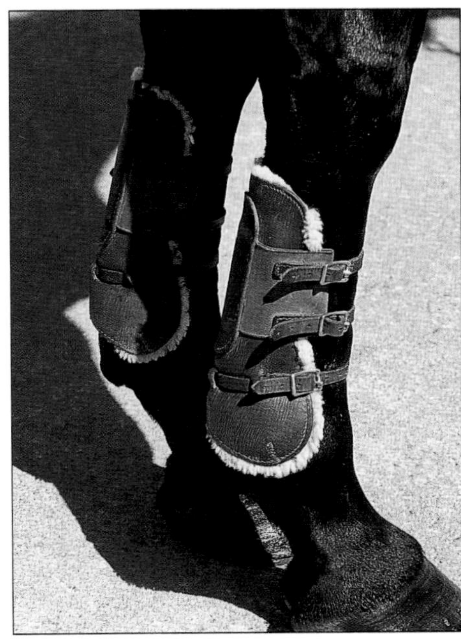

BELOW
Synthetic tendon boots are cheaper and easier to clean than the leather boots.

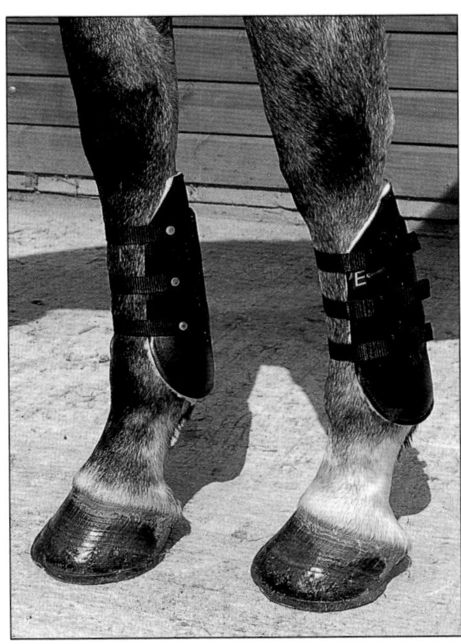

Fetlock boots are shortened versions of brushing boots, fitted to the hindlegs. **Skid boots** are used for Western riding, and are fitted to prevent fetlock injuries which can occur when the horse makes sliding halts.

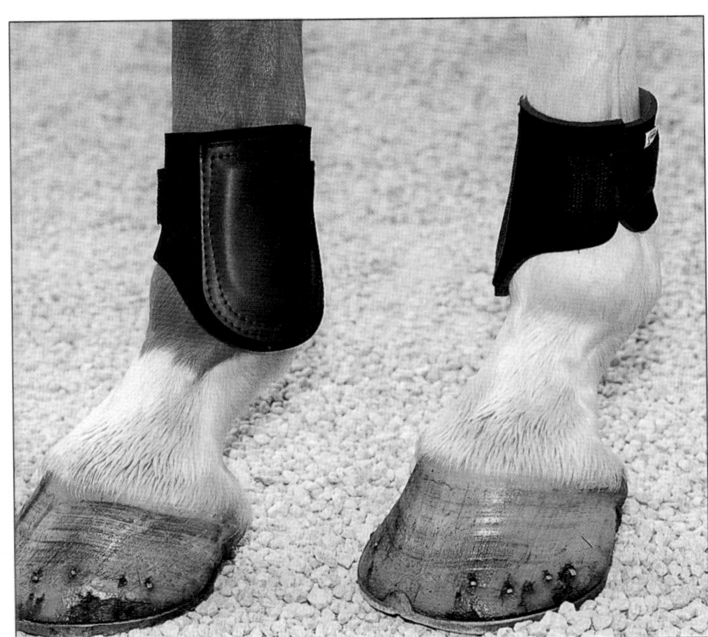

Fetlock boots. These are a shortened version of the brushing boot, and are normally fitted to the hindlegs only.

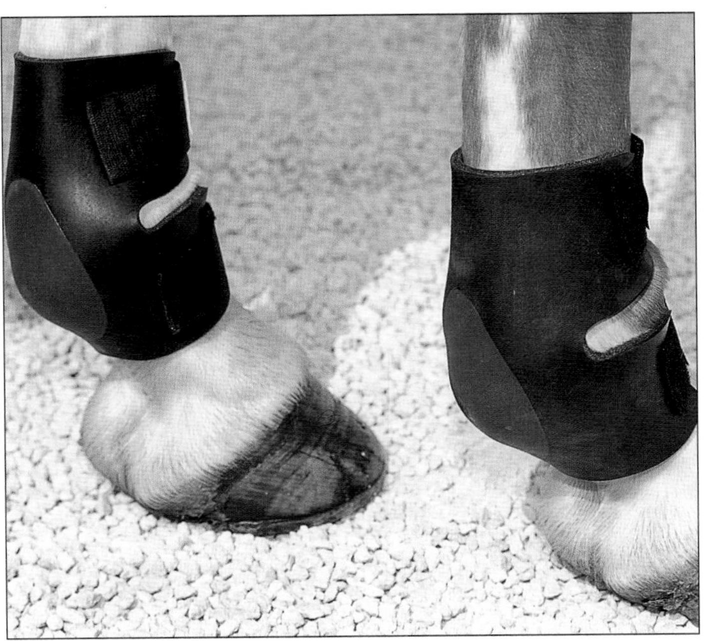

Skid boots. These are fitted to prevent injuries to the fetlock when the horse comes to a sliding halt.

Free knee boots prevent damage to the horse's knees when jumping. Because of their design – they can flip up – they are not suitable for road work or travelling. **Skeleton knee boots** have a lower strap fitted which prevents the pad from flipping up in the event of the horse falling. They are not suitable for jumping as there is a risk that the horse could get a hoof caught in the back strap.

The **coronet ring**, also called an anti-brushing ring, is fitted to one of a pair of legs to prevent brushing injuries. A **sausage boot**, also referred to as a **shoe-boil boot**, is used on stabled horses to prevent injury to the elbow when the horse lies down.

Overreach boots, or **bell boots**, prevent overreach injuries. An overreach is caused by the toe of the hind foot striking into the heel or coronet of the front foot. **Pull-on rubber overreach boots** can be difficult to get on but, once on, stay in place well. A disadvantage of this type of overreach boot is that they can flip up, in which case they will not protect the heel and coronet. **Velcro-fastened rubber overreach boots** are easier to put on and take off. **Petal boots** are less likely to flip up because of their segmented design. They are made up of a series of tough plastic segments or petals which are attached to a strap fitted around the coronet.

Covering boots are felt shoes which fit over the mare's hind feet. They are used on mares being covered, to avoid risking injury to the stallion should the mare try to kick him.

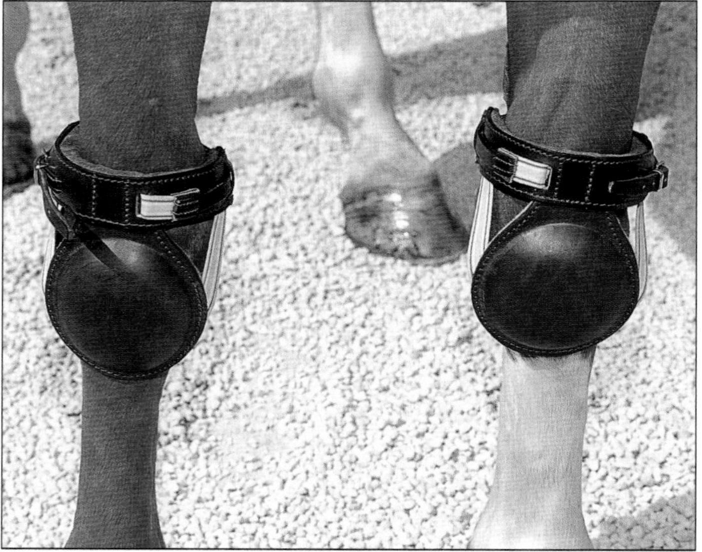

LEFT
Free knee boots. Because of their design, these boots are not suitable for roadwork or travelling.

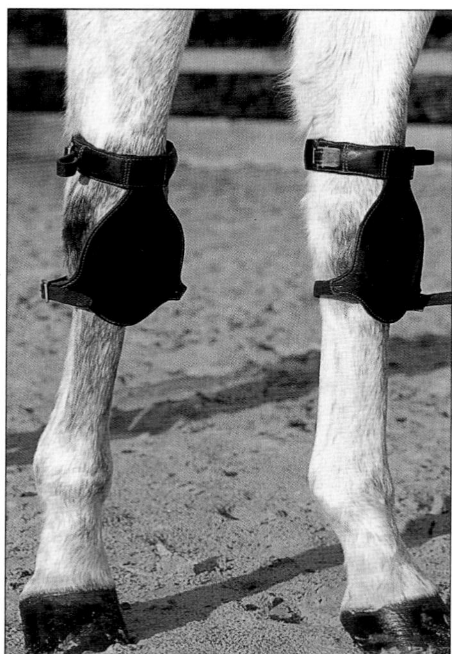

ABOVE
Skeleton knee boots. These have a lower strap fitted which prevents the pad flipping up.

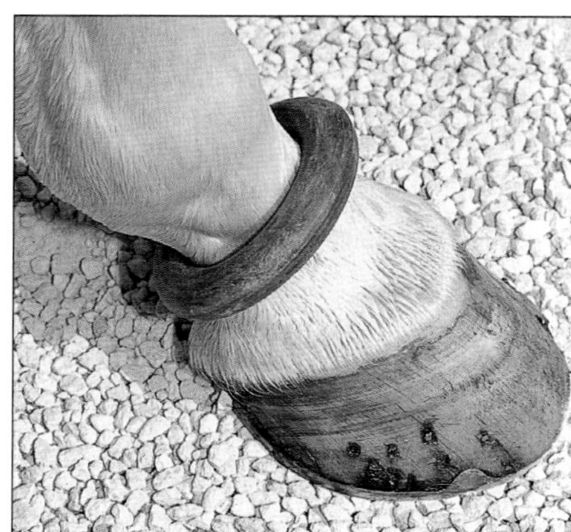

ABOVE
Coronet ring. This is fitted to one leg to prevent brushing injuries.

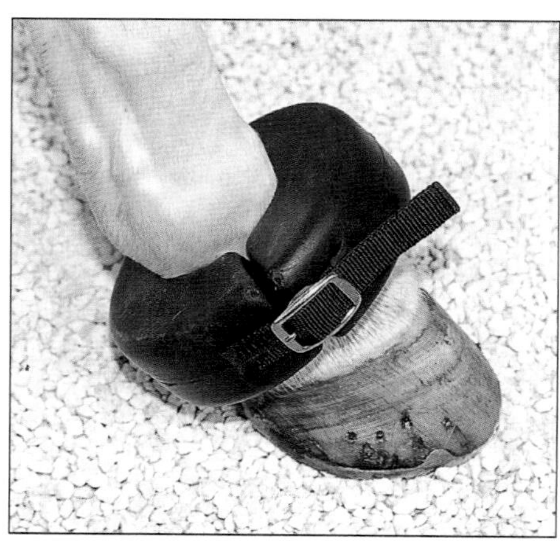

RIGHT
Sausage boot. These are used on stabled horses to prevent injuries to the elbow.

LEFT
Protection is necessary to guard against the hazards encountered during the cross-country phase of a one-day event. Because the horse is jumping fixed objects, it is vital that his legs are protected with boots or bandages.

ABOVE
Mare's covering boots. These felt shoes are fitted over the mare's hind feet to protect the stallion should she lash out at him.

ABOVE
Velcro-fastened rubber overreach boots. This type is easier to put on and take off than the pull-on variety of overreach boot.

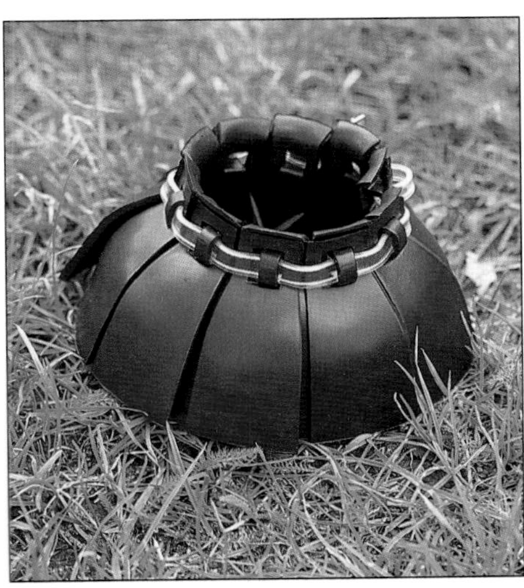

RIGHT
Pull-on rubber overreach boots. These moulded boots will sit securely on the hoof, but they do flip up easily and can offer no protection when this happens.

LEFT
Petal boots are made up of a series of tough plastic segments which are attached to a strap.

EXERCISE BOOTS

Exercise boots, such as brushing boots, are much more convenient to use than exercise bandages (polo wraps) as they are quicker and easier to put on.

BELOW
Skid boots are worn by reining horses to protect the base of the fetlock joint from injury as he comes to a sliding halt.

FITTING BRUSHING BOOTS

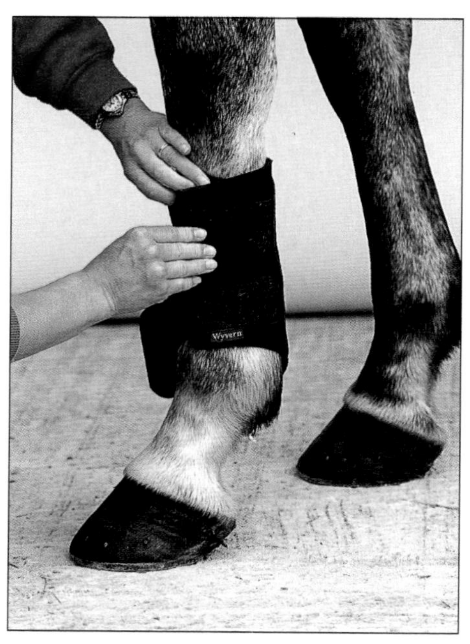

1 Never kneel down when putting on or taking off boots – always crouch so that you can get out of the way quickly should the horse suddenly move. When fitting boots with two straps, fasten the top strap first.

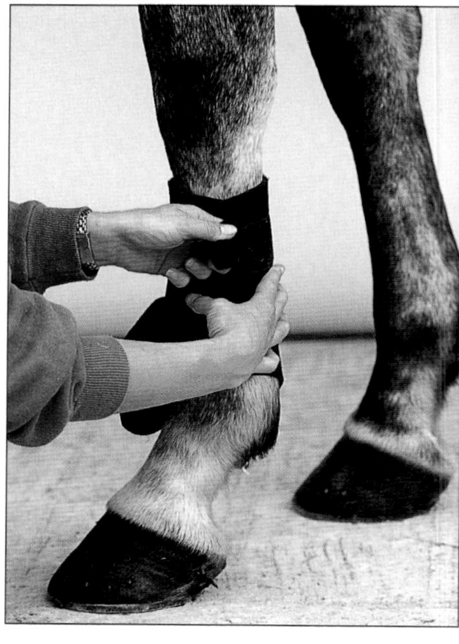

2 On most boots, straps fasten from the front to the back. For boots with more than two straps, fasten the middle strap first, then the top strap and finally the bottom strap or straps.

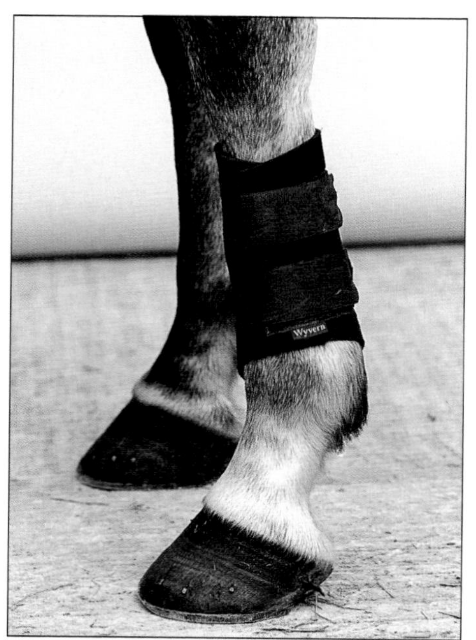

3 Be careful not to over-tighten boots as this is uncomfortable for the horse and can damage the tendons in his lower legs.

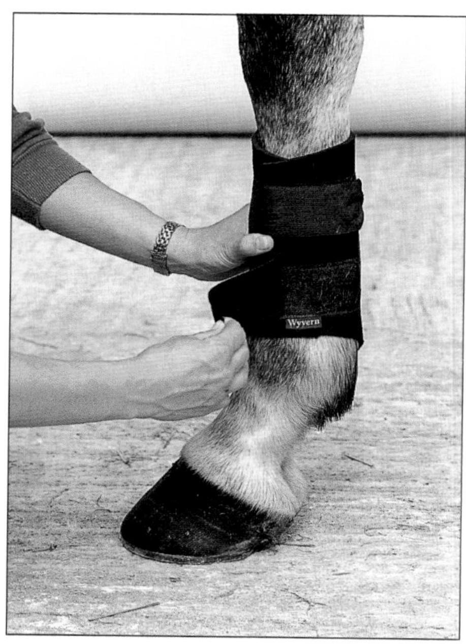

4 When removing boots, undo the bottom strap before unfastening the top one.

THERAPY BOOTS

These boots are designed to keep in place poultices, which are used to draw out dirt from a wound, and otherwise to assist in the treatment of injuries.

Rubber over-shoes fit over the horse's foot. One of these can be used to cover a foot bandage or poultice, or to protect the unshod hoof during ridden work. The **Tenderfoot sox** is used to hold a foot poultice in place.

A **tendon-hosing boot** fitted to the horse's lower leg allows cold water to be trickled down the leg to help reduce swelling caused by stresses, strains or injuries. If something more than a trickle is needed **aqua boots**, covering the entire lower leg and foot, are attached to a compressor which forces water to move around inside, massaging the lower leg.

Magnetic therapy boots are available in various designs. They incorporate thin, flexible magnetic pads which, when placed over the injured area, are said to assist in the repair of muscle, tendon or bone damage.

LEFT
rubber over-shoe

LEFT
magnetic therapy boots

BELOW LEFT
tendon-hosing boot

BELOW RIGHT
aqua boots.

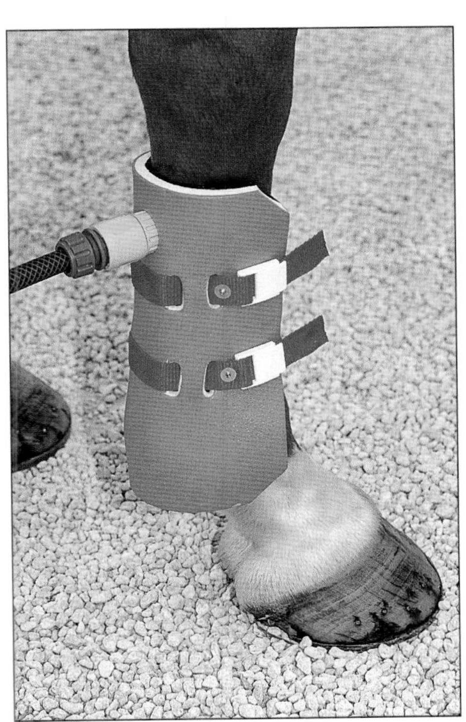

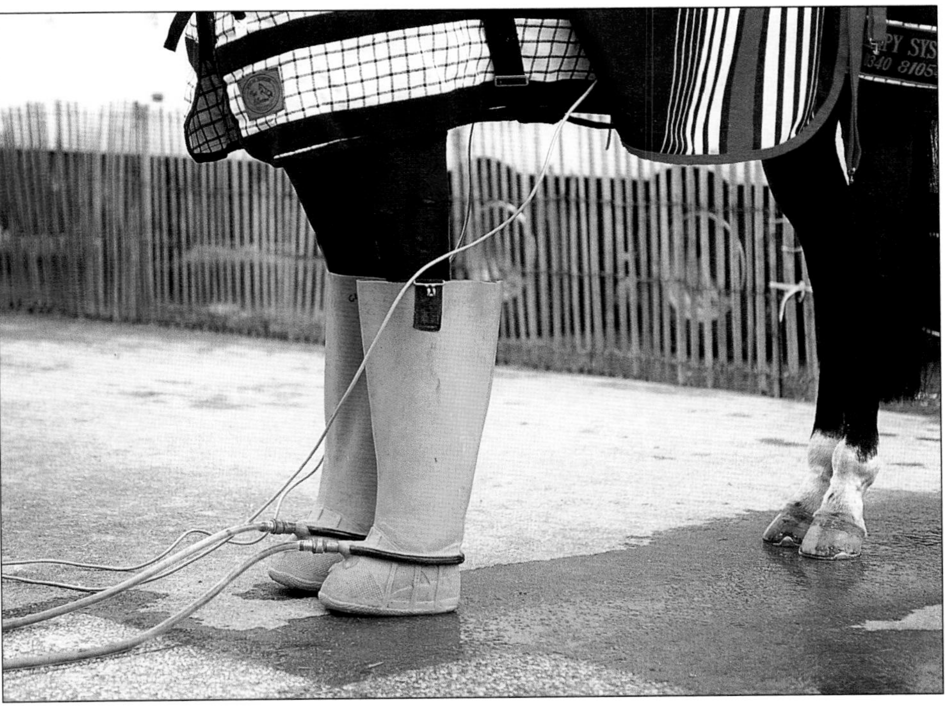

Bandages and Pads

BANDAGES

Like boots, bandages can be used to protect the horse's legs during exercise or travelling as well as for first-aid purposes.

Travelling or **stable bandages** are non-stretch bandages usually made of wool or acrylic and used for warmth and protection. To prevent pressure sores developing on the leg, they should always be used with padding underneath.

Exercise or **tail bandages** are lighter in weight than stable bandages. They are usually slightly elasticated and are held in place with ties. When used to protect the leg during competitions, in particular horse trials, they can be stitched in place. They will help to smooth the tail hair down as well as protecting the tail while the horse is travelling to the competition.

Polo wraps are made from strong, shock-absorbent felt. Unlike traditional bandages, polo wraps do not require padding underneath.

A **cohesive bandage** is a stretchy bandage which sticks to itself. It can be used as an alternative to an exercise bandage or for holding dressings and poultices in place.

PADS

Bandages should never be applied directly to the leg (except for polo bandages) but should be used with bandage pads to help reduce the risk of pressure sores developing on the legs.

Felt pads are hardwearing and shock absorbent, but they do not mould easily to the shape of the horse's leg. **Cotton quilted pads** are easily washable and hardwearing but, like felt, do not mould easily to the horse's leg. **Porter boots** are hard-shelled leg protectors which mould to the shape of the horse's leg and are held in place with an exercise bandage. They are used instead of pads to protect the leg from injury during competitions.

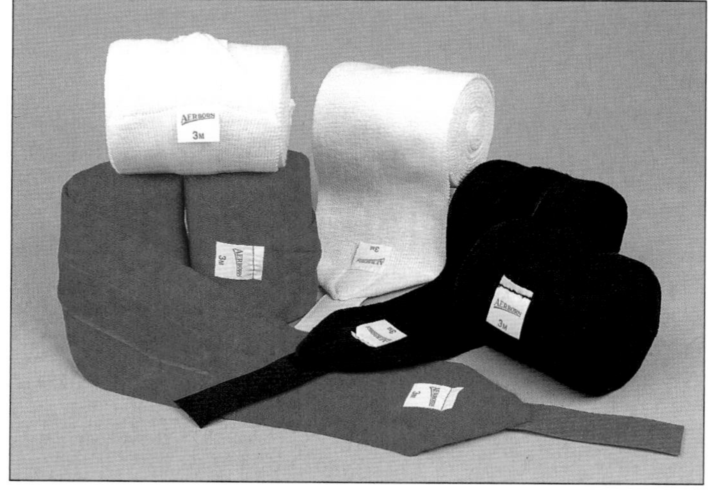

LEFT travelling or stable bandages

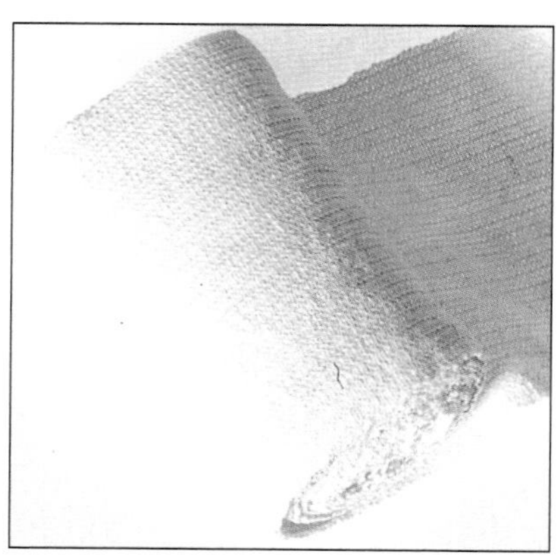

BELOW LEFT exercise or tail bandage

BELOW RIGHT polo wraps

ABOVE LEFT stable bandages

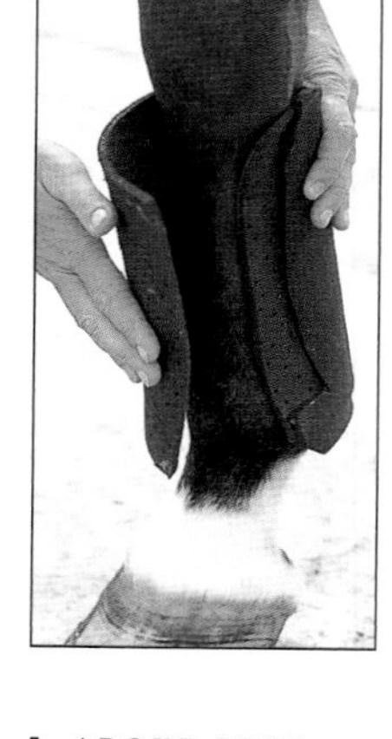

ABOVE RIGHT Porter protector

LEFT cohesive bandage

EXERCISE BANDAGES

Exercise bandages and polo wraps are used to protect the horse's legs during exercise or work. A great deal of skill is required to apply bandages which are neither too tight (which can lead to damaged tendons), nor too loose (when they can unravel and cause the horse to fall). Exercise bandages must always be applied over some sort of padding, such as a Gamgee, Fybagee or Porter boot.

PUTTING ON AN EXERCISE BANDAGE

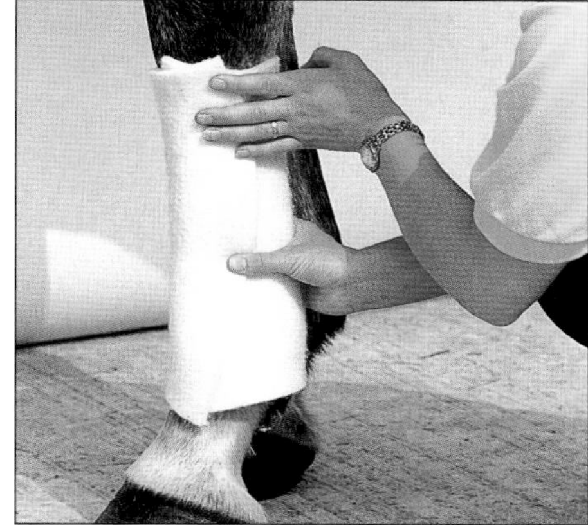

1 Place the padding around the leg, making sure that the edge of the pad lies between the tendons, on the outside of the leg. The padding should start just below the knee or hock and finish just below the fetlock joint. Wrap the pad around the leg firmly, from front to back, making sure that there are no lumps or wrinkles.

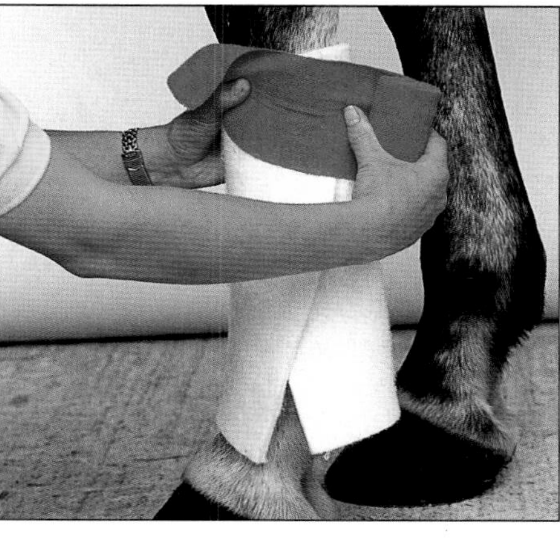

2 Bandage in the same direction as the padding and start just below the padding at the top.

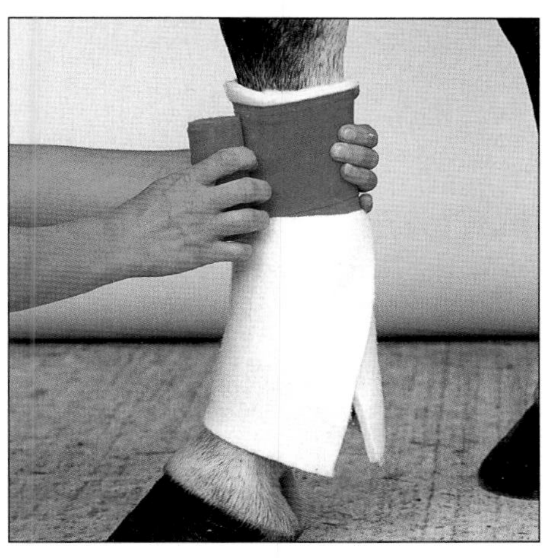

3 Do one complete turn with the bandage around the top of the padding before working down the leg. Exercise bandages are elasticated so be careful not to pull the bandage in too tightly.

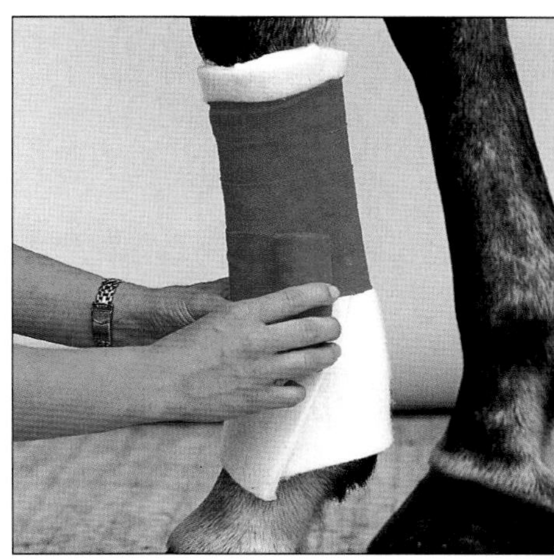

4 Make sure that the bandage stays smooth and that the tension is even.

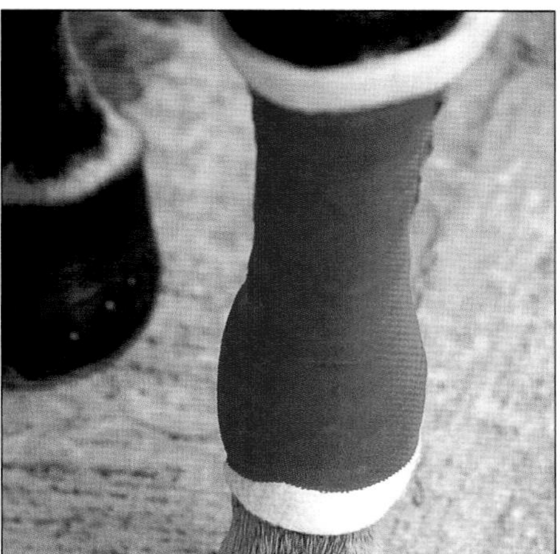

5 At the bottom of the leg the bandage should follow the same angle as the fetlock joint so that it forms a V at the front of the leg. This will ensure that the movement of the fetlock is not restricted.

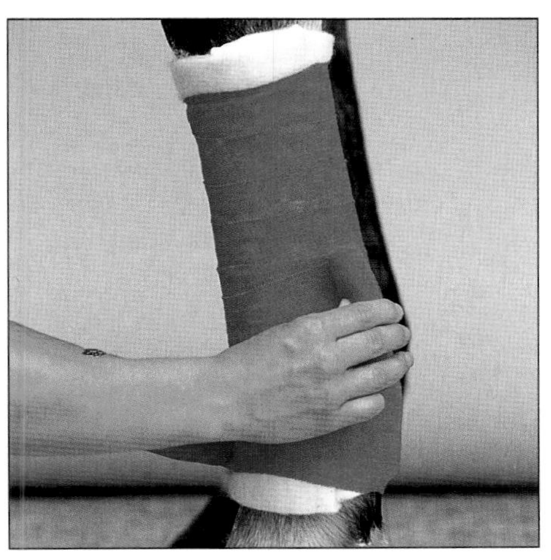

6 Continue to wrap the bandage around the leg, working back up to the top of the padding.

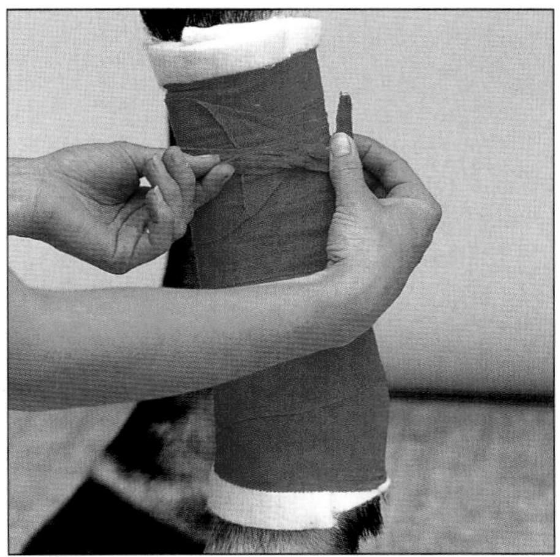

7 Secure the bandage by fastening the ties with a simple knot. The knot should be flat and sit on the outside of the leg. For competitions, stitch the bandage to ensure that it stays in place. Cover the stitched end with insulating tape.

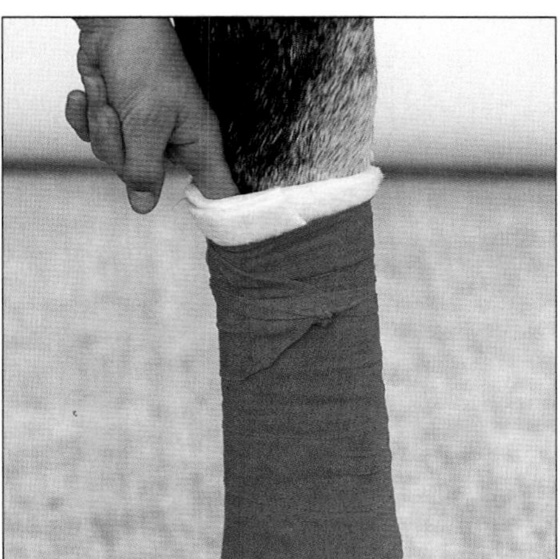

8 The bandage should be firm enough not to slide down but not so tight that it could damage the tendons. You should just be able to slide your finger inside the bandage.

RIGHT
padded tail guard

Travelling Equipment

Special clothing can be used to protect the horse from injuries incurred during transportation in a horse truck or trailer.

A **tail guard** prevents the horse from rubbing his tail when travelling. Linen and cotton tail guards are secured with strips tied to the surcingle. The padded tail guard is fitted with Velcro fastenings.

Shaped travel boots can be used instead of travelling bandages to protect the front and hindlegs, from the coronet up to the knee and hock. **Travel boots** are simple square wraps which give protection to the lower leg.

Hock boots, made from leather and felt, are fitted over the top of travel bandages to protect the hock from injury, in the same way that **knee pads** are used to protect the knees. **Felt travel pads** under travel bandages will do the same job.

A **poll guard**, made from leather with a felt lining, provides protection for the sensitive poll area of the horse's head. It is attached to the headcollar or halter.

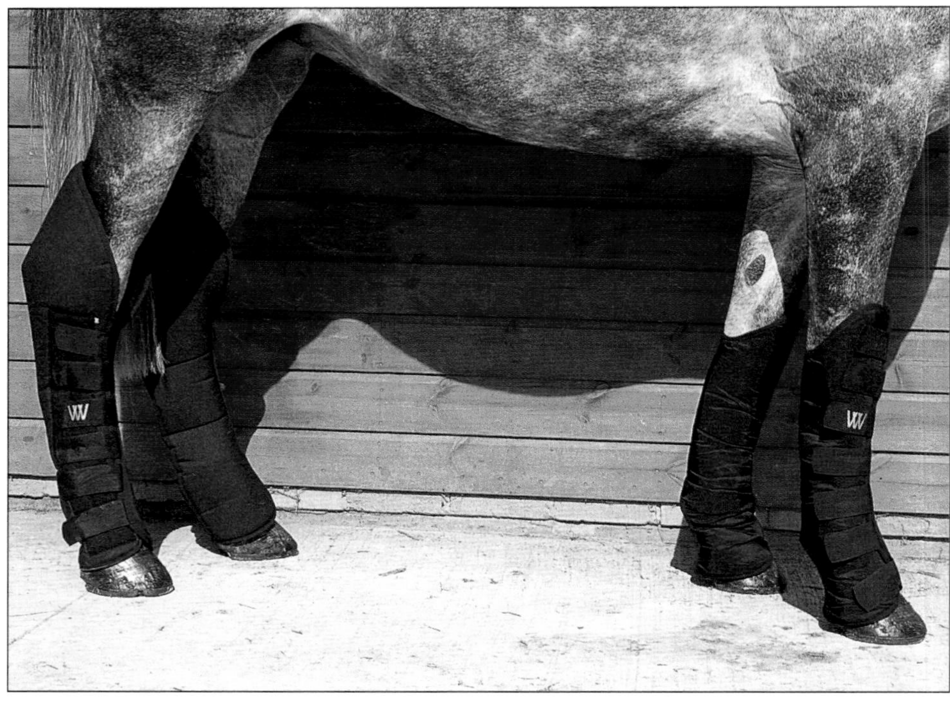

Shaped travel boots. These are designed for front or hindlegs to protect them from the coronet right up to the knee or hock.

Travel boots. These simple square padded wraps are effective in protecting the lower leg.

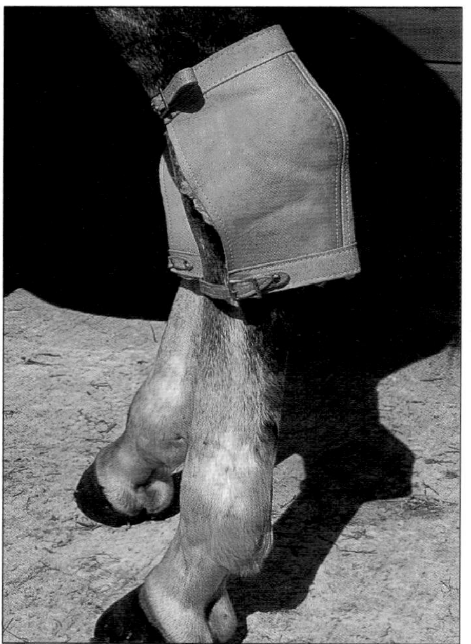

Hock boots. These are fitted to protect the hock joint from injury during transit.

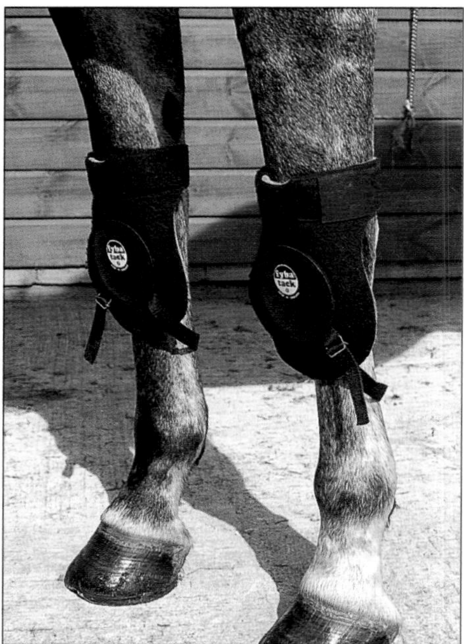

Knee pads. These can be used with travel bandages to protect the knees from damage.

HORSE DRESSED FOR TRAVELLING

Leather headcollar or halter – safer for travelling than a nylon headcollar because it will break more easily in the event of an accident.

Poll guard – protects the poll region of the horse's head whilst in transit.

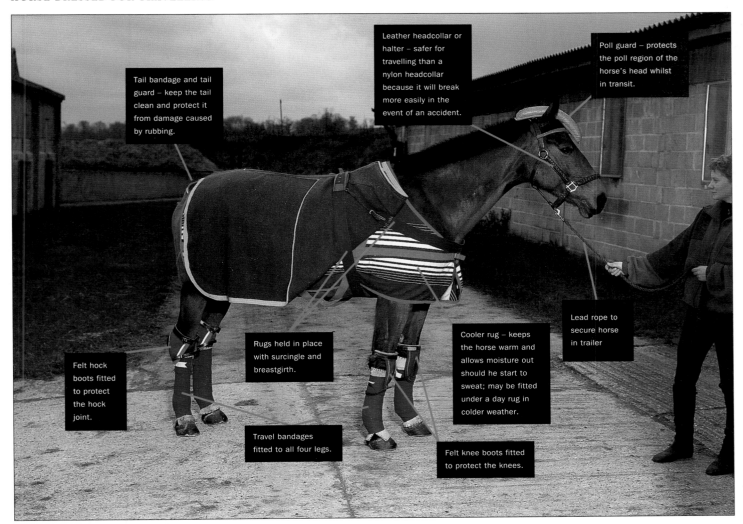

Tail bandage and tail guard – keep the tail clean and protect it from damage caused by rubbing.

Lead rope to secure horse in trailer

Cooler rug – keeps the horse warm and allows moisture out should he start to sweat; may be fitted under a day rug in colder weather.

Rugs held in place with surcingle and breastgirth.

Felt hock boots fitted to protect the hock joint.

Travel bandages fitted to all four legs.

Felt knee boots fitted to protect the knees.

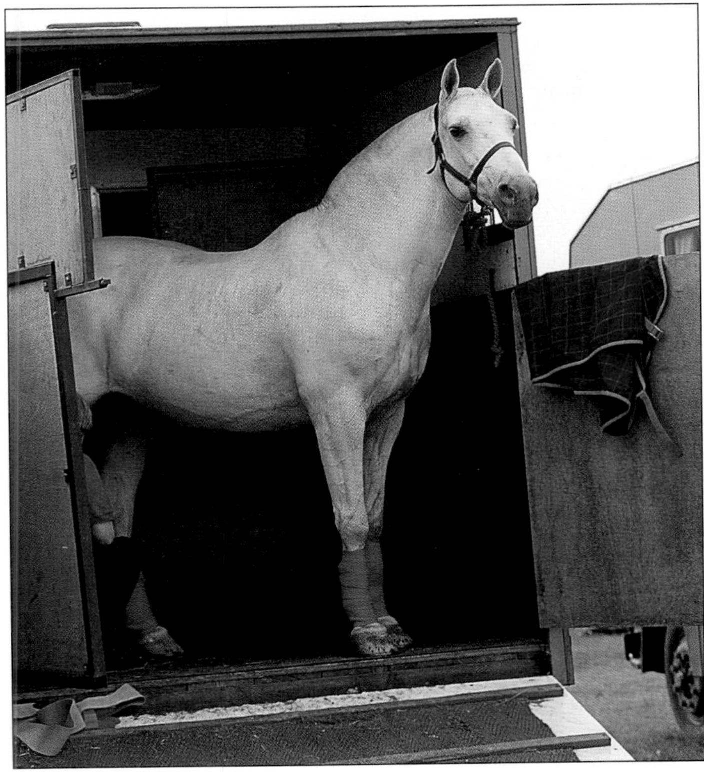

LEFT
Horses are very vulnerable to minor injuries when travelling on the roads. While a complete set of travelling equipment is not always necessary, your horse should be fitted with leg protection and a rug. Regular safety checks should also be made on the trailer itself.

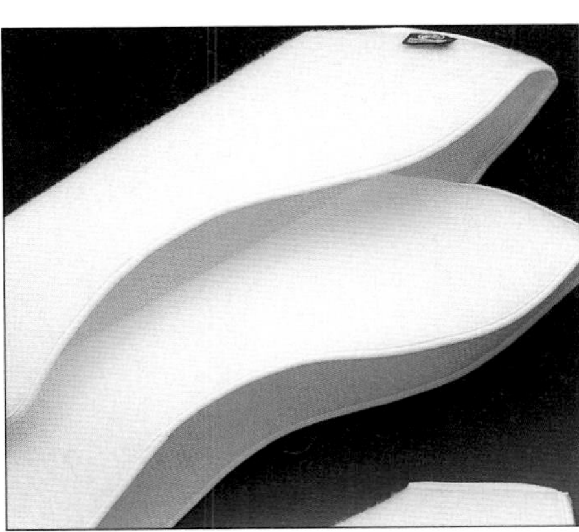

Shaped travel pads can be used in conjunction with travel bandages to protect specific parts of the legs when the horse is in transit.

Corrective Equipment

The following pieces of equipment may be used on the horse to discourage or prevent bad habits when he is stabled or turned out to grass.

A **plastic muzzle** may be used on a horse who is on a strict diet but needs to be turned out. The muzzle prevents him from eating large amounts of food, while the holes in the design allow him to breathe and drink. Plastic muzzles are also useful for horses who bite, chew their rugs or eat their bedding. The design of the **leather muzzle**, made of thick strips, allows the horse to breathe and drink but, like the plastic muzzle, it prevents him from nibbling his rug and biting.

A **bib** is attached to the headcollar and sits below the horse's chin. Like the muzzle, it is fitted to prevent the horse from chewing his rugs or bandages. A much more restrictive item is the **neck cradle**, which should be used only as a last resort to stop a horse from chewing.

A **cribbing collar** is a strong leather strap which is fitted tightly around the horse's throat to prevent him from crib biting and wind-sucking. The collar will not cure the condition, but will stop him doing it while it is fitted.

The design of the leather muzzle allows the horse to breathe and drink but will not allow him to bite and chew.

A plastic muzzle may be used on a horse on a diet who nonetheless needs to be turned out.

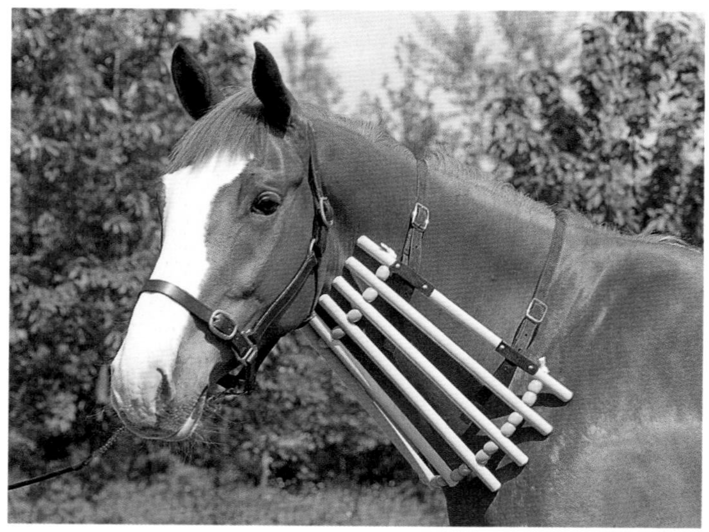

LEFT
The neck cradle offers a last ditch attempt to stop a horse chewing rugs or bandages.

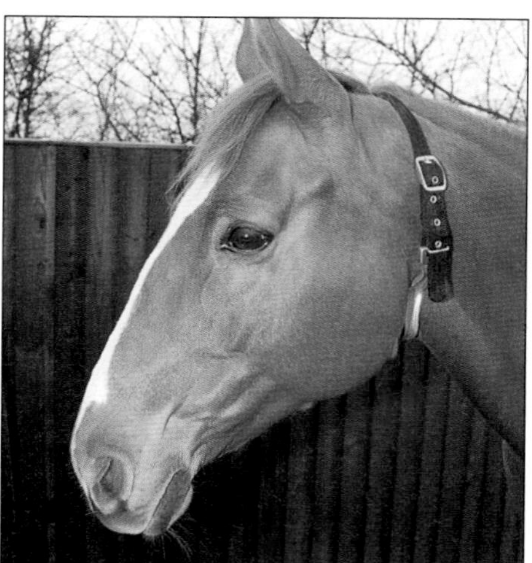

Cribbing collar. This is fitted around the horse's throat to prevent crib biting and wind-sucking.

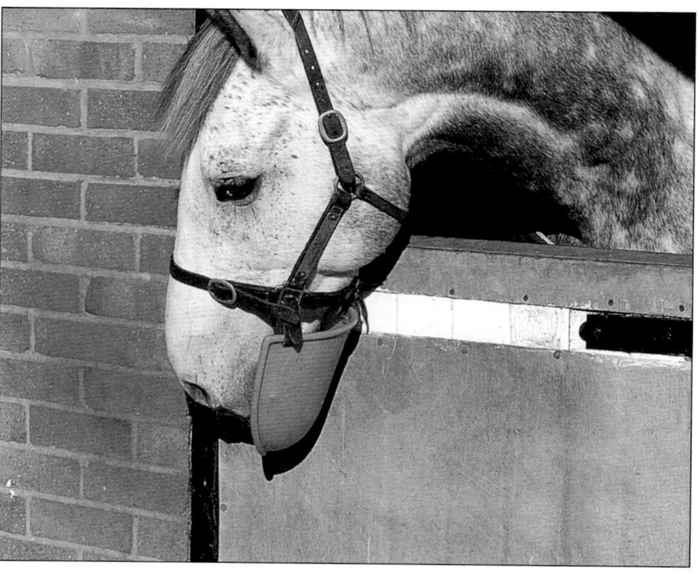

LEFT
The plastic bib is a mildly restrictive piece of equipment which will help to dissuade the horse from chewing his clothing.

What are Vices?

There are a number of pieces of equipment used on horses to prevent or discourage vices (as described on the opposite page) but what are vices and what causes a horse to exhibit them? A vice is chronic, habitual behaviour displayed by the horse, for example box walking, weaving (when the horse rocks from side to side swaying its head), windsucking (the horse sucks in air and swallows it) or crib biting (similar to windsucking except that the horse will also take hold of an object with his teeth).

Most vices are displayed by stabled horses (although not exclusively) and are thought to be a result of boredom or nervousness on the part of the horse. It is also possible that vices are copied by one horse from another.

Before resorting to equipment to stop a vice, it is always worth investigating the possible causes. For example, if a horse is bored being kept in his stable for long periods, try turning him out for part of the day, or increasing the amount of hay in his diet to keep him occupied.

If a horse persistently chews his rugs or bandages it is possible that they may be irritating him in some way. His bandages may have been applied too tightly or his rug may be irritating his skin. In any case it is always worth trying to eliminate the possible causes of a vice before trying to treat the symptoms.

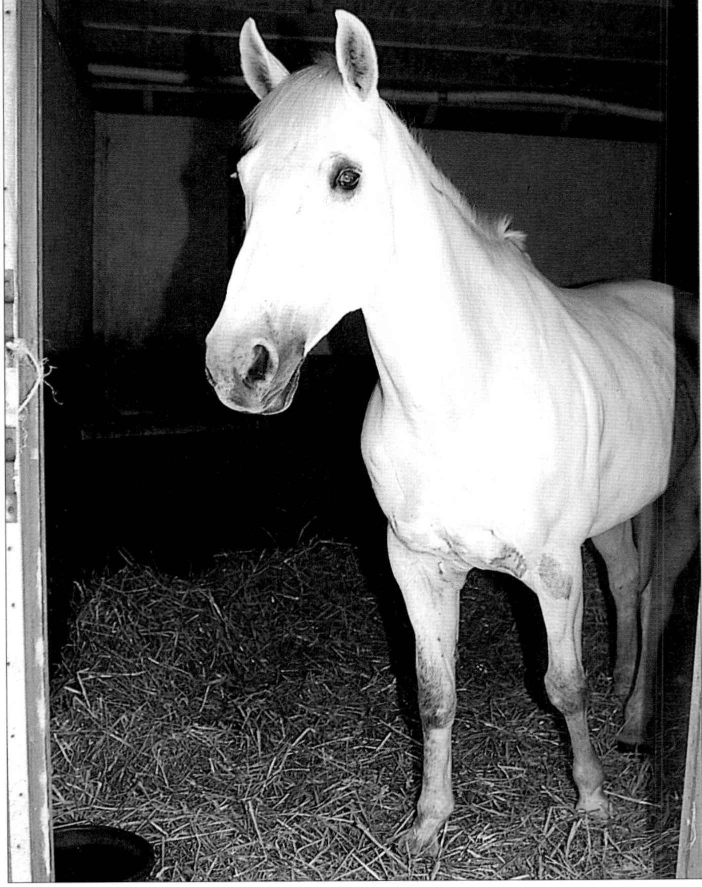

LEFT
It is always better to prevent vices rather than deal with them once the bad habits have formed. Horses can easily get bored if they are kept in a stable all day, and this can lead to chronic stress-induced behaviour. Make sure your horse is turned out as much as possible, to give him exercise and to add variety to his routine.

ABOVE
If your horse is stabled for long periods, make sure he has fresh supplies of hay. This is not only good for his diet, but will also keep him occupied.

BELOW
Check your horse and his rugs. If they are chewed, it may be a sign that the horse is uncomfortable or that his skin is irritated. It may help to remove the rug for a time, loosen it, or try a different material.

The Rider's Clothes

Like the horse, the rider requires specialist clothing for his or her safety and comfort. There is a wide variety of riding clothing available, with new designs and developments always coming on to the market. However, there are a few basic items which are essential for anyone who rides. A protective riding hat should always be worn when riding, lungeing or long reining horses, to reduce the risk of injury to the head. The wearing of a body protector is also a sensible precaution when jumping or riding horses which you know to be unpredictable. Riding boots (short or long) should be worn, because they are designed to prevent the rider's foot getting caught in the stirrup in the event of a fall. Many riders choose to wear gloves: those which have non-slip palms are better as they prevent the reins from slipping through the hands. Gloves, however, should always be worn when lungeing, long reining or leading horses by hand, to prevent injury to the hands should the horse suddenly pull away. Jodhpurs or breeches are a sensible choice for riding as their design prevents rubbing caused by the saddle or stirrup leathers.

Clothes

When working with horses, whether you are on the ground or riding, safety is the keynote. Horses are big, strong animals and there is always an element of danger, however calm and placid they might normally be. Therefore care should be taken even when choosing clothes for mundane, everyday chores such as mucking out.

Neat clothing which is well fitting without being too tight is the easiest to move around in. A long-sleeved shirt with a sweatshirt or sweater, depending on the weather, and a pair of comfortable trousers, jeans or jodhpurs are ideal for stable work. Avoid overtight trousers as they make bending down difficult. Dark colours will stay looking smart longer. Long sleeves are preferable to short ones since they give some protection from nips from equine teeth. Sleeveless suntops and vests should definitely be avoided.

Footwear is of great importance since a misplaced hoof can do a great deal of damage to a human foot. "Trainers" give little protection, nor do most rubber boots, though sturdy Wellingtons are as good as anything for mucking out, particularly if you wear thick walking-boot socks inside. At other times a pair of leather jodhpur boots will probably afford the best protection and will certainly enable you to move more quickly than when wearing Wellingtons. Some boots are now fitted with protective toecaps.

Coats and body warmers, when worn, should be kept fastened – a flapping coat can frighten a nervous horse and there is also the danger that it might become caught up on some "foreign body". Some horses are nervous of noisy waterproof fabrics, so avoid wearing them around the stables.

Long hair should be tied up, again to avoid the possibility of scaring a horse or becoming caught up. This is particularly important in windy weather. Avoid wearing jewellery: rings, earrings, noserings and the like can all cause nasty injuries if they become caught up.

Most well-trained horses are safe to lead about, in and out of their stables, down to the paddock, etc. But if you have any doubts whatsoever about a horse's good behaviour (when handling a young horse, for example) take precautions: wear a hard hat, correctly fastened, in case he rears up and strikes out, boots to protect your feet and a pair of gloves.

ABOVE
A sweatshirt, breeches, boots and a hard hat make a suitable outfit for everyday exercise.

LEFT
Neat, workmanlike clothes enable you to carry out daily chores in comfort and safety.

Safety Gear

Riding has always been and always will be a risk sport. But modern safety equipment is constantly improving and everyone who rides should ensure that they wear the best available protective gear, which includes hat, body protector and boots.

The most vulnerable part of the rider is the head and it is irresponsible to get on to a horse, or to lunge or long rein or otherwise handle an unpredictable young horse, without wearing a **hard hat** securely fastened with a **chin strap**. Your country's national federation (for example in Britain the British Horse Society, in the United States the American Horse Shows Association) will advise on the most up-to-date safety standards. The **jockey skull**, or **crash hat**, is generally considered to give maximum protection and is therefore recommended (and obligatory under the rules of most sports) for all riding which involves fast work or jumping. The **chin harness** must be correctly adjusted and fastened at all times. It may be worn on the point of the chin, with a chin cup, or under the chin, whichever is most comfortable. The alternative is the traditional **hunting cap** which must have a soft peak (a hard peak can cause facial, head or neck injuries in a fall). All riding hats should be correctly fitted (many retailers are trained in hat fitting).

Body protectors are designed to protect the torso and the shoulders in the event of a fall. They should fit well, feel comfortable and not restrict the rider's movement.

Riding boots and **jodhpur boots** are designed to prevent the foot from sliding right through the stirrup iron or otherwise becoming caught up in the iron in the event of a fall – a potentially fatal situation. They have smooth soles and a clearly defined heel. Leather boots afford the best protection from knocks, for example when riding across country, but rubber ones fashioned in the same style are suitable for everyday riding. Wellington boots, trainers and other boots or shoes with ridged soles and little or no heel should never be worn for riding.

LEFT
Fluorescent clothing is a wise safety precaution when riding on the roads. The message on the tabard helps to alert drivers.

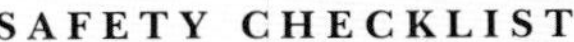

SAFETY CHECKLIST

- Wear a correctly fitting hard hat with the chin strap fastened at all times when mounted.
- Replace a hat that has been subjected to impact in a fall – it may not give sufficient protection next time.
- Always ride in your own hat – a borrowed hat is unlikely to fit you correctly.
- Wear safe footwear at all times when mounted.
- Always use the correct stirrup iron size – about 1 inch (2.5cm) wider than your boot – to prevent your foot becoming stuck.
- Wear fluorescent garments – hat cover, tabard/body warmer etc – fitted with retro-reflective strips when riding on the roads and fit your horse with similar high visibility leg bands.
- Avoid riding on the roads in poor visibility and after dark.
- Never ride in jewellery.
- Always fasten tiepins horizontally or at an angle, never vertically.
- Always ride with your coat fastened.
- Never take off a coat or sweater while mounted – while you are taking your arms out of the sleeves you will have no control over the horse should he make an unexpected move.
- If you have less than perfect eyesight, wear soft contact lenses if possible. If not, seek your optician's advice on the safest type of spectacles.

LEFT
A body protector should be worn when jumping fixed fences and by people needing special protection (for example, an older person with more brittle bones).

LEFT
A jockey skull or "crash hat", with a correctly adjusted chin harness, gives the head maximum protection. It is fitted with a silk cover.

Riding Clothes

By and large all riding clothes are designed for comfort and protection. Only with the odd item of equipment (such as the top hat for dressage) is clothing dictated by fashion.

Most riding clothes are based on hunting attire, which evolved over a long period and led to the design of an entire outfit which would give protection from wet, cold and the many knocks experienced when travelling at speed across country. Long leather boots keep the feet and lower legs dry and give maximum protection from painful encounters with gateposts or other fixed objects. Breeches keep the upper legs warm and dry and protect the insides of the knees from chafing against the saddle. A well-fitting jacket made of a good stout tweed or twill gives warmth and a certain amount of waterproofing while at the same time affording complete freedom of movement – essential for all riding, but particularly for jumping and riding at speed. Gloves keep the hands warm and dry and give a secure grip on the reins. A hunting tie or stock helps protect the neck in the event of a fall. A hard hat, correctly secured with a chin harness, protects the most vulnerable part of all, the head.

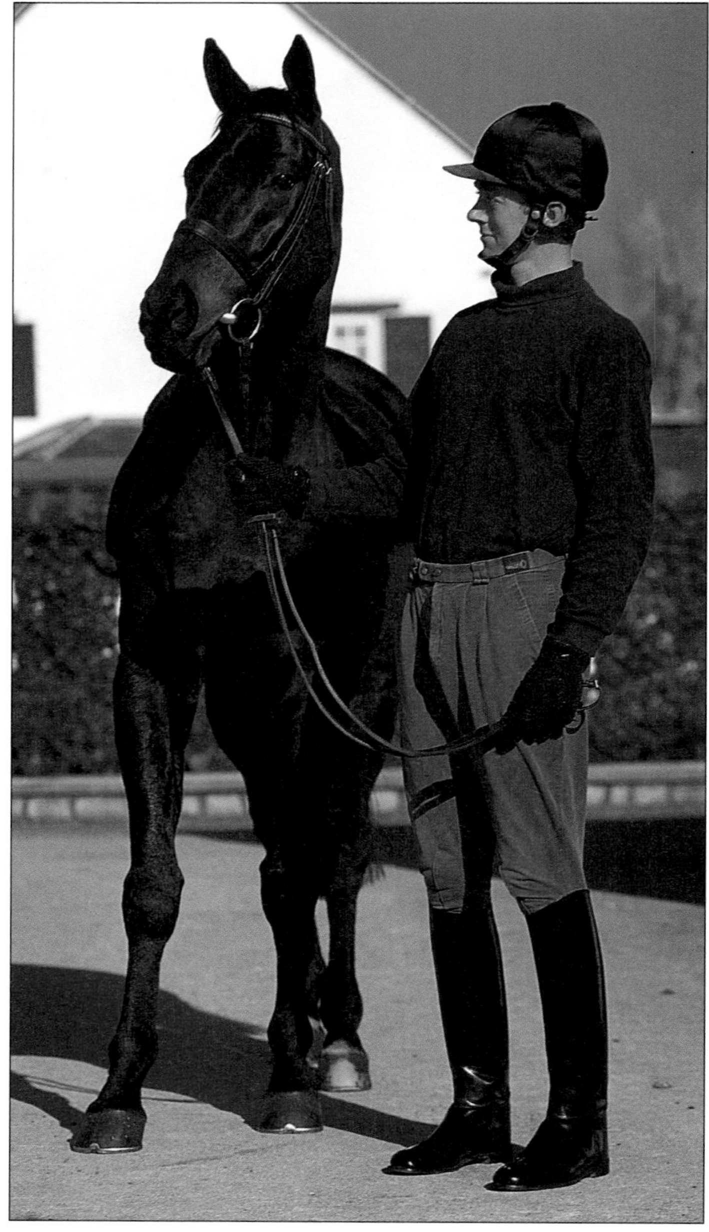

LEFT
Everyday riding clothes should be neat and safe. Dark colours are more practical than the light shades worn with traditional hunting dress.

BELOW LEFT
Chaps are a good alternative to boots. This rider is prepared for roadwork – note the fluorescent tabard and the horse's protective boots.

For everyday riding there is a wealth of suitable clothing to choose from which is both cheaper than more formal attire and suited to frequent immersion in the washing machine. **Jodhpurs**, which extend down the leg to the ankle, and are usually worn with short, elastic-sided leather jodhpur boots, are cooler in summer than breeches and long boots. They come in a range of materials, from lightweight cotton suitable for hot climates to thermal material for wear in extremes of cold. Instead of jodhpur boots, jodhpurs may be worn with **half-chaps**, which cover the leg from below the knee to the foot, or with full **chaps**, which extend up to the thigh.

Close-fitting **riding trousers** are also suitable for everyday wear. Like jodhpurs, they come with "strappings" – reinforcements at the knee and thigh. Some garments are also fitted with an inset seat panel made in an extra-grip material.

Rubber **riding boots** are a cheaper alternative to leather ones, though they can be cold in winter, when an inner sole or an extra pair of socks may be required.

Casual **riding coats** such as waxed or quilted jackets, blousons and body warmers are fine for everyday riding and may be worn with a shirt and/or sweatshirt or sweater. Modern waterproof materials are light and comfortable to wear and the more expensive ones have the advantage of being "breathable". Waterproofs come in a range of lengths and may have added features such as storm collar and cuffs, fleecy lining and pommel flap. Noisy waterproof materials should be avoided as horses tend to be frightened of them, particularly on a windy day.

There are **gloves** for every occasion, specially designed for the rider. Special features include reinforced rein fingers, pimple palm grips and lycra inserts for extra flexibility.

Clothes for Competition

For most forms of competitive riding it is usual to wear a riding coat with breeches and boots, a shirt with a collar and tie or collarless shirt with a hunting tie or stock. The rules of some sports also stipulate the wearing of spurs. A hat is obligatory and although the bowler hat (derby) is still seen in show classes and the top hat in dressage, the trend is more and more to the safer type of hunting cap and, even more so, the jockey skull. The latter is usually worn with a dark-coloured silk cover.

For cross-country riding the jacket is replaced by a sweater or shirt, according to the weather, which may be in the rider's own colours, as may the hat silk.

Endurance riding is one area where tradition holds less sway, partly because the sport is of fairly recent origin (at least in an organized competitive way) and also because at the higher echelons riders are not only in the saddle for very long periods but also spend some of the time on their feet, running alongside their horses to give them a breather. Breeches and boots would be too hot and uncomfortable so this is the one sport where runningshoes are permitted. However, as a safety precaution, riders are required to use enclosed-type stirrup irons to prevent their feet slipping right through.

LEFT
Correct dress for top-level dressage includes a top hat, tail coat and waistcoat.

BELOW
Most riding gear, for women as well as men, is based on clothes developed for the hunting field.

BOTTOM LEFT
The clothes worn for endurance riding are less formal than in other competitive sports.

Whips and Spurs

Whips and spurs (referred to as artificial aids) can be used by the rider to reinforce the leg aids.

The rider uses a whip just behind his or her leg if the horse does not respond to a command from the leg. Whips should only be used in these circumstances and not as an alternative to the leg, or as a punishment.

Shorter, thicker whips are used for show jumping and cross country. Longer, finer whips are ideal for schooling horses on the flat, because they can be used to give a gentle flick without the rider having to take his or her hands off the reins.

Hunting whips are not used on the horse, but are traditionally carried out hunting. They usually have a bent top which is very useful for pulling gates shut, and a plaited leather thong and cord lash which is carried looped round. For showing horses, a simple malacca or leather-covered cane is often carried.

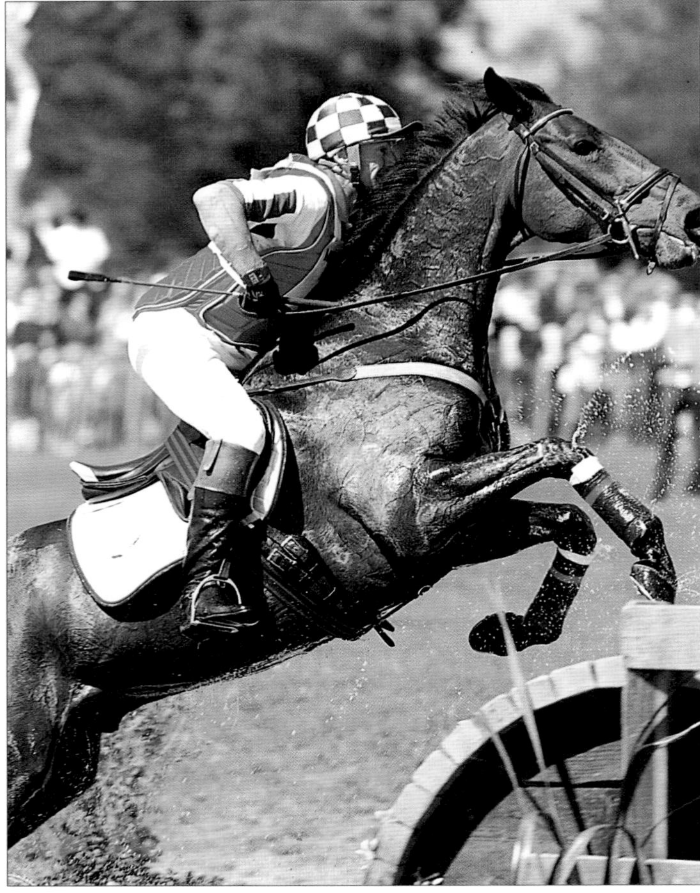

LEFT
This cross-country rider is carrying a short, thick whip, only to be used if the horse does not respond to a command from the leg.

Spurs can be worn to emphasize the rider's leg aids. The most common type of spur used for English riding is called a Prince of Wales spur. It has a short blunt-ended neck which, when fitted, points downward. The spur fits snugly around the back of the rider's boot and is held in place with a strap. Spurs are also available with rowels (small metal discs fitted to the tip of the spurs) which give them a much sharper action. Spurs should only be used by experienced riders who have an independent seat and can maintain control when the spur is applied to the horse.

LEFT
A dressage whip is longer and allows the rider to use the whip without letting go of the reins.

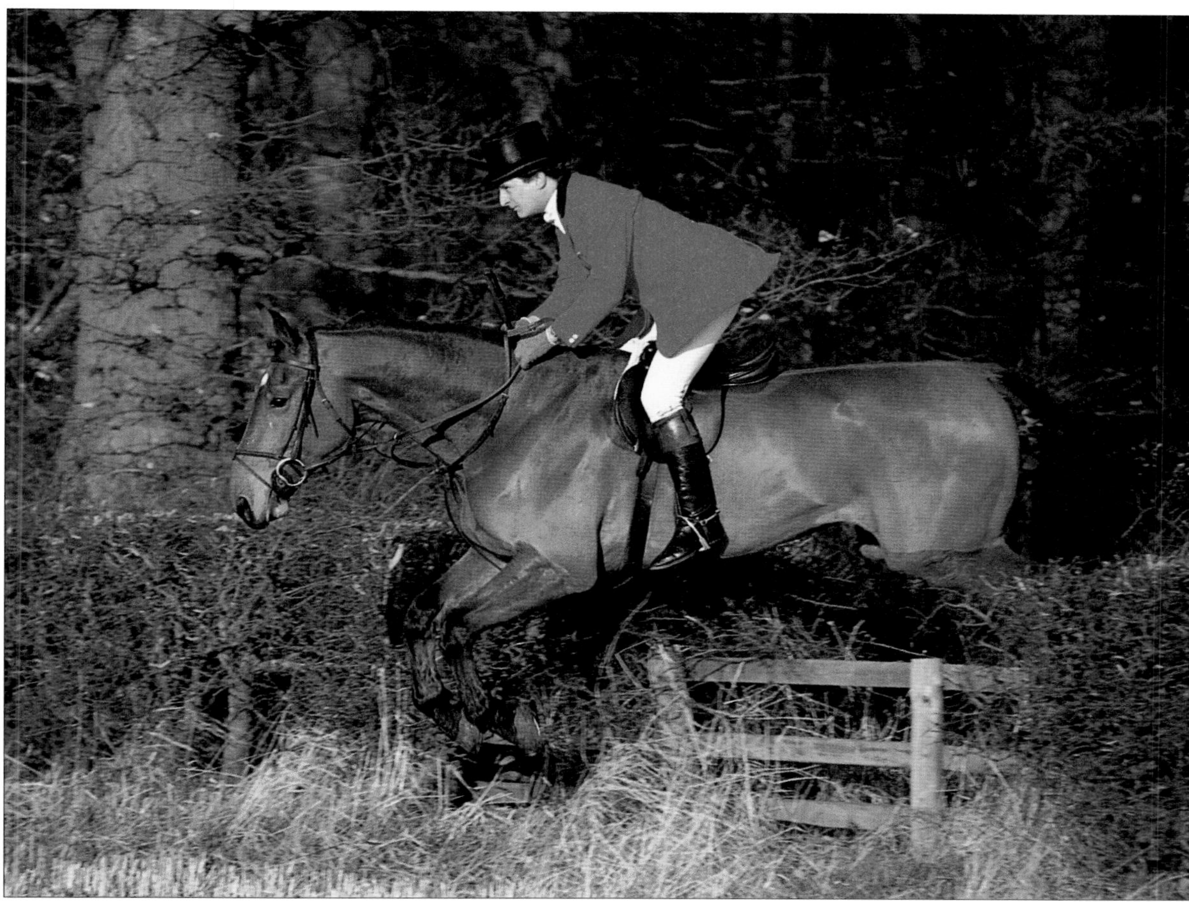

LEFT
The hunting whip is not used on the horse, but is carried as a hunting tradition, and is sometimes used for pulling gates shut. It is much longer than the show-jumping or cross-country whip.

ABOVE
Spurs, like whips, can be used to emphasize the rider's leg aids. They should only be used by experienced riders.

RIGHT
A show-jumping whip, used for encouraging the horse to move forward if he doesn't respond to the rider's leg aids.

Suppliers and Acknowledgements

The authors would like to thank the many individuals and breed societies who kindly provided information for use in the breeds section of this book, particularly:

The American Morgan Horse Association, Inc; The American Paint Horse Association; The American Saddlebred Horse Association, Inc; The British Spotted Pony Society; Vivienne Burdon; The Cleveland Bay Horse Society; The Clydesdale Horse Society of Great Britain and Ireland; The Exmoor Pony Society; The Hackney Horse Society; The Haflinger Society of Great Britain; The Highland Pony Society; The Irish Draught Horse Society (GB); Sylvia Loch (author of *The Royal Horse of Europe*, J.A. Allen, 1986); The Lusitano Breed Society of Great Britain; The Palomino Horse Association of America, Inc; The Pinto Horse Association of America, Inc; Valerie Russell; The Suffolk Horse Society; The Walkaloosa Horse Association; The Walking Horse Owners' Association of America, Inc; The Welsh Pony and Cob Society.

We are grateful to the following for allowing their horses, ponies and stables to be photographed:

HORSES: EUROPE

Arab – Sariah Arabians, Dorking, Surrey
Barb – Haras Regional de Marrakech, Morocco
Thoroughbred – Mrs M Blackburn, c/o Catherston Stud, Whitchurch, Hampshire
Anglo-Arab – Woodlander Stud, Raglan, Gwent
Danish Warmblood – Catherston Stud, Whitchurch, Hampshire
Ariègeois – Bob Langrish, photographer
Norman Cob – Haras National Le Lion d'Angers, Loire, France
Camargue – Laurent Serre, Camargue, France
Selle Français – Haras National Le Lion d'Angers, Loire, France
French Trotter – Haras National Le Lion d'Angers, Loire, France
Percheron – Haras National Le Lion d'Angers, Loire, France
Breton – Haras National Le Lion d'Angers, Loire, France
Hanoverian – Mrs S Bray, Nuneaton, Warwickshire
Holstein – Mr Luetzow, Wokingham, Berkshire
Oldenburg – I Brendel, Trenthide, Dorset
Westphalian – Marlow Building Co Ltd, Marlow, Buckinghamshire
Hackney – Georgina Turner, Ipswich, Suffolk
Shire – Lingwood Shire, Brentwood, Essex
Suffolk – Randy Hiscock, Shaftesbury, Dorset
Shagya Arab – Sonia Lindsay, Okehampton, Devon
Icelandic – Edda Hestar, Salisbury, Wiltshire
Friesian – Harrods, London
Gelderland – Mr Luetzow, Wokingham, Berkshire
Dutch Warmblood – Mrs C Hughes, Doncaster
Don – Russian Horse Society, Epsom, Surrey (standing) Mrs June Connolly, Droitwich, West Midlands (action)
Budenny – Mrs Marcus, Beoley, Redditch, Hereford & Worcester (action)
Kabardin – Mrs June Connolly, Droitwich, West Midlands
Orlov – George Bowman Jnr, Penrith, Cumbria
Vladimir – Russian Horse Society, Epsom, Surrey
North Swedish – Jan Gyllensten, photographer, Sweden
Akhal-Teke – Viscountess Bury, Plumpton, Sussex
Knabstrup – Mrs Ann Peruzzi-Smith, Diss, Norfolk

HORSES: UNITED STATES

Morgan – Betty Gray, Orange Lake, Florida
Quarter Horse – Quiet Oaks Farm, Ocala, Florida & Derby Daze Farm, Ocala, Florida
Saddlebred – Boca Raton Equestrian Center, Del Ray Beach
Standardbred – David McDuffee & Tom Walsh Jnr, South Florida Trotting Center
Missouri Fox Trotter – Sandy Hart, Winter Haven, Florida
Tennessee Walking Horse – Mrs Carol Worsham, Dunnellon, Florida
Mustang – Cindy Bowman, Dunnellon, Florida
Peruvian Paso – Annette Ward, Alachua, Florida
Pony of the Americas – Cynthia Bunnell, Eustis, Florida
American Shetland – Caroline Proctor, Ocala, Florida
Palomino – Holmes Quarter Horses, Brandon, Florida
Appaloosa – Classic Acres Farm, Ocala, Florida
Paint – Brooke Hamlin, Ocala, Florida

PONIES

Haflinger – Millslade Farm Stud, Bridgwater, Somerset
Exmoor – Mrs J Freeman, Wareside, Hertfordshire
New Forest – Shirley Young, Salisbury, Wiltshire
Shetland – Mr & Mrs E House, Bincombe Shetlands, Bridgwater, Somerset
Dales – Mrs B Powell, Farnham, Surrey
Connemara & Welsh Cob – Miss S Clark, Dorking, Surrey
Fjord – Mrs Murray, Ottery St Mary, Devon
Caspian – Henden Caspian Stud, Chippenham, Wiltshire

STABLE MANAGEMENT

Catherston Stud, Whitchurch, Hampshire
Stretcholt Farm Stud, Bridgwater, Somerset.

We would also like to thank the following for facilities and equipment, and for riding for photographs:

FACILITIES AND EQUIPMENT

Philip Wellon for the use of land at Vine Farm; Aubiose UK Ltd for the outdoor arena; HAC TAC Ltd for supplying close-contact breeches.

RIDERS
Amanda Colbourne, Thomas Cooper, Janine Cornish, Charles Daniel, Kate Eckley, Janice Peglar, Sarah Rees-Elford, and Jeremy Russell.

The following companies supplied the tack and equipment featured in this book:

UNITED KINGDOM

Aerborn Equestrian Ltd
Pegasus House
198 Sneiton Dale
Nottingham NG2 4HJ

Albion Saddlemakers Co Ltd
Albion House
55 Caldmore Road
Walsall
West Midlands WS1 3NA

Clyst Equestrian Ltd
Teko House
Furnham Road
Chard
Somerset TA20 1AX

Keenthorne Saddlery
Nether Stowey
Bridgwater
Somerset

Miller Crosby Ltd
30 Birchbrook Industrial Estate
Shenstone
Nr Lichfield
Staffordshire WS14 0DT

Proteq™ Worldwide Ltd
Graingers
West Ashling
Chichester
West Sussex PO18 8DN

The Royal Mews
Buckingham Palace
London SW1W

Shires Equestrian Products
15 Southern Avenue
Leominster
Herefordshire HR6 0QF

Stylo Matchmakers
International Ltd
Holybrook Mill
Harrogate Road
Greengates
Bradford
West Yorkshire BD10 0QW

Wychanger Barton Saddlery
The Haywain
Burlescombe
Nr Tiverton
Devon EX16 7JY

UNITED STATES

Whitman Saddle Manufacturing
5272 West Michigan
Kalamazoo
MI 49006

Libertyville Saddle Shop Inc.
P.O. Box M
Libertyville
IL 60048-4913

Fennell's Horse Supplies
Red Mile Road
Lexington
KY 40504

Drury's Saddlery and Supplies
1638 Danville Road
Harrodsburg
KY 40330

We are also grateful to the following for allowing their equipment, horses and stables to be photographed:

Betty Howett
Bossington Stables
Bossington
Nr Minehead
Somerset

Mrs Mary King
School House
Salcombe Regis
Devon EX10 0JQ

Bob Mayhew
Dumpford Manor Farm
Trotton
Hampshire GU31 5JR

Lynn Russell
Durfold Farm
Plaistow Road
Surrey EV8 4PQ

Sarah Rowe
4 Cleal Cottages
Broadway
Ilminster
Somerset TA19 9RD

Margaret Swords
White Horse Lodge
Over Stowey
Bridgwater
Somerset

Hannah Washer
Fulbrook Cottage
Fiddington
Nr Bridgwater
Somerset

Megan Williams
The Moat House
Longdon
Nr Tewkesbury
Gloucestershire

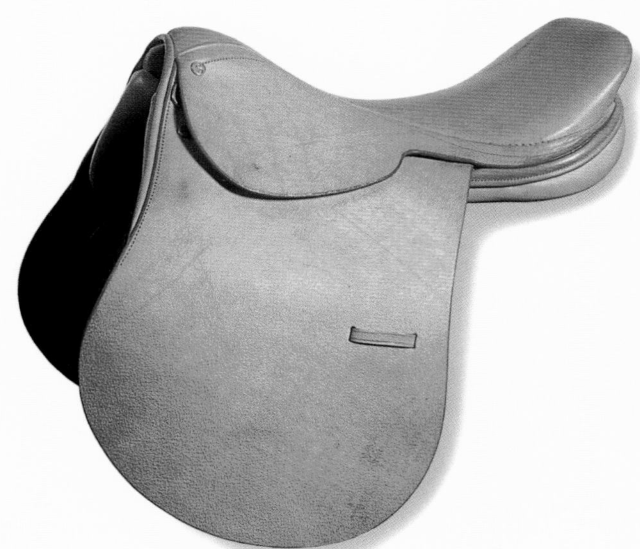

Index

Page numbers in *italic* refer to the illustrations

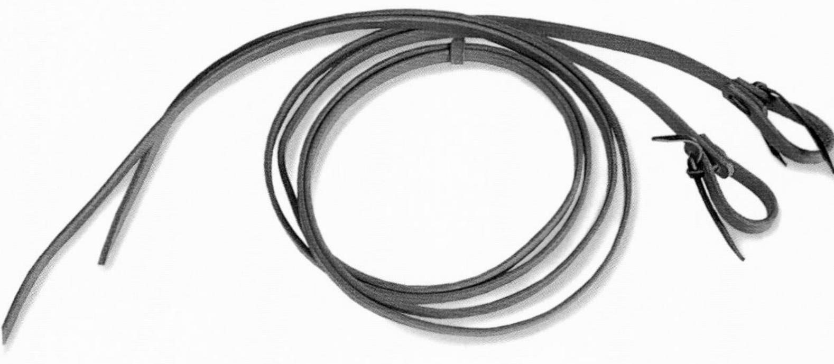

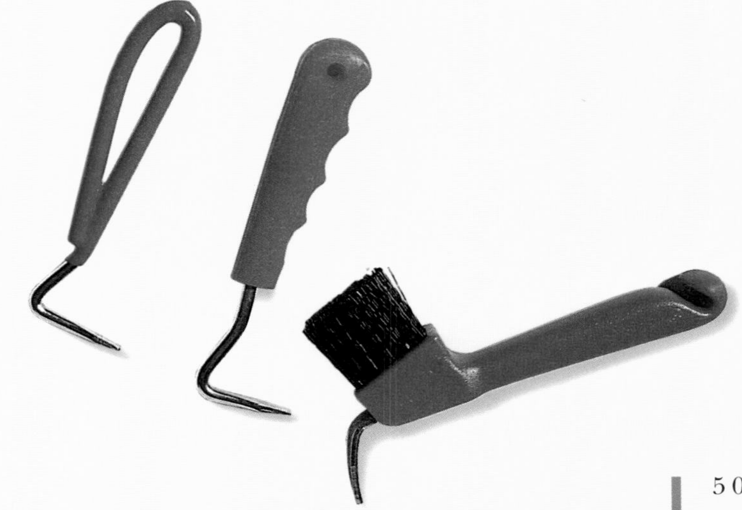

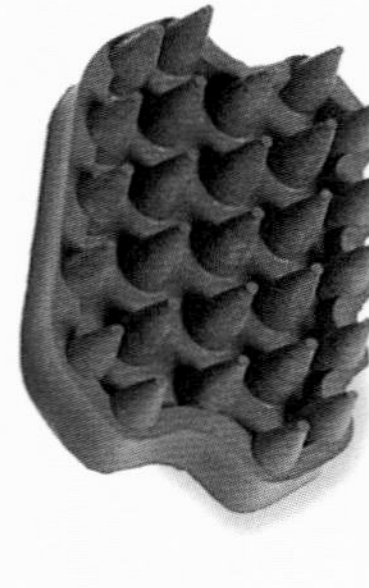

M

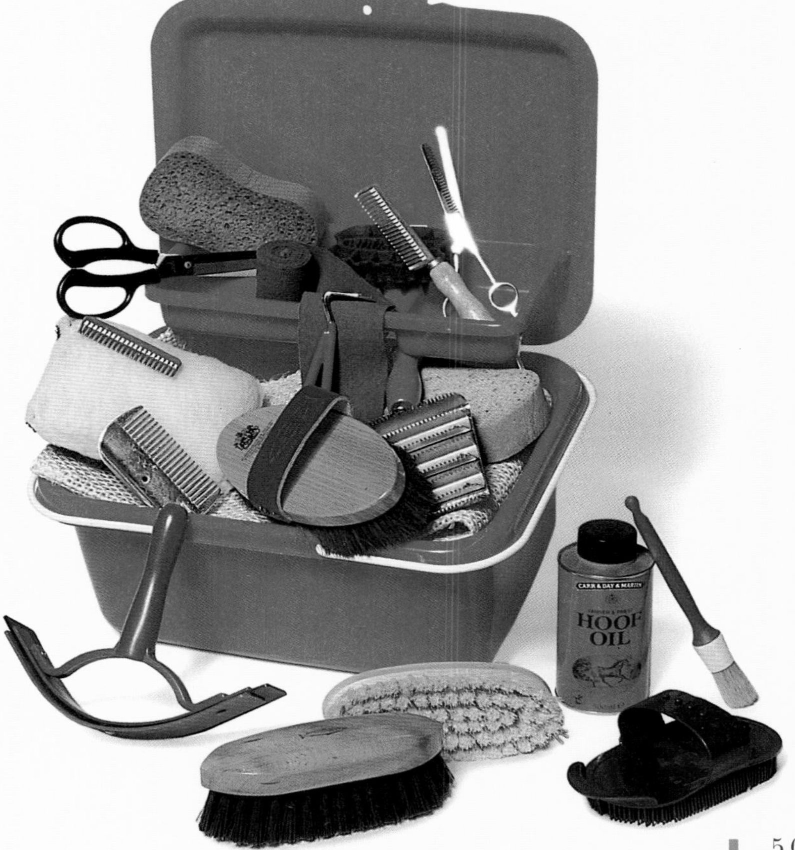